A Delco Advanced Suspension System commands top performance on the road, and that means top satisfaction for your consumers.

At Delco, advanced suspensions begin with the modular strut assembly delivered just in time and in sequence —assuring an accurate, high-quality build.

Next is the Delco Automatic Level Control System which maintains the designed vehicle attitude under varying load. Assures a level ride for smooth vehicle handling.

Add to these features the Delco Computer Command Ride System and you can truly produce the car for tomorrow. The Delco Computer Command Ride System, available with automatic road sensing, detects the type of road surface being traveled and adjusts for optimum suspension damping characteristics. This means impressive ride and handling over all road surfaces. An interface is provided to permit driver selection of specific driving modes whether it's a cushioned ride home from the office or responsive handling on a lonely country road. Delco Computer Command Ride offers a complete ride system utilizing high-technology electronics custom designed for your vehicle.

Delco advanced suspensions also include total air suspension systems to let you provide flexibility and value in your product for today's discriminating consumer.

Delco Products
Division of General Motors Dayton, Ohio 45401

A dynamic leader in systems solutions...worldwide.

Cars International

 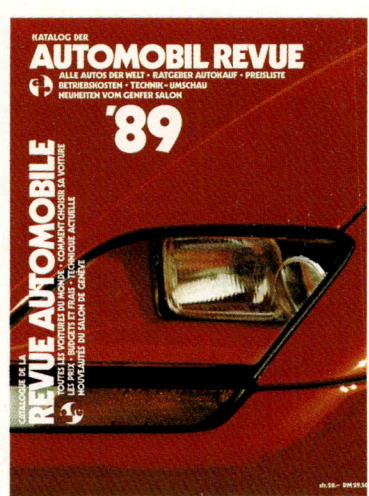

Cars International is the result of a joint agreement by PRS Publishing Ltd, London and Hallwag AG, Berne, to produce an English language edition of Hallwag's 'Automobil Revue' for marketing worldwide. Hallwag have published 'Automobil Revue' for over 40 years, as a German/French edition. The publication contains specifications on over 1500 vehicles, produced worldwide, plus editorials on future trends, concept vehicles, new technology and motor racing. The following summarises some of the technical advancements made in vehicle design over the past twenty years of 'Automobil Revue'.

Twenty years separate these two covers of the French/German language 'Automobil Revue' catalogue. Two decades – which is reason enough to give some thought to the development of car technology in that period. The 1969 edition illustrates the front section of the fascinating Ferrari 365 GTB/4 (Daytona); this top of the range model was first shown at the Paris Motor Show in 1968, and represented the ultimate sports car with its 4.4 litre twin–cam V12 engine, transaxle drive and Pininfarina–designed and Scaglietti–built body. The unique styling included Plexiglas stripes which lay across the whole of the headlight section.

The cover of the 1989 edition shows the 2–seater BMW Roadster Z1, which made its debut at the end of last year. The notable characteristics of this "impractical" car, which according to its builders is designed purely to provide driving pleasure, includes new technology plastic bodywork, as well as vertically opening and closing electric doors.

What can be seen from these two similar pictures? More than one would think! Automotive technology has made significant progress in the last twenty years: cleaner, more powerful and efficient engines, safer chassis, ABS brakes, improved crash protection, more corrosion–free bodywork. There is much more to describe, but all of these factors are far less obvious than aerodynamic body–styling and futuristic interior design.

The headlamp units of the Ferrari Daytona and the BMW Z1, both with glass covers, serve as a small example that only keen observers are aware of the continual stream of technical development underlying the industry. Small changes in the perceived "look" do not provide any indication of the invisible advances made. The very strong and widely–used Halogen lamps are scarcely distinguishable from an early Bilux lamp.

More obvious in this context is the DB–light, which is used in the BMW Z1 and which can be recognised by the small ellipsoid–lens and the absence of a conventional, grooved spreader glass.

A still more intensive light yield is expected of a completely new headlight which possesses extremely complex forms of computer–designed reflector–surfaces; it also works without the conventional diffusing lens, but at first glance this headlight does not differ vastly from the types normally used today.

There will be further progress in the future, though whether this will fundamentally change the "look" of the cars is a question which cannot be answered today.

Max Notzli

English Language Edition:

Publisher:	Simon Cannon
Editorial:	Arthur Way, Stephen Cox
Project Manager:	Stephen Cox
Production:	Vanessa Williamson, Claire Hider, Zuleika Robson
Advertising:	Elaine Boyden (Europe), BWB (Europe), Patricia Cresswell (USA)
Advertising Coordination:	Sally Donlevy
With special thanks to:	Christine Robertshaw and Marianne Korteweg

"Cars International 1989" is the first English language edition of "Automobil Revue/Revue Automobile", published by PRS Publishing Ltd, London. The original edition in German/French is published annually as 'Katalog der Automobil Revue/Catalogue de la Revue Automobile im Hallwag Verlag Bern (Schweiz)'. World rights: Hallwag AG Bern.

World copyright © Hallwag AG Bern, 1989.

Copyright for English edition: PRS Publishing Ltd, London

Available in Hardback: ISBN 0 906237 45 9
　　　　　　 Softback: ISBN 0 906237 46 7

CONTENTS

Eastern Temptations For Western Markets

American and West European car manufacturers are about to face stronger competition from Eastern suppliers. East European car companies are developing an increasingly sophisticated range of models at the lower end of the market and, from the Far East, Japanese producers are gearing up for an attack in the luxury car market.

– Arthur Way

Concept–cars 1988

Despite the fact that cars are now being designed by computers, there is still potential for innovative design thinking. In 1988 about 40 concept cars from 10 countries were introduced to test public reaction and tantalise the car buying public.

– Roger Gloor

Road Tests 1988

Based on the 60 models tested by the weekly Swiss magazine Automobil Revue in 1988, the current emphasis is on better performance but in a way that does not conflict with the growing concern over the environment. Multi–valve engines are becoming an increasingly common feature, four wheel drive is growing in popularity, and fun and enjoyment can be had with a cabriolet.

– "AR" Test Team

A Sport Governed by Numerous Rules

Motor racing in its purest form – Formula 1 – is big business and highly professional, but should also be fun. However, at this level, and other lesser categories too, participating is bedevilled by numerous and, at times, seemingly illogical rule changes by the sport's governing body.

– Adriano Cimarosti

Gags and Gadgets

It used to be that people merely wanted their cars to take them from A to B, but now they are regarded as an extension to their home and as such are kitted out with a whole range of items that add to comfort and convenience. Already there is quite a list of features – many fitted as standard – and more are on the way.

– Max Notzli

Power trip: Muscle is back on US streets

With fuel shortages now a dim and distant memory, American drivers are responding eagerly to the growing number of high performance cars which are being introduced on to the market by US producers and importers alike. Bigger, more powerful engines are selling cars once again.

– Michael G Sheldrick

Automobile Technology Today and Tomorrow

The pace of technological change has never been greater with various influences shaping the course of research and development activities. The recent strength of the motor industry has instilled a new confidence which is giving the vehicle manufacturers plenty of excuses to indulge in innovative thinking.

– Olaf von Fersen

A Sports Car in View

Illustrates some of the Sports derivatives that are now in the market place, with high performance engines and luxurious interior. Also shown are sporty versions of Saloon/Sedans. Coupes, compact cars and the larger 'space' vehicles.

– Martin Wyler

Specifications

Details of over 1,500 vehicles produce worldwide, comprising information on body weight, engine data, engine construction, transmission, gear ratios, dimensions and performance.

Price Guides

Guides for USA and UK markets.

Index

Complete index of contents including advertisers list can be found at the rear of this publication.

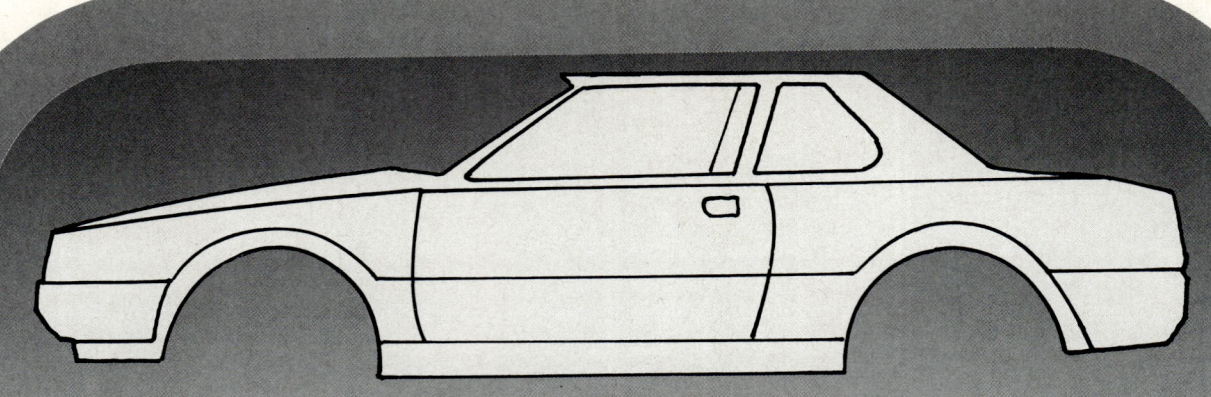

SAIAG GROUP

THE EUROPEAN SPECIALIST FOR RUBBER AND PLASTICS COMPONENTS

13 PLANTS IN EUROPE

32 LICENSEES IN EUROPE, AMERICA, ASIA, AFRICA, AUSTRALIA

ONE HUNDRED SAIAG COMPONENTS

saiag spa - Via Torino 178 - 10093 Collegno (Turin) Italie - Tel. (11) 4111666 - Tx 210461 - Fax (11) 4118092

ALFA 164. SIMPLY NOT COMMON.

3.0 V6

From Alfa Romeo's heritage of superb performance and handling comes the new Alfa 164. A truly incomparable sports saloon. Styled by Pininfarina, the 164's sports-inspired profile has the best aerodynamic rating in its category: CX 0.30. For increased speed, stability and mileage. Elegant materials and obsessive attention to detail have made the 164's interior as luxurious as it is spacious. Active safety features, such as ABS, plus Alfa's legendary road-holding combine security with performance. To provide a unique driving experience. Its 3-litre V6 power plant develops 192 HP, producing exceptional torque of 25 kg/m at 4,000 rpm. More than sufficient to ensure spectacular acceleration, even in high gear, and a top speed of over 230 kph. Also available with automatic transmission. If you prefer, there is a 2-litre Twin Spark engine (148 HP, torque of 19 kg/m at 4,000 rpm and a top speed of over 210 kph). The Alfa 164. Simply not common. From every point of view.

LuK for the best.

Clutches. Lock-up clutches for torque converters. Brake bands for automatic transmissions. All developed and produced by LuK with the precision and innovation which have made LuK famous throughout the world. That's why LuK clutches are to be found in vehicles made by:

Audi, BMW, Chrysler, Citroën, Daimler-Benz, Ford, GM, Jaguar, Nissan, Opel, Peugeot, Toyota, Vauxhall and VW.

In the 1960s, LuK introduced the diaphragm-spring clutch to Europe. Today, LuK has the dual-mass flywheel which offers a new dimension in motoring for cars with manual transmission. This flywheel absorbs noise and vibrations of power transmission to an amazing extent. The result is first-class motoring comfort.

Every year the confidence of our customer in us, is justified by 8 million clutches.

Once again, LuK's products and efficiency have been awarded distinctions by renowned automobile manufacturers throughout the world.

Headquarters Aftermarket worldwide:
AS Autoteile-Service GmbH & Co
Paul-Ehrlich-Str. 21 · POB 1105
D-6070 Langen · Telephone (06103) 753-0
Telex 4185777 · Telefax (06103) 753-295

Head Office and Main Plant Bühl:
LuK GmbH & Co
Industriestr. 3 · POB 1360 · West Germany
D-7580 Bühl/Baden · Tel. (07223) 285-0
Telex 78764 · Telefax (07223) 26950

Eastern Temptations For Western Markets

Eastern Bloc Cars Are Becoming More Sophisticated

With North America and Western Europe representing the two main centres of worldwide car demand, it comes as no surprise that a growing number of car manufacturers from other regions are actively assessing opportunities for entering or expanding their presence in these markets. For many years certain Western countries have been happy hunting grounds for producers from elsewhere, and particularly for Japanese and Eastern Bloc companies. Typically they offered products at low prices, sometimes with many "optional" features as standard equipment. The success of Japanese car producers in export markets was heavily dependent in the early days on offering good value for money to motorists on a limited budget. The same goes for the East Europeans who have provided cars with few frills and a low technical content but at highly competitive prices.

In addition, car industries are becoming established in an increasing number of Far Eastern countries. In order to justify the investment involved, these industries need to export a sizeable proportion of output and, again, rich Western markets provide the obvious target. The success of South Korea in recent years is a classic example of how a motor industry can develop on the back of an export drive and suggests that the country has the makings of another Japan. Other countries in the Far East have similar ambitions – for example, Malaysia, which has developed a car industry with the assistance of Mitsubishi, is beginning to export cars to the USA and Europe.

Japan Is Moving Upmarket

Meanwhile, Japan itself has undergone a major transformation and is no longer regarded as a source of cheap "entry level" cars.

Available in 1990, from Nissan, the Infiniti M30 convertible with 3 litre V6 engine and a host of luxury features.

This is all changing, however. The East European countries are no longer prepared to settle for second best and are shopping around for partners rather than remain dependent on antiquated technology. Their motor industries are undergoing substantial modernisation programmes which mean that the technological gap between a car from the USSR or Poland and one from, for example, France or Italy will not be so great in the future. In this process various Western and Japanese companies are lending a hand – with names such as Bertone, Fiat, Ford and Porsche to the fore.

Its car producers have established a reputation for technical inventiveness and excellence – as seen in their application of four wheel steering and multi-valve engines. Moreover, they have entered niche markets with single-minded determination – as their competitors in the sporting coupe market would agree. More recently it has become clear that the Japanese producers intend to tackle the market for purpose-built, 2-seater sports cars of the type that British manufacturers produced for the world in the 1960s and 1970s. Now their attention is being directed to the lucrative and fast expanding luxury car market. Already Honda has made a strong impact with its Acura division and Nissan (with Infiniti) and Toyota (with Lexus) have set up all-new marques to take on the likes of BMW, Jaguar and Mercedes-Benz.

What does this mean to the car buyer and how will choice be widened? The answer to these and related questions is illustrated by some of the current projects taking shape among the East European and Far Eastern car manufacturers.

Big Expansion Planned For Russian Car Output

Developments in the USSR point to a substantial expansion in car production – from the current annual rate of 1m or so to 2.3m in 1992 – with growing involvement on the part of European, American and Japanese companies. For example, discussions have taken place with Ford concerning the possibility of the forthcoming Scorpio notchback replacing the Volga sedan which is currently produced at the GAZ plant in Gorky. It is probable that built-up cars would be exported to the USSR initially, and Ford would help in re-equipping the Russian plant to make Scorpios. This model is intended for the domestic Russian market, but a series of new models looks set to boost the country's competitive position in world markets. Lada's hatchback Samara, with front wheel drive, serves notice on other manufacturers of the new approach. Over 100,000 Samaras were exported to Western Europe in its first year of production and Canada has become a promising outlet. For this model assistance was received from Porsche. A saloon version of the Samara is scheduled for 1990. A new Riva is expected to arrive in Europe in 1992 featuring, among other things, better aerodynamics. With the new spirit of cooperation that appears to be developing between the world's two superpowers, Lada believes that the US will provide a potentially important export market.

Moskvich is another Russian company which is targeting to increase its exports. Its latest 2141 model has been designed in cooperation with Renault. Again, the US market has been identified as a promising area for the export version. The 2141 has front wheel drive and a five speed gearbox.

There are indications that a major new manufacturing facility for minicars is being planned, with suggestions that Japanese companies – Mitsubishi and Suzuki – are potential partners. Fiat is also involved in proposals to establish new car production facilities in the country.

Poland's Car Industry Is Modernising With Fiat's Help

Fiat has also been closely associated with the development of the Polish motor industry. The new front wheel drive Fiat Topolino is expected to be presented at the end of 1989, with production due to commence two years later in Poland. It is understood that there will be two engine options – one a two cylinder and the other a four cylinder – and the body is likely to bear a close resemblance to the Lancia Y10 with a steeply sloping bonnet. The car features all round independent suspension with disc brakes at the front and drums at the rear. A high level of exports to the West will be essential to pay for the project's investment. FSO has a new hatchback under development. This is interesting insofar as it is possible that the model will be powered by a range of engines from Fiat's Tipo line-up.

A New Model From Skoda

In Czechoslovakia, Skoda is preparing a new car called the Favorit. This model's introduction has been delayed, reportedly due to parts shortages, but is scheduled to enter the market during 1989.

The Yugo 65 GVW – the world's cheapest carbriolet with a power hood.

The company is determined that the new model's impact will not be weakened by a poor reputation and hence special attention has been given to quality control. This has led to various components being returned for not meeting strict quality standards.

There is a version of the Favorit which conforms with US emission standards and Skoda is developing variants – notchback, coupe, estate car, delivery van and pickup – for the 1990s. A luxury version of the model is expected to be announced shortly after the standard model is released. Skoda has received a great deal of assistance from Western companies including Bertone, which helped with the styling, and Porsche. The company sells about 60,000 cars a year in the West, its main markets being Benelux, Scandinavia and the UK.

remain an important factor in the market place – but more on endowing its models with modern features, attractive styling and good performance.

Japan's Entry Into The Luxury Car Market

Meanwhile, the Japanese – faced with growing competition at the lower end of the market from these developing motor industries with their lower production costs – are moving more and more into the specialist and luxury car territory. As incomes rise in the developed nations the expectation is that demand for luxury cars will increase in parallel. The Japanese sense that the Europeans are pricing themselves out of the American market and believe therefore that they can take a sizable slice of the BMW/Mercedes customer base.

Coming in 1989, the 103 Model from Yugo, designed by Giugiaro

From the West's standpoint Yugoslavia has been the most visible Eastern Bloc car producer. This is because the country's motor industry, like South Korea's, has expanded through a commitment to a high level of exports. Zastava earmarked the USA and selected West European countries as priority markets for its Yugo model, and has enjoyed a good measure of success in penetrating Western markets, despite various recent setbacks which have resulted in falling sales. The company is maintaining momentum and has some tempting new models in the pipeline. A cabriolet (ragtop) version of the Yugo is coming soon in the form of the Yugo 65 GVC; this is noteworthy because it will be the smallest and cheapest cabriolet on the market with a powered hood. A completely new car from Zastava – the 103 model – is on schedule for a launch in the West later in 1989. The model has been designed by Giugiaro and is a four door family hatchback in the Escort mould. There will be a choice of 1300cc and 1600cc engines and options will apparently include a five speed gearbox and four wheel drive. In future Zastava intends that its appeal to car buyers will rest not so much on low prices – although this will obviously

Toyota has formed a new division called Lexus which will concentrate on exclusive, low volume cars with a high level of specification. Already Lexus models have been exhibited in the USA and sales are set to begin later in 1989 with prices in the $20,000–40,000 range. The entry level model is the ES250, a front wheel drive, four door sports luxury model with room for five people. The chassis is based on the Camry and the engine is a 24 valve V6 of 2.5 litres. There is only one trim level but this is very high. Standard equipment includes: power windows and locks, air conditioning, cruise control, driver's side airbag, power steering which is variably assisted, 15 inch alloy wheels, anti–lock disc brakes on all four wheels, maple console and luxury in–car entertainment including six speakers. As might be imagined, the list of options will be limited but includes a leather package and compact disc player. Transmission is through a five speed manual gearbox or four speed automatic. Details have also been released on the LS400 which is a bigger vehicle powered by a 4 litre 32 valve V8 engine delivering 250hp. Again there is a heavy emphasis on high technology together with refinement and quality.

The first model from Toyota's Lexus marque – the LS 400.

Nissan's contenders in the luxury car sector are to be marketed under the Infiniti marque. Two models have been announced – the M30 and Q45. The M30 will be available in two forms: a sports coupe due in the autumn of 1989 and a convertible which follows in 1990. The Q45 is a luxury four door sedan which enters the market at the same time as the M30 sports coupe. In 1991 a third model, a mid-size four door sedan, is scheduled to enter the market.

slip differential, multi-link front and rear suspension, cruise control and power assisted operation of windows, door locks, fuel lid opener, trunk release, outside mirrors and seat position. Particular attention has been paid to the interior with, for example, the instruments lit through electro-luminescence for good night time clarity and reduced eye fatigue. With regard to styling, Nissan's main objective was to secure satisfactory air management in order to facilitate high speed stability rather than seek optimum

The Infiniti Q45 – Nissan's contender in the BMW/Mercedes market.

As with Lexus, the emphasis is on performance, styling and comfort. The Q45 is equipped with an all-new 4.5-litre 32 valve V8 engine valves which produces 270hp. The drivetrain incorporates a computer controlled four speed overdrive automatic transmission system which is interactively linked with the engine. Among the standard features are anti-lock brakes, viscous limited

aerodynamic qualities. The M30, with a 3-litre V6 engine which delivers 165hp, and is similarly well equipped.

For the next few years therefore, car manufacturers in the West will come under increasing attack at both ends of the market. Bad news for them, but good news for the motorist. The range of choice – both in terms of models and options – will be wider than ever.

Just picture our global automotive resources.

If one picture is worth a thousand words, then United Technologies Automotive could write a book on automotive solutions.

As a worldwide supplier with over 50 years of experience, we know that it takes an innovative systems approach to put our customers on the inside track.

Take our headliner, for example. We designed and developed a one-piece modular unit that makes installation a literal snap.

And our multiplex electrical systems help reduce wire harness bulk by as much as 75 percent.

In fact, with design and manufacturing capabilities around the world, we produce over 422 different product lines... from motors, switches and hose assemblies to interior trim.

Of course, there's more to United Technologies Automotive than meets the eye. Like the quality we build into every component. Or the engineering and manufacturing expertise we share with our customers.

There's one thing you will see, though. That's a dedicated effort to provide you with the best in automotive technology. For more information write: United Technologies Automotive, 5200 Auto Club Drive, Dearborn, Michigan 48126. Or call (313) 593-9600.

Solutions For The Road Ahead

See Us At SAE Booth 903

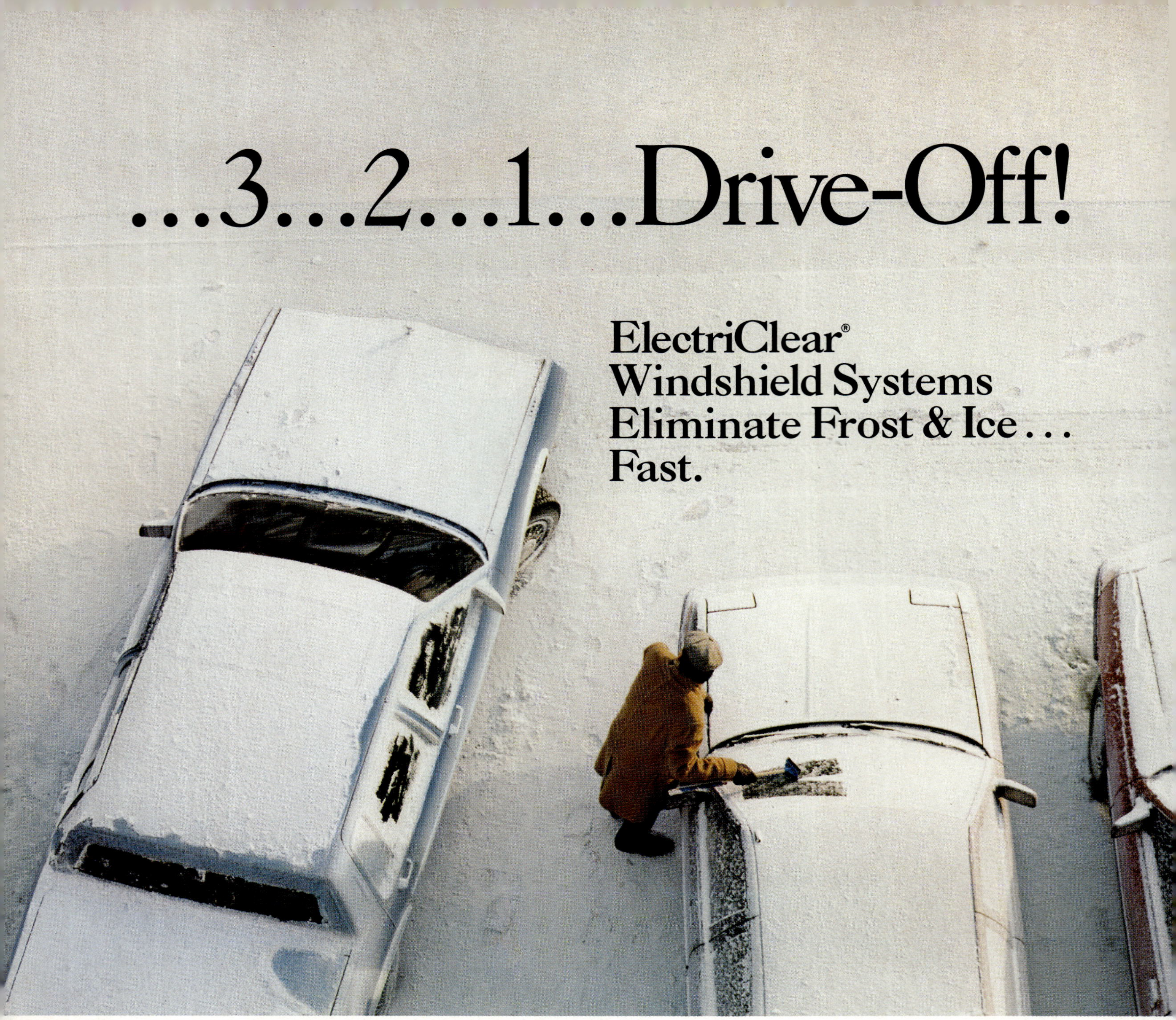

...3....2....1...Drive-Off!

ElectriClear® Windshield Systems Eliminate Frost & Ice... Fast.

Developed jointly by LOF and Delco Remy, the new ElectriClear® Heated Windshield Systems use some of the world's most advanced electronic technology to clear frosty winter windshields three to five times faster than conventional defrost systems. And unlike others, ElectriClear Windshield Systems look just like conventional tinted glass, with no distracting metallic sheen, color, or wire grid to impair vision.

ElectriClear Heated Windshield Systems are designed and engineered to meet specific needs and backed by the uncompromising quality and innovation of LOF and Delco Remy, world-class automotive suppliers. Find out more by calling your LOF or Delco Remy representative.

ElectriClear Heated Windshield Systems. The right choice becomes clear...very, very quickly.

Copyright 1988 Libbey-Owens-Ford/Delco Remy

ElectriClear® Systems
Libbey-Owens-Ford
811 Madison Avenue
P.O. Box 799
Toledo, Ohio 43695

Concept–cars 1988

Forty unique models from 10 countries

Plymouth Slingshot

This car's unusual shape may well remind you of the youthful instrument which its name implies.
The pavilion–part can be lifted up in one piece for entry and exit, and the tail–part was developed as a power–driven modulus.

It conceals a 2.2 litre 16–valve turbo engine with 225hp capacity. A number of Design–College students helped to create the shape, and the Slingshot – with its carbon–fibre chassis, adjustable single wheel suspension and flexible fenders – is meant to embody an economical means of transport for the future.

As in 1987, 1988 has seen around forty concept–cars or style–studies officially introduced to the car world. They originated in no less than ten countries, and this time Italy, with a dozen creations, lay marginally ahead of the USA with its eleven.

While Japan had dominated 1987 with 22 models, the Far Eastern car manufacturers had only one vehicle to their credit in the past year, and that originated in the USA. For the very first time, however, Russia and Korea were represented (see table).

It is understandable that most of the concept cars – which, after all, represent a manufacturers innovative and technological abilities – are always shown at domestic motor shows. In this way the usual two year rotation of most of the international motor shows had its effect. While in 1987 the IAA Frankfurt and Tokyo had their turn, last year it was Turin, Paris and Birmingham. In particular Turin, home of the best known independent car design studios, yielded a rich harvest. Ital-Design, as two years ago, once again proposed three models.

In the USA it became evident that General Motors was trying to attract corporate attention through concept cars. However, when introduced at the important American motor shows at the beginning of 1988, they were still somewhat "unfinished symphonies". But they nevertheless served both as good publicity as well as an opportunity to gauge public reaction. Such models are normally developed in far greater numbers behind closed doors for purely internal study purposes.

Apart from the need to demonstrate the future stylistic and technical possibilities, several of these prototypes are also used as test models. This was, for example, clearly emphasised at the presentation of the Renault Megane, which has been crammed with a multitude of technological ideas for the future. Certain of these vehicles also serve to test new construction materials, such as the Lancia ECV 2, which has been formulated as Rallye–Bolide, or the Vectra by General Electric Plastics. Racing ambitions are pursued not only by Lancia, but by other makes too: while the latest C–Form–Colani is meant to become a record car, the Peugeot Oxia is already directed towards a possible future group C car.

Ford Bronco DM-1

This is a cross country car, which was designed by a team of students from the Art Design Centre in Pasadena (California). It is meant to seat 5 people comfortably in its spacious, yet functional interior.
The steel-reinforced synthetic carriage has a heavily glass-enclosed (vitrified) tail; the tail hatch swivels/tilts into the roof when opened.

The Sbarro Robur, however, was designed as a customer car and the Italo-Swiss company has created other models in earlier forms which can definitely be described as design studies. Last year there was a particularly large number of future studies in the shape of four wheel drive leisure cars.

Some studies, such as the Lagonda Rapide by Zagato or the DD-Coupe by Tom Tjaarda, were merely design cars, while numerous others could be wheeled around but not yet driven.

There were, however, also those models which were already driveable, and one example was the Peugeot Oxia, which had been introduced in the company-owned test grounds in the French Jura.

Further examples are the Ital-designed Aztec, the Michelotti Pura and the Bertone Genesis, which were test driven by 'Automobil Revue'.

These models awakened the as yet unfulfilled hope for speedy mass production.

Model	Style	1st Shown
Chevrolet Corv. Indy 2	Coupe	(1987)
Ford SVO Mustang	Coupe	(1987)
Ford Bronco DM-1	4x4	Los Angeles
Mitsubishi X2S	Cabriolet	Los Angeles
Plymouth Slingshot	Coupe	Los Angeles
Dodge Intrepid	Coupe	Detroit
Buick Lucerne	Coupe	New York
Cadillac Voyage	Saloon/Sedan	New York
Chevrolet Venture	Saloon/Sedan	New York
GMC Centaur	Pick-up	New York
Pontiac Banshee	Coupe	New York
Lincoln Machete	Coupe	Chicago
Ghia Saguaro	4x4	Geneva
Nami Ohta Lada	Estate/Sation Wagon	Geneva
Sbarro Robur	Coupe	Geneva
Zagato Lagonda Rapide	Coupe	Geneva
Baur TC 3	Coupe	Stuttgart
FHS Pforzheim Xenon	Coupe	Pforzheim
Kia KMX-90	Saloon/Sedan	Seoul
Bertone Genesis	Estate/Station Wagon	Turin
IAD Royale	Saloon/Sedan	Turin
IAD Hunter	4x4	Turin
Ilca-Maggiora AC	4x4	Turin
Ital-Design Aztec	Cabriolet	Turin
Ital-Design Aspid	Coupe	Turin
Ital-Design Asgard	Estate/Station Wagon	Turin
Lancia ECV 2	Competition	Turin
Martin/Savio Freely	4x4	Turin
Michelotti Pura	Cabriolet	Turin
Pininfarina Hit	Coupe	Turin
Tjaarda/Dimensione/PPG	Coupe	Turin
GE Plastics Vector	Saloon/Sedan	Geneva
Colani C-Form	Competition	Berne
Citroen Activa	Saloon/Sedan	Paris
ENSCI Pix Band	Saloon/Sedan	Paris
Heuliez AX Evasion	Estate/Station Wagon	Paris
Peugeot Oxia	Competition	Paris
Renault Megane	Saloon/Sedan	Paris
Vecco Astro 2	Coupe	Paris
Jaguar XJ 220	Coupe	Birmingham

Michelotti Pura

This prototype has already been tested and is seriously intended to go into production. It is a highly original sportscar with a dome roof made of plexi glass, which slides backwards on rollers for entry and exit and to drive with the roof open.
It is powered by an Alfa Romeo 1.8 litre turbocharged engine, mounted centrally. The PURA is the very first car wholly conceived by Michelotti.

Ital–Design Aztex

The Spider was realised at the same as the ultra low Coupe Aspid and the "Space Wagon" Asgard, but in contrast to these, it is fully equipped. It is based on the five cylinder from the Audi 200 Turbo Quattro, with the power increased to 250 horsepower, together with its permanent four wheel drive. Entry and exit via sideways lifting of the cockpit tops.
Futuristic dashboard layout and code push buttons at the sides are some further key features applicable to this open central engine sports car prototype.

Pininfarina Hit

This Coupe is a model which sports car enthusiasts might wish for as the successor to the Lancia Fulvia Coupe, Beta Coupe and HPE: a comfortable four seater of individual style. "Hit" stands for High Italian Technology; while the car structure was manufactured from the most modern sandwich construction method, with Nomex, carbon fibre and other synthetic materials, the whole of the drive train, with unchanged wheelbase, is that of the Lancia Delta Integrale.

VECTOR: THE SHAPE OF THINGS TO COME.

There's no time like the present for looking to the future – and the way ahead for the automotive industry can now be seen in the shape of the GE Vector: *the* prototype plastic car.

GE Plastics and the motor industry have the same goal of the highest possible manufacturing, quality and design standards for tomorrow's car and plastic is the material setting these standards.

Large car body areas are already being clad in plastic, but these hybrids are only the beginning. Thermoplastic bumpers are a known fact. Mass production front fenders are on their way. Selective production of plastic tailgates has begun.

To the consumer, the plastic advantage is obvious. It means body panels that not only refuse to rust, but spring back out after a nasty prang.

Now, industry accountants are looking at their sums and coming to a similar conclusion.

For example, the production of a steel fender requires a set of tools – sometimes as many as eight per side – costing as much as £2m for full production. A single injection mould tool for plastic parts costs a tenth of that and is capable of producing 120,000 components a year; that's 600 cars a day.

Through collaboration with the motor industry, GE have produced the first running prototype plastic car to provide a development platform to address, resolve and dispense with the kind of problems standing in the way of a showroom-ready all plastic car.

In design terms, the Vector is not some conceptual flight of fancy. It is a standard, four-seater, small to medium sized saloon – everything about it aimed at a 600 per day production vehicle.

When it was launched at the SITEV automotive exhibition in Geneva in May, the Vector sported a variety of thermo-plastic body panels and components.

Over the next two years, the design will be expanded to include all possible plastic applications leading to the all plastic car of the future. That means side doors, bonnet, roof, major interior parts such as dashboard carrier, seating, door and roof liners and ultimately, a composite frame construction.

In the meantime, this first Vector prototype demonstrates plastics and plastic composites for rear quarter panels, the tailgate, and front fenders as well as the under-bonnet valve cover and oil sump components.

Technically speaking, we are talking about a rear quarter panel injection moulded in NORYL GTX 910. It provides a Class A surface finish straight from the mould and its high temperature capability means it can be painted on line with adjoining steel components.

Panel fixing was the first obstacle here. The panel had to be attached in such a way to allow it to expand and return to its original and set position during the paint cycle. Primary fixings allowing the B pillar to move backwards and a simple sliding clip enable the panel to stay in place during the paint cycle, after which secondary fixings can be attached.

The tailgate – one of the most complicated engineering enclosures with electrics, mechanics and glass to contend with – is a two shell construction.

It comprises of an injection moulded NORYL GTX outer skin for a perfect finish, bonded to a compression moulded AZDEL TPS inner shell for component toughness.

The Vector fender was put through the most rigorous of thermal expansion tests – complete temperature cycles to establish component reactions under various conditions faced by a plastic part attached to a steel carrier.

Under the bonnet, Vector's engine valve cover, unlike its steel counterpart, has a built in breather pipe – so no time consuming separate welding operations here.

With the Vector project, every component presents a challenge, and every new challenge met is a step closer to the all plastic dream – with the reduced assembly operations and cost savings that come with it.

For more information on the GE Vector contact:
GE Plastics Automotive Centre, PO Box 117, 4600 AC Bergen op Zoom, The Netherlands.
Tel: (31) 1640 56560.

Chevrolet Venture

Described as an "aerodynamic sports sedan for 4 people", this family limousine of the future has a remarkably elegant shape.
The glass-sections of the pavilion can be lifted off, so that the illusion of a cabriolet can be achieved. As with other glass-enclosed constructions, a liquid crystal film darkens the visibility surfaces during direct sunlight, for the purpose of heat protection.
It is powered by a 3.1 litre V6 engine.

Pontiac Banshee

It could indeed suggest the design of a future Pontiac Firebird. The 2 + 2 seater Coupe is in fact designed in an impressively sporty shape. A great deal of effort has been invested in its futuristic interior and control design, which naturally exhibit an impressive amount of electronics.
At the GM–Exhibition at the Waldorf Astoria Hotel in New York, a whole range of future studies was shown at the beginning of 1988.

Ghia Saguaro

This is a particularly conspicuously shaped vehicle which combines a somewhat "long–legged" cross–country suitability with precision aerodynamics; the drag co–efficient is quoted as 0.29, which is excellent for this type of vehicle: this concept vehicle from Ford's design centre in Turin an all–wheel drive Limosine, in which there is sufficient room for five adults and two children. The back seats can be folded down as in a Station Wagon.

Nami Ohta Lada

This Russian concept-car, which had arrived at the last minute before the opening of the Geneva Motor Show, created a small sensation. This car is a kind of large scale station wagon, with five to seven folding seats; it was developed in collaboration with the Scientific Research Institute Nami in Moscow and the design centre in Leningrad. It is based on the front wheel drive Lada Samara.

Baur TC 3

This is a 2 + 2 coupe which was developed at the automobile works in Baur, Stuttgart in collaboration with the small scale manufacturers 'Isdera', as early as 1987, but which was not made public until Spring 1988. It is based on a tube frame structure, and uses the BMW 325i transmission.
Were it not for the existence of the BMW Z1, the TC 3 might have been produced in small scale series production. As it is, however, it will have to remain an attractive unique ,model.

Pforzheim Xenon

This is the result of a study conceived and realised by both students and professors at the College for Design in Pforzheim, and may well be produced in the near future. The body consists of reinforced glass fibre and is fully equipped, it has a drag co-efficient of 0.28.
The chassis was developed in collaboration with the Technical College, Esslingen, and the project was also supported by German supply companies.

Kia KMX–90

The South Korean company Kia, who also collaborate with Mazda and Ford, created a surprise in 1988 with its futurisitc limousine called KMX–90 which, apart from its futuristic shape also offers folding doors. The front wheel shrouds pivot when turning into curves.
It is powered by a relatively modest 1.2 litre engine, and a certain number of functions are carried out by computer controls.

Bertone Genesis

This futuristic vehicle is perhaps best described as a sports car with the capacity of a large Station Wagon. The luxuriously equipped interior incorporates 5 comfortable seats,
It is powered by a front mounted engine, with rear wheel drive, a feature belied by its external appearance. The model is based on a Lamborghini Espada V12, with a new chassis.

IAD Royale

An absolutely realistic and non–futuristic luxury limousine, both practical and elegant, and developed by the distinguished England design company IAD. This model could in fact be a Jaguar or Bentley limousine of the future, but it is based on the Subaru XT 6 Alcyone, which was extended by 80cm, and is powered by the six cylinder version of the XT Coupe with permanent four wheel drive transmission. There are also original and novel design features all around the driver's seat.

Colani forme C

The latest realisation of the C-Form patented for Colani in 1967, with negatively inverted airfoil, a truly spectacular model indeed.
This central engine coupe with its individual slotted wing-front is intended to be used during the record-trials in North America this year.
Its Wenko engine, which also originated in Switzerland, is a 32 valve V8 engine whose block comes from the Chevrolet Corvette.

Citroen Activa

At the Paris Motor Show, Citroen surprised the public with a high-tech saloon/sedan, which up until now had only been given its "Premiere" at the Tokyo Motor Show (1987) by the Japanese manufacturers.
Apart from its individual shape, the Activa also boasts permanent four-wheel drive and four-wheel steering. This works fully electronically for all four wheels and without mechanical connection.
This is carried out by computer controlled high pressure hydraulics which also control the hydro-pneumatic suspension as well as various other functions. The Activa has a high efficiency V-6 engine and its interior is extremely luxurious and elaborate.

Heuliez Ax Evasion

The French production and design company Heuliez (who also manufactures the Citroen BX Break), also emerged in 1988 with some studies.
The 'Evasion' is a seven-seater small station wagon with a large area, which has 2-doors on its right side, one on its left, and a hatch-back. This construction was based on the extended base of a Citroen AX.

Peugeot OXIA

This is a car of the same calibre as the Porsche 959 or the Ferrari F40, whose mobility was proven even before the opening of the Paris Motor Show, at the Peugeot high speed oval/track. As with the Citroen Activa, a 24 valve high efficiency version of the PRV-V6 is used for power.
Mounted centrally, the engine is located on the right hand side, and permanently powers all four wheels. Four wheel steering has not been forgotten either. The cockpit, with its analogous - and digital readings, has been kept in rather a traditional sporty style.

Renault Megane

This luxury saloon/sedan was built to enable the long-term testing of its individual system. It has a PRV 3 litre V6 turbo engine.
Its individual characteristics number permanent four wheel drive, electronic four wheel steering, sliding doors at the front and back, a rear window which can be slid backwards by 35cm (change from graduated to inclined rear window with increased interior space), a trunk in the form of a drawer, futuristic communication systems and further electronic specialities.

Jaguar XJ 220

At its presentation at the British International Motor Show in Birmingham during October 1988, it was already reported that this "supercar" could "possibly" one day be manufactured in small scale series by Jaguar Sports Ltd and thus might act as a counterpart to the Ferrari F 40 and the Porsche 959.
Its central engine is of course a V-12, which has also helped to win the World Cup with the XJR-racing coupes; in this case, however, in connection with FF-four wheel drive.
Four wheel steering is envisaged but has not yet been fitted.

Road Tests 1988

Porsche 959

Cars Are Becoming More Friendly With The Environment

1988 saw the weekly Swiss magazine Automobil Revue carry out testing on cars which were for the most part "environment-friendly". A total of 60 models were tested, of which a mere two failed to satisfy the US–83 Exhaust Emission Regulations which have been applicable in Switzerland since October 1987; these were at one extreme the small, economy orientated test car Vesta II from Renault, of which only a few were produced, and at the other extreme the Porsche 959 which has a top speed in excess of 186mph/300kmh. All of the other 58 cars were equipped with a three-way catalyst and lambda probe, thereby ensuring a well regulated supply of lead-free fuel to the engine as well as an optimum clean-up of emissions by means of the catalytic converter installed in the exhaust system.

The most efficient engine control is achieved through multi-point injection; the effectiveness of this method has been considerably enhanced by the development and application of advanced electronics. Single/central point injection systems, which are typically used in smaller capacity engines, show certain irregularities during the warming up phase, but are nevertheless better than electronically controlled carburettor engines. On balance, though, it would appear that the engineers responsible for the research and development efforts have obtained satisfactory solutions in terms of fuel injection and exhaust emissions.

Big Performance from Small Cars

Of course, there is nothing new in the knowledge that the application of electronics with fuel injection works extremely well, but the widespread belief that cars with catalytic converters use more fuel than those without them is less easy to disprove. However, it is quite clear that the use of electronic systems to perform the threefold task of preparing the air/fuel mixture, providing optimum ignition timing and analysing exhaust emissions leads to some encouraging results when assessing a car's performance and fuel consumption.

The light-weight Citroen AX GT, for example, showed remarkably good performance. Its acceleration of 0–62mph/100kmh in 10 seconds compared with the original VW Golf GTi 1.6, yet its fuel consumption during the test of only 7.1L/100km (39.8mpg) [33.1US mpg] made it exceptionally economical. The Renault 5 GTE with a 1.7 litre engine performed better still, but the car's larger engine and heavier weight had the effect of increasing fuel consumption by about 1 litre per 100km.

The noticeably less rapid Fiat Uno 45 i.e. was slightly more economical than the AX, while the Lancia Y10 1.3 i.e. proved to be a quick and nimble car with good all-round qualities.

Praise for the New Volvos

There are good reports on the new Volvo series. The 480 Coupe is attractively styled and has advanced technical features, while the 440 saloon offers a pleasant interior design coupled with comfort and convenience. It is possible to achieve a good driving performance with the 1.7 litre (94hp) engine, and the 118hp turbo engine has excellent acceleration characteristics.

The Seat Ibiza provided good driving performance in both 1.5i and (especially) turbocharged form. The Fiat Tipo impressed with different qualities, notably the above average interior space and compact exterior dimensions. Overall the aerodynamically advanced Tipo offered a high level of comfort and benefited from the quietness of its 1400cc engine – although the same is not true of the 1600cc engine. With regard to both driving performance and fuel consumption, however, the Tipo did not earn the highest marks.

Saab 9000 CD

Toyota Camry V6

The same also applies to the 16–valve Toyota Carina II 2.0i, but this Japanese mid–range car impressed with its consistently good running qualities. Its price increase to the level of European competitors did not pass unnoticed.

Competition in the Middle Range

Cars with a "Made in Germany" badge are invariably positioned at the upper end of the price spectrum. Volkswagen's new Passat with transverse engine is a case in point – not only have its dimensions grown, but also its price. But experience shows that motorists are prepared to pay for good build quality and pleasant driving characteristics, and the Passat combines these with fuel economy and versatility.

Talking of versatility, hatchback cars and station wagons score a definite advantage over models such as the Chevrolet Corsica or the Toyota Camry, yet these of course have their own appeal. The Toyota's six cylinder engine is particularly pleasing.

The V6 engines as fitted to the Renault 25, Honda Legend and Rover 827 have their two banks of cylinders inclined at 90 degrees rather than the more usual 60 degrees, but they cannot match the smoothness of the Toyota engine. However, all three cars offer better driving performance and fuel economy. It is also noticeable that the 3 litre, six cylinder engine of the Opel Senator and the 3 litre V6 of the US–built Ford Taunus are not particularly smooth runners. But the Opel nevertheless manages to impress with its sheer quality, while the Taunus offers a lot of room and can cope with up to eight passengers. The same comments essentially apply to the Lancia Thema Station Wagon and the Saab 9000 CD Limousine; both provide a great deal of space for four to five passengers but are somewhat let down by having turbo engines of only four cylinders.

The sleek Honda Prelude and Mazda 626 coupes are also equipped with four cylinder engines which give a good account of themselves. Interestingly, both feature four wheel steering, but during the everyday use conditions which prevailed during the short tests carried out by Automobil Revue, this feature came across as being neither a positive nor a negative attribute.

Newcomers In The Large Car Class

Once again, there was the opportunity to test one of Europe's most luxurious models – Mercedes–Benz's S–Class Limousine. Among its outstanding characteristics were long distance comfort, detail to quality in every respect and excellent 4.2 litre V8 engine. The 7 Series BMW, tuned by Alpina and producing 250PS, also left a

Reliant Scimitar 1800 T.i.

Chrysler Voyager 3.0-V6

favourable and lasting impression. But this was equalled by the new BMW 535i which is more than 100kg lighter. Even though the new 5 Series is noticeably heavier than its predecessor, the application of advanced aerodynamic principles means that top speeds remain high and acceleration is up to the typically rapid BMW standard.

BMW is operating in a market sector which is growing increasingly competitive, a fact that was borne out by the cars that were tested during the year. The new Alfa 164 positively revelled in its 3 litre V6 engine; this power unit had already impressed the testers with its superb temperament and frugal fuel thirst in the Alfa 75. The Alfa 164 also impressed on a number of other counts: lots of room for passengers and luggage, an extremely well designed body by Pininfarina and a highly competitive price.

The Lancia Thema is based on the same chassis as the Alfa 164. With a 3 litre V8 Ferrari engine, the top model – the 8.32 – provides exhilarating motoring for the young and the "young at heart". As far as acceleration is concerned the Alfa and the Lancia are equally matched, but when making a judgment on the basis of top speed and fuel consumption the Alfa is the clear winner.

A Trend Towards Multi-Valved Engines

Trends in car design are currently being directed first and foremost towards better performance – unlike a few years ago when the emphasis was on fuel economy to the exclusion of almost everything else. The introduction of engines with four valves per cylinder represents a major step towards increasing performance and, at the same time, providing good fuel economy and low exhaust emissions due to optimum combustion characteristics.

A good example of what can be achieved is provided by the Daihatsu GTi whose 3–cylinder engine of 1 litre capacity not only uses four valves per cylinder but also a turbocharger with the result that the power output is in excess of 100PS. This gives the car a 0–62mph/100kmh time of 8.6 seconds, a top speed of 117mph/189kmh and a fuel consumption of 9L/100km (31.4mpg) [26.1US mpg] – very commendable for a four seater compact car.

The Opel Kadett GSi 16V likewise impressed, with a 0–62mph/100kmh time of 7.9 seconds, and a top speed of 136mph/219kmh.

From France the Citroen BX GTi16V and Peugeot 405 MI16 are both powered by the 16 valve 1.9 litre engine which develops about 148hp. The BX showed slightly faster acceleration, but the Peugeot had a higher top speed (by a marginal 1mph/2kmh) and was more economical on fuel (by 0.2L/100km).

Ford Bronco II

Jaguar XJ-S V12 Convertible

Growing Popularity of Four Wheel Drive

Thanks to their better traction abilities, four wheel drive cars have become very popular in Alpine countries.

Apart from passenger cars such as the Subaru and Volkswagen Golf/Jetta models, the specifications of minibuses – like the Mitsubishi L300 and Isuzu Wagon – are increasingly incorporating four wheel drive. In similar manner to light cross country cars – of the type exemplified by the Chevrolet Blazer and Ford Bronco II – these models always combine a relatively heavy weight with a large frontal area, which inevitably has an adverse impact on both driving performance and fuel economy. This new minibus category includes the Renault Espace, which was tested by Automobil Revue in Quadra form with four wheel drive, as well as the front wheel drive Chrysler Voyager. Where space and the ability to carry an above average number of passengers are necessary qualities, Coleman Milne of England has carried out a competent job of elongating a Ford Granada/Scorpio to provide comfortable seating accommodation for up to eight people.

Fun And Enjoyment With A Cabriolet/Convertible

Driving, though, is also about having fun and enjoyment. Testing the Reliant Scimitar brought back to life the much loved roadsters for which British manufacturers were once deservedly famous. The experience also prompted the thought that this is a sector of the market that the international motor industry should pay more attention to.

With regard to enjoyable driving in the open air, which has special appeal whether carried out in town or country, a convertible/cabriolet (soft–top) is a first choice. There are now a variety of possibilities available ranging from a mass production model such as the Ford Escort to a purpose built sports car in the Porsche 911 mould and a luxury orientated grand tourer such as the Jaguar XJ-S V12.

Big Names in the Fast Lanes

In the fast lanes of today's automotive technology, four names are out in front—the four Allied-Signal brand names.

Do you need brake systems or components? Ask for Bendix, the most respected name in brakes and friction materials.

For air bag or seat belt restraint systems, Bendix is the total system supplier.

If you need advanced turbochargers ask for Garrett, the world's leading manufacturer of charge-air systems for diesel and gasoline engines.

Spark plugs? Autolite spark plugs and oxygen sensors are built for exceptional durability and reliability.

Filters? Fram is the best-known and most preferred name in air, oil, fuel and transmission filters for cars, trucks and other vehicles.

Bendix, Fram, Autolite and Garrett are names that have earned a leadership position.

With advanced design, engineering and manufacturing capabilities, Allied-Signal is positioned around the globe to give you complete automotive technology support.

Stay in the fast lanes—with Allied-Signal.

Allied-Signal Automotive
World Headquarters
P.O. Box 5029
Southfield, Michigan 48086

ZF. The Driving Force.

Today's cars, commercial vehicles, agricultural and construction machines are now much more comfortable to drive, safer to operate and more economical to run.

This quiet revolution is the result of many improvements. Not least the continual design advantages incorporated in ZF transmissions, axles and steering systems.

The continual success of the ZF Group stems from the innovative expertise and comprehensive know-how of its workforce, which now numbers 32,000 employees. And with an annual turnover exceeding DM 5 billion, it is not surprising that ZF is the world's leading transmission and steering system specialist.

To find out more about ZF products just quote "ZF. The Driving Force." and write to:

Zahnradfabrik Friedrichshafen AG, Postfach 25 20, D-7990 Friedrichshafen 1.

Transmissions, Axles, Steering Systems

Whether in twos,

four of them,

five of them,

six of them,

eight of them,

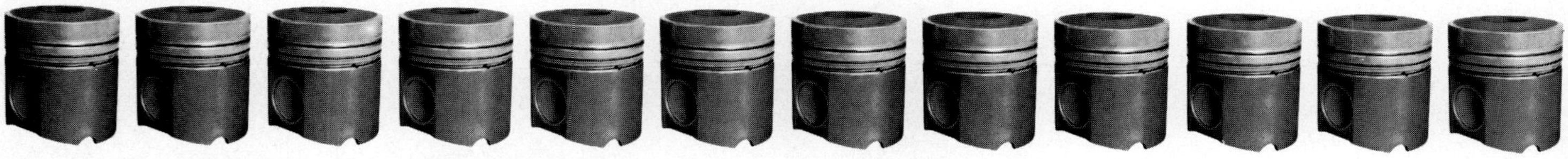

twelve of them

or alone –
MAHLE pistons put engines in motion worldwide.

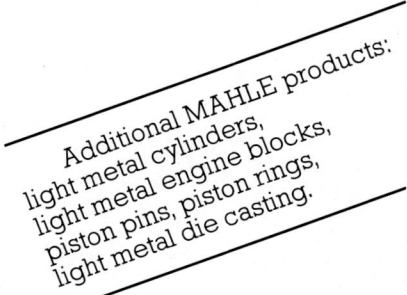

Additional MAHLE products: light metal cylinders, light metal engine blocks, piston pins, piston rings, light metal die casting.

MAHLE

MAHLE GMBH D–7000 Stuttgart 50 (Bad Cannstatt)

Next time you hit the brakes, what else will you hit?

When it's a matter of life or death, your brakes have to be able to transmit forces measured in tonnes, reliably and safely. To do so they need brake components that are designed, developed and manufactured as parts of a system, geared exactly towards the particular type of vehicle. Original ATE brake components meet these criteria. And they meet the highest quality standards of the international automotive industry.

<u>Original ATE brake pads are 100% asbestos free</u>, reliable environmentally safe, with an exemplary friction coefficient. And with General Certification, of course.

<u>Original ATE brake fluid</u> is noted for its extensive safety reserves. With ATE Super DOT 4, for example, the brake fluid only needs changing every two years.
<u>Original ATE brake discs</u> are precision-engineered for guaranteed safety to produce maximum efficiency in all other components in the braking system.

Alfred Teves GmbH · Guerickestrasse 7
D-6000 Frankfurt 90 · Tel. 0 69/76 03-1   **ITT TEVES**

Play it safe with  Brakes.

A Sport Governed by Numerous Rules

Formula 1 - World Champion Ayrton Senna in a McLaren 4/4 Honda

The period of transition from one racing season to the next seems to be a suitable moment to cast a swift glance at the categories or groups of cars. The rules and regulations applicable to motor sport are already complicated and extensive; they are constantly subject to change, however, because of the technical advances being made. It is known, though, that the car manufacturers would wish to achieve more stable and permanent rules and regulations in order to be able to establish a long term programme.

All over the world (apart from the USA), motor sport is characterised by a certain imbalance whereby the "Class of Kings", i.e. Formula 1, takes on too much importance in comparison with the other categories.

Sponsors of Formula 1 teams and meetings are prepared to invest vast sums because the races are broadcast by TV in numerous countries, enabling the Grand Prix races to be watched by several hundred million people. With regard to advertising, the sponsors thus count on maximum impact. Furthermore, the media report on Formula 1 in great detail, while reports on races for sport prototypes or Formula 3000 are kept rather short as a rule, or even omitted completely.

Formula 3000 - Roberto Moreno (Formula 3000 World Champion 1988) in a Reynard RD 88-Cosworth.

Many Rule Alterations

In the past few years the various commissions of the FIA (or FISA) have not always been noted for their vision, competence or logic: racing categories have been invented for which there was no call and, on the other hand, there have been sudden rule alterations in already existing categories.

Following the vaguely announced (and soon cancelled) Group S rally prototypes, another striking example of muddled thinking can be seen in the cancelled Silhouette Cars or Pro-Car Autos. After the creation of the Pro-Car-Group had become public, the manufacturers' interest was negligible, which resulted in the FIA, after a lot of hesitation, discreetly removing this category from the racing calendar.

The FIA's race alterations were also quite bizarre concerning the Group A cars, touring championship. Only a few weeks before the first qualifying races the teams were forced to pay a horrendously high deposit before being allowed to participate in the championships.

The world championship was accompanied by disharmony and was abolished again after its first meeting and in effect replaced by the traditional European championships which, in 1987, had been overshadowed by the world championships. But, with a view to 1989, the Touring Car European Championships, which had been in existence for a quarter of a century, were cancelled, and most of the teams were compelled to make do with national championships, resulting in the withdrawal of sponsors.

Apart from the national championships, the group A cars also take part in the ever popular rallys. Here, however, the four wheel drive models are most prominent, but they are in less demand in the circuit races.

The inconsistent and unpredictable line adopted by the FIA also became evident with regard to the sport prototypes in group C since the FIA was convinced that the silhouette cars have a most promising future. In the summer of 1988 the Sports Council finally felt compelled to admit its error: now the Pro-Car-Series was no longer talked of, and quite a turn-about took place. All of a sudden the category of the Sport-Prototypes was reinstated, now strongly supported by the men in Paris with a once unimaginable goodwill. Yet just two years before, the FIA intended to let Group C quite gradually slip back onto its deathbed. Various coincidences, which have proved to be quite fortuitous for motor sport, have now led to a much brighter looking future for the Group C of the Sport-prototypes, not least because the FIA has finally promised a permanence for rules and regulations of at least ten years.

FORMULA 1: *Stronger Than Ever*

The turbo–era in Formula 1 came to an end with the Grand Prix of Australia in November 1988. It had begun in July 1977 with the introduction of the turbocharged Renault V6 engine. However as from the 1989 season turbocharging is no longer allowed, and Formula 1 races have to be run exclusively with naturally aspirated engines of a maximum 3.5 litres cubic capacity. While a car's fuel per race, in the case of the 1.5-litre turbos had been limited to 150 litres, in order to stem the enormous deployment of power, the naturally aspirated engined cars have been allowed to consume unlimited fuel (of max 102 ROZ) since 1988. However, a designer is still interested in modest consumption (the 3.5-litre engines in 1988 used in excess of 30 litres more fuel than the 1.5-litre turbos) for example, 10 litres additional fuel on board amounts to as much as 7.5 kilos in added weight.

The fact that the pedals in the cockpit had to be mounted behind the front wheel since 1988, for reasons of safety, poses new problems for the chassis-designers with regard to weight distribution: a short engine and a short fuel tank offer more free space, and it is of paramount importance to locate the heavy parts of the vehicle as close to the centre of gravity as possible.

On paper a V12-engine achieves the highest power output, but it is also the longest assembly, and with regard to weight distribution it is the least advantageous.

As a rule a V8 engine produces less horsepower than a 12-cylinder but its advantage can be seen above all in its compactness which allows for an optimum weight distribution, which again is of advantage to the car's driving characteristics.

Several car manufacturers have decided on a compromise between the V8 and the V12 engine, and have built a V10 (Honda and Renault; Alfa Romeo's V10 is not intended for Formula 1), but the experts maintain that the second-grade vibrations which are to be expected, would be rather difficult to control.

In Formula 1 there are other important regulations: since 1972 the engines must not exceed 12-cylinders; since 1981 vehicles with more than four wheels are no longer permitted to race (in 1975, Tyrrell designed and introduced a Monoposto with six wheels), and since then four-wheel drive has also been forbidden; since 1988 vehicles with naturally aspirated engines have had to weigh a minimum of 500 kilos (last year's turbo-cars still had to weigh at least 540 kilos).

Last year most of the top teams still used turbo-engines to do battle but the new naturally aspirated engine era has not missed its impact and attraction with the large manufacturers. The variety of makes planning to take part is larger than ever: Ford, Cosworth, Judd, Renault, Honda, Yamaha, Subary-Motori Moderni, Ferrari, Lamborghini and Life have supplied naturally aspirated engines, and others are expected to follow suit. The high revving, short-stroke engines, which are equipped with an elaborate electronic engine-management system ought to reach a power output in the region of between 580 and 650 horsepower during this season; after tests, the Honda V10 has already been credited with an output of around 700 horsepower, which corresponds to the amazing capacity of 200 horsepower per litre.

FORMULA 3000: *Antichamber*

In 1985 Formula 3000 succeeded the erstwhile Formula 2 (2000cc). The cars have engines of a maximum 3000cc and have to weigh dry a minimum of 540 kilos. In order to slow down the deployment of efficiency - and with it also the costs - engine speeds are limited to 9000rpm by means of an engine speed-limiter, so that the 3-litre engines can thus achieve about 460 horsepower. Formula 3000 is regarded as the logical breeding ground for Formula 1, although the teams, have to operate within much more modest budgets. For a start it is much more difficult to find sponsors for this category. There are spectacular races between young and aspiring drivers, largely because these young lions want to make a name for themselves at all costs, in particular as there is the possibility that the best will move into Formula 1 during the next season.

All competitors line up with V8 engines which are manufactured by Cosworth, Judd or Mugen.

CART: Very Popular In The USA

In European racing circles it is often thought that the US CART-series (Championship Auto Racing Teams) of the Indy-racing cars does not correspond to the pinnacle of technology and driving ability which is evident in Formula 1 and that it furthermore provides some kind of opportunity for rejected Formula 1 drivers. However, it is not a simple matter to become a front runner in CART racing. This is clear from the experience of Porsche, which has been concentrating on this series since 1987 and, despite allocating a great deal of technological resources, has encountered many problems (chassis, aerodynamics and engine) which have had to be put right.

With few exceptions V8 turbo engines of 2.65 litre capacity are used for CART-races (boost pressure limit 45 inches Hg or 1.52 bar) whereby only a turbo engine is permissible for these four camshaft machines. Boost intercooling is not permitted, and the engines are fuelled with methyl alcohol (lower heat value coefficient) and thus lower engine power than with petrol; intercooling effect, higher consumption, as well as lower danger of fire risk. Also permitted are push rod engines which have a capacity limit of 3.4 litres (identical supercharge pressure limit).

More and more CART races are being transferred from the classic oval race tracks of the traditional kind to city race tracks, which obviously need to be repaired and made safe at great expense. But in this way the CART organisation manages to attract the public more easily to its races. After a long supremacy of the Cosworth DFX engine, which won the 500 mile Indianapolis race between 1978 and 1987 without a break, the most famous car race in the world was won in 1988 for the first time by the new Chevrolet V8. This car was produced in England by Ilmor under commission by Chevrolet, whereby the former Cosworth employee, Mario Illien, born in Bunden, was responsible for the engine construction. After Porsche, a second respected car manufacturer from Europe enters into the prestigious US series, i.e. Alfa Romeo. The debut by the Milanese 8-cylinder engine, which was also built into a March (MAILANDER) chassis, is planned for the 500 mile race at Indianapolis in 1989.

Long Lasting Formula 3

A perpetually successful class in the international Monoposto-hierarchy is represented by Formula 3, which has existed in its present day form since 1974.

Here the engines which are fitted to the cars have been derived from large scale production, and their size is a maximum 2000cc. The number of cylinders is limited to four. For many years the maximum output has been around 170–275PS; this is virtually no longer possible as the intake volume of air is limited by the 24mm diameter of the "narrow collar". The power units normally used are either from Alfa Romeo or VW, although recently the four cylinder Toyota engine has appeared on the scene. Because of the limited air intake the engine speeds are not particularly high, and mechanical wear is reduced.

The kerbweight of the relatively advanced new generation of Formula 3 cars has to be at least 455kg. The once popular Formula 3 European championship has not existed since 1985, and the supporting race at the Monaco Grand Prix represents the climax of Formula 3 racing. There is a Formula 3 European cup, which is contested by the best drivers of the various national championships, but this trophy has long since lost its importance. The most significant championships are the English and Italian.

Sports Prototypes

The two-seater Group C long distance races have been running since 1982 and are now officially called Sports Prototypes. Long-distance racing lost public interest in the mid-1970s, and did not recover after 1982 with the introduction of Group C. The superiority of Porsche threatened to dominate this type of racing. At the same time the technically interesting and advanced formula based on fuel consumption without engine size regulations did not go down well with the public. The competing drivers were forced to worry continually about fuel consumption and sometimes eased off with the right foot to avoid running out of fuel. The sports prototypes are only allowed 190 litres of fuel over a 360 kilometre course, the classic 1000 kilometres distance has to be driven with 510 litres and in a 24 hour race a C1 car can only contend with 2550 litres with a minimum weight of 850kg. In the small C2 category there is a maximum allowance of 130 litres for 360km, 365 litres for 1000km, and 1815 litres for a 24 hour race. On average, this means that a C1 car can only consume 51 litres per 100km. These regulations will be valid until the end of 1990, but from 1989 cars with 3.5 litre naturally aspirated engines will be allowed to compete under these conditions, and from 1991 only naturally aspirated engines will be permissible with a reduced minimum weight of 750kg.

Since the Jaguar and Clean Mercedes–Benz models have successfully been taking part in long-distance racing and Porsche no longer has a monopoly of winning in the field, interest in this category has increased again. Both Peugeot and Alfa Romeo intend to start competing with sports-prototypes in 1990, with the result that there will be an impressive variety of models in this sector. As from 1989, the classic 1000km racing distance is no longer featured and has been shortened to 400–500 kilometres in the hope that the races will become more suitable for television screening; the exception is the Le Mans 24–hour race.

Competitions with mass production cars are very popular. However, when they line up on the starting grid they are different from the cars found on the world's roads. There are two groups: Group A (official designation: mass production touring cars); and, in limited prepared form Group N (series mass production touring cars). In order for a model to become homologated in Group N, a minimum of 5,000 have to be produced and this principle also applies to Group A. Since the FIA banned Group B cars from rallys

Car Racing – Indianapolis – winner Rick Mears in a Penske PC 17– Chevrolet

Formula 3 – Enrico Bertaggia in a Dallara 388– Alfa Romeo, winner of the Grand Prix Monaco Formula 3 1988

in 1987 because they had gained far too much importance, the Group A exponents are fighting for total victory at the big rallys, while the Group N cars, being generally of a much lower capacity, fight for victory in their category. Following the bad experience with the dominance of the Group B cars (1982–86), the FIA intends to keep an eye on the record achievements of the Group A cars which take part in rallys, and a maximum of 300PS (horsepower) will be tolerated.

The FIA intends to introduce certain limits from 1990 onwards by equipping supercharged models with a flow control which has a limited 40mm diameter.

For models with naturally aspirated engines, a cubic capacity limited to 3 litres is envisaged. As far as models with more than 2 valves per cylinder are concerned, the cubic capacity is limited to only 2500cc. The Touring Car European Championships for Group A cars have been abolished by the FIA at the stroke of a pen,

Group C – Sports Prototype World Champion Jaguar with the XJR9

Group A – Rally World Champion Massimo Biasion in a Lancia Delta Integrale

using the excuse that national championships were to be promoted instead. Particular popularity is enjoyed by the National Touring Car Championships in France, England, Germany and Italy, whereby the rules and regulations differ in part from the international Group A norms.

New Generation Formula

Motor sport needs to develop new generation formulas in order to promote and encourage fresh young talent to develop. Several manufacturers have launched their own formula during the past two decades; a good example is Vau, who became popular in the mid–1960s both in Europe and also in the USA.

*Group N –
VW Golf 16 V*

*Formula Ford –
Van Diemen RF 88*

Ford, Renault, Fiat/Lancia and, more recently, Alfa Romeo and Opel/Vauxhall followed this example with their own Monoposto–Classes, which are based on the use of specially tuned–up production engines. A world–wide success was achieved by the Ford Formula with its 1.6 litre Monopostas (there is also a 2 litre class, which is not as widely used), in which numerous top champions have earned their first achievements.

Gags and Gadgets

When reviewing the technical progress of cars it is usual to think in terms of engines, transmissions, the chassis and so on – items which are subject to non-stop development and refinement. But the prevailing spirit of automotive technology is also reflected to a large extent in design trends and interior fittings. As in many other areas, the application of electronics has influenced the type of "accessories" that are incorporated into contemporary cars. It is worth taking a (rather light-hearted) look therefore at these items which are meant to add to the general comfort and convenience of the driver and his passengers.

Since the first car was produced more than 100 years ago, the type of equipment fitted as standard has expanded enormously. Items which today are regarded as standard equipment simply were not available not so long ago, at any price. It is true that luxury cars of the 1920s and 1930s were lavishly equipped even by present day standards, but the popular cars of the pre-war era – and, indeed, for quite a number of the immediate post-war years – were very spartan. In those days the important thing was to have a car and hence mobility, and never mind that the heating system (incidentally, still an extra in the 1950s) did not work, the ventilation could not be relied upon and the radio (where fitted) could be heard only with difficulty.

The move towards cars which were more than mere transport was led by the Americans during the 1950s and 1960s. For example, electrically operated roofs were widely used on cabriolets/convertibles (soft tops). In some cases the roof would close automatically as soon as rain was felt on the seatcovers. Electric motors became of great use, being used to power windows, seats, aerials and a lot more besides. Other items which were warmly received by customers included air-conditioning, cigarette lighters and tinted glass.

The concept high level equipment fitted as standard was then taken a step further by the Japanese who started to offer small to medium sized cars with many "extras". With a well thought out marketing strategy, the Japanese soon started to make inroads into the market share held by European manufacturers. Many features which were traditionally found only in the most expensive vehicles became a standard fitting in much cheaper Japanese cars. Although Japanese cars in the early days were far from being technically impressive, no-one could deny that their equipment was better than the average. Coupled with highly competitive prices it was a recipe for success. European manufacturers had no choice but to fall into line.

The result is that within a few years features such as heated rear windows, intermittent windscreen wipers, tinted windows and colour coordinated carpets have become an essential part of a car's basic specification. What might be termed "more exotic features" including electric widows, central locking and adjustable seat height are now fitted as a matter of course in mid-range cars. As if these are not enough, still more advanced features are being developed which no doubt will soon become indispensible to the ordinary motorist.

Even before there is any bodily contact with a car, elaborate installations carry out certain tasks. By means of infra-red remote control on the keyring, the doors are unlocked and, at the same time, the interior lighting comes on. The remote-control mechanism can be adjusted in such a way that the touch of a button can light up the car lamps which cuts out time consuming searches at night in large car parks. Then there is the door release mechanism which required the punching of a personal code – how much longer will it be before the first door lock will be marketed which will examine the car owner's fingerprints before releasing the locks?

Anyone who has ever had to fumble around in the dark until he found the door lock (perhaps even scratching the paintwork in the process) will appreciate those keys which are fashioned like miniature torches. Equally useful are illuminated locks or small strip lamps which light up as soon as the door latch is activated. And in some cars the ignition switch remains illuminated (for example by irridescent green circle) until the engine is running.

Reading lights are welcome – particularly where their lighting angle can be adjusted – as are interior lamps, which remain alight for a few seconds after leaving the car, thereby facilitating a check to be made of the inside.

Many years ago, in the so-called "dream-cars", revolving seats where a common feature. These offered themselves invitingly when the doors where open. In today's safety conscious age, car seats are, in general, firmly built in; there are, though, exceptions in the case of some large capacity limousines, where individual passenger seats can be made to face backwards.

When sitting in a car, the correct seating position becomes important. Electrically adjustable seats have been available for many years, and the "memory-button" for storage and recall of individual seating positions is also fitted to certain models.

Less common, however, is the pneumatic or electro-pneumatic lumbar supports, especially if it can be adjusted upwards. There are still further elaborate features for car seats: seat cushions which can be adjusted lengthwise, side bulges on cushions and armrests which can be adjusted for optimum support according to the individual needs of driver or passenger. Head rests are of course of no use on unoccupied seats and can be a nuisance in so far as they obstruct vision; therefore, one manufacturer has developed rear seat head rests, which can be removed at the touch of a button. There is even a system whereby the rear seat head rests automatically pop up when somebody sits down in the back of the car.

Revolving seats are nowadays exclusively found in luxury large capacity limousines. Many concept-cars thus prove how up-to-date they are. Here the Renault Megane, which was first introduced at the Paris Motor Show.

A real sports car must have well-contoured seats, which will assure sufficient side support when driving fas through road bends, and the seats should additionally be covered with slip resistant material, which is demonstrated by the Nissan 200 SX.

Still on the subject of comfort, under seat heating systems can be activated by way of a switch, while some are thermostatically controlled and automatically switched on and off.

In Illinois, an a could get rich helpin Or vic

Illinois is in the middle of a war zone. A no-holds-barred struggle for automobile supremacy.

And it's a perfectly lovely place for an auto parts manufacturer to be.

On one side, you've got Ford, GM and Chrysler.

On the other, the imports. Nissans are being made in Tennessee.

Mazdas in Michigan. Mitsubishi/Chrysler has a joint venture within our very borders.

All around us, hatchbacks and mini-vans are rolling from assembly lines mobilized for battle.

In total, over 85% of all cars built in America are now assembled within 500 miles of Illinois. Perhaps

*Comparative Analysis of Interstate Variation in Manufacturing Industry Business Costs. School of Public and Environmental Affairs. Indiana University. 1984.

uto parts maker
g Detroit beat Japan.
e versa.

 owhere else are so many customers o close at hand.

And proximity isn't our nly virtue.

In a study they wish we'd never uncovered,* the University of ndiana concluded that costs of manufacturing motor vehicles and equipment are the lowest in Illinois of all Great Lakes states (Ohio, Michigan, Wisconsin, Indiana).

For details, call Rich Funderburk at the Illinois Department of Commerce and Community Affairs (217-782-6861).

As the battle heats up, Illinois parts manufacturers won't have to take sides, just orders. **Illinois**

Illinois Department of Commerce and Community Affairs © 1988

TRW

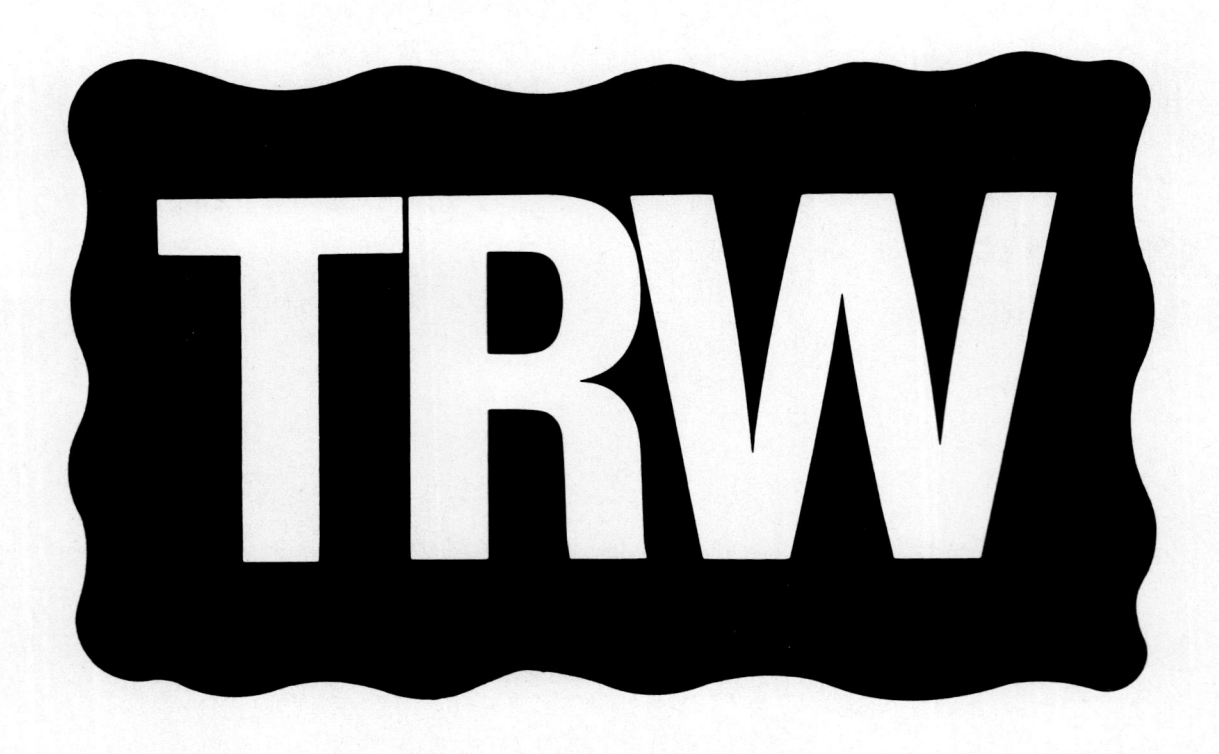

A leader in...

steering systems,

engine components,

occupant restraints,

electrical and electronic controls,

fasteners...

worldwide.

TRW

**TRW Automotive Sector
TRW Occupant Restraint
Systems**

© TRW Inc., 1988
TRW is the name and mark of TRW Inc.

To achieve the correct driving position, it is important to have a steering wheel which comes easily and comfortably to hand. Where it is possible to adjust the steering wheels position, movement is usually restricted to up and down. It is preferable, though, to have a combination with axial movement, which is already available via a small electronic motor. In the case of cars with only limited space for entry, there are "turn up" steering wheels, which afterwards slot back into their previous position.

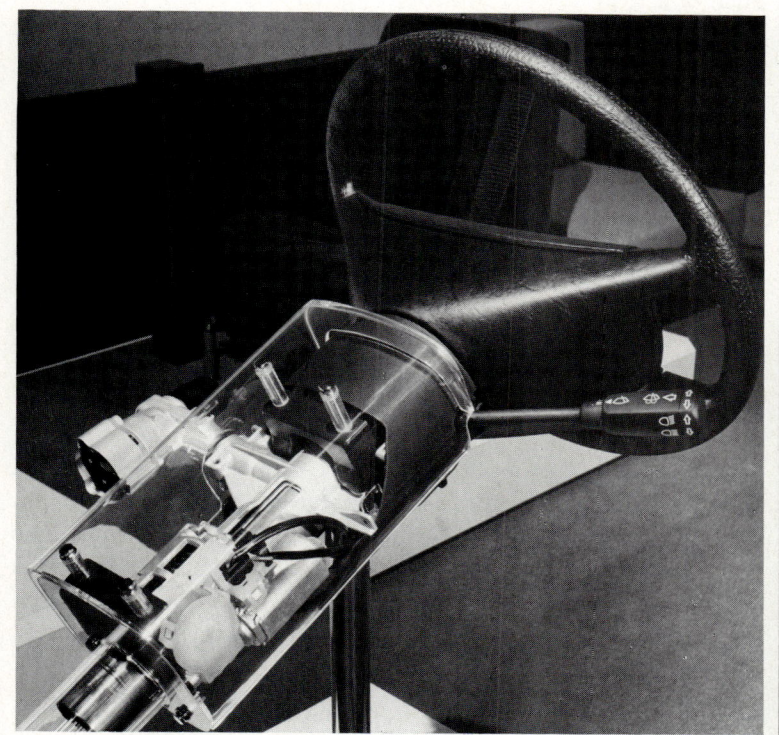

One of the Mercedes–Benz special features specialities is the electrically adjustable steering–column, which can be adjusted lengthwise by a maximum of 60cm. It can even be combined with the memory–control of the driver's seat.

Today even low priced cars are equipped with electrically adjustable wing mirrors, some of which even interact with the car's seating memory. Some wing mirrors are electrically heated, with the switching mechanism linked with the heated rear window function. The latest feature is a wing mirror which tilts inwards when a button is pressed, and with these "flattened ears" driving through narrow spaces should become easier.

Electrically adjusted wing mirror of the BMW Z1 which is connnected to the heated screen and tilts down when reverse gear is engaged.

There is more: in the case of a top class limousine, the passenger wing mirror adjusts downwards as soon as reverse gear is selected; thus enabling the driver to gain a better view of the kerb during his manoeuvre. Other mechanisms can also be connected with reverse gear – for example, the rear windscreen wiper in the case of rain or snow.

Back seat passengers have also gained in importance. This is evident not only from the fact that they can normally enjoy the same degree of comfort as front seat passengers with ash trays, cigarette lighters, head and arm rests, separate outlets for heating, ventilation or air conditioning, but also from the fact that the rear seats are equally well equipped for optimum seating comfort. A relatively new refinement can be seen in the adjustable rear seats and manually or electrically adjustable arm rests.

Rear seat passengers are no longer mere "back benchers", since numerous features have been designed with them in mind, ie reading lamps (here the Alfa Romeo 164), and adjustable head rests, to name but the most basic.

In hatchback cars, the rear seats are designed to fold down (and increasingly also in graduated hatchback limousines) and another version is the so–called "openings" or skiing sacks, which make it possible to transport a pair of skis without the need for a roof rack; these versions, although less practical, are rather popular.

Strong sunlight can be counteracted by sun blinds or curtains, and here again, if so desired, the help of an electric motor can be summoned. In the case of low sunlight, mini–sun blinds at the front windows are rather useful and popular; these may be pulled out or hinged and can also cover the space above the inside rear view mirror.

Large station wagons are sometimes equipped with additional hinged child seats, and special straps are also very useful in order to secure heavy pieces of luggage – thus ensuring the passengers' safety in the event of emergency braking.

Important Atmosphere

It used to be quite difficult to create a comfortable atmosphere inside the car. However, elaborate and easily adjustable instruments are now quite common, and the ventilation systems often impress with their considerable air flow. Genuine air conditioning systems with cold compressors have meanwhile become available on many mid-range cars. Today's aerodynamically styled cars with their large glass area generate a great deal of internal heat during sunshine, making this luxury feature almost indispensible in certain climates.

Fully automatic air conditioning systems, which operate with one or more thermostats – and which continuously adapt to the temperature required for the inside of the car – are very practical, but are at present still very expensive and therefore to be found only in top range models.

Stationary heating systems, which warm up the car before driving, are built in only as an afterthought. Depending on the design, they heat up the cooling system so that the engine as well as the interior will be warm and warm air will be available from the journeys start.

By means of a time switch the start-up time of the stationary heating system can be pre-selected – for example, half an hour before driving off in the morning and this can even be done by remote control, if the car is not too far away. There is even an electrically-heated steering wheel cover but so far this has been available only as an extra. Electric window lifters have already been mentioned, but it is worth noting that the Japanese have designed systems with continuous action which means that the button no longer has to be pressed down permanently. In Italy, a specialised type of electric window was launched, whereby the rear side windows can be opened or closed at the touch of a button.

Manual work is no longer required in other areas either. After boot lids and hatchbacks which can be unlocked from the inside at the touch of a button or lever, there have more recently been those which automatically close and lock by means of a small electric motor.

The latest design in sun roofs, has been developed by Sekurit. It incorporates solar cells which provide power to open the roof for ventilation when parked in direct sunlight.

Sun roofs have developed from prestige to everyday design features. Many cars today are equipped with electrically operated sliding sunroofs (often glass) as standard, while glass sunroofs are also available as an optional extra and, because of their low cost, are extremely popular. In many cases, however, these do not slide and can only be lifted up (hence they are often descibed as "lifting roof"); in some instances they can be completely removed and stored. The latest development is a glass roof which incorporates solar cells to produce sufficient power for a fresh air blower which prevents a closed car from over heating even when parked in direct sunlight.

From openings in roofs it is a small step to open cars and here a clear preference towards lightweight roof-mechanisms is obvious; indeed, some of the lowest priced convertible/cabriolets are equipped with an electrically operated cover.

Today even the lowest priced car has a heated rear window. However, since these use up a lot of power they have been fitted with a time switch, which automatically turns off after a few minutes. Meanwhile, heated front windows are becoming increasingly popular.

More mundane features concern the various can holders, which have been exactly designed for standard aluminium drink containers, and special compartments for audio cassette tapes. The discerning driver has a specially built-in compartment for his compact discs. With regard to layout and design of coin compartments for parking and telephones, the designers' imagination seem to be running away with them at times.

Designers will have to devise dash boards which incorporate all the required information without distraction to drivers. This photo shows the BMW design solution, with air conditioning, CD player and Bord computer.

The first standard use of fibre optics in passenger cars originated in the USA. These ultra-fine light conductors are responsible for currentless control of the car's lighting system; a weak glowing of the fibre end signifies that the lights are working perfectly. The dashboard provides a particularly appropriate and visable area for the application of new technology, and far reaching developments in micro-electronics have introduced significant changes. For example, onboard computers have become highly efficient, owing to the use of advanced sensors and signal transmitters. These modern features become annoying only if they inform the driver about certain irregularities of secondary importance on an unasked and insistent basis – perhaps in a squeaking computerised voice or by way of nerve racking signals. One of the most crucial tasks for automobile engineers will be to develop instruments and systems which provide the driver with the right measure of meaningful information, and in a way that can be most easily and rapidly absorbed. Operating simplification is also an important subject for the designers of future cars. This applies equally to the various functions of an electronic cruise control, as well as for the operation of lights, windscreen wipers and so on – and also to the controls of the cars radio which is fast developing into a sophisticated traffic information system.

Who knows what the future has in store? Perhaps the operation of cars by means of spoken commands, which is already the case with specially equipped car telephones?

Let's wait and see!

A glass roof which changes colour according to external brightness – what an interesting concept. This feature was already realised some time ago in the concept–car Ford Eltec, but also in the Nissan CUE–X, illustrated here.

The Natural Choice

REAL LEATHER   CERTIFICATION TRADE MARK

Resilient, durable and luxuriously comfortable. These natural features are available for the interior of your car with Easirider lambswool car seat covers and floor rugs.

<u>**Car Seat Covers**</u> — a thick wool cushion keeps you warm in winter yet cool in summer. Easirider covers reduce travel fatigue. Easy to fit and keep clean by washing or dry cleaning.

<u>**Floor Rugs**</u> — tailor-made for a perfect fit. CAT CLAWS© anti slip design fitted for extra safety. A special "shoe friendly" heel pad is easily removed for valeting or replacement. All Easirider car seat covers and floor rugs are available in 14 fast colour options, selected for their special wool density. Materials used meet world automotive flame retardancy regulations.

Contact us today for your complimentary colour brochure and lambswool samples.

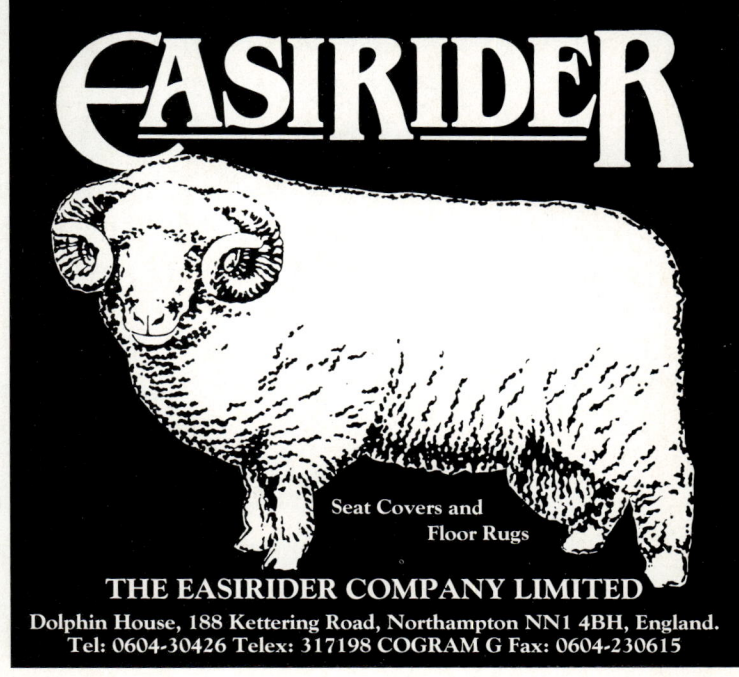

EASIRIDER

Seat Covers and Floor Rugs

THE EASIRIDER COMPANY LIMITED
Dolphin House, 188 Kettering Road, Northampton NN1 4BH, England.
Tel: 0604-30426 Telex: 317198 COGRAM G Fax: 0604-230615

When you have a perfect understanding of the function you can better design the product.

ECIA, a major new force in the automotive component field, resulting from merger between "A.O.P. Equipements Automobiles" and "Cycles Peugeot". A firmly established experience of exterior trim, interior trim and engine support systems.

ECIA

COMPLETE AUTOMOTIVE FUNCTIONS

ÉQUIPEMENTS ET COMPOSANTS POUR L'INDUSTRIE AUTOMOBILE
35, rue Paul-Vaillant-Couturier
92305 Levallois-Perret - France
Tél. (1) 47.58.13.93

PRS

PRS PUBLISHING LTD

OTHER PRS AUTOMOTIVE AND ENGINE YEARBOOKS

World Automotive Digest 1988 (Second Edition) - Price £195

The most comprehensive market reference to the world automotive industry. It provides detailed statistical information on production, demand and trade trends in the worldwide motor industry; analyses and comments on the main commercial and technical developments; identifies the main features which have shaped the individual companies within the automotive sector during the past year, and forecasts the automotive industry's future prospects.

World Components Digest 1989 (First Edition) Publication July 1989 - Price £195

A comprehensive review of important commercial and technical developments in the worldwide automotive components industry, together with an assessment of the current major issues. The Digest also contains top level viewpoints, company profiles and a statistical analysis.

Who's Who in Western European Automotive Components Markets 1988/89 (Second Edition) - Price £95

A unique reference containing information on over 500 automotive component manufacturers throughout Western Europe, including the materials and electronics field.

World Engine Digest 1989 (Ninth Edition) - Price £195

The World Engine Digest provides an up-to-date, comprehensive and detailed statement of world engine production with market data forecast to 1992. It also contains profiles of major engines and component companies; the major company, product and technical news in 1988; a world calendar of events for 1989/90 and a directory of companies.

Who's Who in World Engine and Component Markets 1988/89 (Fourth Edition) - Price £95

The standard company reference for engine and component manufacturers and their suppliers containing concise profiles of over 1500 engine and component companies.

For further information contact:

Elaine Boyden
PRS Publishing Ltd
44-48 Dover Street, London W1X 3RF
Tel: (01) 409 1635   Tlx: 23442   Fax: (01) 629 0221

Power trip: Muscle is back on US streets

Ford Taurus

Not since the mid–1960s, when the so–called Pony cars thundered out of Detroit, has the auto industry seriously touted high–performance cars. But now, memories of fuel queues seem part of the past and even the most pessimistic energy analysts see no fuel shortages on the horizon. In addition, the Environmental Protection Agency is relaxing the rigorous fuel economy standards it developed during the darkest days of the 1970's oil crisis. Suddenly a new US horsepower race is underway.

Unlike the 1960s, when US automakers fought the horsepower race among themselves, a clutch of potent foreign competitors are joining the fray to peddle power to US car buyers – who are responding eagerly.

Consider the following:

- US car buyers, when offered the option, are choosing bigger, more powerful engines. In the 1988 model year, for example, V6 installation rates in domestic models jumped to 35% of all cars produced, up from just 27% in 1987. Most of that gain came at the expense of 4–cylinder engines.

- Sales of Mustang, one of the original Pony cars, have increased dramatically in recent years. The present incarnation of this rear–drive car was earmarked for phaseout in 1989, but thanks to the sales resurgence, particularly of the hot GT model– which boasts a hefty 5.0L engine, the Mustang is likely to live on through the 1990s.

- Hypermuscular models from US car-makers that will be introduced in 1989 include a 380hp Chevrolet Corvette, turbocharged Pontiac Trans Am and Grand Am models, supercharged Ford Thunderbirds and Mercury Cougars and a high–performance Ford Taurus SHO (for super high output).

- Foreign car-makers are not being outdone by any means. Their offerings include a 16–valve Volvo, more powerful BMWs and Nissans, Audi's first V8–equipped car, and new mini–muscle models from Diamond–Star Motors Corp – a US joint–venture between Chrysler and Mitsubishi Motors Corp.

Even in non–high–performance applications, engine displacements and horsepower outputs are creeping up. General Motors Corp increased the size of two of its V6s and its Cadillac Allante V8 for 1989 and Ford squeezed more out of its 3.8L V6 by switching to sequential port fuel injection, friction–fighting roller tappets and lighter weight components.

Car buyers do not yet have the best of both worlds, but at least some of today's improved performance is being achieved without significant fuel economy penalties, thanks to improved technology, including multivalve engines – powerplants with more than two valves per cylinder – and advanced engine electronics. Also, modern muscle cars are smaller and lighter than their 1960's predecessors.

An estimated 25% of all engines made in Japan in 1988 were multivalve powerplants, compared with 11% in 1987. In Europe, multivalve installations doubled during the same period. And in the US, where the technology has lagged a bit, no fewer than three new 4–valve–per–cylinder domestically built engines were introduced for the 1989 model year. One study predicts 20–25% of all cars will have dual–overhead–cam heads by 1995. Several automakers, Ford Motor Co and Daimler–Benz among them, vow to offer 4–valve engines across the board. Importer Toyota Motor Sales USA Inc already offers multivalve engines in every car it sells.

Even some formerly staid manufacturers are getting in on the act. Japan's Honda Motor Co Ltd, primarily a builder of bread–and–butter cars until it broke into the luxury market with its Acura Division, is now reportedly readying a competitor to such high–performance marques as Ferrari, Lamborghini and Lotus. The mid–engine 2–seater due some time in 1989 is likely to be powered by a 2.7L V6 engine – probably with variable valve timing for optimum performance at both ends of the engine speed range. Toyota Motor Corp and Nissan Motor Co Ltd say they are working on performance coupes and saloons/sedans for their new luxury divisions, as well.

Honda and the other Japanese automakers have moved away from near total dependence on 3– and 4–cylinder engines and are launching small V6s and V8s of their own. In 1987, more than 80% of all imports sold in the US were equipped with 4–cylinder engines. But a wave of small–block V6s – like Daihatsu Motor Co Ltd's experimental 130hp 1L V6 – is expected from Japan in the early 1990s. Toyota, Nissan and Honda already offer V6s in some of their cars and are set to debut V8s later in 1989.

Infiniti V8

V12 engines are back in vogue, thanks primarily to West Germany's BMW AG 1987 introduction of the ultra–luxurious 750i. Now Daimler–Benz and Japan's Fuji Heavy Industries Ltd reveal that V12 engines are under development for the 1990s, and Cadillac says it is eyeing a programme of its own. Chrysler Motors Corp confirms it has a V10 under development for trucks and possibly cars.

This year's high–performance crown goes to Chevrolet's new special–edition ZR1 Corvette. Known during its developmental days as the "King of the Hill", the limited–run ZR1 packs a powerful punch with its 32–valve 5.7L V8 engine designed by Chevrolet and GM's UK–based affiliate Group Lotus plc. The quad–cam engine is GM's first multivalve V8. The aluminium–intensive powerplant – both block and head are made of the light–weight metal – generates a generous 380hp and 375lbft (508Nm) of torque. Chevrolet has not yet released official performance numbers, but best guesses place the car's 0–60mph (0–97kmh) time at slightly more than 4 seconds.

"For 35 years, Corvette has been at the leading edge," says Fred J. Schaafsma, Chevrolet's chief engineer. "GM has a commitment to maintain Corvette as a world leader in high–performance street machines. We want to have the fastest accelerating production car in the world. But it must still be driveable – a pussy cat and tiger personality (blended together)," he adds.

Although the new V8 has the same displacement as Corvette's standard engine, only the rear main–bearing seals are common between the two. The high–performance version has a narrower bore and longer stroke. There's also a narrower 22–degree angle between the heads that enabled Chevrolet to squeeze the multivalver into the Corvette's existing engine compartment. A distributorless ignition, with four coils triggering the spark at each of the eight cylinders, is included in the special sequentially fuel–injected LT5 engine package.

The ZR1 Corvette makes some concessions towards fuel economy, chiefly through the addition of an electronically controlled 6–speed manual transmission and a unique three–stage throttle control system.

The Zahradfabrik–Friedrichshafen AG–supplied 6–speed boasts overdrive in its two top gears and a sophisticated control mechanism that forces the driver to shift from first directly to fourth under certain conditions to conserve fuel. The one–four shift comes only when coolant temperature tops 120F (49C), vehicle speed is between 12–19mph (19–31kmh) and the throttle is at 35% capacity or less.

The throttle system employs 16 fuel injectors, each positioned over one of the 16 intake valves. In the full–power mode, all 16 injectors feed fuel to the engine. But in a fuel–saving setting, which the driver can activate via a key–lock switch – called the "Power Valet" – in the centre console, only half the valves and injectors function fully. However, even in the economy state, all 16 injectors and 48 valves will kick in if the accelerator is punched firmly.

Chevrolet rounds out the ZR1 features with a 3–mode electronic suspension system, that offers "Touring, Sport and Competition" settings. The electronic controls automatically adjust shock damping at one of six levels for each of the three modes depending on vehicle speed.

Chevrolet ZR1

Except for special badging, styling goes largely unaltered on the ZR1.

Ford entered the muscle-car arena in 1989, unveiling a supercharged, V6-equipped Thunderbird and Mercury Cougar, along with a 24-valve, high-output Taurus.

The Thunderbird/Cougar 3.8L V6 employs an Eaton Corp supercharger to pump horsepower up to 210 and send the cars from 0–60mph (0–97kmh) in a quick-for-its-class 7.5 seconds.

As with the ZR1, the supercharged 3.8L has little in common with the engine on which it is based. The blown version incorporates a stronger block, reinforced cylinder heads, more durable hypereutectic aluminium-alloy pistons and a tougher, austempered ductile iron crankshaft.

For packaging reasons, the exhaust system also is unique. Dual piping converges into a single channel at about the midpoint of the car, then splits back into two runners after the fuel tank is cleared just forward of the rear axle.

The 90cu ft (1.5L) Eaton Roots-type supercharger weighs 12lbs (5.4kg) and is driven by a V-belt off the crankshaft. It delivers a maximum boost of about 12psi (0.8bar) and reaches peak output at an engine speed of about 4,000 rpm.

The high-powered engine is mated to a totally revamped Thunderbird/Cougar platform that features a longer wheelbase, but shorter overall length, and a fully independent suspension – a first for a rear-drive car from Ford. Styling continues along the aerodynamic theme the automaker inaugurated with the last-generation Thunderbird, but this time the sheet metal has a more tapered, refined appearance.

Meanwhile, Ford called on Japan's Yamaha Motor Co Ltd for help in transforming its sedate, front-wheel-drive Taurus sedan into a wolf in sheep's clothing. Yamaha's contribution is a 24-valve, quad-cam 3L V6 that generates 220hp. The limited-edition Taurus SHO hits 60mph from a standing start in under 8 seconds.

The port-fuel-injected V6 features die-cast aluminium head covers and oil pan and a forged steel crankshaft and connecting rods. Pistons are made of high-pressure die-cast aluminium and spark plugs are platinum tipped for greater durability.

The Yamaha engine incorporates a variable intake system with two runners per cylinder. A throttle valve in each of the shorter, high-speed channels remains closed until the engine hits 4,000 rpm – a setup Ford says provides smooth, constant torque all the way to the V6's 7,300 rpm speed limit.

Ford adds a stiffer suspension, four-wheel disc brakes, speed-rated tyres and cast aluminium wheels. The performance model is available only with a 5-speed manual. Like the ZR1, the Taurus SHO has few distinguishing marks, save for an upgraded interior and slightly altered instrumentation.

Getting new life in 1989 is the engine that once made the now-defunct Buick Grand National the fastest production car in the world. This time the 245hp turbocharged 3.8L V6 finds a home in a special 20th anniversary edition of the Pontiac Trans Am. The turbocharged engine makes for the fastest Firebird ever – 0–60mph (0–97kmh) in 5 seconds–plus, a quarter-mile in under 14 seconds and a top speed of more than 150mph (241kmh). Only 1,500 will be built.

Pontiac Turbo Grand Prix

Also joining the horsepower war is Pontiac's year-old Grand Prix, which is offered with an optional turbocharged 3.1L V6 with intercooler. The McLaren Turbo Grand Prix's boosted engine will crank out 200hp to drive the front wheels through a 4-speed automatic transaxle.

A couple of other high-tech features will be included with the McLaren package: head-up display instrumentation, which projects speedometer readings at the windshield in the driver's line of sight, and antilock brakes.

Distinguishing the turbo model from base Grand Ams are unique front and rear fascias, modified fenders and larger tyres, deep aerodynamic side skirts and functional hood/bonnet louvres – all of which give it a muscle-car look.

Chrysler gets help from Shelby Automobiles Inc in turning its Dodge Shadow into a performance coupe. Most noticeable additions include the rear spoiler, styled composite wheels, special blackout trim and rocker panel cladding. But what makes the Shadow a Shelby is the 2.2L 4-cylinder engine with variable-geometry turbocharger – the first application on a US car. The variable turbo virtually eliminates boost lag, so that peak output comes on some 1,000 rpm sooner.

Except for special vehicles like these, turbochargers seem to have fallen out of favour with US engineers. From a high 4% in 1987 turbocharger installation fell in 1988 to under 3%, and most experts predict a further decline. The reason: better performance is available from multivalve engines and larger displacement engines at lower cost and without the annoyance of "turbo lag," and a host of service and warranty problems.

The year's hottest cars imported into the USA include a new sports coupe from Volkswagen AG, Porsche AG's first "full-production" 4-wheel-drive performance car, a high-powered saloon/sedan from BMW AG and a handful of competitive models from Japan.

VW's Corrado is a 2-door fastback 2+2 derived from Golf mechanicals. Its supercharged 1.8L 4-cylinder engine makes it capable of a top speed of 140mph (225kmh). A V6 had been planned for the Corrado, but proved impossible to package.

Volkswagen Corrado

The Corrado's fast-track image is enhanced with the addition of an adjustable rear spoiler that sits flush with the tailgate surface at moderate speeds but rises 2in (5cm) once the car reaches 75mph (121kmh). In the upright position, the spoiler cuts rear-end lift by 66lbs (294N), VW says. "We wanted to give the driver a clear rear vision when parking, without sacrificing the benefits of 64% less rear-end lift at higher speeds," explains Christian Hildebrandt, VW's head of body engineering.

Porsche pulls out all the high-performance stops with its new 911 Carrera 4. The car links a 250hp version of Porsche's venerable 3.6L 6-cylinder engine to an all-wheel-drive system borrowed from the automaker's limited run, $300,000-plus 959 exoticar. In addition, the Carrera 4 adds a differential slip control device that limits slip individually at all four wheels.

Even France's Peugeot SA has stepped into the performance ring with a 16-valve rendition of its new compact 405 saloon/sedan. Along with the twin-cam, 150hp engine, the 405 Mi 16 includes a fully independent suspension, 4-wheel disc brakes, rear spoiler, halogen headlamps and leather-wrapped sport seats.

Joining the ranks of the "pocket-rocket" segment – consisting of small cars that pack a big punch – are a number of new-for-1989 Japanese makes. Among them:

- The Daihatsu Charade 16-valve. Daihatsu Motor Co Ltd adds a fourth cylinder and two extra valves per chamber to pump up the performance in its Charade minicar. The 16-valve 1.3L puts 80 horses at the reins of the driver, nearly 30hp more than the car's standard 1L 3-cylinder.

- Isuzu I-Mark with "Handling by Lotus." Isuzu Motors Ltd gets help from Lotus in turning its utilitarian I-Mark 4-door into a fully-fledged small sports saloon/sedan with a decidedly European flavour. Lotus revises the I-Mark's suspension and steering to give the car a firmer ride and more responsive handling. For power, Isuzu goes the multivalve route, with a 16-valve 1.6L 4-cylinder that puts out a class-leading 133hp at 7,200 rpm.

Mitsubishi Eclipse GS Turbo

- Mitsubishi Eclipse/Plymouth Laser. These two sporty 2-door hatchbacks derived from Mitsubishi Motors Corp's front-drive Galant platform are actually built in the US by Diamond-Star Motors Corp, a joint venture between Mitsubishi and Chrysler. In full performance dress, the Eclipse/Laser comes fitted with a 2L 16-valve 4-cylinder equipped with an intercooled turbocharger. The package stokes up 190hp and 203lbft (275Nm) of torque, a wealth of power for a car that weighs just 2,660lbs (1,207kg). The performance theme is carried over in the styling department, where the cockpit-like interior suggests a familial link to more exotic, mid-engine sports cars.

Of course, all-out performance cars are not the only models boasting extra strength in 1989. A number of highly powerful, yet refined saloons/sedans also make debuts.

Among the leaders in this class is BMW's reworked 5 series. The top-of-the-line model, the M5, is the West German automaker's interpretation of what muscle cars are all about. The M5 is powered by a 3.6L, 24-valve, in-line six that puts out a monstrous 315hp. Top speed is a regulated– yes, regulated– 155mph (245kmh). Special "aero" wheels efficiently cool the brakes– a necessity for 155-to-0 stops. Oddly, the car is a bit of a laggard off the line. It does 0 to 100kmh (62mph) in 6.3 sec.

Audi's contribution to the horsepower race is its new V8 saloon/sedan. The V8 shares styling features of Audi's 100-200 saloons/sedans, but it is a uniquely engineered vehicle. At the heart is a new 32-valve, all-aluminium, 3.6L V8, best described as two Volkswagen 16-valve 4-cylinder GTI engines put together.

The 250hp engine gives the $55,000 Audi a top speed of 146mph (235kmh) and takes it to 62mph (100kmh) from a standstill in a respectable 9.2 seconds.

The car, equipped with 4-speed electronically controlled automatic, full-time 4-wheel drive and antilock brakes is a prime example of a growing class of luxury vehicles that offer high-power and high-technology at a high price.

"We are trying to offer a completely new idea in performance cars where acceleration and top speed are not so important," says Jurgen Stockmar, Audi vice chairman and head of research and development. "It's not a sports car we are selling, but a kind of executive express, like an express train, offering a lot of comfort even at high speed."

The list goes on and on. Sweden's Volvo adds a 16-valve 4-cylinder to its 740 line and Mitsubishi does the same with its new Galant.

Nissan and Toyota branch off to create luxury car divisions, dubbed Infiniti and Lexus respectively, both of which plan to offer new V8-powered saloons/sedans in 1989.

Now that the new Corvette, supercharged Thunderbird and Corrado and turbocharged Eclipse and Laser have put the high-performance trend back in full swing, the key question is, how long will the movement last? Remember, it was only six years ago that fuel economy ratings played a prominent role in most car manufacturers' advertising copy.

Because the muscle-car market is highly dependent on fuel prices, and the world oil market is potentially and unpredictably volatile, it is anybody's guess as to when consumer demand may swing back towards economy cars. But, all things being equal, the industry appears confident that the next decade will be a good one for fast cars.

Infiniti

In a year-old Delphi study by the University of Michigan's Transportation Research Institute, auto executives polled predicted that fuel prices in the USA would rise only modestly between now and the year 2000. Projections indicate unleaded fuel will average $1.20 in 1990, $1.40 in 1995 and $1.75 by 2000 (in 1986 dollars), modest gains considering only seven years ago experts thought prices would hit $3.61 a gallon by 1990.

Future muscle cars will have another thing going for them besides plenty of fuel at relatively low prices – advanced technology. Again, those surveyed by the University of Michigan predicted heavy design activity in improvements to drivetrain and powertrain efficiency, which means performance cars of the 1990s will not cost their owners so much for fuel.

Even today's muscle cars return adequate fuel economy numbers. The ZR1 Corvette is capable of 10.4L/100km (27.2mpg) [22.5US mpg] – giving the car the best performance-to-fuel-economy ratio of any production vehicle, according to Chevrolet. Manual versions of the supercharged Thunderbird get 9.8L/100km (28.8mpg) [24US mpg] on the highway. Even that stinginess is outdone by the Taurus SHO, which gets 9L/100km (31.4mpg) [26US mpg].

These are respectable figures by any measure and they lead many auto executives to play down any comparison of today's performance cars with the extravagant fuel-gulping muscle cars of the 1960s. "I don't really agree with the term muscle cars," says Thomas J. Wagner, Ford vice president and general manager of the Ford Division. "Today's performance cars are not equivalent to the 1960s muscle cars. They handle better, have more safety features and get better fuel economy."

Whatever the designation – muscle cars or high-performance economy cars – the renaissance of power caught industry forecasters flatfooted. In 1981, only about 19% of the buyers of US-made cars opted for engines with displacements of 5L and above, compared with more than 75% just four years earlier. That plunge had many pundits forecasting the end of the 8-cylinder engine.

Three years later, as copious amounts of cheap fuel were again available, automakers began designing new V8s for the first time in years. General Motors and Ford both have major multivalve V8 programmes underway, and of course carmakers such as Honda, Audi, Nissan and Toyota are bringing out their first V8s ever.

The Delphi study indicates that auto executives remain bullish on the V8. Though displacements are likely to shrink in future new V8s, the powerplant is expected to account for up to 17% of the US car market by 1995. Six-cylinder powerplants have an even healthier future. According to the study they will account for 30–40% of sales in 1995.

Mitsubishi Eclipse GS Turbo

Electronics would give automakers the flexibility to handle any fuel crisis that might occur, by allowing them to optimise engines for economy. There might be some modest sacrifice in performance, but little if any deterioration in driveability, which was the curse of the cars of the 1970s.

"Of course the (performance car) market will vary depending on fuel prices and availability and insurance rates," sums up J. Michael Losh, GM vice president and general manager of the Pontiac Division. Indeed, stratospheric insurance rates could be the undoing of high-performance cars: monthly insurance costs for some high-risk owners – young males for whom muscle cars are a kind of badge of virility, for example – are sometimes higher than their car payments, even for $20,000-plus cars. But few buyers are asking the price, so they must be able to afford it. That gives Losh and other auto executives confidence that the market for performance cars "won't ever go away. I think it is going to remain strong going into the 1990s," he predicts boldy.

Pontiac Trans Am

NOW RE

The systems behind the sophistication!

Today, AC's leadership in the research, design, and manufacture of components for the sophisticated vehicle system applications is recognized internationally.

This is due, in no small measure, to six sophisticated AC systems which contribute to reliable operation.

❶ Fluid Handling Systems
AC produces mechanical and electric fuel pumps, providing increased efficiency and performance requirements for advanced *fluid handling systems.*

❷ Filtration Systems
AC assembles a variety of air, oil, fuel and transmission filters for numerous vehicle *filtration systems.*

...VEALED!

⑤ Control Systems
AC builds the Cruise Control and a vast array of temperature and pressure switches/sensors for a variety of engine *control systems.*

⑥ Induction Systems
AC makes the mass airflow sensor and air cleaner assemblies for vehicle *induction systems.*

Do you have a project that could benefit from AC's leadership in research, design and manufacture? We would welcome your enquiry. AC engineers work in close cooperation with their design and production counterparts at automotive companies all over the world.

AC MAKES MORE PARTS FOR MORE VEHICLES THAN ANY OTHER COMPANY IN THE WORLD.

③ Ignition Systems
AC manufactures an extensive line of spark plugs meeting the diversity of performance specifications for engine *ignition systems.*

④ Exhaust Emission Control Systems
AC supplies catalytic converters to vehicle manufacturers worldwide for advanced automotive *exhaust emission control systems.*

AC SPARK PLUG OVERSEAS CORPORATION · PO BOX 336 · SENTRY HOUSE
500 AVEBURY BOULEVARD · MILTON KEYNES MK9 2NH

Automobile Technology Today and Tomorrow

Technical innovations are mostly triggered by external influences, such as the economy, politics, and ecology as well as the indefinable "Spirit of the Times". The world's economic situation is obviously good. The people of the Western world, at any rate, are able to afford the things they want.

At present, where cars are concerned, they want higher performance and a more stylish design, and the number of families owning two or more cars is on the increase. Increased competition is forcing manufacturers to economize. The current trend is towards lower priced and more highly automated production while applying the "just in time" principle to supply. Large automobile manufacturers increasingly use outside companies for development of their top series models.

Variety In Engine Manufacture

Current trends point towards growth: in higher cubic capacity, increased performance and superior top–technology.

Amongst the top–range models, most design limitations have now been exceeded. Over the past twelve months BMW has broken new ground with its 300–PS twelve cylinder light–alloy engine.

Today, performance alone is no longer sufficient. Since Daimler–Benz announced the development of its V12 with four valves per cylinder, this type of cylinder head design has become the most popular means of obtaining the all important additional 50 horsepower. Porsche caused a stir with their 959, 450PS turbo engine, Ferrari's 478PS F40 model took up the challenge; and last but not least Aston Martin and Jaguar, with still higher performances, entered the race in the fast lane.

Today, untold sums are spent on oil paintings and old cars; it should come as no surprise, then, that the models described here should command almost indecent prices.

The average customer, indeed, has a great deal of quality to choose from. There are two new eight–cylinder models worthy of attention. One is produced by Audi, the other by Lotus, the European subsidiary of GM. The latter is the top model of the Chevrolet–Corvette series. Both of these eight–cylinder cars are constructed mainly of light–alloy, their 32 valves being operated by four camshafts. Subsequently, Ford USA asked Yamaha to supply them with their own remarkable high–tech engine: this 3 litre V6 is intended for the Taurus SHO model, but it could also one day find a European home under the bonnet of a Granada/Scorpio.

Let us look at the mass produced models. With the bore/stroke ratio of four and six cylinder engines, everything is obviously geared towards the centre of square design. Technological advances are exemplified by the light cast technique as well as the growing proportion of light–alloy also used for the cylinder block (eg. Audi V8, Lotus LT5, Corvette ZR1 etc).

Made To Measure

Lotus, a subsidiary of GM, have developed the ZR1 which currently ranks top of the Corvette Series. It has a 5.7 litre V8 engine with 4 camshaft, 32 valves, 530Nm torque and approximately 390PS output.
One particularly impressive feature is that 8 of the 16 inlet valves only open above 3000rpm.

Ford with Yamaha Engine

Yamaha have supplied a V6 engine of 3 litre cubic capacity with 4 camshafts and 24 valves; Ford have installed this in the Taurus SHO (super–high output model), whose maximum performance is 223PS at 6000rpm.

The most popular method of construction for the cylinder block uses multi-cylinders: reducing both total length and weight. This is particularly important for the transverse engines increasingly used in front wheel drive vehicles.

Cylinder heads made of cast iron are only found in the older designs: a light-alloy is now widely used. The valve seats are often made of sinter steel: a result of the reduction in lead added to fuel, which prevented valve seat regression.

The toothed-belt driven camshaft is now virtually a world standard; and the addition of a second camshaft seems poised to become even more widespread. As four-valve technology has spread, the optimum combustion chamber form has changed. The hemispheric combustion chamber must now make room for the more flatter design – with corresponding rounded edges. Both allow the spark plug to occupy the central position which is important for short flame propagation and clean combustion.

Four valves per cylinder no longer identify solely sports engines.

Apart from prestige models their justification is increasingly seen in the possiblity of achieving a smoother engine torque curve. The valves alone, however, cannot acheive this. There are two recent development trends: firstly there are varying length intake tracts which produce good fuel injection in the lower speed range, with the aid of long tract, and increased output at higher speed; and secondly there are variable valve timing systems.

In the case of the latter, three different development approaches can be observed: firstly unvaried control periods, but with phase shift, secondly unvaried control periods, phase shift and variable valve stroke, and thirdly electronically controlled adjustment of phase and stroke. The trend towards narrower V angles between intake and exhaust valves has not continued, presumably because of space. Heat dissipation via the water jacket, and the placement of the cylinder head bolts also play a role here.

Hydraulic lash compensation has increased greatly. The hydraulic components in cup tappets, valve rockers and drag levers have become small and light in the meantime. All this, as well as measures to avoid oil frothing, nowadays make it possible to use hydraulic tappets for high revolution engines.

A particularly interesting example of the new trend towards interrelated action between valve stroke and phasing is the Lotus LT5 eight cylinder engine. The two intake valves of each cylinder are opened for different control periods and the opening valves not only differ in length but also in port diameter.

The primary system with the shorter open period supplies the engine during light load operation. If a higher output is required, the other eight valves come into operation. The change over can be prevented by a locking mechanism in the centre console.

In this position the engine produces a comfortable 200PS. When the second phase becomes active after approximately 3500rpm the maximum output should be somewhere around 390PS.

Exhaust systems with resonance volume and shift from long to short exhaust paths can be found, amongst others, in the six cylinder engines by Honda and Mazda, the Yamaha V6 for Ford, and the eight cylinder Porsche models.

Compact Square Cube

Audi's 200 model has a 3.6 litre V8 engine whose 32 valves are activated with a narrow forked angle of 25deg by 4 toothed belt, or chain driven camshafts.
The mixture preparation of the 250PS is delivered by the Bosch Monotronic M 2.4.

Foreseeable future developments will place great emphasis on both valve control mechanism and variable exhaust pipes.

Diesel engine popularity has waned over the past year – most notably in the Federal Republic of Germany. One of the reasons for this is current uncertainty about emissions; especially regarding particulates. Added to this, was political discord and a failure to come up with effective particulate traps. Meanwhile the quite respectable drop in fuel consumption of petrol/gasoline engines may also insignificant Leading diesel manufacturers are at present working on a new generation of self ignition engines with electronically controlled direct injection, higher revolution levels and even four valve technology.

The fact that the "lean burn" engine has had little mention at present should not lead us to presume that this means of achieving a less noxious engine has been abandoned.

At least one of the larger Japanese manufacturers is presently running long term tests on passenger cars with "lean burn" engines, and these cars also meet stringent American emissions standards without a three way catalyst.

But it will probably be two or three years before such models are mass produced.

Development is speedier in the field of mechanical supercharging. VW have started the ball rolling with the spiral supercharger and others are expected to follow.

Pierburg – part of the Rheinmetall has recently introduced a displacement supercharger, whose main parts consist of extruded profiles. Through disks of varying material width a whole range of superchargers can be developed quite economically.

A second type of supercharger design originates from the Friedrichshafen Gear Wheel factory. The supercharger turbine is brought to high revolutions via planetary gearing.

In addition there is variable drive, which controls the working speed either through centrifugal force or with the aid of vacuum, air or oil pressure in such a way as to supply high charging pressure when performance is desired, while reducing during partial load operation.

Mixture and Ignition Systems

As regards fuel mixture, the trend is undoubtedly towards fuel injection: but the carburettor has developed to a point at which its survival appears safe.

Electronics have become important where both these systems are concerned, and they are also a pre-requisite for the lambda regulated catalyst. Today there are hardly any operating differences between the mixture preparation by a modern carburettor with control electronics and central/single point injection. The systems will both be widely used with cars in the popular price ranges. More elaborate engine designs mostly use sequential injection into the intake system of the individual cylinders.

Meanwhile, every function is amazingly well carried out even for the smallest cylinder-units: for example with the sequential multi-point injection system of the Honda-530 cc three cylinder engine. Apart from the fuel metering, various other functions are also carried out by these control units, which are equipped with three dimensional spark maps.

The next step – already taken by some manufacturers – leads to complete engine management, which includes control of ignition, fuel transmission and auxiliary engine driven system. With regard to ignition systems, the old contact breaker coil ignition has almost completely vanished. It is replaced by electronic systems without contacts and occasionally systems with several coils (eg Saab and Oldsmobile Quad 4) are used.

Longer periods between each service caused manufacturers to develop multi-purpose, long-life spark plugs.

Transmission Development

Four-speed transmission exists today almost exclusively in some light cars. Five is world standard, and the arrival of six-speed transmissions for sports cars can be expected. Porsche and General Motors have already set this trend with top models such as the 959 and the Corvette ZR1; others will undoubtedly follow. The fact that approximately 80% of all passenger car designs have front wheel drive has greatly influenced transmission design. Transverse engines require particularly compact gear/differential units. Asbestos content has almost completely vanished from the clutch friction lining, and the new two-way clutch is an interesting innovation.

Mechanical Charging

The Gear Wheel Factory in Friedrichshafen has developed a mechanically driven super charging system, which brings a small centrifugal air pump to high revolutions with planetary gearing without the use of exhaust gas.

Metal in Place of Ceramic Monolith

Larger specific surface, lower valve opening resistance, smaller dimensions, faster response time as well as higher temperature and vibration strength are the special advantages of such metals.

Widespread use of automatic controls means mechanical torque converter-bridging is prevalent. Automatic transmissions nowadays are four-speed, while a fifth is already heralded. CVT systems marketed by Fiat, Ford and Subaru in some of their models, are slowly gaining popularity with customers. Currently available automatic controls may face an economical competitor in the load isolating controls with two-way friction clutch. Several manufacturers are presently at work on designs for which conventional gear sets can also be used.

Six Speed Transmission

Optimum adaptation to the various kinds of road resistance by the forces operating at the drive gears can be achieved through the highest possible number of reduction gears. This illustration shows the new ZF design with locking synchronization at all stages.

Concept of the Opel Vectra 4x4

Viscous coupling and separate disc clutch are interlocked with the gear unit as a "bolt on" unit. During each braking action above a speed of 15.5mph/25kmh, the hydraulic disc clutch automatically uncouples the rear wheels from the power transmission.

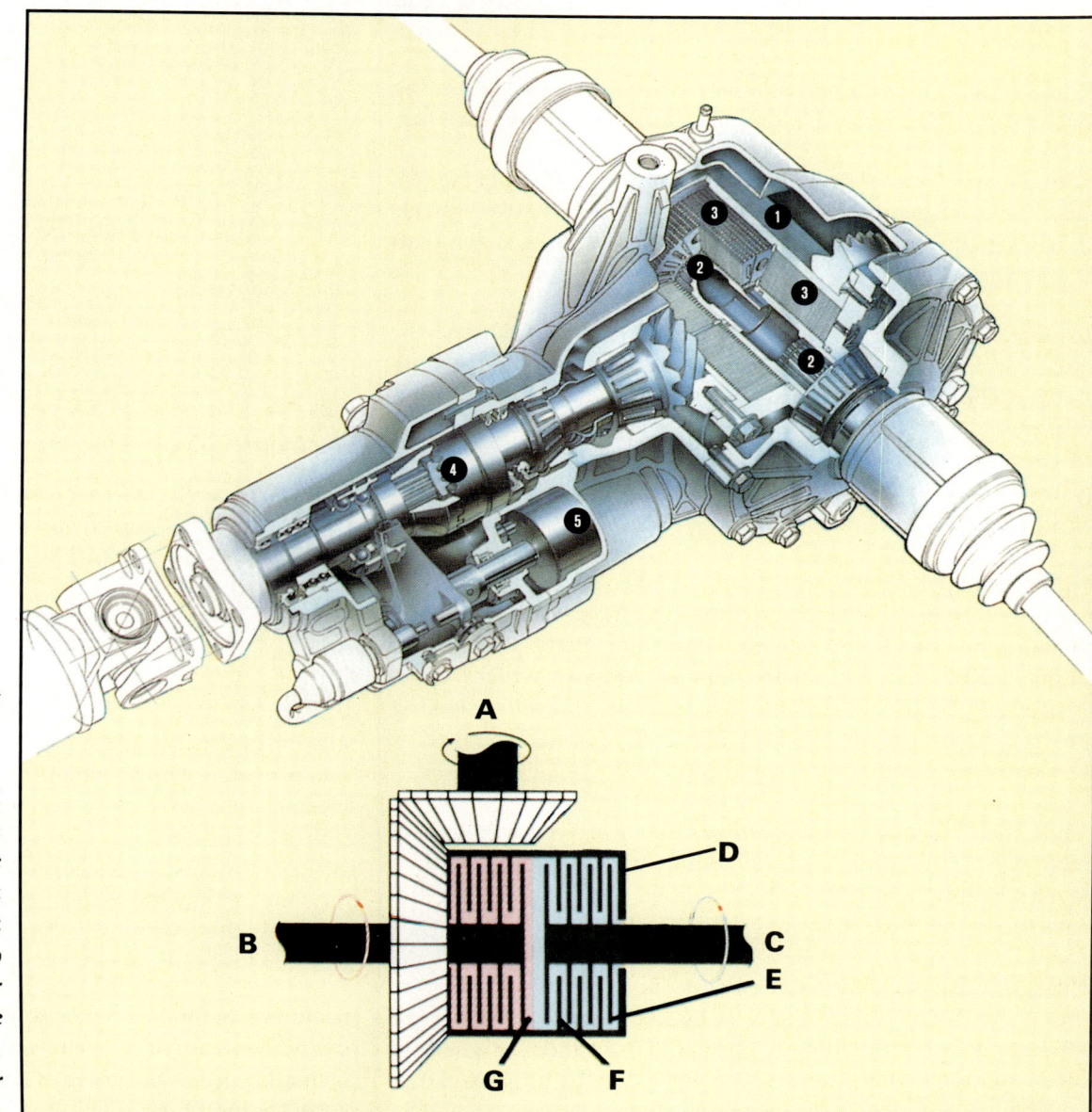

Torque Transfer Without Slip

The Innovative Traction Control System (Intrac) from Honda features two drive shafts for the rear axle which are connected by a viscous coupling. On braking a solenoid releases a jaw clutch to disengage drive – A, propellor shaft, B and C, right and left drive shafts, D, viscous coupling, E, interior segments, F, exterior segments, G, silicon filling.

Four-Wheel Drive And Steering

Four-wheel drive units for passenger cars had been quietly gaining in popularity for some years; until, that is, they gained prestige through the racing successes of the Audi Quattro, and managed to escape the cross country car image. In the meantime, the basic design has changed greatly. The primitive design with manual control of the secondary drive axle has been replaced by elaborate constructions with automatically variable torque-distribution.

During the initial period, locks for both the central differential and the rear differential gearing of the rear wheels had to be manually operated. Nowadays, viscous couplings or a single direction Torsen differential operate automatically by distributing the driving force as a function of the slip-conditions to the wheels in a variable ratio.

A four-wheel drive system not only improves traction, it also helps to achieve a mainly neutral self-steering action, and reduces any load transferral reaction to a minimum. The latest production of the Steyr-Daimler-Puch Fahrzeugtechnik AG is called "Viscomatic" and operates with electronically controlled hydraulics. The connection between the driven front axle and the rear differential is achieved by a combination of Planetary gearing and a viscous clutch.

However, as long as the rear differential does not contain a locking mechanism in the case of a "slipping" rear wheel, the torque is lost.

With the new "Intrac" (Innovative Traction Control) from Honda, the differential gearing of the rear wheels consists of two viscous clutches in the same housing: each is connected to the clutch shaft of one rear wheel, thus avoiding one-sided slippage.

To make the system lock compatible during braking, the rear-wheel drive is disengaged by an electro-magnetic claw clutch. The anti lock capacity in other systems (VW synchro, Viscomatic etc) is also achieved with a similar dividing-clutch which may be standard or optional. The progressive driving systems adapt the various torques to the wheels for individual requirement.

With the Opel Vectra, for example, the power distribution front/back, on dry roads, corresponds to a ratio of 72:25. If there is slippage at the front wheels, then the back wheels are automatically supplied with higher torque, which could theoretically be as high as 100%. Electronically controlled steering and hydraulically activated disc clutches have been developed by Mercedes-Benz and Porsche amongst others.

When the first four wheel steering models arrived from Japan, even experts at European type-testing stations were stretched beyond their limits. They had neither the methods nor the expertise to test these new arrivals.

Without a doubt, the combined front and rear wheel steering offers considerably more safety at higher speeds. Whether the difficulty of opposing the steering of both front and rear wheels at lower speeds (in the interest of a smaller turning circle) is worthwhile, will have to be examined more closely.

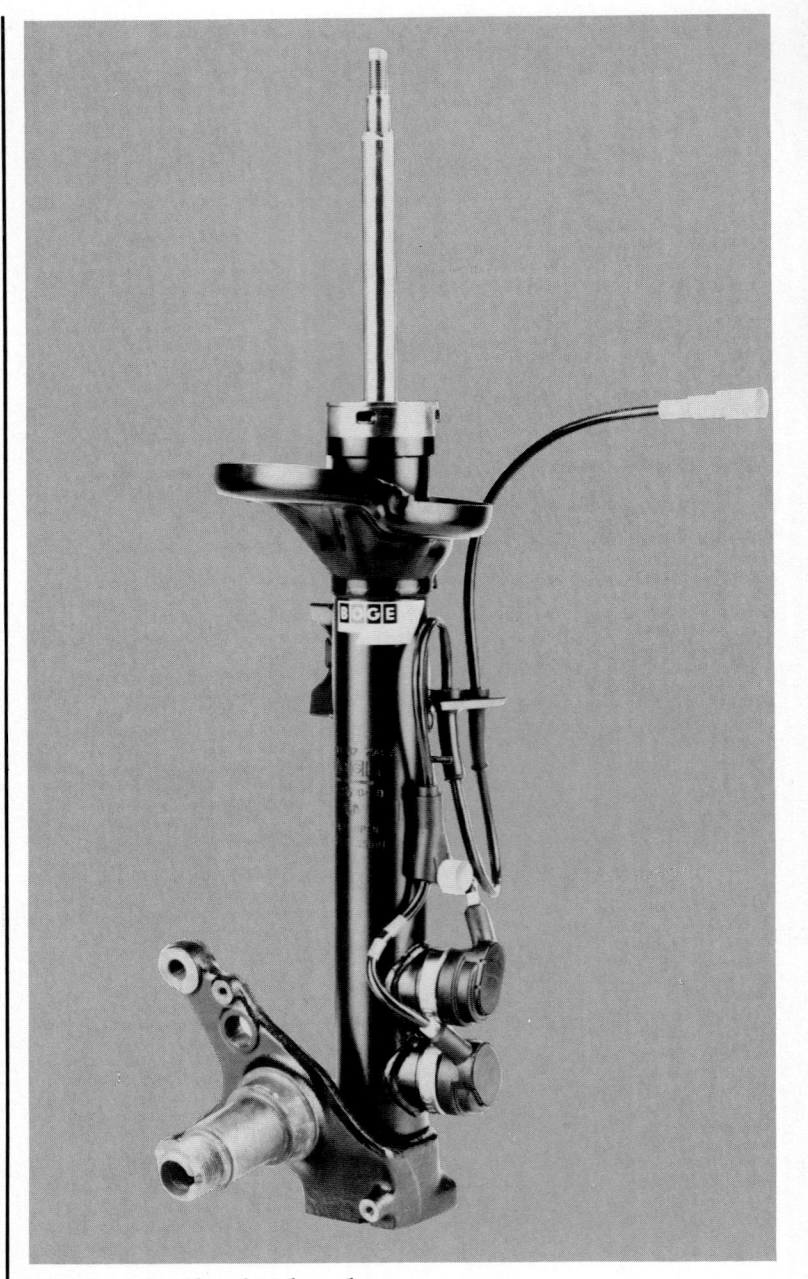

Electronic Shock Absorbers

While the conventional shock absorber represents a compromise, which should cover all existing driving conditions, the electronically controlled version immediately adapts the absorption-factor to any road surface.

Mitsubishi was the courageous first with their top model in the Galant design series: combining four-wheel drive, four wheel steering and a braking-system with four disc brakes and anti-lock control in a one design. Here, the steering of the rear wheels is of particular interest, on a steering-arm with limited mobile steering link and transverse steering controls. Through the clever geometry, the rear wheels when cornering, are simultaneously steered with the front wheels by a small angle.

In addition to this active rear wheel steering there is also an active part with two hydraulic circles. Circle 1, from the servo control (system), receives the energy for the shift of the servo-valve spool in the steering hydraulics of the rear wheels, the energy for the equiaxial steering is contributed as circle 2 by a differential-driven pump, dependent on velocity. Here opposing steering in order to improve manoeuvering capability deliberately omitted, while the 4WS-systems made by Honda, Mazda and Nissan have also taken care of greater mobility – which, however, is only possible at low driving speeds.

Trends In Chassis Design

On first inspection no new trends are discernible. With most of the front-wheel drive models, the designers have relied upon the tried and tested shock-absorber struts using variations of the original by Earle McPherson.

More imagination was used by experts from East and West for the rear wheels: torsion-elastic axle tubes, crankshafts, transverse steering formation, shock absorber struts with variable steering controls and much more. Where rear wheels are powered, oblique steering, or transverse steering formations, are paramount. Interesting fringe developments have also emerged: ie the space rod at Daimler-Benz, multiple steering at Nissan and the Weissach-axle at Porsche.

For several years, manufacturers, research enterprises and some of the large suppliers of chassis components have been experimenting with shock absorption systems which were used between 1987 and 1988 in Formula 1 racing cars. Electronically controlled, they regulate rolling, pitching and yawing.

In England Lotus are considering an active suspension which may eventually be adopted by General Motors in one of their prestige models. Both continental European, as well as Japanese manufacturers are striving for improved comfort. In practice, however, no one has yet managed to advance beyond controllable shock-absorbers.

The problem is made more difficult because of the need to pre-empt reactive amendments and to find a way to predict road conditions and the result of steering manoeuvres.

Where braking systems are concerned, anti-lock systems will become more widely used, and as a result of lower production costs, these will also be introduced to the lower price brackets.

Some experts, however, do not regard electronic steering in present systems, as the optimum solution. Good adaptability and high control frequency are also required.

Wheel brakes have their shortcomings: space becomes limited in the wheel pans and the power of the engines requires wider tyres. Furthermore, there are cooling problems as a result of the spoiler trimmed body This leads to an increase in rim diameter with a corresponding decrease in tyre height.

The question of wheel-tyre-brakes, requires new solutions. Perhaps the latest design by Audi/ATE points towards new freedom as on the Audi V8?

For one of their power models, BMW revived an old idea: double wheel hubs with coding blades, which pass a neat air current through the narrow wheel spokes to the brake disc.

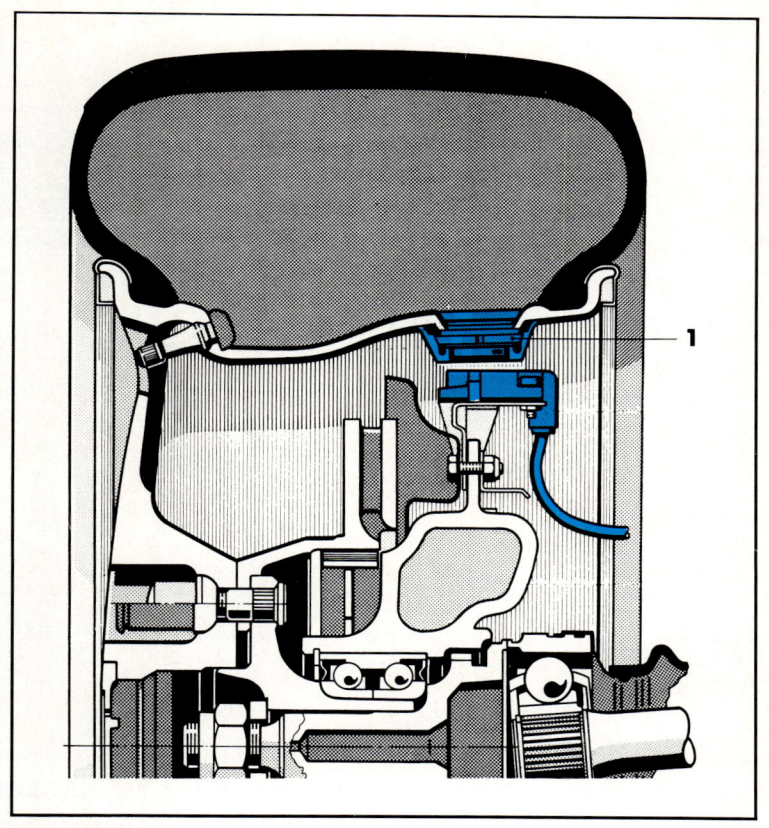

Tyre Pressure Checking

Porsche fits the 928 S4 series with a tyre pressure control unit, which features 2 sensors (1) per wheel. The sensors monitor changes in tyre pressure and temperature and alert the driver when pressure is lost.

In the field of tyre technology, there appears to be a certain stagnation. Although safety tyres have been discussed at length the only result has been the emergency wheel; and many feel this to be less than satisfactory.

The CTS tyre system (Conti Tyre System) by Continental received lavish advance praise, but in spite of this little interest has been shown to date.

The main objection against this tyre, which envelops the rim from the outside, is presumably the need for a close formed distribution network. Furthermore, the necessity to switch production over to a new type of wheel may well pose problems.

It is debateable whether another new product, the twin tyre, will have even a remote chance. Where tyre research is concerned it is said that at present every effort is being made to develop rubber mixtures with improved grip in rain and snow. At the same time, anti roll should be decreased, and durability increased.

Accessories, Safety Etc

General improvement in the standard of living is reflected in the accessory market. Even small cars now offer electrically operated windows and sun roofs, digital clocks, in-car computers, adjustable sports seats (often with heating). Unfortunately, these extras are not always 100% reliable, mechanical defects with windows and central locking occur at regular intervals.

PRS

PRS CONSULTANCY SERVICES

STRATEGIES FOR AUTOMOTIVE BUSINESS DEVELOPMENT

Through continuous original research across the Automotive Industry in three Continents, PRS can assist with:

- Strategy planning
- Technology tracking & forecasting
- Competitor analyses
- Acquisition search & evaluation
- Market & product planning

Areas of expertise:

- Engines/components
- New materials/plastics
- Electronics

For further information contact:

Vanessa Scholfield
PRS Business Consultancy Services Ltd
Premier House
44-48 Dover Street
London, W1X 4RF

Tel: 441 409 1635
Fax: 441 629 0221
Telex: 23442 PRSLON G

DEVELOPING ELECTRONICS ON LINE WITH YOUR THINKING

1. **COMPONENTS** AB is an experienced and long standing supplier of an extensive range of custom design products including switches, sensors, actuators, connectors, electronic modules, dimmer and balance controls.

2. **SYSTEMS** The range of custom designed systems now in production includes Microprocessor Controlled Switching, Central Timing Modules, Driver Information Systems and Lamp Monitoring and Switching Units. Recent innovations include a unique low-cost ASIC microcontroller designed specifically for Automotive applications, and a low current switching system offering significant weight savings.

3. **DESIGN** Fully networked advanced computer aided engineering ready to go on line with your thinking. Our systems and components are incorporated in the vehicles of many leading Automotive Manufacturers.

4. **MANUFACTURING** Substantial manufacturing investment has placed AB amongst the European leaders in electronic assembly with extensive state of the art surface mount capability. Comprehensive "burn-in" facilities provide full range dynamic temperature cycling.

5. **QUALITY** Statistical Process Control (SPC), Failure Mode Effect Analysis (FMEA) together with in circuit and functional testing enable AB to maintain an objective of zero defects manufacture.

For further information please contact

AB Automotive Electronics Ltd.

Forest Farm Industrial Estate, Whitchurch, Cardiff CF4 7YS, Great Britain.
Telephone 0222 692929 Telex: 497014 Fax: 0222 616826

A company in the AB Electronic Products Group PLC.

The Source of Professional Electronics.

Dodge Viper R/T 10

A Sports Car in View

The oil crisis of the 'Seventies and the speed limits imposed as a result had an adverse effect on the sports car market for some time. Almost overnight, the highly popular English roadster vanished from the roads and Italian classic sports car producers invested enormous effort in coping with the stringent emissions regulations. By contrast the German manufacturers exploited their engineering strengths and soon developed the necessary technology to produce engines with increased power and lower emissions.

The 'Eighties saw a sales boom in the car market worldwide and demand has been reawakened not only for the "Hot Cars" but also thoroughbred sports cars. In every country car manufacturers are investing in their sports ranges and a number of new models will make their debuts in the near future. One exception to this is the simply produced, clean–lined roadster which has lost its appeal of the 'Fifties and 'Sixties. Today's driver demands a super fast, low sprung, technically advanced vehicle with all the expense that this implies. Multi–valve technology, with or without turbocharging;

Mercedes-Benz SL

four wheel drive and four wheel steering; luxury with an abundance of electronics, these set the tone for the new generation of sports cars. Even large capacity engines with eight, ten, twelve or sixteen cylinders and up to eight litres capacity are about to go on sale. In performance terms, the sports car of today should be significantly superior to the increasingly fast Hatchbacks and Coupes already on the market. But this is easier said than done when one considers that the leading manufacturers have limited the top speed of their fastest Coupes to 160mph. This was not an entirely free decision as there are continuing problems with tyre development for such fast, heavy vehicles, even the new super sports cars are causing complications for tyre manufacturers as heavy chassis are now preferred to lightweight bodies.

Improved injection systems, more effective catalyst systems, new speed limits and above all the prohibitive price levels are serving to protect the environment and natural oil resources.

Martin Wyler.

Aston Martin Virage

Cizeta Moroder V16T

High Profile And Expensive.

The sports car sector is currently being promoted to counter the attention being given to the fast luxury Coupes. In the future several new developments will be introduced, even at the top of the market, to improve performance for sports car enthusiasts. One thing is certain, manufacturers will be making considerable investment in technical development, luxury and dynamic body styling. Only the best is good enough for the elite sports car fraternity.

Nissan ZX

Mazda MX-5

Honda NS-X

Chevrolet Corvette ZR1

Ferrari Mondial T

Manufacturers may well produce the occasional two seater, and it would be good to see a success in this area.

Porsche 911 Carrera 4

68

Ford Fiesta

Compact And Multi Faceted.

Normally cars in the lower to middle price range are designed for long production periods, so that low costs can be achieved in this highly competitive area. The well styled small car, with the accent on economy, finds favour with the public especially with the flexibility introduced by a choice of hatchback, diesel or sports models.

Ford Fiesta

Volvo 440

Renault 19 16V

Renault 19

Lancia Dedra

MVS Venturi Cabriolet

The Return Of The Coupe

It may seem now that European manufacturers have handed the lucrative coupe category over to their Japanese and American competitors. However, the latest designs from Germany and Italy clearly show that there is increasing interest in this sector of the market with styling and design of paramount importance.

Volkswagen Corrado

Alfa Romeo 75 Coupé SZ

71

Opel Vectra 4 × 4

Opel Vectra 4 × 4

The buyer expecting relatively inexpensive models, is going to be disappointed and may turn to a similarly elegantly shaped, but cheaper, saloon/sedan, which will probably have four wheel drive!

Audi Coupé quattro 20 V

The Path To The Top

Some producers of lower and middle range cars are now making their move into the top class previously occupied by a elite marques (most of them European). The Japanese are trying to project themselves into this market with new, previously unknown, model names, while Europeans adopt a more gradually approach. Only time will tell if all participants can hold their places in the elite market. The battle for market share is now beginning in the United States and sooner or later will spread to Europe.

Infiniti (Nissan)

Lexus (Toyota)

Thunderbird SC

73

Audi V8

Bentley Turbo R

Cadillac DeVille

It's travel time!

The international programme with new ideas for more comfort in travelling.

Updated information, extraordinary clearness and easy to use: This is the trademark of Hallwag road maps. Have a pleasant journey!

Hallwag
SWISS MADE
The Road Maps

Mitsubishi Eclipse/Plymouth Laser

Something For Everybody

The comprehensive range of vehicles now on offer leaves barely a gap. However, occasionally marketing strategists expose areas not yet exploited. With the aid of mass produced components, profitable production is now possible for any major manufacturer. It is in this way that varying constructed and designed vehicles come into being which have a specific attraction for many car lovers and also offer driving enjoyment and performance.

Subaru Justy 4WD ECVT

Suzuki Vitara/Geo Tracker

76

Pontiac Grand Prix Turbo

Mercury Capri

These developments provide a range of vehicles appealing to the whole spectrum of car lovers.

Plymouth Acclaim

Pontiac Trans Sport

Large Space Vehicles

At the beginning of the Eighties, the Large Space Vehicle became very fashionable in the USA and drew the interest of both manufacturers and consumers. In the short or medium term the sales success of these models will inevitably be at the expense of the traditional Kombi.

Mazda MPV

Nissan Prairie

WHAT DIFFERENCE COULD ONE FAULTY SHOCK ABSORBER MAKE TO THIS CAR?

8.5 ft

You're looking at the answer.

And for the owner of a car like this the damage can be far greater than the 'damage' of replacing a faulty shock.

To prove a point – and proof needs facts – we commissioned an impartial test from an organisation called TUV Rheinland: a German authority responsible for testing the safety of many varied products.

The result they came back with was astonishing.

A standard family car travelling at 50mph on a straight, dry, uneven road can increase its stopping distance by 8.5 ft because of just one faulty shock absorber.

A detailed report of this and other tests is available free from any Monroe dealer.

As you can see that distance can be critical. And by driving on faulty shocks it could have as easily been you.

So do yourself a favour and have your shocks tested. If you need replacements, naturally we'd recommend our best, the Monroe Gas Matics.®

After all, Monroe, more than any other manufacturer, know the difference one faulty shock can make.

MONROE
Gas-Matic® shock absorbers

MONROE. KEEPING YOUR CAR WHERE IT SHOULD BE – ON THE ROAD.

Now what?

When answers aren't coming up and stress levels hit new highs, put GenCorp Automotive to the test.

Our strength lies in polymer technology, and for 75 years our thrust has been converting these technologies into automotive polymer products.

Work with us. Think with us. Draw on our research, application engineering, production capacities, our intellectual horsepower and real-world experience. In sum, a "center of excellence" to help build reliability and quality into your products.

Give us your problems and we'll give you answers. The caliber of answers that have made GenCorp Automotive a leading designer, manufacturer and supplier of engineered polymer products for the automotive industry.

Talk with us.

GenCorp AUTOMOTIVE

Engineering the future through polymer technology.

GenCorp Automotive, 34975 West Twelve Mile Road, Farmington Hills, MI 48333-9067. (313) 553-5120.

PRS

PRS CONSULTING GROUP INC

North American office of Planning Research & Systems plc
Specialising in Automotive Research & Consulting

ENGINE, AUTOMOTIVE & COMPONENT CONCENTRATION

Customised Databases - primarily derived from original research

- Diesel Engine Production & Application
- Vehicle Production Car, Truck Engine & other components

Data stored by make and model and covers USA and Canada. It is delivered electronically for use on either a mainframe or micro computer systems in the client's offices.

CONSULTING

Strategy planning services:
- Corporate or Business Strategy
- Market & Product Positioning
- Product Planning
- Developing New Earnings (acquisition, diversification, joint venture)
- Technology Tracking & Forecasting

In these areas:
- vehicles
- components
- construction equipment
- marine power
- agricultural equipment
- industrial equipment
- power equipment
- aftermarket

PUBLICATIONS

- World Automotive Digest 1988 ($350)
- World Components Digest 1989 ($350)
- Who's Who in Western European Automotive Component Markets 1988/9 ($170)
- World Engine Digest 1989 ($350)
- Who's Who in World Engine and Component Markets 1988/89 ($170)
- World Diesel News (10 issues/year) ($225)
- Diesel Cars in the 1990s ($850)
- Automotive Powertrain in Western Europe ($1750)
- World Engine Study 1988 ($950)
- Future for Diesel Engines 1984-92 ($3150)

For further information contact:

D William Pumphrey
PRS Consulting Group Inc
PO Box 1001, Darien, Connecticut 06820, USA
Tel: 203/656 1505   Fax: 203/655 1171

SPECIFICATIONS

Data for 1989 Passenger Vehicles

Explanations

Model Lists

Production Statistics

Data Explanation

This section contains technical data and information on passenger vehicles, sports cars and rough terrain vehicles. Data and information was obtained direct from the manufacturers and the Swiss importers, edited and compiled in an easy to read form.

Vehicles are listed by manufacturer, model name and engine size. The model names relate, in most cases, to Europe, however to assist in finding the appropriate vehicle where the territory marketing name changes, the chart in the index lists the manufacturer, territory, and marketing name of the vehicle. Refer to the highlighted name for data, where necessary.

The following details the type of information to be found under the vehicle name: where possible all data is given; however for some variants complete data was not available.

Body, Weight
1) Body style – Saloon/Sedan, Coupe, Estate/ Station Wagon etc.
2) Number of doors.
3) Number of seats.
4) Kerbweight (DIN) in kilogrammes – kg. DI–Norm 70020 – full fluid levels (oil, water and fuel tank), spare wheel and equipment supplied by the manufacturer. Weight for the USA – mass kerbweight, as the vehicle leaves the manufacturer.
5) Gross vehicle weight, in kilogrammes – kg. Maximum recommended weight.

Engine data
6) Number of cylinders
7) Cylinder configuration – in–line, V or horizontally opposed/flat (Boxer engine)
8) Cylinder bore in millimetres – mm
9) Cylinder stroke in millimetres – mm
10) Cylinder capacity in cubic centimetres – cm^3
11) Compression ratio
12) Power output in kilowatts (kW), horsepower USA (hp) and horsepower (PS).
In brackets at the start of the data is the testing method, from which the power output is calculated. DIN (German Industry Norm), SAE (Society of Automotive Engineers), JIS (Japanese Industry Standard), ECE (Economic Commission for Europe).

$$1kW = 1,36PS/1,34hp$$
$$1PS = 0,7355kW$$

13) Maximum power output speed, in engine rpm.
14) Power output relative to fuel usage, in kW/L, hp and PS/L (L = 1 litre of fuel)
15) Maximum engine torque in Newton metres (Nm) and pounds force feet (lbft)

$$1lbft = 0,738Nm$$

16) Speed at which maximum torque is obtained in rpm
17) Grade and type of fuel recommended – regular or premium grade, leaded or unleaded

Engine construction
18) Engine name
19) Engine location and installation, eg. front, transverse
20) Valve operation
21) Number of valves per cylinder and valve configuration
22) Number and location of camshaft/s
23) Camshaft drive method
24) Cylinder head material
25) Cylinder block material
26) Type of cylinder liners
27) Number of crankshaft main bearings
28) Oil filter type or oil cooler fitted
29) Oil capacity in Litres (L) and US quarts (US qt)

$$1Litre = 0.946 \text{ US quarts}$$

30) Fuel system type
31) Supplier of fuel system
32) Air cleaner type
33) Turbo/Supercharger supplier, type and maximum boost pressure (bars)
34) Battery size and capacity in volts (V) and amperes (Ah)
35) Type of charging system and maximum output in Watts (W) or amps (A)
36) Method of engine cooling
37) Cooling system capacity in Litres (L) and US quarts (US qt)

Transmission
38) Drive axle or axles
39) Type of transmission
40) Number of forward gears
41) Number of synchronised gears
42) Selector/shift lever location
43) Reduction gears, where fitted
44) Drive split and type of coupling
45) Final drive ratio
46) Limited slip differential or differential lock

Gear Ratios
47) All gear ratios
48) Torque multiplication in converter

Chassis
49) Chassis and body construction
50) Front suspension linkage
51) Front suspension springing
52) Rear suspension linkage
53) Rear suspension springing
54) Stabilisor type
55) Damper type

56) Method of brake operation
57) Number of brake circuits
58) Method of brake assistance and control
59) Type of brake pressure regulator
60) Type of brakes, disc or drum and disc diameter in centimetres (cm)
61) Method of parking brake operation
62) Steering type
63) Steering assistance type
64) Fuel tank capacity in Litres (L), UK Gallons (Gal) and US Gallons (US Gal)

$$1 Gal = 4.55L$$
$$1 US Gal = 3.785L$$

65) Tyre width and rating
66) Tyre diameter

Dimensions

68) Wheelbase in centimetres (cm). The distance between the front and rear wheels in centimetres
69) Track/Tread, front and rear in centimetres (cm). The distance measured between the centre of the front tyres, and rear tyres (where necessary)
70) Ground clearance in centimetres (cm). The minimum ground clearance of an unladen vehicle
71) Turning circle in metres (m). Measured from the extreme body components in an arc
72) Theoretical load space in cubic feet (cu ft) and cubic deci-metres (dm^3)

$$1 cu\ ft = 0.0353 dm^3$$

Performance

76) Maximum vehicle speed in miles per hour (mph) and kilometres per hour (kmh)

$$1\ mile = 1,609 km$$

77) Theoretical vehicle speed at an engine speed of 1000rpm in the gear specified, in miles per hour (mph) and kilometres per hour (kmh). This is dependant on tyre size and final drive ratio, it is usually a purely calculated figure.
78) Acceleration time from zero to the speed specified in seconds (secs), with two people on board
79) Standing start to 1 kilometre (km) in seconds (secs) with two people on board. This cannot be calculated into time taken over 1 mile
80) Power to weight ratio in kilogrammes per kilowatt (kg/kW) and kilogrammes per horsepower (kg/PS)
81) Fuel consumption in Litres per 100 kilometres (L/100km), miles per UK gallon (mpg) and miles per US gallon (mpg)

$$1 mpg = \frac{282.48}{L/100km}$$
$$1\ USmpg = 0.83267 mpg$$

The method used for calculating fuel consumption may be indicated before the actual figures. DIN is an average drive cycle of town and touring motoring. ECE; the first figure is at a constant 56mph/90kmh, the second is at a constant 75mph/120kmh and the last figure is town driving

Measuring Performance using Different Testing Norms

Engine performance is a crucial factor when judging a car and its overall performance. In a number of countries it also serves as a means of grading the car into its relevant tax and insurance class. Unfortunately, the norms generally used to rate engine performance do not in many cases correspond directly to one another, however certain units of measurement do indicate a definite relationship e.g.

Kilowatt (kW) 1kW = 1,35962PS = 1.34102hp
Pferdestarke (PS) 1hp = 1,0139PS
US-horsepower (hp)

The Kilowatt has in this respect been widely adopted, despite the fact that figures for performance are calculated using different norms and test specifications. The following institutions have devised their own methods for measuring engine performance, which show only the occasional slight difference. In a number of cases, certain methods have been abolished to achieve greater correspondence in test results.

DIN   Deutsches Institut Normung
ECE   Economic Commission for Europe
EG   Europaeische Gemeinschaft
ISO   International Standardisation Organisation
JIS   Japanese Industrial Standard
SAE   Society of Automotive Engineers (USA)

Engine performance is generally calculated using the following formula:

$$P = Tn$$

where P = engine performance, T = engine torque and n = engine speed. Engine torque T is calculated using the following formula:

$$P = F.I.n$$

where F is the Force acting on Lever I. The process of measuring these units in order to determine the engine's performance takes place not in the vehicle itself but on the engine test-bench, using eddy-current brakes, fluid brakes or dynomometer. The work done by the engine during such a test is converted to heat. In order to achieve the engine performance curve characteristic of a fully-loaded engine, the engine speed is generally measured at intervals of between 250-500min -1. Here, two essential procedures are to be distinguished:

Net Performance
"disposable performance"
Test-engine equipment including other plant accessories e.g. generator, intake silencer, engine ventilator, silencer etc.

Gross Peformance
"work performance"
Test-engine equipment excluding plant accessories. (These figures correspond to the former SAE-performance figures, which exceed the Net Performance by around 10-20%). Both Net and Gross Performance are referred to as "effective performance":

P eff = established engine performance
P red = P eff . k
P red = performance reduced/corrected to a specific reference level
k   = correction to the reference level

Reference Level Depending on differences in air density – atmospheric air pressure, air temperature and air humidity – the air drawn in by the engine is "heavier" or "lighter", thereby causing either more or less fuel/air mixture to enter the engine. Differences in atmospheric test conditions are, following correction, recalculated to a specific reference level. Engine performance, for example, drops around 1% per 100m altitude increase; 100m = approx 8mbar air pressure. The various norms and test specifications provide for different reference levels and methods of calculation to correct engine performance levels ascertained according to the atmospheric conditions on that particular day:

	DIN 70020	EG 80/1269	ECE–R 15 ISO 1585
t	20deg C	25deg C	25deg C
p	1013mbar	990mbar	990mbar
k	$\dfrac{1013}{P}\sqrt{\dfrac{273+t}{293}}$	$\left[\dfrac{990}{p-pw}\right]\left[\dfrac{273+t}{298}\right]^{0.5}$	$\left[\dfrac{990}{p-pw}\right]^{1.2}\left[\dfrac{273+t}{298}\right]^{0.6}$

p = atmospheric air pressure
pw = water load pressure
t = temperature deg C

This correction procedure however applies exclusively to Otto engines; more complicated formulae are used in the case of Diesel engines. In contrast to engine performance levels calculated according to DIN, performance is reduced by 1–3% under the EG and ISO/ECE guidelines as a result of differing methods of correction. Former major differences in performance results between either JIS and SAE and DIN were due to the use of Net Performance and a combination of Kd Gross/Net Performance norms. Even today, the definition as to which auxiliaries are powered by the engine varies according to the norm used. Thus: EG: Visco–ventilator minimal slip ECE/ISO: Visco–ventilator maximal slip. On account of these differences, performances may vary by up to around 10% depending on the type of ventilator used. There is however an increasing tendency to bring current norms into line with the revised 1585 ISO (Net Performance) norm, so that former major differences (up to 25%) no longer occur.

Harald Pissor –Franke

Engine Test Bed

AC · Acura

AC   GB

AC Cars Ltd, Brooklands Industrial Park, Weybridge, Surrey KT13 OYU, England

British sports car marque, recently relocated to Surrey. Since Autumn 1987 part of Ford Motor Company.

AC Ace

AC Ace Prototype of a 2+2-seater sports car based on Ford's 4x4 Sierra/Scorpio with 4-cylinder turbo-engine or V6-engine; light-alloy body. Launch Birmingham 1986. Provisional data.

```
2 Litre Turbo
150/167kW–201/224hp–204/227PS
Fuel Injection
```

Body, Weight: Coupe 2-door, 2+2-seater; kerbweight (DIN) approx 910–1020kg (depending on engine).

Engine data (DIN): 4-cylinder in-line (90.82 x 76.95mm), 1994cm3; compression ratio 8:1; 150kW (201hp) [204PS] at 6000rpm, 75.2kW/L (101hp/L) [102.3PS/L]; 276Nm (203.7lbft) at 4500rpm; leaded premium grade.

Engine construction: Valves in V 45deg (4 per cylinder), hydraulic tappets; 2 overhead camshafts (toothed belt); light-alloy cylinder head; oil cooler; Weber-Marelli electronic fuel injection; 1 Garrett T3 or T31/T04 exhaust turbocharger, 12V 43Ah battery, approx 55A alternator; cooling system capacity approx 9L (8.5US qt).

Transmission (to all wheels): Ferguson 4WD system with viscous clutches (distribution front 34% – rear 66%); 5-speed manual, final drive ratio 3.62.

Gear ratios: 1st 2.952; 2nd 1.937; 3rd 1.336; 4th 1; 5th 0.804; R 2.755; or: 1st 3.358; 2nd 1.808; 3rd 1.258; 4th 1; 5th 0.825; R 3.37; or: 1st 3.61; 2nd 2.08; 3rd 1.36; 4th 1; 5th 0.83.

Chassis: Sheet-steel Monocoque and light-alloy body, independent suspension front and rear, control arms front, compression strut and stabilizer, rear semi-trailing arm, stabilizer, coil springs and telescopic damper. Servo/power disc brakes (front ventilated), disc diameter front 28.3cm, rear 27.2cm, mechanical hand brake to rear wheels; rack and pinion steering, with optional power assistance; fuel tank 65L (14Gal) [17US Gal]; tyres 225/45 VR 16, wheel rims 7J.

Dimensions: Wheelbase 247.5cm, track 160/155cm. Length 396 cm, width 181.5cm, height 117cm.

AC Ace

Performance: Max speed over 140mph/225kmh (manufacturers test specifications), speed at 1000rpm in 5th gear 23mph/37kmh; acceleration from 0 – 62mph/100kmh in under 7secs; power to weight ratio from 5.5kg/kW (4.0kg/PS); consumption approx 9–15L/100km (31–19mpg) [26–16US mpg].

```
2.8/2.9 V6
110.5/106.5kW–148/143hp–150/145PS
Fuel Injection
```

As 2 Litre, except:

Engine data (DIN): 2.8 V6 (93 x 68.5mm), 2792cm3; compression ratio 9.2:1; 110.5kW (148hp) [150PS] at 5800rpm, 39.5kW/L (53hp/L) [53.7PS/L]; 219Nm (161.6lbft) at 3000rpm; leaded premium grade.
2.9 V6: (93 x72mm), 2935cm3; compression ratio 9.5:1; 110.5 kW (148hp) [150kW] at 5700rpm, 37.6kW/L (50.4hp/L) [51.1PS/L]; 233Nm (172lbft) at 3000rpm.
With : Compression ratio 9:1; 106.5kW (143hp) [145PS] at 5500rpm, 36.3kW/L (48.6hp) [49.4PS/L]; 222Nm (163.8lbft) at 3000rpm; unleaded regular grade.

Engine construction: With Catalyst and hydraulic tappets; central camshaft (gear driven), crankshaft with 4 bearings, oil capacity 4.25L (4.1US qt); Bosch LE-Jetronic electronic fuel injection.

Performance: Max speed over 134mph/215kmh; power to weight ratio from 8.2kg/kW (6.1kg/PS); consumption approx 9–16L/100 km (31–18mpg) [26–15US mpg].

AC Cobra Mk IV

Roadster with light-alloy body, 4.9 Litre V8 Ford engine with Catalyst, 5-speed manual and independent suspension. Successor of the AC Cobra Mk III.

AC Cobra Mk IV

```
4.9 Litre V8
168kW–225hp–228PS
Fuel Injection
```

Body, Weight: Roadster 2-door, 2-seater; kerbweight (DIN) 1190kg, gross vehicle weight 1340kg.

Engine data (SAE net): 8-cylinder in V 90deg (101.6 x 76.2mm), 4942cm3; compression ratio 9.2:1; 168kW (225hp) [228PS] at 4200rpm, 34kW/L (45.5hp/L) [46.1PS/L]; 407Nm (300lbft) at 3200rpm; unleaded premium grade.

Engine construction: Ford V8 302 HO designation. Hydraulic tappets, central camshaft (chain); 5 bearing crankshaft; oil capacity 4.7/7L (4.4/6.6US qt); electronic fuel injection. 12V 65Ah battery, 72A alternator; cooling system capacity approx 14L (13US qt).

Transmission (to rear wheels): 5-speed manual, final drive ratio 3.08, limited slip differential.

Gear ratios: 1st 3.50; 2nd 2.14; 3rd 1.36; 4th 1; 5th 0.78; R 3.39.

Chassis: Tubular frame chassis; independent suspension front and rear with A-arms, antiroll bar, coil springs and telescopic damper. Servo/power disc brakes (front ventilated), disc diameter front 29.3cm, rear 27.3cm, mechanical hand brake to rear wheels; rack and pinion steering; fuel tank approx 70/75L (15/16.5Gal) [18.5/20US Gal]; tyres front 225/50 VR 16, rear 255/50 VR 16, wheel rims 7.5/9.5 or 7/8 inches.

Dimensions: Wheelbase 228.5cm, track 142/152.5cm. Turning circle approx 12m. Length 411.5cm, width 173.5cm, height 124.5cm.

Performance: Max speed 134mph/215kmh (manufacturers test specifications), speed at 1000rpm in 5th gear 31.4mph/50.6kmh; acceleration from 0 – 62mph/100kmh in 5.2secs; power to weight ratio from 7.1kg/kW (5,2kg/PS); consumption approx 12–18 L/100km (23.5–16mpg) [19.5–13US mpg].

ACURA   J

Integra and Legend models from Honda are sold in the United States under the name Acura. For technical details see Honda.

Acura Legend

Alfa Romeo

ALFA ROMEO I

Alfa-Lancia Industriale SpA, Viale Alfa Romeo, 20020 Arese, Italia

Famous Italian manufacturer of high-performance cars. Since November 1986 part of the Fiat Group.

MODEL RANGE
Sprint – Alfa 33/33 4x4 – Spider – Alfa 75 – Alfa 164 – E30

Alfa Romeo Sprint

Alfa Romeo Sprint 1.3 – 1.7 Quadrifoglio Verde

Coupe with tail gate and front wheel drive, 4-cylinder horizontally opposed engine. Launch September 1976. Autumn 1987: with 1.7L instead of 1.5L engine.

```
1351cm3
63.5kW-85hp-86PS
Twin 2V Carbs
```

Engine for 1.3L

Body, Weight: Coupe 3-door (with tail gate), 4/5-seater; kerbweight (DIN) 915–930kg, gross vehicle weight 1340kg.

Engine data (DIN): 4-cylinder, horizontally opposed engine (80 x 67.2mm), 1351cm3; compression ratio 9.7:1; 63.5kW (85hp) [86PS] at 5800rpm, 47kW/L (63hp/L) [63.7PS/L]; 119Nm (87.8lbft) at 4000rpm; leaded premium grade 98(R). Some countries: 63kW (84.4hp) [85PS].

Engine construction: 2 x 1 overhead camshaft (toothed belt); light-alloy cylinder heads; 3 bearing crankshaft; oil capacity 4.6L (4.4US qt); 2 downdraught 2V carbs. 12V 50Ah battery, 55A alternator; cooling system capacity 7.3L (6.9US qt).

Transmission (to front wheels): 5-speed manual, final drive ratio 4.111 (9/37).

Gear ratios: 1st 3.143; 2nd 1.864; 3rd 1.323; 4th 1.027; 5th 0.854; R 3.091

Alfa Romeo Sprint

Chassis: Integral body; front McPherson struts, control arms, compression strut and coil springs, rigid rear axle with side bar fixed both in front and behind axle (Watt-linkage). Panhard rod and coil springs, front antiroll bar, telescopic damper. Servo/power brakes, front discs, rear drums, disc diameter 23.9cm, mechanical handbrake to rear wheels; rack and pinion steering; fuel tank 50L (11Gal) [13USGal], 6.5L (1.4Gal) [1.7US Gal] reserve; tyres 165/70 SR 13, wheel rims 5.5J.

Dimensions: Wheelbase 246.5 cm, track 136/136cm, clearance 16.5cm, turning circle 10.4m, load space 11.5cu ft (325dm3). Length 402.5cm, width 162cm, height 130.5cm.

Performance: Max speed 107.5mph/173kmh (manufacturers test specifications), speed at 1000rpm in 5th gear 18.3mph/29.5kmh; acceleration from 0 – 62mph/100kmh in 10.3secs, standing km 32.3secs; power to weight ratio 14.4kg/kW (10.6kg/PS); fuel consumption (ECE) 5.7/7.8/10.3L/100km (49.6/36.2/27.4mpg) [41.3/30.2/22.8US mpg].

```
1717cm3
87/77kW-116.5/103hp-118/105PS
Twin 2V Carbs/Fuel Injection
```

Engine for 1.7 Quadrifoglio Verde

As 1351cm3, except:

Engine data (DIN): 4-cylinder, horizontally opposed engine (87 x 72.2mm), 1717cm3, compression ratio 9.5:1; 87kW (116.5hp) [118PS] at 5800rpm, 50.6kW/L (67.8hp/L) [68.7PS/L]; 147Nm (108.5lbft) at 3500rpm.
For some countries: 84.5kW (113hp) [115PS].
With Catalyst and Bosch LE 3.1-Jetronic fuel injection: 77kW (103hp) [105PS] at 5500rpm, 44.8kW/L (60hp/L) [61.2PS/L]; 145Nm (107lbft) at 4500 rpm; unleaded premium grade (95R).

Engine construction: Hydraulic tappets

Transmission: Final drive ratio 3.7 (10/37) or 3.89 (9/35).

Chassis: Front antiroll bar; ventilated disc brakes; tyres 185/60 HR 14, wheel rims 5.5J.

Dimensions: Track 136.5/136.5cm.

Performance: Max speed 122mph/196kmh, Catalyst 117mph/188kmh (manufacturers test specifications), speed at 1000rpm in 5th gear 20.8mph/33.4kmh; acceleration from 0 – 62mph/100kmh 9.0secs, Catalyst approx 9.7secs; standing km 30.0secs, Catalyst 31.1secs; power to weight ratio 10.5kg/kW (7.8kg/PS); fuel consumption (ECE) 5.9/8.2/11.4L/100km (47.8/34.4/24.8mpg) [39.9/28.7/20.6US mpg].

Alfa Romeo Alfa 33 – 33 4x4

1.3 – 1.3 S – 1.5 – 1.7 – 1.8 TD

Medium-range car with tail gate, 4-cylinder horizontally opposed engine and front wheel drive, optional selectable 4 wheel drive. Launch: saloon/sedan May/June 1983, 4x4 Frankfurt 1983, 4x4 sports car Geneva 1984. Since October 1986 also with 1.7L horizontally opposed engine and 1.8L 3-cylinder turbo-diesel engine. Early Spring/Summer 1988: New model range.

```
1351cm3
58kW-77.7hp-79PS
One 2V Carb
```

Engine for 1.3L

Body, Weight: Saloon/Sedan 5-door (with tail gate), 5-seater; kerbweight (DIN) 910kg, gross vehicle weight 1335kg.

Engine data (DIN): 4-cylinder, horizontally opposed engine (80 x 67.2mm), 1351cm3; compression ratio 9:1; 58kW (77.7hp) [79PS] at 6000 rpm, 43kW/L (57.6hp/L) [58.5PS/L]; 111Nm (81.9lbft) at 3500rpm; leaded premium grade (98/95R).
For some countries: 55kW (73.7hp) [75PS] or 1186cm3, 50kW (67hp) [68PS].

Alfa Romeo Alfa 33 1.3

Engine construction: 2 x 1 overhead camshafts (toothed belt); light-alloy cylinder heads; 3 bearing crankshaft; oil capacity 4.6L (4.4US qt); 1 Weber downdraught 2V carb 32 DIR 61/100 or 81/250. 12V 50Ah battery, 55A alternator; cooling system capacity 7.3L (6.9US qt).

Transmission (to front wheels): 5-speed manual, final drive ratio 4.11 (9/37).

Gear ratios: 1st 3.143; 2nd 1.864; 3rd 1.323; 4th 1.027; 5th 0.854; R 3.091

Chassis: Integral body; independent front suspension, McPherson struts, track control arm, compression strut, antiroll bar and coil springs, rigid rear axle with side bar fixed in front and behind axle (Watt-linkage), Panhard rod and coil springs, telescopic damper. Servo/power assisted brakes, front discs rear drums mechanical handbrake to rear wheels; rack and pinion steering; fuel tank 50L (11Gal) [13.2US Gal], of which 6.5L (1.4Gal) [1.7US Gal] reserve; tyres 165/70 SR 13, wheel rims 5.5J.

Alfa Romeo

Dimensions: Wheelbase 246.5cm, track 136.5/136.5cm, clearance 12cm, turning circle 10.4/11m. Load space 14.1/42.4cu ft (400/1200dm3). Length 401.5cm, width 161cm, height 134.5cm.

Performance: Max peed 104mph/167kmh (manufacturers test specifications), speed at 1000rpm in 5th gear 18.3mph/29.5kmh; acceleration from 0 – 62mph/100kmh in 11.5secs, standing km 33.7secs; power to weight ratio 15.7kg/kW (11.5kg/PS); fuel consumption (ECE) 5.7/8.2/10.1L/100km (49.6/34.4/28.0mpg) [41.3/28.7/23.3US mpg].

```
1351cm3
63.5kW–85hp–86PS
Twin 2V Carbs
```

Engine for 1.3 S and 1.3 S Sports Wagon

As 1.3L 58kW–77.7hp–79PS, except:

Body, Weight: Saloon/Sedan 5–door, 5–seater; kerbweight (DIN) 910kg, gross vehicle weight 1335kg; Sports Wagon 5–door, 5–seater; kerbweight (DIN) 925kg, gross vehicle weight 1350kg.

Engine data (DIN): 4–cylinder horizontally opposed engine (80 x 67.2mm), 1351cm3; compression ratio 9.5:1; 63.5kW (85hp) [86PS] at 5800rpm, 46.8kW/L (62.7hp/L) [63.7PS/L]; 119Nm (87.8lbft) at 4000rpm.

Engine construction: Twin 2V carbs.

Dimensions: Sports car: load space 15.2/47.7cu ft (430/1350dm3); length 414cm.

Performance: Max speed 107.5mph/172kmh (manufacturers test specifications), speed at 1000rpm in 5th gear 17.7mph/29.5kmh; acceleration from 0 – 62mph/100kmh in 10.3/10.7secs, standing km 32.3secs; power to weight ratio 14.4kg/kW (10.6kg/PS); consumption (ECE) 5.7/7.8/10.3L/100km (49.6/36.2/27.4mpg) [41.3/30.2/22.8US mpg].

Alfa Romeo Alfa 33 1.3S Sport Wagon

```
1490cm3
77kW–103hp–105PS
Twin 2V Carbs
```

Engine for 1.5 TI, 1.5 4x4 and 1.5 4x4 Sports Wagon

As 1.3L 58kW–77.7hp–79PS, except:

Body, Weight: Saloon/Sedan 5–door, 5–seater; kerbweight (DIN) 910kg, gross vehicle weight 1335kg. Saloon/Sedan 4x4 5–door, 5–seater; kerbweight (DIN) 970kg, gross vehicle weight 1335kg. Sports Wagon 4x4 5–door, 5–seater, kerbweight (DIN) 990kg, gross vehicle weight 1415kg.

Engine data (DIN): 4–cylinder horizontally opposed engine (84 x 67.2mm), 1490cm3; compression ratio 9.5:1; 77kW (103hp) [105PS] at 5600rpm, 51.6kW/L (69.1hp/L) [70.5PS/L]; 133Nm (98.2lbft) at 4000rpm.

Engine construction: 2 Weber downdraught 2V carbs. 50 or 55Ah battery.

Transmission: Final drive ratio 3.89 (9/35); 4x4 with selectable 4-wheel drive, final drive ratio 3.89 (9/35) or 4.11 (9/37).

Gear ratios: 1st 3.143; 2nd 1.864; 3rd 1.323; 4th 1,027; 5th 0.854; R 3.091; 4x4: 1st 3.75; 2nd 2.05; 3rd 1.387; 4th 1.027; 5th 0.825; R 3.091.

Chassis: Fuel tank 50L (11Gal) [13.2US Gal], 4x4 53L (11.7Gal) [14US Gal]; tyres 175/70 TR 13.

Dimensions: Track 136.5/136.5cm, 4x4 136/137.5cm. Clearance Sports Wagon/4x4 16cm. Load space 14.1/42.4cu ft (400/1200dm3), 4x4 8.8/37.1cu ft (250/1050dm3), 4x4 Sports Wagon 12.4/42.4cu ft (350/1200 dm3). Length 401.5cm, Sports Wagon 414cm.

Performance: Max speed 115mph/185kmh, 4x4 113–112mph/182–180kmh (manufacturers test specifications), speed at 1000rpm in 5th gear (3.89) 21mph/31.8kmh, all 4x4 20.6mph/31.1kmh; acceleration from 0 – 62mph/100kmh in 9.8, 4x4 in 10.5secs, standing km 31.3, 4x4 in 32.3secs; power to weight ratio from 11.8kg/kW (8.7kg/PS); fuel consumption (ECE) 6.1/8.0/10.7L/100km (46.3/35.3/26.4mpg) [38.6/29.4/22US mpg], 4x4 6.0/8.1/10.7L/100km (47.1/34.9/26.4mpg) [39.2/29/22US mpg], 4x4 Sports Wagon 6.1/8.3/11.1L/100km (46.3/34/25.4mpg) [38.6/28.3/21.2US mpg]

Alfa Romeo Alfa 33 1.7S Sport Wagon

```
1717cm3
87/81/77kW–116.6/108.5/103.2hp
118/110/105PS
Twin 2V Carbs/Fuel Injection
```

Engine for 1.7 Quadrifoglio Verde, 1.7IE also 1.7 Sports Wagon and 1.7 Sports Wagon 4x4

As 1.3L 58kW–77.7hp–79PS, except:

Body, Weight: Saloon/Sedan 5–door, 5–seater; kerbweight (DIN) 910–940kg, gross vehicle weight 1335/1355kg; Sports Wagon 5–door, 5–seater; kerbweight (DIN) 925/945kg, gross vehicle weight 1350kg; Sports Wagon 4x4 5–door, 5–seater; kerbweight (DIN) 1010kg, gross vehicle weight 1435kg.

Engine data (DIN): 4–cylinder horizontally opposed engine (87 x 72.2mm), 1717cm3; compression ratio 9.5:1; 87kW (116.6hp) [118PS] at 5800 rpm, 50.6kW/L (67.8hp/L) [68.7PS/L]; 147Nm (108.5lbft) at 3500rpm.
For some countries: 84.5kW (113.2hp) [115PS].
With fuel injection (IE): 81kW (108.5hp) [110PS] at 5800rpm, 47.2kW/L (63.2hp/L) [64.1 PS/L]; 148Nm (109.2lbft) at 4500rpm.
With Catalyst and fuel injection: 77kW (103.2hp) [105PS] at 5500rpm, 44.9kW/L (60.2kW/L) [61.1PS/L]; 145Nm (107lbft) at 4500 rpm; unleaded premium grade (95R).

Engine construction: Hydraulic tappets, 2 downdraught 2V carbs or Bosch LE 3.2-Jetonic electronic fuel injection. 50 or 55Ah battery, 55A or 65A alternator.

Transmission: Final drive ratio 3.7 (10/37) or 3.89 (9/35).

Chassis: Front ventilated disc brakes. Tyres 185/60 HR 14 or 175/70 TR 13, wheel rims 5.5J.

Dimensions: Track 136.5/136.5cm, 4x4 136/137.5cm or 136.5/136cm, clearance Sports Wagon/4x4 16cm. Load space 14.1/42.4cu ft (400/1200dm3), Sports Wagon 15.2/42.5cu ft (430/1200dm3). Length 401.5cm, Sports Wagon 414cm.

Performance: Max speed 122mph/196kmh, IE 117mph/188kmh, IE Catalyst 115–117mph/185–188kmh, sports car 113–111mph/182–178kmh (manufacturers test specifications), speed at 1000rpm in 5th gear 20.8/19.9mph, 33.4/32kmh; acceleration from 0 – 62mph/100kmh in 9secs, IE 9.4–10secs, Catalyst 97–9.9secs; standing km 30.0secs; IE 31–31.7secs; power to weight ratio 10.5kg/kW (7.7kg/PS); fuel consumption (ECE) 5.9/8.2/11.4L/100km (47.9/34.4/24.8mpg) [39.9/28.7/20.6US mpg], IE 6.0/7.6/9.7L/100km (47.1/37.2/29.1mpg) [39.2/30.9/24.2US mpg).

Alfa Romeo Alfa 33 1.7IE

Alfa Romeo

> 1779cm3 Diesel
> 54.5kW–73hp–74PS
> Turbo/Injection Pump

Engine for 1.8 TD and 1.8 TD Sports Wagon

As 1.3L 58kW–77.7hp–79PS, except:

Body, Weight: Saloon/Sedan 5–door, 5–seater; kerbweight (DIN) 1010kg, gross vehicle weight 1435kg; Sports Wagon 5–door, 5–seater; kerbweight (DIN) 1025kg, gross vehicle weight 1450kg.

Engine data (DIN): 3–cylinder in–line (92 x 89.2mm), 1779 cm3; compression ratio 22:1; 54.5kW (73hp) [74PS] at 4000rpm, 30.6kW/L (41hp/L) [41.6PS/L]; 153Nm (112.9lbft) at 2400rpm.

Engine construction: VM HRT 392 designation. Engine in–line, tilted at 30deg, light-alloy cylinder–head, valves parallel; 4 bearing crankshaft; 1 side camshaft (toothed wheel); counterbalance shaft; oil capacity 5.5L (5.2US qt); Bosch VE 3/10 injection pump, 1 exhaust turbocharger KKK 14, max charge–air pressure 0.9bar. 12V 70Ah battery, 65A alternator; cooling system capacity approx 7.5L(7.1US qt).

Transmission: Final drive ratio 3.182 (11/35).

Gear ratios: 1st 3.75; 2nd 2.05; 3rd 1.387; 4th 1.027; 5th 0.825; R 3.091.

Chassis: Tyres 175/70 TR 13

Dimensions: Wheelbase 245.5cm, track 139.5/136.5cm. Load space 14.1/42cu ft (400/1200dm3), Sports Wagon 15.2/47.7cu ft (430/1350dm3). Length 404cm, Sports Wagon 416.5cm.

Performance: Max speed 102.5mph/165kmh (manufacturers test specifications), speed at 1000rpm in 5th gear 25mph/40.2kmh; acceleration from 0 – 62mph/100kmh in 14secs, standing km 35.6secs; power to weight ratio 18.5kg/kW (13.6kg/PS); Fuel consumption (ECE) 4.9/6.9/7.3L/100km (57.6/40.9/38.7mpg) [48/34.1/32.2US mpg], Sports Wagon 4.9/7.1/7.3L/100km (57.6/39.8/38.7mpg) [48/33.1/32.2US mpg].

Alfa Romeo Spider

1.6 – 2.0 – 2.0 Quadrifoglio Verde

Convertible derived from the former Giula Super. Launch Junior 1300 May 1968, Junior 1600 Summer 1972 and Veloce 2000 June 1971. Spring 1986: body and interior modified.

> 1567cm3
> 76.5/75kW–102.5/100.5hp–104/102PS
> Twin 2V Carbs

Engine for 1.6L

Body, Weight: Convertible (Pininfarina) 2–door, 2–seater; kerbweight (DIN) 1020kg, gross vehicle weight 1340kg.

Engine data (DIN): 4–cylinder in–line (78 x 82mm), 1567cm3; compression ratio 9:1; 76.5kW (102.5hp) [104PS] at 5500rpm, 48.8kW/L (65.4hp/L) [66.4PS/L]; 137Nm (101.1lbft) at 4300rpm; leaded premium grade.
For some countries: 76kW (102.5hp) [103PS] or 75kW (100.5hp) [102PS].

Engine construction: Overhead valves (in V 80deg), 2 overhead camshafts (chain); light–alloy cylinder head and cylinder block, wet cylinder liners; 5 bearing crankshaft; oil capacity 6.5L (6.1US qt); 2 Weber horizontal 2V carbs. 12V 50Ah battery, 40A alternator; cooling system capacity 7.5L (7.1US qt).

Alfa Romeo Spider

Transmission (to rear wheels): 5–speed manual, floor shift; final drive ratio 4.55 (9/41), optional limited slip differential.

Gear ratios: 1st 3.30; 2nd 1.99; 3rd 1.35; 4th 1; 5th 0.79; R 3.01.

Chassis: Integral body; front upper and lower wishbones with reactor struts, coil springs, rigid axle with coil springs, torsion bar and wishbones; front and rear antiroll bars and telescopic dampers. Servo/power disc brakes; disc diameter 27.2cm front, 26.7cm rear, mechanical handbrake to rear wheels; ZF worm and wheel steering or Burman–recirculating ball; fuel tank 46L (10.1Gal) [12.2US Gal]; tyres 165 SR/HR 14, optional 185/70 HR or 195/60 HR 15, wheel rims 5.5J.

Dimensions: Wheelbase 225cm, track 132.5/127.5cm, clearance 12.5cm, turning circle 10.7m, Load space 10.6 - 7.1cu ft (300 - 200dm3), length 424.5cm, width 163cm, height 129cm.

Performance: Max speed 112mph/180kmh (manufacturers test specifications); speed at 1000rpm in 4th gear 15.7mph/25.2kmh, in 5th gear 19.8mph/31.8kmh; acceleration from 0 – 62mph/100kmh in 10.1secs, standing km 32.8secs; power to weight ratio 13.3kg/kW (9.8kg/PS); fuel consumption (ECE) 7.4/9.7/11.2L/100km (38.2/29.1/25.2mpg) [31.8/24.2/21US mpg] or 7.8/9.8/11.6L/100km (36.2/28.8/24mpg) [30.2/24/20.3US mpg].

> 1962cm3
> 94/86kW–126/113.2hp–128/115PS
> Twin 2V Carbs

Engine for 2.0 and 2.0 Quadrifoglio Verde As 1567cm3, except:

Body, Weight: Convertible (Pininfarina) 2–door, 2–seater; kerbweight (DIN) 1040–1090kg (USA 1155kg), gross vehicle weight 1360/1390kg.

Engine data (DIN): 4–cylinder in–line (84 x 88.5mm), 1962 cm3; compression ratio 9:1; 94kW (126hp) [128PS] at 5400rpm; leaded premium grade.
For some countries: 92kW (123.3hp) [125PS].
With Catalyst: Fuel injection; 84.5kW (113hp) [115PS] at 5500rpm; 162Nm (119.6lbft) at 3000rpm; unleaded regular grade (91R).
For some countries: 86kW (115.2hp) [117PS].

Engine construction: 2 Weber horizontal 2V carbs or fuel injection. 12V 50 or 60Ah battery.

Transmission: Final drive ratio 4.1 (10/41) or 4.3 (10/43), limited slip differential.

Chassis: Tyres 185/70 HR 14/15 or 195/60 HR 15, wheel rims 5.5J.

Dimensions: Length USA 428cm.

Performance: Max speed 118mph/190kmh, Catalyst 115mph/185kmh (manufacturers test specifications), speed at 1000rpm in 5th gear 21.9/20.8mph, 35.2/33.4kmh; acceleration from 0 – 62mph/100kmh in 9secs; power to weight ratio 13.1kg/kW (9.6kg/PS); fuel consumption (ECE) 6.9/9.4/13.1L/100km (40.9/30.1/21.6mpg) [34.1/25/18US mpg] or 6.6/8.6/13.3L/100km (42.8/32.8/21.2mpg) [35.6/27.4/17.7].

Alfa Romeo Alfa 75

1.6 – 1.8 IE – 2.0 T Spark – 2.5 V6 – 3.0 V6 – 1.8T – 2.0TD – 2.4TD

Successor of the Giulietta. Saloon/Sedan with 1.6 – 2.5 litre engines, 2 litre turbo–diesel engine, rear mounted transmission with differential, De–Dion rear axle. Launch May 1985, 1.8 turbo March 1986. February 1987: new models "Twin Spark 2.0" and "6V 3.0".

> 1567cm3
> 81kW–108.5hp–110PS
> Twin 2V Carbs

Engine for 1.6L

Body, Weight (DIN): Saloon/Sedan 4–door, 5–seater; kerbweight (DIN) 1060kg, gross vehicle weight 1485kg.

Engine data (DIN): 4–cylinder, in–line (78 x 82mm), 1567cm3; compression ratio 9:1; 81kW (108.5hp) [110PS] at 5800rpm, 51.6kW/L (69.1hp/L) [70.2PS/L]; 146Nm (107.7lbft) at 4000rpm; leaded premium grade (98/95R).

Engine construction: 116.50 designation. Overhead valves (in V80 deg), 2 overhead camshafts (chain); light–alloy cylinder head and block, wet cylinder liners; 5 bearing crankshaft; oil capacity 5.5L (5.2US qt); 2 Weber/Dell'Orto DHLA 40 H horizontal 2V carbs. 12V 50Ah battery, 55A alternator; cooling system capacity 8L (7.6US qt).

Transmission (to rear wheels): Rear mounted 5–speed manual with differential; floor shift; final drive ratio 4.556 (9/41).

Gear Ratios: 1st 2.875; 2nd 1.720; 3rd 1.226; 4th 0.946; 5th 0.780; R 3.

Chassis: Integral body; lower A–arms, upper single control arm with flexible tension strut, longitudinal antiroll bar, cornering stabilizer front; De–Dion axle

Alfa Romeo

with semi-trailing arms, Watt linkage, coil springs and rear antiroll bar, telescopic dampers rear and front. Servo/power brakes, rear discs alongside differential, disc diameter 25cm, mechanical handbrake to rear wheels; rack and pinion steering, also available with power assistance; fuel tank 49L (10.8Gal) [12.9US Gal], of which 8L (1.7Gal) [2.1US Gal] are reserve; tyres 185/70 SR/TR 13, wheel rims 5.5J.

Alfa Romeo Alfa 75 1.6

Dimensions: Wheelbase 251cm, track 137/136cm, clearance 12cm, turning circle 10.9m. Load space 17.6cu ft (500dm3). Length 433cm, width 163cm, height 140cm.

Performance: Max speed 112mph/180kmh (manufacturers test specifications), speed at 1000rpm in 5th gear 19.1mph/30.7kmh; acceleration from 0 – 62mph/100kmh in 10.7secs, standing km 32.5secs; power to weight ratio 13.5kg/kW (9.9kg/PS); consumption (ECE) 6.9/9.4/11.8L/100km (40.9/30.1/23.9mpg) [34.1/25/19.9US mpg].

```
1779cm3
90kW–120hp–122PS
Fuel Injection
```

Engine for 1.8 IE

As 1567 cm3, except:

Weight: Kerbweight (DIN) 1110kg, gross vehicle weight 1525kg.

Engine data (DIN): 4-cylinder in-line (80 x 88.5mm), 1779cm3; compression ratio 9.5:1; 90kW (120hp) [122PS] at 5500rpm, 50.6kW/L (67.8hp/L) [68.6PS/L]; 160Nm (118lbft) at 4000rpm.

Engine construction: Bosch Motronic ML 3.3 fuel injection. 12V 55Ah battery, 65A alternator.

Transmission: Final drive ratio 4.3 (10/43).

Chassis: Tyres 185/70 HR 13.

Performance: Max speed 118mph/190kmh (manufacturers test specifications), speed at 1000rpm in 5th gear 20.2mph/32.5kmh; acceleration from 0 – 62mph/100kmh in 10.4secs, standing km 31.9secs; power to weight ratio 12.2kg/kW (8.8kg/PS); fuel consumption (ECE) 6.9/8.9/10.5L/100km (40.9/31.7/26.9mpg) [34.1/26.4/22.4US mpg]. .

```
1962cm3
109/107kW–146/143.4hp–148/145PS
Fuel Injection
```

Engine for Twin Spark 2.0

As 1567cm3, except:

Weight: Kerbweight (DIN) 1120 – 1145kg, gross vehicle weight 1545 – 1570kg.

Engine data (DIN): 4-cylinder in-line (84 x 88.5mm), 1962cm3; compression ratio 10:1; 109kW (146hp) [148PS] at 5800rpm, 55.6kW/L (74.5hp/L) [75.4PS/L]; 186Nm (137.3lbft) at 4000 rpm. With Catalyst: 107kW (143.4hp) [145PS] at 5800rpm, 54.5kW/L (73hp/L) [73.9PS/L]; 178Nm (131.4lbft) at 3000rpm or 186Nm (137.3lbft) at 4700rpm; unleaded premium grade (95R).

Engine construction: Electronic fuel injection Bosch Motronic ML4.1. 2 spark plugs per cylinder; 12V 55Ah battery, 65A alternator.

Transmission: Final drive ratio 4.1 (10/41). Limited slip differential.

Chassis: Servo/power disc brakes (front ventilated) also available with ABS, disc diameter 26.5cm front, 25cm rear; optional power steering; tyres 195/60 VR 14, wheel rims 6.5J.

Dimensions: Track 139.5/138cm; width 163/166cm, length 433/442cm.

Performance: Max speed 127mph/205kmh, with Catalyst 125–126mph/202–204kmh (manufacturers test specifications) at 1000rpm

Alfa Romeo Alfa 75 2.0 T. Spark

in 5th gear 21.2mph/34.1kmh, acceleration from 0 – 62mph/100kmh in 8.2 secs – with Catalyst 8.7/8.7secs, standing km 29.2secs – with Catalyst 29.7/30.1secs; power to weight ratio 10.6kg/kW (7.8kg/PS); fuel consumption (ECE) 6.0/8.4/9.9L/100km (47.1/33.6/28.8mpg) [39.2/28/23.8US mpg] – with Catalyst 6.2/8.6/10.2L/100km (45.6/32.8 27.7mpg) [37.9/27.4/23.1US mpg].

```
2492cm3 V6
114.5kW–153.4hp–156PS
Fuel Injection
```

Engine for 2.5L V6

As 1567cm3, except:

Weight: Kerbweight (DIN) 1160kg, gross vehicle weight 1585kg.

Engine data (DIN): 6-cylinder in V60 deg (88 x 68.3mm), 2492cm3; compression ratio 9:1; 114.5kW (153.4hp) [156PS] at 5600rpm, 46.kW/L (61.6hp/L) [62.6PS/L]; 210Nm (155lbft) at 4000rpm.

With Catalyst: 114.5kW (153.4hp) [156PS] at 5500rpm; 206Nm (152lbft) at 3200rpm.

For some countries: 110kW (147.4hp) [150PS]

Engine construction: 119/11 designation. Light-alloy cylinder head and block; valves in V 46deg; 2 x 1 overhead camshafts (toothed belt); 4 bearing crankshaft; oil capacity 6.4L (6.1US qt); Bosch L-Jetronic electronic fuel injection. 12V 66Ah battery, 840W alternator; cooling system capacity 10L (9.5US qt).

Transmission: Final drive ratio 4.1 (10/41).

Chassis: Servo/power assisted disc brakes (front ventilated), disc diameter 26.5cm front, 25cm rear; power steering; fuel tank 49/68/75L (10.8/15/16.5Gal) [13/18/19.8US Gal]; tyres 195/60 VR 14 or 195/55 VR 15, wheel rims 5.5J.

Performance: Max speed 130.5mph/210kmh (manufacturers test specifications), speed at 1000rpm in 5th gear 21mph/33.8kmh, acceleration from 0 – 62mph/100kmh in 8.2secs; standing km 29.0secs; power to weight ratio 10.1kg/kW (7.4kg/PS); fuel consumption (ECE) 6.8/9.0/13.0L/100km (41.5/31.4/21.7mpg) [34.6/26.1/18.1US mpg]. With Catalyst: Max speed 127mph/205kmh; acceleration from 0 – 62mph/100kmh in 9 secs.

```
2959cm3 V6
138136kW–185/182hp–188/185PS
Fuel Injection
```

Engine for 3.0L V6

As 1567cm3, except:

Weight: Kerbweight (DIN) 1250 – 1340kg, gross vehicle weight 1675 – 1765kg.

Engine data (DIN): 6-cylinder in V60 deg (93 x 72.6mm), 2959cm3; compression ratio 9.5:1; 138kW (185hp) [188PS] at 5800rpm, 46.6kW/L (62.4hp/L) [63.6PS/L]; 250Nm (184.5lbft) at 4500rpm.

With Catalyst: 136kW (182hp) [185PS] at 5800rpm, 46kW/L (61.6hp/L) [62.5PS/L]; 246Nm (181.5lbft) at 4500rpm; unleaded premium grade (95R).

Engine construction: 119/11 designation, light-alloy cylinder head and block in V 46deg; 2 x 1 overhead camshaft (toothed belt); 4 bearing crankshaft; oil capacity 6.4L (6.1US qt); Bosch L-Jetronic electronic fuel injection.

Transmission: Final drive ratio 3.545 (11/39). Limited slip differential.

Chassis: Servo/power assisted disc brakes (front ventilated) also available with ABS, disc diameter 26.5cm front, 25cm rear; optional power steering; fuel tank 68L (15Gal) [18US Gal]; tyres 195/60 VR 14 or 195/55 VR 15, wheel rims 6.5J.

Alfa Romeo

Dimensions: Track 139.5/138cm. Load space 13.4cu ft (380dm3). Length 442cm, width 166cm.

Performance: Max speed 136.7mph/220kmh (manufacturers test specifications), speed at 1000rpm in 5th gear 24.5mph/39.4kmh, acceleration from 0–62mph/100kmh in 7.3secs, standing km 28secs; power to weight ratio 9.4kg/kW (6.9kg/PS); fuel consumption (ECE) 7.4/9.2/12.9L/100km (38.2/30.7/21.9mpg) [31.8/25.6/18.2US mpg]. With Catalyst: Max speed 134–135.5mph/216–218kmh (manufacturers test specifications); acceleration from 0–62mph/100kmh in 7.4–7.9secs, standing km 28.2–28.4secs; power to weight ratio 9.6kg/kW (7.0kg/PS); consumption (ECE) 7.6/9.4/13.2L/100km (37.2/30.1/21.4mpg) [30.9/25/17.8US mpg].

Alfa Romeo Alfa 75 3.0 V6

```
1779cm3 Turbo
114kW–153hp–155PS
Fuel Injection
```

Engine for 1.8L Turbo

As 1567cm3, except:

Weight: Kerbweight (DIN) 1240kg, gross vehicle weight 1665kg.

Engine data (DIN): 4–cylinder in–line (80 x 88.5mm), 1779cm3; compression ratio 7.5:1; 114kW (153hp) [155PS] at 5800rpm, 64.1kW/L (85.9hp/L) [87.1PS/L]; 226Nm (166.8lbft) at 2600rpm; leaded premium grade (98R).

Engine construction: Bosch LE2–Jetronic fuel injection; 1 Garrett T3 exhaust turbocharger, max charge–air pressure 0.75bar, charge–air cooler, 12V 55/60Ah battery, 65A alternator.

Transmission: Final drive ratio 3.909 (11/43). Limited slip differential.

Chassis: Servo/power assisted disc brakes (front ventilated), disc diameter 26.5cm front, 25cm rear; fuel tank 68L (14.9Gal) [18US Gal]; tyres 195/60 VR 14, wheel rims 6.5J.

Dimensions: Track 138/139.5cm; load space 13.4cu ft (380dm3). Length 442cm, width 166cm.

Performance: Max speed 130.5mph/210kmh (manufacturers test specifications), speed at 1000rpm in 5th gear 22mph/35.7kmh, acceleration from 0–62mph/100kmh in 7.6secs, standing km 28.5secs; power to weight ratio 10.0kg/kW (8.0kg/PS); consumption (ECE) 7.0/9.0/9.7L/100km (40.4/31.4/29.1mpg) [33.6/26.1/24.2US mpg].

Alfa Romeo Alfa 75 1.8 Turbo

```
2.0L Turbo–Diesel
70kW–93.8hp–95PS
Injection Pump
```

Engine for 2.0L TD

As 1567cm3, except:

Weight: Kerbweight (DIN) 1220kg, gross vehicle weight 1645kg.

Engine data (DIN): 4–cylinder in–line (88 x 82mm), 1995cm3; compression ratio 22:1; 70kW (93.8hp) [95PS] at 4300rpm, 35.0kW/L (46.9hp/L) [47.6PS/L]; 192Nm (141.7lbft) at 2300rpm.

Engine construction: VM 80A designation. Diesel engine, cast iron cylinder block; light–alloy head, parallel valves, 1 side camshaft (gear wheels); oil capacity 6.6L (6.2US qt); Bosch VE 4/10 diesel injection pump, KKK 16 exhaust turbocharger; max charge–air pressure 0.9bar, charge–air cooler. 12V 70/77/88/92Ah battery, 55A alternator; cooling system capacity approx 10L (9.5US qt).

Transmission: Final drive ratio 3.545 (11/39).

Gear ratios: 1st 3.500; 2nd 1.956; 3rd 1.258; 4th 0.946; 5th 0.780; R 3.

Chassis: Power assisted steering.

Performance: Max speed 109mph/175kmh (manufacturers test specifications), speed at 1000rpm in 5th gear 24.6mph/39.6kmh; acceleration from 0–62mph/100kmh in 12.4secs; standing km 34.5secs; power to weight ratio 17.4kg/kW (12.8kg/PS); fuel consumption (ECE) 5.5/7.9/9.0L/100km (51.4/35.8/31.4mpg) [42.8/29.8/26.1US mpg].

```
2.4L Turbo–Diesel
82kW–110hp–112PS
Injection Pump
```

Engine for 2.4L TD

As 1567cm3, except:

Weight: Kerbweight (DIN) 1260kg, gross vehicle weight 1685kg.

Engine date (DIN): 4–cylinder in–line (92 x 90mm), 2392cm3, compression ratio 22:1; 82kW (110hp) [112PS] at 4200rpm, 34.3kW/L (45hp/L) [46.8PS/L]; 240Nm (177lbft) at 2400rpm.

Engine construction: Diesel engine, cast iron cylinder block, light–alloy head, parallel valves, 1 side camshaft (gear wheels); oil capacity 6.6L (6.2US qt); Bosch VE 4/10 diesel injection pump, KKK 16 exhaust turbocharger, max charge–air pressure 0.9bar, charge air cooler. 12V 70Ah battery, 55A alternator; cooling system capacity approx 10L (9.5US qt).

Alfa Romeo Alfa 75 2.4TD

Transmission: Final drive ratio 3.077 (13/40).

Chassis: Disc brakes, disc diameter front 26.1cm, rear 25cm; power assisted steering; tyres 195/60 VR 14, wheel rims 6.5 J.

Dimensions: Max speed 115mph/185kmh (manufacturers test specifications), speed at 1000rpm in 5th gear 28.3mph/45.5kmh; acceleration 0–100kmh 11.7secs; standing km 33.2secs; power to weight ratio 15.4kg/kW (11.2kg/PS); fuel consumption (ECE) 5.5/7.4/8.9L/100km (51.4/38.2/31.7mpg) [42.8/31.8/26.4US mpg].

Alfa Romeo Alfa 164

Upper medium–range high–performance luxury saloon/sedan, FWD, transverse front engines, 5–speed transmission, independent suspension.

Alfa Romeo

Pininfarina body design, cd 0.30. Launched Frankfurt 1987, 3.0 automatic Spring 1989.

Alfa Romeo Alfa 164 T. Spark

> 1962cm3
> 109/105kW–146/141hp–148/143PS
> Fuel Injection

Engine for 164 T. Spark

Body, Weight: Saloon/Sedan 4–door, 5–seater; kerbweight (DIN) 1200kg, gross vehicle weight 1625kg.

Engine data (DIN): 4–cylinder in–line (84 x 88.5mm), 1962cm3; compression ratio 10:1; 109kW (146hp) [148PS] at 5800rpm, 55.6kW/L (74.5hp/L) [75.4PS/L]; 186Nm (137.3lbft) at 4000rpm; leaded premium grade.
With Catalyst: 105kW (141hp) [143PS] at 5800rpm, 53.5kW/L (71.6hp/L) [72.9PS/L]; 188Nm (138.7lbft) at 4700rpm; unleaded premium grade (95R).

Engine construction: Front transverse engine. Overhead valves (in V 80deg), 2 overhead camshafts (chain); light–alloy cylinder head and block, wet cylinder liners; 5 bearing crankshaft; oil capacity 5.5L (5.2US qt); Bosch Motronic ML 4.1 electronic fuel injection. 2 spark plugs per cylinder; 12V 50Ah battery, 85A alternator; cooling system capacity 8L (7.6US qt).

Transmission (to front wheels): 5–speed manual, floor shift; final drive ratio 3.421 (19/65).

Gear ratios: 1st 3.750; 2nd 2.235; 3rd 1.518; 4th 1.132; 5th 0.928; R 3.583.

Chassis: Integral body with front sub–frame; independent suspension front and rear, McPherson struts and antiroll bar front. Rear McPherson struts with double control arms and tension strut, antiroll bar, coil springs and telescopic dampers. Servo/power assisted disc brakes (front ventilated) and optional ABS (Bosch system), disc diameter 28.4cm or 25.7cm front, 25.1cm rear, mechanical handbrake to rear wheels; power assisted rack and pinion steering; fuel tank 70L (15.4Gal) [18.5US Gal]; tyres 185/70 VR 14 or 195/60 VR 15, wheel rims 5.5 or 6J.

Dimensions: Wheelbase 266cm, track 151.5/149cm, clearance 14cm, turning circle 10.8m. Load space (VDA) 17.8cu ft (505dm3), length 455.5cm, width 176cm, height 140cm.

Performance: Max speed over 130.5mph/210kmh, Catalyst 126mph/207kmh (manufacturers test specifications), speed at 1000rpm in 5th gear 22.2mph/35.8kmh; acceleration from 0 – 62mph/100kmh in 9.2secs, Catalyst 9.8secs; standing km 30.2secs; power to weight ratio 11.0kg/kW (8.1kg/PS); fuel consumption ECE 6.5/8.5/10.0L/100km (43.5/33.2/28.2mpg) [36.2/27.7/23.5US mpg] or 6.5/8.5/9.2L/100km (43.5/33.2/30.7mpg) [36.2/27.7/25.6US mpg]

> 2 Litre Turbo
> 128.5kW–172hp–175PS
> Fuel Injection

Engine for 164 Turbo

As 109kW–146hp–148PS, except:

Weight: Kerbweight (DIN) 1250kg, gross vehicle weight 1675kg.

Engine data (DIN): 4–cylinder in–line (84 x 90mm), 1995cm3; compression ratio 8:1; 128.5kW (172hp) [175PS] at 5250rpm, 64.4kW/L (86.3hp/L) [87.7PS/L]; 265Nm (195.6lbft) at 2500rpm. With Overboost: 284Nm (209.6lbft) at 2500rpm.

Engine construction: Valves in V 65deg; 2 overhead camshafts (toothed belt); Graugus cylinder block; oil capacity 7L (6.6US qt); 1 exhaust Garrett T3/50 turbocharger, max charge pressure 0.84, with Overboost 1.08 bar; charge air cooler; Bosch LE2– Jetronic electronic fuel injection. Cooling system capacity 9.6L (9.1US qt).

Transmission: Final drive ratio 3.095 (21/65).

Chassis: Optional level control system rear; disc diameter 28.4cm front; tyres 195/60 VR 15 or 205/55 VR 15, wheel rims 6 or 6.5J.

Performance: Max speed 138mph/220kmh (manufacturers test specifications), speed at 1000rpm in 5th gear 24.6mph/39.6kmh; acceleration from 0 – 62mph/100kmh in 7.2secs; standing km 28.2secs; power to weight ratio 9.7kg/kW (7.1kg/PS); fuel consumption ECE 6.3/8.2/9.9L/100km (44.8/34.4/28.5mpg) [37.3/28.7/23.8US mpg].

> 2959cm3 V6
> 141/135kW– 190/181hp–192/184PS
> Fuel Injection

Engine for 164 3.0L V6

As 109kW–146hp–148PS, except:

Weight: Kerbweight (DIN) 1 300kg, gross vehicle weight 1725kg.

Engine data (DIN): 6–cylinder in V 60deg (93 x 72.6mm), 2959cm3; compression ratio 9.5:1; 141kW (190hp) [192PS] at 5600rpm, 47.7kW/L (63.9hp/L) [64.9PS/L]; 245Nm (180.8lbft) at 3000rpm.
For some countries: 138kW (185hp) [188PS] or 136kW (182hp) [185PS].
With Catalyst: 135kW (181hp) [184PS] at 5600rpm, 45.6kW/L (61.1hp/L) [62.3PS/L]; 258Nm (190.4lbft) at 4400rpm.

Engine construction: Designated 119/11. Valves in V 46deg; 2 x 1 overhead camshaft (toothed belt); 4 bearing crankshaft; oil capacity 7.5L (7.1US qt). 12V 60/66Ah battery; cooling system capacity 10L (9.5US qt).

Transmission: a) 5–speeed manual, final drive ratio 2.944 (18/53).
b) ZF 4 HP–22 automatic, hydraulic torque converter and 4–speed Planetary gear set.

Gear ratios: a) 5–speed manual. 1st 3.500; 2nd 2.235; 3rd 1.518; 4th 1.132; 5th 0.928; R 3.583.
b) Automatic: Max torque multiplication 2 times, Planetary gear set ratios: 1st 2.48; 2nd 1.48; 3rd 1; 4th 0.73; R 2.08.

Chassis: Rear level control system; front disc diameter 28.4cm; 195/60 VR 15 or 205/55 VR 15 tyres, wheels 6 or 6.5J.

Performance: Max speed over 143mph/230kmh, Catalyst 141mph/227kmh (manufacturers test specifications), speed at 1000rpm in 5th gear 25.9mph/41.6kmh; acceleration from 0 – 62mph/100kmh in 7.7secs, Catalyst 7.9secs; standing km 28.0secs; power to weight ratio 9.2kg/kW (6.8kg/PS); fuel consumption ECE 7.2/9.1/12.8L/100km (39.2/31/22.1mpg) [32.7/25.8/18.4US mpg] or 7.2/9.1/11.4L/100km (39.2/31/24.8mpg) [32.7/25.8/20.6US mpg]

Alfa Romeo Alfa 164 3.0 V6

> Diesel 2500cm3
> 86kW–115hp–117PS
> Turbo/Injection Pump

Engine for 164 TD

As 109kW–146hp–148PS, except:

Weight: Kerbweight (DIN) 1320kg, gross vehicle weight 1745kg.

Engine data (DIN): 4–cylinder in–line (92 x 94mm), 2500cm3; compression ratio 22:1; 86kW (115hp) [117PS] at 4200rpm, 33.6kW/L (45hp/L) [46.8PS/L]; 258Nm (190.4lbft) at 2500rpm.
For some countries: 84kW (112.5hp) [114PS] at 4200rpm; 260Nm (191.9lbft) at 2200rpm.

Engine construction: Designated VM. Diesel front–chamber. Graugus cylinder block; parallel valves, 1 overhead camshaft (toothed wheel); oil capacity 7.2L (6.8US qt); Bosch fuel injection pump, exhaust turbocharger KKK (K 16/2267),

max. charge pressure 0.9bar; charge air cooler. 12V 70Ah battery; cooling system capacity approx 10L (9.5US qt).
Transmission: Final drive ratio 3.190 (21/67)
Gear ratios: 1st 3.750; 2nd 2.235; 3rd 1.379; 4th 0.976; 5th 0.761; R 3.583.
Chassis: Rear level control system; front disc diameter 28.4cm; tyres 185/65 HR 15 or 195/60 HR/VR 15, wheels 6J.
Performance: Max speed 124.3mph/200kmh (manufacturers test specifications), speed at 1000rpm in 5th gear 29.1mph/46.8kmh; acceleration from 0 – 62mph/100kmh in 10.8secs; standing km 32.2secs; power to weight ratio 15.3kg/kW (11.3kg/PS); fuel consumption ECE 5.3/6.5/8.6L/100km (53.3/43.5/32.8mpg) [44.4/36.2/27.4US mpg].

Alfa Romeo Alfa 164TD

Alfa Romeo 75 SZ Coupe

New model. Sports coupe is based on the Alfa 75 3.0 V6 with a Zagato plastic body. Launch Geneva 1989. Provisional data.

3.0 Litre V6
152kW–204hp–207PS
Fuel Injection

Body, Weight: Coupe 2–door, 2–seater; kerbweight (DIN) approx 1260kg, gross vehicle weight approx 1430kg.
Engine data (with Catalyst, DIN): 6–cylinder in V 60deg (93 x 72.6mm), 2959cm3; compression ratio 9.5:1; 152kW (204hp) [207PS] at approx 6200rpm, 51.9kW/L (69.5hp/L) [70PS/L]; approx 245Nm (181lbft) at 4500rpm; premium grade unleaded.

Alfa Romeo 75 SZ Coupe

Engine construction: Designated 119/11. Light–alloy cylinder head and block; valves in V 46deg; 2x1 overhead camshaft (toothed belt); 4 bearing crankshaft; oil cooler, oil capacity 7.9 (7.5US qt); Bosch Motronic ML 4.1 fuel injection.12V 60Ah battery, 70A alternator; cooling system capacity approx 10L (9.5US qt).
Transmission (to rear wheels): 5–speed manual in rear, with built–in differential; final drive ratio 3.727 (11/41). Limited slip differential.

Gear ratios; 1st 3.5; 2nd 1.956; 3rd 1.258; 4th 0.946; 5th 0.780; R 3.
Chassis: Integral body; front A arm, coil springs and antiroll bar, rear De–Dion axle with semi–trailing arms, Watt–linkage, coil springs and antiroll bar, front and rear telescopic dampers.
Servo/power assisted disc brakes (ventilated), inboard rear discs, disc diameter front 28.4cm, rear 25cm, mechanical handbrake on rear; power assisted rack and pinion steering; fuel tank 68L (14.9Gal) [18.0US Gal]; front tyres 205/55 ZR 16, rear 225/50 ZR 16, front wheel rims 7", rear 8".
Dimensions: Wheelbase 251cm, track 140/140cm, clearance 12cm, turning circle 11m. Load space 17.7cu ft (500dm3). Length approx 400cm, width 170cm, height 130cm.
Performances: Max speed 152mph/245kmh (manufacturers test specification); speed at 1000rpm in 5th gear 24.7mph/39.8kmh acceleration 0 – 60mph/100kmh 7secs, standing km 27.4secs; power to weight ratio 8.3kg/kW (6.1kg/PS); fuel consumption (ECE) 7.2/9.2/13.2L/100km (39.2/30.7/21.4mpg) [32.7/25.6/17.8US mpg].

ALPINE RENAULT   F

Automobiles Alpine, 3 Boulevard Foch, Epinay–sur–Seine (93), France
Small manufacturer of sports cars, based in France, part of the Renault Group.

Alpine Renault V6 GT – V6 Turbo

2 + 2–seater sports Coupe with plastic body and rear mounted 2.85 Litre V6 PRV engine with 158hp or 2.5 litre V6 turbo with 198hp. Debut Winter 1985. For technical data refer to Renault France.

Alpine Renault V6 Turbo

ARO   R

Intreprinderae Mecanica Muscal, Strade Vasile Roaita 173, Cimpulung–Muscel, Romania

Rumanian manufacturer of rough terrain motor vehicles.
MODEL RANGE
10S – 24

ARO 10 S

10.0 – 10.1 – 10.3 – 10.4

Rough terrain vehicle with a 1.4 Litre engine or 1.6 Litre Diesel Renault engine. Independent front and rear suspension, with four wheel drive and reduction transmission. Export version marketed as the Duster.

1.4 Litre
49KW–65HP–66PS
1 Carb

ARO

Body, Weight: Convertible Estate/Station Wagon 10.0, 2–door, 2–seater; kerbweight (DIN) 1120kg, gross vehicle weight 1630kg.
Convertible Estate/Station Wagon 10.1, 2–door, 5–seater; kerbweight (DIN) 1130kg, gross vehicle weight 1630kg.
Estate/Station Wagon 10.3 with Hardtop, 2–door, 2–seater; kerbweight (DIN) 1160kg, gross vehicle weight 1630kg.
Estate/Station Wagon 10.4 with Hardtop, 2–door, 5–seater; kerbweight (DIN) 1180kg, gross vehicle weight 1630kg.

Engine data (DIN): 4 cylinder in–line (76 x 77mm), 1397cm3; compression ratio 9.5:1; 49kW (65hp) [66PS] at 5500rpm, 35.1kW/L (47hp/L) [47.2PS/L]; 103Nm (76lbft) at 3300rpm; leaded premium grade.
Some countries: 46kW (61hp) [62PS].

Engine construction: Designated IAP 810–R–99. Side camshaft (chain); light–alloy cylinder head; wet cylinder liners; 5 bearing crankshaft; oil capacity 3L (2.8US qt); 1 Solex 32 BIS or Zenith 32 IF2 downdraught carb. Battery 12V 36Ah, 50A alternator; cooling system capacity approx 5L (4.7US qt).

Transmission (to all wheels): 4–speed manual, final drive ratio 4.571. Rear limited slip differential, engageable four wheel drive; 2–speed reduction gear, 1st 1.047; 2nd 2.249.

Gear ratios: 1st 4.376; 2nd 2.445; 3rd 1.514; 4th 1; R 3.66.

Chassis: Box section frame with cross member, front and rear independent suspension, front lower control arm, coil springs, rear rigid axle with trailing arm and laminated spring, front and rear, telescopic damper. Sero/power assisted brakes, front discs, rear drums. Handbrake on rear wheels; recirculating ball steering. Fuel tank 49L (10.8Gal) [12.9US Gal]; tyres 175 SR 14, wheels 5.5 J.

Dimensions: Wheelbase 240cm, track 133/133cm, clearance 24cm, turning circle 11.5m, load space 55.4cu ft (1570dm3), length 383cm, width 160–164cm, height 165–172cm.

Performance: Maximum speed 78mph/125kmh (manufacturers test specification), speed at 1000rpm in 4th gear 13.4mph/21.5kmh with reduction gear 6mph/10kmh; power to weight ratio from 23kg/kW (17kg/PS); consumption at 56mph/90kmh – 11.1L/100km (25.4mpg) [21.2US mpg].

ARO 10 S

```
1.6 Litre
55kW–74hp–75PS
1 2V Carb
```

As 1.4L, except:

Weight: Kerbweight (DIN) from 1365kg.

Engine data (DIN): 4–cylinder in–line (81.0 x 77.4mm), 1595cm3; compression ratio 9.0:1; 55kW (74hp) [75PS] at 5000rpm, 34.5kW/L (46.4hp/L) [47PS/L]; 127Nm (93.7lbft) at 3200rpm; leaded regular grade (91R).

Engine construction: Hydraulic tappets, 1 overhead camshaft (toothed belt); light–alloy cylinder head; 5 main bearing crankshaft; oil capacity 4L (3.8US qt); 1 Solex 2V carb
12V 45Ah battery, cooling system capacity 4.5L (4.3US qt).

Chassis: Tyres 195 R 14.

Performances: Max speed at 87mph/140kmh (manufacturers test specifications), speed at 1000rpm in 4th gear 17.5mph/28.2kmh, with reduction gear 13.1km/h; power to weight ratio from 24.8kg/kW (18.2kg/PS); consumption at 56mph/90kmh 9.7L/100km (29.1mpg) [24.2US mpg].

```
1.6 Litre Diesel
39.5/59kW–53/79hp–54/80PS
Turbo/Fuel Injection Pump
```

As petrol/gasoline engine, except

Weight: Kerbweight (DIN) 1285–1345kg.

Engine data (DIN): 4–cylinder in–line (76.5 x 86.4mm), 1588cm3, compression ratio 23:1; 39.5kW (53hp) [54PS] at 4800rpm, 24.9kW/L (33.4hp/L) [34PS/L]; 100Nm (73.8lbft) from 2300–2900rpm.
With Turbo: 51.5kW (59hp) [70PS] at 4500rpm, 32.5kW/L (43.6hp/L) [44.1PS/L]; 133Nm (98.1lbft) from 2500–2900rpm
With Turbo and Charge Air Cooler: 59kW (79hp) [80PS] at 4500rpm, 32.5kW/L (43.6hp/L) [44.1PS/L]; 155Nm (114.4lbft) at 2600rpm.

Engine construction: Diesel engine turbulence chamber from VW/Audi. Oil capacity 3.5L (3.3US qt), oil cooler. Bosch VE fuel injection pump distributor, mechanical centrifugal governor, timing device, cold start accleration; also available with exhaust turbocharger (max charge air pressure 0.7bar) and charge–air cooler.

Performances: Max speed approx 71–90mph/115–145kmh; power to weight ratio from 21.8kg/kW (16,1kg/PS); consumption approx 5–10L/100km (56.5–28.2mpg) [47–23.5US qt].

ARO 24

240 – 243 – 244

Rough terrain vehicle with 3/5 doors, convertible or Hardtop. 4–cylinder, 2.5 Litre engine, 4–speed transmission with reduction gear. 1980: 2.5 and 2.7 Litre diesel engines.

```
2.5 Litre
61KW–82hp–83PS
1 Carb
```

Body, Weight: 240: Estate/Station Wagon 2–door, 2–seater; kerbweight (DIN) 1600kg, gross vehicle weight 2350kg; 243: Estate/Station Wagon 3–door, 2–seater; kerbweight (DIN) 1670kg, gross vehicle weight 2350kg; 244: Estate/Station Wagon 5–door, 5–seater; kerbweight (DIN) 1670kg, gross vehicle weight 2350kg.

Engine data (DIN): 4–cylinder in–line (97 x 84.4mm), 2405cm3, compression ratio 8.1; 61kW (82hp) [83PS] at 4800rpm, 24.4kW/L (32.7hp/L) [33.3PS/L]; 170Nm (125.5lbft) at 2900rpm; leaded regular grade.

Engine construction: Designated ARO L–25. Side camshaft; 5 bearing crankshaft; 1 downdraught carb. Battery 12V 66Ah, alternator 500W; water cooled.

Transmission (to all wheels): 4–speed manual, final drive ratio 4.125; two or four wheel drive; in reduction gear 2.127.

Gear ratios: 1st 4.644; 2nd 2.532; 3rd 1.651; 4th 1; R 4.795.

Chassis: Chassis with frame side member and cross member; front independent suspension with coil springs, rear rigid axle with leaf springs, telescopic damper. Front drum brakes, mechanical handbrake to rear wheels; worm and wheel steering; fuel tank 95L (20.9Gal) [25.1US Gal]; tyres 6.50–16; 78–15.

ARO 244

Dimensions: Wheelbase 235cm, track 144.5/144.5cm, clearance minimum 25cm, turning circle 12m, length 414cm, width 177.5cm, height 188/198cm.

Performance: Maximum speed (manufacturers test specification) 68–72mph/110–115kmh, speed at 1000rpm in 5th gear 20.4mph/32.8kmh; power to weight ratio 26.2kg/kW (19.3kg/PS); consumption (touring) approx 12–20L/100km (23.5–14.1mpg) [19.6–11.7US mpg].

ARO • Aston Martin

2.5/2.7 Litre Diesel
53/61kW–71/82hp–72/83PS
Injection Pump

As petrol/gasoline engine, except:

Weight: With diesel engine 75–125kg heavier.

Engine data (DIN): 4–cylinder in–line (94 x 90mm), 2498cm3; compression ratio 23.1; 53kW (71hp) [72PS] at 4100rpm, 21.2kW/L (28.4hp/L) (28.8PS/L); 149Nm (109.7lbft) at 2000rpm.
Or: (97 x 90mm). 2660cm3; compression ratio 20.8.1; 61kW (82hp) [83PS] at 4100rpm 22.9kW/L (30.7hp/L) [31.2PS/L]; 142Nm (104.5lbft) at 2250rpm.

Engine construction: 2.1 Litre; Designated Peugeot XD3P/Aro L27D. Cylinder block inclined 20deg to the right. Oil capacity 5L (4.7US qt); Bosch injection pump EP/VAC. Battery 2x12V 65Ah; cooling system capacity 10L (9.4US qt).

Performance: Maximum speed 71.5mph/115kmh (manufacturers test specification); power to weight ratio from 27.5kg/kW (20.2kg/PS); consumption approx 8–16L/100km (35.3–17.7mpg) [29.4–14.7US mpg].

3.1 Litre Diesel
48kW–64hp–65PS
Injection Pump

As petrol/gasoline engine, except

Weight: Kerbweight from 1745/1785kg.

Engine data (DIN): 4–cylinder in–line (95 x 110mm), 3119cm3; compression ratio 17:1; 48kW (64hp) [65PS] at 3200rpm, 15.4kW/L (20.8PS/L); 186Nm (137.3lbft) at 1800rpm.

Engine construction: Designated ARO D–127. Cylinder block inclined approx 20deg to the right. Oil capacity 5L (4.7US qt); Bosch EP/VAC fuel injection pump.
2x12V 65Ah batteries, cooling system capacity 10L (9.5US qt).

Transmission (to all wheels): 4–speed manual, final drive ratio 3.72.

Chassis: Tyres JR 78–15.

Performances: Max speed 68mph/110kmh (manufacturers test specifications); power to weight ratio from 36.3kg/kW (26.8kg/PS); consumption approx 9–18L/100km (31.4–15.7mpg) [26.1–12.6US qt].

ASTON MARTIN — GB

Aston Martin Lagonda Limited, Tickford Street, Newport Pagnall, Buckinghamshire MK16 9AN, England

English manufacturer of luxury sport cars in a special class. Subsidiary of Ford Motor Company.

Aston Martin Virage

New Model. Luxury high performance car with 5.3 Litre V8 four–valve engine, 5–speed manual or automatic and light–alloy body. Replaced in mid–1989 with V8 Coupe. Debut Birmingham (October) 1989.

5.3 V8/32V
246kW–330hp–335PS
Fuel Injection

Body, Weight: Coupe 2–door, 4–seater; kerbweight (DIN) 1790kg.

Engine data (with catalyst, DIN): 8–cylinder in V 90deg (100 x 85mm), 5341cm3; compression ratio 9.5:1; 246kW (330hp) [335PS] at 5300rpm, 46.1kW/L (61.8hp/L) [62.7PS/L]; 494Nm (364.6lbft) at 4000rpm; regular grade.

Engine construction: Valves in V 27deg, 2x2 overhead camshaft (chain); light–alloy cylinder head and block; wet cylinder liners; 5 bearing crankshaft; oil cooler, oil capacity 11.4L (10.8US qt); electronic fuel injection.
12V 68Ah (also available with 75Ah) battery, 75A alternator; cooling system capacity approx 18L (17US qt).

Transmission (to rear wheels): a) ZF 5–speed manual, central gear lever, final drive ratio 3.062.
b) Chrysler Torqueflite automatic; hydraulic torque converter and 3–speed Planetary gear set, central selector lever positions P–R–N–D–2–L, final drive ratio 3.062. Limited slip differential.

Aston Martin Virage

Gear ratios: a) 5–speed manual: 1st 2.9; 2nd 1.78; 3rd 1.22; 4th 1; 5th 0.845; R 2.63
b) Automatic: Max torque multiplication 2 times; Planetary gear ratios: 1st 2.45; 2nd 1.45; 3rd 1; R 2.2.

Chassis: Platform type frame with light–alloy body; front A arm and coil springs, rear De–Dion axle (light–alloy tube) with Watt linkage and semi–trailing arms, coil springs, front antiroll bar, telescopic damper.
Servo/power assisted disc brakes (front ventilated), disc diameter front approx 30.2cm, rear approx 27.9cm, mechanical handbrake on rear; power assisted rack and pinion steering; fuel tank 113L (24.8Gal) [29.9US Gal]; tyres 255/60 VR 16, wheel rims 8 J.

Dimensions: Wheelbase 261cm, track approx 150/150cm, clearance approx 13cm, turning circle approx 12m. Load space 11.5cu ft (325dm3). Length 473.5cm, width 185.5cm, height 132cm.

Performances: Max speed (automatic) 155mph/250kmh (manufacturers test specifications), speed at 1000rpm in direct gear approx 26.7mph/43kmh; acceleration from 0 – 60mph/97kmh (automatic) 6secs; power to weight ratio from 7.3kg/kW (5.3kg/PS); consumption approx 14–22L/100km (20.2–12.8mpg) [16.8–10.7US mpg].

Aston Martin Virage

Aston Martin V8 – V8 Volante

High performance car with a 5.3 Litre V8 engine and De–Dion rear axle. ZF 5–speed manual or Chyrsler Torqueflite automatic transmission. Debut 1969. 1974: Four 2V Carb instead of fuel injection system. Summer 1978: 'Volante' Convertible/Cabriolet. Autumn 1983: Detail modifications. January 1986: With fuel injection and revised bonnet/hood.

5.3 Litre V8
227.5kW–305hp–309PS
Fuel Injection

Body, Weight: Coupe 2–door, 4–seater; kerbweight (DIN) 1820, USA 1860kg. Cabriolet "Volante" 2–door, 4–seater; kerbweight (DIN) approx 1850kg.

Engine data (DIN): 8–cylinder in V 90deg (100 x 85mm), 5341cm3; compression ratio 9.3:1; 227.5kW (305hp) [309PS] at 5500rpm, 42.6kW/L (57.0hp/L) (57.9PS/L); 434Nm (319.4lbft) at 4000rpm.

Aston Martin

With Catalyst: 197kW (264hp) [268PS] at 5000rpm; 36.8kW/L (49.3hp/L) [50.1PS/L].

Engine construction: Valves in V 64deg, 2x2 overhead camshafts (chain); light–alloy cylinder head and block; wet cylinder liners; 5 bearing crankshaft; 2 oil coolers, oil capacity 11.4L (10.8US qt). Electronic Weber fuel injection, electronic fuel pump. Battery 12V 68, optional 75Ah, alternator 75A; cooling system capacity approx 18.2L (16US qt).

Aston Martin V8

Transmission (to rear wheels): a) 5–speed manual ZF, floor shift; final drive ratio 3.54.
b) Chrysler torqueflite automatic; hydraulic torque converter and 3–speed Planetary gear set, central selector lever positions P– R–N–D–2–L, final drive ratio 3.06 or 3.54. Limited slip differential.

Gear ratios: a) 5–speed manual: 1st 2.9; 2nd 1.78; 3rd 1.22; 4th 1; 5th 0.845; R 2.63.
b) Automatic; Max torque multiplication in converter 2 times. Planetary gear set ratios: 1st 2.45; 2nd 1.45; 3rd 1; R 2.2.

Chassis: Platform type frame with light–alloy body; front A arm and coil springs, rear De–Dion axle with Watt linkage and trailing arms, coil springs, front antiroll bar, telescopic damper. Servo assisted front disc brakes (ventilated), front disc diameter 27.3cm, rear 26.3cm, mechanical handbrake at rear wheels; power assisted rack and pinion steering; fuel tank 104.5L (23Gal) [27.6US Gal], Cabriolet 97.5L (21.4Gal) [27.6US Gal], 12L (2.6Gal) [3.2US Gal] reserve; tyres GR 235/70 VR 15 or 255/60 VR 15/16, wheel rims 7J.

Dimensions: Wheelbase 261cm, track 150/150cm, clearance 14cm, turning circle 11.6m, load space 9cu ft(255dm3), length 466.5, USA 482cm, width 183cm, height 132.5cm, Volante 137cm.

Performance: Maximum speed 146mph/235kmh, automatic 137mph/220kmh (manufacturers test specification), speed at 1000rpm in 5th gear 27mph/43.5kmh; acceleration at 0 – 60mph/97kmh 6.6secs; power to weight ratio from 8.0kg/kW (5.9kg/PS); consumption (touring) approx 15–22L/100km (18.8–12.8mpg) [15.7–10.7US mpg].

Aston Martin V8 Volante

Aston Martin V8 Vantage – V8 Vantage Volante

Debut February 1977. Autumn 1983: modifications to interior. Birmingham 1986: Introduction of Convertible.

Aston Martin V8 Vantage

```
5.3 Litre V8
298kW–400hp–405PS
4 2V Carb
```

Body, Weight: Coupe 2–door, 4–seater; kerbweight (DIN) 1820kg; Cabriolet "Volante" 2–door, 4–seater; kerbweight (DIN) approx 1850kg.

Engine data (DIN): 8–cylinder in V 90deg (100 x 85mm), 5341cm3; compression ratio 10.2.1; 298kW (400hp) [405PS] at 6250rpm, 55.8kW/L (74.7hp/L) [76.0PS/L]; 529Nm (389.3lbft) at 5000rpm. Premium grade.
Optional 322kW (431hp) [438PS] at 6200rpm; 536Nm (394.5lbft) at 5100rpm.

Engine construction: Valves in V 64deg, 2x2 ovehead camshafts (chain); light–alloy cylinder head and block; wet cylinder liners; 5 bearing crankshaft; 2 oil coolers, oil capacity 11.4L (10.8US qt); 4 Weber downdraught 2V carbs 48 IDF 3/150 electronic fuel pump. Battery 12V 68, optional 75Ah, alternator 75A; cooling system capacity, approx 18.2L (17.2US qt).

Transmission (to rear wheels): a) 5–speed manual: 1st 2.9; 2nd 1.78; 3rd 1.22; 4th 1; 5th 0.845; R 2.63.
b) Automatic: Max torque multiplication in converter 2 times; planetary gear set ratios: 1st 2.45; 2nd 1.45; 3rd 1; R 2.2.

Aston Martin V8 Vantage Volante

Chassis: Platform type frame with light–alloy body; front A arm and coil springs, rear De–Dion axle with Watt linkage and trailing arm, coil springs, front antiroll bar, telescopic damper. Servo/power assisted front disc brakes (ventilated), front disc diameter 27.3cm, rear 26.3cm, mechanical handbrake to rear wheels; power assisted rack and pinion steering; fuel tank 104.5 (23Gal) [27.6US Gal]. Cabriolet 97.5L (21.4Gal) [25.7US Gal], 12L reserve; tyres 255/50 VR 16, wheel rims 8J.

Dimensions: Wheelbase 261cm, track 150/150cm, clearance 14cm, turning circle 11.6m, load space 9cu ft (255dm3),length 466.5cm, width 189cm, height 132.5cm, Cabriolet 137.5cm.

Performance: Maximum speed approx 162–174mph/260–280kmh (manufacturers test specification), speed at 1000rpm in 5th gear 25.2mph/40.5kmh; acceleration 0 – 60mph/97kmh 5.2secs, 0 – 62mph/100kmh 5.5secs; power to weight ratio fromt 5.7kg/kW (4.2kg/PS); consumption (touring) approx 17–25L/100km (16.6–11.3mpg) [13.8–9.4US mpg].

Aston Martin Zagato

Body designed by Zagato Italy. Production limited to 50 Coupes and 25 Convertibles. Launch Geneva 1986, Convertible 1987.

Aston Martin • Audi

Aston Martin Zagato Volante

5.3 Litre V8
322kW/227.5kW–432/305HP–438/309PS
4 2V Carbs/Fuel Injection

Body, Weight: Coupe 2–door, 2–seater; kerbweight (DIN) 1650kg; Cabriolet "Volante" 2–door, 2–seater; kerbweight (DIN) 1650kg.

Engine data (DIN): 8–cylinder in V 90deg (100 x 85mm), 5341cm3; compression ratio 10.5.1; 322kW (432hp) [438PS] at 6200rpm, 60.3kW/L (80.1hp/L) [82PS/L]; 536Nm (394.5lbft) at 5100rpm.
Engine for Cabriolet Volante: Compression ratio 9.3 or 9.5.1; 227.5kW (305hp) [309PS] at 5000rpm, 42.6kW/L (57.5hp/L) [57.9PS/L]; 434Nm (319.4lbft) at 4000rpm.
With Catalyst: 197kW (264hp) [268PS] at 5000rpm; 36.8kW/L (49.3hp/L) [50.1PS/L].

Engine construction: Valves in V 64deg, 2x2 overhead camhshafts (chain); light–alloy cylinder head and block; wet cylinder liner; 5 bearing crankshaft; 2 oil coolers; oil capacity 11.4L (10.8US qt); 4 Weber downdraught 2V carbs 48 IDF 3/150 or electronic fuel injection, electronic fuel pump. Battery 12V 68, optional 75Ah, alternator 75A; cooling system capacity approx 18.1L (9.1US qt).

Gear ratios (to rear wheels): a) 5–speed manual ZF, floor shift; final drive ratio 3.06. b) Chrysler Torqueflite automatic; hydraylic torque converter and 3–speed Planetary gear set, central selector lever with positions P–R–N–D–2–L, final drive ratio 3.06. Limited slip differential.

Gear ratios: a) 5–speed manual: 1st 2.9; 2nd 1.78; 3rd 1.22; 4th 1; 5th 0.845; R 2.63. b) Automatic; Max torque multiplication in converter 2 times; Planetary gear set ratios: 1st 2.45; 2nd 1.45; 3rd 1; R 2.2.

Chassis: Platform type frame with light–alloy body; front A arm and coil springs, rear De–Dion axle with Watt linkage and trailing arm, coil springs, front antiroll bar, telescopic damper. Front servo/power assisted disc brakes (ventilated), front disc diameter 27.3cm, rear 26.3cm, mechanical handbrake to rear wheels; power assisted rack and pinion steering; fuel tank 104.5L (23Gal) [27.6US Gal] and 12L (2.7Gal) [3.2US Gal] reserve; tyres 255/50 VR 16, wheel rims 8J.

Dimensions: Wheelbase 261cm, track 152/154cm, clearance 13.5cm, turning circle 11.6m, load space 9cu ft (255dm3), length 439cm, Volante 448cm, width 186cm, height 129.5cm, Volante 130cm.

Performance (Coupe with 432hp Engine): Maximum speed approx 186mph/300kmh (manufacturers test specification), speed at 1000rpm in 5th gear 29.2mph/47kmh; acceleration 0 – 62mph/100kmh approx 5secs; power to weight ratio 5.1kg/kW (3.8kg/PS); consumption (touring) approx 17–28L/100km (16.6–9.8mpg) [13.8– 8.4US mpg].

Aston Martin Lagonda

Luxury high performance touring car with digital instrumentation. Launched in London 1976. 1983 modification to interior. Autumn 1984: digital instrumentation. Geneva 1986: fuel injection. 1987: body modifications.

5.3 Litre V8
227.5kW–305hp–309PS
Fuel Injection

Body, weight: Saloon/Sedan 4–door, 4–seater; kerbweight (DIN) 2095kg; Long wheel base Saloon/Sedan, 4–door, 4–seater (DIN) approx 2200kg.

Engine data (DIN): 8–cylinder in V 90deg (100 x 85mm), 5341cm3; compression ratio 9.5.1; 227.5kW (305hp) [309PS] at 5500rpm, 42.6kW/L (57.01hp/L) [57.9PS/L]; 434Nm (319.4lbft) at 4000rpm.
With Catalyst: 197kW (264hp) [268PS] at 5000rpm; 36.8kW/L (49.3hp/L) [50.1PS/L].

Engine construction: Valves in V 64deg, 2x2 overhead camshafts (chain); light–alloy cylinder head and block, wet cylinder liners; 5 bearing crankshaft; 2 oil coolers, oil capacity 11.4L (10.8US qt); electronic Weber fuel injection, electronic fuel pump. Battery 12V 102Ah, alternator 100A; cooling system capacity approx 18L (17US qt).

Transmission (to rear wheels): Chrysler Torqueflite automatic; hydraulic torque converter and 3–speed Planetary gear set, central selector lever, final drive ratio 3.06. Limited slip differential.

Gear ratios: Automatic; max torque multiplication in converter 2 times; Planetary gear set ratios: 1st 2.45; 2nd 1.45; 3rd 1; R 2.2.

Chassis: Platform type frame with light–alloy body; front A arm and coil springs, rear De–Dion axle with Watt linkage and trailing arm, coil springs, front antiroll bar, telesopic damper, rear level control system. Servo/power assisted front disc brakes (ventilated), front disc diameter 27.3cm, rear 26.3cm, mechanical hand brake to rear wheels; power assisted rack and pinion steering; fuel tank 128L (28.2Gal) [33.8US Gal]. of which 23L (5.1Gal) [6.1US Gal] reserve; tyres 255/60VR, wheel rims 7J.

Dimensions: Wheelbase 291.5cm, track 150/150cm, clearance 14cm, turning circle 11.6cm, load space 13cu ft (370dm3), length 528.5cm, width 179cm, height 135cm.

Performance: Maximum speed 143mph/230kmh (manufacturers test specification), speed at 1000rpm in top gear 26.1mph/42kmh; acceleration from 0 – 60mph/97kmh 8.8secs; power to weight ratio from 9.4kg/kW (6.9kg/PS); consumption approx 16–25L/100km (17.7– 11.3mpg) [14.7–9.4US mpg].

Aston Martin Lagona

AUDI D

Audi NSU Auto Union Ag, 8070 Ingolstadt, Deutschland

Old marque reintroduced in 1965 as a successor to DKW; part of the VW Group.

MODEL RANGE
80 – 90 - Coupe – 200 – quattro – V8

Audi 80/90 – 80/90 quattro

Medium size front wheel drive car. 3 body styles, 4–door, with in–line engine. The Audi 80 is available with 4–cylinder engines and the Audi 90 with 5–cylinder engines. The four wheel drive variant incorporates a Torsen central differential. The Audi 80 was launched in September 1986 and the Audi 90 in May 1987. February 1988: 90 quattro 20V (4 valves per cylinder, Catalyst version launched June 1988. Autumn 1988: modifications to 4–cylinder engine.

1.6/1.8 S
51/55kW–68/74hp–70/75PS
2V Carb

Engine for 80

Body, Weight: 4–door Saloon/Sedan, 5–seater; kerbweight (DIN) 1030kg, gross vehicle weight 1490kg.

Engine data: 4–cylinder in–line engine (81 x 86.4mm), 1781cm3; compression ratio 9.0:1; 55kW (74hp) [75PS] at 4500rpm, 30.9kW/L (41.4hp/L) [42.1PS/L]; 140Nm (103.3lbft) at 2500rpm; leaded regular grade.
Engine for some countries - 1.6 Litre (Catalyst, DIN): 4–cylinder in–line (81 x 77.4mm), 1595cm3; compression ratio 9.0:1; 51kW (68hp) [70PS] at 5200rpm; 118Nm (87lbft) at 2700rpm; unleaded regular grade.

Audi

Without Catalyst: 55kW (74hp) [75PS] at 4500rpm; 140Nm (103.3lbft) at 2500rpm; leaded regular grade.

Engine construction: Front engine tilted to the right; hydraulic tappets, 1 overhead camshaft (toothed belt); light-alloy cylinder head, crankshaft with 5 bearings; oil capacity 3L (2.8US qt); 1 downdraught 2V two stage carb. Battery 12V 40/63Ah, alternator 65A; cooling system capacity, 6.5L (6.1US qt).

Transmission (to front wheels): a) 4-speed manual, final drive ratio 4.111 (9/37).
b) 5-speed manual, final drive ratio 4.111.
c) Automatic, hydraulic torque converter and 3-speed Planetary gear set, final drive ratio 3.250.

Gear ratios: a) 4-speed manual: 1st 3.545; 2nd 1.857; 3rd 1.156; 4th 0.838; R 3.500.
b) 5-speed manual: 1st 3.545; 2nd 1.857; 3rd 1.156; 4th 0.838; 5th 0.683; R 3.500.
c) Automatic: Max torque multiplication in converter 2.44 times, Planetary gear set ratios: 1st 2.714; 2nd 1.5; 3rd 1; R 2.429.

Chassis: Integral body with front sub-frame; front McPherson struts with A-arm, antiroll bar, rear torsion crank axle (trailing arm, axle tube) with diagonal Panhard rod and coil springs, antiroll bar, telescopic damper. Servo/power assisted brakes, front disc, rear drums (Automatic, rear discs), rear mechanical handbrake; rack and pinion steering, optional power assisted steering; fuel tank 68L (14.9Gal) [18US Gal], including 5L Reserve; tyres 175/70 SR 14, wheels 5J.

Dimensions: Wheelbase 254.5cm, track 141/143cm, clearance 13cm, turning circle approx 10.3m; load space VDA 15cu ft (425dm3), length 439.5cm, width 169.5cm, height 139.5cm.

Audi 80

Performance: 74hp; Max speed 108mph/174kmh, automatic 104mph/167kmh (manufacturers test specifications), speed at 1000rpm in 5th gear 24.5mph/39.5kmh; acceleration 0 – 62mph/100kmh 13.7secs, automatic 16.0secs; power to weight ratio from 18.7kg/kW (13.7kg/PS); consumption (ECE) 4- speed 5.8/7.2/10.1L/100km (48.7/39.2/28mpg) [40.6/32.7/23.3US mpg], 5-speed 5.4/6.7/10.1 (52.3/42.2/28mpg) [43.6/35.1/23.3US mpg], automatic 6.3/7.7/10.6L/100km (44.8/36.7/26.6mpg) [37.3/30.5/22.2US mpg].
1.6 Litre with Catalyst: Max speed 104.5mph/168kmh; acceleration 0 – 62mph/100kmh in 14.1secs; consumption (ECE) 5-speed 5.4/6.7/9.6L/100km (51.4/42.2/29.4mpg) [43.6/35.1/24.5US mpg].

Audi 80

```
1.8 S
66kW-88.5hp-90PS
Injection/2V Carb
```

Engine for 80 and 80 quattro

As 74hp, except:

Weight: Kerbweight (DIN) from 1030kg, gross vehicle weight 1490kg.
80 quattro: Kerbweight (DIN) from 1130kg, gross vehicle weight 1590kg.

Engine data (Catalyst, DIN): 4-cylinder in-line (81 x 86.4mm), 1781cm3, compression ratio 9.0:1; 66kW (88.5hp) [90PS] at 5400rpm; 37.1kW/L (49.7hp/L) [50.5PS/L]; 142Nm (104.7lbft) at 3250rpm; unleaded regular grade.
Without Catalyst: Compression ratio 10.0:1; 66kW (88.5hp) [90PS] at 5200rpm; 150Nm (110.6lbft) at 3300rpm; leaded premium grade.
With unregulated Catalyst: Compression ratio 9:1; 66kW (89hp) [90PS] at 5200rpm; 142Nm (104.7lbft) at 3300rpm.

Engine construction: Catalyst version with Bosch central/single point fuel injection (Mono-Jetronic). Battery 40/54Ah, alternator 65/90A.

Transmission (to front wheels, for quattro to all wheels): a) 4-speed manual; final drive ratio 4.111.
b) 5-speed manual; final drive ratio 4.111.
c) Automatic; final drive ratio 3.250.
For quattro: 5-speed manual, permanent all wheel drive, central Torsen differential, rear differential, manual diff-lock; final drive ratio 4.556.

Gear ratios: a) 4-speed manual: as 74hp.
b) 5-speed manual: as 74hp.
c) Automatic: as 74hp.
For quattro: 1st 3.545; 2nd 105; 3rd 1.300; 4th 0.889; 5th 0.725; R 3.500.

Chassis: Tyres 175/70 HR 14. For quattro: Rear independent suspension with A-arm and McPherson struts. Servo/power assisted disc brakes, front ventilated, Bosch ABS; fuel tank 70L (15.4Gal) [18.5US Gal].

Dimensions: 80 quattro: Wheelbase 253.5cm, track 141/142.5cm; load space VDA 11.3cu ft (320dm3).

Performance: Max speed 113mph/182kmh, automatic 111mph/178kmh (manufacturers test specifications), speed at 1000rpm in 5th gear 24.5mph/39.5kmh (quattro 20.1mph/33.6kmh); acceleration 0 – 62mph/100kmh 12.4secs, automatic 14.7secs, quattro 13.6secs; power to weight ratio from 15.6kg/kW (11.4kg/PS); consumption ECE 5.8/7.4/10.6L/100km (48.7/38.2/26.6mpg) [40.6/31.8/22.2US mpg], 5-speed 5.4/6.9/10.6L/100km (52.3/40.9/26.6mpg) [43.6/34.1/22.2US mpg], automatic 6.3/7.9/11.2L/100km (44.8/35.8/25.2mpg) [37.3/29.8/21US mpg], quattro 6.4/8.0/11.9L/100km (44.1/35.3/23.7mpg) [36.8/29.4/19.8US mpg].

```
2.0 E/1.8 E
83/82kW-111/110hp-113/112PS
Fuel Injection
```

Engine for 80 and 80 quattro

As 74hp, except:

Weight: Kerbweight (DIN) from 1080, gross vehicle weight 1540kg, USA 1165kg, quattro 1170, gross vehicle weight 1630kg.

Engine data (Catalyst, DIN): 4-cylinder in-line (82.5 x 92.8mm), 1984cm3; compression ratio 10.5:1; 83kW (111hp) [113PS] at 5800rpm, 41.8kW/L (56hp/L) [57PS/L]; 170Nm (125.5lbft) at 3400rpm; unleaded premium grade, minimum regular grade.
USA Version (SAE net): 81kW (108.5hp) [110PS] at 5300rpm; 164Nm (121lbft) at 3200rpm.
Without Catalyst: (81 x 86.4mm) 1781cm3; compression ratio 10:1; 82kW (110hp) [112PS] at 5800rpm, 160Nm (118lbft) at 3400rpm; leaded premium grade.

Engine construction: Oil capacity 3.5L (3.3US qt), oil cooler; Bosch KE-Jetronic fuel injection.

Transmission (to front wheels, for quattro to all wheels): a) 5-speed manual, final drive ratio 4.111.
b) Automatic, final drive ratio 3.25.
For quattro: 5-speed manual, permanent all wheel drive, central Torsen differential, rear differential, manual diff-lock, final drive ratio 4.556.

Gear ratios: a) 5-speed manual: 1st 3.545; 2nd 2.105; 3rd 1.300; 4th 0.943; 5th 0.789; R 3.500.
b) Automatic: as 74hp.
For quattro: 1st 3.545; 2nd 2.105; 3rd 1.300; 4th 0.889; 5th 0.725; R 3.500.

Chassis: Servo/power assisted disc brakes (front ventilated), optional ABS (Bosch); tyres 175/70 HR 14, optional 195/60 HR 14 with 6J wheels. For quattro: Rear independent suspension with A-arm and McPherson struts. Servo/power assisted disc brakes (front ventilated), Bosch ABS; fuel tank 70L (15.4Gal) [18.5US Gal].

Dimensions: Length USA 448cm. 80 quattro: Wheelbase 253.5cm, track 141/142.5cm, turning circle 12.5cm; load space VDA 11.3cu ft (320dm3).

Performace: Max speed 122mph/196kmh, automatic 121mph/195kmh (manufacturers test specifications), speed at 1000rpm in 5th gear 21mph/34kmh, quattro 20.7mph/33kmh; acceleration 0 – 62mph/100kmh 10.9secs, automatic/quattro 13.1secs; power to weight ratio from 13kg/kW (9.6kg/PS); consumption (ECE, Catalyst variants) 5.3/6.8/10.4L/100km (53.3/41.5/27.2mpg)

Audi

[44.4/34.6/22.8US mpg], automatic 6.2/7.8/10.9L/100km (45.6/36.2/25.9mpg) [37.9/30.2/21.6US mpg], quattro 5.8/7.4/12.3L/100km (48.7/38.2/23mpg) [40.6/31.8/19.1US mpg].

Audi 80 quattro

```
1.6 Litre Diesel
40kW–53.5hp–54PS
Injection Pump
```

Engine for 80

As 74hp, except:

Weight: Kerbweight (DIN) 1050kg, gross vehicle weight 1510kg.

Engine data (DIN): 4–cylinder in–line (76.5 x 86.4mm), 1588cm3; compression ratio 23:1; 40kW (53.5hp) [54PS] at 4800rpm, 25.2kW/L (33.8hp/L) [34PS/L]; 100Nm (73.8lbft) at 2700rpm.

Engine construction: Swirl chamber diesel engine; oil capacity 3.5L (3.3US qt); Bosch VE distributor–injection pump, mechanical centrifugal governor, injection distributor pump with cold start enrichment device. Battery 12V 63Ah, alternator 65A; cooling system capacity, 6.5L (6.1US qt).

Transmission: a) 4–speed manual, final drive ratio 4.111.
b) 5–speed manual, final drive ratio 4.111.
c) Automatic, final drive ratio 3.727.

Performance: Max speed 95mph/153kmh (manufacturers test specifications), speed at 1000rpm in 5th 24.6mph/39.5kmh; acceleration 0 – 62mph/100kmh in 22.0secs; power to weight ratio 26.6kg/kW (19.4kg/PS); consumption (ECE) 4.5/6.2/6.7L/100km (62.8/45.6/42.2mpg) [52.3/37.9/35.1US mpg], 5– speed 4.2/5.8/6.7L/100km (67.3/48.7/42.2mpg) [56/37.9/35.1US mpg].

```
1.6 Litre Diesel
59kW–79hp–80PS
Turbo/Injection Pump
```

Engine for 80 and 90

As 74hp, except:

Weight: Kerbweight (DIN) 1090kg, gross vehicle weight 1550kg.

Engine data (DIN): 4–cylinder in–line (76.5 x 86.4mm), 1588cm3; compression ratio 23:1; 59kW (79hp) [80PS] at 4500rpm, 32.5kW/L (43.5hp/L) [44.1PS/L]; 155Nm (114.3lbft) at 2600rpm.

Engine construction: Swirl chamber diesel engine; oil capacity 3.5L (3.3US qt), oil cooler; Bosch VE fuel injection pump, mechanical centrifugal governor, cold start enrichment device; exhaust turbocharger (max boost pressure 0.7 bar), charge air cooler. Battery 12 V 63Ah; alternator 65A; cooling system capacity 6.5L (6.1US qt).

Transmission: 5–speed manual, final drive ratio 4.111.

Gear ratios: 1st 3.545; 2nd 1.857; 3rd 1.156; 4th 0.789; 5th 0.643; R 3.500.

Performance: Max speed 107mph/172kmh (manufacturers test specifications), speed at 1000rpm in 5th gear 24.5mph/39.5kmh; acceleration 0 – 62mph/100kmh in 14.6secs; power to weight ratio from 18.5kg/kW (13.6kg/PS); consumption ECE 3.8/5.3/6.9L/100km (74.3/53.3/40.9mpg) [61.9/44.4/34.1US mpg].

```
2.0 Litre
5–cylinder 115PS
Fuel Injection
```

Engine for 90

As 74hp, except:

Weight: Kerbweight (DIN) 1170kg, gross vehicle weight 1630kg.

Engine data (Catalyst, DIN): 5–cylinder in–line (81.0 x 77.4mm), 1994cm3; compression ratio 10:1; 85kW (114hp) [115PS] at 5400rpm, 42.6kW/L (57hp/L) [57.7PS/L]; 172Nm (126.9lbft) at 4000rpm; unleaded premium grade.

Without Catalyst: Identical data.

Engine construction: Crankshaft with 5 bearings; oil capacity 3.5L (3.3US qt); Bosch KE–Jetronic mechanical electronic fuel injection. Battery 12 V 63Ah, alternator 90A; cooling system capacity 8L (7.6US qt).

Transmission: 5–speed manual, final drive ratio 3.7.

Gear ratios: 1st 3.545; 2nd 2.105; 3rd 1.3; 4th 1.029; 5th 0.838; R 3.500.

Chassis: All round disc brakes (front ventilated), optional ABS (Bosch); tyres 195/60 HR 14.

Performance: Max speed 122mph/196kmh (manufacturers test specifications), speed at 1000rpm in 5th gear 21.4mph/34.5kmh; acceleration 0 – 62mph/100kmh in 10.2secs; power to weight ratio from 13.8kg/kW (10.2kg/PS); consumption (ECE) 6.1/7.8/11.4L/100km (46.3/36.2/24.8mpg) [38.6/30.2/20.6US mpg].

```
2.3 E 5–cylinder
100kW–134hp–136PS
Fuel Injection
```

Engine for 90 2.3 E, 90 quattro and 80 quattro (USA)

As 74hp, except:

Weight: Kerbweight (DIN) 1170, quattro 1280kg, gross vehicle weight 1630, quattro 1740kg; USA 1240kg, quattro from 1320kg.

Engine data (Catalyst, DIN): 5–cylinder in–line (82.5 x 86.4mm), 2309cm3; compression ratio 10.0:1; 100kW (134hp) [136PS] at 5700rpm, 43.3kW/L (58hp/L) [58.9PS/L]; 190Nm (140.1lbft) at 4500rpm; unleaded premium grade, minimum regular grade.
USA version: 97kW (130hp) [132PS] at 5700rpm, 190Nm (140.1lbft) at 4500rpm.
Without Catalyst: (81 x 86.4mm), 2226cm3; compression ratio 10:1; 100kW (130hp) [36PS] at 5700rpm, 186Nm (137.2lbft) at 3500rpm; leaded premium grade.

Engine construction: Crankshaft with 6 bearings; oil capacity 3.5L (3.3US qt); Bosch KE–Jetronic mechanical electronic fuel injection. Battery 12V 63Ah, alternator 90A; cooling system capacity 8L (7.6US qt).

Transmission (to front wheels, for quattro to all wheels): a) 5–speed manual, final drive ratio 3.7.
b) Automatic, final drive ratio 3.083.
For quattro: 5–speed manual, permanent all wheel drive, central Torsen differential, rear differential manual lock; final drive ratio 4.111.

Gear ratios: a) 5-speed manual: 1st 3.545; 2nd 2.105; 3rd 1.3; 4th 1.029; 5th 0.838; R 3.5.
b) Automatic: As 74hp.
For quattro: 1st 3.545; 2nd 2.105; 3rd 1.300; 4th 0.943; 5th 0.769 (USA 0.796); R 3.500.

Chassis: All round disc brakes (front ventilated), optional ABS (Bosch); power assisted steering; tyres 195/60 VR 14, wheels (USA) 6J. For quattro: Rear independent suspension with A–arm and McPherson struts. Front ventilated disc brakes, Bosch ABS; fuel tank 70L.

Dimensions: Length USA 448cm. Quattro: Wheelbase 253.5cm, track 141/142.5cm; load space VDA 11.3cu ft (320dm3).

Audi 90 quattro

Performance: Max speed 128mph/206kmh, automatic 126mph/202kmh (manufacturers test specifications), speed at 1000rpm in 5th gear 21.6mph/34.8kmh, quattro 21.3mph/34.2kmh; acceleration 0 – 62mph/100kmh in 9.2secs, automatic 11.5secs; power to weight ratio from 11.7kg/kW (8.6kg/PS); consumption (ECE, Catalyst variants) 6.3/8.3/11.8L/100km (44.8/34/23.7mpg) [37.3/28.3/19.1US mpg], automatic 7.2/9.3/12.4L/100km (39.2/30.4/22.8mpg) [32.7/25.3/19US mpg], quattro 6.7/8.8/12.6L/100km (42.2/32.1/22.4mpg) [35.1/26.7/18.7US mpg].

Audi

2.3/2.0 E 20V
125/118kW–168/158hp–170/160PS
Fuel Injection

Engine for 90 20V and quatrro 20V

As 74hp, except:

Weight: Kerbweight (DIN) 1200kg, quattro 1320kg, max gross vehicle weight 1660kg, quattro.

Engine data (Catalyst DIN): 5-cylinder in-line (82.5 x 86.4mm), 2309cm3; compression ratio 10.3:1; 125kW (168hp) [170PS] at 600rpm, 54.1kW/L (72.5hp/L) [73.6PS/L]; 220Nm (162.4lbft) at 4500rpm; unleaded premium grade.
Without Catalyst: (81.0 x 77.4mm), 1994cm3; compression ratio 10.3:1; 118kW (158hp) [160PS] at 6200rpm; 200Nm (162.4lbft) at 4500rpm.

Audi 90 quattro 20V

Engine construction: 4 valves per cylinder (in V 25deg); 2 overhead camshafts (chain); 6 bearing crankshaft; oil capacity 4.5L (4.3US qt), oil cooler; Bosch Motronic injection system (fuel/ignition). 12V 63Ah Battery, 90A alternator; cooling system capacity 8L (7.6US qt).

Transmission (front wheel drive, quattro all wheel drive): 5-peed manual, final drive ratio 3.700.
For quattro: Permenant all wheel drive, central Torsen differential, rear differential with manual lock bar; final drive ratio 4.111.

Gear ratios: 1st 3.545; 2nd 2.105; 3rd 1.3; 4th 0.943; 5th 0.796; R 3.500.
For quattro: 1st 3.545; 2nd 2.105; 3rd 1.3; 4th 0.889; 5th 0.725; R 3.500.
Without Catalyst, 2WD.

Chassis: All round disc brakes (front ventilated) Bosch ABS, power assisted steering; fuel tank capacity 70L (15.4Gal) [18.5US Gal]; tyres 205/50 VR 15, wheels 6J, without Catalyst 195/60 VR 14 with 5.5J.
Quattro: Rear indepent suspension with transverse arms and spring strut.

Dimensions: For quattro, wheelbase 253.5cm, track 142.5/143cm, load space VDA 11.3cu ft (320dm3). Height 137cm.

Performance: Max speed 136mph/218kmh, speed at 1000rpm in 5th gear 23.4mph/37.7kmh, quattro 22.4mph/36kmh; acceleration 0 - 62mph/100kmh 8.6secs, quattro 8.4secs; power to weight ratio 9.6kg/kW (7.1kg/PS); consumption ECE 6.9/8.4/13.2L/100km (40.9/33.6/21.4mpg) [34.1/28/17.7US mpg], quattro 7.3/8.9/13.7L/100km (38.7/31.7/20.6mpg) [32.2/26.4/17.2US mpg].
Without Catalyst: Max speed 134mph/215kmh; acceleration 0 - 62mph/100kmh 8.9secs; consumption 6.6/8.5/13.3L/100km (42.8/33.2/21.2mpg) [35.6/27.7/17.7US mpg].

Audi Coupe – Coupe quattro

New model 5-seater Coupe based on the 80/90 model. Available as quattro, with permanent four wheel drive. 2.3 Litre engine with 134 or 168hp. Launched Birmingham 1988.

2.3 E 5–cylinder
100kW–134hp–136PS
Fuel Injection

Engine for Coupe and Coupe quattro

Body, Weight: Coupe 3-door, 5-seater; kerbweight (DIN) 1170kg, quattro 1280kg, max gross vehicle weight 1630kg, quattro 1740kg.

Engine data (Catalyst, DIN): 5-cylinder in-line (82.5 x 86.4mm), 2309cm3; compression ratio 10:1; 100kW (134hp) [136PS] at 5700rpm, 43.3kW/L (58hp/L) [58.9PS/L]; 190Nm (140.2lbft) at 4500rpm; unleaded premium/regular grade.
Without Catalyst: (81 x 86.4mm), 2226cm3; compression ratio 10:1; 100kW (134hp) [136PS] at 5700rpm; 186Nm (137.3lbft) at 3500rpm; leaded premium grade.

Engine construction: Front engine inclined 20deg to the right. Hydraulic tappets, 1 overhead camshaft (toothed belt); light-alloy cylinder block; 6 bearing crankshaft; oil capacity 3.5L (3.3US qt); Bosch KE-Jetronic fuel injection. 12V 63Ah Battery, 90A alternator; cooling system capacity 8L (7.6US qt).

Transmission (front wheel drive, quattro all wheel drive): 5-speed manual, final drive ratio 3.889.
For quattro: 5-speed manual, permanent all wheel drive, central Torsen differential, rear manual differential lock bar. Final drive ratio 4.111.

Gear ratios: 1st 3.545; 2nd 2.105; 3rd 1.429; 4th 1.029; 5th 0.838; R 3.500.

Chassis: Integral body with front sub-frame; front McPherson strut with lower A arm, antiroll bar, rear compound axle (longitudinal arms and trsion tube) with diagonal Panhard rods, coil springs, antiroll bar and telescopic damper. Servo/power assisted disc brakes (front ventilated), optional ABS, mechanical handbrake to rear; power assisted rack and pinion steering; fuel tank 70L (15.4Gal) [18.5US Gal]; tyres 205/60 VR 15, 6J wheels.
For quattro: Rear independent suspension with lower arms and spring struts; Bosch ABS.

Audi Coupe

Dimensions: Wheelbase 255.5cm, track 145.5/144.5cm, clearance 11cm, turning circle 11.1m. Load space VDA 10.6/34.6cu ft (300/980dm3). Length 436.5cm, width 171.5cm, height 137cm.
For quattro: Wheelbase 255cm, track 145.5/143.5cm. Load space VDA 8.7/32.7cu ft (245/925dm3. Height 136.5cm.

Performance (Catalyst): Max speed 128mph/206kmh (manufacturers test specification), speed at 1000rpm in 5th gear 21.5mph/34.6kmh, quattro 20.4mph/32.8kmh; acceleration 0 - 62mph/100kmh 9.2secs; power to weight ratio 11.7kg/kW (8.6kg/PS); consumption ECE 6.3/8.3/11.8L/100km (44.8/34/23.9mpg) [37.3/28.3/19.9US mpg], quattro 6.7/8.8/12.6L/100km (42.2/32.1/22.2mpg) [35.1/26.7/18.7US mpg]

2.3 E 20V
125kW–168hp–170PS
Fuel Injection

Engine for Coupe quattro 20V

As 134hp, except:

Weight: Kerbweight (DIN) 1320kg, gross vehicle weight 1780kg.

Engine data (Catalyst, DIN): 5-cylinder in-line (82.5 x 86.4mm), 2309cm3; compression ratio 10.3:1; 125kW (168hp) [170PS] at 6000rpm, 54.1kW/L (72.5hp/L) [73.6PS/L]; 220Nm (162.4lbft) at 4500rpm; unleaded premium grade.

Engine construction: 4 valves per cylinder (in V 25deg); 2 overhead camshafts (belt/chain); oil capacity 4.5L (4.3US qt), oil cooler; Bosch Motronic feul injection (fuel/ignition).

Transmission (all wheeel drive): 5-speed manual, permanent all wheel drive, central Torsen differential, rear manual differential lock bar; final drive ratio 4.111.

Chassis: Rear independent suspension with lower A arm and spring struts, Bosch ABS.

Dimensions: Wheelbase 255cm, track 145.5/143.5cm. Load space 8.6/32.7cu ft (245/925dm3). Height 136.5cm.

Performance: Max speed 137mph/220kmh (manufacturers test specifications), speed at 1000rpm in 5th gear 20.4mph/32.8kmh; acceleration 0 - 62mph/100kmh 8.4secs; power to weight ratio 10.6kg/kW (7.8kg/PS); consumption ECE 7.6/9.2/13.7L/100km (37.2/30.7/20.6mpg) [30.9/25.6/17.2US mpg].

Audi

Audi Coupe quattro 20V

Audi 100/200 – 100/200 Avant

Luxury car available with 4 or 5–cylinder engine and diesel engine. Front wheel drive or four wheel drive. The 200 version with interior refinements and a 5–cylinder turbocharged engine. Launched September 1982, Avant March 1983, 200 June 1983. January 1988, quattro with central Torsen differential. Turbodiesel with increased power.

```
1.8 Litre
66kW–88.5hp–90PS
Injection/ 2V Carb
```

Engine for 100, Avant and quattro

Body, Weight: 4–door Saloon/Sedan, 5–seater; kerbweight (DIN) from 1160kg, gross vehicle weight 1710kg, quattro 1270kg, gross vehicle weight 1820kg; 5–door Estate/Station Wagon, 5/7–seater; kerbweight (DIN) from 1200kg, gross vehicle weight 1750kg, quattro 1310kg, gross vehicle weight 1860kg.

Engine data (Catalyst, DIN): 4–cylinder in–line (81 x 86.4mm), 1781cm3; compression ratio 9.0:1; 66kW (88.5hp) [90PS] at 5500rpm; 37.1kW/L (49.7hp/L) [50.5PS/L]; 142Nm (104.7lbft) at 3250rpm; unleaded regular grade.
Without Catalyst: Compression ratio 10.0:1; 66kW (88.5hp) [90PS] at 5200rpm; 150Nm (110.6lbft) at 3300rpm; leaded premium grade.
With unregulated Catalyst: Compression ratio 9:1; 66kW (89hp) [90PS] at 5500rpm; 142Nm (104.8lbft) at 3300rpm.

Engine construction: Front engine tilted 20deg to the right. Hydraulic tappets, 1 overhead camshaft (toothed belt); light– alloy cylinder head; crankshaft with 5 bearings; oil capacity 3L (2.8US qt); with regulated Catalyst, Bosch Mono–Jetronic electronic central injection, other versions with 1 downdraught 2V two stage carb. Battery 12 V 40Ah, alternator 65Ah; cooling system capacity 7L (6.6US qt).

Transmission (to front wheels, quattro to all wheels): a) 5–speed manual, final drive ratio 4.111.
b) Automatic; hydraulic torque converter and 3–speed Planetary gear set, final drive ratio 3.417.
For quattro: 5–speed manual, permanent all wheel drive, central Torsen differential, rear differential manual lock; final drive ratio 4.556.

Gear ratios: a) 5–speed manual: 1st 3.545; 2nd 2.105; 3rd 1.300; 4th 0.943; 5th 0.789; R 3.5.
b) Automatic; maximum torque multiplication in converter 2.4 times, Planetary gear set ratios: 1st 2.714; 2nd 1.5; 3rd 1; R 2.429.
For quattro: 1st 3.545; 2nd 2.105; 3rd 1.300; 4th 0.889; 5th 0.725; R 3.500.

Chassis: Integral body with front sub–frame; front McPherson strut with control arm and antiroll bar, rear torsion crank axle (trailing arm, axle tube) with Panhard rod and coil springs, some versions antiroll bar, telescopic damper (some models optional level control system). Servo/power assisted brakes, Avant–front ventilated disc, rear drums, rear mechanical handbrake; rack and pinion steering, optional power assisted steering; fuel tank 80L (17.6Gal) [21.1US Gal]; tyres 185/70 SR 14; wheels 5.5J. For quattro: Rear independent suspension with lower A–arm, upper single control arm, coil springs and coaxial telescopic damper. Servo/power assisted disc brakes, front ventilated, Bosch ABS; power assisted steering.

Dimensions: Wheelbase 268.5cm, track 147/148.5cm – quattro 147/149cm, turning circle 11.6m; load space VDA 20.1cu ft (570dm3), Avant 26.4–64.9cu ft (784–1837dm3), length 479.5cm, width 181.5cm, height 142cm.

Performance: (Catalyst variants) Max speed 109.4mph/176kmh, Avant 107.5mph/174kmh, automatic 107.5–106.3mph/173–171kmh (manufacturers test specifications), speed at 1000rpm in 5th gear 21.6mph/34.8kmh, quattro 21.3mph/34.2kmh, acceleration 0 – 62mph/100kmh 12.6secs, automatic 14.7secs, quattro 13.2secs, Avant 12.9/15/13.5secs; power to weight ratio from 17.6kg/kW (12.9kg/PS); consumption (ECE) 5.9/7.6/10.9L/100km (47.9/37.2/25.9mpg) [39.9/30.9/21.6US mpg], automatic 6.6/8.5/11.4L/100km (42.8/33.2/24.8mpg) [35.6/27.7/20.6US mpg], quattro 6.5/8.4/12.3L/100km (43.5/33.6/23mpg) [36.2/28/19.1US mpg].

Audi 100

```
2.0 5–Cylinder
85kW–114hp–115PS
Fuel Injection
```

Engine for 100 and Avant

As 1.8 Litre, except:

Weight: Kerbweight (DIN) 1250 (Avant 1290)kg, gross vehicle weight 1800 (1840)kg.

Engine data (Catalyst, DIN): 5–cylinder in–line (81.0 x 77.4mm), 1994cm3; compression ratio 10:1; 85kW (114hp) [115PS] at 5400rpm; 42.6kW/L (57hp/L) [57.7PS/L]; 172Nm (126.9lbft) at 4000rpm; unleaded premium grade, minimum regular grade.
Without Catalyst: 85kW (114hp) [115PS] at 5200rpm; 170Nm (125.4lbft) at 3000rpm; leaded premium grade.

Engine construction: Crankshaft with 6 bearings; oil capacity 4.5L (4.3US qt); Bosch KE–Jetronic mechanical electronic fuel injection. Cooling system capacity 8.1L (7.7US qt).

Transmission: a) 5–speed manual, final drive ratio 3.889.
b) Automatic, final drive ratio 3.455.

Audi 100 Avant

Gear ratios: a) 5–speed manual: 1st 3.545; 2nd 2.105; 3rd 1.429; 4th 1.029; 5th 0.838; R 3.500.
b) Automatic: as 1.8L.

Chassis: Front ventilated disc brakes; power assisted steering; tyres 185/70 HR 14.

Performance: (Catalyst variants) Max speed 118mph/190kmh, automatic 115.6mph/186kmh, Avant 116.8–114.4mph–188–184kmh (manufacturers test specifications), speed at 1000rpm in top gear 21.6mph/34.7kmh; acceleration 0 – 62mph/100kmh 10.7secs, automatic 12.6secs, Avant 10.9/12.8secs; power to weight ratio from 14.7kg/kW (10.9kg/PS); consumption ECE 6.7/8.5/11.4L/100km

Audi

(42.2/33.2/24.8mpg) [35.1/27.7/20.6US mpg], automatic 7.2/9.1/11.9L/100km (39.2/31/23.7mpg) [32.7/25.8/19.8US mpg].

2.3 E/2.2 E
100/101kW–134/135.4hp–136/138PS
Fuel Injection

Engine for 100, Avant and quattro

As 1.8 Litre, except:

Weight: Kerbweight (DIN) 1250kg (Avant 1290kg), gross vehicle weight 1800kg (Avant 1840kg), USA 1290kg (Avant 1340kg), quattro 1360kg (Avant quattro 1400kg), gross vehicle weight 1910kg (Avant quattro 1950kg), USA 1500kg.

Engine data (Catalyst, DIN): 5–cylinder in–line (82.5 x 86.4mm), 2309cm3; compression ratio 10.0:1; 100kW (134hp) [136PS] at 5600rpm, 45.4kW/L (60.8hp/L) [62PS/L]; 190Nm (140.1lbft) at 4000rpm; unleaded premium grade, minimum regular grade.
USA Version: (SAE net): 97kW (130hp) [132PS] at 5600rpm; 190Nm (140.1lbft) at 4000rpm.
Without Catalyst: (81 x 86.4mm), 2226cm3; compression ratio 10.0:1; 101kW (135.4hp) [138PS] at 5700rpm; 188Nm (138.7lbft) at 3500rpm; leaded premium grade.

Engine construction: Crankshaft with 6 bearings; oil capacity 4.5L (4.3US qt); Bosch KE–Jetronic electronic fuel injection. Battery 12V 63Ah, alternator 90-110A; cooling system capacity 8.1L (7.7US qt).

Transmission (to front wheels, quattro to all wheels): a) 5–speed manual, final drive ratio 3.889.
b) Automatic, final drive ratio 3.250.
For quattro: 5–speed manual, final drive ratio 4.111.

Gear ratios: a) 5–speed manual: 1st 3.545; 2nd 2.105; 3rd 1.429; 4th 1.029; 5th 0.838; R 3.500.
For quattro: As above.
b) Automatic: As 1.8 Litre.

Chassis: Servo/power assisted disc brakes, front ventilated, optional ABS; power assisted steering; tyres 185/70 HR 14 or 205/60 VR 15, wheels 5.5 or 6J.

Dimensions: Length (USA) 489.5cm.

Performance: (Catalyst variants) Max speed 125mph/201kmh, Avant 124mph/199kmh, automatic 123–122mph/198–196kmh (manufacturers test specifications), speed at 1000rpm in 5th gear 21.6mph/34.7kmh, quattro 20.4mph/32.9kmh; acceleration 0 – 62mph/100kmh 9.8secs (Avant 10.0secs), automatic 11.5secs (Avant 11.7secs) quattro 10.0secs (Avant quattro 10.2secs); power to weight ratio from 12.5kg/kW (9.2kg/PS); consumption (ECE) 6.7/8.5/11.4L/100km (42.2/33.2/24.8mpg) [35.1/27.7/20.6US mpg], automatic 7.2/9.1/11.9L/100km (39.2/31/23.7mpg) [32.7/25.8/19.9US mpg], quattro 6.9/8.8/11.9L/100kmh (40.9/32.1/23.7mpg) [34.1/26.4/19.9US mpg].

Audi 100 Avant 2.3 quattro

2.2 Turbo
121/147kW–162/197hp–165/200PS
Fuel Injection

Engine for 100/200, Avant and quattro

As 1.8 Litre, except:

Weight: Kerbweight (DIN) 1300kg (Avant 1340kg), gross vehicle weight 1850kg (Avant 1890kg), quattro 1410kg (Avant quattro 1450kg), gross vehicle weight 1960kg (Avant quattro 2000kg); USA: 1400kg, quattro 1520kg (Avant quattro 1560kg).

Engine data (Catalyst, DIN): 5–cylinder in–line (81 x 86.4mm), 2226cm3; compression ratio 7.8:1; 121kW (162hp) [165PS] at 5500rpm, 54.4kW/L (72.9hp/L) [74.1PS/L]; 240Nm (177lbft) at 3000rpm; unleaded premium grade, min regular grade.
Without Catalyst: Compression ratio 8.6:1; 147kW (197hp) [200PS] at 5800rpm, 66kW/L (88.5hp/L) [89.8PS/L]; 270Nm (199.3lbft) at 3000rpm; leaded premium grade.
For 200 automatic: 140kW (188hp) [190PS] at 5800rpm; 270Nm (199.3lbft) at 3000rpm.

Engine construction: Crankshaft with 6 bearings; oil capacity 4.5L (4.3US qt); oil cooler; Bosch KE–Jetronic electro/mechanical fuel injection; exhaust turbocharger KKK, charge-air cooler. Battery 12V 63Ah, alternator 90-110A; cooling system capacity 8.1L (7.7US qt).

Transmission (to front wheels, quattro to all wheels): a) 5–speed manual, final drive ratio 3.889.
b) Automatic, final drive ratio 3.083.

Gear ratios: a) 5–speed manual: 1st 3.600; 2nd 2.125; 3rd 1.360; 4th 0.967; 5th 0.778; R 3.500. For quattro and USA: 5th 0.730.
b) Automatic as 1.8 Litre.

Audi 200 Turbo quattro

Chassis: Servo/power assisted disc brakes, front ventilated discs and Bosch ABS; power assisted steering; tyres 205/60 VR 15, tyres 6J.

Dimensions: Length (USA) 489.5cm.

Performance: (Catalyst variants) Max speed 134.2mph/216kmh, automatic 132mph/212kmh (Avant 132.4–130mph/213–209kmh (manufacturers test specifications), speed at 1000rpm in 5th gear 23.3mph/37.5kmh, quattro 23.6mph/37.9kmh; acceleration 0 – 62mph/100kmh 8.0secs (Avant 8.2secs), automatic 9.2secs (Avant 9.4secs), quattro 8.0secs (Avant 8.2secs); power to weight ratio from 10.7kg/kW (7.9kg/PS); consumption (ECE) 7.2/9.4/13.2L/100km (39.2/30.1/21.4mpg) [32.7/25/17.8US mpg], automatic 7.9/10.3/14.4L/100km (35.8/27.4/19.6mpg) [29.8/22.8/16.3US mpg], quattro 7.7/9.9/14.9L/100km (36.7/28.5/19mpg) [30.5/23.8/15.8US mpg].
Without Catalyst: Max speed 143.6mph/231kmh, automatic 139mph/224kmh; acceleration 0 – 62mph/100kmh 7.5secs, automatic 8.5secs, quattro 7.5secs, power to weight ratio from 8.8kg/kW (6.5kg/PS); consumption 6.9/8.9/13.2L (34.1/31.7/21.4mpg) [34.1/26.4/17.8US mpg], automatic 7.6/9.7/13.7L/100km (37.2/29.1/20.6mpg) [30.9/24.2/17.2US mpg], quattro 7.4/9.4/14.6L/100km (38.2/30.1/19.3mpg) [31.8/25/16.1US mpg].

Audi 200 Avant quattro

2.0 Diesel
51kW–68.3hp–70PS
Injection Pump

Engine for 100 and Avant

As 1.8 Litre, except:

Audi

Weight: Kerbweight (DIN) 1250 (Avant 1290)kg, gross vehicle weight 1800 (Avant 1840)kg.

Engine data (DIN): 5–cylinder in–line (76.5 x 86.4mm), 1986cm3; compression ratio 23:1; 51kW (68.3hp) [70PS] at 4800rpm, 25.7kW/L (34.4hp/L) [35.2PS/L]; 123Nm (90.7lbft) at 2800rpm.

Engine construction: Swirl chamber diesel engine; crankshaft with 6 bearings; oil capacity 5L (4.7US qt); Bosch VE distributor injection pump, mechanical centrifugal governor, cold start enrichment device. Battery 12V 88Ah, alternator 55A; cooling system capacity 9.4L (8.9US qt).

Transmission: a) 5–speed manual, final drive ratio 4.778.
b) Automatic, final drive ratio 3.455.

Gear ratios: a) 5–speed manual: 1st 3.600; 2nd 1.882; 3rd 1.185; 4th 0.844; 5th 0.684; R 3.500.
b) Automatic: as 1.8 Litre.

Chassis: Power assisted steering.

Performance: Max speed 98mph/158kmh, Avant 97mph/156kmh, automatic 96–94.5mph/154–152kmh (manufacturers test specifications), speed at 1000rpm in 5th gear 21.5mph/34.6kmh; acceleration 0 – 62mph/100kmh 18.6secs (Avant 19.3secs), automatic 21.8 (Avant 22.5secs); power to weight acceleration from 24.5kg/kW (17.9kg/PS); consumption ECE 4.6/6.5/9.0L/100km (61.4/43.5/31.4mpg) [51.1/36.2/26.1US mpg], automatic 5.9/7.9/9.0L/100km (47.9/35.8/31.4mpg) [39.9/29.8/26.1US mpg].

```
2.0 Turbo Diesel
74kW–98hp–100PS
Injection Pump
```

Engine for 100 and Avant

As 1.8 Litre, except:

Weight: Kerbweight (DIN) 1300kg (Avant 1340kg), gross vehicle weight 1850kg (Avant 1890kg).

Engine data (DIN): 5–cylinder in–line (76.5 x 86.4mm), 1986cm3; compression ratio 23:1; 74kW (98hp) [100PS] at 4500rpm, 37.3kW/L (50hp/L) [50.4PS/L]; 192Nm (141.7lbft) at 2200rpm.

Engine construction: Swirl chamber diesel engine; crankshaft with 6 bearings; oil capacity 5L (4.7US qt), oil cooler; Bosch VE distributor injection pump, mechanical centrifugal governor, cold start enrichment device, exhaust turbocharger, charge-air cooler. Battery 12V 88Ah, alternator 55A; cooling system capacity 9.4L (8.9US qt).

Transmission: 5–speed manual, final drive ratio 4.111.

Gear ratios: a) 5–speed manual: 1st 3.600; 2nd 1.882; 3rd 1.185; 4th 0.844; 5th 0.684; R 3.500.

Chassis: Power assisted steering.

Performance: Max speed 115mph/185kmh (Avant 114mph/183kmh), speed at 1000 in 5th gear 24.7mph/39.8kmh; acceleration 0 – 62mph/100kmh 12.3secs (Avant 12.8secs); power to weight from 17.6kg/kW (13kg/PS); consumption ECE 4.9/6.6/8.7L/100km (57.6/42.8/32.5mpg) [48/35.6/27US mpg].

Audi quattro

Performance Coupe with a 5–cylinder engine; permanent four wheel drive, 5–speed manual transmission and independent suspension. Launched Geneva 1980. Autumn 1983; quattro Sport with extended wheelbase and 4 valves per cylinder engine. Frankfurt 1987: 2.2 Litre engine. Geneva 1989: 20V version developing 217hp

```
2.2 Litre
146/162kW–197/217hp–220/220PS
Fuel Injection/Turbo
```

Body, Weight: 2–door Coupe, 5–seater; kerbweight (DIN) 1300kg, gross vehicle weight 1760kg.

Engine data (DIN): 5–cylinder in–line (81.0 x 86.4mm), 2226cm3; compression ratio 8.6:1; 147kW (197hp) [200PS] at 5800rpm, 66kW/L (88.5hp/L) [89.8PS/L]; 270Nm (199.3lbft) at 3000rpm; leaded premium grade.
With Catalyst: Compression ratio 7.8:1; 121kW (162hp) [165PS] at 5500rpm; 240Nm (177lbft) at 3000rpm; unleaded premium, minimum regular grade.
'20V' with 4 valves per cylinder. Compression ratio 9.3:1; 162kW (217hp) [220PS] at 5900rpm; 72.8kW/L (97.5hp/L) [98.8PS/L]; 309Nm (228lbft) at 1950rpm.

Engine construction: Front engine, tilted 20deg to the right; 1 or 2 overhead camshafts (toothed belt); light–alloy cylinder head; crankshaft with 6 bearings; oil capacity 4L (3.8US qt), oil cooler; Bosch K–Jetronic mechanical fuel injection 20V–Motronic; 1 exhaust turbocharger KKK; max boost pressure 0.85 bar; charge-air cooler. Battery 12 V 63Ah, alternator 90A; cooling system capacity 9.3L (8.8USqt).

Transmission (to all wheels): 5–speed manual, permanent all wheel drive, central Torsen differential, rear differential manual lock, final drive ratio 3.889.

Audi quattro 20V

Gear ratios: 1st 3.600; 2nd 2.125; 3rd 1.458; 4th 1.071/0.967; 5th 0.778; R 3.500.

Chassis: Integral body with front sub–frame; all round independent suspension, front and rear McPherson struts with A– arms and antiroll bars. Servo/power assisted disc brakes, front ventilated, Bosch ABS, mechanical handbrake to rear wheels; power assisted rack and pinion steering; fuel tank 90L (19.8Gal) [23.8US Gal]; tyres 215/50 VR 15, wheels 8J.

Dimensions: Wheelbase 252.5cm, track 146/149.5cm, clearance 11.5cm, turning circle 11.3m; load space VDA 11.6cu ft (330dm3); length 440.5cm, width 172.5cm, height 134.5cm.

Performance: 197hp; Max speed 137mph/220kmh (manufacturers test specifications), speed at 1000rpm in 5th gear 22.2mph/35.7kmh; acceleration 0 – 62mph/100kmh in 6.7secs; power to weight ratio 8.8kg/kW (6.5kg/PS); consumption ECE 7.6/9.7/13.4L/100km (37.2/29.1/21.1mpg) [30.9/24.2/17.6US mpg].
20V: Max speed 143mph/230kmh (manufacturers test specifications); acceleration 0–62mph/100kmh 6.7secs; consumption ECE 7.8/9.9/14.5L/100km (36.2/28.5/19.5mpg) [30.2/23.8/16.2US mpg].

Audi V8

New model. High performance Saloon/Sedan based on the Audi 100 with a new 3.6 Litre V8 engine (4 valves per cylinder), permanent four wheel drive with integrated ABS and 4-speed automatic transmission. Launched September 1988.

Audi V8

```
3.6 Litre V8
184kW–247hp–250PS
Fuel Injection
```

Body, Weight: Saloon/Sedan 4-door, 5-seater; kerbweight (DIN) 1710kg, gross vehicle weight 2310kg.

Engine data (Catalyst, DIN): 8-cylinder in V 90deg (81,0 x 86.4mm), 3562cm3; compression ratio 10.6:1; 184kW (247hp) [250PS] at 5800rpm, 51.7kW/L (69.3hp/L) [70.2PS/L]; 340Nm (250.9lbft) at 4000rpm; unleaded regular grade.

Engine construction: Hydraulic tappets; 4 valves per cylinder (in V 25deg), 2 overhead camshafts per cylinder bank (belt/chain); light–alloy engine assembly; 5

bearing crankshaft; oil capacity 9.5L (9US qt), oil cooler; Bosch Motronic M2.4 fuel injection (fuel/ignition). 12V 450A Battery, 110A alternator; cooling system capacity 10.5L (9.9US qt).

Transmission (all wheel drive): ZF automatic, hydraulic torque converter and 4-speed Planetary gear set, programme control E/S/M. Permanent all wheel drive, central differential (50/50% drive split) with electronic traction control, rear Torsen differential; final drive ratio 4.111.

Gear ratios: Max torque multiplication in converter 2 times, Planetary gear set ratios: 1st 2.48; 2nd 1.48; 3rd 1; 4th 0.73; R 2.09.

Chassis: Integral body with front sub-frame; front McPherson strut with control arm and antiroll bar; rear independent suspension with lower A arms and upper control arms, coil springs and coaxial telescopic dampers. Servo/power assisted disc brakes (ventilated), ABS (Bosch), mechanical handbrake to rear; power assisted rack and pinion steering; fuel tank 80L (17.6Gal) [21.1US Gal]; tyres 215/60 VR 15, 7.5J wheels.

Dimensions: Wheelbase 270cm, track 151.5/153cm, turning circle 11.5m. Load space 20.1cu ft (570dm3). Length 486cm, width 181.5cm, height 142cm.

Performance: Max speed 146mph/235kmh (manufacturers test specifications), speed at 1000rpm in 4th gear 24.2mph/39kmh; acceleration 0 – 62mph/100kmh 9.2secs; power to weight ratio 9.3kg/kW (6.8kg/PS); consumption ECE 8.9/10.9/17.1L/100km (31.7/25.9/16.5mpg) [26.4/21.6/13.8US mpg].

AUSTIN — GB

Austin Rover Group Ltd, Canley Road, Canley, Coventry CV5 6QX, England.

Famous British mark; earlier the largest English car manufacturer, then a member of BMC, then BL Limited and later BL Cars. 1988: Privatised and incorporated in British Aerospace

MODEL RANGE
Mini – Metro –Maestro – Montego

Mini

Four-seater, two-door small car with transverse mounted engine and front wheel drive. ADO 15 factory designation. Debut Summer 1959. Summer/Autumn 1980: A-Plus engine. Summer/Autumn 1984: 12-inch wheels and front disc brakes. Versions in England: City and Mayfar

```
998cm3
30/32.5kW–40/43.5hp–41/44PS
1 Carb
```

Body, Weight: 2-door Saloon/Sedan, 4-seats; kerbweight (DIN) 625 to 675kg, gross vehicle weight 930 to 1000kg.

Engine data (DIN): 4-cylinder in-line (64.58 x 76.2mm), 998cm3; compression ratio 10.3:1; 30kW (40hp) [41PS] at 5000rpm, 30.1kW/L (40.3hp/L) [41.1PS/L]; 69Nm (50.9lbft) at 2500rpm; leaded premium grade.
For some export countries: 32.5kW (43.5hp) [44PS] or 31kW (41.5hp) [42PS] at 5250rpm; 67Nm (49.4lbft) at 2600rpm.
Japanese edition: Compression ratio 9.6:1, 28.5kW (38hp) [39PS] at 4750rpm; 70Nm (51.6lbft) at 2000rpm.

Engine construction: A-Plus designation. Front engine together with transverse mounted transmission. Side-mounted camshaft (chain); crankshaft with 3 bearings; oil (engine and transmission in same oil bath) 4.8L (4.5US qt); 1 SU/ARG HS 4 semi-downdraught carb; battery 12V 30/32/48Ah, alternator 34A; cooling system capacity 3.6L (3.4US qt).

Transmission (to front wheels):
a) 4-speed manual, floor shift; final drive ratio 3.11 or 2.95.
b) Optional automatic; hydraulic torque converter and 4-speed bevel gear, pistol-grip selector lever with P-R-N-1-2-3-D; final drive ratio 3.27.

Gear ratios: a) 4-speed manual: 1st 3.647; 2nd 2.185; 3rd 1.425; 5th 1; R 3.667.
b) Automatic: Max torque multiplication in converter 2 times; gear ratios: 1st 2.69; 2nd 1.845; 3rd 1.46; 4th 1; R 2.69.

Chassis: Integral body with front and rear sub-frames; front independent suspension with control arms, rear with longitudinal arms; rubber spring elements and front and rear telescopic dampers. Front disc brakes, diameter 21.3cm, rear drums, mechanical handbrake to rear wheels; rack and pinion steering; fuel tank 34L (7.5Gal) [9US Gal]; tyres 145/70SR 12, wheel rims 4.5 inches.

Dimensions: Wheelbase 203.5cm, track 126.5/121.5 or 124/119cm, clearance 15cm, turning circle 8.7m. Load space 4.2cu ft (120dm3). Length 305/307cm, width 141/144cm, height 135cm.

Performance: Max speed 80–82mph/129–132kmh, automatic 78mph/126kmh (manufacturers test specifications), speed at 1000rpm in 4th gear 18.7–19.7mph/30.1–31.7kmh; acceleration 0 – 60mph/97kmh 17.9, automatic 21.9secs; power to weight ratio from 19.2kg/kW (14.2kg/PS); consumption (ECE) 4.7/6.4/6.2L/100km (60.1/44.1/45.6mpg) [50/36.8/37.9US mpg], automatic 6.1/8.9/6.9L/100km (46.3/31.7/40.9mpg) [38.6/26.4/34.1US mpg].

Mini Mayfair

Metro

Lower middle-of-the-range Saloon/Sedan with front wheel drive and tail gate, 1 or 1.3 Litre engine capacities. Debut October 1980. July 1981 1.3 and automatic models. October 1984: Detail modifications, also available in the 5-door Saloon/Sedan. Summer 1987: reduced noise level. Birmingham 1988: New versions GTa, Sport and GS

```
1 Litre
34.5/33/31kW–46/44/41.5hp–47/45/42PS
1 Carb
```

Engine for 1.0

Body, Weight: 3-door Saloon/Sedan, 5-seats; kerbweight (DIN) 750 to 810kg, gross vehicle weight 1100/1225kg/ 5-door Saloon/Sedan, 5-seats; kerbweight (DIN) 795 to 820kg, gross vehicle weight 1140/1275kg.

Engine data (DIN): 4-cylinder in-line (64.58 x 76.2mm), 998cm3; compression ratio 10.3:1; 34.5kW (46hp) [47PS] at 5500rpm, 34.6kW/L (46.4hp/L) [47.1PS/L]; 73Nm (53.8lbft) at 3250rpm; leaded premium grade; also 35kW (48PS) or compression ratio 9.6:1; 33kW (44) [45PS] at 5250rpm, 33.1kW/L (44.4hp/L) [45.1PS/L]; 70Nm (51.6lbft) at 3000rpm; optional compression ratio 8.3:1; 31kW (41.5hp) [42PS] at 5000rpm, 31.1kW/L (41.7hp/L) [42.4PS/L]; 69Nm (50.9lbft) at 2500rpm; leaded regular grade.

Engine construction: A-Plus designation. Front engine with transmission transversely mounted in the body. Side-mounted camshaft (chain); crankshaft with 3 bearings; oil (engine and gearbox in the same oil bath) 4.8L (4.5US qt); 1 SU/ARG HIF 38 semi-downdraught carburettor,.
Battery 12V 30Ah, alternator 45A; cooling system capacity 4.9L (4.6US qt).

Transmission (to front wheels): 4-speed manual, floor shift, final drive ratio 3.647 or 3.11.

Gear ratios: 1st 3.647; 2nd 2.185; 3rd 1.425; 4th 1; R 3.667; or: 1st 4.004; 2nd 2.307; 3rd 1.435; 4th 1;R 4.026.

Chassis: Integral body, front and rear sub-frames, front control arm and antiroll bars, rear longitudinal arms, hydragas– suspension with nitrogen gas–spring cushions and rear auxiliary coil springs. Servo/power assisted brakes, front discs (ventilated), diameter 21.3cm, rear drums, mechanical handbrake to rear wheels, rack and pinion steering; fuel tank 35.5L (7.8Gal) [9.9US Gal]; tyres 160/65R 315; wheel rims 105–315.

Dimensions: Wheelbase 225cm, track 130/129.5cm, clearance 17/11cm, turning circle 10.2m. Load space 8.1/33.7cu ft (230/955dm3). Length 340.5cm, width 155cm, height 136/138cm.

Performance: Max speed 87–89mph/140–144kmh (manufacturers test specifications), speed at 1000rpm in 4th gear 16.3mph/26.2kmh; acceleration 0 – 60mph/97kmh 17.9 to 19secs; power to weight ratio from 21.8kg/kW (16.0kg/PS); consumption (ECE) 4.7/7.0/6.2L/100km (60.1/40.4/45.6mpg) [50/33.6/37.9US mpg], 4.7/6.0/5,8L/100km (60.1/47.1/48.7mpg) [50/39.2/40.6US mpg] or 4.2/6.1/5.9L/100km (67.3/46.3/47.9mpg) [56/38.6/39.9US mpg]. With compression ratio 8.3:1: Max speed 83.9mph/135kmh; acceleration 0 – 62mph/97kmh 19.5secs;

Austin

power–to–weight ratio from 24.2kg/kW (17.9kg/PS); consumption (ECE) 5.1/7.1/6.7L/100km (55.4/39.8/42.2mpg) [46.1/33.1/35.1US mpg].

```
1.3 Litre
46.5/45.5/44kW–62/61/59hp–63/62/60PS
1 Carb
```

Engine for 1.3 and 1.3 automatic

As 1.0 Litre, except:

Weight: Kerbweight (DIN) 785 to 870kg, gross vehicle weight 1140/1270kg.

Engine data (DIN): (70.61 x 81.28mm), 1275cm3; compression ratio 9.75:1; 46.5kW (62hp) [63PS] at 5300rpm, 36.5kW/L (48.9hp/L) [49.4PS/L]; 98Nm (72.3lbft) at 3200rpm; leaded premium grade.
GS: 45.5kW (61hp) [62PS]; premium grade unleaded.
Some countries: 44kW (59hp) [60PS] at 5250rpm; 93Nm (68.6lbft) at 3000rpm.

Metro 1.3

Engine construction: 1 SU/ARG HIF 44 carb; battery 12V 40Ah.

Transmission: a) 4–speed manual; final drive ratio 3.44, 3.21 or 2.95.
b) AP automatic; hydraulic torque converter and 4–speed bevel gear, central selector lever, final drive ratio 3.44, 3.21, 3.11 or 2.95.

Gear ratios: a) 4–speed manual: 1st 3.647; 2nd 2.185; 3rd 1.425; 4th 1; R 3.667; or 1st 4.004; 2nd 2.307; 3rd 1.435; 4th 1; R 4.026;
b) Automatic; Max torque multiplication in converter 2 times; gear ratios: 1st 2.69; 2nd 1.845; 3rd 1.46; 4th 1; R 2.69.

Performance: Max speed 97mph/156kmh, 61hp 95mph/153kmh, 59hp 90mph/145kmh, Automatic 92mph/148kmh, 61hp 90mph/144kmh (manufacturers test specifications), speed at 1000rpm in 4th gear 17.2mph/27.7kmh, 3.21:1 18.5mph/29.8kmh; acceleration 0 – 60mph/97kmh 12.9–13.9secs, Automatic 15.5–16.8secs; power to weight ratio 16.9kg/kW (12.5kg/PS); consumption (ECE) 5.0/6.8/7.0L/100km (56.5/41.5/40.4mpg) [47/34.6/33.6US mpg] or 5.1/7.1/8.4L/100km (54.4/39.8/33.2mpg) [46.1/33.1/28US mpg], Automatic 6.0/8.1/8.0L/100km (47.1/34.9/35.3mpg) [39.2/29/29.4US mpg].

Metro 1.3 GTa

```
1.3 Litre
53.5/51.5kW–72/69hp–73/70PS
1 Carb
```

Engine for 1.3 Sport and 1.3 GTa

As 1.0 Litre, except:

Weight: Kerbweight (DIN) 790 to 870kg, gross vehicle weight 1140/1220kg.

Engine data (DIN): 4–cylinder in–line (70.61 x 81.28mm), 1275cm3; compression ratio 10.5:1; 53.5kW (72hp) [73PS] at 6000rpm, 42kW/L (56.3hp/L) [57.3PS/L]; 99Nm (73lbft) at 4000rpm; leaded premium grade. For some countries: 51.5kW (69hp) [70PS] or 51kW (68hp) [69PS].

Engine construction: 1 SU/ARG HIF 44 carb; battery 12V 40Ah.

Transmission: 4–speed manual; final drive ratio 3.44.

Gear ratios: 4–speed manual: 1st 3.647; 2nd 2.185; 3rd 1.425; 4th 1; R 3.667.

Chassis: Tyres 165/65 R 315 or 185/55 R 13.

Performance: Max speed 101–103mph/163–166kmh, automatic 92mph/148kmh (manufacturers test specifications), speed at 1000rpm in 4th gear 17.2mph/27.7kmh; acceleration 0 – 60mph/97kmh 10.9secs, automatic 15.5secs; power–to–weight ratio from 15.1kg/kW (11.1kg/PS); consumption (ECE) 5.0/6.9/8.1L/100km (56.5/40.9/34.9mpg) [47/34.1/29US mpg], automatic 6.0/8.1/8.0L/100km (47.1/34.9/35.3mpg) [39.2/29/29.4US mpg].

Maestro

Saloon/Sedan with tailgate, transverse engine and front wheel drive. 1.3 and 1.6–litre engine capacities, 4 and 5–speed gearboxes. Allegro successor. Debut 1 March 1983, Autumn 1984: 'S' series instead of 'R' 1.6 Litre engine.

```
1.3 Litre
50.5kW–68hp–69PS
1 Carb
```

Engine for 1.3

Body, Weight: 5–door Saloon/Sedan, 5–seats: Kerbweight (DIN) 875 to 940kg, gross vehicle weight 1370kg.

Engine data (DIN): 4–cylinder in–line (70.64 x 81.28mm), 1275cm3; compression ratio 9.75:1; 50.5kW (68hp) [69PS] at 5600rpm, 39.6kW/L (53hp/L) [54.1PS/L]; 102Nm (75.2lbft) at 3500rpm; leaded premium grade.
For some countries: 45.5kW (61hp) [62PS], 47.5kW (64hp) [65PS] or 48.5kW (65hp) [66PS].

Engine construction: A–Plus designation. Transverse mounted engine. Side–mounted camshaft; oil approx 3.5L (3.3US qt); 1 ARG or SU HIF 44 carb. Unipart GSP 163 spark plugs; battery 12V 36/40/45/66Ah, alternator 37/45/55A; cooling system capacity approx 6.5L (6.1US qt).

Transmission (to front wheels): a) 4–speed manual; final drive ratio 4.17 or 4.25 or 3.89.
b) 5–speed manual; final drive ratio 4.17 or 4.25 or 3.94.

Gear ratios: a) 4–speed manual: 1st 3.45; 2nd 1.94; 3rd 1.29; 4th 0.91; R 3.17. or 1st 3.45; 2nd 1.75; 3rd 1.07; 4th 0.70; R 3.17.
b) 5–speed manual: 1st 3.45; 2nd 1.94; 3rd 1.29; 4th 0.91; 5th 0.71; R 3.17.

Chassis: Integral body; front control arms and McPherson struts with coil springs, compound axle with semi–trialing arms and cross linkage, McPherson struts and coil springs, optional front antiroll bar, telescopic dampers. Servo/power assisted brakes, front discs, rear drums, disc diamter 24cm, mechanical handbrake to rear wheels; rack and pinion steering; fuel tank 50/54L (11/12Gal) [13.2/15.6US Gal]; tyres 145 SR 13, 155 SR 13 or 165 SR 13, wheel rims 4.5 or 5J.

Metro 1.3 Special

Dimensions: Wheelbase 251cm, track 146.5/144cm, clearance 14cm, turning circle 10.3m. Load space 10.6/23/38.5cu ft (300/650/1090dm3). Length 400 to 405cm, width 169cm, height 142cm.

Austin

Performance: Max speed 97mph/156kmh (manufacturers test specifications), speed at 1000rpm in 4th gear 17.3mph/27.8kmh; acceleration 0 – 60mph/97kmh 12.5secs; power to weight ratio from 17.3kg/kW (12.7kg/PS); ECE consumption 5.4/7.8/7.8L/100km (52.3/36.2/36.2mpg) [43.6/30.2/30.2US mpg], 5-speed 4.9/6.9/7.8L/100km (57.6/40.9/36.2mpg) [48/34.1/30.2US mpg].

```
1.6 Litre
63/61kW –84.5/82hp–86/83PS
1 Carb
```

Engine for 1.6

As 1.3 Litre, except:

Weight: Kerbweight (DIN) 945 to 1010kg; gross vehicle weight 1440kg.

Engine data (DIN): 4-cylinder in-line (76.2 x 87.6mm), 1598cm3; compression ratio 9.7:1; 63kW (84.5hp) [86PS] at 5600rpm, 39.4kW/L (52.8hp/L) [53.8PS/L]; 132Nm (97.4lbft) at 3500rpm.
Some countries: 61kW (82hp) [83PS].

Engine construction: 'S' Series designation. 1 overhead camshaft (toothed belt); crankshaft with 5 bearings.

Transmission: a) 5-speed manual; final drive ratio 3.89 or 3.94.
b) Automatic; hydraulic torque converter and 3-speed Planetary gear set, central selector lever, final drive ratio 3.57.

Gear ratios: a) 5-speed manual: 1st 3.45; 2nd 1.94; 3rd 1.29; 4th 0.91; 5th 0.71; R 3.17.
b) Automatic; Max torque multiplication in converter 2.44 times, Planetary gear set ratios: 1st 2.55; 2nd 1.45; 3rd 1; R 2.46.

Chassis: Front antiroll bars; optional power assisted steering; tyres 165 SR 13, wheel rims 5J.

Dimensions: Clearance 15cm. Length 405cm, height 143cm.

Performance: Max speed 104mph/167kmh, automatic 99mph/159kmh (manufacturers test specifications), speed at 1000rpm in 4th gear 19.2mph/30.9kmh, in 5th gear 24.5mph/39.4kmh; acceleration 0 – 60mph/97kmh 10.5secs, automatic 12.8secs; power to weight ratio from 15.0kg/kW (11.0kg/PS); ECE consumption 5.9/8.0/8.8L/100km (47.9/35.3/31.7mpg) [39.9/29.4/26.7US mpg], 5-speed 5.3/7.3/8.9L/100km (53.3/38.7/31.7mpg) [44.4/32.2/26.4US mpg], automatic 6.5/9.3/9.1L/100km (43.5/30.4/31mpg) [36.2/25.3/25.8US mpg].

Maestro 1.6SL

Montego

Middle-of-the-range notchback or Estate/Station Wagon, front wheel drive and transverse engine (1.3 to 2 Litre); closely related to the Austin Maestro. Saloon/Sedan debut 25 April 1984, Estate/Station Wagon October 1984.
Birmingham 1988: Available with direct injection 2.0 Turbo Diesel.

```
1.6 Litre
63/61kW –84/82hp–86/83PS
1 Carb
```

Engine for 1.6

Body, Weight: 4-door Saloon/Sedan, 5-seats; kerbweight (DIN) 965 to 1045kg, gross vehicle weight 1460kg; 5-door Estate/Station Wagon, 5/7-seats; kerbweight (DIN) 1050 to 1105kg, gross vehicle weight 1630/1700kg.

Engine data (DIN): 4-cylinder in-line (76.2 x 87.6mm), 1598cm3; compression ratio 9.7:1; 63kW (84hp) [86PS] at 5600rpm, 39.4kW/L (52.8hp/L) [53.8PS/L]; 132Nm (97.4lbft) at 3500rpm. Unleaded premium grade.
Some countries: 61kW (82hp) [83.5PS] at 5600rpm; 129Nm (95.2lbft) at 3500rpm.
Export 1.3: (70.64 x 81.82mm), 1275cm3; compression ratio 9.75:1; 50.5kW (68hp) [69PS] at 5600rpm, 39.6kW/L (53.5hp/L) [54.1PS/L]; 102Nm (74.2lbft) at 3500rpm; premium grade.

Engine construction: 'S' Series designation. 1 overhead camshaft (toothed belt); crankshaft with 5 bearings, oil approx 3.5L (3.3US qt). 1 ARG/SU HIF 44 E carb. Battery 12V 44/66Ah; cooling system capacity approx 8.5L (8US qt).

Transmission: a) 5-speed manual, final drive ratio 4.06.
b) Automatic: hydraulic torque converter and 3-speed Planetary gear set, central selector lever, final drive ratio 3.41.

Gear ratios: a) 5-speed manual: 1st 2.92; 2nd 1.75; 3rd 1.14; 4th 0.85; 5th 0.65; R 3.0.
b) Automatic: Max torque multiplication in converter 2.4 times, Planetary gear set ratios: 1st 2.55; 2nd 1.45; 3rd 1; R 2.46.

Chassis: Integral body; front control arm and McPherson strut with coil springs, rear compound axle (trailing arms with transverse control arms), McPherson strut and coil springs, front antiroll bar, telescopic dampers
Servo/power assisted brakes, front discs, rear drums. Disc diameter 24.1cm, mechanical handbrake on rear; rack and pinion steering, optional power assisted. Fuel tank 50/53L (11.0Gal) [13.2US Gal], tyres 165 SR 13, wheels 5 J. Optional tyres 180/65 R 365.

Dimensions: Wheelbase 257cm, track 146.5/144 or 148.5/146cm, clearance 15.5cm, turning circle 10.5m. Load space 18.4cu ft (520dm3), Estate/Station Wagon 17.7/60cu ft (500/1700dm3). Length 447cm, width 171cm, height 142cm, Estate/Station Wagon 144.5cm.

Performance: Max speed 102.5mph/165kmh, automatic 98mph/158kmh (manufacturers test specifications), speed at 1000rpm in 4th gear 19.7mph/31.7kmh, in 5th gear 24.5mph/41.4kmh; acceleration 0 – 60mph/97kmh 10.9secs, Automatic 13.2secs; power to weight ratio 15.3kg/kW (11.2kg/PS); consumption (ECE) 5.1/6.8/9.1L/100km (55.4/41.5/31mpg) [46.1/34.6/25.8US mpg], Automatic 6.3/8.2/9.7L/100km (44.8/34.4/29.1mpg) [37.3/28.7/24.2US mpg].
1.3: Max speed 96mph/154kmh (manufacturers test specifications); acceleration 0–60mph/97kmh 13secs; consumption (ECE) 4.8/6.8/7.8L/100km (58.8/41.5/36.2mpg) [49/34.6/30.2US mpg].

Montego 2.0 GTi

```
2.0 Litre
76.5/86/83kW–102.5/115/111hp
–104/117/113PS
1 Carb/Fuel Injection
```

Engine for 2.0 and 2.0 GTi/GS

As 1.6 Litre, except:

Body, Weight: 4-door Saloon/Sedan, 5-seats; kerbweight (DIN) 1020 to 1105kg, gross vehicle weight 1560kg; 5-door Estate/Station Wagon 5/7-seats kerbweight (DIN) 1085 to 1165kg, gross vehicle weight 1700kg.

Engine data (DIN): 4-cylinder in-line (84.46 x 89mm), 1994cm3; compression ratio 9.1:1; 76.5kW (102.5hp) [104PS] at 5500rpm, 38.4kW/L (51.5hp/L) [52.2PS/L]; 164Nm (121lbft) at 3000rpm.
Some countries: 73.5kW (98.5hp) [100PS].
With fuel injection: 86kW (115hp) [117PS] at 5500rpm, 43.1kW/L (57.7hp/L) [58.7PS/L]; 182Nm (134.2lbft) at 2800rpm.
Some countries: 83kW (111hp) [113PS] at 5500rpm, 41.6kW/L (55.7hp/L) [56.7PS/L]; 178Nm (131.3lbft) at 2800rpm.

Engine construction: 'O'-Series designation. 1 overhead camshaft (toothed belt); light-alloy cylinder head; crankshaft with 5 bearings; oil approx 4L (3.8US qt). Battery 12V 44/66Ah; cooling system capacity 8.5L (8US qt).

Austin • Autobianchi • Avanti

Montego Estate 2.0

Transmission: a) 5-speed manual; final drive ratio 3.875 or 3.94.
b) ZF 4 HP 14 automatic; hydraulic torque converter and 4-speed Planetary gear set, central selector lever; final drive ratio 3.94.

Gear ratios: a) 5-speed manual: 1st 3.25; 2nd 1.75; 3rd 1.15; 4th 0.866; 5th 0.657; R 3. or: 1st 2.71; 2nd 1.89; 3rd 1.33; 4th 1.04; 5th 0.852; R 3.
Or: 1st 2.92; 2nd 1.75; 3rd 1.14; 4th 0.848; 5th 0.648/0.757; R 3/3.33.
b) Automatic; max torque multiplication in converter 2 times, Planetary gear set ratios: 1st 2.41; 2nd 1.368; 3rd 1; 4th 0.739; R 2.825.

Chassis: Front ventilated disc brakes; tyres 180/65 R 365. wheel rims 120x365.

Dimensions: Track 148.5/146cm. Estate/Station Wagon; load space 17.6/60cu ft (500/1700dm3), height 144.5cm.

Performance: Max speed 108mph/174kmh, automatic 102.5mph/165kmh (manufacturers test specifications), speed at 1000rpm in 4th gear 20.3mph/32.6kmh, in 5th gear 26.8mph/43.1kmh; acceleration 0 - 60mph/97kmh 9.8secs, automatic 13secs; automatic power to weight ratio 13.3kg/kW (9.8kg/PS); ECE consumption 6.3/8.5/10.4L/100km (50.4/37.2/27.6mpg) [42/30.9/22.6US mpg], manual 5.6/7.6/10.0L/100km (44.8/33.2/28mpg) [37.3/27.7/23.3US mpg].
With fuel injection (2.0 GSi/GTi): Max speed 112mph/180kmh (manufacturers test specifications), speed at 1000rpm in 5th gear 20.7mph/33.3kmh; acceleration 0 - 60mph/97kmh 9.2secs; ECE consumption 6.2/8.1/10.5L/100km (45.6/34.9/26.9mpg) [37.9/29/22.4US mpg], automatic 6.5/9.2/11.6L/100km (43.5/30.7/24.4mpg) [36.2/25.6/20.3].

```
2.0 Turbo Diesel
60kW-80hp-81PS
Direct Injection
```

Engine for 2.0 DL and 2.0 DSL

As 1.6, except

Body, Weight:
Saloon/Sedan 4-door, 5-seater; kerbweight (DIN) 1100–1120kg, gross vehicle weight 1560kg.
Estate/Station Wagon 5-door, 5/7-seater; kerbweight (DIN) 1160–1180kg, gross vehicle weight 1700kg.

Montego 2.0 DSL

Engine data (DIN): 4-cylinder in-line (84.46 x 89mm), 1994cm3; compression ratio 18:1; 60kW (80hp) [81PS] at 5500rpm, 30.1kW/L (40.3hp/L) [40.6PS/L]; 158Nm (116.6lbft) at 3000rpm.

Engine construction: Designated Parkins Prima 80T. 1 overhead camshaft (toothed belt); light-alloy cylinder head; 5 bearing crankshaft; oil capacity 5L (4.7US qt); diesel fuel injection, Garrett T2 turbocharger, max charge-air pressure 0.9bar

12V 66Ah battery; cooling system capacity approx 9L.

Transmission: a) 5-speed manual, final drive ratio 3.875 or 3.94.
b) ZF Automatic 4 HP 14, hydraulic torque and 4-speed Planetary gear set, selector lever in middle; final drive ratio 3.94.

Chassis: Front ventilated disc brakes; tyres 180/65 R 365, wheel rims 120x365.

Dimensions: Track 148.5/146cm.

Performances: Max speed 101mph/163kmh, automatic 96mph/155kmh (manufacturers test specifications); acceleration 0 - 60mph/97kmh 12.5secs, automatic 14.5secs; power to weight ratio 18.3kg/kW (13.6kg/PS); consumption (ECE) 3.8/5.5/5.8L/100km (74.3/51.4/48.7mpg) [61.9/42.8/40.6US mpg].

AUTOBIANCHI   I

Autobianchi del Gruppo Automobili Fiat/Lancia, Via Vincenzo Lancia 27,10141, Turin, Italy.

Founded from the previous Bianchi company (1885–1955) by Fiat and Pirelli in 1955. Passenger car production with Fiat components and its own bodies. Under Fiat control since 1967 and under Lancia since 1975.

Autobianchi Y 10

Luxury small car with transverse front engine, 5-speed manual, front wheel drive and tail gate; 999cm3 (Fire), 1049 and 1297cm3 engines. Sold in some countries as the Lancia Y 10. Geneva 1985 debut. January 1986: new Fire LX edition with superior fittings. Autumn 1987: Fire i.e. with catalyst, 1.3 i.e. new. For technical data see Lancia.

Autobianchi/Lancia Y 10

AVANTI   USA

Avanti Motor Corporation, 726 War Avenue, Youngstown, Ohio 44505, USA

Company founded in 1965 to restart production of earlier Studebaker Avanti. Has changed proprietor many times

Avanti

Sporty coupe with synthetic body by Raymond Loewy, Chevrolet V8 engine. For 1985: body and chassis changes, more power, optional 5-speed manual and also available as convertible. For 1988: long Coupe with 20cm increased wheelbase. For Spring 1989: Saloon/Sedan will be available with 294cm instead of 277cm wheelbase.

Avanti Coupe

Avanti • Bentley

5 Litre V8
127kW–170hp–172PS
Fuel Injection

Body, Weight (laden): 2–door Coupe, 4/5–seats; approx 1610kg. 2–door long Coupe, 4/5–seats; approx 1610kg. 2–door convertible, 4/5–seats; approx 1610kg.

Engine data (SAE net): 8–cylinder in V 90deg (94.89 x 88.39mm), 5001cm3; compression ratio 9.3:1; 127kW (170hp) [172PS] at 4400rpm, 25.4kW/L (34hp/L) [34.4PS/L]; 346Nm (255lbft) at 2400rpm; regular grade.

Engine construction: Chevrolet 305–V8 designation. Hydraulic tappets, central camshaft (chain); crankshaft with 5 bearings; oil capacity 4.7L (4.4US qt); 1 Rochester Quadrajet downdraught 4V carb; double exhaust. Battery 12V 74Ah, alternator 85A; cooling system capacity 16L (15.1US qt).

Transmission (to rear wheels): Automatic 'Turbo Hydra–Matic'; hydraulic torque converter and 4-speed Planetary gear set with Overdrive, final drive ratio 2.87 or 2.73. Limited slip differential.

Gear ratios: Automatic: Max torque multiplication 1.9 times, Planetary gear ratios: 3.06, 1.63, 1, 0.70, R 2.29

Chassis: Sub–frames with cross–members; front swinging A arms, coil springs and antiroll bar; rear rigid axle with longitudinal and semi–trailing arms, coil springs and antiroll bar, telescopic dampers. Servo/power assisted brakes, front discs (ventilated), 26.7cm diameter, rear drums, mechanical handbrake to rear wheels; power assisted ball and nut steering; fuel tank 72/83/95L (15.8/18.2/20.9Gal) [19/21.9/25.1US Gal]; tyres P 205/75 R 15, wheel rims 7J, optional tyres 215/60 R 15 and 245/60 R 15.

Dimensions: Wheelbase 277cm, track 151.5/149cm, clearance approx 12cm, turning circle 11.4m. Load space 11.8cu ft (335dm3). Length 490.5cm, width 179cm, height 139cm. Saloon/Sedan: Wheelbase 294.5cm, track 154/151.5cm, turning circle approx 12.5cm. Length 508cm, width 186.5cm.

Performance: Max speed over 124mph/200kmh, speed at 1000rpm in direct gear 27.1mph/44.2kmh; power to weight ratio 12.7kg/kW (9.4kg/PS); consumption approx 12–20L/100km (23.5–14.1mpg) [19.6–11.8US mpg].

Avanti Convertible

BENTLEY   GB

Bentley Motors Ltd, Crewe, Cheshire, CW1 3PL, England
The elite English marque, part of the Rolls Royce group.

Bentley Mulsanne S – Eight

Bentley Mulsanne S–Eight Saloon/Sedan of top class quality, with 6.75 litre V8 light–alloy in–line engine. Built Rolls Royce Silver Spirit/Silver Spur specification. Integral body. Independent suspension front and rear, automatic level regulation. Debut Paris Mulsanne 1980, July 8 1984. Autumn 1986: with fuel injection and ABS. Autumn 1987: Mulsanne S with modified accessories. For 1989 with round headlamps

6.75 Litre V8
173/158/147kW–232/212/197hp–
233/212/200PS
Fuel Injection

Body, Weight: 4–door Saloon/Sedan, 5–seater; kerbweight (DIN) 2290–2320kg, gross vehicle weight 2700kg; Saloon/Sedan with long wheelbase 4–door, 5–seater; kerbweight (DIN) 2340 with separation 2430kg, gross vehicle weight 2725/2815kg.

Bentley Eight

Engine data (DIN): 8–cylinder in V 90deg (104.14 x 99.06mm) 6750cm3; compression ratio 9:1 for leaded premium grade (97) (compression ratios 8:1 or 7.3:1). No official information on power to weight ratio or torque. Compression ratio 9:1; approx 173kW (232hp) [233PS] at 4300rpm; approx 450Nm (332lbft) at 1500rpm.
With Catalyst: Compression ratio 8:1; approx 158kW (212hp) [215PS] at 4200 rpm; approx 460Nm (339.5lbft) at 1500rpm.
USA version: approx 147kW (197hp) [200PS].

Engine construction: L4101 designation. Hydraulic tappets, central camshaft (gearwheel). Light–alloy cylinder heads and cylinder block; wet cylinder liners; 5 bearing crankshaft; oil capacity 9.9L (9.4US qt); fuel injection Bosch K/KE–Jetronic, 2 electronic fuel pumps. Spark plugs NGK BPR 5 EV; battery 12V 68/71Ah, alternator 108A; cooling system capacity approx 18L (17US qt).

Transmission (to rear wheels): Turbo–Hydra–Matic GM 400 (hydraulic torque converter and 3–speed Planetary gear set).

Gear ratios: Max 2 times torque multiplication in converter, Planetary gear set ratios: 1st 2.48; 2nd 1.48; 3rd 1; R 2.08.

Chassis: Independent suspension front and rear subframe; twin wishbones, coil springs and telescopic damper, rear independent suspension and hydro–pneumatic McPherson/damper struts. Automatic level control system; front and rear antiroll bars. Servo/power assisted disc brakes (front ventilation) with ABS (Bosch System). Disc diameter 27.9 cm. Rear wheel parking brake. Power assisted rack and pinion steering; 108L (23.7Gal) [28.5US Gal] fuel tank; tyres 235/70 HR/VR 15, wheel rims 6/6.5J.

Dimensions: Wheelbase 306cm. Track 155/155cm, clearance 16.5cm, turning circle 13.1m, load space 14.5cu ft (410dm3). Length 527cm, width 188.5cm, height 148.5cm. Long wheelbase: Wheelbase 316cm, turning circle 12.1m, length 537cm.

Performance: Max speed 129mph/208kmh approx.
With Catalyst 121mph/195kmh (manufacturers test specifications). Speed up to 1000rpm, in top gear 30mph/48.3kmh. Acceleration 0 – 60mph/97kmh in 10secs; consumption (ECE) 15.6/17.5/23.6L/100km (18/16/12mpg) [15/13.5/10US mpg].

Bentley Mulsanne S

Bentley Turbo R

Extremely powerful, high performance model 6.75L V8 engine. Launch Mulsanne Turbo Geneva 1982, Turbo R (R meaning Road holding) Geneva 1985. Autumn 1987: Fuel injection and ABS. For l989 with charge-air cooler, Bosch-Motronic and round head lamps.

6.75 Litre V8 Turbo
245/230kW–328/308hp–333/313PS
Fuel Injection

As Mulsanne Eight, except:

BENTLEY · BERTONE · BITTER

Body, Weight: Kerbweight (DIN) 2320-2420kg max up to 2770/2795kg.

Engine data: Compression ratio 8:1. No official information on power to weight ratio or torque. Approx 245kW (328hp) [333PS] at 4500rpm, 658Nm (485.6lbft) at 2250rpm.
With Catalyst: 230kW (308hp) [313PS] at 4200rpm.

Engine construction: Designated L410IT; Bosch KE–Motronic fuel injection; Garret Airesearch T 04B exhaust turbocharger, max boost pressure 0.49bar, knock sensor, charge-air cooler.

Transmission: Final drive ratio 2.28 or 2.69.

Chassis: Tyres 255/65VR 15, wheel rims 7.5J.

Dimensions: Clearance 16cm. Height 148cm.

Perfomance: Max speed 145mph/233kmh (manufacturers test specifications), speed at 1000rpm in top gear 35.6mph/57.3kmh or (2.69) 30.1mph/48.5kmh; acceleration 0 – 60mph/97kmh under 7secs; consumption (ECE) 13.5/17.3/24.8L/100km (21/16.3/11.4mpg) [17.5/13.6/9.5US mpg].

Bentley Turbo R

Bentley Continental

2-door convertible from H J Mulliner/Park Ward with the Corniche hallmark. Launch March 1971. Spring 1977: modifications to body and interior; rack and pinion steering. July 1984: new hallmark "Continental". 1987: Fuel injection and ABS.

6.75 Litre V8
177kW–237hp–240PS (approx)
Fuel Injection

As Mulsanne/Eight, except:

Body, Weight: Convertible, 2–door, 4/5–seater (H J Mulliner/Park Ward); Kerbweight (DIN) 2370-2420kg, gross vehicle weight 2760kg.

Engine data: As Mulsanne Eight

Chassis: Wheel rims 6 1/2J.

Dimensions: Wheelbase 306cm, track 155/155cm, clearance 15cm, turning circle 12.9m, load space 14.1cu ft (400dm3). Length 520/526cm, width 183.5cm, height 152cm.

Performance: Max speed 127mph/205kmh. With Catalyst approx 121mph/195kmh (manufacturers test specifications), speed at 1000rpm in top gear 30mph/48.3kmh; consumption ECE 15.6/18.2/25.4L/100km (18/15.5/11mpg) [15/13/9.3US mpg].

Bentley Continental

BERTONE   I

Carrozzeria Bertone SpA, C Canonico Allamano 40/46, 10095 Gruliasco, Torino, Italy

Famous designer from Turin renowned for unique body workshops specialising in the production of convertibles (Opel Kadett).

Bertone X 1/9

Bertone X 1/9

Middle range, 2–seater Saloon/Sedan, axle assembly by Fiat. Launch 26 November 1972. 1978, 1.5L Birmingham Motor Show.

1.5 Litre
62.5/56kW–83.7/75hp–85/76PS
1 2V Carb/Fuel Injection

Body, Weight: 2–door coupe with removable roof, 2–seater; kerbweight (DIN) 920, USA 965kg, gross vehicle weight 1120kg.

Engine data (DIN): 4–cylinder in–line (86.4 x 63.9mm), 1499cm2; compression ratio 9.2:1; 62.5kW (83.7hp) [85PS] at 6000rpm, 41.7kW/L (55.9hp/L) [56.7PS/L]; 118Nm (87lbft) at 3200rpm; leaded premium grade.
With Bosch L–Jetronic fuel injection and Catalyst: Compression ratio 8.5:1; 56kW (75hp) [76PS] at 5500rpm, 37.4kW/L (50.1hp/L) [50.7PS/L]; 108Nm (79.7lbft) at 3000rpm; unleaded regular grade.
Other countries: 55kW (73.7hp) [75PS]

Engine construction: Designated 128 AS.000. Transverse mounted mid–motor at 11deg tilt to front. 1 overhead camshaft (toothed belt); light–alloy cylinder heads; 5 bearing crankshaft; oil capacity 4.5L (4.3US qt); 1 Weber downdraught 2V carb 34 DATR 7/250. Marelli sparkplugs CW 78 LPR, Bosch WR 6 D or Champion RN; 12V 45Ah battery, alternator 33A; cooling system capacity 11.6L (11US qt).

Transmission (to rear wheels): 5–speed manual (without direct drive), floor shift; final drive ratio 4.077 (13/53).

Gear ratios: 1st 3.83; 2nd 2.235; 3rd 1.454; 4th 1.042; 5th 0.863; R 3.174

Chassis: Integral body; front independent suspension with slanting lower McPherson strut single control arm and compression strut; rear independent suspension, lower A–arm with adjustable auxiliary control arm; coil springs and telescopic dampers. 4-wheel disc brakes, diameter 22.7cm, rear mechanical handbrake; rack and pinion steering; fuel tank capacity 48L (12.7Gal) [15.3US Gal]; tyres 165/70SR 13, wheel rims 5J.

Dimensions: Wheelbase 20cm, track 135.5/135cm, clearance 13cm, turning circle 10m, load space 5.5/4.4cu ft (155/125dm3). Length 397cm, width 157cm, height 118cm.

Performance: Max speed over 112mph/180kmh, with Catalyst approx 106mph/170kmh (manufacturers specification). Speed at 1000rpm in 5th gear 18.3mph/29.4kmh; acceleration 0 – 62mph/100kmh 11.7 secs. With Catalyst approx 13secs; standing km 33.2secs; power to weight ratio 14.7kg/kW (10.8kg/PS); consumption ECE 6.0/7.7/10.6L/100km (47.1/36.7/26.6mph) [39.2/30.5/22.US mpg].

BITTER   D

Bitter Automobile GmbH & Co. KG Berliner–Strasse 57, 5830C Schwelm, Germany.

German producer of small series luxury coupes.

Bitter • BMW

Bitter Type 3 Cabriolet

Bitter Type III

Two seater convertible based on the Opel Omega 3000; 5-speed manual or automatic. Launched in Frankfurt 1987.

3 Litre
130kW–174hp–177PS
Fuel Injection

Body, Weight: 2-door Coupe/Convertible, 2-seater; kerbweight weight (DIN) from 1490kg, gross vehicle weight 1810kg.

Engine data (Catalyst DIN): 6-cylinder in-line (95 x 69.8mm), 2969cm3; compression ratio 9.4:1; 130kW (174hp) [177PS] at 5800rpm, 43.9kW/L (58.8hp/L) [59.6PS/L]; 240Nm (177lbft) at 4200rpm; unleaded premium grade.

Engine construction: Hydraulic tappets; 1 side camshaft (chain) in cylinder head; 7 bearing crankshaft; oil capacity 5.5L (5.2US qt); digitally distributed Bosch Motronic fuel injection. 12V 66Ah battery, alternator 90A; cooling system capacity 10.2L (9.6US qt).

Transmission (to rear wheels): a) 5-speed manual, final drive ratio 3.70. b) Automatic (hydraulic torque converter and 4-speed Planetary gear set). Final drive ratio 3.70; limited slip differential (45%).

Gear ratios: a) 5-speed manual: 1st 4.044; 2nd 2.265; 3rd 1.434; 4th 1; 5th 0.842; R 3.748.
b) Automatic: Max torque multiplication in converter approx 2.35 times, Planetary gear set ratios: 1st 2.45; 2nd 1.45; 3rd 1; 4th 0.69; R 2.21.

Chassis: Integral body; front and rear independent suspension; front McPherson strut and control arms, rear swinging arms and transverse cross member, front and rear coil springs and telescopic damper. Servo/power assisted disc brakes (front ventilated). Disc diameter 28cm, Bosch ABS System, rear wheel mechanical handbrake. Power assisted recirculating ball steering. Fuel tank capacity 75L (16.5Gal) [19.8US Gal]; tyres 215/55 VR 15; wheel rims 7.5J.

Dimensions: Wheelbase 238cm, track 148/150cm, clearance 14cm, turning circle 10.8m. Length 445cm, width 176.5cm, height 139.5cm.

Performance: Max speed 141mph/227kmh, automatic 137mph/220kmh (manufacturers specification). Speed at 1000rpm in 5th gear 23.4mph/37.7kmh; acceleration 0 – 62mph/100kmh 7.6secs, automatic 8.4secs; power to weight ratio from 11.5kg/kW (8.4kg/PS); consumption (DIN) 7.5/9.2/13.9L/100km (37.7/30.7/20.3mpg) [31.4/25.6/16.9US mpg].

BMW D

Bayerische Motoren-Werke AG, Munchen, Germany. German Car and motorcycle manufacturers.
MODEL RANGE
3 – Z 1 – 5 – 6 – 7

316i–318i–320i–325–325i–324d–324td

Compact vehicles with a sporty note. Launch November 1982. Autumn 1983: also 4-door. July 1985: new model 325i, also for convertible and with 4-wheel drive; 324d with 2.4 Litre diesel engine. August 1987: body modifications and new 5-cylinder model: Estate/Station Wagon (Touring) production began in Spring 1988. Autumn 1988: 316i with new 1.6 Litre engine. From March 1989 Touring also with 1.8 Litre.

316i
73/75kW–98/101hp–100/102PS
Fuel Injection

Body, Weight: 2-door Saloon/Sedan, 5-seater; unladen weight (DIN) 1065kg, gross vehicle weight 1525kg; 4-door Saloon/Sedan, 5-seater: unladen weight (DIN) 1085kg, gross vehicle weight 1545kg; automatic models 20kg heavier.

Engine data (Catalyst DIN): 4-cylinder in-line (84 x 72mm), 1596cm3; compression ratio 9:1; 73kW (98hp) [100PS] at 5500rpm, 45.7kW/L (61.2hp/L) [62.7PS/L]; 141Nm (104.1lbft) at 4250rpm; unleaded regular grade. Without Catalyst: Compression ratio 9:1; 75kW (101hp) [102PS] at 5500rpm; 143Nm (105.5lbft) at 4250rpm; leaded premium grade.

BMW 316i

Engine construction: Front mounted engine, inclined at around 30deg to right. Valves in V 14deg, hydraulic tappets; 1 overhead camshaft (toothed belt); light-alloy cylinder head; 5 bearing crankshaft; Oil capacity 4.0L (3.8US qt); digitally distributed Bosch Motronic (fuel injection/ignition). 12V 46Ah Battery, alternator 65A; cooling system capacity approx 6.0L.

Transmission (to rear wheels): a) 5-speed manual, final drive ratio 4.27. b) ZF-Automatic 4 HP–22 (hydraulic torque converter and 4-speed Planetary gear set), final drive ratio 4.45. Also available with limited slip differential.

Gear ratios: a) 5-speed manual: 1st 3.7; 2nd 2.02; 3rd 1.32; 4th 1; 5th 0.80; R 3.45.
b) Automatic ZF 4 HP–22; max torque multiplication in torque converter 2 times, Planetary gear set ratios: 1st 2.73; 2nd 1.56; 3rd 1; 4th 0.73; R 2.09; With carb; 1st 2.48; 2nd 1.48; 3rd 1; 4th 0.73; R 2.09.
Without Catalyst: 1st 2.48; 2nd 1.48; 3rd 1; 4th 0.73; R 2.09.

Chassis: Integral body; front McPherson strut with single control arm and tension strut, rear independent suspension with semi-trailing arm and coil springs, also with A-arm and telescopic damper. Servo/power assisted brakes, front disc and rear drums, handbrake to rear wheels. Power assisted rack and pinion steering; fuel tank capacity 55L (12Gal) [14.5US Gal] including 7L (1.5Gal) [1.8US Gal] reserve; tyres 175/70 TR 14, wheel rims 5.5J.

Dimensions: Wheelbase 257cm, track 140.5/141.5cm, clearance 12.5cm, turning circle 10.5m, load space (VDA) 15cu ft (425dm3). Length 432.5cm, width 164.5cm, height 138cm.

Performance: (Catalyst Version) Max speed 113mph/182kmh automatic 110mph/177kmh (manufacturers test specifications). Speed at 1000rpm in 5th gear 20.2mph/32.5kmh; acceleration 0 – 62mph/100kmh 12.1secs, automatic 14.1secs; power to weight ratio from 14.6kg/kW (10.6kg/PS); consumption (ECE) 6.7/8.6/10.3L/100km (42.2/32.8/27.4mpg) [35.1/27.4/22.8US mpg], automatic 6.9/8.8/10.5L/100km (40.9/32.1/26.9mpg) [34.1/26.7/22.4US mpg].

318i
83/85kW–111/114hp–113/115PS
Fuel Injection

As 316i, except:

Body, Weight: Saloon 2/4-door; kerbweight (DIN) 1065/1085kg, gross vehicle weight 1525/1545kg; Estate/Station Wagon (Touring): 5-door, 5-seater; kerbweight (DIN) approx 1170kg, gross vehicle weight approx 1650kg.

Engine data (Catalyst, DIN): 4-cylinder in-line (84 x 81mm), 1796cm3; compression ratio 8:8.1; 83kW (111hp) [113PS] at 5500rpm, 46.2kW/L (61.9kW/L) [62.9PS/L]; 162Nm (119.6lbft) at 4250rpm; unleaded regular grade. Without Catalyst: Compression ratio 8.8:1; 85kW (114hp) [115PS] at 5500rpm; 165Nm (121.8lbft) at 4250rpm; leaded regular grade.

Transmission: a) 5-speed manual, final drive ratio 4.1, Touring 4.27. b) Automatic, final drive ratio 4.45.

Gear ratios: a) 5-speed manual; as 316i.
b) Automatic: 1st 2.48; 2nd 1.48; 3rd 1; 4th 0.73; R 2.09.

BMW

BMW 318i

Chassis: Tyres 195/65 HR 14

Dimensions: Touring load space 13–39.7cu ft (370–1125dm3).

Performance: Catalyst version, max speed 116.8mph/188kmh, automatic 115.6mph/186kmh (manufacturers test specifications), speed at 1000rpm in 5th gear 21.1mph/34.0kmh; acceleration 0 – 62mph/100kmh 10.8secs, automatic 12.0secs. Standing km 32.2secs, automatic 33.9secs; power to weight ratio 12.8kg/kW (9.4kg/PS) consumption (ECE) 6.7/8.6/10.3L/100km (42.2/32.8/27.4mpg) [35.1/27.4/22.8US mpg], automatic 7.0/8.9/10.6L/100km (40.4/31.7/26.6mpg) [33.6/31.7/22.2US mpg].

```
320i
95kW–127hp–129PS
Fuel Injection
```

BMW 320i Touring

As 316i except:

Body, Weight: 2/4 door Saloon/Sedan; kerbweight (DIN) 1125/1145kg, gross vehicle weight 1585/1605kg; 2–door Convertible, 4–seater; kerbweight (DIN) 1280kg gross vehicle weight 1680kg. 5–door Estate/Station Wagon (Touring), 5–seater; kerbweight (DIN) 1230kg gross vehicle weight 1710kg.

Engine data (Catalyst DIN): 6–cylinder in–line (80 x 66mm), 1991cm3; compression ratio 8.8:1; 95kW(127hp) [129PS] at 6000rpm, 47.7kW/L (63.9hp/L) [64.8PS/L]; 164Nm (121lbft) at 4300rpm; unleaded regular grade.
Without Catalyst: Compression ratio 9.4:1; 95kW (127hp) [129PS] at 6000rpm; 174Nm (128.4lbft) at 4000rpm; leaded premium grade.

Engine construction: Valves in V 44deg, without hydraulic tappets; 1 overhead camshaft (toothed belt); 7 bearing crankshaft; oil capacity 4.25L (4US qt); Bosch Motronic digital engine electronic control (injection/ignition) 50Ah or 63Ah Battery, 80A alternator; cooling system capacity approx 10.5L (9.9US qt).

Transmission: a) 5-speed manual, final drive ratio 4.1, Convertible and Estate/Station Wagon 4.27.
b) Automatic, optional with programme EH, final drive ratio 4.45.

Gear Ratios: a) 5-speed manual as 316i.
b) Automatic: 1st 2.48; 2nd 1.48; 3rd 1; 4th 0.73; R 2.09.

Chassis: Front ventilated disc brakes, Convertible and Touring with rear disc brakes; fuel tank capacity 62L (13.6Gal) [16.4US Gal]; tyres 195/65 HR 14, Touring wheel rims 6J.

Dimensions: Convertible load space 11cu ft (312dm3), Touring 13-39.7cu ft (370-1125dm3). Convertible height 137cm.

Performance: Catalyst version, max speed 122mph/197kmh, Convertible 121.2mph/195kmh, Touring 122mph/196kmh. Automatic 121-121-121mph/195-194-195kmh (manufacturers test specifications). Speed at 1000rpm in 5th gear 21.1mph/34kmh, Convertible and Touring 20.3mph/32.6kmh; acceleration 0 – 62mph/100kmh 10.6secs, Convertible 11.5secs, Touring 11.5secs, automatic 12.3/13.3/13.2secs; standing km 31.7secs, Convertible 32.5secs, Touring 32.5secs, automatic 34.0/34.5/34.5secs; power to weight ratio from 11.8kg/kW (8.7kg/PS); consumption (ECE) 7.5/9.5/12.8L/100km (37.7/29.7/22.1mpg) [31.4/24.8/18.4US mpg], automatic 7.7/9.7/13.4L/100km (36.7/29.4/21.1mpg) [30.5/24.2/17.6US mpg].

```
325i
125/126kW–168/169hp–170/171PS
Fuel Injection
```

As 316i except:

Body, Weight: 2/4–door Saloon/Sedan: Kerbweight (DIN) 1180/1200kg (USA 1275/1295kg), gross vehicle weight 1640/1660kg. iX: 1280/1300kg (USA 1365kg),gross vehicle weight 1740/1740kg. 2–door Convertible: 4–seater, kerbweight (DIN) 1310kg (USA 1365/1385kg), gross vehicle weight 1710kg. Touring 5–door 5–seater, kerbweight (DIN) 1270kg gross vehicle weight 1750kg. iX: 1350kg, gross vehicle 1810kg.

Engine data (Catalyst DIN): 6–cylinder in–line (84 x 75mm), 2494cm3; compression ratio 8.8:1; 125kW (168hp) [170PS] at 5800rpm, 50.1kW/L (67.1hp/L) [68.2PS/L]; 222Nm (163.7lbft) at 4300rpm; unleaded regular grade.
American version: Data is identical.
Without Catalyst: Compression ratio 9.4:1; 126kW (169hp) [171PS] at 5800rpm; 226Nm (166.7lbft) at 4000rpm; leaded premium grade.

BMW 325i

Engine construction: Valves in V 44deg, without hydraulic tappets; 1 overhead camshaft (toothed belt); 7 bearing crankshaft; oil capacity 4.75L (4.5US qt); oil cooler; Bosch Motronic digital electronic engine control (fuel injection/ignition). Battery 12V 65Ah (Convertible 50Ah), 80A alternator; cooling system capacity approx 10.5L (9.9US qt).

Transmission (to rear wheels, 325i to all wheels): a) 5–speed manual, final drive ratio 3.73, Touring 3.91, without Catalyst 3.64.
b) 5–speed manual Sport, final drive ratio 3.91.
c) Automatic, also available with EH–Program, final drive ratio 3.73, Touring 3.91, without Catalyst 3.64. 325iX, permanent 4 wheel drive, central Planetary differentials (torque distribution front/rear 37/63%). Viscous coupling (Ferguson system) for central and rear differentials; final drive ratio, 5–speed 3.91 (without Catalyst 3.64, with sport gear change 3.91). Automatic 3.91, Touring 4.1, without Catalyst 3.73.

Gear ratios: a) 5–speed manual: 1st 3.83; 2nd 2.20; 3rd 1.40; 4th 0.81; R 3.46.
b) 5–speed manual, Sport: 1st 3.76; 2nd 2.33; 3rd 1.61; 4th 1.23; 5th 1; R 4.10.
c) Automatic: 1st 2.48; 2nd 1.48; 3rd 1; 4th 0.73; R 2.09.

BMW 325i Cabrio

Chassis: Front and rear antiroll bar; 325i front A–arm. All round disc brakes (front ventilated), also available with Bosch ABS; Convertible and iX with power assisted steering; fuel tank capacity 62L (13.6Gal) [16.4US Gal]. Tyres 195/65VR 14 (USA iX 205/55VR 15), Wheel rims Convertible, iX, Touring 6 (USA 6, iX 7) J.

BMW

Dimensions: Load space 14.3cu ft (404dm3), Convertible 11cu ft (312dm3), Touring 13-39.7cu ft (370-1125dm3); Convertible height 137cm. 325iX: Track 142/141.5cm, turning circle 11.1m, width 166cm, height 140cm.

Performance (Catalyst version), max speed – manufacturers test specifications; 135mph/218kmh (automatic 132mph/212kmh). Convertible 134mph/216kmh (automatic 130.5mph/210kmh). Touring 133mph/214kmh (automatic 132mph/212kmh). Speed at 1000rpm in 5th gear 22.9mph/36.9kmh, Touring 21.9mph/ 35.2kmh. Acceleration 0 – 62mph/100kmh ; 8.3secs (automatic 9.9secs). Convertible 8.7secs (automatic 10.5secs). Touring 8.8secs (10.1secs). iX 9.2secs (11.3secs). Standing km 29.0secs (automatic 30.8secs), Convertible 29.5secs (automatic 31.5secs), Touring 29.6secs (31.3secs). Power to weight ratio 9.4kg/kW (6.9kg/PS); consumption (ECE) 7.2/9.0/12.9L/100km (39.2/31.4/21.9mpg) [32.7/26.1/18.2US mpg], Sport 7.3/9.1/13.1L/100km (38.7/31/21.6mpg) [32.2/25.8/18US mpg], automatic 7.3/9.2/13.3L/100km (38.7/30.7/21.2mpg) [32.2/25.6/17.7US mpg].

With four wheel drive iX: Max speed 132mph/212kmh (automatic 128mph/206kmh), Touring 129mph/208kmh (automatic 128mph/206kmh), speed at 1000rpm in 5th gear 21.9mph/35.2kmh; acceleration 0 - 62mph/100kmh; 9.2secs (automatic 11.2secs), standing km 30.1secs (automatic 32.4secs), Touring 30.7secs (automatic 32.6secs); Power to weight ratio from 10.2kg/kW (7.5kg/PS); consumption ECE 7.8/9.8/13.6L/100km (36.2/28.8/20.8mpg) [30.2/24/17.3US mpg], automatic 7.9/9.9/13.5L/100km (35.8/28.5/20.9mpg) [29.8/23.8/17.4US mpg].

BMW 325 iX

```
324d
63kW–84hp–86PS
Injection Pump
```

As 316i, except:

Body, Weight: 4–door Saloon/Sedan, kerbweight (DIN) 1195kg, gross vehicle weight 1655kg.

Engine data (DIN): 6–cylinder in–line (80 x 81mm), 2443cm3; compression ratio 22:1; 63kW (84hp) [86PS] at 4600rpm, 25.8kW/L (34.6hp/L) [35.2PS/L]; 153Nm (112.9lbft) at 2500rpm.

Engine construction: Diesel engine swirl chamber. Parallel valves; without hydraulic tappets; 1 overhead camshaft (toothed belt); 7 bearing camshaft; oil capacity 5.25L (5US qt); diesel injection pump. 12V 85Ah battery; 80A alternator; cooling system capacity approx 12L (11.4US qt).

Transmission: a) 5–speed manual, final drive ratio 3.45.
b) Automatic, final drive ratio 3.45.

Chassis: Front ventilated disc brakes.

Performance: Max speed 102mph/165kmh, automatic 98mph/158kmh; acceleration 0 – 62mph/100kmh 16.1secs, automatic 18.5secs; power to weight ratio 19kg/kW (13.9kg;PS); consumption (ECE) 5.0/6.9/8.7L/100km (56.5/40.9/32.5mpg) [47/34.1/27US mpg]. Automatic 5.3/7.1/9.6L/100km (53.3/39.8/29.4mpg) [44.4/33.1/24.5US mpg].

```
324td
85kW–114hp–115PS
Turbo Injection Pump
```

As 316i, except:

Body, Weight: 4–door Saloon/Sedan, kerbweight (DIN) 1260kg, gross vehicle weight 1720kg; 5–door Touring, 5–seater; kerbweight (DIN) 1300kg, gross vehicle weight 1780kg.

Engine data (DIN): 6–cylinder in–line (80 x 81mm), 2443cm3; compression ratio 22:1; 85kW (114hp) [115PS] at 4800rpm, 34.8kW/L (46.6hp/L) [47.1PS/L]; 220Nm (162.3lbft) at 2400rpm.

Engine construction: Diesel engine swirl chamber, parallel valves, without hydraulic tappets; 1 overhead camshaft (toothed belt); 7 bearing crankshaft; oil capacity 5.25L (5US qt); digital electronic diesel fuel injection pump, 1 exhaust turbocharger. 12V 85Ah Battery; 80A alternator; cooling system capacity approx 12L (11.4US qt).

Transmission: a) 5–speed manual, final drive ratio 3.25.
b) Automatic, final drive ratio 3.25.

Gear ratios: a) 5–speed manual: 1st 3.83; 2nd 2.20; 3rd 1.40; 4th 1; 5th 0.81; R 3.46;
b) Automatic: As 316i.

Chassis: All round disc brakes (front ventilated); power assisted steering; tyres 195/65 HR 14, Touring wheel rims 6 J.

Dimensions: Touring load space 13-39.7cu ft (370-1125dm3).

Performance: Max speed 116mph/187kmh, automatic 113mph/182kmh, speed at 1000rpm in 5th gear 26.4mph/42.4kmh; acceleration 0 – 62mph/100kmh 11.9secs, (Automatic 12.8), Touring 12.3secs (13.3secs), standing km 33.4secs (34.4secs), Touring 33.7secs (34.8secs); power to weight ratio 14.8kg/kW (11kg/PS); consumption (ECE) 5.2/6.9/8.9L/100km (54.3/40.9/31.7mpg) [45.2/34.1/26.4US mpg].

BMW M3

High powered version based on the 3 Series. 4–cylinder engine with 4 valves per cylinder. Announced July 1985, Production began in the Summer of 1986. 1988: Version Evolution and Convertible/Cabriolet.

BMW M3

```
2.3 Litre
143/147kW–192/197hp–195/200PS
Fuel Injection
```

As 316i, except:

Body, Weight: 2–door Saloon/Sedan, 4–seater; kerbweight (DIN) 1200kg (USA 1240kg), gross vehicle weight 1600kg.
Convertible/Cabriolet: 2-door, 4-seater; kerbweight (DIN) 1360kg, gross vehicle weight 1720kg.
320is, Italy only: 2/4–door Saloon/Sedan (normal 3 Series) kerbweight (DIN) 1180kg.

Engine data (Catalyst DIN): 4–cylinder in–line (93.4 x 84mm), 2302cm3; compression ratio 10.5: 1; 143kW (192hp) [195PS] at 6750rpm, 62.1kW/L (83.2hp/L) [84.7PS/L]; 230Nm (169.6lbft) at 4750rpm; unleaded premium grade.
Without Catalyst: 147kW (197hp) [200PS] at 6750rpm, 240Nm (177lbft) at 4750rpm; leaded premium grade.
Evolution Version: Compression ratio 11.1; 162kW(217hp) [220PS] at 6750rpm, 245Nm (180.8lbft) at 4750rpm.
320is (only in Italy): (72.65 x 93.4mm), 1990cm3; 141kW (189hp) [192PS] at 6900rpm; 210Nm (155lbft) at 4900rpm.

Engine construction: Overhead valves in V 38 deg (4 per cylinder), without hydraulic tappets; 2 overhead camshafts (chain); oil capacity 5L (4.7US qt), oil cooler; Bosch Motronic digital electronic engine control (fuel injection/ignition). 12V 65Ah Battery, 90A alternator; cooling system capacity approx 9L (8.5US qt).

Transmission: 5–speed manual, final drive ratio 3.25; Evolution 3.15; limited slip differential 25%.

Gear ratios: 1st 3.72; 2nd 2.40; 3rd 1.77; 4th 1.26; 5th 1.00; R 4.23.

Chassis: Front and rear antiroll bar. All round disc brakes (front ventilated) with Bosch ABS; power assisted steering; fuel tank 70L (15.4Gal) [18.5US Gal], Convertible/Cabriolet 62L (13.6Gal) [16.4US Gal]; tyres 205/55 VR 15, wheel rims 7J, Evolution 225/45 ZR 16, 7.5J.

Dimensions: Wheelbase 256.5cm, track 141/142.5cm, Evolution 142/143cm. Turning circle 11.1m, load space VDA 148cu ft (420dm3), Convertible/Cabriolet 10.7cu ft (303dm3) ; length 434.5cm. width 168cm, height 137cm.

Performance: Max speed 143mph/230kmh, Convertible/Cabriolet 142mph/228kmh (manufacturers test specifications), speed at 1000rpm in 5th

BMW

gear 21.3mph/34.2kmh; acceleration 0 – 62mph/100kmh 6.9secs, Convertible/Cabriolet 7.5secs; standing km 27.6secs, Convertible/Cabriolet 28.1secs; power to weight ratio 8.4kg/kW (6.2kg/PS); consumption (ECE) 6.2/7.8/12.4L/100km (45.6/36.2/22.8mpg) [37.9/30.2/19US mpg].
Without Catalyst: Max speed 146mph/235kmh; acceleration 0 – 62mph/100kmh 6.7secs, Evolution 6.7secs; standing km 27.2secs, Evolution 27.1secs; consumption ECE 5.8/7.5/11.6L/100km (48.7/37.7/24.4mpg) [40.6/31.4/20.3US mpg], Evolution 5.7/7.2/11.0L/100km (49.6/39.2/25.7mpg) [41.3/32.7/21.4US mpg].
320is: Max speed 141mph/227kmh; acceleration 0 – 62mph/100kmh 7.9secs, standing km 28.5secs; consumption ECE 6.3/8.0/12.8/100km (44.8/35.3/22.1mpg) [37.3/29.4/18.4US mpg].

BMW M3 Cabriolet

BMW Z1

Sporty 2–seater roadster with sunken doors. Prototype launched in August 1986, final version launched at Frankfurt, 1987. Production began in October 1988.

2.5 Litre 6–Cylinder
125kW–168hp–170PS
Fuel Injection

Body, Weight: 2–door roadster, 2–seater; kerbweight over 1100kg.
Engine data (Catalyst, DIN): 6–cylinder in–line (84 x 75mm), 2BMW Z1494cm3; compression ratio 8.8:1; 125kW (168hp) [170PS] at 5800rpm, 50.1kW/L (67.1hp/L) [68.2PS/L]; 222Nm (163.7lbft) at 4300rpm; unleaded regular grade.
Engine construction: Front engine, mounted behind the front axle, inclined 20deg to the right. Valves in V44deg, 1 overhead camshaft (toothed belt); light alloy cylinder head; 7 bearing crankshaft; oil capacity 4.75L (4.5US qt); oil cooler; Bosch Motronic digital engine electronic control (injection/ignition). 12V 65Ah Battery, 80A alternator, cooling system capacity approx 10L (9.5US qt).
Transmission (to rear wheels): 5–speed manual transaxle, final drive ratio 3.64; limited slip differential.

BMW Z1

Gear ratios: 1st 3.83; 2nd 2.20; 3rd 1.40; 4th 1; 5th 0.81; R 3.46.
Chassis: Integral body, plastic body components. Independent suspension, front McPherson struts and control, rear trailing arm, two control arms and coil springs, front and rear antiroll bar and telescopic damper. Servo/power assisted disc brakes, front ventilated; power assisted rack and pinion steering; fuel tank capacity 58L (12.7Gal) [15.3US Gal]; tyres 225/45VR 16, optional 205/55 VR 15, wheel rims 7.5J.
Dimensions: Wheelbase 244.5cm, track 145.5/147cm, turning circle 10.3m, load space 9.2cu ft (VDA 260dm3). Length 392cm, width 169cm, height 127.5cm.
Performance: Max speed 140mph/225kmh (manufacturers test specifications), speed at 1000rpm in 5th gear 23.4mph/37.7kmh; acceleration 0 – 62mph/100kmh 7.9secs; standing kmh 28.8secs; power to weight ratio from 10.0kg/kW (7.3kg/PS); consumption ECE 6.7/8.2/12.6L/100km (42.2/34.4/22.4mpg) [35.1/28.7/18.7US mpg].

BMW Z1

BMW 520i–525i–530i–535i–524td

Luxury Saloon/Sedan with 6–cylinder engine from 2.0 to 3.5 Litre engine displacement, also with Turbo–diesel. First launched in 1972. June 1981: New body. January 1988: revised edition with reworked body and mechanics.

520i
95kW–127hp–129PS
Fuel Injection

Body, Weight: 4–door Saloon/Sedan, 5 seater; kerbweight (DIN) 1400kg, gross vehicle weight 1910kg. Automatic 20kg heavier.
Engine data (with Catalyst, DIN): 6–cylinder in–line (80 x 66mm), 1991cm3; compression ratio 8.8:1; 95kW (127hp) [129PS] at 6000rpm, 47.7kW/L (63.9hp/L) [64.8PS/L]; 164Nm (121lbft) at 4300rpm; unleaded regular grade.
Without Catalyst: Compression ratio 9.4:1; 95kW (127hp) [129PS] at 6000rpm; 174Nm (128.3lbft) at 4000rpm; leaded premium grade.

BMW 520i

Engine construction: Front engine inclined to the right. Valves in V 44deg, 1 overhead camshaft (toothed belt); light–alloy cylinder heads; 7 bearing crankshaft; oil capacity 4.25L (4US qt); Bosch Motronic digital engine electronics. 12V 50Ah Battery, 80A alternator; cooling system capacity approx 10.5L (9.9US qt).

BMW

Transmission (to rear wheels): a) 5-speed manual, final drive ratio 4.45. b) ZF-Automatic 4 HP-22 (hydraulic torque converter and 4-speed Planetary gear set), optional with EH-Program, final drive ratio 4.45. Optional limited slip differential.

Gear ratios: a) 5-speed manual: 1st 3.72; 2nd 2.02; 3rd 1.34; 4th 1; 5th 0.80; R 3.45. b) Automatic; Max torque multiplication in converter 2 times, Planetary gear set ratios: 1st 2.48; 2nd 1.48; 3rd 1; 4th 0.73; R 2.08.

Chassis: Integral body; independent suspension; front McPherson strut, lower control arm, diagonal pressure strut and antiroll bar, rear semi-trailing arm, auxiliary steering, coil springs with co-axial shock absorbers, starting torque equilibrium and antiroll bar, telescopic damper; optional rear level control system. Servo/power assisted disc brakes (front ventilated), optional with ABS (Bosch), mechanical handbrake to rear wheels; power assisted recirculating ball steering; fuel tank capacity 80L (17.6Gal) [21.1US Gal]; tyres 195/65HR 15, wheel rims 6J.

Dimensions: Wheelbase 276cm, track 146.5/148.5cm, turning circle 11m, load space VDA 16.25cu ft (460dm3). Length 472cm, width 175cm, height 141cm.

Performance: Catalyst Version: Max speed 126mph/203kmh, automatic 123mph/198kmh (manufacturers test specifications), speed at 1000rpm in 5th gear 20.3mph/32.6kmh; acceleration 0 – 62mph/100kmh 11.9secs, automatic 13.9secs; standing km 32.8secs, automatic 35.5secs; power to weight ratio 14.7kg/kW (10.9kg/PS); consumption DIN 7.5/9.2/13.6L/100km (37.7/30.7/20.8mpg) [31.4/25.5/17.3USmpg], automatic 7.7/9.4/13.9L/100km (36.7/30.1/20.3mpg) [30.5/25/16.9US mpg].

BMW 520i

```
525i
125kW–168hp–170PS
Fuel Injection
```

As 520i, except:

Weight: Kerbweight (DIN) 1450kg (USA 1540kg), gross vehicle weight 1960kg.

Engine data (with Catalyst, DIN): 6-cylinder in-line (84 x 75mm), 2494cm3; compression ratio 8.8:1; 125kW (168hp) [170PS] at 5800rpm, 50.1kW/L (67.1hp/L) [68.2PS/L]; 222Nm (163.7lbft) at 4300rpm; unleaded regular grade. Without Catalyst: Identical data.

Transmission: a) 5-speed manual, final drive ratio 3.73. b) Automatic, final drive ratio 3.91, USA 4.1.

Gear ratio: a) 5-speed manual: 1st 3.83; 2nd 2.20; 3rd 1.40; 4th 1; 5th 0.81; R 3.46; b) Automatic: as 520i.

BMW 525i

Chassis: Disc brakes front ventilated, ABS standard; Tyres 195/65 VR 15, USA

Performance: Max speed 137mph/221kmh, automatic 140mph/217kmh (manufacturers test specifications), speed at 1000rpm in 5th gear 23.9mph/38.4kmh; acceleration 0 – 62mph/100kmh 9.5secs, automatic 11.3secs; standing km 30.5secs, automatic 32.3secs; power to weight ratio 11.6kg/kW (8.5kg/PS); consumption DIN 7.0/8.5/13.1 (40.4/33.2/21.6mpg) [33.6/27.7/18US mpg], automatic 7.2/8.8/13.3L/100km (39.2/32.1/21.2mpg) [32.7/26.7/17.7US mpg].

```
530i
138kW–185hp–188PS
Fuel Injection
```

As 520i, except:

Weight: Kerbweight (DIN) 1510kg, gross vehicle weight 2020kg.

Engine data (with Catalyst, DIN): 6-cylinder in-line (89 x 80), 2986cm3; compression ratio 9.0:1; 138kW (185hp) [188PS] at 5800rpm, 46.2kW/L (61.9hp/L) [63PS/L]; 260Nm (191.9lbft) at 4000rpm; unleaded regular grade. Without Catalyst: Identical data.

Engine construction: Valves in V 52deg, 1 overhead camshaft (chain); oil capacity 5.75L (5.5US qt). 12V 75Ah Battery, 90A alternator; cooling system capacity approx 12L (11.4US qt).

Transmission: a) 5-speed manual; final drive ratio 3.64; b) Automatic; final drive ratio 3.73.

Gear ratios: a) 5-speed manual: 1st 3.83; 2nd 2.20; 3rd 1.40; 4th 1; 5th 0.81; R 3.46. b) Automatic as 520i.

Chassis: Front disc brakes front ventilated, ABS standard; tyres 205/60 VR 15, wheel rims 6.5J.

Performance: Catalyst Version: Max speed 141mph/227kph, automatic 139/224kmh (manufacturers test specifications), speed at 1000rpm in 5th gear 24.2mph/38.9kmh; acceleration 0 – 62mph/100kmh 8.6secs, automatic 10.8secs; standing km 29.4secs, automatic 31.6secs; power to weight ratio 10.9kg/kW (8.0kg/PS); consumption DIN 7.4/9.2/15.9L/100km (38.2/30.7/17.8mpg) [31.8/25.6/14.8US mpg], automatic 7.4/9.2/16.8L/100km (38.2/30.7/16.8mpg) [31.8/25.6/14US mpg).

```
535i
155kW–208hp–211PS
Fuel Injection
```

As 520i, except:

Weight: Kerbweight (DIN) 1525kg, USA 1600kg, gross vehicle weight 2035kg.

Engine data (with Catalyst, DIN): 6-cylinder in-line (92 x 86mm), 3430cm3; compression ratio 9:1; 155kW (208hp) [211PS] at 5700rpm, 45.2kW/L (61hp/L) [61.5PS/L]; 305Nm (225lbft) at 4000rpm; unleaded regular grade. Without Catalyst: Identical data.

BMW 535i

Engine construction: Valves in V 52deg, 1 overhead camshaft (chain); oil capacity 5.75L (5.5US qt). 12V 75Ah Battery, 90A alternator; cooling system capacity approx 12L (11.4US qt).

Transmission: a) 5-speed manual; final drive ratio 3.45. b) Automatic with EH-Program, final drive ratio 3.64, USA 3.91. Optional differential lock (ASC).

Gear ratios: a) 5-speed manual: 1st 3.83; 2nd 2.20; 3rd 1.40; 4th 1; 5th 0.81; R 3.46; b) Automatic: as 520i.

Chassis: Disc brakes front ventilated, ABS standard; Tyres 225/60VR 15, wheel rims 7J.

Performance: Catalyst Version: Max speed 146mph/235kmh, automatic 143.6mph/231kmh (manufacturers test specifications), speed at 1000rpm in 5th gear 26.5mph/42.6kmh; acceleration 0 – 62mph/100kmh 7.7secs, automatic

BMW

9.1secs; standing km 28.5secs, automatic 29.7secs; power to weight ratio 9.9kg/kW (7.3kg/PS); consumption DIN 7.6/9.6/16.6L/100km (37.2/29.4/17mpg) [30.1/24.5/14.2US mpg], automatic 7.6/9.6/17.4L/100km (37.2/29.4/16.2mpg) [30.1/24.5/13.5US mpg].

524td
85kw–114hp–115PS
Injection Pump

As 520i, except:

Weight: Kerbweight (DIN) 1480kg, gross vehicle weight 1990kg.

Engine data (DIN): 6–cylinder in–line (80 x 81mm), 2443cm3; compression ratio 22:1; 85kW (114hp) [115PS] at 4800rpm, 34.8kW/L (46.6hp/L) [47.1PS/L]; 220Nm (162.4lbft) at 2400rpm.

Engine construction: Diesel engine swirl chamber. Parallel valves, 1 overhead camshaft (toothed belt); light–alloy cylinder head; oil capacity 5.25L (5US qt); Bosch diesel injection pump, electronically controlled; exhaust turbocharger. 12V 85Ah Battery; 80A alternator; coolant capacity approx 12L (11.4US qt).

Transmission: a) 5–speed manual, final drive ratio 3.25.
b) Automatic, final drive ratio 3.46.

Gear ratios: a) 5–speed gear: 1st 4.35; 2nd 2.33; 3rd 1.39; 4th 1; 5th 0.81; R 3.73.
b) Automatic, Planetary gear set ratios: 1st 2.73; 2nd 1.56; 3rd 1; 4th 0.73; R 2.09.

Performance: Max speed 119mph/192kmh, automatic 118mph/190kmh, speed at 1000rpm in 5th gear 27.4mpg/44.1kmh; acceleration 0 – 62mph/100kmh 12.9secs, automatic 13.9secs, standing km 34.3secs, automatic 35.5secs; power to weight ratio from 17.4kg/kW (12.9kg/PS); consumption ECE 5.1/6.6/9.5 (55.4/42.8/29.7mpg) [46.1/35.6/24.8US mpg].

BMW M 5

New model. High performance of the Series 5 with 3.5Litre 6 cylinder engine. Produced by Motorsport GmbH. Launched September 1988.

3.5 Litre 24V
232kW–311hp–315PS
Fuel Injection

As 520i, except:

Body, Weight: Saloon/Sedan 4-door, 4-seater; kerbweight (DIN) 1670kg, gross vehicle weight 2100kg.

Engine data (Catalyst, DIN): 6 cylinder in-line (93.4 x 86mm), 3535cm3; compression ratio 10.1; 232kW (311hp) [315PS] at 6900rpm, 65.7kW/L (88hp/L) [89.2PS/L]; 360Nm (265.7lbft) at 4750rpm; leaded premium grade.
Without Catalyst: Identical data.

Engine construction: 4-cylinder in V 38deg, 2 overhead camshafts (chain); oil capacity 8L (7.6US qt), oil cooler; electronic digital engine control Bosch M 1.2. Battery 12V 85Ah, alternator 115A; cooling system capacity approx 12L (11.4US qt).

Transmission: 5-speed manual, final drive ratio 3.91; differential brakes 25 deg.

Gear ratios: 1st 3.51; 2nd 2.08; 3rd 1.35; 4th 1; 5th 0.81; R 3.71.

Chassis: Rear level control system. Front ventilated disc brakes, diameter 31.5cm, ABS Bosch system; fuel tank 90L (19.8Gal) [23.8US Gal]; tyres 235/45 ZR 17, wheel rims 8J, optional rea tyres 255/40 ZR 17, wheel rims 9J.

Dimensions: Track 147/149.5cm, height 139cm.

Performance: Catalyst Version: Max speed 155mph/250kmh (manufacturers test specification), speed at 1000rpm in 5th gear 23.3mph/37.5kmh, acceleration 0 - 62mph/100kmh 6.3secs; power to weight ratio 7.2kg/kW (5.3kg/PS); consumption DIN 8.2/9.4/17.1L/100km (34.4/30.1/16.5mpg) [28.7/25.0/13.8US mpg].

BMW M5

BMW 635 CSi – M 635 CSi

Luxury sports coupe with 6–cylinder engine. Launched at Geneva in 1976. Summer 1982: Amended details to Body and Chassis. Summer 1983: high performance version M 635 CSi with 4–valve engine. Catalyst available from Summer 1987 with improved power and fuel efficiency.

635 CSi
155/162kW–208/217hp–211/220PS
Fuel Injection

Body, Weight: 2–door Coupe, 4–seater; kerbweight (DIN) 1460/1475kg, USA 1600kg, gross vehicle weight 1880/1895kg. Automatic 20kg heavier.

Engine data (Catalyst DIN): 6–cylinder in–line (92 x 86mm), 3430cm3; compression ratio 9.0:1; 155kW (208hp) [211PS] at 5700rpm, 45.2kW/L (60.6hp/L) [61.5PS/L]; 304Nm (224.3lbft) at 4000rpm; unleaded regular grade.
US Version: Identical data.
Without Catalyst: Compression ratio 9.2:1; 162kW (217hp) [220PS] at 5700rpm; 315Nm (232.5lbft) at 4000rpm; leaded premium grade.

Engine construction: Valves in V 52deg, 1 overhead camshaft (chain); light–alloy cylinder head; 7 bearing crankshaft; oil capacity 5.75L (5.5US qt); oil cooler; Bosch Motronic digital engine electronic control (fuel injection/ignition). 12V 65Ah Battery, 90A Alternator; cooling system capacity approx 12L (11.4US qt).

Transmission (to rear wheels): a) 5–speed manual, final drive ratio 3.64.
b) ZF Automatic 4 HP–22, hydraulic torque converter and 4–speed Planetary gear set, with EH–Program, selector lever in the middle with positions, P–R–N–D–3–2–1; final drive ratio 3.64, USA 3.91. Optional limited slip differential.

Gear ratios: a) 5 speed manual: 1st 3.83; 2nd 2.20; 3rd 1.40; 4th 1; 5th 0.81; R 3.46.
b) Automatic: max torque multiplication in torque converter 2 times. Planetary gear set ratios: 1st 2.48; 2nd 1.48; 3rd 1; 4th 0.73; R 2.09.

Chassis: Integral body; front McPherson strut, lower control arm, tension strut and antiroll bar; rear independent suspension, with semi–trailing arm, coil springs, starting torque equaliser and antiroll bar, telescopic damper, optional rear level control system. Servo/power assisted disc brakes (front ventilated), Bosch ABS mechanicals. Handbrake to rear wheels; ZF Gemmer power assisted steering. Fuel tank capacity 70L (15.4Gal) [18.5US Gal], with 8L (1.8Gal) [2.1US Gal] reserve; tyres 225/60VR 15, optional 220/55 VR 390 (TRX); wheel rims 7J, optional 165 TR 390.

Dimensions: Wheelbase 262.5cm, track 143.5/146.5cm, clearance 14cm, turning circle 11.7m, load space VDA 14.6cu ft (413dm3). Length 481.5cm, width 172.5cm, height 136.5cm.

Performance (Catalyst version): Max speed 140mph/225kmh, Automatic 137mph/220kmh (manufacturers test specifications), speed at 1000rpm in 5th gear 25.1mph/40.4kmh; acceleration 0– 62mph/100kmh 8.1secs, Automatic 9.0secs, standing km 28.7secs, Automatic 29.7secs; power to weight ratio from 9.5kg/kW (7.0kg/PS); consumption (ECE) 8.2/10.3/12.0L/100km (34.4/27.4/23.5mpg) [28.7/22.8/19.6US mpg], Automatic 8.0/10.2/17.5L/100km (35.3/27.7/16.1mpg) [29.4/23.1/13.4US mpg].
Without Catalyst: Max speed 143mph/230kmh, Automatic 140mph/225kmh; acceleration 0– 62mph/100kmh 7.4secs, Automatic 8.4secs; consumption 7.9/9.9/16.8L/100km (35.8/28.5/16.8mpg) [29.8/23.8/14US mpg], Automatic 7.8/9.8/16.9L/100km (36.2/28.8/16.7mpg) [30.2/24/13.9US mpg].

BMW 635 CSi

BMW

M 635 CSi
191/210kW–256/281hp–260/286PS
Fuel Injection

As M 635CSi, except:

Weight: Kerbweight (DIN) 1500/1515kg, USA M6 1620, gross vehicle weight 1880/1895kg.

Engine data (Catalyst DIN); 6–cylinder in–line (93.4 x 84mm), 3453cm3; compression ratio 9.8:1; 191kW (256hp) [260PS] at 6500rpm, 55.3kW/L (74.1hp/L) [75.3PS/L]; 330Nm (243.5lbft) at 4500rpm; unleaded premium grade. Without Catalyst: Compression ratio 10.5:1; 210kW (281hp) [286PS] at 6500rpm, 60.8kW/L (81.5PS/L) [82.8PS/L]; 340Nm (251lbft) at 4500rpm; leaded premium grade.

Engine construction: Valves in V 38deg,(4 per cylinder), 2 overhead camshafts (chain); oil capacity 8L (7.6US qt), oil cooler. 12V 85Ah Battery.

Transmission: 5–speed manual, final drive ratio 3.91, without Catalyst 3.73; limited slip differential.

Gear ratios: 1st 3.51; 2nd 2.08; 3rd 1.35; 4th 1; 5th 0.81; R 3.71.

Chassis: Optional level control system; tyres 220/55VR 390, optional (and USA) 240/45 VR 415, wheel rims 165 TR 390, optional 195 TR 415.

BMW M 635 CSi

Dimensions: Track 143/146.5cm; load space VDA 11.8cu ft (335dm3). Height 135.5cm.

Performance (Catalyst version): Max speed 152mph/245kmh (manufacturers test specifications), speed at 1000rpm in 5th gear 22.7mph/36.6kmh; acceleration 0 – 62mph/100kmh 6.9secs; standing km 26.8secs; power to weight ratio from 7.9kg/kW (5.8kg/PS); consumption (ECE) 8.1/10.1/17.6L/100km (35/28/16mpg) [29/23.3/13.4US mpg]. Without Catalyst: Max speed 158.5mph/255kmh; acceleration 0 – 62mph/100kmh 6.4secs; standing km 26.4secs; power to weight ratio 7.1kg/kW (5.2kg/PS); consumption 7.8/9.7/16.5L/100km (36.2/29.1/17.1mpg) [30.2/24.2/14.3US mpg].

BMW 730i–735i–750i

Revised edition of the luxury sports 7 series model with a larger body, re–worked chassis and 6–cylinder in–line engine with 3 and 3.5 Litre engine displacement. The top model is the 750i, introduced in July 1987 with new V12 5 Litre engine. Launched Autumn 1986.

730i
138kW–185hp–188PS
Fuel Injection

Body, Weight: 4–door Saloon/Sedan, 5–seater; kerbweight (DIN) from 1600kg, gross vehicle weight 2130kg. Automatic 20kg heavier.

Engine data (Catalyst DIN): 6–cylinder in–line (89 x 80mm), 2986cm3; compression ratio 9:1; 138kW (185hp) [188PS] at 5800rpm, 46.2kW/L (61.9hp/L) [63PS/L]; 260Nm (192lbft) at 4000rpm; unleaded regular grade. Without Catalyst: Identical data.

Engine construction: Valves in V 52deg, 1 overhead camshaft (chain); light–alloy cylinder heads; 7 bearing crankshaft; oil capacity 5.75L (5.5US qt). Bosch Motronic digital electronic engine control (injection/ignition). 12V 75Ah Battery, 90A Alternator; cooling system capacity approx 12L (11.4US qt).

Transmission (to rear wheels): a) 5–speed manual, final drive ratio 3.64.

b) ZF–Automatic 4 HP–22, hydraulic torque converter and 4–speed Planetary gear set; optional EH–Program; final drive ratio 4.10. Optional differential lock (ASC).

Gear ratios: a) 5–speed manual: 1st 3.83; 2nd 2.20; 3rd 1.40; 4th 1; 5th 0.81; R 3.46.

b) Automatic: Max torque multiplication in torque converter 2 times, Planetary gear set ratios: 1st 2.48; 2nd 1.48; 3rd 1; 4th 0.73; R 2.09.

BMW 730i

Chassis: Integral body; independent suspension; front McPherson strut, lower control arm, diagonal pressure struts and antiroll bar, rear semi–trailing arm, auxiliary steering, coil springs with co–axial shock absorbers, starting torque equaliser and antiroll bar; optional rear level control system. Servo/power assisted disc brakes (front ventilated), disc diameter, front 29.6cm, rear 30cm, Bosch ABS. Mechanical handbrake to rear wheels; power assisted recirculating ball steering; fuel tank capacity 90/102L (19.8/22.4Gal) [23.8/27US Gal]; tyres 205/65 VR 15, optional 225/60 VR 15, wheel rims 6.5J, optional 7J.

Dimensions: Wheelbase 283cm, track 152.5/155cm, clearance 12cm, turning circle 11.6m, load space VDA 17.6cu ft (500dm3). Length 491cm, width 184.5cm, height 141cm.

Performance (Catalyst version): Max speed 138mph/222kmh, Automatic 138mph/222kmh (manufacturers test specifications); speed at 1000rpm in 5th gear 39.5kmh; acceleration 0 – 62mph/100kmh 9.3secs, Automatic 10.6ecs, standing km 30.1secs, Automatic 31.9secs; power to weight ratio from 11.6kg/kW (8.5kg/PS); consumption (ECE) 7.6/9.4/16.3L/100km (37.2/30.1/17.3mpg) [30.9/25/14.4US mpg], Automatic 7.9/9.8/17.3L/100km (35.8/28.8/16.3mpg) [29.8/24/13.6US mpg].

735i
155kW–208hp–211PS
Fuel Injection

As 730i, except:

Body, Weight: Saloon/Sedan 735i, kerbweight (DIN) 1600kg USA 1740kg gross vehicle weight 2150kg; Saloon/Sedan 735iL (long.) 5–seater; kerbweight (DIN) 1660kg gross vehicle weight 2180kg.

Engine data (Catalyst DIN): 6–cylinder in–line (92 x 86mm), 3430cm3; compression ratio 9:1; 155kW (208hp) [211PS] at 5700rpm, 45.2kW/L (60.6hp/L) [61.5 PS/L]; 305Nm (225lbft) at 4000rpm; unleaded regular grade. Without Catalyst: Identical data.

BMW 735i

Transmission: a) 5–speed manual, final drive ratio 3.45, USA 3.64.
b) Automatic with EH–Program, final drive ratio 3.91, optional 3.64.

Chassis: Fuel tank iL 102L (22.4Gal) [26.9US Gal]; tyres 225/60 VR 15. wheel rims 7J.

Dimensions: Long version 735iL: Wheelbase 294.5cm, turning circle 12m, length 502.5cm.

Performance (Catalyst version): Max speed 143mph/230kmh, Automatic 143mph/230kmh (manufacturers test specifications), speed at 1000rpm in 5th

BMW D • BMW SA • Bristol

gear 26.5mph/42.6kmh; acceleration 0 – 62mph/100kmh 8.3secs, Automatic 9.1secs, standing km 29.8secs, Automatic 30.5secs; power to weight ratio from 10.3kg/kW (7.6kg/PS); consumption (ECE) 7.7/9.7/16.8 (36.7/29.1/16.8mpg) [30.5/24.2/14US mpg], Automatic 8.1/10.2/17.9L/100km (34.9/27.7/15.8mpg) [29/23.1/13.1US mpg].

BMW 735iL

```
750i V12
220kW–295hp–300PS
Fuel Injection
```

As 730i, except:

Body, Weight: Saloon/Sedan 750i: Kerbweight (DIN) from 1800kg, gross vehicle weight 2320kg; Saloon/Sedan 750iL, 5–seater: Kerbweight (DIN) 1860kg, USA 1920kg, gross vehicle weight 2380 kg.

Engine data (Catalyst DIN): 12–cylinder in V 60deg; (84 x 75mm), 4988cm3; compression ratio 8.8:1; 220kW (295hp) [300PS] at 5200rpm, 44.1kW/L (59hp/L) [60.1PS/L]; 450Nm (332lbft) at 4100rpm; unleaded regular grade. Without Catalyst: Identical data.

Engine construction: 1 overhead camshaft (chain), valves in V (14deg), hydraulic tappets; light–alloy cylinder heads and cylinder block; 7 bearing crankshaft; oil capacity 7.5L (7.1US qt); Bosch Motronic electronic engine control. 12V 85Ah Battery, 140A alternator; cooling system capacity approx 12L (11.4US qt).

Transmission: Automatic with EH–Program, final drive ratio 3.15.

Chassis: Rear level control system, all round disc brakes (ventilated) disc diameter, front 30.2cm, rear 30cm; fuel tank capacity 102L (22.4Gal) [26.9US Gal]; tyres 225/60VR 15, wheel rims 7J.

Dimensions: Wheelbase 283.5cm, track 153/155.5cm, height 140cm. Saloon/Sedan iL; wheelbase 294.5cm, turning circle 12m, length 502.5cm.

Performance: Max speed 155.5mph/250kmh (manufacturers test specifications), speed at 1000rpm in top gear 32.2mph/51.8kmh; acceleration 0 – 62mph/100kmh 7.4secs, standing km 27.3secs; power to weight ratio from 8.2kg/kW (6.0kg/PS). Consumption (ECE) 8.8/10.9/19.8L/100km (32.1/25.9/14.3mpg) [26.7/21.6/11.9US mpg], without Catalyst 8.9/11.1/19.8L/100km (31.7/25.4/14.3mpg) [26.4/21.2/11.9US mpg].

BMW 750i

```
BMW                                          SA
```

BMW (South Africa) (Pty) Ltd, PO Box 2955, Pretoria, South Africa.

South African Assembly works of BMW AG Munich. Construction of 3, 5 and 7 series models with slight variations (316, 318i, 320i, 325i, 325S, 525i, 535i, 730i, 735i, 750iL).

```
BRISTOL                                      GB
```

Bristol Cars Ltd, 368/370 Kensington High Street, London W14 8NL, England

Small English manufacturer of Elite models.

Bristol Britannia – Brigand Turbo

Successor to the Bristol 603 with light alloy body; engine and transmission from Chrysler (USA). Launched 1st October 1976. October 1982.

Bristol Britannia

```
5.9 Litre V8
1 4V Carb
```

Body, Weight: 2–door Saloon/Sedan, 4–seater; kerbweight (DIN) 1745kg.

Engine data (SAE net): 8–cylinder in V 90deg (101.6 x 90.93mm), 5898cm3. No information on power or torque. Brigand available with exhaust turbocharger.

Engine construction: Hydraulic tappets, central camshaft (chain); 5 bearing crankshaft; oil capacity 4.7L; 1 4V Carter downdraught carb. 12V 71Ah battery, 60/65A alternator; cooling system capacity approx 16.5L (15.6US qt).

Transmission (to rear wheels): Chrysler Torqueflite automatic, hydraulic torque converter and 3–speed Planetary gear set; central selector lever, final drive ratio 2.88 or 3.07. Limited slip differential.

Gear ratios: Max torque multiplication in torque converter 2.23 times; Planetary gear set ratios: 1st 2.45; 2nd 1.45; 3rd 1; R 2.2.

Chassis: Transverse box section frame; front wishbone and coil springs, rear rigid axle with torsion bar and automatic Watt linkage. Level control system, front A arm, telescopic damper (adjustable). Servo/power assisted disc brakes, disc diameter, front 27.7cm, rear 27cm, mechanical handbrake to rear wheels; ZF Power assisted recirculating ball steering; fuel tank capacity 82L, with 16L reserve; tyres 215/70VR 15, wheel rims 6J.

Dimensions: Wheelbase 290cm, track 138.5/141cm, clearance 12.5cm, turning circle 12m, load space 19.1cu ft (540dm3). Length 490cm, width 176cm, height 143cm.

Performance: Britannia: Max speed 140mph/225kmh (manufacturers test specifications), speed at 1000rpm in top gear 26.9mph/43.3kmh; acceleration 0 – 60mph/97kmh 7.2secs; consumption 14–25L/100km (20.2–11.3mpg) [16.8–9.4US mpg].
Brigand with exhaust turbocharger: Max speed 149mph/240kmh (manufacturers test specifications), acceleration 0 – 60mph/97kmh 5.9secs; consumption 16–28L/100km (17.7–10.1mpg) [14.7–8.4US mpg].

Bristol Brigand Turbo

Bristol • Buick

Bristol Beaufighter – Beaufort

Luxury convertible with supercharged Chrysler 5.9 Litre V8 engine. The Beaufighter was launched (with safety roll cage) in January 1980; the Beaufort Convertible in Autumn 1984.

```
5.9 Litre V8 Turbo
1 4V Carb.
```

As Britannia/Brigand, except:

Body, Weight: 2–door convertible with or without safety roll cage, 4–seater; kerbweight (DIN) 1750kg, gross vehicle weight 2130kg.

Engine data: 5.9 Litre V8 with turbocharger, no information on power/torque.

Transmission: Final drive ratio 2.88 or 3.07.

Chassis: Fuel tank capacity 95/140L (20.9/33Gal) [25.1/39.5US Gal].

Dimensions: Load space 21.9cu ft (620dm3). Length 494cm.

Performance: Max speed 149mph/240kmh (manufacturers test specifications); acceleration 0 – 60mph/97kmh 5.9secs; consumption (cruising) approx 16–28L/100km (17.7–10.1mpg) [14.7– 8.4US mpg].

Bristol Beaufort

BUICK — USA

Buick Motor Division, General Motors Corp., 1051 E Hamilton Avenue, Flint 2, Michigan, USA.

Part of the General Motors Group, pioneers of torque converters.

MODEL SERIES
Skyhawk – Skylark – Century – Regal – Le Sabre – Electra – Riviera - Reatta.

Buick Skyhawk

Compact with 2–Litre, 4–cylinder transverse engine and front wheel drive, 5–speed manual or automatic, built as part of the J– car family from General Motors. Available as Saloon/Sedan, Convertible and Estate/Station Wagon. Launched February 1982. For 1983 a new Coupe the "T Type" and a new Estate/Station Wagon. For 1989, only with 2–Litre engine.

Buick Skyhawk Coupe S/E

```
2 Litre
67kW–90hp–91PS
Central/Single Point Injection
```

Body, Weight (laden): 4–door Saloon/Sedan, 4/5 seater, 1020kg; 2–door Coupe, 4/5 seater, 1100kg; 5–door Estate/Station Wagon, 4/5 seater, 1155kg.

Engine data (SAE net): 4–cylinder in–line (89 x 80mm), 1991cm3; compression ratio 9.0:1; 67kW (90hp) [91PS] at 5600rpm, 33.6kW/L (45hp/L) [45.7PS/L]; 147m (108.5lbft) at 3200rpm; unleaded regular grade.

Engine construction: Designated LL 8. Transverse front engine, hydraulic tappets, 1 overhead camshaft (chain); light alloy cylinder head; 5 bearing crankshaft; oil capacity 3.8L (3.6US qt); electronic central fuel injection. Battery 12 V 54Ah, alternator 74A; cooling system capacity approx 7.4L (7US qt).

Transmission (to front wheels): a) 5–speed manual, floor shift, final drive ratio 3.45.
b) THM 125 Automatic, hydraulic torque converter and 3-speed Planetary gear set; final drive ratio 3.18.

Gear ratios: a) 5–speed manual: 1st 3.91; 2nd 2.15; 3rd 1.45; 4th 1.03; 5th 0.74; R 3.58.
b) Automatic: Max torque multiplication in torque converter 2.4 times, Planetary gear set ratios: 2.84; 1.6; 1; R 2.07.

Chassis: Integral body. Front sub–frame, front McPherson struts and lower control arm, antiroll bar; rear independent swinging arm suspension, optional antiroll bar, coil springs and telescopic damper front and rear. Servo/power assisted brakes, front disc (ventilated), diameter 24.7cm, rear drums; parking brake to rear wheels; power assisted rack and pinion steering; fuel tank capacity 51.5L (11.1Gal) [13.6US Gal]; tyres 185 R 13 optional 205/70 R 13, 215/60 R 14, wheel rims 5.5 or 6J.

Dimensions: Wheelbase 257cm, track 141/140cm, clearance min 16cm, turning circle approx 11.3m. Load space 13.4cu ft(380dm3), Coupe 12.5cu ft (355dm3), Estate/Station Wagon 64.5cu ft (1825dm3). Length: Saloon/Sedan and Coupe 456cm, Estate/Station Wagon 461.5cm, width 165cm. Height 137cm, Coupe 133cm, Estate/Station Wagon 138cm.

Performance: Max speed 93-99mph/150-160kmh, speed in 5th gear at 1000rpm 27.7mph/44.6kmh; power to weight ratio from 16.4kg/kW (121.1kg/PS); consumption approx 8-13L/100km (35.3-21.7mpg) [29.4-18.1US mpg].

Buick Skyhawk Sedan

Buick Skylark

Luxury sports Coupe with front wheel drive, 2.5 Litre four- cylinder or 3.0L V6 engine, Automatic. Launched August 1984. 1986 Saloon/Sedan version added to the range. 1988 2.3 Litre 4–Valve engine "Quad 4" with 2 overhead camshafts. 1989 with new 3.3Litre V6 '3300'.

```
2.5 Litre
82kW–110hp–112PS
Central/Single Point Injection
```

Body, Weight (laden):
Skylark Custom: 2–door Coupe, 5–seater; approx 1170kg. 4–door Saloon/Sedan, 5–seater; approx 1195kg.
Skylark Limited: 2–door Coupe, 5–seater; approx 1180kg. 4–door Saloon/Sedan, 5–seater;approx 1205kg.

Engine data (SAE net): 4–cylinder in–line (101.6 x 76.2mm), 2471cm3; compression ratio 9:1; 82kW (110hp) [112PS] at 5200rpm, 33.2kW/L (44.5hp/L) [45.3PS/L]; 183Nm (135lbft) at 3200rpm; unleaded regular grade.

Engine construction: Designated L 68. Transverse engine, hydraulic tappets, side camshaft (toothed belt); 5 bearing crankshaft; oil capacity 3.8L (3.6US qt); Rochester (TBI) electronic fuel injection. 12V 54Ah Battery, 74A alternator; cooling system capacity approx 7.4L (7US qt).

Transmission (to front wheels): Automatic THM 125, hydraulic torque converter and 3- speed Planetary gear set, final drive ratio 2.84.

Gear ratios: Max torque multiplication in converter 2.48 times, Planetary gear set ratios: 2.84; 1.6; 1; R 2.07.

Buick

Buick Skylark Limited Coupe

Chassiss: Integral body. Front sub–frame, front McPherson struts and lower control arms, antiroll bar; coil springs and telescopic damper front and rear. Servo/power assisted brakes, front discs (ventilated), diameter 24.7cm, rear drums; parking brake on rear wheels; power assisted rack and pinion steering; fuel tank 51.5L (11.3Gall) [13.6US mpg]; tyres 185 R 13, 205/70 R 13, 215/60 R 14, wheel rims 5.5 or 6J.

Dimensions: Wheelbase 262.5cm, track 141/140cm, clearance 17cm, turning circle approx 11.5m, load space 13.4cu ft (380dm3). Length 457.5cm, width 169.5cm, height 132.5cm.

Performance: Max speed approx 112mph/180kmh, speed at 1000rpm in OD gear 24.9mph/40.1kmh; power to weight ratio from 14.3kg/kW (10.4kg/PS); consumption approx 8–14L/100km (35.3–20.2mpg) [29.4– 16.8US mpg].

Buick Skylark Limited Sedan

```
2.3 Litre DOHC 16V
112kW–150hp–152PS
Fuel Injection
```

Engine for Quad 4

As 2.5Litre, except:

Weight: 25kg heavier.

Engine data (SAE net): 4–cylinder in–line (92 x 85mm), 2260cm3, compression ratio 9.5:1; 112kW (150hp) [152PS] at 5200rpm, 49.6kW/L (66.5hp/L) [67.3PS/L]; 217Nm (160lbft) at 4000rpm.

Engine construction: Designated LD 2. 4–Valves per cylinder; light-alloy cylinder head; 2 overhead camshafts (chain); Rochester electronic fuel injection. Spark plugs AC FR 3LS; 85/100A alternator; cooling system capacity approx 7.2L (6.8US qt).

Performance: Max speed approx 124mph/200kmh; power to weight ratio from approx 10.7kg/kW (7.9kg/PS); consumption approx 8– 15L/100km (35.3–18.8mpg) [29.4–15.7US mpg].

```
3.3 Litre V6
119kW–160hp–162PS
Fuel Injection
```

As 2.5 Litre, except:

Weight: 40kg heavier.

Engine data (SAE net): 6–cylinder in V 90deg (93.98 x 80.26mm), 3340cm3; compression ratio 9:1; 119kW (160hp) [162PS] at 5200rpm, 35.6kW/L (47.7hp/L) [48.5PS/L]; 251Nm (185.2lbft) at 2400rpm.

Engine construction: Designated LG 7. Central camshaft (chain); 4 bearing crankshaft; Rochester electronic fuel injection. Spark plugs AC R44-LTS6; 74A alternator; cooling system capacity approx 9.4L (8.9US qt).

Transmission: Automatic, final drive ratio 2.39.

Performance: Max speed approx 131mph/210kmh, speed at 1000rpm in OD gear 29.6mph/47.7kmh; power to weight ratio from 10.2kg/kW (7.5kg/PS); consumption approx 9–15L/100km (31.4–18.8mpg) [26.1– 15.7US mpg].

Buick Century

Model series with front wheel drive, 4–cylinder V6 engine; automatic gear change. Internal designation "A Body", mechanicals based on the compact X–bodies. Launched December 1981. 1983: New sports series "T Type". 1984: Estate/Station Wagon version. 1988: 2.5 Litre engine with counter-balance shaft. 1989 with new 3.3Litre V6 and body modifications.

Buick Century Custom Coupe

```
2.5 Litre
73kW–98hp–99PS
Central/Single Point Injection
```

Body, Weight (laden):
Century Custom: 4–door Saloon/Sedan, 6–seater; 1255kg; 2–door Coupe, 6–seater; 1235kg; 5–door Estate/Station Wagon, 6/8–seater; approx 1320kg. Century, Limited: 4–door Saloon/Sedan, 6–seater 1265kg; Estate/Station Wagon 5-door, 6/8–seater approx 1325kg. Increased Weight for air-conditioning unit 25kg.

Engine data (SAE net): 4–cylinder in–line (101.6 x 76.2mm), 2471cm3; compression ratio 8.3.1; 73kW (98hp) [99PS] at 4800rpm, 29.5kW/L (39.5hp/L) [40.1PS/L]; 183Nm (135lbft) at 3200rpm; unleaded regular grade.

Engine construction: Designated LR 8. Transverse engine. Hydraulic tappets, side camshaft (toothed belt); 5 bearing crankshaft; oil capacity 2.8L (2.6US qt); Rochester electronic central injection (TBI). Spark plugs AC R44TSX; 12V 90Ah battery, 56/66/78A alternator; cooling system capacity approx 9.2L (8.7US qt).

Transmission (to front wheels): Automatic THM 125, hydraulic torque converter and 3-speed Planetary gear set, final drive ratio 2.84.

Gear ratios: Max torque multiplication in converter 2.35 times, Planetary gear set ratios; 2.84; 1.6; R 2.07.

Chassis: Integral body. Front sub–frame, front McPherson strut and lower control arm, antiroll bar; rear rigid axle with semi– trailing arms, torsion bar, Panhard rod, coil spring and telescopic damper, antiroll bar. Servo/power assisted brakes, front disc (ventilated), diameter 24.7 or 26.0cm, rear drums; parking brake to rear wheels; power assisted rack and pinion steering; fuel tank capacity 59.5L (13.1Gal) [15.7US Gal]; tyres 185/75R 14, wheel rims 5.5J; optional tyres 195/70R 14; 215/60 R 14, wheel rims 5.5 or 6.5J.

Buick Century Custom Sedan

Dimensions: Wheelbase 266.5cm, track 149/144cm, clearance min 16cm, turning circle 13m, load space capacity 16.2cu ft (460dm3), Estate/Station Wagon 74.3cu ft (2105dm3). Length 480.5cm (Estate/Station Wagon 485cm), width 176cm, height 137.5cm (Coupe 136.5cm).

Buick 119

Performance: Max speed approx 99.5mph/160kmh, speed at 1000rpm in OD gear 25.smph/40.6kmh; power to weight ratio from 16.9kg/kW (12.5kg/PS); consumption approx 9–14L/100km (31.4–20.2mpg) [26.1– 16.8US mpg].

```
3.3 Litre
119kW–160hp–162PS
Fuel Injection
```

As 2.5 Litre except:

Weight: Max 55kg.

Engine data (SAE net): 6-cylinder in V 90deg (93.98 x 80.26mm), 3340cm3; compression ratio 9.1; 119kW (160hp) [162PS] at 5200rpm, 35.6kW/L (47.7hp/L) [48.5PS/L]; 251Nm (185.2lbft) at 2000rpm.

Engine construction: Designated LG 7. Central camshaft (chain); 4 bearing crankshaft; Rochester electronic fuel injection. Spark plugs AC R44-LTS6; 74A alternator; cooling system capacity approx 9.4L (8.9US qt).

Transmission: a) Automatic, final drive ratio 2.73; 2.84.
b) 4-speed automatic, final drive ratio 2.73; 3.06; 3.33.

Gear ratios: a) Automatic; max torque multiplication in converter 2.35 times, Planetary gear set ratios: 2.84; 1.6; 1; R 2.07.
b) Automatic with overdrive; max torque multiplication in converter 1.95 times, Planetary gear set ratios: 1st 2.92; 2nd 1.56; 3rd 1; OD 0.7: R 2.38.

Performance: Max speed approx 124mph/200kmh; power to weight ratio from 10.8kg/kW (8.0kg/PS); consumption approx 10-16L/100km (28.2-17.7mpg) [23.5-13.3US mpg].

Buick Century Estate Wagon

Buick Regal

New model. Coupe version of the 2–door Buick, now with front wheel drive and V6 engine. Launched at the Los Angeles Show (January 1987), on sale in Autumn 1987. Also available in 1989 2.8 V6 engine replacing 3.1Litre engine.

```
2.8/3.1 V6
97/104kW–130/140hp–132/142PS
Fuel Injection
```

Body, Weight (laden): 2–door Coupe, 4/5/6–seater; approx 1425kg.

Engine data (SAE net): 6–cylinder in V 60deg (88.9 x 76.2mm), 2838cm3; compression ratio 8.9: 1; 97kW (130hp) [132PS] at 4500rpm, 34.2kW/L (45.8hp/L) [46.5PS/L]; 231Nm (170.5lbft) at 3600rpm; unleaded regular grade.
Later: (88.9 x 84mm), 3128cm3; compression ratio 8.8:1; 104kW (140hp) [142PS] at 4500rpm, 33.2kW/L (44.5hp/L) [45.4PS/L]; 258Nm (190.4lbft) at 3600rpm.

Buick Regal Custom

Engine construction: Designated LB 6/LH 0. Transverse front engine. Hydraulic tappets, central camshaft (chain); light-alloy cylinder head; 4 bearing camshaft; oil capacity 3.8L (3.6US qt); Rochester electronic fuel injection. Spark plugs AC R43CTLSF; 12V 54/69Ah battery, 108/120A alternator; cooling system capacity 10.7L (10.1US qt).

Transmission (to rear wheels): a) 5–speed manual, final drive ratio 3.61.
b) Automatic "Turbo Hydra-Matic" 440-T4, hydraulic torque converter and Planetary gear set, 4–speed/Overdrive, selector lever at steering wheel, final drive ratio 3.33.

Gear ratios: a) 5–speed manual: 1st 3.5; 2nd 2.05; 3rd 1.38; 4th 0.94; 5th 0.72; R 3.41.
b) Automatic: Max torque multiplication in converter 1.95 times, Planetary gear set ratios: 2.92; 1.57; 1; OD 0.7; R 2.38.

Chassis: Integral body with front sub-frame; front and rear independent suspension; front McPherson strut (coil springs), lower longitudinal control arm, longitudinal antiroll bar, rear control arm, shock absorber strut, transverse leaf springs, anti– rollbar, optional level control system; telescopic damper. Servo/power assisted disc brakes, optional with ABS (Delco-Moraine), disc diameter, front ventilated 26.7cm, rear 25.6cm; pedal actuated parking brake to rear wheels; power assisted rack and pinion steering; fuel tank capacity 64.5L (14.1Gal) [16.9US Gal]; tyres 205/70R 14, or 215/60 R 16, wheel rims 5.5 or 6.5".

Dimensions: Wheelbase 273cm, track 151/147cm, clearance 15cm, turning circle 12.5m. Load space capacity 15.5cu ft (440dm3). Length 488cm, width 184cm, height 134.5cm.

Performance: Max speed approx 115mph/185kmh; speed at 1000rpm in 5th gear 28.5mph/45.9kmh; power to weight ratio from 14.7kg/kW (10.8kg/PS); consumption approx 9–15L/100km (31.4–18.8mpg) [26.1- 15.7US mpg].

Buick Regal Gran Sport

Buick LeSabre

Saloon/Sedan and Coupe with front wheel drive and 3.8 Litre V6 engine, Overdrive–Automatic gear shift. Launched Autumn 1985. 1988: Introduction of optional more powerful engine with balance shaft.

Body, Weight (laden):
LeSabre Custom 2–door Coupe, 6–seater: 1465kg; 4–door Saloon/Sedan, 6–seater: 1480kg.
LeSabre Limited 2–door Coupe, 6–seater: 1480kg; 4–door Saloon/Sedan, 6–seater: 1495kg.

```
3.8 Litre V6
123kW–165hp–167PS
Fuel Injection
```

Buick Le Sabre Limited Sedan

Look at Vec

The all-new Opel Vectra. Graceful in form. Fitness in function. Backed by the worldwide resources of General Motors. Designed and engineered by Opel.

The all-new Vectra extends Opel's commitment to design and manufacturing innovation to new and higher levels. A sleek new shape designed with the applica-

tra. Look at Opel now.

tion of the latest super computer technology from the aerospace industry gives Vectra a Cd of 0.29.

Vectra has the latest front-wheel drive technology and improved front and rear suspension geometry. An entirely new 4×4 system is available that progressively activates and disengages automatically during braking. Anti-Lock Brakes (ABS) are also available.

A range of powerful, yet fuel-efficient engines (from 1.4-litre to 2.0-litre gasoline and a 1.7-litre diesel) provide lively performance.

With Vectra comes even higher levels of fit and finish. A new 10-step quality protection program includes waxing the underbody and galvanized or zinc-nickel alloy coating of all body panels.

The all-new Opel Vectra. New evidence of General Motors and Opel's commitment to quality, durability and reliability.

Look at Opel now!

OPEL

BACKED BY THE WORLDWIDE RESOURCES OF GENERAL MOTORS.

Buick

Engine data (SAE net): 6–cylinder in V 90deg, (96.52 x 86.36mm), 3791cm3; compression ratio 8.5:1; 123kW (165hp) [167PS] at 5200rpm, 32.4kW/L (43.4) [44.1PS/L]; 285Nm (210.3lbft) at 2000rpm; unleaded regular grade.

Engine construction: Designated LN 3 '3800'. Transverse front engine. Hydraulic tappets, central camshaft (chain); 4 bearing crankshaft; 1 counter-balance shaft; oil capacity 3.8L (3.6US qt); Bosch electronic fuel injection. Sparkplugs AC R44LTS; 12V 54/69Ah battery, 105A alternator; cooling system capacity 11.7L (11.1US qt).

Transmission (to front wheels): Automatic "Turbo Hydra-Matic" 440-T4 hydraulic torque converter and Planetary gear set, 4- speed/Overdrive, selector lever at steering wheel, final drive ratio 2.84; 2.97.

Gear ratios: Max torque multiplication in converter 1,68 times, Planetary gear set ratios: 2.92; 1.57; 1; OD 0.7; R 2.38.

Buick Le Sabre T-Type Coupe

Chassis: Integral body with front sub-frame, front and rear independent suspension; front McPherson struts, lower control arm and antiroll bar; rear shock absorber struts lower A-arm and antiroll bar; coil springs, telescopic damper; optional level control system. Servo/power assisted brakes, optional with ABS (ITT Teves), front discs (ventilated) diameter 25.6cm, rear drums; pedal actuated parking brake to rear wheels; power assisted rack and pinion steering; fuel tank capacity 68L (14.9Gal) [18US Gal]; tyres 205/75R 14, for T-type 215/65 R 15, wheel rims 6J.

Dimensions: Wheelbase 281.5cm, track 153/152cm, clearance 14cm, turning circle 13.0m, load space capacity 16.4cu ft (465dm3), Coupe 15.7cu ft (445dm3). Length 500cm, width 184cm, height 141cm, Coupe 139cm.

Performance: Max speed approx 121mph/195kmh; speed at 1000rpm in direct gear 26.5mph/42.6kmh; power to weight ratio from 11.9kg/kW (8.8kg/PS); consumption approx 11-18L/100km (25.7-15.7mpg) [21.4-13.1US mpg].

Buick Electra

Luxury model with front wheel drive, transverse engine and Overdrive-Automatic transmission. Internal designation "C-body". Launched April/May 1984. 1986 available only with 3.8 Litre V6 engine. 1989 new luxury model 'Ultra'.

Buick Electra Ultra

```
3.8 Litre V6
123kW-165hp-167PS
Fuel injection
```

Body, Weight (laden): Electra Limited 4-door Saloon/Sedan, 6-seater; 1490kg.
Electra Park Avenue 4-door Saloon/Sedan, 6-seater; 1510kg.
Electra T Type 4-door Saloon/Sedan, 5-seater; 1535kg.
Electra Ultra 4-door Saloon/Sedan, 6-seater; 1555kg.

Engine data (SAE net): 6–cylinder in V 90deg, (96.52 x 86.36mm), 3791cm3; compression ratio 8.5:1; 123kW (165hp) [167PS] at 5200rpm, 32.4kW/L (43.4hp/L) [44.1PS/L]; 285Nm (210.3lbft) at 2000rpm; unleaded regular grade.

Engine construction: Designated LN 3 "3800." Transverse front engine. Hydraulic tappets, central camshaft (chain); 4 bearing crankshaft; counter-balance shaft. Oil capacity 3.8L (3.6US qt); Bosch electronic fuel injection. Spark plugs AC R44LTS; 12V 54/69 Ah battery, 105A alternator; cooling system capacity 11.7L (11.1US qt).

Transmission (to front wheels): Automatic "Turbo Hydra-Matic" 440-T4 hydraulic torque converter and Planetary gear set, 4 speed/Overdrive, selector lever at steering wheel, final drive ratio 2.84; 2.97.

Gear ratios: Max torque multiplication in converter 1.68 times, Planetary gear set ratios: 2.92; 1.57; 1; OD 0.7; R 2.38.

Chassis: Integral body with front sub-frame. Front and rear independent suspension, front McPherson strut lower control arm and antiroll bar, rear shock absorber strut, lower A-arm and antiroll bar; coil springs, telescopic damper, level control system. Servo/power assisted brakes, optional with ABS (ITT Teves), front discs (ventilated) diameter 25.6cm, rear drums; pedal actuated parking brake to rear wheels; power assisted rack and pinion steering; fuel tank capacity 68L (15Gal) [18US Gal]; tyres 205/75 R 14, Ultra 205/70 R 15, T Type 215/65 R 15, wheel rims 6J.

Dimensions: Wheelbase 281.5cm, track 153/152cm, clearance 15cm, turning circle 13.0m, load space capacity 16.4cu ft (465dm3). Length 500cm, width 184cm, height 138cm.

Performance: Max speed approx 121mph/195kmh; speed at 1000rpm in direct gear 26.5mph/42.6kmh; power to weight ratio from 12.1kg/kW (8.9kg/PS); consumption approx 11-17L/100km (25.7-16.6mpg) [21.4- 13.8US mpg].

Buick LeSabre/Electra Estate Station Wagon

Estate/Station Wagon from the oldest series: LeSabre with rear wheel drive, 5 Litre V8 engine. 1988: improved equipment.

Buick Le Sabre Estate Wagon

Body, Weight (laden):
LeSabre Estate/Station Wagon: 5-door Estate/Station Wagon, 6-seater 1910kg.
5-door Estate/Station Wagon, 8-seater 1925kg.
Electra Estate/Station Wagon: 5-door Estate/Station Wagon, 6-seater 1935kg.
5-door Estate/Station Wagon, 8-seater 1950kg.

```
5 Litre V8
104kW-140hp-142PS
1 4V Carb
```

Engine data (SAE net): 8–cylinder in V 90deg, (96.52 x 85.98mm), 5033cm3; compression ratio 8:1; 104kW (140hp) [142PS] at 3200rpm, 20.7kW/L (27.7hp/L) [28.2PS/L]; 346Nm (255.3lbft) at 2000rpm; unleaded regular grade.

Engine construction: Designated LV 2. Hydraulic tappets, central camshaft (toothed belt); 5 bearing crankshaft; oil capacity 4.7L (4.4US qt); 1 Rochester downdraught 4V carb. Spark plugs AC FR3LS6; 12V 54Ah battery, 78A alternator; cooling system capacity approx 14.8L (14US qt).

Transmission (to rear wheels): Automatic "Turbo Hydra-Matic" 440- T4 hydraulic torque converter and 4-speed Planetary gear set, selector lever at steering wheel, final drive ratio 2.93; 3.23.

Gear ratios: Max torque multiplication in converter 1.9 times, Planetary gear set ratios: 2.74; 1.57; 1; OD 0.67; R 2.07.

Buick 123

Chassis: Box section frame with cross members; front upper wishbone, lower wishbone and tension struts, coil springs, front antiroll bar; rear rigid axle with coil springs, lower trailing arm and semi-trailing arm, differentail stabiliser bar optional antiroll bar, telescopic damper, optional pneumatic rear level control system. Servo/power assisted brakes, front discs (ventilated), diameter 30.1cm, rear drums; pedal actuated parking brake to rear wheels; power assisted recirculating ball steering; fuel tank capacity 83L (18.2Gal) [22US Gal], tyres 225/75 R 15, wheel rims 7J.

Dimensions: Wheelbase 294.5cm, track 158/162.5cm, clearance 20.5cm, turning circle 13.5m, load space capacity 87.9cu ft (2490dm3). Length 560cm, width 201.5cm, height 150.5cm.

Performance: Max speed approx 99–106mph/160–170kmh, speed at 1000rpm in OD 41.5mph/66.8kmh; power to weight ratio from 18.4kg/kW (13.4kg/PS); consumption approx 12–19L/100km (23.5– 14.9mpg) [19.6–12.4US mpg].

Buick Riveria

Prestige Coupe from the Buick Division. 1986: new model launched with transverse engine, front wheel drive and more compact body. Launched in Autumn 1986. 1989 26cm longer.

3.8 Litre V6
123kW–165hp–167PS
Fuel Injection

Buick Riviera

Body, Weight (laden): 2–door Coupe, 4/5–seater approx 1560kg.

Engine data (SAE net): 6–cylinder in V 90deg (96.52 x 86.36mm), 3791cm3; compression ratio 8.5:1; 123kW (165hp) [167PS] at 5200rpm, 32.4kW/L (43.4hp/L) [44.1PS/L]; 285Nm (2210.3lbft) at 2000rpm; regular unleaded regular grade.

Engine construction: Designated LN 3 "3800." Transverse front engine. Hydraulic tappets, central camshaft (chain); 4 bearing crankshaft; counter–balance shaft; oil capacity 3.8L (3.6US qt); electronic fuel injection. 12V 54/69Ah Battery, 108/120A alternator; cooling system capacity 11.7L (11.1US qt).

Transmission (to front wheels): Automatic "Turbo Hydra–Matic" 440–T4, hydraulic torque converter and 4-speed Planetary gear set; final drive ratio 2.73; 2.84.

Gear ratios: Max torque multiplication in converter 1.68 times, Planetary gear set ratios: 2.92; 1.57; 1; OD 0.7; R 2.38.

Chassis: Integral body with front sub–frame; front and rear independent suspension, front McPherson strut (coil springs), lower longitudinal control arm, antiroll bar, rear control arm, shock absorber strut, fibre glass transverse leaf spring and level control system; telescopic damper. Servo/power assisted disc brakes (ventilated),optional with ABS (Teves), diameter, front 26.0cm, rear 25.4cm, optional ABS Teves system; pedal actuated parking brake to rear wheels; power assisted rack and pinion steering; fuel tank capacity 69L (15.2Gal) [18.2US Gal]; tyres 205/70 R 15, T type 215/65 R 15, wheel rims 6J.

Buick Riviera

Dimensions: Wheelbase 274.5cm, track 152/152cm, clearance 15cm, turning circle 12.8m, load space capacity 13.8cu ft (390dm3). Length 477cm, width 182cm, height 136cm.

Performance: Max speed approx 124mph/200kmh; speed at 1000rpm in direct gear (2.84) 26.4mph/42.4kmh; power to weight ratio from 14.4kg/kW (10.6kg/PS); consumption approx 11–17L/100km (25.7– 16.6mpg) [21.4–13.8US mpg].

Buick Reatta

Luxury 2–seater Hardtop Coupe with a 3.8 Litre V6 engine. Four wheel disc brakes, ABS, Automatic. Launched February 1988. Convertible prevue 1990.

3.8 Litre V6
123kW–165hp–167PS
Fuel Injection

Buick Reatta

Body, Weight (laden): 2–door Coupe, 2–seater; approx 1540kg.

Engine data (SAE net): 6–cylinder in V 90deg (96.52 x 86.36mm), 3791cm3; compression ratio 8.5:1; 123kW (165hp) [167PS] at 5200rpm, 32.4kW/L (43.4hp/L) [44.1PS/L]; 285Nm (29.0lbft) at 2000rpm; unleaded regular grade.

Engine construction: Designated LN 3 "3800." Transverse front engine. Hydraulic tappets, central camshaft (chain); 4 bearing crankshaft; counter–balance shaft; oil capacity 3.8L (3.6US qt); electronic fuel injection. 12V 54/69Ah Battery, 120A alternator; cooling system capacity 11L (10.4US qt).

Transmission (to rear wheels): Automatic "Turbo Hydra–Matic" 440– T4, hydraulic torque converter and 4-speed Planetary gear set, 4– speed/Overdrive, central selector lever, final drive ratio 2.97.

Gear ratios: Max torque multiplication in converter 1.68 times, Planetary gear set ratios: 2.92; 1.57; 1; OD 0.7; R 2.38.

Chassis: Integral body with front sub–frame; front and rear independent suspension; front McPherson strut (coil springs) lower longitudinal control arm, antiroll bar, rear control arm, shock absorber strut, fibre glass transverse leaf spring and level control system; telescopic damper. Servo/power assisted disc brakes, front ventilated, diameter, front 26.4cm, rear 25.9cm, Teves ABS system; pedal actuated parking brake to rear wheels; power assisted rack and pinion steering; fuel tank capacity 69L (15.2Gal) [18.2US Gal]; tyres 215/65 R 15, wheel rims 6J.

Dimensions: Wheelbase 250cm, track 153/153cm, clearance 15cm, turning circle 12.1m, load space capacity 10.2cu ft (290dm3). Length 466cm, width 185cm, height 130cm.

Performance: Max speed above 124mph/200kmh; speed at 1000rpm in OD 35mph/56.3kmh; acceleration 0 – 60mph/97kmh under 10secs; power to weight ratio from 12.5kg/kW (9.2kg/PS); consumption approx 11–17L/100km (25.7–16.6mpg) [21.4–13.8US mpg].

Buick Reatta

Cadillac

CADILLAC — USA

Cadillac Motor Car Division, 2860 Clark Avenue, Detroit, Michigan 48232, USA

Top of the General Motors Corporation range. The largest constructor of luxury models.

Model range
Seville – De Ville – Fleetwood Brougham – Eldorado – Allante

Cadillac Seville

Luxurious Saloon/Sedan with front wheel drive and independent suspension, V8 engine. Autumn 1979: new body, front wheel drive. Autumn 1985: new body, compact dimensions. 1988: new 4.5 Litre V8 engine. Modifications to details of car body. 1989: Seville Touring Saloon/Sedan (STS) with shorter final drive ratio.

Cadillac Seville STS

4.5 Litre V8
115kW–155hp–157PS
Central/Single Point Injection

Body, Weight (unladen): 4–door, 5–seater Saloon/Sedan; approx 1575kg.

Engine data (SAE net): 8–cylinder in V 90deg (92 x 84mm), 4467cm3; compression ratio 9:1; 115kW (156hp) [157 PS] at 4000rpmm 25.7kW/L (34.4hp/L) [35.1PS/L]; 326Nm (240.6lbft) at 2800rpm; unleaded regular grade.

Engine construction: Designated LR6. Transverse mounted front engine, hydraulic tappets, central camshaft. Light–alloy cylinder block; crankshaft with 5 bearings; oil capacity 4.7L (4.4US qt); Rochester electronic central/single point fuel injection. AC R44LTS6K spark plugs; 12V 45Ah Battery, alternator 120A; cooling system capacity approx 11.4L (10.8US qt).

Transmission (on front wheels): Automatic; "Turbo Hydra-Matic" 440–T4, hydraulic torque converter with 4–speed Planetary gear set, final drive ratio 2.97, STS 3.33

Gear ratios: Max torque multiplication in converter 1.63 times, Planetary gear ratios: 2.92; 1.57; 1; OD 0.7; R 2.38.

Cadillac Seville

Chassis: Integral body with front sub frame; independent suspension front and rear; front McPherson strut (coil springs), control arm and antiroll bar, rear control arm, damper, fibreglass transverse leaf spring and level control system, optional rear antiroll bar; telescopic damper. Servo/power assisted disc brakes, disc diameter front 26.0cm, rear 25.4cm. ABS System (Teves ITT II); pedal actuated parking brake system at rear wheels; power assisted rack and pinion steering; fuel tank capacity 71L (15.6Gal) [18.8US Gal]; tyres 205/75 R 15, wheel rims 6 J, optional 215/65 R 15.

Dimensions: Wheelbase 274.5cm, track 152/152cm, clearance 15cm, turning circle 12.8m, load space 14.1cu ft (400dm3). Length 484.5cm, width 180cm, height 136.5cm.

Performance: Max speed over 115mph/185kmh, speed at 1000rpm in top gear 32.5-36.5mph/52.3-58.7kmh; acceleration 0 – 60mph/97kmh 9.9secs; power to weight ratio from 13.7kg/kW (10kg/PS); consumption approx 11–16L/100km (25.7-17.7mpg) [21.4-14.7US mpg].

Cadillac De Ville–Sixty Special–Fleetwood

De-Luxe model with front wheel drive. Transverse engine (V8 injection and Overdrive automatic transmission. Designated "C- Body". Launch April/May 1984. The diesel version has not been available since 1986. 1988: 4.5 instead of 4.1 Litre-V8. 1989 with greater dimensions and modifications to body.

Cadillac De Ville Sedan

Body Weight (unladen):
De Ville: 4–door, 6–seater Saloon/Sedan: 1575kg. 2–door, 6–seater Coupe: 1540kg.
Fleetwood: 4–door, 6–seater Saloon/Sedan; approx 1610kg; 2 door Coupe, 6–seater; 1570kg.
Fleetwood Sixty Special: 4–door, 6–seater Saloon/Sedan; approx 1635kg.

4.5 Litre V8
115kW–155hp–157PS
Central/Single Point Injection

Engine data (SAE net): 8–cylinder in V 90deg (92 x 84mm), 4467cm3; compression ratio 9:1; 115kW (155hp) [157PS] at 4000/min, 25.7kW/L (34.4hp/L) [35.1PS/L]; 326Nm (240.6lbft) at 2800/min; unleaded regular grade.

Engine construction: Designated LR 6. Transverse mounted front engine. Hydraulic tappets, central camshaft; light–alloy cylinder block; crankshaft with five bearings; oil capacity 4.7L (4.4US qt); Rochester electronic central/single point injection. AC R44LTS6K spark plugs; 12V 69Ah battery, alternator 120A; cooling system capacity approx 11.4L (10.8US qt).

Transmission (on front wheels): Automatic; "Turbo Hydra-Matic" 440–T4, hydraulic torque converter and 4–speed Planetary gear set, selector lever at steering wheel; final drive ratio 2.97.

Cadillac Fleetwood Sedan

Gear ratios: Max torque multiplication in converter 1.63 times, Planetary gear set ratios: 2.92; 1.57; 1; OD 0.7; R 2.38.

Chassis: Integral body with front sub-frame; independent suspension front and rear; front McPherson struts lower control arm and antiroll bar, rear shock

Cadillac

absorber, lower control arm and antiroll bar; coil springs, telescopic damper; level control system. Servo/power assisted brakes, front ventilated discs, diameter 25.6cm, rear drums, optional ABS–Teves System; pedal actuated rear wheel parking brake; power assisted rack and pinion steering; fuel tank capacity 68L (14.9Gal) [18US Gal]; tyres 205/70 R 14, wheel rims 6J.

Dimensions: Coupe: wheelbase 281.5cm, track 153/152cm, clearance 14cm, turning circle approx 12.2m. Load space 18cu ft (510dm3). Length 515cm, width 184cm, height 139.5cm.
Saloon/Sedan: Wheelbase 289cm. Load space 18.4cu ft (520dm3). Length 522.5cm.

Performance: Max speed approx 115mph/185kmh; speed at 1000rpm in top gear 36.2mph/58.3kmh; acceleration 0 – 60mph/97kmh 9.9secs; power to weight ratio from 13.4kg/kW (9.7kg/PS); consumption approx 10–16L/100km (28.2–17.7mpg) [23.5–14.7US mpg].

Cadillac Fleetwood Coupe

Cadillac Brougham

Very well known de–luxe model, in 1985 it was the only line produced by Cadillac with rear wheel drive. 1986 saw the 5 Litre V8 engine, built to Saloon/Sedan specifications with modified equipment. Restyling for 1989.

```
5 Litre V8
104–127kW–140/170hp–142/172PS
1 4V Carb
```

Body, Weight: 4–door, 6–seater Saloon/Sedan; approx 1935kg.

Engine data (SAE net): 8–cylinder in V 90deg (96.52 x 85.98mm), 5033cm3; compression ratio 8:1; 104kW (140hp) [142PS] at 3200rpm, 20.7kW/L (27.7hp/L) [28.2PS/L]; 346Nm (255.3lbft) at 2000rpm; unleaded regular grade.
Or: (94.89 x 88.39mm), 5001cm3; compression ratio 8.0:1; 127kW (170hp) [172PS] at 4000rpm, 25.4kW/L (34hp/L) [34.4PS/L]; 339Nm (250.2lbft) at 2600/min.

Engine construction: Designated LV 2/LG8. Hydraulic tappets, central camshaft (gearwheels); crankshaft with 5 bearings; oil capacity 4.7L (4.4US qt); 1 Rochester downdraught 4V carb. AC FR3LS6 spark plugs; 12V 69Ah Battery, alternator 100A; cooling system capacity 14.4L (13.6US qt).

Transmission (rear wheels): a) Automatic; "Turbo Hydra–Matic" 200–4R, hydraulic torque converter and 4–speed Planetary gear set. Selector lever at steering wheel, final drive ratio 2.73: 3.23.
b) For 170hp; 3–speed THM 400, hydraulic torque converter and 3– speed Planetary gear set. Selector lever at steering wheel, final drive ratio 3.73.

Gear ratios: a) Automatic OD; Max torque multiplication in converter 1.9 times, Planetary gear set ratios; 1st 2.74; 2nd 1.57; 3rd 1; OD 0.67; R 2.07.
b) 3–Speed automatic; Max torque multiplication in converter 2 times; Planetary gear set ratios; 1st 2.48; 2nd 1.48; 3rd 1; R 2.08.

Cadillac Brougham

Chassis: Box section chassis; front upper A arm, lower single control arm with tension strut and coil springs, front antiroll bar; rear rigid axle with coil springs; rear lower control arm and upper semi–trailing arm leading to differential, antiroll bar, telescopic damper also with rear pneumatic level control system. Servo/power assisted brakes, front ventilated discs, diameter 29.8cm, rear drums; pedal operated parking brake system to rear wheels; power assisted recirculating ball steering; fuel tank capacity 95L (20.9Gal) [25.1US Gal]; tyres 225/75 R 15, wheel rims 6J.

Dimensions: Wheelbase 308.5cm, track 157/154cm, clearance 14cm, turning circle 13.4m, load space 19.6cu ft (555dm3). Length 561.5cm, width 194cm, height 144cm.

Performance: Max speed approx 112–118mph/180–190kmh, speed at 1000rpm in top gear (2.63) 41.4mph/66.7kmh; acceleration 0 – 60mph/97kmh 14.3secs; power to weight ratio from 14kg/kW (11kg/PS); consumption approx 11–18L/100km (25.7–15.7mpg) [21.4– 13.1US mpg].

Cadillac Eldorado

Luxury American coupe with front wheel drive. Autumn 1978: new edition with petrol or diesel engine and smaller body. 1983: more powerful petrol engine. More compact dimensions for 1986. New 4.5 Litre V8 engine for 1988.

Cadillac Eldorado

```
4.5 Litre V8
115kW–155hp–157PS
Central/Single Point Injection
```

Body, Weight (unladen): 2–door Saloon/Sedan, 5–seater; approx 1550kg.

Engine data (SAE net): 8–cylinder in V 90deg (92 x 84mm), 4467cm3; compression ratio 9:1; 115kW (155hp) [157PS] at 4200rpm, 25.7kW/L (34.4hp/L) [35.1PS/L]; 326Nm (240.6lbft) at 2800rpm; unleaded regular grade.

Engine construction: Designated LR6. Transverse front engine. Hydraulic tappets, central camshaft (chain); light–alloy cylinder block; crankshaft with 5 bearings; oil capacity 4.7L (4.4US qt); Rochester electronic central/single point injection. AC R44LTS6K spark plugs; 12V 69Ah Battery, alternator 120A; cooling system capacity 11.4L (10.8US qt).

Transmission (to front wheels): Automatic "Turbo Hydra–Matic" 440–T4; hydraulic torque converter and 4-speed Planetary gear set), final drive ratio: 2.97; 3.33

Cadillac Eldorado

Gear ratios: Max torque multiplication in converter 1.68 times, Planetary gear set ratios: 2.92; 1.57; 1; OD 0.7; R 2.38.

Cadillac • Carbodies

Chassis: Integral body with front sub-frame; front and rear independent suspension; front McPherson struts (coil springs), lower longitudinal arm and control arm, antiroll bar, rear control arm, shock absorber strut, fibreglass transverse leaf spring and level control system, also available with antiroll bar; telescopic damper. Servo/power assisted ventilated disc brakes, diameter 26.0cm, rear 25.4cm, also available with ABS Teves ITT II system; pedal actuated parking brake system to rear wheels; power assisted rack and pinion steering; fuel tank capacity 71L (15.6Gal) [18.8US gal]; tyres 205/70 R 15, wheel rims 6 J, with tyres 215/65 R 15.

Dimensions: Wheelbase 274.5cm, track 152/152cm, clearance 15cm, turning circle 12.8m, load space 14cu ft (400dm3). Length 486cm, width 182cm, height 136.5cm.

Performance: Max speed above 115mph/185kmh. Speed at 1000rpm in top gear 36.5mph/58.7kmh; acceleration 0 – 60mph/97kmh 9.9secs; power to weight ratio from 13.5kg/kW (9.9kg/PS); consumption approx 11–16L/100km (25.7–17.7mpg) [21.4–14.7USmpg].

Cadillac Allante

Two door Convertible/Coupe Hardtop with Cadillac-Mechanic body and Pininfarina interior. Launch September 1986. 1989, 4.5 Litre V8 engine with 200hp.

```
4.5 Litre V8
149kW-200hp-203PS
Fuel Injection
```

Cadillac Allante

Body, Weight (unladen): 2-door Convertible/Coupe Hardtop, 2-seater; approx 1585kg.

Engine data (SAE net): 8-cylinder in V 90deg (92 x 84mm), 4467cm3; compression ratio 9:1; 149kW (200hp) [203PS] at 4400rpm, 33.4kW/L (44.7hp/L) [45.4PS/L]; 366Nm (270.1lbft) at 3200rpm; unleaded premium grade.

Engine construction: Designated LQ 6. Transverse front engine. Hydraulic tappets, central camshaft (chain); light-alloy cylinder block; crankshaft with 5 bearings; oil capacity 5.7L (5.4US qt); electronic fuel injection SPFI. ACR44LTS6K spark plugs; 12V 69Ah Battery, 120A alternator; cooling system capacity 11.4L (10.8US qt).

Transmission (to front wheels): Automatic "Turbo Hydra-Matic" F7, hydraulic torque converter and 4-speed Planetary gear set, final drive ratio 2.95.

Gear ratios: Max torque multiplication in converter 1.63 times, Planetary gear set ratios: 2.92; 1.57; 1; OD 0.7; R 2.38.

Cadillac Allante

Chassis: Integral body with front sub-frame; front and rear independent suspension; front McPherson strut (coil springs) lower longitudinal arm and control arm, shock absorber strut, fibreglasss cross leaf spring and telescopic damper. Servo/power assisted disc brakes (front ventilated), diameter front 26.0cm, rear 25.4cm, ABS Bosch System III; pedal actuated parking brake system to rear wheels; power assisted rack and pinion steering; fuel tank capacity 83L (18.2Gal) [21.9US Gal]; tyres 225/55VR 16, wheel rims 7J.

Dimensions: Wheelbase 252.5cm, track 153.5/153.5cm, clearance 16cm, turning circle 11.6m, load space 16.2cu ft (460dm3). Length 453.5cm, width 186.5cm, height 132.5cm.

Performance: Max speed above 124mph/210kmh, speed at 1000rpm in top gear 32.8mph/52.8kmh; acceleration 0 – 62mph/97kmh 8.5secs; power to weight ratio from 10.6kg/kW (7.8kg/PS); consumption approx 11–18 L/100km (28.2–15.7mpg) [23.5–13.1US mpg].

CARBODIES GB

Carbodies Sales and Service Ltd, Holyhead Road, Coventry CV5 8JJ, England.

English manufacturer, specialising in the manufacture of the London Black Cab.

Carbodies Taxi FX 4 R/S

Robust Saloon/Sedan with 6 or 7-seater. Built to specifications of Taxi or Car-Hire firms. Launch London 1958. Birmingham, 1982: Rover diesel engine and transmission.

```
2.3/2.5 Diesel
45/50kW-60/67hp-61/68PS
Injection Pump
```

Body, Weight: 4-door Saloon/Sedan, 6/7-seater: kerbweight (DIN) 1560kg.

Engine data (DIN): 4-cylinder in-line (90.47 x 88.9mm), 2286cm3; compression ratio 23:1; 45kW (60hp) [61PS] at 4000rpm, 19.6kW/L (26.3hp/L) [26.7PS/L]; 139Nm (102.5lbft) at 1800rpm. Engine for FX 4 S: (90.47 x 97mm), 2494cm3; compression ratio 21:1; 50kW (67hp) [68PS] at 4000rpm, 20.1kW/L (26.9hp/L) [27.3PS/L]; 155Nm (114.3lbft) at 1800rpm.

Engine construction: Land Rover prechamber diesel engine (Ricardo Comet V); side camshaft (chain); crankshaft with 3/5 bearings; oil capacity 6.25L (6US qt); CAV-injection pump. KLG glow plugs; 12V 68Ah Battery, alternator; cooling system capacity approx 10L (9.5US qt).

Carbodies Taxi FX 4 R/S

Transmission (to rear wheels): a) 5-speed manual (Rover); floor shift, final drive ratio 3.91 or 4.8.
b) Borg Warner Automatic; hydraulic torque converter and 3-speed Planetary gear set, final drive ratio 3.91 or 4.8.

Gear ratios: a) 5-speed manual: 1st 3.321; 2nd 2.087; 3rd 1.396; 4th 1; 5th 0.79; R 3.428.
b) Automatic: Max torque multiplication in converter 2.1 times, Planetary gear set ratios; 1st 2.39; 2nd 1.45; 3rd 1; R 2.09.

Chassis: Cross brace box section frame, with A-arm and coil springs, rear rigid axle with semi-elliptic spring, rear antiroll bar, piston type damper. Servo/power assisted drum brakes, mechanical handbrakes to rear wheels; power assisted worm and wheel steering; fuel tank capacity 52L (11.4Gal) [13.7US Gal]; tyres 175R 16, 185 R 16 or 6.00-16.

Dimensions: Wheelbase 281cm, track 142/142cm, turning circle 7.6m. Length 458cm, width 174cm, height 177cm.

Performance: Max speed (according to engine) 65–78mph/105–125kmh (manufacturers test specifications), speed at 1000rpm in direct gear 19.3–15.7mph/31–25.3kmh; power to weight ratio 34.7kg/kW (25.6kg/PS); comsumption (average) 8–10L/100km (35.3–28.2mpg) [29.4–23.5US mpg] –manufacturers test specifications.

PRS

PRS DATABASE SERVICES LTD

BUILD YOUR INFORMATION BASE WITH PRS

INTRODUCTION TO A UNIQUE SERVICE:

The PRS Automotive Database is the most comprehensive and detailed available. Over the past four years, more than £3 million has been invested in its development. Now in its fifth year of supplying data to the automotive industry, PRS has built up a client base comprising over 65 of the world's leading vehicle manufacturers and component companies.

The majority of these companies used to carry out their data analysis requirement in-house. PRS' database division provides a service which eliminates the duplication, throughout the industry, of data collection and analysis.

By using the PRS database service, market analysis costs are reduced and more time becomes available for the essential task of planning. Trends can be identified, new competitors tracked and changes in technology highlighted. Awareness of such developments is vital in a world of interesting competitiveness.

THE SERVICE

FEATURES
- Coverage: cars, trucks, buses, diesel engines and components.
- Type of data: production, registrations, vehicle population and specifications (history & forecasts).
- Geographic areas include Western Europe (17 countries) USA, Japan, South America and South Korea.
- Frequency annual and monthly.
- PRS provides a friendly software "package" solution for either pc or mainframe systems.
- Delivery can be on diskette, on-line, magnetic tape or hard copy.
- Developed by industry specialists.
- Sources include recognised government and trade association data enhanced by contiuous original research programmes and further supported by PRS exchange agreements with vehicle and component manufacturers.
- Customisation to suit your needs is PRS' speciality.
- Assistance to fully exploit the databases is given via PRS' customer services department.

BENEFITS
- Whichever sector of the automotive industry you are in, PRS can provide you with the information you need.
- Whether you are involved with after-market or original equipment planning, PRS can assist.
- European or even global market analysis is now possible.
- Regular updates of your data are assured.
- PRS data can be used with any hard/software combination.
- PRS' software provides an immediately usable, fast and flexible means of providing the desired output.
- High quality data are guaranteed.
- Data to the highest level of detail and accuracy possible are developed.
- The database can be extended to incorporate information specific to your product range.
- A help line between PRS and the client is provided at all times in case of queries.

For further information contact:

Bill Pumphrey
PRS Consulting Group Inc
PO Box 1001, Darien,
Connecticut 06820
Tel: 010 1 203 656 1505

Marie Lester, PRS Database Services Ltd
44-48 Dover Street, London,
W1X 3RF
Tel: 409 1635   Fax: 629 0221

Kuni Fukui
PRS Asia Pacific Ltd
Azabudai Uni-House 104
1-1-20 Azabudai
Minato-Ku, Tokyo 106
Tel: 010 81 3 582 0096

CATERHAM — GB

Caterham Car Sales and Coachworks Ltd, Seven House, Town End, Caterham Hill, Surrey CR3 5UG, England.

Small English manufacturer, continuing production of the early Lotus Seven.

Caterham Super Seven

Successor of the Lotus Seven having certain differences to the Ford engine and plastic body. Autumn 1986: new quality version with Ford–Cosworth with four valves per cylinder.

```
1600 GT
62kW–83hp–84PS
1 2V Carb
```

Engine for 1600 GT

Body, Weight: No–door Roadster, 2–seater: kerbweight (DIN) from 580 kg, gross vehicle weight 820kg.

Engine data (DIN): 4–cylinder in-line (80.98 x 77.62mm), 1599cm3; compression ratio 9:1; 62kW (83hp) [84PS] at 5500rpm, 38.6kW/L (51.7hp/L) [52.5PS/L]; 125Nm (92.2lbft) at 3500rpm; leaded premium grade.
With Catalyst: 1.6 injection OHC, (79.96 x 79.52mm), 1598cm3; compression ratio 8.5:1; 70kW (94hp) [95PS] at 5800rpm; 123Nm (90.7lbft) at 4600rpm; unleaded regular grade.
With turbocharger: 97kW (130hp) [132PS] at 5700rpm; approx 180Nm (132.8lbft) at approx 2800rpm.

Engine construction: Ford "Kent" side camshaft, crankshaft with 5 bearings; oil capacity 3.6L (3.4US qt); 1 Weber downdraught 2V carb 32 DGAV; Motorcraft AGR 12 spark plugs; 12V 40 Ah Battery, alternator 35/45 A; cooling system capacity 5.7L (5.4US qt).

Transmission (to rear wheels): 4 or 5–speed manual; final drive ratio 3.636 or 3.92. Optional limited slip differential.

Gear ratios: a) 4–speed manual: 1st 3.337; 2nd 1.995; 3rd 1.418; 4th 1; R 3.867. b) 5–speed manual: 1st 3.358; 2nd 1.809; 3rd 1.258; 4th 1; 5th 0.825; R 3.37.

Chassis: Tubular frame with keystone A-arm, coil springs and antiroll bar, rear De Dion axle or rigid axle with twin trailing arms and one reaction arm, coil springs, and optional antiroll bar; telescopic damper. Front disc and rear drum brakes, or four wheel disc brake, disc diameter 22.9cm, mechanical handbrake to rear wheels; rack and pinion steering; fuel tank capacity 36L (7.9Gal) [9.5US Gal]; tyres 185/70HR 13 or 185/60HR 14, wheel rims 6 or 7J.

Caterham Super Seven

Dimensions: Wheelbase 225cm, track 127/132cm, clearance 11cm, turning circle 10.4m, load space 2.7cu ft (75dm3). Length 338cm, width 158cm, height 104/109cm.

Performance: Max speed 100mph/161kmh (manufacturers test specifications), speed at 1000rpm in 4th gear 18.5–20.2mph/29.7–32.5kmh; acceleration 0–62mph/100kmh 7.8secs; power to weight ratio 9.4kg/kW (6.9kg/PS); consumption approx 8–10L/100km (35.3–28.2mpg) [29.4–23.5US mpg].

```
Sprint
81/99.5kW–108.5/133hp–110/135PS
2 2V Carbs
```

Engine for 1600 Sprint and 1700 Super Sprint.

As 1600 GT except:

Engine data (DIN): 4–cylinder in-line (80.98 x 77.62mm), 1599cm3; compression ratio 9:1; 81kW (108.5hp) [110PS] at 6000rpm, 50.7kW/L (68hp/L) [68.8PS/L]; 143Nm (105.5lbft) at 4800rpm. 1700 Super Sprint: (83.27 x 77.62mm), 1690cm3; compression ratio 10.5:1; 99.5kW (133hp) [135PS] at 6000rpm; 58.9kW/L (78.9hp/L) [79.9PS/L]; 171Nm (126.1lbft) at 4500rpm.

Engine construction: 2 horizontal-Weber 2V carbs 40 DCOE. NGK BP7ES or B8ECS spark plugs.

Chassis: Tyres 185/70 HR 13, wheel rims 6J.

Performance: Max speed 105–112mph/169–180kmh (manufacturers test specifications); acceleration 0–62mph/100kmh 6.9 and 5.9secs.

```
1600/1700
110.5/125kW–148/167.5hp–150/170PS
2 2V Carbs
```

Motor for Cosworth 1600/1700 4 valve BDR.

As 1600 GT, except:

Engine data (DIN): 4–cylinder in-line (80.98 x 77.62mm), 1599cm3; compression ratio 11:1; 110.5kW (148hp) [150PS] at 6500rpm, 69.2kW/L (92.7hp/L) [93.9PS/L]; 176Nm (129.8lbft) at 5500rpm. 1700: (83.27 x 77.62mm), 1690cm3; 125kW (167.5hp) [170PS] at 6500rpm.

Engine construction: Ford Cosworth 1600/1700 BDR 16. Light alloy cylinder heads, 4 valves per cylinder, valves in V, 2 overhead camshafts; 2 horizontal Weber 2V carbs 40 and 45 DCOE. NGK B8ECS (1600) spark plugs.

Transmission: 1700 only available with 5–speed manual, final drive ratio 3.62 or 3.92. Limited slip differential.

Chassis: 1700; available only with De Dion axle and rear antiroll bar; tyres 185/60HR 14, wheel rims 6J.

Performance: Max speed 115mph/185kmh, 1700–120mph/193kmh (manufacturers test specifications); acceleration 0–62mph/100kmh 5.6secs, approx 5secs with 1700 engine.

CHEVROLET — USA

Chevrolet Motor Division, Engineering Centre, 30003 Van Dyke, Warren, Michigan, USA.

General Motors' top and best known marque in the USA.

MODEL RANGE
Cavalier – Corsica–Beretta – Celebrity – Camaro – Caprice – Corvette – Blazer – Lumina.

Chevrolet Cavalier RS

Chevrolet

Chevrolet Cavalier

Compact vehicle with front wheel drive and 2 Litre 4 cylinder transverse engine, 4-speed manual or Automatic: part of General Motors' J-car family. Launched April 1981. New front end, 1984. 1985 sports model Z24 with 2.8 Litre V6 engine. 1987: 2.8-Litre- engine with more power. 1988 modifications to body details. 1989: modifications to interior.

Chevrolet Calavier Station Wagon

Body, Weight (laden):Cavalier: 4-door Saloon/Sedan, 5-seater; 1100kg; 2-door Coupe, 5-seater; 1095kg; 5-door Estate/Station Wagon, 5-seater; 1125kg. Cavalier Z24: 2-door Coupe, 5-seater; 1175kg; 2-door Convertible/Cabriolet, 5-seater; 1240kg.

2 Litre
67kW-90hp-91PS
Central/Single Point Injection

Engine data (SAE net): 4-cylinder in-line (89 x 80mm), 1991cm3; compression ratio 9.0:1; 67kW (90hp) [91PS] at 5600rpm, 33.6kW/L (45hp/L) [45.7PS/L]; 147Nm (108.4lbft) at 3200rpm; unleaded regular grade.

Engine construction: Designated LL 8. Transverse front engine, hydraulic tappets, side camshaft (chain); crankshaft with 5 bearings; light-alloy cylinder head; oil capacity 3.8L (3.6US qt); Rochester electronic central/single point fuel injection. AC FR3LM spark plugs, 12V 54Ah battery, 74A alternator; cooling system capacity approx 7.5L (7.1US qt).

Transmission (to front wheels): a) 5-speed manual; final drive ratio 3.45.
b) Automatic THM 125; hydraulic torque and 3-speed Planetary gear set, mid selector lever, final drive ratio 3.18.

Gear ratios: a) 5-speed manual: 1st 3.91; 2nd 2.15; 3rd 1.45; 4th 1.03; 5th 0.74; R 3.58.
b) Automatic: Max torque multiplication in converter 2.7 times, Planetary gear set ratios;: 2.84; 1.6; 1; R 2.07.

Chassis: Integral body. Front sub-frame, front McPherson struts and lower control arms, antiroll bar; rear independent suspension with swinging arms, optional antiroll bar, coil springs and telescopic damper at front and rear. Servo/power assisted brakes, front discs (ventilated), diameter 24.7cm, rear drum; parking brake to rear wheels; power assisted rack and pinion steering; fuel tank capacity 51L (11.2Gal) [13.2US Gal]; tyres 185 R 13, also at 215/60 R 14, wheel rims 5.5/6J.

Chevrolet Cavalier Z24 Coupe

Dimensions: Wheelbase 257cm, track 141/140cm, minimum clearance 14cm, turning circle approx 11.3m, load space 13.6cu ft (385dm3). Length 454cm, width 168cm, height 136cm. Coupe: load space 13.2cu ft (375dm3), convertible 10.4cu ft (295dm3); height 132cm. Station wagon: load space 64.4cu ft (1825dm3), height 138cm.

Performance: Max speed approx 96–102.5mph/155–165kmh, speed at 1000rpm in 5th gear 27.7mph/44.6kmh; power to weight ratio from 16.3kg/kW (12kg/PS); consumption approx 8–13L/100km (35.3– 21.7mpg) [29.4–18.1US mpg].

2.8 Litre V6
93/97kW - 125/130hp - 127/132PS
Fuel Injection

Also for Z24 and Station Wagon

As 2 Litre, except:

Weight: Heavier by 40kg

Engine data (SAE net): 6-cylinder in V 60deg (88.9 x 76.2mm), 2838cm3; compression ratio 8.9:1; 93kW (125hp) [127PS] at 4500rpm, 32.8kW/L (43.9hp/L) [44.8PS/L]; 217Nm (160.1lbft) at 3600rpm.
Z24: 97kW (130hp) [132PS]; 224Nm (165.3lbft).
Wagon: 95kW (127hp) [129PS]; 217Nm (160.1lbft)

Engine construction: Designated LB 6. 4 bearing crankshaft; central camshaft; Rochester electronic fuel injection; AC R43LTSE sparkplugs; cooling system capacity 10.5L (9.9 US qt).

Transmission: a) 5-speed manual, final drive ratio 3.61.
b) Automatic, final drive ratio 3.18; 2.84

Gear ratios: a) 5-speed manual: 1st 3.50; 2nd 2.05; 3rd 1.38; 4th 0.94; 5th 0.72; R 3.42.
b) Automatic: As 2 Litre.

Performance: Max speed above 112mph/180kmh, speed at 1000rpm in 5th gear 27.3mph/44.0kmh; power to weight ratio from 11.5kg/kW (17.6hp/L) [8.5kg/PS]; consumption approx 11–16L/100km (25.7– 17.7mpg) [21.4–14.7US mpg].

Chevrolet Cavalier Z24 Convertible

Chevrolet Corsica – Beretta

Compact vehicle with front wheel drive, transverse built-in 2-litre-four cylinder or 2.8-litre-V6, 5 speed gear or Automatic, also available as Corsica Saloon/Sedan or Beretta Coupe. Launched at the beginning of 1987. 1989 Corsica also available in a five door version.

Body, Weight (unladen): Beretta: 2-door Coupe, 5-seater; approx 1195kg. Corsica: 4 door Saloon/Sedan, 5-seater; approx 1175kg; 5 door Saloon/Sedan, 5-seater; approx 1185kg

2 Litre
67kW-90hp-91PS
Central/Single Point Injection

Engine data (SAE net): 4-cylinder in-line (99 x 80mm), 1991 cm3; compression ratio 9.0:1; 67kW (90hp) [91PS] at 5600rpm, 33.6kW/L (45hp/L) [45.7PS/L]; 147Nm (108.5lbft) at 3200rpm; unleaded regulard grade.

Engine construction: Designated LL8. Transverse front engine, hydraulic tappets, side camshafts (chain); light alloy cylinder heads; 5 main bearing crankshaft; oil capacity 3.8L (3.6US qt); Rochester electronic central/single point injection. AC FR3LM sparkplugs; 12V 45/55 Ah battery, 42 A alternator; cooling system capacity approx 8.2L (3.6US qt).

Transmission (to all wheels): a) 5-speed manual, final drive ratio 3.83.
b) Automatic THM 125, hydraulic torque converter and 3-speed Planetary gear set, final drive ratio 3.18.

Gear ratios: a) 5-speed manual: 1st 3.73; 2nd 2.15; 3rd 1.33; 4th 0.92; 5th 0.74; R 3.50.

Chevrolet

b) Automatic: Max torque multiplication 2.7 times, lower in Planetary gear set: 2.84; 1.6; 1; R 2.07.

Chevrolet Beretta

Chassis: Integral body. Front sub–frame, front McPherson struts and lower A–arm, anti-roll bar; rear independent suspension with trailing arms, anti–roll bars, coil springs and telescopic damper front and rear. Servo/power assisted brakes, front discs (ventilated), diameter 24.2cm, rear drums; parking brake to rear wheels; power assisted rack and pinion steering; fuel tank capacity 51.5L (11.3Gal) [13.6US Gal]: tyres 185/75 R 13 optional 195/70 R 14, wheel rims 55J. Beretta tyres 195/70 R 14 optional 206/60 R 14, wheel rims 6J.

Dimensions: Wheelbase 262.5cm, track 142/140cm, clearance 15cm, turning circle approx 11.6m, load space 13.4cu ft (380dm3). Length 466, Coupe 475.5cm, width 173.5cm, height 143, Coupe 140.5cm.

Performance: Max speed above 106mph/170kmh, speed at 1000rpm in 5th gear (185/75 R 13) 25.2mph/40.6kmh; power to weight ratio from 17.5kg/kW (12.9kg/PS); consumption approx 8–13L/100km (35.5-21.7mpg) [29.4-18.1US mpg].

Chevrolet Corsica Hatchback

```
2.8 Litre V6
97kW–130hp–132PS
Fuel Injection
```

As 2–Litre, except:

Weight: Heavier by 45kg

Engine data (SAE net): 6-cylinder in V 60deg (88.9 x 76.2mm), 2838cm3; compression ratio 8.9:1; 97kW (130hp) [132PS] at 4700rpm, 34.2kW/L (45.8hp/L) [46.5PS/L]; 217Nm (160.1lbft) at 3600rpm.

Engine construction: Designated LB6. 4 main bearing crankshaft; central camshaft: Rochester electronic fuel injection; AC R43CTLSE spark plugs; cooling system capacity 10.7L (10.1US qt).

Transmission: a) 5-speed manual, final drive ratio 3.61.
b) Automatic, final drive ratio 3.18.

Gear ratios: a) 5-speed manual 1st 3.50; 2nd 2.05; 3rd 1.38; 4th 0.94; 5th 0.72; R 3.42.
b) Automatic: As 2 Litre.

Performance: Max speed above 115mph/185kmh; speed at 1000rpm in 5th gear 27.3mph/44kmh; power to weight ratio 12.6kg/kW (9.2kg/PS). Consumption approx 11 – 16L/100km (25.7-17.7mpg) [21.4-14.7US mpg].

Chevrolet Beretta GTU

Chevrolet Celebrity

Model series with front wheel drive, 4–cylinder and V6 engine: 4–speed manual or automatic transmission. Internally designated "A–body". Launched in December 1981. 1984: new Estate/Station Wagon. 1989 will see the introduction of a 2.5-Litre engine with more power and anti-vibration arms.

```
2.5 Litre
73kW–98hp–99PS
Central/Single Point Injection
```

Body, Weight: 4–door Saloon/Sedan, 5–seater; kerbweight (DIN) 1250kg. 5–door Estate/Station Wagon, 5–seater; kerbweight (DIN) 1310kg. Heavier by 25kg with air conditioning.

Engine data (SAE net): 4–cylinder in–line (101.6 x 76.2mm), 2471cm3; compression ratio 8.3:1; 73kW (98hp) [99PS] at 4800rpm, 29.5kw/L (39.5hp/L) [40.1PS/L]; 183Nm (135.1lbft) at 3200rpm; unleaded regular grade. Later: 82kW (111hp) [112PS].

Engine construction: Designated LR 8. Transverse front engine. Hydraulic tappets, side camshaft (toothed belt); 5 bearing crankshaft; oil capacity 2.8L (2.6US qt); Rochester electronic central/single point injection. 12V 54Ah Battery, 85A alternator; cooling system capacity approx 9.2L (8.7US qt).

Transmission (to front wheels): Automatic THM 125, hydraulic torque converter and 3–speed Planetary gear set, selector lever at steering column, final drive ratio 2.84.

Chevrolet Celebrity Eurosport

Gear ratios: Max torque multiplication in converter 2.35 times, Planetary gear set ratios: 2.84; 1.6; 1; R 2.07.

Chassis: Integral body. Front sub–frame, front McPherson struts and lower A arm, antiroll bar; rear rigid axle with trailing arm, torsion bar spring, Panhard rod, coil springs and telescopic damper. Servo/power assisted brakes, front discs (ventilated), diameter 24.7cm, rear drums; pedal actuated parking brake to rear wheels; power assisted rack and pinion steering; fuel tank capacity 59L (13Gal) [15.6US Gal]; tyres 185/75 R 14, optional 195/75 or 195/70 R 14, wheel rims 5.5".

Dimensions: Wheelbase 266.5cm, track 149/144.5cm, clearance min 14cm, turning circle 12.2m, load space 16.2cu ft (460dm3). Length 478.5cm, width 176cm, height 137.5cm. Estate/Station Wagon: Load space 75cu ft (2125dm3), length 484.5cm.

Performance: Max speed approx 99mph/160kmh, speed at 1000rpm in top gear 25mph/40.2kmh; power to weight ratio from 16.8kg/kW (12.4kg/PS); consumption approx 9–14L/100km (31.4–20.2mpg) [26.1– 16.8US mpg].

```
2.8 Litre V6
93kW–125hp–127PS
Fuel Injection
```

As 2.5 Litre, except:

Chevrolet

Weight: Heavier by 38kg.

Engine data (SAE net): 6–cylinder in V 90deg (88.9 x 76.2mm), 2838cm3; compression ratio 8.9:1; 93kW (125hp) [127PS] at 4500rpm, 32.8kW/L (43.9hp/L) [44.8PS/L]; 217Nm (160.1lbft) at 3600rpm.

Engine construction: Designated LB6. 4 bearing crankshaft; oil capacity 3.8L (3.6US qt); Rochester electronic fuel injection. AC R43LTSE sparkplugs; 85/100A Alternator; cooling system capacity approx 11.8L (11.2US qt).

Transmission: a) Automatic, final drive ratio 2.84
b) Automatic 4–speed, final drive ratio 3.33.

Gear ratios: a) Automatic: Max torque multiplication in converter 2.35 times, Planetary gear set ratios: 2.84; 1.6; 1; R 2.07.
b) 4-speed Automatic: Max torque multiplication in converter 1.95 times, Planetary gear set ratios: 1st 2.92; 2nd 1.56; 3rd 1; OD 0.7; R 2.38.

Performance: Max speed approx 109–115mph/175–185kmh, speed at 1000rpm in 5th gear 27.3mph/43.9kmh; power to weight ratio from 13.5kg/kW (9.9kg/PS); consumption approx 10–17L/100km (28.2– 16.6mpg) [23.5–13.8US mpg].

Chevrolet Celebrity Eurosport Wagon

Chevrolet Lumina

New model. Front wheel drive, transverse engine and Automatic gear shift, all round independent suspension, four wheel disc brakes, categorised between the Celebrity and the Caprice. Launched in January 1989. Provisional data.

Chevrolet Lumina

2.5 Litre
82kW-110hp-112PS
Central/Single Point Injection

Body, Weight: 4–door Saloon/Sedan, 5/6-seater; kerbweight (DIN) approx 1360kg; 2–door Coupe, 5/6-seater; kerbweight (DIN) approx 1340kg.

Engine data (SAE net): 4–cylinder in-line (101.6 x 76.2mm), 2471cm3; compression ratio 9:1; 82kW (110hp) [112PS] at 5200rpm, 33.2kW/L (44.5hp/L) [45.3PS/L]; 183Nm (135lbft) at 3200rpm; unleaded regular grade.

Engine construction: Designated LR 8. Transverse front engine. Hydraulic tappets, side camshaft (toothed belt); 5 bearing crankshaft; oil capacity 2.8/3.8L (2.6/3.6US qt); Rochester electronic central injection (EFI). AC R44TSX spark plugs; battery 12V 54Ah, alternator 56-78A; cooling system capacity approx 9.2L (8.7US qt).

Transmission (to front wheels): Automatic THM 125, hydraulic torque and 3 speed Planetary gear set, selector lever at centre or at steering wheel, final drive ratio 2.84.

Gear ratios: Automatic; max torque multiplication in converter 2.35, Planetary gear set ratios: 2.84; 1.6; 1; R 2.07.

Chassis: Integral body with front sub-frame; independent suspension front and rear; front McPherson struts (coil springs), lower longitudinal control arm, and antiroll bar, rear control arm, shock absorber struts, transverse leaf spring, antiroll bar, telescopic dampers. Servo/power assisted brakes optionally with ABS (Delco-Moraine), disc diameter front (ventilated) 26.7cm, rear 25.6cm; pedal actuated parking brake to rear wheels; power assisted rack and pinion steering; fuel tank capacity approx 65L (14.3Gal) [17.2US Gal]; tyres 195/70 R 14, 205/70 R 14 or 215/60 R 16, wheel rims 5.5 or 6.5".

Dimensions: Wheelbase 273cm, track 151/147cm, clearance 15cm, turning circle 12.5m. Load space approx 15.9cu ft (450dm3). Length approx 490cm, width approx 185cm, height approx 135cm.

Performance: Max speed approx 102.5mph/165kmh. Speed at 1000rpm in direct gear 25.5mph/41kmh; power to weight ratio from 16.3kg/kW (12.0kg/PS); consumption approx 9-14L/100km (31.4-20.2mpg) [26.1-16.8US mpg].

Chevrolet Lumina

3.1 Litre V6
104kW-140hp-142PS
Fuel Injection

As 2.5-Litre, except:

Weight: Heavier by approx 40kg

Engine data (SAE net): 6-cylinder in V 60deg (80.9 x 84mm), 3128cm3; compression ratio 8.8:1; 104kW (140hp/L) [142PS] at 4800rpm, 33.2kW/L (44.5hp/L) [45.4PS/L]; 251Nm (185.2lbft) at 3200rpm.

Engine construction: Designated LH 0. 4 bearing crankshaft; central camshaft (chain); oil capacity 3.8L (3.6US qt); Rochester electronic fuel injection. Alternator 66-97A; cooling system capacity approx 12L (11.4US qt).

Transmission: a) Automatic, final drive ratio 2.84;
b) 4-speed Automatic, final drive ratio 3.33.

Gear ratios: a) Automatic: max torque multiplication in converter 2.35, Planetary gear set ratios: 2.84; 1.6; 1; R 2.07;
b) 4-speed Automatic: max torque multiplication in converter 1.95, Planetary gear set ratios: 1st 2.92; 2nd 1.56; 3rd 1; OD 0.7; R 2.38.

Performance: Max speed approx 118mph/190kmh; acceleration 0-60mph/97kmh 10.6s; power to weight ratio from 13.3kg/kW (9.7kg/PS); consumption approx 10-16L/100km (28.2-17.7mpg) [23.5-14.7US mpg].

Chevrolet Camaro

Sports Coupe – Iroc-Z – Convertible

Four seater with a sporty note and tail gate. Engine from 2.8, 5.0 and 5.7 Litre engine displacement, manual and automatic transmission. Launched in December 1981, as "High–Output" 5 Litre V8 (Corvette) engine, 191hp with additional power. 1988: V8 engine with more power; also available for the Convertible. 1989, a new body version, the "RS".

2.8 Litre V6
101kW-135hp-137PS
Fuel Injection

Body, Weight: 3–door Sport Coupe, 4-seater; kerbweight (DIN) 1400kg; 2–door Convertible, 4-seater; kerbweight (DIN) 1480kg. Weight increased by 20kg with air conditioning.

Not available for Iroc-Z

Chevrolet

Engine data (SAE net): 6–cylinder in V 60deg (88.9 x 76.2mm), 2838cm3; compression ratio 8.9:1; 101kW (135hp) [137PS] at 4900rpm, 35.5kW/L (47.6hp/L) [48.3PS/L]; 217Nm (160.1lbft) at 3900rpm; unleaded regular grade.

Engine construction: Designated LB 8. Hydraulic tappets, central camshaft (chain); 4 bearing crankshaft; oil capacity 3.8L (3.6US qt). Rochester electronic fuel injection. AC R42CTS sparkplugs 12V 54Ah Battery, 85/100A alternator; cooling system capacity approx 12.2L (11.5US qt).

Transmission (to rear wheels): a) 5–speed manual, final drive ratio, 3.42.
b) Automatic, hydraulic torque and 4 speed Planetary gear set, final drive ratio 3.42
Optional limited slip differential.

Gear ratios: a) 5–speed manual: 1st 4.03; 2nd 2.37; 3rd 1.50; 4th 1; 5th 0.76; R 3.76.
b) Automatic with OD: Max torque multiplication in converter 2.35 times, Planetary gear set ratios: 1st 3.06; 2nd 1.63; 3rd 1; OD 0.7; R 2.29.

Chevrolet Camaro RS

Chassis: Integral body; front lower A arm, shock absorber struts, coil springs and antiroll bar, rear rigid axle with trailing arms, coil springs and Panhard rod, antiroll bar, front and rear telescopic dampers. Servo/power assisted brakes, front discs (ventilated), diameter 26.7cm, rear drums; mechanical handbrake to rear wheels; power assisted recirculating ball steering; fuel tank capacity 59L (13Gal) [15.6US Gal]; tyres 215/65 R 14, wheel rims 7 J.

Dimensions: Wheelbase 256.5cm, track 152.5/155cm, clearance min 13cm, turning circle 12m. Load space 12.4/31cu ft (350/880dm3), Convertible 5.1cu ft (145dm3). Length 488cm, width 185cm, height 128cm.

Performance: Max speed approx 106–112mph/170–180kmh, speed at 1000rpm in 5th gear 28.8mph/46.4kmh; power to weight ratio from 13.9kg/kW (10.2kg/PS); consumption approx 10–15L/100km (28.2– 18.8mpg) [23.5–15.7US mpg].

```
5 Litre V8
127kW–170hp–172PS
Fuel Injection
```

Available for Iroc-Z on demand.

As 2.8 Litre, except:

Weight: Kerbweight from 1470kg, Iroc-Z from 1405kg.

Engine data (SAE net): 8–cylinder in V 90deg (94.89 x 88.39mm), 5001cm3; compression ratio 9.3:1; 127kW (170hp) [172PS] at 4400rpm, 25.4kW/L (34hp/L) [34.4PS/L]; 346Nm (255.3lbft) at 2400rpm.

Engine construction: Designated LO 3. 5 bearing crankshaft; oil capacity 4.5L(4.3US qt); Rochester electronic fuel injection; AC R45TS sparkplugs; cooling system capacity approx 15.5L(14.7US qt).

Chevrolet Camaro Iroc-Z Convertible

Transmission: a) 5–speed manual, final drive ratio, 3.08.
b) 4-speed Automatic, final drive ratio 2.73.

Gear ratios: a) 5–speed manual: 1st 2.95; 2nd 1.94; 3rd 1.34; 4th 1; 5th 0.63; R 2.76.
b) Automatic: Max torque multiplication in converter 1.91 times, Planetary gear set ratios: 1st 3.06; 2nd 1.63; 3rd 1; OD 0.7; R 2.29.

Performance: Max speed approx 115–121mph/185–195kmh, speed at 1000rpm in 5th gear 39mph/62.1kmh; power to weight ratio from 11.1kg/kW (8.5kg/PS); consumption approx 10–18L/100km (28.2– 15.7mpg) [23.5-13.1US mpg].

```
5 Litre V8
146/164/171kW-195/220/230hp-
198/223/233PS
Fuel Injection
```

Engine for Iroc-Z

As 2.8 Litre, except:

Body, Weight: Kerbweight (DIN) from 1480kg.

Engine data (SAE net): 8–cylinder in V 90deg (94.89 x 88.39mm), 5001cm3; compression ratio 9.3:1.
With Automatic: 146kW (195hp) [198PS] at 4000rpm, 29.2kw/L (39.1hp/L) [39.6PS/L]; 400Nm (295.2lbft) at 2800rpm.
With 5–speed manual: 164kW (220hp) [223PS] at 4400rpm, 32.8kW/L (43.9hp/L) [44.6PS/L]; 393Nm (290lbft) at 3200rpm.
With dual exhaust: 171kW (230hp) [233PS] at 4600rpm, 34.2kW/L (45.8hp/L) [46.6PS/L]; 407Nm (300.4lbft) at 3200rpm.

Engine construction: Designated LB9. 5 main bearing crankshaft; oil capacity 4.5L (4.3US qt); Bosch electronic fuel injection. AC R45TS sparkplugs; 105A Alternator; cooling system capacity approx 16.8L (15.9US qt).

Transmission: a) 5–speed manual, final drive ratio 3.08; 230hp 3.45.
b) 4-speed Automatic, final drive ratio 2.73.

Gear ratios: a) 5–speed manual: 1st 2.95; 2nd 1.94; 3rd 1.34; 4th 1; 5th 0.63; R 2.76.
230hp: 1st 2.75; 2nd 1.94; 3rd 1.34; 4th 1; 5th 0.74; R 2.76.
b) Automatic with OD: Max torque multiplication in converter 2.15 times, Planetary gear set ratios: 1st 3.06; 2nd 1.63; 3rd 1; OD 0.7; R 2.29.

Chevrolet Camaro Iroc-Z

Chassis: Iroc-Z with four wheel disc brakes, disc dia front 30.1cm, rear 29.6cm; tyres optionally 245/50 ZR 16, wheel rims 8 J.

Performance: Max speed approx 131–143mph/210–230kmh, speed at 1000rpm in 5th gear (0.63:1) 38.6mph/62.1kmh; power to weight ratio from 8.7kg/kW (6.3kg/PS); consumption approx 11–20L/100km (25.7– 14.1mpg) [21.4–11.8US mpg].

```
5.7 Litre V8
171kW–230hp–233PS
Fuel Injection
```

Only available for Iroc-Z

As 2.8 Litre, except:

Weight: Kerbweight (DIN) from 1520kg

Engine data (SAE net): 8–cylinder in V 90deg (101.6 x 88.39), 5733cm3; compression ratio 9.3:1; 171kW (230hp) [233PS] at 4400rpm, 29.8kW/L (39.9hp/L) [40.6PS/L]; 448Nm (331lbft) at 3200rpm.
With dual exhaust: 179kW (240hp) [243PS] at 4400rpm, 31.2kW/L (41.8hp/L) [42.4PS/L]; 468Nm (345.4lbft) at 3200rpm

Engine construction: Designated L 98. 5 bearing crankshaft; oil capacity 4.5L(3.6US qt); Bosch electronic fuel injection. AC R45TS sparkplugs 105A Alternator; cooling system capacity approx 16.8L (15.9US qt).

Transmission: 4-speed Automatic, final drive ratio 2.77; 240hp 3.27.

Chevrolet 133

Chevrolet Camaro Iroc–Z Convertible

Gear ratios: Max torque multiplication in converter 1.85 times, Planetary gear set ratios: 1st 3.06; 2nd 1.63; 3rd 1; OD 0.7; R 2.29.

Chassis: Optionally with four wheel disc brakes, disc diameter front 30.1cm, rear 29.6cm; tyres optionally with 245/50 ZR 16, wheel rims 6 J.

Dimensions: Iroc–Z; track 154/154cm.

Performance: Max speed above 137mph/225kmh, speed at 1000rpm in 4th gear (2.77) 38.6mph/62.1kmh; power to weight ratio from 8.5kg/kW (6.3kg/PS); consumption approx 11–20L/100km (25.7–14.1mpg) [21.4– 11.8US mpg].

Chevrolet Caprice

A very common model in the USA. Available with 6–cylinder and V8 engines. 1984: modifications to body and interior; model series enlarged with the addition of a Coupe. 1985: new 4.3 Litre base engine. 1988 now Saloon/Sedan and Estate/Station Wagon available. 1989 5-Litre-V8 also available.

Chevrolet Caprice Brougham LS

Body, Weight (laden):

Caprice: 4–door Saloon/Sedan, 6–seater; approx 1675kg.
Caprice Classic: 4–door Saloon/Sedan, 6–seater; approx 1685kg. 5–door Estate/Station Wagon, 8–seater; approx 1900kg.
Caprice Classic Brougham: 4–door Saloon/Sedan, 6–seater; approx 1710kg.

```
5 Litre V8
127/104kW-170/140hp-172/142PS
Central-Single Point Injection/Carb
```

Engine data (SAE net): 8–cylinder in V 90deg (94.89 x 88.39mm), 5001cm3; compression ratio 9.3:1; 127kW (170hp) [172PS] at 4400rpm, 25.4kW/L (34hp/L) [34.4PS/L]; 346Nm (35.3mkp) at 2400rpm.
Engine for Estate/Station Wagon (with carb): (96.52 x 85.98mm), 5033cm3; compression ratio 8:1; 104kW (140hp) [142PS] at 3200rpm, 20.7kW/L (27.7hp/L) [28.2PS/L]; 346Nm (255.3lbft) at 2000rpm.

Engine construction: Designated LO 3/LV2. Hydraulic tappets, central camshaft (chain); 5 bearing crankshaft; oil capacity 4.5L (4.3US qt); Rochester electronic central injection/1 carb. AC R45TS spark plugs; Battery 12V 42Ah, Alternator 84A; cooling system capacity approx 15L (14.2US qt).

Transmission (to rear wheels): Automatic hydraulic torque and 4-speed Planetary gear set, selector level at steering wheel, final drive ratio 2.73; 3.08; Estate/Station Wagon 2.93; 3.23. Optional limited slip differential.

Gear ratios: Max torque multiplication in converter 1.91 times, Planetary gear set ratios: 1st 2.74; 2nd 1.57; 3rd 1; 4th 0.67 R 2.07.

Chevrolet Caprice Classic Station Wagon

Chassis: Box section frame with cross members; front upper trailing A arm, lower single control arm with elastic torsion struts and coil springs, antiroll bar; rear rigid axle with coil springs, lower longitudinal arms and upper axle control arms, optional antiroll bar. Servo assisted brakes, disc dia front (ventilated) 27.9, Station Wagon 30.1cm, rear drums; pedal actuated parking brake to rear wheels; Servo/power assisted recirculating ball steering; fuel tank capacity 95, Station Wagon 83L; tyres 205/75 R 15, wheel rims 6 J, Station Wagon 225/75 R 15, wheel rims 7 J.

Dimensions: Wheelbase 294.5cm, track 157/154cm, clearance 15cm, turning circle 13.6m. Load space 20.8cu ft (590dm3). Length 539/540cm, width 191.5cm, height 143.5cm.
Station Wagon: Track 158/163cm, clearance 20cm, turning circle 13.8m. Load space 88cu ft (2490dm3). Length 548.5cm, width 201.5cm, height 148cm.

Performance: Max speed approx 106-115mph/170-185kmh, speed at 1000rpm in 4th gear 38.6mph/62.1kmh; power to weight ratio from 13.2kg/kW (9.7kg/PS); consumption (touring) approx 14-20L/100km (20.2-14.1mpg) [16.8-11.8US qt].

Chevrolet Corvette

Sports car with plastic body, rear independent suspension, four wheel disc brakes, electronic fuel injection, Overdrive, Automatic transmission and tail gate. Coupe launched in February 1983, convertible in January 1986. Autumn 1986: more power. 1989: 6-speed transmission and new high performance version, the ZR1 with 385HP.

Chevrolet Corvette

```
5.7 Litre V8
179/182kW–240/245hp–243/248PS
Fuel Injection
```

Body, Weight (laden): 3–door Sports Coupe, 2–seater; approx 1460kg. 2–door Convertible, 2–seater; approx 1480kg.

Engine data (SAE net): 8–cylinder in V 90deg (101.6 x 88.39mm), 5733cm3; compression ratio 9.5:1; 179kW (240hp) [243PS] at 4000rpm, 31.2kW/L (41.8hp/L) [42.4PS/L]; 454Nm (335.1lbft) at 3200rpm.
With twin exhausts: 182kW (245hp) [248PS] at 4300rpm, 31.7kW/L (42.4hp/L) [43.3PS/L]; 461Nm (340.2lbft) at 3200rpm; unleaded regular grade.

Engine construction: Designated L 98. Hydraulic tappets, central camshaft (chain); light–alloy cylinder heads; 5 bearing crankshaft; oil capacity 3.8L(3.6US qt); Bosch electronic fuel injection; dual exhaust. AC FR5LS sparkplugs 12V 54Ah Battery, 105A alternator; cooling system capacity 13.8L (13.1US qt).

Chevrolet

Transmission (to rear wheels): a) 6-speed manual, final drive ratio 3.54; later 3.33;
b) Automatic, hydraulic torque and 4-speed Planetary gear set, final drive ratio 2.59; 2.73; 3.09.
"Positraction" limited slip differential.

Gear ratios: a) 6 speed manual: 1st 2.68; 2nd 1.80; 3rd 1.29; 4th 1; 5th 0.50; R 2.50;
b) Automatic; max torque in converter 1.85, Planetary gear set ratios: 3.06; 1.63; 1; 0.70; R 2.29.

Chassis: Integral body frame with front and rear axle support, all round independent suspension, front upper A arm, rear trailing arm, control arm and steering tie rod; front and rear fibre glass leaf spring, antiroll bar and telescopic damper. Servo/power assisted (ABS Bosch) disc brakes (ventilated), disc diameter front 30.2/32.7cm, rear 30.2cm with pedal actuated parking brake to rear wheels; power assisted rack and pinion steering; fuel tank capacity 76L (16.7Gal) [20.1US Gal]; tyres 275/40 ZR 17 optional rear 315/35 ZR 17, wheel rims 9.5 or 11 J.

Dimensions: Wheelbase 244.5cm, track 151.5/153.5cm, clearance min 12cm, turning circle 12.6cm. Load space 18cu ft (510dm3), Convertible 6.7cu ft (190dm3). Length 448.5cm, width 180.5cm, height 118.5cm, convertible 118cm.

Performance: Max speed above 146mph/1235kmh, speed at 1000rpm in 5th gear 28.2mph/45.4kmh, in 6th gear 42.4mph/68.3kmh; power to weight ratio from 8.0kg/kW (5.9kg/PS); consumption (touring) approx 12–20L/100km (23.5–14.1mpg) [19.6–11.8US mpg].

Chevrolet Corvette Convertible

```
5.7 Litre V8/32V
287kW-385hp-390PS
Fuel Injection
```

Engine for ZR1

As 240/245 HP, except:

Body, Weight (laden): 3–door Coupe, 2-seater; approx 1550kg.

Engine data (SAE net): 8–cylinder in V 90deg (99 x 93mm), 5727cm3; compression ratio 11.25: 1; 287kW (385hp) [390PS] at 5800rpm, 50.1kW/L (67.1hp/L) [68.1PS/L]; 529Nm (390.4lbft) at 5200rpm.

Engine construction: designated LT5. 4 valves (in V22deg) per cylinder, 2 x 2 overhead camshafts (chain), light alloy cylinder heads and block.

Transmission: 6-speed manual, final drive ratio 3.54.

Gear ratios: 1st 2.68; 2nd 1.80; 3rd 1.29; 4th 1; 5th 0.751; 6th 0.50; R 2.50.

Chassis: Disc brakes, disc diameter front 32.7cm, rear 30.2cm; tyres front 275/40 ZR 17, rear 315/35 ZR 17.

Chevrolet Corvette ZR1

Dimensions: Width 188cm

Performance: Max speed approx 180mph/290kmh, speed at 1000rpm in 5th gear 28.2mph/45.4kmh, in 6th gear 43.4mph/69.9kmh; acceleration 0-60mph/97kmh approx 4.2s; power to weight ratio from 5.4kg/kW (4.0kg/PS); consumption (touring) approx 12-23L/100km (23.5-12.3mpg) [19.6-10.2US mpg].

Chevrolet Lumina APV

New model. Part of a series of vehicles in multiple use by GM. Fibreglass body, 3 sliding doors and tailgate, 5 to 7 seater; 3.1-Litre V6 engine, front wheel drive, Automatic gearshift. Data is provisional and incomplete.

```
3.1 Litre V6
90kW-120hp-122PS
Central/Single Point Injection
```

Body, Weight: 3–door Wagon with tailgate, 5-7-seater; kerbweight approx 1550kg.

Engine data (SAE net): 6-cylinder in V60deg (88.9 x 84mm), 3128cm3; compression ratio 8.8:1; 90kW (120hp) [122PS] at 4500rpm, 28.8kW/L (38hp/L) [39PS/L]; 231Nm (170.5lbft) at 3200rpm; unleaded regular grade.

Engine construction: Designated LH0. Transverse front engine. Hydraulic tappets, central camshaft (chain); 4 bearing crankshaft; light-alloy cylinder heads; oil capacity 3.8L (3.5US qt); Rochester electronic central/single point injection. AC R43CTLSE spark plugs; battery 12V 54/69 Ah, alternator 108/120A; cooling system capacity 10.7L (10.2US qt).

Transmission (to front wheels): Automatic THM 125, hydraulic torque and 3-speed Planetary gear set, selector lever at steering wheel or central console, final drive ratio 2.84.

Gear ratios: Max torque multiplication in converter 2.35, Planetary gear set ratios: 2.84; 1.6; 1; R 2.07.

Chassis: Box section frame with cross members; front independent suspension with coil springs, A arm and antiroll bar; rear rigid axle, longitudinal control arm, optionally with rear antiroll bar, telescopic damper. Servo/power assisted disc brakes, disc diameter front (ventilated) 26.7cm, rear drums, pedal actuated parking brake to rear wheels; power assisted rack and pinion steering; fuel tank capacity 76L (16.7Gal) [20.1US Gal]; tyres 205/70 R 14; 195/70 R 15, wheel rims 6 J.

Dimensions: Wheelbase 279cm, track 155/152cm clearance 18cm, turning circle 12.5m. Load space max 123.6cu ft (3500dm3). Length 491cm, width approx 185cm, height approx 165cm.

Performance: Max speed above 102mph/165kmh, speed at 1000rpm in top gear 25.5mph/41kmh; power to weight ratio from 17.2kg/kW (12.7kg/PS); consumption (touring) approx 10-16L/100km (28.2-17.7mpg) [23.5-14.7US mpg].

Chevrolet Lumina APV

Chevrolet Blazer S

All terrain vehicle with rear wheel and optional all wheel drive. 2.5 Litre or 2.8 Litre V6 engine. Launched in September 1982. 1986: V6 with fuel injection. From April 1988 also available with 4.3 Litre V6.

```
2.8 Litre V6
93kW-125hp-127PS
Central/Single Point Injection
```

Weight: 3–door Estate/Station Wagon, 4-seater, kerbweight 1430-1850kg.

Engine data (SAE net): 6–cylinder in V 60deg (88.9 x 76.2mm), 2838cm3; compression ratio 8.9:1; 93kW (125hp) [127PS] at 4800rpm, 32.9kW/L (44.1hp/L) [44.8PS/L]; 204Nm (151.5lbft) at 2400rpm; unleaded regular grade. Optionally for 2 wheel drive: 4-cylinder in-line (101.6 x 76.2mm), 2471cm3; compression ratio 8.3:1; 73kW (98hp) [99PS] at 4800rpm; 176Nm (129.9lbft) at 3200rpm.

Engine construction: Designated LR 2. Hydraulic tappets, central camshaft (chain); 4 bearing crankshaft; oil capacity 3.8L (3.5US qt); electronic central injection. AC R 42 CTS sparkplugs, battery 12 V 45/55 Ah, Alternator 85A; water coolant capacity approx 10L (9.5US qt).

Transmission (to rear or all wheels): a) 5-speed manual; final drive ratio 3.42; if required 3.73;
b) Automatic, hydraulic torque and 4-speed Planetary gear set, selector lever at steering wheel, final drive ratio, as a).
Optional limited slip differential. Engageable four wheel drive with limited slip central differential; reduction gears 2.72.

Gear ratios: a) 5-speed manual: 1st 3.76; 2nd 2.18; 3rd 1.36; 4th 1; 5th 0.86; R 3.76; Automatic: max torque multiplication in converter 1.9, Planetary gear set ratios: 1st 3.06; 2nd 1.63; 3rd 1; OD 0.7; R 2.29.

Chevrolet Blazer S

Chassis: Box section frame with crossmembers; front upper A arm, torsion bar, antiroll bar; rear rigid axle with semi elliptic springs, front and rear telescopic dampers. Servo/power assisted brakes with ABS to rear, front discs, parking brake to rear wheels; power assisted recirculating ball steering; fuel tank capacity 50L (11Gal) [13.2US Gal], optionally 76L (16.7Gal) [20.1US Gal]; tyres 195/75 R 15 optionally to 235/75 R 15.

Dimensions: Wheelbase 255cm, track 141.5/137.5cm, clearance 17.5cm, turning circle 10.8m, length 432.5cm, width 164.5cm, height 162.5cm.

Performance: Max speed approx 93–99mph/150–160kmh; speed at 1000rpm in top gear (3.42) 35.8mph/57.6kmh; power to weight ratio from 15.4kg/kW (11.4kg/PS); consumption approx 12–18L/100km (23.5–15.7mpg) [19.9–13.1US mpg].

```
4.3 Litre V6
119kW–160hp–162PS
Central/Single Point Injection
```

As 2.8 Litre, except:

Weight: Heavier by approx 75kg.

Engine data (SAE net): 6–cylinder in V 90deg (101.6 x 88.39mm), 4300cm3; compression ratio 9.3:1; 119kW (160hp) [162PS] at 4000rpm, 27.7kW/L (37.1hp/L) [37.7PS/L]; 312Nm (230.2lbft) at 2400rpm.

Chevrolet Blazer S 4x4

Engine construction: Designated LB 4. Bosch electronic central/single point injection. Cooling system capacity 12.3L (11.6US qt).

Performance: Max speed approx 106mph/170kmh; power to weight ratio from 12kg/kW (8.8kg/PS); consumption approx 12–22L/100km (23.5-12.8mpg) [19.6-10.7US mpg].

Chevrolet GMC Jimmy S 15

Identical car to the Chevrolet Blazer S 10, see there for technical data.

Chevrolet Blazer V

All terrain vehicle with four wheel drive (K10) or only to rear wheels. C10 4–speed or automatic transmission, V8 engine. For 1982 new V8 Diesel engine with 6.2 Litre displacement. 1987 fuel engine with injection.

```
5.7 Litre V8
157kW–210hp–213PS
Fuel Injection
```

Body, Weight: C10, 2–door 5–seater; 1880kg. K10, 2–door 5–seater; 2075kg.

Engine data (SAE net): 8–cylinder in V90deg (101.6 x 88.39mm), 5733cm3; compression ratio 9.3:1; 157kW (210hp) [213PS] at 4000rpm, 27.4kW/L (36.7hp/L) [37.2PS/L]; 407Nm (300.4lbft) at 2800rpm; unleaded regular grade.

Engine construction: Designated LS 9. Central camshaft (chain); 5 bearing crankshaft; oil capacity 5.7L (5.4US qt); optional oil cooler; electronic fuel injection. 61Ah Battery, 37/66A alternator; cooling system capacity 16.3L (15.4US qt).

Transmission (to rear wheels or all wheels): a) 4–speed manual, final drive ratio 2.73; 3.08.
b) Automatic, hydraulic torque converter and 3-speed Planetary gear set with OD, selector lever at steering column, final drive 2.73; 3.08. Optional limited slip differential, connection to four wheel drive (only for K10) with central limited slip differential, cross country reduction 2.0.

Gear ratios: a) 4–speed manual: 1st 6.32; 2nd 3.09; 3rd 1.69; 4th 1; R 7.44.
b) Automatic: Max torque multiplication in converter 1.9 times, Planetary gear set ratios: 2.74; 2nd 1.57; 3rd 1; OD 0.67; R 2.07.

Chassis: Box section frame with 5 cross members; front and rear rigid axles with semi–elliptic springs, front optional antiroll bar; telescopic dampers. C10 with front independent suspension. Servo/power assisted brakes, front discs (ventilated), diameter 30.1cm, rear drums; pedal actuated parking brake to rear wheels; power assisted recirculating ball steering; fuel tank capacity 95L (20.9Gal) [25.1US Gal], optionally 117L (25.7Gal) [30.9US Gal]; tyres 235/75 R 15, wheel rims 7 J.

Chevrolet Blazer V

Dimensions: Wheelbase 270.5cm, track 168/160cm, clearance 18cm, turning circle 13.1m. Length 469.5cm, width 202cm, height 187.5cm.

Performance: Max speed approx 106mph/170kmh, power to weight ratio from 12.0kg/kW (8.8kg/PS); consumption (touring) approx 12–25L/100km (23.5–11.3mpg) [19.6–9.1US mpg].

Chevrolet USA • Chevrolet BR

6.2L V8 Diesel
97kW–130hp–132PS
Injection Pump

As 210hp, except:

Weight: Heavier by 65kg

Engine data (SAE net): 8–cylinder in V90deg (101 x 97mm), 6217cm3; compression ratio 21.3:1; 97kW (130hp) [132PS] at 3600rpm, 15.6kW/L (20.9hp/L) [21.2PS/L]; 326Nm (241.1lbft) at 2000rpm.

Engine construction: Designated LH 6. Central camshaft (chain); 5 bearing crankshaft; oil capacity 8L (7.6US qt); diesel injection pump. Cooling system capacity 17L (16.1US qt).

Transmission: Automatic, final drive ratio 3.08; 3.42; 3.73.

Performance: Max speed approx 90mph/145kmh; power to weight ratio from 22.1kg/kW (16.2kg/PS); consumption approx 12–22L/100km (23.5–12.8mpg) [19.6–10.7US mpg].

Chevrolet GMC Jimmy V

Identical vehicle to the Chevrolet Blazer V, see there for technical data.

CHEVROLET BR

General Motors do Brasil SA, Av. Goias, 1805 Sao Caetano do Sul, Sao Paulo, Brasil.

General Motors' factory in Brasil.

MODEL RANGE
Chevette – Monza – Opala – Comodoro – Diplomata

Chevrolet Chevette

Brazilian version of the early Opel Kadett with 1.6 Litre four cylinder engine. The L and SL are regular exports. Launched on April 24th 1973, the four door Saloon/Sedan followed in October 1978 and the Estate/Station Wagon, "Marajo" in September 1980. Not available in Europe. Available additionally as an Automatic in 1985.

1.6 Litre
54/60kW–72/81hp–73/82hp
1 2V Carb

Body, Weight: 2–door Saloon/Sedan, 5–seater; kerbweight (DIN) 920kg gross vehicle weight 1340kg. 4–door Saloon/Sedan, 5–seater; kerbweight (DIN) 920kg gross vehicle weight 1340kg. 3–door Estate/Station Wagon, 5–seater; kerbweight (DIN) 960kg gross vehicle weight 1410kg.

Engine data (SAE net): (82 x 75.7mm), 1599cm3; compression ratio 8.5:1; 54kW (72hp) [73PS] at 5200rpm, 33.8kW/L (45.3hp/L) [45.7PS/L]; 123Nm (90.7lbft) at 3000rpm; leaded regular grade.
Operating with ethyl alcohol: compression ratio 12:1; 60kW (81hp) [82PS] at 5200rpm; 128Nm (94.4lbft) at 2800rpm.

Chevrolet Chevette SL

Engine construction: 1 overhead camshaft (toothed belt); 5 bearing crankshaft; oil capacity 3.5L (3.3US qt); 1 Weber downdraught 2V carb, 288L (1.4 Litre: 1 Weber downdraught 2V carb, 228). 12V 36Ah Battery, 32A alternator; cooling system capacity approx 7L (6.6US qt).

Transmission (to rear wheels): a) 4–speed manual (only for export), final drive ratio 4.188.
b) 5–speed manual, final drive ratio 3.8.
c) Optional Automatic "Turbo Hydra–Matic", hydraulic torque converter and 3–speed Planetary gear set, central selector lever, final drive ratio 3.54.

Gear ratios: a) 4–speed manual: 1st 3.746; 2nd 2.157; 3rd 1.378; 4th 1; R 3.815.
b) 5–speed manual: 1st 3.746; 2nd 2.157; 3rd 1.378; 4th 1; 5th 0.84; R 3.815.
c) Automatic "Turbo Hydra–Matic": Max torque multiplication in converter 2.25 times, Planetary gear set ratios: 2.4; 1.48; 1; R 1.92.

Chassis: Integral body; front A–arm and coil springs, rear rigid axle with longitudinal Panhard rod and coil springs, front and rear antiroll bar and telescopic damper. Brakes with optional Servo/power assistance, front discs, rear drums, disc diameter 23.8cm; mechanical handbrake to rear wheels; rack and pinion steering; fuel tank capacity 58L (12.7Gal) [15.3US Gal]; tyres 165–13 or 165 SR 13 on wheel rims 5.5J, optional tyres 175/70 SR 13.

Dimensions: Wheelbase 239.5cm, track 130/130cm, clearance 14cm, turning circle 9.8m. Load space 11.5cu ft (325dm3), Estate/Station Wagon max 53.3cu ft (1510dm3). Length 418.5cm, Wagon 421.5cm, width 157cm, height 132.5, Estate/Station Wagon 138.5cm.

Performance: Max speed 90–99.5mph/145–160kmh (manufacturer's test specifications), speed at 1000rpm in 5th gear 21.3mph/34.2kmh; power to weight ratio from 15.3kg/kW (11.2kg/PS); consumption (touring) approx 7–12L/100km (40.4–23.5mpg) [33.6–19.6US mpg].

Chevrolet Chevette Marajo SL/E

Chevrolet Monza

Compact vehicle with front wheel drive, part of General Motors' J–Car family. Saloon/Sedan with tailgate launched in April 1982 and tail step/notchback Saloon/Sedan in March 1983. 1986 saw the 1.8 and 2 Litre engine introduced. 1989 Tail gate model is no longer in production.

1.8 Litre
70kW–94hp–95PS
1 2V Carb

Body, Weight: 2/4–door Saloon/Sedan, 5–seater; kerbweight (DIN) 1030/1060kg gross vehicle weight 1540/1560kg.

Engine data (SAE net): 4–cylinder in–line (84.8 x 79.5mm), 1796cm3; compression ratio 8.8:1; 70kW (94hp) [95PS] at 5800rpm, 39.0kW/L (52.3hp/L) [52.9PS/L]; 140Nm (103.3lbft) at 3000rpm; leaded regular grade (86R).
Operating with ethyl alcohol: compression ratio 12:1; 70kW (94hp) [95PS] at 5600rpm, 148Nm (109.2lbft) at 3000rpm.

Engine construction: Transverse engine. Light–alloy cylinder head. Hydraulic tappetts, 1 overhead camshaft (toothed belt); 5 bearing crankshaft; oil capacity 3L (2.8US qt); 1 Weber downdraught 2V carb 288L. 12V 36/54Ah Battery, 35/65A alternator; cooling system capacity approx 7L (6.6US qt).

Transmission (to front wheels): 5–speed manual; final drive ratio 4.188; SR 3.72.

Gear ratios: 1st 3.42; 2nd 1.95; 3rd 1.28; 4th 0.89; 5th 0.71; R 3.333.
For SR 1st 3.42; 2nd 2.16; 3rd 1.48; 4th 1.12; 5th 0.89; R 3.33.

Chassis: Integral body; front A arm and McPherson strut (negative steering offset), rear swinging arm and compound linkage to rear axle, front and rear coil springs, telescopic damper; front antiroll bar and optional rear. Servo/power assisted brakes, front discs, diameter 23.3cm, rear drums, mechanical handbrake to rear wheels; rack and pinion steering; fuel tank capacity 61L (13.4Gal) [16.1US Gal]; tyres 165 SR 13 or 185/70 SR 13, wheel rims 5.5J, for SR optionally 195/60 HR 14.

Chevrolet BR

Dimensions: Wheelbase 257.5cm, track 140.5/140.5cm, clearance 17cm, turning circle 11m. Load space 19.6–53cu ft (555-1500dm3), VDA 15.4–41.8cu ft (435–1180dm3). Length 436.5cm, width 167cm, height 135.5cm.

Performance: Max speed 99.5mph/160kmh (manufacturer's test specifications), speed at 1000rpm in 5th gear 22.9mph/36.8kmh; acceleration 0 – 62mph/100kmh 14.5secs (manufacturer's test specifications); power to weight ratio 14.7kg/kW (10.8kg/PS); consumption approx 7–10km (40.4-28.2mpg) [33.6-23.5US mpg].

Chevrolet Monza SL/E

```
2 Litre
73/81kW–98/108.5hp–99/110PS
1 2V Carb
```

As 94hp, except:

Engine data (SAE net): 4–cylinder in–line (86 x 86mm), 1998cm3; compression ratio 8.8:1; 73kW (98hp) [99PS] at 5600rpm, 36.5kW/L (48.9hp/L) [49.5PS/L]; 159Nm (117.3lbft) at 3500rpm; leaded regular grade. Operating with ethyl alcohol: compression ratio 12:1; 81kW (108.5hp) [110PS] at 5600rpm, 40.5kW/L (54.3hp/L) [55PS/L]; 170Nm (125.4lbft) at 3000rpm.

Transmission (to front wheels): a) 5–speed manual; final drive ratio 3.94. b) Automatic; hydraulic torque converter and 3–speed Planetary gear set; final drive ratio 3.333.

Gear ratios: a) 5–speed manual: 1st 3.42; 2nd 1.95; 3rd 1.28; 4th 0.89; 5th 0.71; R 3.333.
For SR: 1st 3.42; 2nd 2.16; 3rd 1.48; 4th 1.12; 5th 0.89; R 3.33.
b) Automatic; Max torque multiplication in converter 2.4 times, Planetary gear set ratios: 1st 2.84; 2nd 1.60; 3rd 1; R 2.07.

Dimensions: SR; length 426.5cm, height 135cm.

Performance: Max speed 102.5–109mph/165–175kmh (manufacturer's test specifications), speed at 1000rpm in 5th gear 24.3/39.1kmh; acceleration 0 – 62mph/100kmh 12.6/10.1secs (manufacturer's test specifications); power to weight ratio 14.1kg/kW (10.4kg/PS); consumption approx 7–11L/100km (40.4-25.7mpg) [33.6-21.4US mpg].

Chevrolet Monza Classic

Chevrolet Opala – Comodoro – Diplomata

Based on the Opel Rekord C with 4 or 6–cylinder Chevrolet engine. The Opala was launched in Sao Paulo in 1968, the Comodoro in Autumn 1970, and the Diplomata in November 1979.

```
2.5 Litre
62/65kW–83/87hp–84/88PS
1 2V Carb
```

Body, Weight: 4–door Saloon/Sedan, 5/6–seater; kerbweight (DIN) 1175kg gross vehicle weight 1595kg. 3–door Estate/Station Wagon, 5/6–seater; kerbweight (DIN) 1240kg, gross vehicle weight 1660kg.

Engine data (SAE net): 4–cylinder in–line (101.6 x 76.2mm), 2471cm3; compression ratio 8:1; 62kW (83hp) [84PS] at 4400rpm, 25.1kW/L (33.6hp/L) [34.0PS/L]; 164Nm (121lbft) at 2000rpm.
Operating with ethyl alcohol: compression ratio 11:1; 65kW (87hp) [88PS] at 4000rpm, 190Nm (140.1lbft) at 2500rpm.

Engine construction: Designated GMB 151. Hydraulic tappets, side camshaft (toothed belt); 5 bearing crankshaft; oil capacity 3.5L (3.3US qt); 1 Weber downdraught 2V carb 288L. 12V 45Ah Battery, 32A Alternator; cooling system capacity approx 8.6L (8.1US qt).

Transmission (to rear wheels): a) 4 or 5–speed manual, steering wheel or floor shift, final drive ratio 3.54.
b) Available with ZF Automatic, hydraulic torque and 4–speed Planetary gear set, final drive ratio 3.54 or 3.25.
Optional limited slip differential.

Gear ratios: a) 4–speed manual: 1st 3.40; 2nd 2.16; 3rd 1.38; 4th 1; R 3.81. 5–speed manual: 1st 2.48, 2nd 1.48, 3rd 1, 4th 0.73, R 2.09.
b) Automatic: Max torque multiplication in converter 2.4 times, Planetary gear set ratios; 4–speed: 1st 2.48; 2nd 1.48; 3rd 1; 4th 0.73; R 2.09.

Chevrolet Diplomata

Chassis: Integral body; front upper keystone A arm., lower single control arm with elastic tension strut and coil springs, rear rigid axle with longitudinal A arm and coil springs, antiroll bar, telescopic damper. Servo/power assisted brakes, front disc (ventilated), rear drums, disc diameter 26.6cm; mechanical handbrake to rear wheels; worm and wheel steering, optional power assisted; fuel tank capacity 84L (18.5Gal) [22.2US Gal], with 5L (1.1Gal) [1.3US Gal] reserve; tyres 175SR 14, optional 195/70 SR 14, wheel rims 6J.

Dimensions: Wheelbase 267cm, track 143/141cm, clearance 15cm, turning circle 11.5m. Load space 12.2cu ft (347dm3), Estate/Station Wagon max 41.3/68.8cu ft (1170/1950dm3). Length 480, Estate/Station Wagon 481cm, width 176cm, height 141cm, Coupe 138cm. **Performance:** Max speed 92.5mph/149kmh (manufacturer's test specifications), speed at 1000rpm in top gear (3.54:1) 20.4mph/32.8kmh; power to weight ratio from 18.1kg/kW (13.3kg/PS); consumption (touring) approx 9–12L/100km (31.4– 23.5mpg) [26.1-19.6US mpg].

```
4.1 Litre
87/99.5kW–116.5/133hp–118/135PS
Carb
```

Chevrolet Diplomata Caravan

As 2.5 Litre, except:

Weight: 6–cylinder engine 60kg heavier.

Chevrolet BR • Chrysler

Engine data (SAE net): 6–cylinder in-line (98.4 x 89.6mm), 4093cm3; compression ratio 8:1; 87kW (116.5hp) [118PS] at 4000rpm, 21.3kW/L (28.5hp/L) [28.8PS/L]; 275Nm (203lbft); leaded regular grade (70R).
With 2V carb.: 92.5kW (124hp) [126PS] at 4400rpm; 273Nm (201.5lbft) at 2300rpm. Operating with ethyl alcohol: compression ratio 10:1; 99.5kW (133hp) [135PS] at 4000rpm; 295Nm (217.7lbft) at 2000rpm.

Engine construction: Designated GMB 250; 7 bearing crankshaft; oil capacity 5L (4.7US qt); cooling system capacity approx 10.2L (9.6US qt).

Transmission: Final drive ratio 2.73, Automatic 3.08.

Gear ratios: 4-speed manual; 1st 3.07; 2nd 2.02; 3rd 1.39; 4th 1; R 3.81.
Automatic: as 4-cylinder version.

Chassis: Tyres 195/70SR 14.

Performance: Max speed 118mph/190kmh (manufacturer's test specifications), speed at 1000rpm in top gear (2.73:1) 26.7mph/42.9kmh; power to weight ratio from 12.5kg/kW (9.2kg/PS); consumption (touring) approx 10–15L/100km (28.2–18.8mpg) [23.5-15.7US mpg].

CHRYSLER — USA

Chrysler–Plymouth Division, 1220 E Jefferson, Detroit, Michigan 48215, USA.

Third greatest manufacturer of cars in the United States of America. Factory base for the Chrysler Corporation.

MODEL RANGE
ES – GS Turbo 2 – GTS – LeBaron – New Yorker – Fifth Avenue – TC by Maserati – Voyager

Chrysler ES

Export version of the Dodge Shadow and Plymouth Sundance. Compact Saloon/Sedan with tailgate and front wheel drive; 2.5 Litre 4-cylinder engine or 2.2 Litre Turbo. Launched in March 1986 For 1989 2.5 Litre Turbo.

**2.5 Litre
72kW–96.5hp–98PS
Central/Single Point Injection**

Body, Weight (laden): 3/5-door Saloon/Sedan, 5-seater; approx 1175kg.

Engine data (Catalyst DIN): 4-cylinder in-line (87.5 x 104mm), 2501cm3; compression ratio 9:1; 72kW (96.5hp) [98PS] at 4400rpm, 28.8kW/L (38.6hp/L) [39.2PS/L]; 180Nm (132.8lbft) at 2800rpm; regular unleaded grade.

Engine construction: Transverse front engine. Hydraulic tappets, 1 overhead camshaft (toothed belt); light-alloy cylinder head; 5 bearing crankshaft; 2 counter-balance shafts; oil capacity 3.8L (3.6US qt); Bosch/Holley electronic central/single point fuel injection. 12V 66Ah Battery, 90/120A alternator; cooling system capacity approx 8.5L (8US qt).

Transmission (to front wheels): a) 5-speed manual, final drive ratio 2.51.
b) Automatic "Torqueflite"; hydraulic torque converter and 3- speed Planetary gear set, selector lever central or at steering wheel, final drive ratio 3.02.

Chrysler ES

Gear ratios: a) 5-speed manual: 1st 3.29; 2nd 2.08; 3rd 1.45; 4th 1.04; 5th 0.72; R 3.14; b) Automatic: Max torque multiplication in converter 2 times, Planetary gear set ratios: 2.69; 1.55; 1; R 2.1.

Chassis: Integral body. Front McPherson strut and A-arm, rear rigid axle with longitudinal arms and Panhard rod, front and rear coil springs, telescopic damper and antiroll bar. Servo/power assisted brakes, front disc (ventilated), diameter 23.6cm, rear drums; pedal actuated parking brakes to rear wheels; power assisted rack and pinion steering; fuel tank capacity 53L (11.6Gal) [14US Gal]; tyres 195/60 HR, 205/50 VR 15, wheel rims 6J.

Dimensions: Wheelbase 246.5cm, track 146.5/145.5cm, clearance min. 11.5cm. Turning circle 11.0m. Load space 13.2/33.4cu ft (375/945dm3), Hatchback 13.1/33cu ft (370/935dm3). Length 436cm, width 171cm, height 134cm.

Performance: Max speed approx 99.5–106mph/160–170kmh, speed at 1000rpm in 5th gear 36.9mph/59.4kmh; power to weight ratio from 16.3kg/kW (12.0kg/PS); consumption approx 7–12L/100km (40.4– 23.5mpg) [33.6–19.6US mpg].

**2.5 Litre Turbo
107kW–144hp–146PS
Fuel Injection**

Engine for Turbo As 96.5hp, except:

Weight (laden): 25kg heavier.

Engine data (SAE nett): 4-cylinder in-line (87.5 x 104mm), 2501cm3; compression ratio 7.8:1; 107kW (144hp) [146PS] at 4800rpm, 42.8kW/L (57.3hp/L) [58.4PS/L]; 244Nm (108lbft) at 2000rpm; unleaded premium or regular grade.

Engine construction: Electronic fuel injection (multiport), 1 exhaust turbocharger M.H.I.

Chassis: Front disc brakes, diameter 25.6cm.

Performance: Max speed approx 115–121mph/185–195kmh; power to weight ratio from 11.2kg/kW (8.2kg/PS); consumption approx 9– 14L/100km (31.4–20.2mpg) [26.1–16.8US mpg].

Chrysler GS Turbo 2

Export version of the Dodge Daytona. Sport Coupe with front wheel drive and tail gate, 2.2 Litre Turbo engine with intercooler. Launched August 1983.

Chrysler GS Turbo 2

**2.2 Litre Turbo
130kW–174hp–177PS
Fuel Injection**

Body, Weight (laden): 3-door Coupe, 4-seater; approx 1195–1300kg.

Engine data (Catalyst DIN): 4-cylinder in-line (87.5 x 92mm), 2213cm3; compression ratio 8.2:1; 130kW (174hp) [177PS] at 5200rpm, 58.6kW/L (78.5hp/L) [80PS/L]; 276Nm (203.7lbft) at 3200rpm; unleaded premium grade.

Engine construction: Transverse front engine. Hydraulic tappets, 1 overhead camshaft (toothed belt); light-alloy cylinder heads; 5 bearing crankshaft; oil capacity 3.8L (3.6US qt); Bosch/Holley electronic fuel injection; 1 Garrett T3 exhaust turbocharger; intercooler. 12V 66Ah Battery, 90/120A alternator; cooling system capacity approx 8.5L (8US qt).

Transmission (to front wheels): 5-speed manual, final drive ratio 2.74.

Gear ratios: 1st 3.00; 2nd 1.89; 3rd 1.28; 4th 094; 5th 0.71; R 3.14.

Chassis: Integral body. Front McPherson strut and A arm, rear rigid axle with longitudinal arms and Panhard rod, front and rear coil springs, telescopic damper and antiroll bar. Servo/power assisted brakes, front disc (ventilated) diameter 25.6cm, rear drums; pedal actuated parking brake to rear wheels;

power assisted rack and pinion steering; fuel tank capacity 53L (11.6Gal) [14US Gal]; tyres 205/60 HR 15, 225/50 VR 15 or 205/50 VR 15 wheel rims 6J.

Dimensions: Wheelbase 246.5cm, track 146.5/146.5cm, clearance min. 11cm, turning circle 12.4m. Load space 17.1cu ft (485dm3). Length 447cm, width 177.5cm, height 129cm.

Performance: Max speed approx 137mph/220kmh, speed at 1000rpm in 5th gear 36.6mph/58.9kmh; power to weight ratio from 9.2kg/kW (6.8kg/PS); consumption approx 10–17L/100km (28.2–16.6mpg) [23.5– 13.8US mpg].

Chrysler GTS

Saloon/Sedan with front wheel drive and tail gate based on the K– car with extra long Wheelbase. 2.2 Litre four cylinder, Turbo if required, technical details as Dodge Lancer. Launched Autumn 1984. 1989 with 2.5 Litre Turbo and 2.2 Litre Intercooler

```
2.2 Litre
69kW–93hp–94PS
Central/Single Point Injection
```

Body, Weight (laden): 5–door Saloon/Sedan, 5–seater; approx 1230kg.

Engine data (SAE Net): 4–cylinder in–line (87.5 x 92mm), 2213cm3; compression ratio 9.5:1; 69kW (93hp) [94PS] at 4800rpm, 31.2kW/L (41.8hp/L) [42.5PS/L]; 165Nm (122.4lbft) at 3200rpm; unleaded regular grade.

Engine construction: Transverse front engine. Hydraulic tappets, 1 overhead camshaft (toothed belt); light–alloy cylinder head; 5 bearing crankshaft; oil capacity 3.8L (3.6US qt); Bosch/Holley electronic central/single point injection. 12V 66Ah Battery, 90/120 alternator; cooling system capacity approx 8.5L (8US qt).

Transmission (to front wheels): a) 5–speed manual, final drive ratio 2.51. b) Automatic "Torqueflite"; hydraulic torque converter and 3– speed Planetary gear set; final drive ratio 3.02.

Gear ratios: a) 5–speed manual: 1st 3.29; 2nd 2.08; 3rd 1.45; 4th 1.04; 5th 0.72; R 3.14.
b) Automatic: Max torque multiplication in converter 2.1 times, Planetary gear set ratios: 2.69; 1.55; 1; R 2.1.

Chassis: Integral body. Front McPherson strut and A arm, rear rigid axle with trailing arm and Panhard rod, front and rear antiroll bar, coil springs, telescopic damper. Servo/power assisted brakes, front discs (ventilated), rear drums, disc diameter 25.5cm; pedal actuated parking brake to rear wheels; power assisted rack and pinion steering; fuel tank capacity 53L (11.6Gal) [14US GAL]; tyres 195/70 R 14, also available with 205/60 R 15, wheel rims 5.5 or 6".

Dimensions: Wheelbase 262cm, track 146.5/145.5cm, clearance minimum 12cm, turning circle 11.8m. Load space 18.4/33cu ft (520/935dm3). Length 458cm, width 173.5cm, height 134.5cm.

Performance: Max speed approx 102.5mph/165kmh, speed at 1000rpm in 5th gear 39.4mph/63.4kmh; power to weight ratio from 17.8kg/kW (13.1kg/PS); consumption approx 8–14L/100km (35.3–20.2mpg) [29.4– 16.8US mpg].

Chrysler GTS

```
2.5 Litre
74kW–100hp–101PS
Central/Single Point Injection
```

As 2.2 Litre, except:

Weight: Kerbweight approx 1280kg

Engine data (SAE net): 4–cylinder in–line (87.5 x 104mm), 2501cm3; compression ratio 9:1; 74kW (100hp) [101PS] at 4800rpm, 29.8kW/L (39.9hp/L) [40.4PS/L]; 183Nm (135lbft) at 2800rpm.

Engine construction: 2 counter–balance shafts.

Performance: Max speed approx 106-112mph/170–180kmh, power to weight ratio from 17.3kg/kW (12.7kg/PS); consumption approx 9– 14L/100km (31.4–20.2mpg) [26.1–16.8US mpg].

```
2.5 Litre Turbo
112kW-150hp-152PS
Fuel Injection
```

As 2.2 Litre, except:

Weight: Kerbweight approx 1300kg

Engine data (SAE net): 4-cylinder in-line (87.5 x 104mm), 2501cm3; compression ratio 7.8:1; 112kW (150hp) [152PS] at 4800rpm, 44.8kW/L (60hp/L) [60.8PS/L]; 244Nm (180lbft) at 2000rpm; premium or regular grade.
For some countries: 107kW (144hp) [146PS] or 108kW (145hp) [148PS]

Engine construction: 2 anti-vibration arms; Holley electronic fuel injection, 1 MHI exhaust gas turbocharger

Performance: Max speed approx 115-121mph/185-195kmh; power to weight ratio from 11.6kg/kW (8.6kg/PS); consumption approx 9-15L/100km (31.4-18.8mpg) [26.1-15.7US mpg].

```
2.2 Litre Turbo
129kW–174hp–176PS
Fuel Injection
```

Engine for Lancer Shelby

As 2.2 Litre, except:

Weight: Kerbweight approx 1330kg.

Engine data (SAE net): 4-cylinder in-line (87.5 x 92mm), 2213cm3; compression ratio 8.1:1; 129kW (174hp) [176PS] at 5200rpm, 58.3kW/L (78.1hp/L) [79.5PS/L]; 271Nm (200lbft) at 2400rpm; leaded premium or regular grade.
For some countries: 130kW (174hp) [177PS].

Engine construction: Bosch/Holley electronic fuel injection, 1 Garrett T3 exhaust turbocharger; charge-air cooler.

Transmission: 5-speed manual, final drive ratio 2.74.

Gear ratios: 1st 3.0; 2nd 1.89; 3rd 1.28; 4th 0.94; 5th 0.71; R 3.14.

Chassis: Disc diameter front 28cm, rear 28.6cm; tyres 205/60 VR 15, wheels 6J.

Performance: Max speed approx 137mph/220kmh; speed at 1000rpm in 5th gear 36.5mph/58.7kmh; power to weight ratio from 11.1kg/kW (8.2kg/PS); consumption 10-17L/100km (28.2-16.6mpg) [23.5-13.8US mpg].

Chrysler LeBaron

Coupe and convertible based on the old design of the LeBaron, 2.5 Litre normally aspirated and 2.2 Litre Turbo engine. Launched September 1986. 1989: 2.2 Turbo intercooler.

```
2.5 Litre
74kW–100hp–101PS
Central/Single Point Injection
```

Body, Weight (laden): 2–door Coupe, 5–seater; approx 1275kg. 2–door Coupe Premium, 5–seater; approx 1335kg. 2–door Convertible, 4–seater; approx 1330kg. 2–door Convertible Premium, 4–seater; approx 1380kg.
Automatic model heavier by 14–17kg.

Chrysler LeBaron Coupe

Engine data (SAE net): 4–cylinder in–line (87.5 x 104mm), 2501cm3; compression ratio 9:1; 74kW (100hp) [101PS] at 4800rpm, 29.6kW/L (39.7hp/L) [40.4PS/L]; 183Nm (135lbft) at 2800rpm.

Chrysler

For some countries: 71kW (95hp) [97PS].

Engine construction: Transverse front engine. Hydraulic tappets, 1 overhead camshaft (toothed belt); light-alloy cylinder head; 5 bearing crankshaft; 2 counter-balance shafts; oil capacity 3.8L (3.6US qt); Bosch/Holley electronic central/single point injection. 12V 66Ah Battery, 90A alternator; cooling system capacity approx 8.5L (8US qt).

Transmission (to front wheels): a) 5-speed manual, final drive ratio 2.51. b) Automatic "Torqueflite", hydraulic torque converter and 3- speed Planetary gear set, central selector lever, final drive ratio 3.02.

Gear ratios: a) 5-speed manual: 1st 3.29; 2nd 2.08; 3rd 1.45; 4th 1.04; 5th 0.72; R 3.14.
b) Automatic: Max torque multiplication in converter 2 times, Planetary gear set ratios: 2.69; 1.55; 1; R 2.1.

Chassis: Integral body. Front McPherson strut and A-arm; negative steering offset; rear rigid axle with trailing arm and Panhard rod, front and rear independent suspension, telescopic damper and antiroll bar. Servo-assisted brakes, front disc (ventilated), diameter 25.5cm, rear 26.8cm ; pedal actuated parking brakes to rear wheels; power assisted rack and pinion steering; fuel tank capacity 53L (11.6Gal) [14US Gal]; tyres P 195/70 R 14 optional 205/60 R 15, wheel rims 5.5 or 6J.

Dimensions: Wheelbase 254.5cm, track 146.5/146.5cm, clearance 12cm, turning circle 11.6/12.2m. Load space 13.9cu ft (395dm3). Length 469.5cm, width 174cm, height 129.5cm. Convertible: Wheelbase 255cm, Load space 10.2cu ft (290dm3), height 132.5cm.

Performance: Max speed approx 102.5-109mph/165-175kmh, speed at 1000rpm in top gear 38.5mph/62.0kmh; power to weight ratio from 17.2kg/kW (12.6kg/PS); consumption approx 9-14L/100km (31.4- 20.2mpg) [26.1-16.8US mpg].

Chrysler LeBaron Convertible

```
2.5 Litre Turbo
129kW-150hp-152PS
Fuel Injection
```

As 100hp, except:

Weight: Heavier by 5kg.

Engine data (SAE net): 4-cylinder in-line (87.5 x 104mm), 2501cm3; compression ratio 7.8:1; 112kW (150hp) [152PS] at 4800rpm, 44.8kW/L (60hp/L) [60.8PS/L]; 244Nm (180lbft) at 2000rpm; leaded premium or regular grade.
For some countries: 107kW (144hp) [146PS] or 108kW (145hp) [147PS]

Engine construction: Holley electronic fuel injection, 1 M.H.I. exhaust turbocharger

Performance: Max speed approx 115-121mph/185-195kmh; power to weight ratio from 11.4kg/kW (8.4kg/PS); consumption approx 9- 15L/100km (31.4-18.8mpg) [26.1-15.7US mpg].

```
2.2 Litre Turbo
129kW-174hp-176PS
Fuel Injection
```

As 100hp, except:

Weight: Kerbweight, Coupe GTC from 1375kg, Convertible GTC from 1405kg.

Engine data (SAE net): 4-cylinder in-line (87.5 x 92mm), 2213cm3; compression ratio 8.1:1; 129kW (174hp) [176PS] at 5200rpm, 58.3kW/L (78.1hp/L) [79.5PS/L]; 271Nm (200lbft) at 2400rpm; premium or regular unleaded.
For some countries: 130kW (174hp) [177PS]

Engine construction: Without anti-vibration arms; Bosch/Holley electronic fuel injection; 1 Garrett T3 exhaust turbocharger; charge-air cooler.

Transmission: 5 speed manual, final drive ratio 2.74
Gear ratios: 1st 3.0; 2nd 1.89; 3rd 1.28; 4th 0.94; 5th 0.71; R 3.14.
Chassis: Disc diameter, front (ventilated) 28cm, rear 28.6cm; tyres 205/55 VR 16, wheel rims 6J.
Performance: Max speed approx 137mph/220kmh, speed at 1000rpm in 5th gear 38.2mph/61.5kmh; power to weight ratio from 10.7kg/kW (7.8kg/PS); consumption approx 10-17L/100km (28.2-16.6mpg) [23.5-13.8US mpg].

Chrysler LeBaron Coupe GTC

Chrysler New Yorker/Landau

Saloon/Sedan with front wheel drive, available with Mitsubishi 3 Litre V6 engine. Technically compatible with the Dodge Dynasty. Launched in September 1987. More power and new automatic transmission for 1989.

```
3 Litre V6
105kW-141hp-143PS
Fuel Injection
```

Body, Weight (laden): 4-door Saloon/Sedan, 6-seater; approx 1465kg, Landau 1495kg.

Engine data (SAE net): 6-cylinder in V 60deg., (91.1 x 76.0mm), 2972cm3; compression ratio 8.9:1; 105kW (141hp) [143PS] at 5000rpm, 35.3kW/L (47.3hp/L) [48.1PS/L]; 232Nm (171.2) at 2800rpm; unleaded regular grade.

Chrysler New Yorker

Engine construction: Designated Mitsubishi 6 G 72. Transverse front engine; valves in V, hydraulic tappets, 2x1 overhead camshaft (toothed belt); light alloy cylinder heads; 4 bearing crankshaft; oil capacity 3.8L (3.6US qt); Bosch/Holley electronic fuel injection. 12V 66Ah Battery, 90A alternator; cooling system capacity 9.0L (8.5US qt).

Transmission (to front wheels): Automatic "Torqueflite", hydraulic torque converter and 4-speed Planetary gear set, selector lever at steering wheel, final drive ratio 3.75.

Gear ratios: Max torque multiplication in converter 1.8 times, Planetary gear set ratios: 2.84; 1.57; 1; 0.69 R 2.21.

Chassis: Integral body. Front McPherson strut and A-arm; negative steering offset; rear rigid axle with trailing arm and Panhard rod, front and rear coil springs, telescopic damper and antiroll bar, optional level control system. Servo/power assisted brakes, front discs (ventilated), rear drums, disc diameter 25.6cm, optional four wheel disc brakes and ABS (Bosch); pedal actuated parking brake to rear wheels; power assisted rack and pinion steering; fuel tank capacity 61L (13.4Gal) [16.1US Gal]; tyres 195/75 R 14, wheel rims 5.5J.

Dimensions: Wheelbase 265cm, track 146.5/146.5cm, clearance min 12.5cm, turning circle 11.9m. Load space 16.3cu ft (465dm3). Length 492cm, width 174cm, height 136cm.

Performance: Max speed approx 121mph/195kmh, speed at 1000rpm in OD gear 28.3mph/45.6kmh; power to weight ratio from 13.9kg/kW (10.2kg/PS); consumption approx 12–17L/100km (23.5–16.6mpg) [19.6–13.8US mpg].

Chrysler New Yorker Landau

Chrysler Fifth Avenue

Luxury Saloon/Sedan with V8 engine and rear wheel drive. 1989 fitted with Airbag as standard.

Body, Weight (laden): 4-door Saloon/Sedan, 6-seater; approx 1710kg.

> 5.2 Litre V8
> 104kW–140hp–142PS
> 1 2V Carb

Engine data (SAE net): 8–cylinder in V 90deg, (99.31 x 84.07mm), 5210cm3; compression ratio 9.0:1; 104kW (140hp) [142PS] at 3600rpm, 20.0kW/L (26.8hp/L) [27.3PS/L]; 359Nm (264.9lbft) at 2000rpm; unleaded regular grade. Export version: 132.5kW (177.5hp) [180PS] at 4000rpm.

Engine construction: Hydraulic tappets, central camshaft (chain); 5 bearing crankshaft; oil capacity 3.8L (3.6US qt); 1 Holley downdraught carb 6280. 12V battery 66/70Ah, 90A alternator; cooling system capacity approx 14.7/15.6L.

Transmission (to rear wheels): Automatic "Torqueflite"; hydraulic torque converter and 3–speed Planetary gear set, selector lever at steering wheel, final drive ratio 2.26; 2.24; 2.76; 2.94. Optional limited slip differential.

Gear ratios: Max torque mulitplication in converter 2 times, Planetary gear set ratios: 2.74; 1.54; 1; R 2.22.

Chassis: Integral body; front upper A arm, lower single control arm with elastic bearing tension strut and transverse torsion bar, front antiroll bar; rear rigid axle with semi–elliptic leafspring; telescopic damper. Servo/power assisted brakes, front discs (ventilated), rear drums, disc diameter 27.5cm; pedal actuated parking brake to rear wheels; power assisted recirculating ball steering; fuel tank capacity 68L (14.9Gal) [18US Gal]; tyres 205/75 R 15 wheel rims 7 J.

Dimensions: Wheelbase 286cm, track 153.5/152.5cm, clearance 15cm, turning circle 13.3m, load space 15.5cu ft (440dm3). Length 525cm, width 184cm, height 140cm.

Performance: Max speed approx 112mph/180kmh, speed at 1000rpm in top gear 34.5mph/55.5kmh; power to weight ratio from 16.4kg/kW (12kg/PS); consumption (touring) approx 12–17L/100km (23.5– 16.6mpg) [19.6–13.8US mpg].

Chrysler Fifth Avenue

Chrysler's TC by Maserati

Turbo II – 16V–DeTomaso

Sporty convertible with 2.2 Litre transverse engine and front wheel drive; produced in collaboration with Maserati. Prototype launched in Winter 1985/86. Series model for Summer 1988.

> 2.2 Litre Turbo
> 129kW - 173hp - 176PS
> Fuel Injection

Engine for Turbo II

Body, Weight (laden): 2–door Convertible, 2/2–seater; approx 1450kg.

Engine data (SAE net): 4–cylinder in–line (87.5 x 92mm), 2213 cm3; compression ratio 8.1:1; 129kW (173hp) [176PS] at 5200rpm, 58.3kW/L (78.1hp/L) [79.5PS/L]; 271Nm (200lbft) at 2400rpm; premium or regular grade. Also: 121kW (162hp) [164PS]; 232Nm (171.2lbft).

Chrysler's TC by Maserati

Engine construction: Transverse front engine. Hydraulic tappets, 1 overhead camshaft (toothed belt); light–alloy cylinder head; 5 bearing crankshaft; oil capacity 3.8L (3.6US qt); electronic fuel injection (multiport), 1 exhaust turbocharger, intercooler. Champion RA 8 HC spark plugs, 12V 66Ah battery, 120A alternator; cooling system capacity approx 8.5L (8US qt).

Transmission (to front wheels): Automatic "Torqueflite", hydraulic torque converter and 3–speed Planetary gear set, final drive ratio 3.02.

Gear ratios: Automatic; Max torque multiplication in converter 2 times, Planetary gear set ratios: 2.69; 1.55; 1; R 2.1.

Chassis: Integral body. Front McPherson strut and A–arm, rear rigid axle with trailing arm and Panhard rod, front and rear coil springs, telescopic damper and antiroll bar. Servo/power assisted disc brakes with ABS (Teves) (front ventilated), disc diameter 25.6cm, rear 27.1cm. Parking brake to rear wheels; power assisted rack and pinion steering; fuel tank capacity 53L (11.6Gal) [14US Gal]; tyres 205/60 VR 15, wheel rims 6".

Dimensions: Wheelbase 236cm, track 146/146.5cm, clearance minimum 16.5cm, turning circle approx 11.3m, load space 12 + 2.8cu ft (340 + 80dm3), length 446.5cm, width 174cm, height 132cm.

Performance: Max speed above 130mph/210kmh, speed at 1000rpm in 5th gear 25.5mph/41kmh; power to weight ratio from 11.2kg/kW (8.2kg/PS); consumption approx 9–16L/100km (31.4– 17.7mpg) [26.1–14.7US mpg]

> 2.2 Litre Turbo 16V
> 149kW-200hp-203PS
> Fuel Injection

Engine for 16V–Maserati

As 173hp, except:

Body, Weight (laden): 2-door Convertible, 2-seater; approx 1475kg.

Engine data (SAE net): 4-cylinder in-line (87.5 x 92mm), 2213cm3; compression ratio 7.3:1; 149kW (200hp) [203PS] at 5500rpm, 67.3kW/L (90.2hp/L) [91.7PS/L]; 298Nm (219.9lbft) at approx 3400rpm.

Engine construction: 4 valves per cylinder, 2 overhead camshafts.

Transmission: 5–speed manual, final drive ratio 3.47.

Gear ratios: 1st 3.54; 2nd 2.05; 3rd 1.37; 4th 1.03; 5th 0.76; R 3.03.

Chrysler • Citroen

Performance: Max speed above 137mph/220kmh, speed at 1000rpm in 5th gear 27mph/43.4kmh; power to weight ratio 9.9kg/kW (7.3kg/PS); consumption approx 9–16L/100km (31.4–17.7mpg) [26.1–14.7US mpg].

Chrysler's TC by Maserati

Chrysler Voyager

Export version of the Dodge Caravan and the Plymouth Voyager. Extremely roomy Saloon/Sedan with front wheel drive, between 5 and 8 seats, 2.5 or 3 Litre engine displacement, available with 2 different wheelbases. 1989 also available with 2.5 Litre Turbo.

2.5 Litre
74kW–99hp–101PS
Central/Single Point Injection

Body, Weight (laden): 5–door Saloon/Sedan, 5/8–seater; approx 1385kg; 5–door Grand Saloon/Sedan SE, 5/8–seater; approx 1475kg.

Engine data (SAE net): 4–cylinder in–line (87.5 x 104mm), 2501cm3; compression ratio 9:1; 74kW (99hp) [101PS] at 4800rpm, 29.6kW/L (39.6hp/L) [40.4PS/L]; 183Nm (135lbft) at 2800rpm; unleaded regular grade.

Engine construction: Transverse front engine. Hydraulic tappets, 1 overhead camshaft (toothed belt); light–alloy cylinder head; 2 counter–balance shafts; 5 bearing crankshaft; oil capacity 3.8L (3.6US qt); Bosch/Holley electronic central/single point injection. 12V 66Ah battery, 90A alternator; cooling system capacity approx 8.1L (7.7US qt).

Transmission (to front wheels): a) 5–speed manual, final drive ratio 2.76.
b) Automatic "Torqueflite", hydraulic torque converter and 3–speed Planetary gear set, selector lever at steering wheel, final drive ratio 3.22.

Chrysler Voyager LE

Gear ratios: a) 5–speed manual; 1st 3.29; 2nd 2.08; 3rd 1.45; 4th 1.04; 5th 0.72; R 3.14.
b) Automatic; Max torque multiplication in converter 2 times, Planetary gear set ratios: 2.69; 1.55; 1; R 2.1.

Chassis: Integral body. Front McPherson strut, coil springs and A arm, rear rigid axle with cross leaf spring, front and rear telescopic damper. Servo/power assisted brakes, front discs (ventilated), optional rear disc diameter 28cm rear drums, disc diameter 25.6cm; pedal actuated parking brake to rear wheels; rack and pinion steering with optional power assistance; fuel tank capacity 57/75L (12.5/16.5Gal) [15.1/19.8US Gal]; tyres 195/75R 14; wheel rims 5.5J, optional 205/70 R 14, wheel rims 5.5/6 J.

Dimensions: Wheelbase 284.5cm, track 152/158cm, clearance minimum 10cm, turning circle 12.5m, load space max 115.1cu ft (3260dm3). Length 447/450cm,
width 183.5cm, height 163.5cm. Grand Saloon/Sedan: Wheelbase 302.5cm, turning circle 13.1m, load space 139.1cu ft (3940dm3). Length 484cm.

Performance: Max speed approx 90–96mph/145–155kmh, speed at 1000rpm in 5th gear 36.8mph/59.3kmh; power to weight ratio from 18.7kg/kW (13.7kg/PS); consumption approx 10–16L/100km (28.2–17.7mpg) [23.5–14.7US mpg].

2.5 Litre Turbo
112kW–150hp–152PS
Fuel Injection

As 2.5 Litre, except:

Weight: Heavier by 15kg.

Engine data (SAE net): 4-cylinder in-line (87.5 x 104mm), 2501cm3; compression ratio 7.8:1; 112kW (150hp) [152PS] at 4800rpm, 44.8kW/L (60hp/L) [60.8PS/L]; 244Nm (180lbft) at 2000rpm; leaded super or regular grade.
For some countries: 107kW (143hp) [146PS]

Engine construction: Holley electronic fuel injection, 1 exhaust gas turbocharger.

Performance: Max speed approx 112mph/180kmh; power to weight ratio from 12.4kg/kW (9.1kg/PS); consumption approx 9–16L/100km (31.4–17.7mpg) [26.1-14.7US mpg].

Chrysler Grand Voyager

3 Litre V6
105kW–141hp–143PS
Fuel Injection

As 2.5 Litre, except:

Weight: Kerbweight (DIN) from 1410kg.

Engine data (SAE net): 6–cylinder in V 60deg (91.1 x 76.0mm), 2972cm3; compression ratio 8.9:1; 105kW (141hp) [143PS] at 5200rpm, 35.3kW/L (47hp/L) [48.1PS/L]; 232Nm (171.2lbft) at 2800rpm.

Engine construction: Designated Mitsubishi 6G 72. Valves in V ; 1 overhead camshaft (toothed belt); 4 bearing camshaft; without counter–balance shaft; ECI electronic fuel injection. Cooling system capacity approx 9.5L (9US qt).

Transmission: a) Automatic "Torqueflite", hydraulic torque converter and 3-speed Planetary gear set, final drive ratio 3.02.
b) Automatic "Torqueflite" A604, hydraulic torque converter and 4-speed Planetary gear set, final drive ratio 2.36.

Gear ratios: a) Max torque multiplication in converter 2 times, Planetary gear set ratios: 2.69; 1.55; 1; R 2.1.
b) Max torque in converter 1.8 times, Planetary gear set ratios: 2.84; 1.57; 1; 0.69; R 2.21.

Performance: Max speed approx 109mph/175kmh, speed at 1000rpm in top gear 30.1mph/49.9kmh; power to weight ratio from 13.4kg/kW (9.8kg/PS); consumption approx 12–17L/100km (23.5–16.6mpg) [19.6–13.8US mpg].

CITROEN   F

Automobiles Citroen, 62, boulevard Victor–Hugo, F–92208 Neuilly–sur–Seine, France.

Prominent representative of the front wheel drive concept. Pioneer of the new suspension system. 1965: absorption of the Panhard works, top marque in 1967. After the end of co–operation with Fiat, Citroen joined the Peugeot Group in 1974.

Hallwag Euro Guide – the travel planner for Europe.

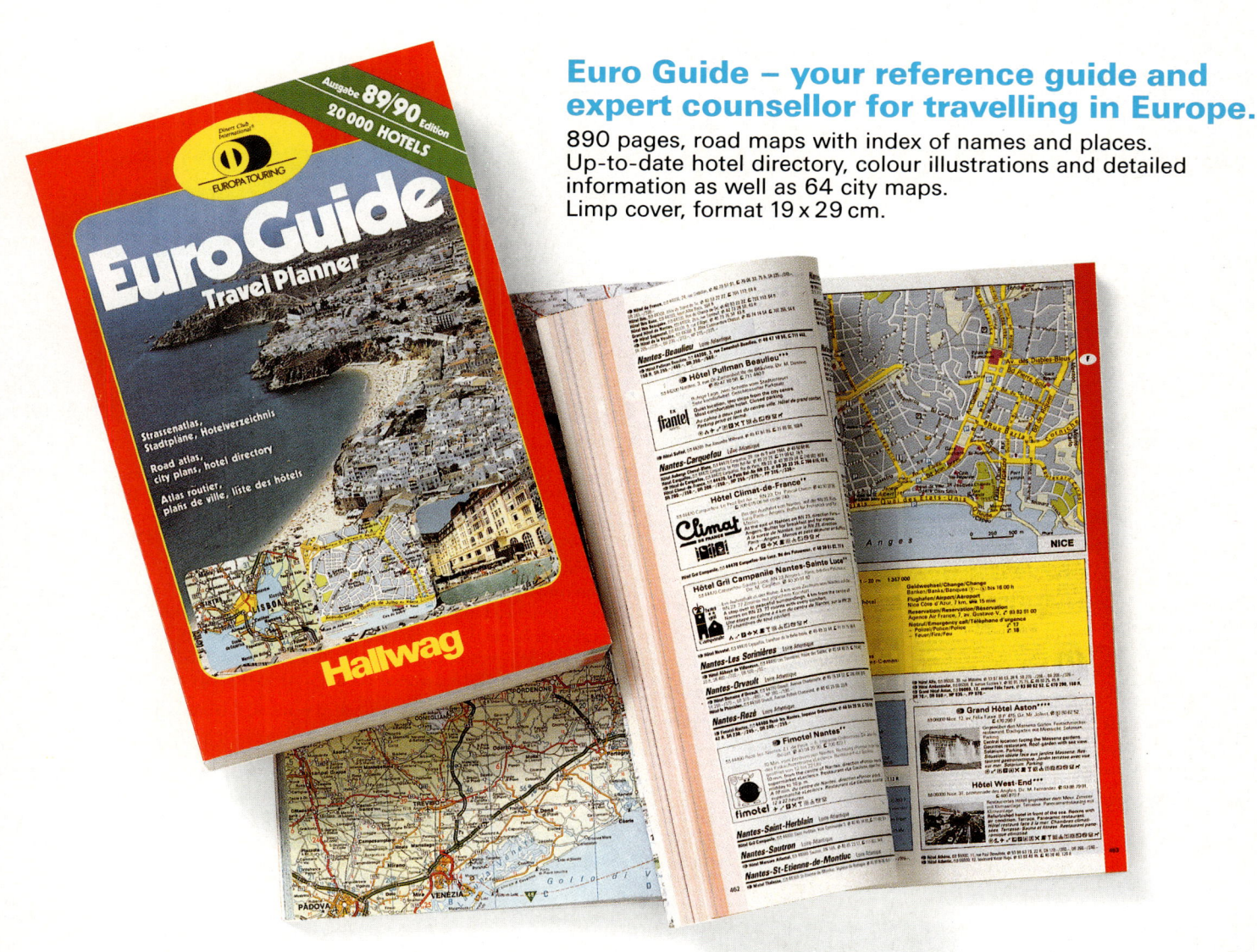

Euro Guide – your reference guide and expert counsellor for travelling in Europe.

890 pages, road maps with index of names and places. Up-to-date hotel directory, colour illustrations and detailed information as well as 64 city maps.
Limp cover, format 19 x 29 cm.

Europe à la carte

The Euro Guide provides up-to-date information on the European road network and a number of useful tourist hints – everything you need when travelling.
- For trip preparation, the planning map with all of Europe's main traffic routes in the scale of 1 : 4,5 million.
- Road maps from the North Cape down to the Mediterranean in the scale of 1 : 1 million.
- The Alps from Marseille to Vienna, presented in a special scale of 1 : 600 000.

With an index of more than 75 000 names and places.

Hotel directory with touring information and city maps

This very useful reference section contains information on accomodation in no fewer than 20 000 hotels throughout Europe. Prices, hotel categories and facilities available are mentioned.

You will find 64 city maps and a lot of valuable touring information in this comprehensive reference work.

For planning and travelling

Hallwag

Citroen

MODEL RANGE
2CV 6 – AX – Visa – Axel/Oltcit – BX – CX - XM

Citroen 2 CV 6

Special – Club – Charleston

Small economical model with front wheel drive and 2–cylinder Boxer engine. Launched in Paris 1948. Summer 1979: only available with 602cm3 engine. Autumn 1980: modified carb, altered consumption. Autumn 1983: optional tail gate version. Autumn 1985: optional modified engine compression.

602cm3
21.5/20.5kW–28.8/27.5hp–29/28PS
1 Compound Carb

Body, Weight: 4 optional 5–door Saloon/Sedan, 4–seater; kerbweight (DIN) from 585kg, gross vehicle weight 930kg.

Engine data (DIN): 2–cylinder Boxer engine (74 x 70mm), 602cm3, compression ratio 8.5:1; 21.5kW (28.8hp) [29PS] at 5750rpm, 35.8kW/L (48hp/L) [48.2PS/L]; 39Nm (28.8lbft) at 3500rpm; leaded premium grade.
Some countries: Compression ratio 7.9:1; 20.5kW (27.5hp) [28PS]; leaded regular grade.

Engine construction: Designated A 06/635 or A 06/664. Valves in V, central camshaft (toothed belt); light–alloy cylinder heads and cylinder block, grey cast iron dry cylinder liners; 2 bearing crankshaft; gauze filter; oil cooler, oil capacity 2.3L (2.2US qt); 1 Solex 26/35 CSIC downdraught compound carb. Bosch W5 A or Champion L 85 or Eyquem 755 spark plugs; 12V 25/30Ah battery, 28A 400 alternator; air cooled with fan.

Transmission (to front wheels): 4–speed manual, gear shift lever at dashboard; final drive ratio 4.125 (8/33).

Gear ratios: 1st 5.203; 2nd 2.657; 3rd 1.786; 4th 1.316; R 5.203.

Chassis: Platform type frame; all–round independent suspension with longitudinal radius arm connecting to front and rear. Suspension elements through horizontal coil springs, telescopic damper. Front disc brakes, rear drums, disc diameter 24.4cm, handbrake to front wheels; rack and pinion steering; fuel tank capacity 25L (5.5Gal) [6.6US Gal]; tyres 125R 15, wheel rims 4J.

Dimensions: Wheelbase 240cm, track 126/126cm. Clearance 15cm, turning circle 11.2m. Load space 7.8cu ft (220dm3) – net 5.6cu ft (160dm3) to 44.1cu ft (1250dm3). Length 383cm, width 148cm, height 160cm.

Performance: Max speed 71.5–68.5mph/115–110kmh (manufacturer's test specification), speed at 1000rpm in 4th gear 12.6mph/20.3kmh; acceleration 0 – 62mph/100kmh 33.5secs, standing km 44.5secs; power to weight ratio 27.2kg/kW (20.2kg/PS); consumption ECE 5.4/–/6.8L/100km (52.3/–/41.5mpg) [43.6/–/34.6US mpg] or 6.0/–/7.0L/100km (47.1/–/40.4mpg) [39.2/–/33.6US mpg].

Citroen 2 CV 6 Special

Citroen AX

10 - 11 - 14 - GT - Sport - 14 Diesel

Compact Saloon/Sedan with tail gate, 4–cylinder transverse engine and front wheel drive, all round independent suspension; favourable kerbweight (from 640kg) and aerodynamic body (cd 0.31). Launched Summer/Autumn 1986, Paris Sport, Saloon/Sedan with 5–doors and GT Autumn 1987. A 1.4 Litre Diesel version was introduced at the Paris Show in 1988.

954cm3
33/31kW–44/41.5hp–45/42PS
1 Carb

Engine for 10E, 10RE and 10TRE

Body, Weight: 3–door Saloon/Sedan, 5–seater; kerbweight (DIN) 640kg, gross vehicle weight 1055kg; 5–door Saloon/Sedan, 5–seater; kerbweight (DIN) 655kg, gross vehicle weight 1070kg.

Citroen AX 10 RE

Engine data (DIN): 4–cylinder in–line (70 x 62mm), 954cm3; compression ratio 9.4:1; 33kW (44hp) [45PS] at 5200rpm, 34.7kW/L (46.5hp/L) [47.1PS/L]; 71Nm (52.4lbft) at 2400rpm; leaded premium grade.
For some countries: Compression ratio 8.2:1; 31kW (41.5hp) [42PS]; leaded regular grade.

Engine construction: Designated TU9. Transverse engine. Valves in V (approx 35deg), 1 overhead camshaft (toothed belt); light–alloy cylinder head and block, wet cylinder liners; 5 main bearing crankshaft; oil capacity 3.5L (3.3US qt); 1 Weber 32 ISBH 16 carb. Champion C9 YCK Eyquem FC 52 L3 spark plugs; 12V 25Ah battery, 650/750 alternator; cooling system capacity approx 4.8L (4.5US qt).

Transmission (to front wheels): 4–speed manual, final drive ratio 3.764 (17/64).

Gear ratios: 1st 3.417; 2nd 1.81; 3rd 1.129; 4th 0.814; R 3.584.

Chassis: Integral body; front McPherson strut (coil spring and co–axial telescopic damper) with lower A arm, rear independent suspension with trailing arm, transverse torsion bar spring and telescopic damper. Servo/power assisted brakes, front discs, diameter 23.8cm, rear drums, mechanical handbrake to rear wheels; rack and pinion steering; fuel tank capacity 36/43L (7.9/9.5Gal) [9.5/11.4US Gal]; tyres 135/70 SR 13, wheel rims 4".

Dimensions: Wheelbase 228.5cm, track 138/130cm, clearance 11cm, turning circle 9.6m, load space 9.7/23.7/41.3cu ft (275/670/1170dm3). Length 350cm, width 156cm, height 135cm.

Citroen AX 11 TRE

Performance: Max speed 90–87mph/145–140kmh (manufacturer's test specifications), speed at 1000rpm in 4th gear 19.3mph/31kmh; acceleration 0 – 62mph/100kmh 17.9/20.8secs, standing km 38.5/40.2secs; power to weight ratio from 19.4kg/kW (14.2kg/PS); consumption ECE 3.9/5.6/5.6L/100km (72.4/50.4/50.4mpg) [60.3/42/42US mpg]. Or 4.1/5.9/6.0L/100km (68.9/47.9/47.1mpg) [57.4/39.9/39.2US mpg].

Citroen 145

> 1124cm3
> 40kW–54hp–55PS
> 1 Carb

Engine for 11E, 11RE and 11 TRE

As 954cm3, except:

Weight: Kerbweight (DIN) from 645/660kg, gross vehicle weight 1085/1100/1120kg.

Engine data (DIN): 4–cylinder in–line (72 x 69mm), 1124cm3; compression ratio 9.4:1; 40kW (54hp) [55PS] at 5800rpm, 35.6kW/L (47.7hp/L) [48.9PS/L]; 89Nm (65.6lbft) at 3200rpm.
With Catalyst: 40kW (53.6hp) [55PS] at 5500rpm; 83Nm (61.2lbft) at 3500rpm; unleaded premium grade.

Engine construction: Designated TU 1. One Solex 32 PBISA 16 carb.

Transmission: a) 4–speed manual, final drive ratio 3.444 (18/62).
b) 5–speed manual, final drive ratio 3.444 (18/62).

Gear ratios: a) 4–speed manual: 1st 3.147; 2nd 1.81; 3rd 1.129; 4th 0.814; R 3.584.
b) 5–speed manual: 1st 3.417; 2nd 1.95; 3rd 1.357; 4th 1.054; R 3.584.

Chassis: Optional 135/70 SR 13 or 155/70 SR 13 tyres, wheel rims 4 or 4.5".

Performance: Max speed 98–100mph/158–161kmh (manufacturer's test specifications), speed at 1000rpm in 4th gear 21.1mph/34kmh, in 5th gear 20.1mph/32.4kmh; acceleration 0 – 62mph/100kmh 13.2/12.9secs, Catalyst 14.6secs; standing km 34.9/34.7secs, Catalyst 35.8secs; power to weight ratio from 15.9kg/kW (11.7kg/PS); consumption ECE 3.9/5.6/5.7L/100km (72.4/50.4/49.6mpg) [60.3/42/41.3US mpg], Catalyst variants 4.8/6.5/7.6L/100km (58.8/43.5/37.2mpg) [49/36.2/30.9US mpg].

Citroen AX 14 TZS

> 1361cm3
> 51.5/44/48kW-69/59/64hp-70/60/65PS
> 1 Carb

Engine for 14TRS and 14TZS

As 954cm3, except:

Weight: Kerbweight (DIN) from 695/710kg, gross vehicle weight 1115/1130kg.

Engine data (DIN): 4–cylinder in–line (75 x 77mm), 1361cm3; compression ratio 9.3:1; 51.5kW (69hp) [70PS] at 5600rpm, 37.8kW/L (50.6hp/L) [51.4PS/L]; 111Nm (81.9lbft) at 3400rpm.
With Catalyst: Compression ratio 8.8:1; 44kW (59hp) [60PS] or 48kW (64hp) [65PS] at 5200rpm, 32.3/35.3kW/L (43.3/47.3hp/L) [44.1/47.8PS/L]; 103Nm (76lbft) at 3000rpm; unleaded premium grade.

Engine construction: Designated TU 3A. 1 Weber 34 TLP 3/100 carb.

Transmission: 5–speed manual, final drive ratio 3.444 (18/62).

Gear ratios: 1st 3.417; 2nd 1.95; 3rd 1.357; 4th 1.054; 5th 0.854; R 3.584.

Chassis: Front antiroll bar; fuel tank capacity 43L (95Gal) [11.4US Gal]; tyres 155/70 SR 13, wheel rims 4.5".

Dimensions: Turning circle 10.5m.

Performance: Max speed 106mph/170kmh, Catalyst 102.5mph/165kmh (manufacturer's test specifications), speed at 1000rpm in 5th gear 21.2mph/34.1kmh; acceleration 0 – 62mph/100kmh 10.8secs, Catalyst 13.1secs, standing km 32.7secs; power to weight ratio from 13.5kg/kW (9.9kg/PS);

R10

consumption ECE 4.2/6.0/6.9L/100km (67.3/47.1/40.9mpg) [56/39.2/34.1US mpg]. Or 4.4/6.2/7.3L/100km (64.2/45.6/38.7mpg) [53.5/37.9/32.2US mpg], Catalyst 5.2/6.2/7.9L/100km (54.3/45.6/35.8mpg) [45.2/37.9/29.8US mpg].

> 1361cm3
> 62.5/55/59kW-84/74/79hp-85/75/80PS
> 1 2V Carb/Central-Single
> Point Injection

Engine for GT

As 954cm3, except:

Body, Weight: 3–door Saloon/Sedan, 5–seater; kerbweight (DIN) 720kg, gross vehicle weight 1160kg.

Citroen AX GT

Engine data (DIN): 4–cylinder in–line (75 x 77mm), 1361cm3; compression ratio 9.3:1; 62.5kW (84hp) [85PS] at 6400rpm, 45.9kW/L (61.5hp/L) [62.5PS/L]; 116Nm (85.6lbft) at 4000rpm.
With Catalyst and Central/single point injection (Bosch): 55kW (74hp) [75PS] or 59kW (79hp) [80PS] at 6200rpm, 40.4/43.4kW/L (54.1/58.1hp/L) [55.2/58.8PS/L]; 109Nm (80.4lbft) at 4000rpm; unleaded premium grade.

Engine construction: Designated TU 3S or TU 3 M. 1 Solex 32–3 Z2 downdraught 2V carb or Bosch central/single point injection. Eyquem FC 62 LS spark plugs, 12V 25/29Ah battery.

Transmission: 5–speed manual, final drive ratio 3.938 (16/63).

Gear ratios: 1st 3.147; 2nd 1.95; 3rd 1.357; 4th 1.054; 5th 0.854; R 3.584.

Chassis: Front and rear antiroll bar; fuel tank capacity 43L (9.5Gal) [11.4US Gal]; tyres 165/65 SR 13, wheel rims 5".

Dimensions: Track 139/131cm, turning circle 10.5m, length 350cm, width 160cm, height 134cm.

Performance: Max speed 112mph/180kmh (manufacturer's test specifications), speed at 1000rpm in 5th gear 18.3mph/29.4kmh; acceleration 0 – 62mph/100kmh 9.3secs, standing km 31.2secs; power to weight ratio 10.2kg/kW (7.5kg/PS); consumption ECE 4.9/6.6/7.L/100km (57.6/42.8/37.2mpg) [48/35.6/30.9US mpg].
With Catalyst: Max speed 110.5mph/178kmh, acceleration 0-62mph/100kmh 9.7secs, standing km 31.8secs.

> 1294cm3
> 70kW–94hp–95PS
> 2 2V Carbs

Engine for Sport

As 954cm3, except:

Body, Weight: 3–door Saloon/Sedan, 4–seater; kerbweight (DIN) 735kg, gross vehicle weight 1065kg.

Engine data (DIN): 4–cylinder in–line (75 x 73.2mm) 1294cm3; compression ratio 9.6:1; 70kW (94hp) [95PS] at 6800rpm, 54.1kW/L (72.5hp/L) [73.4PS/L]; 113Nm (83.8lbft) at 5000rpm.

Engine construction: Designated TU 2/4. 2 Solex 40 ADDHE horizontal 2V carbs. Eyquem FC 82 LS spark plugs, 12V 29Ah Battery.

Transmission: 5–speed manual, final drive ratio 4.285 (14/60).

Gear ratios: 1st 3.417; 2nd 1.95; 3rd 1.357; 4th 1.054; 5th 0.854; R 3/584.

Chassis: Front and rear antiroll bar; disc diameter 25.8cm; fuel tank capacity 43L (9.5Gal) [11.4US Gal]; tyres 165/60 HR 14, wheel rims 5 or 5.5".

Dimensions: Track 140/132cm, turning circle 10.6m, length 350cm, width 160cm, height 129cm.

Citroen

Performance: Max speed 116mph/186kmh (manufacturer's test specifications), speed at 1000rpm in 5th gear 17mph/27.5kmh; acceleration 0 – 62mph/100kmh 8.8secs, standing km 30.8secs; power to weight ratio 10.5kg/kW (7.7kg/PS); consumption ECE 5.7/7.7/9.7L/100km (49.6/36.7/29.1mpg) [41.3/30.5/24.2US mpg].

Citroen AX Sport

```
1361cm3 Diesel
39kW-52hp-53PS
Injection Pump
```

Engine for 14D, 14RD and 14 TRD

As 954cm3, except:

Body, Weight: 3-door Saloon/Sedan 5-seater; kerbweight (DIN) 710kg, gross vehicle weight 1150kg; 5-door Saloon/Sedan, 5-seater; kerbweight (DIN) 725kg, gross vehicle weight 1165kg.

Engine data (DIN): 4-cylinder in-line (75 x 77mm), 1361cm3; compression ratio 22:1; 39kW (52hp) [53PS] at 5000rpm, 28.7kW/L (38.5hp/L) [38.9PS/L]; 84Nm (70lbft) at 2500rpm.

Engine construction: Designated TUD3. Parallel valves; CAV RotoDiesel or Bosch diesel pump. 12V battery approx 50 Ah.

Transmission: 5-speed manual, final drive ratio 3.938 (16/63)

Gear ratios: 1st 3.418; 2nd 1.81; 3rd 1.276; 4th 0.975; 5th 0.767; R 3.584.

Chassis: Front antiroll bar; fuel tank capacity 43L; tyres 145/70 SR 13, wheel rims 4.5".

Dimensions: Turning circle 10.5m, width 160cm.

Performance: Max speed 96mph/155kmh, speed at 1000rpm in 5th gear 43.8mph/32.7kmh; acceleration 0 - 62mph/100kmh in 14.3secs; standing km 36.2secs; power to weight ratio 18.2kg/kW (13.4kg/PS); consumption ECE 3.6/5.0/5.2L/100km (78.5/56.5/54.3mpg) [65.3/47/45.2US mpg].

Citroen AX 14 TRD

Citroen Visa

Visa – 10E – 11RE – GTi –17D/RD

Compact Saloon/Sedan with front wheel drive and five doors (tail gate). Choice of: air cooled twin cylinder Boxer with 652cm3 or four cylinder engine. Launched September 1978. Spring 1984 available with 1.7 Litre diesel engine; GTi launched Paris 1984.

```
652cm3
25kW-33.5hp-34PS
1 2V Carb
```

Engine for Visa

Body, Weight: 5–door Saloon/Sedan, 4/5–seater; kerbweight (DIN) 755kg, gross vehicle weight 1090kg.

Engine data (DIN): 2-cylinder Boxer engine (77 x 70mm), 652cm3; compression ratio 9.5:1; 25kW (33.5hp) [34PS] at 5500rpm, 38.3kW/L (51.3hp/L) [52.2PS/L]; 49Nm (36.2lbft) at 3500rpm; leaded premium grade.
For some countries: compression ratio 8.4:1; 24.5kW (32.8hp) [33PS] at 5250rpm; 48Nm (35.4lbft) at 3750rpm; leaded regular grade.

Engine construction: Designated V06/644. Valves in V 70deg, central camshaft (toothed belt); light–alloy cylinder heads and block, dry liners; 3 bearing crankshaft; oil cooler, oil capacity 3L (2.8US qt); 1 Solex 26/35 CSIC/244 or Weber 32/34 DMTC 2/100 downdraught 2V carb. Champion BN6 Y or Eyquem 800LJS spark plugs. 12V 29/35Ah Battery, 33A/462 W alternator; air cooled.

Transmission (to front wheels): 4-speed manual (without direct drive), floor shift; final drive ratio 3.889 (9/35).

Gear ratios: 1st 4.55; 2nd 2.5; 3rd 1.64; 4th 1.15; R 4.18.

Chassis: Integral body; front McPherson struts with lower control arm and antiroll bar, rear independent suspension, with McPherson struts and trailing arms, front and rear coil springs and telescopic damper. Front disc brakes, rear drums, disc diameter 24.5cm, mechanical handbrake to rear wheels; rack and pinion steering; fuel tank capacity 40L (8.8Gal) [10.6US Gal]; tyres 135 SR 13, wheel rims 4".

Dimensions: Wheelbase 243cm, track 129/124cm, clearance 13cm, turning circle 9.9m, load space 10.6–24.4cu ft (300–690dm3). Length 372cm, width 153cm, height 140cm.

Performance: Max speed 78mph/125kmh (manufacturer's test specifications), speed at 1000rpm in 4th gear 14mph/22.5kmh; acceleration 0 – 62mph/100kmh 26.2secs; standing km 42.8secs; power to weight ratio 30.2kg/kW (22.2kg/PS); consumption ECE 5.2/–/6.5L/100km (54.3/–/43.5mpg) [45.2/–/36.2US mpg] 5.6/–/6.7L/100km (50.4/–/42.2mpg) [42/–/35.1US mpg].

```
954cm3
33kW–44hp–45PS
1 Carb
```

Engine for 10E

As 652cm3, except:

Body, Weight: 5–door Saloon/Sedan, 4/5–seater; kerbweight (DIN) 810kg, gross vehicle weight 1235kg.

Engine data (DIN): 4–cylinder in–line (70 x 62mm), 954cm3; compression ratio 9.3:1; 33kW (44hp) [45PS] at 6000rpm, 34.7kW/L (46.5hp/L) [47.1PS/L]; 69Nm (50.9lbft) at 2750rpm; leaded premium grade.
For some countries: 31kW (41.5hp) [42PS].

Engine construction: Designated 108C–XV 8. Engine and transmission in one unit, inclined 72deg to rear. Overhead valves in V (approx 35deg), 1 overhead camshaft (chain); light–alloy cylinder head and block, wet cylinder liners; 5 bearing crankshaft; oil capacity 4.5L (4.3US qt); 1 Solex 32 PBISA 12 horizontal carb. Champion S 281 YC spark plugs; 462 or 750 alternator; cooling system capacity approx 7.5L (7.1US qt).

Transmission: Final drive ratio 3.87 (15/58).

Gear ratios: 1st 3.88; 2nd 2.07; 3rd 1.38; 4th 0.94; R 3.57.

Chassis: Front and rear antiroll bar; optional servo/power assisted brakes; tyres 145 SR 13, wheel rims 4.5".

Dimensions: Wheelbase 242cm.

Performance: Max speed 83mph/133kmh (manufacturer's test specifications), speed at 1000rpm in 4th gear 17.6mph/28.3kmh; acceleration 0 – 62mph/100kmh 19.8secs; standing km 39.7secs; power to weight ratio 24.6kg/kW (18kg/PS); consumption ECE 5.5/7.6/6.8L/100km (51.4/37.2/41.5mpg) [42.8/30.9/34.6US mpg].

```
1124cm3
37kW–49.6hp–50PS
1 Carb
```

Engine for 11RE

As 652cm3, except:

Body, Weight: 5–door Saloon/Sedan, 4/5–seater; kerbweight (DIN) 810kg, gross vehicle weight 1235kg.

Engine data (DIN): 4–cylinder in–line (72 x 69mm), 1124cm3; compression ratio 9.7:1; 37kW (49.6hp) [50PS] at 5500rpm, 32.7kW/L (43.8hp/L) [44.5PS/L]; 84Nm (62lbft) at 2500rpm; leaded premium grade.
Optional compression ratio: 8.2:1; 35.5kW (47.6hp) [48PS] at 5750rpm; 78Nm (57.5lbft) at 2500rpm; or compression ratio 9.2:1; 42kW (56hp) [57PS].

Engine construction: Designated 109/5F. Engine and transmission in one unit, inclined 72deg to rear. Valves in V approx 35deg, 1 overhead camshaft; light–alloy cylinder head and block, wet cylinder liners; 5 bearing crankshaft; oil capacity 4.5/5L (4.3/4.7US qt); 1 Solex 32 PBISA 12 A/341 downdraught carb. Champion S281 YC or Eyquem C62 LJS Sparkplugs. 462 or 750W alternator; cooling system capacity approx 6.5/7.5L (6.1/7.1US qt).

Transmission: a) 4–speed manual, final drive ratio 3.56 (16/57) or 3.35 (17/57). b) 5–speed manual, final drive ratio 3.87 (15/58).

Gear ratios: a) 4–speed manual: 1st 3.88; 2nd 2.07; 3rd 1.38; 4th 0.94; R 3.57. b) 5–speed manual: 1st 3.88; 2nd 2.29; 3rd 1.50; 4th 1.12; 5th 0.90; R 3.57.

Chassis: Front and rear antiroll bar; Servo/power assisted brakes; tyres 145 SR 13, wheel rims 4.5".

Dimensions: Wheelbase 242cm.

Performance: Max speed 87–89mph/140–143kmh (manufacturer's test specifications), speed at 1000rpm in 4th gear 19.1mph/30.7kmh in 5th gear 18.3mph/29.5kmh; acceleration 0 – 62mph/100kmh 16.6secs; standing km 37.9secs; power to weight ratio 21.9kg/kW (16.2kg/PS); consumption ECE 4.8/6.3/6.3L/100km (58.8/44.8/44.8mpg) [49/37.3/37.3US mpg], 5–speed, 4.8/6.3/6.8L/100km (58.8/44.8/41.5mpg) [49/37.3/34.6US mpg].

```
1580cm3
84.5–113hp–115PS
Fuel Injection
```

Engine for GTi

As 652cm3, except:

Body, Weight: 5–door Saloon/Sedan 4/5–seater; kerbweight (DIN) 870kg, gross vehicle weight 1210kg.

Engine data (DIN): 4–cylinder in–line (83 x 73mm), 1580cm3; compression ratio 9.8:1; 84.5kW (113hp) [115PS] at 6250rpm, 53.5kW/L (71.7hp/L) [72.8PS/L]; 133Nm (98.1lbft) at 4000rpm.

Engine construction: Designated B6D–XU5 J. Transverse engine, parallel valves, 1 overhead camshaft (toothed belt); oil capacity 5L (4.7US qt); Bosch LE2–Jetronic electronic fuel injection. Bosch H6 DC, Champion S279 YC or Eyquem C72 LJS sparkplugs. 12V 29/35/45Ah Battery, 750W alternator; cooling system capacity 6.6L (6.2US qt).

Transmission: 5–speed manual, final drive ratio 3.866 (16/63).

Gear ratios: 1st 3.308; 2nd 1.882; 3rd 1.360; 4th 1.069; 5th 0.865; R 3.333.

Chassis: Front and rear antiroll bar; Servo/power assisted brakes, front ventilated discs, diameter 24.7cm; fuel tank capacity 43L (9.5Gal) [11.4US Gal]; tyres 185/60 HR 13, wheel rims 5.5".

Dimensions: Wheelbase 242cm, track 139/127cm, turning circle 10.6m. Load space 6.4/23.8/27.6cu ft (265/675/780dm3). Width 160cm, height 137cm.

Performance: Max speed 119.3mph/192kmh (manufacturer's test specifications), speed at 1000rpm in 5th gear 18.3mph/29.5kmh; acceleration 0 – 62mph/100kmh 8.8secs; standing km 30.5secs; power to weight ratio 10.3kg/kW (7.6kg/PS); consumption ECE 6.1/8.0/9.2L/100km (46.3/35.3/30.7mpg) [38.6/29.4/25.6US mpg].

```
1769cm3 Diesel
44kW–59hp–60PS
Injection Pump
```

Engine for 17D and 17RD

As 652cm3, except:

Body, Weight: 5–door Saloon/Sedan, 5–seater; kerbweight (DIN) 890kg, gross vehicle weight 1300kg.

Engine data (DIN): 4–cylinder in–line (80 x 88mm), 1769cm3; compression ratio 23:1; 44kW (59hp) [60PS] at 4600rpm, 24.9kW/L (33.4hp/L) [33.9PS/L]; 112Nm (82.6lbft) at 2000rpm.

Engine construction: Designated XUD7. Transverse engine, parallel valves, grey cast iron cylinder block; 1 overhead camshaft (toothed belt); oil capacity 4.2/4.6L (4/4.4US qt); CAV Roto– Diesel or Bosch diesel injection pump. 12V 35/42/50/60Ah Battery; 675/750W alternator; cooling system capacity 7.5L (7.1US qt).

Transmission: a) 4–speed manual, final drive ratio 3.588 (17/61). b) 5–speed manual, final drive ratio 3.938 (16/63).

Gear ratios: a) 4–speed manual; 1st 3.308; 2nd 1.882; 3rd 1.148; 4th 0.800; R 3.333.

b) 5–speed manual; 1st 3.308; 2nd 1.882; 3rd 1.28; 4th 0.969; 5th 0.757; R 3.333.

Chassis: Front and rear antiroll bar; Servo/power assisted brakes, diameter 24.7cm; fuel tank 43L (9.5Gal) [11.4US Gal]; tyres 145 SR 13, wheel rims 4.5".

Dimensions: Wheelbase 242cm, track 135/125cm; turning circle 10.6m.

Performance: Max speed 94.5–95.7mph/152–154kmh (manufacturer's test specifications), speed at 1000rpm in 4th gear 22.4mph/36.1kmh, in 5th gear 21.6mph/34.7kmh; acceleration 0 – 62mph/100kmh in 15.6–15.9secs; standing km 36.4–36.8secs; power to weight ratio 20.2kg/kW (14.8kg/PS); consumption ECE 4.3/5.9/5.5L/100km (65.7/47.9/51.4mpg) [54.7/39.9/42.8US mpg), 5– speed manual 4.6/6.2/6.0L/100km (57.6/45.6/47.1mpg) [51.1/37.9/39.2US mpg].

Citroen Axel/Oltcit

Compact Saloon/Sedan with front wheel drive and tail gate; produced in Rumania. Choice of three engines: two–cylinder Boxer with 652cm3 or 1.1 Litre; 1.3 Litre four cylinder Boxer; and the Rumanian designation, Oltcit, known in Western Europe as the Export Axel. Launched in 1981.

```
652cm3
25kW–33.5hp–34PS
1 2V Carb
```

Engine for Special

Body, Weight: 3–door Saloon/Sedan, 4/5–seater; kerbweight (DIN) 835kg, gross vehicle weight (overall) 1235kg.

Engine data (DIN): 2–cylinder Boxer engine (77 x 70mm), 652cm3; compression ratio 9:1; 25kW (33.5hp) [34PS] at 5250, 38.4kW/L (51.5hp/L) [52.1PS/L]; 50Nm (36.9lbft) at 3500rpm; leaded premium grade.

Engine construction: Designated V 06/630. Valves in V 70deg, central camshaft (toothed belt); light–alloy cylinder heads and blocks, light–alloy dry cylinder liners; 3 bearing crankshaft; oil cooler; oil capacity 3L (2.8US qt); 1 Solex 26/35 CSIC downdraught 2V carb. Champion BN 6 Y, AC 42 LTS, Marchal SCGT 34–5H spark plugs; 12V 25/35 Ah Battery, 460W alternator; air cooled.

Transmission (to front wheels): 4–speed manual (without direct drive), floor shift, final drive ratio 4.375 (8/35).

Gear ratios: 1st 4.55; 2nd 2.50; 3rd 1.64; 4th 1.15; R 4.18.

Chassis: Integral body; front transverse engine with longitudinal torsion bar, rear independent suspension with transverse torsion bar and longitudinal radius arm, front and rear telescopic damper. Four wheel disc brakes (front ventilated), diameter 25.2 or 27.0cm, rear 20.8cm, mechanical handbrakes to rear wheels; rack and pinion steering; fuel tank capacity 42L (9.2Gal) [11.1US Gal]; tyres 145 SR 13, wheel rims 4".

Citroen Axel

Dimensions: Wheelbase 237cm, track 132/124cm, clearance 15cm, turning circle 9.8m, load space 10.4–21.9cu ft (295/620dm3). Length 372cm, width 154cm, height 142cm.

Citroen

Performance: Max speed 73.7mph/118kmh (manufacturer's test specifications), speed at 1000rpm in 4th gear 12.8mph/20.6kmh; acceleration 0 – 62mph/100kmh 35.5secs; standing km 44.6secs; power to weight ratio 33.4kg/kW (24.6kg/PS); consumption ECE 6.0/–/7.3L/100km (47.1/–/38.7mpg) [39.2/–/32.2US mpg].

```
1129cm3
42kW–56hp–57PS
1 2V Carb
```

Engine for Oltcit Club, Axel and Axel 11RE

As 652cm3, except:

Body, Weight: 3–door Saloon/Sedan, 4/5–seater; kerbweight (DIN) 860kg, gross vehicle weight 1260kg.

Engine data (DIN): 4–cylinder Boxer engine (74 x 65.6mm), 1129cm3; compression ratio 9:1; 42kW (56hp) [57PS] at 6250rpm, 37.2kW/L (49.8hp/L) [50.5PS/L]; 79Nm (58.3lbft) at 3500rpm.

Engine construction: Designated G 11/631. 2 x 1 overhead camshaft (toothed belt); oil capacity 3.5L (3.3US qt); 1 Solex 28 CIC CIT 234 downdraught 2V carb. Champion BN 7Y or Eyquem 800LJS spark plugs; 12V 45Ah battery, 40A/550W alternator.

Transmission: Final drive ratio 4.125 (8/33) or 3.89 (9/35).

Gear ratios: 1st 3.818; 2nd 2.294; 3rd 1.50; 4th 1.031; R 4.182.

Performance: Max speed 150kmh (manufacturer's test specifications), speed at 1000rpm in 4th gear 15–16mph/24.2– 25.8kmh; acceleration 0 – 62mph/100kmh 15/2/15.4secs; standing km 37.1secs; power to weight ratio 20.5kg/kW (15.1kg/PS); consumption ECE 6.0/8.0/8.9L/100km (47.1/35.3/31.7mpg) [39.2/29.4/26.4US mpg].

```
1299cm3
45kW–60hp–61PS
1 2V Carb
```

Engine for Axel 12 TRS

As 652cm3, except:

Body, Weight: 3–door Saloon/Sedan, 4/5–seater; kerbweight (DIN) 875kg, gross vehicle 1275kg.

Engine data (DIN): 4–cylinder Boxer engine (79.4 x 65.6mm), 1299cm3; compression ratio 8.7:1; 45kW (60hp) [61PS] at 5500rpm, 34.7kW/L (46.5hp/L) [47.0PS/L]; 96Nm (70.8lbft) at 3250rpm.

Engine construction: Designated T13/653. 2 x 1 overhead camshafts (toothed belt); oil capacity 3.5L (3.3US qt); 1 Solex 28 CIC CIT 361 downdraught 2V carb.

Transmission: 5–speed manual, final drive ratio 3.89 (9/35).

Gear ratios: 1st 3.818; 2nd 2.294; 3rd 1.50; 4th 1.133; 5th 0.912; R 4.182.

Chassis: Optional 160/65 HR 340 tyres, wheel rims 120 TR 340.

Performance: Max speed 98–99.5mph/157–160kmh (manufacturer's test specifications), speed at 1000rpm in 5th gear 18.1/29.2kmh; acceleration 0 – 62mph/100kmh 13.1secs; standing km 35.3secs; power to weight ratio 19.5kg/kW (14.4kg/PS); consumption ECE 5.7/7.7/8.6L/100km (49.6/36.7/32.8mpg) [41.3/30.5/27.4US mpg].

Citroen BX

14/11 – 15 – 16 – 19 – 19GTI – 19GTI 16V – Diesel - Turbo-Diesel

Five seater vehicle with tail gate, transverse engine, front wheel drive and hydro–pneumatic suspension. Launched 23 September 1982. Diesel version introduced in Frankfurt, 1983 and the Break in June 1985. In June 1986: modifications to the body and interior (dashboard), GTi with 125 PS, new catalyst model. April 1987: "16V". Paris: 1988: "4 x 4" with permanent all wheel drive.

```
1361/1124cm3
53kW-71hp-72PS
1 Carb/Central-Single Point Injection
```

Engine for BX, BX 14 E/RE and BX 11

Body, Weight: 5–door Saloon/Sedan, 5–seater; kerbweight (DIN) 900-930kg, gross vehicle weight 1360/1380kg; 5–door Estate/Station Wagon (Break), 5–seater; kerbweight (DIN) 930, gross vehicle weight 1445kg.

Engine data (DIN): 4-cylinder in-line (75 x 77mm), 1361cm3; compression ratio 9.3:1; 53kW (71hp) [72PS] at 5600rpm, 39kW/L (52hp/L) [53PS/L]; 111Nm (81.9lbft) at 3000rpm; premium unleaded.

For some countries: 50/51kW (67/68hp) [68/69PS]; or compression ratio 8:1; 45kW (60hp) [61PS].

With Catalyst and central/single point injection (Bosch): 55 or 59kW (74 and 84hp) [75 and 80PS] at 6200rpm, 40.4kW (54.5hp) [55PS] at 5800rpm; 89Nm (65.7lbft) at 4000rpm.

For some countries: (72 x 69mm), 1124cm3; compression ratio 9.4:1; 40kW (54hp) [55PS] at 5800rpm; 89Nm (119lbft) at 3400rpm.

Citroen BX Break

Engine construction: Designated TU 3A. Transverse engine. Valves in V (approx 35deg), 1 overhead camshaft (toothed belt), light-alloy cylinder head and block, wet cylinder liners; 5 bearing crankshaft; oil capacity 3.2/3.5L (3/3.3US qt); 1 Solex 34 PBISA downdraught carb or Weber 34 TLP. Champion C9 YCX or Eyquem FC 52 LS; battery 12V 29/35 Ah, alternator 50A; cooling system capacity approx 6.5L (6.1US qt).

Transmission (front wheels): a) 5-speed manual, final drive ratio 4.538 (13/59), Catalyst 3.867 (15/58).
b) 4-speed manual, final drive ratio 4.286 (14/60)

Gear ratios: a) 5-speed manual: 1st 3.417; 2nd 1.81; 3rd 1.275; 4th 0.975; 5th 0.767; R 3.584.
b) 4-speed manual: 1st 3.417; 2nd 1.81; 3rd 1.129; 4th 0.814; R 3.584.

Chassis: Integral body, hydropneumatic suspension with automatic level control system; independent suspension; front McPherson struts and A arm, rear trailing arms, front and rear antiroll bar. Servo/power assisted four wheel disc brakes, diameter front 26.6cm, rear 22.4cm, mechanical handbrake to front wheels; rack and pinion steering; fuel tank capacity 44/52L; tyres 145SR 14, wheel rims 4.5", optionally tyres 165/70 SR 14, wheel rims 5".

Dimensions: Wheelbase 265.5cm, track 141/135cm, clearance 16cm, turning circle 10.9m, load space 15.7-51.4cu ft (445-1455dm3), Break 18/30.4/63.7cu ft (510/860/1805dm3). Length 424, Break 440cm, width 168cm, height 136cm, Break 141-143cm.

Performance: Max speed 104mph/167kmh, Break 100mph/161kmh, speed at 1000rpm in top gear 19.2mph/31kmh; acceleration 0 - 62mph/100kmh 13.1-13.8secs, standing km 35-35.5secs; power to weight ratio from 17.0kg/kW (12.5kg/PS); consumption ECE 5.5/7.1/8.1L/100km (51.4/39.8/34.9mpg) [42.8/33.1/29US mpg] , Break 5.8/7.7/8.5L/100km (48.7/36.7/33.2mpg) [40.6/30.5/27.7US mpg].

With Catalyst: Max speed 104mph/168kmh; acceleration 0 - 62mph/100kmh 12.2secs, standing km 34secs.

With 1124cm3 engine: Max speed 96mph/154kmh; consumption ECE 5.1/6.9/7.8L/100km (55.4/40.9/36.2mpg) [46.1/34.1/30.2US mpg].

```
1580cm3
59/55kW–79/74hp–80/75PS
1 Carb
```

Engine for 15RE/TRE and 16RS/TRS and 16RS

As 1361 cm3 except:

Body, Weight: 5-door Saloon/Sedan, 5-seater; kerbweight (DIN) 950kg, gross vehicle weight 1405/1430kg; 5-door Saloon/Sedan (Break), 5-seater; kerbweight (DIN) 995kg, gross vehicle weight 1540kg.

Engine data (DIN): (83 x 73mm), 1580cm3; compression ratio 9.3:1; 59kW (79hp) [80PS] at 5600rpm, 37.3kW/L (50hp/L) [50.6PS/L]; 132Nm (97.4lbft) at 2800rpm.
With unregulated Catalyst: Compression ratio 8.65:1; 53kW (71hp) [72PS] at 5600rpm; 123Nm (90.8lbft) at 2800rpm.
With Catalyst and electronic controlled Carb: Compression ratio 8.65:1; 55kW (74hp) [75PS] at 5600rpm, 34.8kW/L (46.6hp/L) [47.4PS/L]; 120Nm (88.5lbft) at 3500rpm.

Adapting to the tides of change.

Today's rapid development is present in every aspect of life. To adapt to new conditions without losing the essential identity is of vital importance. Continual adjustment leads to new capabilities and strengths. The natural principle of adaptation is a living synergistic process which is simulated in the concept of systematic thinking. Evolution is the driving force.

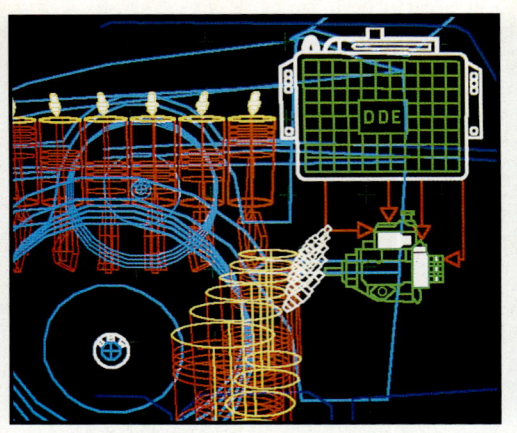

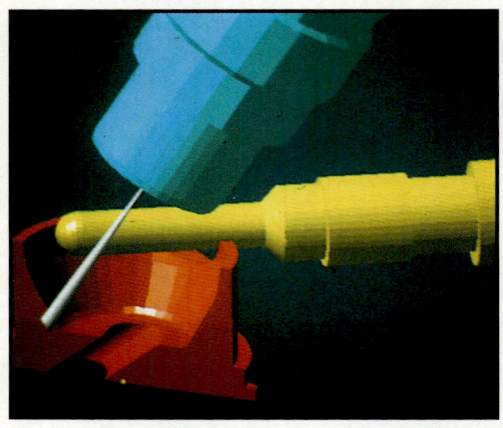

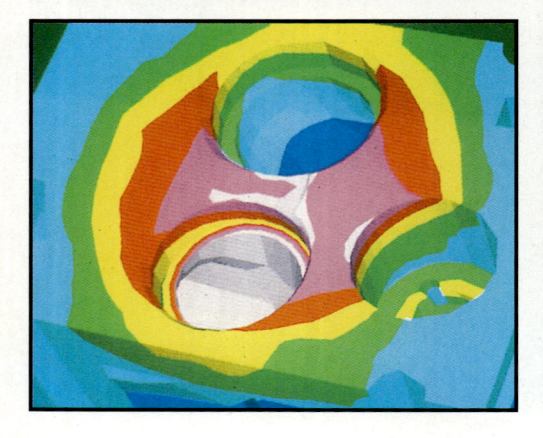

Evolution creates new power.

A vital aspect of BWM's strategy is to be a leader in developing and manufacturing excellent engines. The Engine Sales and Marketing Division of BWM creates complete powering solutions tailored to the customer's requirements. Adapting and customizing engines at BMW means applying the same art of engineering as with every BMW in-house innovation. Yet nothing of the distinguishing BMW engine character is lost. Our engineers are competent partners who offer their expertise in a cooperative spirit to those seeking a complete powering solution. Systematic engineering and close human relationships make BMW's adaptation philosophy what it is – the evolution of power.

BMW Motoren Gesellschaft m.b.H.
Engine Sales and Marketing
P.O.Box 44
A-4400 Steyr
Austria

Tel.: (Austria) 72 52/655-57
Telex: (Austria) 28 2 36
Telefax: (Austria) 72 52/63 3 70

Citroen

Engine construction: Designated 89A–XU 51C. Transverse engine inclined 30deg to rear. Parallel valves, 1 overhead camshaft (toothed belt); oil capacity 4.75/5L (4.5/4.7US qt); 1 Solex 36TLP also 34TBIA. Battery 12V 33/35/45A.

Transmission: 5-speed manual, final drive ratio 4.188 (16/67).

Gear ratios: 1st 3.25; 2nd 1.85; 3rd 1.280; 4th 0.969; 5th 0.757; R 3.333.

Chassis: Optional ABS (Teves); optional power assisted steering; fuel tank capacity 52L (11.4Gal) [13.7US Gal]; tyres 165/70 SR 14, wheel rims 5".

Dimensions: Track 142/136cm.

Performance: Max speed 106mph/170kmh, Catalyst 104mph/167kmh, Break Catalyst 101mph/162kmh (manufacturer's test specifications), speed at 1000rpm in 5th gear 21.2mph/34.1kmh; acceleration 0 – 62mph/100kmh 12.6secs, catalyst 14.9/16.2secs, standing km 34.4secs, Catalyst 35.7secs; power to weight ratio from 16.1kg/kW (11.9kg/PS); consumption ECE 5.6/7.5/8.9L/100km (50.4/37.7/31.7mpg) [42/31.4/26.4US mpg], Catalyst 6.4/8.4/10.7L/100km (44.1/33.6/26.4mpg) [36.8/28/22US mpg].

Citroen BX 16 TRS

```
1580 cm3
69/85kW-93/114hp-94/115PS
1 2V Carb/Fuel Injection
```

Engine for 16S/RS/TRS/TRI/GTi

As 1361 cm3 except:

Body, Weight: 5-door Saloon/Sedan, 5-seater; kerbweight (DIN) 950–1015kg, gross vehicle weight 1450kg. 5-door Estate/Station Wagon (Break), 5-seater; kerbweight (DIN) 990–1045kg, gross vehicle weight 1530–1580kg.

Engine data (DIN): (83 x 73mm), 1580cm3; compression ratio 9/9.5:1; 69kW (93hp) [94PS] at 6000rpm, 43.8kW/L (58.7hp/L) [59.5PS/L]; 137Nm (101.1lbft) at 2800rpm.
For some countries: 66kW (88.5hp) [90PS] or compression ratio 8.4:1; 65.5kW (87.8hp) [89PS].
With Bosch LE2-Jetronic injection: compression ratio 9.8:1; 85/83kW (114/111hp) [115/113PS] at 6250rpm; 131Nm (96.7lbft) at 3000rpm.

Engine construction: Designated 171 C–XU 5S. Transverse engine, inclined 30deg to rear. Parallel valves, 1 overhead camshaft (toothed belt); oil capacity 4.75/5L (4.5/4.7US qt); 1 Solex 32– 34 Z1/319 or Weber 32–34 DRTC 100W downdraught 2V carb. Bosch H6DC, Champion S279 YC or Eyquem C72LJS sparkplugs, 12V 33/35/45Ah.

Transmission: a) 5-speed manual, final drive ratio 4,188 (16/67) or 4.43 (14/62).
b) Automatic ZF 4 HP 14, hydraulic torque converter and 4-speed Planetary gear set, central selector lever; final drive ratio 3.688 (16/59).

Gear ratios: a) 5-speed manual: 1st 3.25; 2nd 1.85; 3rd 1.280; 4th 0.969; 5th 0.757; R 3.333.
b) Automatic; max torque multiplication in converter 2 times, Planetary gear set ratios: 1st 2.78; 2nd 1.577; 3rd 1.15; 4th 0.851; R 3.258.

Chassis: Optional ABS (Teves); optional power assisted steering; fuel tank capacity 52L (11.4Gal) [13.7US Gal]; tyres 165/70HR 14, wheel rims 5".

Dimensions: Track 142/136cm.

Performance: Max speed 109.4mph/176kmh. Break and Automatic 106mph/170kmh (manufacturer's test specifications), speed at 1000rpm in 5th gear 21.2mph/34.1kmh; acceleration 0 – 62mph/100kmh 11.3secs, Automatic 13.8secs, standing km 32.9secs, Automatic 35.6secs; power to weight ratio from 14kg/kW (10.3kg/PS); consumption ECE 5.5/7.0/8.9L/100km (51.4/40.4/31.7mpg) [42.8/33.6/26.4US mpg]; Break 5.8/7.5/8.9L/100km (48.7/37.7/31.7mpg) [40.6/31.4/26.4US mpg], Automatic 5.8/7.6/8.7L/100km (48.7/37.2/32.5mpg) [40.6/30.9/27US mpg].
With Injection: Max speed 120mph/194kmh.

```
1905cm3
77/79/80kW-103/106/107hp-105/107/109PS
12V Carb/Fuel Injection
```

Engine for 19TRS, 19RI and 19 TRI

As 1361cm3 except:

Body, Weight: 5-door Saloon/Sedan, 5-seater; kerbweight (DIN) 995–1000kg, gross vehicle weight 1460 - 1480kg.
Saloon/Sedan 4x4 5-door, 5-seater; kerbweight (DIN) 1105kg, gross vehicle weight 1570kg.
Estate/Station Wagon (Break) 5-door, 5-seater; kerbweight (DIN) 1035–1050kg, gross vehicle weight 1570–1600kg.
Estate/Station Wagon 4x4 5-door, 5-seater; kerbweight (DIN) 1145kg, gross vehicle weight 1690kg.

Citroen BX 19 TRS

Engine data (DIN): 4-cylinder in–line (83 x 88mm), 1905cm3; compression ratio 9.3:1; 77kW (103hp) [105PS] or 79kW (106hp) [107PS] at 5600rpm, 40.5kW/L (54.3hp/L) [55.1PS/L]; 162Nm (119.5lbft) at 3000rpm.
Some countries: 75kW (101hp) [102PS].
With Catalyst and fuel injection: Compression ratio 9.2:1; 80kW (107hp) [109PS] at 6000rpm, 42kW/L (56.3hp/L) [57.2PS/L]; 162Nm (119.5lbft) at 3000rpm; unleaded regular grade.

Engine construction: Designated D2A–XU9 2C also XU9M. Transverse engine, inclined 30 deg to rear. Parallel valves, 1 overhead camshaft (toothed belt); oil capacity 4.75/5L (4.5/4.7US qt); 1 Solex 34Cl–SAC Z1 2V carb also Solex-Fenix 1B central injection. Bosch H6 DC, Champion C9 YCX or Eyquem FC52 LS sparkplugs, 12V 33/45/50Ah battery.

Transmission (to front wheels or 4x4 permanent all wheels): a) 5-speed manual, final drive ratio 3.688 (16/59) 4.429 (14/62) or (Break) 4.063 (16/65).
b) Automatic ZF 4 HP 14, hydraulic torque converter and 4-speed Planetary gear set, central selector lever; final drive ratio 3.15.
c) 4x4 only with 5-speed manual, final drive ratio 4.429 (14/62); permanent four wheel drive (distribution front/rear 53/47%), manual lock central Planetary differential. Rear limited slip differential, with ABS-Torsen differential.

Citroen BX 19 4x4

Gear ratios: a) 5-speed manual: 1st 3.308; Catalyst: 2.923, 4x4 3.454; 2nd 1.85; 3rd 1.28; 4th 0.969; 5th 0.757; R 3.333.

Citroen

b) Automatic; Max torque multiplication in converter 2 times, Planetary gear set ratios: 1st 2.78; 2nd 1.577; 3rd 1.15; 4th 0.85; R 3.258.

Chassis: Optional ABS (Teves); power assisted steering; fuel tank capacity 66L (14.5Gal) [17.4US Gal). Tyres 165/70HR 14, wheel rims 5".

Dimensions: Track 142/136cm, turning circle 11.2m.

Performance: Max speed 115mph/185kmh, Break 113mph/182kmh, Automatic 112–110mph/180–177kmh (manufacturer's test specifications), speed at 1000rpm in 5th gear 21.1mph/33.9kmh. Break 21.8mph/35.1kmh; acceleration 0 - 62mph/100kmh 10secs, Break 10.4secs, Automatic 11.8secs; standing km 32secs, Break 32.5secs, Automatic 33.4/35.2secs power to weight ratio from 12.9kg/kW (9.5kg/PS); consumption ECE 6.0/7.6/9.5L/100km (47.1/37.2/29.7mpg) [39.2/30.9/24.8US mpg], Automatic 6.1/7.6/9.5L/100km (46.3/37.2/29.7mpg) [38.6/30.9/24.8US mpg], Break 5.9/7.8/9.4L/100km (47.9/36.2/30.1mpg) [39.9/30.2/25US mpg], Automatic 6.1/7.8/9.5L/100km (46.3/36.2/29.7mpg) [38.6/30.2/24.8US mpg].
4x4: Max speed 114mph/183kmh, Break 112mph/180kmh; acceleration 0 - 62mph/100kmh 10.7secs, break 11.2secs; consumption ECE 6.6/8.5/10.5 (42.8/33.2/26.9mpg) [35.6/27.7/22.4US mpg].
With Catalyst: Max speed 118mph/189kmh; acceleration 0 – 62mph/100kmh 10.8secs, standing km 32.8secs; consumption ECE 6.9/8.8/10.9L/100km (40.9/32.1/25.9mpg) [34.1/26.7/21.6US mpg].

1905cm3
92kW–123hp–125PS
Fuel Injection

Engine for 19 GTI and 19 RI/TRI break

As 1361cm3, except:

Body, Weight: 5–door Saloon/Sedan, 5-seater; kerbweight (DIN) 1025kg, gross vehicle weight 1480 - 1515kg.
Estate/Station Wagon (Break) 5-door, 5-seater; kerbweight (din) 1045 - 1060kg, gross vehicle weight 1510 - 1640kg.

Engine data (DIN): 4–cylinder in–line (83 x 88mm), compression ratio 9.3:1; 92kW (123hp) [125PS] at 5500rpm, 48.3kW/L (64.8hp/L) [65.6PS/L]; 175Nm (129.1lbft) at 4500rpm.
With Catalyst: Compression ratio 9.2:1; 90 or 88kW (121 or 118hp) [122 or 120PS] at 6000rpm; 47.3/46.2kW/L (63.4/62hp/L) [64.1/63.0PS/L]; 153Nm (112.9lbft) at 3000rpm; unleaded premium grade.

Engine construction: Designated D6A–XU9 J2. Transverse engine inclined 30deg to rear. Parallel valves, 1 overhead camshaft (toothed belt); oil capacity 4.75/5L (4.4/4.7US qt); Bosch LE 3– Jetronic electronic fuel injection, Catalyst-Motronic M1-3. Eyquem FC62LS spark plugs or FC52 LS; 12V 45Ah battery.

Transmission: a) 5–speed manual, final drive ratio 3.588 (17/61), 3.688 (16/59), Break 4.2 (15/63), 4.286 (14/62) also 4.188 (16/67).
b) Automatic ZF 4 HP 14, hydraulic torque converter and 4-speed Planetary gear set, central selector lever; final drive ratio 3.825 (17/65).

Gear ratios: a) 5-speed manual, 1st 3.308/3.25; 2nd 1.882/1.85; 3rd 1.36; 4th 1.069; 5th 0.865; R 3.333 or 1st 3.25; 2nd 1.85; 3rd 1.28; 4th 0.969; 5th 0.757/0.865; R 3.333.
b) Automatic, Max torque multiplication in converter 2 times, Planetary gear ratios: 1st 2.51; 2nd 1.425; 3rd 1.04; 4th 0.769; R 2.944.

Chassis: Optional ABS (Teves); power assisted steering; fuel tank 66L (14.5Gal) [17.4US Gal]; tyres 185/60HR 14 or 165/70 HR 14, wheel rims 5.5".

Dimensions: Track 143/138cm, turning circle 11.2m.

Citroen BX 19 GTi

Performance: Max speed 123mph/198kmh, Break 119mph/192kmh (manufacturer's test specifications), speed at 1000rpm in 5th gear 21.1mph/34kmh; acceleration 0 – 62mph/100kmh 8.9secs, Automatic 10.3secs; standing km 30.5secs, Automatic 31.9secs; power to weight ratio 11.1kg/kW (8.2kg/PS); consumption ECE 6.1/8.2/10.4L/100km (46.3/34.4/27.2mpg) [38.6/28.7/22.6US mpg], Automatic 6.4/8.2/11.1L/100km (44.1/34.4/25.4mpg) [36.8/28.7/21.2US mpg].
With Catalyst: Max speed 122mph/196kmh, Break 118mph/189kmh, Automatic 119-116mph/192-186kmh; acceleration 0 - 62mph/100kmh 9.8secs, Break 10.3secs; standing km 31.3secs, Break 32.1secs.

1905cm3 16V
117.5/110kW–157.5/147hp–160/150PS
Fuel Injection

Engine for 19GTI 16 V

As 1361cm3 except:

Body, Weight: 5–door Saloon/Sedan, 4/5–seater; kerbweight (DIN) 1070 - 1120kg, gross vehicle weight 1490/1535kg.

Engine data (DIN): 4-cylinder in–line (83 x 88mm), 1905cm3; compression ratio 10.4:1; 117.5kW (157.5) [160PS] at 6500rpm, 61.7kW/L (82.7hp/L) [84PS/L]; 181Nm (133.5lbft) at 5000rpm.
With Catalyst: Compression ratio 9.7:1; 108kW (145hp) [148PS] or 110kW (147hp) [150PS] at 6400rpm, 56.7/57.8kW/L (76/77.5hp/L) [76.2/78.8PS/L]; approx 180Nm (132.8lbft) at 5000rpm; octane req premium grade.

Engine construction: Designated D6A–XU9 J4b/J4/Z. Transverse engine inclined 30deg to rear. 4 valves per cylinder (in V), hydraulic tappets, 2 overhead camshafts (toothed belt); oil capacity 4.75/5L (4.5/4.7US qt); Bosch Motronic electronic fuel injection. Eyquem FC62LS sparkplugs, 12V 45Ah Battery, 90A alternator; cooling system capacity 8L (7.6US qt).

Transmission: 5–speed manual, final drive ratio 4.43 (14/62).

Gear ratios: 1st 2.923; 2nd 1.85; 3rd 1.28; 4th 0.969; 5th 0.757; R 3.333.

Chassis: Disc brakes, front ventilated, ABS (Teves); power assisted steering; fuel tank capacity 66L (14.5Gal) [17.4US Gal]; tyres 195/60VR 14, wheel rims 6".

Dimensions: Track 144/138cm, turning circle 11.2m. Width 169cm.

Performance: Max speed 135.5mph/218kmh (manufacturer's test specifications), speed at 1000rpm in 5th gear 20.2mph/32.3kmh; acceleration 0 – 62mph/100kmh 7.9secs; standing km 28.8secs; power to weight ratio 9.1kg/kW (6.9kg/PS); consumption ECE 6.6/8.1/11.3L/100km (42.8/34.9/25mpg) [35.6/29/20.8US mpg].
With Catalyst: Max speed 132mph/213kmh; acceleration 0 – 62mph/100kmh 8.9secs, standing km 29.7secs; consumption ECE 6.8/8.5/12.0L/100km (41.5/33.2/23.5mpg) [34.6/27.7/19.6US mpg].

Citroen BX 19 GTi 16 Valve

1.9/1.8 Diesel
52/48/44kW–70/64/59hp–71/65/60PS
Injection Pump

Engine for 19RD/TRD and 19 D/RD Break. D/17 RD

As 1361cm3 except:

Body, Weight: 5–door Saloon/Sedan, 5–seater; kerbweight (DIN) 990–1020kg gross vehicle weight 1500kg; 5–door Estate/Station Wagon (Break), 5-seater; kerbweight (DIN) 1035–1050kg gross vehicle weight 1580kg.

Engine data (DIN): 4–cylinder in–line (83 x 88mm), 1905cm3; compression ratio 23:1; 52kW (70hp) [71PS] at 4600rpm, 27.4kW/L (36.7hp/L) [37.3PS/L]; 123Nm (90.7lbft) at 2000rpm.
Some countries: 48kW (64hp) [65PS] at 4600rpm, 25.3kW/L (33.9hp/L) [34.1PS/L]; 120Nm (88.5lbft) at 2000rpm.
1.8 Litre Diesel: (80 x 88mm), 1769cm3; compression ratio 23:1; 44kW (59hp) [60PS] at 4600rpm, 24.9kW/L (33.4hp/L) [33.9PS/L]; 110Nm (81.1lbft) at 2000rpm.

Citroen

Engine construction: Designated 162-XUD9/161 A-XUD7. Transverse engine inclined 30deg to rear. Parallel valves, 1 overhead camshaft (toothed belt); grey cast iron cylinder block; oil capacity 4.5/5L (4.4/4.7US qt); CAV Roto diesel or Bosch diesel injection pump. Glow plugs, 12V 50/60/83Ah Battery.

Transmission: a) 5-speed manual, final drive ratio 3.94 (16/63) or 4.25 (16/68), Break 4.063 (16/65), 1.8 4.188 (16/67).
b) Automatic ZF 4 HP 14, hydraulic torque converter and 4-speed Planetary gear set, central selector lever with Positions P-R-N-A-3-2-1; final drive ratio 3.825 (17/65).

Gear ratios: a) 5-speed manual, 1st 3.25/3.308; 2nd 1.85/1.882; 3rd 1.28; 4th 0.969; 5th 0.757; R 3.333.
b) Automatic; Max torque multiplication in converter 2 times, Planetary gear set ratios: 1st 2.51; 2nd 1.425; 3rd 1.425; 4th 0.769; R 2.944.

Citroen BX 19 TRD

Chassis: Optional ABS (Teves); optional power assisted steering; fuel tank capacity 52L (11.4Gal) [13.7US Gal]; tyres 165/70 TR 14, wheel rims 5".

Dimensions: Track 142/136cm; turning circle 11.2m.

Performance: Max speed 102.5mph/165kmh, Break 101mph/162kmh (manufacturer's test specifications), speed at 1000rpm in 5th gear 22.5mph/36.2kmh, Break 21.8mph/35.1kmh; acceleration 0 – 62mph/100kmh 13.8secs, Break 14.5secs, standing km 35.3secs, Break 36.3secs; power to weight ratio from 19.0kg/kW (13.9kg/PS); consumption ECE 4.6/6.1/6.5L/100km (61.4/46.3/43.5mpg) [51.1/38.6/36.2US mpg], Break 4.8/6.6/6.5L/100km (58.8/42.8/43.5mpg) [49/35.6/36.2US mpg].
With 64PS: Max speed 98–96mph/157–155kmh; acceleration 0 – 62mph/100kmh 15.5/16/3secs, standing km 36.9/37.6secs; consumption ECE 4.7/6.2/6.5L/100km (60.1/45.6/43.5mpg) [50/37.9/36.2US mpg], Break 5.0/6.7/6.5L/100km (56.5/42.2/43.5mpg) [47/35.1/36.2US mpg].
1.8-Diesel: Max speed 97mph/155kmh; acceleration 0 – 62mph/100kmh 17.2secs, standing km 37.9secs; consumption ECE 4.6/6.4/6.4L/100km (61.4/44.1/44.1mpg) [51.1/36.8/36.8US mpg].

```
1.8 Turbo Diesel
66kW-88hp-90PS
Injection Pump
```

Engine for RD/TRD Turbo

As 1361cm3 except:

Body, Weight: Saloon/Sedan 5-door, 5-seater; kerbweight (DIN) from 1025kg, gross vehicle weight 1500kg.
Estate/Station Wagon (Break) 5-door, 5-seater; kerbweight (DIN) from 1075kg, gross vehicle weight 1620kg.

Engine data: 4-cylinder in-line (80 x 88mm), 1769cm3; compression ratio 22:1; 66kW (88hp) [90PS] at 4300rpm, 37.3kW/L (50hp/L) [50.9PS/L]; 182Nm (134.3lbft) at 2100rpm.

Engine construction: Designated XUD 7TE. Transverse front engine inclined 30deg to rear. Parallel valves, 1 overhead camshaft (toothed belt); greycast iron cylinder head; oil capacity 5L (4.7US qt); diesel injection pump; 1 turbocharger KKK K14 or Garrett T2; max charge-air pressure 0.8 bar, charge-air cooler; glow plugs, 12V 50/60/83Ah battery.

Transmission: 5-speed manual, final drive ratio 3.938 (16/63).

Gear ratios: 1st 3.25; 2nd 1.85; 3rd 1.148/1.28; 4th 0.829; 5th 0.658; R 3.333.

Chassis: Optional ABS (System Teves); Power/assisted steering; fuel tank 66L (14.5Gal) [17.4US Gal]; tyres 165/70 TR 14, wheel rims 5".

Dimensions: Track 142/136cm; turning circle 11.2m.

Performance: Max speed 112mph/180kmh, Break 108mph/174kmh (manufacturers test specification), speed at 1000rpm in top gear 25.9mph/41.7kmh; power to weight ratio from 15.6kg/kW (11.4kg/PS); consumption ECE 4.5/6.3/6.9L/100km (62.8/44.8/40.9mpg) [52.3/37.3/34.1US mpg], Break 4.8/6.8/6.9L/100km (58.8/41.5/40.9mpg) [49/34.6/34.1US mpg].

Citroen BX TRD Turbo Break

Citroen CX

20 – 22 – 25 – 25 Turbo 2 – 25 D – 25 D Turbo 2

Top of the Mid-Class category with front wheel drive and transverse engine. Launched in August 1974. June 1979: 2 Litre light-alloy engine. September 1979: Diesel Saloon/Sedan long wheelbase. April 1983 with Turbo Diesel and June 1983, with 2.5 fuel injection. September 1984: 2.5 Turbo with 165.5hp. July 1985: modifications to body, also with 2.2. Autumn 1986 Turbo with catalyst (157.5hp) and early in 1987 Turbo Diesel with increased power.

Citroen CX 20 RE

```
CX 20
78/75kW-104.5/100.5hp-106/102PS
1 2V Carb
```

Engine for 20RE/TRE and 20 RE Break/Family

Body, Weight: 4-door Saloon/Sedan, 5-seater; kerbweight (DIN) from 1220kg, gross vehicle weight 1780kg. 5-door Estate/Station Wagon "Break/Family", 5/8-seater; kerbweight (DIN) 1390/1400kg, gross vehicle weight 2080kg.

Engine data (DIN): 4-cylinder in-line (88 x 82mm), 1995cm3; compression ratio 9.2:1; 78kW (104.5hp) [106PS] at 5500rpm, 39.1kW/L (52.4hp/L) [53.1PS/L]; 166Nm (122.4lbft) at 3250rpm; leaded premium grade.
Or 75kW (100.5hp) [102PS]; 162Nm (119.5lbft).

Engine construction: Front transverse engine, designated 829-A5. Valves in V 33deg, 1 overhead camshaft (toothed belt); light-alloy engine block and cylinder head, wet cylinder liners; 5 bearing crankshaft; oil capacity 5L (4.7US qt); 1 Solex 34 CICF/214 or Weber 34DMTR 46/250 downdraught 2V carb. Bosch H7 DC, Champion S281 YC or Eyquem C72 LJS sparkplugs. 12V 45 or 60Ah Battery, 72A/972W alternator; cooling system capacity 9.6L (9.1US qt).

Transmission (to front wheels): 4 or 5-speed manual, floor shift, final drive ratio 4.36 (14/61).

Gear ratios: 4-speed manual: 1st 3.166; 2nd 1.833; 3rd 1.133; 4th 0.8; R 3.153.

Chassis: Integral body with bolted auxiliary frame; hydro-pneumatic suspension with hydraulic support, automatic level control system, front control

Citroen

arm, rear trailing arm, front and rear antiroll bar. Servo/power assisted disc brakes, diameter front (ventilated) 26cm, rear 22.4cm, Break 23.5cm, mechanical handbrake to front wheels; power assisted rack and pinion steering; fuel tank capacity 68L (14.9Gal) 18US Gal); tyres front (Break front and rear) 195/70TR 14, rear 185/70 TR 14, wheel rims 5.5"J.

Dimensions: Saloon/Sedan: Wheelbase 284.5cm, track 152/137cm, clearance 15.5cm, turning circle 12.5m, load space 17.8cu ft (505dm3) - net 11.6cu ft (330dm3). Length 465cm, width 177cm, height 136cm. Estate/Station Wagon: Wheelbase 309.5cm, track 151/139 or 152/140cm, clearance 15.5cm turning circle 13.4m. Load space 41- 76.6cu ft (1160-2170dm3). Length 493cm, width 177cm, height 146cm.

Performance: Max speed 109mph/175kmh, Break 103mph/165kmh (manufacturer's test specifications), speed at 1000rpm in 4th gear 20.8mph/33.4kmh in 5th 22.5mph/36.2kmh; acceleration 0 - 62mph/100kmh 12.4secs, standing km 33.6secs; power to weight ratio from 15.6kg/kW (11.5kg/PS); consumption ECE 6.9/9.0/12.0L/100km (40.9/31.4/23.5mpg) [34.1/26.1/19.6US mpg].

```
CX 22
84.5kW-113hp-115PS
1 2V Carb
```

Engine for 22 TRS and 22 RS Break/Family.

As CX 20, except:

Body, Weight: 4-door Saloon/Sedan, 5-seater; kerbweight (DIN) from 1245kg gross, vehicle weight 1780kg; 5-door Estate/Station Wagon "Break/Family" 5/8-seater; kerbweight (DIN) 1390/1400kg, gross vehicle weight 2080kg.

Engine data (DIN): 4-cylinder in-line (88 x 89mm), 2165cm3; compression ratio 9.8:1; 84.5kW (113hp) [115PS] at 5600rpm, 39.1kW/L (52.4hp/L) [53.1PS/L]; 178Nm (131.3lbft) at 3250rpm.

Engine construction: Designated J6 TA 500. 1 Weber 34 DMTR 110/100 downdraught twin 2V carb. Champion S 279 YC or Eyquem C 72 LJS sparkplugs; cooling system capacity 12L (11.4US qt).

Chassis: Optional ABS (Bosch)

Performance: Max speed 116mph/186kmh, Break 112mph/180kmh (manufacturer's test specifications), speed at 1000rpm in 5th gear 22.5mph/36.2kmh; acceleration 0 - 62mph/100kmh 10.6secs, standing km 32.5secs, Break 33.5secs; power to weight ratio 15.1kg/kW (11.1kg/PS); consumption ECE 6.6/8.5/12.0L/100km (42.8/33.2/23.5mpg) [35.6/27.7/19.6US mpg], Break 7.1/9.1/12.0L/100km (39.8/31/23.5mpg) [33.1/25.8/19.6US mpg].

Citroen CX 22 RS Break/Familiale

```
CX 25
101.5/90.5kW-136/121hp-138/123PS
Fuel Injection
```

Engine for GTi and Prestige as Break/Family TRI/RI

As CX 20, except:

Body, Weight: 4-door RI/GTi Saloon/Sedan, 5-seater; kerbweight (DIN) 1310-1370kg, gross vehicle weight 1885kg; 4-door long wheelbase Prestige Saloon/Sedan, 5-seater; kerbweight (DIN) 1430/1455kg, gross vehicle weight 1910kg; 5-door Break and Family Estate/Station Wagon, 5/8-seater; kerbweight (DIN) 1420/1480kg, gross vehicle weight 2165kg.

Engine data (DIN): (93 x 92mm), 2500cm3; compression ratio 8.75:1; 101.5kW (136hp) [138PS] at 5000rpm, 40.6kW/L (54.4hp/L) [55.2PS/L]; 211Nm (155.6lbft) at 4000rpm.

With Catalyst: compression ratio 8:1; 90.5kW (121hp) [123PS] at 5000rpm, 36.2kW/L (48.5hp/L) [49.2PS/L]; 187Nm (137.9lbft) at 4000rpm; unleaded regular to premium grade.

For some countries: 88.5kW (118.5hp) [120PS] or 89kW (119hp) [121PS].

Engine construction: Designated M25/659, Valves in V 60deg, side camshaft (chain); light-alloy cylinder head, grey cast iron block, wet cylinder liners; oil capacity 4.75L (4.5US qt); Bosch LE2-/LU2-Jetronic fuel injection. Champion L 82 Y or Eyquem 755 SX sparkplugs, 12V 60/70Ah battery, 80A alternator; cooling system capacity 12.3L (11.6Us qt).

Transmission: a) 5-speed manual, final drive ratio 4.07 (15/61) or 4.21 (14/59). b) ZF-Automatic, hydraulic torque converter and 3-speed Planetary gear set, central selector lever; final drive ratio 4.77 (13/62).

Gear ratios: a) 5-speed manual: 1st 3.166; 2nd 1.833; 3rd 1.25; 4th 0.939; 5th 0.733; R 3.153.
b) ZF-Automatic; Max torque multiplication in converter 2 times, Planetary gear set ratios: 1st 2.478; 2nd 1.478; 3rd 1; R 2.085.

Chassis: Optional ABS (Bosch); tyres 195/70HR 14, wheel rims 5.5", optional tyres 190/65 HR 390, wheel rims 150TR 390

Dimensions: Prestige (long wheelbase Saloon/Sedan): wheel base 309.5cm, turning circle 13.4m. Length 490cm, width 177cm, height 137.5cm.

Performance: Max speed 125.5mph/202kmh, Automatic 121mph/195kmh, Break 121-119mph/195-191kmh (manufacturer's test specifications), speed at 1000rpm in 5th gear 23.3mph/37.5kmh or 24.1mph/38.8kmh; acceleration 0 - 62mph/100kmh 9.2-9.7secs, Automatic 11.7- 12.3secs, standing km 31.1-31.7secs, Automatic 33.5-33.9secs; power to weight ratio from 12.9kg/kW (9.5kg/PS); consumption ECE 7.3/9.0/13.6L/100km (38.7/31.4/20.8mpg) [32.2/26.1/17.3US mpg], Automatic 8.5/10.2/13.0L/100km (33.2/27.7/21.7mpg) [27.7/23.1/18.1US mpg] or 9.1/11.1/13.0L/100km (31/25.4/21.7mpg) [25.8/21.2/18.1US mpg].
With Catalyst: Max speed 121mph/195kmh, Automatic 117mph/188kmh, Break 118-113mph/190-182kmh (manufacturer's test specifications); acceleration 0 - 62mph/100kmh 11.3secs, Automatic 14.2secs, Break 12.5/16.3secs; consumption ECE 8.5/9.9/14.7L/100km (33.2/28.5/19.2mpg) [27.7/23.8/16US mpg], Automatic 9.6/11.9/13.8L/100km (29.4/23.7/20.5mpg) [24.5/19.8/17US mpg].

Citroen CX 25 GTi Turbo 2

```
CX 25 Turbo
123.5/117.5kW-165.5/157.5hp-168/160PS
Fuel Injection
```

Engine for GTi Turbo 2 and Prestige Turbo 2.

As CX 20, except:

Body, Weight: 4-door Saloon/Sedan, 5-seater; kerbweight (DIN) 1370-1385kg gross vehicle weight 1885kg; 4-door Long Saloon/Sedan, 5-seater; kerbweight (DIN) 1440-1455kg gross vehicle weight 1920kg.

Engine data (DIN): (93 x 92mm), 2500cm3; compression ratio 8.5: 1; 123.5kW (167.5hp) [168PS] at 5000rpm, 49.4kW/L (66.2hp/L) [67.4PS/L]; 294Nm (217lbft) at 3250rpm; leaded premium grade.
With Catalyst: Compression ratio 7.75: 1; 117.5kW (157.5hp) [160PS] at 4750rpm, 47kW/L (63hp/L) [64PS/L]; 270Nm (199.2lbft) at 3250rpm; unleaded regular grade.

Engine construction: Designated M 25/662/EN 5 TE. Valves in V 60deg, side camshaft (chain); light-alloy cylinder head, grey cast iron block, wet cylinder liners; oil capacity 4.85L (4.5US qt); Bosch LE/LU2-Jetronic electronic fuel injection, 1 Garret TO3 exhaust turbocharger, Max boost pressure 0.7bar, charge-air cooler; electronic fuel pump. Champion L82, Eyquem 755X sparkplugs, 12V 60/70Ah battery, 80A/1080W alternator; cooling system capacity 13L (12.3US qt).

Transmission: 5-speed manual, final drive ratio 3.93 (15/59) or 4.214 (14/59).

Gear ratios: 1st 3.417; 2nd 1.944; 3rd 1.25; 4th 0.882; 5th 0.674; R 3.154.

Dimensions: Prestige (Long wheelbase Saloon/Sedan); wheelbase 309.5cm, turning circle 13.4m. Length 490cm, width 177cm, height 137.5cm.

Performance: Max speed 139mph/223kmh (manufacturer's test specifications), speed at 1000rpm in 5th gear 27mph/43.5kmh; acceleration 0 – 62mph/100kmh 7.8–8secs, standing km 29–29.3secs power to weight ratio from 11.1kg/kW (8.2kg/PS); consumption ECE 7.8/9.6/13.8L/100km (36.2/29.4/20.5mpg) [30.2/24.5/17US mpg]. With Catalyst: Max speed 134mph/215kmh (manufacturer's test specifications); acceleration 0 – 62mph/100kmh 9.2secs, standing km 30.7secs; consumption ECE 8.2/10.2/14.5L/100km (34.4/27.7/19.5mpg) [28.7/23.1/16.2US mpg].

Citroen CX 25 Prestige Turbo 2

```
CX 25 Diesel
55kW–74hp–75PS
Injection Pump
```

Engine for 25RD/TRD and 25 RD Break/Family

As CX 20, except:

Body, Weight: Saloon/Sedan: kerbweight (DIN) 1330kg, gross vehicle weight 1890kg; Estate/Station Wagon Break and Family (8–seater); kerbweight (DIN) 1455kg gross, vehicle weight 2190kg.

Engine data (DIN): (93 x 92mm), 2500cm3; compression ratio 22.25: 1; 55kW (74hp) [75PS] at 4250rpm, 22kW/L (29.5hp/L) [30PS/L]; 153Nm (112.9lbft) at 2000rpm.

Engine construction: Designated M 25/660. Parallel valves, side camshaft (toothed belt); grey cast iron block, light–alloy cylinder head; oil capacity 4.6L (4.4US qt); injection pump. Heater plugs; 12V 88Ah battery; 72/80A alternator; cooling system capacity 12.3L (11.6US qt).

Transmission: Final drive ratio 4.36 (14/61).

Performance: Max speed 98mph/158kmh, Break 95mph/153kmh (manufacturer's test specifications), speed at 1000rpm in top gear 22.5mph/36.2kmh; acceleration 0 – 62mph/100kmh 16.8secs, Break 17.8secs, standing km 37.7secs, Break 38.6secs; power to weight ratio 24.2kg/kW (17.8kg/PS); consumption ECE 5.5/7.5/8.4L/100km (51.4/37.7/33.6mpg) [42.8/31.4/29US mpg].

```
CX 25 Turbo Diesel
88/78kW–118/104.5hp–120/106PS
Injection Pump
```

Engine for RD/TRD Turbo 2, Saloon/Sedan D Turbo 2 and TRD Turbo 2 Break/Family.

As CX 20, except:

Body, Weight: Saloon/Sedan; kerbweight (DIN) 1360–1420kg, gross vehicle weight 1905kg. 4–door long wheelbase Saloon/Sedan, 5–seater; kerbweight (DIN) 1400kg, gross vehicle weight 1920kg: Estate/Station Wagon (Break/Family); kerbweight (DIN) 1480–1520kg, gross vehicle weight 2200kg.

Engine data (DIN): (93 x 92mm), 2500cm3; compression ratio 21.25: 1; 88kW (118hp) [120PS] at 3900rpm, 35.2kW/L (47.2hp) [48PS/L]; 256Nm (188.9lbft). Some countries: Compression ratio 21:1; 78kW (104.5hp) [106PS] at 3900rpm, 31.2kW/L (41.8hp/L) [42.4PS/L]; 258Nm (190.4lbft) at 2250rpm.

Engine construction: Designated M25/648 parallel valves, side camshaft (toothed belt); light–alloy cylinder head, grey cast iron block; oil capacity 4.6/4.8L (4.4/4.5US qt); Diesel injection pump; 1 Garrett TO25/TO3 exhaust turbocharger, boost pressure 0.8/0.68 bar. Bosch heater plugs; 12V 88Ah Battery, 80A alternator; cooling system capacity 13L (12.3US qt).

Transmission: Final drive ratio 3.625 (16/59).

Gear ratios: 1st 3.417; 2nd 1.944; 3rd 1.25; 4th 0.882; 5th 0.674; R 3.154.

Chassis: Optional ABS (Bosch); tyres 195/70 TR/HR 14, wheel rims 5.5", Saloon/Sedan 6", optional tyres 190/65 HR 390, wheel rims 150 TR 390.

Citroen CX 25 TRD Turbo 2 Break/Familiale

Dimensions: Long wheelbase Saloon/Sedan: wheelbase 309.5cm, turning circle 13.4m. Length 490cm, width 177cm, height 137.5cm.

Performance: Max speed 121mph/195kmh, Break 117mph/188kmh (manufacturer's test specifications), speed at 1000rpm in 4th gear 22.4mph/36kmh, in 5th gear 28.9mph/46.5kmh; acceleration 0 – 62mph/100kmh 10.5–12.6secs, standing km 32.3secs power to weight ratio 15.6kg/kW (11.4kg/PS); consumption ECE 4.9/6.6/8.5L/100km (57.6/42.8/33.2mpg) [48/35.6/27.7US mpg], Break 5.4/7.4/8.5L/100km (52.3/38.2/33.2mpg) [43.6/31.8/27.7US mpg]. 104.5hp. Version 157.5PS: Max speed 114.5mph/184kmh, Break 111mph/178kmh; acceleration 0–100kmh; 13.1–14.2secs, standing km 34.8–35.9secs consumption ECE 5.6/7.4/8.6L/100km (50.4/38.2/32.8mpg) [42/31.8/27.4US mpg], Break 6.1/7.9/8.6L/100km (46.3/35.8/32.8mpg) [38.6/29.8/27.4US mpg].

Citroen XM

New model. Successor to the CX Saloon/Sedan with semi-active hydropneumatic system, tail gate, front wheel drive, 4-cylinder or V6 engine, from 2-3 Litre capacity (Performance approx 168hp) with Diesel and Turbodiesel. Launched during March 1989.

Citroen XM

CITROEN R

Soaetatea Mixta Oltcit SA, Craiova, SR Rumanien

Factory founded in collaboration with the Rumanian State.

Citroen Oltcit

For technical data see under Citroen in France.

CIZETA   I

Cizeta Motors SRL, Via dei Tipografi 6/B, 41100 Modena, Italy.
New manufacturer, constructing Sports cars in small quantity series.

Cizeta Moroder V16T

New model. High efficiency Sports car with central engine 6 Litre V16 (total 64 valves), 552hp and 5-speed manual transmission. Launched Los Angeles Auto show January 1989.

```
6.0 V16 64V
412kW-552hp-560PS
Fuel Injection
```

Body, Weight: Coupe 2-door, 2-seater; kerbweight (DIN) 1700kg.
Engine Data (DIN): 16 cylinder in V 90deg (86 x 64.5mm), 5995cm3; compression ratio 9.3:1; 412kW (552hp) [560PS] at 8000rpm, 68.7kW/L (92.1hp/L) [93.3PS/L]; 540Nm (398.5lbft) at 6000rpm; premium grade.
Engine construction: Transverse central engine. 4 valves for cylinder (total 64 valves), per cylinder bank 2 overhead camshafts, total 8 camshafts (toothed belt); light-alloy cylinder head and cylinder block, wet cylinder liners; 2x5 bearing crankshafts; oil capacity approx 18L (17US qts); 2 Bosch k-Jetronic fuel injectors. 12V 80Ah battery, 115W alternator; cooling system capacity.
Transmission (to all wheels): 5-speed manual, floor shift, final drive ratio 4.22; optional differential brakes.
Gear ratios: 1st 2.42: 2nd 1.61; 3rd 1.14; 4th 0.846; 5th 0.704; R 2.86.
Chassis: Space chassis with light-alloy body; front and rear independent suspension with swinging A-arms, coil springs, telescopic damper, rear twin compression struts and twin dampers, front antiroll bar. Power/assisted disc brakes (ventilated), disc diameter 33.2cm, mechanical handbrake to rear wheels; Servo/assisted rack and pinion steering; 2 fuel tanks capacity 60L (13.2Gal) [15.9US Gal], total 120L (26.4Gal) [31.7US Gal]; front tyres 245/40 ZR 17, rear 335/35 ZR 17, wheel rims 9 also 13J.
Dimensions: Wheelbase 269cm, track 161/166.5cm, clearance approx 12cm, turning circle 12.9m, load space 12.4cu ft (350dm3), length 444cm, width 206cm, height 111.5cm.
Performance: Max speed 204mph/328kmh (manufacturers test specification), speed at 1000rpm in 5th gear 25.5mph/41kmh; acceleration 0 - 62mph/100kmh 4.5secs; power to weight ratio 4.1kg/kW (3.0kg/PS); consumption ECE 9.6/11.3/24L/100km (29.4/25/11.8mpg) [24.5/20.8/9.8US mpg].

Cizeta Moroder V16T

DACIA   R

Uzina de Autoturisme Pitesti, Progresul, Ploiesti, St. Gangeni 99, Rumania
Rumanian manufacturer building Renault vehicles under license since 1968.

Dacia 1210/1310/1410

Production of the Renault 12 under license in Romania since 1969, allowed to export model since 1977. November 1984: also available as a 2-door Coupe. For 1989, new fastback model being prepared.

```
4-cylinder
35.5/39.5/48kW-47.5/53/64hp-48/54/65PS
1 Carb
```

Body, Weight: 4-door Saloon/Sedan, 5-seater; kerbweight (DIN) 910–940kg, gross vehicle weight 1360kg. 2-door Coupe, 4/5-seater; kerbweight (DIN) 900kg, gross vehicle weight approx 1320kg. 5-door Fastback-Saloon/Sedan 5-seater; kerbweight (DIN) approx 900kg, gross vehicle weight 1360kg. 5-door Estate/Station Wagon, 5-seater; kerbweight (DIN) 980kg, gross vehicle weight 1380kg.

Dacia Fastback

Engine data (DIN): 4-cylinder in-line; 1210: (70 x 77mm), 1185cm3; compression ratio 8.5:1; 35.5kW (47.5hp) [48PS] at 5300rpm, 29.8kW/L (39.9hp/L) [40.5PS/L]; 80Nm (59lbft) at 3000rpm; leaded regular grade.
Export version: 37kW (49.5hp) [50PS]. 1310: (73 x 77mm), 1289cm3; compression ratio 8.5:1; 39.5kW (53hp) [54PS] at 5250rpm, 30.8kW/L (41.3hp/L) [41.9PS/L]; 88Nm (64.9lbft) at 3000rpm; leaded regular grade. 1410: (76 x 77mm), 1397cm3; compression ratio 9.5:1; 48kW (64hp) [65PS] at 5500rpm, 34.4kW/L (46.1hp/L) [46.5PS/L]; 100Nm (73.8lbf) at 3300rpm; leaded premium grade.
For some countries: 45.4kW (61hp) [62PS].
Engine construction: Engine fitted in front of front axle. Side-mounted camshaft (chain); light-alloy cylinder head; wet cylinder linings; crankshaft with 5 bearings; oil capacity 3L (2.8US qt); 1 Solex 32 or Zenith 32 downdraught carb. Battery 12V 45Ah, alternator 36/50A; cooling system capacity 5L (4.7US qt).
Transmission (to front wheels): 4 or 5-speed manual, floor shift, final drive ratio 3.78 (9/34).
Gear ratios: a) 4-speed manual: 1st 3.62; 2nd 2.26; 3rd 1.48; 4th 1.032; R 3.08. b) 5-speed manual: 1st 4.091; 2nd 2.176; 3rd 1.409; 4th 1.030; 5th 0.861; R 3.545.
Chassis: Integral body, front lower A arms, upper single control arms with torsion struts and coil springs, rear rigid axle with longitudinal arms, middle A rods and coil springs, front and rear antiroll bars, telescopic dampers. Brakes; optional servo/power assisted, front discs, rear drums, disc 22.8cm diameter, mechanical handbrake to rear wheels; rack and pinion steering; fuel tank 43/49L (9.5/10.8Gal) [11.4/12.9US Gal]; tyres 155 SR 13, 165 SR 13, 175/70 SR 13, wheel rims 4.5inches.
Dimensions: Wheelbase 244cm, track 131/133cm, Estate/Station Wagon 131/131cm, clearance 11cm, turning circle 10.8m. Load space 14.8cu ft (420dm3), Estate/Station Wagon 32–58.3cu ft (910– 1650dm3). Length 435cm – Fsatback and Estate/Station Wagon 440.5cm, width 163.5cm, height 143.5 –Estate/Station Wagon 145.5cm.
Performance: Max speed 84–87–93mph/135–140–150kmh (manufacturers test specifications), speed at 1000rpm in 4th gear 16.8mph/27kmh; standing km 43/41/38secs; power to weight ratio from 19.0kg/kW (14.0kg/PS). Consumption at 80kmh/urban 1210: 6.25/8.7L/100km (45.2/32.5mpg) [37.6–27US mpg], 1310: 6.25/8.7L/100km (45.2/32.5mpg) [37.6–27US mpg], 1410: 7.25/9.25L/100km (40/30.6mpg) [32.5–25.5US mpg] (manfuacturers test specifications).

```
1.6 Litre Diesel
51kW–68hp–70PS
Injection Pump/Turbo
```

As 47.5/53/64hp, except:

Weight: Kerbweight (DIN) approx 1040kg, gross vehicle weight 1440kg.
Engine data (DIN): 4-cylinder in-line (76.5 x 86.4mm), 1588cm3; compression ratio 23:1; 51kW (68hp) [70PS] at 4500rpm, 133Nm (98.2lbft) from 2500–2900rpm.

Dacia • Daewo • Daihatsu

Engine construction: Turbulence chamber diesel; oil capacity 4L (3.8US qt); turbocharger; Bosch BE injection pump, centrifugal governor, cold start enrichment device. Battery 12V 63Ah, alternator 45A.

Transmission: 5–speed manual, final drive ratio 3.67.

Gear ratios: 1st 3.82; 2nd 2.24; 3rd 1.48; 4th 0.97; 5th 0.76; R 3.4.

Performance: Max speed 99mph/160kmh; acceleration 0–62mph/100kmh 19secs; consumption ECE 5.2/7.2/7.8L/100km (54.3/39.2/36.2mpg) [45.2/32.7/30.2US mpg].

DAEWOO KO

Daewoo Motor Co. Ltd., Namdaemun–No 5–Ga, Chung–Gu, Seoul, South Korea

South Korean heavy industry group; assembly of the Opel Kadett under license in a new factory in Pupyong with 50 per cent GM participation.

Daewoo LeMans

LeMans – LeMans SE – LeMans GLE/GSE

Korean assembly of the Opel Kadett sold in South Korea as Daewoo LeMans with 1.5 Litre engine and as Pontiac LeMans in the USA with a 1.6 Litre engine. 1989 with 1.6 or 2.0 Litre engine.

> 1.6 Litre
> 55kW–74hp–75PS
> 1 Central/Single Point Injection

Engine for LeMans GLE/GSE

Body, Weight: 3–door Saloon/Sedan, 5–seater; kerbweight (DIN) 970kg, LE 990kg, GSE 1045kg. Saloon/Sedan L 4-door, 5-seater; kerbweight (DIN) 1015kg, SE 1070kg.

Engine data (DIN): 4–cylinder in–line (79 x 81.5mm), 1598cm3; compression ratio 8.6:1; 55kW (74hp) [75PS] at 5600rpm, 34.5kW/L (46.2hp/L) [46.9PS/L]; 122Nm (90lbft) at 2800rpm; regular grade

Engine construction: Front transverse mounted engine; light–alloy cylinder head; hydraulic tappets, 1 overhead camshaft (toothed belt); crankshaft with 5 bearings, oil capacity 3.75L (3.5US qt); Rochester central/single point injection. Battery 12V 44/55Ah, alternator 65A; cooling system capacity approx 7.7L (7.3US qt).

Transmission (to front wheels): a) 4–speed manual, final drive ratio 3.72.
b) 5–speed manual, final drive ratio 3.72.
c) Automatic THM 125, hydraulic torque converter and 3-speed Planetary gear set, final drive ratio 3.43.

Daewoo LeMans

Gear ratios: a) 4–speed manual: 1st 3.42; 2nd 1.95; 3rd 1.283; 4th 0.89; R 3.308.
b) 5–speed manual: 1st 3.55; 2nd 1.95; 3rd 1.28; 4th 0.89; 5th 0.71; R 3.308.
c) Automatic: Max torque multiplication in converter 2.4 times, Planetary gear set ratios 2.84; 1.6; 1; R 2.07.

Chassis: Integral body; front control and longitudinal arms and McPerhson struts (negative steering offset), rear compound axle (longitudinal arms with cross–linkage), front and rear coil springs, telescopic dampers, optional front and rear antiroll bars. Servo/power assisted brakes, front discs 23.6cm diameter, rear drums, 322cm2 active brake area, mechanical handbrake to rear wheels; rack and pinion steering; fuel tank 50/52L (11/11.4Gal) [13.2/13.7US Gal]; tyres 155 SR 13, 165 SR 13, wheel rims 5 or 5.5J.

Dimensions: Wheelbase 252cm, track 140/140.5cm, clearance minimum 13.5cm, turning circle 10.6m. Load space 18.4–34.8cu ft (520– 985dm3). Length 438cm, Coupe 416cm, width 167cm, height 136.5cm. 3-door; load space 18.9cu ft (535dm3). Length 416cm, width 166.5cm, height 136cm.

Performance: Max speed 106mph/170kmh (manufacturers test specifications), speed at 1000rpm in 5th gear 24.9mph/40.1kmh; acceleration 0 – 62mph100kmh 14secs; power to weight ratio from 17.6kg/kW (12.9kg/PS); consumption 6-10L/100km (47.1-28.2mpg) [39.2-23.5US mpg] (manufacturers test specifications).

> 2 Litre
> 71kW-96hp-97PS
> Central/Single Point Injection

As 1.6 Litre, except:

Engine data (SAE): 4-cylinder in-line (86 x 86mm), 1998cm3; compression ratio 8.8:1; 71kW (96hp) [97PS] at 4800rpm, 35.5kW/L (47.6hp/L) [48.5PS/L]; 160Nm (118lbft) at 3600rpm; unleaded regular grade.

Tranmission: a) 5–speed manual, final drive ratio 3.72.
b) Automatic, final drive ratio 3.18.

Gear ratios: a) 5–speed manual: 1st 3.55; 2nd 2.16; 3rd 1.48; 4th 1.13; 5th 0.89; R 3.308.
b) Automatic; Max torque multiplication in converter 2.4 times; Planetary gear set ratios: 2.84; 1.6; 1; R 2.07.

Chassis: Front ventilated discs, daimeter 25.6cm.

Performance: Max speed 115mph/185kmh, automatic 112mpg/180kmh; speed at 1000rpm in 5th gear 20mph/32.1kmh; power to weight ratio from 13.7kg/kW (10kg/PS); consumption approx 7–12L/100km (40.4-23.5mpg) [33.6-19.6US mpg].

Pontiac LeMans GSE

DAIHATSU J

Daihatsu Kogyo Co. Ltd., 1 Daihatsu–Cho, Ikeda City, Osaka, Prefecture Japan

Japanese car manufacturer belonging to the Toyota Group.

MODEL RANGE
Cuore – Leeza – Charade – Rugger/Rocky

Daihatsu Cuore

Cuore – Mira – Mira Turbo – Mira 4WD – Mira Turbo 4WD – Cuore 44

Small car with water–cooled 3–cylinder engines and rear independent suspension. Debut May 1976. Summer 1985 with new engine generation and longer wheelbase. Domino designation in some countries. Autumn 1987: small body modifications and Mira Turbo with fuel injection and permanent all–wheel–drive.

Daihatsu

```
548cm3
24kW-32hp-32PS
1 Compound Carb
```

Not available for export

Body, Weight: 3-door Saloon/Sedan, 4-seater; kerbweight (DIN) from 530kg, 4WD from 610kg. 5-door Saloon/Sedan, 4-seater; kerbweight (DIN) from 550kg, 4WD from 630kg.

Engine data (JIS net): 3-cylinder in-line (62 x 60.5mm), 548cm3; compression ratio 10:1; 24kW (32hp) [32PS] at 6000rpm, 43.8kW/L (58hp/L) [58.4PS/L]; 43Nm (31.6lbft) at 3500rpm.

Engine construction: EB designation. Transverse engine. Valves (in V), 1 overhead camshaft (toothed belt), light-alloy cylinder head; crankshaft with 4 bearings; oil 2.9L (2.7US qt) 1 downdraught-compound carb. Battery 12V 35Ah, alternator 560W; cooling system capacity 2.8L (2.1US qt).

Transmission (to front wheels, 4WD): a) 4-speed manual, final drive ratio 4.733 or 5.333.
b) 5-speed manual, final drive ratio 4.733, 4.588 or 5.33.
c) Automatic, hydraulic torque converter and 3-speed gear set, final drive ratio 4.651.
4WD: Engageable rear-wheel-drive, 5-speed manual, final drive ratio 6.545.

Gear ratios: a) 4-speed manual: 1st 3.583; 2nd 2.1; 3rd 1.392; 4th 0.971; R 3.538.
b) 5-speed manual: 1st 3,538; 2nd 2.1; 3rd 1.392 (4WD 1.464); 4th 0.971; 5th 0.82; R 3.583.
c) Automatic; Max torque multiplication in converter 1.7 times, Planetary gear set ratios: 1st 2.727; 2nd 1.536; 3rd 1; R 2.222.

Daihatsu Cuore

Chassis: Integral body; front McPherson struts, single control arm and antiroll bar, rear independent suspension with semi- trailing arms and coil springs, 4WD rigid axle with longitudinal arms, telescopic dampers. Servo/power assisted brakes, front discs, rear drums (some versions four-wheel drum brakes), mechanical handbrake to rear wheels; rack and pinion steering; fuel tank 28 (6.2Gal) [7.4US Gal] 4WD 30 (6.6Gal) [7.9US Gal]; tyres 5.20-10 or 145/70 SR 12, 4WD 5.95-12 or 145 SR 12.

Dimensions: Wheelbase 225cm, track 121.5/120.5cm, 4WD 121.5/121cm, clearance 15.5-17cm, turning circle 9-9.2m. Load space 3.5-10.2cu ft (98-288dm3). Length 319.5cm, width 139.5cm, height 141.5cm, 4WD 146.5cm.

Performance: Max speed approx 68mph/110kmh, speed at 1000rpm in 5th gear (4.733:1) 15mph/24.1kmh; power to weight ratio from 22.1kg/kW (16.6kg/PS); consumption approx 5-8L/100kmh (56.5- 35.3mpg) [47.0-29.4US mpg].

```
548cm3
47/37kW-63/49hp-64/50PS
Turbo/Injection/Carb
```

As 32hp version, except:

Body, Weight: 3-door Saloon/Sedan; kerbweight (DIN) from 560kg, 4WD from 630kg.

Engine data (JIS net): 3-cylinder in-line (62 x 60.5mm), 548cm3; compression ratio 8.0:1; 47kW (63hp) [64PS] at 7000rpm, 85.8kW/L (115hp/L) [116.8PS/L]; 76Nm (56lbft) at 4000rpm.
With Carb: Compression ratio 8.3:1; 37kW (49hp) [50PS] at 6500rpm; 69Nm (50.9lbft) at 4000rpm.

Engine construction: EB Turbo designation. Electronic fuel injection, 49hp version with 1 downdraught compound carburettor, 1 turbocharger with charge-air cooler.

Transmission: a) 5-speed manual, final drive ratio 5.333 (63hp), 4.733 or 5.285.
b) Automatic (49hp only), final drive ratio 4.705.
4WD: 63hp: Permanent all-wheel-drive with visco-coupling. 49hp version: Engageable rear-wheel-drive, 5-speed manual, final drive ratio 5.909.

Gear ratios: a) 5-speed manual: 1st 3.307; 2nd 2.1; 3rd 1.392; 4th 0.971; 5th 0.794; R 3.538.
4WD: 1st 3.583; 2nd 2.1; 3rd 1.392; 4th 0.971; 5th 0.743 (63hp) or 0.794 (49hp).
b) Automatic, as 32hp.

Chassis: Front disc brakes; tyres 145/70 SR 12, 4WD 145 SR 13 or 145 SR 12.

Dimensions: Track 121.5/120.5cm-121cm or 122/121cm (63hp). Height 140cm, 4WD 145cm.

Performance: Max speed over 87mph/140kmh, speed at 1000rpm in 5th gear (FWD 5.333:1) 13.7mph/22.1mh; power to weight ratio from 12.5kg/kW (9.2kg/PS); consumption approx 6-9L/100kmh (47.1- 31.4mpg) [39.2-26.1US mpg].

```
847cm3
32kW-43hp-44PS
1 Carb
```

Engine for export

As 32hp, except:

Weight: Kerbweight (DIN) from 595kg, gross vehicle weight 970kg.

Engine data (DIN): 3-cylinder in-line (66.6 x 81mm), 847cm3; compression ratio 9.5:1; 32kW (43hp) [44PS] at 5500rpm, 37.8kW/L (50.7hp/L) [52.0PS/L]; 68Nm (50lbft) at 3200rpm.
With Catalyst (DIN): 32kW (42hp) [43PS] at 5500rpm; 68Nm (50lbft) at 3200rpm.

Engine construction: ED-10 designation. Oil 2.8L (2.6US qt); 1 downdraught carb, Catalyst version electronically controlled. Battery 12V 35Ah, alternator 45A, cooling system capacity 2.8L (2.6US qt).

Transmission: a) 4-speed manual, final drive ratio 3.947.
b) 5-speed manual, final drive ratio 3.947.
c) Automatic, final drive ratio 4.26.

Gear ratios: 5-speed manual 4WD: 1st 3.583; 2nd 2.1; 3rd 1.392; 4th 0.971; 5th 0.795; R 3.538.

Chassis: Tyres 145/70 SR 12, wheel rims 4J, 4WD 145 SR 12, wheel rims 3.5J.

Performance: Max speed 84mph/135kmh (manufacturers specifications), speed at 1000rpm in 5th gear 18.0mph/28.9kmh; acceleration 0 - 62mph/100kmh 15.7secs; power to weight ratio from 18.6kg/kW (13.5kg/PS); consumption (ECE) 5-speed 4.0/6.3/5.8L/100kmh (70.6/44.8/48.7mpg) [58.8/37.3/40.6US mpg].

Daihatsu Coure 44

Daihatsu Leeza

2 + 2-seater small car on shortened Cuore chassis with aerodynamic body, front-wheel-drive and independent suspension. Debut December 1986. Currently not for export. January 1989: available with increased power Turbo engine.

```
548cm3
24/37kW-32/49hp-32/50PS
1 Compound Carb/Turbo
```

Body, Weight: 3-door Coupe, 2+2-seater; kerbweight (DIN) 570-600kg.

Daihatsu

Engine data (JIS net): 3–cylinder in–line (62 x 60.5mm), 548cm3; compression ratio 10.1; 24kW (32hp) [32PS] at 6000rpm, 43.8kW/L (58hp/L) [58.4PS/L]; 43Nm (31.6lbft) at 3500rpm.
Without turbocharger: Compression ratio 8.3:1; 37kW (49hp) [50PS] at 6500rpm, 67.5kW/L (90.4hp/L) [91.2PS/L]; 69Nm (50.9lbft) at 3500rpm.

Engine construction: EB designation. Transverse engine; valves in V, 1 overhead camshaft (toothed belt), light–alloy cylinder head; crankshaft with 4 bearings; oil 2.9L (2.7US qt); 1 downdraught compound carb; turbo engine with charge–air cooling. Battery 12V 35Ah, alternator 560W; cooling system capacity 3.5L (3.3US qt).

Transmission (to front wheels): a) 4–speed manual, final drive ratio 5.333.
b) 5–speed manual (Turbo), final drive 5.333.
c) Semi–automatic, hydraulic torque converter and 2–speed Planetary gear set, central selector lever, P–R–N–D–L positions; final drive ratio 5.081, Turbo 4.705.
d) Automatic (not for 32hp), hydraulic torque converter and 3-speed Planetary gear set, final drive ratio, 4.651.

Gear ratios: a) 4–speed manual: 1st 3.583; 2nd 2.1; 3rd 1.392; 4th 0.971; R 3,538.
b) 5–speed manual: 1st 3.307; 2nd 2.1; 3rd 1.392; 4th 0.971; 5th 0.82; R 3.538.
c) Semi–automatic; Max torque multiplication in converter 1.3 times, Planetary gear set ratios: 1.821; 1; R 1.821.
d) Automatic: Max torque multiplication in converter 1.7 times, Planetary gear set ratios; 1st 2.727; 2nd 1.536; 3rd 1; R 2.222.

Chassis: Integral body; front McPherson struts, single control arms and antiroll bar, rear independent suspension with semi– trailing arms and coil springs, telescopic dampers. Servo/power assisted brakes, front discs, rear drums, mechanical handbrake to rear wheels; rack and pinion steering, optoinal power assisted; fuel tank 28L (6.2Gal) [7.4US Gal]; tyres 5.20–10, 145/70 SR 12 or 155/70 SR 12 (Turbo).

Dimensions: Wheelbase 213cm, track 121.5/120.5cm, clearance 16.0– 16.5cm, turning circle 9m. Length 319.5cm, width 139.5cm, height 133.5cm.

Performance: Max speed approx 75mph/120kmh (Turbo approx 87mph/140kmh), speed at 1000rpm in 5th gear (5.285:1) 11.3mph/18.2kmh; power to weight ratio from 16.2kg/kW (12kg/PS); consumption approx 5–9L/100kmh (56.5–31.4mpg) [47.0–26.1US mpg].

```
548cm3
47kW-63hp-64PS
Turbo/Fuel Injection
```

As 32hp, except:

Engine data (JIS): 3-cylinder in-line (62 x 60.5mm), 548cm3; compression ratio 8.0:1; 47kW (63hp) [64PS] at 7000rpm, 85.8kW/L (115hp/L) [116.8PS/L]; 76Nm (56lbft) at 4000rpm.

Engine construction: Designated EB Turbo. Electronic injection, 1 turbocharger with charge-air cooler.

Transmission: 5-speed manual, final drive ratio 5.333.

Chassis: Tyres 155/70 SR 12.

Performance: Max speed 90mph/145kmh, speed at 1000rpm in 5th gear 13.7mph/22.1kmh; power to weight ratio 13kg/kW (9.5kg/PS); consumption 6-9L/100km (47.1-31.4mpg) [34.1-26.1US mpg]

Daihatsu Charade

Compact Saloon/Sedan with transverse mounted 3–cylinder engine and front–wheel–drive. Debut October 1977. January 1987: new edition with aerodynamic body and modified suspension. Sporty version with super–charged DOHC–four-valve engine. 1988: version with four cylinder (16 valves, fuel injection) 1.3– Litre capacity and engageable four wheel drive.

```
993cm3
40kW-54hp-55PS
Compound Carb/Fuel Injection
```

Body, Weight: 3–door Saloon/Sedan, 4/5–seater; kerbweight (DIN) from 680kg. 5–door Saloon/Sedan, 4/5–seater; kerbweight (DIN) from 690kg.

Engine data (JIS net): 3-cylinder in-line (76 x 73mm), 993cm3; compression ratio 9.5:1; 40kW (54hp) [55PS] at 5600rpm, 40.3kW/L (54hp/L) [55.4PS/L]; 78Nm (57.4lbft) at 3600rpm; leaded regular grade.
Or: 37kW (49hp) [50PS] at 5600rpm, 75Nm (55.3lbft) at 3200rpm.
European version (DIN): 38kW (51hp) [52PS] at 5600rpm, 38.5kW/L (51.6hp/L) [52.3PS/L]; 75Nm (55.3lbft) at 3200rpm.

With Catalyst (fuel injection, DIN): 40kW (53hp) [54PS] at 5200rpm; 80Nm (59lbft) at 3600rpm.

Engine construction: CB 36/37 designation, CB 90 with Catalyst. Front transversely–mounted engine. Valves (in V), overhead camshaft (toothed belt); light–alloy cylinder head; 1 counter-balance shaft; crankshaft with 4 bearings; oil 3.0L (2.8US qt); 1 Aisin downdraught compound carb, electronic fuel injection with Catalyst. Battery 12V 36Ah, alternator 45A; cooling system capacity 3.5 or 3.7L (automatic) (3.3 or 3.5US qt).

Transmission (to front wheels): a) 4–speed manual; final drive ratio 4.933 or 4.500.
b) 5–speed manual; final drive ratio 4.235, 4.500, 4.642 (Catalyst) or 4.933.
c) Automatic, hydraulic torque converter and 3-speed Planetary gear set; final drive ratio 3.872.

Gear ratios: a) 4–speed manual: 1st 3.09; 2nd 1.842; 3rd 1.23; 4th 0.864; R 3.142.
b) 5–speed manual: 1st 3.09; 2nd 1.842; 3rd 1.23; 4th 0.864; 5th 0.707; R 3.142.
c) Automatic; Max torque multiplication in converter 2.5 times, Planetary gear set ratios: 1st 2.810; 2nd 1.549; 3rd 1; R 2.296.

Chassis: Integral body; all–round independent suspension , front McPherson struts, lower single control arms and antiroll bar, rear McPherson struts with double lower control arms and single longitudinal arms, some models with antiroll bar, telescopic dampers. Servo/power assisted brakes, front discs, rear drums, mechanical handbrake to rear wheels; rack and pinion steering, optional with servo; fuel tank 37L (8.1Gal) [9.8US Gal] tyres 6.00–12, 145 SR 13 or 155 SR 13, optional 165/70 SR 13, wheel rims 4 or 4.5J.

Dimensions: Wheelbase 234cm, track 138.5/136.5cm, clearance 16cm, turning circle 9.4m. Load space 6.1–13.6cu ft (173–385dm3). Length 361cm, width 160–161.5cm, height 138.5cm.

Performance: (ECE versions) top speed 90mph/145kmh, automatic 81mph/130kmh (manufacturers test specifications), speed at 1000rpm in 5th gear (tyres 155–13, 4.500:1) 20.7mph/33.3kmh; acceleration 0 – 62mph/100kmh 14secs; power to weight ratio from 16.8kg/kW (12.4kg/PS); consumption (ECE) 4.2/6.2/6.7L/100km (67.3/45.6/42.2mpg) [56.0/37.9/35.1US mpg], automatic 5.2/7.2/7.7L/100kmh (54.3/39.2/36.7mpg) [45.2/32.7/30.5US mpg].

Daihatsu Charade

```
993cm3
77kW-103hp-105PS
Turbo/Fuel Injection
```

As 54hp, except:

Body, Weight: 3–door Saloon/Sedan, 4–seater; kerbweight (DIN) from 800kg.

Engine data (JIS net): 3–cylinder in–line (76 x 73mm), 993cm3; compression ratio 7.8:1; 77kW (103hp) [105PS] at 6500rpm, 77.5kW/L (103.9hp/L) [105.7PS/L]; 130Nm (95.7lbft) at 3500rpm.
European version (DIN): 74kW (99hp) [101PS] at 6500rpm; 130Nm (95.7lbft) at 3500rpm; leaded regular grade.
With Catalyst (DIN): Identical data.

Engine construction: CB–70 desgination. 4 valves per cylinder, 2 overhead camshafts (toothed belt); oil–cooler, electronic fuel injection, 1 IHI, RHB 51 exhaust turbocharger, max boost pressure 0.75bar, charge-air cooler. Alternator 50A.

Transmisson: 5-speed manual, final drive ratio 4.642.

Gear ratios: 1st 3.09: 2nd 1.750; 3rd 1.23; 4th 0.916; 5th 0.750; R 3.142.

Chassis: Front and rear antiroll bars; four-wheel disc brakes (ventilated at front); fuel tank 40L (8.8Gal) [10.6US Gal] tyres 175/60 HR 14, optional 185/60 HR 14, wheel rims 5J.

DANIEL STEENSTRA

shape of things to come

michelotti
STUDIO TECNICO
DESIGN CARROZZERIA

TORINO - ITALY - TEL. 349.72.91 - FAX 349.01.21

Daihatsu

Performance: Max speed 124mph/200kmh (manufacturers test specifications), speed at 1000rpm in 5th gear 18.5mph/29.7kmh; acceleration 0 – 62mph/100kmh 8.2secs; power to weight ratio from 10.4kg/kW (7.6kg.PS); consumption (ECE) 5.2/7.5/7.6L/100kmh (54.3/37.7/37.2mpg) [45.2/31.4/30.9US mpg].

Daihatsu Charade GTti

```
1295cm3
69kW-93hp-94PS
Fuel Injection
```

As 54hp, except:

Body, Weight: Salonn/Sedan 3-door; kerbweight (DIN) 740kg, 5-door 750kg, gross vehicle weight 1240kg; 4WD kerbweight 810kg, gross vehicle weight 1295kg.
Engine data (JIS): 4-cylinder in-line (76 x 71.4mm), 1295cm3; compression ratio 9.5:1; 69kW (93hp) [94PS] at 6500rpm, 53.3kW/L (71.4hp/L) [72.6PS/L]; 108Nm (79.7lbft) at 5000rpm.
With Catalyst (DIN): 66kW (89hp) [90PS] at 6500rpm; 105Nm (77.5lbft) at 5000rpm.
Engine construction: Designated HC-E. 4 valves per cylinder, 1 overhead camshaft (toothed belt); light-alloy cylinder head and block, 5 bearing crankshaft; oil capacity 3L (2.8US qt); electronic fuel injection. Alternator 50A.
Transmission (to front or rear wheels): a) 5-speed manual, final drive ratio 4.642. b) Automatic, final drive ratio 3.872.
4WD: Permanent all wheel drive with central differential (50/50% split) and viscous coupling. 5-speed manual, final drive ratio 5.076.
Gear ratios: a) 5-speed manual: 1st 3.09; 2nd 1.842; 3rd 1.23; 4th 0.916; 5th 0.750; R 3.142.
4WD: 1st 3.09; 2nd 1.842; 3rd 1.23; 4th 0.864; 5th 0.707; R 3.142.
b) Automatic, as 54hp.
Chassis: Rear antiroll bar; fuel tank 40L (8.8Gal) [10.6US Gal], 4WD 37L (8.1Gal) [9.8US Gal]; tyres 165/70 SR 13 or 155 HR 13, optional 175/60 HR 14, wheels 4.5 or 5J.
Dimensions: 4WD; track 138/136.5cm. Height 140cm.
Performance: Max speed 106mph/170kmh, speed at 1000rpm in 5th gear 18.5mph/29.8kmh, 4WD 17.9mph/28.8kmh; power to weight ratio 10.7kg/kW (7.9kg/PS); consumption 6-10L/100km (47.1-28.2mpg) [39.2-23.5US mpg].

Daihatsu Charade 1300 4WD

```
993cm3 D
37/28kW-49/36hp-50/38PS
Turbo/Pump Injection
```

As 54hp, except:

Weight: Kerbweight (DIN) from 750kg.

Engine data (JIS net): 3-cylinder in-line (76 x 73mm), 993cm3; compression ratio 21.5:1; 37kW (49hp) [50PS] at 4800rpm, 37.3kW/L (49.9hp/L) [50.4PS/L]; 90Nm (66.2lbft) at 3000rpm.
European version (DIN): 35kW (47hp) [48PS] at 4800rpm; 85Nm (62.7lbft) at 2900rpm.
With Turbo (JIS): 28kW (37hp) [38PS] at 5000rpm; 61Nm (45lbft) at 3200rpm.
European version (DIN): 27kW (36hp) [37PS] at 4800rpm; 60Nm (44.3lbft) at 3200rpm.
Engine construction: Swirl chamber turbulence diesel engine. CL 70/61 designation. Nippondenso/Bosch VE diesel injection pump, Aisin AMT 30 exhaust turbocharger, max boost pressure 0.7bar. Battery 12V 60Ah, alternator 40A.
Transmission: a) 5-speed manual; final drive ratio 4.642 or 5.076, with Turbo 4.933.
b) Automatic (not Turbo), final drive ratio 3.872.
Performance: Max speed 87mph/140kmh, Turbo 75mph/120kmh (manufacturers test specifications), speed in 5th gear at 1000rpm (4.642) 19.6mph/31.5kmh; acceleration 0 – 62mph/100kmh 17secs; power to weight ratio from 20.3kg/kW (15kg/PS); consumption (ECE) 3.6/5.7/4.9L/100kmh (78.5/49.6/57.6mpg) [65.3/41.3/48.0US mpg], with Turbo 3.6/6.6/4.9L/100km (78.5/42.8/57.6mpg) [65.3/35.6/48US mpg].

Daihatsu Rocky 4WD

Medium-sized rough terrain vehicle with new 2 Litre petrol engine or 2.8 Litre diesel engine with or without turbo-charging. Taft successor. 'Rugger' desgination in Japan, also 'Fourtrak' in some countries. Debut June 1984. 1987: modifications to the body and mechanics.

```
2 Litre
67/65kW–90/87hp–91/88PS
Fuel Injection/Compound Carb
```

Petrol/Gasoline engine for export

Body, Weight: 3-door Estate/Station Wagon, 5/7-seater; kerbweight (DIN) from 1330kg, gross vehicle weight 1895kg. 3-door short Soft top, 4/5-seater; kerbweight (DIN) 1230kg, gross vehicle weight 1680kg; 3-door long Soft top, 6/8-seater; kerbweight (DIN) 1270kg, gross vehicle weight 1895kg. 3-door Hard top, 6-seater; kerbweight (DIN) 1240kg, gross vehicle weight 1680kg.
Engine data (Catalyst, DIN): 4-cylinder in-line (86 x 86mm), 1998cm3; compression ratio 8.8:1; 67kW (89hp) [91PS] at 4400rpm, 33.5kW/L (44.9hp/L) [45.5PS/L]; 163Nm (120.1lbft) at 3400rpm.
With carb (DIN): 65kW (87hp) [88PS] at 4600rpm, 157Nm (115.8lbft) at 3000rpm.
Some countries (SAE net): 63kW (84hp) [86PS]; 153Nm (112.9lbft).
Engine construction: 3 Y desgination. Hydraulic tappets, 1 side-mounted camshaft (chain); light-alloy cylinder head; crankshaft with 5 bearings; oil-cooler, oil 3.5L (3.3US qt); electronic fuel injection or 1 Nippon downdraught compound carb. Battery 12V 40Ah, alternator 40-45A; cooling system capacity 9L (8.5US qt).

Daihatsu Rocky 4WD

Transmission (to rear wheels); Rear wheel drive with engageable four wheel drive, with reduction gears, final drive ratio on-road 1.297, off-road 2.370.
a) 4-speed manual, final drive ratio 3.363 or 3.909.

Daihatsu

b) 5-speed manual, final drive ratio 3.363 or 3.909. Some models with rear limited slip differential or mechanical differential lock.

Gear ratios: a) 4-speed manual: 1st 3.647; 2nd 2.136; 3rd 1.484; 4th 1; R 4.351.
b) 5-speed manaul: 1st 3.647; 2nd 2.136; 3rd 1.484; 4th 1; 5th 0.86; R 4.351.

Chassis: Sub-frames with cross-members, body screwed onto frames; front and rear rigid axles with leaf springs, front Panhard rod and antiroll bar, telescopic dampers. Servo/power assisted brakes, front discs, rear drums, manual parking brake to rear wheels; reciculating ball steering, optional power assisted; fuel tank 60L (13.2Gal) [15.9US Gal]; tyres 6.00-16, H78-15 or 215 R 15, wheel rims 6J, optional 7J.

Dimensions: Wheelbase 220.5cm, track 132/130cm, clearance 21cm. Length 371.5-377.5cm, width 158cm, height 183-184cm; Estate/Station wagon and long Soft top: Wheelbase 253cm, length 404-410cm, height 182.5-191.5cm.

Performance: (87hp) Max speed 81mph/130kmh (manufacturers test specifications), speed at 1000rpm in 5th gear (axle 3.909) 18.5mph/29.8kmh; acceleration 0 - 62mph/100kmh 26.4secs; power to weight ratio from 19.1kg/kW (14.0kg/PS); consumption (ECE) 9.4/14.7/14.0L/100kmh (30.1/19.2/20.2mpg) [25.0/16.0/16.8US mpg].

```
2.8 Litre Diesel
54kW-72hp-73PS
Injection Pump
```

As 2 Litre, except:

Weight: Diesel engine excess weight 125kg.

Engine data (DN): 4-cylinder in-line (92 x 104mm), 2765cm3; compression ratio 21.2:1; 54kW (72hp) [73PS] at 3600rpm, 19.5kW/L (26.1hp/L) [26.4PS/L]; 170Nm (125.1lbft) at 2200rpm.
Some countries (SAE net): 56kW (75hp) [76PS] at 3800rpm.
Japanese version (JIS net): 58kW (78hp) [79PS] at 3800rpm; 172Nm (126.6lbft) at 2200rpm.

Daihatsu Rocky 4WD Turbo Diesel

Engine construction: Swirl chamber turbulance diesel engine. (Toyota) DL designation. Side-mounted camshaft (gear driven), grey cast-iron cylinder head; oil 5.5L (5.2US qt) Nippondenso diesel injection pump (Bosch license). Battery 12V 80 or 100Ah, alternator 45A; cooling system capacity 10L (9.4US qt).

Transmission: Final drive ratio 3.363.

Performance: Max speed 81mph/130kmh (manufacturers test specifications), speed in 5th gear at 1000rpm 21.5mph/34.6kmh; acceleration 0 - 62mph/100kmh 25.7secs; power to weight ratio from 25.3kg/kW (18.6kg/PS); consumption (ECE) 8.1/13.8/10.5L/100kmh (34.9/20.5/26.9mpg) [29.0/17.0/19.3US mpg].

```
2.8 Litre Diesel
67kW-90hp-91PS
Turbo/Injection Pump
```

As 2 Litre, except:

Weight: Turbodiesel engine weight 150kg heavier.

Engine data (DIN): 4-cylinder in-line (92 x 104mm), 2765cm3; compression ratio 21.2:1; 67kW (90hp) [91PS] at 3400rpm, 24.2 kW/L 32.4hp/L] [32.9PS/L]; 223Nm (164.1lbft) at 2200rpm.
Or: 65kW (87hp) [88PS] at 3600rpm; 211Nm (155.7lbft) at 2200rpm.
Japanese version (JIS net): 69kW (92hp) [94PS] at 3400rpm, 226Nm (166.3lbft) at 2200rpm.

Engine construction: Swirl chamber turbulence diesel engine. (Toyota) DL desgination. Side-mounted camshaft (gear driven), grey cast-iron cylinder head; oil 5.5L (5.2US qt) oil-cooler; Nippondenso diesel injection pump (Bosch license), max boost pressure 0.5bar. Battery 12V 80 or 100Ah, alternator 45A; cooling system capacity 11L (10.4US qt).

Transmission: 5-speed manual, final drive ratio 3.363.

Gear ratios: 1st 3.447; 2nd 2.037; 3rd 1.317; 4th 1; 5th 0.82; R 4.148.

Chassis: Optional front internally-cooled disc brakes.

Performance: Max speed 84/135kmh (manufacturers test specifications), speed at 1000rpm in 5th gear 22.6mph/36.3kmh; power to weight ratio from 20.9kg/kW (15.3kg/PS); consumption (ECE) 7.8/13.7/9.8L/100kmh (36.2/20.6/28.8mpg) [30.2/17.2/24.0US mpg].

Daihatsu Feroza 4WD

New model. Compact rough terain vehicle, derived from the large Rocky variant. 1.6 Litre, 4 valves per cylinder engine. Engageable four wheel drive for rough terian operation, with reduction gears. Front independent suspension and rigid rear suspension. Launched Autumn 1988.

Daihatsu Feroza

```
1600 16V
70/63kW-94/85hp-95/86PS
Fuel Injection/Carb
```

Body, Weight: 3-door, Convertible Saloon/Sedan, 4-seater; kerbweight (DIN) 1100kg, gross vehicle weight 1580kg. 3-door Hardtop, 4-seater; kerbweight (DIN) 1125kg, gross vehicle weight 1580kg.

Engine data (Catalyst, DIN): 4-cylinder in-line (76 x 87.6mm), 1590cm3; compression ratio 9.5:1; 70kW (94hp) [95PS] at 5700rpm, 44kW/L (59hp/L) [59.7PS/L]; 128Nm (94.5lbft) at 4800rpm; unleaded regular grade.
With Carb (without Catalyst, DIN): 63kW (85hp) [86PS] at 6000rpm; 126Nm (93lbft) at 3500rpm.

Engine construction: Designated HD-C, with injection HD-E. 4 valves per cylinder (in V), 1 overhead camshaft (toothed belt); light-alloy cylinder head and block; 5 bearing crankshaft; oil capacity 3.5L (3.3US qt). Fuel injection or 1 down-draught 2V Carb. 12V 28-36Ah battery, 45-50A alternator; water cooled.

Transmission (to rear wheels or all wheels): Engageable four wheel drive, optional front free-wheel hub, reduction gears, road going 1, rough terrain 1.754. 5-speed manual, final drive ratio 5.285; optional rear limited slip differential.

Gear ratios: 1st 3.752; 2nd 2.182; 3rd 1.428; 4th 1 (Carb - 1.529); 5th 0.865; R 3.942.

Chassis: Box section frame with cross members, independent body; front independent suspension with upper and lower A arms, torsion bar and antiroll bar, rear rigid axle with leaf springs, telescopic dampers. Servo/power assisted brakes, front discs (optional ventilated), diameter 27.7cm, rear drums; recirculating ball steering, optional power assisted; fuel tank 60L (13.2Gal) [15.9US Gal]; tyres 195 SR 15, wheels 5.5J.

Dimensions: Wheelbase 217.5cm, track 132/132cm, clearance 20.5cm, turning circle 10m. Length 368.5cm, width 158cm, height 172cm.

Performance (94hp): Max speed 93mph/150kmh, speed at 1000rpm in 5th gear 17.5mph/28.2kmh; acceleration 0 - 62mph/100kmh 11.7secs; power to weight ratio 16kg/kW (11.8kg/PS); consumption ECE 7.6/11.9/10.5L/100km (37.2/23.7/26.9mpg) [30.9/19.8/22.4US mpg].

DAIMLER GB

Jaguar Cars Limited, Browns Lane, Allesley, Coventry CV5 9DR, England

Oldest English car factory. Part of Jaguar Cars Limited and as a result connected with BMC since 1966 and with BLMC/British Leyland since 1968. 1984: reprivatised with Jaguar.

MODEL RANGE
3.6 – Double–Six – Saloon/Sedan

Daimler 3.6

Daimler 3.6

New edition of the Saloon/Sedan 4.2 built since 1969 with a new 3.5 litre six cylinder engine. Debut October 1986. Winter 87/88: higher performance for Catalyst version.

> 3.6 Litre 6–cylinder
> 165/149kW–221/200hp–224/202PS
> Fuel Injection

Body, Weight: 4–door Saloon/Sedan, 5–seats; kerbweight (DIN) 1770kg, gross vehicle weight 2190kg.

Engine data (DIN): 6–cylinder in–line (91 x 92mm), 3590cm3; compression ratio 9.6:1; 165kW (221hp) [224PS] at 5000rpm, 46kW/L (61.6hp/L) [62.4PS/L]; 337Nm (248.7lbft) at 4000rpm; leaded premium grade.
Some countries: 156kW (209hp) [212PS]; 324Nm (239.1lbft).
With Catalsyt: compression ratio 9.6:1; 149kW (200hp) [202PS] at 5250rpm, 41.5kW/L (55.6hp/L) [56.3PS/L]; 302Nm (222.9lbft) at 4000rpm; unleaded regular grade (95R).
Or compression ratio 8.1:1; 135kW (184PS) at 4750rpm, 37.6kW/L (50.8hp/L) [51.3PS/L]; 300Nm (221.4lbft) at 3750rpm; unleaded regular grade (91R).

Daimler 3.6

Engine construction: AJ6 designation. 4 valves per cylinder, in V 46deg 40', 2 overhead camshafts (chain); light-alloy cylinder block and head, dry cylinder liners; crankshaft with 7 bearings; oil–cooler, oil capacity 8.5L (8US qt); indirect electronic fuel injection (Lucas/Bosch digital), electronic fuel pump.
Champion RC 12 YC spark plugs; battery 12V 68Ah, alternator 60A; cooling system capacity 11.6L (11US qt).

Transmission (to rear wheels): a) 5–speed manual, floor shift, final drive ratio 3.54/3.58.
b) ZF automatic 4 HP 22, hydraulic torque converter and 4–speed Planetary gear set, central selector lever with P–R–N–D/D–3–2 positions; final drive ratio 3.54/3.58.
Limited slip differential.

Gear ratios: a) 5–speed manual: 1st 3.57; 2nd 2.06; 3rd 1.39; 4th 1; 5th 0.76; R 3.46.
b) Automatic; Max torque multiplication in converter 2.1 times, Planetary gear set ratios: 1st 2.48; 2nd 1.48; 3rd 1; 4th 0.73; R 2.09.

Chassis: Integral body with front and rear sub–frames; front swinging A–arms, antiroll bar, coil springs and telescopic dampers, rear lower A–arms, upper support arms semi–floating axle, coil springs and telescopic dampers, level control system. Servo/power assisted disc brakes with ABS (Bosch system), front disc diameter (ventilated) 28.4cm, rear 26.3cm, mechanical handbrake to rear wheels; power assisted rack and pinion steering; fuel tank 89L (19.6Gal) [23.5US Gal]; tyres 220/65 VR 390; wheel rims 198mm.

Dimensions: Wheelbase 287cm, track 150/150cm, clearance 13cm, turning circle 12.9m. Load space 15.2cu ft (430dm3). Length 499cm, width 180cm, height 138cm.

Performance: Max speed 136mph/219kmh, automatic 135mph/217kmh (manufacturers test specifications), speed at 1000rpm in 5th gear 28.3mph/45.6kmh, automatic in 4th gear 29.5mph/47.5kmh; acceleration 0–60mph/97kmh 7.4secs, automatic 8.8secs; power to weight ratio 10.7kg/kW (7.9kg/PS), consumption (ECE) 7.9/9.5/15.2L/100km (35.8/29.7/18.6mpg) [29.8/24.8/15.5US mpg], automatic 7.8/9.3/15.1L/100km (36.2/30.4/18.7mpg) [30.2/25.3/15.6US mpg].
With Catalyst and automatic: Max speed 130.5mph/210kmh; acceleration 0–62mph/100kmh approx 9.9secs.

Daimler Double–Six

Luxury Saloon/Sedan with V12 5.3 Litre engine. Debut July 1972, with fuel injection May 1975, with GM automatic spring 1977. July 1981: H.E. (High Efficiency) with 'May–Fireball'– combustion chamber.

> 5.3 Litre V12
> 217/195kW–291/261hp–295/265PS
> Fuel Injection

Body, Weight: 4–door Saloon/Sedan, 5–seats; kerbweight (DIN) 1930kg, gross vehicle weight 2350kg.

Engine data (DIN): 12–cylinder in 60deg V (90 x 70mm), 5343cm3; compression ratio 12.5:1; 217kW (291hp) [295PS] at 5500rpm, 40.6kW/L (54.4hp/L) [55.2PS/L]; 432Nm (318.8lbft) at 3250rpm; leaded premium grade (97).
With Catalyst: Compression ratio 11.5:1; 195kW (261hp) [265PS] at 5000rpm, 36.5kW/L (48.9hp/L) [49.6PS/L]; 389Nm (287lbft) at 3000rpm; unleaded premium grade.

Engine construction: V12 H.E. (May–Fireball), designation. 2x1 overhead camshafts (chain); light–alloy cylinder block and heads, wet cylinder liners; crankshaft with 7 bearings; oil–cooler, oil capacity 10.8L (10.2US qt); indirect electronic digital D– Jectonic (Bosch–Bendix–Lucas) fuel injection, electric fuel pump. Champion BN 5 spark plugs; battery 12V 68Ah, alternator 60A; cooling system capacity 21L (19.9US qt).

Transmission (to rear wheels): GM 'Turbo Hydra–Matic 400' automatic, hydraulic torque converter and 3–speed Planetary gear set, central selector lever with P–R–N–D–2–1 positions; final drive ratio 2.88; limited slip differential.

Gear ratios: Max torque multiplication in converter 2.4 times; Planetary gear set ratios: 1st 2.48; 2nd 1.48; 3rd 1; R 2.08.

Chassis: Integral body; front swinging A–arms, coil springs and telescopic dampers, rear independent with lower forked leading arms, upper support arms, semi–floating axle and longitudinal arms (differential housing with inside disc brakes in flexibly suspended sub–frames), each side with two coil springs with inside telescopic dampers, front antiroll bar. Servo/power assisted disc brakes, front (ventilated) disc, diameter 28.4cm, rear 26.3m, mechanical handbrake to rear wheels; rack and pinion steering; fuel tank (2 compartments) 91L (20Gal) [24US Gal]; tyres 215/70 VR 15, wheel rims 6J.

Dimensions: Wheelbase 286.5cm, track 148/149.5cm, clearance 13cm, turning circle 13.4m. Load space 13.8cu ft (390cm3). Length 496cm, width 177cm, height 137.5cm.

Daimler • De la Chapelle • Dodge

Performance: Max speed 146mph/235kmh (manufacturers test specifications), speed at 1000rpm in top gear 27mph/43.5kmh; acceleration 0 – 60mph/97kmh 8.1secs; power to weight ratio from 8.9kg/kW (6.5kg/PS); consumption (ECE) 10.6/13.1/18.8L/100km (26.6/21.6/15mpg) [22.2/18/12.5US mpg].

Daimler Double–Six

Daimler Limousine

Eight–seater prestige limousine with 4.2 Litre engine and front and rear independent suspension from Jaguar. Debut June 1968. 1986: new 'Executive' edition.

Body, Weight: 4–door Saloon/Sedan, 8–seats; kerbweight (DIN) 2140kg; 4–door Landaulette Saloon/Sedan, 8–seats; kerbweight (DIN) 2160kg.

> 4.2 Litre 6–cylinder
> 121/131kW–162/175.5hp–164/178/PS
> 2 Carbs/Fuel Injection

Engine data (DIN): 6–cylinder in–line (92.07 x 106mm), 4235cm3; compression ratio 7.5:1; 121kW (162hp) [164PS] at 4250rpm, 28.5kW/L (38.2hp/L) [38.8PS/L]; 309Nm (228lbft) at 3000rpm; leaded premium grade (97R). With fuel injection (SAE net): Compression ratio 8.1:1; 131kW (175.5hp) [178PS] at 4750rpm, 30.9kW/L (41.4hp/L) [42PS/L]; 297Nm (219.2lbft) at 2500rpm; regular grade (91R).

Engine construction: Jaguar 4.2L desgination. Overhead valves (in 70deg V), 2 overhead camshafts (chain); light–alloy cylinder head; dry cylinder liners; crankshaft with 7 bearings; oil capacity 6.75L (6.4US qt); 2 horizontal SU HD 8 carbs; 2 electronic SU fuel pumps. Champion N 11 Y spark plugs, battery 12V 60Ah, alternator 45A; cooling system capacity 15L (14.2US qt).

Daimler Limousine

Tranmission (to rear wheels): Automatic Borg–Warner; hydraulic torque converter and 3–speed Planetary gear set, selector lever on steering wheel with P–R–N–2–1–L positions; final drive ratio 3.54 or 3.31; limited slip differential.

Gear ratios: Max torque multiplication in converter 2 times; Planetary gear set ratios: 1st 2.40; 2nd 1.457; 3rd 1; R 2.00.

Chassis: Integral body, front A–arms and coil springs, rear independent suspension with forked leading arms, upper support arms, semi–floating axle and longitudinal arms (differential housing on flexibly suspended sub–frames), each side with 2 coil springs, front antiroll bars, telescopic dampers. Servo/power assisted disc brakes, front disc diameter 28.4cm (ventilated), rear 26.3cm, mechanical handbrake to rear wheels; power assisted recirculating ball steering; fuel tank (2 compartments) 92L (20.2Gal) [24.4US Gal]; tyres 205/70 HR 15 or H 70 HR 15, wheel rims 6J.

Dimensions: Wheelbase 358cm, track 147/147cm, clearance 18cm, turning circle 14m. Length 574cm, width 199.5cm, height 162cm.

Performance: Max speed 110mph/177kmh (manufacturers test specifications), speed at 1000rpm in top gear 21.6mph/34.8kmh; acceleration 0 – 50mph/80kmh 9.2secs and 0 – 100mph/160kmh 43.5secs; standing mile 19.5secs; power to weight ratio from 17.7kg/kW (13.0kg/PS); consumption (ECE) 13.4/18.2/19.9L/100km (21.1/15.5/14.2mpg) [17.7/12.9/11US mpg].

DE LA CHAPELLE   F

Automobiles De La Chapelle, Chemin de Sacuny, 69530 Brignais (Lyon), France.

French construction of small series replicas.

De La Chapelle Bugatti 55/II/III

Reproduction of the Bugatti 55 with plastic body and mechanics of the BMW. Launched Geneva 1978. Summer 1980: Wheelbase lengthened. Series II without, Series III with doors.

As BMW model 3 with 6–cylinder engine, also:

Body, Weight: Roadster with 2–seater and plastic body. kerbweight (DIN) 1050kg.

Engine: 6–cylinder engine with fuel injection of BMW, 2-2.7Litre capacity, 95-154kW (127-206hp) [129-210PS].

Chassis: Central chassis. Fuel tank 50L (11Gal) [13.2US Gal]; tyres 205/65HR, wheel rims 6J.

Dimensions: Wheelbase 280cm, track 145/145cm. Load space 8.8cu ft (250dm3). Length 410cm, width 175cm, height 128cm.

De La Chapelle Bugatti 55 III

DODGE   USA

Dodge Divison, Chrysler Corporation, Detroit, Michigan 48231, USA

Chrysler Corporation mark

MODEL RANGE
Omni – Shadow – Daytona – Aries – Lancer – Spirit – Dynasty – Diplomat – Caravan – Ramcharger

Dodge Omni

Compact model with 2.2 Litre engine, front wheel drive, technically identical to Plymouth Horizon. Saloon/Sedan debut December 1977, Charger Coupe Autumn 1983. 1987 still only available with 2.2 Litre engine. 1988 only available as Omni Saloon/Sedan.

> 2.2 Litre
> 69kW–93hp–94PS
> Central/Single Point Injection

Dodge

Body, Weight (laden): 5-door Saloon/Sedan, 5-seats; approx 1040kg.
Engine data (SAE net): 4-cylinder in-line (87.5 x 92mm), 2213cm3; compression ratio 9.5:1; 69kW (93hp) [94PS] at 4800rpm, 31.2kW/L (41.8hp/L) [42.5PS/L]; 165Nm (121.7lbft) at 3200rpm; unleaded regular grade.
Engine construction: Transverse mounted engine tilting backwards. Hydraulic tappets; 1 overhead camshaft (toothed belt); light- alloy cylinder head; crankshaft with 5 bearings; oil capacity 3.8L (3.6US qt); electronic Bosch/Holley central/single point fuel injection. Battery 12V 60/66Ah, alternator 90A; cooling system capacity 8.5L (8US qt);
Transmission (to front wheels): a) 5-speed manual, final drive ratio 2.55.
b) Automatic 'Torqueflite', hydraulic torque converter and 3- speed Planetary gear set, final drive ratio 2.78.
Gear ratios: a) 5-speed manual: 1st 3.29; 2nd 2.08; 3rd 1.45; 4th 1.04; 5th 0.72; R 3.14.
b) Automatic: Max torque multiplication in converter 2 times; Planetary gear set ratios: 2.69; 1.55; 1; R 2.1.

Dodge Omni

Chassis: Integral body (floor-pan assembly) with welded body; front A-arms and McPherson struts with coil springs, rear independent suspension with drawn longitudinal A-swinging arms and coil springs, front antiroll bar, telescopic dampers. Servo/power assisted brakes, front discs (ventilated) diameter 22.8cm, rear drums, mechanical handbrake to rear wheels; rack and pinion steering, optional power assisted; fuel tank 49L (10.8Gal) [12.9US Gal], tyres 165 R 13, wheel rims 5J.
Dimensions: Wheelbase 251.5cm, track 142.5/141/5cm, clearance 12cm. Turning circle 12.1m. Load space 10.4/33cu ft (295/935dm3). Length 414.5cm, width 168cm, height 134.5cm.
Performance: Max speed approx 96-102.5mph/155-165kmh, speed at 1000rpm in 5th gear 36.5mph/58.8kmh; power to weight ratio from 15.1kg/kW (11.1kg/PS); consumption approx 7-13L/100km (40.4- 21.7mpg) [33.6-18.1US mpg].

Dodge Shadow

Compact Saloon/Sedan with tail gate and front wheel drive, 3- and 5-door, 2.2 Litre engine with or without turbo. Parallel model to the Plymouth Sundance. Debut March 1986. Designation for export: Chrysler ES. 1989: available with 2.5 Litre Turbo engine.

2.2 Litre
69kW - 93hp - 94 PS
Central/Single Point Injection

Body, Weight (laden): 3-door Saloon/Sedan, 5-seats; approx 1180kg; 5-door Saloon/Sedan, 5-seats; approx 1200kg.
Engine data (SAE net): 4-cylinder in-line (87.5 x 92mm), 2213cm3; compression ratio 9.5:1; 69kW (93hp) [94PS] at 4800rpm, 31.2kW/L (41.8hp/L) [42.5PS/L]; 165Nm (121.8lbft) at 3200rpm; unleaded regular grade.
Engine construction: Transverse engine. Hydraulic tappets, 1 overhead camshaft (toothed belt); light-alloy cylinder head; crankshaft with 5 bearings, oil capacity 3.8L (3.6US qt); Bosch/Holley central/single point fuel injection. Battery 12V 60Ah, alternator 90A; cooling system capacity 8.5L (8US qt).
Transmission (to front wheels): a) 5-speed manual, final drive ratio 2.51.
b) Automatic 'Torqueflite', hydraulic torque converter and 3- speed Planetary gear set, final drive ratio 3.02.
Gear ratios: a) 5-speed manual: 1st 3.29; 2nd 2.08; 3rd 1.45; 4th 1.04; 5th 0.72; R 3.14.
b) Automatic; Max torque multiplication in converter 2.1 times, Planetary gear set ratios: 2.69; 1.55; 1; R 2.1.
Chassis: Integral body. Front McPherson struts and A-arms, rear rigid axle with longitudinal arms and Panhard rods, front and rear coil springs, telescopic dampers and antiroll bars. Servo/power assisted brakes, front discs (ventilated), 25.5cm diameter, rear drums, pedal-activated parking brake to rear wheels; power assisted rack and pinion steering; fuel tank 53L (11.6Gal) [14US Gal]; tyres 175 R 13 or 185/70 R 14, wheel rims 5.5J, optional tyres 195/60 VR 15, wheel rims 6J.
Dimensions: Wheelbase 246.5cm, track 146.5/145.5cm, minimum clearance 11.5cm, turning circle 11.0m. Load space 13.2/33.4cu ft (375/945dm3), hatchback 13.1/33cu ft (370/935dm3). Length 436cm, width 171cm, height 134cm.
Performance: Max speed approx 99-103mph/160-165kmh, speed at 1000rpm in 5th gear 38.1mph/61.4kmh; power to weight ratio from 17.1kg/kW (12.6kg/PS); consumption approx 7-12L/100km (40.4- 23.5mpg) [33.6-19.6US mpg].

Dodge Shadow ES

2.5 Litre
74kW-100hp-101PS
Central/Single Point Injection

As 2.2 Litre, except:
Weight: 15kg heavier.
Engine data (SAE net): 4-cylinder in-line (87.5 x 104mm), 2501cm3; compression ratio 9:1; 74kW (100hp) [101PS] at 4800rpm, 29.6kW/L (39.7hp/L) [40.4PS/L]; 183Nm (135lbft) at 2800rpm.
Export version: 77kW (103hp) [105PS] at 4800rpm or 71kW (95hp) [96PS].
Engine construction: 2 counter-balance shafts.
Performance: Max speed approx 106-112mph/170-180kmh, power to weight ratio from 16.1kg/kW (11.8kg/PS); consumption approx 9- 14L/100km (31.4-20.2mpg) [26.1-16.8US mpg].

Dodge Shadow ES

2.5 Litre Turbo
112kW - 150hp - 152PS
Fuel Injection

As 2.2 Litre, except:
Weight: 25kg heavier.
Engine data (SAE net): 4-cylinder in-line (87.5 x 104mm), 2501cm3; compression ratio 7.8:1; 112kW (150hp) [152PS] at 4800rpm, 44.8kW/L (60hp/L) [60.8PS/L]; 244Nm (180lbft) at 2000rpm; unleaded premium or regular grade.
For some countries: 107kW (143hp) [146PS].

Dodge

Engine construction: 2 anti vibration arms; Holley electronic fuel injection, 1 M.H.I exhaust turbocharger.
Performance: Max speed approx 115–121mph/185–195kmh; power to weight ratio from 10.8kg/kW (7.9kg/PS); consumption approx 9–14L/100km (31.4– 20.2mpg) [26.1–16.8US mpg].

Engine construction: Holley electronic fuel injection, 1 M.H.I. exhaust turbocharger.
Performance: Max speed approx 115–121mph/185–195kmh, speed at 1000rpm in 5th gear 39.2mph/63.1kmh; power to weight ratio from 11.4kg/kW (8.4kg/PS); consumption approx 9–16L/100km (31.4– 17.7mpg) [26.1–14.7US mpg].

Dodge Daytona

Daytona – Daytona ES – Daytona Shelby
Sporty coupe with transverse engine, front wheel drive and tail gate; 2.2 Litre four cylinder with injection or with injection and exhaust turbo. Debut August 1983. For 1987 also with intercooler. Chrylser GS Turbo 2 export designation. 1989: new front and stronger 2.5 Litre turbo engine.

2.5 Litre
74kW–100hp–101PS
Central/Single Point Injection

Engine for Daytona
Body, Weight (laden): 3–door Coupe, 4–seats; approx 1250kg.
Engine data (SAE net): 4–cylinder in–line (87.5 x 104mm), 2501cm3; compression ratio 9:1; 74kW (100hp) [101PS] at 4800rpm, 29.6kW/L (39.6hp/L) [40.4PS/L]; 183Nm (135lbft) at 2800rpm.
Export version: 77kW (103hp) [105PS] at 4800rpm or 71kW (95hp) [96PS].
Engine construction: Transverse mounted front engine. Hydraulic tappets, 1 overhead camshaft (toothed belt); light-alloy cylinder head; crankshaft with 5 bearings; 2 counter–balance shafts; oil capacity 3.8L (3.6US qt); electronic Bosch/Holley central/single point fuel injection. Battery 12V 66Ah, alternator 90/120A; cooling system capacity 8.5L (8US qt).
Transmission (to front wheels): a) 5–speed manual, final drive ratio 2.51. b) Automatic 'Torqueflite', hydraulic torque converter and 3– speed Planetary gear set, selector lever central or at steering wheel, final drive ratio 3.02.
Gear ratios: a) 5-speed manual: 1st 3.29; 2nd 2.08; 3rd 1.45; 4th 1.04; 5th 0.72; R 3.14.
b) Automatic; Max torque multiplication in converter 2 times, Planetary gear set ratios: 2.69; 1.55; 1; F 2.1.
Chassis: Integral body. Front McPherson struts and A–arms, rear rigid axle with longitudinal arms and Panhard rods, front and rear coil springs, telescopic dampers and antiroll bars. Servo/power assisted brakes, front discs (ventilated), diameter 25.5cm, rear discs 26.8cm diameter, rear drums; pedal– activated parking brake to rear wheels; power assisted rack and pinion steering; fuel tank 53L (11.6Gal) [14US Gal]; tyres 185/70 R 14, wheel rims 5.5J; optional tyres 205/60 HR 15; 205/60 HR 15; wheel rims 6 J.
Dimensions: Wheelbase 246.5cm, track 146.5/146.5cm, minimum clearance 11cm, turning circle 11.3m. Load space 9.5/33cu ft (270/935dm3). Length 455cm, width 176cm, height 127.5cm.
Performance: Max speed approx 102.5–109mph/165–175kmh, speed at 1000rpm in 5th gear 38.5mph/62kmh; power to weight ratio from 16.9kg/kW (12.4kg/PS); consumption approx 9–14L/100km (31.4– 20.2mpg) [26.1–16.8US mpg].

Dodge Daytona

Dodge Daytona ES

2.2 Litre Turbo
129kW–174hp–176PS
Fuel Injection

Engine for Daytona and Shelby Z
As 100hp, except:
Weight: Kerbweight from approx 1330kg.
Engine data (SAE net): 4–cylinder in–line (87.5 x 92mm), 2213cm3; compression ratio 8.1:1; 129kW (174hp) [176PS] at 5200rpm, 58.3kW/L (78.1hp/L) [79.5PS/L]; 271Nm (200lbft) at 2400rpm; premium or regular grade.
Engine construction: Without counter–balance shafts; electronic fuel injection (multiport), 1 Garrett T3 exhaust turbocharger; charge-air cooler.
Transmission: 5–speed manual, final drive ratio 2.74.
Gear ratios: 1st 3.0; 2nd 1.89; 3rd 1.28; 4th 0.94; 5th 0.71; R 3.14.
Chassis: All round disc brakes, front diameter 28cm, rear 28.6cm, tyres 205/55 VR 15, wheel rims 6J.
Performance: Max speed approx 137mph/220kmh, speed at 1000rpm in 5th gear 36.7mph/59.1kmh; power to weight ratio from 9.9kg/kW (7.3kg/PS); consumption approx 10–17L/100km (28.2–16.6mpg) [23.5– 13.8US mpg].

Dodge Daytona Shellby

2.5 Litre Turbo
112kW - 150hp - 152PS
Fuel Injection

As 100hp, except:
Weight: Kerbweight approx 1280kg.
Engine data (SAE net): 4–cylinder in–line (87.5 x 104mm), 2501cm3; compression ratio 7.8:1 112kW (150hp) [152PS] at 4800rpm, 44.8kW/L (60hp/L) [60.8PS/L]; 244Nm (180lbft) at 2000rpm; premium or regular grade.
For some countries: 107kW (144hp) [146PS].

Dodge Aries

Aries – Aries LE
Smaller compact Amercian model with front wheel drive and four cylinder engine, 5–speed manual or automatic, available as two and four–door Saloon/Sedan as well as five–door Estate/Station Wagon. Debut Autumn 1980. Face lift for 1985. 1986 with new Chrysler 2.5 Litre engine. From 1989 the Estate/Station Wagon will no longer be produced.

2.2 Litre
69kW - 93hp - 94PS
Central/Single Point Injection

Body, Weight (laden): 2–door Saloon/Sedan, 6–seats; approx 1100kg. 4–door Saloon/Sedan, 6–seats; approx 1100kg.

Dodge

Engine data (SAE net): 4–cylinder in–line (87.5 x 92mm), 2213cm3; compression ratio 9.5:1; 69kW (93hp) [94PS] at 4800rpm, 31.2kW/L (41.8hp/L) [42.5PS/L]; 165Nm (121.8lbft) at 3200rpm; unleaded regular grade.

Engine construction: Transverse mounted front engine. Hydraulic tappets, 1 overhead camshaft (toothed belt); light–alloy cylinder head; crankshaft with 5 bearings; oil capacity 3.8L (3.6US qt); Bosch/Holley electronic central/single point fuel injection. Battery 12V 60/66Ah, alternator 90A; cooling system capacity 8.5L (8US qt).

Dodge Aries LE

Transmission (to front wheels): a) 5-speed manual, final drive ratio 2.51. b) Automatic 'Torqueflite', hydraulic torque converter and 3- speed Planetary gear set, final drive ratio 3.02.

Gear ratios: a) 5–speed manual: 1st 3.29; 2nd 2.08; 3rd 1.45; 4th 1.04; 5th 0.72; R 3.14.
b) Automatic; Max torque multiplication in converter 2.1 times, Planetary gear set ratios: 2.69; 1.55; 1; R 2.1.

Chassis: Integral body. Front McPherson struts and A–arms, rear rigid axle with longitudinal arms and Panhard rods, front and rear coil springs, telescopic dampers and antiroll bars. Servo/power assisted brakes, front discs (ventilated), rear drums, disc diameter 23.6cm or 25.5cm; pedal–activated parking brake to rear wheels; rack and pinion steering, optional power assisted; fuel tank 53L (11.6Gal) [14US Gal]; tyres 175 R 13, wheel rims 5J, optional tyres 185/70 R 14, wheel rims 5.5J.

Dimensions: Wheelbase 255cm. Track 146/145cm, minimum clearance 12cm, turning circle 11.4m. Load space 15cu ft(425dm3)– Estate/Station Wagon 35.3–67.6cu ft (1000–1915dm3). Length 454cm, width 173cm, height 133/134cm.

Performance: Max speed approx 99mph/160kmh, speed at 1000rpm in 5th gear 38.1mph/61.4kmh; power to weight ratio from 15.9kg/kW (11.7kg/PS); consumption approx 8–13L/100km (35.3– 21.7mpg) [29.4–18.1US mpg].

> **2.5 Litre**
> **74kW–100hp–101PS**
> **Central/Single Point Injection**

As 2.2 Litre, except:

Weight: 30kg heavier.

Engine data (SAE net): 4–cylinder in–line (87.5 x 104mm), 2501cm3; compression ratio 9:1; 74kW (100hp) [101PS] at 4800rpm, 29.7kW/L (39.8hp/L) [40.4PS/L]; 180Nm (132.8lbft) at 2800rpm.

Engine construction: 2 counter–balance shafts.

Transmission: Automatic, final drive ratio 3.02.

Performance: Max speed approx 106–112mpg/170–180kmh, speed at 1000rpm in direct gear 22.8mph/36.7kmh; power to weight ratio from 15.3kg/kW (11.2kg/PS); consumption approx 9–14L/10km (31.4– 20.2mpg) [26.1–16.8US mpg].

Dodge Aries LE

Dodge Lancer

Lancer – Lancer ES - Lancer Shelby

Saloon/Sedan with front wheel drive and tail gate based on K–car with lengthened wheelbase. 2.2 Litre four cylinder, optional with exhaust turbocharger. Debut August 1984. Since 1989 also with 2.5 Litre-Turbo engine and Lancer Shelby with 174hp engine.

> **2.2 Litre**
> **69kW - 93hp - 94PS**
> **Central/Single Point Injection**

Body, Weight (laden): 5–door Saloon/Sedan, 5–seats; approx 1230kg.

Engine data (SAE net): 4–cylinder in–line (87.5 x 92mm), 2213cm3; compression ratio 9.5:1; 69kW (93hp) [94PS] at 4800rpm, 31.2kW/L (41.8hp/L) [42.5PS/L]; 165Nm (121.8lbft) at 3200rpm; unleaded regular grade.

Engine construction: Transverse mounted front engine. Hydraulic tappets, 1 overhead camshaft (toothed belt); light–alloy cylinder head; crankshaft with 5 bearings; oil capacity 3.8L (3.6US qt); Bosch/Holley electronic central/single point fuel injection. Battery 12V 66Ah, alternator 90/120A; cooling system capacity 8.5L (8US qt).

Transmission (to front wheels): a) 5-speed manual, final drive ratio 2.51. b) Automatic 'Torqueflite', hydraulic torque converter and 3- speed Planetary gear set, final drive ratio 3.02.

Gear ratios: a) 5–speed manual: 1st 3.29; 2nd 2.08; 3rd 1.45; 4th 1.04; 5th 0.72; R 3.14.
b) Automatic; Max torque multiplication in converter 2 times, Planetary gear set ratios: 2.69; 1.55; 1; R 2.1.

Chassis: Integral body. Front McPherson struts and A–arms, rear rigid axle with longitudinal arms and Panhard rods, front and rear coil springs, telescopic dampers and antiroll bars. Servo/power assisted brakes, front discs (ventilated), rear drums, disc diameter 25.5cm; pedal–activated parking brake to rear wheels; power assisted rack and pinion steering, fuel tank 53L (11.6Gal) [14US Gal]; tyres 195/70 R 14, optional 205/60 R 15, wheel rims 5.5 or 6 inches.

Dimensions: Wheelbase 262cm, track 146.5/145.5cm, minimum clearance 12cm, turning circle 11.8m. Load space 10.8–33cu ft (305/935dm3). Length 458cm, width 173.5cm, height 134.5/133cm.

Performance: Max speed approx 102mph/165kmh, speed at 1000rpm in 5th gear 39.4mph/63.4kmh; power to weight ratio from 17.8kg/kW (13.1kg/PS); consumption approx 8–14L/100km (35.3–20.2mpg) [29.4– 16.8US mpg].

> **2.5 Litre**
> **74kW–100hp–101PS**
> **Central/Single Point Injection**

As 2.2 Litre, except:

Weight: Kerbweight approx 1235kg, ES 1245kg.

Engine data (SAE net): 4–cylinder in–line (87.5 x 104mm), 2501cm3; compression ratio 9:1; 74kW (100hp) [101PS] at 4800rpm, 29.8kW/L (39.9hp/L) [40.4PS/L]; 183Nm (135lbft) at 2800rpm.

Dodge Lancer ES

Engine construction: 2 counter–balance shafts.

Performance: Max speed approx 106–112mph/170–180kmh; power to weight ratio from 16.7kg/kW (12.2kg/PS); consumption approx 9– 14L/100km (31.4–20.2mpg) [26.1–16.8US mpg].

Dodge

2.5 Litre
112kW - 150hp - 152PS
Fuel Injection

As 2.2 Litre, except:

Weight: Kerbweight approx 1255kg, ES 1260kg.

Engine data (SAE net): 4–cylinder in-line (87.5 x 104mm), 2501cm3; compression ratio 7.8:1; 112kW (150hp) [152PS] at 4800rpm, 44.8kW/L (60hp/L) [60.8PS/L]; 244Nm (180lbft) at 3600rpm; premium or regular grade.
For some countries: 107kW (144hp) [146PS]

Engine construction: 2 anti vibration arms; Holley electronic fuel injection, 1 M.H.I exhaust turbocharger.

Performance: Max speed approx 115–121mph/185–195kmh; power to weight ratio from 11.2kg/kW (8.3kg/PS); consumption approx 9– 15L/100km (31.4–18.8mpg) [26.1–15.7US mpg].

Dodge Lancer Shelby

2.2 Litre Turbo
129kW–174hp–176PS
Fuel Injection

Engine for Lancer Shelby

As 2.2 Litre, except:

Weight: Kerbweight from approx 1355kg.

Engine data (SAE net): 4–cylinder in-line (87.5 x 92mm), 2213cm3; compression ratio 8.1:1; 129kW (174hp) [176PS] at 5200rpm, 58.3kW/L (78.1hp/L) [79.5PS/L]; 271Nm (200lbft) at 2400rpm; premium or regular grade.

Engine construction: Bosch/Holley electronic fuel injection, 1 Garrett T3 exhaust turbocharger; charger-air cooler.

Transmission: 5–speed manual, final drive ratio 2.74.

Gear ratios: 1st 3.0; 2nd 1.89; 3rd 1.28; 4th 0.94; 5th 0.71; R 3.14.

Chassis: All round disc brakes, front disc diameter 28cm, rear 28.6cm; tyres 205/60 VR 15, wheel rims 6J.

Performance: Max speed approx 137mph/220kmh, speed at 1000rpm in 5th gear 36.5mph/58.7kmh; power to weight ratio from 10.5kg/kW (7.7kg/PS); consumption approx 10–17L/100km (28.2–16.6mpg) [23.5– 13.8US mpg].

Dodge Spirit

New model. Four door Saloon/Sedan based on the A-car, with front wheel drive, 2.5 or 3 Litre engine; replaces the "600" model. Launched Winter, 1988.

2.5 Litre
74kW - 100hp - 101PS
Central/Single Point Injection

Not available for ES

Body, Weight (laden): 4-door Saloon/Sedan, 5/6-seater, approx 1255kg.

Engine data (SAE net): 4-cylinder in-line (87.5 x 104mm), 2501cm3; compression ratio 9:1; 74kW (100hp) [101PS] at 4800rpm, 29.6kW/L (39.7hp/L) [40.4PS/L]; 185Nm (136.5lbft) at 2800rpm; regular unleaded.

Engine construction: Transverse front engine. Hydraulic tappets, 1 overhead camshaft (toothed belt); light-alloy cylinder head; 2 antivibration arms; 5 main bearing crankshaft; oil capacity 3.8L (3.6US qt); Holley electronic central injection. 12V Battery 66Ah, Alternator 90A; cooling system capacity approx 8.5L (8US qt).

Dodge Spirit ES

Transmission (to front wheels): a) 5-speed manual, final drive ratio 2.51.
b) Automatic "Torqueflite", hydraulic torque converter and 3-speed Planetary gear set, selector lever at centre or at steering column, final drive ratio 3.02.

Gear ratios: a) 5-speed manual: 1st 3.29; 2nd 2.08; 3rd 1.45; 4th 1.04; 5th 0.72; R 3.14.
b) Automatic: Max torque multiplication in converter 2.1 times, Planetary gear set ratios: 2.69; 1.55; 1; R 2.1.

Chassis: Integral body. Front McPherson struts and A-arm, rear rigid axle with trailing arm and Panhard rod, front and rear coil springs, telescopic dampers and antiroll bar. Servo/power assisted brakes, disc diameter front (ventilated) 25.5cm, rear drums; pedal actuated parking brakes to rear wheels; Power assisted rack and pinion steering; fuel tank capacity 61L (13.4Gal) [16.1US Gal]; tyres 195/70 R 14, SE 205/60 R 15, wheel rims 5.5/6 J.

Dimensions: Wheelbase 262.5cm, track 146/145.5cm, clearance min 12cm, turning circle 11.9m. Load space (14.5cu ft) [410dm3]. Length 460cm, width 173cm, height 141cm.

Performance: Max speed approx 121mph/165kmh, speed at 1000rpm in 5th gear 39.4mph/63.4kmh; power to weight ratio from 17kg/kW (12.4kg/PS); consumption approx 10-15L/100km (28.2-18.8mpg) [23.5-15.7US mpg].

2.5 Litre Turbo
112kW - 150hp - 152PS
Fuel Injection

As 2.5 Litre, except:

Weight: Kerbweight approx 1265 ES 1315kg

Engine data (SAE net): 4-cylinders in-line (87.5 x 104mm), 2501cm3; compression ratio 7.8:1; 112kW (150hp) [152PS] at 4800rpm, 44.8kW/L (60hp/L) [60.8PS/L]; 244Nm (180lbft) at 2000rpm; premium or regular.
For some countries: 107kW (144hp) [146PS]

Engine construction: Holley electronic fuel injection, 1 MHI exhaust turbocharger.

Performance: Max speed approx 115-121mph/185-195kmh; power to weight from 11.3kg/kW (8.3kg/PS); consumption approx 9-15L/100km (31.4-18.8mpg) [26.1-15.7US mpg].

3-Litre V6
105kW - 141hp - 143PS
Fuel Injection

As 2.5 Litre, except:

Weight: Kerbweight (DIN) from 1355kg.

Engine data (SAE net): 6-cylinder in V 60deg (91.1 x 76.0mm), 2972cm3; compression ratio 8.9:1; 105kW (141hp) [143PS] at 5000rpm, 35.3kW/L (47.3hp/L) [48.1PS/L]; 232Nm (171.2lbft) at 2800rpm.

Engine construction: Designated Mitsubishi 6G 72, Valves in V; 1 overhead camshaft (toothed belt); 4 main bearing crankshaft; without antivibration arms; Holley electronic fuel injection. Cooling system capacity 9L (8.5US qt).

Transmission: Automatic "Torqueflite", hydraulic torque converter and 4-speed Planetary gear set, selector lever at steering column, final drive ratio 2.36.

Gear ratios: Automatic: Max torque multiplication in converter 1.8 times, Planetary gear set ratios: 2.84; 1.57; 1; 0.69; R 2.21.

Performance: Max speed approx 121mph/195kmh, speed at 1000rpm in top gear 43.5mph/70.1kmh; power to weight ratio from 12.9kg/kW (9.5kg/PS); consumption approx 12-17L/100km (23.5-16.6mpg) [19.6-13.8US mpg].

Dodge

Dodge Spirit ES

Dodge Dynasty

Dynasty – Dynasty LE

Saloon/Sedan with front wheel drive, available with 2.5 Litre four cylinder or 3 Litre V6 engine. Technically related to the Chrysler New Yorker. Debut September 1987.

```
2.5 Litre
74kW–100hp–101PS
Central/Single Point Injection
```

Body, Weight (laden): 4–door Saloon/Sedan, 6–seats: approx 1355kg.

Engine data (SAE net): 4–cylinder in–line (87.5 x 104mm), 2501cm3; compression ratio 9:1; 74kW (100hp) [101PS] at 4800rpm, 29.6kW/L (39.7hp/L) [40.4PS/L]; 183Nm (138lbft) at 2800rpm; unleaded regular grade.

Engine construction: Transverse mounted front engine. Hydraulic tappets, 1 overhead camshaft (toothed belt); light–alloy cylinder head; 2 counter–balance shafts; crankshaft with 5 bearings; oil capacity 3.8L (3.6US qt); Bosch/Holley electronic central/single point fuel injection. Battery 12V 66Ah, alternator 90A; cooling system capacity 8.5L (8US qt).

Transmission (to front wheels): Automatic 'Torqueflite', hydraulic torque converter and 3–speed Planetary gear set, selector lever on steering wheel, final drive ratio 3.02.

Gear ratios: Automatic; Max torque multiplication in converter 2 times, Planetary gear set ratios: 2.69; 1.55; 1; R 2.1.

Dodge Dynasty

Chassis: Integral body. Front McPherson struts and A–arms; negative steering offset; rear rigid axle with longitudinal arms and Panhard rods, front and rear coil springs, telescopic dampers and antiroll bars. Servo/power assisted brakes, front discs (ventilated), rear drums, disc diameter 25.6cm, optional rear disc brakes, diameter 25.5cm ABS (Bosch); pedal actuated parking brake to rear wheels; power assisted rack and pinion steering; fuel tank 61L(13.4Gal) (15.9US Gal); tyres 195/75 R 14, wheel rims 5.5J.

Dimensions: Wheelbase 265cm, track 146.5/146.5cm, minimum clearance 12.5cm, turning circle 11.9m. Load space 16.4cu ft (465dm3), length 487.5cm, width 174cm, height 136cm.

Performance: Max speed approx 102.5mph/165kmh, speed at 1000rpm in top gear 25mph/40.2kmh; power to weight ratio from 19.0kg/kW (14.0kg/PS); consumption approx 10–15L/100km (28.2–18.8mpg) [23.5–15.7US mpg].

```
3 Litre V6
105kW - 141hp - 143PS
Fuel Injection
```

As 2.5 Litre, except:

Weight: Kerbweight (DIN) from approx 1390kg.

Engine data (SAE net): 6–cylinder in 60deg V (91.1 x 76.0mm), 2972cm3; compression ratio 8.9:1; 105kW (141hp) [143PS] at 5000rpm, 35.3kW/L (47.3hp/L) [48.1PS/L]; 232Nm (171.2lbft) at 2800rpm.

Dodge Dynasty LE

Engine construction: Mitsubishi 6G 72 designation. Valves in V; 2x1 overhead camshaft (toothed belt); crankshaft with 4 bearings; without counter–balance shafts; EC1 electronic fuel injection. Cooling system capacity 9.5L (9US qt).

Transmission: Automatic "Torqueflite", hydraulic torque converter and 4-speed Planetary gear set, final drive ratio 2.36.

Gear ratios: Automatic; Max torque multiplication in converter 1.8 times, Planetary gear set ratios: 2.84; 1.57; 1; 0.69; R 2.21.

Performance: Max speed approx 118mph/190kmh; speed at 1000rpm in top gear 45mph/72.4kmh; power to weight ratio from 13.2kg/kW (9.7kg/PS); consumption approx 10–15L/100km (28.2–18.8mpg) [23.5–15.7US mpg].

Dodge Diplomat

Luxurious car with a V8 engine and automatic transmission. 1985; increased power output. Production will be suspended during 1989.

```
5.2 Litre V8
104kW–140hp–142PS
1 2V Carb
```

Body, Weight (laden): Diplomat Saloon/Sedan; 4–door, 5/6–seats; approx 1625kg. Diplomant SE; 4–door Saloon/Sedan, 5/6–seats; approx 1695kg.

Engine data (SAE net): 8–cylinder in 90deg V (99.31 x 84.07), 5210cm3; compression ratio 9.0:1; 104kW (140hp) [142PS] at 3600rpm, 20.0kW/L (26.8hp/L) [27.3PS/L]; 360Nm (265.71lbft) at 2000rpm; unleaded regular grade.
Police version (with 4V carb): 130kW (174hp) [177PS] at 4000rpm, 25.0kW/L (33.5hp/L) [34.0PS/L]; 339Nm (250.2lbft) at 3200rpm.
Export version: 132.5kW (177.5hp) [180PS] at 4000rpm.

Engine construction: Hydraulic tappets, central camshaft (chain); crankshaft with 5 bearings; oil capacity 3.8L (3.6US qt); 1 Holley 6280 downdraught 2V carb. Battery 12V 66Ah, alternator 90A; cooling system capacity 14.7L (13.9US qt).

Transmission (to rear wheels): Automatic 'Torqueflite', hydraulic torque converter and 3–speed Planetary gear set, selector on steering wheel, final drive ratio 2.26; 2.74; 2.76; 2.94. Optional limited slip differential.

Dodge Diplomat

Gear ratios: Max torque multiplication in converter 2 times, Planetary gear set ratios: 2.74; 1.54; 1; R 2.22.

Dodge • Donkervoort

Chassis: Integral body; front upper swinging A arms, lower single control arm with elastically-mounted torsion struts and two transverse torsion bars, antiroll bars, rear rigid axle with semi-elliptical springs, telescopic dampers. Servo/power assisted brakes, front discs (ventilated), rear drums, disc diameter 27.5cm; parking brake to rear wheels; power assisted recirculating ball steering; fuel tank 68L (14.9Gal) [18US Gal], tyres 205/75 R 15, wheel rims 7 inches.

Dimensions: Wheelbase 286cm, track 153.5/152.5cm, clearance 15cm, turning circle 13.3m. Load space 15.5cu ft (440dm3). Length 519.5cm, width 184cm, height 140cm.

Performance: Max speed approx 109-115mph/175-185kmh, speed at 1000rpm in top gear 34.5mph/55.5kmh; power to weight ratio 15.6kg/kW (11.5kg/PS); consumption (touring) approx 13-20L/100km (21.7-14.1mpg) [18.1-11.8US mpg].

Dodge Caravan

Roomy vehicle with front wheel drive, 5 to 8-seats, 2.5 and 3 Litre engine capacities, 2 different wheelbases. Parallel model to Plymouth Voyager. Chrysler Voyager export desgination; for technical data see Chrysler Voyager.

Dodge Caravan

Dodge Ramcharger

Rough terrain vehicle with rear wheel or four wheel drive. 1989: 5.9 Litre with fuel injection.

5.2 Litre V8
127kW-170hp-172PS
Central/Single Point Injection

Body, Weight: 3-door Estate/Station Wagon, 5-seats; kerbweight from approx 1800kg, gross vehicle weight approx 2500kg.

Engine data (SAE net): 8-cylinder in 90deg V (99.31 x 84.07mm), 5210cm3; compression ratio 9.2:1; 127kW (170hp) [172PS] at 4000rpm, 24.4kW/L (32.7hp/L) [33.0PS/L]; 353Nm (260.5lbft) at 2000rpm; regular grade.

Dodge Ramcharger

Engine construction: Hydraulic tappets, central camshaft (chain); crankshaft with 5 bearings; oil capacity 3.8L (3.6US qt); electronic fuel injection. Battery 12V 60Ah, alternator 60A; cooling system capacity 14.7/15.6L (13.9-14.8US qt).

Transmission (to rear or all wheels): a) 4-speed manual, final drive ratio 3.21 or 3.55.

b) Automatic 'Loadflite', hydraulic torque converter and 3-speed Planetary gear set, selector lever on steering wheel with P-R-N- D-2-1 positions, final drive ratio 2.94. Limited slip differential; engageable four-wheel-drive; central differential with engageable reduction gear, final drive ratio 2.01.

Gear ratios: a) 4-speed manual: 1st 6.68; 2nd 3.34; 3rd 1.66; 4th 1; R 8.26.
or 4-speed manual: 1st 4.56; 2nd 2.28; 3rd 1.31; 4th 1; R 4.07.
or 4-speed manual: 1st 3.09; 2nd 1.67; 3rd 1; 4th 0.73; R 3.
b) Automatic: Max torque multiplication in converter 1.9 times, Planetary gear set ratios: 2.45; 1.45; 1; R 2.2.

Chassis: Sub-frames with 5 cross-members; front and rear rigid axles with semi-elliptical springs, telescopic dampers. Servo/power assisted brakes, front discs, diameter 29.8cm, rear drums; pedal-activated parking brake to rear wheels; recirculating ball steering, optional power assisted; fuel tank 132L (29Gal) [35US Gal]; tyres 235/75 R 15 (7 inches).

Dimensions: Wheelbase 269cm, track 167/167cm, clearance 20cm, turning circle 12m. Length 469cm, width 202cm, height 179-187cm.

Performance: Max speed approx 99.5mph/160kmh, speed at 1000rpm in top gear 24.4mph/39.3kmh; power to weight ratio from 14.2kg/kW (10.4kg/PS); consumption (touring) approx 14-25L/100km (20.2- 11.3mpg) [16.8-9.4US mpg].

Dodge Ramcharger 4x4

5.9 Litre V8
142kW - 190hp - 193PS
Central/Single Point Injection

As 5.2 Litre, except:

Weight: Kerbweight approx 1800kg.

Engine data (SAE net): 8-cylinder in 90deg V (101.6 x 90.93mm), 5898cm3; compression ratio 9.2:1; 142kW (190hp) [193PS] at 4000rpm, 24.1kW/L (32.3hp/L) [32.7PS/L]; 400Nm (295.2lbft) at 2000rpm.

Engine construction: Hydraulic tappets, central camshaft; crankshaft with 5 bearings; cooling system capacity 15.1L (14.3US qt), engageable cooler-ventilator.

Performance: Max speed approx 106mph/170kmh; power to weight ratio from 12.7kg/kW (7.0kg/PS); consumption (touring) approx 16- 24L/100km. (17.7-11.8mpg) [14.7-9.8US mpg].

DONKERVOORT　　NL

Joop Donkervoort, Nieuw Loosdrechtsedijk 205a, 1231 KT Nieuw Loosdrecht, Holland

Small manufacturer in Holland building replicas of the earlier Lotus Seven in slightly changed form.

Donkervoort Super Eight-S8A

Two-seater roadster in the style of the Lotus Super Seven with 2 Litre Ford engine and light-alloy/synthetic body; S8A model with fuel injection and rear independent suspension. Debut Amsterdam 1985.

2 Litre
77kW-103hp-105PS
1 2V Carb

Donkervoort • Eagle

Engine for Super Eight

Body, Weight: 2–door roadster, 2–seats: kerbweight (DIN) 585–610kg, gross vehicle weight.

Engine data (DIN): 4–cylinder in–line (90.82 x 76.95), 1994cm3; compression ratio 9.2:1; 77kW (103hp) [105PS] at 5400rpm, 38.7kW/L (51.9hp/L) [52.7PS/L]; 155Nm (114.3lbft) at 4000rpm; leaded premium grade.

Engine construction: Valves in 15deg V, 1 overhead camshaft (toothed belt); crankshaft with 5 bearings; oil capacity 3.8L (3.6US qt); 1 downdraught Weber 32/36 DGAV carb. Battery 12V 55Ah, alternator 45A; cooling system capacity 7L (6.6US qt).

Transmission (to rear wheels): 5–speed manual, final drive ratio 3.44. Optional limited slip differential.

Gear ratios: 1st 3.651; 2nd 1.968; 3rd 1.368; 4th 1; 5th 0.820; R 3.660.

Chassis: Tubular frame; front swinging A arms, coil springs and antiroll bar, rear rigid axles with 4 longitudinal arms and one Panhard rod as well as coil springs, telescopic dampers. Front disc, rear drum–brakes, disc diameter 22.8cm, mechanical handbrake to rear wheels; rack and pinion steering; fuel tank 40L (8.8Gal) [10.6US Gal], tyres 195/60 HR 14, wheel rims 7J.

Dimensions: Wheelbase 230.5cm, track 132/144cm, clearance 10cm, turning circle 7.8m. Length 356cm, width 164cm, height 99/110cm.

Performance: Top speed 118mph/190kmh (manufacturers test specifications), speed at 1000rpm in 5th gear 23.8mph/38.3kmh, acceleration 0 – 62mph/100kmh in 6.2secs; power to weight ratio 7.6kg/kW (5.6kg/PS); consumption (touring) 7–12L/100km (40.4–23.5mpg) [33.6–19.6US mpg].

```
2 Litre
86/12.5kW–115/168hp–117/170PS
Fuel Injection
```

Engine for S8A

Weight: Kerbweight (DIN) 675kg, gross vehicle weight 925kg.

Engine data: 4–cylinder in–line (90.82 x 76.95), 1994cm3; compression ratio 9.2:1; 86kW (115hp) [117PS] at 5500rpm, 43.2kW/L (57.9hp/L) [58.7PS/L]; 163Nm (120.2lbft) at 4000rpm.
With Catalyst (DIN): Compression ratio 8.5:1; 78kW (104hp) [106PS] at 5100rpm, 152Nm (112.2lbft) at 4000rpm; unleaded grade.
Available with turbocharger: Compression ratio 8:1; 125kW (168hp) [170PS] at 5500rpm; 230Nm (169.7lbft) at 4000rpm
With Catalyst: 119kW (160hp) [162PS].

Engine construction: Bosch KE–Jetronic mechanical fuel injection. Garrett T3 turbocharger and charge air cooler.

Transmission: 5–speed manual, final drive ratio 3.62 or 3.45.

Gear ratios: 1st 3.36; 2nd 1.81; 3rd 1.26; 4th 1; 5th 0.82; R 3.66.

Chassis: Rear independent suspension with double A–arms and longitudinal arms. Front ventilated disc brakes; fuel tank 45/47L (9.9/10.3Gal) [11.9/12.4US Gal] tyres 205/50 HR 15 and 225/50 HR 15, wheel rims 8J.

Dimensions: Track 136/147cm or 140/147cm. Length 360cm, width 173cm.

Performance: Max speed 127.4mph/205kmh (manufacturers test specifications), turbocharger: 137–135mph/220–217kmh; speed at 1000rpm in 5th gear 22.5mph/36.2kmh; acceleration 0 – 62mph/100kmh 6secs; power to weight ratio 7.8kg/kW (5.8kg/PS); consumption (touring) approx 7–12L/100km (40.4–23.5mpg) [33.6–19.6US mpg], turbocharger 6–4.8L/100km (47.1–58.8mpg) [39.2–49US mpg].

Donkervoort S8A

Donkervoort D10

New model. Super sports version with 2.2 Litre Turbo (188hp), max speed 150mph/242kmh, acceleration 0–62mph/100kmh 4.5secs. Debut Paris 1988.

Donkervoort D10

EAGLE   USA

Jeep–Eagle Division, Chrysler Corporation, Detroit, Michigan 48231, USA.

Jeep–Eagle is a new division of Chrysler.

Eagle Premier

Four door Saloon/Sedan with front wheel drive available in four cylinder 2.5 Litre or 3 Litre V6 engines with five speed manual or automatic transmission. Launched summer 1987. 1989 only available with automatic.

```
2.5 Litre
83kW–111hp–113PS
Central/Single Point Injection
```

Body, Weight: 4–door Saloon/Sedan, 5–seater; kerbweight (DIN) 1310kg, gross vehicle weight 1865kg.

Engine data (SAE net): 4–cylinder in–line (98.42 x 80.97mm), 2464cm3; compression ratio 9.2:1; 83kW (111hp) [113PS] at 4750rpm, 33.6kW/L (45hp/L) [45.9PS/L]; 193Nm (142.4lbft) at 2500rpm; unleaded regular grade.

Engine construction: In–line engine, hydraulic tappets, side camshaft (chain); 5 bearing crankshaft; oil capacity 3.8L (3.6US qt); Weber central/single point electronic fuel injection. Champion M12Y spark plugs; 12V 66Ah battery, 105A alternator; cooling system capacity approx 8.2L (7.8US qt).

Eagle Premier ES

Transmission (to front wheels): Electronic controlled automatic, hydraulic torque converter and 4–speed Planetary gear set, selector lever on steering wheel; final drive ratio 2.62.

Gear ratios: Max torque multiplication in converter 2 times; Planetary gear set ratios: 1st 2.71; 2nd 1.55; 3rd 1; 4th 0.68; R 2.11.

Eagle • Ecosse • Engesa

Chassis: Integral body, all round independent suspension, front (negative camber angle) McPherson strut (coil spring and co–axial telescopic damper) with wishbone and stabiliser bar, rear trailing arms and transverse torsion bar, stabiliser bar and telescopic dampers. Servo/power assisted brakes, front ventilated discs, 26.5cm dia, rear drum brakes, mechanical handbrake on rear; power assisted rack and pinion steering; 64L (14.5Gal) [17US Gal] fuel tank; tyres 195/70 R14, 205/70 R14 or 215/60 R 15, 5.5 or 6 inch wheels.

Dimensions: Wheelbase 269.5cm, track 148/145cm. Clearance 12cm, turning circle 11.9m, load space 16.2cu ft (460dm3). Length 490cm, width 178cm, height 136cm.

Performance: Max speed approx 109mph/175kmh, speed at 1000rpm in top gear 40.5mph/65.2kmh, power to weight ratio from 15.8kg/kW (11.6kg/PS); consumption approx 10–13L/100km (28.2–21.7mpg) [23.5–18.1US mpg].

Eagle Premier LX

```
3 Litre V6
112kW–150hp–152PS
Fuel Injection
```

As 2.5 Litre, except:

Weight: Kerbweight (DIN) from 1380kg, gross vehicle 1950kg.

Engine data (SAE net): 6–cylinder in 90deg V (93 x 73mm), 2975cm3; compression ratio 9.3:1; 112kW (150hp) [152PS] at 5000rpm, 37.6kW/L (51.1PS/L); 232Nm (171.1lbft) at 3600rpm.

Engine construction: 2 x 1 overhead camshaft (chain); light–alloy cylinder block; wet cylinder liners; 4 bearing crankshaft; oil capacity 4.8L [4.5US qt]; fuel injection Bosch K–Jetronic. 96A alternator; cooling system capacity approx 9.8L (9.3US qt).

Transmission: Automatic: ZF 4 HP 18, final drive ratio 2.66.

Gear ratios: Max torque multiplication in converter 2.6 times; Planetary gear set ratios; 1st 2.58; 2nd 1.41; 3rd 1; 4th 0.74; R 2.88.

Performance: Max speed approx 121mph/195kmh; speed at 1000rpm in top gear 36.6mph/59kmh; power to weight ratio 12.3kg/kW (9.1kg/PS); consumption approx 11–15L/100km (27.5–18.8mpg) [21.4– 15.7US mpg].

ECOSSE   GB

Ecosse Car Company plc, Nup End, Knebworth, Hertfordshire, SG3 6QL

Small English car manufacturing plant, based on the old AC 3000 ME 2–seater sports car.

Ecosse Signature

New model. 2–seater mid–engine coupe with plastic body and Fiat 2 Litre turbo. Chassis from old AC 3000 ME. Debut Birmingham 1988. Provisional data.

```
2 Litre Turbo
121kW–162hp–165PS
Fuel Injection
```

Body, Weight: Coupe 2–door, 2–seater; kerbweight (DIN) 950kg.

Engine data (DIN): 4–cylinder in–line (84 x 90mm), 1995cm3; compression ratio 8:1; 121kW (162hp) [165PS] at 5500rpm, 60.6kW/L (81.2hp/L) [82.7PS/L]; 284Nm (209.6lbft) at 2750rpm; premium grade.

Ecosse Signature

Engine construction: Fiat transverse mid–engine. Valves in V65 deg, 2 overhead camshafts (toothed belt); light–alloy cylinder head, 5 bearing crankshaft; oil capacity 7L (6.6US qt); Bosch LE 2 Jetronic electronic fuel injection; 1 Garrett T3 exhaust turbocharger, max charge–air pressure 0.53bar; charge–air cooler. 12V 70Ah battery, 65/85A alternator; cooling system capacity 9.6L (9.1US qt).

Transmission (to rear wheels): 5–speed manual, final drive ratio 3.944 (18/53).

Gear ratios: 1st 3.750; 2nd 2.235; 3rd 1.518; 4th 1.132; 5th 0.928; R 3.583.

Chassis: Platform/box–type frame; front and rear independent suspension with A arm, antiroll bar, coil springs and telescopic dampers. Servo/power assisted disc brakes (front ventilated), disc diameter 28.3cm, rear 27.2cm, mechanical handbrake to rear; power assisted rack and pinion steering; fuel tank capacity 64L (14.1Gal) [16.9US Gal]; tyres 205/50 VR 15, wheel rims 6.5 J.

Dimensions: Wheelbase 229cm, track 146.5/150cm, turning circle 9.5m. Load space 10cu ft (285dm3). Length 409cm, width 167.5cm, height 120cm.

Performances: Max speed over 145mph/233kmh (manufacturers test specifications), speed at 1000rpm in 5th gear 24.8mph/39.9kmh; acceleration 0–60mph/97kmh 6.2secs; power to weight ratio from 7.8kg/kW (5.8kg/PS); consumption approx 8–13L/100km (35.3–21.7mpg) [29.4–18.1US mpg].

Ecosse Signature

ENGESA   BR

Engesa – Engenheiros Especialisados SA, Av Tucunare, 25 (Cai postal 152), 06400 Barueri, Brazil

Enterprise making specialised cars for the army and agricultural markets.

Engesa 4

Rough–terrain vehicles with canvas hoods, Chevrolet Opala 2.5 Litre engine, rear wheel drive with engageable 4 wheel drive. In preparation for 1989 a Perkins diesel engine.

```
2.5 Litre
64.5kW–87hp–88PS
1 2V Carb
```

Engesa • Envemo • Excalibur

Body, Weight: 2-door convertible roadster, 4-seater, kerbweight (DIN) 1500kg, gross vehicle weight 2000kg.

Engine data (DIN): 4-cylinder in-line (101.6 x 76.2mm), 2471cm3; compression ratio 11:1; 64.5kW (87hp) [88PS] at 4000rpm, 26.2kW/L (35.1hp/L) [35.6PS/L]; 190Nm (140.1lbft) at 2500rpm; ethyl alcohol.
Available with petrol/gasoline engine.
Perkins diesel engine: (98.4 x 127mm), 3863cm3; compression ratio 16:1; 66kW (89hp) [90PS] at 2800rpm, 17.1kW/L (22.9hp/L) [23.3PS/L]; 276Nm (203.7lbft) at 1600rpm.

Engine construction: Designated GMB 151, hydraulic tappets, side camshaft (gear driven), 5 bearing crankshaft; oil capacity 3.5L (3.3US qt); 1 downdraught 2V Weber 446 carb. Bosch NGK 44 N spark plugs, 12V 45 battery, 32A alternator; cooling system capacity 8.5L (8US qt).

Transmission (to rear wheels or all wheels): 5-speed manual, final drive ratio 3.92, front 3.91, diesel 3.07; with front wheel drive engaged. Limited slip differential.

Engesa 4

Gear ratios: 1st 6.89; 2nd 3.92; 3rd 2.34; 4th 1.49; 5th 1; R 6.99.

Chassis: Box-type frame with tubular steel members, front and rear beam axle with transverse tie rods, coil springs and telescopic dampers. Servo/power assisted brakes, front ventilated discs, rear drum brakes, 29cm dia, mechanical handbrake on rear; worm and peg steering, 90L (19.8 Gall) [23.8 US Gall] fuel tank, 10L (2.2Gal) [2.6US Gal] reserve tank, tyres 7.5 x 16, also available with 215/80 R 16, 5 or 6J wheels.

Dimensions: Wheelbase 226cm, track 145.5/145.5cm, clearance 23cm, turning circle 12m. Length 376cm, width 167cm, height 185cm.

Performance: Max speed 79.5mph/128kmh, speed 1000rpm in 5th gear 22.1mph/35.5kmh, power to weight ratio 23.2kg/kW (17.0kg/PS); consumption approx 13-18L/100km (21.7-15.7mpg) [18.1-13.1US mpg].

ENVEMO — BR

Envemo-Engenharia de Veiulos e Motores Ltda, Av Nacoes Unidas, 167 37, 04794 Sao Paulo, Brazil

A small factory known for rebuilding and for special vehicles.

Envemo Camper 4 x 4

3-door Estate/Station Wagon with Chevrolet-Opala engine, rear wheel drive and engagable four wheel drive.

2.5 Litre
64kW-86hp-88PS
1 2V Carb

Body, Weight: Estate/Station Wagon 3-door, 5-seater; kerbweight (DIN) 1500kg, gross vehicle weight 2100kg.

Engine data (DIN): 4-cylinder in-line (101.6 x 76.2mm), 2471cm3; compression ratio 11.1:1; 64kW (86hp) [88PS]; 190Nm (140lbft) at 2500rpm; with ethyl alcohol.

Petrol/gasoline engine: Compression ratio 8:1; 63kW (84hp) [85PS]; 177Nm (130.6lbft); leaded regular grade.
With 6-cylinder engine: 6-cylinder in-line (98.4 x 89.6mm), 4093cm3; compression ratio 8:1; 87kW (117hp) [118PS] at 4000rpm, 21.3kW/L (28.5hp/L) [28.8PS/L]; 275Nm (203lbft) at 2000rpm; unleaded regular grade.
With 2V Carb: 92.5kW (124hp) [126PS] at 4400rpm; 274Nm (202.2lbft) at 2300rpm.
Ethyl alcohol: Compression ratio 10:1; 99.5kW (133hp) [135PS] at 4000rpm; 295rpm (217.7lbft) at 2000rpm.

Engine construction: Designated GMB 151. Hydraulic tappets, side camshaft (toothed belt); 5 bearing crankshaft; oil capacity 3.5L (3.3US qt); 1 Weber 446 downdraught 2V carb.
12V 48Ah battery, 55A alternator; cooling system capacity 8.5L (8US qt).

Transmission (to rear or all wheels): 5-speed manual, final drive ratio rear 3.92, front 3.91; with front wheel drive engaged. Limited slip differential.

Gear ratios: 1st 6.89; 2nd 3.92; 3rd 2.34; 4th 1.49; 5th 1; R 6.99.

Chassis: Box-type frame with tubular steel members, front and rear beam axle with transverse tie rods, coil springs and telescopic dampers.
Servo/power assisted disc brakes, disc diameter (ventilated) 25.4cm, rear drums; mechanical handbrake to rear; worm and peg steering; fuel tank capacity 90L (19.8Gal) [23.8US Gal], 10L (2.2Gal) [2.6US Gal] reserve tank; tyres 255 R 15, wheel rims 7 J.

Dimensions: Wheelbase 247cm, track 149/149cm, clearance 23cm, turning circle 13.2m. Length 415cm, width 179cm, height 173cm.

Performances: Max speed 87mph/140kmh (manufacturers test specifications), speed at 1000rpm in 5th gear 22mph/35.5kmh; power to weight ratio from 23.4kg/kW (17.1kg/PS); consumption approx 12.5-15L/100km (22.6-18.8mpg) [18.8-15.7US mpg].

Envemo Camper 4x4

EXCALIBUR — USA

Excalibur Automobile Corporation, 1735 South 106th Street, Milwaukee, Wisconsin 53214, USA.

Small American enterprise, founded in 1964. Under new ownership since 1986.

Excalibur Series V

Imitation of the Mercedes 500/540K (1937 to 1938) sports car according to the drawings of Brooks Stevens. Summer 1985: Series V with modifications to the chassis and the bodywork; additional variants Royale and Limited. Autumn 1988: Grand Saloon/Sedan with 519cm wheelbase.

Excalibur Series V Roadster

Excalibur • Farus

```
5/5.7 Litre V8
146/171kW–196/229hp–198/233PS
1 4V Carb
```

Body, Weight: 2–door Roadster, 2+2–seater, 2110kg; 2–door Phaeton, 4–seater, 2110kg; 4–door Royale Saloon/Sedan, 5–seater, 2175kg; 4–door Limited Saloon/Sedan, 2355kg; gross vehicle weight 2750–3000kg; 4–door Grand Saloon/Sedan, 8–seater; 2585kg.

Engine data (SAE net): 8–cylinder V90 deg (94.89 x 88.39mm), 5001cm3; compression ratio 9.3:1; 146kW (196hp) [198PS] at 4000rpm, 29.2kW/L (39.1hp/L) [39.6PS/L] 400Nm (295.2lbft) at 2800rpm; regular grade.
Or (101.6 x 88.39mm) 5733cm3; compression ratio 9.3:1; 171kW (229hp) [233PS] at 4400rpm, 29.8kW/L (39.9hp/L) [40.6PS/L]; 448Nm (330.6lbft) at 3200rpm.
Also available with 7.4 Litre V8: (107.98 x 101.60mm), 7443cm3; compression ratio 7.9:1; 171kW (229hp) [233PS] at 3600rpm, 23.0kW/L (30.8hp/L) [31.3PS/L]; 522Nm (385lbft) at 1600rpm.

Excalibur Series V Phaeton

Engine construction: Designated Chevrolet LB9/L98. Hydraulic tappets, central camshaft (chain); 5 bearing crankshaft; oil capacity 4.7L (4.45US qt); Bosch electronic fuel injection; 12V 73Ah battery, 94A alternator; cooling system capacity 20.8L (19.7US qt).

Transmission (to rear wheels): 'Turbo–Hydra–Matic' automatic; hydraulic torque converter and 3–speed Planetary gear set (plus overdrive), selector lever position to centre console; final drive ratio 2.73 or 3.07. Standard and with limited slip differential.

Gear ratios: Max torque multiplication in converter 2 times, Planetary gear set ratios: 2.74; 1.57; 1; OD 0.67; R 2.07.

Chassis: Transverse box–type frame, front A arm, rear independent suspension with 2 longitudinal side arms, fixed differential, front and rear torsion stabilising bar and antiroll bar, telescopic dampers.
Some Models: Rear rigid axle with longitudinal arms and semi–trailing arms, alround coil springs and telescopic dampers.
Servo/power assisted disc brakes, disc brakes 29.8cm diameter; Grand Saloon/Sedan rear disc brakes, manual parking brake to rear; power assisted recirculating ball steering, 83L (18.2Gal) [21.9US Gal] fuel tank; tyres 235/75 R 15, 7/8 J wheels.

Excalibur Series V Grand Limousin

Dimensions: Wheelbase 315cm, track 162.5/162.5cm, clearance 18cm, turning circle 12.2m. Length 518cm, width 193cm, height 150cm. Royale–Saloon/Sedan: Wheelbase 376cm, track 166/162.5cm. Length 580cm, width approx 195cm, height 155cm. Limited–Saloon/Sedan: Wheelbase 436cm, track 166/162.5cm. Length 640cm, width approx 195, height 155cm.
Grand Saloon/Sedan: Wheelbase 518cm, track 163/163cm. Length 721cm, width approx 195cm, height 163cm.

Performance: Max speed approx 112–124mph/180–200kmh, speed at 1000rpm in top gear 21–19.5mph/69–63kmh; power to weight ratio 12.4kg/kW (9.1kg/PS); consumption approx 16–23L/100km (17.7– 12.3mpg) [14.7–10.2US mpg].

FARUS   BR

TECVAN - Tecnologia de Vanguarda Ltda., Rua Camilio Flamrion 311, 32210 Contagem (Minas Gerais), Brasil.

Produces Sports cars in small series.

FARUS

Beta - Cabriolet - Quadro

2-seater Coupe and Cabriolet with plastic body, engine with 2 Litre capacity from VW or Chevrolet. 1988: For Export with 2.2 Litre Engine of Chrysler LeBaron Turbo. 1989: Quadro with 4-seater and front wheel drive.

Farus Quadro

```
2 Litre
82/73kW-110/98hp-112/99PS
1 2V Carb
```

Body, Weight: Coupe/Cabriolet 2-door, 2-seater; kerbweight (DIN) 910kg, gross vehicle weight 1250kg.
Coupe Quadro 2-door, 4-seater; kerbweight (DIN) 1060kg, gross vehicle weight 1460kg.

Engine data (DIN): 4-cylinder in-line (82.5 x 92.8mm) 1984cm3.
Operating on ethyl alcohol (DIN): Compression ratio 12:1; 82kW (110hp) [112PS] at 5200rpm, 41.3kW/L (55.3hp/L) [56.4PS/L]; 170Nm (125.5lbft) at 3400rpm.
b) Petrol/Gasoline engine: Compression ratio 8:1; 73kW (98hp) [99PS] at 5200rpm, 36.8kW/L (49.3hp/L) [49.9PS/L]; 159 Nm (117.3lbft) at 3400rpm; leaded regular grade.

Engine construction: Central engine (Beta/Cabriolet), front engine (Quadro); 1 overhead camshaft (toothed belt); light-alloy cylinder head; 5 bearing crankshaft; oil capacity 4L (3.8US qt); 1 Brosol-Pierburg 2E7 downdraught carb. 12V 54Ah battery, 65A alternator; cooling system capacity approx 14.5L (13.7US qt), Quadro 6.7L (6.3US qt).

Transmission (to rear, Quadro to front wheels) : 5-speed manual, final drive ratio 4.11.

Gear ratios: 1st 3.45; 2nd 1.94; 3rd 1.29; 4th 0.97; 5th 0.8; R 3.17.

Chassis: Central frame; front and rear independent suspension, McPherson struts and control arm. Front disc brakes; mechanical hand brake to rear wheels; rack and pinion steering; fuel tank 70L (15.4Gal) [18.5US Gal], Quadro 75L (16.5Gal) [19.8US Gal]; tyres 185/70SR 13, wheel rims 7, Quadro 6J.

Dimensions: Wheelbase 240cm, track 143/146cm, clearance 15cm, turning circle 10.2m, length 405cm, width 168.5cm, height 110cm.
Quadro: Track 141/142cm, turning circle 11m, length 430cm, width 170.5cm, height 129cm.

Performance: Max speed approx 124mph/200kmh, speed at 1000rpm in 5th gear 20.7mph/33.3kmh; power to weight ratio 11.1kg/kW (8.1kg/PS); consumption approx 8-12L/100km (35.3-23.5mpg) [29.4-19.6US mpg].

```
2 Litre
81/73kW-108/98hp-110/99PS
1 2V Carb
```

Farus • Ferrari

Engine for Beta and Cabriolet

As 110/98hp, also:

Weight: Kerbweight (DIN) 830kg, gross vehicle weight 1170kg.

Engine data (DIN): 4-cylinder in-line (86 x 86mm) 1998cm3. Operating on ethyl alcohol: Compression ratio 12:1; 81kW (108hp) [110PS] at 5600rpm, 40.5kW/L (54.3hp/L) [55.0PS/L]; 170Nm (125.5lbft) at 3000rpm. Petrol/Gasoline: 73kW (98hp) [99PS] at 5600rpm, 36.7kW/L (49.2hp/L) [49.6PS/L]; 159 Nm (117.3lbft) at 3500 rpm; octane requirement 86 ROZ.

Engine construction: Transverse engine. Designated Chevrolet. Hydraulic tappets, side camshaft (chain). Oil capacity 3.0L (2.8US qt).

Transmission: 5-speed manual, final rive ratio 3.94.

Gear ratios: 1st 3.42 2nd 2.16; 3rd 1.48; 4th 1.12 5th 0.89 R 3.33.

Chassis: Fuel capacity 65L (14.3Gal) [17.2US Gal].

Performance: Max speed 124mph/200kmh, speed at 1000rpm in 5th gear 19.4mph/31.2kmh; power to weight ratio from 10.3kg/kW (7.5kg/PS); consumption approx 8-12L/100km (35.3-23.5mpg) [29.4-19.6US mpg].

```
2.2 Litre Turbo
109kW-146hp-148PS
Central/Single Point Injection
```

Engine for Export USA (Beta and Cabriolet).

As 112/99PS, except:

Weight: Kerbweight 1070kg.

Engine data (SAE net): 4-cylinder in-line (87.5 x 92mm), 2213cm3; compression ratio 8.1:1; 109kW (146hp) [148PS] at 5200rpm, 49.3kW/L (66hp/L) [66.9PS/L] at 3600rpm; premium or regular grade.

Engine construction: Transverse central engine. Hydraulic tappets, 1 overhead camshaft (toothed belt); light-alloy cylinder head; 5 bearing crankshaft; oil capacity 3.8L (3.6US qt); Bosch/Holley electronic central fuel injection. 12V 66Ah battery, 90/120A alternator; cooling system capacity 8.5L (8US qt).

Transmission: 5-speed manual, final drive ratio 4.21; 3.56.

Gear ratios: 1st 3.29; 2nd 1.89; 3rd 1.21; 4th 0.88; 5th 0.72; R 3.14.

Chassis: Front tyres 185/60R 14, rear 195/ R 14.

Performance: Max speed 122mph/196kmh, speed at 1000rpm in 5th gear 22.1mph/35.6kmh; acceleration 0 - 60.2mph/97kmh 7.2secs; power to weight ratio from 9.9kg/kW (7.2kg/PS); consumption approx 9-15L/100km (31.4-18.8mpg) [26.1-15.7US mpg].

Farus Cabriolet

FERRARI I

Ferrari SpA, Viale Trento Trieste 31, 41100 Modena, Italy

Celebrated classic Italian built racing car. Nine times winner of the Le Monde 24 Hour Race. Joined the Fiat Group in 1969.

MODEL RANGE
328 GTB/GTS – GTB/GTS Turbo – Mondial T/Mondial T Cabriolet – 412 – Testarossa – F40

Ferrari 328 GTB/GTS

2–door Coupe with mechanics of the Dino 308 GT 4: V8 transverse mid engine with 2x2 overhead camshaft. Coupe launched September 1975, Spider GTS September 1977. Autumn 1980: with fuel injection. Autumn 1982: new cylinder head with four valves per cylinder; Frankfurt 1985: 3.2 Litre engine with 266hp.

Ferrari 328 GTB

```
3.2 Litre V8
198.5/187.5kW–266/251hp–270/255PS
Fuel Injection
```

Body, Weight: 2–door Coupe (Pininfarina), 2–seater; kerbweight (DIN) 1265kg, USA 1425kg. 2–door Spider (Pininfarina), 2–seater; kerbweight (DIN) 1275kg, USA 1440kg.

Engine data (DIN): 8-cylinder in V90deg (83 x 73.6mm), 3186cm3; compression ratio 9.8:1; 198.5kW (266hp) [270PS] at 7000rpm. 62.3kW/L (83.5hp/L) [84.8PS/L]; 304Nm (224.5lbft) at 5500rpm; leaded premium grade.
With Catalyst: 187.5kW (251hp) [255PS] or 194kW (260hp) [264PS] at 7000rpm; 289Nm (213.3lbft) at 5500rpm.

Engine construction: Designated F105 CB000. Transverse mid–engine with transmission and differential in one unit. Valve in V33.5 deg, 4 valves per cylinder, 2x2 overhead camshaft (toothed belt); light metal cylinder head and cylinder block, wet cylinder liner; 5 bearing crankshaft; oil cooler, oil capacity approx 10L (9.5US qt); Bosch K/KE-Jetronic mechanical fuel injection, electronic pump. Champion A6G spark plugs, 12V 66Ah battery, 85A alternator; cooling system capacity 22L (21US qt).

Transmission (to rear wheels): 5-speed manual, final drive ratio 3,706 (17/63); ZF limited slip differential.

Gear ratios: 1st 3.419; 2nd 2.353; 3rd 1.693; 4th 1.244; 5th 0.919; R 3.248.
Or: 1st 3,305; 2nd 2.274; 3rd 1.637; 4th 1.203; 5th 0.889; R 3.14.

Chassis: Space frame, front and rear independent suspension with keystone wishbone and coil spring, front and rear antiroll bar, telescopic dampers. Servo/Power assisted four-wheel disc brakes (ventilated), front disc diameter 28.2cm, rear 28cm, mechanical handbrake on rear; rack and pinion steering; 74L (16.3Gal) [19.6US Gal] tank capacity; front tyres 205/55VR 16, rear 250/50VR 16, 7" front wheels, 8" rear.

Dimensions: Wheelbase 235cm, track 148.5/146.5cm, clearance approx 12cm, turning circle 12m, load space 7cu ft (200dm3). Length 425.5cm, USA 428.5cm, width 173cm, height 113cm.

Performance: Max speed 164mph/263kmh (manufacturers test specification), speed at 1000rpm in 5th gear 21.1mph/34.1kmh; acceleration 0 – 62mph/100kmh 6.4secs; standing start km 25.7secs; power to weight ratio 6.4kg/kW (4/7kg/PS); consumption ECE 9.0/10.4/17.9L/100km (31.4/27.2/15.8mpg) [26.1/22.6/13.1US mpg].

Ferrari 328 GTS

Ferrari

Ferrari GTB/GTS Turbo

Model with exhaust turbocharger, only delivered in Italy. Launched 1982 in Turin. From Turin in 1986 with intercooler and multi power output.

```
2 Litre V8 Turbo
187kW–247hp–254PS
Fuel Injection
```

Body, Weight: 2–door Coupe and Spider, 2–door; kerbweight (DIN) 1265/1275kg.

Engine data (DIN): 8-cylinder in V90 deg (66.8 x 71mm), 1991cm3, compression ratio 7.5:1; 187kW (247hp) [254PS] at 6500rpm, 93.8kW/L (126.1hp/L) [127.6PS/L]; 329Nm (243lbft)) at 4100rpm.

Engine construction: Designated F106 N000. Valves in V46 deg, 2 valves per cylinder; Bosch K–Jetronic, IHI turbocharger, charge-air pressure 1.05 bar; intercooler; Champion N2G spark plugs, 70A alternator.

Performance: Max speed 157mph/253kmh (manufacturers test specification); acceleration 0 – 62mph/100 kmh 6.3secs; standing start km 25.7secs; power to weight ratio 6.8kg/kW (5.0kg/PS); consumption ECE 7.8/10.0/15.6L/100km (36.2/28.2/18.1mpg) [30.2/23.5/15.1US mpg].

Ferrari Mondial T

Coupe and Cabriolet with V8 mid–engine. 2 + 2-seater. Body according to the design from Pininfarina. Launched 3 Litre 1980 in Geneva. Autumn 1982: Cylinder head with four valves per cylinder; higher performance. Since 1984 a Cabriolet has been available. Frankfurt 1985: 3.2 Litre engine with 266hp. 1989: Mondial T with longitudinal instead of transverse engine, 3.4 Litre V8, 300PS.

```
3.4 Litre V8
221kW–296hp–300PS
Fuel Injection
```

Body, Weight: Coupe (Pininfarina) 2-door. 2 + 2-seater; kerbweight (DIN) 1505kg, gross vehicle weight 1825kg.
Cabriolet (Pininfarina) 2-door, 2 + 2-seater; kerbweight (DIN) 1535kg, gross vehicle weight 1825 kg.

Engine data (DIN): 8-cylinder in V90 deg (85 x 75mm), 3405cm3, compression ratio 10.4:1; 221kW (296hp) [300PS] at 7200rpm, 65kW/L (87.1hp/L) [88.2PS/L]; 323Nm (238.4lbft) at 4200rpm.

Engine construction: Designated F. Longitudinal T-formed engine and transmission as one assembly. Valves in V 32.5deg, 4 valves per cylinder, 2x2 overhead camshaft (toothed belt), light–alloy cylinder head and cylinder block, wet cylinder liners; 5 main bearing crankshaft; dry sump lubrication; oil cooler, oil capacity 12L (11.4US qt); Bosch 2.5 Motronic electronic fuel injection. 12V 66Ah battery, 105A alternator; cooling system capacity approx 24L (23US qt).

Transmission (on rear wheels): 5–speed manual, central gear lever; final drive ratio 3.823 or 3.706; ZF limited slip differential.

Ferrari Mondial T

Gear ratios: 1st 3.214 2nd 2.105; 3rd 1.146; 4th 1.094; 5th 0.861; R 2.786.

Chassis: Space frame; front and rear independent suspension with keystone wishbone and coil spring, front and rear antiroll bar, telescopic damper. Servo/power assisted disc brakes (ventilated) and ABS (ATE), front disc diameter 28.2cm, rear 28cm, mechanical handbrake on rear; rack and pinion steering; fuel tank 96L (21.1Gal) [25.4US Gal], Cabriolet 86L (18.9Gal) [22.7US Gal], from 20L (4.4Gal) [5.3US Gal] Reserve; front tyres 7", rear 8", optional front tyres 220/55 VR 390, rear 240/55 VR 390, wheel rims front 165 and rear 180TR.

Dimensions: Wheelbase 265cm, track 152/156cm, clearance min 12.5cm, turning circle 11.9m. Load space 10.6cu ft (300dm3). Length 453.5cm, width 181cm, height 123.5, Cabriolet 126.5cm.

Performance: Max speed 159mph/255kmh (manufacturers test specification), speed at 1000rpm in 5th gear 20.2mph/32.5kmh; acceleration 0 – 62mph/100kmh 6.3secs; standing km 25.8secs USA 26.0secs; power to weight ratio 6.8kg/kW (5.0kg/PS); consumption ECE 9.5/11.9/21.4L/100km (29.7/23.7/13.2mpg) [24.8/19.8/11US mpg].

Ferrari 412

Successor to the 400i, modifications to the motor, body and interior. Debut Geneva 1985.

```
4.9 Litre V12
250/239kW–335/320hp–340/325PS
Fuel Injection
```

Body, Weight: 2–door Coupe (Pininfarina) 2 + 2 seater; kerbweight (DIN) at 1805kg, gross vehicle weight 2200kg.

Engine data (DIN): 12-cylinder in V 60deg (82 x 78mm), 4943cm3; compression ratio 9.6:1, 250kW (335hp) [340PS] at 6000rpm, 50.6kW/L (68hp/L) [68.8PS/L]; 451Nm (333lbft) at 4200rpm; leaded premium grade.
With Catalyst: 239kW (320hp) [325PS].

Engine construction: Designated 101 E070 (automatic) or F101 E010 (5–speed manual). Overhead valves in V 46deg; 2x2 overhead camshaft (chain); light–alloy cylinder head and cylinder block; wet cylinder liners; 7 main bearing crankshaft; 2 oil filters; oil capacity 13L (12.3US qt); Bosch K/KE–Jetronic mechanical fuel injection, 2 electrical fuel pumps. Champion N 6 GY spark plugs, 12V 90Ah battery, 2x65A alternators; cooling system capacity approx 18L (17US qt).

Transmission (on rear wheels): a) 'Turbo–Hydra–Matic' automatic, hydraulic torque converter and 3–speed Planetary gear set, cental gear lever with positions P–R– N–D–2–1; final drive ratio 3.250 (12/39).
b) 5-speed manual, final drive ratio 4.3 (10/43). ZF limited slip differential (40%).

Gear ratios: a) Automatic; Max torque mulitiplication in converter 2.2 times, Planetary gear set ratios: 2.48; 1.481; 1; R 2.077.
b) 5-speed manual: 1st 2.837; 2nd 1.707; 3rd 1.254; 4th 1.12; 5th 0.759; R 2.315.

Chassis: Space frame; front and rear independent suspension with keystone wishbone and coil spring, rear level control system, front and rear antiroll bar, Koni telescopic dampers. Servo/power assisted disc brakes with ABS (ventilated), front disc dia 30.1cm, rear 29.6cm, mechanical handbrake on rear; worm and peg power assisted steering; 116L (25.5Gal) [30.6US Gal] fuel tank, 20L (4.4Gal) [5.3US Gal] reserve tank capacity; tyres 240/55VR 16, 7.5" wheels; or tyres 240/55VR 415, 180TR wheels.

Dimensions: Wheelbase 270cm, track 147.5/151cm, clearance 13cm, turning circle 12.2m. Load space 17.6cu ft (500dm3). Length 481cm, width 180cm, height 131.5cm.

Performance: Max speed 159mph/255kmh, automatic 155mph/250kmh (manufacturers test specification), speed at 1000rpm in top automatic gear 23.9mph/38.5kmh, in 5th gear 24.2mph/39.2kmh; acceleration 0 – 62mph/100kmh 6.7secs, automatic 8.3secs, standing start km 26.4secs, automatic 27.7secs; power to weight ratio 7.2kg/kW (5.3kg/PS); consumption ECE 13.3/15.9/29.1L/100km (21.1/17.8/9.7mpg) [17.7/14.8/8.1US mpg], automatic 13.2/15.3/26.4L/100km (21.4/18.5/10.7mpg) [17.8/15.4/8.9US mpg].

Ferrari 412

Ferrari   177

Ferrari Testarossa

Successor to the BB 512i. High performance Coupe with 4.9 Litre twin cylinder engine with 4 valves per cylinder and Pininfarina body. Debut Salon, Paris 1984.

Ferrari Testarossa

```
4.9 Litre 12 cylinder
287/272kW–385/365hp–390/370PS
Fuel Injection
```

Body, Weight: 2–door Coupe, 2–seater; kerbweight (DIN) 1505kg, USA 1660kg, gross vehicle weight 1860kg.

Engine data (DIN): 12-cylinder flat engine (180deg), (82 x 78mm), 4942cm3; compression ratio 9.2:1; 287kW (385hp) [390PS] at 6300rpm, 58.1kW/L (77.9hp/L) [78.9PS/L]; 490Nm (362lbft) at 4500rpm; leaded premium grade. With Catalyst: 272kW (365hp) [370PS] at 6000rpm, 55kW/L (74hp/L) [74.9PS/L]; 451Nm (333lbft) at 4600rpm; unleaded premium grade.

Engine construction: Designated F113 A000. Mid–engine, mounted longitudinally; 4 valves per cylinder in V 41deg; 2x2 overhead camshaft (toothed belt); light-alloy cylinder block and cylinder head, wet cylinder liners; 7 main bearing crankshaft; dry sump lubrication, oil cooler, oil capacity 15.5L (14.8US qt); Bosch K/KE–Jetronic mechanical fuel injection. 12V 66Ah battery, 120A alternator, cooling system capacity approx 20L (19US qt).

Transmission (on rear wheels): 5–speed manual, final drive ratio 3.214 (14/45).

Gear ratios: 1st 3.140; 2nd 2.014; 3rd 1.526; 4th 1.167; 5th 0.875; R 2.532. Or 1st 3.035; 2nd 1.947; 3rd 1.476; 4th 1.129; 5th 0.849; R 2.448.

Ferrari Testarossa

Chassis: Space frame; front and rear independent suspension with keystone wishbone and coil spring (rear double), front and rear antiroll bar, telescopic dampers (rear 4). Servo/power assisted disc brakes (ventilated), front disc dia 30.9cm, rear 31cm, mechanical handbrake on rear; 115L (25.3Gal) [30.4US Gal] fuel tank, USA 100L (22.0Gal) [26.4US Gal]; front tyres 225/50VR 16, rear 255/50VR 16, 8" front wheels, 10" rear; or front tyres 240/45VR 415, rear 280/45VR 415, 210TR front wheels, rear 240TR.

Dimensions: Wheelbase 255cm, track 152/166cm, turning circle 12m. Length 448.5cm, width 197.5cm, height 113cm.

R12

Performance: Max speed 180mph/290kmh (manufacturers test specification), speed at 1000rpm in 5th gear 26.5mph/42.6kmh; acceleration 0 – 62mph/100kmh 5.8secs, standing start km 24.1secs; power to weight ratio 5.2kg/kW (3.9kg/PS); consumption ECE 9.9/11.8/23.7L/100km (28.5/23.9/11.9mpg) [23.8/19.9/9.9US mpg].

Ferrari F40

Competition sport style with 471hp mid–engine; derived from the GTO. 3 Litre V8 engine with 2x2 overhead camshaft and 2 turbochargers. Tubular frame chassis and body of Karbon/Kevlar. Debut July 1987. Production begins 1988.

Ferrari F40

```
2936cm3
351.5kW–471hp–478PS
2 Turbos/Fuel Injection
```

Body, Weight: 2–door Coupe (Pininfarina), 2–seater; kerbweight (DIN) 1100kg, gross vehicle weight 1400kg.

Engine data (DIN): 8-cylinder in V 90deg (82 x 69.5mm), 2936cm3; compression ratio 7.8:1; 351.5kW (471hp) [478PS at 7000rpm, 119.7kW/L (160.4hp/L) [162.8PS/L]; 577Nm (426lbft) at 4000rpm; leaded premium grade.

Engine construction: Designated F120 A000. Longitudinal mid– engine, with transmission and differential in one unit. 4 valves per cylinder in V 35.5deg, 2x2 overhead camshaft (toothed belt); light–alloy cylinder head and block, 5 main bearing crankshaft; dry sump lubrication, 2 oil coolers, oil capacity 12.5L (11.8US qt); Weber/Marelli IAW electronic engine (fuel injection/ignition), 2 IHI turbochargers, max boost pressure 1.1 bar, 2 intercoolers. 12V battery, 70A alternator; water cooled.

Transmission (on rear wheels): 5–speed manual, final drive ratio 2.727 (11/30). Limited slip differential.

Gear ratios: 1st 2.769; 2nd 1.722; 3rd 1.227; 4th 0.963; 5th 0.767; R 2.461. With additional differential gear reduction: 1st 3.678; 2nd 2.296; 3rd 1.636; 4th 1.284; 5th 1.021; R 3.28.

Chassis: Tubular steel frame reinforced with carbon fibre/Kevlar elements, independent suspension, front lower and upper A arm, rear lower and upper keystone wishbone, front and rear antiroll bar all round coil spring with coaxial shock absorber, automatic self–levelling suspension. Servo/power assisted brakes (internal ventilation), disc diameter 33cm, mechanical handbrake on rear; rack and pinion steering; 2 x 60L (13.2Gal) [15.9US Gal] fuel tanks; front tyres 245/40ZR 17, rear 335/35ZR 17; 8" front wheels, rear 13".

Dimensions: Wheelbase 245cm, track 159.5/161cm, clearance 12.5cm, turning circle 12m. Length 443cm, width 198cm, height 113cm.

Performance: Max speed 201mph/324kmh (manufacturers test specification), speed at 1000rpm in 5th gear approx 28.6mph/46kmh; acceleration 0 – 124mph/200kmh 12secs; standing start km 21.0secs; power to weight ratio 3.1kg/kW (2.3kg/PS); consumption approx 17–35L/100km (16.6– 8.1mpg) [13.8–6.7US mpg].

Ferrari F40

FIAT   I

FIAT SpA, Corso Marconi, 10, 10125 Torino, Italy

Important producer of automobiles in Europe, manufacturer of passenger, truck and also industrial vehicles. Activites in the country include aeronautical, naval, mechanical construction and civil engineering. 1969: Revival of Lancia and Ferrari and November 1986 of Alfa Romeo.

MODEL RANGE
126 – Panda – Uno – X1/9 – Duna – Tipo – Regata – Croma – Campagnola

Fiat 126 Bis

Small car produced in Pologne with a 2 cylinder rear engine. Debut with 594cm3 Turin 1972, with 652cm3 July 1977. September 1987: tail gate and water cooled, horizontally mounted 2-cylinder rear engine, 704cm3, 25hp DIN.

```
704cm3
19kW–25hp–26PS
1 2V Carb
```

Body, Weight: 3–door Saloon/Sedan, 4–seater; kerbweight (DIN) 620kg, gross vehicle weight 965/980kg.

Engine data (DIN): 2-cylinder in–line (80 x 70mm), 704cm3; compression ratio 8.6:1; 19kW (25hp) [26PS] at 4500rpm, 27kW/L (36.1hp/L) [37PS/L]; 49Nm (36.2lbft) at 2000rpm; leaded regular grade.

Engine construction: Rear engine, horizontally mounted. Designated 126 A2.000. Side camshaft (chain); light-alloy cylinder head and engine block; dry cylinder liners; 2 main bearing crankshaft; oil capacity 2.5L (2.4US qt); 1 Weber 30DGF 3/150 downdraught 2V carb. 12V 34Ah battery, 45A alternator; cooling system capacity approx 4.5/4.8L (4.3/4.5US qt).

Transmission (on rear wheels): 4-speed manual, 2nd, 3rd and 4th syncronized gears, final drive ratio 4.33 (9/39).

Fiat 126 Bis

Gear ratios: 1st 3.25; 2nd 2.067; 3rd 1.3; 4th 0.872; R 0.872.

Chassis: Integral body; front upper A arm and lower control arm transverse leaf spring; rear independent suspension with oblique A arm and coil spring, telescopic dampers. All round drum brakes, mechanical handbrake on rear; rack and pinion steering; 21L (4.6) [5.5US Gal] fuel tank, 3.5–5L (0.8–0.9Gal) [0.9–1.3US Gal] reserve tank; 135/70SR 13 tyres, 4L wheels.

Dimensions: Wheelbase 184cm, track 113.5/117cm, clearance 12.5/17cm, turning circle 8.6/9.2m. Front load space 1.9cu ft (55dm3), rear 3.9/9.5/17.7cu ft (110/270/500dm3). Length 310.5cm, width 137.5cm, height 134.5cm.

Performance: Max speed 72.1mph/116kmh (manufacturers test specification), speed at 1000rpm in 5th gear 15.7mph/25.2kmh; acceleration 0 – 62mph/100kmh 33secs, standing start km 43secs; power to weight ratio 32.6kg/kW (23.8kg/PS); consumption ECE 4.4/–/5.8L/100km (64.2/–/48.7mpg) [53.5/–/40.6US mpg].

Fiat Panda

750 – 1000 – 1300D

2–door small car, tail gate and front wheel drive. Debut Geneva in 1980. New palet engine (Fire, 770 and 999cm3), "Omega" rear axle with modifications to the body and interior. April 1986: Also available with a 1.3 Litre diesel engine.

```
750
25kW–33hp–34PS
1 Carb
```

Body, Weight: 3–door Saloon/Sedan, 5–seater, kerbweight (DIN) 715kg, gross vehicle weight 1100/1150kg.

Engine data (DIN): 4 cylinder in–line (65 x 58mm), 770cm3; compression ratio 9.2/9.4:1; 25kW (33hp) [34PS] at 5250rpm, 32.5kW/L (43.5hp/L) [44.2PS/L]; 57Nm (5.8mkp) at 3000rpm; leaded premium/regular.

Engine construction: Designated 156 A4.000. Transverse mounted front engine, 12deg to the rear. 1 overhead camshaft (toothed belt); light-alloy cylinder head; 5 main bearing crankshaft; oil capacity 3.75L (3.6US qt); 1 Weber 32 TLF 6/250 or TLF 24 downdraught carb. 12V 30Ah, 36A or 40Ah battery, 45A alternator; cooling system capacity approx 5.2L (4.9US qt).

Transmission (on front wheels): a) 4–speed manual, final drive ratio 4.23. b) 5–speed manual, final drive ratio 4.23.

Gear ratios: a) 4–speed manual: 1st 3.909; 2nd 2.056; 3rd 1.344; 4th 0.978; R 3.727. b) 5–speed manual: 1st 3.909; 2nd 2.056; 3rd 1.344; 4th 0.978; 5th 0.837; R 3.727.

Chassis: Integral body; front independent suspension with McPherson struts, rear "Omega" shaped axle casing with central anchor and sloping trailing arm, coil springs; telescopic damper. Servo/power assisted brakes, front disc diameter 22.7cm, rear drum brake, mechanical handbrake on rear; rack and pinion steering; 40/43L (8.8/9.5Gal) [10.6/11.4US Gal] fuel tank, 135SR 13 tyres, also available 155/65SR 16, 4" or 4.5" wheels.

Dimensions: Wheelbase 216cm, track 126/126.5cm, clearance 13cm, turning circle 9.4m. Load space 9.5/22.2/38.5cu ft (270/630/1090dm3). Length 341cm, width 149.5cm, height 142/144cm.

Performance: Max speed 78mph/125kmh (manufacturers test specification), speed at 1000rpm in 4th/5th gear 14.9–17.5mph/24–28.2kmh; acceleration 0–62mph/100kmh 23secs, standing start 41.1secs; power to weight ratio 28kg/kW (20.6kg/PS); consumption ECE 5.0/–/6.2L/100km (56.5/–/45.6mpg) [47.0/–/37.9US mpg], 5-speed 4.6/–/6.2/L100km (61.4/–/45.6Gal) [51.1/–/37.9US mpg].

```
1000/1000 ie
33kW–44hp–45PS
1 Carb/Central–Single Point Injection
```

As 750, except:

Engine data (DIN): 4–cylinder in–line (70 x 64.9mm), 999cm3; compression ratio 9.8:1; 33kW (44hp) [45PS] at 5000rpm, 33kW/L (44.2hp/L) [45PS/L; 80Nm (59lbft) at 2750rpm.

Some countries: Compression ratio 9.2:1; 32.5kW (43.5hp) [44PS]; 76Nm (56.1lbft).

With Catalyst and central/single point injection (Bosch Mono–Jetronic): Compression ratio 9/9.5:1; 33kW (44hp) [45PS] at 5250rpm; 75Nm (55.4lbft) at 3250rpm.

Engine construction: Designated 156 A2.000, with central/single point injection and Catalyst 156 A/2246.

Transmission: 4 or 5–speed manual, final drive ratio 3.733 or 3.867.

Fiat Panda 1000 S

Performance: Max speed 87mph/140kmh, 43.5hp 44PS 85mph/138kmh (manufacturers test specification), speed at 1000rpm in 4th/5th gear 16.4/19.1mph26.4/30.8kmh; acceleration 0 – 62mph/100kmh 16secs; standing start km 37.4secs; power to weight ratio from 21.2kg/kW (15.6kg/PS); consumption ECE 5.0/6.8/6.3 (56.5/41.5/44.8mpg) [47/34.6/37.3US mpg], 5-speed 4.6/6.5/6.3L/100km (61.4/43.5/44.8mpg) [51.1/36.2/37.3US mpg], 44PS (5.4/7.3/6.8 [52.3/32.2/34.6US mpg], catalyst 4.9/7.0/6.7L/100km (57.6/40.4/35.1US mpg).

Fiat

1302cm3 Diesel
27kW–36hp–37PS
Injection Pump

As 750, except

Weight: Kerbweight (DIN) 810kg, gross vehicle weight 1210kg.

Engine data (DIN): 4–cylinder in–line (76.1 x 71.5mm), 1302cm3, compression ratio 20:1; 27kW (36hp) [37PS] at 4000rpm, 20.9kW/L (28hp/L) [28.4PS/L]; 71Nm (52.4) at 2500rpm.

Engine construction: Designated 156 A5.000. Pre–chamber diesel, 1 overhead camshaft (toothed belt); light-alloy cylinder head; 5 main bearing crankshaft; oil capacity 4.3L (4.1US qt); Bosch fuel injection pump. 12V 50Ah battery, 55A alternator; cooling system capacity approx 5.6L (5.3US qt).

Transmission: 5–speed manual, final drive ratio 3.867.

Gear ratios: 1st 3.909; 2nd 2.056; 3rd 1.344; 4th 0.978; 5th 0.780; R 3.727.

Chassis: 32L (7.0Gal) [8.5US Gal] fuel tank.

Performance: Max speed 81mph/130kmh (manufacturers spec), speed at 1000rpm in 4th/5th gear 16.4–20.6mph/26.4–33.1kmh; acceleration 0 – 62mph/100kmh 25secs, standing start km 41.1secs; power to weight ratio 29.8kg/kW (21.9kg/PS); consumption ECE 4.6/6.5/5.5L/100km (61.4/43.5/51.4mpg) [51.1/36.2/42.8US mpg].

Fiat Panda 4 x 4

Small car, derived from the Panda. Front wheel drive with limited slip differential on rear wheels. Debut June 1983. January 1986: With 'Fire' engine.

Fiat Panda 4x4

1000
37/33kW–49/44hp–50/45PS
1 Carb/Central–Single Point Injection

As 750, except

Weight: Kerbweight (DIN) 790-805kg, gross vehicle weight 1190/1200kg.

Engine data (DIN): 4–cylinder in–line (70 x 64.9mm), 999cm3; compression ratio 9.8:1; 37kW (49hp) [50PS] at 5500rpm, 37kW/L (49.6hp/L) [50.1PS/L]; 78Nm (58.1lbft) at 3000rpm.
Some countries: Compression ratio 9/9.2:1; 32.5kW (43.5hp) [44PS]; 76Nm (56.1lbft).
With Catalyst and Bosch Mono–Jetronic central/single point injection: Compression ratio 9:1; 33kW (43.5hp) [45PS] at 5250rpm; 75Nm (55.4lbft) at 3250rpm.

Engine construction: Designated 156 A3.000, Bosch Mono–tronic central/single point injection and Catalyst 156 A2.246. 1 Weber 32TLF 8/250 downdraught carb.

Transmission (on front wheels or all wheels): 5–speed manual, final drive ratio 5.455 (11/60).

Gear ratios: 1st 3.909; 2nd 2.056; 3rd 1.344; 4th 0.978; 5th 0.780; R 3.727.

Chassis: Integral body; front indepedent suspension with McPherson strut (coil spring), control arm and tension strut, rear rigid axle with semi–elliptic spring, telescopic dampers. 35/30L (7.7/6.6Gal) [9.2/7.9US Gal] fuel tank; 145R 13 tyres, 4.5J wheels.

Dimensions: Wheelbase 217cm, track 125/126 or 128/128.5cm, clearance 18cm, turning circle 9.2m. Load space 9.5–38.5cu ft (270–1090dm3). Length 341cm, width 150cm, height 147/148.5cm.

Performance: Max speed 81–84mph/130–135kmh, Catalyst 78mph/125kmh (manufacturers test specifications), speed at 1000rpm in 4th/5th gear 12.1–15.1mph/19.4–24.3kmh; acceleration 0 – 62mph/100km 17.5secs; standing start km 38secs; power to weight ratio 21.4kg/kW (15.8kg/PS); consumption ECE 6.1/8.2/7.0L/100km (46.3/34.4/40.4mpg) [38.6/28.7/33.6US mpg].

Fiat Uno

MODEL RANGE
45 – 60 – Selecta – 70 – 75 i.e. – D – Turbo D

Compact Saloon/Sedan with front wheel drive, transverse mounted 4 cylinder engine (903–1698cm3), 3 or 5–door, 4 or 5–speed manual transmission. Debut January 1983, Diesel May 1983, with Catalyst Geneva 1985, 'Fire' June 1985, Turbo–Diesel April 1986 and 1700– Diesel September 1986. For 1988 also with CVT transmission.

999/903cm3
33kW–44hp–45PS
1 Carb/Central–Single Point Injection

Engine for Uno 45 and 45 i.e.

Body, Weight: 3–door Saloon/Sedan, 5–seater; kerbweight (DIN) 700-735kg, gross vehicle weight 1110kg; 5–door Saloon/Sedan, 5– seater; kerbweight (DIN) 720–755kg, gross vehicle weight 1200kg.

Engine data (DIN): 4–cylinder in–line (70 x 64.9mm), 999cm3; compression ratio 9.8:1; 33kW (44hp) [45PS] at 5000rpm; 33kW/L (44.2hp/L) [45PS/L]; 80Nm (59lbft) at 2750rpm.
Or: 32.5kW (43hp) [44PS]; 76Nm (56.1lbft).
Some countries with 903cm3 (side camshaft): (65 x 68mm), 903cm3; compression ratio 9:1; 33kW (44hp) [45PS] at 5600rpm, 36.6kW/L (49hp/L) [49.9PS/L]; 67Nm (49.4lbft) at 3000rpm; leaded premium grade.
With Catalyst and Bosch Mono–Jetronic central/single point injection: (70 x 64.9mm) 999cm3; compression ratio 9/9.5:1; 33kW (44hp) [45PS] at 5250rpm; 75Nm (55.4lbft) at 3250rpm; unleaded premium grade.

Engine construction: Designated 156 A2.000. Transverse mounted front engine to the rear; 1 overhead camshaft (toothed belt); light-alloy cylinder head; 5 main bearing crankshaft; oil capacity 3.9L (3.7US qt); 1 Weber 32TLF4 downdraught carb. 12V 30/40Ah battery, 45A alternator; cooling system capacity approx 4.6L (4.4US qt).

Transmission (on front wheels): a) 4–speed manual, final drive ratio 3.733, 903cm3, 4.071.
b) 5–speed manual, final drive ratio 3.733.

Gear ratios: a) 4–speed manual: 1st 3.909; 2nd 2.055; 3rd 1.342; 4th 0.964; R 3.615.
b) 5–speed manual: 1st 3.909; 2nd 2.056; 3rd 1.344; 4th 0.978; 5th 0.780; R 3.727.

Chassis: Integral body; front independent suspension with McPherson strut and control arm, rear semi–rigid axle (trailing arms and cross arms); coil spring and telescopic dampers. Brakes, disc dia 22.7cm, rear drum; mechanical handbrake on rear; rack and pinion steering; 42/40L (9.2/8.8Gal) [11.1US Gal] fuel tank; 135SR 13 tyres, also available 155/70SR 13 tyres, 4.5J wheels.

Dimensions: Wheelbase 236cm, track 133/130cm, clearance approx 15cm, turning circle approx 9.8m. Load space 8–34.2cu ft (225/970dm3). Length 364.5cm, width 155cm, height 142.5cm.

Performance: Max speed 87–90mph/140–145kmh (manufacturers spec), speed at 1000rpm in 4th gear 17.2mph/27.7kmh, in 5th gear 21.3mph/34.2kmh; acceleration 0 – 62mph/100km 16.2/17.5secs; standing start km 37.2/37.8secs; power to weight ratio 15.5kg/kW (21.2kg/PS); consumption ECE 4.5/5.9/6.2L/100km (62.8/47.9/45.6mpg) [52.3/39.9/37.9US mpg] 903cm3 5.0/6.6/7.1L/100km (56.5/42.8/39.8mpg) [47.0/35.6/33.1US mpg], 5–speed 4.1/5.4/6.2L/100km (68.9/ 52.3/45.6mpg) [57.4/43.6/37.9US mpg], Catalyst 4.6/6.4/6.7L/100km (61.4/44.1/42.2mpg) [51.1/36.8/35.1US mpg].

Fiat Uno 45

Fiat

1116cm3
42.5kW–57hp–58PS
1 2V Carb

Engine for Uno 60 and Uno Selecta

As 999cm3, except:

Body, Weight: 3–door Saloon/Sedan, 5–seater; kerbweight (DIN) 770-800kg, gross vehicle weight 1160/1200/1250kg; 5–door Saloon/Sedan, 5–seater; kerbweight (DIN) 780-810kg, gross vehicle weight 1170/1200/1260kg.

Engine data (DIN): 4–cylinder in–line (80 x 55.5mm), 1116cm3; compression ratio 9.2:1; 42.5kW (57hp) [58PS] at 5700rpm. 38.1kW/L (51hp/L) [52PS/L]; 87Nm (64.2lbft) at 3000rpm.

Engine construction: Designated 146A4.048. Oil capacity 4.4L (4.2US qt); 1 Weber 30/32 DMTE 10/150 or Solex C 30/32 downdraught twin barrel carb. Cooling system capacity 6/6.2L (5.7/5.9US qt).

Transmission: a) 5–speed manual, final drive ratio 3.867.
b) For "Selecta"; continuous Automatic transmission with metal drive belt; central selector lever, final drive ratio 5.843.

Gear ratios: a) 5–speed manual: 1st 3.909; 2nd 2.056; 3rd 1.344; 4th 0.978; 5th 0.780; R 3.727.
b) Automatic; continous variable between 14.076 and 2.409; R 14.076.

Chassis: Servo/power assisted brakes, disc diameter 22.7cm, Selecta 24cm; tyres 155/70 SR 13.

Performance: Max speed 96mph/155kmh (manufacturers test specifications), speed at 1000rpm in 4th gear 16.2mph/26.1kmh, in 5th gear 20.6mph/33.1kmh; acceleration 0 – 62mph/100kmh 15secs; standing km 36.3secs; power to weight ratio 18.1kg/kW (13.3kg/PS); consumption ECE 4.8/6.1/7.5L/100km (58.8/46.3/37.7mpg) [49/38.6/31.4US mpg]. Selecta: Max speed 92mph/148kmh; acceleration 0 – 62mph/100kmh 15.5secs; consumption ECE 4.8/6.5/7.6L/100km (58.8/43.5/37.2mpg) [49/36.2/30.9US mpg].

Fiat Uno 60

1302/1499cm
3 48/55kW–64/74hp–65/75PS
1 2V Carb/Injection

Engine for Uno 70 and 75 i.e.

As 999cm3, except:

Body, Weight: 3–door Saloon/Sedan, 5–seater; kerbweight (DIN) from 770-830kg, gross vehicle weight 1170/1250kg. 5–door Saloon/Sedan, 5–seater; kerbweight (DIN) from 780/840kg, gross vehicle weight 1180/1250kg.

Engine data (DIN): 4–cylinder in–line (86.4 x 55.5mm), 1302cm3; compression ratio 9.5:1; 48kW (64hp) [65PS] at 5600rpm, 36.9kW/L (49.4hp/L) [49.9PS/L]; 100Nm (73.8lbft) at 3000rpm.
With Catalyst (and Bosch Mono–Jetronic central/single point fuel injection): (86.4 x 63.9mm), 1499cm3; compresssion ratio 9.2:1; 55kW (74hp) [75PS] at 5600rpm, 36.7kW/L (49.2hp/L) [50PS/L]; 113Nm (83.4lbft) at 3000rpm.

Engine construction: Designated 149A 7.000. Oil cooler, oil capacity 4.4L(4.2US qt); 1 Weber DMTE 12/150 downdraught twin barrel carb. 12V 40/45Ah Battery; cooling system capacity 6.2L (5.9US qt).

Transmission: 5–speed manaul, final drive ratio 3.733 or 3.867; Catalyst 3.353.

Gear ratios: 1st 3.909; 2nd 2.056; 3rd 1.344; 4th 0.978; 5th 0.780; R 3.727.
With Catalyst: 1st 3.909; 2nd 2.267; 3rd 1.44; 4th 1.029; 5th 0.824; R 3.714.

Chassis: Servo/power assisted brakes; tyres 145 SR 13, 155/70 SR 13 or 165/65 SR 13, wheel rims 4.5 J.

Performance: Max speed 103mph/165kmh, Catalyst 106mph/170kmh (manufacturers test specifications), speed at 1000rpm in 4th/5th gear 17.0-21.4mph/27.4-34.4kmh; acceleration 0 – 62mph/100kmh 11.5secs, Catalyst 12secs; standing km 33.8secs; power to weight ratio 16.1kg/kW (11.9kg/PS); consumption ECE 4.9/6.4/7.7 (57.6/44.1/36.7mpg) [48/36.8/30.5US mpg], Catalyst 5.5/7.0/8.4L/100km (51.4/40.4/33.6mpg) [42.8/33.6/28US mpg].

Fiat Uno D

1302cm3 Diesel
33kW–44hp–45PS
Injection Pump

Engine for Uno D/DS

As 999cm3, except:

Body, Weight: 3–door Saloon/Sedan, 5–seater; kerbweight (DIN) 800kg, gross vehicle weight 1200kg. 5–door Saloon/Sedan, 5–seater; kerbweight (DIN) 810kg, gross vehicle weight 1210kg.

Engine data (DIN): 4–cylinder in–line (76.1 x 71.5mm), 1302cm3; compression ratio 20:1; 33kW (44hp) [45PS] at 5000rpm, 25.4kW/L (34hp/L) [34.6PS/L]; 75Nm (55.4lbft) at 3000rpm.

Engine construction: Designated 127 A5.000. Pre–chamber diesel; oil cooler; oil capacity 4.4L (4.2US qt); Bosch diesel injection pump. 12V 55Ah Battery, 55A alternator; cooling system capacity 8L (7.6US qt).

Transmission: 5–speed manual, final drive ratio 4.071.

Gear ratios: 1st 3.909; 2nd 2.055; 3rd 1.342; 4th 0.964; 5th 0.831; R 3.615.

Chassis: Servo/power assisted brakes; tyres 155/70 SR 13, wheel rims 4.5J.

Performance: Max speed 87mph/140kmh (manufacturers test specifications), speed at 1000rpm in 5th gear 18.4mph/29.6kmh; acceleration 0 – 62mph/100kmh 20.6secs, standing km 39.5secs; power to weight ratio from 24.2kg/kW (17.8kg/PS); consumption ECE 4.7/6.5/6.3L/100km (60.1/43.5/44.8mpg) [50/36.2/37.3US mpg].

1367cm3 Diesel
51.5kW–69hp–70PS
Turbo/Injection Pump

Engine for Uno Turbo D

As 999cm3, except:

Body, Weight: 3–door Saloon/Sedan, 5–seater; kerbweight (DIN) 870kg, gross vehicle weight 1270/1320kg. 5–door Saloon/Sedan, 5–seater; kerbweight (DIN) 880kg, gross vehicle weight 1280/1320kg.

Engine data (DIN): 4–cylinder in–line (78 x 71.5mm), 1367cm3; compression ratio 20:1; 51.5kW (69hp) [70PS] at 4800rpm, 37.7kW/L (50.5hp/L) [51.2PS/L]; 115Nm (85.1lbft) at 3000rpm.

Engine construction: Pre–chamber diesel; oil cooler; oil capacity 4.4/5L (4.2/4.3US qt); Bosch diesel injection; 1 Garrett T2 exhaust turbocharger, max boost pressure 0.7bar; charge–air cooler. 12V 55Ah Battery, 55A alternator; cooling system capacity 8/8.9L (7.6/8.4US qt).

Transmission: 5–speed manual, final drive ratio 3.588 (17/61).

Gear ratios: 1st 4.091; 2nd 2.235; 3rd 1.469; 4th 1.043; 5th 0.827; R 3.714.

Chassis: Front antiroll bar; Servo/power assisted brakes, front ventilated discs, disc diameter 24cm; tyres 155/70 SR 13, wheel rims 4.5J.

Dimensions: Track 134/131cm, width 156cm, height 142cm.

TIPO. CAR OF THE YEAR 1989.

Fiat

Performance: Max speed 103mph/165kmh (manufacturers test specifications), speed at 1000rpm in 5th gear 20.9mph/33.7kmh; acceleration 0 – 62mph/100kmh 12.4/13secs, standing km 34secs; power to weight ratio from 15.9kg/kW (11.7kg/PS); consumption ECE 4.0/5.8/5.6L/100km (70.6/48.7/50.4mpg) [58.8/40.6/42US mpg].

Fiat Uno Turbo D

```
1698cm3 Diesel
44/42kW - 59/56hp - 60/57PS
Injection Pump
```

Export engine for Uno D/DS

As 999cm3, except:

Body, Weight: 3–door Saloon/Sedan, 5–seater; kerbweight (DIN) 860kg, gross vehicle weight 1260/1320kg. 5–door Saloon/Sedan, 5–seater; kerbweight (DIN) 870kg, gross vehicle weight 1270/1320kg.

Engine data (DIN): 4–cylinder in–line (82.6 x 79.2mm), 1698cm3; compression ratio 20:1; 44kW (59hp) [60PS] at 4500rpm, 26.0kW/L (34.8hp/l) [35.3PS/L]; 103Nm (76lbft) at 3000rpm.
Or: 42kW (56hp) [57PS] at 4600rpm; 98Nm (72.3lbft) at 2900rpm.

Engine construction: Designated 149 B3.000. Pre–chamber diesel; oil cooler; oil capacity 4.4/4.9L (4.2/4.6US qt); Bosch diesel injection pump. 12V 55Ah Battery, 45/55A alternator; cooling system capacity 8.9L (8.4US qt).

Transmission: 5–speed manual, final drive ratio 3.588.

Gear ratios: 1st 4.090; 2nd 2.235; 3rd 1.469; 4th 1.034; 5th 0.827; R 3.714.

Chassis: Front antiroll bar; Servo/power assisted brakes, disc diameters 24.0cm; tyres 155/70 SR 13, wheel rims 4.5J.

Dimensions: Track 134/131cm. Width 156cm, height 142cm.

Performance: Max speed 96.3mph/155kmh (manufacturers test specifications), speed at 1000rpm in 5th gear 20.9mph/33.7kmh; acceleration 0 – 62mph/100kmh 15secs, standing km 36secs; power to weight ratio from 19.5kg/kW (14.3kg/PS); consumption ECE 4.0/5.7/5.4L/100km (70.6/49.6/52.3mpg) [58.8/41.3/43.6US mpg].

Fiat Uno Turbo i.e.

Sports version of the Fiat Uno with turbocharger and electronic fuel injection. Launched in April 1985. November 1987: available with ABS "Antiskid"

Fiat Uno Turbo i.e.

```
1301cm3
77/73.5kW–103/99hp–105/100PS
Turbo/Fuel Injection
```

As Uno 999cm3, except:

Body, Weight: 3–door Saloon/Sedan, 5–seater; kerbweight (DIN) 845–905kg, gross vehicle weight 1245–1280kg.

Engine data (DIN): 4–cylinder in–line (80.5 x 63.9mm), 1301cm3; compression ratio 8:1; 77kW (103hp) [105PS] at 5750rpm, 59.1kW/L (79.2hp/l) [80.6PS/L]; 147Nm (108.5bft) at 3200rpm.
With Catalyst: Compression ratio 7.7:1; 73.5kW (99hp) [100PS] at 6000rpm, 56.5kW/L (76hp/L) [76.8PS/L]; 142Nm (105.1lbft) at 3500rpm.

Engine construction: Designated 146 A2.000/246. Oil capacity 4L (3.8US qt); Bosch LE2–Jetronic electronic fuel injection, Catalyst LU–Jetronic; 1 IHI VL–2 exhaust turbocharger, max boost pressure 0.6bar, charge–air cooler. 12V 45Ah Battery, 65A alternator; cooling system capacity 6.5/6.9L (6.1/6.5US qt).

Transmission: 5–speed manual, final drive ratio 3.588 (17/61), Catalyst 3.562.

Gear ratios: 1st 4.091; 2nd 2.235; 3rd 1.469; 4th 1.034/1.043; 5th 0.827 (0.863); R 3.714.
Catalyst: 1st 3.909; 2nd 2.264; 3rd 1.44; 4th 1.029; 5th 0.875; R 3.909.

Chassis: Front antiroll bar; Servo/power assisted four wheel disc brakes (front ventilated), disc diameters front 24cm, rear 22.7cm; ABS "Antiskid"; fuel tank capacity 50/46L (11/10.1Gal) [13.2/15.9US Gal]; tyres 175/60HR 13, wheel rims 5.5J.

Dimensions: Track 134.5/131cm. Width 156cm, height 137cm.

Performance: Max speed approx 137mph/200kmh, Catalyst 118mph/190kmh (manufacturers test specifications), speed at 1000rpm in 5th gear 20mph/32.2kmh; acceleration 0 – 62mph/100kmh 8.3secs, Catalyst 8.5secs; standing km 29.8secs; power to weight ratio 11.0kg/kW (8.0kg/PS); consumption ECE 5.8/7.6/8.9L/100km (48.7/37.2/31.7mpg) [40.6/30.9/26.4US mpg], Catalyst 5.6/7.8/9/2L/100km (50.4/36.2/30.7mpg) [42/30.2/25.8US mpg].

Fiat Duna

Four–door Saloon/Sedan and five–door Estate/Station Wagon, 1.1 or 1.3 Litre or 1.7 Litre diesel. Technically compatible with the Brasilian Fiat Premio. Launched in January 1987.

Fiat Duna 60

```
1116cm3
42.5kW–57hp–58PS
1 2V Carb
```

Engine for 60

Body, Weight: 4–door Saloon/Sedan, 5–seater; kerbweight (DIN) 875, gross vehicle weight 1275kg. 5–door Estate/Station Wagon, 5–seater; kerbweight (DIN) 890kg, gross vehicle weight 1350kg.

Engine data (ECE): 4–cylinder in–line (76 x 61.5mm), 1116cm3; compression ratio 9.35:1; 42.5kW (57hp) [58PS] at 5500rpm, 38.2kW/L (51.2hp/L) [52PS/L]; 85Nm (63lbft) at 2750rpm; leaded premium grade.

Engine construction: Designated 146 A6.000. Transverse front engine. 1 overhead camshaft (toothed belt); light–alloy cylinder head; 5 bearing crankshaft; oil capacity 3.7L (3.5US qt); 1 Weber 30/32 DMTE28/150 downdraught twin barrel carb. 12V 34Ah Battery, 45A alternator; cooling system capacity 4.8L (4.5US qt).

Transmission (to front wheels): 5–speed manual, final drive ratio 3.765 (17/64).

Gear ratios: 1st 4.091; 2nd 2.235; 3rd 1.469; 4th 1.043; 5th 0.863; R 3.714.

Chassis: Integral body; front independent suspension with McPherson struts, lower single control arm and compression struts/antiroll bar, rear independent suspension with A arm, shock absorber strut and self-stabilising transverse leaf spring, telescopic dampers. Servo/power assisted brakes, front discs, rear drums, disc diameter 24cm, mechanical handbrake to rear wheels; rack and pinion steering; fuel tank capacity 54L (11.9Gal) [14.3US Gal], with 8L (1.8Gal) [2.1US Gal]; reserve; tyres 165/70 SR 13, wheel rims 4.5J.

Dimensions: Wheelbase 236cm, track 131.5/132.5cm, clearance approx 14cm, turning circle approx 9.8m. Load space 17.8cu ft (505dm3). Length 403.5cm, width 155.5cm, height 143cm. Weekend: Track 131.5/131.5cm, load space 17.3–50.5cu ft (490–1430dm3), height 145cm.

Performance: Max speed 93mph/150kmh (manufacturers test specifications), speed at 1000rpm in 5th gear 19.4mph/31.2kmh; acceleration 0 – 62mph/100kmh 16.0secs; standing km 37.5secs; power to weight ratio from 20.5kg/kW (15.1kg/PS); consumption ECE 5.1/7.5/8.1L/100km (55.4/37.7/34.9mpg) [47/31.4/29US mpg].

```
1301cm3
49.5kW–66hp–67PS
1 2V Carb
```

Engine for 70

As 1116cm3, except:

Engine data (ECE): 4–cylinder in–line (76.1 x 71.5mm), 1301cm3; compression ratio 9.3:1; 49.5kW (66hp) [67PS] at 5500rpm, 37.9kW/L (50.7hp/L) [51.5PS/L]; 101Nm (75lbft) at 2500rpm.

Engine construction: Designated 146 A5.000. 1 Weber DMTE27/150 downdraught twin barrel carb. Cooling system capacity 5L (4.7US qt).

Transmission: 5–speed manual, final drive ratio 3.765 (17/64).

Gear ratios: 1st 4.091; 2nd 2.235; 3rd 1.469; 4th 0.959; 5th 0.811; R 3.714.

Chassis: Tyres 165/70 SR 13.

Performance: Max speed 96mph/155kmh (manufacturers test specifications), speed at 1000rpm in 5th gear 21mph/33.8kmh, acceleration 0 – 62mph/100kmh 13.2secs; standing km 35.2secs; power to weight ratio 17.8kg/kW (13.1kg/PS); consumption ECE 5.2/7.1/8.3L/100km (54.3/39.8/34mpg) [45.2/33.1/28.3US mpg].

Fiat Duna Weekend DS

```
1698cm3 Diesel
44kW–59hp–60PS
Injection Pump
```

Engine for DS

As 1116cm3, except:

Body, Weight: 4–door Saloon/Sedan, 5–seater; kerbweight (DIN) 935kg, gross vehicle weight 1335kg. 5–door Estate/Station Wagon, 5–seater; kerbweight (DIN) 950kg, gross vehicle weight 1410kg.

Engine data (ECE): 4–cylinder in–line (82.6 x 79.2mm), 1697cm3; compression ratio 20.5:1; 44kW (59hp) [60PS] at 4500rpm, 26.0kW/L (34.8hp/L) [35.3PS/L]; 103Nm (76lbft) at 3000rpm.

Engine construction: Designated 149B3.000. pre–chamber diesel engine. Oil capacity 5.7L (5.4US qt); Bosch VER 256 diesel injection pump. 12V 66Ah Battery, 55A alternator; cooling system capacity 5L (4.7US qt).

Transmission: 5–speed manual, final drive ratio 3.765.

Gear ratios: 1st 4.091; 2nd 2.235; 3rd 1.469; 4th 0.959; 5th 0.811; R 3.714.

Performance: Max speed 93mph/150kmh (manufacturers test specifications), speed at 1000rpm in 5th gear 21mph/33.8kmh; acceleration 0 – 62mph/100kmh 18.0secs, standing km 38.0secs; power to weight ratio 21.2kg/kW (15.6kg/PS); consumption ECE 4.5/6.8/6.5L/100km (62.8/41.5/43.5mpg) [52.3/34.6/36.2US mpg].

Fiat Tipo

New five–door Saloon/Sedan with front wheel drive and transverse engine (1100 to 1900cm3 displacement) also Diesel and Turbo diesel. Successor of the Ritmo. Launched in January 1988.

```
1108cm3
41kW–55hp–56PS
1 Carb
```

Body, Weight: 5–door Saloon/Sedan, 5–seater; kerbweight (DIN) 905/925kg, gross vehicle weight 1450kg.

Engine data (DIN): 4–cylinder in–line (70 x 72mm), 1108cm3; compression ratio 9.6:1; 41kW (55hp) [56PS] at 5500rpm, 37kW/L (49.6hp/L) [50.6PS/L]; 89Nm (66.1lbft) at 2900rpm; leaded premium grade.

Engine construction: Designated 160A3000. Transverse engine; 1 overhead camshaft (toothed belt); light–alloy cylinder head; 5 bearing crankshaft; oil capacity 3.75L (3.6US qt); 1 Weber 32 TLF 12/250 downdraught carb. 12V 32Ah Battery, 55A alternator; cooling system capacity 4.5L (4.3US qt).

Transmission (to front wheels): 5–speed manual, final drive ratio 3.765.

Gear ratios: 1st 3.909; 2nd 2.267; 3rd 1.44; 4th 1.029; 5th 0.875; R 3.909.

Chassis: Integral body with front and rear sub–frame; front independent suspension with McPherson struts and lower A arm, rear independent suspension with trailing arm, front and rear antiroll bar, coil springs and telescopic dampers. Servo/power assisted brakes, front discs, rear drums, disc diameter 24cm, mechanical handbrake to rear wheels; rack and pinion steering; fuel tank capacity 55/53L (12.1/11.6Gal) [14.5/17.4US Gal], with 5–8L (1.1–1.8Gal) [1.3–2.1US Gal] reserve; tyres 165/70 SR 13 or 165/65 SR 14, wheel rims 5".

Dimensions: Wheelbase 254cm, track 143/141.5cm, clearance approx 15cm, turning circle approx 10.7m, load space 12.3/25/38.8cu ft (350/710/1100dm3). Length 396cm, width 170cm, height 144.5cm.

Performance: Max speed 93mph/150kmh (manufacturers test specifications), speed at 1000rpm in 4th gear 16.6mph/26.7kmh, in 5th gear 19.5mph/31.4kmh; acceleration 0 – 62mph/100kmh 17.2secs, standing km 37.2secs; power to weight ratio from 22.1kg/kW (16.2kg/PS); consumption ECE 4.7/6.5/7.5L/100km (60.1/43.5/37.7mpg) [50/36.2/31.4US Gal].

Fiat Tipo

```
1372cm3
53/51kW - 71/69hp - 72/70PS
1 2V Carb
```

As 1108cm3, except:

Weight: Kerbweight (DIN) 945-1000kg, gross vehicle weight 1490kg.

Engine data (DIN): 4–cylinder in–line (80.5 x 67.4mm), 1372cm3; compression ratio 9.2:1; 53kW (71hp) [72PS] at 6000rpm, 38.6kW/L (51.7hp/L) [52.5PS/L]; 108Nm (80lbft) at 2900rpm.

Fiat

Or: 51kW (69hp) [70PS] and 50kW (67hp) [68PS]
With Catalyst and Bosch Mono-Jetronic central/single point injection: 51kW (69hp) [70PS] at 6000rpm, 37.2kW/L (49.8hp/L) [51PS/L]; 106Nm (78.2lbft) at 3000rpm.

Engine construction: Designated 160A1000. Oil capacity 4.25L (4.1US qt); 1 Weber 32/34TLDE 4/150 downdraught twin barrel carb. 12V 40/45Ah Battery; cooling system capacity 6.5L (6.1US qt).

Transmission: 5-speed manual, final drive ratio 3.765.

Gear ratios: 1st 3.909; 2nd 2.267; 3rd 1.44/1.469; 4th 1.029/1.043; 5th 0.827; R 3.909.

Chassis: Optional power assisted steering.

Performance: Max speed 100mph/161kmh (Manufacturers test specifications), speed at 1000rpm in 4th gear 16.4mph/26.4kmh, in 5th gear 20.6mph/33.2kmh; acceleration 0 – 62mph/100kmh 13secs; standing km 34.7secs; power to weight ratio from 19.4kg/kW (14.1kg/PS); consumption ECE 5.2/7.1/8.5L/100km (54.3/39.8/33.2mpg) [45.2/33.1/27.7US mpg].

Fiat Tipo

```
1580/1585cm3
61/66kW–82/88hp–83/90PS
1 2V Carb/Injection
```

As 1108cm3, except:

Weight: Kerbweight (DIN) 970-1050kg, gross vehicle weight 1500kg.

Engine data (DIN): 4-cylinder in-line (86.4 x 67.4mm), 1580cm3; compression ratio 9.2:1; 61kW (82hp) [83PS] at 6000rpm, 38.6kW/L (51.7hp/L) [52.5PS/L]; 132Nm (97.4lbft) at 4000rpm.
With Catalyst: DOHC engine with GM-Delco central/single point injection: (84 x 71.5mm), 1585cm3; compression ratio 9.5:1; 66kW (88hp) [90PS] at 6250rpm, 41.6kW/L (55.7hp/L) [56.8PS/L]; 123Nm (91.1lbft) at 4250rpm.

Engine construction: Designated 160A2000, injection 138 AR 000. Oil capacity 4.25/5.3L (4.1/5.0US qt). 1 Weber 32/34 TLDE 5/150 2V barrel carb. GM-Delco central/single point fuel injection. 12V 45Ah Battery; cooling system capacity 6.5/7.5L (6.1–7.1US qt).

Transmission: 5-speed manual, final drive ratio 3.563 or 3.765.

Gear ratios: 1st 3.909; 2nd 2.267; 3rd 1.44; 4th 1.029; 5th 0.827; R 3.909.

Chassis: Optional Servo/power assisted steering.

Performance: Max speed 107mph/172kmh (manufacturers test specifications), speed at 1000rpm in 4th gear 17.5mph/28.2kmh, in 5th 21.8mph/35.1kmh; acceleration 0 – 62mph/100kmh 12secs; standing km 33.9secs; power to weight ratio 15.9kg/kW (11.7kg/PS); consumption ECE 5.0/6.9/8.9L/100km (56.5/40.9/31.7mpg) [47/34.1/26.4US mpg] or 5.3/7.4/9.3L/100km (53.3/38.2/30.4mpg) [44.4/31.8/25.3US mpg].
With Catalyst: Max speed 178kmh; acceleration 0 – 62mph/100kmh approx 12s.

```
1697cm3 Diesel
43kW–57hp–58PS
Injection Pump
```

Engine for ds

As 1108cm3, except:

Weight: Kerbweight (DIN) 1030/1040kg, gross vehicle weight 1550kg.

Engine data (DIN): 4-cylinder in-line (82.6 x 79.2mm), 1697cm3; compression ratio 20.0:1; 43kW (57hp) [58PS] at 4600rpm, 25.3kW (33.9hp/L) [34.2PS/L]; 100Nm (74lbft) at 2900rpm.

Engine construction: Designated 149B4000. Pre-chamber Diesel engine. Oil capacity 5.6L (5.3US qt); Bosch VER 308 diesel injection pump. 12V 60/65Ah Battery; cooling system capacity 8L (7.6US qt).

Transmission: 5-speed manual, final drive ratio 3.765.

Gear ratios: 1st 3.909; 2nd 2.267; 3rd 1.44; 4th 1.029; 5th 0.827; R 3.909.

Chassis: Optional servo/power assisted steering.

Performance: Max speed 93mph/150kmh (manufacturers test specifications), speed at 1000rpm in 4th gear 16.6mph/26.7kmh, in 5th gear 20.6mph/33.2kmh, acceleration 0 – 62mph/100kmh 17.8secs, standing km 38.0secs; power to weight ratio 24.0kg/kW (17.8kg/PS); consumption ECE 4.9/6.7/6.7L/100km (57.6/42.2/42.2mpg) [48/35.3/35.1US Gal].

Fiat Tipo

```
1929cm3 Diesel
68kW–91hp–92PS
Injection Pump/Turbo
```

Engine for turbo ds

As 1108cm3, except:

Weight: Kerbweight (DIN) 1110kg, gross vehicle weight 1620/1660kg.

Engine data (DIN): 4-cylinder in-line (82.6 x 90mm), 1929cm3; compression ratio 19.2:1; 68kW (91hp) [92PS] at 4100rpm, 35.2kW/L (47.2hp/L) [47.7PS/L]; 191Nm (141.1lbft) at 2400rpm.

Engine construction: Designated 160A6000. Diesel engine swirl chamber. Oil capacity 6L (5.7US qt); Oil cooler; 1 KKK K16 exhaust turbocharger, max boost pressure 0.8bar; charge-air cooler; Bosch VE 4/9F diesel injection pump. 12V 65Ah Battery, 65A alternator; cooling system capacity 8.8L (8.3US qt).

Transmission: 5-speed manual, final drive ratio 3.052.

Gear ratios: 1st 3.545; 2nd 2.267; 3rd 1.523; 4th 1.142; 5th 0.794; R 3.909.

Chassis: Disc brakes, diameter 25.7cm, optional four wheel disc brakes with ABS (System Bosch); power assisted steering; tyres 175/65 TR 14, wheel rims 5.5J.

Performance: Max speed 109mph/175kmh (manufacturers test specifications), speed at 1000rpm in 4th gear 18.5mph/29.7kmh, in 5th 26.1mph/42.7kmh; acceleration 0 – 62mph/100kmh 12.0secs; standing km 34.0secs; power to weight ratio 16.3kg/kW (12.1kg/PS); consumption ECE 4.9/6.6/6.2L/100km (57.6/42.8/45.6mpg) [48/35.6/37.9US mpg].

Fiat Tipo 16V

Fiat Tipo 16V

New model. High performance version of the Tipo. Sixteen valve engine, for the Italian market, with 1750cm3 engine displacement and 148hp at 6000rpm; kerbweight 1110kg; graduated five speed transmission and all round disc brakes; max speed above 210kmh, acceleration 0-100kmh in less than 8 secs. Preview presentation in Spring 1989.

Fiat Regata

70 – 75/85 – 100/90 – D – DS – Turbo DS

Mid–class vehicle with transverse engine and front wheel drive. Technically derived from the Ritma. Saloon/Sedan launched in September 1983, Estate/Station Wagon Weekend in Turin in 1984. June 1986: new engine series and modifications to body and interior.

```
1.3 Litre
48kW–64hp–65PS
1 2V Carb
```

Engine for 70, 70S and 70C.A.

Body, Weight: 4–door Saloon/Sedan, 5–seater; kerbweight (DIN) 890, automatic 920kg, gross vehicle weight 1290/1400kg. 5–door Estate/Station Wagon, 5–seater; kerbweight (DIN) 930kg, gross vehicle weight 1430kg.

Engine data (ECE): 4–cylinder in–line (86.4 x 55.5mm), 1302cm3; compression ratio 9.5:1; 48kW (64hp) [65PS] at 5600rpm, 36.7kW/L (49.2kW/L) [49.9PS/L]: 100Nm (73.8lbft) at 3000rpm; leaded premium grade.
Engine for automatic: (86.4 x 55.4mm), 1299cm3; compression ratio 9.4:1.

Engine construction: Designated 149A 3.000. Transverse front engine front inclined. 1 overhead camshaft (toothed belt); light– alloy cylinder head; 5 bearing crankshaft; oil capacity 4.4L (4.2US qt); 1 Weber 30/32 DMTR 80/250 or Solex C30/32 CIC–1, ES; Weber 30/32 DMTE 1/250 downdraught twin barrel carb. 12V 40Ah Battery, 55A alternator; cooling system capacity 6.9L (6.5US qt).

Transmission (to front wheels): a) 5–speed manual, final drive ratio 3.765 (17/64). b) Automatic, hydraulic torque converter and 3–speed Planetary gear set, central selector lever with positions P–R–N–D–2–1, final drive ratio 3.409 (22/75).

Gear ratios: a) 5–speed manual: 1st 4.091; 2nd 2.235; 3rd 1.469; 4th 1.043; 5th 0.827; R 3.714.
b) Automatic; Max torque multiplication in converter 2.5 times, Planetary gear set ratios: 1st 2.714; 2nd 1.5; 3rd 1; R 2.43.

Chassis: Integral body; front independent suspension with McPherson struts, lower single control arm and semi trailing arm and antiroll bar, rear independent suspension with A arm, shock absorber struts and self stabilising transverse leaf springs, telescopic dampers. Servo/power assisted brakes, front discs, rear drums, disc diameter 22.7, Weekend 25.7cm, mechanical handbrake to rear wheels; rack and pinion steering; fuel tank capacity 55L (12.1Gal) [14.5US Gal], with 5–8L (1.1–1.8Gal) [1.3–2.1] reserve; tyres 155 SR 13, 165/70 SR 13 or 165/65 SR 14, wheel rims 4.5J or 5.5J.

Fiat Regata

Dimensions: Wheelbase 245.5cm, track 138.5/139cm, clearance 14.5cm, turning circle 10.3/11.0, automatic 10.7/11.2m. Load space 18.2cu ft (515dm3). Length 426cm, width 165cm, height 142cm. Weekend: track 140/138cm, clearance approx 15cm, turning circle 10.3m. Load space 16.2–49.4cu ft (460–1400dm3). Length 426.5cm, width 165cm, height 145/146cm.

Performance: Max speed above 96mph/155kmh, automatic 93mph/150kmh (manufacturers test specifications), speed at 1000rpm in 4th gear 16.7mph/26.8kmh, in 5th gear 21mph/33.8kmh; acceleration 0 – 62mph/100kmh 13.5secs, automatic 16.5secs; standing km 35secs, automatic 38secs; power to weight ratio from 18.6kg/kW (13.7kg/PS); consumption ECE 5.3/7.0/8.5L/100km (53.3/40.4/33.2mpg) [44.4/33.6/27.7US mpg], Automatic 6.5/8.5/9.0L/100km (43.5/33.2/31.4mpg) [36.2/27.7/26.1US mpg].

```
1.5/1.6 Litre
55/60.5kW–73/81hp–75/82PS
1 Carb/Central–Single Point Injection
```

Engine for 75/75i.e. and 85

As 1.3 Litre, except:

Weight: Kerbweight (DIN) 905/955kg, Weekend 945/975kg, gross vehicle weight 1300 to 1580kg.

Engine data (DIN): (86.4 x 63.9mm) 1499cm3; compression ratio 9:1; 55–60.5kW (73–81hp) [75–82PS] at 5700rpm, 36.7–40.4kW/L (49.2–54.1hp/L) [50–54.8PS/L]; 117Nm (86.3lbft) at 3000rpm.
Some countries: 1.6 Litre engine with 60.5kW (81hp) [82PS]; 124Nm (91.5lbft). With Catalyst (1499cm3, Bosch Mono–Jetronic fuel injection); compression ratio 9.2:1; 55kW (73hp) [75PS] at 5600rpm, 113Nm (83.4lbft) at 3000rpm; unleaded premium grade.

Engine construction: Designated 138 B 3.0482. 1 Weber 30/32 DMTR downdraught twin barrel carb. 12V 40/45Ah Battery; cooling system capacity 7L (6.6US qt).

Transmission: a) 5–speed manual, final drive ratio 3.765 or 3.588/3.571/3.368. b) Automatic, hydraulic torque converter and 3–speed Planetary gear set, central selector lever with Positions P–R–N–D–2–1, final drive ratio 3.565, 3.409 or 2.695.

Gear ratios: a) 5–speed manual: 1st 4.09; 2nd 2.235; 3rd 1.461; 4th 1.034; 5th 0.827; R 3.714. Or 1st 3.909; 2nd 2.267; 3rd 1.44; 4th 1.029; 5th 0.825; R 3.909.
b) Automatic; Max torque multiplication in converter 2.5 times, Planetary gear set ratios: 1st 2.55; 2nd 1.45; 3rd 1; R 2.46.

Chassis: Automatic; antiroll bar at front. Tyres 155 SR 13, 165/70 AR 13 or 165/65 SR 14, wheel rims 4.5 or 5.5J.

Dimensions: Track 140/139, Weekend 140/138cm.

Performance: Max speed 99–106mph/160–170kmh, automatic 96–99mph/155–160kmh, speed at 1000rpm in 5th gear 20.6mph/33.1kmh; acceleration 0 – 62mph/100kmh 12.4–12.0secs, Automatic 14.5–15.0secs; standing km 33.5secs, automatic 36secs; power to weight ratio from 16.5kg/kW (12.1kg/PS); consumption ECE 5.4/7.4/9.2L/100km (52.3/38.2/30.7mpg) [43.6/31.8/25.6US mpg] or 5.4/7.2/9.4L/100km (52.3/39.2/30.1mpg) [43.6/32.7/25US mpg], automatic 7.6/9.8/10.7L/100km (37.2/28.8/26.4mpg) [30.9/24.0/22.0US mpg] or 6.6/8.9/9.2L/100km (42.8/31.7/30.7mpg) [35.6/26.4/25.6US mpg]. With Catalyst: Max speed 99mph/160kmh; acceleration 0 – 62mph/100kmh ; 12/15secs; consumption ECE 5.6/7.7/9.3L/100km (50.4/36.7/30.4mpg) [42.0/30.5/25.3US mpg], automatic 6.8/9.8/9.7L/100km (41.5/28.8/29.1mpg) [34.6/24.0/24.2US mpg].

```
1.6 Litre
73.5/66kW–99/88hp–100/90PS
Central/Single Point Injection
```

Engine for 100/90 S i.e.

As 1.3 Litre, except:

Weight: Kerbweight (DIN) 970/995, Weekend 1010/1045kg, gross vehicle weight 1370/1400, Weekend 1510/1580kg.

Engine data (ECE): 4–cylinder in–line (84 x 71.5mm), 1585cm3; compression ratio 9.7:1; 73.5kW (99hp) [100PS] at 6000rpm, 46.4kW/L (62.2hp/L) [63.1PS/L]; 128Nm (94.5lbft) at 4000rpm.
With Catalyst and central/single point injection: compression ratio 9.5:1; 66kW (88hp) [90PS] at 6250rpm; 41.6kW/L (56hp/L) [56.8PS/L]; 123Nm (91.1lbft) at 4250rpm; unleaded premium grade.

Engine construction: Designated 149A 2.000, with Catalyst 149 C2.000. Valves in V (65deg), 2 overhead camshafts (toothed belt); oil capacity 5.3L (5US qt); SPI electronic central/single point injection. 55/65A Alternator; cooling system capacity 7.5L (7.1US qt).

Transmission: 5–speed manual, final drive ratio 3.21 (19/61) or 3.33.

Gear ratios: 1st 4.091; 2nd 2.235; 3rd 1.533; 4th 1.163; 5th 0.960; R 3.92. Or 1st 3.909; 2nd 2.267; 3rd 1.524; 4th 1.143; 5th 0.968; R 3.909.

Chassis: Front antiroll bar. Disc diameter 25.7cm; optional power assisted steering; tyres 165/65 SR/TR 14, wheel rims 5.5J.

Fiat

Fiat Regata 100/90 i.e. Weekend

Dimensions: Track 140.5/139, Weekend 140.5/138cm.

Performance: Max speed 112mph/180kmh (manufacturers test specifications), speed at 1000rpm in 5th gear 20.9mph/33.7kmh; acceleration 0 – 62mph/100kmh 10secs; standing km 32secs; power to weight ratio from 13.2kg/kW (9.7kg/PS); consumption ECE 5.3/6.8/9.8L/100km (53.3/41.5/28.8mpg) [44.4/34.6/24.0US mpg]. With Catalyst: Max speed 109–112mph/175–180kmh; acceleration 0 – 62mph/100kmh 11–12secs; consumption ECE 6.0/7.7/10.0L/100km (47.1/36.7/28.2mpg) [39.2/30.5/23.5US mpg].

```
1.7 Litre Diesel
44kW–59hp–60PS
Injection Pump
```

Engine for D

As 1.3 Litre, except:

Weight: Kerbweight (DIN) 980, Weekend 1020kg, gross vehicle weight 1380/1400, Weekend 1520/1580kg.

Engine data (ECE): 4–cylinder in–line (82.6 x 79.2mm), 1697cm3; compression ratio 20.0:1; 44kW (59hp) [60PS] at 4500rpm, 26.0kW/L (35hp/L) [35.3PS/L]; 103Nm (76lbft) at 3000rpm.

Engine construction: Designated 149B3.000. Front chamber diesel engine. Oil capacity 5.5L (5.2US qt); Bosch VER 207 diesel injection pump. 12V 66Ah Battery; cooling system capacity 7.5L (7.1US qt).

Transmission: 5–speed manual, final drive ratio 3.765 (17/64).

Gear ratios: 1st 4.091; 2nd 2.235; 3rd 1.469; 4th 1.043; 5th 0.863; R 3.714.

Chassis: Front antiroll bar; tyres 155 SR 13 or 165/65 SR/TR 14, wheel rims 4.5 or 5.5J.

Dimensions: Track 139/139, Weekend 140/138cm.

Performance: Max speed 93mph/150kmh (manufacturers test specifcations), speed at 1000rpm in 5th gear 20.1mph/32.4kmh; acceleration 0 – 62mph/100kmh 18.9secs; standing km 38secs; power to weight ratio from 22.2kg/kW (16.3kg/PS); consumption ECE 5.2/7.1/6.7L/100km (54.3/39.8/42.2mpg) [45.2/33.1/35.1US mpg].

```
1.9 Litre Diesel
48kW–64hp–65PS
Injection Pump
```

Engine for DS

As 1.3 Litre, except:

Weight: Kerbweight (DIN) 1000, Weekend 1040/1050kg, gross vehicle weight 1400/1430, Weekend 1540/1580kg.

Engine data (ECE): 4–cylinder in–line (82.6 x 90mm), 1929cm3; compression ratio 21:1; 48kW (64hp) [65PS] at 4600rpm, 24.8kW/L (33.2hp/L) (33.2hp/L) [33.7PS/L]; 119Nm (87.8lbft) at 2000rpm.

Engine construction: Designated 149 A1.000. Diesel engine swirl chamber. Oil capacity 5.5L (5.2US qt); Bosch VER 141 Diesel injection pump. 12V 66Ah Battery, 55/66A alternator; cooling system capacity 7.5L (7.1US qt).

Transmission: 5–speed manual, final drive ratio 3.588 (17/61).

Gear ratios: 1st 4.091; 2nd 2.235; 3rd 1.469; 4th 1.043; 5th 0.827; R 3.714/3.917.

Chassis: Front antiroll bar; disc diameter 25.7cm; optional power assisted steering; tyres 165/65 SR/TR/HR 14, wheel rims 5.5J.

Dimensions: Track 140/139cm, Weekend 140.5/138cm.

Performance: Max speed above 96mph/155kmh (manufacturers test specifications), speed at 1000rpm in 5th gear 21.8mph/35kmh; acceleration 0 – 62mph/100kmh 16secs; standing km 37secs; power to weight ratio from 20.9kg/kW (15.4kg/PS); consumption ECE 4.5/6.5/7.1L/100km (62.8/43.5/39.8mpg) [52.3/36.2/33.1US mpg].

```
1.9 Litre Diesel
59kW–79hp–80PS
Turbo/Injection Pump
```

Engine for Turbo DS

As 1.3 Litre, except:

Weight: Kerbweight (DIN) 1050, Weekend 1090/1100kg, gross vehicle weight 1450/1480, Weekend 1590/1630kg.

Engine data (DIN): 4–cylinder in–line (82.6 x 90mm), 1929cm3; compression ratio 20:1; 59kW (79hp) [80PS] at 4200rpm, 30.6kW/L (41hp/L) [41.5PS/L]; 172Nm (126.9lbft) at 2400rpm.

Engine construction: Designated 831D 1.000. Diesel engine swirl chamber. Oil capacity 5L (4.7US qt); oil cooler; 1 KKK K16 exhaust turbocharger, max boost pressure 0.8bar; charge–air cooler; Bosch VER 234 diesel injection pump. 12V 60/66Ah Battery, 55/65A alternator; cooling system capacity 7/7.5L (6.6/7US qt).

Transmission: 5–speed manual, final drive ratio 3.048 (21/64).

Gear ratios: 1st 3.583; 2nd 2.235; 3rd 1.524; 4th 1.154; 5th 0.838; R 3.667.

Chassis: Front antiroll bar; disc brakes diameter 25.7cm; optional power assisted steering; tyres 165/65 SR/TR/HR 14, wheel rims 5.5J.

Dimensions: Track 140/139, Weekend 140/138.5cm.

Performance: Max speed 106mph/170kmh (manufacturers test specifications), speed at 1000rpm in 5th gear 25.3mph/40.7kmh; acceleration 0 – 62mph/100kmh 12.9secs; standing km 34.4secs; power to weight ratio from 17.8kg/kW (13.1kg/PS); consumption ECE 4.4/6.1/6.3L/100km (64.2/46.3/44.8mpg) [53.5/38.6/37.3US mpg].

Fiat Regata DS

Fiat Croma

1600 – CHT – i.e. – Turbo i.e. – TD–ID – Turbo D

Top of the middle range Saloon/Sedan, with notchback or tail gate, transverse engine, front wheel drive and independent suspension. Launched December 1985. Turin 1988: Also with 1.9 Litre direct injection turbo diesel.

```
1.6 Litre
61kW–82hp–83PS
1 2V Carb
```

Engine for Croma 1600

Body, Weight: 5–door Saloon/Sedan, 5–seater; Kerbweight (DIN) 1095kg, gross vehicle weight 1595kg.

Engine data (DIN): 4–cylinder in–line (84 x 71.5mm), 1585cm3; compression ratio 9.75:1; 61kW (82hp) [83PS] at 5600rpm, 38.5kW/L (52.1hp/L) [52.4PS/L]; 128Nm (94.5lbft) at 2800rpm; leaded premium grade.

Engine construction: Transverse engine. 1 overhead camshaft (toothed belt); light–alloy cylinder head; 5 bearing crankshaft; oil capacity 5.4L (5.1US qt); 1 Weber 32–34DAT 52/250 downdraught twin barrel carb. 12V 45Ah Battery; 55A alternator; cooling system capacity 8.9L (8.4US qt).

Transmission (to front wheels): 5–speed manual, floor shift; final drive ratio 3.933 (15/59).

Gear ratios: 1st 3.750; 2nd 2.235; 3rd 1.379; 4th 0.976; 5th 0.814; R 3.583.

Fiat

Chassis: Integral body; front and rear independent suspension, front McPherson struts, A arm and antiroll bar, rear McPherson struts, single control arm, steering tie rod and tension struts, coil springs and telescopic dampers. Servo/power assisted brakes, discs front and rear, front diameter 25.7cm, rear 25.1cm; mechanical handbrake to rear wheels; rack and pinion steering with optional power assistance; fuel tank capacity 70L (15.4Gal) [18.5US Gal]; tyres 175/70TR 14, wheel rims 5.5J.

Fiat Croma 1600

Dimensions: Wheelbase 266cm, track 148/147cm, clearance 14cm, turning circle 11.1m, load space 17.7/31.8/49.4cu ft (500/900/1400dm3). Length 449.5cm, width 176cm, height 143.5cm.

Performance: Max speed approx 106mph/170kmh (manufacturers test specifications), speed at 1000rpm in 4th gear 17.7mph/28.4kmh, in 5th gear 21.6mph/34.8kmh; acceleration 0 – 62mph/100kmh 14.0secs; standing km 35.0secs; power to weight ratio 18.0kg/kW (13.2kg/PS); consumption ECE 5.8/7.6/8.8L/100km (48.7/37.2/32.1mpg) [40.6/34.6/26.7US mpg].

```
2 Litre
66kW–88hp–90PS
1 2V Carb
```

Engine for Croma CHT

As 1.6 Litre, except:

Weight: Kerbweight (DIN) 1110kg, gross vehicle weight 1610kg.

Engine data (DIN): 4–cylinder in–line (84 x 90mm), 1995cm3; compression ratio 9.5:1; 66kW (88hp) [90PS] at 5500rpm, 33.1kW/L (44.3hp/L) [45.1PS/L]; 169Nm (124.7lbft) at 2800rpm.

Engine construction: Valves in V (65deg), 2 overhead camshafts (toothed belt); oil capacity 6.5L (6.1US qt); 1 Weber 34 DAT 54/250 downdraught twin barrel carb. Cooling system capacity 9L (8.5US qt).

Transmission: Final drive ratio 3.421 (19/65).

Chassis: Power assisted steering; tyres 175/70 TR 14 optional 195/60 HR 14, wheel rims 5.5bzw 6J.

Performance: Max speed above 112mph/180kmh (manufacturers test specifications), speed at 1000rpm in 4th gear 20.6mph/33.2 in 5th gear 24.7mph/39.8kmh; acceleration 0 – 62mph/100kmh 11.8secs; standing km 33.0secs; power to weight ratio 16.8kg/kW (12.3kg/PS); consumption ECE 5.5/7.2/8.5L/100km (51.4/39.2/33.2mpg) [42.8/32.7/27.7US mpg].

```
2 Litre
88.5/84.5kW–119/113hp–120/115PS
Fuel Injection
```

Engine for Croma i.e.

As 1.6 Litre, except:

Weight: Kerbweight (DIN) 1120–1195kg, gross vehicle weight 1620kg. Automatic heavier by 25kg.

Engine data (DIN): 4–cylinder in–line (84 x 90mm), 1995cm3; compression ratio 9.75:1; 88.5kW (119hp) [120PS] at 5250rpm, 44.4kW/L (59.5hp/L) [60.2PS/L]; 167Nm (123.2lbft) at 3300rpm.
With Catalyst: Compression ratio 9.5:1; 84.5kW (113hp) [115PS] at 5600rpm, 42.4kW/L (56.8hp/L) [57.6PS/L]; 162Nm (119.5lbft) at 4000rpm.

Engine construction: Valves in V (65deg), 2 overhead camshafts (toothed belt); oil capacity 6.5L (6.1US qt) ; Weber IAW electronic fuel injection, Bosch LU Jetronic (Catalyst). 12V 45, 60Ah Automatic, Battery; 65/70/85A alternator; cooling system capacity 9.0L (8.5US qt).

Transmission: a) 5–speed manual, final drive ratio 3.421 (19/65).
b) Automatic, hydraulic torque converter and 3–speed Planetary gear set, central selector lever, final drive ratio 3.166 (15/59).

Gear ratios: a) 5–speed manual: 1st 3.750; 2nd 2.235; 3rd 1.379; 4th 0.976; 5th 0.814; R 3.583.
Catalyst: 1st 3.75; 2nd 2.235; 3rd 1.518; 4th 1.132; 5th 0.929; R 3.583.
b) Automatic; Max torque multiplication in converter 2.4 times, Planetary gear set ratios: 1st 2.612; 2nd 1.446; 3rd 1; R 2.612.

Chassis: Optional ABS System Bosch; power assisted steering; tyres 175/70HR 14 optional 195/60 HR, wheel rims 5.5J or 6J.

Performance: Max speed 119mph/192kmh, automatic 117mph/188kmh (manufacturers test specifications), speed at 1000rpm in 4th gear 20.7mph/33.2kmh, in 5th gear 24.7mph/39.8kmh; acceleration 0–62mph/100kmh 9.9secs, automatic 11.8secs; standing km 31.1secs, automatic 32secs; power to weight ratio 12.7kg/kW (9.3kg/PS); consumption ECE 6.0/7.6/9.2L/100km (47.1/37.2/30.7mpg) [39.2/30.9/25.6US mpg], automatic 7.0/8.6/9.4L/100km (40.4/32.8/30.1mpg) [33.6/27.4/25 US mpg].
With Catalyst: Max speed 118mph/190kmh, automatic 115mph/186kmh; acceleration 0–62mph/100kmh 10.4secs, automatic 12.3secs; consumption ECE 6.5/8.5/9.6L/100km (43.5/33.2/29.4mpg) [36.2/27.7/24.5US mpg].

Fiat Croma i.e.

```
2 Litre Turbo
114/110.5kW–153/148hp–155/150PS
Fuel Injection
```

Engine for Croma Turbo i.e.

As 1.6 Litre, except:

Weight: Kerbweight (DIN) 1180–1220kg, gross vehicle weight 1680kg.

Engine data (DIN): 4–cylinder in–line (84 x 90mm), 1995cm3; compression ratio 8:1; 114kW (153hp) [155PS] at 5250rpm, 57.1kW/L (76.5hp/L) [77.7PS/L]; 235Nm (173.4lbft) at 2350rpm.
With Catalyst: Compression ratio 7.5:1; 110.5kW (148hp) [150PS] at 5500rpm, 55.4kW/L (74.2hp/L) [75.2PS/L]; 247Nm (182.3lbft) at 2750rpm.

Engine construction: Valves in V (65deg), 2 overhead camshafts (toothed belt); oil capacity 7L (6.6US qt); Bosch LE 2 Jetronic fuel injection, LU Jetronic (Catalyst); 1 Garrett T3 exhaust turbocharger, max boost pressure 0.53bar; charge–air cooler. 12V 70Ah Battery, 65/85A alternator; cooling system capacity 9.6L (9.1US qt).

Transmission: Final drive ratio 2.944 (18/53).

Gear ratios: 1st 3.750; 2nd 2.235; 3rd 1.518; 4th 1.132; 5th 0.928; R 3.583.

Chassis: Disc brakes front ventilated; also available with ABS System Bosch; power assisted steering; tyres 195/60 VR 14, wheel rims 6J.

Dimensions: Track 149.5/148.5cm.

Performance: Max speed above 131mph/210kmh (manufacturers test specifications), speed at 1000rpm in 5th gear 24.8mph/39.9kmh; acceleration 0 – 62mph/100kmh 7.6secs, Catalyst 7.9secs; standing km 29.0secs; power to weight ratio 10.3kg/kW (7.6kg/PS); consumption ECE 6.3/8.3/9.9L/100km (44.8/34/28.5mpg) [37.3/28.3/23.8US mpg]; Catalyst 6.4/8.4/10.2L/100km (36.8/33.6/27.7mpg) [36.8/28/23.1US mpg].

```
1.9 Litre Diesel
68kW–91hp–92PS
Turbo/Direct Injection
```

Engine for 1900 TD–ID

As 1.6 Litre, except:

Weight: Kerbweight (DIN) 1230kg, gross vehicle weight 1730kg.

Fiat

Engine data (DIN): 4–cylinder in–line (82.6 x 90mm), 1929cm3; compression ratio 18:1; 68kW (91hp) [92PS] at 4200rpm, 35.2kW/L (47.2hp/L) [47.7PS/L]; 190Nm (118lbft) at 2500rpm or 66kW (88hp) [90PS].

Engine construction: Diesel engine with direct injection, oil capacity 5.6L (5.3US qt); oil cooler; 1 KKK K16 exhaust turbocharger, max charge–air pressure 0.8bar; charge air cooler; Bosch VE diesel fuel injection pump.
12V 70Ah battery, 65A alternator; cooling sytem capacity 9.6L (9.1US qt).

Transmission: 5–speed manual, final drive ratio 3.562 (16/57).

Gear ratios: 1st 3.75; 2nd 2.176; 3rd 1.379; 4th 0.976; 5th 0.761; R 3.583

Chassis: Front ventilated disc brakes; available with ABS System Bosch; power assisted steering; tyres 175/70 TR 14, available with 185/65 TR 14 or 195/60 HR 14, wheel rims 5.5–6J.

Performances: Max speed 112mph/180kmh (manufacturers test specifications), speed at 1000rpm in 5th gear 25.4mph/40.9kmh; acceleration 0–62mph/100kmh 12.5secs; standing km 33.5secs; power to weight ratio 18.1kg/kW (13.4kg/PS); consumption ECE 3.9/5.5/6.0L/100km (72.4/51.4/47.1mpg) [60.3/42.8/39.2US mpg].

Fiat Croma 1900 TD–ID

```
2.5 Litre Diesel
55kW–74hp–75PS
Injection Pump
```

Engine for Croma D

As 1.6 Litre, except:

Weight: Kerbweight (DIN) 1210kg, gross vehicle weight 1710kg.

Engine data (DIN): 4–cylinder in–line (93 x 92mm), 2499cm3; compression ratio 22:1; 55kW (74hp) [75PS] at 4200rpm, 22kW/L (29.5hp/L) [30PS/L]; 162Nm (120.1lbft) at 2200rpm.

Engine construction: Swirl chamber Diesel engine. Oil capacity 7.8L (7.4US qt); Bosch VER 214 injection pump. 12V 70Ah Battery; cooling system capacity 9L (8.5US qt).

Transmission: Final drive ratio 2.944 (18/53).

Gear ratios: Power assisted steering.

Performance: Max speed 103mph/165kmh (manufacturers test specifications), speed at 1000rpm in 4th gear 24mph/38.6kmh, in 5th gear 28.8mph/46.4kmh; acceleration 0–62mph/100kmh 16.5secs; standing km 36.5secs; power to weight ratio 22kg/kW (16.1kg/PS); consumption ECE 4.7/6.3/7.6L/100km (64.2/44.8/37.2mpg) [50.0/37.3/37.2US mpg].

```
2.45 Litre Diesel
73.5kW–98hp–100PS
Turbo/Injection Pump
```

Engine for Croma Turbo D

As 1.6 Litre, except:

Weight: Kerbweight (DIN) 1240kg, gross vehicle weight 1740kg.

Engine data (DIN): 4–cylinder in–line (93 x 90mm), 2445cm3; compression ratio 22:1; 73.5kW (98.5hp) [100PS] at 4100rpm, 30.1kW/L (40.3hp/L) [40.9PS/L]; 217Nm (22.1lbft) at 2300rpm.

Engine construction: Diesel engine swirl chamber. Oil capacity 6.4L (6.1US qt); Bosch VER 192 injection pump, 1 exhaust turbocharger (KKK K26), max boost pressure 0.87bar, charge air cooler. 12V 70Ah Battery, 65/85A alternator; cooling system capacity 9L (8.5US qt).

Transmission: Final drive ratio 3.19 (21/67).

Gear ratios: 1st 3.750; 2nd 2.235; 3rd 1.379; 4th 0.976; 5th 0.761; R 3.583.

Chassis: Disc brakes, front ventilated; optional ABS System Bosch; power assisted steering; tyres 185/65TR 14 optional 195/60HR 14 wheel rims 5.5 or 6J.

Performance: Max speed 115mph/185kmh (manufacturers test specifications), speed at 1000rpm in 5th gear 27.9mph/44.9kmh; acceleration 0 – 62mph/100kmh 11.9secs; standing km 33.2secs; power to weight ratio 16.9kg/kW (12.4kg/PS); consumption ECE 5.2/6.9/8.5L/100km (54.3/40.9/33.2mpg) [45.2/34.1/27.7US mpg].

Fiat Campagnola

Light all terrain vehicle with all wheel drive and independent suspension. 2 Litre engine, 79hp DIN. Launched June 1974. November 1979: modification to body, 5–speed manual, optional diesel engine. Built at the demand and to the specifications of the Military services.

Fiat Campagnola

```
2 Litre
59kW–79hp–80PS
1 2V Carb
```

Body, Weight: 3–door Estate/Station Wagon, 3/7–seater; kerbweight (DIN) 1670, with metal roof 1740kg, gross vehicle weight 2420/2490kg. Long Estate/Station Wagon, 3/9–seater; kerbweight (DIN) 1730, with metal roof 1780kg, gross vehicle weight 2480/2530kg.

Engine data (DIN): 4–cylinder in–line (84 x 90mm), 1995cm3; compression ratio 8.6:1; 59kW (79hp) [80PS] at 4600rpm, 20.6kW/L (27.6hp/L) [28.8PS/L]; 151Nm (111.4lbft) at 2800rpm; (recommended) leaded premium grade.

Engine construction: Designated 6132 AZ 2000. Side camshaft (chain); light–alloy cylinder head; 5 bearing crankshaft; oil capacity 5.3L (5.0US qt); 1 Solex C 32 PHHE–1RM downdraught twin barrel carb. 12V 55Ah Battery, 55A alternator; cooling system capacity 8.9L (8.4US qt).

Transmission (to all wheels): 5–speed manual and 2 reduction gears; front and rear final drive ratio 5.375 (8/43); reduction gears 1.1 (Street) and 3.87 (Country). Optional front limited slip differential.

Gear ratios: 1st 3.615; 2nd 2.043; 3rd 1.363; 4th 1; 5th 0.838; R 3.419. Or 1st 3.612; 2nd 2.045; 3rd 1.357; 4th 1; 5th 0.834; R 3.434.

Chassis: Integral body; front and rear independent suspension with shock absorber struts (doubled at rear), transverse compression struts and torsion bar spring. Servo/power assisted drum brakes, diameter front and rear 28cm, mechanical handbrakes to rear wheels; worm and wheel steering with optional power assistance; fuel tank capacity 57L (12.5Gal) [15.1US Gal]; tyres 7.00R 16 C, wheel rims 5".

Dimensions: Wheelbase 230cm, track 136.5/140.5cm, clearance (when laden) 27.5cm, turning circle 10.8m. Length 377.5cm, long version 402.5cm, width 158cm, height 197.5/202.5cm.

Performance: Max speed above 75mph/120kmh (manufacturers test specifications), speed at 1000rpm in 5th gear 17.7mph/28.4kmh; acceleration 0 – 62mph/100kmh 41secs; standing km 43secs; power to weight ratio from 28.3kg/kW (20.9kg/PS). Consumption ECE 12.5/–/16.8L/100km (22.6/–/16.8mpg) [18.8/–/14.0US mpg].

```
2.4 Litre Diesel
53kW–71hp–72PS
Injection Pump
```

Fiat I • Fiat BR • Fiat RA

As 2 Litre, except:

Weight: Heavier by 150kg.

Engine data (DIN): (93 x 90mm), 2445cm3; compression ratio 22:1; 53kW (71hp) [72PS] at 4200rpm, 21.7kW/L (29.1hp/L) (29.4PS/L); 147Nm (108.4lbft) at 2400rpm.

Engine construction: Designated Sofim 8142.61. 1 overhead camshaft (chain/toothed belt); oil capacity 6.7L (6.3US qt); Bosch or CAV injection. 88Ah Battery; cooling system capacity 9.6L (9.1US qt).

Chassis: Power assisted steering.

Performance: Max speed 72mph/115kmh (manufacturers test specifications); acceleration 0 – 62mph/100kmh 43secs, standing km 47secs; power to weight ratio 34.3kg/kW (25.3kg/PS); consumption ECE 12.5/–/14.6L/100km (22.6/–/19.3mpg) [18.8/– /12.2US mpg].

FIAT   BR

Fiat Automotives SA, Rodovia Fernao Dias, km 429, 32500 Belim (Minas Gerais), Brasil.

Fiat Uno – Premio – Elba

Saloon/Sedan derived from the Italian Uno. Series: other engines available (1.3 and 1.5), larger hood. Spare wheel in rear of engine compartment. Launched in August 1984. March 1985: Premio. April 1986 also available as Estate/Station Wagon "Elba".

```
1.3 Litre
42.5/44kW–57/59hp–58/60PS
1 Carb
```

Body, Weight: 4-door Saloon/Sedan, 5-seater; kerbweight (DIN) approx 800kg, gross vehicle weight approx 1220kg. 3-door Saloon/Sedan (with tailgate), 5-seater; kerbweight (DIN) 790–795kg, gross vehicle weight 1210kg. 2-door Saloon/Sedan, 5-seater; kerbweight (DIN) 835–850kg, gross vehicle weight 1260kg. 3/5-door Estate/Station Wagon, 5-seater; kerbweight (DIN) from 865kg, gross vehicle weight 1270kg.

Engine data (DIN): 4-cylinder in-line (76 x 71.5mm), 1297cm3; compression ratio 8:1; 42.5kW (57hp) [58PS] at 5200rpm, 32.8kW/L (43.9hp/L) [44.7PS/L]; 98Nm (72.3lbft) at 3000rpm.
Running on ethyl alcohol: Compression ratio 10.6:1; 44kW (59hp) [60PS] at 5200rpm; 98Nm (72.3lbft) at 2600rpm

Engine construction: Transverse front engine. 1 overhead camshaft (toothed belt); light-alloy cylinder head; 5 bearing crankshaft; oil capacity 4L (3.8US qt); 1 Weber 32 ICEV downdraught carb. 12V 45Ah Battery, 45A alternator; cooling system capacity 5.5/6.3L (5.2/6.0US qt).

Transmission (to front wheels): 4 or 5-speed manual, final drive ratio 3.765 (17/64); 4.417 (12/53).

Gear ratios: a) 4-speed manual: 1st 4.091; 2nd 2.235; 3rd 1.469; 4th 0.967; R 3.714.
b) 5-speed manual: 1st 4.091; 2nd 2.235; 3rd 1.469; 4th 0.96; 5th 0.811; R 3.714.

Fiat Premio

Chassis: Integral body; front independent suspension with McPherson struts, lower single control arm and compression struts/antiroll bar, rear independent suspension with A arm, shock absorber struts and self stabilising transverse leaf springs, telescopic dampers. Brakes with optional servo/power assistance, front discs, rear drums, disc diameter 24cm; mechanical handbrake to rear wheels; rack and pinion steering; fuel tank capacity 52L (11.4Gal) [13.7US Gal] with 8L (1.8Gal) [2.1US Gal] reserve; tyres 145SR 13 or 165/70SR 13, wheel rims 4.5J.

Dimensions: Wheelbase 236cm, track 132/134cm, clearance approx 14cm, turning circle approx 10m, load space 102.–36.4cu ft (290– 1030dm3). Length 364.5cm, width 155cm, height 144.5cm. Premio: Load space 18.7cu ft (530dm3); length 403.5cm. Elba: Load space 21.5/52.3cu ft (610/1480dm3). Length 403.5cm.

Performance: Max speed 93mph/150kmh (manufacturers test specifications), speed at 1000rpm in 4th gear 17.7mph/28.4kmh; power to weight ratio from 15.2kg/kW (11.1kg/PS); consumption (touring) approx 6–10L/100km (47.1–28.2mpg) [39.2–23.5US mpg].

```
1.5 Litre
52/63kW–70/84hp–71/86PS
1 2V Carb
```

As 1.3 Litre, except:

Engine data (DIN): 4-cylinder in-line (86.4 x 63.9mm), 1499cm3; compression ratio 8:1; 52kW (70hp) [71PS] at 5500rpm, 34.8kW/L (46.4hp/L) [47.2PS/L]; 121Nm (89.3lbft) at 3000rpm.
Running on ethyl alcohol: Uno 1.5R; compression ratio 11.5; 63kW (84hp) [86PS] at 6000rpm; 126Nm (93.1lbft) at 3500rpm.
Premio and Elba; compression ratio 11:52kW (70hp) [71PS] at 5500rpm; 121Nm (89.3lbft) at 3000rpm.

Engine construction: Oil capacity 4.3L (4.1US qt); 1 Weber 30/34 DMTB/103 downdraught twin barrel carb. Cooling system capacity 6.3L (6.0US qt).

Transmission: 5-speed manual, floor shift; final drive ratio 4.417 (12/53).

Gear ratios: 1st 4.091; 2nd 2.235; 3rd 1.461; 4th 0.967; 5th 0.811; R 3.714.

Chassis: Tyres 165/70 SR 13.

Performance: Max speed 99mph/160kmh (manufacturers test specifications); power to weight ratio from 16.0kg/kW (11.8PS); consumption (touring) approx 8–11L/100km (35.3–25.7mpg) [29.4– 21.4US mpg].

Fiat Elba

```
1698cm3 Diesel
44kW–59hp–60PS
Injection Pump
```

See Italian Fiat Uno. Manufactured exclusively for export.

FIAT   RA

Sevel Argentina SA, Humberto 1st No 1001, (1682) Villa Bosch, Buenos Aires, Argentina.

Argentinian manufacturers working under license from Fiat. Factories in Buenos Aires, Cordoba and Santa Fe. Safrar Peugeot and Fiat Automobiles merged in 1981 to form Sevel Argentina S.A.

Fiat RA • Ford USA

Fiat 147 Spazio/Brio

Derived from 127/147 Fiat, with 1.1 Litre engine, front wheel drive and tail gate. Launched January 1982, the Spazio in November 1984.

```
1116cm3
39kW–52hp–53PS
1 Carb
```

Body, Weight: 3–door Saloon/Sedan (with tailgate), 5–seater; kerbweight (DIN) 780kg, gross vehicle weight 1180kg.

Engine data (DIN): 4–cylinder in–line (80 x 55.5mm), 1116cm3; compression ratio 9.2:1; 39kW (52hp) [53PS] at 6150rpm, 34.9kW/L (46.8hp/L) [47.5PS/L]; 79Nm (58.3lbft) at 3200rpm; leaded premium grade.

Engine construction: Designated 128A 038. Transverse front engine inclined 20deg to front. 1 overhead camshaft (toothed belt); light–alloy cylinder head; 5 bearing crankshaft; oil capacity 4.25L (4.1US qt); 1 Weber 32 ICEV 14/250 downdraught carb. Champion N 9 Y or Bosch W 175 T 30 spark plugs; 12V 34/45Ah Battery, 38/45A alternator; cooling system capacity 6.5L (6.1US qt).

Transmission (to front wheels): 5–speed manual (without direct drive), final drive ratio 3.764 (17/64).

Gear ratios: 1st 3.583; 2nd 2.235; 3rd 1.454; 4th 1.042; 5th 0.863; R 3.714.

Chassis: Integral body; front independent suspension with McPherson struts, lower single control arm and antiroll bar, rear independent suspension with A arm, shock absorber struts and self stabilising transverse leaf spring, telescopic dampers. Servo/power assisted brakes, front discs, rear drums, disc diameter 22.7cm, at rear 215cm2, total 343cm3, mechanical handbrake to rear wheels; rack and pinion steering; fuel tank capacity 37L (8.1Gal) [9.8US Gal]; tyres 145 SR 13, wheel rims 4.5J.

Dimensions: Wheelbase 222.5cm, track 127.5/130cm, clearance 14cm, turning circle 10.4m. Load space 12.9–37.8cu ft (365– 1070dm3). Length 374.5cm, width 154.5cm, height 135cm.

Performance: Max speed 84mph/135kmh (manufacturers test specifications), speed at 1000rpm in 5th gear 19.9mph/32kmh; acceleration 0 – 62mph/100kmh; 19.9secs; standing km approx 39.7secs; power to weight ratio 20kg/kW (14.7kg/PS); consumption approx 6–9L/100km (47.1–31.4mpg) [39.2–26.1US mpg].

Fiat 147 Spazio

Fiat 128

Licensed production of the early 128 with 5–speed manual, also available as Station Wagon. For 1984: front and rear modifications. For data see Zastava 101.

Fiat Duna

Argentinian version of the Duna with 1.3 Litre Engine and 61hp, 1.5 Litre 81hp as 1.3 Litre Diesel with 44hp. For data see Italian Fiat/Brasilian.

Fiat Regata

Mid–Class vehicle with transverse 1.5 or 2 Litre front engine, derived from the Italian model. Launched in July 1985. For data on 1500 see Fiat Regata under Italian entry.

```
2 Litre
81kW–109hp–110PS
1 2V Carb
```

As Fiat Regata 1.3 Litre, except:

Weight: Kerbweight (DIN) 1000kg, gross vehicle weight 1510kg.

Engine Data (DIN): 4–cylinder in–line (84 x 90mm), 1995cm3; compression ratio 9.5:1; 81kW (109hp) [110PS] at 5000rpm, 40.6kW/L (54.4hp/L) [55.1PS/L]; 163Nm (120.3lbft) at 3000rpm.

Engine construction: Valves in V (65deg), 2 overhead camshafts (toothed belt); oil capacity 6.5L (6.1US qt); 1 Weber 34 DAT 54/250 downdraught twin barrel carb. Cooling system capacity 9L (8.5US qt).

Transmission: 5–speed manual, final drive ratio 3.421 (19/65).

Chassis: Power assisted steering; tyres 175/70 TR 13, wheel rims 5.5J.

Performance: Max speed 115mph/185kmh (manufacturers test specifications), speed at 1000rpm in 5th gear 22.4mph/36.0kmh; acceleration 0 – 62mph/100kmh; power to weight ratio 12.3kg/kW (9.1kg/PS); consumption approx 5–9L/100km (56.5–31.4mpg) [47.0– 26.1US mpg].

Fiat Regata 2000

FORD USA

Ford Motor Company Inc, P.O. Box 2053, Dearborn, Michigan, USA

The second largest automobile producer in the World. This is the parent producer of the Ford Motor Company.

MODEL RANGE
Festiva – Escort – Tempo – Probe – Mustang – Taurus – Taurus SHO – LTD Crown Victoria – Thunderbird – Aerostar – Bronco II – Bronco

Ford Festiva

Ford Festiva

3–door small vehicle with front wheel drive and 1.3 Litre engine. Original concept from Mazda, built in Korea. For technical data see Mazda/Ford.

Ford USA — 191

Ford Escort/EXP

Escort Pony – Escort LX – Escort GT

Vehicle with transverse engine. Front wheel drive and tail gate. 3 and 5–door Saloon/Sedan. 5–door Estate/Station Wagon as 3–door Coupe EXP model with mechanical or automatic transmission. Launched in September 1980. 1987: fuel injection engine. 1989: modifications to the body.

Ford Escort Wagon

**1.9 Litre
67kW–90hp–91PS
Central/Single Point Injection**

Not available for GT

Body, Weight (laden):
Escort Pony: 3–door Saloon/Sedan, 4–seater; approx 1015kg.
Escort LX: 3–door Saloon/Sedan, 4–seater; approx 1015kg. 5–door Saloon/Sedan, 4–seater; approx 1050kg. 5–door Estate/Station Wagon, 4–seater; approx 1050kg.

Engine data (SAE net): 4–cylinder in–line (82 x 88mm), 1859cm3; compression ratio 9:1; 67kW (90hp) [91PS] at 4600rpm, 36.0kW/L (48.2hp/L) [49.0PS/L]; 144Nm (106.3lbft) at 3400rpm; unleaded regular grade.

Engine construction: Designated CVH. Front transverse engine; hydraulic tappets; 1 overhead camshaft (toothed belt); light– alloy cylinder heads; 5 main bearing crankshaft; oil capacity 3.8L (3.6US qt); Ford electronic central/single point injection. 12V 48/58Ah Battery, 60A alternator; cooling system capacity approx 7.5L (7.1US qt).

Transmission (to front wheels): a) 4–speed manual, final drive ratio 2.85; 3.52. b) 5–speed manual, final drive ratio 3.52. c) Automatic: hydraulic torque converter and 3–speed Planetary gear set, central selector lever, final drive ratio 3.26.

Gear ratios: a) 4–speed manual: 1st 3.21 (Pony 3.46); 2nd 1.81; 3rd 1.15; 4th 0.78; R 3.27.
b) 5–speed manual: 1st 3.60; 2nd 2.21; 3rd 1.39; 4th 1.02; 5th 0.75; R 3.62.
c) Automatic: Max torque multiplication in converter 2.37 times, Planetary gear set ratios: 1st 2.81; 2nd 1.60; 3rd 1; R 2.03.

Chassis: Integral body; front McPherson struts (coil springs), lower single control arm and antiroll bar, rear independent suspension with shock absorber struts, control arm, tension struts and coil springs, telescopic damper, antiroll bar. Servo/power assisted brakes, rear drums, front disc diameter 23.4cm (ventilated); mechanical handbrake to rear wheels; rack and pinion steering with optional power assistance; fuel tank capacity 49L (10.8Gal) [12.9US Gal]; tyres 175/70 SR 13, wheel rims 5J, also available with 5.5J.

Ford Escort LX

Dimensions: Wheelbase 239.5cm, track 139/142cm, clearance 13cm, turning circle 11m. Load space 28.2–38.5cu ft (800–1090dm3), Estate/Station Wagon 19.2–59.3cu ft (545–1680dm3), length 430cm, width 167.5cm, height 136.5cm.

Performance: Max speed approx 96–103mph/155–165kmh, speed at 1000rpm in 5th gear 26mph/41.8kmh; power to weight ratio from 15.1kg/kW (11.1kg/PS); consumption approx 7–12L/100km (40.4– 23.5mpg) [33.6–23.5US mpg].

**1.9 Litre
82kW–110hp–112PS
Fuel Injection**

Only available for GT:

As 90hp, except:

Body, Weight: 3–door Saloon/Sedan GT, 4–seater; approx 1110kg.

Engine data (SAE net): 4–cylinder in–line (82 x 88mm), 1859cm3; compression ratio 9:1; 82kW (110hp) [112PS] at 5400rpm, 44.1kW/L (59.1hp/L) [60.2PS/L]; 156Nm (115.1lbft) at 4200rpm.

Engine construction: Bosch electronic fuel injection.

Transmission: 5–speed manual, final drive ratio 3.73.

Gear ratios: 1st 3.60; 2nd 2.12; 3rd 1.39; 4th 1.02; 5th 0.75; R 3.62.

Chassis: Tyres 195/60 HR 15, wheel rims 6J.

Performance: Max speed approx 115–118mph/185–190kmh, speed at 1000rpm in 5th gear 24.9mph/40.1kmh; power to weight ratio from 13.5kg/kW (9.9kg/PS); consumption approx 7–13L/100km (40.4– 21.7mpg) [33.6–18.1US mpg].

Ford Escort GT

Ford Tempo

GL – GLS – LX – All Wheel Drive

2 and 4–door Saloon/Sedan with front wheel drive, 2.3–Litre cylinder engine, 5–speed manual or automatic. Launched in 1983. At request, in 1987 the 4–door Saloon/Sedan also availble with all wheel drive (AWD). 1989: Also available with airbag.

**2.3 Litre
73kW–98hp–99PS
Fuel Injection**

Body, Weight: Tempo GL: 2–door Saloon/Sedan, 5–seater; approx 1150kg. 4–door Saloon/Sedan, 5–seater; approx 1170kg. Tempo LX: 4–door Saloon/Sedan, 5–seater; approx 1190kg.

Engine data (SAE net): 4–cylinder in–line (93.47 x 83.8mm), 2300cm3; compression ratio 9:1; 73kW (98hp) [99PS] at 4400rpm, 31.7kW/L (42.5hp/L) [43.0PS/L]; 168Nm (124.1lbft) at 2200rpm; unleaded regular grade.

Engine construction: Transverse front engine. Hydraulic tappets; side camshaft (chain); 5 main bearing crankshaft; oil capacity 3.8L (3.6US qt); Ford electronic fuel injection. 12V 58Ah Battery, 65–75A alternator; cooling system capacity 7.6L (7.2US qt).

Transmission (to front wheels): a) 5–speed manual, final drive ratio 3.40.
b) Automatic: hydraulic torque converter and 3–speed Planetary gear set, final drive ratio 3.07.

Gear ratios: a) 5–speed manual: 1st 3.6; 2nd 2.12; 3rd 1.39; 4th 1.02; 5th 0.75; R 3.62.
b) Automatic: Max torque multiplication in converter 2.2 times, Planetary gear set ratios: 1st 2.81; 2nd 1.60; 3rd 1; R 2.03.

Chassis: Integral body; front McPherson struts (coil springs), lower single control arm and antiroll bar, rear independent suspension with shock absorber struts; control arm, tension struts and coil springs, telescopic dampers. Servo/power assisted brakes, front discs (ventilated), disc diameter 23.4cm, rear drums; mechanical handbrake to rear wheels; power assisteed rack and pinion

Ford USA

steering; fuel tank capacity 58L (12.7Gal) [15.3US Gal]; tyres 185/70 R 14, wheel rims 6J.

Dimensions: Wheelbase 254cm, track 139.5/146cm, clearance 13cm, turning circle 11.8m, load space 12.9cu ft (365dm3), 2–door 13.2cu ft (375dm3). Length 449, width 173.5, height 134cm.

Performance: Max speed approx 95–102mph/155–165kmh, speed at 1000rpm in 5th gear 27.3mph/43.9kmh; power to weight ratio from 15.7kg/kW (11.6kg/PS); consumption approx 7–12L/100km (40.4–23.5mpg) [33.6–19.6US mpg].

Ford Tempo LX

```
2.3 Litre
74kW–100hp–101PS
Fuel Injection
```

Engine for GLS and AWD

As 98hp, except:

Body, Weight: GLS: 2–door Saloon/Sedan, 5–seater; approx 1155kg. 4–door Saloon/Sedan, 5–seater; approx 1180kg. All Wheel Drive: 4–door Saloon/Sedan, 5–seater; approx 1265kg.

Engine data (SAE net): 4–cylinder in–line (93.47 x 83.8mm), 2300cm3; compression ratio 9:1; 74kW (100hp) [101PS] at 4400rpm, 32.2kW/L (43.1hp/L) [43.9PS/L]; 176Nm (130.1lbft) at 2600rpm.

Transmission (to front wheels or all wheels): a) 5–speed manual, final drive ratio 3.73.
b) Automatic: hydraulic torque converter and 3–speed Planetary gear set, central selector lever, final drive ratio 3.26.
All Wheel Drive 3.07; engageable rear wheel drive.

Gear ratios: a) 5–speed manual: 1st 3.21; 2nd 2.12; 3rd 1.39; 4th 1.02; 5th 0.75; R 3.62.
b) Automatic: Max torque multiplication in converter 2.2 times, Planetary gear set ratios: 1st 2.81; 2nd 1.60; 3rd 1; R 2.03.

Chassis: Fuel tank for AWD 54L (11.9Gal) [14.3US Gal]; wheel rims 5.5J.

Performance: Max speed approx 99–106mph/160/170kmh, speed at 1000rpm in 5th gear 24.8mph/40kmh; power to weight ratio from 15.6kg/kW (11.4kg/PS); consumption approx 7–11L/100km (40.4–25.7mpg) [33.6–21.4US mpg].

Ford Tempo GLS

Ford Probe

GL – LX – GT

2–door Coupe with tail gate, 2.2 Litre engine with and without turbo charger; transmission, bodywork and loading area identical to the Mazda MX–6. Produced by Mazda in Flat Rock/USA. Launched in February 1988.

```
2.2 Litre
82kW–110hp–112PS
Fuel Injection
```

Engine for GL and LX

Body, Weight: 3–door Coupe GL/LX, 4–seater; kerbweight (DIN) 1230kg.

Engine data (SAE net): 4–cylinder in–line (86 x 94mm), 2184cm3; compression ratio 8.6:1; 82kW (110hp) [112PS] at 4700rpm, 37.5kW/L (50.1hp/L) [51.3PS/L]; 176Nm (130.1lbft) at 3000rpm; unleaded regular grade.

Engine construction: Transverse front engine. 3 valves per cylinder; 1 overhead camshaft (toothed belt); light–alloy cylinder head; 5 main bearing crankshaft; oil capacity 4.6L (4.4US qt); Mazda electronic injection. Nippon Denso AGSP 33C spark plugs; 12V 51Ah Battery; 70A alternator; cooling system capacity approx 7.5L (7.1US qt).

Ford Probe

Transmission (to front wheels): a) 5–speed manual, final drive ratio 4.1.
b) Automatic, hydraulic torque converter and 4–speed Planetary gear set, final drive ratio 3.7.

Gear ratios: a) 5 speed gear: 1st 3.307; 2nd 1.833; 3rd 1.233; 4th 0.914; 5th 0.717; R 3.166.
b) Automatic: Max torque multiplication 1.8 times; Planetary gear set: 1st 2.80; 2nd 1.54; 3rd 1; OD 0.70; R 2.33.

Chassis: Integral body; all round independent suspension; front McPherson struts with lower control arms, rear McPherson struts, twin control arms, trailing arms, front and rear antiroll bars, telescopic dampers. Servo/power assisted brakes, front ventilated discs, diameter 26.2cm, rear drums, mechanical handbrake to rear wheels, power assisted rack and pinion steering; fuel tank capacity 57L (12.5Gal) [15.1US Gal]; tyres 185/70 R 14, wheel rims 5.5J.

Dimensions: Wheelbase 251.5cm, track 145.5/146.5cm, clearance 13cm, turning circle 10.6m. Load space 12/40.6cu ft (340/1150dm3). Length 449.5cm, width 172.5cm, height 131.5cm.

Performance: Max speed approx 115–118mph/185–190kmh, speed at 1000rpm in 5th gear 24.2mph/38.9kmh; power to weight ratio from 15kg/kW (11.0kg/PS); consumption 8–12L/100km (35.3–23.5mpg) [29.4–19.6US mpg].

Ford Probe GT

Ford USA

2.2 Litre Turbo
108kW–145hp–147PS
Fuel injection

Engine for GT

As 110hp, except:

Weight: Kerbweight approx 1300kg.

Engine data (SAE net): 4–cylinder in–line (86 x 94mm), 2184cm3; compression ratio 7.8:1; 108kW (145hp) [147PS] at 4300rpm, 49.5kW/L (66.3hp/L) [67.3PS/L]; 258Nm (190.4lbft) at 3500rpm.

Engine construction: 1 exhaust turbocharger IHI, Max boost pressure 0.5–0.65bar, charge–air cooler.

Transmission: 5-speed manual, final drive ratio 4.1.

Gear ratios: 1st 3.25; 2nd 1.772; 3rd 1.194; 4th 0.926; 5th 0.711; R 3.461.

Chassis: Servo/power assisted disc drive, optionally with ABS (Sumimoto), diameter front 26.2, rear 25.7cm; tyres 195/60 VR 15, wheel rims 6J.

Dimensions: Width 174cm.

Performance: Max speed approx 124mph/200kmh, speed at 1000rpm in 5th gear 24mph/38.6kmh; power to weight ratio form 12kg/kW (8.8kg/PS); consumption approx 9–14L/100km (31.4–20.2mpg) [26.1– 16.8US mpg].

Ford Mustang LX – GT

Luxurious and sporty four–seater; engine from 2.3 and 4.9 Litre capacity. Launched in July 1978. Available, if required, with 5– speed manual. 1983, also with 4.9 Litre HO–V8 engine and available as convertible. 1989: V8 also for LX.

Ford Mustang LX

2.3 Litre
67kW–90hp–91PS
Fuel Injection

Only available for LX

Body, Weight (laden): 2–door Coupe, 4–seater; kerbweight 1250kg. 3–door Coupe, 4–seater; kerbweight 1280kg. 2–door Convertible, 4–seater; kerbweight 1345kg.

Engine data (SAE net): 4–cylinder in–line (96.04 x 79.4mm), 2301cm3; compression ratio 9.5:1; 67kW (90hp) [91PS] at 3800rpm, 29.1kW/L (39.1hp/L) [39.5PS/L]; 176Nm (130.1lbft) at 2800rpm; unleaded regular grade.

Engine construction: Valves in V; hydraulic tappets, 1 overhead camshaft (toothed belt); 5 main bearing crankshaft; oil capacity 4.7L (4.4US qt); electronic fuel injection. 12V 48/58Ah Battery, 75A alternator; cooling system capacity 8.2L (7.8US qt).

Transmission (to rear wheels): a) 5–speed manual, final drive ratio 3.45.
b) Automatic, hydraulic torque converter and 4–speed Planetary gear set ratio, central selector lever, final drive ratio 3.73. Optional limited differential.

Gear ratios: a) 5 speed gear: 1st 3.97; 2nd 2.34; 3rd 1.46; 4th 1; 5th 0.79; R 3.71.
b) Automatic: Max torque multiplication in converter 2.6 times, Planetary gear set ratios: 1st 2.47; 2nd 1.47; 3rd 1; 4th 0.75; R 2.11.

Chassis: Integral body; front upper A arm, lower single control arm with elastic tension struts, coil springs, rear rigid axle with coil springs, lower trailing arm and upper semi–trailing arm, front optional rear antiroll bar, telescopic dampers. Servo/power assisted brakes, front discs (ventilated), rear drums, disc diameter 25.6/27.5cm; mechanical handbrake to rear wheels; power assisted rack and pinion steering; fuel tank capacity 58L (12.7Gal) [15.3US Gal]; tyres 195/75 R 14, wheel rims 5J, also avilable with 5.5J

Dimensions: Wheelbase 255.5cm, track 144/145cm, clearance 11.5cm, turning circle 11.8m. Load space 10cu ft (285dm3), with tail gate max 30cu ft (850dm3), convertible 6.4cu ft (180dm3). Length 456cm, width 175.5cm, height 132cm.

R13

Ford Mustang LX Convertible

Performance: Max speed approx 93.2–99mph/150–160kmh, speed at 1000rpm in 5th gear 27.3mph/44.0kmh; power to weight ratio from 18.7kg/kW (13.7kg/PS); consumption approx 9–14L/100km (31.4– 20.2mpg) [26.1–16.8US mpg].

4.9 Litre V8
168kW–225hp–228PS
Fuel Injection

As 90hp, except:

Weight: Heavier by approx 1380kg.

Engine data (SAE net): 8–cylinder in V 90deg (101.6 x 76.2mm), 4942cm3; compression ratio 9:1; 168kW (225hp) [228PS] at 4200rpm, 34.0kW/L (45.6hp/L) [46.1PS/L]; 407Nm (300.1lbft) at 3200rpm.

Engine construction: Central camshaft (chain). 12V 58Ah Battery; cooling system capacity approx 13.3L (12.6US qt).

Transmission: a) 5–speed manual, final drive ratio 2.73; 3.08.
b) Automatic, "Automatic Overdrive", hydraulic torque converter and 4–speed Planetary gear set, final drive ratio 2.73; 3.27.
Limited slip differential.

Gear ratios: a) 5–speed manual: 1st 3.35; 2nd 1.93; 3rd 1.29; 4th 1; 5th 0.68; R 3.15.
b) Automatic, "Automatic Overdrive", Max torque multiplication in converter 2.53 times; Planetary gear set ratios: 2.40; 1.47; 1; 0.67; R 2.

Chassis: Front and rear antiroll bar. Disc diameter 27.5cm; tyres 225/60 VR 15, wheel rims 7J.

Performance: Max speed over 137mph/220kmh, speed at 1000rpm in OD 39.9mph/64.2kmh; power to weight ratio from 8.2kg/kW (6.1kg/PS); consumption approx 12–20L/100km (23.5– 14.1mpg) [19.6–11.8US Gal].

Ford Mustang GT

Ford Taurus

L – GL – LX

Mid class vehicle with front wheel drive and transverse engine, 2.5 Litre four cylinder or 3 Litre V6, Saloon/Sedan or Estate/Station Wagon with aerodynamic body. Launched in February 1985. In 1988 also available with 3.8 Litre V6 engine.

Ford USA

2.5 Litre
67kW–90hp–91PS
Central/Single Point Injection

Not available for Estate/Station Wagon

Body, Weight: 4–door Saloon/Sedan, 5/6–seater; kerbweight from 1315kg.

Engine data (SAE net): 4–cylinder in–line (93.47 x 91mm), 2498cm3; compression ratio 9.0:1; 67kW (90hp) [91PS] at 4400rpm, 26.8kW/L (35.9hp/L) [36.4PS/L]; 176Nm (130.1lbft) at 2600rpm; unleaded regular grade.

Engine Construction: Transverse front engine. Hydraulic tappets, overhead camshaft (chain); 5 bearing crankshaft; oil capacity 3.8L (3.5US qt); central/single point injection. Motorcraft AWSF–52 spark plugs; 12V 58–84Ah battery, 75–100A alternator; cooling system capacity 8.0L (7.6US qt).

Transmission (to front wheels): Automatic, hydraulic torque converter and 3–speed Planetary gear set, central selector lever, final drive ratio 3.26.

Gear ratios: Max torque multiplication in converter 2.2 times, Planetary gear set ratios: 1st 2.81; 2nd 1.60; 3rd 1; R 2.03.

Chassis: Integral body; front McPherson struts (coil springs), lower single control arm, tension struts and antiroll bar, rear independent suspension with single control and semi trailing arms, coil springs and telescopic dampers (Saloon/Sedan with McPherson struts), antiroll bar. Servo/power assisted brakes, front discs, rear drums, disc diameter 25.7cm; mechanical handbrake to rear wheels; power assisted rack and pinion steering; fuel tank capacity 61L (13.4Gal) [16.1US Gal], also available 70L (15.4Gal) [18.5US Gal]; tyres P 205/70 R 14, tyres 5.5J, optional 205/65 R 15, wheel rims 6J.

Dimensions: Wheelbase 269.5cm, track 156.5/153.5cm, clearance 13cm, turning circle 12.1m. Load space 17cu ft (480dm3). Length 478.5cm, width 180cm, height 138cm. Estate/Station Wagon: load space 80.9cu ft (2290dm3). Length 487.5cm, height 140cm.

Performance: Max speed approx 96mph/155kmh, speed at 1000rpm in 5th gear 21.9mph/35.3kmh; power to weight ratio from 19.6kg/kW (14.4kg/PS); consumption 10–14L/100km (28.2–20.2mpg) [23.5–16.8US mpg].

Ford Taurus LX

3 Litre V6
104kW–140hp–142PS
Fuel Injection

As 2.5 Litre, except:

Body, Weight: 4–door Saloon/Sedan, 5/6 Seater; kerbweight from L 1370kg, GL 1380kg, LX 1395kg. 5–door Estate/Station Wagon, 5/6–seater; kerbweight from L 1445kg, GL 1445kg, LX 1460kg.

Engine data (SAE net): 6–cylinder in V 60deg (88.9 x 80mm), 2979cm3; compression ratio 9.3:1; 104kW (140hp) [142PS] at 4800rpm, 34.9kW/L (47.1hp/L) [47.7PS/L]; 217Nm (160.1lbft) at 3000rpm.

Engine construction: Central camshaft (chain); 4 main bearing crankshaft; oil capacity 4.2L (4US qt); Ford electronic fuel injection. Motorcraft AWSF–32C spark plugs; 85Ah battery, 100A alternator; cooling system capacity approx 9.5L (9.0US qt).

Transmission: Automatic "Automatic Overdrive", hydraulic torque converter and 4–speed Planetary gear set, central or steering column selector lever, final drive ratio 3.37.

Gear ratios: Max torque multiplication in converter 2.2 times; Planetary gear set ratios: 2.77; 1.54; 1; 0.69; R 2.26.

Performance: Max speed approx 109–115mph/175–185kmh, speed at 1000rpm in OD 30.1mph/49.5kmh; power to weight ratio from 13.2kg/kW (9.6kg/PS); consumption (touring) approx 10–15L/100km (28.2–18.8mpg) [23.5–12.5US mpg].

Ford Taurus LX Wagon

3.8 Litre V6
104kW–140hp–142PS
Fuel Injection

As 2.5 Litre, except:

Body, Weight: 4–door Saloon/Sedan, 5/6–seater; kerbweight from L 1380kg, GL 1390kg, LX 1425kg. 5–door Estate/Station Wagon, 5/6–seater; kerbweight from L 1450kg, GL 1460kg, LX 1485kg.

Engine data (SAE net): 6–cylinder in V 90deg (96.52 x 86.36mm), 3791cm3; compression ratio 9.0:1; 104kW (140hp) [142PS] at 3800rpm, 27.4kW/L (36.7hp/L) [37.5PS/L]; 292Nm (215.5lbft) at 2400rpm.

Engine construction: Central camshaft (chain); light–alloy cylinder heads; 4 main bearing crankshaft; electronic fuel injection. Motorcraft AWSF–44C spark plugs; 100A alternator; cooling system capacity approx 11.5L (10.9US qt).

Transmission: Automatic: "Automatic Overdrive", hydraulic torque converter and 4–speed Planetary gear set, selector lever at centre or steering column, final drive ratio 3.19.

Gear ratios: Max torque multiplication in converter 1.9 times; Planetary gear set ratios: 2.77; 1.54; 1; 0.69; R 2.26.

Performance: Max speed approx 111–118mph/180–190kmh, speed at 1000rpm in OD 32.5mph/52.3kmh; power to weight ratio from 13.3kg/kW (9.7kg/PS); consumption (touring) approx 11–17L/100km (25.7–16.6mpg) [21.4–13.8US mpg].

Ford Taurus SHO

New model. High performance version of the Saloon/Sedan Taurus with a Yamaha 3 Litre V8 engine. Debut Autumn 1988.

3 Litre V6
164kW - 220hp - 223PS
Fuel Injection

Body, Weight: 4–door Saloon/Sedan, 5–seater, kerbweight from 1395kg.

Engine data (SAE net): 6–cylinder V60 deg (88.9 x 80mm), 2979cm3; compression ratio 9.8:1; 164kW (220hp) [223PS] at 6000rpm, 55kW/L (73.7hp/L) [74.9PS/L]; 271Nm (200lbft) at 4800rpm; unleaded premium grade.

Engine construction: Transverse front engine, hydraulic tappets; 4 valves per cylinder; light–alloy cylinder head; 1 overhead camshaft (chain and toothed belt), 4 bearing crankshaft; oil capacity 4.2L; Nippon Denso electronic fuel injection. Motorcraft AGSP–32P spark plugs, 12V 72Ah battery, 90A alternator; cooling system capacity approx 9.5L.

Ford Taurus SHO

Transmission (to front wheels): 5–speed manual, final drive ratio 3.74.

Gear ratios: 1st 3.21; 2nd 2.09; 3rd 1.38; 4th 1.02; 5th 0.73; R 3.14.

Ford USA

Chassis: Integral body; front McPherson strut (coil springs), lower single control arm and antiroll bar, rear independent suspension with single control and semi trailing arms, McPherson struts, antiroll bar. Servo/power assisted brakes, disc diameter (ventilated), front and rear 25.5cm; mechanical handbrake to rear; power assisted rack and pinion steering; fuel tank capacity 70L (15.4Gal) [18.5US Gal]; tyres 215/65 VR 15, wheel rims 6J.

Dimensions: Wheelbase 269.5cm, track 156.5/153.5cm, clearance 13cm, turning circle 12.1m. Load space 17cu ft (480dm3). Length 478.5cm, width 180cm, height 138cm.

Performance: Max speed approx 137mph/220kmh, speed at 1000rpm in 5th gear 26.1mph/42.1km/h; acceleration 0–60mph/97km/h 7.3secs; power to weight ratio from 8.5kg/kW (6.3kg/PS); consumption approx 10–16L/100km (28.2-17.7mpg) [23.5–14.7US mpg].

Ford Taurus SHO

Ford LTD Crown Victoria

LTD Crown Victoria – LTD Crown Victoria LX – Wagons

1979: New structuring of the Model series with smaller dimensions and lower weight. For 1983 base engine: 4.9 Litre V8 with fuel injection. 1988: 2–door no longer available.

```
4.9 Litre V8
112/119kW–150/160hp–152/162PS
Fuel Injection
```

Body, Weight (laden): LTD Crown Victoria: 4–door Saloon/Sedan, 6–seater; approx 1690kg. 5–door Estate/Station Wagon, 6–seater; approx 1785kg. 5–door Estate/Station Wagon Country Squire, 6–seater; approx 1785kg
LTD Crown Victoria LX: 4–door Saloon/Sedan, 6–seater; approx 1710kg. 5–door Estate/Station Wagon 6–seater; approx 1775kg. 5–door Estate/Station Wagon Country Squire, 6–seater; approx 1820kg.

Engine data (SAE net): 8–cylinder in V 90deg (101.6 x 76.2mm), 4942cm3; compression ratio 8.9:1; 112kW (150hp) [152PS] at 3200rpm, 22.6kW/L (30.3hp/L) [30.8PS/L]; 366Nm (270.1lbft) at 2000rpm; unleaded regular grade.
With dual exhaust: 119kW (160hp) [162PS] at 3400rpm, 24.1kW/L (32.3hp/L) [32.8PS/L]; 380Nm (280.4lbft) at 2200rpm.
Police version (5.8–351 V8): Compression ratio 8.3:1; 135kW (181hp) [183PS] at 3600rpm; 387Nm (285.6lbft) at 2400rpm.

Ford LTD Crown Victoria LX

Engine construction: Hydraulic tappets, central camshaft (chain); 5 main bearing crankshaft; oil capacity 4.7L (4.4US qt); electronic fuel injection. 12V 58–84Ah Battery, 65–100A alternator; cooling system capacity approx 13.6L (12.9US qt).

Transmission (to rear wheels): Automatic "Automatic Overdrive", hydraulic torque converter and 4–speed Planetary gear set, selector lever at steering column, final drive ratio 2.73; 3.08; 3.27; 3.55. Optional limited slip differential.

Gear ratios: Automatic; "Automatic Overdrive", max torque multiplication in converter 2.30 times; Planetary gear set ratios: 2.40; 1.47; 1; 0.67; R 2.

Chassis: Box section frame with cross members; front coil springs, upper and lower keystone A–arms, antiroll bar; rear rigid axle with coil springs, lower trailing arm, upper semi–trailing arm, antiroll bar, telescopic dampers, optional level control system. Servo/power assisted brakes, front discs (ventilated), rear drums, disc diameter 27.9cm; pedal actuated parking brake to rear wheels; power assisted recirculating ball steering; fuel tank capacity 68L (14.9Gal) [18.0US Gal], tyres 215/70 R 15, wheel rims 6 optional 6.5J.

Dimensions: Wheelbase 290cm, track 158/157.5cm, clearance 13cm, turning circle 13.1m. Load space 22.4cu ft (635dm3). Length 536cm, width 197cm, height 141cm. Estate/Station Wagon: Load space 88.1cu ft (2495dm3). Length 548.5cm, width 201.5cm, height 145cm.

Performance: Max speed approx 112–118mph/180–190kmh, speed at 1000kmh in top gear 37.5mph/60.4kmh; power to weight ratio from 14.2kg/kW (10.4kg/PS); consumption (touring) approx 12–18L/100km (23.5–15.7mpg) [19.6–13.1US mpg].

Ford LTD Crown Victoria Country Squire

Ford Thunderbird

Standard – LX – Super Coupe

Luxury touring version based on the American sporty model. Autumn 1979: new smaller body. Autumn 1988: New edition with longer wheelbase and 3.8 Litre V6 engine with and without compressor. Drag co–efficient 0.31.

Ford Thunderbird

```
3.8 Litre V6
104kW–140hp–142PS
Fuel Injection
```

Not available for Super Coupe

Body, Weight (laden): 2–door Coupe, 4/5–seater; approx 1610kg, LX 1615kg.

Engine data (SAE net): 6–cylinder in V 90deg (96.52 x 86.36mm), 3791cm3; compression ratio 9:1; 104kW (140hp) [142PS] at 3800rpm, 27.4kW/L (36.7hp/L) [37.5PS/L]; 292Nm (215.5lbft) at 2400rpm.

SIEMENS

And when the road
becomes an ice rink –
what then?

Keep your grip when the going is critical: rain, snow, ice and non-metalled roads mean maximum alert for driver and car.

Active help is at hand from Siemens electronics. In a fraction of a second the automatic 4WD option designed to slip into gear when the going gets tough or the automatic limited-slip differential option provide straight-line stability and optimum traction. Often before the driver is even aware of the danger and has had time to react!

Two systems for more safety – for the occupants and for the car.

These are just two examples of the innovative automotive systems from Siemens. They are typical of the wide variety of developments, which are making today's cars more economical, safer, more reliable and comfortable, e.g.:

- **Engine and power train management systems**
- **Electronic body components**
- **Plastics, heating and air-conditioning systems**
- **Vehicle wiring systems/Bergmann Kabelwerke AG**
- **Electric motors**
- **Sensors**

I would like to find out more about automotive systems from Siemens. Please send me your publication with an overview.

☐ in English
(order No. A19100-J71-A1-X-7600)
☐ in German
(order No. A19100-J71-A1)

Write to:
Siemens AG
Infoservice 221/Z545
Postfach 2348, D-8510 Fürth
Germany

**Drive with Experience:
Automotive Technology
from Siemens**

Ford USA

Engine construction: Central camshaft (chain); light–alloy cylinder heads; hydraulic tappets, 4 main bearing crankshaft; oil capacity 4.3L (4.1US qt), electronic fuel injection. Motorcraft AWSF–44C spark plugs; 12V 48Ah Battery, 65A alternator; cooling system capacity approx 10.1L (9.6US qt).

Transmission: Automatic "Automatic Overdrive", hydraulic torque converter and 4–speed Planetary gear set, final drive ratio 3.27. Optional limited slip differential.

Gear ratios: Max torque multiplication in converter 2.53 times; Planetary gear set ratios 2.40; 1.47; 1; 0.67; R 2.11.

Chassis: Integral body; front and rear independent suspension, front upper A arm, lower single control arm with tension struts, antiroll bar; rear lower A arm and upper single control arm and antiroll bar; coil springs, telescopic damper. Servo/power assisted brakes, front disc diameter (ventilated) 25.4cm, rear drum; pedal actuated parking brake to rear wheels; power assisted rack and pinion steering; fuel tank capacity 72 or 64L (15.8 or 14.1Gal) [19 or 17US Gal]; tyres 205/70 R 15 or 215/70 R 15, wheel rims 6 or 6.5".

Dimensions: Wheelbase 287cm, track 156/153cm, clearance 14cm, turning circle 12m. Load space 14.7cu ft (415dm3). length 505cm, width 185cm, height 134cm.

Performance: Max speed approx 112mph/180kmh, speed at 1000rpm in OD 34.8mph/56kmh; power to weight ratio from 15.4kg/kW (11.3kg/PS); consumption (touring) approx 10–16L/100km (28.2-17.7mpg) [23.5-14.7US mpg].

Ford Thunderbird

3.8 Litre V6
157kW - 210hp - 213PS
Compressor/Fuel Injection

Engine for Super Coupe

As 140hp, except:

Weight: Kerbweight from 1680kg.

Engine data (SAE net): 6–cylinder in V90 deg (96.52 x 86.36mm), 3791cm3; compression ratio 8.2:1; 157kW (210hp) [213PS] at 4000rpm, 41.4kW/L (55.5hp/L) [56.3PS/L]; 427Nm (315lbft) at 2600rpm; premium grade.

Engine construction: Roots (Eaton) mechanical compressor, max charge-air pressure 0.8bar; charge-air cooler. Motorcraft AWSF–34P spark plugs; 12V 58/72/75Ah battery, 110A alternator; cooling system capacity 12L (11.4US qt).

Transmission: a) 5–speed manual, final drive ratio 2.73.
b) Automatic "Automatic Overdrive", hydraulic torque converter and 4–speed Planetary gear set, final drive ratio 3.08 or 3.27.

Gear ratios: a) 5–speed manual: 1st 3.75; 2nd 2.32; 3rd 1.43; 4th 1; 5th 0.75; R 3.26; b) Automatic "Automatic Overdrive", max torque multiplication 2.3 times; Planetary gear set ratios 2.40; 1.47; 1; 0.67; R 2.

Chassis: Servo/power assisted brakes with ABS (Teves), front disc diameter (ventilated) 27.5cm, rear 25.5cm; tyres 225/60 VR 16, wheel rims 7".

Ford Thunderbird Super Coupe

Performance: Max speed over 137mph/220kmh, speed at 1000rpm in 5th gear 37.3mph/60.1km/h; acceleration 0–60mph/97km/h 7.5secs, automatic 8secs; power to weight ratio from 10.7kg/kW (7.9kg/PS); consumption approx 10–18L/100km (28.2-15.7mpg) [23.5-13.1US mpg].

Ford Aerostar Wagon

Large capacity Saloon/Sedan with 5 to 7–seats, 3 side–doors and tail gate, 3 Litre V6 Engine, 5–speed manual or automatic. 1989: lengthened version.

Ford Aerostar Wagon

3 Litre V6
108kW–145hp–147PS
Fuel Injection

Body, Weight: 3–door Wagon with tailgate, 5–7-seater; kerbweight approx 1520/1590kg.

Engine data (SAE net): 6–cylinder in V 60deg (88.9 x 80mm), 2979cm3; compression ratio 9.3:1; 108kW (145hp) [147PS] at 4800rpm, 36.3kW/L (48.6hp/L) [49.3PS/L]; 224Nm (165.3lbft) at 3600rpm; unleaded regular grade.

Engine construction: Hydraulic tappets; central camshaft (chain); 4 main bearing crankshaft; oil capacity 3.8L (3.6US qt); electronic fuel injection. Motorcraft ASF–32C sparkplugs; 12V 72Ah Battery; 60A alternator; cooling system capacity approx 9.5L (9.0 US qt).

Transmission (to rear wheels): a) 5–speed manual, final drive ratio 3.08.
b) Automatic, "Automatic Overdrive", hydraulic torque converter and 4–speed Planetary gear set, selector lever at steering column with positions P–R–N–D–D–1; final drive ratio 3.37. Limited slip differential.

Gear ratios: a) 5–speed manual: 1st 3.72; 2nd 2.20; 3rd 1.50; 4th 1; 5th 0.79; R 3.42.
b) Automatic, " Automatic Overdrive", max torque multiplication in converter 2.53 times; Planetary gear set ratios: 2.47; 1.47; 1; 0.75; R 2.

Chassis: Box section frame with cross members, front coil springs, upper and lower keystone A arm, antiroll bar; rear rigid axle with coil springs, lower trailing arms, upper semi–trailing arm, optional rear antiroll bar, telescopic dampers. Servo/power assisted brakes, front discs (ventilated), rear drums, pedal actuated parking brakes to rear wheels; power assisted rack and pinion steering; fuel tank capacity 64L (14.1Gal) [16.9US Gal], also available with 79L (17.4Gal) [21US Gal]; tyres 185/75 R 14, 205/75 R 14, 215/70 R 14, wheel rims 6, optionally 6.5J.

Ford Aerostar Wagon "extended"

Dimensions: Wheelbase 302cm, track 156/152.5cm, clearance 18cm, turning circle 12.9m. Load capacity max 140.2cu ft (3970dm3). Length 444cm, width 182cm, height 185cm.
"Extended": Length 483cm, width 183cm.

Ford USA

Performance: Max speed approx 99.4–105.7mph/160–170kmh, speed at 1000rpm in OD 27.3mph/44.0kmh; power to weight ratio from 14.1kg/kW (10.3kg/PS); consumption (touring) approx 11–16L/100km (25.7– 17.7mpg) [21.4–14.7US mpg].

Ford Bronco II

Compact, all terrain vehicle with European 2.8 Litre V6 Engine. Launched in January 1983. For 1985 also available with 2.3 Litre Turbo diesel. 1986: 2.9 Litre V6 Engine; also available without four wheel drive. 1989 modifications to details of the body and the interior.

Body, Weight: 3–door Estate/Station Wagon, 4–5 seater; kerbweight approx 1435kg.

2.9 Litre V6
104kW–140hp–142PS
Fuel Injection

Engine data (SAE net): 6–cylinder in V 60deg (93 x 72mm), 2935cm3; compression ratio 9:1; 104kW (140hp) [142PS] at 4600rpm, 35.6kW/L (48hp/L) [48.4PS/L]; 231Nm (170.4lbft) at 2600rpm; unleaded regular grade.

Engine construction: Central camshaft (toothed belt); 4 main bearing crankshaft; oil capacity approx 4.7L (4.4US qt); electronic fuel injection. Motorcraft spark plugs; 12V 72Ah Battery, 60A alternator; cooling system capacity approx 10L (9.5US qt).

Transmission (to rear wheels or all wheels): Connected to all wheels, optional front and rear limited slip differentials, cross country reduction 2.48.
a) 5–speed manual, final drive ratio 3.45, 3.73.
b) Automatic; "Automatic Overdrive", hydraulic torque converter and 4–speed Planetary gear set, selector lever at steering column with Positions P–R–N–D–D–1; final drive ratio 3.45; 3.73.

Gear ratios: a) 5–speed manual: 1st 3.72; 2nd 2.20; 3rd 1.50; 4th 1; 5th 0.79; R 3.42 or 1st 3.77; 2nd 2.21; 3rd 1.52; 4t 1; 5th 0.81; R 3.40.
b) Automatic; "Automatic Overdrive", Max torque multiplication in converter 2.53 times; Planetary gear set ratios; 2.47; 1.47; 1; 0.75; R 2.1.

Chassis: Box section frame with cross members; front independent suspension with two crossed axle beams, coil springs and antiroll bar; rear rigid axle with leaf springs and antiroll bar, telescopic dampers. Servo/power assisted brakes, front discs (ventilated), diameter 27.6cm, rear drums, pedal actuated parking brake to rear wheels; power assisted recirculating ball steering; fuel tank capacity 87L (19.1Gal) [23US Gal]; tyres 205/75 R 15, wheel rims 6".

Dimensions: Wheelbase 239cm, track 144.5/144.5cm, clearance approx 20cm, turning circle approx 11.5m, load space 25.6/44.7/63.7cu ft (725/1265/1805dm3). Length 411cm, width 173cm. Height 174cm.

Performance: Max speed approx 99mph/160kmh; power to weight ratio from 14.3kg/kW (10.5kg/PS); consumption (touring) approx 12–19L/100km (23.5–14.9mpg) [19.6–12.4US mpg].

Ford Bronco II

Ford Bronco

Cross country vehicle from Ford; 6–cylinder, or V8 engine; for 1987, six cylinder engine with injection.

Body, Weight: 3–door Estate/Station Wagon, 2–6 seater; kerbweight Standard model approx 1985kg; gross vehicle weight to 2635– 2835kg.

4.9 Litre 6–cylinder
108kW–145hp–147PS
Fuel Injection

Engine data (SAE net): 6–cylinder in–line (101.6 x 101.09mm), 4917cm3; compression ratio 8.8:1; 108kW (145hp) [147PS] at 3400rpm, 22.0kW/L (29.5hp/L) [29.9PS/L]; 360Nm (265.7lbft) at 2000rpm; regular grade.

Engine construction: Hydraulic tappets, side camshaft (chain); 7 main bearing crankshaft; oil capacity 4.7L (4.4US qt); electronic fuel injection. Motorcraft AWSF–42 spark plugs; 12V 45/71Ah Battery, 60A alternator; cooling system capacity approx 13L (12.3US qt).

Transmission (to all wheels): a) 4–speed manual, final drive ratio 3 or 3.5; optional limited slip differentials; four wheel drive; reduction 1.96.
b) Automatic "Cruise–O–Matic" C6, hydraulic torque converter and 3–speed Planetary gear set, central selector lever with Positions P–R–N–D–L2–L1; final drive ratio 3 or 3.5; connected to all wheel drive; reduction 2.
c) Automatic "Automatic Overdrive", hydraulic torque converter and 4–speed Planetary gear set, selector lever at steering column with Positions P–R–N–D–3–1; final drive ratio 3.08; 3.42; 3.55.

Gear ratios: a) 4–speed manual: 1st 6.32; 2nd 3.09; 3rd 1.69; 4th 1; R 7.44.
b) 5-speed manual: 1st 3.9; 2nd 2.25; 3rd 1.49; 4th 1; 5th 0.8; R3.41.
c) Automatic: Max torque multiplication in converter 2.14 times, Planetary gear set ratios: 2.46; 1.46; 1; R 2.18.
d) Automatic " Automatic Overdrive"; max torque mulitplication in converter 2.29 times; Planetary gear set ratios: 2.40; 1.46; 1; 0.67; R 2.

Chassis: Box section frame with cross members; front independent suspension with 2 crossed axle beams, coil springs and antiroll bar; rear rigid axle with leaf springs, optional antiroll bar, front and rear telescopic dampers. Servo/power assisted brakes, front discs, diameter 29.6cm, rear drums, pedal actuated parking brake to rear wheels; power assisted recirculating ball steering; fuel tank capacity 95L (20.9Gal) [25.1UA Gal], optional 121L (27Gal) [32US Gal]; tyres 235/75–15 or L 78–15, wheel rims 5.5", optional LR 78–15.

Dimensions: Wheelbase 266cm, track 165.5cm, clearance 20cm, turning circle 11.4m. Length 451cm, width 196cm, height 186cm.

Performance: Max speed approx 87mph/140kmh; power to weight ratio from 18.4kg/kW (13.5kg/PS); consumption (touring) approx 14-20L/100km (20.2-14.1mpg) [16.8–11.8US Gal].

Ford Bronco

4.9 Litre V8
138.5kW–185hp–188PS
Fuel Injection

As 145hp, except:

Weight: 4.9 Litre V8 Engine heavier by 48kg.

Ford USA • Ford EUR

Engine data (SAE net): 8-cylinder in V 90deg (101.6 x 76.2mm), 4942cm3; compression ratio 9:1; 138.5kW (185hp) [188PS] at 3800rpm, 27.9kW/L (37.4hp/L) [38.0PS/L]; 366Nm (270.1lbft) at 2400rpm.

Engine construction: Central camshaft; 5 main bearing crankshaft; electronic fuel injection, cooling system capacity 13.8L (13.1US qt).

Transmission: a) 4-speed manual, final drive ratio 3.45; 3.73.
b) Automatic "Automatic Overdrive", hydraulic torque converter and Planetary gear set, selector lever at steering column with Positions P-R-N-D-D-1; final drive ratio 3.45; 3.73.

Performance: Max speed approx 96-102mph/155-165kmh; power to weight ratio from 14.7kg/kW (10.8kg/PS); consumption approx 13-20L/100km (21.7-14.1mpg) [18.1-11.8US mpg].

Ford Bronco

```
5.8 Litre V8
157kW-210hp-213PS
1 4V Carb
```

As 145hp, except:
Weight: 5.8 Litre V8 engine heavier by 65kg.
Engine data (SAE net): 8-cylinder in V 90deg (101.6 x 88.9mm), 5766cm3; compression ratio 8.8:1; 157kW (210hp) [213PS] at 3800rpm, 27.2kW/L (36.4hp/L) [36.9PS/L]; 427Nm (315.1lbft) at 2800rpm.

Engine construction: Central camshaft; 5 main bearing crankshaft; 1 Ford downdraught four barrel carb; cooling system capacity 15L (14.2US qt).

Transmission: Automatic "Cruise-O-Matic", hydraulic torque converter and 3-speed Planetary gear set, selector lever at steering column, optional at central console with Positions P-R-N-D-2-1; final drive ratio 3.45.

Performance: Max speed approx 103-109mph/165-175kmh; power to weight ratio from 12.6kg/kW (9.3kg/PS); consumption approx 15-25L/100km (18.8-11.3mpg) [15.7-9.4US mpg].

FORD   EUR

Ford Werke AG, 5 Koln 21, Deutschland
Ford Motor Co Ltd, Brentwood, Essex CM 13 3BW, England.

European Automobile Manufacturer, affiliated to Ford Motor Company Inc USA.

MODEL RANGE
Fiesta – Escort – Orion – Sierra – Scorpio

Ford Fiesta

C – CL – CLX - S – Ghia – XR2i – Popular – Popular Plus – L – Ghia – 1.4S – XR2i

Compact Saloon/Sedan with transverse engine, front wheel drive and tailgate. Launched June 1976. 1989 Geneva: Series totally remodelled, dimensions enlarged, 3 + 5 doors, new generation of engine, modernised suspension and new interior. By Summer 1989 a sporty model XR2i and by the end of the year a Turbo version.

```
1 Litre
33kW-44hp-45PS
1V Carb
```

Body, Weight: 3-door Saloon/Sedan, 5-seater; kerbweight (DIN) from 770kg, gross vehicle weight approx 1200kg.

Engine data (DIN): 4-cylinder in-line (68.7 x 67.5mm), 1001cm3; compression ratio 9.5:1, 33kW (44hp) [45PS] at 5000rpm, 33kW/L (44.2hp/L) [45PS/L]; 74Nm (54.6lbft) at 3000rpm; leaded regular grade.

Engine construction: Designated HCS. Front transverse engine. Side camshaft (chain); 3 main bearing crankshaft; oil capacity 3.25L (3.1US qt); 1 Weber downdraught carb. 12V 27/35Ah Battery, 28/55A alternator; cooling system capacity approx 5.4L (5.1US qt).

Transmission (to front wheels): 4-speed manual, final drive ratio 4.06.

Gear ratios: 4-speed manual: 1st 3.583; 2nd 2.043; 3rd 1.32; 4th 0.951; R 3.769.

Chassis: Integral body; front McPherson struts (coil springs and coaxial telescopic dampers), lower A arm (negative steering offset) and longitudinal struts, rear rigid axle with trailing arms, Panhard rod, coil springs, telescopic dampers. Servo/power assisted brakes, optional ABS, front disc diameter 24cm (with ABS ventilated);rear drums; mechanical handbrake to rear wheels; rack and pinion steering; fuel tank capacity 42L (9.2Gal) [11.1US Gal], tyres 135SR, wheel rims 4.5 or 5J.

Dimensions: Wheelbase 244.5cm, track 139/138.5cm, clearance 14cm, turning circle 9.8m, load space (VDA) 8.8-32.8cu ft (250-930dm3). Length 374cm, width 161cm, height 132.5cm.

Performance: Max speed 86mph/139kmh (manufacturers test specifications), speed at 1000rpm in 4th gear 15.4mph/24.7kmh, acceleration 0 – 62mph/100kmh 20.2secs. Power to weight ratio 23.3kg/kW (17.1kg/PS); consumption (ECE) 4.6/6.5/6.1L/100km (61.4/43/546/3mpg) [51.1/36.2/38.6US mpg].

Ford Fiesta C

```
1.1 Litre
40/37kW-54/49hp-55/50PS
1 2V Carb
```

As 1.0, except:
Weight: Kerbweight (DIN) from 785kg, gross vehicle weight 1210kg.

Engine data (DIN): 4-cylinder in-line (68.7 x 75.5mm), 1119cm3; compression ratio 9.5:1, 40kW (54hp) [55PS] at 5200rpm, 35.7kW/L (47.8hp/L) [48.5PS/L]; 86Nm (63.5lbft) at 2700rpm.
Also: 40kW (53hp) [54PS].
With Catalyst (5-speed): Compression ratio 8.8:1; 37kW (49hp) [50PS] at 52000rpm, 33.2kW/L (44.5hp/L) [44.7PS/L]; 83Nm (61.3lbft) at 3000rpm.

Engine construction: 1 twin barrel carb.

Transmission: a) 4-speed manual, final drive ratio 4.06.
b) 5-speed manual, final drive ratio 4.06.
c) Continuous Automatic CTX, central selector lever, final drive ratio 3.84.

Gear ratios: a) 4-speed manual: 1st 3.583; 2nd 2.043; 3rd 1.32; 4th 0.951; R 3.769.
b) 5-speed manual: 1st 3.583; 2nd 2.043; 3rd 1.32; 4th 0.951; 5th 0.756l R 3.615.
c) Variable continuous automatic between 3.84 and 0.66; R 4.26.

Chassis: S; Rear antiroll bar; Tyres 145 SR 13, 155/70 SR 13 or 165/65 SR 13.

Performance: Max speed 93mph/149kmh (manufacturers test specifications), speed at 1000rpm in 4th gear 16.7mph/26.8kmh, in 5th gear 20.8mph/33.5kmh; acceleration 0 – 62mph/100kmh 16.3secs; power to weight ratio from 19.6kg/kW (14.3kg/PS); consumption (ECE) 4.6/6.6/6.1L/100km (57.6/41.5/45.6mpg) [48.0/34.6/37.9US mpg], 5- speed manual 4.3/6.1/6.1L/100km (65.7/46.3/46.3mpg) [54.7/38.6/38.6US mpg].
With CTX: Max speed 88mph/142kmh; acceleration 0 – 62mph/100kmh 18secs; consumption ECE 4.5/6.9/6.6L/100km (62.8/40.9/42.8mpg) [52.3/34.1/35.6US mpg].
With Catalyst: Max speed 89mph/143kmh; acceleration 0 – 62mph/100kmh 18.1secs; consumption ECE 4.7/6.5/6.8L/100km (60.1/43.5/51.5mpg) [50/36.2/34.6US mpg].

Ford EUR

Ford Fiesta CLX

1.4 Litre
55/54/52kW–74/72/70hp–75/73/71PS
1 2V Carb/Fuel Injection

As 1.0, except:

Weight: Kerbweight (DIN) from 815kg, gross vehicle weight 1280kg.

Engine data (DIN): 4–cylinder in–line (77.2 x 74.3mm), 1391cm3; compression ratio 9.5:1; 55kW (74hp) [75PS] at 5600rpm, 39.5kW/L (52.9hp/L) [53.9PS/L]; 109Nm (80.4lbft) at 4000rpm; leaded premium grade.
Also: 54kW (72hp) [73PS].
With Catalyst: Compression ratio 8.5:1; 52kW (70hp) [71PS] at 5500rpm, 37.4kW/L (50.1hp/L) [51S/L]; 103Nm (76lbft) at 4000rpm; unleaded regular/premium grade.

Engine construction: Designated CVH. Valves in V (45deg), hydraulic tappets, 1 overhead camshaft (toothed belt); light-alloy cylinder head; 5 bearing crankshaft; oil capacity 3.5L (3.3US qt); 1 Weber DFM downdraught 2V carb. Central/single point injection for Catalyst. 12V 43Ah Battery; cooling system capacity approx 7.5L (7.1US qt).

Transmission: a) 5–speed manual, final drive ratio 4.06, Catalyst 3.84.
b) Continuous Automatic CTX, final drive ratio 3.84.

Gear ratios: 1st 3.15; 2nd 1.91; 3rd 1.28; 4th 0.95; 5th 0.76; R 3.62.
With Catalyst: 1st 3.583; 2nd 2.043; 3rd 1.32; 4th 0.951; 5th 0.756; R 3.615.

Chassis: Rear antiroll bar; tyres 155/70 SR 13 or 165/65 SR 13.

Performance: Max speed 103mph/165kmh (manufacturers test specifications), speed at 1000rpm in 5th gear 20.8mph/33.5kmh; acceleration 0 – 62mph/100kmh in 12.2secs, power to weight ratio from 14.8kg/kW (10.9kg/PS); consumption ECE 5.2/6.7/8.6L/100km (54.3/42.2/32.8mpg) [45.2/35.1/27.4US mpg].
With CTX: Max speed 99mph/160kmh; acceleration 0 - 62mph/100kmh 12.6secs; consumption ECE 5.1/7.1/8.7L/100km (55.4/39.8/32.5mpg) [46.1/33.1/27US mpg].
With Catalyst: Max speed 101mph/162kmh; acceleration 0 – 62mph/100kmh 13secs; consumption ECE 5.6/7.3/8.8L/100km (50.4/38.7/32.1mpg) [42/32.2/26.7US mpg].

Ford Fiesta S

1.6 Litre
66kW–88hp–90PS
1 2V Carb

As 1.0, except:

Weight: Kerbweight (DIN) 840kg, gross vehicle weight 1270kg.

Engine data (DIN): 4-cylinder in–line (80 x 79.5mm), 1598cm3; compression ratio 9.5:1; 66kW (88hp) [90PS] at 5800rpm, 41.3kW/L (55.3hp/L) [56.3PS/L]; 133Nm (98.2lbft) at 4000rpm; leaded premium grade.

Engine construction: Designated CVH. Valves in V (45deg), hydraulic tappets, 1 overhead camshaft (toothed belt); light– alloy cylinder head; 5 bearing crankshaft; oil capacity 3.5L (3.3US qt); 1 Weber downdraught compound carb. 12V 43Ah Battery; cooling system capacity 8L (7.6US qt).

Transmission: 5–speed manual; final drive ratio 3.82.

Gear ratios: 1st 3.154; 2nd 1.913; 3rd 1.275; 4th 0.951; 5th 0.756; R 3.615.

Chassis: S: Front antiroll bar. Tyres 145 SR 13, 155/70 SR 13 or 165/65 SR 13.

Dimensions: Track 138.5/134cm; length 371cm, width 162cm.

Performance: Max speed 108mph/174kmh (manufacturers test specifications), speed at 1000rpm in 5th gear 22.1mph/35.6kmh; acceleration 0 – 62mph/100kmh 10.3secs; power to weight ratio 12.6kg/kW (9.3kg/PS); consumption ECE 5.4/7.0/8.8L/100km (52.3/40.4/32.1mpg) [43.6/33.6/26.7US mpg].

1.6 Litre EFI
81/76kW–109/102hp–110/104PS
Fuel Injection

Engine for XR2i

As 1.0, except:

Weight: Kerbweight (DIN) from 890kg, gross vehicle weight approx 13kg.

Engine data: 4-cylinder in-line (80 x 79.5mm), 1598cm3; compression ratio 9.75:1; 81kW (109hp) [110PS] at 6000rpm, 50.7kW/L (67.9hp/L) [68.8PS/L]; 138Nm (101.8lbft) at 2800rpm.
With Catalyst: 76kW (102hp) [104PS] at 6000rpm, 47.6kW/L (63.8hp/L) [65.1PS/L]; 135Nm (99.6lbft) at 2800rpm.

Engine construction: Designated CVH. Valves in V 45 deg, hydraulic valve tappets, 1 overhead camshaft (toothed belt); light-alloy cylinder head; 5 bearing crankshaft; oil capacity 3.5L (3.3US qt); mechanical/electronic fuel injection. 12V 43Ah; cooling system capacity, approx 8L (7.6US qt).

Transmission: 5-speed manual, final drive ratio 4.06.

Gear ratios: 1st 3.154; 2nd 1.913; 3rd 1.275; 4th 0.951; 5th 0.756; R 3.615.

Chassis: Front antiroll bar; tyres 185/60HR 13, wheel rims 5.5J.

Dimensions: Track 141/138cm. Length 380cm, width 163cm.

Performance: Max speed 119mph/192kmh (manufacturers test specifications), speed at 1000rpm in 5th gear 20.4mph/32.9mph; acceleration 0 - 62mph/100kmh 9.8secs; power to weight ratio from 11kg/kW (8.1kg/PS); consumption ECE 5.7/7.4/9.9L/100km (49.6/38.2/28.5mpg) [41.3/31.8/23.8US mpg].
With Catalyst: Max speed 116mph/187kmh; acceleration 0 - 62mph/100kmh 10.1secs; consumption 6.1/7.8/10.4L/100km (46.3/36.2/27.2mpg) [38.6/30.2/22.6US mpg].

Ford Fiesta CLX 1.8 D

Diesel 1.8 Litre
44kW–59hp–60PS
Injection Pump

Ford EUR

As 1.0, except:

Weight: Kerbweight (DIN) from 870kg, gross vehicle weight approx 1310kg.

Engine data (DIN): 4-cylinder in-line (82.5 x 82mm), 1753cm3; compression ratio 21.5:1; 44kW (59hp) [60PS] at 4800rpm, 25.1kW/L (33.6hp/L) [34.2PS/L]; 110Nm (81.2lbft) at 2500rpm.

Engine construction: Diesel engine Ford/KHD swirl chamber turbulence. Parallel valves, 1 overhead camshaft (toothed belt); 5 bearing crankshaft; oil capacity 5L (4.7US Gal), diesel injection pump. 12V 63Ah; cooling system capacity, approx 8.5L (8.0US qt).

Transmission: 5-speed manual, final drive ratio 3.59.

Gear ratios: 1st 3.15; 2nd 1.913; 3rd 1.275; 4th 0.951; 5th 0.756; R 3.615.

Chassis: Tyres 145 SR 13.

Performance: Max speed 95mph/152kmh (manufacturers test specifications), speed at 1000rpm in 5th gear 15.4mph/29.7kmh; acceleration 0 – 62mph/100kmh 16secs; power to weight ratio from 19.8kg/kW (14.5kg/PS); consumption ECE 4.0/5.6/5.8L/100km (70.6/50.4/48.7mpg) [58.8/42.0/40.6US mpg].

Ford Escort

C – CL – Ghia – XR3i – RS Turbo – Popular – L – GL – Ghia – XR3i – RS Turbo

Spacious model at the lower end of the mid class range with transverse engine and front wheel drive. Saloon/Sedan and Estate/Station Wagon, engine series from 1.1 to 1.6 litre displacement. Launched September 1980, XR3i (103hp) Paris 1982, 5-door Combi at Geneva 1983, convertible at Frankfurt 1981/83, RS Turbo Autumn 1984. January 1986: modifications to body and interior, new 1.4 Litre engine. Autumn 1986: RS Turbo engine, body and interior alterations.

Ford Escort GL

```
1.1 Litre
37kW–49hp–50PS
1 Carb
```

Body, weight; 3–door Saloon/Sedan, 5–seater; kerbweight (DIN) from 825kg, gross vehicle weight 1300kg. 5–door Saloon/Sedan, 5–seater; kerbweight (DIN) from 845kg, gross vehicle weight 1300kg. 2–door Convertible, 4/5–seater; kerbweight (DIN) 925kg, gross vehicle weight 1350kg. 5–door Estate/Station Wagon, 5–seater; kerbweight (DIN) from 870kg, gross vehicle weight approx 1375kg.

Engine data (DIN): 4-cylinder in-line (73.96 x 64.98mm), 1117cm3; compression ratio 9.5:1; 37kW (49hp) [50PS] at 5000rpm, 33.1kW/L (44.4hp/L) [44.8PS/L]; 83Nm (61.3lbft) at 2700rpm; leaded premium grade.

Engine construction: Front transverse engine; side camshaft (chain); 3 bearing crankshaft; oil capacity 3.25L (3.1US qt); 1 Ford Motorcraft VV carb. 12V 35/43Ah Battery; 45/55/70A alternator; cooling system capacity 6.7L (6.3US qt).

Transmission (to front wheels): 4 or 5-speed manual, final drive ratio 3.84 or 4.06 optional 4.29.

Gear ratios: a) 4-speed manual: 1st 3.58; 2nd 2.04; 3rd 1.32; 4th 0.95; R 3.77. b) 5-speed manual: 1st 3.58; 2nd 2.04; 3rd 1.32; 4th 0.95; 5th 0.76; R 3.77.

Chassis: Integral body; front McPherson struts (coil springs), lower single control arm and antiroll bar, rear independent suspension with shock absorber struts, control arm, longitudinal struts and coil springs, telescopic dampers. Servo/power assisted brakes, front discs, rear drums, disc diameter 23.9cm; optional mechanical Lucas/Girling ABS System; mechanical handbrake to rear wheels; rack and pinion steering; fuel tank capacity 48L (10.5Gal) [12.7US Gal]: tyres 145 SR 13, 155 SR 13 or 175/70 SR/HR 13, wheel rims 4.5 or 5J.

Dimensions: Wheelbase 240cm, track 140.5/142.5cm, clearance 14cm, turning circle 10.6m. Load space 12.7–36.4cu ft (360–1030), Estate/Station Wagon 12.7–42.4cu ft (360–1200dm3). Length 402/406cm, Estate/Station Wagon 408cm, width 164cm, height 137cm.

Performance: Max speed 90mph/145kmh (manufacturers test specifications), speed at 1000rpm in 4th gear (145 SR 13, 3.84:1) 17.7mph/28.4kmh in 5th gear 22.1mph/35.6kmh; acceleration 0 – 62mph/100kmh 18.2secs; power to weight ratio from 22.3kg/kW (16.5kg/PS); consumption (ECE) 5.1/6.9/7.5L/100km (55.4/40.9/37.7mpg) [46.1/34.1/31.4US mpg], 5-speed manual 4.7/6.5/7.5L/100km (60.1/43.5/37.7mpg) [50.0/36.2/31.4US mpg].

```
1.3 Litre
46/44kW–62/59hp–63/60PS
1 Carb
```

As 1.1 Litre, except:

Weight: Heavier by 15kg.

Engine data (DIN): 4-cylinder in-line (73.96 x 75.48mm), 1297cm3; compression ratio 9.5:1; 46kW (62hp) [63PS] at 5000rpm, 35.5kW/L (47.6hp/L) [48.6PS/L]; 101Nm (74.5lbft) at 3000rpm.
With 1V Carb: Compression ratio 9.3:1; 44kW (59hp) [60PS] at 5000rpm, 33.9kW/L (45.4hp/L) [46.3PS/L]; 97Nm (71.6lbft) at 3000rpm.

Engine construction: 5 bearing crankshaft. Cooling system capacity approx 7.6L (7.2US qt).

Transmission: 4 or 5-speed manual, final drive ratio 3.84.

Gear ratios: a) 4-speed manual: 1st 3.15; 2nd 1.91; 3rd 1.28; 4th 0.95; R 3.62. b) 5-speed manual: 1st 3.15; 2nd 1.91; 3rd 1.28; 4th 0.95; 5th 0.76; R 3.62.

Performance: Max speed 98mph/157kmh; speed at 1000rpm in 4th gear 17.6mph/28.3kmh, in 5th gear 22.1mph/35.6kmh; acceleration 0 – 62mph/100kmh 15.4secs; power to weight ratio from 18.3kg/kW (13.3kg/PS); consumption (ECE) 5.6/7.1/7.4L/100km (50.4/39.8/38.2mpg) [42/33.1/31.8US mpg], 5-speed manual 4.9/6.5/7.4L/100km (57.6/43.5/38.2mpg) [48.0/36.2/31.8US mpg], with 59hp 5.3/7.1/8.2L/100km (53.3/39.8/34.3mpg) [44.4/33.1/28.7US mpg].

```
1.4 Litre
55/54kW–74/72hp–75/73PS
1 2V Carb/Injection
```

As 1.1 Litre, except:

Weight: Heavier by approx 25kg.

Engine data (DIN): 4-cylinder in-line (77.24 x 74.3mm), 1392cm3; compression ratio 9.5:1; 55kW (74hp) [75PS] at 5600rpm, 39.5kW/L (52.9hp/L) [53.9PS/L]; 109Nm (146lbft) at 4000rpm.
With Catalyst: Compression ratio 8.5:1; 54kW (72hp) [73PS] at 5600rpm, 38.8kW/L (51.9hp/L) [52.4PS/L]; 103Nm (76lbft); unleaded premium grade.

Engine construction: Designated CVH. Valves in V (45deg), hydraulic tappets, 1 overhead camshaft (toothed belt); light- alloy cylinder heads; 5 main bearing crankshaft; oil capacity 3.5L (3.3US qt); 1 Weber DFM downdraught 2V carb. Central/single point injection for Catalyst. Cooling system capacity approx 7.6L (7.2US qt).

Ford Escort CL Station Wagon

Ford EUR

Transmission: 5-speed manual, final drive ratio 3.84.
Gear ratios: 1st 3.15; 2nd 1.91; 3rd 1.28; 4th 0.95; 5th 0.76; R 3.62.
With Catalyst: 1st 3.583; 2nd 2.043; 3rd 1.32; 4th 0.951; 5th 0.756; R 3.615.
Chassis: Front vetilated disc brakes; tyres 155 SR 13 or 175/70 SR 13, wheel rims 5J.
Performance: Max speed 103mph/165kmh, speed at 1000rpm in 4th gear 17.9mph/28.8kmh, in 5th gear 22.5mph/36.2kmh; acceleration 0 – 62mph/100kmh 12.7secs; power to weight ratio from 15.9kg/kW (11.7kg/PS); consumption (ECE) 4.9/6.4/8.1L/100km (57.6/44.1/34.9mpg) [48/36.8/29US mpg].
With Catalyst: Max speed 103mph/165kmh; acceleration 0 - 62mph/100kmh 13.3secs; consumption ECE 6.0/7.6/8.9L/100km (47.1/37.2/31.7mpg) [39.2/30.9/26.4US mpg].

```
1.6 Litre
66kW–88hp–90PS
1 2V Carb
```

As 1.1 Litre, except:
Weight: Heavier by approx 35kg.
Engine data (DIN): 4-cylinder in-line (79.96 x 79.52mm), 1598cm3; compression ratio 9.5:1; 66kW (88hp) [90PS] at 5800rpm, 41.3kW/L (55.3hp/L) [56.4PS/L]; 133Nm (98.2lbft) at 4000rpm.
Engine construction: Designated CVH. Valves in V (45deg), hydraulic tappets, 1 overhead camshaft (toothed belt); light- alloy cylinder head; 5 bearing crankshaft; oil capacity 3.5L (3.3US qt); 1 Weber DFM downdraught 2V carb. Cooling system capacity approx 7.8L (7.4US qt).
Transmission: a) 5-speed manual, final drive ratio 3.58.
b) Automatic, hydraulic torque converter and 3-speed Planetary gear set, central selector lever, final drive ratio 3.36, 3.31 or 3.58.
Gear ratios: a) 5-speed manual: 1st 3.15; 2nd 1.91; 3rd 1.28; 4th 0.95; 5th 0.76; R 3.62.
b) Automatic: Max torque multiplication in converter 2.35 times, Planetary gear set ratios: 1st 2.79; 2nd 1.61; 3rd 1; R 1.97.
Chassis: Disc brakes, front ventilated; tyres 155 SR 13 or 175/70 SR 13.
Performance: Max speed 111mph/179kmh, automatic 108mph/174kmh (manufacturers test specifications), speed at 1000rpm in 5th gear 24.2mph/38.8kmh; acceleration 0 – 62mph/100kmh 10.8secs, automatic 12.5secs; power to weight ratio from 13kg/kW (9.6kg/PS); consumption (ECE) 5.1/6.9/8.3L/100km (55.4/40.9/34.0mpg) [46.1/34.1/28.3US mpg]. Automatic 5.9/7.8/9.1L/100km (47.9/36.2/31.0mpg) [39.9/30.2/25.8US mpg].

Ford Escort XR3i

```
1.6 Litre
77/66kW–103/88hp–105/90PS
Fuel Injection
```

Engine for XR3i, Convertible i and 1.6i.
As 1.1 Litre, except:
Weight: Kerbweight (DIN) from approx 880kg, XR3i 945kg, Convertible 995kg, gross vehicle weight 1325/1400kg.
Engine data (DIN): 4-cylinder in-line (79.96 x 79.52mm), 1598cm3; compression ratio 9.5:1; 77kW (103hp) [105PS] at 6000rpm, 48.3kW/L (64.7hp/L) [65.7PS/L]; 138Nm (101.8lbft) at 4800rpm; leaded premium grade.
With Catalyst and KE Jetronic: Compression ratio 8.5:1; 66kW (88hp) [90PS] at 5800rpm, 41.3kW/L (55.3hp/L) [56.4PS/L]; 123Nm (90.8lbft) at 4600rpm; unleaded regular grade.
Engine construction: Designated CVH. Valves in V (45deg), hydraulic tappets, 1 overhead camshaft (toothed belt); light- alloy cylinder head; 5 bearing crankshaft; oil capacity 3.5L (3.3US qt); mechanical Bosch K/KE-Jetronic injection. 12V 43Ah Battery, 55/70A alternator; cooling system capacity approx 7.8L (7.4US qt).

Transmission: 5-speed manual, final drive ratio 4.27 Catalyst 3.82.
Gear ratios: 1st 3.15; 2nd 1.91; 3rd 1.28; 4th 0.95; 5th 0.76; R 3.62.
Chassis: Front ventilated disc brakes; Lucas/Girling ABS System; tyres (XR3i and Convertible i) 185/60 HR 14, wheel rims 6", optional 5.5"; tyres for 1.6i 555 SR 13, 175/70 SR 13 or 175/65 HR 14, wheel rims 5J.
Performance: Max speed 115mph/185kmh (manufacturers test specifications), speed at 1000rpm in 5th gear 20.3mph/32.6kmh, acceleration 0 – 62mph/100kmh 10.5secs; power to weight ratio 11.4kg/kW (8.4kg/PS); consumption ECE 6.2/7.6/10.2L/100km (45.6/37.2/27.7mpg) [37.9/30.9/23.1US mpg]. With Catalyst: Max speed 111mph/178kmh (manufacturers test specifications); acceleration 0 – 62mph/100kmh 11.5secs; consumption ECE 5.9/7.7/10.0L/100km (47.9/36.7/28.2mpg) [39.9/30.5/23.5US mpg].

Ford Escort XR3i Cabriolet

```
1.6 Litre
97kW–130hp–132PS
Fuel Injection/Turbo
```

Engine for RS Turbo
As 1.1 Litre, except:
Body, Weight: 3-door Saloon/Sedan; kerbweight (DIN) 965kg, gross vehicle weight 1400kg.
Engine data (DIN): 4-cylinder in-line (82.5 x 82mm), 1753cm3; compression ratio 22.1:1; 44kW (59hp) [60PS] at 4800rpm, 25.1kW/L (33.6hp/L) [34.2PS/L]; 110Nm (81.2lbft) at 2500rpm.
Engine construction: Designated CVH. Valves in V (45deg), hydraulic tappets, 1 overhead camshaft (toothed belt); light- alloy cylinder head; 5 bearing crankshaft; oil cooler, oil capacity 4L (3.8US qt); Bosch KE-Jetronic fuel injection; Garrett T3 exhaust turbocharger, max boost pressure 0.5bar, charge-air cooler. 12V 43Ah Battery, 55/70A alternator; cooling system capacity approx 8L (7.6US qt).
Transmission: 5-speed manual, final drive ratio 3.59 or 3.84.
Gear ratios: 1st 3.15; 2nd 1.91; 3rd 1.28; 4th 0.95; 5th 0.76; R 3.62.
Chassis: Lower single control arm and front longitudinal struts, antiroll bar front and rear; front ventilated disc brakes, diameter 26cm; Lucas/Girling ABS System; tyres 195/50 VR 15, wheel rims 6J.

Ford Escort RS Turbo

Dimensions: Track 142.5/144cm. Length 406cm, width 165cm, height 135cm.

Ford EUR

Performance: Max speed 94mph/151kmh (manufacturers test specifications), speed at 1000rpm in 5th gear 24.1mph/38.8kmh; acceleration 0 – 62mph/100kmh 16.8secs; power to weight ratio 20.7kg/kW (15.2kg/PS); consumption ECE 4.2/5.7/6.3L/100km (67.3/49.6/44.8mpg) [56/41.3/37.3US mpg].

```
1.8 Litre Diesel
44kW–59hp–60PS
Injection Pump
```

As 1.1 Litre, except:

Weight: Heavier by 85kg.

Engine data (DIN): 4–cylinder in–line (80 x 80mm), 1753cm3; compression ratio 21.5:1; 44kW (59hp) [60PS] at 4800rpm, 25.1kW/L (33.6hp/L) [34.2PS/L]; 110Nm (81.2lbft) at 2500rpm.

Engine construction: Ford/KHD diesel engine swirl chamber. 1 overhead camshaft (toothed wheels/toothed belt); 5 bearing crankshaft; oil capacity 5L (4.7US qt); diesel injection pump. 12V 63/66Ah Battery; cooling system capacity 9.3L (8.8US qt).

Transmission: 5–speed manual, final drive ratio 3.59 0r 3.84.

Gear ratios: 1st 3.58; 2nd 1.91; 3rd 1.28; 4th 0.95; 5th 0.76; R 3.77.

Chassis: Tyres 155 SR 13 or 175/70 SR 13, wheel rims 5J.

Performance: Max speed 94mph/151kmh (manufacturers test specifications), speed at 1000rpm in 5th gear 24mph/38.8kmh; acceleration 0 – 62mph/100kmh 18.9secs; power to weight ratio from 20.7kg/kW (15.2kg/PS); consumption (ECE) 4.2/5.7/6.3L/100kmh (67.3/49.6/44.8mpg) [56/42/37.3US mpg].

Ford Orion

L – CL/GL – Ghia – Ghia Injection

Vehicle of lower mid–class, with notchback, based on the Ford Escort 1.3 and 1.6 Litre engines and 1.6 Litre diesel engine. Launched in July 1983. January 1986: modifications to body and interior.

```
1.3 Litre
46kW–62hp–63PS
1 Carb
```

Body, Weight: 4–door Saloon/Sedan, 5–seater; kerbweight (DIN) 875kg, gross vehicle weight 1325kg.

Engine data (DIN): 4–cylinder in–line (73.96 x 75.48mm), 1297cm3; compression ratio 9.5:1; 46kW (62hp) [63PS] at 5000rpm, 35.5kW/L (47.6hp/L) [48.6PS/L]; 101Nm (74.5lbft) at 3000rpm.

Engine construction: Transverse front engine; side camshaft (chain); 5 bearing crankshaft; oil capacity 3.25L (3.1US qt); 1 Ford–Motorcraft VV Carb. 12V 35 or 43Ah battery; 45/55/70A alternator; cooling system capacity 6.7/7.6L (6.3/7.2US qt).

Transmission (to front wheels): 5–speed manual, final drive ratio 3.84.

Gear ratios: Integral body; front McPherson struts (coil springs), lower single control arm and antiroll bar, rear independent suspension with shock absorber struts, control arm, longitudinal struts and coil springs, telescopic dampers. Servo/power assisted brakes, front discs, rear drums, disc diameter 23.9cm, mechanical handbrake to rear wheels; rack and pinion steering; fuel tank capacity 48L (10.5Gal) [12.7US Gal]; tyres 155 SR 13 or 175/70 SR 13, wheel rims 4.5 or 5J.

Dimensions: Wheelbase 240cm, track 140.5/142.5cm, clearance 14cm, turning circle 10.6m. Load 15.9cu ft (450dm3) (VDA). Length 421.5cm, width 164cm, height 139.5cm.

Performance: Max speed 98mph/157kmh (manufacturers test specifications), speed at 1000rpm in 4th gear 17.6mph/28.3kmh, in 5th gear 22.1mph/35.6kmh; acceleration 0 – 62mph/100kmh 15.8secs; power to weight ratio 19.9kg/kW (13.9kg/PS); consumption ECE 4.5/6.2/6.4L/100km (62.8/45.6/44.1mpg) [52.3/37.9/36.8US mpg].

```
1.4 Litre
55/54kW–74/72hp–75/73PS
1 2V Carb
```

As 1.3 Litre, except:

Weight: Heavier by approx 5kg.

Engine data (DIN): 4–cylinder in–line (77.24 x 74.3mm), 1392cm3; compression ratio 9.5:1; 55kW (74hp) [75PS] at 5600rpm, 39.5kW/L (52.9hp/L) [53.9PS/L]; 109Nm (80.4lbft) at 4000rpm.
With Catalyst: Compression ratio 8.5:1; 54kW (72hp) [73PS] at 5600rpm, 38.8kW/L (52hp/L) [52.4PS/L]; 103Nm (76lbft) at 4000rpm; regular unleaded grade.

Engine construction: Designated CVH. Valves in V (45deg), hydraulic tappets, 1 overhead camshaft (toothed belt); light– alloy cylinder head; oil capacity 3.5L (3.3US qt); 1 Weber DFM downdraught 2V carb. Cooling system capacity approx 7.6L (7.2US qt).

Transmission: 5–speed manual, final drive ratio 3.84.

Gear ratios: 1st 3.58; 2nd 2.04; 3rd 1.32; 4th 0.95; 5th 0.76; R 3.77.

Chassis: Front ventilated disc brakes; tyres 155 SR 13 or 175/70 SR 13; 185/60 HR 14.

Performance: Max speed 103mph/165kmh, speed at 1000rpm in 4th gear 17.9mph/28.8kmh, in 5th gear 22.5mph/36.2kmh; acceleration 0 – 62mph/100kmh 13.2secs; power to weight ratio from 16kg/kW (11.7kg/PS); consumption (ECE) 4.7/6.1/8.1L/100km (60.1/46.3/34.9mpg) [50/38.6/29US mpg].

```
1.6 Litre
66kW–88hp–90PS
1 2V Carb
```

As 1.3 Litre, except:

Weight: Kerbweight (DIN) from 890kg, gross vehicle weight 1350kg.

Engine data (DIN): 4–cylinder in–line (79.96 x 79.52mm), 1598cm3; compression ratio 9.5:1; 66kW (88hp) [90PS] at 5800rpm, 41.3kW/L (55.3hp/L) [56.4PS/L]; 133Nm (98.1lbft) at 4000rpm.

Ford Orion 1.6i

Engine construction: Designated CVH. Valves in V (45deg), hydraulic tappets, 1 overhead camshaft (toothed belt); light– alloy cylinder head; oil capacity 3.5L (3.3US qt); 1 Weber DFM downdraught twin barrel carb. Cooling system capacity approx 7.8L (7.4US qt).

Ford Orion CL

Ford EUR

Transmission: a) 5–speed manual, final drive ratio 3.58.
b) Automatic, hydraulic torque converter and 3–speed Planetary gear set, central selector lever with Positions P–R–N–D–2–1; final drive ratio 3.31 or 3.26.

Gear ratios: a) 5–speed manual: 1st 3.15; 2nd 1.91; 3rd 1.28; 4th 0.95; 5th 0.76; R 3.62.
b) Automatic; Max torque multiplication in converter 2.35 times, Planetary gear set ratios: 1st 2.79; 2nd 1.61; 3rd 1; R 1.97.

Chassis: Front ventilated disc brakes; tyres 155 SR 13 or 175/70 SR 13; 185/60 HR 14.

Performance: Max speed 111mph/179kmh, automatic 108mph/174kmh (manufacturers test specifications), speed at 1000rpm in 5th gear 24.1mph/38.8kmh; acceleration 0 – 62mph/100kmh 11secs, automatic 12.8secs; power to weight ratio from 13.5kg/kW (9.9kg/PS); consumption (ECE) 5.2/6.7/8.3L/100km (54.3/42.2/34.0mpg) [45.2/35.1/28.3US mpg], Automatic 5.7/7.5/9.1L/100km (49.6/37.7/31.0mpg) [41.3/31.4/25.8US mpg].

```
1.6 Litre
77/66kW/103/88hp–105/90PS
Fuel Injection
```

As 1.3 Litre, except:

Weight: Kerbweight (DIN) from approx 920kg, gross vehicle weight 1375kg.

Engine data (DIN): (79.96 x 79.52mm), 1598cm3; compression ratio 9.5:1; 77kW (105PS) at 6000rpm, 48.3kW/L (64.7hp/L) [65.7PS/L]; 138Nm (101.8lbft) at 4800rpm; leaded premium grade.
With Catalyst and KE–Jetronic: Compression ratio 8.5:1; 66kW (88hp) [90PS] at 5800rpm, 41.3kW/L (54.3hp/L) [55.4PS/L]; 123Nm (90.8lbft) at 4600rpm.

Engine construction: Designated CVH. Valves in V (45deg), hydraulic tappets, 1 overhead camshaft (toothed belt); light– alloy cylinder head; oil capacity 3.5L (3.3US qt); Bosch K/KE– Jetronic mechanical injection. 12V 43Ah Battery, 55A alternator; cooling system capacity approx 7.8L (7.4US qt).

Transmission: 5–speed manual, final drive ratio 3.82.

Gear ratios: 1st 3.15; 2nd 1.91; 3rd 1.28; 4th 0.95; 5th 0.76; R 3.62.

Chassis: Front and rear antiroll bar; disc brakes, front ventilated; tyres 155 SR 13; 185/60 HR 14, wheel rims 5.5 or 6J.

Performance: Max speed 115mph/185kmh (manufacturers test specifications), speed at 1000rpm in 5th gear 22.6mph/36.4kmh; acceleration 0 – 62mph/100kmh 10.3secs; power to weight ratio 11.9kg/kW (8.8kg/PS); consumption ECE 5.5/7.2/10.0L/100km (51.4/39.2/28.2mpg) [42.8/32.7/23.5US mpg]. With Catalyst: Max speed 111mph/179kmh (manufacturers test specifications), acceleration 0 – 62mph/100kmh 11.7secs; consumption ECE 5.8/7.6/10.0L/100km (48.7/37.2/28.2mpg) [40.6/30.9/23.5US mpg].

```
1.8 Litre Diesel
44kW–59hp–60PS
Injection Pump
```

As 1.3 Litre, except:

Weight: Kerbweight (DIN) 935kg, gross vehicle weight 1375kg.

Engine data (DIN): 4-cylinder in-line (82.5 x 82mm), 1753cm3; compression ratio 22:1; 44kW (59hp) [60PS] at 4800rpm, 25.1kW/L (33.6hp/L) [34.2PS/L]; 110Nm (81.2lbft) at 2500rpm.

Engine construction: Ford/KHD diesel engine swirl chamber. Parallel valves, mechanical tappets, 1 overhead camshaft (toothed wheel/toothed belt); 5 bearing crankshaft; oil capacity 5L (4.7US qt); diesel injection pump. 12V 63/66Ah Battery; cooling system capacity 9.3L (8.8US qt).

Transmission: 5–speed manual, final drive ratio 3.84.

Gear ratios: 1st 3.58; 2nd 1.91; 3rd 1.28; 4th 0.95; 5th 0.76; R 3.62.

Chassis: Tyres 155 SR 13 or 175/70 SR 13.

Performance: Max speed 94mph/151kmh (manufacturers test specifications), speed at 1000rpm in 5th gear 24.1mph/38.8kmh; acceleration 0 – 62mph/100kmh 16.8secs; power to weight ratio from 21.2kg/kW (15.6kg/PS); consumption (ECE) 4.1/5.5/6.3L/100km (68.9/51.4/44.8mpg) [57.4/42.8/37.3US mpg].

Ford Sierra

C – CL – GL – Ghia – S – XR 4x4

Saloon/Sedan – L – LX – GL – GLS – Ghia – XR4x4

Mid class aerodynamic vehicle with different engines, from 1.3 to 2.8/2.9 Litre displacement, four cylinder, or V6, Diesel from Peugeot, 4 and 5–speed manual or Automatic; rear independent suspension. Launched Autumn 1982, 3–door Saloon/Sedan, Autumn 1983. 1.8 Litre Autumn 1984, XR4x4 and 2.0 injection Spring 1985 (Geneva), Estate/Station Wagon 4x4 Geneva 1986. February 1987: also available as four–door Saloon/Sedan (GB: Sapphire); modifications to body.

```
1.6 Litre
55kW–74hp–75PS
1 2V Carb
```

Body, Weight: 3–door Saloon/Sedan, 5–seater; kerbweight (DIN) from 995kg, gross vehicle weight 1575kg; 4–door Saloon/Sedan, 5–seater; kerbweight (DIN) from 1025kg, gross vehicle weight 1575kg; 5–door Saloon/Sedan, 5–seater; kerbweight (DIN) 1035kg, gross vehicle weight 1575kg; 5–door Estate/Station Wagon, 5–seater; kerbweight (DIN) from 1065kg, gross vehicle weight 1600kg.

Engine data (DIN): 4-cylinder in-line (81.3 x 76.95mm), 1598cm3; compression ratio 9.5:1; 55kW (74hp) [75PS] at 4900rpm, 34.5kW/L (46.2hp/L) [46.9PS/L]; 123Nm (90.8lbft) at 2900rpm; leaded premium grade.

Engine construction: Valves in V 15deg, 1 overhead camshaft (toothed belt); 5 bearing crankshaft; oil capacity 3.75L (3.6US qt); 1 Weber downdraught compound carb. 12V 35/43/54Ah, Battery, 55A alternator; cooling system capacity 8L (7.6US qt).

Transmission (to rear wheels): a) 4–speed manual, final drive ratio 3.92 or 3.62.
b) 5–speed manual, final drive ratio 3.92 or 3.62.

Gear ratios: a) 4–speed manual: 1st 3.34; 2nd 1.99; 3rd 1.42; 4th 1; R 3.87. Or 1st 3.58; 2nd 2.01; 3rd 1.40; 4th 1; R 3.32. Or 1st 3.65; 2nd 1.97; 3rd 1.37; 4th 1; R 3.66.
b) 5–speed manual: 1st 3.65; 2nd 1.97; 3rd 1.37; 4th 1; 5th 0.82; R 3.66. Or 1st 3.89; 2nd 2.08; 3rd 1.34; 4th 1; 5th 0.82.

Chassis: Integral body; front and rear independent suspension, front McPherson struts, control arm and antiroll bar, rear semi– trailing arm, coil springs and telescopic dampers; Estate/Station Wagon with rear optional level control system. Servo/power assisted brakes, front discs (ventilated, except Saloon/Sedan 1.6), diameter 24cm, rear drums; optional ABS with four wheel disc brakes, mechanical handbrake to rear wheels; rack and pinion steering; fuel tank capacity 60L (13.2Gal) [15.9US Gal); tyres 165 SR/TR 13, 185/70 SR/TR 13 or 195/65 HR 14, wheel rims 5.5J, Estate/Station Wagon, tyres 175SR/TR 13.

Dimensions: Wheelbase 261cm, track 145/147cm, clearance approx 12cm, turning circle 10.6m. Load space 13.8–42.4cu ft (390– 1200dm3). Length 442.5cm, width 169.5/172cm, height 136cm. 4–door Saloon/Sedan: Load space 14.8cu ft (420dm3). Length 446.5cm, width 170cm. Estate/Station Wagon: Track 145/146cm. Load space 15.2/37.8/69.2cu ft (430/1070/1960dm3). Length 451cm, height 138.5cm.

Performance: Max speed 103-101mph/165-162kmh (manufacturers test specifications), speed at 1000rpm in 4th gear (3.62:1) 18.6mph/29.9kmh; acceleration 0 – 62mph/100kmh 14.2/14.7secs; power to weight ratio from 18.0kg/kW (13.3kg/PS); consumption ECE 6.1/7.7/8.9L/100km (46.3/36.7/31.7mpg) [46.3/36.7/31.7US mpg], 5– speed manual 5.5/7.1/8.9L/100km (51.4/39.8/31.7mpg) [38.6/30.9/26.4US mpg], Catalyst 5.7/7.4/8.9L/100km (49.6/38.2/31.7mpg) [49.6/31.8/26.4US mpg].

Ford Sierra GL

```
1.8 Litre
65/66kW–87/89hp–88/90hp
1 2V Carb
```

As 1.6 Litre, except:

Weight: Kerbweight (DIN) from 1045kg; gross vehicle weight 1600/1650kg.

Engine data (DIN): 4-cylinder in-line (86.2 x 76.95mm), 1796cm3; compression ratio 9.5:1; 65kW (87hp) [88PS] at 5400rpm, 36.2kW/L (48.5hp/L) [49.0PS/L]; 134Nm (98.9lbft) at 3500rpm.

Ford EUR

Without unregulated Catalyst: 1.8 Litre-CVH (80 x 88mm), 1769cm3; compression ratio 9.3:1; 66kW (89hp) [90PS] at 5250rpm; 147Nm (108.5lbft) at 3000rpm.

Engine construction: 1 Pierburg 2 E-3 downdraught compound carb. 43/54Ah Battery, optional 66Ah.

Transmission: a) 5-speed manual, final drive ratio 3.62, 3.92 or 3.38.
b) Automatic A4LD "Automatic 4-speed-Lock-up-Overdrive", hydraulic torque converter and Planetary gear set, selector lever at central console, final drive ratio 3.62.

Gear ratios: a) 5-speed manual: 1st 3.65; 2nd 1.97; 3rd 1.37; 4th 1; 5th 0.82; R 3.66.
Or 1st 3.89; 2nd 2.08; 3rd 1.34; 4th 1; 5th 0.83.
b) Automatic: Max torque multiplication in converter 2.1 times, Planetary gear set ratio: 1st 2.474; 2nd 1.474; 3rd 1; 4th 0.750; R 2.111.

Performance: Max speed 107mph/172kmh, automatic 106mph/170kmh (manufacturers test specifications), speed at 1000rpm in 4th gear 18.6mph/29.9kmh; acceleration 0 – 62mph/100kmh, 12.2secs, automatic 15secs; power to weight ratio from 15.8kg/kW (11.6kg/PS); consumption ECE 5.5/7.2/9.1L/100km (51.4/39.2/31mpg) [42.8/32.7/25.8US mpg], Automatic 5.9/7.7/9.2L/100km (47.9/36.7/30.7mpg) [39.9/30.5/25.6US mpg].

Ford Sierra Ghia

2.0 Litre
77/74kW–103/99hp–105/100PS
1 2V Carb

As 1.6 Litre, except:

Weight: Kerbweight (DIN) from 1055kg; gross vehicle weight 1650kg.

Engine data (DIN): 4-cylinder in-line (90.82 x 76.95mm), 1993cm3; compression ratio 9.2:1; 77kW (103hp) [105PS] at 5200rpm, 38.6kW/L (51.7hp/L) [52.7PS/L]; 157Nm (115.8lbft) at 4000rpm.
With unregulated Catalyst: 74kW (99hp) [100PS] at 5400rpm; 153Nm (112.9lbft) at 4000rpm.

Engine construction: 1 Weber downdraught 2V compound carb. 43/54Ah Battery.

Transmission: a) 5-speed manual, final drive ratio 3.62 or 3.38.
b) Automatic A4LD; "Automatic 4-speed-Lock-up-Overdrive", hydraulic torque converter and Planetary gear set, selector lever at central console, final drive ratio 3.38.

Gear ratios: a) 5-speed manual: 1st 3.65; 2nd 1.97; 3rd 1.37; 4th 1; 5th 0.82; R 3.66.
Or 1st 3.89; 2nd 2.08; 3rd 1.34; 4th 1; 5th 0.82; R 3.66.
b) Automatic: Max torque multiplication in converter 2.11 times, Planetary gear set ratios: 1st 2.474; 2nd 1.474; 3rd 1; 4th 0.750; R 2.111.

Chassis: Optional power assisted steering; TR/HR-tyres.

Ford Sierra GLS (Sapphire)

Performance: Max speed 113mph/182kmh, automatic 111mph/179kmh (manufacturers test specifications), speed at 1000rpm in 5th gear 22.7mph/36.6kmh; acceleration 0 – 62mph/100kmh 10.4secs, automatic 12.9secs; power to weight ratio from 13.7kg/kW (10kg/PS); consumption ECE 5.8/7.4/10.3L/100km (48.7/38.2/27.4mpg) [40.6/31.8/22.8US mpg], automatic 6.1/7.7/10.6L/100km (46.3/36.7/26.6mpg) [38.6/30.5/22.2US mpg].

With unregulated Catalyst and 5-speed manual: Max speed 111mph/178kmh, 0 – 62mph/100kmh 10.8secs; consumption ECE 6.2/8.0/11.3L/100km (45.6/35.3/25.0mpg) [37.9/29.4/20.8US mpg].

2.0 Litre
85/74kW–114/99hp–115/100PS
Fuel Injection

As 1.6 Litre, except:

Weight: Kerbweight (DIN) from 1060kg, gross vehicle weight 1650/1715kg.

Engine data (DIN): 4-cylinder in-line (90.82 x 76.95mm), 1993cm3; compression ratio 9.2:1; 85kW (114hp) [115PS] at 5500rpm, 42.6kW/L (57.1hp/L) [57.6PS/L]; 160Nm (118.1lbft) at 4000rpm.
With Catalyst: Compression ratio 8.5:1; 74kW (99hp) [100PS] at 5100rpm, 37.2kW/L (50hp/L) [50.7PS/L]; 148Nm (109.2lbft) at 4000rpm; unleaded regular grade.

Engine construction: Bosch L-Jetronic electronic fuel injection. 43/55Ah Battery, 55/70A alternator.

Transmission: a) 5-speed manual, final drive ratio 3.92 or 3.62 (Catalyst).
b) Automatic A4LD; "Automatic 4-speed-Lock-up-Overdrive", hydraulic torque converter and Planetary gear set, selector lever at central console, final drive ratio 3.62.

Gear ratios: a) 5-speed manual: 1st 3.65; 2nd 1.97; 3rd 1.37; 4th 1; 5th 0.82; R 3.66.
Or 1st 3.89; 2nd 2.08; 3rd 1.34; 4th 1; 5th 0.82; R 3.66.
b) Automatic: Max torque multiplication in converter 2.11 times, Planetary gear set ratios: 1st 2.474; 2nd 1.474; 3rd 1; 4th 0.750; R 2.111.

Chassis: Optional power assisted steering; tyres TR/HR "S" 195/60 HR 14.

Performance: Max speed 118mph/190kmh, automatic 114mph/184kmh (manufacturers test specifications), speed at 1000rpm in 5th gear 20.9–22.7mph/33.7–36.6kmh; acceleration 0 – 62mph/100kmh 9.9secs; automatic 12secs; power to weight ratio from 12.6kg/kW (9.2kg/PS); consumption ECE 6.5/8.4/10.8L/100km (43.5/33.6/26.2mpg) [36.2/28.0/21.8US mpg], automatic 5.8/7.5/10.8L/100km (48.7/37.7/26.2mpg) [40.6/31.4/21.8US mpg]. With Catalyst: Max speed 112mph/181kmh, automatic 111mph/178kmh; acceleration 0 – 62mph/100kmh 11.2secs, automatic 13.4secs; consumption ECE 6.0/7.8/11.8L/100km (47.1/36.2/23.9mpg) [39.2/30.2/19.9US mpg], automatic 7.0/8.9/12.0L/100km (40.4/31.723.5mpg) [33.6/26.4/19.6US mpg].

Ford Sierra Wagon/Turnier 4x4

2.9 Litre V6
110.5/106.5kW–148/143hp–150/145PS
Fuel Injection

Engine for XR4x4 and Estate/Station Wagon 4x4, in some countries, also GL and Ghia.

As 1.6 Litre, except:

Weight: Kerbweight (DIN) from 1270kg, gross vehicle weight 1775kg.

Engine data (DIN): 6-cylinder in V 60deg (93 x 72mm), 2935cm3; compression ratio 9.5:1; 110.5kW (148hp) [150PS] at 5700rpm, 37.6kW/L (50.4hp/L) [51.1PS/L]; 233Nm (172lbft) at 3000rpm.
With Catalyst: Compression ratio 9:1; 106.5kW (143hp) [145PS] at 5500rpm, 36.3kW/L (48.6hp/L) [49.4PS/L]; 222Nm (163.7lbft) at 3000rpm; unleaded regular grade.

Engine construction: Central camshaft (chain); 4 main bearing crankshaft; oil capacity 4.25L (4.1US qt); Bosch K- Jetronic or LE Jetronic fuel injection. 12V 44/55 Battery optional 66Ah, 70A alternator; cooling system capacity 8.5L (8.0US qt).

Transmission: a) 5–speed manual, final drive ratio 3.36.
b) 5–speed manual for 4x4; Ferguson System 4 wheel drive with viscous couplings (power division: front 37/34%, rear 63/66%), final drive ratio 3.62.

Gear ratios: 1st 3.61; 2nd 2.08; 3rd 1.36; 4th 1; 5th 0.83; R 3.26.

Chassis: Front and rear antiroll bar; four wheel disc brakes (front ventilated), diameter front 26cm, rear 25.2cm; power assisted steering; tyres 195/60 VR 14, wheel rims 5.5J.

Dimensions: Track 147.5/148.5cm.

Performance: Max speed 127kmh/205kmh, Estate/Station Wagon 124mph/200kmh, speed at 1000rpm in 5th gear 22.4mph/36.1kmh; acceleration 0–62mph/100kmh 8.8secs, Estate/Station Wagon 9.2secs; power to weight ratio 11.5kg/kW (8.5kg/PS); consumption ECE 7.5/9.3/15.5L/100km (37.7/30.4/18.2mpg) [31.4/25.3/15.2US mpg].

Ford Sierra XR 4x4

```
2.3 Litre Diesel
49kW–66hp–67PS
Injection Pump
```

As 1.6 Litre, except:

Weight: Kerbweight (DIN) from 1165kg; gross vehicle weight 1700/1775kg.

Engine data (DIN): 4–cylinder in–line (94 x 83mm), 2304cm3; compression ratio 22.2:1; 49kW (66hp) [67PS] at 4200rpm, 21.3kW/L (28.5hp/L) [29.1PS/L]; 139Nm (102.5lbft) at 2000rpm.

Engine construction: Designated LXD2. Cylinder block inclined 20deg to right. Side camshaft (chain), light–alloy cylinder heads; oil capacity 5.6L (4.7US qt); Bosch EP/VAC injection pump. 12V 68/88Ah Battery; 70/55A alternator; cooling system capacity 9.5L (9.5US qt).

Transmission: 5–speed manual, final drive ratio 3.14 or 3.38.

Gear ratios: 1st 3.91; 2nd 2.32; 3rd 1.40; 4th 1; 5th 0.82; R 3.66.

Chassis: Optional power assisted steering.

Performance: Max speed 95–96mph/153–155kmh (manufacturers test specifications), speed at 1000rpm in 5th gear 26.2–24.4mph/42.2–39.2kmh; acceleration 0–62mph/100kmh 19.1secs; power to weight ratio from 23.8kg/kW (17.4kg/PS); consumption ECE 4.9/6.5/8.6L/100km (57.6/43.5/32.8mpg) [48.0/36.2/27.4USmpg].

Ford Sierra Cosworth

Ford Sierra Cosworth

Sporty export version with 2 Litre Cosworth engine, exhaust turbocharger, 201hp. Launched as a 3–door Saloon/Sedan in Frankfurt in 1985; limited production for the motor racing homologation, Group A (5000 vehicles). July 1987; evolution version badged as the RS 500. January 1988; New version based on the Saloon/Sedan with boot/trunk, Catalyst version under preparation.

```
2000 DOHC
150kW–201hp–204PS
Turbo/Fuel Injection
```

As Sierra, 1.6 Litre, except:

Body, Weight: 4–door Saloon/Sedan, 5–seater; kerbweight (DIN) 1250/1230kg, gross vehicle weight 1700kg.

Engine data (DIN): 4–cylinder in–line (90.8 x 77.0mm), 1994cm3; compression ratio 8:1; 150kW (201hp) [204PS] at 6000rpm, 75.2kW/L (100.8hp/L) [102.3PS/L]; 276Nm (203.8lbft) at 4500rpm; leaded premium grade.

Engine construction: Valves in V 45deg (4 per cylinder), hydraulic tappets; 2 overhead camshafts (toothed belt); light– alloy cylinder head; oil cooler; Weber Marelli electronic fuel injection; 1 Garrett TO3 B exhaust turbocharger, max boost pressure approx 0.55bar, charge-air cooler. Battery 12V 43 Ah, Alternator 90A.

Transmission: 5–speed manual, final drive ratio 3.64; limited slip differential (viscous coupling).

Gear ratios: 1st 2.952; 2nd 1.937; 3rd 1.336; 4th 1; 5th 0.804; R 2.755.

Chassis: Integral body; front and rear independent suspension, front McPherson struts, control arm and antiroll bar, coil springs and telescopic dampers. Servo/power assisted disc brakes (front ventilated), diameter front 28.3cm, rear 27.2cm, ABS (Teves) mechanical handbrake to rear wheels; power assisted rack and pinion steering; fuel tank capacity 60L (13.2Gal) [15.9US Gal), RS 500 65L (14.3Gal) [17.2US Gal] L; tyres 205/50 VR 15, wheel rims 7J.

Dimensions: Track 144.5/146cm, load space 14.7cu ft (415dm3). Length 449.5cm, width 170cm, height 137cm.

Performance: Max speed 150mph/242kmh, RS 500 153mph/246kmh (manufacturers test specifications), speed at 1000rpm in 5th gear 22.8mph/36.7kmh; acceleration 0–62mph/100kmh 6.5secs, RS 500 6.2secs; power to weight ratio 8.3kg/kW (6.1kg/PS), RS 500 7.4kg/kW (5.5kg/PS); consumption ECE 8.0/10.2/12.8L/100km (35.3/27.7/22.1mpg) [29.4/23.1/18.4US mpg].

Ford Scorpio/Granada

CL – GL – Ghia
GB Granada: L – GL – Ghia – Scorpio

Successor to the Granada with aerodynamic body, front engine, rear wheel drive; Saloon/Sedan with tailgate, four wheel disc brakes and antilock system. Launched on March 20 1985. Frankfurt, 1985: Scorpio 4 x 4; from January 1986 also available with 2.5 Litre Peugeot diesel engine. For 1987: 2.4 and 2.9 Litre V6 engines.

```
2 Litre
77kW–103hp–105PS
1 2V Carb
```

Body, Weight: 5–door Saloon/Sedan, 5–seater; kerbweight (DIN) from 1185kg; gross vehicle weight 1750/1775kg.

Engine data (DIN): 4–cylinder in–line (90.82 x 76.95mm), 1993cm3; compression ratio 9.2:1; 77kW (103hp) [105PS] at 5200rpm, 38.6kW/L (51.7hp/L) [52.7PS/L]; 157Nm (115.9bft) at 4000rpm.
With unregulated Catalyst: 74kW (99hp) [100PS] at 5400rpm; 153Nm (112.9lbft) at 4000rpm.

Ford Scorpio GL

Engine construction: Valves in V 15deg, 1 overhead camshaft (toothed belt); 5 main bearing crankshaft; oil cooling system capacity 3.5/3.75L (3.3/3.5US qt); 1 Weber downdraught compound carb. 12V 43/48Ah Battery, 55/90A alternator; cooling system capacity 8L (7.5US qt).

Ford EUR

Transmission (to rear wheels): a) 5–speed manual, final drive ratio 3.92, 3.62 or 3.36; with limited slip differential 3.64.
b) Automatic A4LD; "Automatic 4–speed–Lock–up–Overdrive", hydraulic torque converter and Planetary gear set, selector lever at central console, final drive ratio 3.62; 3.64.

Gear ratios: a) 5–speed manual: 1st 3.65; 2nd 1.97; 3rd 1.37; 4th 1; 5th 0.82; R 3.66.
Or 1st 3.89; 2nd 2.08; 3rd 1.34; 4th 1; 5th 0.82.
b) Automatic: Max torque multiplication in converter 2.11 times, Planetary gear set ratios: 1st 2.474; 2nd 1.474; 3rd 1; 4th 0.750; R 2.111.

Chassis: Integral body; front and rear independent suspension, front McPherson struts, control arm and antiroll bar, coil springs and telescopic dampers; optional rear level control system. Power assisted disc brakes (front ventilated) with ABS (Teves System), disc diameter front 26cm, rear 25.3cm, mechanical handbrake to rear wheels; rack and pinion steering with optional power assistance; fuel tank capacity 70L (15.4Gal) [18.5US Gal]; tyres 175 TR/HR 14 optional 185/70 HR 14, wheel rims 5.5J, optional 6J.

Dimensions: Wheelbase 276cm, track 147.5/147.5cm, clearance approx 12cm, turning circle 11.0m. Load space 15.5/29.5/47.7cu ft (440/835/1350dm3) 440/835/1350dm3. Length 467cm, width 176cm, height 144cm.

Performance: Max speed 117mph/188kmh, automatic 114mph/184kmh (manufacturers test specifications), speed at 1000rpm in 5th gear (3.92:1) 22.4mph/36kmh; acceleration 0 – 62mph/100kmh 11.5secs, automatic 14.2secs; power to weight ratio from 15.4kg/kW (11.3kg/PS); consumption ECE 6.2/7.7/10.8L/100km (45.6/36.7/26.2mpg) [37.9/30.5/21.8US mpg], automatic 5.8/7.4/10.9L/100km (48.7/38.2/25.9mpg) [40.6/31.8/21.6US mpg], With unregulated catalyst and 5–speed manual: Max speed 113mph/181kmh; 0 – 62mph/100kmh 12secs; consumption ECE 6.5/8.5/11.9L/100km (43.5/33.2/23.7mpg) [36.2/27.7/19.8US mpg].

---

2 Litre
85/74kW–114/99hp–115/101PS
Fuel Injection

Weight: Kerbweight (DIN) from 1200kg, gross vehicle weight 1750/1800kg.

Engine data (DIN): 4–cylinder in–line (90.82 x 76.95mm), 1993cm3; compression ratio 9.2:1; 85kW (114hp) [115PS] at 5500rpm, 42.6kW/L (57.1hp/L) [57.6PS/L]; 160Nm (118.1lbft) at 4000rpm.
With Catalyst: Compression ratio 8.5:1; 74kW (99hp) [101PS] at 5100rpm, 37.2kW/L (49.6hp/L) [50.7PS/L]; 148Nm (109.2lbft) at 4000rpm; unleaded regular grade.

Ford Scorpio "Exclusive"

Engine construction: Bosch L–Jetronic electronic fuel injection. 43/48/54Ah Battery, 90A Alternator.

Chassis: Power assisted steering; tyres 185/70 HR 14 or 195/65 HR 15, wheel rims 6J.

Performance: Max speed 120mph/193kmh, automatic 118mph/189kmh (manufacturers test specifications), speed at 1000rpm in 5th gear (3.92:1) 21.5mph/35.6kmh; acceleration 0 – 62mph/100kmh 10.6secs, automatic 13.5secs; power to weight ratio from 14.1kg/kW (10.4kg/PS); consumption ECE 6.6/8.2/11.1L/100km (42.8/34.3/25.4mpg) [35.6/28.7/20.5US mpg], automatic 6.2/8.2/11.5L/100km (45.6/34.4/24.6mpg) [37.9/28.7/20.5US mpg]. With Catalyst: Max speed 113mph/181kmh, automatic 110mph/177kmh; acceleration 0 –62mph/100kmh 12.4secs, automatic 15.3secs; consumption ECE 7.1/9.0/12.6L/100km (40.4/31.4/22.4mpg) [33.6/26.1/18.7US mpg], automatic 6.7/8.9/12.7L/100km (42.2/31.7/22.2mpg) [35.1/26.4/18.5US mpg].

2.4 Litre V6
96/92kW–129/123hp–130/125PS
Fuel Injection

Engine for 2.4i
As 2.0 Litre 103hp, except:

Body, Weight: Kerbweight (DIN) 1265–1335kg, gross vehicle weight 1800–1850kg.

Engine data (DIN): 6–cylinder in V 60deg (84 x 72mm), 2394cm3; compression ratio 9:1; 96kW (129hp) [130PS] at 5800rpm, 40.1kW/L (53.7hp/L) [54.3PS/L]; 193Nm (142.4lbft) at 3000rpm; leaded premium grade.
With Catalyst: Compression ratio 9.5:1; 92kW (123hp) [125PS] at 5800rpm, 38.4kW/L (51.5hp/L) [52.2PS/L]; 182Nm (143.3lbft) at 3500rpm.

Engine construction: Central camshaft (chain); 4 main bearing crankshaft; oil capacity 4.25/4.5L (4.1/4.3US qt); Bosch L/LE–Jetronic fuel injection. 12V 43/48Ah Battery, 90A alternator; cooling system capacity 8.5L (8.0US qt).

Transmission: Final drive ratio 3.64/3.92.

Gear ratios: 1st 3.89; 2nd 2.08; 3rd 1.34; 4th 1; 5th 0.82; R 3.26.

Chassis: Power assisted steering; tyres 185/70 HR 14, wheel rims 6J, optional tyres 195/65 HR 15.

Performance: Max speed 121mph/195kmh, Catalyst 118/190kmh, automatic 119mph/191kmh (manufacturers test specifications), speed at 1000rpm in 5th gear 23.9mph/38.5kmh; acceleration 0 – 62mph/100kmh 9.9secs, Catalyst 11secs, automatic 12.3secs; power to weight ratio from 13.2kg/kW (9.7kg/PS); consumption ECE 6.5/8.1/12.9L/100km (43.5/34.9/21.9mpg) [36.2/29.0/18.2US mpg], automatic 6.6/8.1/12.9L/100km (42.8/34.9/21.9mpg) [35.6/29.0/18.2US mpg].

Ford Scorpio GL 4x4

2.9 Litre V6
110.5/106.5kW–148/143hp–150/145PS
Fuel Injection

Engine for 2.9i and 4x4
As 2.0 Litre 103hp, except:

Body, Weight: Kerbweight (DIN) 1315–1385kg, gross vehicle weight 1850–1900kg. Saloon/Sedan 4x4 kerbweight (DIN) 1345–1450kg, gross vehicle weight 1900kg.

Engine data (DIN): 6–cylinder in V 60deg (93 x 72mm), 2935cm3; compression ratio 9.5:1; 110.5kW (148hp) [150PS] at 5700rpm, 37.6kW/L (50.4hp/L) [51.1PS/L]; 233Nm (171.9lbft) at 3000rpm.
With Catalyst: Compression ratio 9:1; 106.5kW (143hp) [145PS] at 5500rpm, 36.3kW/L (48.6hp/L) [49.4PS/L]; 222Nm (163.7lbft) at 3000rpm; unleaded regular grade.

Engine construction: (With Catalyst hydraulic tappets); central camshaft (chain); 4 main bearing crankshaft; oil capacity 4.25/4.5L (4.1US qt); Bosch L/LE Jetronic electronic fuel injection. 12 V 43/48Ah Battery, 90A alternator; cooling system capacity 8.5L (8.0US qt).

Transmission: a) 5–speed manual, final drive ratio 3.64 or 3.36.
b) Automatic A4LD; "Automatic 4–speed–Lock–up–Overdrive", hydraulic torque converter and Planetary gear set, selector lever at central console, final drive ratio 3.64 or 3.36.
c) 4x4: 5–speed manual, Ferguson System four wheel drive with viscous couplings (transmission division: 37/34% front 63/66% rear), final drive ratio 3.62.

Gear ratios: a) 5–speed manual: 1st 3.61; 2nd 2.08; 3rd 1.36; 4th 1; 5th 0.83; R 3.26.
b) Automatic: Max torque multiplication in converter 2.11 times, Planetary gear set ratios: 1st 2.474; 2nd 1.474; 3rd 1; 4th 0.749; R 2.111.

Chassis: Power assisted steering; tyres 185/70 VR 14 or 195/65 VR 15, wheel rims 6J; 4x4 tyres 205/60 VR 15.

Ford EUR • Ford AUS

Ford Scorpio 2.9i GL

Dimensions: 4x4; wheelbase 276.5cm, track 147.5/148cm, height 143.5cm.

Performance: Max speed 129mph/208kmh, automatic 127mph/204kmh, 4x4 5-speed manual 126mph/203kmh (manufacturers test specifications), speed at 1000rpm in 5th gear 23.9mph/38.5kmh; acceleration 0 – 62mph/100kmh 9.0secs, automatic 11.0secs, 4x4 5-speed manual 9.5secs; power to weight ratio from 11.9kg/kW (8.7kg/PS); consumption ECE 7.1/8.9/14.2L/100km (39.8/31.7/19.9mpg) [33.1/26.4/16.6US mpg], automatic 7.0/8.8/14.5L/100km (40.4/32.1/19.5mpg) [33.6/26.7/16.2US mpg], 4x4 5-speed manual 7.5/10.1/14.8L/100km. With Catalyst: Max speed 127mph/204kmh, automatic 124mph/200kmh, 4x4 5-speed manual, 125mph/201kmh; acceleration 0 - 62mph/100kmh 9.4secs, automatic 11.4secs, 4x4 5-speed manual approx 10secs, consumption 7.4/9.3/14.8L/100km (38.2/30.4/19.1mpg) [31.8/25.3/15.9US mpg], Automatic 7.5/9.5/15.2L/100km (37.7/29.7/18.6mpg) [31.4/24.8/15.5US mpg].

```
2.5 Litre Diesel
51/68kW-68/91hp-69/92PS
Injection Pump/Turbo
```

As 2.0 Litre 103hp, except:

Weight: Kerbweight (DIN) 1325/1355kg, gross vehicle weight 1850kg.

Engine data (DIN): 4–cylinder in–line (94 x 90mm), 2498cm3; compression ratio 23:1; 51kW (68hp) [69PS] at 4200rpm, 20.4kW/L (27.3hp/L) [27.6PS/L]; 148Nm (109.2lbft) at 2000rpm.
With Turbocharger (Garrett AiResearch T.03): Compression ratio 21:1; 68kW (91hp) [92PS] at 4150rpm, 27.2kW/L (36.5hp/L) [36.8PS/L]; 204Nm (150.5lbft) at 2250rpm.

Engine construction: Designated Peugeot XD 3, cylinder block inclined to right; parallel valves; side camshaft (chain); oil capacity 5.6L (5.3US qt); Bosch EP/VAC injection pump. 12V 68/88Ah Battery, 70A alternator; cooling system capacity 11L (10.4US qt).

Transmission: 5–speed manual, final drive ratio 3.92, 3.62 or 3.36.

Gear ratios: Turbo: 1st 3.61; 2nd 2.08; 3rd 1.36; 4th 1; 5th 0.83; R 3.26.

Chassis: Power assisted steering.

Performance: Max speed 117mph/158kmh, Turbo 107mph/173kmh (manufacturers test specifications), speed at 1000rpm in 5th gear 24.3mph/39.1kmh; acceleration 0 – 62mph/100kmh 19.4secs, Turbo approx 13.7secs; power to weight ratio from 26.0/19.5kg/kW (19.2/14.4kg/PS); consumption ECE 6.1/7.8/9.4L/100km (46.3/36.2/30.1mpg) [38.6/30.2/25.0US mpg], Turbo 5.7/7.4/8.8L/100km (49.6/38.2/32.1mpg) [41.3/31.8/26.7US mpg].

```
FORD                                              AUS
```

Ford Motor Company of Australia Limited, Private Bag 6, Campbellfield, Victoria 3061, Australia.

Australian enterprise operating under license from Ford Motor Company Inc.

Ford Laser

Licensed production of the Mazda 323 as Ford Laser in Australia. Launched in Autumn 1980. For technical data see Mazda 323.

Ford Telstar

Licensed production of the new Mazda 626 as Ford Telstar in Australia. For technical data see Mazda 626.

Ford Telstar

Ford Falcon–Fairmont–Fairlane–LTD

New model, new six cylinder engine with 3.2 and 3.9-Litre capacity. New body and new all-round suspension. Launched in June 1988.

Body, Weight: 4–door Saloon/Sedan, 5–seater; kerbweight from 1420; Fairlane 1555, LTD 1610kg. 5–door Estate/Station Wagon, 6–seater; kerbweight from 1510kg; Automatic versions 10kg heavier.

```
3.2 Litre
90kW-120hp-122PS
Central/Single Point Injection
```

Engine data (DIN): 6–cylinder in–line (91.86 x 79.4mm), 3157cm3; compression ratio 8.8:1; 90kW (120hp) [122PS] at 4000rpm, 28.5kW/L (38.2hp/L) [38.6PS/L]; 235Nm (173.4lbft) at 2200rpm; unleaded regular grade.

Engine construction: Hydraulic tappets, overhead camshaft (toothed belt), light–alloy cylinder heads; 7 main bearing crankshaft; oil capacity 4.5L (4.3US qt); electronic central/single point injection. 12V 61Ah Battery, 38/55A alternator; cooling system capacity 10L (9.5US qt).

Transmission (to rear wheels): a) 4–speed manual, floor shift, final drive ratio 2.92.
b) 5–speed manual, floor shift, final drive ratio 3.23.
c) Automatic, hydraulic torque and 3–speed Planetary gear set, selector lever at steering column or in centre; final drive ratio 2.77, Estate/Station Wagon 2.92. Optional limited slip differential.

Ford Falcon

Gear ratios: a) 5–speed manual: 1st 3.50; 2nd 2.14; 3rd 1.39; 4th 1; 5th 0.78; R 3.39.
b) Automatic: Max torque multiplication in converter 2 times, Planetary gear set ratios: 2.39; 1.45; 1; R 2.09.

Chassis: Integral body; front upper keystone A arm, lower single control arm with tension struts, antiroll bar; rear rigid axle, four trailing arms, watt–linkage and antiroll bar, coil springs and telescopic dampers; Estate/Station Wagon has semi elliptic springs. Ghia with level control system. Servo/power assisted brakes, front discs (ventilated) diameter 28.7cm, rear drums optional four wheel disc brakes for some models, pedal actuated parking brakes to rear wheels; rack and pinion steering, optional power assistance; fuel tank capacity 68L (14.9Gal) [18US Gal]; tyres 185/75 HR 14, wheel rims 5.5 J.

Dimensions: a) Falcon: Wheel base 279.5cm, track 154.5/153.5cm, clearance 14cm, turning circle 10.7m. Load space 16.6cu ft (470dm3). Length 481cm, width 185.5cm, height 140cm.
b) Fairlane/LTD: Wheelbase 292cm, track 156/154.5cm, turning circle 11.4m. Load space 17cu ft (481dm3). Length 502cm, width 185.5cm, height 142cm.

Ford AUS • Ford BR

c) Station Wagon: Wheelbase 292.5cm, track 154.5/153.5cm, turning circle 11.4m. Load space max 92.5cu ft (2620dm3). Length 500.5cm, width 185.5cm, height 148,5cm.

Performance: Max speed above 99mph/160kmh, speed at 1000rpm in top gear (3.23:1) 22.2mph/35.7kmh; power to weight ratio from 15.8kg/kW (11.6kg/PS); consumption (touring) approx 10–14L/100km (28.2–20.2mpg) [23.5–16.8US mpg].

```
3.9 Litre 6 cylinder
120kW-161hp-163PS
Central/Single Point Injection
```

As 3.2 Litre, except:

Weight: Heavier by 10-15kg.

Engine data (DIN): 6–cylinder in–line (91.86 x 99.3mm), 3949cm3; compression ratio 8.8:1; 120kW (161hp) [163PS] at 4250rpm, 30.4kW/L (40.7hp/L) [41.3PS/L]; 311Nm (229.5lbft) at 3250rpm.

Transmission: a) 5–speed manual, final drive ratio 3.23.
b) Automatic, final drive ratio 2.77 or 2.92.
Optional limited slip differential.

Chassis: Tyres 195 HR 14, 205/65 HR 14 or 215/65 HR 14.

Performance: Max speed above 112mph/180kmh, speed at 1000rpm in top gear (2.92:1) 24.2mph/39.0kmh; power to weight ratio from 11.9kg/kW (8.8kg/PS); consumption approx 11-15L/100km (25.7–18.8mpg) [21.4–15.7US mpg].

Ford Fairlane

```
3.9 Litre 6-cylinder
139kW-186hp-189PS
Fuel Injection
```

As 3.2 Litre, except:

Weight: Heavier by 10-15kg

Engine data (DIN): 6–cylinder in–line (91.86 x 99.3mm), 3949cm3; compression ratio 8.8:1; 139kW (186hp) [189PS] at 4250rpm, 35.2kW/L (47.2hp/L) [47.9PS/L]; 338Nm (249.4lbft) at 3500rpm.

Engine construction: Bosch LE2–Jetronic electronic fuel injection.

Transmission: a) 5–speed manual, final drive ratio 2.92.
b) Automatic, final drive ratio 2.77.

Chassis: Tyres 195 HR 14, 205/65 HR 14 or 215/65 HR 14.

Performance: Max speed over 148mph/200kmh; speed at 1000rpm in top gear (2.92:1) 25.2mph/40.6kmh; power to weight ratio from 10.4kg/kW (7.6kg/PS); consumption approx 12–16L/100km (23.5–17.7mpg) [19.6–14.7US mpg].

Ford LTD

FORD — BR

Ford Brasil SA, Rua Manoelito de Ornellas, 303–0479 Sao Paulo, Brasil.

Ford Brasil SA was formed in 1976 as a result of the fusion of Ford Motor do Brasil and Willys–Overland do Brasil. Autumn 1986: merger with VW do Brasil under the name "Autolatina".

MODEL RANGE
Escort – Del Rey

Ford Escort

Escort L - Escort GL - Escort Ghia - Escort XR3 - Escort Convertible.

Spacious vehicle of the lower–mid class with transverse engine and front wheel drive. 3 and 5–door Saloon/Sedan, engine with 1.6 Litre displacement. Launched in July 1983. Modifications to body details for 1988.

```
1555cm3
54.5/55kW-73/74hp-74/75PS
1 2V Carb
```

Body, Weight: 3/5–door Saloon/Sedan and 2–door Convertible, 5– seater; kerbweight (DIN) 855–935kg, gross vehicle weight 1350kg.

Engine data (DIN): 4–cylinder in–line (77 x 83.5mm), 1555cm3; compression ratio 9:1; 54.5kW (73hp) [74PS] at 5200rpm, 35.0kW/L (46.9hp/L) [50.6PS/L]; 124Nm (91.5lbft) at 2400rpm.
With ethyl alcohol: Compression ratio 12:1; 55kW (74hp) [75PS] at 5200rpm; 129Nm (95.2lbft) at 2400rpm.

Engine construction: Front transverse engine; side camshaft (chain); light–alloy cylinder heads, wet cylinder liners; 5 main bearing crankshaft; oil capacity 3.5L (3.3US qt); 1 Weber DMTB 38 (XR3: DMTB 32) downdraught twin barrel carb. 12V 43Ah Battery, 45/55A alternator; cooling system capacity 5.8L (5.5US qt).

Transmission (to front wheels): 5–speed manual, lower 4.29; 3.84.

Gear ratios: 1st 3.15; 2nd 1.91; 3rd 1.27; 4th 0.95; 5th 0.75; R 3.62.

Chassis: Integral body, front McPherson struts (coil springs), lower single control arm and tension struts, rear independent suspension with shock absorber struts, control arm, tension struts and coil springs, telescopic dampers, front and rear antiroll bars. Brakes with optional Servo/power assistance, front discs (ventilated), rear drums, disc diameter 24cm; mechanical handbrake to rear wheels; rack and pinion steering; fuel tank capacity 48L (10.5Gal) [12.7US Gal], XR3 65L (14.3Gal) [17.2US Gal]; tyres 175/70 SR 13, wheel rims 4.5 or 5J.

Dimensions: Wheelbase 240cm, track 140/142.5cm, clearance 12cm, turning circle 10.5m. Load space 12.7–37.1cu ft (360–1050dm3). Length 402cm, XR3 406cm, width 164cm, height 132.5cm.

Performance: Max speed 96-105-110mph/155-169-177kmh (manufacturers test specifications), speed at 1000rpm in 5th gear (4.29:1) 20.4mph/32.9kmh; acceleration 0 – 62mph/100kmh 12.8/12.3secs; power to weight ratio from 13.5kg/kW (9.9kg/PS); consumption (touring) 7.5–10.5L/100km (37.7–26.9mpg) [31.4–22.4US mpg] (manufacturers test specifications).

Ford Escort L

Ford BR • Ford RA

1555cm3
61kW–82hp–83PS
1 2V Carb

Engine for XR3

As 73/74hp version, except:

Weight: Kerbweight (DIN) approx 900kg.

Engine data (DIN): 4–cylinder in–line (77 x 83.5mm), 1555cm3. With ethyl alcohol: compression ratio 12:1; 61kW (82hp) [83PS] at 5600rpm, 39.2kW/L (52.5hp/L) [53.4PS/L]; 125Nm (92.3lbft) at 4000rpm.

Chassis: Tyres 185/60 HR 14

Performance: Max speed 107mph/172kmh (manufacturers test specifications); power to weight ratio from 14.8kg/kW (10.8kg/PS); consumption approx 8–12L/100km (35.3–23.5mpg) [29.4– 19.6US mpg].

Ford Escort XR3 Cabriolet

Ford Del Rey

Del Rey L – Del Rey GL – Del Rey GLX – Del Rey Ghia – Belina L – Belina GLX – Belina Ghia – Belina 4 x 4

Luxury version of the old Corcel with 1.6 Litre engine. Also available as 4x4.

1.6 Litre
55/53.5kW–74/72hp–75/73PS
1 2V Carb

Body, Weight: 2–door Saloon/Sedan, 5–seater; kerbweight (DIN) 1050kg, gross vehicle weight 1450kg. 4–door Saloon/Sedan, 5–seater; kerbweight (DIN) 1055kg, gross vehicle weight 1455kg. 5–door Estate/Station Wagon, 5–seater; kerbweight (DIN) 1100kg.

Ford Del Rey GLX

Engine data (DIN): 4–cylinder in–line (77 x 83.5mm), 1555cm3; compression ratio 9:1; 55kW (74hp) [75PS] at 5200rpm, 35.4kW/L (47.4hp/L) [48.2PS/L]; 126Nm (93.1lbft) at 2400rpm.

With ethyl alcohol: Compression ratio 12:1; 53.5kW (72hp) [73PS] at 4800rpm; 127Nm (93.7lbft) at 2400rpm.

Engine construction: Side camshaft (chain); light–alloy cylinder head; wet cylinder liners; 5 main bearing crankshaft; oil capacity 3.5L (3.3US qt); 1 Solex 34 SIE downdraught twin carb. 12V 36/42Ah Battery, 55A alternator; cooling system capacity 4.5L (4.3US qt), thermostatically regulated ventilator.

Transmission (to front wheels, 4x4): a) 5–speed manual, final drive ratio 3.84; 3.875.
b) Automatic, electronic control, hydraulic torque converter and 3–speed Planetary gear set, central selector lever, lower 3.865.

Gear ratios: Integral body; front lower A arm, upper single control arm with tension strut, coil springs and telescopic dampers; rear rigid axle with torsion bars and central A arms, coil springs and telescopic dampers, front and rear antiroll bars. Servo/power assisted brakes, front discs, rear drums 22.7cm; hand brake to rear wheels; rack and pinion steering; fuel tank capacity 57L (12.5Gal) [15.1US Gal], Belina 63L (13.8Gal) [16.6US Gal]; tyres 185/70 SR 13, 195/60 HR 14, wheel rims 4.5 or 5J.

Dimensions: Wheelbase 244cm, track 136.5/133.5cm. Clearance 13cm, turning circle 11.7m, load space 13.8cu ft (390dm3), Estate/Station Wagon 60.4cu ft (1710dm3). Length 450cm, width 167.5cm, height 134.5cm.

Performance: Max speed 91.4mph/147kmh (manufacturers test specifications), speed at 1000rpm in 4th gear 18.6mph/30kmh; acceleration 0 – 62mph/100kmh 14.8secs; power to weight ratio 19.1kg/kW (14.0kg/PS); consumption (touring) 10–12L/100km (28.2– 23.5mpg) [23.5–19.6US mpg] (manufacturers test specifications.)

Ford Del Rey Belina 4x4

FORD RA

Ford Motor Argentina SA, Casilla de Correo 696, Correo Central, 1000 Buenos Aires, Argentina.

Argentinian enterprise working under Ford Motor Company Inc USA license.

MODEL RANGE
Escort - Sierra – Falcon/Futura

Ford Escort

Licensed producer of the Brazilian Escort with 1555cm3 engine. For data see Ford Escort BR.

Ford Escort

Ford RA

Ford Sierra

L – Ghia – Ghia S – Rural – XR4

Licensed version of the Ford Sierra with 1.6 or 2.3 Litre four cylinder engine; also available as XR4 Coupe. Launched in Summer 1984, XR4 Autumn 1984, Estate/Station Wagon "Rural" in September 1985.

```
              1.6 Litre
          55kW–74hp–75PS
             1 2V Carb
```

Engine for Sierra L and Sierra GL

Body, Weight: 5–door Saloon/Sedan, 5–seater; kerbweight (DIN) 1115kg.
Engine data (DIN): 4–cylinder in–line (87.65 x 66mm), 1593cm3; compression ratio 9.2:1; 55kW (74hp) [75PS] at 5000rpm, 34.5kW/L 46.2hp/L [47.1PS/L]; 123Nm (90.7lbft) at 3000rpm; leaded premium grade.
Engine construction: Valves in V 15deg, 1 overhead camshaft (toothed belt); 5 main bearing crankshaft; oil capacity 3.75L (3.6US qt); 1 downdraught twin barrel carb. 12V 45Ah Battery, 55A alternator; cooling system capacity 8L (7.6US qt).
Transmission (to rear wheels): a) 4–speed manual, final drive ratio 3.62.
b) 5–speed manual, final drive ratio 3.62.
Gear ratios: a) 4–speed manual: 1st 3.65; 2nd 2.14; 3rd 1.37; 4th 1; R 3.66.
b) 5–speed manual: 1st 3.65; 2nd 2.14; 3rd 1.37; 4th 1; 5th 0.82; R 3.66.
Chassis: Integral body; front and rear independent suspension, front McPherson struts, control arm and antiroll bar, rear semi– trailing arm, coil springs and telescopic dampers. Servo/power assisted brakes, front discs (ventilated), disc diameter 24cm, rear drums, mechanical handbrake to rear wheels; rack and pinion steering; fuel tank capacity 60L (13.2Gal) [15.9US Gal]; tyres 165 SR 13 or 185/70 SR 13, wheel rims 5.5J.
Dimensions: Wheelbase 261cm, track 145/146cm, clearance approx 12m, turning circle 10.6m. Load space 12.5–51.7cu ft (355–1465dm3). Length 445.5cm, width 172.5cm, height 142.5cm.
Performance: Max speed 103mph/165kmh (manufacturers test specifications), speed at 1000rpm in 4th gear (3.62:1) 18.8mph/30.2kmh; acceleration 0–62mph/100kmh 14secs; power to weight ratio from 20.3kg/kW (14.9kg/PS); consumption approx 8–11L/100km (35.3–25.7mpg) [29.4–21.4US mpg].

Ford Sierra Ghia S

```
              2.3 Litre
     77/88kW–103/118hp–105/120PS
             1 2V Carb
```

Engine for Ghia, Ghia S, Rural and XR4
As 1.6, except:
Body, Weight: 5–door Saloon/Sedan, 5–seater; kerbweight (DIN) 1165kg, gross vehicle weight 1585kg. 3–door Coupe XR4, 5–seater; kerbweight (DIN) 1165kg, gross vehicle weight 1585kg. 5–door Estate/Station Wagon, "Rural", 5–seater; kerbweight (DIN) 1215kg, gross vehicle weight 1715kg.
Engine data (DIN): (96.04 x 79.4mm); 2301cm3; compression ratio 9:1; 77kW (103hp) [105PS] at 5000rpm, 33.5kW/L (44.9hp/L) [45.6PS/L]; 167Nm (123.2lbft) at 2500rpm; leaded premium grade.
Engine for Ghia S and XR4: 88kW (118hp) [120PS] at 5500rpm, 38.2kW/L (51.2hp/L) [52.2PS/L]; 177Nm (131lbft) at 3500rpm.
Engine construction: Hydraulic tappets; oil capacity 4.7L (4.4US qt); 1 Solex downdraught twin barrel carb. 12V 53Ah Battery, 70/75/90A alternator.
Transmission (to rear wheels): a) 4–speed manual, final drive ratio 3.14 or 3.38.
b) 5–speed manual, final drive ratio 3.14 or 3.38, XR4 3.62.
c) Automatic C3; hydraulic torque converter and 3–speed Planetary gear set, selector lever at central console, final drive ratio 3.14 or 3.38.
Gear ratios: a) 4–speed manual: 1st 3.65; 2nd 2.14; 3rd 1.37; 4th 1; R 3.66.
b) 5–speed manual: 1st 3.65; 2nd 2.14; 3rd 1.37; 4th 1; 5th 0.82; R 3.66.
c) Automatic: Max torque multiplication in converter 2 times, Planetary gear set ratios: 1st 2.47; 2nd 1.47; 3rd 1; R 2.11.
Chassis: Optional power assisted steering; tyres 185/70 SR 13, XR4 195/60 HR 14, wheel rims 5 or 5.5J.
Dimensions: Height XR4 141cm. Estate/Station Wagon; track 145/147cm. Load space 37.8/69.2cu ft (1070/1960dm3). Length 463cm, width 173cm, height 145cm.
Performance: Max speed 112mph/180kmh, Rural 108.1mph/174kmh, XR4 118.1mph/190kmh (manufacturers test specifications); acceleration 0–62mph/100kmh 12, Rural 12.4secs, XR4 9.9secs; power to weight ratio from 13.3kg/kW (9.7kg/PS); consumption approx 8–12L/100km (35.3–23.5mpg) [29.4-19.6US mpg].

Ford Sierra Rural

Ford Falcon/Futura

Models produced under license from Falcon America with different engines and details. From 1983: also available with 2.3–Litre– four–cylinder engine.

```
              2.3 Litre
          66kW–88hp–90PS
             1 2V Carb
```

Body, Weight: 4–door Saloon/Sedan, 5/6–seater; kerbweight (DIN) approx 1190–1225kg. 5–door Rural Estate/Station Wagon, 5/6–seater; kerbweight (DIN) approx 1310kg; gross vehicle weight 1600kg.
Engine data (DIN): 4–cylinder in–line (96.04 x 79.4mm), 2301cm3; compression ratio 7.5:1; 66kW (88hp) [90PS] at 5000rpm, 28.7kW/L (38.5hp/L) [39.1PS/L]; 155Nm (114.4lbft) at 2500rpm; leaded regular grade.
Engine construction: Valves (in V), 1 overhead camshaft (toothed belt); 5 main bearing crankshaft; oil capacity 4.5L (4.3US qt); 1 downdraught twin barrel carb. 12V 45Ah Battery, 38 or 55A alternator; cooling system capacity 7.9L (7.5US qt).
Transmission (to rear wheels): 4–speed manual, final drive ratio 3.54 or 3.73.
Gear ratios: 1st 3.65; 2nd 2.13; 3rd 1.37; 4th 1; R 3.66.

Ford Falcon

Ford RA • Ford SA

Chassis: Integral body; front upper A arm and lower single control arm, elastic longitudinal compression struts and coil springs, rear rigid axle with semi elliptic springs, front antiroll bar, telescopic dampers. Servo/power assisted brakes, front discs, diameter 27.8cm, rear drums, mechanical handbrake to rear wheels, recirculating ball steering with optional power assistance; fuel tank capacity 61L (13.4Gal) [16.1US Gal], Estate/Station Wagon 67.5L (14.8Gal) [17.9US Gal]; tyres 6.95 S 14 or 175 SR 14.

Dimensions: Wheelbase 278cm, track 141/138.5cm, clearance 18cm, turning circle 11.5m. Length 471.5cm, Estate/Station Wagon 472.5cm, width 178cm, height 140cm.

Performance: Max speed approx 96–99mph/155–160kmh, speed at 1000rpm in 3rd gear 20.1mph/32.4kmh; acceleration 18kg/kW (13.2kg/PS); consumption approx 10–14L/100km (28.2–20.2mpg) [23.5–16.8US mpg].

Ford Falcon Rural

```
3.1 Litre
62kW–83hp–84PS
1 Carb
```

As 2.3, except:

Weight: Heavier by approx 50kg.

Engine data (DIN): 6–cylinder in-line (93.47 x 74.67mm), 3081cm3; compression ratio 7.4:1; 62kW (83hp) [84PS] at 4000rpm, 20.1kW/L (26.9hp/L) [27.3PS/L]; 183Nm (135.1lbft) at 2000rpm; leaded regular grade.

Engine construction: Side camshaft (chain): 7 main bearing crankshaft; oil capacity 4.5L (4.3US qt); 1 Holley downdraught carb. 12V 45/55Ah Battery, cooling system capacity 8.7L (8.2US qt).

Transmission: a) 3–speed manual, final drive ratio 3.07/ 3.31.
b) 4–speed manual, final drive ratio 3.07/ 3.31.
c) Automatic, hydraulic torque converter and 3–speed Planetary gear set, selector lever optional at central console; final drive ratio 3.07 or 3.31.

Gear ratios: a) 3–speed manual: 1st 3.26; 2nd 1.91; 3rd 1; R 3.46.
b) 4–speed manual: 1st 3.11; 2nd 2.2; 3rd 1.47; 4th 1; R 3.11.
c) Automatic: Max torque multiplication in converter 2 times, Planetary gear set ratios: 1st 2.45; 2nd 1.45; 3rd 1; R 2.18.

Performance: Max speed 95mph/153kmh (manufacturers test specifications), speed at 1000rpm in 3rd gear (3.07:1) 23.2mph/37.4kmh; power to weight ratio 20kg/kW (14.8kg/PS); consumption 12L/100km (23.5mpg) [19.6US mpg] (manufacturers test specifications)

```
3.6 Litre
79.5/103kW–107/138hp–108/140PS
1 Carb
```

As 2.3, except:

Weight: Heavier by approx 50kg.

Engine data (DIN): 6–cylinder in-line (93.47 x 87.88mm), 3620cm3; compression ratio 8.2:1; 79.5kW (107hp) [108PS] at 4000rpm, 22kW/L (29.5hp/L) [29.9PS/L]; 235Nm (173.4lbft) at 1500rpm; leaded premium grade.
SP with twin carb: 103kW (138hp) [140PS] at 4500rpm, 28.5kW/L (38.2hp/L) [38.7PS/L]; 251Nm (185lbft) at 2500rpm.

Transmission: a) 3–speed manual, final drive ratio 2.87/3.07.
b) 4–speed manual, final drive ratio 2.87/3.07.
c) Automatic, hydraulic torque converter and 3–speed Planetary gear set, selector lever optional at central console; final drive ratio 2.87 or 3.07.

Gear ratios: a) 3–speed manual: 1st 3.26; 2nd 1.91; 3rd 1; R 3.46.
b) 4–speed manual: 1st 3.11; 2nd 2.2; 3rd 1.47; 4th 1; R 3.11.
c) Automatic: Max torque multiplication in converter 2 times, Planetary gear set ratios: 1st 2.474; 2nd 1.474; 3rd 1; R 2.111.

Performance: Max speed 99–112mph/160–180kmh (manufacturers test specifications), speed at 1000rpm in top gear (6.95–14, 2.87:1) 24.9mph/40kmh; power to weight ratio from 12kg/kW (8.9kg/PS); consumption (touring) 13L/100km (21.7mpg) [18.1US mpg], manufacturers test specifications.

FORD SA

Ford Motor Company of South Africa (Pty), Limited, Albany Road, P.O. Box, Port Elizabeth 6000, South Africa.

South African enterprise working under license from the Ford Motor Company and Toyo Kogyo (Mazda). Production of various models from both Ford (Escort and Sierra) and Mazda (323 Laser and Meteor).

Ford Sierra

Licensed production of Sierra with 4 cylinder engine from 1.6 Litre (Kent, 79hp) to 2 Litre OHC (104hp). For technical data, with the exception of the 1.6 Litre, see Ford Europe.

```
1.6 Litre
59kW–79hp–80PS
1 2V Carb
```

As Sierra (Europe) 1.6, except:

Engine data (DIN): 4–cylinder in-line (80.98 x 77.62mm), 1598cm3; compression ratio 9.2:1; 59kW (79hp) [80PS] at 5500rpm, 36.8kW/L (49.3hp/L) [50PS/L]; 120Nm (88.5lbft) at 2800rpm.

Engine construction: Side camshaft (chain); 5 bearing crankshaft; oil capacity 4.25L (4.1US qt); 1 Weber downdraught compound carb. 12V 40/50 Ah Battery, 45A Alternator; cooling system capacity 8L (7.6US qt).

Transmission: 4-speed manual, final drive ratio 3.7 or 3.89.

Gear ratios: 1st 3.65; 2nd 1.97; 3rd 1.37; 4th 1; R 3.66.

Performance: Max speed 107mph/172kmh (manufacturers test specifications), speed at 1000rpm in top gear 18.4mph/29.6kmh; power to weight ratio from 18.2kg/kW (13.4PS); consumption approx 7–12L/100km (40.4–23.5mpg) [33.6–19.6US mpg].

Ford Sierra XR6

Ford Sierra 3.0 V6 – XR6

Licensed to produce Sierras. Sports version with 3 Litre engine "Essex"; XR6 with 138hp or 154hp. Launched in Summer 1984.

```
3 Litre V6
103/115kW–138/154hp–140/156PS
1 2V Carb
```

As Sierra (Europe), except:

Body, Weight: 5–door Saloon/Sedan, 5–seater: Kerbweight (DIN) 1285–1320kg, gross vehicle weight 1715kg. 5–door Estate/Station Wagon, 5–seater; kerbweight (DIN) 1295kg, gross vehicle weight 1740kg.

Engine data (DIN): 6–cylinder in V 60deg (93.67 x 72.42mm), 2993cm3; compression ratio 9:1; 103kW (138hp) [140PS] at 5000rpm, 34.4kW/L (46hp/L) [46.8PS/L]; 237Nm (175lbft) at 3000rpm; leaded premium grade.
XR6–Engine: Compression ratio 10.1:1; 115kW (154hp) [156PS].

Ford SA • FSO

Engine construction: Central camshaft (toothed belt); 4 bearing crankshaft; oil capacity 5.65L (5.4US qt); 1 Weber 38/38 EGAS downdraught carb. 12V 65Ah Battery, 55A alternator; cooling system capacity 10.2L (9.6US qt).

Transmission: a) 5-speed manual, final drive ratio 3.36.
b) Automatic A4LD "Automatic 4-speed-Lock-up-Overdrive", hydraulic torque converter and 4-speed Planetary gear set, selector lever at central console, final drive ratio 3.08 or 3.36.

Gear ratios: a) 5-speed manual: 1st 3.36; 2nd 1.81; 3rd 1.26; 4th 1; 5th 0.82; R 3.66.
b) Automatic: Max torque multiplication in converter 2.1 times, Planetary gear set ratios: 1st 2.474; 2nd 1.474; 3rd 1; 4th 0.749; R 2.111.

Chassis: Front and rear antiroll bar. Front ventilated disc brakes, diameter 25.6cm, rear drums diameter 25.4cm. Tyres 195/60HR 14 or 185/70HR, wheel rims 5.5/6J.

Performance: Max speed 123mph/198kmh, XR6 127mph/205kmh (manufacturers test specifications), speed at 1000rpm in 5th gear 24.2mph/39kmh; acceleration 0 - 62mph/100kmh 10.2secs, XR6 9.1secs; power to weight ratio 11.2kg/kW (8.2kg/PS); consumption approx 9-15L/100km (31.4-18.8mpg) [26.1-15.7US mpg].

FSO   PL

Fabryka Samochodow Osobowych (FSO), AL. Stalingradzka 50, Warszawa 03-215, Poland.

Polish factory producing under license from, among others, Fiat.

FSO 125 P

1.3 MC/ME - 1.5 MC/ME - 1.5 Wagon

Five-seater. Licensed production from Fiat, engine, transmission and suspension derived from the old 1300/1500 model. Type 125 body modified with twin headlamps. Launched in Summer 1968, Estate/Station Wagon in 1972.

> 1.3 Litre
> 48kW-64hp-65PS
> 1 2V Carb

Body, Weight: 4-door Saloon/Sedan, 5-seater; kerbweight (DIN) 1020kg, gross vehicle weight 1445kg; 5-door Saloon/Sedan, 5-seater; kerbweight (DIN) 1065kg, gross vehicle weight 1540kg.

Engine data (DIN): 4-cylinder in-line (72 x 79.5mm) 1295cm3; compression ratio 9:1; 48kW (64hp) [65PS] at 5600rpm, 37.1kW/L (49.7hp/L) [50.2PS/L]; 93Nm (69lbft) at 3400rpm; leaded regular grade.

Engine construction: Valves in V 48deg, side camshaft (chain); light-alloy cylinder head; 3 bearing crankshaft; oil capacity 3.5L (3.3US qt); 1 FOS 34S2C14 downdraught compound carb. 12V 48Ah Battery, 53A alternator; cooling system capacity 6.7L (6.3US qt).

Transmission (to rear wheels): a) 4-speed manual, final drive ratio 4.1 (10/41).
b) 5-speed manual, final drive ratio 4.1.

FSO 125 P

Gear ratios: a) 4-speed manual: 1st 3.75; 2nd 2.30; 3rd 1.49; 4th 1; R 3.87.
b) 5-speed manual: 1st 3.778; 2nd 1.944; 3rd 1.307; 4th 1; 5th 0.803; R 3.867.

Chassis: Integral body; front A arm and coil springs, rear rigid axle with semi-elliptic springs and longitudinal compression struts, front antiroll bar, telescopic dampers. Servo/power assisted disc brakes, diameter 22.7; mechanical handbrake to rear wheels; worm and wheel steering; fuel tank capacity 45L (9.9Gal) [11.9US Gal]; tyres 165 S 13/165 SR 13, wheel rims 4.5J; Wagon 175 SR 13, wheel rims 5J.

Dimensions: Wheelbase 250.5cm, track 130/127.5cm or 131.5/129cm, clearance 14cm, turning circle 10.8m. Load space 13.6cu ft (385dm3), Estate/Station Wagon 38.8-54.7cu ft (1100-1550dm3). Length 422.5cm, Estate/Station Wagon 423.5cm, width 163cm, height 144, Estate/Station Wagon 147.5cm.

Performance: Max speed 90mph/145kmh (manufacturers test specifications), speed at 1000rpm in 4th gear 16.4mph/26.4kmh; acceleration 0 - 62mph/100kmh 20secs; power to weight ratio from 21.9kg/kW (16.2kg/PS); consumption ECE 6.6/9.3/10.3L/100km (42.8/30.4/27.4mpg) [35.6/25.3/22.8US mpg].

FSO 125 P Kombi

> 1.5 Litre
> 55/60kW-74/80hp-75/82PS
> 1 2V Carb

As 1.3 Litre, except:

Engine data (DIN): (77 x 79.5mm), 1481cm3;
a) Compression ratio 9.2:1; 55kW (74hp) [75PS] at 5200rpm, 37.1kW/L (50hp/L) [50.6PS/L]; 115Nm (84.8lbft) at 3200rpm.
b) Compression ratio 9.2-9.5:1; 60kW (80hp) [82PS] at 5200rpm, 40.5kW/L (54.3hp/L) [55.4PS/L]; 114Nm (84.1lbft) at 3400rpm; leaded regular grade.

Engine construction: 1 FOser 34S2C12 downdraught compound carb.

Performance: Max speed 96mph/155kmh (manufacturer's test specifications); acceleration 0 - 62mph/100kmh 17secs; power to weight ratio from 17.0kg/kW (12.8kg/PS); consumption ECE 6.5/9.0/10.0L/100km (43.5/31.4/28.2mpg) [36.2/26.1/23.5US mpg], Estate/Station Wagon 6.6/9.1/10.2L/100km (42.8/31.0/27.7mpg) [35.6/25.8/23.1US mpg].

FSO Polonez

1.5 C/L/LE/SLE - 1.6 LE/SLE

Saloon/Sedan with tailgate, mechanics based on the Polish Fiat 125, engine with 1500cm3 capacity. Launched in May 1978, three-door version in 1980. Birmingham 1986: prototype with modernised body. 1987 also available with 1.6 Litre engine.

> 1.5 Litre
> 60kW-80hp-82PS
> 1 2V Carb

Body, Weight: 3/5-door Saloon/Sedan, 5-seater; kerbweight approx 1125kg, gross vehicle weight 1590kg.

Engine data (DIN): 4-cylinder in-line (77 x 79.5mm), 1481cm3; Compression ratio 9.2:1; 60kW (80hp) [82PS] at 5200rpm, 40.5kW/L (54.3hp/L) [55.4PS/L]; 114Nm (84.1lbft) at 3200rpm.

FSO • Geo

Engine construction: Valves in V 48deg, side camshaft (toothed belt), light–alloy cylinder head; 3 bearing crankshaft; oil capacity 3.5L (3.3US qt); 1 Weber 34 DCMP2/300 downdraught compound carb. 12V 48Ah Battery, 40A alternator; cooling system capacity 7.5L (7.1US qt).

FSO Polonez

Transmission (to rear wheels): 5-speed manual, final drive ratio 4.1.

Gear ratios: 1st 3.778; 2nd 1.944; 3rd 1.307; 4th 1; 5th 0.803; R 3.526.

Chassis: Integral body; front A arm and coil springs, rear rigid axle with semi-elliptic springs and longitudinal compression struts, front antiroll bar, telescopic dampers. Servo/power assisted disc brakes, disc diameter 22.7cm; mechanical handbrake to rear wheels; worm and wheel steering; fuel tank capacity 45L (9.9Gal) [11.9US Gal], reserve 4.5–7L (1.0–1.5Gal) [1.2–1.8US Gal]; tyres 175 SR 13, wheel rims 5J.

Dimensions: Wheelbase 251cm, track 121.5/120cm, clearance 13cm, turning circle 10.8m. Length 432cm, width 165cm, height 138cm.

Performance: Max speed 96mph/155kmh (manufacturers test specifications), speed at 1000rpm in 5th gear 19mph/30.6kmh; acceleration 0 – 62mph/100kmh 17secs or 16secs; power to weight ratio from 18.7kg/kW (13.7kg/PS); consumption ECE 6.6/9.1/10.2L/100km (42.8/31/27.7mpg) [35.6/25.8/23.1US mpg].

```
1.6 Litre
64kW–86hp–87PS
1 2V Carb
```

As 1.5 Litre, except:

Engine data (DIN): 4–cylinder in–line (80 x 79.5mm), 1598cm3; compression ratio 9.5:1; 64kW (86hp) [87PS] at 5200rpm, 40kW/L (54hp/L) [54.4PS/L]; 132Nm (97.4lbft) at 3800rpm; unleaded regular grade.

Engine construction: 1 FOS 34 S2C16 downdraught compound carb.

Transmission: 5–speed manual, final drive ratio 3.9.

Gear ratios: 1st 3.778; 2nd 1.940; 3rd 1.31; 4th 1; 5th 0.803; R 3.526.

Performance: Max speed 96.3mph/155kmh (manufacturer's test specifications), speed at 1000rpm in 5th gear 22.1mph/35.5kmh; power to weight ratio 17.8kg/kW (13.1kg/PS); consumption ECE 6.0/8.5/9.5L/100km (47.1/33.2/29.7mpg) [39.2/27.7/24.8US mpg].

FSO Polonez Prima

GEO — USA/J

Geo/Chevrolet Motor Division, General Motors Corporation, 30 007 Van Dyke Avenue, Warren, Michigan 48090, USA.

A new marque from General Motors and Chevrolet Motors Division, distributor of Far Eastern models from Suzuki, Isuzu and Toyota under the Geo badge.

Geo Metro

US export version of the new edition of the Suzuki Swift. For tecnical data see under Suzuki Japan.

Geo Spectrum

US export version of the new Isuzu Gemini model with front wheel drive. For technical data see Isuzu Japan.

Geo Prizm

Middle class vehicle with front wheel drive, based on the Toyota Corolla, and available as Saloon/Sedan or Liftback; 1.6 Litre DOHC engine with four valves per cylinder; it is produced in California.

Geo Prizm Sedan/Liftback

```
1587cm3
76kW-102hp-103PS
Fuel Injection
```

Body, Weight: 4-door Saloon/Sedan, 5-seater; kerbweight (DIN) from 1050kg; 5-door Liftback, 5-seater; kerbweight (DIN) from 1075kg.

Engine data (SAE net): 4-cylinder in-line (81 x 77mm), 1587cm3; compression ratio 9.5:1; 76kW (102hp) [103PS] at 5800rpm, 47.9kW/L (64.2hp/L) [64.9PS/L]; 137Nm (101lnft) at 4800rpm; premium unleaded.

Engine construction: Front inclined engine. Designated 4A-GEL. 4 valves (in V) per cylinder; 2 x overhead camshaft (toothed belt); light-alloy cylinder head; 5 main bearing crankshaft; oil capacity 3.7 (3.5US qt); electronic fuel injection (license Bosch). Battery 12V 60Ah, 60 Alternator; cooling system capacity approx 6L (5.7US qt).

Transmission (to front wheels): 5-speed manual, final drive ratio 3.722.

Gear ratios: 1st 3.166; 2nd 1.904; 3rd 1.310; 4th 0.969; 5th 0.815; R 3.25.

Chassis: Integral body. Front and rear independent suspension with McPherson struts, front lower A-arm, rear parallel control arm and trailing arm, front and rear antiroll bar. Servo/power assisted brakes, front discs, rear drums, mechanical handbrake to rear wheels; rack and pinion steering, optionally with power assistance; fuel tank capacity 50L (1Gal) [13.2US Gal]; tyres 175/70 SR 13, wheel rims 5J.

Dimensions: Wheelbase 243cm, track 143/141cm, clearance 15.5cm, turning circle 10.2m. Load space, Liftback 17.1/13.2cu ft (485/910dm3), Saloon/Sedan 12cu ft (340dm3). Length FX 434cm, width 166cm, height 133cm.

Geo · Ginetta · Gurgel

Performance: Max speed approx 115mph/185kmh, speed at 1000rpm in 5th gear 21.7mph/35kmh; power to weight ratio from 13.8kg/kW (10.2kg/PS); consumption approx 8-12L/100km (35.3-23.5mpg) [29.4-19.6US mpg].

Geo Tracker

US export version of the Suzuki Escudo/Vitara. For technical details see Suzuki Japan.

Geo Tracker

GINETTA — GB

Ginetta Cars Limited Dunlop Way, Queesway Industrial Estate, Scunthorpe, South Humberside DN16 3RN, England.

English sports car manufacturer, earlier producer of "Kit-car" and now also of completed models.

Ginetta G32

Middle class vehicle based on the Ford Fiesta with two seats and plastic body, and a 1.6-Litre engine. Prototype launched in Autumn 1986 and as production model at Birmingham, 1988.

```
1.6-Litre
71kW-103hp-105PS
Fuel Injection
```

Body, Weight: 2-door Coupe (with plastic body), 2-seater; kerbweight (DIN) 800kg, gross vehicle weight approx 1000kg.

Engine data (DIN): 4-cylinder in-line (79.96 x 79.52mm), 1598cm3; compression ratio 9.5:1; 77kW (103hp) [105PS] at 6000rpm, 48.3kW/L (64.7hp/L) [65.7PS/L]; 138Nm (101.8lbft) at 4800rpm; premium grade.
With Catalyst and KE-Jetronic: Compression ratio 8.5:1; 66kW (88hp) [90PS] at 5800rpm, 41.3kW/L (55.3hp/L) [49.4PS/L]; 123Nm (90.8lbft) at 4600rpm; regular unleaded.

Ginetta G32

Engine construction: Designated CVH; transverse mid-engine. Valves in V(45deg), hydraulic tappets, 1 overhead camshaft (toothed belt); light-alloy cylinder head; 5 bearing crankshaft; oil capacity 3.5L (3.3US qt); Bosch K/KE Jetronic mechanical injection. Battery 12V 43Ah, Alternator 55/70 A; cooling system capacity approx 8L (7.6US qt).

Transmission (to rear wheels): 5-speed manual, floor shift, final drive ratio 3.82 or 4.27.

Gear ratios: 1st 3.15; 2nd 1.91; 3rd 1.28; 4th 0.95; 5th 0.76; R 3.62.

Chassis: Tubular space frame; front independent suspension with upper single control arm and antiroll bar; rear independent suspension with McPherson struts and lower control arm; coil springs and telescopic damper. Four wheel disc brakes, disc diameter, front (ventilated) 24.1cm, rear 24.7cm, mechanical handbrakes to rear wheels; rack and pinion steering; fuel tank capacity 45.5L (10Gal) [12US Gal]; tyres 185/60HR 14 wheel rims 6".

Dimensions: Wheelbase 221cm, track approx 140/140cm, clearance 12cm, turning circle 10m. Load space 8.8cu ft (250dm3). Length 376cm, width 165cm, height 117cm.

Performance: Max speed approx 124mph/200kmh, speed at 1000rpm in 5th gear 22.7-20.3mph/36.5-32.7kmh; acceleration 0 - 62mph/100kmh approx 9secs; power to weight ratio 10.4kg/kW (7.6kg/PS); consumption approx 6-11L/100km (47.1-25.7mpg) [29.2-21.4US mpg].

GURGEL — BR

Gurgel sa Industrial Com de Veiculos, Rodovia Washington Luiz, km 171, 13500 Rio Claro, S.P (Caixa Postol 98), Brazil

Small manufacturer of vehicles, company owned by and named after Dr. Gurgel.

Gurgel BR-800

Small, economical vehicle with 2 horizontally opposed-cylinder Boxer engine, 792cm3, plastic body. Launched in August 1987. Data incomplete.

```
792cm3
23.5kW-31.5hp-32PS
1 Carb
```

Body, Weight: Saloon/Sedan (plastic body) 2-door, 4-seater; kerbweight (DIN) approx 550kg, gross vehicle weight 900kg.

Engine data (DIN): 2-cylinder horizontally opposed engine (85.5 x 69mm), 792cm3; compresssion ratio 8.5:1 23.5kW (31.5hp) [32PS] at 4500rpm 29.7kW/L (38.8hp/L) [40.4PS/L]; 57Nm (42lbft) at 2800rpm; leaded regular grade.

Engine construction: Front engine, central camshaft (gears) light-alloy cylinder head and block; wet cylinder liners; 3 bearing crankshaft; oil capacity 2.5L (2.4US qt), downdraught carb Brosol H35 Alfa 1 28. Battery 12 V 32Ah, alternator 350W; water cooled.

Transmission (to rear wheels): 4-speed manual, floor shift; final drive ratio 4.1.

Gear ratios: 1st 3.07; 2nd 2.02; 3rd 1.39; 4th 1; R 3.57.

Gurgel BR-800

Chassis: Plastic body secured to steel frame chassis; front swinging axle, lower wishbone and upper control arm, 'Spring-Shocks' telescopic damper, rear rigid axle with leaf spring, telescopic damper. Front disc, rear drum brake; mechanical handbrake to rear wheels; rack and pinion steering; 40L (8.8Gal) [10.6US Gal] fuel tank; tyres 145 SR 13, wheel rims 5J.

Dimensions: Wheelbase 191cm, track 128.5/128.8cm, clearance 15cm, turning circle 9m, length 319.5cm, width 146cm, height 146cm.

Performance: Max speed 68.5mph/110kmh (manufacturers test specifications), speeds at 1000rpm in 4th gear 15.6mph/25.2kmh ; power to weight ratio from 23.4kg/kW (17.2kg/PS); consumption (touring) 4–7L/100kmh (70.6–40.4mpg) [58.8–33.6US mpg].

Gurgel X-12 Tocantins

Open 4–seater, derived from the Volkswagen, with 1600cm3 engine. Model 'TR' with Hardtop.

```
1.6 Litre
37kW–49.6hp–50PS
1 Carb
```

Body, Weight: Plastic Body, 4–seater; kerbweight (DIN) 800kg, 'TR' with Hardtop 830kg, gross vehicle weight 1150kg.

Engine data: (DIN) 4–cylinder, horizontally opposed engine (85.5 x 69mm), 1584 cm3; compression ratio 7.2:1; 37kW (49.6hp) [50PS] at 4200rpm, 23.4kW/L (31.4hp/L) [31.5PS/L]; 108Nm (79.7lbft) at 2200rpm; leaded regular grade.

Engine construction: Rear mounted engine, central camshaft (gear), light–alloy cylinder head and block; 4 bearing crankshaft; oil capacity 2.5L (2.4US qt), oil cooler; 1 downdraught carb Solex H30 FC; oil-bath air cleaner. Battery 12V 36Ah, Dynamo 350W; air cooled engine.

Transmission (to rear wheels): 4–speed manual, final drive ratio, 4.125 or 4.375. Optional limited slip differential.

Gear ratios: 1st 3.8; 2nd 2.06; 3rd 1.32; 4th 0.89; R 3.88.

Chassis: Steel chassis in plastic body, front double-crank arm suspension with torsion bar. Rear independent suspension with swinging axle, transverse leaf spring and antiroll bar, telescopic damper. Front disc, rear drum brake, mechanical handbrake at rear wheels; worm and wheel steering; fuel tank 41L (9Gal) [10.8US Gal]; tyres 7.35–14, wheel rims 5.5".

Dimensions: Wheelbase 204cm, track 138.5/138.5cm, clearance 24cm, turning circle 9.5m. Load space 1.8cu ft (50dm3). Length 348cm, width 167cm, height 156/160cm.

Performance: Max speed 81mph/130kmh (manufactures test specifications), speed at 1000rpm in 4th gear 20mph/32.2kmh; power to weight ratio from 21.6kg/kW (16kg/PS); consumption (touring) 8L/100kmh (35.3mpg) [29.4US mpg].

Gurgel X–12 Tocantins

Gurgel Carajas

Open or closed wagon with 1.8 Litre or 1.6 Litre diesel engine, based on the VW Passat, rear wheel drive. Launched November 1984.

```
1.8 Litre
63/68KW–84/91HP–85/92PS
1 2V Carb
```

Body, Weight: 3/5 door Station Wagon, 4/5–seater; kerbweight (DIN) 1200–1270kg, gross vehicle weight 2020kg.

Engine data (DIN): 4–cylinder in–line (81 x 86.4mm), 1781cm3; compression ratio 8.3:1; 63kW (84hp) [85PS] at 5000rpm, 35.4kW/L (47hp/L) [47.7PS/L]; 146Nm (107.7lbft) at 2600rpm; leaded regular grade (86R).

Engine for operation on Ethyl Alcohol: Compression ratio 12.1; 68kw (91hp) [92PS] at 5000rpm, 38.2kW/L (51.2hp/L) [51.7PS/L]; 149Nm (110lbft) at 2600rpm.

Engine construction: Front transverse engine. 1 overhead camshaft (toothed belt); light alloy–cylinder head; 5 bearing crankshaft; oil capacity 3.5L (3.3US qt); 1 downdraught 2V carb, Brosol–Pierburg 2E7. Battery 12V 65Ah alternator 35A; cooling system capacity approx 7.1L (6.7US qt).

Transmission (to rear wheels): 4–speed manual, final drive ratio 5.143.

Gear ratios: 1st 3.8; 2nd 2.06; 3rd 1.32; 4th 0.89; R 3.88.

Chassis: Steel chassis in plastic body, front torsion bar, antiroll bar, rear semi trailing arm, coil spring, telescopic damper. Front disc, rear drum brake, mechanical handbrake on rear wheels; worm and wheel steering; fuel tank 80L (17.6Gal) [21.1US Gal]; tyres 7.35 x 14.6, wheel rims 5.5 J.

Dimensions: Wheelbase 255cm, track 131/141.5cm, clearance 29cm. Load space 17–58.2cu ft (480–1650dm3). Length 411.5cm, width 170.5cm, height 177.5cm. 5-door: Length 436.5cm, height 187cm.

Performance: Max speed 81mph/130kmh (manufacturers test specifications), speed at 1000rpm in 4th gear 16mph/25.8kmh; power to weight ratio 17.6kg/kW (13kg/PS); consumption (touring) 8–12L/100km (35.3–23.5mpg) [29.4–19.6US mpg].

Gurgel Carajas

```
1.6 Litre Diesel
37kW–49.6hp–50PS
Injection Pump
```

As 1.8 Litre except:

Engine data (SAE): 4–cylinder in–line (76.5 x 86.4mm), 1588cm3; compression ratio 23.5:1; 37kW (49.6hp) [50 PS] at 4500rpm, 23.2kW/L (31hp/L) [31.5PS/L]; 93Nm (68.6lbft) at 3000rpm.

Engine construction: Swirl chamber diesel engine. Overhead camshaft (toothed belt); light–alloy cylinder block, 5 bearing crankshaft; oil capacity 3,5L (3.3US qt). Bosch VE distributor pump, centrifugal govenor, cold start system. Bosch heater plugs, 12V 63Ah battery, 45/65A alternator. Cooling system capacity 5.6L (5.3US qt).

Performance: Max speed approx 75mph/120kmh; power to weight ratio 27.2kg/L (20kg/PS); consumption 6–10L/100km (47–28mpg) [39–23.5US mpg].

HINDUSTAN   IND

Hindustan Motors Limited, 9/1 R N Mukherjee Road, Culcutta 700 001, India.

Indian Firm. Manufacturer of medium size vehicles, with BMC mechanicals.

Hindustan Ambassador Mark 4

Mid–size car with 1.5 Litre engine and 4–speed manual transmission. Mark 4 with higher performance and modifications to the body and interior. Launched with Morris Oxford Series 11 May 1954.

```
1.5 Litre
37kW–49hp–50PS
1 Carb
```

Body, Weight: Saloon/Sedan, 4–door, 5–seater; kerbweight (DIN) from 1160kg, gross vehicle weight 1525kg.

Engine data (DIN): 4–cylinder in–line (73.025 x 88.9mm), 1489cm3; compression ratio 7.2:1; 37kW (49.6hp) [50 PS] at 4400rpm, 24.9kW/L (33.4hp/L) [34.3PS/L]; 103Nm (76lbft) at 2500rpm; leaded regular grade. Also available with 1.8 Litre diesel engine.

Hindustan • Hofstetter

Engine construction: Side camshaft (chain); 3 bearing crankshaft; oil capacity 4.25L (4US qt); 1 downdraught carb. Battery 12V 60/62Ah Dynamo 297W; cooling system capacity approx (without heating system) 8L (7.6US qt).

Transmission (to rear wheels); 4–speed manual, 2nd, 3rd, and 4th gear synchromesh; final drive ratio 4.555.

Gear ratios: 1st 3.807; 2nd 2.253; 3rd 1.506; 4th 1; R 3.807.

Chassis: Integral body; front swinging arm suspension with torsion bar. Rear rigid axle with semi–elliptic leaf spring, telescopic damper. Drum brakes (optional servo/power assisted), mechanical handbrake to rear wheels. Rack and pinion steering; fuel tank 54.5L (12Gal) [14.3US Gal]; tyres 5.90–15, wheel rims 4J.

Dimensions: Wheelbase 246.5cm, track 136/135cm, clearance 16cm, turning circle 10.9m. Load space 15.9cu ft (450dm3). Length 431cm, width 167.5cm, height 160cm.

Performance: Max speed 78mph/125kmh (manufacturers test specifications), speed at 1000rpm in 4th gear 16.4mph/26.4kmh. Power to weight ratio from 31.4kg/kW (23.2kg/PS); consumption (DIN) 9.7L/100km (29mpg) [24.2US mpg].

Hindustan Ambassador Mark IV

Hindustan Contessa

Saloon/Sedan based on the Vauxhall Victor (1972) with a 4-cylinder engine. Start of production 1984.

```
1.5/1.8 Litre
65/37kW–87/49hp–88/50PS
1 Carb
```

Body, Weight: Saloon/Sedan 4–door, 5–seater, kerbweight (DIN) 1140kg, gross vehicle weight 1590kg.

Engine data (DIN): 4–cylinder in–line (84 x 82mm), 1818cm3; compression ratio 8.5:1; 65kW (87hp) [88PS] at 5000rpm, 35.7kW/L (47.8hp/L) [48.4PS/L]; 136Nm (100.4lbft) at 3000rpm; unleaded regular grade.
Optional with 1.5 Litre engine: (73.25 x 88.9mm), 1489cm3; compression ratio 7.2:1; 37kW (49hp) [50PS] at 4400rpm; 100Nm (73.8) at 2500rpm.
Or compression ratio 8.3:1; 39.5kW (53hp) [54PS].

Engine construction: Overhead and side camshaft (chain); 3 bearing crankshaft; oil capacity 4.25L (4US qt); 1 downdraught carb. Battery 12V 60/62Ah, dynamo 297W; cooling system capacity approx 8L (7.6US qt).

Transmission (to rear wheels): 4–speed manual, final drive ratio 3.4 or 4.56.

Gear ratios: 1st 3.807; 2nd 2.253; 3rd 1.506; 4th 1; R 3.807.

Chassis: Integral body; front semi–swinging arm suspension with coil springs, rear rigid axle, trailing arms, Panhard rod and coil springs, telescopic damper. Drum brakes, (optional servo/power assisted), mechanical handbrake on rear wheels; rack and pinion steering; fuel tank 65L (14.3Gal) [17.2US Gal]; tyres 175 SR 13 or 6.40-13, wheel rims 5J.

Dimensions: Wheelbase 266.5cm, track 142/140cm, clearance 15/16cm, turning circle 11.5m, load space 21.2cu ft (600dm3). Length 457cm, width 170cm, height 137.5cm.

Performance: Max speed approx 99mph/160kmh or 78mph/125kmh, speed at 1000rpm in 4th gear 20.4/15.2mph/32.8/24.5kmh; power to weight ratio from 17.5kg/kw (13.0 kg/PS). Consumption approx 9–12L/100kmh (31.4–23.5mpg) [26–19.6US mpg].

Hindustan Contessa

HOFSTETTER BR

Tecnodesign Mecanica Ind e Com Ltda, Rua Gomes de Carvalho 1165, 04547 Sao Paulo, Brasil.

Small manufacturer of sports cars, using VW mechanics.

Hofstetter Turbo

Mid–engine with Gull–Wing doors. 2.0 Litre VW engine. Prototype shown November 1984 at Sao Paulo show.

Hofstetter Turbo

```
2.0 Litre
129/199kW–173/267hp–175/270PS
1 2V Carb
```

Body, Weight: 2–door Coupe, 2–seater; kerbweight (DIN) 1030kg.

Engine data (DIN): a) Garrett–Turbocharged engine for operation on Ethyl Alcohol: 4–cylinder in–line (82.5 x 92.8mm), 1984cm3; compression ratio 12:1; 129kW (173hp) [175PS] at 4950rpm, 65kW/L (87.1hp/L) [88.2PS/L]; 280Nm (1206.6lbft) at 3600rpm.
b) "S" with intercooler: Compression ratio 9:5; 199kW (267hp) [270PS], 100.3kW/L (134.4hp/L) [136.1PS/L].
c) Petrol/Gasoline engine: Compression up to 73–82kW (98-110hp) [99-112PS]; unleaded regular grade (86R).

Engine construction: Mid–engine, inclined to the right, 1 overhead camshaft (toothed belt); light–alloy cylinder block; 5 bearing camshaft; oil capacity 3.5L (3.3US qt); 1 downdraught 2V carb Brosol Pierburg 2E7. Garrett turbocharger, max charge-air pressure 1.3 bar. 12V 60Ah, alternator 65A; cooling system capacity, approx 12L (11.4US qt).

Transmission (to rear wheels): 5–speed manual, final drive ratio 4.11.

Gear ratios: 5–speed manual: 1st 3.45; 2nd 1.94; 3rd 1.29; 4th 0.97; 5th 0.8; R 3.17.

Chassis: Tubular frame chassis; front upper wishbone, lower control arm, coil spring and telescopic damper; rear rigid axle with trailing arm and control arm, McPherson strut with coil spring, antiroll bar, telescopic damper. Servo/power assisted disc brakes, front ventilated; disc diameter. front 23.8cm, rear 23.9cm, mechanical handbrake to rear wheels; rack and pinion steering. Fuel tank 51L (11.2Gal) [13.5US Gal]. Tyres; front 205/60 VR 14, rear 255/55 VR 14. Wheel rims 7.5J.

Dimensions: Wheelbase 234cm, track 136/140cm, clearance 14cm, length 418cm, width 174cm, height 108cm.

Performance (173hp): Max speed 143mph/230kmh (manufacturers test specifications), speed at 1000rpm in 5th gear 21.2mph/34.1kmh; acceleration 0 – 62mph/100kmh 7.5secs; power to weight ratio from 8kg/kW (5.9Kg/PS); consumption 14.5L/100km (19.5mpg) [16.2US mpg].

Hofstetter Turbo

HOLDEN — AUS

General Motors–Holden's, 241 Salmon St, PO Box 1714, Melbourne 3001, Australia.

Australian manufacturer, a subsidiary General Motors. A distributor of various imported vehicles: Barina (Suzuki Swift), Gemini (Isuzu), Astra (Nissan Cherry, also with Opel engine).

Holden Camira

Compact Saloon/Sedan of General Motors J–Car familiy, with a 1.6 Litre carb or 1.8 Litre injection engine. For technical data refer to the Opel Ascona and Vauxhall Cavalier (Estate/Station Wagon).

Holden Commodore/Calais

Executive - S/SL - Berlina - Calais

New model. Derived from the Opel Senator with a 3.8 Litre 6–cylinder or 5 Litre V8 engine; rear disc brakes; Calais series with luxurious fittings. Launched October 1978.

Holden Commodore

```
3.8 Litre V6
125kW–167hp–170PS
Fuel Injection
```

Body, Weight: Saloon/Sedan; 4–door, 5–seater, kerbweight (DIN) 1310kg. Saloon/Sedan Calais; 4–door, 5–seater, kerbweight (DIN) 1380kg Estate/Station Wagon; 5–door, 5–seater kerbweight (DIN) 1300– 1350kg.

Engine data (DIN): 6–cylinder in–V 90deg (96.52 x 86.36mm), 3791cm3. Compression ratio 8.5:1; 125kW (167hp) [170PS] at 4800rpm, 33.0kW/L (44.2hp/L) [44.8PS/L]; 292Nm (215.5lbft) at 3200rpm; unleaded regular grade.

Engine construction: Designated Buick LN 3 "3800". Hydraulic tappets, 1 overhead camshaft (chain); light–alloy cylinder head; 7 bearing crankshaft; oil capacity 3.8L (3.6US qt); electronic fuel injection. Battery 12V 54/69Ah, alternator 105A; Cooling system capacity approx 11.7L (11.1US qt).

Transmission: (to rear wheels): a) 5–speed manual, final drive ratio 3.08. b) Automatic THM 700 hydraulic torque converter and 4–speed Planetary gear set with OD, selector lever in the middle; final drive ratio 3.08. Also available with limited slip differential.

Gear ratios: a) 5–speed manual: 1st 3.25; 2nd 1.99; 3rd 1.29; 4th 1; 5th 0.72; R 3.382.
b) Automatic: Max torque multiplication in torque converter 2 times; Planetary gear set ratios: 1st 3.06; 2nd 1.63; 3rd 1; OD 0.7; R 2.182.

Chassis: Integral body; front McPherson Strut and control arm with tie bar, rear rigid axle with trailing arms and Panhard rod. Front and rear (not on Saloon/Sedan) antiroll bar, coil spring and telescopic damper. Servo/power assisted brakes, front discs (ventilated), rear drums, discs diameter. 26.8cm, mechanical handbrake to rear wheels. Rack and pinion steering, (optional power assisted); fuel tank 63L (13.8Gal) [16.6US Gal], optional 85L (18.7Gal) [22.5US Gal], Estate/Station Wagon 68L (14.9Gal) [18US Gal]. Tyres 185/75 HR 14, wheel rims 6J (optional tyres 205/65 HR 15).

Dimensions: Wheelbase 273cm, Estate/Station Wagon 282cm, track 145/148cm, clearance 14.5cm, turning circle 10.4m. Load space 17.7cu ft (500dm3), Estate/Station Wagon 51.4cu ft (1455dm3). Length 485cm, width 179.5cm, height 140.5cm – Estate/Station Wagon 139cm.

Performance: Max speed 115–121mph/185–195kmh, speed at 1000rpm in 5th gear 32.7mph/52.6kmh; acceleration 0 – 62mph/100kmh 8.3secs, Automatic 8.5secs; power to weight ratio from 10.5kg/kW (7.7kg/PS); consumption approx 11–16L/100km (25.7–17.7mpg) [21.4–14.7US mpg].

Holden Commodore Wagon

```
5 Litre V8
122/140kW–163/188hp–166/190PS
1 4V Carb
```

As 3.8 Litre, except:

Weight: Kerbweight (DIN) 1380kg.

Engine data (DIN): 8–cylinder in V 90deg (101.6 x 77.77mm), 5044cm3; compression ratio 9.4:1; 122kW (163hp) [166PS] at 4400rpm, 24.2kW/L (32.4hp/L) [32.9PS/L]; 323Nm (238.4lbft) at 3200rpm.
With fuel injection: 140kW (188hp) [190PS] at 5000rpm.

Engine construction: Designated GMH 308. Hydraulic tappets, central camshaft (chain); 5 bearing crankshaft; oil capacity 5L (4.7US qt); 1 downdraught Rochester or fuel injection. Battery 12V 62Ah, alternator 45/60A; cooling system capacity approx 12.5/13.4L (11.8/12.7US qt).

Transmission: Automatic, final drive ratio 3.08.

Chassis: Front disc diameter 28.9cm, rear 26.8cm; tyres 205/55 VR 16, wheel rims 7".

Performance: Max speed 118mph/190kmh, speed at 1000rpm top gear 23mph/37kmh; power to weight ratio from 9.9kg/kW (7.3kg/PS); consumption 12–19L/100km(23.5–14.9mpg)[19.6–12.4USmpg].

Holden • Honda

Holden Calais V8

HONDA   J

Honda Motor Co Ltd, No 5.5–Chome, Yeasu, Chuo–Ku, Tokyo, Japan

Largest manufacturer of motorcycles in the world. Started to produce motor vehicles in 1964. Some models also assembled in the USA. Integra and Legend Series even sold under other marque designation (Acura)

MODEL RANGE
Today - City - Civic/Ballade - Quint Integra - Concerto - NS–X – Accord/Vigor - Prelude - Legend

Honda Today

Small 3 door vehicle with a 2–cylinder engine. Front wheel drive. Launched September 1985. Spring 1988 3–cylinder replaced by 2–cylinder with four valve heads. Modification to body front and rear.

```
0.55 Litre
32/26kW–43/35hp–44/36PS
1 2V Carb
```

Body, Weight: Saloon/Sedan, 3–door, 2/4–seater; kerbweight (DIN) 580/650kg.

Engine data (JIS Nett): 3–cylinder in–line (62.5 x 59.5mm), 547cm3; compression ratio 9.8:1; 32kW (42hp) [44PS] at 8000rpm; 58.5kW/L (78.4hp/L) [80.4PS/L]; 45Nm (33.2lbft) at 4500rpm; leaded regular grade.
Automatic: 31kW (41hp) [42PS]; 46Nm (33.9lbft).
With central injection: 31kW (41hp) [42PS]; 45Nm (33.2lbft).
With carb: 26kW (35hp) [36PS] at 6500rpm; 44Nm (32.5lbft) at 5200rpm.

Engine construction: Designated E 05A. Transverse front engine inclined 60deg to the right. 4 valves in V 54 deg per cylinder. 1 overhead camshaft (toothed belt), light–alloy cylinder head, 4 bearing crankshaft; oil capacity 2.9L (2.7US qt); Electronic fuel injection, central injection or sliding pressure carb. Battery 12V 32Ah, alternator 35A; cooling system capacity approx 3.L (2.8US qt).

Transmission (to front wheels): a) 4–speed manual (35hp), final drive ratio 5.214.
b) 5-speed manual, final drive ratio 5.692 or 5.214.
c) Automatic, hydraulic torque converter and 3-speed Planetary gear set, final drive ratio 5.357.

Honda Today

Gear ratios: a) 4–speed manual: 1st 3.916; 2nd 2.235; 3rd 1.461; 4th 1.031; R 3.909.
b) 5-speed manual: 1st 3.916; 2nd 2.235; 3rd 1.461; 4th 1.064; 5th 0.857; R 3.909.
c) Automatic: Max torque multiplication in converter 1.3 times, Planetary gear ratios: 1st 2.647; 2nd 1.515; 3rd 0.930; R 2.047 or (36PS) 1st 2.444; 2nd 1.441; 3rd 0.930; R 2.047.

Chassis: Integral body; front independent suspension with McPherson strut and control arm; rear torsion crank axle (longitudinal tube axle) with Panhard rod and coil springs. Front disc, rear drum brakes; mechanical handbrake to rear wheels; rack and pinion steering; fuel tank 30L (6.6Gal) [7.9US Gal]; tyres 145/65 SR 13, 36PS 135 SR 12 or 145/70 SR 12, wheel rims 4J.

Dimensions: Wheelbase 233cm, track 122.5/123cm, clearance 15.5cm, turning circle 9.8m. Length 319.5cm, width 139.5cm, height 132cm.

Performance: Max speed approx 81-90mph/130-145kmh speed at 1000rpm in 5th gear 12.2mph/19.6kmh; power to weight ratio from 19.1kg/kW (13.9kg/PS); consumption 4–7L/100km (70.6–40.4mpg) [58.8–33.6US mpg].

Honda City

Small front wheel drive 3–door vehicle with independent suspension. 5–speed manual or automatic transmission. Launched November 1986. Autumn 1988: More powerful engine.

```
1.2 Litre
56kW–75hp–76PS
1 Carb
```

Body, Weight: Saloon/Sedan, 3–door, 5–seater; kerbweight 680– 700kg.

Engine data (JIS Nett): 4–cylinder in–line (72 x 76mm), 1238cm3, compression ratio 9.5:1; 56kW (75hp) [76PS] at 6500rpm, 45.2kW/L (60.6hp/L) [61.4PS/L]; 98Nm (72.3lbft) at 4000rpm.

Engine construction: Designated D12A, transverse front engine, 4 valves per cylinder, 1 overhead camshaft (toothed belt); 5 bearing crankshaft; oil capacity 4.2L (4US qt); 1 downdraught two stage electronic controlled carb. Battery 12 V 35/47Ah, alternator 35/45A; cooling system capacity approx 4.2L (4US qt).

Transmission (to front wheels): a) 5–speed manual, final drive ratio 4.266.
b) Automatic, hydraulic torque converter and 4–speed Planetary gear set, final drive ratio 3.933.

Gear ratios: a) 5–speed manual: 1st 3.181; 2nd 1.750; 3rd 1.166; 4th 0.852; 5th 0.710; R 2.916.
b) Automatic; Planetary gear set ratios: 1st 2.647; 2nd 1.480; 3rd 0.972; 4th 0.731; R 2.047.

Chassis: Integral body; front independent suspension with McPherson struts, track control arm and antiroll bar; rear torsion crank axle (longitudinal tube axle) with Panhard rod and coil springs. Servo/power assisted brakes, front disc, rear drums; mechanical handbrake on rear wheels; rack and pinion steering (optional power assisted). Fuel tank 40L (8.8Gal) [10.6US Gal]; Tyres 165/70 SR 12 or 175/60 SR 13, wheel rims 4.5 or 5J.

Dimensions: Wheelbase 240cm, track 140/141cm, clearance 16cm, turning circle 9.2m. Length 360.5cm, width 162cm, height 133.5cm.

Performance: Max speed 93.2mph/150kmh, speed at 1000rpm in 5th gear 20.4mph/32.9kmh; power to weight ratio from 12.2kg/kW (8.9kg/PS); consumption 5–8L/100km (56.5–35.3mpg) [47–29.4US mpg].

Honda City EE

Honda

```
1.3 Litre
73/60kW–98/80hp–100/82PS
Injection/Carb
```

As 1.2 Litre, except:

Weight: Kerbweight (DIN) 760–820kg, version with carb 730–800kg.

Engine data (JIS Nett): 4-cylinder in-line (73.7 x 76mm), 1296cm3; compression ratio 9.6:1; 73kW (98hp) [100PS] at 6500rpm, 56.3kW/L (75.4hp/L) [77.2PS/L]; 114Nm (84.1lbft) at 5500rpm.
With Carb: 60kW (80hp) [82PS] at 6500rpm; 103Nm (76lbft) at 4000rpm.

Engine construction: Designated D 13 C. PGM-FI electronic fuel injection.

Transmission: a) 5-speed manual, final drive ratio 4.500, 80hp 4.266.
b) Automatic, final drive ratio 3.866.

Gear ratios: a) 5-speed manual: 1st 3.181; 2nd 1.764; 3rd 1.200; 4th 0.896; 5th 0.718; R 2.916.
80hp as 1.2 Litre.
b) Automatic, Planetary gear set ratios: 1st 2.647; 2nd 1.480; 3rd 1.028; 4th 0.775; R 2.047.
80hp as 1.2 Litre.

Chassis: 98hp: Front ventilated disc brakes; servo/power assisted steering; tyres 175/60 SR 13.

Performance: Max speed approx 112mph/180kmh. Speed at a 1000rpm in 5th gear 19mph/30.5kmh; power to weight ratio from 10.4kg/kW (7.6kg/PS); consumption approx 6-10L/100km (47.1-28.2mpg) [39.2-23.5US mpg].

Honda Civic-Ballade

Front wheel drive hatchback with a 1.3 or 1.6 Litre transverse engine. Available in Saloon/Sedan, Shuttle Wagon and Coupe CRX. In some countries badged as the Ballade. Launched Autumn 1983, modifications to the interior and suspension in September 1987, also a new 4-valve engine. "Real Time" four wheel drive for Saloon/Sedan and Shuttle.

```
1.3 Litre
55kW–74hp–75PS
1 2V Carb
```

Not available for Shuttle and CRX

Body, Weight: Saloon/Sedan; 3–door, 5–seater; kerbweight (DIN) 800kg. Sallon/Sedan; 4–door, 5–seater; kerbweight (DIN) 870kg. Estate/Station Wagon; 5–door, 5–seater; kerbweight (DIN) 900kg. Coupe; 3–door, 2+2–seater; kerbweight (DIN) 830kg.

Engine data (DIN): 4–cylinder in–line (76 x 76mm), 1343cm3; compression ratio 9.0:1; 55kW (74hp) [75PS] at 6300rpm, 41KW/L (54.9hp/L) [55.8PS/L]; 102Nm (75.2lbft) at 3100rpm; leaded regular grade.
Japanese Version (JIS nett): 60kW (80.4hp) [82PS] at 6300rpm, 44.7kW/L (59.9hp/L) [61.1PS/L]; 104Nm (176.7lbft) at 3500rpm.

Engine constuction: Transverse front engine, 4–valves (in V) per cylinder, 1 overhead camshaft (toothed belt); light-alloy cylinder head and block, 5 bearing crankshaft; oil capacity 3.5L (3.3US qt); downdraught two stage carb, electronic engine management. Battery 12V 35/47Ah, alternator 45-65A; cooling system capacity approx 4.4-5.0L (4.2-4.7US qt).

Transmission (to front wheels): a) 5-speed manual, final drive ratio 4.058 or 4.250.
b) Automatic, hydraulic torque converter 4-speed Planetary gear set and lock-up, final drive ratio 3.933.

Gear ratios: a) 5-speed manual: 1st 3.250; 2nd 1.894; 3rd 1.259; 4th 0.937; 5th 0.771; R 3.153.
b) Automatic; Planetary gear set ratios: 1st 2.705; 2nd 1.560; 3rd 1.027; 4th 0.780; R 1.954.

Chassis: Integral body; all–round independent suspension with coil springs and air adjustable shock absorbers, front upper A–arm, lower control arm and antiroll bar; rear trailing arms with upper and lower control arms. Servo/power assisted brakes, front ventilated discs, rear drums, mechanical handbrake on rear wheels; rack and pinion steering (optional power assisted). Fuel tank 45L (9.9Gal) [11.9US Gal]; tyres 155 SR 13, (optional 165/70 SR 13), wheel rims 4.5J (optional 5J).

Dimensions: a) Saloon/Sedan 3–door, wheelbase 250cm, track 145/145.5cm, clearance 16cm, turning circle 10.4m; load space 8.8cu ft (250dm3). Length 396.5cm, width 168cm, height 133cm.

b) Saloon/Sedan 4–door: wheelbase 250cm, track 145/145.5cm, clearance 16cm, turning circle 10.4m; load space 13.5cu ft (383dm3). Length 423cm, width 169cm, height 136cm.

Performance: Max speed Saloon/Sedan 3–door 104.4mph/168kmh (manufacturers test specifications) speed at 1000rpm in 5th gear 21mph/33.8kmh (4.058:1); acceleration 0 – 62mph/100kmh 11secs; power to weight ratio from 13.3kg/kW (9.8kg/PS); consumption (ECE) 5.1/6.8/7.5L/100km (55.4/41.5/37.7mpg) [46.1/34.6/31.4US mpg].

Honda Civic Hatchback

```
1.5 Litre
69kW–93hp–94PS
Central/Single point Injection – 1/2 Carbs
```

As Civic 1300, except:

Body, Weight: a) Saloon/Sedan 3–door 825–895kg.
b) Saloon/Sedan 4–door 885–955kg.
c) Shuttle 5–door 900kg.
d) Coupe CRX 830kg.

Engine data (Catalyst DIN): 4–cylinder in–line (75 x 84.5mm), 1493cm3; compresion ratio 9.2:1; 69kw (93hp) [94PS] at 6000rpm, 46.2kW/L (61.9hp/L) [63.0 PS/L]; 121Nm (89.2lbft) at 4500rpm; unleaded regular grade.
USA version: Identical data.
Japanese version (JIS nett): 1493cm3; 77kW (103hp) [105PS] at 6500rpm; 130Nm (95.9lbft) at 4500rpm.
With automatic or 4WD: 73.5kW (98.4hp) [100PS] at 6300rpm; 126Nm (92.9lbft) at 4500rpm.
With 1 carb (3–door Shuttle): 67kW (89.8hp) [91PS] at 6000rpm; 119Nm (87.8lbft) at 4000rpm.
European Version without Catalyst (DIN): (75 x 79mm), 1396cm3; compression ratio 9.3:1; 66kW (88.4hp) [90PS] at 6300rpm; 112Nm (82.6lbft) at 4500rpm.
For CRX HF (USA) 2 valves, 1 carb (SAE nett): 1493cm3; 46kW (61.6hp) [62PS] at 4500rpm; 122Nm (90lbft) at 2000rpm.

Engine construction: Electronic central/single point injection (catalyst version). 2 horizontal draught constant pressure carbs or 1 down draught carb. Battery 42-60Ah, cooling system capacity 5.1L (4.8US qt).

Transmission (to front wheels, 4WD): a) 5-speed manual, final drive ratio 4.058, 4.250, USA also 3.89 (CRX HF 2.95).
b) Automatic, final drive ratio 3.933.
Saloon/Sedan and Shuttle 4WD (73.4kW engine), permanent four– wheel–drive with viscous coupling. 5-speed manual with range change, final drive ratio 4.428

Gear ratios: a) 5-speed manual: As 1300.
For 4WD: 1st 3.384; 2nd 1.950; 3rd 1.275; 4th 0.941; 5th 0.783; R 3.000; Low range 4.512.
b) Automatic: As 1300.

Chassis: Tyres 165/70 SR 13 or 175/70 SR 13 (optional 185/60 SR/HR 14), wheel rims 5J.

Dimensions: Shuttle: Wheelbase 250cm, track 144.5/145.5cm (4WD 144/145cm). Load space 22.9cu ft (648dm3), length 410.5cm width 169cm, height 147cm, 4WD 151.5cm. Coupe CRX: Wheelbase 230cm, track 145/145.5cm, clearance 10.5cm, turning circle 9.8m. Load space 6.9cu ft (196dm3), length 375.5cm, width 167.5cm, height 127cm.

Performance: Max speed 3–door 111mph/178kmh, 4-door 109mph/175kmh, Shuttle 107mph/172kmh. With automatic 107–105– 103mph/172–168–165kmh (manufacturers test specifications). Speed at 1000rpm in 5th gear (4.058:1) 21.1mph/33.9kmh; power to weight ratio from 10.7kg/kW (7.9kg/PS); consumption 6–10L/100km (47.1– 28.2mpg) [39.2–23.5US mpg]

Honda

Honda Civic Sedan 4WD

1.6 Litre
79kW–106hp–107PS
Fuel Injection

Not for CRX (except USA) As Civic 1300 except:

Body, Weight: Saloon/Sedan 3–door 850–910kg. Saloon/Sedan 4–door 900–970kg, 4WD 1040kg. Shuttle 5–door 940kg, 4WD 1080kg. CRX (USA) 915kg.

Engine data (Catalyst DIN): (75 x 90mm), 1590cm3; compression ratio 9.1:1; 79kW (106hp) [107PS] at 6300rpm, 49.7kW/L (66.6hp/L) [67.3PS/L]; 133Nm (98.1bft) at 5200rpm; unleaded regular grade.
USA version: 81kW (109hp) [110PS] at 6000rpm; 135Nm (99.6lbft) at 5000rpm.
European version (DIN): 85kW (114hp) [116PS] at 6300rpm; 141Nm (104lbft) at 5300rpm.
Japanese version (JIS nett): 88kW (118hp) [120PS] at 6300rpm 55.3kW/L (74.1hp/L) [75.5PS/L]; 142Nm (104.7lbft) at 5500rpm.

Engine construction: Electronic fuel–injection PGM–Fl. Battery 60Ah.

Transmission (to front wheels, 4WD): a) 5–speed manual, final drive ratio 4.058/4.250.
b) Automatic, final drive ratio 3.933.
Sedan and Shuttle 4WD, permanent four–wheel–drive with viscous coupling. 5–speed manual with range change, final drive ratio 4.928/4.428.

Gear ratios: a) 5–speed manual: As 1300.
For 4WD: 1st 3.384; 2nd 1.950; 3rd 1.275; 4th 0.941; 5th 0.783; R 3.000; range change 4.512.
b) Automatic: As 1300.

Chassis: Rear antiroll bar. Some models with four wheel disc brakes (front ventilated), Shuttle rear drums; tyres 175/70 SR 13, 175/65 SR 13 185/60 HR 14 or 185/65 HR 14. 4WD 165 SR 13 or 175/65 SR 14, wheel rims 5J.

Dimensions: Shuttle; wheelbase 250cm, track 144.5/145.5cm, (4WD 144/145cm). Max load space 22.9cu ft (648dm3). Length 410.5cm, width 169cm, height 147cm, 4WD 151.5cm.

Performance: Max speed Saloon/Sedan 118mph/190kmh, Shuttle 4WD 107mph/172kmh (manufacturers test specifications), speed at 1000rpm in 5th gear (4.058:1) 21.1mph/33.9kmh; acceleration 0 – 62mph/100kmh (80kW) 8.9secs; power to weight ratio from 9.7/kW (7.1kg/PS); consumption 6–11L/100km (47.1–25.7mpg) [39.2–21.4US mpg].

Honda Civic Shuttle

1.6 Litre DOHC
96kW–128hp–130PS
Fuel Injection

Engine for Civic Si (3–door) and CRX As Civic 1300, except:

Body, Weight: Saloon/Sedan 3–door – 910kg. Coupe CRX 890 – 925kg.

Engine data (DIN): 4–cylinder in–line (75 x 90mm), compression ratio 9.5:1; 96kW (128hp) [130PS] at 6800rpm, 60.4kW/L (80.9hp/L) [81.8PS/L]; 143Nm (105.5lbft) at 5700rpm.
With Catalyst (DIN): 88kW (118hp) [120PS] at 6800rpm; 135Nm (99.6lbft) at 5700rpm; unleaded regular grade.
Japanese version (JIS nett): 96kW (128hp) [130PS]; 144Nm (106.2lbft).

Engine construction: Designated ZC. 2 overhead camshafts (toothed belt); oil capacity 4L (3.8US qt), electronic fuel injection PGM–Fl. Battery 12V 47Ah, alternator 60A, cooling system capacity 4.5L (4.3US qt).

Transmission: a) 5–speed manual, final drive ratio 3.888, with Catalyst 4.250.
b) Automatic, hydraulic torque converter and 4–speed Planetary gear set with lock–up, selector lever in the middle, final drive ratio 3.933.

Gear ratios: a) 5–speed manual; 1st 3.250; 2nd 1.944; 3rd 1.346; 4th 1.033; 5th 0.878; R 3.153.
With Catalyst; 1st 3.250; 2nd 1.894; 3rd 1.259; 4th 0.937; 5th 0.771; R 3.153.
b) Automatic; Planetary gear set ratios: 1st 2.705; 2nd 1.560; 3rd 1.027; 4th 0.780; R 1.954.

Chassis: All–round disc brakes (front ventilated); tyres 185/60 HR/VR 14, wheel rims 5 or 5.5J.

Dimensions: Coupe CRX; wheelbase 230cm, track 145/145.5cm, clearance 16cm, turning circle 9.8m. Load space 6.9cu ft (196dm3). Length 375.5cm, width 167.5cm, height 127cm.

Performance: Max speed CRX 132mph/212kmh (manufaturers test specifications), speed at 1000rpm in 5th gear 19.3mph/31.0kmh; acceleration 0 – 62mph/100kmh 7.5secs; power to weight ratio from 9.2kg/kW (6.8kg/PS); consumption ECE 5.4/6.8/8.3L/100km (52.3/41.5/34mpg) [43.6/34.6/28.3US mpg].
With Catalyst: Max speed 127mph/205kmh, speed at 1000rpm in 5th gear 20.1mph/32.3kmh; power to weight ratio 10.5kg/kW (7.7kg/PS); consumption 5.8/7.5/6.7L/100km (48.7/37.7/42.2mpg) [40.6/31.4/35.1US mpg].

Honda Civic CRX

Honda Quint Integra

Medium size front wheel drive vehicle, with a 1.6 Litre 16–valve engine. Available with carb or injection. Launched February 1985, Saloon/Sedan October. Sold in the USA as the Acura Integra. 4– door version launched Autumn 1986.

1.6 Litre
73kW–98hp–100PS
1 2V Carb

Body, Weight: Saloon/Sedan; 4–door, 5–seater; kerbweight (DIN) from 900kg. Saloon/Sedan; 5–door, 5–seater; kerbweight (DIN) from 920kg. Coupe; 3–door, 5–seater; kerbweight (DIN) from 890kg.

Engine data (JIS Nett): 4–cylinder, in–line (75 x 90mm), 1590cm3; compression ratio 9.3:1; 73kW (98hp) [100PS] at 6500rpm, 45.9kW/L (61.5hp/L) [62.9PS/L]; 126Nm (93lbft) at 4000rpm.
1 OHC engine: (74 x 86.5mm), 1488cm3; 56kW (75hp) [76PS] at 6000rpm; 116Nm (85.6lbft) at 3500rpm.

Engine construction: Designated ZC. Transverse front engine, 4 valves per cylinder, 2 overhead camshafts (toothed belt); light– alloy cylinder head and

Honda

block; oil capacity 3.5L (3.3US qt); 1 Downdraught 2V two-stage carb. 1.5-litre with 3 valves per cylinder and 1 overhead camshaft. Battery 12V 47Ah, alternator 65A; cooling system capacity 5.6L (5.3US qt).

Transmission (to front wheels): a) 5-speed manual, final drive ratio 4.400. b) Automatic, hydraulic torque converter, 4-speed Planetary gear set and lock-up, final drive ratio 4.214.

Gear ratios: a) 5-speed manual: 1st 2.916; 2nd 1.764; 3rd 1.192; 4th 0.866; 5th 0.718; R 2.916.
b) Automatic; Planetary gear set ratios: 1st 2.500; 2nd 1.407 or 1.500; 3rd 9.969; 4th 0.681 or 0.729; R 1.954.

Honda Quint Integra

Chassis: Integral body; front independent suspension with McPherson strut and control arms, antiroll bar; rear torsion crank axle (longitudinal tube axle) with Panhard rod and coil springs, some models with antiroll bar. Servo/power assisted brakes, front ventilated discs, rear drums; mechanical handbrake on front wheels; rack and pinion steering (optional power assisted); fuel tank 50L (11Gal) [13.2US Gal]; tyres 165 SR13 (optional 185/70 SR 13), wheel rims 5J.

Dimensions: Saloon/Sedan; wheelbase 252cm, track 142/143.5cm, clearance 16.5cm, turning circle 9.8m; load space 9-15.2cu ft (255-430dm3). Length 438cm, 5 door 435cm, width 166.5cm, height 134.5cm. Coupe; wheelbase 245cm, turning circle 9.6m, length 428cm.

Performance: Max speed 106mph/170kmh; speed at 1000rpm in 5th gear 21.5mph/34.6kmh; power to weight ratio from 12.1kg/kW (8.9kg/PS); consumption approx 6-10L/100km (47.1-28.2mpg) [39.2- 23.5US mpg].

```
1.6 Litre
88kW-118hp-120PS
Fuel Injection
```

As 98hp carb version, except:

Body, Weight: Kerbweight (DIN) Saloon/Sedan from 990kg (USA 1070kg), Coupe from 940kg (USA 1050kg).

Engine data (JIS nett): 4-cylinder in-line (75 x 90mm), 1590cm3; compression ratio 9.3:1; 88kW (118hp) [120PS] at 6500rpm, 55.3kW/L (74.1hp/L) [75.5PS/L]; 137Nm (101.1lbft) at 5500rpm.
USA version (SAE nett): Compression ratio 9.5:1; 88kW (118hp) [120PS]; 139Nm (102.5lbft); unleaded regular grade.
Export Versions (DIN): Compression ratio 9.5:1; 92kW (123hp) [125PS]; 140Nm (103.3lbft).

Engine construction: Oil capacity 3.8L (3.6US qt), oil cooler. Electronic fuel injection PGM-Fl.

Transmission: a) 5-speed manual, final drive ratio 4.066, USA 4.214.
b) Automatic, final drive ratio 4.214.

Honda Quint Integra

Gear ratios: a) 5-speed manual, 1st 3.181; 2nd 1.944; 3rd 1.304; 4th 0.937; 5th 0.771; R 3.000.
Or 1st 3.181; 2nd 1.944; 3rd 1.347; 4th 1.033; 5th 0.878; R 3.0.
b) Automatic; As 98hp carb version, or 1st 2.705; 2nd 1.560; 3rd 1.027; 4th 0.780; R 1.954.

Chassis: Antiroll bar front and rear. Servo/power assisted disc brakes (front ventilated); power assisted steering; tyres 185/60 HR 14 (optional 195/60 HR 14), wheel rims 5.5J.

Performance: Max speed 115mph/185kmh; speed at 1000rpm in 5th gear 21mph/33.8kmh; power to weight ratio from 10.7kg/kW (7.8kg/PS); consumption 7-11L/100km (40.4-25.7mpg) [33.6-21.4US mpg].

Honda Concerto

New model. 4 or 5-door Saloon/Sedan with transverse 1.5 or 1.6 front engine, 5-speed manual or automatic optionally two different four wheel drive systems. Launched in June 1988. Will be widely available in Europe by the end of 1989.

Honda Concerto

```
1.5 Litre
67kW-90hp-91PS
1 2V Carb
```

Body, Weight: 4/5-door Saloon/Sedan, 5-seater; kerbweight (DIN) from 950kg; automatic heavier by 20kg.

Engine data (JIS Nett): 4-cylinder in-line (75 x 84.5mm), 1493cm3; compression ratio 9.2:1; 67kW (90hp) [91PS] at 6000rpm, 44.9kW/L (60.2hp/L) [61PS/L]; 119Nm (87.8lbft) at 4000rpm.

Engine construction: Transverse front engine. Designated D 15B. 4 valves (in V) per cylinder, 1 overhead camshaft (toothed belt); light-alloy cylinder head and block, 5 bearing crankshaft; oil capacity 3.5L (3.3US qt); 1 downdraught compound carb. Battery 12V 35-47Ah, alternator 55-70A; cooling system capacity approx 5L (4.7US qt).

Transmission (to front wheels): a) 5-speed manual, final drive ratio 3.888.
b) Automatic, hydraulic torque, 4-speed Planetary gear set and Lock-up, final drive ratio 3.933.

Gear ratios: a) 5-speed manual: 1st 3.250; 2nd 1.894; 3rd 1.259; 4th 0.937; 5th 0.771; R 3.153.
b) Automatic, Planetary gear set ratios: 1st 2.705; 2nd 1.500; 3rd 0.972; 4th 0.738; R 1.954.

Chassis: Integral body; all round independent suspension with coil springs and coaxial shock absorbers, front upper control arm, torsion strut, upper A arm, antiroll bar; rear lower trailing arm with additional track correction trailing arms; lower and upper control arms. Servo/power assisted brakes front ventilated discs, rear drums, handbrake to rear wheels; rack and pinion steering optionally servo assisted; fuel tank capacity 45L (9.9Gal) [11.9US Gal]; tyres 175/70 SR 13, wheel rims 5J.

Dimensions: Wheelbase 255cm, track 145/145.5cm, clearance 15cm, turning circle 9.8m; load space (VDA) 14.8cu ft (420dm3), 5-door 13-29cu ft (370-821dm3). Length 441.5cm, 5-door 427cm, width 169cm, height 139.5cm.

Performance: Max speed approx 106mph/170kmh, speed at 1000rpm in 5th gear 22mph/35.4kmh; power to weight ratio from 14.2kg/kW (10.4kg/PS); consumption approx 6-9L/100km (47.1-31.4mpg) [39.2-26.1US mpg].

Honda

1.6 Litre
77kW–103hp–105PS
2 Carbs

As 1.5 Litre, except:

Weight: Kerbweight (DIN) from 990kg, 4WD (only 4-door) from 1090kg.

Engine Data (JIS Nett): 4-cylinder in-line (75 x 90mm), 1590cm3; compression ratio 9.1:1; 77kW (103hp) [105PS] at 6300rpm, 48.4kW/L (64.9hp/L) [66PS/L]; 135Nm (99.6lbft) at 4500rpm.

Engine construction: Designated ZC. Oil capacity 3.8L (3.6US qt), oil cooler; 2 horizontal constant carbs.

Transmission (to front wheels, 4WD to all wheels):
a) 5-speed manual, final drive ratio 4.250.
b) Automatic, final drive ratio 3.933.
4WD "real time": Permanent all wheel drive with intregal viscous coupling. 5-speed manual with rough terrain transmission, final drive ratio 4.428.

Gear ratios: a) 5-speed manual: as 1500; for 4WD; 1st 3.384; 2nd 1.950; 3rd 1.275; 4th 0.941; 5th 0.783; R 3.000; rough terrain 4.512.
b) Automatic: 1st 2.705; 2nd 1.560; 3rd 1.027; 4th 0.780; R 1.954.

Chassis: Servo/power assisted steering; tyres 175/65 HR 14.

Dimensions: 4WD: Track 144.5/145.5cm; clearance 16cm, height 141.5cm.

Performance: Max speed approx 112mph/180kmh; speed at a 1000rpm in 5th gear 20.3mph/32.6kmh, 4WD 19.1mph/30.8kmh; power to weight ratio from 12.9kg/kW (9.4kg/PS); consumption approx 7-12L/100km (40.4-23.5mpg) [33.6-19.6US mpg].

Honda Concerto

1.6 Litre
88kW–118hp–120PS
Fuel Injection

As 1.5 litre, except:

Weight: Kerbweight (DIN) from 1020kg, 4WD (4-door only) from 1110kg.

Engine data (JIS net): 4-cylinder in-line (75 x 90mm), 1590cm3; compression ratio 9.1:1; 88kW (118hp) [120PS] at 6300rpm, 55.3kW/L (74.1hp/L) [75.5PS/L]; 142Nm (104.8lbft) at 5500rpm.

Engine construction: Designated ZC. Oil capacity 3.8L (3.6US qt), oil cooler; PGM-FI electronic fuel injection.

Transmission (to front wheels, 4WD to all wheels):
a) 5-speed manual, final drive ratio 4.250.
b) Automatic, final drive ratio 3.933.
4WD: Permanent all wheel drive.
"real time" with integral viscous coupling;
"Intrac" with two viscous couplings with a front conventional differential, free wheel hub for ABS braking.
5-speed manual with all terrain transmission, final drive ratio 4.428;
Automatic (two program): Final drive ratio 4.333

Gear ratios: a) 5-speed manual: As 1500; for 4WD; 1st 3.384; 2nd 1.950; 3rd 1.275; 4th 0.941; 5th 0.783; R 3.000; rough terrain 4.512.
b) Automatic: 1st 2.705; 2nd 1.500; 3rd 1.027; 4th 0.780; R 1.954; for 4WD: 1st 2.529; 2nd 1.428; 3rd 0.974; 4th 0.733; R 1.954.

Chassis: Rear stabiliser (not for the 4WD). 4-wheel disc brakes (front ventilated), 4WD "Intrac" with ABS (4WD "real time" rear drums); power assisted steering; tyres 175/65 HR 14.

Dimensions: 4WD: Track 144.5/145.5cm; clearance 16cm, height 141.5cm.

Performance: Max speed approx 115-118mph/185-190kmh; speed at 1000rpm in 5th gear 20.3mph/32.6kmh, 4WD 19.1mph/30.8kmh; power to weight 11.6kg/kW (8.5kg/PS); consumption approx 7-12L/100km (40.4-23.5mpg) [33.6-19.6US mpg].

Honda NS-X

New model. Prototype sports car with central V6 engine and aluminium chassis. Incomplete data. Debut Chicago Show February 1989. Production to begin during 1990.

Honda NS-X

3.0 Litre V6 24V
184kW–247hp–250PS
Fuel Injection

Body, Weight: 2–door, 2–seater Coupe; kerbweight (DIN) 1300kg.

Engine data (Catalyst): 6–cylinder in V 90deg, (90 x 78mm), 2977cm3; over 184kW (247hp) [250PS].

Engine construction: Central mounted transverse engine with gearbox and differential in one assembly. Four valves (in V) per cylinder, 2x2 overhead camshaft (toothed belt), light-alloy cylinder head and block, 4 bearing crankshaft; oil cooler, electronic fuel injection PGM-FI, water cooled.

Transmission (to rear wheels): a) 5–speed manual.
b) 4–speed automatic, anti–slip device.

Chassis: Monocoque body with chassis, front and rear independent suspension, front and rear upper and lower control arms, coil springs and anti-roll bar. Servo/power assisted disc brakes with ABS, handbrake to rear wheels; power assisted rack and pinion steering; tyres front 205/50 ZR 15, rear 225/50 ZR 16.

Dimensions: Wheelbase 250cm, track 151/152.5cm, length 431.5cm, width 180cm, height 117cm.

Performance: Max speed over 155mph/250kmh (manufacturers test specifications), acceleration 0–62mph/100kmh under 6secs; standing quarter mile under 14secs; power to weight ratio 7kg/kW (5.2kg/PS).

Honda NS-X

Honda

Honda Accord – Vigor

Accord – Vigor – Aerodeck 130a

Medium size front wheel drive vehicle. Launched September 1981, revised in June 1985. Available in 4-door Saloon/Sedan and 3-door Coupe Aerodeck with a 1.8 Litre 3-valves per cylinder engine and 1.8 and 2.0 Litre 4-valves per cylinder DOHC. Coupe hatchback launched in the USA in 1987.

```
1.8 Litre
81kW–109hp–110PS
1 2V Carb
```

Body, Weight: Saloon/Sedan; 4-door, 5-seater; kerbweight (DIN) from 1050kg. Coupe Aerodeck; 3-door, 5-seater; kerbweight (DIN) from 1050kg.

Engine data (JIS): 4-cylinder in-line (80 x 91mm), 1830cm3, compression ratio 9.0:1; 81kW (109hp) [110PS] at 5800rpm, 44.2kW/L (59.2hp/L) [60.1PS/L]; 149Nm (109.9lbft) at 3500rpm.
Export version (DIN): (80 x 79.5mm), 1598cm3; compression ratio 9.0:1; 65kW (87hp) [88PS] at 6000rpm, 40.4kW/L (54.1hp/L) [55.1PS/L]; 122Nm (90lbft) at 3500rpm; leaded regular grade.

Engine construction: Designated A18A. Transverse front engine; 3 valves (in V) per cylinder, 1 overhead camshaft (toothed belt); light-alloy cylinder head, 5 bearing crankshaft; oil capacity 3.5L (3.3US qt); 1 downdraught 2V two-stage carb. Battery 12V 47Ah, alternator 50-70A; cooling system capacity 6L (5.7US qt).

Transmission (to front wheels): a) 5-speed manual, final drive ratio 4.066.
b) Automatic, hydraulic torque converter and 4-speed Planetary gear set, final drive ratio 3.933.

Gear ratios: a) 5-speed manual; 1st 3.181; 2nd 1.842; 3rd 1.208; 4th 0.878; 5th 0.694; R 3.
Or; 1st 3.181; 2nd 1.842; 3rd 1.250; 4th 0.937; 5th 0.0771; R 3.
b) Automatic; Planetary gear set ratios; 1st 2.421; 2nd 1.56; 3rd 1.064; 4th 0.729; R 1.954. or 1st 2.421; 2nd 1.56; 3rd 0.969; 4th 0.729; R 1.954.

Chassis: Integral body; independent suspension with lower and upper control arms, longitudinal tie bars, coil springs and telescopic shock absorbers, front and optional rear antiroll bars. Servo/power assisted brakes, front ventilated discs, rear drums; mechanical handbrake on rear wheels; rack and pinion steering, (optional power assisted). Fuel tank 60L (13.2Gal) [15.9US Gal]; tyres 165 SR 13, wheel rims 5J.

Honda Accord Aerodeck

Dimensions: Wheelbase 260cm, track 148/147.5cm, clearance 16cm, turning circle 10.6m, load space 16.6cu ft (470dm3), Coupe 10– 17.9cu ft (280-507dm3). Length 453.5–456.5cm, Coupe 433.5– 436.5cm, width 169.5cm, height 135.5cm, Coupe 133.5cm.

Performance: Max speed 109mph/175kmh (manufacturers test specifications), speed at 1000rpm in 5th gear 24.1mph/38.7kmh; power to weight ratio from 13.0kg/kW (9.6kg/PS); consumption ECE (1.6L) 5.6/7.4/9.4L/100km (50.4/38.2/30.1mpg) [42/31.8/25US mpg]. Automatic 5.7/7.3/8.9L/100km (49.6/38.7/31.7mpg) [41.3/32.2/26.4USmpg].

```
1800 16V
96kW–129hp–130PS
2 Carbs
```

As 1.8 Litre 108.5hp, except:

Body, Weight: Kerbweight Saloon/Sedan from 1100kg – Coupe 1090kg.

R15

Engine data (JIS nett): 4-cylinder in-line (81 x 89mm), 1834cm3 compression ratio 9.4:1; 96kW (129hp) [130PS] at 6000rpm, 52.3kw/L (70hp/L) [70.9PS/L]; 162Nm (119.5lbft) at 4000rpm.

Engine construction: Designated B18A. 2 overhead camshafts; 4 valves (in V 52deg) per cylinder; light-alloy cylinder head and block; oil capacity 3.9L (3.7US qt), oil cooler. 2 horizontal carbs. Cooling system capacity 7.8L (7.4US qt).

Transmission: a) 5-speed manual, final drive ratio 4.066.
b) 4-speed automatic, final drive ratio 4.066.

Gear ratios: a) 5-speed manual; 1st 3.181; 2nd 1.842; 3rd 1.25; 4th 0.937; 5th 0.771; R 3.
b) Automatic; Planetary gear set ratios: 1st 2.529; 2nd 1.481; 3rd 1.060; 4th 0.743; R 1.904.

Chassis: Tyres 185/70 SR 13.

Performance: Max speed 115mph/185kmh, speed at 1000rpm in 5th gear 21.7mph/34.9kmh; power to weight ratio from 11.4kg/kW (8.4kg/PS); consumption 8–13L/100km (35.3–21.7mpg) [29.4–18.1US mpg].

Honda Accord EX 2.0

```
2 Litre
75/83kW–100.5/111hp–102/113PS
Carb/Fuel Injection
```

Engine for export

As 1.8 Litre 108.5hp, except:

Body, Weight: Kerbweight (DIN) Saloon/Sedan from 1100 kg (USA from 1135kg); Coupe Aerodeck from 1070kg; 2-door Coupe (USA), 5-seater; kerbweight from 1130kg; 3-door Coupe Hatchback (USA), 5-seater; kerbweight from 1140kg.

Engine data (Catalyst DIN): 4-cylinder in-line (82.7 x 91mm), 1955cm3; compression ratio 9.1:1; 75kW (100.5hp) [102PS], Automatic 76kW (101.8hp) [103PS] at 5500rpm. 38.4kW/L (51.5hp/L) [52.2PS/L]; 154Nm (113.6lbft) at 3500rpm; unleaded regular grade (91R).
Japanese version (JIS nett): 77kW (103.2hp) [105PS]; 152Nm (112.1lbft).
USA version (SAE nett): 73kW (97.8hp) [99PS]; 148Nm (109.2lbft).
Without Catalyst (DIN): 78kW (104.5hp) [106PS]; 153Nm (112.9lbft).
Injection: With Catalyst (DIN): Compression ratio 8.8:1; 83kW (111hp) [113PS] at 5500rpm; 42.5kW/L (57hp/L) [57.8PS/L]; 160Nm (118lbft) at 4500rpm; unleaded regular grade (91R).
USA version (SAE nett): Compression ratio 9.3.1; 90kW (120.6hp) [122PS] at 5800rpm; 166Nm (122.4lbft) at 4000rpm.
Without Catalyst: Compression ratio 9.4:1; 90kW (120.6) [122PS] at 5500rpm; 166Nm (122.4lbft) at 5000rpm; leaded premium grade.

Engine construction: Oil cooler for automatic version. 1 downdraught 2V two-stage carb or electronic fuel injection PGM- Fl. Cooling system capacity 6.3-6.9L (6-6.5US qt).

Transmission: a) 5-speed manual, final drive ratio 4.066. USA also 3.87 (97.8hp).
b) 4-speed automatic, final drive ratio 4.066.

Gear ratios: a) 5-speed manual; 1st 3.181; 2nd 1.842; 3rd 1.250; 4th 0.937; 5th 0.771; R 3.
Or: 1st 3.27; 2nd 1.842; 3rd 1.208; 4th 0.878; 5th 0.694; R 3.
b) Automatic; Planetary gear set ratios: 1st 2.529; 2nd 1.481; 3rd 1.060/1.030; 4th 0.743/0.700; R 1.904.

Chassis: Injection version: Antiroll bar front and rear, all-round disc brakes (front ventilated), power assisted steering; tyres 185/70 HR 13, 185/60HR 14 or 195/60 HR/VR 14, wheel rims 5 or 5.5J.

Dimensions: Coupe USA; length, 2-door 456.5cm, 3-door, 444cm, height 134 or 133.5cm.

Honda

Performance (Catalyst versions): Max speed 114mph/184kmh, Injection 119mph/191kmh, Coupe 112–118mph/180– 189kmh (manufacturers test specifications) speed at 1000rpm in 5th gear 21.7mph/34.9kmh; acceleration 0 – 62mph/100kmh (111hp) 9.7secs; power to weight ratio from 13.9kg/kw (10.2kg/PS); consumption ECE (111hp) Saloon/Sedan and Coupe 6.9/8.7/10.5L/100km (40.9/32.5/26.9mpg) [34.1/27/22.4US mpg]. Automatic 7.3/8.8/11.5L/100km (38.7/32.1/24.6mpg) [32.2/26.7/20.5US mpg].

Honda Accord Coupe

```
2 Litre 16V
98/101kW–131/135hp–134/137PS
Fuel Injection
```

As 1.8 Litre 108.5hp, except

Body, Weight: Kerbweight Saloon/Sedan and Hatchback from 1140kg, Coupe Aerodeck from 1100kg.

Engine data: With Catalyst (DIN): 4–cylinder in–line (81 x 95mm), 1958cm3; compression ratio 9.4:1; 98kW (131hp) [134PS] at 6000rpm, 50.1kW/L (67.1hp/L) [68.4PS/L]; 171Nm (126.1lbft) at 5000rpm; unleaded premium grade (95R). Without Catalyst: Compression ratio 9.5:1; 101kW (135hp) [137PS] at 6000rpm; 170Nm (125.4lbft) at 5000rpm; leaded premium grade.
Japanese version (JIS nett): Compression ratio 9.4:1; 107kW (143hp) [145PS] at 6200rpm, 54.6kW/L (73.2hp/L) [74.1PS/L], 173Nm (127.6lbft) at 4000rpm.

Engine construction: Designated B20A; 2 overhead camshafts (toothed belt); 4 valves (in V) per cylinder; light–alloy cylinder head and block; oil capacity 3.9L (3.7US qt); electronic fuel injection PGM FI. Cooling system capacity 7.8L (7.4US qt).

Transmission: a) 5–speed manual, final drive ratio 4.066.
b) 4–speed automatic, final drive ratio 4.066.

Gear ratios: a) 5–speed manual; 1st 3.166; 2nd 1.857/1.772; 3rd 1.259/1.185; 4th 0.967; 5th 0.794; R 3.000.
b) Automatic; Max torque multiplication in converter 2.3 times, Planetary gear set ratios: 1st 2.529; 2nd 1.444; 3rd 1.030; 4th 0.725; R 1.904.

Chassis: Front and rear antiroll bar, disc brakes all round (front ventilated), optional ABS; power assisted steering; tyres 185/70 HR 13 or 195/60 HR 14, wheel rims 5 or 5.5J.

Performance: Catalyst version; Max speed 126.2mph/203kmh (manufacturers test specifications), speed at 1000rpm in 5th gear (195/60HR 14) 20.8mph/33.4kmh; acceleration 0 – 62mph/100kmh 8.9secs; power to weight ratio from 10.4kg/kW (7.7kg/PS); consumption ECE 7.2/8.3/10.9L/100km (39.2/34/25.9mpg) [32.7/28.3/21.6US mpg].

Honda Accord Hatchback

Honda Prelude

Front wheel drive 2–door, 2 + 2 Coupe launched November 1982, revised body and mechanics April 1987. 2 Litre 3 or 4–valves per cylinder. 2.0 Litre with four–wheel steering.

```
2 Litre
81kW–108.5hp–110PS
2 Constant Pressure Carbs
```

Body, Weight: Coupe; 2–door, 2+2–seater, kerbweight (DIN) 1050–1120kg (USA from 1165kg).

Engine data (JIS Nett): 4–cylinder in–line (81 x 95mm), 1958cm3; compression ratio 9.1:1; 81kW (108.5hp) [110PS] at 5800rpm, 41.3kW/L (55.3hp/L) [56.2PS/L]; 152Nm (112.1lbft) at 4000rpm.
With Catalyst (DIN): 80kW (107hp) [109PS] at 5800rpm; 154Nm (113.6lbft) at 4000rpm; unleaded regular grade.
USA version (SAE nett): 77kW (103.2hp) [105PS], with Automatic 78kW (104.5hp) [106PS]; 150Nm (110.6bft).
Without Catalyst (DIN): 84kW (112.6hp) [114PS] at 5800rpm; 157Nm (116lbft) at 4500rpm.

Engine construction: Designated EBA4; transverse front engine, 3 valves (in V) per cylinder, 1 overhead camshaft (toothed belt); light–alloy cylinder head, 5 bearing crankshaft; oil capacity 3.9L (3.7US qt); 2 horizontal 2–stage carbs (electronic control on Catalyst variants). Battery 12V 50-65Ah, alternator 70A; cooling system capacity 6.05L (5.7US qt).

Transmission (to front wheels): a) 5–speed manual, final drive ratio 4.062. USA 4.187.
b) 4–speed automatic, hydraulic torque converter and Planetary gear set, final drive ratio 4.066.

Gear ratios: a) 5–speed manual; 1st 3.166; 2nd 1.857; 3rd 1.259; 4th 0.935; 5th 0.794; R 3.000.
Or; 1st 3.166; 2nd 1.857; 3rd 1.222; 4th 0.906; 5th 0.742; R 3.000.
b) Automatic; Max torque multiplication in converter 2.3 times, Planetary gear set ratios; 1st 2.529; 2nd 1.444/1.393; 3rd 1.030; 4th 0.725/0.763; R 1.904
USA: 1st 2.65; 2nd 1.48; 3rd 1.06; 4th 0.74; R 1.9.

Chassis: Integral body; front and rear independent suspension with upper and lower wishbones, tie bars, coil springs with telescopic shock absorbers, front and rear antiroll bar. Servo/power assisted disc brakes (front ventilated), disc diameter front 24cm, rear 23.7cm, mechanical handbrake on rear wheels; rack and pinion steering, (optional power assisted and mechanical four wheel steering); fuel tank 60L (13.2Gal) [15.9US Gal]; tyres 185/70 HR 13 or 165 SR13 wheel rims 5J.

Dimensions: Wheelbase 256.5cm, track 148/147cm, clearance 14.5cm, turning circle 11.4m, load space (VDA) 12.5-25.8cu ft (353-730dm3). Length 446cm, width 169.5-171cm, height 125-129.5cm.

Performance: Max speed 114.5mph/184kmh, automatic 112.5mph/181kmh (manufacturers test specification), speed at 1000rpm in 5th gear 21.1mph/34.0kmh acceleration 0 – 62mph/100kmh 10.5secs; power to weight ratio from 13.0kg/kW (9.5kg/Ps); consumption ECE 7.1/8.7/9.1L/100km (39.8/32.5/31mpg) [33.1/27/25.8US mpg]. Automatic 7.5/9.2/9.4L/100km (37.7/30.7/30.1mpg) [31.4/25.6/25US mpg].

Honda Prelude 2.0i–16

```
2 Litre 16V
107kW-143hp-145PS
Fuel Injection
```

As 108.5hp, except:

Body, Weight: Kerbweight (DIN) from 1130kg, USA from 1230kg.

Engine data (JIS nett): 4–cylinder in–line (81 x 95mm), 1958cm3; compression ratio 9.4:1; 107kW (143hp) [145PS] at 6000rpm 54.6kW/L (73.2hp/L) [74.0PS/L]; 175Nm (129.1lbft) at 4500rpm.
With Catalyst (DIN): Compression ratio 9.0:1; 101kW (135hp) [138PS] at 6200rpm; 175Nm (129.1lbft) at 4500rpm; unleaded regular grade.
USA version (SAE nett): 101kW (135hp) [137PS]; 172Nm (126.9lbft).
Without Catalyst (DIN): 110kW (147hp) [150PS] at 6000rpm; 180Nm (132.8lbft) at 5500rpm.

Honda

Engine construction: Designated EBAS; 2 overhead camshaft (toothed belt); 4 valves (in V 52deg) per cylinder; light–alloy cylinder head and block; oil cooler. Electronic fuel injection PGM–FI. Cooling system capacity 7.05L (6.6US qt).

Transmission: a) 5–speed manual, final drive ratio 4.062, USA 4.27.
b) 4–speed automatic, final drive ratio 4.066, USA 4.13.

Gear ratios: a) 5–speed manual; 1st 3.166; 2nd 1.772/1.857; 3rd 1.222/1.259; 4th 0.935; 5th 0.794; R 3.000.
b) Automatic; Planetary gear set ratios; 1st 2.529; 2nd 1.393/1.444; 3rd 1.030; 4th 0.763/0.725; R 1.904.

Chassis: Front brake disc dia 26.2cm, (optional ABS); power steering; tyres 195/60 VR/HR 14 wheel rims 5.5 J.

Dimension: Turning circle with 4WS 10.4m.

Performance: Max speed 127mph/204kmh, Automatic 124mph/200kmh (manufacturers test specifications) speed at 1000rpm in 5th gear (0.763) 20.8mph/33.5kmh; acceleration 0 – 62mph/100kmh 8.8secs, automatic 10.2secs; power to weight ratio from 10.6 kg/kW (7.8kg/PS). Consumption ECE 6.9/8.7/9.2L/100km (40.9/32.5/30.7mpg) [34.1/27/25.6US mpg]. Automatic 7.1/9.0/9.4L/100km (39.8/31.4/30.1mpg) [33.1/26.1/25US mpg].

Honda Prelude 2.0i–16

Honda Legend

High class four/two door Saloon/Sedan; front wheel drive with independent suspension and a V6 engine. Built as a joint venture with the Rover Group, marketed in the USA as the Acura. Launched October 1985, engine revised in February 1987. September 1987: 2.7 Litre also available for Saloon/Sedan. Autumn 1988: Saloon/Sedan with modified front (only in Japan), same rear wheel suspension as the Coupe, Turbo version for 2 Litre.

Honda Legend V6 Ti

```
2.0 V6
140/107kW-188/143hp-190/145PS
Turbo/Fuel Injection
```

Also with 2.0 V6 (Japan only)

Body, Weight: 4-door Saloon, 5-seater; kerbweight (DIN) 1320-1360kg, Turbo 1400-1440kg.

Engine data (JIS nett): 6-cylinder in V 90deg (82 x 63mm), 1996cm3; compression ratio 9:1; 140kW (188hp) [190PS] at 6000rpm, 70.1kW/L (94hp/L) [95.2PS/L]; 241Nm (177.9lbft) at 3500rpm; premium grade.
Without Turbocharger: Compression ratio 9.2:1; 107kW (143hp) [145PS] at 6300rpm; 172Nm (126.9lbft) at 5000rpm; regular grade.

Engine construction: Designation E-C20A, 2.5 V6–C25A, 2.0 V6–C250A; transverse front engine; 4 valves per cylinder (in V), hydraulic tappets, 1 overhead camshaft (toothed belt); light–alloy cylinder head and block; 4 bearing crankshaft; oil capacity 5.7L (5.4US qt), 2.5 V6 5.5L (5.2US qt), turbo oil cooler. Electronic fuel injection PGM FI; 1 exhaust turbocharger, charge air cooler. Battery 12V 50/65Ah, alternator 65/70A; cooling system capacity approx 8.1L (7.7US qt).

Transmission (to front wheels): a) 5-speed manual, (not applicable for Turbo) final drive ratio 4.200.
b) Automatic, hydraulic torque converter and 4–speed Planetary gear set, with E/S–program (Turbo), final drive ratio 4.533, Turbo 4.714.

Gear ratios: a) 5-speed manual: 1st 3.250; 2nd 1.857; 3rd 1.346; 4th 1.033; 5th 0.794; R 3.000.
b) Automatic: Planetary gear set ratios: 1st 2.764; 2nd 1.500; 3rd 0.972; 4th 0.707; R 1.904;
Without Turbo: 1st 2.705; 2nd 1.629; 3rd 1.058; 4th 0.750; R 1.904.

Chassis: Intergral Body; all round independent suspension; front with upper and lower control arms, lower tie bars, coil springs and coaxial shock absorbers, rear and upper control arms, lower trailing arms, coil springs, coaxial shock absorbers, front and rear antiroll bars. Four wheel servo/power assisted disc brakes (front ventilated), optionally with ABS, handbrake to rear wheels; power assisted rack and pinion steering; fuel tank capacity 68L (15Gal) [18US Gal]; tyres 195/65 HR 15, without turbo 185/70 SR 14, wheel rims 5/5.5 J.

Dimensions: Wheelbase 276cm, track 147.5/145.5cm, without turbo 148/146cm, clearance 15cm, turning circle 12.5m. Load space (VDA) 16.6cu ft (470dm3). Length 469cm, width 169.5cm, height 139cm.

Performance: Max speed approx 130mph/210kmh, without turbo approx 118mph/190kmh, speed at 1000rpm in 5th gear 21.2mph/34.2kmh; power to weight ratio from 10kg/kW (7.4kg/PS); consumption approx 9-16L/100km (31.4-17.7mpg) [26.1-14.7US mpg], without turbo 7-12L/100km (40.4-23.5mpg) [33.6-19.6US mpg].

Honda Legend

```
2.7 Litre V6
132kW-177hp-180PS
Fuel Injection
```

As 2 Litre, except:

Body, Weight: Saloon/Sedan; kerbweight (DIN) 1390-1430 (USA 1440-1460)kg; 2-door Coupe, 5-seater; kerbweight (DIN) 1395-1420 (USA 1425-1445)kg.

Engine data (JIS net): 6-cylinder in V 90deg (87 x 75mm), 2675cm3; compression ratio 9:1; 132kW (177hp) [180PS] at 6000rpm, 49.3kW/L (66hp/L) [67.3PS/L]; 226Nm (166.8lbft) at 4500rpm.
With Catalyst (DIN): 124kW (167hp) [169PS] at 5900rpm; 225Nm (166lbft) at 4500rpm; regular unleaded.
USA Version (SAE net): 120kW (161hp) [163PS]; 220Nm (162.4lbft).
European Version (Without Catalyst, DIN): 130kW (174hp) [177PS] at 6000rpm; 228Nm (168lbft) at 5000rpm.
Automatic: 128kW (172hp) [174PS].

Engine construction: Designated C27A. Cooling system capacity 8.8L (8.3US qt).

Transmission: a) 5-speed manual, final drive ratio 4.200;
b) Automatic, final drive ratio 4.266.

Gear ratios: a) 5-speed manual: 1st 2.932; 2nd 1.789; 3rd 1.222; 4th 0.909; 5th 0.750 or 0.702; R 3.000.
b) Automatic; Planetary gear set ratios: 1st 2.647; 2nd 1.448; 3rd 1.058; 4th 0.794; R 1.904.
Or (USA, Japan): 1st 2.647; 2nd 1.555; 3rd 1.028; 4th 0.707; R 1.904.

Chassis: Disc brakes, diameter front 28cm, rear 25.8cm, tyres 205/60 VR 15, 195/65 HR 15 or 195/70 HR 14, wheel rims 5.5/6 J.

Dimensions: Saloon/Sedan; track 150/146cm. Length 484cm, width 175cm. Coupe; wheelbase 270.5cm, track 150/150cm, clearance 14.5cm, turning circle 11.1m. Load space 15.5cu ft (440dm3). Length 477.5cm, width 174.5cm, height 137cm.

Performance: Max speed Coupe 132mph/213kmh, Automatic 129mph/207kmh (manufacturers test specifications), speed at 1000rpm in 5th gear (0.750) 22.6mph/36.4kmh; acceleration 0 - 62mph/100kmh 8.8secs, Automatic 9.4secs; power to weight ratio from 10.7kg/kW (7.8kg/PS); consumption ECE 8.2/9.3/12.9L/100km (34.4/30.4/21.9mpg) [28.7/25.3/18.2US mpg], Automatic 9.1/10.2/14.0L/100km (31/27.7/20.8mpg) [25.8/23.1/16.8US mpg].

Honda • Hongki • Hyundai

Honda Legend Coupe

HONGKI TJ

Vehicle manufacturer from The Peoples Republic Of China.

Hongki

Saloon/Sedan, 4–door with a 5.7 Litre V8 engine. Low volume production.

```
5.7 Litre V8
162kW–217hp–220PS
1 2V Carb
```

Body, Weight: Saloon/Sedan (CA 771) 4–door, 6–seater; kerbweight (DIN) 2270kg, gross vehicle weight 2690kg. Saloon/Sedan (CA 773) 4–door, 8–seater; kerbweight (DIN) 2500kg, gross vehicle weight 3060kg; Saloon/Sedan (CA 770) 4–door, 8–seater; kerbweight (DIN) 2650/2730kg, gross vehicle weight 3210/3290kg.

Engine data (SAE gross): 8–cylinder in V 90deg (100 x 90mm), 5655cm3; compression ratio 8.5:1; 162kw (217hp) [220PS] at 4400rpm, 28.6kW/L (38.3hp/L) [38.9PS/L]; 412Nm (304lbft) at 2800rpm; leaded regular grade (86R).

Engine construction: Hydraulic tappets, central camshaft (chain); 5 bearing crankshaft; oil capacity 5.5L (5.2US qt); 1 downdraught 2V carb. Battery 12 V 70Ah, dynamo; water cooled.

Transmission (to rear wheels): Automatic; hydraulic torque converter and 2-speed planetary gear set, final drive ratio 3.55 or 3.90.

Gear ratios: Max torque multiplication in converter 2 times, Planetary gear set ratios: 1st 1.95; 2nd 1; R 1.95.

Chassis: Box section chassis with cross members; front wishbones with coil springs; rear rigid axle with semi–elliptic leaf springs; front and rear telescopic dampers. Servo/power assisted drum brakes; mechanical handbrake on rear wheels: Recirculating ball steering; fuel tank 80L (17.6Gal) [21.1US Gal]; tyres 8.20–15 or 8.90–15.

Dimensions: Wheelbase 307/342/372cm, track 158/155cm, clearance 16cm, turning circle 12.8/14.4/15.1m. Load space 19.4cu ft (550dm3). Length 533/550/598cm, width 199cm, height 164cm.

Performance: Max speed 99–112mph/160–180kmh (manufacturers test specification), speed at 1000rpm in top gear (8.20–15, 3.54:1) 26.7mph/43kmh; power to weight ratio from 14kg/kW (10.3kg/PS); consumption 18–20L/100km (15.7–14.1mpg) [13.1–11.8US mpg] (manufacturers test specification)

Hongki

HYUNDAI KO

Hyundai Motor Company, 140-2 Ke-dong, Chongro-ku, Seoul, South Korea.
Important industrial factory and large scale vehicle manufacturer.

Hyundai Pony/Excel

Medium size Saloon/Sedan vehicle with a 1.3 or 1.5 Litre Mitsubishi engine. Front wheel drive. Automatic transmission available on 1.5 Litre only. Launched October 1985. Marketed in the USA as the Mitsubishi Precis 1.5 Litre

Hyundai Pony R14

```
1.3 Litre
49kW-66hp-67PS
1 2V Carb
```

Body, Weight: Saloon/Sedan; 4–door, 5–seater; kerbweight (DIN) 870–900kg. Saloon/Sedan; 3–door, 5–seater; kerbweight (DIN) 850–870kg; Saloon/Sedan; 5–door, 5–seater; kerbweight (DIN) 850–900kg.

Engine construction (DIN): 4–cylinder in–line (71 x 82mm), 1299cm3; compression ratio 9.8:1; 49kW (66hp) [67PS] at 5500rpm, 37.7kW/L (50.5hp/L) [51.6PS/L]; 97Nm (71.5lbft) at 3500rpm; leaded premium grade.
Engine for some countries: 55kW (74hp) [75PS]; 108Nm (79.7lbft).

Engine construction: Designated Mitsubishi G13B; overhead valves (in V); 1 overhead camshaft (toothed belt); light–alloy cylinder head; 5 bearing crankshaft; oil capacity 4L (3.8US qt); 1 downdraught 2V two-stage carb. Battery 12V 45Ah, alternator 45A; cooling system capacity 7.3L (6.9US qt).

Transmission (to front wheels) a) 4–speed manual, final drive ratio, 3.166. b) 5–speed manual, final drive ratio, 3.166.

Gear ratios: a) 4–speed manual; 1st 4.226; 2nd 2.365; 3rd 1.467; 4th 1.05; R 4.109. b) 5–speed manual; 1st 4.226; 2nd 2.365; 3rd 1.467; 4th 1.05; 5th 0.855; R 4.109.

Chassis: Integral body; front McPherson strut (coil springs) with lower control arms, rear independent suspension with semi– trailing arms, coil springs, front and rear antiroll bar, telescopic damper. Servo/power assisted brakes; front disc, rear drums, mechanical hand brake on rear wheels; rack and pinion steering; fuel tank 40L (8.8Gal) [10.6US Gal], optional 50L (11Gal) [13.2US Gal]; tyres 155 SR 13 (optional) 175SR 13, wheel rims 4.5 or 5J.

Hyundai Pony

Dimensions: Wheelbase 238cm, track 137.5/134cm, clearance 17cm, turning circle 10.4m. Load space 3/5–door max 26cu ft (735dm3), 4–door 11.1cu ft (315dm3). Length 398.5cm, 4–door 416.5cm, width 159.5cm, height 138cm.

Hyundai

Performance: Max speed 96mph/155kmh (manufacturers test specification), speed at 1000rpm in 4th gear 18.8mph/30.3kmh; power to weight ratio from 17.3kg/kW (12.7kg/PS); consumption ECE 6.0/8.1/8.5L/100km (47.1/34.9/33.2mpg) [39.2/29/27.7US mpg]. 5-speed 5.7/7.7/8.5L/100km (49.6/36.7/33.2mpg) [41.3/30.5/27.7US mpg].

```
1.5 Litre
53kW-71hp-72PS
1 2V Carb
```

As 1.3 Litre, except:

Body, Weight: 20kg heavier; USA kerbweight 980-1005kg.

Engine data (DIN): 4-cylinder in-line (75.5 x 82mm), 1468cm3; compression ratio 9.5:1; 53kW (71hp) [72PS] at 5500rpm. 36.1kW/L (48.4hp/L) [49.0 PS/L]; 111Nm (81.9lbft) at 3500rpm.
Engine for some countries: 62.5kW (84hp) [85PS]; 123Nm (90.7lbft).
With Catalyst (SAE nett): Compression ratio 9.4:1; 51kW (68hp) [70PS] at 5500rpm; 111Nm (81.9lbft) at 3500rpm; unleaded regular grade.

Engine construction: Designated Mitsubishi G15B; Catalyst version with electronic controlled carb.

Transmission (to front wheels): a) 4-speed manual, final drive ratio, 3.166; 3.470. b) 5-speed manual, final drive ratio, 3.166; 3.470. c) Automatic, hydraulic torque converter with 3-speed Planetary gear set; selector lever in the middle, final drive ratio 3.166/3.598.

Gear ratios: a) 4-speed manual; 1st 4.226; 2nd 2.365; 3rd 1.467; 4th 1.105; R 4.109.
b) 5-speed manual; 1st 4.226; 2nd 2.365; 3rd 1.467; 4th 1.105 5th 0.855; R 4.109.
c) Automatic; Max torque multiplication in converter 2 times; Planetary gear set ratios; 1st 2.846; 2nd 1.581; 3rd 1; R 2.176.

Chassis: Tyres 175 SR 13 or 175/70 SR 13, wheel rims 5J.

Performance: Max speed 101mph/162kmh, automatic 96mph/155kmh (manufacturers test specifications); power to weight ratio 16.4kg/kW (12.1kg/kW); consumption ECE 5.9/7.9/8.5L/100km (47.9/35.8/33.2mpg) [39.9/29.8/27.7US mpg]. 5-speed 5.9/7.5/8.5L/100km (47.9/37.7/33.2mpg) [39.9/31.4/27.7US mpg]. Automatic 6.6/8.8/9.0L/100km (42.8/32.1/31.4mpg) [35.6/26.7/26.1US mpg].

Hyundai Pony/Excel

Hyundai Stellar

Saloon/Sedan, 4-door, with a 4-cylinder Mitsubishi engine. Launched at the London Motorfair in the Autumn of 1983. 2 Litre engine available from the Autumn of 1986/87.

```
1.6 Litre
56kW-75hp-76PS
1 2V Carb
```

Body, Weight: Saloon/Sedan, 4-door, 5-seater; kerbweight (DIN) 1000kg, GSL 1030kg. Automatic 1055kg.

Engine data (DIN): 4-cylinder in-line (76.9 x 86mm), 1597cm3; compression ratio 8.5:1; 56kW (75hp) [76PS] at 5200rpm, 35kW/L (46.9hp/L) [47.6PS/L]; 137Nm (101.1lbft) at 4000rpm; leaded regular grade fuel.

Engine construction: Designated Mitsubishi G 32B. Overhead valves (in V); 1 overhead camshaft (chain); light-alloy cylinder head; 5 bearing crankshaft; oil capacity 4L (3.8US qt); 1 downdraught 2V carb. Battery 12V 45/60Ah, alternator 45/50A; cooling system capacity 7.2L (6.8US qt).

Transmission (to rear wheels) a) 4-speed manual, final drive ratio 3.909.
b) 5-speed manual, final drive ratio 3.909.
c) Automatic, hydraulic torque converter and 3-speed Planetary gear set, selector lever in the middle with positions P-R-N-D-2-L; final drive ratio 3.909.

Gear ratios: a) 4-speed manual; 1st 3.525; 2nd 2.193; 3rd 1.442; 4th 1; R 3.867.
b) 5-speed manual; 1st 3.444; 2nd 2; 3rd 1.316; 4th 1; 5th 0.853; R 3.667.
c) Automatic; Max torque multiplication in converter 2 times, Planetary gear set ratios; 1st 2.45; 2nd 1.45; 3rd 1; R 2.222.

Chassis: Integral body; front control arms, coil springs and antiroll bar, rear rigid axle with semi-trailing arms, coil springs, telescopic damper. Servo/power assisted brakes; front disc dia 24.8cm; mechanicl handbrake on rear wheels; rack and pinion steering; fuel tank 54L (11.9Gal) [14.3US Gal]; tyres 165SR 13, (optional 185/70 SR 13), wheel rims 4.5/5J.

Dimensions: Wheelbase 258cm, track 144.5/142.5cm, clearance 18cm, turning circle 10.5m, length 441.5/443cm, width 171.5cm, height 137cm.

Performance: Max speed 99mph/160kmh (manufacturers test specification), speed at 1000rpm in top gear 17.3mph/27.9kmh; power to weight ratio 17.9kg/kW (13.2kg/PS); consumption 8-13L/100km (35.3-21.7mpg) [29.4-18.1US mpg].

Hyundai Stellar

```
1.4 Litre
67.5kW-90.5hp-92PS
1 2V Carb
```

As 1.6 Litre, except:

Engine data (JIS): (73 x 86mm), 1439cm3; compression ratio 9:1; 67.5kW (90.5hp) [92PS] at 6300rpm, 47kW/L (63hp/L) [63.9PS/L]; 125Nm (92.2lbft) at 4000rpm.
European version (DIN): 50kW (67hp) [68PS] at 5000rpm. 34.8kW/L (46.6hp/L) [47.2PS/L]; 104Nm (76.7lbft) at 3000rpm.
Engine for some countries: 51.5kW (69hp) [70PS].

Engine construction: Designated Mitsubishi Saturn.

Transmission: Final drive ratio, 4.11.

Performance: Max speed 99mph/160kmh (manufacturers test specifications), speed at 1000rpm in top gear 16.5mph/26.5kmh; power to weight ratio 14.8kg/kW (10.9kg/PS); consumption 7-12L/100km (40.4-23.5mpg) [33.6-19.6US mpg].

```
2 Litre
68kW-91hp-93PS
1 2V Carb
```

As 1.6 Litre, except:

Weight: Kerbweight (DIN) 1230kg.

Engine data (DIN): 4-cylinder in-line (85 x 88mm), 1997cm3; compression ratio 8.5:1; 68kW (91hp) [93PS] at 5500rpm, 34.1kW/L (45.7hp/L) [46.6PS/L]; 151Nm (111.4lbft) at 3000rpm.

Engine construction: Designated Mitsubishi G 63B. Battery 12V 60Ah, alternator 70A.

Transmission (to rear wheels) a) 5-speed manual, final drive ratio 3.583.
b) Automatic, hydraulic torque converter and 4-speed Planetary gear set, final drive ratio 3.909.

Gear ratios: a) 5-speed manual; 1st 3.369; 2nd 2.035; 3rd 1.360; 4th 1; 5th 0.856; R 3.635.
b) Automatic; Max torque multiplication in converter 2 times, Planetary gear set ratios: 1st 2.452; 2nd 1.452; 3rd 1; 4th 0.688; R 212.

Chassis: Tyres 185/70 SR 13.

Hyundai • Infiniti

Dimensions: Length 455.5cm, width 175.5cm, height 138cm.
Performances: Max speed 109mph/175kmh (manufacturers test specifications), speed at 1000rpm in 5th gear 24.2mph/39kmh; power to weight ratio 18.1kg/kW (13.2kg/PS); consumption 8– 14L/100km (35.3–20.2mpg) [29.4–16.8US mpg].

Hyundai Sonata

New model. Middle class Saloon/Sedan with front wheel drive, 1.8 or 2.4 Litre, 4-cylinder engine, based mechanically on the Mitusbishi. Launched in Autumn 1988.

1.8 Litre
73kW-98hp-99PS
Fuel Injection

Body, Weight: 4-door Saloon/Sedan, 5-seater; kerbweight (DIN) from 1200kg.
Engine data (DIN): 4-cylinder in-line (80.6 x 88mm), 1796cm3; compression ratio 8.9:1; 73kW (98hp) [99PS] at 5000rpm, 40.6kW/L (54.4hp/L) [55.1PS/L]; 146Nm (107.7lbft) at 4000rpm.
With Catalyst: Compression ratio 8.8; 70kW (94hp) [95PS] at 5000 rpm, 39kW/L (52.3hp/L) [52.9PS/L]; 143Nm (105.5lbft) at 4000rpm; regular unleaded.
Engine construction: Front-inclined transverse engine. Designated Mitsubishi G 62B. Overhead valves (in V), 1 overhead camshaft (toothed belt); 2 anti vibration arms; light-alloy cylinder head; 5 bearing crankshaft; oil capacity 4 L (3.8US qt); electronic fuel injection. 12V 60Ah Battery, 75A Alternator; cooling system capacity 6.1 L (5.8US qt).
Transmission (to front wheels): a) 5-speed manual, final drive ratio 4.592.
b) Automatic, hydraulic torque converter with 4-speed Planetary gear set, final drive ratio 3.986.
Gear ratios: a) 5-speed manual: 1st 3.363; 2nd 1.947; 3rd 1.285; 4th 0.939; 5th 0.756; R 3.083.
b) Automatic; Max torque multiplication in converter approx 2 times, Planetary gear set ratios: 1st 2.846; 2nd 1.581; 3rd 1; 4th 0.685; R 2.176.
Chassis: Integral body; front McPherson struts with lower A-arm, rear compound axle (trailing arm, suspension tube) with Panhard rod and coil springs, front antiroll bar (in some versions also rear), telescopic dampers. Servo/power assisted brakes, front discs (ventilated), rear drums, mechanical handbrake to rear wheels; power assisted rack and pinion steering; fuel tank capacity 60L (13.2Gal) [16US Gal]; tyres 185/70 SR 14 optionally 195/70 SR 14, wheel rims 5.5J.
Dimensions: Wheelbase 265cm, track 145/144cm, clearance 17cm, turning circle approx 10.5m. Length 468cm, width 175cm, height 141cm.
Performance: Max speed approx 106mph/170kmh, speed at 1000rpm in 5th gear 20.4mph/32.9kmh; power to weight ratio from 16.4kg/kW (12.1kg/PS); consumption ECE 6.7/8.8/11.4L/100km (42.2/32.1/24.8mpg) [35.1/26.7/20.6US mpg], Catalyst 6.4/8.5/10.6L/100km (44.1/33.2/26.6mpg) [36.8/27.7/22.2US mpg], Automatic 6.3/8.7/12.2L/100kmh (44.8/32.5/23.2mpg) [37.3/27/19.3USmpg], Catalyst 6.9/9.4/10.3L/100km (40.9/30.1/27.4mpg) [34.1/25/22.8US mpg].

Hyundai Sonata

2 Litre
76kW-102hp-104PS
Fuel Injection

As 1.8 Litre, except:
Weight: Kerbweight from 1215kg.
Engine data (DIN): 4-cylinder in-line (85 x 88mm), 1997cm3; compression ratio 8.6:1; 76kW (102hp) [104PS] at 5000rpm, 38.1kW/L (51hp/L) [52.1PS/L]; 164Nm (121lbft) at 3500rpm.
With Catalyst: 74kW (99hp) [100PS] at 5000rpm, 37.1kW/L (49.7hp/L) [50.1PS/L]; 159Nm (117lbft) at 4000rpm; premium unleaded.
Engine construction: Designated Mitsubishi 4G 63. Cooling system capacity 6.5L (6.1US qt).
Transmission: a) 5-speed manual, final drive ratio 4.322.
b) Automatic, final drive ratio 3.986.
Performance: Max speed approx 112mph/180kmh, speed at 1000rpm in 5th gear 21.7mph/35.0kmh; power to weight ratio from 16kg/kW (11.7kg/PS); consumption ECE 6.9/8.9/9.4L/100km (40.9/31.7/30.1mpg) [34.1/26.4/25US mpg], Catalyst 6.5/8.6/10.1L/100km (43.5/32.8/28mpg) [36.2/27.4/23.3US mpg], Automatic 6.2/8.3/10.1L/100km (45.6/34/28mpg) [37.9/28.3/23.3US mpg), Catalyst 7.1/9.0/9.5L/100km (39.8/31.4/29.7mpg) [33.1/26.1/24.8US mpg].

Hyundai Sonata

2.35 Litre
86kW-115hp-117PS
Fuel Injection

As 1.8 Litre, except:
Weight: Kerbweight from 1240kg.
Engine data (DIN): 4-cylinder in-line (86.5 x 100mm), 2351cm3; compression ratio 8.6:1; 86kW (115hp) [117PS] at 4500rpm, 36.6kW/L (49hp/L) [49.8PS/L]; 193Nm (142.4lbft) at 3500rpm.
With Catalyst: 83kW (111hp) [113PS] at 4500rpm, 35.3kW/L (47.5hp/L) [48.1PS/L]; 189Nm (139.5cu ft) at 3500rpm; unleaded premium grade
Engine Construction: Designated Mitsubishi 4G 64; oil capacity 4L (3.8US qt). Cooling system capacity 9L (8.5US qt).
Transmission: a) 5-speed manual, final drive ratio 4.067.
b) Automatic, final drive ratio, 3.986.
Gear ratios: a) 5-speed manual: 1st 3.166; 2nd 1.833; 3rd 1.240; 4th 0.896; 5th 0.666; R 3.166.
b) Automatic: Max torque multiplication in converter approx 2 times, Planetary gear set ratios: 1st 2.551; 2nd 1.488; 3rd 1; 4th 0.685; R 2.176.
Performance: Max speed approx 118mph/190kmh, speed at 1000rpm in 5th gear 26.2mph/42.2kmh; power to weight ratio from 14.4kg/kW (10.6kg/PS); consumption ECE 6.3/8.4/12.0L/100km (44.8/33.6/23.5mpg) [37.3/28/19.6US mpg], Catalyst 6.8/8.9/12.4L/100km (41.5/31.7/22.8mpg) [34.6/26.4/19US mpg], Automatic 7.4/9.5/12.6L/100km (38.2/29.7/22.4mpg) [31.8/24.8/18.7US mpg], Catalyst 6.9/9.1/11.2L/100km (40.9/31/25.2mpg) [34.1/25.8/21US mpg].

INFINITI   J

Nissan Motors Co. Ltd., 17-1 Ginza 6-chome, Chuo-ku, Tokyo 104, Japan
New luxury make of car for Nissan Motors, priority is the American market.
MODEL RANGE
Q45 - M30 Coupe - M30 Convertible

Infiniti M30

New model. Luxurious Coupe and Cabriolet with rear wheel drive and V6 engine with 3 litre capacity and 165hp. Engine related to the Nissan Leopard. Launched Winter 1988/89, production begins Autumn 1989, Cabriolet 1990.

3.0 Litre V6
123kW-165hp-167PS
Fuel Injection

Body, Weight: Coupe 2-door, 5-seater; kerbweight from 1495kg. Cabriolet 2-door, 4-seater; kerbweight from 1575kg.

Infiniti • Innocenti

Infiniti M30 Sports Coupe

Engine data (SAE net): 6-cylinder in V 60deg (87 x 83mm), 2960cm3; compression ratio 9:1; 123kW (165hp) [167PS] at 5200rpm; 41.6kW/L (55.7hp/L) [56.4PS/L]; 235Nm (173.4lbft) at 4000rpm; unleaded regular grade.

Engine construction: Designated VG 30E. Valves in V; hydraulic tappets; 1 overhead camshaft (toothed belt), light-alloy cylinder head; 4 bearing crankshaft; oil capacity 4.7L (4.4US qt); electronic fuel injection. 12V 60Ah, alternator 90A, cooling system capacity approx 9L (8.5US Gal).

Transmission (to rear wheels): Automatic with programme, hydraulic torque converter with 4-speed Planetary gear set, final drive ratio 3.917. Optional limited slip differential.

Gear ratios: Automatic; max torque multiplication 2 times; Planetary gear set ratios: 1st 2.784; 2nd 1.544; 3rd 1; 4th 0.694; R 2.272.

Chassis: Integral body; front McPherson struts, control arm, torsion struts and antiroll bar, rear independent suspension with semi-trailing arm, coil springs and antiroll bar. Electronically regulated telescopic dampers. Servo/ power assisted brakes, front ventilated ABS, handbrake to rear wheels; power assisted rack and pinion steering; fuel tank 65L (14.3Gal) [17.2US Gal]; tyres 215/60 HR 15, wheel rims 6.5J.

Dimensions: Wheelbase 261.5cm, track 143.5/143.5cm, clearance approx 13cm, turning circle 10.4m, length 479.5cm, width 169cm, height 137cm.

Performance: Max speed approx 124mph/200kmh, speed at 1000rpm in 5th gear 26.7mph/43.0mph; power to weight ratio from 12.2kg/kW (8.9kg/PS); consumption approx 9-16L/100km (31.4-17.7mpg) [26.1-14.7US mpg].

Infiniti M30 Comvertible

Infiniti Q45

New model. Luxury Saloon/Sedan of superior class. 4.5 Litre V8 engine with 32 valves and above 270hp. 4-speed automatic and rear wheel drive. Launched Winter 1988/89. Production begins Autumn 1989. Data incomplete.

```
4.5 Litre V8
200kW-270hp-273PS
Fuel Injection
```

Body, Weight: Saloon/Sedan 4-door, 5-seater; kerbweight from 1750kg.

Engine data (SAE net): 8-cylinder in V 90deg (93 x 82.7mm), 4494cm3; compression ratio 10.2:1; over 200kW (270hp) [273PS] at 6000rpm, over 44.5kW/L (59.6hp/L) [60.7PS/L]; over 380Nm (280.4lbft) at 4000rpm; unleaded regular grade.

Engine construction: 4 valves in V per cylinder; hydraulic tappets, 2 overhead camshafts (chain); light-alloy cylinder head and engine block; 5 bearing crankshaft; oil capacity 6.6L (6.2US qt); electronic engine management (fuel injection, ignition). 12V battery, 110A alternator; cooling system capacity approx 9.5L (9.0US qt).

Transmission (to rear wheels): Electronic regulated automatic, hydraulic torque converter and 4-speed Planetary gear set, final drive ratio 3.538. Limited slip differential (Visco).

Chassis: Integral body; all round independent suspension, front dual A arms, coil springs and antiroll bar, rear multi pivoting axle, (axial struts, top single control arm, diagonal strut), semi-trailing arm and coaxial telescopic dampers, antiroll bar, optional electronic regulated damper. Servo/power assisted disc brakes with ABS, front ventilated, disc diameter front 27.9cm, rear 29.2cm, handbrake to rear wheels; power assisted rack and pinion steering, optional hydraulic steering Super HICAS; fuel tank 85L (18.7Gal) [22.5US Gal]; tyres 215/65 VR 15, wheel rims 6.5J.

Dimensions: Wheelbase 288cm, track 157/157cm, turning circle 11.4m, load space 15cu ft (425dm3). Length 507.7-509cm, width 182.5cm, height 143cm.

Performance: Max speed 143mph/230kmh (manufacturers test specification); speed 0-60mph/97kmh 7.3secs; power to weight ratio from 8.7kg/kW (6.4kg/PS); consumption approx 10-18L/100km (28.2-15.7mpg) [23.5-13.1US mpg].

Infiniti Q45

INNOCENTI I

Innocenti Nuova Innocenti S.p.A., Via Rubattino 37, 20134 Milano, Italia

Nuova Innocenti, part of the De Tomaso Group, formed in 1976. Innoccenti 990

Innocenti 990/500

900 – 990 Matic – 990 Diesel – Turbo De Tomaso – 650/550

```
1 Litre
39kW-52hp-53PS
1 2V Carb
```

Engine for Matic, 990 SL and 990 SE

Body, Weight: Saloon/Sedan 3–door 5-seats; kerbweight (DIN), SE 695kg, SL 700kg, Matic 715kg, gross vehicle weight 1095–1115kg.

Engine data (DIN): 3–cylinder in–line (76 x 73mm), 993cm3; compression ratio 9.5:1; 39kW (52hp) [53PS] at 5750rpm, 39.3kW/L (52.7hp/L) [53.4PS/L]; 75Nm (55.3lbft) at 3200rpm; leaded premium grade (97R).

Engine construction: Front transverse engine, designated Daihatsu. Overhead valves (in V), 1 overhead camshaft (toothed belt); light-alloy cylinder head, 1 counter–balance shaft, 4 bearing crankshaft; oil capacity 2.9L (2.7US qt); 1 downdraught Aisan 2V two stage carb. Battery 12V 30/35/40Ah, alternator 45A; cooling system capacity 4.3L (4.1US qt).

Transmission (to front wheels): a) 5-speed manual, final drive ratio 4.5.
b) Semi-automatic, hydraulic torque converter and 2-speed Planetary gear set, selector lever in the middle, final drive ratio 4.210.

Gear ratios: a) 5-speed manual; 1st 3.090; 2nd 1.842; 3rd 1.230; 4th 0.864; 5th 0.707; R 3.142.

Innocenti • Irmscher

b) Semi-automatic; Max torque multiplication in converter 2 times; Planetary gear set ratios; 1.821; 1; R 1.821.

Chassis: Integral body; front independent suspension with McPherson strut, lower control arm and tie bar; rear independent suspension with A-arm, damper strut, transverse leaf spring, telescopic dampers. Brakes; front disc, rear drums, mechanical handbrake on rear wheels. Rack and pinion steering; fuel tank capacity 40L (8.8Gal) [10.6US Gal], including 4.5–7L (1Gal) [1.2US Gal] reserve; tyres 135 SR 12 or 155/70 SR 12, wheel rims 4 or 4.5J.

Dimensions: Saloon/Sedan (long); wheelbase 220.5cm, track 124.5/129cm, clearance 13cm, turning circle 9.95m. Load space 10.4–35cu ft (295–990dm3). Length 337.5cm, width 151.5cm, height 137.5cm.

Performance: Max speed 90mph/145kmh (automatic 87mph/140kmh) (manufacturers test specifications); speed at 1000rpm in 5th gear 18.8mph/30.2kmh; acceleration 0 – 62mph/100kmh 16.2secs; standing km 36.3secs; power to weight ratio from 17.8kg/kW (13.1kg/PS). Consumption (ECE) 5.6/7.4/7.6L/100km (50.4/38.2/37.2mpg) [42.0/31.8/30.9US mpg]. Semi-automatic 6.7/9.1/7.5L/100km (42.2/31.0/37.7mpg) [35.1/25.8/31.4US mpg].

Innocenti 990 SL

548cm3
24kW–31hp–32PS
1 2V Carb

Engine for 550.

Body, Weight: Kerbweight (DIN) 650kg, gross vehicle weight, 1050kg.

Engine data (DIN): 3-cylinder in-line (62 x 60.5mm) 548cm3; compression ratio 10:1; 24kW (31hp) [32PS] at 6400rpm. 43.8kW/L (58.7hp/L) [59.6PS/L]; 42Nm (31.9lbft) at 3000rpm.

Engine construction: Designated Daihatsu EB.

Gear ratios: 1st 3.583; 2nd 2.100; 3rd 1.392; 4th 0.971; 5th 0.820; R 3.538.

Transmission: 5-speed manual, final drive ratio 5.333.

Chassis: Tyres 135 SR 12 or 145/70 SR 12.

Dimensions: Wheelbase 204.5cm, track 124.5/130cm, clearance 12cm, turning circle 9.5m, load space 9.9-31.8cu ft (280-900dm3), length 321cm, width 152cm, height 138cm.

Performance: Max speed 75mph/120kmh (manufacturers test specifications), speed at 1000rpm in 5th gear 13.5mph/21.8kmh; power to weight ratio 27.6kg/kW (20.3kg/PS). Consumption ECE 4.4/-/5.6L/100km (64.2/-/50.4mpg) [53.5/-/42.0US mpg].

1 Litre Turbo
53kW–71hp–72PS
1 2V Carb

Engine for Turbo De Tomaso as 52hp except:

Body, Weight: Kerbweight (DIN) 710kg, gross vehicle weight 1060kg.

Engine data (DIN): 3-cylinder in-line (76 x73 mm) 993cm3; compression ratio 8:1; 53kW (71hp) [72PS] at 5700rpm, 53.4kW/L (71.6hp/L) [72.5PS/L]; 104Nm (76.7lbft) at 3500rpm.
With unregulated Catalyst: 50kW (67hp) [68PS] at 5500rpm, 106Nm (78.2lbft) at 3200rpm.

Engine construction: Designation CB-60; 1 2V two stage Aisan carb, 1 exhaust turbocharger IHI RHB 32; max boost pressure 0.5 bar; oil cooler.

Transmission: 5-speed manual, final drive ratio 4.5; 4.642.

Chassis: Antiroll bar front and rear; tyres 160/65 R 315.

Dimensions: Wheelbase 204.5cm, track 125.5/128.5cm, clearance 12cm, turning circle 9.5m, load space 9.9-31.8cu ft (280-900dm3), length 313.5cm, width 152cm, height 134cm.

Performance: Max speed 101mph/162kmh (manufacturers test specification), speed at 1000rpm in 5th gear 18.6mph/30kmh; acceleration 0 – 62mph/100kmh 10.8secs; power to weight ratio from 13.4kg/kW (9.9kg/PS); consumption ECE 6.4/8.7/10.1L/100km (44.1/32.5/28mpg) [36.8/27/23.3US mpg]. With unregulated Catalyst: Max speed 99mph/160kmh.

1 Litre Diesel
27kW–36hp–37PS
Fuel Injection

Engine for Minidiesel and 990 Diesel, as 52hp, except:

Body, Weight: Minidiesel; kerbweight 685kg, gross vehicle weight 1090kg. 990; kerbweight (DIN) 740kg, gross vehicle weight 1140kg.

Engine data (DIN): 3-cylinder in-line (76 x73 mm) 993cm3; compression ratio 21.5:1; 27kW (36hp) [37PS] at 4600rpm, 27.2kW/L (36.4hp/L) [37.3PS/L]; 61Nm (45lbft) at 3000rpm.

Engine construction: Swirl chamber diesel engine. Designated CL10, parallel valves; oil capacity 3.2L (3US qt); Nippondenso Bosch VE injection pump. Battery 12V 55Ah, alternator 40A.

Transmission: 5-speed manual; final drive ratio 4.5.

Performance: Max speed 78mph/125kmh (manufacturers test specification); standing start km 45secs; power to weight ratio from 25.4kg/kW (18.5kg/PS). Consumption ECE 3.7/-/5.8L/100km (76.3/-/48.7mpg) [63.6/-/40.6US mpg].

Innocenti Turbo De Tomaso

IRMSCHER D

Irmscher GmbH, Postfach 1127, 7064 Remshalden 1, Deutschland

German manufacturer, for production of Opel.

Irmscher GT

Coupe on the basis of the Opel Omega 3000 with 3.6 Litre capacity larger engine. Launched prototype in Geneva 1988; production preview. Provisional data and incomplete.

3.6 Litre
147kW–197hp–200PS
Fuel Injection

Body, Weight: Coupe 2-door, 2-seater; kerbweight from 1330kg.

Engine data (with Catalyst DIN): 6-cylinder in-line (95 x 85mm), 3615cm3; compression ratio 9.4:1; 147kW (197hp) [200PS] at 5200rpm, 40.7kW/L (54.5hp/L) [55.3PS/L]; 285Nm (210.3lbft) at 4200rpm; premium unleaded grade.

Engine construction: Hydraulic tappets, side camshaft (chain) in cylinder head; 7 bearing crankshaft; oil capacity 5.5L (5.2US qt); Bosch Motronic digital fuel injection. 12V 55 Ah battery, 70A alternator, cooling system capacity approx 10.2L (9.6US qt).

Transmission (to rear wheels): 5-speed manual, final drive ratio 3.45; limited differential.

Gear ratios: 1st 4.044; 2nd 2.265; 3rd 1.434; 4th 1; 5th 0.842; R 3.748.

Chassis: Integral body; front and rear independent suspension; front McPherson struts and lower A arm, rear semi-trailing arm and coil springs, front and rear antiroll bars; telescopic damper, electronic damper. Servo/power assisted disc brakes with ABS (front ventilated), disc diameter front 28cm, rear 27cm; mechanical handbrake to rear wheels; power assisted recirculating ball steering; fuel tank 75L (16.5Gal) [19.8US Gal]; tyres 245/45VR 16, wheel rims 8J.

Dimensions: Wheelbase 273cm, track 145/147cm, clearance 12cm, turning circle 10.8m, length 459cm, width 178cm, height 134cm.

Performance: Max speed 152mph/245kmh (manufacturers test specification), speed at 100rpm in 5th gear 24.5mph/39.4kmh; speed 0 - 62mph/100kmh 7.9secs; power to weight ratio from 9.0kg/kW (6.6kg/PS); consumption ECE 7.6/9.3/15.1L/100km (37.2/30.4/18.7mpg) [30.9/25.3/15.6US mpg].

Irmscher GT

ISUZU J

Isuzu Motors Ltd 22.10 Minami-oi 6 chome, Shingawa-ku, Tokyo, Japan.

Part of the Hitachi consortium, manufacturers of passenger vehicles and utility vehicles.

MODEL RANGE
Gemini/Spectrum – Aska – Piazza – Rodeo Bighorn – Trooper

Isuzu Gemini/Geo Spectrum

Medium size 4-door vehicle with a 1.5 Litre 4-cylinder engine. 5- speed manual or automatic transmission, marketed in the USA as the Geo Spectrum. Launched in November 1984, introduction of a 5-speed electronic controlled Navi5 transmission and turbo in 1986. Turbo-diesel and four valve engine available in 1988.

Isuzu Gemini

```
1471cm3
54kW–72hp–73PS
1 2V Carb
```

Body, Weight: Coupe; 3-door, 5-seats; kerbweight (DIN) from 870kg. Saloon/Sedan; 4-door, 5-seats; kerbweight (DIN) from 860kg.

Engine data (JIS nett): 4-cylinder in-line (77 x 79mm) 1471cm3; compression ratio 9.8:1; 54kW (72hp) [73PS] at 5600rpm, 36.7kW/L (49.2hp/L) [49.6PS/L]; 116Nm (85.6lbft) at 3600rpm; regular grade.

With Catalyst (US-83): Compression ratio 9.6:1; 52kW (70hp) [71PS] at 5400rpm; 118Nm (87lbft) at 3400rpm.

Engine construction: Designated 4XC1; valves (in V) 1 overhead camshaft (toothed belt); light-alloy cylinder head; 5 bearing crankshaft; oil capacity 2.8L (2.6US qt); 1 downdraught 2V carb. Battery 12V 40/50Ah, alternator 50/60A; cooling system capacity 6.4L (6.1US qt).

Transmission (to front wheels): a) 5-speed manual, also available with Navi5 electronic control; final drive ratio 3.578; 3.833.
b) Automatic, hydraulic torque converter and 3-speed Planetary gear set, selector lever in the middle, final drive ratio 3.526.

Gear ratios: a) 5-speed manual; 1st 3.727, 2nd 2.043; 3rd 1.448; 4th 1.027; 5th 0.829 (Navi5 0.744); R 3.583.
For USA; 1st 3.727; 2nd 2.043; 3rd 1.333; 4th 0.923; 5th 0.744; R 3.583.
b) Automatic; Max torque multiplication in converter 2 times. Planetary gear set ratios; 1st 2.841; 2nd 1.541; 3rd 1; R 2.4.

Chassis: Integral body; front lower control arm and McPherson strut, some variants with antiroll bar, rear compound axle with trailing arm; telescopic dampers. Servo/power assisted brakes, front disc (some models ventilated), disc diameter 22.5cm, rear drums; handbrake on front wheels. Rack and pinion steering (optional power assisted); fuel tank 42L (9.2Gall) [11.1US Gal]; tyres 155 SR 13, 175/70 SR 13 (optional 185/60 HR 14) wheel rims 4.5/5J.

Dimensions: Wheelbase 240cm, track 139/138.5cm, clearance 16.5cm, turning circle 9.6m, load space 3-door 11.3-24cu ft (320-680dm3), 4-door 12-24.7cu ft (340-700dm3), length 3-door 396-399.5cm (USA 401cm), 4-door 403.5-407cm (USA 408cm), width 160- 161.5cm, height 135-140.5cm.

Performance: Max speed 96mph/155kmh (manufacturers test specifications), speed at 1000rpm (3.578) in 5th gear 22.2mph/35.8kmh; acceleration 0 - 62mph/100kmh 13secs; power to weight ratio from 15.9kg/kW (11.8kg/PS); consumption 5–11L/100km (56.5–25.7mpg) [47.0–21.4US mpg].

```
1471cm3
88kW–118hp–120PS
Turbo/Fuel Injection
```

As 72hp, except:

Body, Weight: Kerbweight (DIN); 3-door from 930kg, 4-door from 940kg.

Engine data (JIS nett); 4-cylinder in-line (77 x 79mm) 1471cm3, compression ratio 8.5:1; 88kW (118hp) [120PS] at 5800rpm, 59.8kW/L (80hp/L) [81.6PS/L]; 181Nm (133.5lbft) at 3400rpm. Low boost pressure: 77kW (103hp) [105PS]. USA Version (SAE net): 81kW (109hp) [110PS] at 5400rpm; 163Nm (120.2lbft) at 3500rpm.

Engine construction: Designated 4XC1-UT; electronic central/single point injection, 1 turbocharger, adjustable boost pressure; air to air cooler.

Transmission: a) 5-speed manual, final drive ratio 3.450.
b) Automatic, final drive ratio 3.350.

Gear ratios: a) 5-speed manual: 1st 3.727, 2nd 2.043; 3rd 1.448; 4th 1.027; 5th 0.829; R 3.583.
b) Automatic: As 72hp.

Chassis: Front antiroll bar: front ventilated discs; tyres 185/60HR 14, wheel rims 5J.

Dimensions: Track 141/139cm.

Performance: Max speed 115–118mph/185–190kmh, speed at 1000rpm in 5th gear 23mph/37.0kmh; power to weight ratio from 10.7kg/kW (7.8kg/PS); consumption 8–13L/100km (35.2/21.7mpg) [29.4/18.1US mpg].

Isuzu Gemini GTi

Isuzu

1.6 Litre 16V
99kW–133hp–135PS
Fuel Injection

As 72hp, except:

Body, Weight: Kerbweight (DIN) from 950kg.

Engine data (JIS nett): 4-cylinder in-line (80 x 79mm) 1588cm3; compression ratio 10:1; 99kW (133hp) [135PS] at 7200rpm, 62.3kW/L (83.5hp/L) [85PS/L]; 140Nm (103.3lbft) at 5600rpm.
With Catalyst (DIN): Compression ratio 9.8:1; 92kW (123hp) [125PS] at 6800rpm; 136Nm (100.4lbft) at 5400rpm; unleaded regular grade.

Engine construction: Designated 4XE1. 4 valves in V per cylinder, hydraulic tappets, 2 overhead camshafts (toothed belt);ECM electronic engine management injection/ignition; battery 12V 50Ah, alternator 75A.

Transmission: a) 5-speed manual, final drive ratio 4.117.
b) Automatic, final drive ratio 3.526.

Gear ratios: a) 5-speed manual; 1st 3.727; 2nd 2.043; 3rd 1.448; 4th 1.027; 5th 0.829; R 3.583.
b) Automatic; as 72hp.

Chassis: Antiroll bar front and rear; front ventilated disc brakes; tyres 185/60 HR 14, wheel rims 5J.

Dimensions: Track 141/139cm. Length 3-door 401cm, 4-door 408cm.

Performance (Catalyst version): Max speed 118mph/190kmh (manufacturers test specification), speed at 1000rpm in 5th gear 19.3mph/31.0kmh; power to weight ratio from 10.5kg/kW (7.8kg/PS); consumption approx 7-12L/100km (40.4-23.5mpg) [33.6-19.6US mpg].

1488cm3D
51/38kW-68/51hp-70/52PS
Turbo/Fuel Injection

As 72hp, except:

Weight: Kerbweight (DIN) from 910, Turbo from 960kg.

Engine data (JIS net): 4-cylinder in-line (76 x 82mm), 1488cm3; compression ratio 22:1; 51kW (68hp) [70PS] at 5000rpm, 34.3kW/L (45.9hp/L) [47PS/L]; 132Nm (97.4lbft) at 2500 rpm.
Without Turbo (JIS net): Compression ratio 23:1; 38kW (51hp) [52PS] at 5400rpm; 93Nm (68.6lbft) at 2600rpm.

Engine construction: Designated 4EC1. Swirl chamber turbulence - diesel engine. Parallel valves; diesel injection pump (Bosch VE), version 67PS with 1 exhaust turbocharger, 12V 65Ah battery, 50A alternator.

Transmission: a) 5-speed manual, optional electronic programme selection Navi 5, final drive ratio 3.736, or Turbo 3.833, 4.117.
b) Automatic, as 72hp.

Gear ratios: a) 5-speed manual; 1st 3.909; 2nd 2.150; 3rd 1.448; 4th 1.027; 5th 0.829 (Navi5 0.744); R 3.583.
b) Automatic, as 72hp.

Performance (Turbodiesel): Max speed approx 103mph/165kmh, speed at 1000rpm in 5th gear (axle 3.736) 21.3mph/34.3kmh; power to weight ratio from 18.6kg/kW (13.6kg/PS); consumption (touring) approx 6-9L/100km (47.1/31.4mpg) [39.2-26.1US mpg].

Isuzu Aska

Saloon/Sedan 4-door, front wheel drive, available with 5 different engines. Derived from General Motors J-cars. Launched April 1983. 1985 changed to electronic.Circuit Navi5.

Isuzu Aska

1800
77kW-103hp-105PS
1 2V Carb

Body, Weight: Saloon/Sedan 4-door 5-seats; kerbweight (DIN) 1020kg.

Engine data (JIS): 4-cylinder in-line (84 x 82mm) 1818cm3; compression ratio 9:1; 77kW (103hp) [105PS] at 5600rpm, 42.5kW/L (57hp/L) [57.8PS/L]; 152Nm (112.1lbft) at 3600rpm; leaded regular grade.

Engine construction: Designated 4ZB1. Valves in V; 1 overhead camshaft (toothed belt); light-alloy cylinder head; downdraught Stromberg 2V two stage carb. Battery 12V 35-50Ah, alternator 500W; cooling system capacity 7.5L (7.1US qt).

Transmission (to front wheels): a) 5-speed manual, final drive ratio 3.578.
b) Automatic, hydraulic torque converter and 3-speed Planetary gear set, final drive ratio, 3.431.

Gear ratios: a) 5-speed manual; 1st 3.727; 2nd 2.043; 3rd 1.258; 4th 0.875; 5th 0.704; R 3.583.
b) Automatic; Max torque multiplication in converter 2 times, Planetary gear set ratios; 1st 2.84; 2nd 1.6; 3rd 1; R 2.07.

Chassis: Integral body; front sub-frame; front McPherson strut and lower A-arm, antiroll bar; rear compound axle trailing arm with cross braces, coil springs, optional antiroll bar, telescopic damper. Servo/power assisted brakes, front disc (ventilated) rear drums, mechanical handbrake on front wheels. Rack and pinion steering, optional power assisted; fuel tank 56L (12.3Gal) [14.8US Gal]; tyres 165 SR 13, wheel rims 5J.

Dimensions: Wheelbase 258cm, track 140.5/141cm, clearance 15.5cm, turning circle 10.2m. Length 444cm, width 167cm, height 137.5cm.

Performance: Max speed 96mph/155kmh, speed at 1000rpm in 5th gear 27mph/43.4kmh; power to weight ratio from 14.9kg.kW (11.0kg/PS); consumption 7-11L/100km (40.4-25.7mpg) [33.6-21.4US mpg].

2000
110/81kW–147/109hp-150/110PS
1 2V Carb

As 1800, except:

Weight: Kerbweight (DIN) 1040-1100kg, without Turbo from 1040kg.

Engine data (JIS): 4-cylinder in-line (88 x 82mm) 1995cm3; compression ratio 8.2:1; 110kW (147hp) [150PS] at 5400rpm, 55.1kW/L (73.8hp/L) [75.2PS/L]; 226Nm (166.8lbft) at 3000rpm; leaded regular grade.
Without Turbo, with Carb: Compression ratio 8.8:1; 81kW (109hp) [110PS] at 5400rpm, 40.6kW/L (54.4hp/L) [55.1PS/L]; 167Nm (123.2lbft) at 3400rpm; leaded regular grade.

Engine construction: Designated 4ZC1-T. Electronic fuel injection; 1 exhaust turbocharger, Version 109hp with compound carb.

Transmission: a) 5-speed manual, final drive ratio 3.45 with Navi5 (109hp) 3.578.
b) Automatic (109hp), final drive ratio 3.333.

Gear ratios: a) 5-speed manual: 1st 3.583; 2nd 1.958; 3rd 1.258; 4th 0.875; 5th 0.704; R 3.583.
Or (109hp): 1st 3.583; 2nd 1.958; 3rd 1.448; 4th 1.027; 5th 0.829; R 3.583.
Navi5: 1st 3.727; 2nd 2.043; 3rd 1.258; 4th 0.875; 5th 0.704; R 3.583.
b) Automatic: As 1800.

Chassis: Rear antiroll bar; tyres 195/60 HR 14, wheel rims 5.5, optional 6J.109hp version tyres 185/65 SR 14.

Performance (Turbo): Max speed approx 121mph/195kmh, speed at 1000rpm in 5th gear 27.7mph/44.5kmh; power to weight ratio 10.1kg/kW (7.4kg/PS); consumption approx 10-16L/100km (28.2-17.7mpg) [23.5-14.7US mpg].

2000 Diesel
63kW-84hp-85PS
Turbo/Injection Pump

As 1800, except:

Weight: Kerbweight (DIN) 1130-1190kg. Turbodiesel from 1130kg; diesel from 1100kg.

Engine data (JIS nett): 4-cylinder in-line (84 x 90mm), 1995cm3; compression ratio 21:1; 63kW (84hp) [85PS] at 4500rpm, 31.6kW/L (42.3hp/L) [42.6PS/L] 180Nm (132.8lbft) at 2500rpm.
Without Turbocharger: 51kW (68hp) [70PS] at 4700rpm, 25.6kW/L (34.3hp/L) [35.1PS/L]; 123Nm (90.7lbft) at 2500rpm.

TROOPER 4WD

ALL-AROUND BEST, ALL AROUND THE WORLD

All around the world, leaders help to shape the future. And TROOPER is no exception. This forward-looking multi-purpose 4×4 vehicle combines rugged versatility with remarkably sophisticated good looks. The choice of solid, dependable gasoline or diesel engines, coupled with powerful drive train and braking systems assure strong, steady operation for years. And TROOPER has captured the hearts of drivers and passengers on every continent. Achievers and leaders in communities everywhere have found that TROOPER is the all-around best tool to help them shape their future.

ISUZU

Isuzu

Engine construction: Designated 4FC1. Swirl chamber diesel engine, parallel valves, grey cast iron cylinder head; injection pump.

Transmission: a) 5-speed manual, final drive ratio 3.833.
b) Automatic, final drive ratio 3.341.
Without Turbo 3.737.

Gear ratios: a) 5-speed manaul: 1st 3.500; 2nd 1.916; 3rd 1.333; 4th 0.923; 5th 0.704; R 3.583.
With Navi5: 1st 3.909; 2nd 2.15; 3rd 1.333; 4th 0923; 5th 0.704; R 3.583.
Without Turbo: 1st 3.727; 2nd 2.043; 3rd 1.333; 4th 1.027; 5th 0.744; R 3.583.
b) Automatic: As 1800.

Chassis: Tyres also 185/70 SR 13 or 185/65 SR 14.

Dimensions: Clearance 16cm, length 445cm.

Performance (Turbodiesel): Max speed approx 103mph/165kmh, speed at 1000rpm in 5th gear 25.2mph/40.6kmh; power to weight ratio from 17.3kg/kW (12.7kg/PS); consumption 7–11L/100km (40.4–25.7mpg) [33.6–21.4US mpg].

Isuzu Aska Irmscher

Isuzu Piazza

3-door Coupe designed by Giugiaro. 4-cylinder engine, rear wheel drive. Prototype first shown at Geneva 1979, Piazza June 1981. Successor to the 117 Coupe. Marketed in the USA as the Impulse, also produced in Australia by Holden. Turbo version introduced in 1985.

Isuzu Piazza Turbo

2 Litre OHC
88kW–118hp–120PS
Fuel Injection

Body, Weight: Coupe 3-door 4-seats; kerbweight (DIN) from 1170kg, USA 1235kg.

Engine data (JIS): 4-cylinder in-line (87 x 82mm) 1950cm3; compression ratio 8.8:1; 88kW (118hp) [120PS] at 5800rpm. 45.1kW/L (60.4hp/L) [61.5PS/L]; 162Nm (119.5lbft) at 4000rpm.
USA version (SAE nett): (87 x 94.8mm) 2254cm3; compression ratio 8.3:1; 82kW (110hp) [112PS] at 5000rpm; 172Nm (126.9lbft) at 3000rpm.

Engine construction: Designated G200. Valves in V. 1 overhead camshaft (chain); light-alloy cylinder head, 5 bearing crankshaft; oil capacity 5L (4.7US qt); electronic fuel injection (some models Bosch L-Jetronic). Battery 12V 36/50Ah, alternator 65A; cooling system capacity 9L (8.5US qt).

Transmission (to rear wheels): a) 5-speed manual, final drive ratio 3.583.
b) Automatic, hydraulic torque converter and 4-speed Planetary gear set. Selector lever in the middle, final drive ratio 3.583.
Optional limited slip differential.

Gear ratios: a) 5-speed manual: 1st 3.785; 2nd 2.165; 3rd 1.413; 4th 1; 5th 0.787; R 3.753.
b) Automatic: Max torque multiplication in converter 2 times. Planetary gear set ratios; 1st 2.45; 2nd 1.45; 3rd 1; OD 0.689; R 2.222.

Chassis: Integral body; front wishbones and coil springs; rear rigid axle, short drive shaft and torque tube, trailing arms Panhard rod and coil springs, front and rear antiroll bar, telescopic damper. Servo/power assisted disc brakes (front ventilated), mechanical handbrake on rear wheels; rack and pinion steering, optional power assisted; fuel tank 57L (12.5Gal) [15.1US Gal]; tyres 195/60 HR 14, wheel rims 6J.

Dimensions: Wheelbase 244cm, track 135.5/137cm, clearance 15.5cm, turning circle 9.6m. Length 434cm, USA 438.5cm, width 167.5cm, height 130.5cm.

Performance: Max speed 106–109mph/170–175kmh (manufacturers test specifications), speed at 1000rpm in 5th gear (3.909) 21.8mph/35.1kmh; power to weight ratio from 13.3kg/kW (9.7kg/PS); consumption 8–12L/100km (35.3–23.5mpg) [29.4–19.6US mpg].

2 Litre
110kW–147.5hp–150PS
Turbo/Fuel Injection

As 120hp, except:

Body, Weight: Kerbweight (DIN) from 1220kg, USA 1280kg.

Engine data (JIS nett): 4-cylinder in-line (88 x 82mm), 1995cm3; compression ratio 8.2:1; 110kW (147.5hp) [150PS] at 5400rpm 55.1kW/L (73.8hp/L) [75.2PS/L] 226Nm (166.8lbft) at 3400rpm.
With Catalyst (DIN): Compression ratio 7.9:1; 104kW (139hp) [141PS] at 5400rpm. 225Nm (166lbft) at 3000rpm; unleaded regular grade.

Engine construction: Designated 4ZC1. Oil capacity 4.5L (4.3US qt), oil cooler; 1 exhaust turbocharger, charge-air cooler. Alternator 75A.

Transmission: a) 5-speed manual, final drive ratio 3.909.
b) Automatic, final drive ratio 3.583.
Optional limited slip differential.

Gear ratios: a) 5-speed manual: 1st 3.174; 2nd 1.963; 3rd 1.364; 4th 1; 5th 0.775; R 3.402.
b) Automatic: Max torque multiplication in converter 2 times. Planetary gear set ratios: 1st 2.452; 2nd 1.452; 3rd 1; OD 0.688; R 2.212.

Chassis: Rear double trailing arm; all round ventilated discs; tyres 195/69 VR 14, optional 205/60 HR 14, wheel rims 6J.

Dimensions: Track 135.5/138cm, length 434-438.5cm.

Performance: Max speed 130.5mph/210kmh (manufacturers test specifications), speed at 1000rpm in 5th gear 22.4mph/36.1kmh; acceleration 0 – 62mph/100kmh 9.1secs; power to weight ratio from 11.1kg/kW (8.1kg/PS); consumption from 9–15L/100km (31.4– 18.8mpg) [26.1-15.7US mpg].

Isuzu Piazza Turbo

Isuzu Rodeo Bighorn/Trooper

Rough terrain vehicle, available in 3 body styles and 2 engine capacities, reduction transmission. Export version marketed as the Trooper and sold by General Motors. 5-door version launched Geneva 1985. Increased engine capacity and power output in 1988.

2.6 Litre
84kW–113hp–114PS
Carb/Injection

Isuzu • Jaguar

Isuzu Rodeo Bighorn/Trooper

Body, Weight: Estate/Station Wagon – Convertible 3–door, 5–seats; kerbweight (DIN) 1430/1480kg, gross vehicle weight 2230kg. Estate/Station Wagon 3–door, 5–seats; kerbweight (DIN) 1560kg, gross vehicle weight 2300kg; Estate/Station Wagon (long) 3/5–doors, 5–seats; kerbweight (DIN) 1610kg, gross vehicle weight 2300kg.

Engine data (Catalyst, DIN): 4–cylinder in–line (93 x 95mm) 2559cm; compression ratio 8.3:1; 84kW (113hp) [114PS] at 5000rpm, 32.8kW/L (43.9hp/L) [44.5PS/L]; 195Nm (143.9lbft) at 2500rpm; leaded regular grade.
Japanese Version (JIS net): 88kW (118hp) [120PS] at 5000rpm; 196Nm (144.6lbft) at 2600rpm.
USA version (SAE nett): 90kW (121hp) [122PS] at 4600rpm, 206Nm (152lbft) at 2600rpm.
Without Catalyst (DIN): 85kW (114hp) [116PS] at 4600rpm, 195Nm (143.9lbft) at 2600rpm.
For USA also V6 from Chevrolet (SAE net): 6–cylinder in V60deg (88.9 x 76.2mm), 2838cm3; compression ratio 8.9:1; 93kW (125hp) [127PS] at 4800rpm, 32.9kW/L (44hp/L) [44.8PS/L]; 204Nm (150.5lbft) at 2400rpm.

Engine construction: Designated 4ZEI. Valves in V, 1 overhead camshaft (toothed belt); light–alloy cylinder head; 5 bearing crankshaft; oil capacity 4.9L (4.6US qt); 1 downdraught Nikki 2V two stage carb. 2.6–Litre; electronic fuel injection. Battery 12V 60Ah, alternator 50/55A; cooling system capacity 8L (7.6US qt).

Transmission (to rear wheels or all wheels): Engageable front wheel drive, reduction gears, front free wheel hub.
a) 5–speed manual, final drive ratio 4.3 or 4.55.
b) Automatic hydraulic torque converter and 4–speed Planetary gear set, final drive ratio 4.777.
Optional rear limited slip differential.

Gear ratios: Reduction gears: Road 1, Cross-country 2.283 (Automatic 2.66).
a) 5–speed Manual: 1st 3.767; 2nd 2.314; 3rd 1.404; 4th 1; 5th 0.809; R 3.873.
b) Automatic: 1st 2.804; 2nd 1.532; 3rd 1: OD 0.705; R 2.394.

Chassis: Frame chassis with cross members. Front independent suspension with A–arm, torsion bar supension and antiroll bar; rear rigid axle with leaf spring; front and rear telescopic damper. Servo/power assisted brakes, front ventilated, disc diameter 24.9cm; mechanical handbrake on front wheels; recirculating ball steering, optional power assisted; fuel tank 83L (18.2Gal) [21.9US Gal]; tyres 2125 SR 15, USA 225/75 SR 15, wheel rims 6J.

Dimension: Wheelbase 230cm, track 139/140cm (wide version 145/146cm), clearance minimum 21cm, turning circle 10.6m. Length 407.5cm, width 165cm, height 180/183cm. Estate/Station Wagon (long): Wheelbase 265cm, turning circle 11.8m, length 438-447cm.

Performance: 2.6 Litre – Max speed 93.2mph/150kmh (manufacturers test specifications), speed at 1000rpm in 5th gear 23.7mph/38.1kmh; power to weight ratio from 18.6kg/kW (13.7kg/PS); consumption ECE 10.0/14.0/15.4L/100km (28.2/20.2/18.3mpg) [23.5/16.8/15.3US mpg].

```
2.2/2.8 Litre Diesel
74kW–99hp–100PS
Turbo/Injection Pump
```

As petrol/gasoline engine, except:

Weight: 130kg heavier.

Engine data (DIN): 4–cylinder in–line (93 x 102mm) 2772cm3; compression ratio 18.2:1; 74kW (99hp) [100PS] at 3700rpm, 26.7kW/L (35.8hp/L) [36.1PS/L]; 208Nm (153.5lbft) at 2100rpm.
Engine for some countries: 72kW (96hp) [97PS].

Japanese version (JIS nett): Compression ratio 17.5:1; 85kW (114hp) [115PS] at 3600rpm, 235Nm (172.3lbft) at 2300rpm.

Engine construction: Designated C 4JB1-T; direct injection diesel. Parallel valves; side camshaft; grey cast iron cylinder head; oil capacity 6L (5.7US qt); Bosch injection pump; 1 exhaust turbocharger. Battery 12V 80/100Ah, alternator 50A; cooling system capacity 10.8L (10.2US qt).

Performance: Max speed 87mph/140kmh (manufacturers test specifications); power to weight ratio from 22.8kg/kW (16.9kg/PS); consumption ECE 8.4/12.2/10.0L/100km (33.6/23.2/28.2mpg) [28/19.3/23.5US mpg].

Isuzu Rodeo Bighorn/Trooper

JAGUAR GB

Jaguar Cars Ltd., Browns Lane Allesley, Coventry CV5 9DR, England

Renowned manufacturers of luxury cars. 1960: Take over of the Daimler Marque, 1961 purchase of Guy. 1966 joined with BMC and BMH. 1968 became part of the British Leyland Motor Corporation. 1984 Daimler privatised.

MODEL RANGE
XJ6 –Sovereign V12 –XJ–S

Jaguar XJ6

New edition of the XJ–limousine first launched in 1968, available with a 6 cylinder 2.9 or 3.6 litre in–line engine; with 5 speed manual transmission or 4 speed automatic transmission. Launched October 1986.

```
2.9 Litre
123kW–165hp–167PS
Fuel Injection
```

Engine for the XJ6 2.9 and Sovereign 2.9

Body, Weight: 4–door Saloon/Sedan, 5–seater; kerbweight (DIN) 1720kg, gross vehicle weight 2140kg.

Engine Data (DIN): 6–cylinder in–line (91 x 74.8mm), 2919cm3, Compression ratio 12.6:1; 123kW (165hp) [167PS] at 5600rpm, 42.1kW/L (56.4hp/L) [57.2PS/L]; 239Nm (176.3lbft) at 4000rpm. Leaded premium grade.
Catalyst variant: Under preparation.

Engine construction: Designated AJ6 (May–Fireball). Single overhead camshaft (chain driven); alloy cylinder block with dry liners; 7 bearing crankshaft. Oil capacity 8L (7.6US qt); electronic Bosch LH–Jetronic fuel injection. 12V 68Ah battery, 60A alternator; cooling system capacity, approx 12.3L (11.6US qt).

Transmission (to rear wheels): a) 5–speed manual, final drive ratio 3.7.
b) ZF4 HP22 automatic, hydraulic torque converter and 4– speed Planetary gear set, final drive ratio 4.09.
Also available with limited slip differential.

Gear ratios: a) 5–speed manual: 1st 3.57; 2nd 2.06; 3rd 1.39; 4th 1; 5th 0.76; R 3.46.
b) Automatic: Max torque multiplication in converter 2 times; Planetary gear set ratios: 1st 2.73; 2nd 1.56; 3rd 1; 4th 0.73; R 2.09.

Chassis: Integral chassis with front and rear subframes; front wishbone suspension, antiroll bar, coil springs and telescopic dampers, rear wishbone suspension with flexible drive shafts and suspended axle, coil springs and telescopic damper.

Jaguar

Jaguar XJ 6

Chassis: Also available with self-leveling suspension. Servo/power assisted disc brakes and Bosch ABS system, disc diameter front (ventilated) 28.4cm, rear 26.3cm, mechanical handbrake on rear wheels; power assisted rack and pinion steering; fuel tank capacity 89L (19.6Gal) [23.5US Gal]; 220/65 VR 390 tyres, 180mm wheels.

Dimensions: Wheelbase 287cm, track 150/150cm, clearance 17.5/12cm, turning circle 12.9m, load space 15.2cu ft (430dm3). Length 499cm, width 180cm, height 138/136cm.

Performance: Max speed approx 120mph/193kmh, automatic 118mph/190kmh (manufacturers specifications). Speed at 1000rpm in 5th gear (3.77:1) 26.6mph/42.8kmh, automatic in 4th gear (4.09:1) 25.5mph/41kmh; acceleration 0 – 60mph/97kmh 9.6secs, automatic 10.8secs; power to weight ratio 14kg/kW (10,3kg/PS); Fuel consumption (ECE) 7.3/9.1/14.5L/100km (38.7/31/19.5mpg) [32.2/25.8/16.2US mpg], automatic 7.8/10.3/14.3L/100km (36.3/27.4/19.8mpg) [30.2/22.8/16.4US mpg].

Jaguar Sovereign 3.6

```
3.6 Litre
165/149kW-221/197hp-224/202PS
Fuel Injection
```

Engine for XJ6 3.6 and Sovereign 3.6

As 2.9, except for:

Weight: Kerbweight (DIN) 1770kg, gross vehicle wieght 2190kg.

Engine Data (DIN); 6–cylinder in–line engine (91x92mm), 3590cm3; compression ratio 9.6:1; 165kw (221hp) [224PS] at 5000rpm, 46kW/L (61.6hp/L) [62.4PS/L]; 337Nm (248.7lbft) at 4000rpm. Leaded premium grade.
Some countries: 156kW (209hp) [212PS]; 324Nm (239.1lbft).
With Catalyst: Compression ratio 9.6:1; 149kW (197hp) [202PS] at 5250rpm, 41.5kW/L (55.6hp/L) [56.3PS/L], 337Nm (248.7lbft) at 4000rpm. Unleaded premium grade.
Or 145kW (194hp) [198PS] at 5000rpm; unleaded premium grade.

Engine construction: Designated AJ6. 4 valves per cylinder in V 46degs 40mins, twin overhead camshafts; Bosch/Lucas digital electronic injection.

Transmission: Final drive ratio 3.54/3.58.

Gear ratios: a) 5–speed manual: 1st 3.57; 2nd 2.06; 3rd 1.39; 4th 1; 5th 0.76; R 3.46
b) Automatic: Max torque multiplication in converter 2.1 times, Planetary gear set ratios; 1st 2.48; 2nd 1.48; 3rd 1; 4th 0.73; R 2.09.

Performance: Max speed 136mph/219kmh, automatic 135mph/217kmh (manufacturers specifications), speed at 1000 rpm in 5th gear 28.3–27.9mph/45.6–45.0kmh, automatic in 4th gear 29.5–27.2mph/47.5–47.0kmh; acceleration 0 – 60mph/97kmh 7.4secs, automatic 8.8secs; power to weight ratio 10.7kW/kW (7.9kg/PS); fuel consumption (ECE) 7.9/9.5/15.2L/100km (35.8/29.7/18.6mpg) [29.8/24.8/15.5US mpg], automatic 7.8/9.3/15.1 L/100km (36.2/30.4/18.7mpg) [30.2/25.3/15.6US mpg]. With Catalyst and automatic transmission; max speed 130.5mph/210kmh; acceleration 0 – 62mph/100kmh 9.9secs.

Jaguar Sovereign 3.6

Jaguar Sovereign V12

XJ luxury car with a 5.3 Litre V12 engine fitted with electronic fuel injection. First produced July 1972, fuel injection May 1975, with GM automatic transmission 1977, digital fuel injection for 1981. July 1981: HE (High Efficency) engine, "May–Fireball". Interior modifications October 1982.

Jaguar Sovereign V12

```
5.3 Litre V12
217/195kW-291/261hp-295/265PS
Fuel Injection
```

Body, Weight: 4–door Saloon/Sedan, 4/5–seater; kerbwieght (DIN) from 1920kg to a maximum of 2350kg.

Engine Data (DIN): 12–cylinder in V 60 degreees (90x70mm), 5343cm3; compression ratio 12.5:1; 217kW (291hp) [295PS] at 5500rpm, 40.6kW/L (54.4hp/L) [55.2PS/L]; 432Nm (318.2lbft) at 3250rpm; leaded premium grade.
With Catalyst: Compression ratio 11.5:1; 195kW (261hp) [265PS] at 5000rpm, 36.5kW/L (48.9hp/L) [49.6PS/L]; 389Nm (287lbft) at 3000rpm; unleaded premium grade.

Engine construction: Designated; V12 HE (May–Fireball). 2x1 overhead camshafts (chain driven); alloy cylinder block with wet liners; 7 bearing crankshaft; oil cooler, oil capacity 10.8L (10.2US qt); Bosch/Lucas digital electronic fuel injection, electronic fuel pump. 12V 68Ah battery, 60A alternator, cooling system capacity approx 21L (19.8US qt).

Transmission (to the rear wheels): GM "Turbo Hydra–Matic 400" automatic, hydraulic torque converter and 3–speed Planetary gear set, central selector lever; final drive ratio 2.88; limited slip differential.

Gear ratios: Max torque multiplication in converter 2.4 times; Planetary gear set ratios, 1st 2.48; 2nd 1.48; 3rd 1; R 2.08.

Chassis: Integral body; front swinging arm suspension, coil springs and telescopic dampers. Independent rear suspension with flexible drive shafts, longitudinally support final drive with limited slip differential, coil springs, telescopic dampers and antiroll bar. Servo/power assisted disc brakes, disc dia. front (ventilated) 28.4cm, rear 26.3cm, mechanical handbrake to rear wheels; Power assisted rack and pinion steering; fuel tank capacity (twin tanks) 91L (20Gal) [24US Gal]; tyres 215/70 VR 15, wheel rims 6J.

Dimensions: Wheelbase 286.5cm, track 148/149.5cm, clearance 18/13cm, turning circle 13m. Load space 13.8cu ft (390dm3). Length 496cm, width 177cm, height 137.5cm

Jaguar

Performance: Max speed 146mph/235kmh (manufacturers test specifications), speed at 1000rpm in top gear 27mph/43.5kmh; acceleration 0 – 60mph/97kmh 8.1secs; power to weight ratio 8.9kg/kW (6.5kg/PS); consumption (ECE) 10.6/13.1/18.8L/100km (26.6/21.6/15mpg) [22.2/18/12.5US mpg].

Jaguar Sovereign V12

Jaguar XJ-S

High performance sports car with a 5.3 Litre V12 or 3.6 Litre 6– cylinder engine. Launched September 1975. Available with GM automatic and electronic injection in 1981. July 1981 introduction of the "May–Fireball" high efficency engine. October 1983 introduction of the "SC" Convertible–Coupe and 3.6 Litre engine.

```
3.6 Litre
165kW–221hp–224PS
Fuel Injection
```

Engine for XJ–S 3.6

Body, Weight: 2–door, 4–seater Coupe; kerbweight 1680kg (DIN), gross vehicle weight 2030kg.

Engine data (DIN): 6–cylinder in–line (91 x 92mm), 3590cm3; compression ratio 9.6:1; 165kW (221hp) [224PS] at 5100rpm, 46kW/L (61.6hp/L) [62.4PS/L]; 337Nm (248.7lbft) at 4000rpm; leaded premium grade.
Some countries 162kW (217hp) [220PS].

Engine construction: Designated AJ6. 4 valves per cylinder in V 46deg 40', two overhead camshafts (chain), light–alloy cylinder head and block, dry cylinder liners; 7 bearing crankshaft; oil cooler, oil capacity 8.5L (8US qt); indirect Bosch/Lucas digital electronic injection, electric fuel pump. 12V 68Ah Battery, 60A alternator, cooling system capacity 11.6L (11US qt).

Jaguar XJ S 3.6 Coupe

Transmission (to rear wheels): a) 5–speed manual, central gear shift; final drive ratio 3.54.
b) Automatic ZF 4 HP 22, hydraulic torque converter and 4–speed Planetary gear set, central selector lever; final drive ratio 3.54.
Limited slip differential.

Gear ratios: a) 5–speed manual: 1st 3.57; 2nd 2.06; 3rd 1.39; 4th 1; 5th 0.76; R 3.46.
b) Automatic: Max torque multiplication in converter 2.1 times; Planetary gear set ratios; 1st 2.48; 2nd 1.48; 3rd 1; 4th 0.73; R 2.09.

Chassis: Integral body; front swinging arm suspension with coil springs and telescopic dampers, rear twin longitudinal arms, semi floating axle and control arms. Limited slip differential and rubber mounted axle. Coil springs and coaxial shock absorbers. Front and rear antiroll bar. Servo/power assisted disc brakes, disc diameter front (ventilated) 28.4cm, rear 26.3cm; mechanical handbrake on rear wheels. Rack and pinion steering; 91L (20Gal) [24US Gal] fuel tank; tyres 215/70 VR 15 or 235/60 VR 15, wheel rims 6.5J.

Dimensions: Wheelbase 259cm, track 149/150.5cm, clearance 14cm, turning circle 13/12m. Load space 14.1 10cu ft (400/285dm3). Length 476.5cm, width 179.5cm, height 126cm.

Performance: Max speed 142mph/228kmh, automatic 140mph/225kmh, speed at 1000rpm in 5th gear 28.9–28mph/46.5–45kmh; acceleration 0 – 60mph/97kmh 7.4secs, automatic 8.1secs; power to weight ratio 10.2kg/kW (7.5kg/PS); consumption (ECE) 7.6/8.8/15.2L/100km (37.2/32.1/18.6mpg) [30.9/26.7/15.5US mpg], automatic 7.8/9.3/15.5L/100km (36.2/30.4/18.2mpg) [30.2/25.3/15.2US mpg].

Jaguar XJ S V12 Convertible

```
5.3 Litre V12
217/195kW–291/261hp–295/265PS
Fuel Injection
```

Engine for XJ–S V12 and XJ–SC V12

As 3.6 Litre, except:

Body, Weight: 2–door, 4–seater Coupe; kerbweight 1800kg (DIN), gross vehicle weight 2150kg. 2–door, 2–seater Convertible; kerbweight 1900kg (DIN), gross vehicle weight 2100kg.

Engine data (DIN): 12–cylinder in V 60deg (90 x 70mm), 5343cm3; compression ratio 12.5:1; 217kW (291hp) [295PS] at 5500rpm, 40.6kW/L (54.4hp/L) [55.2PS/L]; 430Nm (317lbft) at 3000rpm; leaded premium grade.
With Catalyst: Compression ratio 11.5:1; 194kW (260hp) [264PS] at 5250rpm, 36.3kW/L (48.6hp/L) [49.4PS/L]; 379Nm (279.7lbft) at 2750rpm; unleaded premium grade.

Engine construction: Designated V12 H.E. (May–Fireball). 2x1 overhead camshafts. Light–alloy cylinder head and block, wet cylinder liners; 7 bearing crankshaft; oil cooler, oil capacity 10L (9.5US qt); Lucas/Bosch digital indirect electronic fuel injection. 12V 68Ah Battery, 60A alternator; cooling system capacity 21.3L (20US qt).

Transmission (to rear wheels): GM "Turbo Hydra–Matic 400" automatic; hydraulic torque converter and 3–speed Planetary gear set, central selector lever; final drive ratio 2.88; limited slip differential.

Jaguar XJ SC V12 Coupe

Jaguar • Jeep

Gear ratios: Max torque multiplication in converter 2.4 times; Planetary gear set ratios: 1st 2.5; 2nd 1.5; 3rd 1; R 2.
Chassis: ABS System Teves; fuel tank 91L (20Gal) [24US Gal], Convertible 82L (18Gal) [21.7US Gal].
Dimensions: Length 476.5cm, USA 487cm.
Performance: Max speed 151mph/243kmh, Convertible 150mph/241kmh, Catalyst 145–143mph/233–231kmh (manufacturers test specifications), speed at 1000rpm in direct gear 43.3/42.5kmh; acceleration 0–62mph/100kmh 7.8secs, Convertible 8.2secs, Catalyst 8.8/9.1secs; power to weight ratio 8.3kg/kW (6.1kg/PS); consumption ECE 10.4/12.6/18.8L/100km (27.2/22.4/15mpg) [22.6/18.7/12.5US mpg], Catalyst 12.0/13.9/20.9L/100km (23.5/20.3/13.5mpg) [19.6/16.9/11.3US mpg].

JEEP — USA

Jeep–Eagle Division, Chrysler Corporation, Detroit, Michigan 48231, USA.
Previously named Willys Motors, Inc., 1970 part of the AMC group. Now called Jeep–Eagle part of the Chrysler Group.

Jeep Wrangler

Successor to the CJ-Model with 4 wheel drive, available with a 2.5 Litre 4-cylinder or 4.2 6-cylinder engine. Launched January 1986 (Geneva).

Jeep Wrangler S

2.5 Litre
88kW–117hp–119PS
Central/Single Point Injection

Body, Weight: Roadster/Wagon, 3–door, 4–seater; kerbweight 1320kg.
Engine data (SAE): 4–cylinder, in–line (98.4 x 81mm), 2464cm3; compression ratio 9.2:1; 88kW (117hp) [119PS] at 5000rpm, 35.7kW/L (47.8hp/L) [48.3PS/L]; 183Nm (135lbft) at 3500rpm; regular grade.
Export version: 76kW (104hp) [106PS]; 180Nm (132.8lbft).
Engine construction: Hydraulic tappets; side camshaft (chain); 5 bearing crankshaft; oil capacity 4.7L (4.4US qt); electronic central/single point injection. Battery 12V 50Ah, alternator 37A; cooling system capacity approx 9L (8.5US qt).
Transmission (to rear wheels or all wheels): Engageable 4 wheel drive, reduction gears (2.72); 5–speed manual, final drive ratio 4.11. Optional limited slip differential.
Gear ratios: 1st 3.93; 2nd 2.33; 3rd 1.45; 4th 1; 5th 0.84; R 3.76.

Jeep Wrangler Sahara

Chassis: Box section frame with cross members; front and rear rigid axle, leaf springs, telescopic dampers and front antiroll bar. Servo/power assisted brakes, front discs (ventilated), rear drums; pedal operated parking brake on rear wheels; recirculating ball steering, optional power assisted; fuel tank 57/76L (12.5/16.7Gal) [15.1/20.1US Gal]; tyres 215/75 R 15 or 225/75 R 15, wheel rims 7J.
Dimensions: Wheelbase 237cm, track 147.5/147.5cm, clearance 21cm, turning circle 10m. Load space 14.1/42.4/53cu ft (400/1200/1500dm3). Length 388cm, width 167.5cm, height 174.5/183cm.
Performance: Max speed 84–90mph/135–145kmh; speed at 1000rpm in direct drive 19.6mph/31.5kmh; acceleration 0–60mph/97kmh 14secs; power to weight ratio 15kg/kW (11.1kg/PS); consumption 10–17L/100km (28.2–16.6mpg) [23.5–13.8US mpg].

4.2 Litre
84kW–112hp–114PS
1 2V Carb

As 2.5 Litre, except:
Weight: Kerbweight 1375kg.
Engine data (SAE): 6–cylinder in–line (95.25 x 99.06mm), 4235cm3; compression ration 9.2:1; 84kW (112hp) [114PS] at 3000rpm; 19.8kW/L (26.5hp/L) [26.9PS/L]; 285Nm (210.1lbft) at 2000rpm; regular grade.
Engine construction: 7 bearing crankshaft; 1 downdraught Carter 2V carb. Cooling system capacity 9.9L (9.4US qt).
Export version: (98.4 x 86.7mm), 3956cm3; compression ratio 9.2:1; 127kW (170hp) [173PS] at 4500rpm, 32.5kW/L (43.7hp/L) [44.2PS/L]; 298Nm (220lbft) at 2500rpm; regular grade.
Transmission: a) 5–speed manual, final drive ratio 3.08 or 3.55.
b) Automatic Chrysler 999, hydraulic torque converter and 3–speed Planetary gear set; final drive ratio 3.08 or 3.55.
Gear ratios: a) 5–speed manual: 1st 3.83; 2nd 2.33; 3rd 1.44; 4th 1; 5th 0.72; R 4.22.
b) Automatic: Max torque multiplication in converter 2.3 times; Planetary gear set ratios: 2.74; 1.55; 1; R 2.2.
Performance: Max speed 81–87mph/130–140kmh; speed at 1000rpm in direct drive (3.08) 26.1mph/42kmh; acceleration 0–62mph/100kmh 12secs; power to weight ratio 16.4kg/kW (12.1kg/PS); consumption 12–20L/100km (23.5–14.1mpg) [19.6–11.8US mpg]. Export Version: Max speed 109mph/175kmh; power to weight ratio 10.8kg/kW (8.0kg/PS); consumption 10–20L/100km (28.2–14.1mpg) [23.5–11.8US mpg].

Jeep Wrangler Islander

Jeep Cherokee – Wagoneer

Rough terrain vehicle. 1984; smaller body, new 2.5 Litre AMC engine and suspension. Also in 1984; Renault 2.1 Litre turbodiesel engine. 1987: 4 Litre 6–cylinder fuel injected engine.

2.5 Litre
90kW–121hp–123PS
Central/Single Point Injection

Body, Weight: Cherokee rear wheel drive, 3/5–door, kerbweight (DIN) 1230kg. Cherokee 4x4, 3/5–door, kerbweight (DIN) 1330kg. Wagoneer 5–door, kerbweight (DIN) 1325kg.
Engine data (SAE): 4–cylinder in–line (98.4 x 81mm), 2464xcm3; compression ratio 9.2:1; 90kW (121hp) [123PS] at 5000rpm, 36.7kW/L (49.2hp/L) [49.9PS/L]; 191Nm (140.9lbft) at 3500rpm; regular grade.
Engine construction: Hydraulic tappets, side camshaft (chain); 5 bearing crankshaft; oil capacity 4.7L (4.4US qt); electronic central/single point injection. Battery 12V 50Ah, alternator 37A; cooling system capacity 7.9L (7.5US qt).

Jeep

Jeep Cherokee Sport

Transmission (rear wheel drive, 4x4): a) 5-speed manual.
b) Automatic, Aisin-Warner 30-40LE, hydraulic torque converter and 4-speed Planetary gear set; steering wheel mounted selector lever. Final drive ratios: 3.07; 3.08; 3.54; 3.55; 4.11; 4.56.
Optional limited slip differential
4x4: Engageable four wheel drive "Selec-Trac". Rear wheel drive or permanent four wheel drive with central differential; reduction gear 2.671.
Gear ratios: a) 5-speed manual: 1st 3.93; 2nd 2.33; 3rd 1.45; 4th 1; 5th 0.85; R 4.47.
b) Automatic: Max torque multiplication in converter 2.3 times; Planetary gear set ratios; 2.80; 1.53; 1; 0.71; R 2.39.

Jeep Cherokee 4x4 Limited

Chassis: Box frame with cross members; front and rear rigid axle; front trailing arm and coil springs, rear leaf springs, front and rear telescopic dampers and antiroll bars. Servo/power assisted brakes, also available with ABS (Bendix), front discs, diameter 27.9cm, rear drums; mechanical handbrake to rear wheels; power assisted recirculating ball steering; fuel tank 76L (16.7Gal) [20.1US Gal]; tyres 195/75 SR 15, or 205/75 SR 15, 215/75 SR 15 or 225/70 R 15, wheel rims 6 or 7J.
Dimensions: Wheelbase 257.5cm, track 145/145cm, clearance 19cm, turning circle 10.9m. Load space 35/71cu ft (990/2010dm3). Length 420cm, width 179cm, height 161cm.
Performance: Max speed 93-99mph/150-160kmh; speed at 1000rpm in direct drive (3.07) 23.9mph/38.4kmh; power to weight ratio 13.7kg/kW (10kg/PS); consumption 10-18L/100km (28.2-15.7mpg) [23.5-13.1US mpg].

```
4 Litre
132kW-177hp-179PS
Fuel Injection
```

As 2.5 Litre, except:
Weight: Increased weight of 65kg.
Engine data (SAE): 6-cylinder in-line (98.4 x 86.7mm), 3956cm3; compression ratio 9.2:1; 132kW (177hp) [179PS] at 4500rpm, 33.4kW/L (44.8hp/L) [45.2PS/L]; 304Nm (224.4lbft) at 2500rpm; regular grade.
Export Version (DIN): 127kW (170hp) [173PS] at 4500rpm, 32.5kW/L (43.6hp/L) [44.2PS/L]; 298Nm (220lbft) at 2500rpm; regular grade.
Some countries: 125kW (167.5hp) [168PS] 294Nm (217lbft).
Engine construction: 7 bearing crankshaft; electronic fuel injection. Cooling system capacity 11.4L (10.8US qt).
Transmission: a) 5-speed manual, final drive ratio 3.07, 3.54 or 4.11.

Jeep Wagoneer 4x4 Limited

b) Automatic, hydraulic torque converter and 4-speed Planetary gear set; final drive ratio 3.07, 3.54 or 4.11.
Gear ratios: a) 5-speed: 1st 3.83; 2nd 2.33; 3rd 1.44; 4th 1; 5th 0.79; R 4.22.
b) Automatic: 1st 3.79; 2nd 2.39; 3rd 1.51; 4th 1; 5th 0.78; R 3.76.
Performance: Max speed 109mph/175kmh; speed at 1000rpm in direct drive (3.08) 26.1mph/42kmh; power to weight ratio 9.8kg/kW (7.2kg/PS); consumption 10-20L/100km (28.2-14.1mpg) [23.5-11.7US mpg].

```
2.1 Litre Diesel
63.5kW-85hp-86PS
Turbo/Injection Pump
```

As 2.5 Litre, except:
Weight: Kerbweight (DIN) 1310-1565kg, gross vehicle weight 2210kg.
Engine data (SAE): 4-cylinder in-line (86 x 89mm), 2068cm3; compression ratio 21.5:1; 63.5kW (85hp) [86PS] at 3750rpm 30.6kW/L (41hp/L) [41.6PS/L]; 179Nm (132lbft) at 2750rpm.
Export version (DIN): 64.5kW (86hp) [88PS] at 4000rpm; 181Nm (133.6lbft) at 2250rpm.
Engine construction: Swirl chamber diesel engine; 1 overhead camshaft (toothed belt); light-alloy cylinder block; oil capacity 6.3L (6US qt); diesel injection pump; turbocharger. Battery 12V 65Ah; cooling system capacity 8.5L (8US qt).
Transmission: 5-speed manual, final drive ratio 4.1 or 4.111.
Gear ratios: 1st 3.93; 2nd 2.33; 3rd 1.45; 4th 1; 5th 0.85; R 4.74.
Performance: Max speed 87mph/140kmh (manufacturers test specifications); speed at 1000rpm in 5th gear 22.4mph/36.1kmh; acceleration 0 – 62mph/100kmh 17.7secs; power to weight ratio 20.3kg/kW (14.9kg/PS); consumption 8-13L/100km (35.3-21.7mpg) [29.4-18.1US mpg].

Jeep Cherokee 4x4 Turbodiesel

```
Jeep Grand Wagoneer V8
```

Rough terrain Estate/Station Wagon with four wheel drive. Servo/power assisted brakes, front discs. 1980: new transmission and transfer box. Designated in the USA as "Grand Daddy".

Jeep • Jensen • Lada • Lafer

```
5.9 Litre V8
107kW–144hp–146PS
1 2V Carb
```

Body, Weight: Wagoneer 5–door; 2045kg.

Engine data (SAE): V8 in 90deg (103.63 x 87.38mm), 5896cm3; compression ratio 8.25:1; 107kW (144hp) [146PS] at 3200rpm; 18.1kW/L (24.3hp/L) [24.8PS/L]; 380Nm (280.4lbft) at 1500rpm; regular grade.

Engine construction: Hydraulic tappets, central camshaft (chain); 5 bearing crankshaft; oil capacity 4.7L (4.4US qt); 1 downdraught 2V Motorcraft carb. Battery 12V 60Ah, alternator 54A, cooling system capacity approx 14.7L (16US qt).

Transmission (to all wheels): Automatic Chrysler 27, hydraulic torque converter and 3–speed Planetary gear set, selector lever on steering wheel; final drive ratio 2.73; 3.31. Optional limited slip differential, engageable four wheel drive; optional "Quadra-Trac" transmission with central limited slip differential; reduction gear 2.61.

Gear ratios: Max torque multiplication in converter 2.3 times; Planetary gear set ratios; 2.45; 1.55; 1; R 2.2.

Chassis: Box frame with 5 cross members; front and rear rigid axle, semi–elliptic leaf springs, front antiroll bar, front and rear telescopic dampers. Servo/power assisted brakes, front discs (ventilated), diameter 30.5cm, rear drums; pedal actuated parking brake on rear wheels; power assisted recirculating ball steering; fuel tank 77L (16.9Gal) [20.3US Gal]; tyres 235/75 R 15, wheel rims 7".

Dimensions: Wheelbase 276cm, track 151/147cm, clearance 18cm, turning circle 11.5cm. Max load space 95.2cu ft (2695dm3). Length 473.5cm, width 190cm, height 168.5cm.

Performance: Max speed 90–93mph/145—150kmh, speed at 1000rpm in top gear 30.6mph/49.2kmh; power to weight ratio 19.1kg/kW (14kg/PS); consumption (touring) approx 16–23L/100km (17.7- 12.3mpg) [14.7–10.2US mpg].

Jeep Grand Wagoneer V8

JENSEN   GB

Jensen Cars Limited, Kelvin Way, West Bromwich, West Midlands B70 7JT, England

A make of utilitarian vehicles founded in 1934. Up until 1976 producer of vehicles with individual character. 1987: new Interceptor put into production.

Jenson Interceptor S4

**Sporty luxury Coupe with Chrysler V8 engine. Prototype launched in Autumn 1965, Coupe in London 1966, Convertible in New York 1974. Autumn 1975 and 1987: new S4 Coupe.

```
5.9 Litre V8
179/138kW–240/185hp–243/188PS
4V Carb
```

Body, Weight: 2–door Coupe (if required with tailgate): 4–seater; kerbweight (DIN) approx 1800kg; 2–door Cabriolet, 4–seater; kerbweight (DIN) approx 1820kg.

Engine data (SAE net): 8–cylinder in V90 deg (101.6 x 90.93mm), 5898cm3; compression ratio 9.0:1; 179kW (240hp) [243PS] at 4400rpm, 30.4kW/L (40.7hp/L) [41.2PS/L]; 410NM (302.6lbft) at 2000rpm; unleaded regular grade.

With Catalyst: Compression ratio 8.1:1; 138kW (185hp) [188PS] at 4000rpm, 23.4kW/L (31.3hp/L) [31.9PS/L]; 384Nm (283.3lbft) at 1600rpm.

With Fuel Injection (without Catalyst): 206kW (276hp) [280PS].

Engine construction: Chrysler V8 (360). Hydraulic tappets, central camshaft (chain); 5 bearing crankshaft; oil capacity 4.8L (4.5US qt); 1 Carter downdraught 4V carb. 12V 69Ah battery, 90A alternator; cooling system capacity 16L (15.1US qt).

Transmission (to rear wheels): Automatic "Torqueflite", hydraulic torque converter and 3–speed Planetary gear set central selector lever, final drive ratio 3.07/2.88. Limited slip differential.

Gear ratios: Max torque multiplication 2 times, Planetary gear ratios 2.45, 1.45; 1; R 2.2.

Chassis: Tubular frame chassis; front indepedent suspension with transverse A arm, rear rigid axle with semi–elliptic springs and Panhard rod, front and rear anti–roll bar, telescopic damper. Servo/power assisted brakes (ventilated), disc diameter 27.3cm; mechanical handbrake to rear; power assisted steering; fuel tank 91L (20Gal) [24US Gal], tyres 225/70 VR 15, wheel rims 7".

Dimensions: Wheelbase 267cm, track 143/145cm, clearance 14cm, turning circle 11.6m. Load space 8.1cu ft (230dm3). Length 477cm, height 175cm, height 135cm.

Performance: Max speed (according to engine) over 130mph/210kmh, speed at 1000rpm in direct gear 25.2mph/40.5kmh; power to weight ratio at 10.1kg/kW (7.4kg/PS); consumption approx 13–20L/100km (21.7–14.1mpg) [18.1–11.8US mpg]..

Jensen Interceptor SA

LADA   SU

Export version of the Shiguli in certain West European countries. For technical data see Shiguli.

Lada Samara

LAFER   BR

Lafer S.A., Garcia Lorca, 301-Villa Pauliceia, 09700 Sao Bernardo do Campo, SP, Brasil.

Furniture factory at Sao Paulo, with special department for the manufacture of cars.

CARO
CAROSSERIEN & ACCESSOIRES

Cabriolets
auf Mercedes Benz-Basis
190 C, 300 CE und 560 SEC,
auf Porsche-Basis
928 S-4 Cabriolet
Langlimousinen
und Sicherheitsfahrzeuge
Verlängerung des Radstandes
von 30 cm bis 112 cm
Wurzelholz-
und Sonder-Innenausstattungen

CARO GmbH · Kohlentwiete 6 · 2000 Hamburg 50 · Telefon 040 850 50 11 · Telex 2 166 366 caro d · Telefax 040 85 60 68

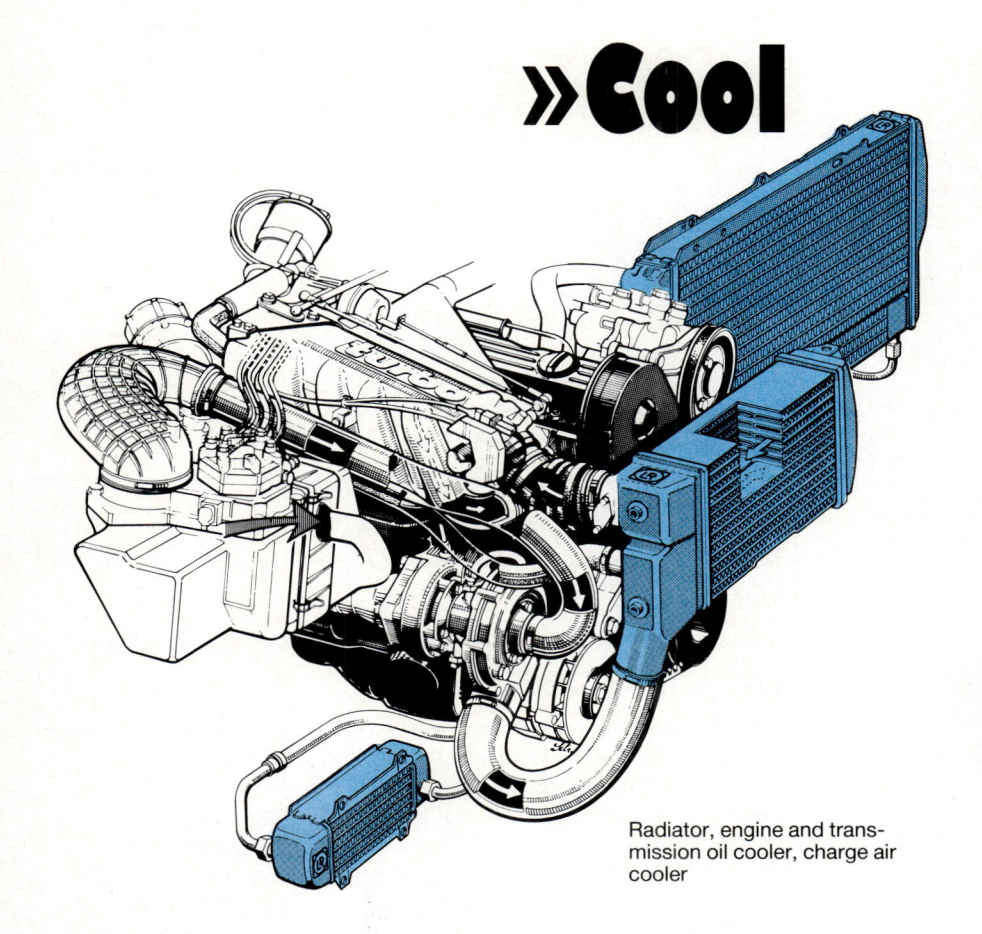

»Cool Solutions«

LÄNGERER & REICH manufactures coolers for vehicles, engines, transmissions and the engineering industry for more than 75 years.

LÄNGERER & REICH, the European leader in charge air coolers is also the best answer to your other cooling problems.

Radiator, engine and transmission oil cooler, charge air cooler

KÜHLERFABRIK LÄNGERER & REICH GMBH & CO. KG

Echterdinger Straße 57, D-7024 Filderstadt
Phone (0711) 7001-0, Telex 7 255 627
Telefax (0711) 7001-297

Lafer • Laforza • Lagonda • Lamborghini

Lafer MP Lafer

Imitation of the MG TD Mark II of 1951, engine based on the VW 1600 from VW Brasil. Launched in spring 1974.

```
1.6 Litre
40kW-53hp-54PS
2 Carbs
```

Body, Weight: 2-door Roadster, 2-seater; kerbweight 760kg.

Engine data (DIN): 4-cylinder Boxer engine (85.5 x 69mm), 1584cm3; compression ratio 7.2:1; 40kW (53hp) [54PS] at 4200rpm, 25.2kW/L (33.4hp/L) [34.1PS/L]; 106Nm (78.2lbft) at 3000rpm; leaded regular grade.
For operation on ethyl alcohol: (77 x 69mm), 1285cm3; compression ratio 10:1; 31kW (41.5hp) [42PS] at 4200rpm, 24.1kW/L (32.3hp/L) [32.7PS/L]; 79Nm (58.3lbft) at 3000rpm.

Engine construction: Designated VW 103. Central camshaft (toothed belt); light-alloy cylinder heads and block; dry cylinder liners; 4 bearing crankshaft; oil cooler; oil capacity 2.5L (2.4US qt); 2 Solex H 32 PDSI 3 downdraught carbs. 12V 36Ah Battery, alternator 350W; air cooled.

Transmission (to rear wheels): 4-speed manual (without direct drive), final drive ratio 4.125 (8/33).

Gear ratios: 1st 3.8; 2nd 2.06; 3rd 1.32; 4th 0.89; R 3.88.

Chassis: Tubular frame, rear fork/cradle with platform bodywork, twin crank steering with transverse torsion bar spring; rear independent suspension with swinging axle, longitudinal arms and transverse torsion bar spring, diagonal compensating spring over the rear axle, front and rear antiroll bar, telescopic damper. Front disc brakes, rear drums, disc diameter 27.8cm; mechanical handbrake to rear wheels; worm and wheel steering; fuel tank capacity 46L (10.1Gal) [12.2US Gal]; tyres 5.60-15, wheel rims 4.5J, optional tyres 175 SR 14, wheel rims 6.5J or tyres, front 185/70 HR 14, rear 195/70 HR 14.

Dimensions: Wheelbase 240cm, track 130.5/135cm, clearance 15cm, turning circle 11m. Length 391cm, width 157cm, height 135cm.

Performance: Max speed 84mph/135kmh (manufacturers test specifications), speed at 1000rpm in 4th gear 19.6mph/31.6kmh; power to weight ratio 19.3kg/kW (14.1kg/PS); consumption 9L/100km (31.4mpg) [26.1US mpg], manufacturers test specifications.

MP Lafer

LAFORZA   USA/I

Laforza Automobiles Inc, 3860 Bay Center Place, Hayward, CA 94545, USA.

New vehicle manufacturer with factory based in California.

Laforza

American version of the Rayton Fissore. Chassis, bodywork and interior from Turin, engine and transmission from Ford USA. Assembly work takes place at Laforza, Hayward, California (USA).

Laforza

```
4.9 Litre V8
138kW-185hp-187PS
Fuel Injection
```

Body, Weight: 5-door Saloon/Sedan, 7-seater; kerbweight (DIN) approx 1850kg, gross vehicle weight 2750kg.

Engine data (SAE net): 8-cylinder in V 90deg (101.6 x 76.2mm), 4942cm3; compression ratio 9.3:1; 138kW (185hp) [187PS] at 3800rpm, 27.9kW/L (37.4hp/L) [37.8PS/L]; 366Nm (270lbft) at 2400rpm; regular unleaded.

Engine construction: Hydraulic tappets, central camshaft (chain); 5 main bearing crankshaft; oil capacity 4.7L (4.4US qt); electronic fuel injection. 12V 85Ah Battery, 100A alternator; cooling system capacity approx 13.6L (12.9US qt).

Transmission (to all wheels): 4-speed manual and 2 speed reduction gears, permanent all wheel drive, optional engageable 4WD; central differential with viscous coupling; final drive ratio front and rear 3.9, reduction gear ratios: 1 (town) and 2.74 (country). Rear limited slip differential.

Gear ratios: Max torque multiplication in converter 2.28 times, Planetary gear set ratios: 2.40; 1.46; 1; 0.67; R 2.

Chassis: Integral body; front independent suspension with shock absorbers (rear doubled), rear compression struts and torsion bar; rear rigid axle with semi-elliptic springs; telescopic damper. Servo/power assisted brakes, front discs, rear drums, mechanical handbrake to rear wheels; power assisted rack and pinion steering; fuel tank capacity 80L (17.6Gal) [21.1US Gal]; tyres 225/75 R 16, wheel rims 7J.

Dimensions: Wheelbase 270cm, track 172/172cm, turning circle 10.5m, clearance 17cm, length 457cm, width 200cm, height 184cm.

Performance: Max speed approx 112mph/180kmh, speed at 1000rpm in 4th gear approx 29.8mph/48kmh; power to weight ratio 13.4kg/kW (9.9kg/PS); consumption approx 12-22L/100km (23.5-12.8mpg) [19.6-10.7US mpg].

LAGONDA   GB

See Aston Martin

LAMBORGHINI   I

Nuova Automobil Feruccio, Lamborghini S.p.A., Via Modena 12, 40019 Sant'Agata Bolognese, Bologna, Italia

Marque created in 1963 out of an Italian mechanical construction and agricultural tractors enterprise. Taken over by Chrysler in 1987.

Lamborghini Countach S quattrovalvole

Power sports car with V12 4.8 Litre Central engine. Bertone body. Launched at Geneva in 1982. Developed from the 400 Model; "quattrovalvole" model with bigger engine and more power, four valves per cylinder.

```
5.2 Litre V12
334.5kW-448hp-455PS
6 2V Carbs/Injection
```

Lamborghini • Lancia

Lamborghini Countach S quattrovalvole

Body, Weight: 2–door Coupe (Bertone), 2–seater; kerbweight (DIN) 1490kg, gross vehicle weight 1680kg.

Engine data (DIN): 12–cylinder in V 60deg (85.5 x 75mm), 5167cm3; compression ratio 9.5:1; 334.5kW (448hp) [455PS] at 7000rpm, 64.8kW/L (86.8hp/L) [88.1PS/L]; 500Nm (369lbft) at 5200rpm; leaded premium grade.
With Catalyst: 314kW (421hp) [426PS] at 7000rpm; 461Nm (340.2lbft) at 5000rpm.

Engine construction: Designated LP 112D. Longitudinal central engine. overhead valves (in V 45deg), 2 x 2 overhead camshaft (chain); light–alloy cylinder heads and cylinder block, wet cylinder liners; 7 bearing crankshaft; lubrication for engine, transmission and differentials; oil cooler, oil capacity 17L (16.1US qt); 6 Weber 44 DCNF horizontal 2V carbs or Bosch K– Jetronic fuel injection; 2 electronic Bendix–fuel pumps. 12V 55Ah Battery, 85/115A alternator; cooling system capacity 17L (16.1US qt).

Transmission (to rear wheels): 5–speed manual, final drive ratio 4.09 (11/45). ZF limited slip differential.

Gear ratios: 1st 2.232; 2nd 1.625; 3rd 1.086; 4th 0.858; 5th 0.707; R 1.96.

Chassis: Tubular frame chassis and light–alloy/steel body; front keystone A arm, coil springs, telescopic damper, rear overhead single control arm and longitudinal strut, twin coil springs and twin dampers, front and rear antiroll bar. Servo/power assisted disc brakes (ventilated), disc diameter, front 30cm, rear 28.4cm; mechanical handbrake to rear wheels; rack and pinion steering; 2 side fuel tanks, capacity up to 60L (13.2Gal) [15.9US Gal]; tyres front 225/50 VR 15, rear 345/35 VR 15; magnesium wheel rims 12".

Dimensions: Wheelbase 250cm, track 153.5/160.5cm. Clearance 10.5cm, turning circle 13m. Load space 8.5cu ft (240dm3). Length 414/420cm, width 200cm, height 107cm.

Performance: Max speed 183mph/295kmh (manufacturers test specifications), speed at 1000rpm in 5th gear 24.7mph/39.8kmh; acceleration 0 – 62mph/100kmh 5.0secs; standing km 23.5secs; power to weight ratio 4.5kg/kW (3.3kg/PS); consumption ECE 12.3/14.3/22.2L/100km (23/19.8/12.7mpg) [19.1/16.4/10.6US mpg].

Lamborghini Countach S quattrovalvole

Lamborghini LM–002

All terrain, high performance vehicle with 5.2 Litre 12–cylinder engine from 444hp power. Five speed manual and cross country reduction transmission. Series version launched in Autumn 1985.

```
5.2 Litre V12
331kW–444hp–450PS
6 2V Carbs
```

Body, Weight: 4–door Estate/Station Wagon, 4 + 4–seater; kerbweight (DIN) 2700-2950kg gross vehicle weight 3500kg.

Engine data (DIN): 12–cylinder in V 60deg (85.5 x 75mm), 5167cm3; compression ratio 9.5:1; 331kW (444hp) [450PS] at 6800rpm, 64.1kW/L (85.6hp/L) [87.1PS/L]; 500Nm (369lbft) at 4500rpm; leaded regular grade.

Engine construction: Designated L 510. Longitudinal front engine. Overhead valves (in V 45deg), 2 x 2 overhead camshafts (chain); light–alloy cylinder heads and cylinder block, wet cylinder liners; 7 bearing crankshaft; lubrication for engine, transmission and differentials; oil cooler, oil capacity 17.5L (16.5US qt); 6 Weber 44 DCNF horizontal 2V carbs, 2 Bendix electronic fuel pumps. 12V 90Ah Battery, 90A alternator; cooling system capacity 17L (16.1US qt).

Transmission (to rear wheels or all wheels): 5–speed manual, final drive ratio 4.111. Front and rear ZF– limited slip differentials. Central differential with lock; rear wheel drive, engageable four wheel drive; reduction gears Town 1.428, Country 4.286.

Gear ratios: 1st 2.99; 2nd 1.9; 3rd 1.33; 4th 1; 5th 0.89; R 2.7.

Chassis: Tubular frame chassis; front A arm, coil springs, rear control arm and coil springs, front and rear telescopic damper. Servo/power assisted brakes, front discs (ventilated), rear drums; power assisted recirculating ball steering; 2 fuel tanks, total capacity 290L (63.8Gal) [76.6US Gal]; tyres 325/65 VR 17 or 345/60 VR 17, wheel rims 11".

Dimensions: Wheelbase 300cm, track 161.5/161.5cm, clearance 29.5cm. Turning circle 12.2m. Length 490/495cm, width 200/204cm, height 185cm.

Performance: Max speed 125mph/201kmh (manufacturers test specifications), speed at 1000rpm in 5th gear 18.4mph/29.6kmh; acceleration 0–62mph/100kmh 8.5secs; power to weight ratio 8.2kg/kW (6.0kg/PS); consumption approx 20–40L/100km (14.1–7mpg) [11.8– 5.7US mpg].

Lamborghini LM–002

LANCIA I

Lancia & Co, Fabbrica Automobili S.p.A., Via Vicenzo Lancia 27, 10141 Torino, Italia.

Italian marque, famous particularly for its technical conceptions. A subsidiary of Fiat since 1969.

MODEL RANGE
Y10 – Delta – Prisma – Thema

Lancia Y 10

Luxurious small car with transverse engine, front wheel drive and tail gate; engine from 999cm3 (fire) to 1301cm3, also Turbo. Available in some countries as Autobianchi Y 10. Launched in Geneva, 1985. September 1986: 4WD version For data see Autobianchi. Detail modifications to body and interior.

```
999cm3
33kW–44hp–45PS
1 Carb/Central/Single Point Injection
```

Engine for Fire

Body, Weight: 3–door Saloon/Sedan, 5–seater; kerbweight (DIN) 780kg, gross vehicle weight 1180kg.

Lancia

Engine data (DIN): 4-cylinder in-line (70 x 64.9mm), 999cm3; compression ratio 9.5:1; 33kW (44hp) [45PS] at 5500rpm, 33kW/L (44hp/L) [45PS/L]; 80Nm (59lbft) at 2750rpm; premium unleaded.
For some countries: 34kW (45hp) [46PS].
With Catalyst and central/single point injection (Bosch Mono-Jetronic); compression ratio 9/9.5: 1; 33kW (44hp) [45PS] at 5250rpm; 74Nm (54.6lbft) at 3250rpm.

Engine data (DIN): Designated 156 A2.000/2.100/2.246. Transverse front engine, inclined 12deg to front, 1 overhead camshaft (toothed belt); light-alloy cylinder head; 5 main bearing crankshaft; oil capacity 3.9L (3.7US qt); 1 Weber 32 TLF4/251 downdraught carb and Bosch Mono-Jetronic central/single point injection. 12V 30Ah Battery, 45A Alternator; cooling system capacity approx 4.6L (4.4US qt).

Transmission (to front wheels): 5-speed manual; final drive ratio 3.733.

Gear ratios: 1st 3.909; 2nd 2.055; 3rd 1.344; 4th 0.978; 5th 0.780; R 3.727.

Chassis: Integral body; front independent suspension with McPherson struts, control arm and antiroll bar, rear "Omega" formed suspension tube with mid-anchor and semi trailing arm, coil springs; telescopic damper. Servo/power assisted brakes, disc diameter, front 22.7cm, rear drums; handbrake to rear wheels; rack and pinion steering; fuel tank capacity 47L (10.3Gal) [12.4US Gal]; tyres 135 SR 13, optionally 155/70 SR/HR 13, wheel rims 4.5/5 J.

Dimensions: Wheelbase 216cm, track 128/128cm, clearance 16cm, turning circle 9.8m. Load space 6.9/29.3cu ft (195/830dm3). Length 339cm, width 151cm, height 144cm.

Performance: Max speed 90mph/145kmh, speed at 1000rpm in 5th gear 21.3mph/34.3kmh; acceleration 0-62mph/100kmh 16secs, standing km 37secs; power to weight ratio 23.6kg/kW (17.3kg/PS); consumption ECE 4.2/5.8/6.4L/100km (67.3/48.7/44.1mpg) [56/40.6/36.8US mpg].

Lancia Y 10 LX ie

```
1108cm3
42kW-56hp-57PS
Central/Single Point Injection
```

Engine for LX ie

As 999cm3, except:

Weight: Kerbweight (DIN) 795kg, gross vehicle weight 1195kg.

Engine data (DIN): 4-cylinder in-line (70 x 72mm), 1108cm3; compression ratio 9.6:1; 42kW (56hp) [57PS] at 5500rpm, 33.4kW/L (44.8hp/L) [51.4PS/L]; 90Nm (66.4lbft) at 3000rpm.

Engine construction: Designated 156C.000. Oil capacity 3.65L (3.5US qt); Bosch Monojetronic central fuel injection. 12V 40Ah Battery.

Performance: Max speed 96mph/155kmh (manufacturers test specifications), speed at 1000rpm in 5th gear 16.9mph/27.3kmh; acceleration 0-62mph/100kmh 15.2secs, standing km 36.5secs; power to weight ratio 18.9kg/kW (13.9kg/PS); consumption ECE 4.4/6.1/7.0L/100km (64.2/46.3/40.4mpg) [53.5/38.6/33.6US mpg].

```
1301cm3
57/54kW-76/73hp-78/74PS
Fuel Injection
```

Engine for GT i.e.

As 999cm3, except:

Weight: Kerbweight (DIN) 885kg, gross vehicle weight 1255kg.

Engine data (DIN): 4-cylinder in-line (76.1 x 71.5mm), 1301cm3; compression ratio 9.5:1; 57kW (76hp) [78PS] at 5750rpm, 43.8kW/L (58.7hp/L) [59.9 PS/L]; 102Nm (75.3lbft) at 3250rpm.
With Catalyst: (76 x 71.5mm), 1297cm3; Compression ratio 9.2:1; 54kW (73hp) [74PS] at 5750rpm, 41.6kW/L (55.7hp/L) [57.2 PS/L]; 100Nm (73.8lbft) at 3250rpm. Or: 53kW (71hp) [72PS].

Engine construction: Designated 156B.000. Oil capacity 3.95L (3.8US qt); Bosch L 3.2-Jetronic electronic fuel injection. 12V 40Ah Battery; cooling system capacity approx 5.6L (5.3US qt).

Transmission: Final drive ratio 3.867.

Gear ratios: 1st 3.909; 2nd 2.055; 3rd 1.344; 4th 0.978; 5th 0.836; R 3.727.

Chassis: Tyres 155/70 SR 13.

Performance: Max speed 109mph/175kmh (manufacturers test specifications), speed at 1000rpm in 5th gear 19.3mph/31kmh; acceleration 0-62mph/100kmh 12secs, standing km 33.5secs; power to weight ratio 15.5kg/kW (11.3kg/PS); consumption ECE 5.7/7.3/7.8L/100km (49.6/38.7/36.2mpg) [41.3/32.2/30.2US mpg].

Lancia Y 10 GT ie

Lancia Y 10 4WD

Small vehicle with engageable four wheel drive, based on the Y 10, 1-Litre "Fire" engine with 49hp Transmission derived from the Fiat Panda 4 x 4, rear wheels with free-wheel hub, with engageable front wheel drive. Launched in September 1986. Autumn 1987: i.e. with Catalyst. 1989 with 1.1 Litre engine.

```
1108/999cm3
42/33kW-56/44hp-57/45PS
Central/Single Point Injection
```

As Y 10 fire, except:

Weight: Kerbweight (DIN) 885kg, gross vehicle weight 1285kg.

Engine data (DIN): 4-cylinder in-line (70 x 72mm), 1108cm3; compression ratio 9.6:1; 42kW (56hp) [57PS] at 5500rpm, 33.4kW/L (44.8hp/L) [45.2PS/L]; 90Nm (9.2mkp) at 3000rpm
With Catalyst: (70 x 64.9mm), 999cm3; compression ratio 9/9.5:1; 33kW (44hp) [45PS] at 5250rpm; 74Nm (99.2lbft) at 3250rpm.

Engine construction: Designated 156C.000/ 156 A3.000. Bosch Mono-Jetronic central/Single point injection.

Transmission (to front or all wheels): Engageable rear wheel drive, free wheel hub to rear wheels, when only front wheels are engaged.
5-speed manual, final drive ratio 5.455 (11/60).

Gear ratios: 1st 3.909; 2nd 2.055; 3rd 1.344; 4th 0.978; 5th 0.731; R 3.727.

Chassis: Rigid rear axle with semi–elliptic springs. Fuel tank 35L (7.7Gal) [9.2US Gal]; tyres 155/70 TR 13, wheel rims 5J.

Dimensions: Wheelbase 218cm, track 127.5/128cm, clearance approx 18cm, turning circle 9.8m. Load space 6.9-29.3cu ft (195-830dm3). Length 339cm, width 153.5cm, height 146cm.

Performance: Max speed 92mph/148kmh, Catalyst 87mph/140kmh (manufacturer's test specifications), speed at 1000rpm in 5th gear 16.1mph/26kmh; acceleration 0-100kmh 17secs; standing km 38secs; power to weight ratio 21.1kg/kW (15.5kg/PS); consumption ECE 5.2/7.0/6.8L/100km (54.3/40.4/41.5mpg) [45.2/33.6/34.6US mpg], Catalyst 5.7/7.9/7.5L/100km (49.6/35.8/37.7mpg) [41.3/29.8/31.4US mpg].

Lancia 247

Lancia Y 10 4WD ie

Lancia Delta

Delta – LX – Automat – GT i.e. – HF Turbo – HF Integrale – Turbo ds

Lower middle class Saloon/Sedan with 5–doors, front wheel drive, all round independent suspension. Related technically to the Fiat Ritmo. Launched in September 1979. May 1986; Turbodiesel. October 1987 Model HF integral with permanent four wheel drive, 183hp, a version with Catalyst is in preparation.

```
1.3 Litre
57kW–76.5hp–78PS
1 2V Carb
```

Engine for Delta and LX

Body, Weight: 5–door Saloon/Sedan, 5–seater; kerbweight (DIN) 950kg gross vehicle weight 1400kg.

Engine data (ECE): 4–cylinder in–line (86.4 x 55.5mm), 1302cm3; compression ratio 9.5:1; 57kW (76.5hp) [78PS] at 5800rpm, 43.8kW/L (58.7hp/L) [59.9PS/L]; 105Nm (77.4lbft) at 3400rpm; leaded premium grade.
For some countries: 55kW (74hp) [75PS].

Engine construction: Designated 831 A.000. Transverse front engine inclined 20deg to front, 1 overhead camshaft (toothed belt); light–alloy cylinder head; 5 bearing crankshaft; oil capacity 4.5L (4.3US qt); 1 Weber 32/34 TLDA1 250 downdraught 2V carb. 12V 40Ah Battery, 45/55A alternator; cooling system capacity 6L (5.7US qt).

Transmission (to front wheels): 5–speed manual, final drive ratio 3.765.

Gear ratios: 1st 4.091; 2nd 2.235; 3rd 1.469; 4th 1.043; 5th 0.863; R 3.714.

Chassis: Integral body; front independent suspension with McPherson struts, lower control arm, rear independent suspension with twin control arms, trailing arms, tension struts, McPherson struts, telescopic damper, front and rear antiroll bar. Servo/power assisted brakes, front discs, rear drums, diameter 22.7cm; mechanical handbrakes to rear wheels; rack and pinion steering; fuel tank capacity 55/57L (12.1/12.5Gal) [14.5/15.1US Gal], with 6–9L (1.6–2Gal) [2.1–2.4US Gal] reserve; tyres 165/70 SR 13 optional 165/65 SR 14, wheel rims 5J.

Dimensions: Wheelbase 247.5cm, track 140/140cm, clearance 14.5cm, turning circle 11.6m. Load space 9.2/35.3cu ft (260/1000dm3). Length 389.5cm, width 162cm, height 138cm.

Performance: Max speed 101mph/163kmh (manufacturers test specifications), speed at 1000rpm in 4th gear 16.4mph/26.4kmh, in 5th gear 19.8mph/31.8kmh; acceleration 0 – 62mph/100kmh 14.3secs, standing km 35.2secs; power to weight ratio from 16.7kg/kW (12.2kg/PS); consumption ECE 5.5/7.4/8.7L/100km (51.4/38.2/32.5mpg) [42.8/31.8/27US mpg].

Lancia Delta

```
1.5 Litre
59kW–79hp–80PS
1 2V Carb
```

Engine for 1.5 Automatic

As 1.3 Litre, except:

Weight: Kerbweight (DIN) 975kg, gross vehicle weight 1425kg.

Engine data (ECE): 4–cylinder in–line (86.4 x 63.9mm), 1499cm3; compression ratio 9.5:1; 59kW (79hp) [80PS] at 5600rpm, 39.3kW/L (52.3hp/L) [53.4PS/L]; 123Nm (90.7lbft) at 3200rpm.

Engine construction: Designated 831 A 1.000. 1 Weber 32/34 TLDA2/250 downdraught 2V carbs. 65A Alternator.

Transmission: Automatic AP, hydraulic torque converter and 3–speed Planetary gear set, central selector lever, final drive ratio 3.595.

Gear ratios: Automatic; max torque multiplication in converter 2.5 times, Planetary gear set ratios: 1st 2.346; 2nd 1.402; 3rd 1; R 2.346.

Performance: Max speed 99.5mph/160kmh (manufacturers test specifications), speed at 1000rpm in top gear 17.9mph/28.8kmh; acceleration 0 – 62mph/100kmh 14.3secs, standing km 35.9secs; power to weight ratio 16.6kg/kW (12.2kg/PS); consumption ECE 7.0/9.2/9.9L/100km (40.4/30.7/28.5mpg) [33.3/25.6/23.8US mpg].

Lancia Delta GT ie

```
1.6 Litre
79/66kW–106/88hp–108/90PS
Fuel Injection
```

Engine for GT i.e.

As 1.3 Litre, except:

Weight: Kerbweight (DIN) 995/1025kg gross vehicle weight 1445/1475kg.

Engine data (ECE): 4–cylinder in–line (84 x 71.5mm), 1585cm3; compression ratio 9.7:1; 79kW (106hp) [108PS] at 5900rpm, 49.8kW/L (66.7hp/L) [68.1PS/L]; 135Nm (99.6lbft) at 3500rpm.
With Catalyst: Central/single point injection; compression ratio 9.5:1; 66kW (88hp) [90PS] at 6250rpm, 41.6kW/L (55.7hp/L) [56.8PS/L]; 123Nm (90.7lbft) at 4250rpm; unleaded premium grade.

Engine construction: Designated 828 B.000. Valves in V; 2 overhead camshafts; oil capacity 5.3L (5US qt); Weber 1AW electronic fuel injection. 65A Alternator; cooling system capacity 7.5L (7.1US qt)

Transmission: 5–speed manual, final drive ratio 3.588, Catalyst 3.571.

Gear ratios: 1st 3.545; 2nd 2.267; 3rd 1.523; 4th 1.142; 5th 0.967; R 3.909.

Chassis: All round disc brakes, diameter, front 25.7cm, rear 22.7cm; tyres 165/65 TR 14, wheel rims 5.5J.

Performance: Max speed 115mph/185kmh, Catalyst 109mph/175kmh (manufacturers test specifications), speed at 1000rpm in 5th gear 18.7mph/30.1kmh; acceleration 0 – 62mph/100kmh 10.0secs, Catalyst 11secs; standing km 31.8secs; power to weight ratio 12.5kg/kW (9.2kg/PS); consumption ECE 6.2/8.0/9.8L/100km (45.6/35.3/28.8mpg) [37.9/29.4/24US mpg], Catalyst 6.4/8.4/10.1L/100km 44.1/33.6/28mpg) [36.8/28/23.3US mpg].

```
1.6 Litre Turbo
103/97kW–138/130hp–140/132PS
Fuel Injection
```

Engine for HF Turbo

As 1.3 Litre, except:

Lancia

Weight: Kerbweight (DIN) 1020/1060kg gross vehicle weight 1470/1500kg.
Engine data (ECE): 4-cylinder in-line (84 x 71.5mm), 1585cm3; compression ratio 8.0:1; 103kW (138hp) [140PS] at 5500rpm, 65kW/L (87hp/L) [88.3PS/L]; 191Nm (140.9lbft) at 3500rpm.
With overboost: 206Nm (151.9lbft) at 3750rpm.
With Catalyst: Compression ratio 7.5:1; 97kW (130hp) [132PS] at 5500rpm; 196Nm (144.6lbft) at 2750rpm; unleaded premium grade.
Engine construction: Valves in V; 2 overhead camshafts (toothed belt); oil capacity 5.9L (5.6US qt); Weber IAW electronic fuel injection; 1 Garrett T2 exhaust turbocharger, max boost pressure 0.85 bar, charge-air cooler, knock sensor. 65A Alternator; cooling system capacity 6.5L (6.1US qt).
Transmission: 5-speed manual (ZF), final drive ratio 3.353.
Gear ratios: 1st 3.583; 2nd 2.235; 3rd 1.542; 4th 1.154; 5th 0.903; R 3.667.
Chassis: All round disc brakes, front ventilated, diameter 25.7cm, rear 22.7cm; tyres 165/65HR 14, wheel rims 5.5J.
Performance: Max speed 126mph/203kmh, Catalyst 123mph/198kmh (manufacturers test specifications), speed at 1000rpm in 5th gear 20.9mph/33.7kmh; acceleration 0 – 62mph/100kmh 8.7secs; standing km 29.5secs; power to weight ratio 9.9kg/kW (7.3kg/PS). Consumption ECE 6.5/8.4/10.0L/100km (43.5/33.6/28.2mpg) [36.2/28/23.5US mpg].

Lancia Delta HF Turbo

Lancia Delta HF Integrale

```
2.0 Litre Turbo
136/147kW-182/197hp-185/200PS
Fuel Injection
```

Engine for HF Integral and Integral 16V
As 1.3 Litre, except:
Weight: Kerbweight (DIN) 1215/1250kg, gross vehicle weight 1665kg.
Engine data (DIN): 4-cylinder in-line (84 x 90mm), 1995cm3; compression ratio 8:1; 136kW (182PS) [185PS] at 5300rpm, 68.2kW/L (91.4hp/L) [92.7PS/L]; 304Nm (224lbft) at 3500rpm.
Integrale 16V: Compression ratio 8:1; 147kW (197hp) [200PS] at 5500rpm, 73.6kW/L (98.6hp/L) [100.1PS/L]; 304Nm (224lbft) at 3000rpm.
Engine construction: Valves in V (2 or 4 per cylinder), 2 overhead camshaft (toothed belt); 2 anti vibration arms; oil capacity 5.9L (5.6US qt); 1 Garrett T3 exhaust turbocharger (16V 60/50), max charge-air pressure 1.0, 16V 0.8-1.2 bar; charge-air cooler; IAW Weber electronic fuel injection. 12V 45Ah Battery, 65A alternator.
Transmission (to all wheels): 5-speed manual, central Planetary differential with viscous coupling, distribution front/rear 56/44, 16V 57/44%, rear Torsen limited slip differential, final drive ratio 3.111.
Gear ratios: 1st 3.50; 2nd 2.235; 3rd 1.518; 4th 1.132; 5th 0.928; R 3.583.
Chassis: Four wheel disc brakes, front ventilated, diameter front 28.4cm, rear 22.7cm; tyres 195/55 VR 15, 16V 205/50 VR 15, wheel rims 6, 16V 7 J.
Dimensions: Track 142.5cm, load space 7-33.2cu ft (200-940dm3). Length 390cm, width 170cm.
Performance: Max speed 134mph/215kmh, 16V 138mph/222kmh (manufacturers test specifications), speed at 1000rpm in 5th gear 23.4mph/37.7kmh; acceleration 0-62mph/100kmh 6.6secs 16V 5.7secs; standing km 27.1secs, 16V 26.1secs; power to weight ratio from 8.5kg/kW (6.3kg/PS); consumption ECE 7.7/10.2/10.8L/100km (36.7/27.7/26.2mpg) [30.5/23.1/21.8US mpg], 16V 7.9/10.5/11.2L/100km (35.8/26.9/25.2mpg) [29.8/22.4/21 US mpg].

```
1.9 Litre Diesel
59kW-79hp-80PS
Turbo/Injection Pump
```

Engine for Turbo ds
As 1.3 Litre, except:
Weight: Kerbweight (DIN) 1060kg, gross vehicle weight 1510kg.
Engine data (ECE): 4-cylinder in-line (82.6 x 90mm), 1929cm3; compression ratio 20:1; 59kW (79hp) [80PS] at 4200rpm, 30.6kW/L (41hp/L) [41.5PS/L]; 172Nm (126.9lbft) at 2400rpm.
Engine construction: Swirl chamber, diesel engine. Oil capacity 5.6L (5.3US qt); oil cooler; 1 exhaust turbocharger KKK K16, max boost pressure 0.8 bar; inter-cooler; Bosch VE diesel injection pump. 12V 70Ah Battery, 65A alternator; cooling system capacity 7L (6.6US qt).
Transmission: 5-speed manual, final drive ratio 3.053.
Gear ratios: 1st 3.545; 2nd 2.267; 3rd 1.523; 4th 1.142; 5th 0.823; R 3.909.
Chassis: Tyres 165/65 TR 14, wheel rims 5.5J.
Performance: Max speed 106mph/170kmh (manufacturers test specifications), speed at 1000rpm in 5th gear 25.2mph/40.5kmh; acceleration 0 – 62mph/100kmh 12.9secs; standing km 34.4secs; power to weight ratio 18.0kg/kW (13.3kg/PS); consumption ECE 4.6/6.4/6.5L/100km (61.4/44.1/43.5mpg) [51.1/36.8/36.2US mpg].

Lancia Prisma

1.3 – 1.5 – 1.6 – 1.6ie – Integrale – Diesel – Turbodiesel
Saloon/Sedan with front wheel drive. 1300, 1500 or 1600cm3 engine, all round independent suspension. Launched in December 1982. June 1984 with 1.9 Litre Turbodiesel. Turin 1986: 1600cm3 with fuel injection and 2 Litre with front wheel drive. Turin 1988 with changes to gear ratios.

```
1.3 Litre
57kW-76.5hp-78PS
1 2V Carb
```

Body, Weight: 4-door Saloon/Sedan, 5-seater; kerbweight (DIN) 950kg, gross vehicle weight 1400kg.
Engine data (DIN): 4-cylinder in-line (86.4 x 55.5mm), 1302cm3; compression ratio 9.5:1; 57kW (76.5hp) [78PS] at 5800rpm, 43.8kW/L (58.7hp/L) [59.9PS/L]; 105Nm (77.4lbft) at 3400rpm; leaded premium grade.
Engine construction: Designated 831 A.000. Transverse front engine, inclined 20deg to front, 1 overhead camshaft (toothed belt); light-alloy cylinder head; 5 bearing crankshaft; oil capacity 4.5L (4.4US qt); 1 Weber horizontal 2V carb. 12V 40Ah Battery, 55A alternator; cooling system capacity approx 6L (5.7US qt).
Transmission (to front wheels): 5-speed manual, final drive ratio 3.765.
Gear ratios: 1st 4.091; 2nd 2.235; 3rd 1.469; 4th 1.043; 5th 0.863; R 3.714.
Chassis: Integral body; front independent suspension with McPherson struts, lower control arm, rear independent suspension with twin control arms, trailing arms, tension struts, McPherson struts, telescopic damper, front and rear antiroll bar. Servo/power assisted brakes, front discs, rear drums, disc diameter 22.7cm; mechanical handbrake to rear wheels; rack and pinion steering; fuel tank capacity 55/57L (12.1/12.5Gal) [14.5/15.1US mpg], with 6-9L (1.3–2Gal) [1.6–2.4US Gal] reserve; tyres 165/70SR 13 optional 165/65 SR 14, wheel rims 5J.
Dimensions: Wheelbase 247.5cm, track 140/140cm, clearance 14.5cm, turning circle 11.6m. Load space 15.9–26.1cu ft (450–740dm3). Length 418cm, width 162cm, height 138.5cm.

Lancia

Performance: Max speed 101mph/163kmh (manufacturers test specifications), speed at 1000rpm in 4th gear 16.4mph/26.4kmh, in 5th gear 19.8mph/31.8kmh; acceleration 0 – 62mph/100kmh 14.3secs, standing km 35.2secs; power to weight ratio 16.7kg/kW (12.2kg/PS); consumption ECE 5.5/7.4/8.7L/100km (51.4/38.2/32.5mpg) [42.8/31.8/27US mpg].

Lancia Prisma

```
1.5 Litre
59kW–79hp–80PS
1 2V Carb
```

As 1.3 Litre, except:

Weight: Kerbweight (DIN) 955kg, gross vehicle weight 1405kg. Automatic heavier by 20kg.

Engine data (DIN): 4–cylinder in–line (86.4 x 63.9mm), 1499cm3; compression ratio 9.5:1; 59kW (79hp) [80PS] at 5600rpm, 39.3kW/L (52.7hp/L) [53.4PS/L]; 123Nm (90.7lbft) at 3200rpm.

Engine construction: Designated 831 A 1.000. 1 Weber horizontal 2V carb. Alternator 55/65 A.

Gear ratios: a) 5–speed manual: As 1.3 Litre.
b) Automatic: Max torque multiplication in converter 2.5 times, Planetary gear set ratios: 1st 2.346; 2nd 1.402; 3rd 1; R 2.346.

Performance: Max speed 103mph/166kmh, automatic 99.5mph/160kmh (manufacturers test specifications), speed at 1000rpm in 5th gear 20.8mph/33.4kmh; acceleration 0 – 62mph/100kmh 12.1secs, automatic 14.3secs, standing km 33.9secs, automatic 35.5secs; power to weight ratio from 16.2kg/kW (11.9kg/PS); consumption ECE 5.5/7.2/9.1L/100km (51.4/39.2/31mpg) [42.8/32.7/25.8US mpg], automatic 7.0/9.2/9.9L/100km (40.4/30.7/28.5mpg) [33.6/25.6/23.8US mpg].

Lancia Prisma

```
1.6 Litre
74kW–99hp–100PS
1 2V Carb
```

As 1.3 Litre, except:

Weight: Kerbweight (DIN) 990kg, gross vehicle weight 1440kg.

Engine data (DIN): 4–cylinder in–line (84 x 71.5mm), 1585cm3; compression ratio 9.7:1; 74kW (99hp) [100PS] at 5900rpm, 46.4kW/L (62.2hp/L) [63.1PS/L]; 127Nm (93.7lbft) at 4000rpm.

Engine construction: Designated 828 B.000. Valves in V; 2 overhead camshafts; oil capacity 4.7L (4.4US qt); 1 Weber 34 DAT 13/250 downdraught 2V carb.

Transmission: 5-speed manual, final drive ratio 3.588

Gear ratios: 1st 3.583; 2nd 2.235; 3rd 1.55; 4th 1.163; 5th 0.959; R 3.714.

Chassis: All round disc brakes, diameter front 25.7cm, rear 22.7cm; tyres 165/65 SR 14, wheel rims 5.5J.

Performance: Max speed 112mph/180kmh (manufacturers test specifications), speed at 1000rpm in 5th gear 18.7mph/30.1kmh; acceleration 0 – 62mph/100kmh 10.4secs; standing km 32.5secs; power to weight ratio 13.4kg/kW (9.9kg/PS); consumption ECE 6.3/8.2/10.0L/100km (44.8/34.4/28.2mpg) [37.3/28.7/23.5US mpg].

```
1.6 Litre
79/66kW–106/88.5hp–108/90PS
Fuel Injection
```

As 1.3 Litre, except:

Weight: Kerbweight (DIN) 995/1025, gross vehicle weight 1445/1475kg.

Engine data (ECE): 4–cylinder in–line (84 x 71.5mm), 1585cm3; compression ratio 9.7:1; 79kW (106hp) [108PS] at 5900rpm, 49.8kW/L (66.7hp/L) [68.1PS/L]; 135Nm (99.6lbft) at 3500rpm.
With Catalyst: Central/single point injection; compression ratio 9.5:1; 66kW (88.5hp) [90PS] at 6250rpm, 41.6kW/L (55.7hp/L) [56.8PS/L]; 123Nm (90.7lbft) at 4250rpm; unleaded premium grade.

Engine construction: Designated 828 B.000. Valves in V; 2 overhead camshafts; oil capacity 4.7L (4.4US qt); Weber IAW electronic fuel injection.

Transmission: 5–speed manual, final drive ratio 3.588.

Gear ratios: 1st 3.545; 2nd 2.267; 3rd 1.523; 4th 1.142; 5th 0.959; R 3.909.
With Catalyst: 1st 3.545; 2nd 2.267; 3rd 1.523; 4th 1.142; 5th 0.967; R 3.909.

Chassis: All round disc brakes, diameter front 25.7cm, rear 22.7cm; tyres 165/65 SR 14, wheel rims 5.5J.

Performance: Max speed 115mph/185kmh, Catalyst 109mph/175kmh (manufacturers test specifications), speed at 1000rpm in 5th gear 18.7mph/30.1kmh; acceleration 0 – 62mph/100kmh 10.0secs, Catalyst 11secs; standing km 31.8secs; power to weight ratio 12.6kg/kW (9.2kg/PS); consumption ECE 6.2/8.0/9.8L/100km (45.6/35.3/28.8mpg) [37.9/29.4/24US mpg], Catalyst 6.4/8.4/10.1L/100km (44.1/33.6/28mpg) [36.8/28/23.3US mpg].

```
2 Litre
85/82kW–114/110hp–115/112PS
Fuel Injection
```

Engine for Integrale

As 1.3 Litre, except:

Weight: Kerbweight (DIN) 1180/1210, gross vehicle weight 1630/1660kg.

Engine data (DIN): 4–cylinder in–line (84 x 90mm), 1995cm3; compression ratio 9.75:1; 85kW (114hp) [115PS] at 5400rpm, 42.6kW/L (57.1hp/L) [57.6PS/L]; 163Nm (120.2lbft) at 3250rpm.
With Catalyst: Compression ratio 9.5:1; 82kW (110hp) [112PS] at 5500rpm, 41.1kW/L (55.1hp/L) [56.1PS/L]; 157Nm (115.8lbft) at 4000rpm; unleaded premium grade.

Lancia Prisma Integrale

Engine construction: Valves in V (65deg), 2 overhead camshafts (toothed belt); 2 counter–balance shafts; light–alloy cylinder head; 5 bearing crankshaft; oil capacity 6.5L (6.1US qt); Weber IAW electronic fuel injection. 12V 45/50Ah Battery, 65A alternator; cooling system capacity 9.0L (8.5US qt).

Transmission (to all wheels): 5–speed manual, central Planetary differential with viscous coupling, power distribution front/rear 56/44%, pneumatic rear differential lock; final drive ratio 3.421.

Gear ratios: 1st 3.750; 2nd 2.235; 3rd 1.518; 4th 1.132; 5th 0.928; R 3.583.

Chassis: All round disc brakes, front diameter 25.7cm, rear 22.7cm; power asssited steering; tyres 185/60 HR 14, wheel rims 5.5J.

Lancia

Dimensions: Track 141/140.5cm, load space 12.7–23cu ft (360–650dm3).
Performance: Max speed 114mph/184kmh, Catalyst 112.5mph/181kmh (manufacturers test specifications), speed at 1000rpm in 5th gear 20.7mph/33.3kmh; acceleration 0–62mph/100kmh 10.5secs; standing km 32.2secs; power to weight ratio 14.0kg/kW (10.3kg/PS); consumption (ECE) 7.8/10.0/11.0L/100km (36.2/28.2/25.7mpg) [30.2/23.5/21.4US mpg], Catalyst 8.0/10.3/11.3L/100km (35.3/27.4/25mpg) [29.4/22.8/20.8US mpg].

1.9 Litre Diesel
48kW–64hp–65PS
Injection Pump

Engine for Diesel
As 1.3 Litre, except:
Weight: Kerbweight (DIN) 1030kg, gross vehicle weight 1480kg.
Engine data (DIN): 4–cylinder in–line (82.6 x 90mm), 1929cm3; compression ratio 21:1; 48kW (64hp) [65PS] at 4600rpm, 24.8kW/L (33.2hp/L) [33.7PS/L]; 119Nm (87.8lbft) at 2000rpm.
Engine construction: Diesel engine, swirl chamber. Oil capacity 5L (4.7US qt); Bosch VE diesel injection pump. 12V 70Ah Battery, 55A alternator; cooling system capacity 7L (6.6US qt).
Transmission: 5–speed manual, final drive ratio 3.588.
Gear ratios: 1st 4.091; 2nd 2.235; 3rd 1.469; 4th 1.043; 5th 0.827; R 3.714.
Performance: Max speed 98mph/158kmh (manufacturers test specifications), speed at 1000rpm in 5th gear 21.7mph/34.9kmh; acceleration 0–62mph/100kmh 16secs; standing km 39.6secs; power to weight ratio 21.5kg/kW (15.8kg/PS); consumption (ECE) 4.6/6.5/7.1L/100km (61.4/43.5/39.8mpg) [51.1/36.2/33.1US mpg].

1.9 Litre Diesel
59kW–79hp–80PS
Turbo/Injection Pump

Engine for Turbo ds
As 1.3 Litre, except:
Weight: Kerbweight (DIN) 1060kg, gross vehicle weight 1510kg
Engine data (ECE): 4–cylinder in–line (82.6 x 90mm), 1929cm3; compression ratio 20:1; 59kW (79hp) [80PS] at 4200rpm, 30.6kW/L (41hp/L) [41.5PS/L]; 172Nm (126.9lbft) at 2400rpm.
Engine construction: Diesel engine, swirl chamber. Oil capacity 5L (4.7US qt); oil cooler; 1 exhaust turbocharger KKK K16, max boost pressure 0.8bar; Intercooler; Bosch VE diesel injection pump. 12V 70Ah Battery, 65A alternator; cooling system capacity 9L (8.5US qt).
Transmission: 5–speed manual, final drive ratio 3.053.
Gear ratios: 1st 3.545; 2nd 2.267; 3rd 1.523; 4th 1.142; 5th 0.823; R 3.909.
Chassis: Tyres 165/65 SR 14, wheel rims 5.5J.
Performance: Max speed 107mph/170kmh (manufacturers test specifications), speed at 1000rpm in 5th gear 25.2mph/40.5kmh; acceleration 0–62mph/100kmh 12.9secs; standing km 34.4secs; power to weight ratio 18.0kg/kW (13.3kg/PS); consumption ECE 4.6/6.4/6.5L/100km (61.4/44.1/43.5mpg) [51.1/36.8/36.2US mpg].

Lancia Dedra

New model. Notchback Saloon/Sedan with 1.6, 1.8 or 2-Litre as well as 1.9 Litre Turbo diesel engine; longer by 4.34 metres, cd 0.29. Launched in May 1989.

Lancia

Lancia Thema

ie – ie turbo – 6V – Limousine – turbo ds – Estate/Station Wagon

Mid range vehicle with front wheel drive and all–round independent suspension, various engine types. 2 Litre with 2 antivibration arms, also turbodiesel version, either manual or automatic. Launched in October 1984. April 1986/Turin Saloon/Sedan: new top model 8.32 with 2.9 Litre Ferrari V8. Summer 1986: also available as Estate/Station Wagon. September "Limousine" with 30cm longer wheelbase. Paris 1988, detail modifications and new engine pallett.

2 Litre
88/85kW–118/114hp–119/115 PS
Fuel Injection

Not available for ie, or Estate/Station Wagon.
Body, Weight: 4–door Saloon/Sedan, 5–seater; kerbweight (DIN) 1230kg, gross vehicle weight 1730kg. Automatic heavier by 25kg.
Engine data (DIN): 4–cylinder in–line (84 x 90mm), 1995cm3; compression ratio 9.5:1; 88kW (118hp) [119PS] at 5250rpm, 44.1kW/L (59.1hp/L) [59.6PS/L]; 165Nm (121.8lbft) at 3300rpm; leaded premium grade.
With Catalyst: 85kW (114hp) [115PS] at 5600rpm, 42.6kW/L (57hp/L) [57.6PS/L]; 162Nm (119.6lbft) at 4000rpm; unleaded premium grade.
Engine construction: Transverse engine inclined to the rear. Valves in V (65deg), 2 overhead camshafts (toothed belt); light–alloy cylinder head; 5 bearing crankshaft; oil capacity 5.5L (5.2US qt); Bosch LE–2–Jetronic (Catalyst LU) electronic fuel injection. 12V 45Ah Battery; 65/85A alternator; cooling system capacity 8.2L (US qt).
Transmission (to front wheels): 5–speed manual, final drive ratio 3.421.
Gear ratios: 1st 3.750; 2nd 2.176; 3rd 1.519; 4th 1.132; 5th 0.929; R 3.545.
Chassis: Integral body; front and rear independent suspension, front McPherson strut, control arm and antiroll bar, rear McPherson struts, single control arm and tension strut, antiroll bar, coil springs and telescopic damper. Servo/power assisted brakes, discs front and rear (front ventilated), front diameter 25.7cm, rear 25.1cm; optional ABS System Bosch; mechanical handbrake to rear wheels; power assisted rack and pinion steering; fuel tank capacity 70L (15.4Gal) [18.5US Gal]; tyres 175/70 HR 14 optional 195/60 HR 14, wheel rims 5.5/6J.
Dimensions: Wheelbase 266cm, track 148/147cm, clearance 14cm, turning circle 11.7m. Load space 19.4–35.3cu ft (550-1000dm3). Length 459cm, width 175cm, height 143.5cm. Station Wagon: Load space 15.5–56.5cu ft (440-1600dm3), height 144cm.
Performance: Max speed 121mph/195kmh, Catalyst 118mph/190kmh; (manufacturers test specifications); speed at 1000rpm in 5th gear 21.7mph/34.9kmh; acceleration 0–62mph/100kmh 10.5secs; standing km 31.9secs; power to weight ratio 14.0kg/kW (10.3kg/PS); consumption ECE 6.5/8.4/9.8L/100km (43.5/33.6/28.8mpg) [36.2/28.0/24.0US mpg].

Lancia Thema ie 16V

2 Litre 16V
110kW–147hp–150PS
Fuel Injection

Engine for ie 16V and Station Wagon
As 118PS, except:
Body, Weight: 4–door Saloon/Sedan, 5–seater; kerbweight (DIN) 1250kg, gross vehicle weight 1750kg; 5–door Estate/Station Wagon, 5–seater; kerbweight (DIN) 1330kg, gross vehicle weight 1930kg.

Lancia

Engine data (DIN): 4-cylinder in-line (84 x 90mm), 1995cm3; compression ratio 9.85:1; 110kW(140hp) [150PS] at 6000rpm, 55.1kW/L (73.8hp/L) [75.2PS/L]; 184Nm (135.8lbft) at 4000rpm.

Engine construction: 4 valves per cylinder; Bosch LE 3.1 Jetronic electronic fuel injection.

Transmission: a) 5-speed manual, final drive ratio 3.421, Estate/Station Wagon 3.562.
b) Automatic: Model ZF, hydraulic torque and 4 speed Planetary gear set, final drive ratio 4.201.

Gear ratios: a) 5-speed manual: 1st 3.750; 2nd 2.176; 3rd 1.519; 4th 1.132; 5th 0.929; R 3.545.
b) Automatic: max torque multiplication in converter 2 times, Planetary gear set ratios: 1st 2.579; 2nd 1.407; 3rd 1; 4th 0.742; R 2.882.

Chassis: Station Wagon, tyres 185/70 HR/VR 14, wheel rims 5.5 J.

Performance: Max speed 127mph/205kmh, Automatic 124mph/200kmh (manufacturers test specifications), speed at 1000rpm in 5th gear 21.7mph/34.9kmh; acceleration 0 - 62mph/100kmh 9.5secs, Automatic 12secs; standing km 30.6secs, Automatic 32secs; power to weight ratio from 11.0kg/kW (8.3kg/PS); consumption ECE 6.4/8.2/10.4L/100km (44.1/34.4/27.2mpg) [36.8/28.7/22.6US mpg], Automatic 6.8/8.4/12.5L/100km (41.5/33.6/22.6mpg) [34.6/28.0/18.8US mpg]. Wagon: Max speed 123mph/198kmh; acceleration 0 - 62mph/100kmh 11secs; consumption ECE 6.8/9.2/10.8L/100km (41.5/30.7/26.2mpg) [34.6/25.6/21.8US mpg].

Lancia Thema ie turbo 16V

Lancia Thema Station Wagon ie turbo 16V

```
2 Litre 16V
136/110kW-182/147hp-185/150PS
Fuel Injection/Turbo
```

Engine for ie Turbo and Estate/Station Wagon

As 118hp, except:

Body, Weight: 4-door Saloon/Sedan, 5-seater: Kerbweight (DIN) 1285kg, gross vehicle weight 1785kg. 5-door Estate/Station Wagon, 5-seater; kerbweight (DIN) 1360kg, gross vehicle weight 1960kg.

Engine data (DIN): 4-cylinder in-line (84 x 90mm), 1995cm3; compression ratio 8:1; 136kW (182hp) [185PS] at 5500rpm, 68.2kW/L (91.3hp/L) [92.7PS/L]; 284Nm (209.6lbft) at 2750rpm.
With Overboost: 320Nm (236.2lbft) at 2500rpm.
With Catalyst: Compression ratio 7.5:1; 110kW (147hp) [150PS] at 5500rpm, 55.1kW/L (73.8hp/L) [75.2PS/L]; 247Nm (182.3lbft) at 2750rpm.

Engine construction: 4 valves per cylinder, 2 with catalyst; 1 Garrett T3 exhaust turbocharger, max boost pressure 0.65-0.9, Catalyst 0.53bar; Intercooler. Cooling system capacity 9.6L (9.1US qt).

Transmission: 5-speed manual, final drive ratio 3.111, Estate/Station Wagon 3.176.

Gear ratios: 1st 3.500; 2nd 2.176; 3rd 1.524; 4th 1.156; 5th 0.917; R 3.545.

Chassis: Disc diameter front 28.4cm; tyres 195/16 VR 15, wheel rims 6J.

Dimensions: Track 149.5/148.5cm.

Performance: Max speed 140mph/225kmh, Wagon 133mph/214kmh (Manufacturers test specifications), speed at 1000rpm in 5th gear 24.5mph/39.4kmh; acceleration 0 - 62mph/100kmh 7.0secs, Wagon 8.0secs; standing km 27.4secs, Wagon 29.0secs; power to weight ratio from 9.4kg/kW (6.9kg/PS) ; consumption ECE 6.7/8.6/10.9L/100km (42.2/32.8/25.9mpg) [35.1/27.4/25.9US mpg), Wagon 7.4/9.6/11.5L/100km (38.2/29.4/24.6mpg) [31.8/24.5/20.5US mpg].
With Catalyst: Max speed 130mph/210kmh.

```
2.85 Litre V6
110kW-147hp-150/147PS
Fuel Injection
```

Engine for 6V and Saloon/Sedan

As 118hp, except:

Weight: Kerbweight (DIN) 1280kg, gross vehicle weight 1780kg. Saloon/Sedan: Kerbweight (DIN) 1380kg, gross vehicle weight 1830kg. Automatic heavier by 30kg.

Engine data (Catalyst DIN): 6-cylinder in V 90deg (91 x 73mm), 2849cm3; compression ratio 9.5:1; 110kW (147hp) [150PS] at 5000rpm, 38.6kW/L (51.7hp/L) [52.7PS/L]; 230Nm (169.7lbft) at 3500rpm.
Swiss version: 108kW (145hp) [147PS]; 226Nm (166.8lbft).

Engine construction: Valves in V; 1 overhead camshaft (Chain); light-alloy cylinder heads and block, wet cylinder liners; 4 bearing crankshaft; oil capacity 6.6L (6.2US qt); Bosch LH 2.2-Jetronic mechanical fuel injection. 12V 60Ah Battery, 85A alternator; Saloon/Sedan 115A; cooling system capacity 6L (5.7US qt).

Transmission: a) 5-speed manual, final drive ratio 2.944.
b) Automatic, final drive ratio 3.046.

Gear ratios: a) 5-speed manual: 1st 3.500; 2nd 2.176; 3rd 1.519; 4th 1.132; 5th 0.929; R 3.545.
b) Automatic: Max torque multiplication in converter 2 times, Planetary gear set ratios: 1st 2.479; 2nd 1.479; 3rd 1; R 2.086.

Lancia Thema 6V

Chassis: Tyres 185/70 VR 14, optional 205/60 VR 14; Saloon/Sedan 195/60 VR 15.

Dimensions: Saloon/Sedan: Wheelbase 296cm, length 489cm.

Performance: Max speed 127mph/205kmh, automatic 124mph/200kmh (manufacturers test specifications), speed at 1000rpm in 5th gear 25.8mph/41.6kmh; acceleration 0 - 62mph/100kmh 8.4secs, automatic 9.4secs; standing km 30.0secs, automatic 31.2secs; power to weight ratio 11.6kg/kW (8.5kg/PS); consumption 7.4/9.4/14.0L/100km (38.2/30.1/20.2mpg) [31.8/25.0/16.8US mpg], Automatic 8.6/10.5/14.3L/100km (32.8/26.9/19.8mpg) [27.4/22.4/16.4US mpg]. Saloon/Sedan: acceleration 0 - 62mph/100kmh, 8.7secs, Automatic 9.7secs.

Lancia • Land Rover

Diesel 2.5 Litre
87kW–117hp–118PS
Turbo/Fuel Injection

Engine for Turbo ds and Estate/Station Wagon.
As 119PS, except:

Body, Weight: 4–door Saloon/Sedan, 5–seater; kerbweight (DIN) 1350kg, gross vehicle weight 1850kg. 5–door Estate/Station Wagon, 5–seater; kerbweight (DIN) 1410kg, gross vehicle weight 2010kg.

Engine data (DIN): 4–cylinder in–line (93 x 92mm), 2500cm3; compression ratio 21:1; 87kW (117hp) [118PS] at 3900rpm, 34.8kW/L (46.6hp/L) [47.2PS/L]; 250Nm (184.5lbft) at 2200rpm.

Engine construction: Diesel engine, swirl chamber. Parallel valves; 1 overhead camshaft (toothed belt), light–alloy cylinder head; oil capacity 6.4L (6.1US qt); Bosch injection pump, 1 exhaust turbocharger KKK K26; max boost pressure 0.87bar. 12V 70Ah Battery, 65/85A alternator; cooling system capacity 9L (8.5US qt).

Transmission: a) 5-speed manual, final drive ratio 3.421, Estate/Station Wagon 3.562.
b) Automatic: Model ZF, hydraulic torque converter and 4-speed Planetary gear set, final drive ratio 3.348.

Gear ratios: a) 5-speed manual: 1st 3.50; 2nd 2.176; 3rd 1.379; 4th 0.976; 5th 0.723; R 3.545.
b) Automatic, max torque multiplication in converter 2 times, Planetary gear set ratios: 1st 2.579; 2nd 1.407; 3rd 1; 4th 0.742; R 2.882.

Chassis: Tyres 185/70 14 optional 195/60 HR 14.

Performance: Max speed 144mph/195, Automatic 139mph/188kmh (Manufacturers test specifications), speed at 1000rpm in 5th gear 28.6mph/46kmh; acceleration 0 - 62mph/100kmh 11secs, Automatic 12.7secs; standing km 32.6secs; power to weight ratio from 15.5kg/kW (11.4kg/PS); consumption ECE 5.3/7.0/8.6L/100km (53.3/40.4/32.8mpg) [44.4/33.6/27.4US mpg], Automatic 6.0/7.8/9.5L/100km (47.1/36.2/29.7mpg) [39.2/30.2/24.8US mpg]. Wagon: Max speed 190/183kmh acceleration 0 - 62mph/100kmh 11.9/12.1secs; consumption ECE 5.7/7.7/9.4L/100km (49.6/36.7/30.1mpg) [41.3/30.5/25.0US mpg], Automatic 6.4/8.5/10.0L/100km (44.1/33.2/28.2mpg) [36.8/27.7/23.5US mpg].

Lancia Thema turbo ds Station Wagon

Lancia Thema 8.32

Version of the Thema with 2.9 Litre Ferrari V8 Engine. Launched in April 1986 at the Turin Salon.

2.9 Litre V8
158/151kW-212/202hp-215/205PS
Fuel Injection

As 119hp, except:

Weight: Kerbweight (DIN) 1400kg, Catalyst 1410kg, gross vehicle weight 1880kg.

Engine data (DIN): 8–cylinder in V 90deg (81 x 71mm), 2927cm3; compression ratio 10.5:1; 158kW (212hp) [215PS] at 6750rpm, 54kW/L (72.4hp/L) [73.5PS/L]; 281Nm (207.4lbft) at 4500rpm.
With Catalyst: Compression ratio 9.5:1; 151kW (202hp) [205PS] at 6750rpm, 51.6kW/L (69.1hp/L) [70PS/L]; 263Nm (194.1lbft) at 5000rpm.

Engine construction: Designated Ferrari F 105L. Valves in V 33.5deg, 4 valves per cylinder, 2 x 2 overhead camshafts (toothed belt); light–alloy cylinder heads and cylinder block, wet cylinder liners (Nicasil); 5 bearing crankshafts; oil capacity approx 7.6L (6.8US qt); Bosch KE–3–Jetronic mechanical/electronic fuel injection. 12V 60Ah Battery, 85A alternator; cooling system capacity approx 9.8L (9.3US qt).

Transmission: 5–speed manual, final drive ratio 3.412 (17/58), Catalyst 3.562 (16/57).

Gear ratios: 1st 3.50; 2nd 2.176; 3rd 1.523; 4th 1.156; 5th 0.916; R 3.545.

Chassis: Disc diameters, front 28.4cm, rear 25.1cm; ABS; tyres 205/55 VR 15, wheel rims 6J.

Performance: Max speed 149mph/240kmh (manufacturers test specifications), speed at 1000rpm in 5th gear 22.1mph/35.6kmh, Catalyst 21.1mph/34kmh; acceleration 0 – 62mph/100kmh 6.8secs; standing km 26.8secs; power to weight ratio 8.9kg/kW (6.5kg/PS); consumption ECE 8.5/10.5/16.0L/100km (33.2/26.9/17.7mpg) [27.7/22.4/14.7US mpg].

Lancia Thema 8.32

LAND ROVER   GB

Land Rover Ltd., Lode Lane, Solihull, West Midlands B92 8NW, GB

English manufacturer of rough terrain vehicles, Land Rover since 1948.

Range Rover

Rough terrain Estate/Station Wagon with a V8 engine and permanent all wheel drive. Launched June 1970. July 1981 4–door version, Paris 1982 automatic available, July 1983 5–speed manual. October 1986 fuel injection and 4–speed automatic, Turin 1986 tubodiesel. November 1988: Catalyst version with 3.9 Litre engine.

Range Rover Vogue

3.5 Litre V8
124kW-166hp-168PS
Fuel Injection

Body, Weight: Estate/Station Wagon 3/5–door, 5–seater; Kerbweight (DIN) 1925kg, gross vehicle weight 2510kg. Increased weight for automatic 45kg.

Engine data (DIN): 8–cylinder in V 90deg (88.9 x 71.12mm), 3532cm3; compression ratio 9.35:1; 124kW (166hp) [168PS] at 4750rpm, 35.1kW/L (47hp/L) [47.6PS/L]; 280Nm (206.6) at 3000rpm; premium grade.
For some countries: 127kW (170hp) [173PS].

Land Rover

Engine construction: Hydraulic tappets; central camshaft (chain). Light–alloy cylinder block; dry cylinder liners; 5 bearing crankshaft. Oil capacity 6.25L (6.0US qt); Lucas M-Electronic electronic fuel injection. Battery 12V 60Ah, alternator 65/80A; cooling system capacity approx 11.3L (10.7US qt).

Transmission (to all wheels): a) 5–speed manual with central differential, gear drive and viscous coupling, torque distribution front and rear 50/50%; reduction gears, final drive 3.538, reduction gears 1.206 or 3.243.
b) Automatic ZF 4 HP 22; hydraulic torque converter and 4–speed Planetary gear set, central selector lever, final drive ratio 3.538; reduction gears: 1st 1.22 2nd 3.320.

Gear ratios: a) 5–speed manual: 1st 3.321; 2nd 2.312; 3rd 1.397; 4th 1; 5th 0.77; R 3.429.
b) Automatic: Max torque multiplication in converter 2.2 times; Planetary gear set ratios: 1st 2.48; 2nd 1.48; 3rd 1; 4th 0.728; R 2.086.

Chassis: Box type frame with cross member; front rigid axle with trailing arm and Panhard rod, rear rigid axle with trailing arm, central, lower longitudinal A arm, coil springs and hydraulic level control system, telescopic damper. Servo/power assisted disc brakes, front diameter 30cm, rear 29cm; mechanical handbrake to propshaft; power assisted recirculating ball steering; fuel tank 79.5L (17.5Gal) [21US Gal]; Radial tyres 205 R 16 XM + S 200, wheel rims 7 J.

Dimensions: Wheelbase 254cm, track 149/149cm, clearance 19cm, turning circle 11.2m, load space 36–70.6cu ft (1020–2000dm3). Length 445cm, width 182cm, height 179cm.

Performance: Max speed approx 106mph/170kmh, speed at 1000rpm in 5th gear 25.5mph/41kmh, in 5th gear with all terrain reduction 9.4mph/15.2kmh; power to weight ratio from 15.5kg/kW (11.5kg/PS); consumption ECE 10.4/13.5/18.3L/100km (27.2/20.9/15.4mpg) [22.6/17.4/12.9US mpg], Automatic 10.8/14.0/19.4L/100km (26.2/20.2/14.6mpg) [21.8/16.8/12.1US mpg].

3.9 Litre V8
134kW-180hp-182PS
Fuel Injection

As 166hp, except:

Body, Weight: 5-door Estate/Station Wagon, 5-seater; kerbweight (DIN) 1930kg, gross vehicle weight 2550kg.

Engine data (Catalyst DIN): 8 cylinder in V 90deg (94 x 71.1mm), 3947cm3; compression ratio 8.1:1; 134kW(180hp) [182PS] at 4750rpm, 33.9kW/L (45.4hp/L) [46.1PS/L]; 308Nm (23.2lbft) at 3500rpm; regular unleaded.

Engine construction: Bosch LH-Jetronic electronic fuel injection.

Transmission (to all wheels): Automatic ZF 4 HP 22, hydraulic torque and 4-speed Planetary gear set, central selector lever, final drive ratio 3.538; reduction gear ratios: 1st 2.058; 2nd 3.2431. 5-speed manual in preparation.

Gear ratios: Max torque multiplication in converter 2.2 times; Planetary gear set ratios: 1st 2.48; 2nd 1.48; 3rd 1; 4th 0.728; R 2.086."

Chassis: Tyres 205 R 16 XM + S 244, wheel rims 7".

Performance: Max speed above 106mph/170kmh (manufacturers test specifications), speed at 1000rpm in top gear 26.9mph/43.3kmh, with reduction 10mph/16.1kmh; power to weight ratio from 14.4kg/kW (10.6kg/PS), consumption approx 15-21L/100km (18.8-13.5mpg) [15.7-11.2US mpg].

Range Rover Vogue

2.4 Litre Diesel
84kW-113hp-114PS
Turbo/Pump Injection

As 166hp except:

Body, Weight: Estate/Station Wagon 3/5–door, 5-seater; kerbweight (DIN) 2015kg. Gross vehicle weight 2510kg. Increased weight for automatic 45kg.

Engine data (DIN): 4–cylinder in–line (92 x 90mm), 2393cm3; compression ratio 21.5:1; 84kW (113hp) [114PS] at 4200rpm; 35.1kW/L (47.0hp/L) [47.6PS/L]; 248Nm (183lbft) at 2400rpm.
Certain countries: 78kW (105hp) [106PS].

Engine construction: Designated VM 81A. Diesel engine, grey cast iron cylinder block; parallel valves; 1 side camshaft (toothed belt). Oil capacity 6.6L (6.2US qt); Bosch diesel injection pump; exhaust turbocharger KKK K 16, charge–air cooler. Battery 12 V 77Ah, alternator 55 A; cooling system capacity approx 10L (9.5US qt).

Transmission: 5–speed manual, final drive ratio 3.583.

Gear ratios: 1st 3.69; 2nd 2.13; 3rd 1.4; 4th 1; 5th 0.77; R 3.43.

Performance: Max speed 90mph/145kmh (manufacturers test specifications), speed at 1000rpm in 5th gear 30.8mph/49.6kmh, acceleration 0 – 62mph/100kmh 19.5secs; power to weight ratio 24kg/kW (17.7kg/PS); Consumption ECE 8.3/11.6/11.0L/100km (34.0/24.4/25.7mpg) [28.3/20.3/21.4US mpg].

Land Rover 90–110

Rough terrain permanent four wheel drive, 2 wheelbases, 4 engines. Model 110 with long wheelbase, launched Geneva 1983, Model 90 June 1984. 1985 also available with 2.5 Litre Diesel, Birmingham 1986; 2.5 Litre Turbo Diesel

Range Rover 90

2.5 Litre 4–cylinder
62kW-83hp-84PS
1 Carb

Body, Weight: Series 90: Estate/Station Wagon 2/3–door, 2–7–seater; unladen weight without additional equipment 1605–1715kg. Series 110: Estate/Station Wagon 3/5–door; Unladen weight 1640–1760kg.

Engine data (DIN): 4–cylinder in–line (90.47 x 97mm) 2494cm3; compression ratio 8.1. 62kW (83hp) [84PS] at 4000rpm, 24.8kW/L (33.5hp/L) [33.7PS/L]; 181Nm (133.6lbft) at 2000rpm; leaded regular grade.

Engine construction: Side camshaft (chain); 5 bearing crankshaft; optional oil cooler; oil capacity 6.25L (6.0US qt); 1 Weber downdraught carb 32/34DMTL, Oil bath air cleaner. Battery 12V 55Ah, alternator 34A; cooling system capacity, approx 8.7L (8.2US qt).

Transmission (to all wheels): 5–speed manual and 2 reduction gears; central differential; manual lock bar; final drive ratio front and rear 3.54.

Gear ratios: 1st 3.585; 2nd 2.301; 3rd 1.507; 4th 1; 5th 0.831; R 3.701.
Reduction gears: 90; 1st 1.411; 2nd 3.32. 110: 1st 1.667; 2nd 3.32.

Chassis: Box type frame with cross member; front rigid axle with trailing arm and Panhard rod, coil springs, rear rigid axle with twin trailing arms, central A arm, coil springs, front and rear telescopic damper. Servo/power assisted front disc brakes, diameter 29.9cm, rear drums, mechanical handbrake on propeller shaft; worm and wheel steering, optional power assisted; fuel tank 55L (12.1Gal) [14.5US Gal]. 110: 80L (17.6Gal) [21.1US Gal]: Tyres 6.00 x 16, 205 R 16, tyres 5.5 or 6J.

Dimensions: a) 90: Wheelbase 236cm, track 149.5/149.5cm, clearance 20cm, turning circle 11.7m, length 372cm, Estate/Station Wagon 388cm, width 179cm, height 199cm.

Land Rover • Lexus

b) 110: Wheelbase 279cm, track 148.5/148.5cm, turning circle 12.8m, length 460cm, width 179cm, height 203/207cm.

Performance: Max speed 72mph/115kmh (manufacturers test specification), speed at 1000rpm in 5th gear 27.8mph/44.7kmh; power to weight ratio from 26.0kg/kW (18.5 kg/PS); consumption ECE 90: 12.4/–/17.3L/100km (22.8/–/16.3mpg) [19.0/–/13.6US mpg]. 110: 13.5/–/19.4L/100km (20.9/–/14.6mpg) [17.4/–/12.1US mpg].

```
2.5 Litre Diesel
50.5kW–68hp–69PS
Injection Pump
```

As 83hp, except:

Weight: Increased weight 40kg.

Engine data (DIN): 4–cylinder in–line (90.47 x 97mm), 2494cm3; compression ratio 21.1; 50.5kW (68hp) [69PS] at 4000rpm, 20.3kW (27.2hp/L) [27.7PS/L]; 158Nm (116.6lbft) at 1800rpm.

Engine construction: Pre–combustion chamber, diesel engine (Ricardo Comet V); CAV fuel injection pump; KLG glow plug filament; battery 12V 95Ah; cooling system capacity approx 8.4L (7.9US qt).

Performance: Max speed from 68mph/110kmh (manufacturers test specification); power to weight ratio from 32.4kg/kW (23.8kg/PS); consumption ECE 90: 10.0/–/10.6L/100km (28.2/–/26.6mpg) [23.5/–/22.2US mpg]. 110: 11.4/–/13.1L/100km (24.8/–/21.6mpg) [20.6/–/18.0US mpg].

```
2.5 Litre Diesel
63.5kW–85hp–86PS
Turbo/Fuel Injection Pump
```

As 83hp, except:

Weight: Kerbweight (DIN) 90: 1745kg, 110: 1920kg.

Engine data (DIN): 4–cylinder in–line (90.47 x 97mm), 2494cm3; compression ratio 21.1; 63.5kW (85hp) [86PS] at 4000rpm, 25.4kW/L (34hp/L) [34.5PS/L]; 204Nm (150.6lbft) at 1800rpm.
Some Countries: Also with 2.3 Litre Turbodiesel or 3.9 Litre diesel.

Engine construction: Pre–combustion chamber, diesel engine (Ricardo Comet V); CAV fuel injection pump; KLG glow plug filament; battery 12V 95Ah; cooling system capacity approx 8.4L (7.9US qt).

Gear ratios: 1st 3.585; 2nd 2.301; 3rd 1.507; 4th 1; 5th 0.831; R 3.701. Reduction gears: 1st 1.411; 2nd 3.32.

Performance: Max speed from 75mph/120kmh (manufacturers test specifications), power to weight ratio from 27.6kg/kw [20.3kg/PS]; consumption ECE 90: 10.6/–/11.9L/100km (28.2/–/23.7mpg) [22.2/–/19.8US mpg]. 110: 11.0/–/12.2 L/100km (25.7/–/23.2mpg) [21.4/–/19.3US mpg].

```
3.5 Litre V8
103kW–138hp–140PS
2 Carbs
```

As 83hp, except:

Weight: Kerbweight (DIN) 1615–1735kg. Gross vehicle weight 3050kg.

Engine data (DIN): 8–cylinder in V 90deg (88.9 x 71.12mm), 3532cm3; compression ratio 8.1.1; 103kW (138hp) [140PS] at 5000rpm, 29.2kW/L (39.1hp/L) [39.6PS/L]; 253Nm (186.7lbft) at 2500rpm.
With Catalyst: Under preparation.

Engine construction: Hydraulic tappets; central camshaft (chain); light–alloy cylinder block; dry cylinder liners; 5 bearing crankshaft; oil capacity 5.1L (4.8US qt); 2 Zenith– Stromberg downdraught carbs 175 CD SE. 12V 60Ah battery, alternator 34/45A; cooling system capacity approx 11.3L (10.7US qt).

Transmission: 5–speed manual with central differential, manual lock bar, reduction gear, final drive ratio 3.54.

Gear ratios: 1st 3.65; 2nd 2.18; 3rd 1.436; 4th 1; 5th 0.795; R 3.824; Reduction gears: 90: 1st 1.122; 2nd 3.32; 110: 1st 1.41; 2nd 3.32.

Performance: Max speed approx 90–93mph/145–150kmh, speed at 1000rpm in 5th gear 25.2mph/40.5kmh; power to weight ratio from 15.7 kg/kW (11.5kg/PS); consumption ECE 90: 12.7/19.0/20.0L/100km (22.2/14.9/14.1mpg) [18.5/12.4/11.8US mpg]. 110: 13.4/19.1/21.7L/100km (21.1/14.8/13.0mpg) [17.6/12.3/10.8US mpg]

Land Rover 110 V8

LEXUS USA/J

Toyota Motor Co., Ltd, Toyota-shi, Aichi-ken, Japan

Luxury vehicle from Toyota.

Lexus ES 250

New model. Luxury version of the Camry with 2.5 Litre V6 engine, each with 2 overhead camshafts, 4 valves per cylinder, 156PS, four wheel disc brakes with ABS. Launched in December 1988. For technical data see Toyota Camry 2.5 V6.

Lexus ES 250

Lexus LS 400

New model. Luxurious Saloon/Sedan with 4 Litre V8 DOHC engine and 247hp power, automatic, four wheel drive with ABS. Launched December 1988. Data is provisional.

```
4L-V8 DOHC 32V
184kW-247hp-250PS
Fuel Injection
```

Body, Weight: 4-door Saloon/Sedan, 5-seater; kerbweight (DIN) approx 1720kg.

Engine data (DIN): 8–cylinder in V 90deg (87.5 x 82.5mm), 3969cm3; compression ratio 10:1; 184kW (247hp) [250PS] at 5600rpm, 46.4kW/L (62.2hp/L) [63PS/L]; 353Nm (260.5lbft) at 4400rpm.

Engine construction: Hydraulic tappets; 4 valves per cylinder; each with 2 overhead camshafts (toothed belt); light–alloy cylinder head and block; 5 bearing crankshaft; oil capacity 5L (4.7US qt); electronic fuel injection. 12V 60Ah Battery, 960W Alternator; cooling system capacity approx 13.4L (12.7US qt).

Transmission (to rear wheels): Automatic, hydraulic torque converter and 4-speed Planetary set, final drive ratio 3.615.

Gear ratios: Max torque multiplication in converter 2.2 times; Planetary gear set ratios: 1st 2.531; 2nd 1.531; 3rd 1; 4th 0.705; R 1.88.

Lexus • Lincoln

Chassis: Integral body; front and rear A-arm, antiroll bar, optional level control system to rear. Servo/power assisted four wheel disc brakes (ventilated) and ABS; handbrake to rear wheels; power assisted rack and pinion steering; fuel tank capacity 85L (18.7Gal) [22.5US Gal]; tyres 205/65 VR 15, wheel rims 6.5J.

Dimensions: Wheelbase 281.5cm, track 156.5/156.5cm, clearance 15cm, turning circle approx 12m. Length 499.5cm, width 182cm, height 140/141cm.

Performance: Max speed above 149mph/240kmh (Manufacturers test specifications), speed at 1000rpm in OD 33mph/53.1kmh; acceleration 0 - 62mph/100kmh approx 8secs; power to weight ratio from 9.3kg/kW (6.9kg/PS); consumption approx 9-16L/100km (31.4-17.7mpg) [26.1-14.7US mpg].

Toyota Lexus LS 400

LINCOLN — USA

Lincoln Division, Ford Motor Company, Dearborn, Detroit 32, Michigan USA

Prestige marque from the Ford Motor Company. Elite American model.

MODEL RANGE
Continental – Town Car – Mark VII

Lincoln Continental

New edition of the luxury four door Saloon/Sedan for 1988, front wheel drive, 3.8 Litre V6 engine, four wheel disc brakes. Launched Autumn 1987. For 1989: shorter final drive ratio, and Airbag.

Lincoln Continental

> 3.8 Litre V6
> 104kW-140hp-142PS
> Fuel Injection

Body, Weight: 4 door Saloon/Sedan, 5/6-seater; kerbweight 1650kg.

Engine data (SAE net): 6–cylinder in V90deg (96.52 x 86.36mm), 3791cm3; compression ratio 9:1; 104kW (140hp) [142PS] at 3800rpm, 27.4kW/L (36.7hp/L) [37.5PS/L]; 292Nm (215.5lbft) at 2200rpm; unleaded regular grade.

Engine construction: Transverse front engine. Hydraulic tappets; central camshaft (chain); 1 counter-balance shaft; 4 bearing crankshaft; oil capacity 4.3L (4.1US qt); Ford electronic fuel injection. Motorcraft AWSF-44C sparkplugs; 12V 84Ah Battery, 100A alternator; cooling system capacity approx 11.5L (10.9US qt).

Transmission (to all wheels): Automatic "AXOD"; hydraulic torque converter and 4-speed Planetary gear set, selector lever at steering column, final drive ratio 3.37.

Gear ratios: Max torque multiplication in converter 1.9 times, Planetary gear set ratios: 1st 2.77; 2nd 1.54; 3rd 1; 4th 0.69; R 2.26.

Chassis: Integral body; front McPherson struts, lower single control arm, tension struts and antiroll bar, rear independent suspension with transverse and longitudinal trailing arm with antiroll bar; pneumatic spring system with level control system. Servo/power assisted disc brakes, front ventilated, disc diameters, front 25.7cm, rear 25.5cm, ABS, mechanical handbrake to rear wheels; power assisted rack and pinion steering; fuel tank 70L (15.4Gal) [18.5US Gal]; tyres 205/70 R 15, wheel rims 6.5J.

Dimensions: Wheelbase 277cm, track 158/155cm, clearance 15cm, turning circle 12.5m. Load space 19.1cu ft (540dm3). Length 521cm, width 185cm, height 141.5cm.

Performance: Max speed approx 115mph/185kmh, speed at 1000rpm in 4th gear 38.7mph/52.4kmh; power to weight ratio from 15.9kg/kW (11.6kg/PS); consumption approx 11-16L/100km (25.7-17.7mpg) [21.4-14.7US mpg].

Lincoln Continental

Lincoln Town Car

Luxury model from the Ford Motor Company. Autumn 1979: new compact body, small V8 engine, Overdrive–Automatic transmission. Also, since 1982, available as Saloon/Sedan. 1986 with fuel injection and more power. Modifications to body and interior for 1989.

> 4.9 Litre V8
> 112/119kW–150/160hp–152/162PS
> Fuel Injection

Body, Weight (laden): 4–door Saloon/Sedan, 6–seater; approx 1835–1860kg.

Engine data (SAE net): 8–cylinder in V 90deg (101.6 x 76.2mm), 4942cm3; compression ratio 8.9:1; 112kW (150hp) [152PS] at 3200rpm, 22.6kW/L (30.3hp/L) [30.8PS/L]; 366Nm (270.1lbft) at 2000rpm; unleaded regular grade. With twin exhaust: 119kW (160hp) [162PS] at 3400rpm, 24.1kW/L (32.3hp/L) [32.8PS/L]; 380Nm (280.4lbft) at 2200rpm.

Engine construction: Hydraulic tappets; central camshaft (chain); 5 bearing crankshaft; oil capacity 4.7L (4.4US qt); Ford electronic fuel injection. Also available with twin exhausts. Motorcraft AWSF-44C sparkplugs; 12V 72Ah Battery, 65/100A alternator, cooling system capacity approx 13.6L (12.9US qt).

Transmission (to rear wheels): Automatic, "Automatic Overdrive", hydraulic torque converter and 4–speed Planetary gear set, selector lever at steering wheel, final drive ratio 3.08; 3.27; 3.55. Optional limited slip differential.

Gear ratios: Max torque multiplication in converter 2.3 times; Planetary gear set ratios: 2.40; 1.47; 1; 0.67; R 2.

Chassis: Transverse box section frame; front coil springs, upper and lower keystone A–arm; rear rigid axle with coil springs, lower trailing arm, upper semi–trailing arm, telescopic damper, optional level control system. Servo/power assisted brakes, front ventilated discs, rear drums, disc diameter 27.9cm; pedal actuated parking brake to rear wheels; power assisted recirculating ball steering; fuel tank capacity 68L (14.9Gal) [18US Gal]; tyres 215/70 R 15, wheel rims 6/6.5J.

Dimensions: Wheelbase 298cm, track 158/157.5cm. Clearance 14cm, turning circle 13.4m. Load space 19.6cu ft (556.5dm3), width 198.5cm, height 142cm.

Performance: Max speed approx 115mph/185kmh, speed at 1000rpm in 4th gear 38mph/61.2kmh; power to weight ratio from 15.4kg/kW (11.3kg/PS). Consumption (touring) approx 12–20L/100km (23.5– 14.1mpg) [19.6–11.8US mpg].

Lincoln • Lotus

Lincoln Town Car

Lincoln Mark VII

Prestige vehicle from the Ford Motor Company with aerodynamic body, electronically controlled pneumatic suspension and 4.9 Litre V8. New version, the Mark VII, Summer 1983, 1989: detail modifications to body.

```
4.9 Litre V8
168kW–225hp–228PS
Fuel injection
```

Body, Weight: 2–door Coupe, 5–seater; approx 1700kg. Weight reduced by approx 15kg for the "Designer Series".

Engine data (SAE net): 8–cylinder in V 90deg (101.6 x 76.2mm), 4942cm3; compression ratio 9:1; 168kW (225hp) [228PS] at 4200rpm, 34.0kW/L (45.6hp/L) [46.1PS/L]; 407Nm (300.4lbft) at 3200rpm; unleaded regular grade.

Engine construction: Hydraulic tappets, central camshaft (chain); 5 bearing crankshaft; oil capacity 4.7L (4.4US qt); electronic fuel injection; twin exhaust. Motorcraft ASF-42C sparkplugs; 12V 84Ah Battery, 100A alternator; cooling system capacity approx 13.3L (12.6US qt).

Transmission (to rear wheels): Automatic, "Automatic Overdrive"' hydraulic torque converter and 4–speed Planetary gear set, central selector level, final drive ratio 3.08; 3.27; optional limited slip differential.

Gear ratios: Max torque multiplication in converter 2.3 times; Planetary gear set ratios: 2.40; 1.47; 1; 0.67; R 2.

Chassis: Integral body; front lower A arm with elastic bearing tension struts, antiroll bar, shock absorber struts, rear rigid axle with lower trailing arm, upper semi–trailing arm and antiroll bar, electronically controlled pneumatic suspension, telescopic damper. Servo/power assisted disc brakes (front ventilated), disc diameter front 27.7cm, rear 28.6cm, ABS; pedal actuated parking brake to rear wheels; power assisted rack and pinion steering; fuel tank capacity 84L (18.5Gal) [22.2US Gal]; tyres 215/70 R 15, wheel rims 6J, optional tyres 225/60 R 16, wheel rims 7J.

Lincoln Mark VII LSC

Dimensions: Wheelbase 275.5cm, track 148.5/150cm, clearance min 13cm, turning circle approx 12.9m, load space 25.2cu ft (400dm3). Length 515cm, width 180cm, height 138cm.

Performance: Max speed approx 137mph/220kmh, speed at 1000rpm in 4th gear 37.4mph/60.2kmh; power to weight ratio 10.1kg/kW (7.5kg/PS); consumption approx 11–18L/100km (25.7–15.7mpg) [21.4– 13.1US mpg].

LOTUS GB

Lotus Cars Limited, Norwich, Norfolk, NR14 8EZ, England

English manufacturer specialising in the construction of sports vehicles. January 1986: taken over by General Motors.

MODEL RANGE
Esprit – Esprit Turbo – Excel

Lotus Esprit

Sports Coupe with 2.2 Litre Central engine and 4 valves per cylinder. Plastic body by Giugiaro. Launched in October 1975. May 1980: new 2.2 or 2 Litre engine. October 1987: modifications to the body and interior, new transmission and greater power.

Lotus Esprit

```
2.2 Litre
128kW–172hp–174PS
2 2V Carbs
```

Body, Weight: 2–door Coupe with plastic body, 2–seater; kerbweight (DIN) fron 1175kg.

Engine data (DIN): 4–cylinder in–line (95.29 x 76.2mm), 2174cm3; compression ratio 10.9:1; 128kW (172hp) [174PS] at 6500rpm, 58.9kW/L (78.9hp/L) [80.1PS/L]; 221Nm (163lbft) at 5000rpm; leaded premium grade.

Engine construction: Designated Lotus 912 S. Central engine inclined 45deg. Valves in V (4 per cylinder); 2 overhead camshafts (toothed belt); light–alloy cylinder head and block; 5 main bearing crankshaft; oil capacity 5.7L (5.4US qt); 2 horizontal Dell'Orto DHLA 45 2V carbs. 12V 44 or 55Ah Battery, 90A Alternator; cooling system capacity 10.8L (10.2US qt).

Transmission (to rear wheels): 5–speed manual, floor shift, final drive ratio 3.88.

Gear ratios: 1st 3.36; 2nd 2.05; 3rd 1.38; 4th 1.03; 5th 0.82; R 3.15.

Chassis: Plastic body and tubular frame chassis; front upper and lower A–arm, coil springs, coaxial telescopic damper and antiroll bar, rear independent suspension with control arm and coaxial telescopic damper. Servo/power assisted disc brakes (front ventilated), diameter front 25.9cm, rear 27.3cm, mechanical handbrake to rear wheels; rack and pinion steering; fuel tank capacity 67L (14.7Gal) [17.7US Gal]; tyres front 195/60 VR 15, wheel rims 7J, rear 235/60 VR 15, wheel rims 8J.

Dimensions: Wheelbase 244cm, track 152.5/155.5cm, clearance 15cm, turning circle 11.8m, load space 8.1cu ft (230dm3). Length 433cm, width 186cm, height 115cm.

Performance: Max speed 138mph/222kmh (manufacturers test specifications), speed at 1000rpm in 5th gear 23.6mph/38kmh; acceleration 0 – 60mph/97kmh 6.5secs; power to weight ratio 9.2kg/kW (6.8kg/PS); consumption ECE 6.9/8.3/16.1L/100km (40.9/34/17.5mpg) [34.1/28.3/14.6US mpg].

Vehicle based on the Esprit S2 model with 2.2 Litre engine and turbocharger. Launched in February 1980. For 1985: front suspension and modifications to body. October 1987: modifications to body and interior, new transmission. Winter 1988/1989: more power for US version with Catalyst and Injection.

Body, Weight: 2 door Coupe with plastic body, 2–seater; kerbweight (DIN) from 1270kg.

Lotus • Luaz

Lotus Esprit Turbo

2.2 Turbo
160/170kW-215/228hp-218/231PS
2 2V Carbs/Injection

Engine data (DIN): 4-cylinder in-line (95.29 x 76.2mm), 2174cm3; compression ratio 8:1; 160kW (215hp) [218PS] at 6000rpm, 73.6kW/L (98.6hp/L) [100.3PS/L]; 298Nm (219.9lbft) at 4250rpm; leaded regular/premium grade.
USA Version (with Catalyst and fuel injection): 170kW (228hp) [231PS] at 6250rpm; 296Nm (218.4) at 5000rpm.

Engine construction: Designated Lotus 910 S. Central engine inclined 45deg. Overhead valves (4 per cylinder); 2 overhead camshafts (toothed belt); light-alloy cylinder head and block, 5 bearing crankshaft; oil capacity 5.7L (5.4US qt); 2 Dell'Orto DHLA 45M horizontal 2V carbs. Bosch KE Jetronic fuel injection. Garrett TBO3 exhaust turbo charger, boost pressure 0.66bar. 12V 44 or 55Ah Battery; 90A alternator; cooling system capacity 12L (11.4US qt).

Transmission (to rear wheels): 5-speed manual, final drive ratio 3.88.

Gear ratios: 1st 2.36; 2nd 2.05; 3rd 1.38; 4th 1.03; 5th 0.82; R 3.15.

Chassis: Plastic body and tubular frame chassis; front upper and lower A arm, coil springs, coaxial telescopic damper and antiroll bar, rear independent suspension with control arm and longitudinal strut, coil springs and coaxial telescopic damper. Servo/power assisted disc brakes (front ventilated), diameter front 25.9cm, rear 27.3cm, mechanical handbrake to rear wheels; rack and pinion steering; fuel tank capacity 79/86L (17.4/18.9Gal) [20.9/22.7US Gal]; tyres front 195/60 VR 15, wheel rims 7J, rear 235/60 VR 15, wheel rims 8J.

Dimensions: Wheelbase 244cm, track 152.5/155.5cm, clearance 15cm, turning circle 11.8m, load space 7.1cu ft (200dm3). Length 433cm, width 186cm, height 115cm.

Performance: Max speed 152/155mph/245/250kmh (manufacturers test specifications), speed at 1000rpm in 5th gear 23.6mph/38kmh; acceleration 0–60mph/97kmh 5.3secs, standing km 26.1secs; power to weight ratio from 7.9kg/kW (5.8kg/PS); consumption (ECE) 8.3/10.6/17.2L/100km (34/26.6/16.4mpg) [28.3/22.2/13.7US mpg].

Lotus Esprit Turbo

Lotus Excel

Excel – Excel SE – Excel SA

4-seater, high performance Coupe; plastic body 2.2 Litre engine with 4 valves per cylinder. Launched as the Elite in May 1974, as the Eclat in October 1974. May 1980: available with 2.2 Litre engine, October 1985: SE with 180hp. October 1986: SA with ZF Automatic. Autumn 1988: modifications to body.

2.2 Litre
116kW-160hp-162PS
2 2V Carbs

Engine for Excel

Body, Weight: 2 door Coupe, 2+2-seater; kerbweight (DIN) 1135kg. Heavier by 34kg with air conditioning.

Engine data (DIN): 4-cylinder in-line (95.29 x 76.2mm), 2174cm3; compression ratio 9.4:1; 119kW (160hp) [162PS] at 6500rpm, 54.7kW/L (73.3hp/L) [74.5PS/L]; 217Nm (160.1lbft) at 5000rpm; leaded premium grade.

Engine construction: Designated Lotus 912. Front engine, inclined 45deg. Valves in V (4 per cylinder); 2 overhead camshafts (toothed belt); light-alloy cylinder head and block, 5 bearing crankshaft; oil capacity 5.7L (5.4US qt); 2 Dell'Orto DHLA 45 E horizontal 2V carbs. 12V 55Ah Battery, optional 60Ah alternator 70A; cooling system capacity 8.5L (8US qt).

Transmission: 5-speed manual, floor shift; final drive ratio 4.1 or 3.73.

Gear ratios: 1st 3.29; 2nd 1.89; 3rd 1.23; 4th 1; 5th 0.78.

Chassis: Plastic body; front and rear cradle zinc central support chassis; front upper A arm and lower single control arm, coil springs, telescopic damper and antiroll bar, rear independent suspension with control arm and torsion strut, coil springs and telescopic dampers. Servo/power assisted disc brakes (ventilated), diameter front 25.8cm and rear 26.6cm; mechanical handbrake to rear wheels; power assisted rack and pinion steering; fuel tank capacity 67L (14.7Gal) [17.7US Gal]; tyres 205/60 VR 14, optional 215/50 VR 14, wheel rims 7J.

Dimensions: Wheelbase 248.5cm, track 146/146cm, clearance 12.5cm, turning circle 10.5m. Load space 13.1cu ft (370dm3). Length 437.5cm, width 181.5cm, height 120.5cm.

Performance: Max speed 134mph/216kmh (manufacturers test specifications), speed at 1000rpm in 5th gear 21.1mph/34.1kmh; acceleration 0–60mph/97kmh 7secs; power to weight ratio from 9.5kg/kW (7.0kg/PS); consumption ECE 7.8/9.6/14.1L/100km (36.2/29.4/20mpg) [30.2/24.5/16.7US mpg].

Lotus Excel

2.2 Litre
134.5kW-180hp-183PS
2 2V Carbs

Engine for Excel SE, and SA

As 2.2 Litre, 160hp, except:

Engine data (DIN): 4-cylinder in-line (95.29 x 76.2mm), 2174cm3; compression ratio 10.9:1; 134.5kW (180hp) [183PS] at 6500rpm, 61.9kW/L (82.9hp/L) [84.2PS/L]; 232Nm (171.1lbft) at 5000rpm.

Engine construction: Designated 912S. 2 Dell'Orto DHLA 45D horizontal 2V carbs.

Transmission: a) 5-speed manual, final drive ratio 4.1.
b) ZF Automatic 4 HP-22, hydraulic torque converter and 4-speed Planetary gear set, central selector lever, final drive ratio 3.727.

Gear ratios: a) 5-speed manual: 1st 3.29; 2nd 1.89; 3rd 1.23; 4th 1; 5th 0.78.
b) Automatic: Max torque multiplication 2 times, Planetary gear set ratios: 1st 2.73; 2nd 1.56; 3rd 1; 4th 0.73; R 2.09.

Chassis: Tyres 215/50 VR/ZR 15, wheel rims 7J.

Performance: Max speed 135mph/217kmh, automatic 130mph/209kmh (manufacturers test specifications), speed at 1000rpm in 5th gear 21.2mph/34.1kmh; acceleration 0–60mph/97kmh 6.8secs, automatic 8.6secs; power to weight ratio from 8.4kg/kW (6.2kg/PS); consumption ECE 6.7/8.6/14.3L/100km (42.2/32.8/19.8mpg) [35.1/27.4/16.4US mpg]. Automatic 7.6/9.0/14.6L/100km (35.8/31.4/19.3mpg) [30.9/26.1/16.1US mpg].

LUAZ   USSR

Russian car factory in Loutsk, Ukraine.

Luaz 4 x 4

Small 5-seater all terrain model with air conditioner, Zaz 968A V4 engine. Known in some countries as the "Volin 969" with Ford engine.

Body, Weight: 2-door Roadster, 4/5-seater; kerbweight (DIN) 950–980kg, gross vehicle weight 1350/1380kg.

Engine data (DIN): 4-cylinder in V 90deg (76 x 66mm), 1196cm3; compression ratio 7.2:1; 29.5kW (39.5hp) [40PS] at 4400rpm, 24.7kW/L (33.1hp/L) [33.4PS/L]; 75Nm (55.3lbft) at 2800rpm; leaded regular grade.

Luaz • Mahindra • Maserati

```
1196cm3
29.5kW-39.5hp-40PS
1 Carb
```

"Powered by Ford": 4-cylinder in-line (74 x 65mm), 1118cm3; compression ratio 9.5:1; 37kW (49hp) [50PS] at 5000rpm, 33.1kW/L (44.4hp/L) [44.7PS/L]; 83Nm (61.3lbft) at 2700rpm.

Engine construction: Overhead valves, central camshaft (toothed belt); light-alloy cylinder heads; 3 bearing crankshaft; centrifugal oil filter, oil capacity 3.3/3.75L (3.1/3.5US qt); 1 downdraught carb (K-127), oil bath air filter. A 6 US or Isolator M14-260 spark plugs; 12V 42/55Ah Battery, 30A alternator; air cooler with axial blower.

Transmission (to all wheels): 4-speed manual (without direct drive), rear wheel drive with engageable four wheel drive; final drive ratio 5.338.

Gear ratios: 1st 3.8; 2nd 2.12; 3rd 1.41; 4th 0.964; R 4.165.

Chassis: Independent suspension, front and rear with trailing arms and torsion bar spring, telescopic damper. Servo/power assisted drum brakes, mechanical handbrake to rear wheels; fuel tank capacity 34L (7.5Gal) [9US Gal]; tyres 5.90-13.

Dimensions: Wheelbase 180cm, track 132.5/132cm, clearance 28cm, turning circle 11m. Length 337/339cm, width 161-164cm, height 177/179cm.

Performance: Max speed 59-68mph/ 95-110kmh (manufacturers test specifications); power to weight ratio from 32.2kg/kW (23.8kg/PS); consumption approx 10-15L/100km (28.2-18.8mpg) [23.5-15.7US mpg].

Luaz 4x4

MAHINDRA   IND

Mahindra CJ

Construction of the licenced Jeep CJ-38, with Peugot diesel engine, two distinct wheelbases. Incomplete data.

```
2.1 Litre Diesel
55kW-74hp-75PS
Injection Pump
```

Body, Weight: 3-door, 4-seater; kerbweight (DIN) from 1300kg, gross vehicle weight 2010kg.

Engine data (SAE net): 4-cylinder in-line (90 x 83mm), 2112cm3; compression ratio 22.2:1; 55kW (74hp) [75PS] at 4500rpm, 26kW/L (34.8hp/L) [35.5PS/L]; 121Nm (89.3hp/L) at 2000rpm.

Engine construction: Designated Peugeot XDPG 4.90. Swirl chamber turbulence diesel engine; side camshaft; light-alloy cylinder head; 5 bearing crankshaft; oil capacity 5L (4.7US qt); injection pump. 12 V 90Ah, 25A alternator; cooling system capacity approx 12L (11.4US qt).

Transmission (to rear wheels or all wheels): Engageable front wheel drive, low range (2.46); 4-speed Planetary gear set, final drive ratio 4.89; 5.38.

Gear ratios: 1st 3.99; 2nd 2.37; 3rd 1.47; 4th 1; R 5.35.

Chassis: Box type frame with cross member; front and rear stabiliser with leaf springs, telescopic damper. Servo/power assisted brakes, front and rear drums; parking brakes to rear wheels; worm and wheel gear steering; fuel tank 40L (8.8Gal) [10.6US], optional 45L (9.9Gal) [11.9US Gal]; tyres 215/75 R 15 or 235/75 R 15, wheel rims 7J.

Dimensions: Wheelbase 203/231cm, track 125/125cm, clearance 21cm, length 340/375cm, width 158cm, height approx 180cm.

Performance: Max speed approx 62-65mph/100-105kmh; power to weight ratio from 23.6kg/kW (17.3kg/PS); consumption approx 8-14L/100km (35.3-20.2mpg) [29.4-16.8US mpg].

Mahindra CJ 4D

MASERATI   I

Officine A Maserati SpA, Viale Ciro Menotti 322, 41100 Modena, Italy
Famous Italian manufacturer for sporty top-performance cars
MODEL RANGE
Biturbo – 228 – Royale

Maserati Biturbo

Sports car with rear wheel drive, V6 engine with 2 exhaust turbochargers, 5-speed or automatic transmission, all-round independent suspension. Introduced as 2 Litre model in December 1981. Autumn 1983 with 2.5 Litre V6 engine. December 1983 as four-door saloon/sedan (425). 1984 Turin Motor Show: Spyder model with 2 Litre engine. Winter 1985/6: 4-door saloon/sedan 420/420 S. December 1987: 430 with 2.8 Litre V6 engine. Geneva 1988: Karif.

```
2 Litre V6 Turbo
164/180kW-220/241hp-223/245PS
Fuel Injection
```

Engine for Coupe 222, Saloon/Sedan 422, Spyder as well as Coupe 2.24V.

Body, Weight: 2-door Coupe, 5-seats; kerbweight (DIN) 1175-1260kg, gross vehicle weight approx 1730kg; 4-door Saloon/Sedan, 5-seats; kerbweight (DIN) 1180-1275kg, gross vehicle weight approx 1730kg. Spyder Cabriolet, 2-door, 2+2-seater; kerbweight (DIN) from about 1100kg. Karif Coupe with 2.8 V6, 2-door, 2 seater; kerbweight (DIN) from 1280kg.

Maserati Biturbo Spyder

Maserati

Engine data (DIN): 6-cylinder in 90deg V (82 x 63mm), 1996cm3; compression ratio 7.8:1; 164kW (220hp) [223PS] at 6250rpm, 82.2kW/L (110.1hp/L) [111.8PS/L]; 262Nm (193.4lbft) at 3500rpm; leaded premium grade.
2.24V (4 valves per cylinder, total 24): 180kW (241hp) [245PS] at 6200rpm, 90.1kW/L (120.7hp/L) [122.6PS/L]; 296Nm (218.4lbft) at 5000rpm.

Maserati Biturbo 2.24V

Engine construction: Biturbo designation. 3 also 4 valves per cylinder, 2x1 overhead camshafts (toothed belt); light-alloy cylinder head and cylinder block, wet nicasil-cylinder liners; 4 bearing crankshaft; oil capacity 7L (6.6US qt); 1 electronic fuel injection. 2 IHI exhaust turbochargers; boost pressure 0.5bar, charge-air cooler. Battery 12V 60Ah, alternator 65A; cooling system capacity 12L (11.4US qt).

Transmission (to rear wheels): a) 5-speed manual, final drive ratio 3.73.
b) ZF-automatic 3 HP-22, hydraulic torque converter and 3-speed Planetary gear set, central selector lever; final drive ratio 3.31. Optional Torsen limited slip differential.

Gear ratios: a) 5-speed manual; 1st 3.42; 2nd 2.08/1.94; 3rd 1.39; 4th 1; 5th 0.87/0.79; R 3.66.
b) Automatic ZF 3 HP-22, max torque multiplication in converter 2.28 times, Planetary gear set ratios; 1st 2.478; 2nd 1.478. 3rd 1; R 2.09.

Chassis: Integral body with front McPherson struts, lower control arms with tension struts and antiroll bar, rear independent suspension with semi-trailing arms, optional antiroll, front and rear coil springs and telescopic dampers. Servo/power assisted disc brakes; mechanical handbrake to the rear wheels; rack and pinion steering, optional power assisted; fuel tank 80/82L (17.6/18Gal) [21.1/21.7US Gal]; tyres 205/55 VR 14 or 205/55 VR 15, wheels 6.5 or 7J.

Maserati Biturbo Coupe

Dimensions: Wheelbase 251.5cm, track 144/145cm, 7 J 146/145.5cm, clearance 12.5cm, turning circle 11.7m, load space 14.1cu ft (400dm3). Length 415.5/419cm, width 171.5cm, height 130.5/125.5cm.
422: Wheelbase 260cm, load space 19.4cu ft (550dm3). Length 440cm, width 173cm, height 131cm. Spyder: Wheelbase 240cm, load space 19.4cu ft (550dm3). Length 404cm, width 171.5cm, height 130.5cm.
Spyder and Karif: Wheelbase 240cm, length 404cm, width 171cm, height 131cm.

Performance: Max speed over 140mph/225kmh, 2.24V 143mph/230kmh (manufacturers test specifications), speed at 1000rpm in 5th gear 20.8–22.9mph/33.4–36.8kmh; acceleration 0 – 62mph/100kmh 6.2/5.9secs, standing km 26.3/26.1secs; power to weight ratio from 6.5kg/kW (4.8kg/PS); fuel consumption approx 9– 17L/100km (31.4–16.6mpg) [26.1–13.8US mpg].

```
2.5 Litre V6 Turbo
138kW–185hp–188PS
Fuel injection
```

Engine for Coupe, Spyder and 425
As 2 Litre V6 Turbo model, except:

Engine data (DIN) (Catalyst): 6-cylinder in V 90deg (91.6 x 63mm), 2491cm3; compression ratio 7.8:1; 138kW (185hp) [188PS] at 5000rpm, 55.4kW/L (74.2hp/L) [75.5PS/L]; 321Nm (236.9lbft) at 3000rpm.

Transmission: a) 5-speed manual; final drive ratio 3.31 or 3.73.
b) Automatic; final drive ratio 3.31.

Performance: Max speed over 134mph/215kmh, catalyst 131mph/210kmh (manufacturers specifications), speed at 1000rpm in 5th gear 23.4–25.8mph/37.7–41.5kmh; acceleration from 0 – 62mph/100kmh 6.9secs, standing km 28.8secs; power to weight ratio 8kg/kW (5.9kg/PS); fuel consumption approx 11–18L/100km (25.7–15.7mph) [21.4–13.1US mpg].

Maserati Biturbo 430

```
2.8 Litre V6 Turbo
184/180kW–247/241hp–250/245PS
Fuel Injection
```

Engine for 430, Karif and Spyder
As 2 Litre V6 Turbo model, except:

Engine data (DIN): 6-cylinder in V 90deg (94 x 67mm), 2790cm3; compression ratio 7.8:1; 184kW (247hp) [250PS] at 5600rpm, 66.0kW/L (88.4hp/L) [89.6PS/L]; 385Nm (284.1lbft) at 3600rpm.
Or: 180kW (241hp) [245PS] also 210kW (281hp) [285PS].
With Catalyst: Compression ratio 7.4:1; 165kW (221hp) [225PS] at 5500rpm, 59.1kW/L (79.2hp/L) [89.6PS/L]; 370Nm (273lbft) at 3500rpm.

Transmission: a) 5-speed manual, final drive ratio 3.31.
b) ZF automatic with overdrive hydraulic torque converter and Planetary gear set, central selector lever; final drive ratio 3.31. Sensitork limited slip differential.

Gear ratios: a) 5-speed manual; 1st 3.42; 2nd 1.94; 3rd 1.39; 4th 1; 5th 0.79; R 3.66.
b) Automatic, max torque multiplication approx 2.28times, Planetary gear set: 1st 2.478; 2nd 1.478; 3rd 1; 4th 0.73; R 2.09.

Chassis: Front ventilated disc brakes; tyres 205/55 VR 15, wheels 6.5J.

Performance: Max speed 149mph/240kmh (manufacturers test specifications), speed at 1000rpm in 5th gear 23–25.5mph/37– 41kmh; acceleration 0 – 62mph/100kmh 5.7secs, standing km 27.5 secs; power to weight ratio from 6.5kg/kW (4.8kg/PS); fuel consumption approx 10–18L/100km (28.2–15.7mpg) [23.5–13.1].

Maserati 228

Luxury sports Coupe with 2.8 Litre V6 engine and 2 exhaust turbochargers; 5-speed manual or 4-speed automatic transmission; all-round independent suspension. Debut December 1984. Fuel injection at end of 1986.

```
2.8 Litre V6 Turbo
184kW–247hp–250PS
Fuel Injection
```

Body, Weight: 2-door Coupe, 5-seats; kerbweight (DIN) 1240kg, gross vehicle weight 1800kg.

Engine data (DIN): 6-cylinder in 90deg V (94 x 67mm), 2790cm3; compression ratio 7.7:1; 184kW (247hp) [250PS] at 6000rpm, 66kW/L (88.4hp/L) [89.6PS/L]; 373Nm (275.3lbft) at 3500rpm; leaded premium grade.
Or: 180kW (241hp) [245PS].
With Catalyst: Compression ratio 7.4:1; 165kW (221hp) [225PS] at 5500rpm, 59.1kW/L (79.2hp/L) [89.6PS/L]; 370Nm (273.1lbft) at 3500rpm.

Maserati • Mazda

Maserati 228

Engine construction: Biturbo designation. 3 valves per cylinder, 2x1 overhead camshafts (toothed belt); light–alloy cylinder head and block, wet cylinder liners; 4 bearing crankshaft; oil capacity 7L (6.6US qt); electronic fuel injection; 2 IHI exhaust turbochargers, boost pressure approx 0.5bar. Battery 12V 60Ah, alternator 65A; cooling system capacity 12L (11.4US qt).

Transmission (to rear wheels): a) 5–speed manual, final drive ratio 3.31. b) ZF–automatic with overdrive, hydraulic torque converter and Planetary gear set, central selector lever; final drive ratio 3.31. Sensitork limited slip differential.

Gear ratios: a) 5–speed manual; 1st 3.42; 2nd 1.94; 3rd 1.39; 4th 1; 5th 0.79; R 3.66. b) Automatic; max torque multiplication in converter 2.28 times, Planetary gear set ratios; 1st 2.478; 2nd 1.478; 3rd 1; 4th 0.73; R 209.

Chassis: Integral body; front McPherson struts, lower control arm with tension struts and antiroll bar, rear independent suspension with semi–trailing arms, front and rear coil springs and telescopic dampers. Servo/power assisted disc brakes, (front ventilated), handbrake to rear wheels; power assisted rack and pinion steering; fuel tank 82L (18Gal) [21.7US Gal]; tyres 225/50 VR 15, wheels 7J.

Dimensions: Wheelbase 260cm, track 154/155cm, minimum clearance 13.5cm, turning circle 11.7cm. Load space 18.7cu ft (530dm3). Length 446cm, width 186.5cm, height 133cm.

Performance: Max speed over 146mph/235kmh (manufacturers test specifications), speed at 1000rpm in 5th gear 26.4mph/42.4kmh, acceleration 0 – 62mph/100kmh 5.8secs, standing km 26.3secs; power to weight ratio 6.7kg/kW (5.0kg/PS); fuel consumption 10– 19L/100km (28.2–14.9mpg) [23.5–21.4US mpg].

Maserati Royale

Maserati Royale

Luxury saloon/sedan with light–alloy V8–engine, 5–speed manual or automatic transmission. Debut at Turin in 1976. Only available with 4.9 Litre engine since 1985. For 1987: Royale with luxury fittings and increased power.

4.9 Litre V8
220.5/206kW–295.5/276hp–300/280PS
4 2V Carbs

Body, Weight: 4–door Saloon/Sedan, 4/5–seats; kerbweight (DIN) 1940–1990kg.

Engine data (DIN): 8–cylinder in 90deg V (93.9 x 89mm), 4930cm3; compression ratio 9.5:1; 220.5kW (296hp) [300PS] at 5600rpm, 44.7kW/L (59.9hp/L) [60.9PS/L]; 402Nm (296.7lbft) at 3000rpm; leaded premium grade.
Some countries: Compression ratio 8.5:1; 206kW (276hp) [280PS]; 392Nm (289.3lbft).

Engine construction: Designated 107.22.49. Overhead valves (in 30deg V), 2x2 overhead camshafts (chain); light–alloy cylinder head and bock, wet cylinder liners; 5 bearing crankshaft; oil capacity 9L (8.5US qt); 4 downdraught Weber 2V carbs 42 DCNF 6, 2 electronic fuel pumps. Battery 12V 75Ah, alternator 90A; cooling system capacity 16L (15.1US qt).

Transmission: a) 5–speed ZF manual, final drive ratio 3.54 or 3.31. b) Automatic, hydraulic torque converter and 3–speed Planetary gear set, central selector lever; final drive ratio 3.07 or 3.54. Sensitork limited slip differential.

Gear ratios: a) 5–speed manual; 1st 2.99; 2nd 1.90; 3rd 1.32; 4th 1; 5th 0.89; R 2.7. b) Automatic; max torque multiplication in converter 2.75 times, Planetary gear set ratios; 1st 2.4; 2nd 1.4; 3rd ; R 2.2.

Chassis: Integral body, front and rear independent suspension; front A–arms and coil springs, rear control and longitudinal arms, semi–rigid axle, coil springs, front and optional rear antiroll bars and telescopic dampers. Servo/power assisted disc brakes (ventilated), disc diameter, front 28.4cm, rear 28.2cm, mechanical handbrake on rear wheels; power assisted rack and pinion steering; fuel tank 100L (22Gal) [26.4US Gal] including 10L (2.2Gal) [2.6US Gal] reserve; tyres 215/70 VR 15 or 225/70 VR 15, wheels 7 or 7.5".

Dimensions: Wheelbase 280cm, track 152.5/152.5cm, minimum clearance 12.5cm, turning circle 12.5m. Load space 21.2cu ft (600dm3). Length 491–507cm, width 189cm, height 138.5cm.

Performance: Max speed 149mph/240kmh, automatic 143mph/230kmh (manufacturers test specifications), speed at 1000rpm in 5th gear (215/70 VR 15) 26.1mph/42.0kmh; acceleration 0 – 62mph/100kmh (automatic) 6.5secs, standing km 30secs; power to weight ratio from 8.6kg/kW (6.5kg/PS); consumption (CUNA) 12.9L/100km (21.9mpg) [18.2US mpg], touring 18–20L/100km (15.7–14.1mpg) [13.1–11.8US mpg].

MAZDA J

Toyo Kogyo Co. Ltd, 6047 Fuchu–Machi, Agi–gun, Hiroshima, Japan

Car brand name of a large Japanese commercial vehicle manufacturer. Wankel engine licensee.

MODEL RANGE
121 – 323 (Familia) – 626 (Capella) – Cosmo/929 (Luce) – RX–7 (Savanna)

Mazda 121

Three–door minicar measuring 3.6m in length. Front wheel drive and transverse mounted four cylinder 1.1/1.3 Litre engines. Mazda concept, built in Korea (at Kia) and in Japan (at Mazda). Sold under the name of Ford Festiva in the USA and Japan. Exported as the Mazda 121. Debut at the 1985 Tokyo Motor Show. Production start–up in Spring 1986. Will also be available in Europe in 1988.

Mazda 121

1.1 Litre
38kW–51hp–52PS
1 2V Carb

Body, Weight: 3–door Saloon/Sedan, 4–seater; kerbweight (DIN) from 700kg.

Engine data (JIS net): 4–cylinder in–line (68x78.4mm), 1138cm3; compression ratio 10:1; 38kW (51hp) [52PS] at 5500rpm; 33.4kW/L (44.8hp/L) [45.7PS/L]; 86Nm (63.4lbft) at 3500rpm.
Export version (DIN): Compression ratio 9.4:1; 41kW (55hp) [56PS] at 5800rpm; 88Nm (64.9lbft) at 3600rpm; leaded regular grade.

Mazda

Engine construction: B 1 designation. Transverse mounted front engine. Valves in V; 1 overhead camsahft (toothed belt);light–alloy cylinder head; crankshaft with 5 bearings; oil 3.4L (3.2US qt); 1 downdraught 2V electronically controlled carb. Battery 12V 50Ah, alternator 45A, cooling system capacity 5L (4.7US qt).

Transmission (to front wheels): a) 4–speed manual, final drive ratio 3.777 or 4.375.
b) 5–speed manual, final drive ratio 4.375.

Gear ratios: a) 4–speed manual; 1st 3.454; 2nd 1.789; 3rd 1.093; 4th 0.810; R 3.583. Or 1st 3.454; 2nd 1.944; 3rd 1.275; 4th 0.861; R 3.583.
b) 5–speed manual; 1st 3.454; 2nd 1.944; 3rd 1.275; 4th 0.861; 5th 0.692; R 3.583.

Chassis: Integral body; front McPherson struts with lower control arms and antiroll bar, rear torsion crank axle (longitudinal arms, axle tube) with coil springs, telescopic dampers. Servo/power assisted brakes, front discs, rear drums, disc diameter 21.9cm, mechanical handbrake to rear wheels; rack and pinion steering; fuel tank 38L (8.4Gal) [10US Gal]; tyres 5.95 12, 145 SR 12, optional 165/70 SR 13, wheels 4, optional 4.5J.

Dimensions: Wheelbase 229.5cm, track 140/138.5cm, clearance 16-18cm, turning circle approx 9m. Load space (SAE) 6.7cu ft (190dm3). Length 347.5cm, width 160.5cm, height 145–146cm, Convertible–Saloon/Sedan 150.5-151.5cm.

Performance: Max speed 93mph/150kmh (manufacturers test specifications), speed at 1000rpm in 4th gear (0.810, axle 3.777) 20.1mph/32.4kmh; acceleration 0 – 62mph/100kmh 13.6secs; power to weight ratio from 17.4kg/kW (12.8kg/PS); consumption 5–9L/100km (56.5–31.4mpg) [47–26.1US mpg].

```
1.3 Litre
47kW–63hp–64PS
1 2V Carb
```

As 1.1 Litre model, except:
Weight: Kerbweight (DIN) 730–785kg, USA 775–795kg.
Engine data (JIS net): 4–cylinder in–line (71x83.6mm), 1323cm3; compression ratio 9.7:1; 47kW (63hp) [64PS] at 5500rpm, 35.5kW/L (47.6hp/L) [48.4PS/L]; 102Nm (75.2lbft) at 3500rpm.
With Catalyst (DIN): 40kW (54hp) [55PS] at 5000rpm; 98Nm (72.3lbft) at 3500rpm.
Export version (DIN): Compression ratio 9.4:1; 49kW (65.5hp) [66PS] at 5600rpm; 103Nm (76lbft) at 3600rpm.
USA version (SAE net): compression ratio 9:1; 43kW (57.5hp) [58PS] at 5000rpm; 99Nm (73lbft) at 3500rpm.

Engine construction: B 3 designation.
Transmission: a) 4–speed manual, final drive ratio 3.777.
b) 5–speed manual, final drive ratio 3.777 or 4.058.
c) Automatic, hydraulic torque converter and 3–speed Planetary gear set, final drive ratio 3.450.

Gear ratios: a) 4–speed manual: 1st 3.454; 2nd 1.944; 3rd 1.275; 4th 0.861; R 3.583.
b) 5–speed manual: 1st 3.454; 2nd 1.944; 3rd 1.275; 4th 0.861 or 0.914; 5th 0.692 or 0.763; R 3.583.
c) Automatic: Max torque multiplication in converter 2 times, Planetary gear set ratios: 1st 2.841; 2nd 1.541; 3rd 1; R 2.400.

Chassis: Tyres 145 SR 12, 165/70 SR 12 or 165/70 SR 13, tyres 4 or 4.5J.
Dimensions: Length 357cm.
Performance: Max speed 93mph/150kmh (manufacturers test specifications), speed at 1000rpm in 5th gear (0.692, axle 4.058) 22mph/35.4kmh; acceleration 0 – 62mph/100kmh 11.6secs; power to weight ratio from 15.5 kg/kW (11.4kg/PS) fuel consumption ECE 5.5/8.1/8.0L/100km (51.4/34.9/35.3mpg) [42.8/29.0/29.4US mpg].

```
1.3 Litre 16V
65kW–87hp–88PS
Fuel Injection
```

As 1.1 Litre model, except:
Weight: Kerbweight (DIN) 770–800kg.
Engine data (JIS net): 4–cylinder in–line (78x67.5mm), 1290cm3; compression ratio 9.4:1; 65kW (87hp) [88PS] at 7000rpm, 50.4kW/L (67.5hp/L) [68.2PS/L]; 98Nm (72.3lbft) at 4500rpm.
Engine construction: B J designation. 4 valves per cylinder, hydraulic tappets; 2 overhead camshafts (toothed belt); oil capacity 3.6L (3.4US qt), oil cooler; electronic fuel injection (Bosch L-Jetronic licence).
Transmission: 5–speed manual, final drive ratio 4.058.
Gear ratios: 1st 3.454; 2nd 1.944; 3rd 1.392; 4th 1.030; 5th 0.810; R 3.583.
Chassis: Front and rear antiroll bars; front ventilated disc brakes; tyres 165/70 SR 12 or 175/60 HR 13, wheels 4.5 or 5J.

Dimensions: Length 358cm, width 161.5cm.
Performance: Max speed approx 109mph/175kmh, speed at 1000rpm in 5th gear (175/60 HR 13)) 18.6mph/30.0kmh; power weight ratio frorm 11.8kg/kW (8.8kg/PS;); consumption approx 7–10L/100km (40.4– 28.2mpg) [33.6–23.5US mpg].

Mazda 323 (Familia) – Etude

Middle class model with front wheel drive, tail gate, 3 or 5-doors or notchback. June 1980 debut. Also sold in Japan and Australia as the Ford Laser and Meteor and in the USA as the Mercury Tracer. January 1985: new body. October 1985: also with permanent four wheel drive; 1.6 Litre DOHC 16 valve turbo–engine. January 1987: Coupe Etude based on the 323. February 1987: face lift, new engines.

Mazda 323/Familia

```
1300
49kW–66hp–67PS
1 2V Carb/Fuel Injection
```

Not available for 4WD model
Body, Weight: 3–door Saloon/Sedan, 5–seater; kerbweight (DIN) from 830kg. 5–door Saloon/Sedan, 5–seater; kerbweight (DIN) from 850kg. 4–door Saloon/Sedan, 5–seater; kerbweight (DIN) from 850kg. 5–door Estate/Station Wagon, 5–seater; kerbweight (DIN) from 890kg.
Engine data (JIS net): 4–cylinder in–line (71x83.6mm), 1323cm3; compression ratio 9.7:1; 49kW (66hp) [67PS] at 5500rpm, 37kW/L (49.6hp/L) [50.6PS/L]; 102Nm (75.2lbft) at 3500rpm.
With Catalyst (fuel injection, DIN): 49kW (66hp) [67PS] at 5000rpm; 100Nm (73.8lbft) at 3500rpm; unleaded fuel.
Without Catalyst (DIN): Compression ratio 9.4:1 50kW (67hp) [68PS] at 5800rpm; 105Nm (77.4lbft) at 3600rpm; or also: 44kW (59hp) [60PS]; 94Nm (69.3lbft).
For some countries (DIN): (77x69.4mm), 1296cm3; compression ratio 9.2:1; 50kW (67hp) [68PS] at 5800rpm; 95Nm (70.1lbft) at 3800rpm; or: (70x69.5mm), 1071cm3; 39kW (53hp) [54PS] at 5800rpm; 79Nm (58.3lbft) at 3600rpm.

Engine construction: B 3 designation. Transverse mounted front engine. Valves in V, hydraulic tappets, overhead camshaft (toothed belt); light–alloy cylinder head; crankshaft with 5 bearings, oil capacity 3.4L (3.2US qt); 1 downdraught 2V carb, catalyst version electronic fuel injection (Bosch L-Jetronic licence). Battery 12V 33-50Ah, alternator 50-60A; cooling system capacity 5L (4.7US qt), automatic 6L (5.7US qt).

Transmission (to front wheels): a) 4–speed manual, final drive ratio 4.105; 3.850.
b) 5–speed manual, final drive ratio 4.105; 3.850.
c) Automatic, hydraulic torque converter and 3–speed Planetary gear set, final drive ratio 3.941; 3.631.

Gear ratios: a) 4–speed manual: 1st 3.416; 2nd 1.842; 3rd 1.29; 4th 0.918; R 3.214.
b) 5–speed manual: 1st 3.416; 2nd 1.842; 3rd 1.29; 4th 0.918; 5th 0.731 or 0.775; R 3.214.
c) Automatic: Max torque multiplication in converter 2 times; Planetary gear set ratios: 1st 2.841; 2nd 1.541; 3rd 1; R 2.4.

Chassis: Integral body; all–round independent suspension; front MacPherson struts with lower A arms, some models with antiroll bars, rear coil springs, longitudinal double control arms, cornering stabilisers, telescopic dampers. Servo/power assisted brakes, front discs (ventilated), rear drums, mechanical handbrake to rear wheels; rack and pinion steering (optional power assisted); fuel tank 48L (10.5Gal) [12.7US Gal], Japan 45L (9.9Gal) [11.9US Gal]; tyres 6.15 13 or 155 SR 13, optional 175/70 SR 13, wheels 4.5 or 5J.

Mazda

Dimensions: Wheelbase 240cm, track 139/141.5cm, turning circle 9.4cm, load space 3/5-door 11.1-19.2cu ft (315-543dm3), 4-door 15.2cu ft (431dm3), Estate/Station Wagon 27cu ft (764dm3). Hatchback length 399cm, 4-door Saloon/Sedan 419.5cm, Estate/Station Wagon 422.5cm, width 164.5cm, height 139cm, Estate/Station Wagon 143cm.

Performance: (Catalyst version) Max speed approx 99.5mph/160kmh (manufacturers test specifications), speed at 1000rpm in 5th gear (4.105:1) 21.9mph/35.3kmh; power to weight ratio from 16.9kg/kW (12.4kg/PS); fuel consumption (urban/off-road/combination) 7.3/5.3/6.5L/100km (38.7/53.3/43.5mpg) [32.2/44.4/36.2US mpg].

```
1500
56kW-75hp-76PS
1 2V Carb
```

As 1300 model, except:

Weight: Excess weight approx 20-30kg, with 4WD from 980kg.

Engine data (JIS net): 4-cylinder in-line (78x78.4mm), 1498cm3; compression ratio 9.5:1; 56kW (75hp) [76PS] at 6000rpm, 37.4kW/L (50.1hp/L) [50.7PS/L]; 112Nm (82.6lbft) at 3500rpm.
European version (DIN); compression ratio 9.1:1; 55kW (74hp) [75PS] at 5700rpm; 115Nm (84.8lbft) at 3200rpm.
Or: 54kW (72hp) [73PS] at 5500rpm; 113Nm (83.3lbft) at 3200rpm.
For some countries (DIN): (77x80mm), 1490cm3; compression ratio 9:1; 55kW (74hp) [75PS] at 5500rpm; 115Nm (84.8lbft) at 3500rpm.

Engine construction: B 5 designation.

Transmission (to front or all wheels): a) 5-speed manual, final drive ratio 4.105; 3.850.
b) Automatic, final drive ratio 3.850 or 3.631.
For 4WD: Permanent all-wheel-drive, central Planetary differential (50/50 per cent split), 5-speed manual, final drive ratio 4.388.

Gear ratios: a) 5-speed manual: as 1300 model.
b) Automatic: as 1300 model.
For 4WD: 5-speed manual, 1st 3.307; 2nd 1.833; 3rd 1.233; 4th 0.914; 5th 0.775; R 3.166.

Chassis: Front antiroll bar, 4WD rear disc brakes; tyres 155 SR 13 or 175/70 SR 13.

Dimensions: 4WD; track 139/142.5cm. Height 140.5cm.

Performance: Max speed 104mph/167kmh (manufacturers test specifications), speed at 1000rpm in 5th gear (3.850) 22.1mph/35.5kmh; acceleration 0-62mph/100kmh 12secs; power to weight ratio from 15.2kg/kW (11.2kg/PS); consumption ECE 5.4/7.5/8.5L/100km (52.3/37.7/33.2mpg) [43.6/31.4/27.7US mpg].

Mazda 323 Station Wagon

```
1600
63/77kW-84.5/103hp-86/105PS
Fuel injection
```

As 1300 model, except:

Weight: Saloon/Sedan kerbweight (DIN) from 935kg (4WD from 1075kg), Estate/Station Wagon from 975kg (4WD approx 1100kg), USA versions 955-1045kg.

Engine data (Catalyst, DIN): 4-cylinder in-line (78x83.6mm), 1598cm3; compression ratio 9.3:1; 63kW (84.5hp) [86PS] at 5000rpm, 39.4kW/L (52.8hp/L) [53.8PS/L]; 123Nm (90.7lbft) at 2500rpm; unleaded regular grade.
Japanese version (JIS net): 62kW (83hp) [85PS] at 5500rpm; 123Nm (90.7lbft) at 2500rpm.
USA version (SAE net): 61kW (82hp) [83PS] at 5500rpm; 125Nm (92.2lbft).
Without Catalyst (DIN): Compression ratio 10.5:1; 77kW (103hp) [105PS] at 6000rpm; 137Nm (101.1lbft) at 4200rpm; leaded premium grade.

Engine construction: B 6 designation. Oil capacity 3.6L (3.4US qt); electronic EGI (Bosch L-Jetronic licence) fuel injection.

Transmission (to front or all wheels): a) 4-speed manual (only USA), final drive ratio 4.105.
b) 5-speed manual, final drive ratio 4.105.
c) 4-speed automatic, final drive ratio 3.700, USA 3.842.
d) For 4WD: Permanent all-wheel-drive, central Planetary differential (50/50% split); 5-speed manual, final drive ratio 4.388; 4-speed automatic, final drive ratio 3.842.

Gear ratios: a) 4-speed manual (USA): as 1300.
b) 5-speed manual: as 1300 or (103hp model): 1st 3.153; 2nd 1.842; 3rd 1.29; 4th 1.028; 5th 0.82; R 3.214.
c) 4-speed automatic, Planetary gear set ratios: 1st 2.800; 2nd 1.540; 3rd 1.000; 4th 1.700; R 2.333.
d) For 4WD model: 5-speed manual: 1st 3.307; 2nd 1.833; 3rd 1.233; 4th 0.914; 5th 0.775; R 3.166; Automatic as 2WD.

Chassis: Front and rear antiroll bars; 103hp version and 4WD rear disc brakes; some models power assisted steering; 4WD fuel tank 50L (11Gal) [13.2US Gal]; tyres 175/70 SR 13 or 185/60 HR 14 (also USA 155 SR 13), wheels 4.5 (USA) 5 or 5.5J.

Dimensions: Length USA; Hatchback 411cm, Saloon/Sedan 431cm, Estate/Station Wagon 431-435.5cm. 4WD: Track 139/142.5cm. Height 140.5cm.

Performance: (Catalyst version) Max speed 106mph/170kmh (manufacturers test specifications), speed at 1000rpm in 5th gear (0.731) 22mph/35.4kmh; power to weight ratio from 14.8kg/kW (10.9kg/PS); consumption approx 7-11L/100km (40.4-25.7mpg) [33.6-21.4US mpg]. With 103hp: Max speed 114.5mph/184kmh (manufacturers test specifications), speed at 1000rpm in 5th gear 19.6mph/31.5kmh; acceleration 0 - 62mph/100kmh 9.5secs; power to weight ratio from 12.5kg/kW (9.2kg/PS); fuel consumption EEC 6.6/8.8/10.9L/100km (42.8/32.1/25.9mpg) [35.6/26.7/21.6US mpg].

Mazda 323

```
1600 16V Turbo
103/110kW-138/147hp-140/150PS
Fuel Injection
```

As 1300 model; except:

Weight: 3/4-door Saloon/Sedan, kerbweight (DIN) from 970kg, without Turbo from 950kg, USA 1180kg, 4WD from 1100kg; 3-door Coupe Etude (without Turbo), 5-seater; kerbweight (DIN) from 980kg.

Engine data (Catalyst, DIN): 4-cylinder in-line (78x83.6mm), 1598cm3; compression ratio 7.9:1; 103kW (138hp) [140PS] at 6000rpm, 64.4kW/L (86.3hp/L) [87.5PS/L]; 185Nm (136.5lbft) at 3000rpm; unleaded premium grade.
USA version (SAE net): 98kW (131hp) [134PS]; 184Nm (135.6lbft).
Japanese version (JIS net): 103kW (138hp) [140PS] at 6000rpm; 186Nm (137.2lbft) at 5000rpm.
Without Catalyst (DIN): 110kW (147hp) [150PS] at 6000rpm, 68.8kW/L (92.2hp/L) [93.9PS/L]; 195Nm (144lbft) at 5000rpm; leaded premium grade.
Without Turbocharger (JIS net): compression ratio 9.4:1; 81kW (108.5hp) [110PS] at 6500rpm; 132Nm (97.4lbft) at 4500rpm.

Engine construction: B 6 designation, DOHC (turbo). 4 valves per cylinder; 2 overhead camshafts (toothed belt); oil capacity 3.6L (3.4US qt), oil-cooler; 1 IHI RHJB exhaust turbocharger, max boost pressure 0.6bar, charge-air cooler; electronic fuel injection (Bosch L-Jetronic licence). Cooling system capacity 6L (5.7US qt).

Transmission (to front or all wheels): a) 5-speed manual, final drive ratio 3.850, without turbo and USA 4.105, Etude 4.388.
b) 4-speed automatic (not for turbo), final drive ratio 3.700. Turbo available with limited slip differential (visco).

Mazda

4WD (only turbo): Permanent all–wheel–drive; central Planetary differential (50/50% split), 5–speed manual, final drive ratio 4.105; optional rear (visco) limited slip differential.

Mazda 323 1.6i 4WD Turbo 16V

Gear ratios: a) 5–speed manual: 1st 3.307; 2nd 1.833; 3rd 1.233; 4th 0.970; 5th 0.795; R 3.166. Without turbo 1st 3.307; 2nd 1.833; 3rd 1.310; 4th 1.030; 4th 0.837; R 3.166.
b) 4–speed automatic, Planetary gear set ratios: 1st 2.800; 2nd 1.540; 3rd 1.000; 4th 0.700; R 2.333.
4WD: 5–speed manual as 2WD model.

Chassis: Front and rear antiroll bars; 4WD optional level control system. Four–wheel disc brakes, ventilated at front; power assisted steering; fuel tank 50L (11Gal) [13.2US Gal]; tyres 185/60 HR/VR 14, wheels 5.5J.

Dimensions: Etude: length 410.5cm, height 135.5cm.
4WD; track 139/142.5cm. Turning circle 10.7m. Height 135.5–139cm.

Performance: (Catalyst version) Max speed 126mph/203kmh, 4WD 124mph/200kmh (manufacturers test specifications), speed at 1000rpm in 5th gear 20.2mph/32.5kmh; power to weight ratio (2WD) from 9.4kg/kW (6.9kg/PS); fuel consumption (urban/off– road/combination) 9.4/7.6/8.6L/100km (30.1/37.2/32.8mpg) [25/30.9/27.4US mpg]. 4WD without Catalyst: Max speed 127mph/205kmh; acceleration 0 – 62mph/100kmh 8.3secs; power to weight ratio from 10kg/kW (7.3kg/PS); EEC consumption 7.6/9.8/11.2L/100km (37.2/28.5/25.2mpg) [30.9/24/21US mpg].

Mazda Etude

1.7 Litre Diesel
43kW–57.5hp–58PS
Injection Pump

As 1300 model, except:

Weight: Kerbweight (DIN) from approx 910kg.

Engine data (JIS net): 4–cylinder in–line (78x90mm), 1720cm3; compression ratio 21.7:1; 43kW (57.5hp) [58PS] at 4700rpm, 25kW/L (33.5hp/L) [33.7PS/L]; 105Nm (77.4lbft) at 3000rpm.
European version (DIN): 43kW (57.5hp) [58PS] at 4700rpm, 107Nm (78.9lbft) at 3000rpm.

Engine construction: PN designation. Swirl chamber diesel engine. Parallel valves, mechanical tappets; oil capacity 3.5L (3.3US qt); Bosch licence injection pump. Alternator 65A, cooling system capacity approx 6L (5.7US qt).

Transmission: a) 4–speed manual, final drive ratio 3.850.
b) 5–speed manual, final drive ratio 3.850.
c) 4–speed automatic, final drive ratio 3.571.

Gear ratios: a) 4–speed manual: 1st 3.416; 2nd 1.842; 3rd 1.29; 4th 0.972; R 3.214.
b) 5–speed manual: 1st 3.416; 2nd 1.842; 3rd 1.29; 4th 0.918 or 0.972; 5th 0.731; R 3.214.
c) 4–speed automatic, Planetary gear set ratios: 1st 2.800; 2nd 1.540; 3rd 1.000; 4th 0.700; R 2.333.

Chassis: Front and rear antiroll bars; tyres 155 SR 13, wheels 4.5J.

Performance: Max speed 91.5mph/145kmh (manufacturers test specifications), speed at 1000rpm in 5th gear (0.731) 23.4mph/37.6kmh; acceleration 0 - 62mph/100kmh 18.4secs; power to weight ratio from 21.1kg/kW (15.7kg/PS); consumption ECE 4.6/6.7/6.0L/100km (61.4/42.2/47.1mpg) [51.1/35.1/39.2US mpg].

Mazda 626 (Capella) – Persona

Middle class vehicle with four cylinder engine and front wheel drive. Autumn 1982 debut. Also sold in Japan and Australia as the Ford Telstar. May 1987: new edition with modified body and new engines and available with four–wheel–steering and all–wheel–drive. Spring 1988: also available as Estate/Station Wagon. Autumn 1988: luxurious "Persona" Hardtop Saloon/Sedan with identical mechanics.

Mazda 626

1.6 Litre
54kW–72hp–73PS
1 2V Carb

Body, Weight: 4–door Saloon/Sedan, 5–seater; kerbweight (DIN) from 1010kg. 5–door Saloon/Sedan, 5–seater; kerbweight (DIN) from 1095kg; 5–door Estate/Station Wagon, 5–seater; kerbweight approx 1100kg.

Engine data (JIS net): 4–cylinder in–line (78x83.6mm), 1597cm3; compression ratio 9.3:1; 54kW (72hp) [73PS] at 5500rpm, 33.8kW/L (45.3hp/L) [45.7PS/L]; 122Nm (90lbft) at 3500rpm; leaded regular grade.
Export version (DIN): (81x77mm), 1587cm3; compression ratio 9:1; 60kW (80.5hp/L) [81PS] at 5500rpm; 120Nm (88.5lbft) at 3800rpm.

Engine construction: B 6 designation. Transverse mounted front engine. Valves in V; 1 overhead camshaft (toothed belt); light– alloy cylinder head; crankshaft with 5 bearings; oil capacity 3.4L (3.2US qt); 1 downdraught 2V carb. Battery 12V 45/60Ah, alternator 50-70A; cooling system capacity approx 6L (5.7US qt).

Transmission (to front wheels): a) 4–speed manual (only export model), final drive ratio 3.850.
b) 5–speed manual, final drive ratio 3.850.
c) Automatic, hydraulic torque converter and 4–speed Planetary gear set, final drive ratio 3.700.

Gear ratios: a) 4–speed manual: 1st 3.307; 2nd 1.833; 3rd 1.233; 4th 0.970; R 3.166.
b) 5–speed manual: 1st 3.307; 2nd 1.833; 3rd 1.233; 4th 0.914; 5th 0.755; R 3.166 or 3.454. Or (export model): 1st 3.307; 2nd 1.833; 3rd 1.310 or 1.233; 4th 1.030 or 0.970; 5th 0.837 or 0.795; R 3.166.
c) Automatic: Max torque multiplication in converter 3 times; Planetary gear set ratios: 1st 2.800; 2nd 1.540; 3rd 1; OD 0.700; R 2.333.

Chassis: Integral body; all–round independent suspension, front McPherson struts with lower A arms, rear coil springs, double control arms, longitudinal arms, front and rear (some models) antiroll bars, telescopic dampers. Servo/power assisted brakes, front ventilated discs, disc diameter 24.2cm, rear drums, mechanical handbrake to rear wheels, rack and pinion steering, optional power assisted; fuel tank 60L (13.2Gal) [15.9US Gal]; tyres 165 SR 13, optional 185/70 SR 13, wheels 4.5 or 5J, optional 5.5J.

Dimensions: Wheelbase 257.5cm, track 146–145.5cm, clearance 15cm, turning circle 10.2–10.6m. Load space (VDA) 4–door 16.5cu ft (467dm3), 5–door 23.3cu ft (660dm3). Length 451.5cm, width 169cm, height 4–door Saloon/Sedan 139.5cm, 5–door Saloon/Sedan 136cm.

Mazda

Performance: Max speed approx 99.5mph/160kmh, speed at 1000rpm in 5th gear 23.4mph/37.6kmh; power to weight ratio from 18.9kg/kW (13.8kg/PS); consumption approx 7–10L/100km (40.4–28.2mpg) [33.6– 23.5US mpg].

Mazda 626

1.8 12 V
60/71kW–80.5/95hp–82/97PS
1 2V Carb/Fuel Injection

As 1.6 Litre model, except:

Body, Weight: 4/5–door Saloon/Sedan, kerbweight from 1070kg. 4-door Hardtop Persona, 5-seater; kerbweight (DIN) from 1170kg; 5-door Estate/Station Wagon; kerbweight from approx 1100kg; 2–door Coupe, 5–seater, kerbweight from 1070kg.

Engine data (JIS net): 4–cylinder in–line (86x77mm), 1789cm3; compression ratio 8.8:1; 60kW (80.5hp) [82PS] at 5500rpm, 33.5kW/L (44.9hp/L) [45.8PS/L]; 133Nm (98.1lbft) at 2500rpm.
With fuel injection: 71kW (95hp) [97PS] at 5500rpm; 143Nm (105.5lbft) at 4500rpm.
Export version (DIN): 2 valves per cylinder; compression ratio 8.6:1; 66kW (88.5hp) [90PS] at 5500rpm; 140Nm (103.3lbft) at 3400rpm.

Engine construction: F8 designation. 3 valves per cylinder, hydraulic tappets. Oil capacity 4.3L (4.1US qt). 95hp version with electronic EGI (Bosch L–Jetronic licence) fuel injection. Cooling system capacity approx 7L (6.6US qt).

Transmission: a) 4–speed manual (export model), final drive ratio 3.850.
b) 5–speed manual, final drive ratio 3.850, Estate/Station Wagon also 4.105, 95hp 4.388.
c) Automatic, final drive ratio 3.700, 95hp model 3.842.

Chassis: Front and rear antiroll bars. Some versions with power assisted steering; 95hp Version (Japan), also with hydraulic four wheel steering (rear suspension: single lower control arm, trailing arm); tyres 165 SR 13 or 185/70 SR 14, optional 195/60 HR 15, wheels 4.5 or 5.5J.

Dimensions: 95hp version; track 145.5/146.5cm. 4–door model height 141cm, 5–door model 137.5cm. Hardtop: track 146/146.5cm, length 455cm, height 133.5cm. Coupe: Wheelbase 251.5cm; track 145.5/146.5cm. Load space 16.1cu ft (457dm3). Length 445cm, width 169cm, height 136cm.

Performance: (88.5hp) Max speed 107mph/172kmh, Estate/Station Wagon 101mph/163kmh (manufacturers test specifications); speed at 1000rpm in 5th gear (3.850) 22.2mph/35.7kmh; acceleration 0 – 62mph/100kmh 13secs; power to weight ratio from 16.4kg/kW (12kg/PS); fuel consumption ECE 6.0/8.0/10.2L/100km (47.1/35.3/27.7mpg) [39.2/29.4/23.1US mpg] Automatic 6.1/8.6/11.0L/100km (46.3/32.8/25.7mpg) [38.6/27.4/21.4US mpg].

Mazda 626 Coupe

2.2/2.0 12V
85/80kW–114/107hp–115/109PS
Fuel Injection/Carb

Export model engine

As 1.6 Litre model, except:

Body, Weight: 4/5–door Saloon/Sedan, kerbweight from 1055kg (USA 1175kg). Estate/Station Wagon, kerbweight from 1120kg. 2–door Coupe, 5–seater, kerbweight from 1090kg (MX-6 USA from 1150kg).

Engine data (Catalyst model, DIN): 4–cylinder in–line (86x94mm), 2184cm3; compression ratio 8.6:1; 85kW (114hp) [115PS] at 5000rpm, 38.9kW/L (52.1hp/L) [52.7PS/L]; 180Nm (132.8lbft) at 3000rpm; unleaded regular grade.
USA version (SAE net): 82kW (110hp) [112PS] at 4700rpm, 176Nm (129.8lbft) at 3000rpm; Also turbo model with intercooler: Compression ratio 7.8:1; 108kW (145hp) [147PS] at 4300rpm; 258Nm (190.4lbft) at 3500rpm.
Without Catalyst (DIN): (86x86mm), 1998cm3; compression ratio 10:1; 80kW (107hp) [109PS] at 5300rpm, 165Nm (121.7lbft) at 3300rpm. Also with 2 valves per cylinder: With Catalyst (DIN): (86x86mm), 1998cm3; compresson ratio 8.6:1; 66kW (88.5hp) [90PS] at 5200rpm; 150Nm (110.7lbft) at 3400rpm; unleaded regular grade.
For some countries (without Catalyst, carb, DIN): 75kW (100.5hp) [102PS] at 5600rpm; 156Nm (115.1lbft) at 3700rpm.

Engine construction: FE designation. 3 valves per cylinder, hydraulic tappets, oil capacity 4.3L (4.1US qt), oil–cooler; catalyst version with electronic EGI (Bosch L–Jetronic licence) fuel injection, 107hp model with compound carb. Cooling system capacity 7L (6.6US qt).

Mazda 626 2.0i Wagon

Transmission: a) 5–speed manual, final drive ratio 4.105 or 3.850.
b) Automatic, final drive ratio 3.700.

Gear ratios: a) 5–speed manual: 1st 3.307; 2nd 1.833; 3rd 1.233; 4th 0.914; 5th 0.717 or 0.755; R 3.166. Or 1st 3.307; 2nd 1.833; 3rd 1.310; 4th 1.030; 5th 0.837; R 3.166. Or 1st 3.307; 2nd 1.833; 3rd 1.233; 4th 0.970; 5th 0.795; R 3.166. Turbo USA: 1st 3.250; 2nd 1.772; 3rd 1.194; 4th 0.926; 5th 0.711; R 3.461.
b) 4–speed automatic: 1.6 Litre model.

Chassis: Front and rear antiroll bars. 26.4cm brake disc diameter; power assisted steering; tyres 185/70 SR/HR 14 or 185/70 SR 13 (USA), Coupe also 195/60 HR 15, wheels 5.5 or 6J. USA turbo: four-wheel disc brakes (ventilated at front), optional ABS; also with hydraulic four–wheel steering (single lower control-arm rear suspension, longitudinal arms); tyres 195/60 HR 14, wheels 6J.

Dimensions: Track 145.5/146.5cm. USA model length 455.5cm, 4–door height 141cm, 5–door 137.5cm. Coupe: Wheelbase 251.5cm; track 145.5/146.5cm. Load space 16.1cu ft (457dm3). Length 445cm (USA 449.5cm), width 169cm, height 136cm.

Performance: (107hp) Max speed approx 115-118mph/186-190kmh, speed at 1000rpm in 5th gear (0.837, axle 3.850) 22mph/35.5kmh; power to weight ratio from 13.5kg/kW (10kg/PS); fuel consumption approx ECE 5.9/7.6/10.9L/100km (47.9/37.2/25.9mpg) [39.9/30.9/21.6US mpg], Automatic 6.4/7.9/12.3L/100km (44.1/35.8/23mpg) [36.8/29.8/19.1US mpg]

Mazda 626 2.0i 16V 4WS

Mazda

2.0 DOHC 16V
103kW–138hp–140PS
Fuel Injection

As 1.6 Litre model, except:

Body, Weight: 4/5–door Saloon/Sedan, kerbweight from 1160kg. 4-door, Hardtop Persona, 5-seater; kerbweight from 1210kg. Estate/Station Wagon; kerbweight from 1200kg. 2–door Coupe, 5-seater, kerbweight from 1140kg.

Engine data (JIS net): 4–cylinder in–line (86x86mm), 1998cm3; compression ratio 9.2:1; 103kW (138hp) [140PS] at 6000rpm, 51.6kW/L (69.1hp/L) [70.1PS/L]; 172Nm (126.9lbft) at 5000rpm.
With Catalyst (DIN): Compression ratio 9.5:1; 103kW (138hp) [140PS] at 6000rpm; 173Nm (127.7lbft) at 4000rpm; unleaded regular grade.
Without Catalyst (DIN): Compression ratio 10.2:1 109kW (146hp) [148PS] at 6000rpm; 182Nm (134.2lbft) at 4000rpm; leaded premium grade.

Engine construction: FE designation. 4 valves (in 32deg V) per cylinder, hydraulic tappets; 2 overhead camshafts (toothed belt); oil capacity 4.3L (4.3US qt), oil–cooler. Electronic EGI (Bosch L–Jetronic licence) fuel injection. Cooling system capacity 7L (6.6US qt).

Transmission (to front or all wheels): a) 5-speed manual, rear drive ratio 3.850 or 4.105.
b) Automatic, rear drive ratio 3.700.
For 4WD (only 4–door Saloon/Sedan): Permanent all–wheel–drive, central Planetary differential (50/50% split); 5–speed manual, final drive ratio 4.388; rear limited slip differential (visco).

Gear ratios: a) 5–speed manual: 1st 3.307; 2nd 1.833; 3rd 1.310; 4th 0.970; 5th 0.755; R 3.166. Or 1st 3.307; 2nd 1.833; 3rd 1.310; 4th 1.030; 5th 0.837; R 3.166.
b) 4–speed automatic: as 1.6 Litre model.

Chassis: Front and rear antiroll bars, front disc diameter 26.4cm, rear 25.9cm, optional ABS; power assisted steering; optional hydraulic four–wheel steering; tyres 185/70 SR/HR 14 or 195/60HR 15, wheels 5.5 or 6J.

Dimensions: Track 145.5/146.5cm. 4-door model height 141cm, 5-door 137.5cm. Hardtop: track 146/146.5cm. Length 455cm, height 133.5cm. Coupe: Wheelbase 251.5cm; track 145.5/146.5cm. Load space 16.1cu ft (457dm3). Length 445cm, width 169cm, height 136cm. 4WD: Track 145/146.5cm, clearance 17cm. Height 139.5cm.

Performance: (Catalyst version); Max speed 128mph/206kmh (manufacturers test specifications), speed at 1000rpm in 5th gear (0.837, axle 3.850, tyres 195/60–15) 21.7mph/34.9kmh, 4WD 21.4mph/34.5kmh; acceleration 0 – 62mph/100kmh 9.4secs; power to weight ratio from 11.1kg/kW (8.1kg/PS); fuel consumption (urban/off–road/combination) 11.0/6.7/8.7L/100km (25.7/42.2/32.5mpg) [21.4/35.1/27US mpg].

Mazda Persona

2 Litre Diesel
60kW–80.5hp–82PS
Comprex/Injection Pump

As 1.6 Litre model, except:

Weight: Kerbweight from (DIN) 1190kg.

Engine data (JIS net): 4–cylinder in–line (86x86mm) 1998cm3; compression ratio 21:1; 60kW (80.5hp) [82PS] at 4000rpm, 30.0kW/L (40.2hp/L) [41PS/L]; 181Nm (133.5lbft) at 2000rpm.
Export model version (without Comprex, DIN): Compression ratio 22.7:1; 55kW (73hp) [74PS] at 4000rpm; 121Nm (89.3lbft) at 2750rpm.

Engine construction: RF designation. Swirl chamber diesel engine, parallel valves; oil capacity 6L (5.7US qt). Bosch injection pump, pressure–wave Comprex compressor. Cooling system capacity approx 9L (8.5US qt).

Transmission: a) 5–speed manual, final drive ratio 4.105, Export 3.850, Estate/Station Wagon also 4.388.
b) Automatic, final drive ratio 3.700.

Gear ratios: a) 5–speed manual: 1st 3.307; 2nd 1.833; 3rd 1.161; 4th 0.861; 5th 0.680; R 3.166. Export model: 1st 3.307 (Estate/Station Wagon 3.666); 2nd 1.833; 3rd 1.233; 4th 0.914; 5th 0.755; R 3.166.
b) Automatic: as 1.6 Litre model.

Chassis: Some versions with power assisted steering; tyres 165 SR 14 or 185/70 SR 14, wheels 5 or 5.5J.

Dimensions: Track 145.5/146.5cm. Height 141cm.

Performance: (Comprex): Max speed approx 102mph/165kmh, speed at 1000rpm in 5th gear 25.3mph/40.7kmh; power to weight ratio from 19.7kg/kW (14.5kg/PS); consumption approx 5-9L/100km (56.5-31.4mpg) [31.4-26.1US mpg].
Export Version: Max speed 149-154kmh; consumption ECE 4.8/7.1/7.1L/100km (58.8/39.8/39.8mpg) [49/33.1/33.1US mpg], Estate/Station Wagon 5.6/7.8/7.4L/100km (50.4/36.2/38.2mpg) [42/30.2/31.8US mpg].

Mazda 929 (Luce)

Middle class car with reciprocating or Wankel engine. 1975 debut in Frankfurt. September 1986: Luce/929 Saloon/Sedan totally revised with 4–cylinder and Wankel engine as well as new V6 engines with and without turbo. Coupe and Estate/Station Wagon no longer part of programme. Autumn 1988: 3 Litre version of the V6, and modifications for Japan.

1998cm3
60kW–80.5hp–82PS
1 2V Carb

Body, Weight: 4–door Saloon/Sedan and Hardtop, 5/6-seater; kerbweight (DIN) from 1230kg.

Engine data (JIS net): 4–cylinder in–line (86x86mm), 1998cm3; compression ratio 8.6:1; 60kW (80.5hp) [82PS] at 5000rpm, 30kW/L (40.2hp/L) [41PS/L]; 149Nm (109.9lbft) at 2500rpm.

Engine construction: FE designation. Valves in V; 1 overhead camshaft (toothed belt); light–alloy cylinder head; crankshaft with 5 bearings; oil capacity 4.1L (3.9US qt); 1 downdraught 2V carb. Battery 12V 45/65Ah, alternator 50/65A; cooling system capacity 7.5L (7.1US qt).

Transmission (to rear wheels): a) 5-speed manual, final drive ratio 3.727.
b) Automatic, hydraulic torque converter and 3-speed Planetary gear set with OD, final drive ratio 3.909.

Gear ratios: a) 5-speed manual: 1st 3.489; 2nd 1.888; 3rd 1.33; 4th 1; 5th 0.859; R 3.758. b) Automatic: Planetary gear set ratios: 1st 2.841; 2nd 1.541; 3rd 1; OD 0.720; R 2.4.

Chassis: Integral body; all–round independent suspension; front McPherson struts with lower control arms and diagonal pressure struts, rear double lower and single overhead control arms, longitudinal arms and coil springs with co–axial shock absorbers; front and rear antiroll bars, telescopic dampers. Servo/power assisted disc brakes (ventilated at front), some models with rear drums, mechanical handbrake to rear wheels; power assisted rack and pinion steering, fuel tank 70L (15.4Gal) [18.5US Gal]; tyres 175 SR 14, optional 195/70 HR/SR 14, wheels 5.5, optional 6J.

Dimensions: Wheelbase 271cm, track 144/145cm, with rear drum brakes 144/140cm. Clearance 17cm, turning circle 10.8m. Load space 15.1cu ft (427dm3); length 469cm, width 169.5–170.5cm, height 142.5–143.5cm, Hardtop 140.5cm.

Performance: Max speed approx 102.5mph/165kmh, speed at 1000rpm in 5th gear 22.6mph/36.3kmh; power to weight ratio from 20.5kg/kW (15.0kg/PS); consumption approx 7–12L/100km (40.4–23.5mpg) [33.6– 19.6US mpg].

Mazda 929

2184cm3
100/85kW–134/112.5hp–136/115PS
Fuel Injection/Carb

Mazda

Engine for export model

As 1998cm3 model, except:

Weight: Kerbweight (DIN) 1310–1380kg.

Engine data (DIN): 4–cylinder in–line (86x94mm), 2184cm3; compression ratio 9.8:1; 100kW (134hp) [136PS] at 5500rpm; 45.8kW/L (61.4hp/L) [62.3PS/L]; 196Nm (144.6lbft) at 4000rpm.
With carb: 85kW (112.5hp) [115PS] at 5000rpm; 181Nm (133.5lbft) at 3500rpm.
With Catalyst: Compression ratio 9.8:1; 85kW (112.5hp) [115PS] at 5000rpm; 180Nm (111.8lbft) at 3900rpm; unleaded regular grade.
2 Litre model: (86x86mm), 1998cm3; compression ratio 10:1; 85kW (112.5hp) [116PS] at 5300rpm; 164Nm (121lbft) at 4500rpm.

Engine construction: Designated F2/F2 EGI. 3 valves (in V) per cylinder, hydraulic tappets; oil capacity 4.5L (4.4US qt); electronic fuel injection (Bosch L–Jetronic licence), 1 downdraught compound carb. Battery 50-65Ah, alternator 65A.

Transmission: a) 5-speed manual, final drive ratio 3.727, 3.909 or 4.100.
b) Automatic, final drive ratio 3.909 or 4.100.

Gear ratios: a) 5-speed manual: 1st 3.489; 2nd 1.888; 3rd. 1.33; 4th 1; 5th 0.816 or 0.765; R 3.758.
b) Automatic; Planetary gear set ratios: 1st 2.826; 2nd 1.493; 3rd 1; OD 0.688; R 2.703. Or 1st 2.452; 2nd 1.452; 3rd 1; OD 0.730; R 2.212.

Chassis: Disc brakes, diameter front 25.5cm, rear 26.6cm; fuel tank 75L (16.5Gal) [19.8US Gal]; tyres 195/70 HR 14, wheels 5.5J.

Dimensions: Length 488.5cm. width 170.5cm, height 142.5cm.

Performance: (134hp model) Max speed 116mph/187kmh (manufacturers test specifications), speed at 1000rpm in 5th gear (0.765, axle 3.909), 24.2mph/38.9kmh; acceleration 0 – 62mph/100kmh 9.9secs; power to weight ratio from 13.4kg/kW (9.8kg/PS); EEC fuel consumption 7.0/9.3/11.1L/100km (40.4/30.4/25.4mpg) [33.6/25.3/21.2US mpg], automatic 7.2/9.6/13.4L/100km (39.2/29.4/21.1mpg) [32.7/24.5/20.6US mpg].

2.0 V6
81/107kW–109/143hp–110/145PS
Fuel Injection (Turbo)

As 2 Litre 80.5hp model, except:

Weight: Kerbweight from 1350kg, turbo from 1420kg.

Engine data (JIS net): 6-cylinder in 60 deg V (74x77.4mm), 1997cm3; compression ratio 9.2:1; 81kW (109hp) [110PS] at 5500rpm, 40.6kW/L (54.4hp/L) [55.1PS/L]; 168Nm (123.9lbft) at 4000rpm.
With turbocharger: Compression ratio 8.0:1; 107kW (143hp) [145PS] at 5000rpm, 53.6kW/L (71.8hp/L) [72.6PS/L]; 231Nm (170.4lbft) at 2500rpm.

Engine construction: JF/Turbo designation. 3 valves (in V) per cylinder, tappets; each with overhead camshaft (toothed belt); crankshaft with 4 bearings; oil capacity approx 5L (4.7US qt); electronic EGI fuel injection; 143hp version with 1 turbocharger. Cooling system capacity approx 9L (8.5US qt).

Transmission: a) 5-speed manual, final drive ratio 4.100.
b) Automatic, final drive ratio 4.300 or 4 .100.

Mazda 929 3.0i V6

Gear ratios: a) 5-speed manual: 1st 3.483; 2nd 2.015; 3rd 1.391; 4th 1; 5th 0.806; R 3.288.
b) Automatic: 4-cylinder model.

Chassis: Optional level-control system; optional ABS; tyres 195/70 SR 14 (119PS) or 195/65 HR 15, wheels 5.5 or 6J.

Dimensions: Track 144/145cm. Height 142.5, Hardtop 139.5cm.

Performance: Max speed approx 115mph/185kmh, turbo approx 124mph/200kmh, speed at 1000rpm in 5th gear 21.8mph/35kmh; power to weight ratio from 13.3kg/kW (9.8kg/PS); consumption approx 8–16L/100km (35.3–17.7mpg) [29.4–14.7US mpg].

2954cm3 V6
118kW–158hp–160PS
Fuel Injection

As 2 Litre 80.5hp model, except:

Weight: Kerbweight (DIN) from 1460kg (USA from 1535kg).

Engine data (JIS net): 6-cylinder in 60deg V (90x77.4mm), 2954cm3; compression ratio 8.5:1; 118kW (158hp) [160PS] at 5500rpm, 40kW/L (53.6hp/L) [54.2PS/L]; 235Nm (173.3lbft) at 4000rpm.
With Catalyst (DIN): Compression ratio 9.2:1; 125kW (167.5hp) [170PS] at 5300rpm; 240Nm (177lbft) at 4000rpm; unleaded fuel.
USA version (SAE net): Compression ratio 8.5:1; 118kW (158hp) [160PS] at 5500rpm, 231Nm (170.4lbft) at 4000rpm.
Without Catalyst (DIN): Compression ratio 10:1; 140kW (188hp) [190PS] at 5500rpm; 255Nm (188.2lbft) at 4200rpm; leaded premium grade.

Engine construction: Designated JE 3. 3 valves (in V) per cylinder, hydraulic tappets; 2x1 overhead camshafts (toothed belt) per cylinder; crankshaft with 4 bearings; oil capacity 5.4L (5.1US qt), electronic fuel injection (Bosch L-Jectronic licence). Battery 50-70Ah, alternator 65-80A, cooling system capacity 9.4L (8.9US qt).

Transmission: a) 5-speed manual, final drive ratio 3.583 or 3.727.
b) Automatic, final drive ratio 3.909 or 3.727.
Optional limited slip differential.

Gear ratios: a) 5-speed manual: 1st 3.483; 2nd 2.015; 3rd 1.391; 4th 1; 5th 0.806 or 0.762; R 3.288.
b) Automatic: As 4-cylinder model.

Chassis: Optional level-control system; some versions (Japan) front and rear ventilated disc brakes, front disc diameter 25.5cm, rear 26.6cm, with ABS; export model fuel tank 75L (16.5Gal) [19.8US Gal]; tyres 205/60 VR 15 or 195/65 HR 15, wheels 6J.

Dimensions: Track 144/145cm. Length 482cm or 488.5cm (USA 490.5cm). Width 170.5cm, height 142.5, Hardtop 139.5cm.

Performance: (Catalyst version) Max speed 127mph/205kmh, automatic 123mph/198kmh (manufacturers test specifications), speed at 1000rpm in 5th gear (0.762, axle 3.727) 25.1mph/40.4kmh; acceleration 0 – 62mph/100kmh 8.6secs; power to weight ratio from 11.7kg/kW (8.6kg/PS); fuel consumption ECE (without Catalyst) 8.1/9.9/15.9L/100km (34.9/28.5/17.8mpg) [29/23.8/14.8US mpg].

Mazda Luce 3000 V6 DOHC

2954cm3-24V
147kW–197hp–200PS
Fuel Injection

As 2-Litre with 80.5hp, except:

Weight: kerbweight (DIN) 1410-1490kg.

Engine data (JIS net): 6-cylinder in V 60deg (90 x 77.4mm), 2954cm3; compression ratio 9.5:1; 147kW (197hp) [200PS] at 6000rpm, 49.8kW/L (66.7hp/L) [67.7PS/L]; 260Nm (26.5mkp) at 4500rpm

Engine construction: Designated JED 4. Valves (in V) per cylinder, hydraulic tappets; 2 overhead camshafts each (toothed belt); 4 main bearing crankshaft; oil capacity 5.4L (5.1US qt), electronic fuel injection (Bosch L-Jetronic: Licence). Battery 50-70Ah, Alternator 65-80A; cooling system capacity approx 9.4L (8.9US qt).

Transmission: Automatic, final drive ratio 4.100.

Chassis: Optional level control system; disc brakes, front and rear ventilated, optional ABS; tyres 195/65HR 15 or 205/60 HR 15, wheel rims 6J.

Dimensions: Track 144/145cm. Length 482cm, height 142.5cm, Hardtop 139.5cm.

Mazda

Performance: Max speed approx 137mph/220kmh, speed at 1000rpm in OD 24.5mph/39.4kmh; power to weight ratio from 9.6kg/kW (7.1kg/PS); consumption approx 9-18L/100km (31.4-15.7mpg) [26.1-13.1US mpg].

> 2.6 Litre Wankel
> 132kW-177hp-180PS
> Turbo/Fuel Injection

As 2 Litre 80.5hp model, except:

Weight: Kerbweight (DIN) 1420-1500kg.

Engine data (JIS net): Double-vane reciprocating Wankel engine, swirl-chamber capacity 654cm3, equivalent engine capacity 2616cm3; compression ratio 8.5:1; 132kW (177hp) [180PS] at 6500rpm, 50.5kW/L (67.8hp/L) [68.8PS/L]; 245Nm (180.7lbft) at 3500rpm.

Engine construction: Light-alloy rotary engine (13B) with 2 rotors; oil capacity 6.2L (5.9US qt), oil-cooler; electronic fuel injection, 1 exhaust turbocharger, charge air cooler. Battery 12V 50/55Ah, alternator 50/70A; cooling system capacity 8.7L (8.2US qt).

Transmission: Automatic, final drive ratio 4.100.

Chassis: Optional level-control system; front and rear ventilated disc brakes; optional ABS; tyres 195/65 HR 15, wheels 6J.

Dimensions: Track 144/145cm. Height 142.5, Hardtop 139.5cm.

Performance: Max speed over 124mph/200kmh, speed at 1000rpm in OD 24.5mph/39.4kmh; power to weight ratio from 10.7kg/kW (7.9kg/PS); fuel consumption approx 9-18L/100km (31.4-15.7mpg) [26.1-13.1US mpg].

Mazda RX-7 (Savanna)

Sporty Coupe with 2+2 seater and rotary engine. March 1987 debut. Autumn 1983: launch of turbocharger. September 1985: new body, rear independent suspension, 2.6 Litre rotary engine with and without turbocharger. August 1987: RX-7 Turbo also available as Convertible.

Mazda RX-7

> 2.6 Litre Wankel
> 110kW-147hp-150PS
> Fuel Injection

Engine for export

Body, Weight: 3-door Coupe, 2+2 seater; kerbweight (DIN) from 1205kg, USA 1190-1235kg; 2-door Convertible (only USA), 2 seater; kerbweight (DIN) approx 1280kg.

Engine data (DIN): Double-vane rotary Wankel engine, chamber volume 654cm3, equivalent engine capacity 2616cm3; compression ratio 9.4:1; 110kW (147hp) [150PS] at 6500rpm, 42kW/L (56.3hp/L) [57.3PS/L]; 182Nm (134.2lbft) at 3000rpm; leaded regular grade.
USA version (SAE net): Compression ratio 9.4:1; 109kW (146hp) [148PS] at 6500rpm; 187Nm (137.9lbft) at 3500rpm.

Engine construction: 13B designation. Light-alloy rotary engine with 2 rotors; oil capacity 6.2L (5.9US qt), oil-cooler; electronic fuel injection. Battery 12V 50/55Ah, alternator 50/70A; cooling system capacity 8.7L.

Transmission (to rear wheels): a) 5-speed manual, final drive ratio 4.300, USA 4.100.
b) For USA: Automatic, hydraulic torque converter and 3-speed Planetary gear set with OD, final drive ratio 3.909.
Optional limited slip differential.

Gear ratios: a) 5-speed manual: 1st 3.475; 2nd 2.002; 3rd 1.366; 4th 1; 5th 0.758, USA 0.711; R 3.493.
b) Automatic (USA): Max torque multiplication in converter 3 times; Planetary gear set ratios: 1st 2.841; 2nd 1.541; 3rd 1; OD 0.720; R 2.400.

Chassis: Integral body; front and rear independent suspension with lower A arms, rear semi-trailing arms, diagonal auxiliary arm and coil springs, front and rear antiroll bars, telescopic dampers. Servo/power assisted disc brakes (ventilated), front disc diameter 27.6cm, rear 27.3cm, optional ABS (Nippon system), mechanical handbrake to rear wheels; rack and pinion steering, some models power assisted; fuel tank 63L (13.8Gal) [16.6US Gal]; tyres 205/60 VR 15, USA also 185/70 HR 14, wheels 6, USA also 5.5J.

Dimensions: Wheelbase 243cm, track 145/144cm, clearance approx 15cm, turning circle 9.8m. Load space 19.4/19.8cu ft (550/560dm3). Length 429-431cm, width 169cm, height 126.5cm.

Performance: Max speed 130.5mph/210kmh (manufacturers test specifications), speed at 1000rpm in 5th gear 21.9mph/35.3kmh; acceleration 0 - 62mph/100kmh 8secs; power to weight ratio from 10.9kg/kW (8.0kg/PS); fuel consumption ECE 8.4/11.3/17.1L/100km (33.6/25/16.5mpg) [28/20.8/13.8US mpg].

> 2.6 Litre Wankel
> 136kW-182hp-185PS
> Turbo/Fuel Injection

As 147hp version, except:

Weight: Coupe, kerbweight (DIN) 1210-1310kg, convertible from 1360.

Engine data (JIS net): Double-vane rotary Wankel engine, chamber volume 654cm3, equivalent engine capacity 2616cm3; compression ratio 8.5:1; 136kW (182hp) [185PS] at 6500rpm, 52.0kW/L (67.7hp/L) [70.7PS/L]; 245Nm (180.7lbft) at 3500rpm.
With Catalyst (DIN): 133kW (178hp) [181PS] at 6500rpm; 247Nm (182.2lbft) at 3500rpm; unleaded fuel.
USA version (SAE net): 136kW (182hp) [185PS]; 248Nm (182.9lbft).

Engine construction: 13B Turbo designation. 1 turbocharger, charge-air cooler.

Transmission: a) 5-speed manual, final drive ratio 4.100.
b) Automatic, final drive ratio 4.100. Limited slip differential.

Gear ratios: a) 5-speed manual: 1st 3.483; 2nd 2.015; 3rd 1.391; 4th 1; 5th 0.806, USA and Catalyst 0.762; R 3.288.
b) Automatic; Planetary gear set ratios: 1st 2.458; 2nd 1.458; 3rd 1; OD 0.720; R 2.181.

Chassis: Power assisted steering in export model; export model fuel tank 72L (15.8Gal) [19US Gal]; tyres 205/55 VR 16 or 205/60 HR 15, wheels 7 or 6J.

Dimensions: Length 431cm, height 126.5-127cm.

Performance: Max speed 142.9mph/230kmh (manufacturer test specifications), speed at 1000rpm in 5th gear (0.762) 23.1mph/37.1kmh; acceleration 0 - 62mph/100kmh 7.2secs; power to weight ratio from 8.9kg/kW (6.5kg/PS); fuel consumption (urban/off-road/combination) 13.7/8.4/11.0L/100km (20.6/33.6/25.7mpg) [17.2/28/21.4US mpg].

Mazda RX-7 Cabriolet

Mazda MX-5 Miata

New model. 2-seater sports car of conventional design. Integral body, 1.6 litre front engine with 16 valves and 118PS. Rear wheel drive. Launched at the Chicago Show in February 1989. Currently available in the United States, and later also in Japan and Europe.

> 1.6 DOHC
> 87kW-117hp-118PS
> Fuel Injection

Body, Weight: 2-door Convertible/Cabriolet, 2-seater; kerbweight (DIN) from 990kg.

Engine data (Catalyst, SAE net): 4-cylinder in-line (78 x 83.6mm), 1598cm3; compression ratio 9.4:1; 87kW (117hp) [118PS] at 6500rpm, 54.4kW/L (72.9hp/L) [73.8PS/L]; 135Nm (99.6lbft) at 5500rpm. Regular grade fuel.

Engine construction: Designated B6 DOHC, 4 valves (in V) per cylinder, hydraulic tappets, 2 overhead camshafts (belt driven); light-alloy cylinder block;

Mazda • Mercedes-Benz

5 bearing crankshaft; oil capacity 3.6L (3.4US qt), oil cooler; electronic fuel injection (Bosch L Jetronic licence); 12V battery, 60A alternator, cooling system capacity 4.7L (4.4US qt).

Transmission (to rear wheels): 5–speed manual, final drive ratio 4.3.

Gear ratios: 1st 3.136; 2nd 1.888; 3rd 1.330; 4th 1; 5th 0.814; R 3.758.

Chassis: Integral body, front and rear independent suspension with upper and lower A arms; coil springs and co-axial telescopic dampers, front and rear anti roll bar. Servo/power assisted disc brakes, front ventilated, handbrake to rear wheels; rack and pinion steering (optional power assistance). Fuel tank 45L (9.9Gal) [11.9US Gal]; tyres 185/60 HR 14, wheel rims 5.5J.

Dimensions: Wheelbase 226.5cm, track 141/143cm, clearance 11.5cm, length 395cm, width 167.5cm, height 122.5cm.

Performance: Max speed 121mph/195kmh, speed at a 1000rpm in 5th gear 18.8mph/30.3kmh; power to weight ratio 11.4kg/kW (8.4kg/PS); consumption 7–13l/100km (40.4–21.7mpg) [33.6–18.1US mpg].

Mazda MX–5 Miata

Mazda MPV

New model. Large capacity Saloon/Sedan with longitudinal engine and rear wheel drive, 2.6 Litre, 4-cylinder or 3 Litre, V6, five speed manual or Automatic transmission. From Spring 1989, V6 with four wheel drive. Launched September 1988. Aimed at the American market.

2.6 Litre
90kW–121hp–123PS
Fuel Injection

Body, Weight: 3-door Saloon/Sedan with tailgate, 5-seater; kerbweight (DIN) from 1570kg. 3-door Saloon/Sedan with tailgate, 7-seater; kerbweight (DIN) from 1600kg. Automatic heavier by 15kg.

Engine data (Catalyst SAE net): 4-cylinder in-line (92 x 98mm), 2606cm3; Compression ratio 8.4:1; 90kW (121hp) [123PS] at 4600rpm, 34.5kW/L (46.2hp/L) [47.2PS/L]; 202Nm (149lbft) at 3500rpm; regular unleaded.

Engine construction: Designated G6. 3 valves (in V 38deg) per cylinder, hydraulic valve play compensation, 1 overhead camshaft (chain); light-alloy cylinder heads; 5 main bearing crankshaft; oil capacity 5.3L (5US qt); 2 anti-vibration arms; electronic fuel injection. Battery 12V 50/65Ah, Alternator 70A; cooling system capacity approx 6.8-7.2L (6.4-6.8US qt).

Transmission (to rear wheels): a) 5-speed manual, final drive ratio 3.727.
b) Automatic, hydraulic torque converter and 3-speed Planetary gear set with OD, final drive ratio 3.909.

Gear ratios: a) 5-speed manual: 1st 3.730; 2nd 2.158; 3rd 1.396; 4th 1; 5th 0.816; R 3.815.
b) Automatic: max torque multiplication in converter 3 times; Planetary gear set ratios: 1st 2.841; 2nd 1.541; 3rd 1; OD 0.720; R 2.400.

Chassis: Integral body, with reinforced sub-frame; front McPherson struts, lower single control arm, torsion strut and antiroll bar; rear rigid axle with coil springs, four trailing arms, Panhard rod and antiroll bar, telescopic damper. Servo/power assisted brakes (ventilated), diameter 25.6cm, rear drums, handbrake to rear; power assisted rack and pinion steering; fuel tank capacity 60L (13.2Gal) [15.9US Gal]; tyres 205/75PR 14, also 215/65 PR 15, wheel rims 5.5 or 6J.

Dimensions: Wheelbase 280.5cm, track 152.5/154cm, clearance 18cm, turning circle 11.6m. Load space 11.1-37.4cu ft (315-1060dm3). Length 446.5cm, width 182.5cm, height 173cm.

Performance: Max speed 106mph/171kmh (manufacturers test specifications), speed at 1000rpm in 5th gear 24.4mph/39.3kmh; acceleration 0-60mph/97kmh, 13secs, Automatic 14secs; power to weight ratio from 17.4kg/kW (12.8kg/PS); consumption approx 9-13L/100km (31.4-21.7mpg) [26.1-18.1US mpg].

Mazda MPV

3 Litre V6
112kW–150hp–152PS
Fuel Injection

As 2.6 Litre, except:

Weight: Kerbweight 5–seater 1595kg, 4WD 1750kg; 7–seater 1625kg, 4WD 1780kg.

Engine data (Catalyst, SAE net): 6-cylinder in V 60deg (90 x 77.4mm), 2954cm3; compression ratio 8.5:1; 112kW (150hp) [152PS] at 5000rpm, 37.9kW/l (50.8hp/L) [51.5PS/L]; 224Nm (165.3lbft) at 4000rpm.

Engine construction: Designated JE-V6. 1 overhead camshaft (toothed belt) per cylinder range; 4 main bearing crankshaft; no anti vibration arms; oil capacity 4.9L (4.6US qt); electronic fuel injection (licenced Bosch L-Jetronic), cooling system capacity 9.4/9.8L (8.9/9.3US qt).

Transmission (to rear wheels or all wheels): a) 5-speed manual, final drive ratio 3.727, 4WD 3.909.
b) Automatic, final drive ratio 3.909, 4WD 4.100.
With 4WD: All wheel drive with manual central locking Planetary differential (simultaneous distribution 50/50%), cross country reduction gears, disengageable front wheel drive (additional free rolling in front differential).

Gear ratios: a) 5-speed manual: As 2.6 litre.
b) Automatic: Planetary gear set ratios: 1st 3.027; 2nd 1.619; 3rd 1; OD 0.694; R 2.272.
With 4WD: Cross country reduction: high 1, low 2.538.

Chassis: Fuel tank capacity 74L (16.3Gal) [19.6US Gal].
4WD: Front A arm. Tyres 215/65 PR 15, wheel rims 6J.

Dimensions: 4WD: Track 154.4/154cm, turning circle 12.6m. Width 183.5cm, height 180cm.

Performance: Max speed 111mph/179kmh (manufacturers test specifications); acceleration 0–60mph/97kmh 11secs, automatic 12secs; power to weight ratio from 14.2kg/kW (10.5kg/PS); consumption approx 10–15L/100km (28.2–23.5mpg) [18.8–15.7US mpg].

MERCEDES–BENZ   D

Daimler–Benz AG, Stuttgart–Untertuerkheim, West Germany

German manufacturer of high quality cars and commercial vehicles. The oldest car producer.

MODEL RANGE
201 – 124 – 126 – 129 – G

Mercedes-Benz 190

201 Series

Luxury middle–class Saloon/Sedan with 4-cylinder engine, 4/5– speed manual or automatic transmission and sophisticated rear axle construction. Debut November 1982. Frankfurt 1983: 2.3 Litre engine with 16 valves and 2 Litre diesel engine. Frankfurt 1985: Available with 2.6 Litre six–cylinder engine. In the course of 1986 also with 190 E 2.3. 2.5 Litre turbo diesel engine. August 1988: the 2.5-16 replaces the 2.3-16.

Mercedes-Benz

```
2 Litre
75kW–100.5hp–102PS
1 Carb
```

Engine for 190

Body, Weight: 4–door Saloon/Sedan, 5–seater; kerbweight (DIN) 1160kg. Gross vehicle weight 1660kg.

Engine data (Catalyst, ECE): 4–cylinder in–line (89 x 80.2mm), 1996cm3; compression ratio 9.1:1, 75kW (100.5hp) [102PS] at 5500rpm, 37.6kW/L (50.4hp/L) [51.1PS/L]; 160Nm (118lbft) at 3000rpm; unleaded premium grade.
For some countries: 73kW (98hp) [99PS]; leaded regular grade.
Without Catalyst/After sale Catalyst conversion: 77kW (103hp) [105PS]; 165Nm (121.7lbft).

Engine construction: M 102 V 20 designation. Engine positioned 15deg to right. Hydraulic tappets; valves in 45deg V, 1 overhead camshaft (chain); light–alloy cylinder head; crankshaft with 5 bearings; oil capacity 5L (4.7US qt); 1 downdraught carb 2EE. Battery 12V 62Ah, alternator 70W; cooling system capacity approx 8.5L (8US qt).

Transmission (to rear wheels): a) 4–speed manual, final drive ratio 3.46.
b) 5–speed manual, final drive ratio 3.46.
c) Mercedes–Benz automatic, hydraulic torque converter and 4– speed Planetary gear set, final drive ratio 3.46.
Optional ASD, automatic traction control.

Gear ratios: a) 4–speed manual: 1st 3.91; 2nd 2.17; 3rd 1.37; 4th 1; R 3.78.
b) 5–speed manual: 1st 3.91; 2nd 2.17; 3rd 1.37; 4th 1; 5th 0.78; R 4.27.
c) Automatic: Planetary gear set ratios: 1st 4.25; 2nd 2.41; 3rd 1.49; 4th 1; R 5.67.

Chassis: Integral body; front and rear independent suspension; front shock absorber struts, coil springs and A arms (negative steering offset), antiroll bar, rear suspended axle with compliance arms, semi–trailing arms, tie rods, coil springs, telescopic dampers and antiroll bar. Servo/power assisted disc brakes, front disc diameter 27.3cm, rear 27.9cm; optional Bosch ABS system; mechanical handbrake to rear wheels; power assisted recirculating ball steering; fuel tank 55L (12.1Gal) [14.5US Gal] including 7.5L (1.6Gal) [2US Gal] reserve; tyres 186/65 HR 15, wheels 6J.

Dimensions: Wheelbase 266.5cm, track 143.5/142cm, clearance 15.5cm, turning circle 10.6m. Load space (VDA) 14.5cu ft (410dm3). Length 445cm, width 169cm, height 139cm.

Performance: Max speed 114mph/183kmh, automatic 111mph/178kmh (manufacturers test specifications), speed at 1000rpm in direct gear 20.4mph/32.9kmh; acceleration 0 – 62mph/100kmh 12.8secs, automatic 13.1secs; power to weight ratio 15.5kg/kW (11.4kg/PS); ECE consumption 5–speed 6.4/8.3/11.5L/100km (44.1/34/24.6mpg) [36.8/28.3/20.5US mpg], automatic 7.4/9.3/11.3L/100km (38.2/30.4/25mpg) [31.8/25.3/20.8US mpg]. Without Catalyst: Max speed +1mph/2kmh, acceleration –0.4secs.

```
2 Litre
87kW–116.5hp–118PS
Fuel Injection
```

Engine for 190 E model

As 2 Litre/100.5hp model, except:

Weight: Kerbweight (DIN) 1170kg, gross vehicle weight 1670kg.

Engine data (Catalyst, ECE): 4–cylinder in–line (89 x 80.2mm), 1996cm3; compression ratio 9.1:1; 87kW (116.5hp) [118PS] at 5100rpm, 43.5kW/L (58.3hp/L) [59.1PS/L]; 172Nm (126.9lbft) at 3500rpm.
Without Catalyst/After sale Catalyst conversion: 90kW (121hp) [122PS]; 178Nm (131.3lbft).

Engine construction: M 102 E 20 designation. Mechanical/electronic Bosch KE–Jetronic fuel injection, electric fuel pump.

Transmission: a) 4–speed manual, final drive ratio 3.23.
b) 5–speed manual, final drive ratio 3.46.
c) Automatic, 3.23.

Performance: Max speed 118mph/190kmh, automatic 115mph/185kmh (manufacturers test specifications), speed at 1000rpm in 5th gear 26.1mph/42.1kmh; acceleration 0 – 62mph/100kmh 10.9secs, automatic 11.5secs; power to weight ratio 13.4kg/kW (9.9kg/PS); ECE consumption 5–speed 6.6/8.3/11.4L/100km (42.8/34/24.8mpg) [35.6/28.3/20.6US mpg], automatic 7.3/9.1/10.9L/100km (38.6/31/25.9mpg) [32.2/25.8/21.6US mpg]. Without Catalyst: Max speed +3mph/5kmh, acceleration –0.5secs.

```
2.3 Litre
97kW–130hp–132PS
Fuel Injection
```

Engine for 190 E 2.3

As 2 Litre/100.5hp model, except:

Weight: Kerbweight (DIN) 1220kg, gross vehicle weight 1720kg.

Engine data (Catalyst, ECE): 4–cylinder in–line (95.5 x 80.25mm), 2298cm; compression ratio 9:1; 97kW (130hp) [132PS] at 5100rpm, 42.2kW/L (56.5hp/L) [57.4PS/L]; 198Nm (146lbft) at 3500rpm.
Without Catylst/After sale Catalyst conversion: 100kW (134hp) [136PS]; 205Nm (151.2lbft).

Engine construction: M 102 E 23 designation. Mechanical/electronic Bosch KE–Jetronic fuel injection, electric fuel pump.

Transmission: a) 5–speed manual, final drive ratio 3.27.
b) Automatic, final drive ratio 3.27.

Gear ratios: a) 5–speed manual: 1st 3.91; 2nd 2.17; 3rd 1.37; 4th 1; 5th 0.78; R 4.27.
b) Automatic: As 190.

Chassis: Front ventilated disc brakes.

Performance: Max speed 122mph/197kmh, automatic 119mph/192kmh (manufacturers test specifications), speed at 1000rpm in 5th gear 27.7mph/44.6kmh; acceleration 0 – 62mph/100kmh 10.6secs, automatic 10.7secs; power to weight ratio 12.6kg/kW (9.2kg/PS); ECE consumption 6.5/8.2/11.4L/100km (43.5/34.4/24.8mpg) [36.2/28.7/20.6US mpg], automatic 7.8/9.3/11.3L/100km (36.2/30.4/25mpg) [30.2/25.3/20.8US mpg]. Without Catalyst: Max speed +1mph/3kmh, acceleration –0.3secs.

```
2.6 Litre 6–cylinder
118kW–158hp–160PS
Fuel Injection
```

Engine for 190 E 2.6

As 2 Litre/100.5hp model, except:

Weight: Kerbweight (DIN) 1270kg, USA 1340kg. Gross vehicle weight 1770kg.

Engine data (Catalyst, ECE): 6–cylinder in–line (82.9 x 80.2mm), 2597cm3; compression ratio 9.2:1; 118kW (158hp) [160PS] at 5800rpm, 45.4kW/L (60.8hp/L) [61.6PS/L]; 220Nm (162.3lbft) at 4600rpm.
Without Catalyst/After sale Catalyst conversion: 122kW (163.5hp) [166PS]; 228Nm (168.2lbft).
Some countries: 115kW (154hp) [156PS].

Engine construction: M 103 E 26 designation. Crankshaft with 7 bearings; oil capacity 6.0L (5.7US qt), mechanical/electronic Bosch KE–Jetronic fuel injection, electric fuel pump. Alternator 980W.

Transmission: a) 5–speed manual, final drive ratio 3.27.
b) Automatic, final drive ratio 3.07.

Gear ratios: a) 5–speed manual: 1st 3.86; 2nd 2.18; 3rd 1.38; 4th 1; 5th 0.80; R 4.22.
b) Automatic: As 190 model.

Chassis: Front ventilated disc brakes; ABS; tyres 185/65 VR 15.

Performance: Max speed 132mph/212kmh, automatic 129mph/207kmh (manufacturers test specifications), speed at 1000rpm in 5th gear 26.3mph/42.3kmh. acceleration 0 – 62mph/100kmh 9.2secs, automatic 9.5secs; power to weight ratio 10.8kg/kW (7.9kg/PS); ECE consumption 7.0/8.9/13.0L/100km (40.4/31.7/21.7mpg) [33.6/26.4/18.1US mpg], automatic 8.2/10.2/12.4L/100km (34.4/27.7/22.8mpg) [28.7/23.1/19US mpg]. Without Catalyst: Max speed +1mph/3kmh, acceleration –0.3secs.

```
2.5 Litre 16V
143kW–192hp–195PS
Fuel Injection
```

Engine for 190 E 2.5–16

As 2 Litre/100.5hp model, except:

Weight: 4–seater, kerbweight (DIN) 1300kg, gross vehicle weight 1800kg.

Engine data (Catalyst, ECE): 4–cylinder in–line (95.5 x 87.2mm), 2498cm3; compression ratio 9.7:1; 143kW (192hp) [195PS] at 6750rpm, 57.2kW/L (76.6hp/L) [78.1PS/L]; 235Nm (173.4lbft) at 5000-5500rpm.
Without Catalyst/After sale Catalyst conversion: 150kW (201hp) [204PS]; 240Nm (177lbft).

Engine construction: Designated M 102. 4 valves per cylinder, valves in 45deg V, 2 overhead camshafts (chain); light–alloy cylinder head; oil–cooler; mechanical/electronic Bosch KE– Jetronic III fuel injection, electric fuel pump. Battery 12V 55Ah.

Mercedes-Benz

Mercedes–Benz 190 E 2.5–16

Transmission: a) 5–speed manual, final drive ratio 3.07.
b) Automatic, final drive ratio 3.07.
ASD traction control.

Gear ratios: a) 5–speed manual: 1st 4.08; 2nd 2.52; 3rd 1.77; 4th 1.26; 5th 1; R 4.16.
b) Automatic: As 190.

Chassis: Rear level control system, optional at front; front ventilated disc brakes; front disc diameter 28.4cm, rear 25.8cm; ABS; fuel tank 70L (15.4Gal) [18.5US Gal] including 8.5L (1.9Gal) [2.2US Gal] reserve; tyres 205/55 ZR 15, wheels 7J.

Dimensions: Track 144.5/143cm, clearance 12.5cm. Load space 13.6cu ft (385dm3). Length 443cm, width 170.5cm, height 136cm.

Performance: Max speed 143mph/230kmh, automatic 140mph/225kmh (manufacturers test specifications), speed at 1000rpm in 5th gear 22.5mph/36.2kmh; acceleration 0 – 62mph/100kmh 7.7secs, automatic 8.1secs; power to weight ratio 9.1kg/kW (6.7kg/PS); consumption ECE 7.8/9.4/13.3L/100km (36.2/30.1/21.2mpg) [30.2/25/17.7US mpg], automatic 7.8/9.0/13.0L/100km (36.2/31.4/21.7mpg) [30.2/26.1/18.1US mpg]. Without Catalyst: Max speed +3mph/5kmh, acceleration –0.2secs.

Mercedes–Benz 190 E 2.5–16

```
2 Litre Diesel
53/55kW–71/74hp–72/75PS
Injection Pump
```

Engine for 190 D

As 2–litre/100.5hp model, except:

Weight: Kerbweight (DIN) 1180kg, gross vehicle weight 1680kg.

Engine data (ECE): 4–cylinder in–line (87 x 84mm), 1997cm3; compression ratio 22:1; 53kW (71hp) [72PS] at 4600rpm, 26.5kW/L (35.5hp/L) [36PS/L]; 123Nm (90.7lbft) at 2800rpm.
New engine generation: 55kW (74hp) [75PS].

Engine construction: OM 601 designation. Hydraulic tappets; oil capacity 6.5L (6.1US qt); Bosch diesel injection pump. Battery 12V 72Ah.

Transmission: a) 4–speed manual, final drive ratio 3.23.
b) 5–speed manual, final drive ratio 3.91.
c) Automatic, final drive ratio 3.23.

Gear ratios: a) 4–speed manual: 1st 4.23; 2nd 2.36; 3rd 1.49; 4th 1; R 4.1.
b) 5–speed manual: 1st 3.91; 2nd 2.17; 3rd 1.37; 4th 1; 5th 0.78; R 4.27.
c) Automatic: As 190.

Performance: Max speed 99.5mph/160kmh, automatic 97mph/156kmh; acceleration 0 – 62mph/100kmh 18.1secs, automatic 18.6secs; power to weight ratio 22.3kg/kW (16.4kg/PS); ECE consumption 5.3/6.9/7.5L/100km (53.3/40.9/37.7mpg) [44.4/34.1/31.4US mpg] , 5–speed 5.3/6.9/7.9L/100km (53.3/40.9/35.8mpg) [44.4/34.1/29.8US mpg], automatic 5.6/7.3/7.6L/100km (50.4/38.7/37.2mpg) [42/32.2/30.9US mpg].

Mercedes–Benz 190 D

```
2.5 Litre 5–cylinder Diesel
66/69kW–88.5/92.5hp–90/94PS
Injection Pump
```

Engine for 190 D 2.5

As 2 Litre/100.5hp model, except:

Weight: Kerbweight (DIN) 1230kg, USA 1340kg, gross vehicle weight 1730kg.

Engine data (ECE): 5–cylinder in–line (87 x 84mm), 2497cm3; compression ratio 22:1; 66kW (88.5hp) [90PS] at 4600rpm, 27.5kW/L (35.5hp/L) [36.0PS/L]; 154Nm (113.6lbft) at 2800rpm.
New engine generation: 69kW (92.5hp) [94PS]

Engine construction: OM 602 designation. Pre–combustion chamber diesel engine; parallel valves; oil capacity 7L (6.6US qt); crankshaft with 6 bearings; Bosch diesel injection. Glow plugs; battery 12V 72Ah; cooling system capacity 8.5L (8US qt).

Transmission: a) 5–speed manual, final drive ratio, 3.64.
b) Automatic, final drive ratio 3.07.

Gear ratios: a) 5–speed manual: 1st 3.91; 2nd 2.17; 3rd 1.37; 4th 1; 5th 0.78; R 4.27.
b) Automatic: As 190.

Performance: Max speed 108mph/174kmh, automatic 106mph/170kmh (manufacturers test specifications), speed at 1000rpm in 5th gear 24.9mph/40.0kmh; acceleration 0 – 62mph/100kmh 15.1secs, automatic 16.1secs; power to weight ratio 18.6kg/kW (13.7kg/PS); ECE consumption 5.5/7.1/8.6L/100km (51.4/39.8/32.8mpg) [42.8/33.1/27.4US mpg], automatic 6.0/7.7/8.3L/100km (47.1/36.7/34mpg) [39.2/30.5/28.3US mpg].

```
2.5 Litre Turbodiesel
90kW–121hp–122PS
Injection Pump
```

Engine for 190 D 2.5 turbo

Mercedes–Benz 190 D 2.5 Turbo

As 2–litre/100.5hp model, except:

Weight: Kerbweight (DIN) 1300kg, gross vehicle weight 1800kg.

Engine data (ECE): 5–cylinder in–line (87x84mm) 2497cm3; compression ratio 22:1; 90kW (121hp) [122PS] at 4600rpm, 36.0kW/L (48.2hp/L) [48.9PS/L]; 225Nm (166lbft) at 2400rpm.

Engine construction: OM 602/T designation. Pre–combustion chamber diesel engine; parallel valves; oil capacity 7L (6.6US qt); crankshaft with 6 bearings; Bosch diesel injection pump; exhaust turbocharger. Glow plugs; battery 12V 72Ah, alternator 980W; cooling system capacity 8.5L (8US qt).

Transmission: Automatic, final drive ratio 2.65.

Gear ratios: Planetary gear set ratios: 1st 4.25; 2nd 2.41; 3rd 1.49; 4th 1; R 5.67.

Chassis: Front ventilated disc brakes.

Performance: Max speed 119mph/192kmh (manufacturers test specifications), speed at 1000rpm in top gear 26.7mph/42.9kmh; acceleration 0 – 62mph/100kmh 11.5secs; power to weight ratio 14.4kg/kW (10.7kg/PS); ECE consumption 6.0/7.9/8.5L/100km (47.1/35.8/33.2mpg) [39.2/29.8/27.7US mpg].

Mercedes-Benz 200 - 300 TD Turbo

124 Series

Luxury upper middle–class Saloon/Sedan with 4 or 6–cylinder engines from 2 to 3 Litre engine capacity; diesel engines from 2 to 3 Litre capacity, 4/5–speed manual or automatic, sophisticated rear axle construction (as 190). November/December 1984 debut. Available as 'T' Estate/Station Wagon since 1985 IAA Frankfurt Motor Show. 1987 Frankfurt: 6–cylinder model with optional 4Matic. 1989 also available as 200 E/TE and 250 Turbo diesel.

```
2 Litre
77kW–103hp–105PS
1 2V Carb
```

Engine for 200 and 200 T

Body, Weight: 4–door Saloon/Sedan, 5–seater; kerbweight (DIN) 1280kg, gross vehicle weight 1800kg. 5–door Estate/Station Wagon, 5/7–seater; kerbweight (DIN) 1400kg, gross vehicle weight 2020kg.

Engine data (Catalyst, ECE): 4–cylinder in–line (89 x 80.2mm), 1996cm3; compression ratio 9.1:1; 77kW (103hp) [105PS] at 5500rpm, 38.7kW/L (51.9hp/L) [52.6PS/L]; 160Nm (118lbft) at 3000rpm; unleaded premium grade. Without Catalyst/After sale Catalyst conversion: 80kW (107hp) [109PS]; 165Nm (121.7lbft).

Mercedes-Benz 200

Engine construction: M 102 V 20 designation. Engine inclined 15deg to right. Valves in 45deg V; hydraulic tappets; 1 overhead camshaft (chain); light–alloy cylinder head; crankshaft with 5 bearings; oil capacity 5.0L (4.7US qt); 1 downdraught 2V compound carb 2EE. Battery 12V 62Ah, alternator 770W; cooling system capacity approx 8.5L (8US qt).

Transmission (to rear wheels): a) 4–speed manual, final drive ratio 3.42; 'T' 3.64.
b) 5–speed manual, final drive ratio 3.42; 'T' 3.64.
c) Mercedes–Benz automatic, hydraulic torque converter and 4– speed Planetary gear set, final drive ratio 3.42; 'T' 3.64.
Optional automatic ASD traction control.

Gear ratios: a) 4–speed manual: 1st 3.91; 2nd 2.71; 3rd 1.37; 4th 1; R 3.78.
b) 5–speed manual: 1st 3.91; 2nd 2.17; 3rd 1.37; 4th 1; 5th 0.78; R 4.27.
c) Automatic: Planetary gear set ratios: 1st 4.25; 2nd 2.41; 3rd 1.49; 4th 1; R 5.67.

Chassis: Integral body; front and rear independent suspension; front shock absorber struts, coil springs on A arms (negative steering offset), antiroll bar, rear suspended axle with compliance arms, control and semi–trailing arms, tie rods, coil springs, telescopic dampers and antiroll bar, optional level control system. Servo/power assisted disc brakes, front disc diameter 28.4cm, rear 25.8cm; optional ABS Bosch system; mechanical foot–operated parking brake to rear wheels; power assisted recirculating ball steering; fuel tank 70L (15.4Gal) [18.5US Gal], 'T' 72L (15.8Gal) [19US Gal] including 9L (2Gal) [2.4US Gal] reserve; tyres 185/65 HR 15, wheels 6J, 'T' tyres 195/65 TR 15, wheels 6.5J.

Dimensions: Wheelbase 280cm, track 150/149cm, clearance 16cm, turning circle 11.2m (4Matic 12.1m). Load space 18.4cu ft (520dm3). Length 474cm, width 174cm, height 144.5cm. Estate/Station Wagon: Load space 18.7/31.3/76.8cu ft (530/885/2175dm3). Length 476.5cm, height 149cm.

Performance: Max speed 115mph/185kmh, automatic 112mph/180kmh (manufacturers test specifications), speed at 1000rpm in 4th gear 20.6mph/33.2kmh; acceleration 0 – 62mph/100kmh 13.0secs, automatic 13.5secs; power to weight ratio 16.6kg/kW (12.2kg/PS); ECE consumption 5–speed 6.4/8.1/11.4L/100km (44.1/34.9/24.8mpg) [36.8/29/20.6 US mpg], automatic 7.6/9.3/11.2L/100km (37.2/30.4/25.2mpg) [30.9/25.3/21US mpg]. 'T': Max speed 107.5mph/173kmh, automatic 104mph/168kmh; acceleration 0 – 62mph/100kmh 14.0secs, automatic 14.5secs. Without Catalyst: Max speed +1mph/2kmh, acceleration –0.4secs.

```
2 Litre
87kW–117hp–118PS
Fuel Injection
```

Engine for 200E and 200TE

As 200, except:

Body, Weight: 4–door Saloon/Sedan, 5–seater; kerbweight (DIN) 1290kg, gross vehicle weight 1810kg. 5–door Estate/Station Wagon, 5/7–seater; kerbweight (DIN) 1410kg, gross vehicle weight 2030kg.

Engine data (Catalyst ECE): 4-cylinder in-line (89 x 80.2mm), 1996cm3; Compression ratio 9.1:1; 87kW (117hp) [118PS] at 5100rpm, 43.5kW/L (58.3hp/L) [59.1PS/L]; 172Nm (127lbft) at 3500rpm.
Without Catalyst/After sale Catalyst conversion: 90kW (120hp) [122PS]; 178Nm (131lbft).

Engine construction: Designated M 102 E 20. Mechanical/electronic Bosch KE-Jetronic fuel injection, electronic fuel pump.

Chassis: Tyres 195/65 HR 15, wheel rims 6.5 J.

Performance: Max speed 131mph/193kmh, Automatic 117mph/188kmh (manufacturers test specifications), speed at 1000rpm in 4th gear 21mph/33.9kmh; acceleration 0 - 62mph/100kmh, 12.0secs, Automatic 12.3secs; power to weight ratio 14.8kg/kW (10.9kg/PS); consumption ECE 5-speed manual 6.5/6.2/11.4L/100km (43.5/45.6/24.8mpg) [36.2/37.9/20.6US mpg], Automatic 7.5/9.3/11.3L/100km (37.7/30.4/25mpg) [31.4/25.3/20.8US mpg].
"T": Max speed 112mph/180kmh, Automatic 109mph/175kmh; acceleration 0-62mph/100kmh 12.9secs, Automatic 13.1secs.
Without Catalyst: Max speed +1mph/2kmh, acceleration 0-62mph/100kmh -0.6secs.

```
2.3 Litre
97kW–130hp–132PS
Fuel Injection
```

Engine for 230E and 230 TE

As 200 model, except:

Body, Weight: 4–door Saloon/Sedan, 5–seater; kerbweight (DIN) 1310kg, gross vehicle weight 1830kg. 5–door Estate/Station Wagon, 5/7–seater; kerbweight (DIN) 1420kg, gross vehicle weight 2040kg.

Engine data (Catalyst, ECE): 4–cylinder in–line (95.5 x 80.2mm), 2298cm3; compression ratio 9:1; 97kW (130hp) [132PS] at 5100rpm, 42.2kW/L (56.5hp/L) [57.4PS/L]; 198Nm (146lbft) at 3500rpm.
Without Catalyst/After sale Catalyst conversion: 100kW (134hp) [136PS]; 205Nm (151.2lbft).

Engine construction: M 102 E 23 designation. Mechanical/electronic Bosch KE–Jetronic fuel injection, electric fuel pump.

Transmission: a) 4–speed manual, final drive ratio 3.27; 'T' 3.46.
b) 5–speed manual, final drive ratio 3.27; 'T' 3.46.
c) Automatic, final drive ratio 3.27; 'T' 3.46.

Chassis: Tyres 195/65 HR 15, wheels 6.5 J.

Mercedes-Benz

Performance: Max speed 124mph/200kmh, automatic 121mph/195kmh (manufacturers test specifications), speed at 1000rpm in 4th gear 22.1mph/35.5kmh; acceleration 0 – 62mph/100kmh 10.6secs; power to weight ratio 13.5kg/kW (9.9kg/PS); ECE consumption 5–speed 6.5/8.2/11.4L/100km (43.5/34.4/24.8mpg) [36.2/28.7/20.6US mpg], automatic 7.8/9.3/11.4L/100km (36.2/30.4/24.8mpg) [30.2/25.3/20.6US mpg]. 'T': Max speed 117mph/188kmh, automatic 114mph/183kmh; acceleration 0 – 62mph/100kmh 11.4secs, automatic 11.5secs. Without Catalyst: Max speed +2mph/3kmh. acceleration –0.2secs.

Mercedes–Benz 230 TE

```
2.6 Litre 6–cylinder
118kW–158hp–160PS
Fuel Injection
```

Engine for 260 E/4Matic

As 200 model, except:

Body, Weight: 4–door Saloon/Sedan, 5–seater; kerbweight (DIN) 1370kg, USA 1455kg, gross vehicle weight 1890kg. 4Matic: Kerbweight 1490kg, gross vehicle weight 2010kg.

Engine data (Catalyst, ECE): 6–cylinder in–line (82.9 x 80.2mm), 2597cm3; compression ratio 9.2:1; 118kW (158hp) [160PS] at 5800rpm, 45.6kW/L (61.1hp/L) [61.6PS/L]; 220Nm (22.4lbft) at 4600rpm.
Without Catalyst/After sale Catalyst conversion: 122kW (163.5hp) [166PS]; 228Nm (168.2lbft).
Some countries: 115kW (154hp) [156PS].

Engine construction: M 103 E 26 designation. Crankshaft with 7 bearings; oil capacity 6L (5.7US qt). Mechanical/electronic Bosch KE–Jetronic fuel injection, electric injection pump. Alternator 980W.

Transmission: a) 5–speed manual, final drive ratio 3.27.
b) Automatic, final drive ratio 3.27.
c) Optional automatically engageable '4Matic' all–wheel– drive; final drive ratio 5–speed manual 3.46, automatic 3.29.

Gear ratios: a) 5–speed manual: 1st 3.86; 2nd 2.18; 3rd 1.38; 4th 1; 5th 0.80; R 4.22.
b) Automatic: Planetary gear set ratios: 1st 4.25; 2nd 2.41; 3rd 1.49; 4th 1; R 5.67.
For 4Matic: 1st 3.87; 2nd 2.25; 3rd 1.44; 4th 1; R 5.59.

Chassis: Front ventilated disc brakes; ABS; tyres 196/65 VR 15, wheels 6.5J.

Performance: Max speed 134mph/215kmh, automatic 131mph/210kmh, 4Matic 129mph/207kmh (manufacturers test specifications), speed at 1000rpm in 5th gear 25.9mph/41.6kmh; acceleration 0 – 62mph/100kmh 9.0secs, 4Matic 10.3secs, automatic 9.8secs, 4Matic 10.8secs; power to weight ratio 11.6kg/kW (8.6kg/PS); ECE consumption 7.2/9.2/12.9L/100km (39.2/30.7/21.9mpg) [32.7/25.6/18.2US mpg], automatic 8.5/10.3/12.6L/100km (33.2/27.4/22.4mpg) [27.7/22.8/18.7US mpg]. Without Catalyst: Max speed +2mph/3kmh, acceleration –0.3secs.

```
3 Litre 6–cylinder
132kW–177hp–180PS
Fuel Injection
```

Engine for 300 E/4Matic and 300 TE/4Matic

As 200 model, except:

Body, Weight: 4–door Saloon/Sedan, 5–seater; kerbweight (DIN) 1370kg, USA 1455kg, gross vehicle weight 1890kg. 4Matic: Kerbweight 1490kg, gross vehicle weight 2010kg. 5–door Estate/Station Wagon, 5/7–seater; kerbweight (DIN) 1480kg, USA 1600kg, gross vehicle weight 2090kg. 4Matic: Kerbweight 1600kg, gross vehicle weight 2180kg.

Engine data (Catalyst, ECE): 6–cylinder in–line (88.5 x 80.2mm), 2960cm3; compression ratio 9.2:1; 132kW (177hp) [180PS] at 5700rpm, 44.6kW/L (59.8hp/L) [60.8PS/L]; 255Nm (188.2lbft) at 4400rpm.
Without Catalyst/After sale Catalyst conversion: 138kW (185hp) [188PS]; 260Nm (191.9lbft).

Mercedes–Benz 300 E 4Matic

Engine construction: M 103 E 30 designation. Crankshaft with 7 bearings; oil capacity 6.0L (5.7US qt). Mechanical/electronic fuel Bosch KE–Jetronic fuel injection, electric fuel pump. Alternator 980W.

Transmission: a) 5–speed manual, final drive ratio 3.07; 'T; 3.27.
b) Automatic, final drive ratio 3.07; 'T' 3.27.
c) Optional '4Matic' automatically engageable all–wheel–drive; final drive ratio 5–speed manual 3.29, 'T' 3.27; automatic 3.07, 'T' 3.27.

Gear ratios: a) 5–speed manual: 1st 3.86; 2nd 2.18; 3rd 1.38; 4th 1; 5th 0.80; R 4.22.
b) Automatic: Max torque multiplication in converter 2 times. Planetary gear set ratios: 1st 3.68; 2nd 2.41; 3rd 1.44; 4th 1; R 5.14.

Chassis: Front ventilated disc brakes; ABS; tyres 195/65 VR 15, wheels 6.5J.

Performance: Max speed 140mph/225kmh, automatic 137mph/220kmh, 4Matic 135mph/217kmh (manufacturers test specifications), speed at 1000rpm in 5th gear 29.4mph/47.3kmh; acceleration 0 – 62mph/100kmh 8.1secs, automatic 8.5secs; power to weight ratio 10.4kg/kW (7.6kg/PS); ECE consumption 7.1/9.1/13.2L/100km (39.8/31/21.4mpg) [33.1/25.8/17.8US mpg], automatic 8.6/10.4/13.3L/100km (32.8/27.2/21.7mpg) [27.4/22.6/18.1US mpg];
'T': Max speed 132mph/212kmh, automatic 129mph/207kmh, 4Matic 127mph/204kmh; acceleration 0 – 62mph/100kmh 8.4secs, automatic 9secs. Without Catalyst: Max speed +2mph/3kmh, acceleration –0.2secs.

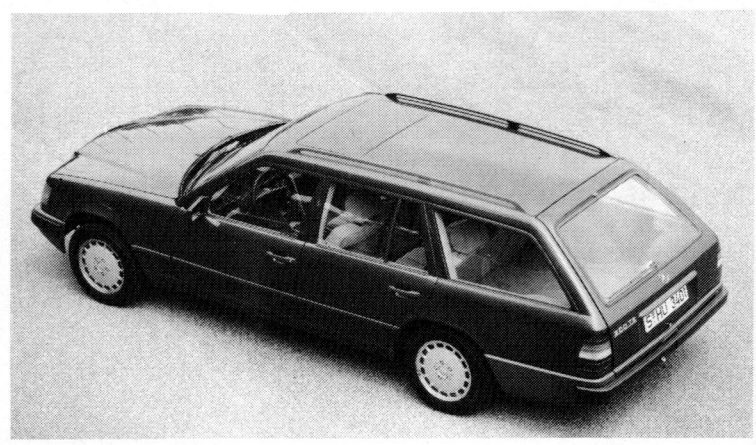

Mercedes–Benz 300 TE

```
2 Litre Diesel
53/55kW–71/74hp–72/75PS
Injection Pump
```

Engine for 200 D and 200 TD

As 200 model, except:

Body, Weight: 4–door Saloon/Sedan, 5–seater; kerbweight (DIN) 1290kg, gross vehicle weight 1810kg. 5–door Estate/Station Wagon, 5/7–seater; kerbweight 1410kg, gross vehicle weight 2030kg.

Engine data (ECE): 4–cylinder in–line (87x84mm), 1997cm3; compression ratio 22:1; 53kW (71hp) [72PS] at 4600rpm, 26.5kW/L (35.5hp/L) [36PS/L]; 123Nm (90.7lbft) at 2800rpm.
New engine generation: 55kW (74hp) [75PS].

Engine construction: OM 601 designation. Pre–combustion chamber diesel engine; parallel valves; oil capacity 6.5L (6.1US qt); Bosch diesel injection pump. Glowplugs; battery 12V 72Ah; cooling system capacity 7.2L (6.8US qt).

Mercedes-Benz

Transmission: a) 4-speed manual (not available for 'T'), final drive ratio 3.42.
b) 5-speed manual, final drive ratio 3.91.
c) Automatic, final drive ratio 3.42; 'T' 3.64.

Gear ratios: a) 4-speed manual: 1st 4.23; 2nd 2.36; 3rd 1.49; 4th 1; R 4.10.
b) 5-speed manual: 1st 3.91; 2nd 2.17; 3rd 1.37; 4th 1; 5th 0.78. R 4.27.
c) Automatic: As 200 model.

Chassis: Tyres 185/65 TR 15, wheels 6J. 'T'; tyres 195/65 TR 15, wheels 6.5J.

Performance: Max speed 99.5mph/160kmh, automatic 96mph/155kmh (manufacturers test specifications), speed at 1000rpm in 5th gear 23.2mph/37.3kmh; acceleration 0 – 62mph/100kmh 18.5secs, automatic 20.4secs; power to weight ratio 24.3kg/kW (17.9kg/PS); ECE consumption 5.3/7.0/7.9L/100km (53.3/40.4/35.8mpg) [44.4/33.6/29.8US mpg], 5-speed 5.0/6.8/8.4L/100km (56.5/41.5/33.6mpg) [47/34.6/28US mpg], automatic 5.7/7.6/8.0L/100km (49.6/37.2/35.3mpg) [41.3/30.9/29.4US mpg]. 'T': Max speed 93mph/150kmh, automatic 90mph/145kmh.

2.5 Litre 5-cylinder Diesel
66kW–88.5hp–90PS
Injection Pump

Engine for 250 D and 250 TD

As 200 model, except:

Body, Weight: 4-door Saloon/Sedan, 5-seater; kerbweight (DIN) 1350kg, gross vehicle weight 1870kg. 5-door Estate/Station Wagon, 5/7-seater; kerbweight (DIN) 1460kg, gross vehicle weight 2080kg.

Engine data (ECE): 5-cylinder in-line (87x84mm), 2497cm3; compression ratio 22:1; 66kW (88.5hp) [90PS] at 4600rpm, 27.5kW/L (37hp/L) [38.0PS/L]; 154Nm (113.6lbft) at 2800rpm.
New engine generation: 69kW (93hp) [94PS].

Engine construction: OM 602 designation. Pre-combustion chamber diesel engine; parallel valves; oil capacity 7L (6.6US qt); crankshaft with 6 bearings; Bosch diesel injection pump. Glow plugs; battery 12V 72Ah; cooling system capacity 8.5L (8US qt).

Transmission: a) 5-speed manual, final drive ratio 3.64; 'T' 3.91.
b) Automatic, final drive ratio 3.07; 'T' 3.23.

Gear ratios: a) 5-speed manual: 1st 3.91; 2nd 2.17; 3rd 1.37; 4th 1; 5th 0.78; R 4.27.
b) Automatic: As 200 model.

Chassis: Tyres 195/65 TR 15, wheels 6.5J.

Performance: Max speed 109mph/175kmh, automatic 106mph/170kmh (manufacturers test specifications), speed at 1000rpm in 5th gear 25.4mph/40.9kmh; acceleration 0 – 62mph/100kmh 16.5secs, automatic 17.0secs; power to weight ratio 20.5kg/kW (15.0kg/PS); ECE consumption 5.4/7.0/8.0L/100km (52.3/40.4/31.7mpg) [43.6/33.6/26.4US mpg], automatic 5.9/7.7/8.6L/100km (47.9/36.7/32.8mpg) [39.9/30.5/27.4US mpg]. 'T': Max speed 102.5mph/165kmh, automatic 99.5mph/160kmh, acceleration 0 – 62mph/100kmh 17.6secs, automatic 18.8secs.

2.5 Litre Turbodiesel
93kW–124hp–125PS
Injection Pump

Engine for 250 D Turbo

As 200, except:

Body, Weight: 4-door Saloon/Sedan, 5-seater; kerbweight (DIN) 1410kg, gross vehicle weight 1930kg.

Engine data (ECE): 5-cylinder in-line (87 x 84mm), 2497cm3; Compression ratio 22:1; 93kW (124hp) [125PS] at 4600rpm, 37.2kW/L (49.8hp/L) [50.1PS/L]; 231Nm (170.5lbft) at 2400rpm.

Engine construction: Designated OM 602/T. Diesel pre-combustion chamber; parallel valves; oil capacity 7.5L (6.6US qt); 6 main bearing crankshaft; Bosch diesel injection pump; turbocharger. Heater plugs; battery 12V 72Ah, Alternator 980W; cooling system capacity 8.5L (8US qt).

Transmission: Automatic, final drive ratio 2.65.

Gear ratios: Planetary gear set ratios, 1st 4.25; 2nd 2.41; 3rd 1.49; 4th 1; R 5.67.

Chassis: Disc brakes, front ventilated; ABS; tyres 196/65 HR 15, wheel rims 6.5 J.

Performance: Max speed 121mph/195kmh (manufacturers test specifications), speed at 1000rpm in top gear 27.2mph/43.8kmh; acceleration 0 – 62mph/100kmh 12.3secs, power to weight ratio 15.2kg/kW (11.3kg/PS); consumption ECE 6.0/7.9/9.2L/100km (47.1/35.8/30.7mpg) [39.2/29.8/25.6US mpg].

Mercedes-Benz 250 D Turbo

---
3 Litre 6-cylinder Diesel
80kW–107hp–109PS
InjectionPump

Engine for 300 D/4Matic and 300 TD

As 200 model, except:

Body, Weight: 4-door Saloon/Sedan, 5-seater; kerbweight (DIN) 1390kg, gross vehicle weight 1910kg. 4Matic: Kerbweight 1510kg, gross vehicle weight 2030kg. 5-door Estate/Station Wagon, 5/7-seater; kerbweight (DIN) 1500kg, gross vehicle weight 2120kg.

Engine data (ECE): 6-cylinder in-line (87 x 84mm), 2996cm3; compression ratio 22:1; 80kW (107hp) [109PS] at 4600rpm, 26.8kW/L (35.9hp/L) [36.4PS/L]; 185Nm (136.5lbft) at 2800rpm.
New engine generation: 83kW (111hp) [113PS].

Engine construction: OM 603 designation. Pre-combustion chamber diesel engine; parallel valves; oil capacity 7.5L (7.1US qt); crankshaft with 7 bearings; Bosch diesel injection pump. Glow plugs; battery 12V 72Ah; cooling system capacity 8.7L (8.2US qt).

Transmission: a) 5-speed manual, final drive ratio 3.46, 'T' 3.67.
b) Automatic, final drive ratio 2.88, 'T' 3.07.
c) Saloon/Sedan with optional automatically engageable '4Matic' all-wheel-drive; final drive ratio 5-speed manual 3.67, automatic 2.87.

Gear ratios: a) 5-speed manual: 1st 3.86; 2nd 2.18; 3rd 1.38; 4th 1; 5th 0.80; R 4.22.
b) Automatic: Planetary gear set ratios: 1st 4.25; 2nd 2.41; 3rd 1.49; 4th 1; R 5.67. For 4Matic: 1st 3.87; 2nd 2.25; 3rd 1.44; 4th 1; R 5.59.

Chassis: ABS; tyres 195/65 TR 15, wheels 6.5J.

Performance: Max speed 118mph/190kmh, 4Matic 114mph/183kmh, automatic 115mph/185kmh; 4Matic 111mph/178kmh (manufacturers test specifications), speed at 1000rpm in 5th gear 26mph/41.9kmh; acceleration 0 – 62mph/100kmh 13.7secs, 4Matic 15.0secs, automatic 14.1secs, 4Matic 16.0secs; power to weight ratio 17.4kg/kW (12.8kg/PS); ECE consumption 5.4/7.0/9.8L/100km (52.3/40.4/28.5mpg) [43.6/33.6/24US mpg], automatic 6.2/7.9/9.3L/100km (45.6/35.8/30.4mpg) [37.9/29.8/25.3US mpg]. 'T': Max speed 112mph/180kmh, automatic 109mph/175kmh, acceleration 0 – 62mph/100kmh 14.6secs, automatic 15.2secs.

---
3 Litre Turbodiesel
105/108kW–141/145hp–143/147PS
Injection Pump

Engine for 300 D Turbo/4matic and 300 TD Turbo/4matic

As 200 model, except:

Body, Weight: 4-door Saloon/Sedan, 5-seater; kerbweight (DIN) 1450kg, gross vehicle weight 1970kg. 4Matic: Kerbweight 1570kg, gross vehicle weight 2090kg. 5-door Estate/Station Wagon, 5/7-seater; kerbweight (DIN) 1560kg, gross vehicle weight 2180kg. 4Matic: Kerbweight 1680kg, gross vehicle weight 2285kg.

Engine data (ECE): 6-cylinder in-line (87 x 84mm), 2296cm3; compression ratio 22:1; 105kW (141hp) [143PS] at 4600rpm, 35.1kW/L (47hp/L) [47.7PS/L]; 267Nm (197lbft) at 2400rpm.
4Matic Saloon/Sedan: 108kW (145hp) [147PS] at 4600rpm, 36kW/L (48.2hp/L) [49PS/L]; 273Nm (201.5lbft) at 2400rpm.

Mercedes-Benz

Engine construction: OM 617 turbo pre-combustion chamber diesel engine. 1 overhead camshaft (chain); grey cast-iron cylinder head; crankshaft with 6 bearings; full-flow and by-pass oil filter, oil capacity 8.0L (7.6US qt), oil-cooler; Bosch 6 plunger-type injection pump and exhaust turbocharger (Garrett). Bosch KE 4677/CA or Beru 383 GK spark plugs; alternator 980W; cooling system capacity 11L (10.4US qt).

Transmission: Only available with automatic, final drive ratio 2.65. Optional automatically engageable '4Matic' all-wheel-drive.

Gear ratios: Planetary gear set ratios: 1st 3.87; 2nd 2.25; 3rd 1.44; 4th 1; R 5.59.

Chassis: Front ventilated disc brakes; ABS; tyres 195/65 HR 15.

Performance: Max speed 125.5mph/202kmh, 4Matic 123kmh/198kmh (manufacturers test specifications), speed at 1000rpm in direct gear 27.2mph/43.8kmh; acceleration 0 – 62mph/100kmh 10.9secs, 4Matic 11.8secs; power to weight ratio from 13.4kg/kW (9.9kg/PS); ECE fuel consumption 6.2/8.1/9.3L/100km (45.6/34.9/30.4mpg) [37.9/29/25.3US mpg]. 'T': Max speed 121mph/195kmh, 4Matic 117mph/188kmh; acceleration 0 – 62mph/100kmh 11.9secs, 4Matic 12.8secs.

Mercedes-Benz 300 TD Turbo

Mercedes-Benz 230 CE – 300 CE

Coupe edition of the new 124 series Saloon/Sedan. 2.3 Litre 4- cylinder or 3 Litre 6-cylinder engine, 5-speed manual or automatic transmission. 1987 debut in Geneva.

```
2.3 Litre
97kW-130hp-132PS
Fuel Injection
```

Engine for 230 CE

Body, Weight: 2-door Coupe, 5-seater; kerbweight (DIN) 1340kg, gross vehicle weight 1790kg.

Engine data (Catalyst, ECE): 4-cylinder in-line (95.5 x 80.25mm), 2299cm3; compression ratio 9:1; 97kW (130hp) [132PS] at 5100rpm, 42.2kW/L (56.6hp/L) [57.4PS/L]; 198Nm (146lbft) at 3500rpm; unleaded premium grade. Without Catalyst/After sale Catalyst conversion: 100kW (134hp) [136PS]; 205Nm (151.2lbft).

Engine construction: M 102 E 23 designation. Engine positioned 15deg to right. Valves in 45deg V; hydraulic tappets; 1 overhead camshaft (chain); light-alloy cylinder head; cranksahft with 5 bearings; oil capacity 5.0L (4.7US qt), mechanical-electronic Bosch KE-Jetronic fuel injection. Battery 12V 62Ah, alternator 770W; cooling system capacity approx 8.5L (8US qt).

Transmission (to rear wheels): a) 5-speed manual, final drive ratio 3.27.
b) Mercedes-Benz automatic, hydraulic torque converter and 4- speed Planetary gear set, final drive ratio 3.27.
Optional automatic ASD traction control.

Gear ratios: a) 5-speed manual: 1st 3.91; 2nd 2.17; 3rd 1.37; 4th 1; 5th 0.78; R 4.27.
b) Automatic: Planetary gear set ratios: 1st 4.25; 2nd 2.41; 3rd 1.49; 4th 1; R 5.67.

Chassis: Integral body; front and rear independent suspension; front shock absorbers struts, coil-sprngs on A arms (negative steering offset), antiroll bar, rear suspended axle with compliance arms, control and semi-trailing arms, tie rods, coil springs, telescopic dampers and antiroll bar, optional level control system. Servo/power assisted disc brakes, ventilated at front, front disc diameter 28.4cm, rear 25.8cm; optional Bosch ABS system; mechanical foot-operated parking brake to rear wheels; power assisted recirculating ball steering; fuel tank 70L (15.4Gal) [18.5US Gal] including 9L (2Gal) [2.3US Gal] reserve; tyres 195/65 HR 15, wheels 6.5J.

Dimensions: Wheelbase 271.5cm, track 150/149cm, clearance 16cm, turning circle 10.9m. Load space 17cu ft (480dm3). Length 465.5cm, width 174cm, height 141cm.

Performance: Max speed 124mph/200kmh, automatic 121mph/195kmh (manufacturers test specifications), speed at 1000rpm in 5th gear 28.3mph/45.5kmh; acceleration 0 – 62mph/100kmh 10.6secs; power to weight ratio 13.8kg/kW (10.2kg/PS); ECE consumption 6.5/8.2/11.4L/100km (43.5/34.4/24.8mpg) [36.2/28.7/20.6US mpg], automatic 7.8/9.3/11.4L/100km (36.2/30.4/24.8mpg) [30.2/25.3/20.6US mpg]. Without Catalyst: Max speed +2mph/3kmh; acceleration –0.2secs.

Mercedes-Benz 230 CE

```
3 Litre 6-cylinder
132kW-177hp-180PS
Fuel Injection
```

Engine for 300 CE

As 230 CE model, except:

Weight: Kerbweight (DIN) 1390kg, USA 1500kg, gross vehicle weight 1840kg.

Engine data (Catalyst, ECE): 6-cylinder in-line (88.5 x 80.25), 2960cm3; compression ratio 9.2:1; 132kW (177hp) [180PS] at 5700rpm, 44.6kW/L (59.8hp/L) [60.8PS/L]; 255Nm (188.2lbft) at 4400rpm.
Without Catalyst/After sale Catalyst conversion: 138kW (185hp) [188PS]; 260Nm (191.9lbft).

Engine construction: M 103 E 30 designation. Cranksahft with 7 bearings; oil capacity 6.0L (5.7US qt). Mechanical/electronic Bosch KE-Jetronic fuel injection, electric fuel pump. Alternator 980W.

Transmission: a) 5-speed manual, final drive ratio 3.07.
b) Automatic, final drive ratio 3.07.

Gear ratios: a) 5-speed manual: 1st 3.86; 2nd 2.18; 3rd 1.38; 4th 1; 5th 0.80; R 4.22.
b) Automatic: Max torque multiplication in converter 2 times, Planetary gear set ratios: 1st 3.68; 2nd 2.41; 3rd 1.44; 4th 1; R 5.14.

Chassis: Tyres 195/65 VR 15, wheels 6.5J.

Performance: Max speed 140mph/225kmh, automatic 137mph/220kmh (manufacturers test specifications), speed at 1000rpm in 5th gear 29.4mph/47.3kmh; acceleration 0 – 62mph/100kmh 8.1secs, automatic 8.5secs; power to weight ratio 10.5kg/kW (7.7kg/PS); ECE consumption 7.1/9.1/13.5L/100km (39.8/31/20.9mpg) [33.1/25.8/17.4US mpg], automatic 8.6/10.4/13.3L/100km (32.8/27.2/21.2mpg) [27.4/22.6/17.7US mpg]. Without Catalyst: Max speed +2mph/3kmh; acceleration –0.2secs.

Mercedes-Benz 300 CE

Mercedes-Benz S

126 Series 5-seater luxury Saloon/Sedan with six-cylinder or light-alloy V8 engine. Debut September 1979. Autumn 1981: lean-burn engines. Frankfurt 1985: new engine series, revised body and interiors. 1988: ABS fitted as standard, increased performance V8 engine. Autumn 1988, 560 SE.

This week from IBM:
Not something to be sneezed at.

GGK

Hold it! Camera! A new creation from the automobile industry first sees the light of day, shaped not only by the creativity of its designers but also to a substantial degree by the computer. To be precise, by an IBM CAE system which, in addition to assisting the designers in their work, will have made life a whole lot easier for the engineers in their design, calculation and production planning.

What's more, a manufacturer can send the rough draft of his design direct to his supplier's CAE system. By computer, from monitor to monitor, enabling the supplier to then fit headlamps, windscreen and rear window, tail-lights or spoilers into the picture with made-to-measure perfection. And when everything is ready, the manufacturer can be sent the geometric data the very same way.

From conception to production, IBM CAE systems thus allow a constant flow of information between all those concerned. This not only saves time and money even at the development stage but in turn helps minimize production costs. And that's not all: significantly fewer prototypes are needed. This way, the first "mystery model" rolls out faster and finer than ever.

Yet IBM CAE systems are used not only in the medium to large-scale motor industry but also in other sectors such as mechanical engineering, plastics and the packaging industry. And IBM not only supplies systems for design or production planning but also expandable solutions for all computer-integrated manufacturing (CIM) applications.

For further details, write to IBM Deutschland GmbH, Informationsservice, Postfach 22 22, 4804 Versmold. Keyword: CAE.

Please send me further details of IBM CAE solutions.
P 32518

Name: _____

Company: _____

Sector: _____

Street: _____

Place/Postal Code: _____

IBM

Mercedes-Benz

2.6 Litre 6-cylinder
118kW–158hp–160PS
Fuel Injection

Engine for 260 SE

Body, Weight: 4–door Saloon/Sedan, 5/6–seater; kerbweight (DIN) 1520kg, gross vehicle weight 2040kg.

Engine data (Catalyst, ECE): 6–cylinder in–line (82.9 x 80.25mm), 2597cm3; compression ratio 9.2:1; 118kW (158hp) [160PS] at 5800rpm, 45.4kW/L (60.8hp/L) [61.6PS/L]; 220Nm (162.3lbft) at 4600rpm.
Without Catalyst/After sale Catalyst conversion: 122kW (163.5hp) [166PS]; 228Nm (168.2lbft).

Engine construction: M 103 E 26 designation. Engine inclined 15deg to right. Valves in 45deg V; hydraulic tappets; 1 overhead camshaft (chain); light-alloy cylinder head; crankshaft with 7 bearings; oil capacity 6.0L (5.7US qt); mechanical/electronic Bosch KE–Jetronic fuel injection, electric fuel pump. Battery 12V 62Ah, alternator 980W; cooling system capacity approx 8.5L (8US qt).

Transmission (to rear wheels): a) 5–speed manual, floor shift, final drive ratio 3.46.
b) Mercedes–Benz automatic; hydraulic torque converter and 4– speed Planetary gear set, central selector lever, final drive ratio 3.46.
Optional limited slip differential or automatic ASD traction control.

Gear ratios: a) 5–speed manual: 1st 3.86; 2nd 2.18; 3rd 1.38; 4th 1; 5th 0.8; R 4.22.
b) Automatic: Max torque multiplication in converter 2.2 times, Planetary gear set ratios: 1st 4.25; 2nd 2.41; 3rd 1.49; 4th 1; R 5.67.

Chassis: Integral body; front and rear single control arm with compression struts, upper single control arm and antiroll bar, coil springs and telescopic dampers; rear independent suspension with swinging arms and coil springs with rubber auxiliary springs and antiroll bar, optional level control system, telescopic dampers. Servo/power assisted disc brakes, front disc diameter (ventilated) 28.6cm, rear 27.9cm; Bosch ABS system; mechanical foot–operated parking brake to rear wheels; power assisted recirculating ball steering; fuel tank 90L (19.8Gal) [23.8US Gal] including 12.5L (2.8Gal) [3.3US Gal] reserve; tyres 205/65 HR/VR 15, wheels 7J.

Dimensions: Wheelbase 293.5cm, track 155.5/153.5cm, clearance 15cm, turning circle 11.8m. Load space 17.8cu ft (505dm3). Length 502cm, width 182cm, height 144.5cm.

Performance: Max speed 124mph/200kmh, automatic 121mph/195kmh (manufacturers test specifications), speed at 1000rpm in 5th gear 26.6mph/42.8kmh; acceleration 0 – 62mph/100kmh 10.5secs, automatic 10.9secs; power to weight ratio 12.9kg/kW (9.5kg/PS); ECE fuel consumption 7.7/10.1/14.3L/100km (36.7/28/19.8mpg) [30.5/23.3/16.4US mpg], automatic 9.1/11.5/13.8L/100km (31/24.6/20.5mpg) [25.8/20.5/17US mpg]. Without Catalyst: Max speed +3mph/5kmh; acceleration –0.3secs.

Mercedes–Benz 260 SE

3 Litre 6-cylinder
132kW–177hp–180PS
Fuel Injection

Engine for 300 SE/300 SEL

As 260 SE model, except:

Body, Weight: SE–Saloon/Sedan: Kerbweight (DIN) 1520kg, gross vehicle weight 2040kg. SEL–Saloon/Sedan: Kerbweight (DIN) 1550kg, USA 1710kg, gross vehicle weight 2070kg.

Engine data (Catalyst, ECE): 6–cylinder in–line (88.5 x 80.2mm), 2960cm3; compression ratio 9.2:1; 132kW (177hp) [180PS] at 5700rpm, 44.6kW/L (59.8) [60.8PS/L]; 255Nm (188.2lbft) at 4400rpm.
Without Catalyst/After sale Catalyst conversion: 138kW (185hp) [188PS]; 260Nm (191.9lbft).

Engine construction: M 103 E 30 designation.

Transmission: a) 5-speed manual, final drive ratio 3.46.
b) Automatic, final drive ratio 3.46

Gear ratios: 5-speed manual: 1st 3.86; 2nd 2.18; 3rd 1.38; 4th 1; 5th 0.80; R 4.22.
Automatic: Max torque mulitplication in converter 2 times; Planetary gear set ratios, 1st 3.87; 2nd 2.25; 3rd 1.44; 4th 1; R 5.59.

Dimensions: SEL; Wheelbase 307.5cm, turning circle 12.3m. Length 516cm, USA 528.5cm, height 144cm.

Performance: Max speed 127mph/205kmh; automatic 124mph/200kmh (manufacturers test specifications); acceleration 0 – 62mph/100kmh 9.3secs, automatic 9.4secs; power-to-weight ratio from 11.5kg/kW (8.4kg/PS); ECE consumption 8.0/10.3/14.5L/100km (31.7/27.4/19.5mpg) [29.4/22.8/16.2US mpg], automatic 9.4/11.8/13.9L/100km (30.1/23.9/20.3mpg) [25.8/19.9/16.9US mpg]. Without Catalyst: Max speed +3mph/5kmh; acceleration –0.2secs.

Mercedes–Benz 420 SE

4.2 Litre V8
165kW–221hp–224PS
Fuel Injection

Engine for 420 SE/420 SEL

As 260 SE model, except:

Body, Weight: SE–Saloon/Sedan: Kerbweight (DIN) 1630kg, gross vehicle weight 2150kg. SEL–Saloon/Sedan: Kerbweight (DIN) 1660kg. USA 1760kg, gross vehicle weight 2180kg.

Engine data (Catalyst, ECE): 8–cylinder in 90deg V (92 x 78.9mm), 4196cm3; compression ratio 10:1; 165kW (221hp) [224PS] at 5400rpm, 39.3kW/L (52.7hp/L) [53.4PS/L]; 325Nm (240lbft) at 4000rpm.
Without Catalyst/After sale Catalyst conversion: 170kW (228hp) [231PS]; 335Nm (247.3lbft).
USA version with Catalyst (SAE net): Compression ratio 9:1; 150kW (201hp) [204PS]; 310Nm (228.8lbft); unleaded regular grade.

Engine construction: M 116 E 42 designation. 1 overhead camshaft (chain) per cylinder bank; light–alloy cylinder head and block; crankshaft with 5 bearings; oil capacity 8L (7.6US qt). Battery 12V 66Ah; alternator 1120W; cooling system capacity 12.5L (11.8US qt).

Transmission: Automatic, final drive ratio, 2.47.
Optional limited slip differential or ASR traction control.

Gear ratios: Automatic: Planetary gear set ratios: 1st 3.87; 2nd 2.25; 3rd 1.44; 4th 1; R 5.59.

Chassis: Optional hydro–pneumatic suspension for SEL model.

Dimensions: SEL; Wheelbase 307.5cm, turning circle 12.3m. Length 516cm, USA 528.5cm, height 144cm.

Performance: Max speed 137mph/220kmh (manufacturers specifications), speed at 1000rpm in 4th gear 29.8mph/48kmh; acceleration 0 – 62mph/100kmh 8.3secs; power to weight ratio from 9.9kg/kW (7.3kg/PS); consumption (ECE) 9.1/11.3/15.4L/100km (31/25/18.3mpg) [25.8/20.8/15.3US mpg]. Without Catalyst: Max speed +1mph/2kmh; acceleration –0.1secs.

5 Litre V8
185kW–248hp–252PS
Fuel Injection

Engine for 500 SE/500 SEL

As 260 SE model, except:

Mercedes-Benz

Body, Weight: SE–Saloon/Sedan: Kerbweight (DIN) 1660kg, gross vehicle weight 2180kg. SEL–Saloon/Sedan: Kerbweight (DIN) 1700kg gross vehicle weight 2220kg.

Engine data (Catalyst, ECE): 8–cylinder in 90deg V (96.5 x 85mm), 4973cm3; compression ratio 10:1; 185kW (248hp) [252PS] at 5200rpm, 37.2kW/L (49.8hp/L) [50.7PS/L]; 390Nm (287.8lbft) at 3750rpm.
Without Catalyst/After sale Catalyst conversion: 195kW (261hp) [265PS] at 5200rpm; 405Nm (298.9lbft) at 4000rpm.

Engine construction: M 117 E 50 designation. 1 overhead camshaft (chain) for each cylinder bank; light–alloy cylinder head and block; crankshaft with 5 bearings; oil capacity 8L (7.6US qt). Battery 12V 66Ah; alternator 1120W; cooling system capacity 13L (12.3US qt).

Transmission: Automatic, final drive ratio 2.24. Optional limited slip differential or ASR traction control.

Gear ratios: Planetary gear set ratios: 1st 3.87; 2nd 2.25; 3rd 1.44; 4th 1; R 5.59.

Chassis: Optional hydro–pneumatic suspension for SEL model, rear starting torque compensation.

Dimensions: SE: Wheelbase 293cm. SEL: Wheelbase 307cm, turning circle 12.3m. Length 516cm, height 144cm.

Performance: Max speed 143mph/230kmh (manufacturers test specifications), speed at 1000rpm in 4th gear 32.6mph/52.9kmh; acceleration 0 – 62mph/100kmh 7.5secs; power to weight ratio from 9.0kg/kW (6.6kg/PS); consumption (ECE) 9.4/11.7/16.2L/100km (30.1/24.1/17.4mpg) [25/20.1/14.5US mpg]. Without Catalyst: Max speed +3mph/5kmh; acceleration –0.3secs.

5.5 Litre V8
205kW–275hp–279PS
Fuel Injection

Engine for 560 SE/560 SEL

As 260 SE model, except:

Body, Weight: SE–Saloon/Sedan; kerbweight (DIN) 1790kg, gross vehicle weight 2250kg. SEL-Limousine; kerbweight (DIN) 1830kg, USA 1850kg, gross vehicle weight 2290kg.

Engine data (Catalyst, ECE): 8–cylinder in 90deg V (96.5 x 94.8mm), 5547cm3; compression ratio 10:1; 205kW (275hp) [279PS] at 5200rpm, 37.0kW/L (49.6hp/L) [50.3PS/L]; 430Nm (317.3lbft) at 3750rpm.
Without Catalyst/After sale Catalyst conversion: 200kW (296hp) [300PS] at 5000rpm; 455Nm (335.8lbft) at 3750rpm.
USA version with Catalyst (SAE net): Compression ratio 9:1; 177kW (237hp) [241PS]; 390Nm (287.8lbft); unleaded regular grade.

Engine construction: M 117 E 56 designation. 1 overhead camshaft (chain) per cylinder bank; light–alloy cylinder head and block; crankshaft with 5 bearings; oil capacity 8L (7.6US qt). Battery 12V 92Ah; alternator 1120W; cooling system capacity 13L (12.3US qt).

Transmission: Automatic, final drive ratio 2.65.
Optional limited slip differential or ASR traction control.

Gear ratios: Planetary gear set ratios: 1st 3.87; 2nd 2.25; 3rd 1.44; 4th 1; R 5.59.

Chassis: Hydro–pneumatic suspension; rear starting torque compensation. Tyres 215/65 VR 15.

Dimensions: SE: Wheelbase 293cm. SEL: Wheelbase 307cm, turning circle 12.3m, length 516cm, height 144cm.

Performance: Max speed 149mph/240kmh (manufacturers test specifications), speed at 1000rpm in 4th gear 28.3mph/45.6kmh; acceleration 0 – 62mph/100kmh 7.2secs; power to weight ratio from 8.9kg/kW (6.6kg/PS); ECE consumption 11.1/13.6/17.6L/100km (25.4/20.8/16mpg) [21.1/17.3/13.4US mpg]. Without Catalyst: Max speed +6/mph10kmh; acceleration –0.3secs.

Mercedes-Benz 560 SEL

Mercedes–Benz SEC

126 Series

Luxury Coupe with light–alloy V8 engine, with 4.2, 5.0 or 5.5 litre engines since Frankfurt 1985 and 4–speed automatic transmission. Debut September 1981. Increased power for 1988.

4.2 Litre V8
165kW–221hp–224PS
Fuel Injection

Engine for 420 SEC

Body, Weight: 2–door Coupe, 5–seater; kerbweight (DIN) 1620kg, gross vehicle weight 2140kg.

Mercedes–Benz 420 SEC

Engine data (Catalyst, ECE): 8–cylinder in 90deg V (92x78.9mm), 4196cm3; compression ratio 10:1; 165kW (221hp) [224PS] at 5400rpm, 39.3kW/L (52.7hp/L) [53.4PS/L]; 325Nm (239.9lbft) at 4000rpm; unleaded premium grade.
Without Catalyst/After sale Catalyst conversion: 170kW (228hp) [231PS]; 335Nm (247.2lbft).

Engine construction: M 116 E 42 designation. Hydraulic tappets; 1 overhead camshaft (chain) per cylinder bank; light–alloy cylinder head and block; crankshaft with 5 bearings; oil capacity 8L (7.6US qt), mechanical/electronic Bosch KE-Jetronic fuel injection, electric fuel pump. Battery 12V 66Ah; alternator 1120W; cooling system capacity 12.5L (11.8US qt).

Transmission (to rear wheels): Mercedes–Benz automatic, hydraulic torque converter and 4–speed Planetary gear set, final drive ratio 2.47.
Optional limited slip differential or ASR traction control.

Gear ratios: Automatic: Max torque multiplication in converter 2.2 times, Planetary gear set ratios: 1st 3.87; 2nd 2.25; 3rd 1.44; 4th 1; R 5.59.

Chassis: Integral body; front lower single control arm with compression struts, upper single control arm and antiroll bar, coil springs and telescopic dampers; rear suspension wheel with swinging arms and coil springs with rubber auxiliary springs and antiroll bar, optional level control system; telescopic dampers. Servo/power assisted disc brakes, front disc (internally ventilated) diameter 28.6cm, rear 27.9cm; Bosch ABS system; mechanical foot–operated parking brake to rear wheels; power assisted recirculating ball steering; fuel tank 90L (19.8Gal) including 12.5L (2.7Gal) [3.3US Gal] reserve; tyres 205/65 VR 15, wheels 7J.

Dimensions: Wheelbase 285cm, track 155.5/153cm, clearance 15.5cm, turning circle 11.5m. Load space 17.8cu ft (505dm3). Length 493.5cm, width 183cm, height 141cm.

Performance: Max speed 137mph/220kmh (manufacturers test specifications), speed at 1000rpm in 4th gear 29.8mph/48kmh; acceleration 0 – 62mph/100kmh 8.3secs; power to weight ratio 9.8kg/kW (7.2kg/PS); consumption (ECE) 9.1/11.3/15.4L/100km (31/25/18.3mpg) [25.8/20.8/15.3US mpg]. Without Catalyst: Max speed +1mph/2kmh; acceleration –0.1secs.

---
5 Litre V8
185kW–248hp–252PS
Fuel Injection

Engine for 500 SEC

As 420 SEC model, except:

Weight: Kerbweight (DIN) 1650kg, gross vehicle weight 2170kg.

Engine data (Catalyst, ECE): 8–cylinder in 90deg V (96.5x85mm), 4973cm3; compression ratio 10:1; 185kW (248hp) [252PS] at 5200rpm, 37.2kW/L (49.8hp/L) [50.7PS/L]; 390Nm (287.8lbft) at 3750rpm.

Mercedes-Benz

Without Catalyst/After sale Catalyst conversion: 195kW (261hp) [265PS] at 5200rpm; 405Nm (298.9lbft) at 4000rpm.

Engine construction: Cooling system capacity 13L (12.3US qt).

Transmission: Final drive ratio 2.24.

Chassis: Rear starting torque compensation.

Performance: Max speed 143mph/230kmh (manufuacturers test specifications), speed at 1000rpm in 4th gear 32.8mph/52.9kmh; acceleration 0 – 62mph/100kmh 7.5secs; power to weight ratio 8.9kg/kW (6.5kg/PS); ECE consumption 9.4/11.7/16.2L/100km (30.1/24.1/17.4mpg) [25/20.1/14.5US mpg]. Without Catalyst: Max speed +3mph/5kmh; acceleration –0.3secs.

Mercedes–Benz 560 SEC

```
5.5 Litre V8
205kW–275hp–279PS
Fuel Injection
```

Engine for 560 SEC

As 420 SEC model except:

Weight: Kerbweight (DIN) 1760kg, USA 1775kg, gross vehicle weight 2220kg.

Engine data (Catalyst, ECE): 8–cylinder in 90deg V (96.5 x 94.8mm), 5547cm3; compression ratio 10:1 205kW (275hp) [279PS] at 5200rpm, 37.0kW/L (49.6hp/L) [50.3PS/L]; 430Nm (43.8lbft) at 3750rpm.
Without Catalyst/After sale Catalyst conversion: 221kW (296hp) [300PS] at 5000rpm; 455Nm (335.8lbft) at 3750 rpm.
USA version with Catalyst (SAE net): Compression ratio 9:1; 177kW (237hp) [241PS]; 390Nm (287.8lbft); unleaded regular grade.

Engine construction: Battery 12V 92Ah; cooling system capacity 13L (12.3US qt).

Transmission: Final drive ratio 2.65.

Chassis: Hydro–pneumatic suspension; rear starting torque compensation. Tyres 215/65 VR 15.

Dimensions: Wheelbase 284.5cm. Length USA 506cm.

Performance: Max speed 149mph/240kmh (manufacturers test specifications), speed at 1000rpm in 4th gear 28.3mph/45.6kmh; acceleration 0 – 62mph/100kmh 7.2secs; power to weight ratio 8.6kg/kW (6.3kg/PS); consumption (ECE) 11.1/13.6/17.6L/100km (25.4/20.8/16mpg) [21.2/17.3/13.4US mpg]. Without Catalyst: Max speed +6mph/10kmh; acceleration –0.3secs.

Mercedes–Benz SL

129 Series

New model range. Sporty vehicle with six–cylinder or V8 engines. Rear suspension multiple arm, with optional level control system; cd 0.31 to 0.33. Launched in Geneva in 1989. Data is provisional.

```
3 Litre 6–cylinder
140kW–188hp–190PS
Fuel Injection
```

Engine for 300 SL

Body, Weight: 2-door Roadster with optional hardtop, 2 + 2 seater; kerbweight (DIN) 1650kg, gross vehicle weight 2040kg.

Engine data (Catalyst, ECE): 6–cylinder in–line (88.5 x 80.20mm), 2960cm3; compression ratio 9.2:1; 140kW (188hp) [190PS] at 5700rpm, 47.3kW/L (63.3hp/L) [64.2PS/L]; 260Nm (191.9lbft) at 4500rpm; unleaded premium grade.

Engine construction: Designated 103.984. Overhead valves in 54deg V, 2 overhead camshafts (chain); light–alloy cylinder head; crankshaft with 7 bearings; oil–cooler, oil capacity 6.8L (6.4US qt); mechanical Bosch KE5–Jetronic fuel injection. Battery 12V 72Ah, alternator 1400W; cooling system capacity 11L (10.4US qt).

Transmission (to rear wheels): a) 5-speed manual, final drive ratio 3.67. b) Mercedes–Benz automatic, hydraulic torque converter and 4-speed Planetary gear set, final drive ratio 3.29.

Gear ratios: a) 5-speed manual: 1st 3.86; 2nd 2.18; 3rd 1.38; 4th 1; 5th 0.8; R 4.15. b) Automatic: Max torque multiplication in converter 2.2 times, Planetary gear set ratios: 1st 3.87; 2nd 2.25; 3rd 1.44; 4th 1; R 5.59.

Chassis: Integral body; independent suspension front and rear; front shock absorber struts, coil springs and A arm, rear suspension with single upper transverse arm and semi trailing arm with tie rod, coil springs, telescopic damper and antiroll bar, optional level control system, front and rear with adaptive shock absorber system (ADS). Servo/power assisted disc brakes (ventilated), front disc diameter 30cm, rear 27.8cm; ABS (Bosch); foot actuated parking brake to rear wheels; power assisted recirculating ball steering; fuel tank 80L (17.6Gal) [21.1US Gal] including 10L (2.2Gal) [2.7US Gal] reserve; tyres 225/55 ZR 16; wheels 8J, optional Conti CTS.

Dimensions: Wheelbase 251.5cm, track 153/152cm, clearance 15cm, turning circle 10.8m. Load space 9.2cu ft (260dm3). Length 446.5cm, width 181cm, height 128.5cm, Hardtop 130.5cm.

Performance: Max speed 142mph/228kmh, automatic 138mph/223kmh (manufacturers test specifications), speed at 1000rpm in 5th gear 25.3mph/40.8kmh; acceleration 0 – 62mph/100kmh 9.3secs, automatic 9.5secs; standing km 30.1secs, Automatic 30.6secs; power to weight ratio from 11.8kg/kW (8.7kg/PS); consumption (ECE) 5–speed 8.5/10.3/15.9L/100km (33.2/27.4/17.8mpg) [27.7/22.8/14.8US mpg], automatic 9.2/10.9/15.5L/100km (30.7/25.9/18.2mpg) [25.6/21.6/15.2US mpg].

Mercedes–Benz 300 SL

```
3 Litre 6-cylinder 24V
170kW–288hp–231PS
Fuel Injection
```

Engine for 300 SL-24

As 300 SL, except:

Weight: Kerbweight (DIN) 1690kg, gross vehicle weight 2080kg.

Engine data (Catalyst ECE): 6-cylinder in-line (88.5 x 80.20mm), 2960cm3; Compression ratio 10:1; 170kW (228hp) [231PS] at 6400rpm, 57.4kW/L (76.9hp/L) [78PS/L]; 272Nm (200.7lbft) at 4600rpm.

Engine construction: Designated M 104.981. 4 valve (50deg) per cylinder; 2 overhead crankshafts; oil capacity 7.5L (7.1US qt).

Transmission: a) 5-speed manual, final drive ratio 3.27 b) Automatic, final drive ratio 3.46.

Gear ratios: a) 5-speed manual: 1st 4.15; 2nd 2.52; 3rd 1.69; 4th 1.24; 5th 1; R 4.15. b) Automatic: As 300 SL.

Performance: Max speed 149mph/240kmh, Automatic 146mph/235kmh (manufacturers test specifications), speed at 1000rpm in 5th gear 22.7mph/36.6kmh; acceleration 0-62mph/100kmh 8.2secs, Automatic 8.5secs; standing km 28.8secs, Automatic 29.1secs; power to weight ratio from 9.9kg/kW (7.3kg/PS); consumption ECE 8.8/10.4/16.2L/100km (32.1/27.2/17.4mpg) [26.7/22.6/14.5US mpg], Automatic 9.4/10.9/15.8L/100km (30.1/25.9/17.9mpg) [25/21.6/14.9US mpg]

Mercedes-Benz D • Mercedes-Benz/Puch D/A

Mercedes-Benz 300 SL-24

5 Litre V8 32V
240kW–322hp–326PS
Fuel Injection

Engine for 500 SL

As 300 SL model, except:

Weight: Kerbweight (DIN) 1770kg, gross vehicle weight 2160kg.

Engine data (Catalyst, ECE): 8–cylinder in V 90deg (96.5 x 85mm), 4973cm3; compression ratio 10:1; 240kW (322hp) [326PS] at 5500rpm, 48.3kW/L (64.7hp/L) [65.5PS/L]; 450Nm (332.1lbft) at 4000rpm.
Without Catalyst/After sale Catalyst conversion: 245kW (328hp) [333PS] at 5500rpm; 460Nm (339.5lbft) at 4000rpm.

Engine construction: Hydraulic tappets; 4 valves (37.7deg) per cylinder; 2 overhead camshafts (chain); light–alloy cylinder head and block; crankshaft with 5 bearings; oil–cooler; oil capacity 8L (7.6US qt). Cooling system capacity 15L (14.2US qt).

Transmission: Automatic, final drive ratio 2.65.

Gear ratios: Planetary gear set ratios: 1st 3.87; 2nd 2.27; 3rd 1.44; 4th 1; R 5.59.

Performance: Max speed 155mph/250kmh (manufacturers test specifications), speed at 1000rpm in direct gear 28mph/45.2kmh; acceleration 0 – 62mph/100kmh 6.2secs; standing km 25.8secs; power to weight ratio from 7.4kg/kW (5.4kg/PS); consumption ECE 10.1/12.0/16.6L/100km (28/23.5/17mpg) [23.3/19.6/14.2US mpg].

Mercedes–Benz 500 SL

MERCEDES–BENZ/PUCH D/A

Daimler–Benz AG, Stuttgart–Untertuerkheim, Deutschland
Steyr–Daimler–Puch AG, Werke Graz, Postfach 823, A–8011 Graz, Austria

Mercedes–Benz G/Puch G

300 GD – 250 GD – 230 GE – 280 GE

Off–road vehicle with two wheelbases and four engines. Mechanical components from Daimler–Benz, frames and body from Puch, assembly in Graz. Sold as Puch in Switzerland, Austria and Eastern Europe and as Mercedes–Benz in other countries. Debut in February 1979. Turin 1982: 230 GE. Frankfurt 1987: 250 GD.

3 Litre 5–cylinder Diesel
64kW–86hp–88PS
Injection Pump

Engine for 300 GD

Body, Weight: a) Shorter wheelbase: 2–door Roadster with sheet metal or folding roof, 5 seater; kerbweight (DIN) 1885kg, gross vehicle weight 2600kg.
3–door Estate/Station Wagon, 5 seater; kerbweight (DIN) 1935kg, gross vehicle weight 2600kg.

b) Longer wheelbase: 5–door Estate/Station Wagon, 5+4 seater; kerbweight (DIN) 2055kg, gross vehicle weight 2800kg.

Engine data (DIN): 5–cylinder in–line (90.0 x 92.4mm), 2998cm3; compression ratio 21:1; 64kW (86hp) [88PS] at 4400rpm, 21.7kW/L (29.1hp/L) [29.4PS/L]; 172Nm (126.9lbft) at 2000rpm.

Engine construction: Mercedes–Benz OM 617 pre–combustion chamber diesel engine. 1 overhead camshaft (chain); grey cast–iron cylinder head; crankshaft with 6 bearings; full–flow oil and by–pass filter, oil capacity 7L (6.6US qt), oil–cooler; Bosch plunger–type injection pump. Battery 12V 88Ah, alternator 55A; cooling system capacity 10.7L (10.1US qt).

Transmission (to the rear or all wheels): a) 4–speed manual, final drive ratio 4.9.
b) 5–speed manual, final drive ratio 4.9.
c) Daimler–Benz automatic, hydraulic torque converter and 4–speed Planetary gear set, central selector lever, final drive ratio 4.9.
All–wheel–drive, standard transfer case, final drive ratio 2.14, optional front and rear differential lock.

Gear ratios: a) 4–speed manual: 1st 4.628; 2nd 2.462; 3rd 1.473; 4th 1; R 4.348.
b) 5–speed manual: 1st 3.822; 2nd 2.199; 3rd 1.398; 4th 1; 5th 0.813; R 3.705.
c) Automatic: Max torque multiplication in converter 2.2 times, Planetary gear set ratios: 1st 4.007; 2nd 2.392; 3rd 1.463; 4th 1; R 5.495.

Chassis: Box–type frame; front and rear rigid axles each with 2 longitudinal arms and 1 control arm and coil springs, front antiroll bar, telescopic dampers. Servo/power assisted brakes, front with 30.3cm diameter discs, rear drums; mechanical handbrake to rear wheels; power assisted rack and pinion steering; fuel tank capacity 81.5L (17.9Gal) [21.2US Gal] including 11L (2.4Gal) [2.9US Gal] reserve; tyres 205 R 16, wheel rims 5.5J, optional tyres 215 R 16, 235/70 HR 15.

Dimensions: Wheelbase 240/285cm, track 142.5/142.5cm, clearance 21cm, turning circle 11.4/13m. Load space 23.3/61.1–47.3/91.5cu ft (745/1730–1340/2590dm3). Length 395.5/440.5cm, width 170cm, height 192.5cm.

Performance: Max speed 79mph/127kmh (manufacturers test specifications), speed at 1000rpm in 4th gear 17.1mph/27.5kmh; power to weight ratio from 29kW/L (21.4PS/L); consumption ECE 11.9/–/14.6L/100km (23.7/–/19.3mpg) [19.8/–/16.1US mpg].

300 GD

2.5 Litre Diesel
62kW–83hp–84PS
InjectionPump

Engine for 250 GD

As 300 GD, except:

Body, Weight: a) Shorter wheelbase: 2–door Roadster with sheet–metal or folding roof, 5 seater; kerbweight (DIN) 1830kg, gross vehicle weight 2600kg.
3–door Estate/Station Wagon, 5 seater; kerbweight (DIN) 1930kg, gross vehicle weight 2600kg.
b) Longer wheelbase: 5–door Estate/Station Wagon, 5+4 seater; kerbweight (DIN) 2050kg, gross vehicle weight 2800kg.

Engine data (DIN): 5–cylinder in–line (87.0 x 84.0mm), 2497cm3; compression ratio 22:1; 62kW (83hp) [84PS] at 4600rpm, 24.8kW/L (33.2hp/L) [33.6PS/L]; 154Nm (113.6lbft) at 2200–2800rpm.

Engine construction: Daimler–Benz OM 602 designation.

Transmission: a) 4–speed manual, final drive ratio 6.17.
b) 5–speed manual, final drive ratio 6.17.
c) Automatic, final drive ratio 6.17.

Gear ratios: a) 4–speed manual: 1st 4.628; 2nd 2.462; 3rd 1.473; 4th 1; R 4.348.
b) 5–speed manual: 1st 3.856; 2nd 2.183; 3rd 1.376; 4th 1; 5th 0.799; R 3.705.

Mercedes-Benz/Puch D/A • Mercury

c) Automatic; Max torque multiplication in converter 2.2 times, Planetary gear set ratios: 1st 4.007; 2nd 2.392; 3rd 1.463; 4th 1; R 5.495.

Performance: Max speed 78mph/125kmh (manufacturers test specifications), speed at 1000rpm in direct drive 13.5mph/21.8kmh; power to weight ratio from 29.5kg/kW (21.8kg/PS); consumption ECE 11.1/–/13.9L/100km (25.4/–/20.3mpg) [21.2/–/17US mpg].

2.3 Litre
92/89.5kW–123/120hp–125/122PS
Fuel Injection

Engine for 230 GE

As 300 GD, except:

Body, Weight: a) Shorter wheelbase: 2–door Roadster with sheet metal or folding roof, 5 seater; kerbweight (DIN) 1830kg, gross vehicle weight 2600kg. 3–door Estate/Station Wagon, 5 seater; kerbweight (DIN) 1880kg, gross vehicle weight 2600kg.
b) Longer wheelbase: 5–door Estate/Station Wagon, 5+4 seater; kerbweight (DIN) 2000kg, gross vehicle weight 2800kg.

Engine data (DIN): 4–cylinder in–line (95.5 x 80.25mm); 2299cm3; compression ratio 9:1; 92kW (123hp) [125PS] at 5000rpm, 40kW/L (53.6hp/L) [54.4PS/L]; 192Nm (141.6lbft) at 4000rpm. Leaded premium grade.
With Catalyst: 89.5kW (120hp) [122PS].
Some countries: (89 x 80.2mm), 1996cm3; compression ratio 9.1:1; 80kW (107hp) [109PS] at 5200rpm, 40.1kW/L (53.7hp/L) [54.6PS/L]; 165Nm (121.7lbft) at 3000rpm; leaded regular grade.

Engine construction: Daimler–Benz M 102 E desgination. Valves in V; light–alloy cylinder head, crankshaft with 5 bearings; oil capacity 6.0L (5.7US qt); electronic Bosch KE–Jetronic fuel injection. Battery 12V 66Ah.

Performance: Max speed 89mph/143kmh, speed at 1000rpm in top gear 17.1mph/27.5kmh; power to weight ratio from 19.9kg/kW (14.6kg/PS); ECE consumption 11.6/15.4/17.0L/100km. (24.4/18.3/16.6mpg) [20.3/15.3/14.2US mpg].

230 GE

2.8 Litre
110kW–147hp–150PS
Fuel Injection

Engine for 280 GE

As 300 GD, except:

Body, Weight: a) Shorter wheelbase: 2–door Roadster with sheet metal or folding roof, 5 seater; kerbweight (DIN) 1895kg, gross vehicle weight 2600kg. 3–door Estate/Station Wagon, 5 seater; kerbweight (DIN) 1945kg, gross vehicle weight 2600kg.
b) Longer wheelbase: 5–door Estate/Station Wagon, 5+4 seater; kerbweight (DIN) 2065kg, gross vehicle weight 2800kg.

Engine data (DIN): 6–cylinder in–line (86x78.8mm), 2746cm3; compression ratio 8:1; 110kW (147hp) [150PS] at 5250rpm, 40.1kW/L (53.7hp/L) [54.6PS/L]; 226Nm (166.7lbft) at 4250rpm; leaded regular grade.

Engine construction: Daimler–Benz M 110 E desgination. Overhead valves in 54deg V, 2 overhead camshafts (chain); light–alloy cylinder head; crankshaft with 7 bearings; oil–cooler, oil capacity 7.5L (7.1US qt); indirect mechanical Bosch K–Jetronic fuel injection. Battery 12V 66Ah.

Transmission: a) 4–speed manual, final drive ratio 4.9.
b) 5–speed manual, final drive ratio 4.9.
c) Automatic, final drive ratio 4.9.

Gear ratios: a) 4–speed manual: 1st 4.043; 2nd 2.206; 3rd 1.381; 4th 1; R 3.787.
b) 5–speed manual; as 300 GD.
c) Automatic; as 300 GD.

Performance: Max speed 96mph/155kmh (manufacturers test specifications); power to weight ratio from 17.2kg/kW (12.6kg/PS); consumption ECE 13.3/17.9/21.5L/100km (21.2/15.8/13.1mpg) [17.7/13.1/10.9US mpg].

280 GE

MERCURY   **USA**

Ford Motor Company, PO Box 2053, Dearborn, Michigan 48121, USA
Branch of Ford Motor Company producing vehicles between Ford and Lincoln class.
MODEL RANGE
Tracer – Topaz – Sable – Cougar – Grand Marquis

Mercury Tracer

Production for Mercury in Hermosillo, North Mexico, under Mazda 323 licence. Went on sale in USA in Spring 1987. See Mazda for technical data.

Mercury Tracer

Mercury Capri

Mercury Capri

New model. 2+2-seater convertible with hardtop on the basis of Mazda 323, transverse engine and front wheel drive, engine 1.6 Litre OHC with or without Turbo. 5-speed manual or automatic. Other characteristics: power assisted steering, front disc brakes, optional air conditioning unit, body design through Ghia and interior design through Ital-design. Production location Broadmeadows, Melbourne, Australia. Prototype launched Spring 1989, production uncertain.

Mercury

Mercury Topaz

GS – LS – XR5 – LS Sport – AWD

2 and 4-door Saloon/Sedan with front-wheel-drive, 2.3 Litre 4- cylinder engine, 5-speed manual or automatic. January 1983 debut. 2 Litre diesel engine option for 1984. Available with engageable all-wheel-drive (AWD) in 1987. Increased performance for 1988. 1989 optional airbag.

```
2.3 Litre
73kW–98hp–99PS
Fuel Injection
```

Not available for XR5, LS Sport and AWD

Body, Weight: Topaz GS: 2–door Saloon/Sedan, 5 seater; approx 1165kg. 4–door Saloon/Sedan, 5 seater; approx 1185kg. Topaz LS: 4–door Saloon/Sedan, 5 seater; approx 1200kg.

Engine data (SAE net): 4–cylinder in–line (93.47 x 83.8mm), 2300cm3; compression ratio 9:1; 73kW (98hp) [99PS] at 4000rpm, 31.7kW/L (42.5hp/L) [43.0PS/L]; 168Nm (123.9lbft) at 2200rpm; unleaded regular grade.

Engine construction: Transverse mounted front engine. Hydraulic tappets; side–mounted camshaft (chain); crankshaft with 5 bearings; oil capacity 4.7L (4.4US qt); electronic Ford fuel injection. Battery 12V 58Ah, alternator 65/75A; cooling system capacity 7.6L (7.2US qt).

Transmission (to front wheels): a) 5–speed manual, final drive ratio 3.40.
b) Automatic, hydraulic torque converter and 3–speed Planetary gear set, central selector lever, final drive ratio 3.07.

Gear ratios: a) 5–speed manual: 1st 3.60; 2nd 2.12; 3rd 1.39; 4th 1.02; 5th 0.75; R 3.62.
b) Automatic: Max torque multiplication in converter 2.2 times, Planetary gear set ratios; 1st 2.81; 2nd 1.60; 3rd 1; R 2.03.

Chassis: Integral body; front McPherson struts (coil springs), lower single control arm and antiroll bar, rear independent suspension with shock absorber struts; control arms, tension struts and coil springs, telescopic dampers. Servo/power assisted brakes, front 23.4cm diameter discs (ventilated), rear drums; mechanical handbrake to rear wheels; rack and pinion steering, optional power assisted; fuel tank 58L (12.7Gal) [15.3US Gal]; tyres 185/70 R 15, wheel rims 5.5J.

Dimensions: Wheelbase 254cm, track 139.5/146cm, clearance 13cm, turning circle 11.8m. Load space 12.9cu ft (365dm3), 2–door 13.2cu ft (375dm3). Length 449.5cm, 2–door 448cm, width 170cm, 2– door 173.5cm, height 134cm.

Performance: Max speed approx 93–101mph/150–165kmh, speed at 1000rpm in 5th gear 29.7mph/47.8kmh; power to weight ratio from 16.0kg/kW (11.8kg/PS); consumption approx 7–12L/100km (40.4– 23.5mpg) [33.6–19.6US mpg].

Mercury Topaz LS

```
2.3 Litre
74kW–100hp–101PS
Fuel Injection
```

Engine for XR5, LS Sport and AWD

As 98hp, except:

Body, Weight: XR5: 2–door Saloon/Sedan, 5 seater, approx 1155kg. LS Sport: 4–door Saloon/Sedan, 5 seater, approx 1225kg. All Wheel Drive: 4–door Saloon/Sedan, 5 seater; approx 1275kg.

Engine data (SAE net): 4–cylinder in–line (93.47 x 83.8mm), 2300cm3; compression ratio 9:1; 74kW (100hp) [101PS] at 4400rpm, 32.2kW/L (43.1hp/L) [43.9PS/L]; 176Nm (129.8lbft) at 2600rpm.

Transmission (to front or all wheels): a) 5–speed manual, final drive ratio 3.80.
b) Automatic; hydraulic torque converter and 3–speed Planetary gear set, central selector lever, final drive ratio 3.26, All Wheel Drive 3.07; engageable rear–wheel–drive.

Gear ratios: a) 5–speed manual; 1st 3.21; 2nd 2.12; 3rd 1.39; 4th 1.02; 5th 0.75; R 3.62.
b) Automatic; Max torque multiplication in converter 2.2 times. Planetary gear set ratios: 1st 2.81; 2nd 1.60; 3rd 1; R 2.03.

Performance: Max speed approx 99-106mph/160-170kmh, speed at 1000rpm in 5th gear 25.2mph/40.5kmh; power to weight ratio from 15.6kg/kW (11.4kg/PS); consumption approx 7–11L/100km (40.4–25.7mpg) [33.6– 21.4US mpg].

Mercury Topaz XR 5

Mercury Sable

Middle range car with front wheel drive and new 3 Litre V6 transverse mounted engine, Saloon/Sedan or Estate/Station Wagon, aerodynamic body. Prototype debut February 1985. Optional 3.8 Litre V6 engine for 1988. 1989 with modifications to body and interior.

Mercury Sable LS

```
3 Litre V6
104kW–140hp–142PS
Fuel Injection
```

Body, Weight: 4–door Saloon/Sedan, 5/6 seater; kerbweight GS from 1410kg, LS 1435kg. 5–door Estate/Station Wagon, 5/6 seater; kerbweight GS from 1455kg, LS 1475kg.

Engine data (SAE net): 6–cylinder in 60deg V (88.9 x 80mm), 2979cm3; compression ratio 9.3:1; 104kW (140hp) [142PS] at 4800rpm, 34.9kW/L (46.8hp/L) [47.7PS/L]; 217Nm (160.1lbft) at 3000rpm; unleaded regular grade.

Engine construction: Transverse mounted front engine. Hydraulic tappets; central camshaft (chain); crankshaft with 4 bearings; oil capacity 4.3L (4.1US qt); electronic Ford fuel injection. Battery 12V 58/84Ah, alternator 100A; cooling system capacity approx 9.5L (9US qt).

Transmission (to front wheels): Automatic 'AOD', hydraulic torque converter and 4–speed Planetary gear set, selector lever on steering wheel or option of central position, final drive ratio 3.37.

Gear ratios: Max torque multiplication in converter 2.2 times, Planetary gear set ratios: 1st 2.77; 2nd 1.54; 3rd 1; 4th 0.69; R 2.26.

Mercury

Chassis: Integral body, front McPherson struts (coil springs), lower single control arm and antiroll bar, rear independent suspension with control arms, coil springs and telescopic dampers (Saloon/Sedan McPherson struts), antiroll bar. Servo/power assisted brakes, front discs (ventilated), rear drums, disc diameter 25.7cm; mechanical handbrake to rear wheels; power assisted rack and pinion steering; fuel tank 61L (13.4Gal) [16.1US Gal], optional 71L (15.6Gal) [18.8US Gal]; tyres 205/70 R 14, wheel rims 5.5J, optional 205/65 R 15, wheel rims 6J.

Dimensions: Wheelbase 269.5cm, track 156.5/153.5cm, clearance 14cm, turning circle 12.2m. Load space 18.5cu ft (525dm3). Length 488cm, width 180cm, height 138cm. Estate/Station Wagon: Load space 80.8cu ft (2290dm3). Length 491.5cm, height 140cm.

Performance: Max speed approx 115mph/185kmh, speed at 1000rpm in 4th 31.3mph/50.4kmh; power to weight ratio from 13.6kg/kW (9.9kg/PS); consumption approx 10–15L/100km (28.2–18.8mpg) [23.5– 15.7US mpg].

Mercury Sable LS Wagon

```
3.8 Litre V6
104kW–140hp–142PS
Fuel Injection
```

As 3 Litre, except:

Body, Weight: 4–door Saloon/Sedan, 5/6 seater; kerbweight GS from 1420kg, LS 1450kg. 5–door Estate/Station Wagon, 5/6 seater; kerbweight GS from 1465kg, LS 1485kg.

Engine data (SAE net): 6–cylinder in 90deg V (96.52 x 86.36mm), 3791cm3; compression ratio 9:1; 104kW (140hp) [142PS] at 3800rpm, 27.4kW/L (36.7hp/L) [37.5PS/L]; 292Nm (215.5lbft) at 2400rpm.

Engine construction: Oil capacity 4.3L (4.1US qt); battery 12V 84Ah; cooling system capacity approx 11.5L (10.9US qt).

Transmission: Automatic 'Automatic Overdrive', final drive ratio 3.19.

Performance: Max speed approx 115mph/185kmh, speed at 1000rpm in 4th 33mph/53.2kmh; power to weight ratio from 13.6kg/kW (10kg/PS); consumption (touring) approx 10–15L/100km (28.2– 18.8mpg) [23.5–15.7US mpg].

Mercury Sable LS

Mercury Cougar

LS – XR7

Sporty luxury coupe from Mercury. Autumn 1988: new body with 3.8–litre–V6– with or without compressor; parallel to the Ford Thunderbird.

```
3.8 Litre V6
104kW–140hp–142PS
Fuel Injection
```

Engine for LS

Body, Weight (laden): 2–door Coupe, 4/5–seater; approx 1615kg.

Engine data (SAE net): 6–cylinder in 90deg V (96.52 x 86.36mm), 3791cm3; compression ratio 9:1; 104kW (140hp) [142PS] at 3800rpm, 27.4kW/L (36.7hp/L) [37.5PS/L]; 292Nm (215.5lbft) at 2400rpm; unleaded regular grade.

Engine construction: Light-alloy cylinder head. Hydraulic tappets; central camshaft (chain); crankshaft with 4 bearings; oil capacity 4.3L (4.1US qt); electronic fuel injection. Sparkplugs Motorcraft AWSF-44C; battery 12V 58/72Ah, alternator 75A; cooling system capacity approx 10.1L (9.6US qt).

Transmission (to rear wheels): Automatic 'AOD', hydraulic torque converter and 4–speed Planetary gear set, selector lever on steering wheel, final drive ratio 3.27. Optional limited slip differential.

Gear ratios: Max torque multiplication in converter 2.53 times, Planetary gear set ratios: 1st 2.40; 2nd 1.47; 3rd 1; 4th 0.67; R 2.11.

Chassis: Integral body; front lower A arm, antiroll bar, shock absorbers struts, coil springs; rear rigid axle with coil springs, lower longitudinal arms and overhead semi–trailing arm, rear antiroll bar, telescopic dampers. Servo/power assisted brakes, front (ventilated) disc–diameter 25.4cm; rear drums; pedal–activated parking brake to rear wheels; power assisted rack and pinion steering; fuel tank 72L or 64L (15.8-14.1Gal) [19-16.9US Gal]; tyres 205 70 R 15 or 215/70 R 15, wheel rims 6 or 6.5J.

Dimensions: Wheelbase 287cm, track 156/153cm, clearance 13cm, turning circle 12m. Load space 14.7cu ft (415dm3). Length 505cm, width 185cm, height 134cm.

Performance: Max speed approx 112mph/180kmh, speed at 1000rpm in 4th gear 34.8mph/56kmh; power to weight ratio from 15.5kg/kW (11.4kg/PS); consumption (touring) approx 10–16L/100km (28.2– 17.7mpg) [23.5–14.7US mpg].

Mercury Cougar LS

```
3.8 Litre V6
157kW–210hp–213PS
Compressor/Fuel Injection
```

Engine for XR7

As 140hp, except:

Weight: Kerbweight approx 1685kg.

Engine data (SAE): 6–cylinder in V 90deg (96.52 x 86.36mm), 3791cm3; compression ratio 8.2:1; 157kW (210hp) [213PS] at 4000rpm, 41.4kW/L (55.5hp/L) [56.3PS/L]; 427Nm (315.1lbft) at 2600rpm. Unleaded premium grade.

Engine construction: Mechanical Roots compressor (Eaton), max charge-air pressure 0.8bar; charge-air cooler. Spark plugs Motorcraft AWSF-34P. Battery 12V 58/72/75Ah, 110A alternator; cooling system capacity approx 12L (11.4US qt).

Mercury Cougar XR7

Transmission: a) 5-speed manual, final drive ratio 2.73.
b) Automatic "Automatic Overdrive", hydraulic torque converter and 4-speed Planetary gear set ratios, final drive ratio 3.08 or 3.27. Limited slip differential.

Gear ratios: a) 5-speed manual: 1st 3.75; 2nd 2.32; 3rd 1.43; 4th 1; 5th 0.75; R 3.26.
b) Automatic "Automatic Overdrive"; max torque multiplication with converter 2.3 times; Planetary gear set ratios: 2.40; 1.47; 1; 0.67; R2.

Mercury • Merkur

Chassis: Servo/power assisted brakes with ABS (Teves), front disc diameter 27.5cm, rear 25.5cm; tyres 225/60 VR 16, wheel rims 7J.
Performance: Max speed over 137mph/220kmh, speed at 1000rpm in 5th gear 37.3mph/60.1kmh; acceleration 0 - 60mph/97kmh 7.5secs, automatic 8secs; power to weight ratio from 10.7kg/kW (7.9kg/PS); consumption (touring) approx 10–18L/100km (28.2– 15.7mpg) [23.5–13.1US mpg].

Mercury Cougar XR7

Mercury Grand Marquis – Colony Park

Large American top–class car. 4.9 Litre V8 with fuel injection and increased performance for 1986. Body changes in 1988. Modifications to body in 1989.

Mercury Grand Marquis

4.9 Litre V8
112/119kW–150/160hp–152/162PS
Fuel Injection

Body, Weight (laden): Grand Marquis: 4–door Saloon/Sedan, 6 seater approx 1715kg.
Grand Marquis LS/GS: 4–door Saloon/Sedan, 6 seater; approx 1710kg.
Colony Park: 5–door Estate/Station Wagon, 6/8 seater; approx 1810kg.
Colony Park LS/GS 5–door Estate/Station Wagon, 6/8 seater; approx 1775kg.
Engine data (SAE net): 8–cylinder in 90deg V (101.6 x 76.2mm), 4942cm3; compression ratio 8.9:1; 112kW (150hp) [152PS] at 3200rpm, 22.6kW/L (30.3hp/L) [30.8PS/L]; 366Nm (270.1lbft) at 2000rpm; unleaded regular grade.
With twin–exhaust: 119kW (160hp) [162PS] at 3400rpm, 24.1kW/L (32.3hp/L) [32.8PS/L]; 380Nm (280.4lbft) at 2200rpm.
Engine construction: Hydraulic tappets, central camshaft (chain); crankshaft with 5 bearings; oil capacity 4.7L (4.4US qt); Ford electronic fuel injection. Battery 12V 72/84Ah, alternator 65/100A; cooling system capacity approx 13.6L (12.9US qt).
Transmission (to rear wheels): Automatic 'Automatic Overdrive'; hydraulic torque converter and 4–speed Planetary gear set, selector lever on steering wheel, final drive ratio 2.73; 3.08; 3.27; 3.55. Optional limited slip differential.
Gear ratios: Max torque multiplication in converter 2.3 times; Planetary gear set ratios: 2.40; 1.47; 1; 0.67; R 2.
Chassis: Box–type frame with cross–members; front coil springs, upper and lower trapeze–A–arms, antiroll bar; rear rigid axle with coil springs, lower longitudinal arms, overhead semi– trailing arms, optional rear antiroll bar, telescopic dampers; optional level–control system. Servo/power assisted brakes, front discs diameter 27.9cm (ventilated), rear drums, disc diameter 27.8cm; pedal–activated parking brake to rear wheels; power assisted recirculating ball steering; fuel tank 68L (14.9Gal) [18US Gal]; tyres 215/70 R 15, wheel rims 6, optional 6.5J.
Dimensions: Wheelbase 290cm, track 158/157.5cm, clearance 13cm, turning circle 13.1m. Load space 22.4cu ft (635dm3). Length 544cm, width 197cm, height 141cm. Estate/Station Wagon: Load space 87.9cu ft (2490dm3). Length 556.5cm, width 201.5cm, height 143.5cm.

Performance: Max speed approx 112–118mph/180–190kmh, speed at 1000rpm in top gear 42.9mph/69.1kmh; power to weight ratio from 14.4kg/kW (10.6kg/PS); consumption (touring) approx 12–18L/100km (23.5–15.7mpg) [19.6–13.1US mpg].

Mercury Colony Park

MERKUR   EUR/USA

Ford–Werke AG, 5 Cologne 21, Germany

The exclusively–Ford products, developed by Ford Europe, are sold under the Merkur name in the USA. Sold through the Lincoln– Mercury–Division.

Merkur XR4Ti

Sporty version of the Ford Sierra with turbocharger for the USA. Assembled at Karmann in Germany. Debut Summer 1984.

Merkur XR4Ti

2.3 Litre Turbo
130/108kW–175/145hp–177/147PS
Fuel Injection

Body, Weight: 3–door Saloon/Sedan, 5 seater; kerbweight (DIN) 1325kg.
Engine data (SAE net): 4–cylinder in–line (96.04 x 79.4mm), 2301cc; compression ratio 8:1; 130kW (175hp) [177PS] at 5000rpm, 56.6kW/L (75.8hp/L) [76.9PS/L]; 271Nm (27.7lbft) at 3000rpm; premium grade.
Automatic model: 108kW (145hp) [147PS] at 4400rpm, 47.0kW/L (63hp/L) [63.9PS/L]; 244Nm (180lbft) at 3000rpm.
Engine construction: Valves in V; hydraulic tappets, 1 overhead camshaft (toothed–belt); crankshaft with 5 bearings; oil capacity 4.7L (4.4US qt); electronic fuel injection; Warner ISHI exhaust turbocharger, charge–air cooler. Sparkplugs Motocraft AWSF 32C; battery 12V 55Ah, alternator 90A, cooling system capacity 9.7L (9.2US qt).
Transmission: a) 5–speed manual, final drive ratio 3.64.
b) Automatic C3, hydraulic torque converter and 3–speed Planetary gear set, selector lever on middle console, final drive ratio 3.36.
Gear ratios: a) 5–speed manual: 1st 3.358; 2nd 1.809; 3rd 1.258; 4th 1; 5th 0.825; R 3.37.
b) Automatic; Max torque multiplication in converter 2.6 times, Planetary gear set ratios: 1st 2.474; 2nd 1.474; 3rd 1; R 2.111.
Chassis: Integral body; front and rear independent suspension, front McPherson struts, control arm and antiroll bar, rear semi– trailing arm, coil springs and telescopic dampers. Servo/power assisted brakes, front discs, 26.0 cm diameter, rear drums; mechanical handbrake to rear wheels; power assisted rack and pinion steering; fuel tank 57L (12.5Gal) [15.1US Gal]; tyres 195/60 HR 15, wheel rims 5.5J.

Merkur • MG

Dimensions: Wheelbase 261cm, track 145/147cm, clearance 11.5cm, turning circle 11.3m. Load space 11.5–35.3cu ft (325–1000dm3). Length 453cm, width 173cm, height 136.5cm.

Performance: Max speed approx 118–127mph/190–205kmh, speed at 1000rpm in 5th gear 23.3mph/37.5kmh; power to weight ratio from 10.2kg/kW (7.5kg/PS); consumption approx 9–15L/100km (31.4– 18.8mpg) [26.1–15.7US mpg].

Merkur Scorpio

2.9 Litre V6 vehicle solely for export to the US, also available as 4x4. See Ford Europe for data.

Merkur Scorpio

MG — GB

Austin Rover Group Limited, Canley Road, Canley, Coventry VC5 QX, England
Marque of the Nuffield Organisation, now part of the Austin Rover Group.
MODEL RANGE
Metro – Maestro – Montego

MG Metro

Derived from the Austin Metro with a 1.3 Litre 4–cylinder engine. Launched May 1982, Turbo version launched at the 1982 Birmingham show. October 1984: modifications to the body and interior.

MG Metro

```
1.3 Litre
53.5kW–72hp–73PS
1 Carb
```

Body, Weight: Saloon/Sedan 3–door, 5–seater; kerbweight 795kg, gross vehicle weight 1140/1225kg.

Engine data (DIN): 4–cylinder in–line (70.61 x 81.28mm), 1275cm3, compression ratio 10.5:1 53.5kW (72hp) [73PS] at 6000rpm, 42kW/L (56.3hp/L) [57.2PS/L]; 99Nm (73.1lbft) at 4000rpm; leaded premium grade.
Some countries: 51.5kW (69hp) [70PS] at 6000rpm; 96Nm (70.8lbft) at 3900rpm.

Engine construction: Designated A–Plus. Engine and transmission in one unit. Side camshaft (chain); 3 bearing crankshaft; Oil capacity (engine and transmission in same oil bath) 4.8L (4.5US qt); 1 semi–downdraught SU HIF–44 carb. Battery 12V 40Ah, alternator A; cooling system capacity 4.9L (4.US qt).

Transmission (to front wheels): 4–speed manual, final drive ratio 3.44.

Gear ratios: 1st 3.647; 2nd 2.184; 3rd 1.425; 4th 1; R 3.666.

Chassis: Integral body; front and rear sub–frames; independent suspension, front control arm and antiroll bar, rear trailing arm; Hydragas–Suspension with Nitrogen gas dampers and rear auxiliary coil springs. Servo/power assisted brakes, front ventilated discs, 21.3cm diameter, rear drums; mechanical handbrake to rear wheels; rack and pinion steering; fuel tank 35.5L (7.8Gal) [9.3US Gal]; tyres 160/60 R 315, wheel rims 120–315 or tyres 185/55 SR 13, wheel rims 5.5J.

Dimensions: Wheelbase 225cm, track 130/129.5cm, clearance 17/11cm, turning circle 10.2m. Load space 8.1/19.4/33.7cu ft (230/550/955dm3). Length 340.5cm, width 155cm, height 137cm.

Performance: Max speed 103–101mph/166–163kmh (manufacturers test specifications). Speed at 1000rpm in 5th gear 17.2mph/27.7kmh; acceleration 0–60mph/97kmh 10.9secs; power to weight ratio 14.9kg/kW (10.9kg/PS); consumption (ECE) 5.1/6.7/8.1L/100km (55.4/42.2/34.9mpg) [46.1/35.1/29US mpg].

```
1.3 Litre Turbo
69kW–93hp–94PS
1 Carb
```

Engine for Metro Turbo
As 72hp, except:
Weight: Kerbweight 850kg, gross vehicle weight 1160kg.
Engine data (DIN): Compression ratio 9.4:1; 69kW (93hp) [94PS] at 6130rpm, 54.3kW/L (72.8hp/L) [73.7PS/L]; 115Nm (84.8lbft) at 2650rpm.
Some countries: 66kW (88.5hp) [90PS].
Engine construction: Oil cooler; 1 Garrett AiResearch T3 turbocharger; maximum boost pressure 0.52bar.
Transmission: 4–speed manual, final drive ratio 3.21.
Chassis: Front and rear antiroll bar; tyres 165/60 HR/VR 13 or 185/55 HR/VR 13, wheel rims 5.5J.
Dimensions: Track 132/128.5cm, clearance 17.5cm. Length 156.5cm, height 138cm.
Performance: Max speed 112mph/180kmh (manufacturers test specifications), speed at 1000rpm in 5th gear 18.7mph/30.1kmh; acceleration 0–60mph/97kmh 9.9secs; consumption ECE 5.3/7.5/8.2L/100km (53.3/37.7/34.4mpg) [44.4/31.4/28.7US mpg].

MG Maestro 2.0i/Turbo

Hatchback Saloon/Sedan, with front wheel drive and transverse engine. Sport version of the Austin Maestro. Launched March 1983, October 1984: 2 Litre engine to replace the 1.6 Litre. Birmingham, October 1988: Also with 2 Litre Turbo engine.

MG Maestro 2.0i

```
2 Litre
86kW–115hp–117PS
Fuel Injection
```

Body, Weight: Saloon/Sedan 5–door, 5–seater; kerbweight 1020kg, gross vehicle weight 1440kg.

Engine data (DIN): 4–cylinder in–line engine (84.46 x 89mm), 1994cm3; compression ratio 9:1; 86kW (115hp) [117PS] at 5500rpm, 43.1kW/L (57.7hp/L) [58.7PS/L]; 182Nm (13.2lbft) at 2800rpm; leaded premium grade.
Some countries: 83kW (111hp) [113PS]; 178Nm (131.6lbft).

Engine construction: Designated O–Series. Transverse engine. 1 overhead camshaft (toothed belt); light–alloy cylinder head; 5 bearing crankshaft; oil capacity 3.5L (3.3US qt); Lucas L electronic fuel injection. Battery 12V 40/45Ah, alternator 55A; cooling system capacity 6.5L (6.1US qt).

MG · Middlebridge

Transmission (to front wheels): 5-speed manual, final drive ratio 3.875 or 3.94.

Gear ratios: 1st 2.71; 2nd 1.89; 3rd 1.33; 4th 1.04; 5th 0.852; R 3.
Or 1st 2.923; 2nd 1.75; 3rd 1.222; 4th 0.935; 5th 0.764; R 3.

Chassis: Integral body; front McPherson strut with control arm and coil spring, rear compound axle (trailing arm and control arm) with coil springs, front and rear antiroll bar, telescopic dampers. Servo/power assisted brakes, front disc, diameter 24.1cm, rear drums. Mechanical handbrake to rear wheels; rack and pinion steering, optional power assisted; fuel tank 54/50L (11.9/11Gal) [14.3/13.2US Gal]; tyres 175/65 HR 14 or 185/55 HR 15, wheel rims 5.5J.

Dimensions: Wheelbase 250.5cm, track 148/145.5cm, clearance 15cm, turning circle 10.3m. Load space 12.9/23/38.5cu ft (365/650/1090dm3). Length 405cm, width 168.5cm, height 142cm.

Performance: Max speed 115mph/185kmh (manufacturers test specifications); speed at 100rpm in 5th gear 21.4mph/34.5kmh; acceleration 0 – 60mph/97kmh 8.5secs; power to weight ratio 11.9kg/kW (8.7kg/PS); consumption (ECE) 6.0/8.1/10.5L/100km (47.1/34.9/26.9mpg) [39.2/29/22.4US mpg].

```
2.0 Turbo
112kW–150hp–152PS
1 Carb
```

Engine for Maestro Turbo

As Maestro 2.0i, except:

Body, Weight: Kerbweight (DIN) approx 1100kg, gross vehicle weight 1550kg.

Engine data (DIN): 4-cylinder in-line (84.46 x 89mm), 1994cm3; compression ratio 8.5:1; 112kW (150hp) [152PS] at 5100rpm, 56.2kW/L (75.3hp/L) [76.2PS/L]; 230Nm (169.7lbft) at 3500rpm; Premium grade.
Some countries: 110kW (147hp) [150PS].

Engine construction: Designated "O" series. 1 semi-constant pressure Carb ARG, 1 Garrett Airesearch T3 turbocharger, charge-air cooler.

Transmission: 5-speed manual, final drive ratio 3.647.

Gear ratios: 1st 2.923; 2nd 1.750; 3rd 1.222; 4th 0.935; 5th 0.764; R 3.0.

Chassis: Power/assisted steering; tyres 190/65 VR 365 or 195/55 VR 15, wheel rims 6J.

Performance: Max speed 126mph/203kmh (manufacturers test specification), speed at 1000rpm in 5th gear 25mph/40.3kmh; acceleration 0 - 60mph/97kmh 7.3secs; power to eight ratio 9.8kg/kW (7.2kg/PS); consumption ECE 6.6/9.2/10L/100km (42.8/30.7/28.2mpg) [35.6/25.6/23.5US mpg].

MG Montego 2.0i/Turbo

Saloon/Sedan sports version of the Montego, available with a 2 Litre injection engine or a 2 Litre Turbo. Launched 25 April 1984, Turbo version April 1985.

MG Montego 2.0i

```
2 Litre
86kW–115hp–117PS
Fuel Injection
```

Engine for the Montego 2.0i

Body, Weight: Saloon/Sedan, 4-door, 5-seater; kerbweight (DIN) 1030kg, gross vehicle weight 1560kg.

Engine data (DIN): 4-cylinder in-line (84.46 x 89mm), 1994cm3; compression ratio 9:1; 86kW (115hp) [117PS] at 5500rpm, 43.1kW/L (57.7hp/L) [58.7PS/L]; 182Nm (134.2lbft) at 2800rpm; leaded premium grade.
Some countries: 83kW (111hp) [113PS]; 178Nm (131.3lbft).

Engine construction: Designated O Series, transverse mounted, 1 overhead camshaft (toothed belt), light–alloy cylinder head; 5 bearing crankshaft; oil capacity 3.5L (3.3US qt); Lucas L electronic fuel injection. Battery 12V 44/66Ah, alternator 55A, cooling system capacity approx 6.5L (6.1US qt).

Transmission (to front wheels): 5-speed manual, final drive ratio 3.875 or 3.94.

Gear ratios: 1st 2.71; 2nd 1.89; 3rd 1.33; 4th 1.04; 5th 0.852; R 3.
Or 1st 2.923; 2nd 1.75; 3rd 1.222; 4th 0.935; 5th 0.764; R 3.

Chassis: Integral body; front McPherson strut, lower control arm and coil spring, rear compound axle (trailing arm and control arm) with coil spring, front and rear antiroll bar and telescopic dampers. Servo/power assisted brakes, front discs (ventilated) rear drums. Disc diameter 24.1cm; rack and pinion steering, optional power assisted; fuel tank 53/50L (11.6/11Gal) [14/13.2US Gal]; tyres 185/65 HR 14/365, wheel rims 5.5J, or tyres 195/55 HR 15, wheel rims 6J.

Dimensions: Wheelbase 256.5cm, track 148.5/146cm, clearance 15.5cm, turning circle 10.8m. Load space 18.4cu ft (520dm3). Length 446.5cm, width 171cm, height 142cm.

Performance: Max speed 116–114mph/186–183kmh (manufacturers test specification), speed at 1000rpm in 5th gear 20.7mph/33.3kmh; acceleration 0 – 60mph/97kmh 8.9/9.2secs; power to weight ratio 12kg/kW (8.8kg/PS); consumption ECE 6.2/8.1/10.4L/100km (45.6/34.9/27.2mpg) [38.6/29/22.6US mpg].

```
2 Litre Turbo
112kW–150hp–152PS
1 Carb
```

Engine for Montego Turbo

As Montego 2.0i, except:

Body, Weight: Kerbweight (DIN) 1100kg, gross vehicle weight 1560kg.

Engine data: 4–cylinder in–line (84.46m x 89mm), 1994cm3; compression ratio 8.5:1; 112kW (150hp) [152PS] at 5100rpm, 56.2kW/L (75.3hp/L) [76.2PS/L]; 230Nm (169.6lbft) at 3500rpm; leaded premium grade.
Some countries: 110kW (147hp) [150PS].

Engine construction: Designated O Series, 1 semi–downdraught constant pressure carb ARG, 1 Garrett AiReseach T3 turbocharger.

Transmission: 5–speed manual, final drive ratio 3.647.

Gear ratios: 1st 2.923; 2nd 1.750; 3rd 1.222; 4th 0.935; 5th 0.764; R 3.

Chassis: Power assisted steering; tyres 190/65 VR 365 or 195/55 VR 15, wheel rims 6J.

Performance: Max speed 126mph/203kmh (manufacturers test specifications), speed at 1000rpm in 5th gear 25mph/40.3kmh; acceleration 0 – 60mph/97kmh 7.3secs; power to weight ratio 9.8kg/kW (7.2kg/PS); consumption (ECE) 6.6/9.2/10L/100km (42.8/30.7/28.2mpg) [35.6/25.6/23.5US mpg].

MG Montego Turbo

MIDDLEBRIDGE — GB

Middlebridge Scimitar Limited, 100 Lilac Grove, Beeston, Nottingham NG9 1RF, England.

Small vehicle manufacturer, producing vehicles based on the early Scimitar GTE.

Middlebridge Scimitar GTE

Sporty Estate/Station Wagon with plastic body and Ford V6 engine. Launched as the Scimitar in October 1986, Middlebridge Birmingham 1988. Provisional data.

Middlebridge · Mini GB · Mini P · Mitsubishi

Middlebridge Scimitar GTE

MINI — GB

See Austin

MINI — P

S.C.I.A. Francisca Battista Russo & Irmao, S.A.R.L., Av. Infante D. Henrique, Il Circular, Cabo Ruivo, 1900 Lisbon, Portugal.

Austin Rover Group Portuguese affiliate.

Mini–Moke

Leisure vehicle based on the English Mini, 1000cm3 engine, front wheel drive, 4–speed manual transmission

Mini–Moke

2.9 Litre V6
110kW–147hp–150PS
Fuel Injection

Body, Weight: Saloon/Sedan with plastic body, 3-door, 4-seater; kerbweight (DIN) from 1265-1310kg, gross vehicle weight 1680kg. Convertible 2-door in preparation.

Engine data (DIN): 6-cylinder in V 60deg (93 x 72mm), 2935cm3; compression ratio 9.5:1; 110kW (147hp) [150PS] at 5700rpm, 37.5kW/L (50.3hp/L) [51.1PS/L]; 233Nm (172lbft) at 3000rpm; regular grade, optional 95 ROZ.

Engine construction: Central camshaft (gear wheel); 4-bearing crankshaft; oil capacity 4.7L (4.4US qt); electronic Bosck K-Jetronic fuel injection. Motorcraft spark plugs; 12 V 71Ah battery, 90A alternator; cooling systemcapacity approx 10L (9.5US qt).

Transmission (to rear wheels): a) 5-speed manual, final drive ratio 3.54.
b) Automatic A4LD "Automatic 4-speed lock up overdrive", hydraulic torque converter and Planetary gear set, central selector lever to centre console, final drive ratio 3.54.

Gear ratios: a) 5-speed manual: 1st 3.358; 2nd 1.809; 3rd 1.258; 4th 1; 5th 0.825; R 3.375.
b) Automatic: Max torque multiplication in converter 2.11 times; Planetary gear set ratios: 1st 2.474; 2nd 1.474; 3rd 1; 4th 0.749; R 2.111.

Chassis: Box frame with cross members; front swinging A arm and coil springs, rear rigid axle with torsion struts, Watt linkage and coil springs, front antiroll bar, telescopic damper. Servo/power assisted brakes, front discs ventilated, rear drums, disc diameter 27.5cm, mechanical handbrake to rear; power assisted rack and pinion steering; fuel tank 91L (20Gal) [24US Gal], tyres 195/65 VR 15, wheel rims 6J.

Dimensions: Wheelbase 263.5cm, track 147.5/142.5cm, clearance approx 14cm, turning circle 11.6m, load space 21/30/40cu ft (595/850/1135dm3), length 443cm, width 172cm, height 132cm.

Performance: Max speed approx 124mph/200kmh, speed at 1000rpm in top gear 24.7mph/39.7kmh; power to weight ratio from 11.5kg/kW (8.4kg/PS); consumption approx 9-15L/100km (31.4-18.8mpg) [26.1-15.7US mpg].

998cm3
29kW–39hp–40PS
1 Carb

Body, Weight: Open vehicle with fabric roof; 4-seater; kerbweight (DIN) 630kg, gross vehicle weight 1030kg.

Engine data (DIN): 4–cylinder in-line (64.58 x 76.2mm), 998cm3; compression ratio 8.3:1; 29kW (39hp) [40PS] at 4750rpm, 29.1kW/L (40hp/L) [40.1PS/L]; 68Nm (50.2lbft) at 2500rpm; leaded regular grade.

Engine construction: A–Plus designation. Transverse mounted front engine and transmission assembly. Side–mounted camshaft (chain); crankshaft with 3 bearings; oil (engine and transmission in same oil bath) 4.8L (4.5US qt); 1 SU HS 4 semi–downdraught carb, electrionic SU fuel pump. Battery 12V 30/32/48Ah, alternator 34A; cooling system capacity 3.6L (3.4US qt).

Transmission (to front wheels): 4–speed manual, final drive ratio 3.11.

Gear ratios: 1st 3.647; 2nd 2.185; 3rd 1.425; 4th 1; R 3.667.

Chassis: Integral body with front and rear sub–frames; front independent suspension with control arms, rear with longitudinal arms; front and rear rubber suspension elements and telescopic dampers. Front disc brakes 21.3cm diameter, rear drums, mechanical handbrake to rear wheels; rack and pinion steering; fuel tank 39L (8.6Gal) [10.3US Gal]; tyres 145/70 SR 12, wheels rim 4.5".

Dimensions: Wheelbase 203.5cm, track 126.5/121.5cm, clearance 19cm, turning circle 9.4m. Length 323cm, width 144cm, height 146cm.

Performance: Max speed approx 81mph/130kmh, speed at 1000rpm in 4th gear 18.7mph/30.1kmh; power to weight ratio 21.7kg/kW (15.8kg/PS); consumption approx 5–9L/100km (56.5-31.4mpg) [47– 26.1US mpg].

Middlebridge Scimitar GTE

MITSUBISHI — J

Mitsubishi Heavy Industries Ltd., 102–chome Marunouchi, Chiyoda– ku, Tokyo, Japan.

Passenger car, product of a large Japanese heavy industry company.

Mitsubishi 289

MODEL RANGE
Minica – Mirage – Colt/Lancer - Lancer Wagon - Precis - Sapporo - Galant/Eterna – Starion Eclipse - Debonair V - Space Wagon/Chariot - Jeep - Pajero

Mitsubishi Minica

New model. 3 or 5-door Minicar with 3-cylinder engine for 550cm3 engine capacities. Towny export designation. Debut Spring 1984. 1985: Engageable 4x4. 1987: now permanent all wheel drive (viscous coupling), new engine. January 1989: New body, with permanent all wheel drive with hydraulic coupling; Sporty version with 5 valves per cylinder and turbocharger.

Mitsubishi Minica

```
548cm3
24/22kW-31.5/29hp-32/30PS
1 2V Carb
```

Body, Weight: Saloon/Sedan 3-door, 2 or 4-seater; kerbweight (DIN) from 560kg, 4WD from 650kg.
b) Saloon/Sedan 5-door, 4-seater; kerbweight (DIN) from 600kg; 4WD from 670kg; Lettuce model with 2-doors left and 1 right.

Engine data (JIS net): 3-cylinder in-line (62.3 x 60mm) 548cm3; compression ratio 9.8:1; 24kW (31.5hp) [32PS] at 6500rpm, 43.8kW/L (58.7hp/L) [59.6PS/L]; 42Nm (31lbft) at 4000rpm.
3-door: 22kW (29hp) [30PS] at 6500rpm; 41Nm (30.3lbft) at 3000rpm.
Export version (ECE): 796cm3; compression ratio 9.0:1; 30kW (40hp) [41PS] at 5500rpm; 65Nm (47.9lbft) at 2500rpm.

Engine construction: Transverse mounted front engine. Designated 3G 81. Overhead valves in V, 1 overhead camshaft (toothed belt); light-alloy cylinder head; 2 counter-balance shafts; crankshaft with 4 bearings; oil capacity approx 3L (2.8US qt); 1 downdraught 2V carb. Battery 12V 24Ah, alternator 180W; cooling system capacity approx 4.5L (4.3US qt).

Transmission (to front wheels, 4WD to all wheels): a) 4-speed manual, final drive ratio 5.571 or 5.200.
b) 5-speed manual, final drive ratio 5.571 or 5.200, 4WD 5.916.
c) Automatic, hydraulic torque converter and 3-speed Planetary gear set; final drive ratio 4.845, 4WD 5.697.
4WD: Permanent all wheel drive with hydraulic coupling.

Gear ratios: a) 4-speed manual: 1st 3.538; 2nd 2.052; 3rd 1.392; 4th 0.970; R 3.500.
b) 5-speed manual: 1st 3.538; 2nd 2.052; 3rd 1.392; 4th 0.970; 5th 0.810; R 3.500.
4WD: 5-speed manual: 1st 3.916; 2nd 2.352; 3rd 1.576; 4th 1.093; 5th 0.888; R 3.909.
c) Automatic: Max torque multiplication in converter 2 times, Planetary gear set ratios: 1st 2.846; 2nd 1.581; 3rd 1; R 2.176.

Chassis: Integral body; front McPherson struts, control arms and coil springs, rear compound axle (axle tube and longitudinal arms), coil springs and Panhard rod, 4WD rigid axle with longitudinal arms; telescopic damper. Servo/power assisted brakes, front discs (some models with drums), handbrake to rear wheels; rack and pinion steering; fuel tank 32L (7Gal) [8.5US Gal]; tyres 135 SR 12 or 145 SR 10.

Dimensions: Wheelbase 226cm, track 121.5/121.5cm, clearance 15.5cm (4WD 16.5cm), turning circle 8.4m. Length 319.5cm, width 139.5cm, height 146.5cm, 4WD 148.5cm.

R19

Performance: Max speed approx 75mph/120kmh, speed at 1000rpm in 5th gear (5.200) 14mph/22.6kmh; power to weight ratio from 25kg/kW (18.8kg/PS); consumption approx 4–7L/100km (70.6– 40.4mpg) [58.8–33.6US mpg].

Mitsubishi Minica

```
548cm3
47kW-63hp-64PS
Turbo/Injection
```

Not available for 4WD

As 29hp, except:

Weight: Saloon/Sedan 3-door; kerbweight (DIN) from 620kg.

Engine data (JIS net): 3-cylinder in-line (62.3 x 60mm), 548cm3; compression ratio 8.5:1; 47kW (63hp) [64PS] at 7500rpm, 85.8kW/L (115hp/L) [116.8PS/L]; 75Nm (55.4lbft) at 4500rpm.

Engine construction: Designated 3G 81 DOHC 5. 5 valves in V per cylinder, hydraulic valve lash adjustment, 2 overhead camshafts (toothed belt); oil cooler; electronic fuel injection; 1 Mitsubishi turbocharger, charge-air cooler.

Transmission: 5-speed manual, final drive ratio 5.538.

Chassis: Larger front disc brakes; tyres 165/60 SR 12.

Dimensions: Track 120.5/120.5cm.

Performance: Max speed over 93mph/150kmh, speed at 1000rpm in 5th gear 13.3mph/21.4kmh; power to weight ratio from 13.2kg/kW (9.7kg/PS); consumption approx 5–9L/100km (56.5–31.4mpg) [47– 26.1US mpg].

Mitsubishi Minica Dangan ZZ

Mitsubishi Mirage – Colt/Lancer

Compact Saloon/Sedan with transverse mounted front engine and front-wheel-drive. Debut Tokyo 1983. Colt/Lancer export designation, in USA also where Dodge and Plymouth sell. October 1987: new 3-door steepback body, new 1.6 Litre four-valve engine with and without turbocharger. January 1988: four-door Saloon/Sedan version, also with permanent all wheel drive (incomplete data). Designated in USA Eagle Summit. 1988: Also when 5-door Saloon/Sedan Lancer obtainable.

```
1.3 Litre
49kW-66hp-67PS
1 2V Carb
```

Mitsubishi

Body, Weight: 3–door Saloon/Sedan, 5–seater; kerbweight (DIN) from 850-985kg, gross vehicle weight 1465kg.
4–door Saloon/Sedan, 5–seater; kerbweight (DIN) from 880-985kg, gross vehicle weight 1465kg.
5-door Saloon/Sedan, 5-seater; kerbweight (DIN) from 920kg.
Engine data (JIS net): 4–cylinder in–line (71 x 82mm), 1299cm3; compression ratio 9.7:1; 49kW (66hp) [67PS] at 5500rpm, 37.7kW/L (50.5hp/L) [51.6PS/L]; 104Nm (76.7lbft) at 3500rpm.
With Catalyst (DIN): 50kW (67hp) [68PS] at 6000rpm; 101Nm (74.5lbft) at 4000rpm; unleaded grade.
Or: 44kW (59hp) [60PS] at 5500rpm; 96Nm (70.8lbft) at 3000rpm.
Without Catalyst (DIN): 53kW (71hp) [72PS] at 5500rpm; 105Nm (77.5lbft) at 3500rpm.

Mitsubishi Colt

Engine construction: 4G 13 B designation. Overhead valves in V, 1 overhead camshaft (toothed belt); light–alloy cylinder head; crankshaft with 5 bearings; oil capacity 3.4L (3.2US qt); 1 electronically controlled Aisan 2V compound carb. Battery 12V 45-60Ah, alternator 50-60A; cooling system capacity approx 5L (4.7US qt).
Transmission (to front wheels): a) 4–speed manual, final drive ratio 4.021.
b) 5–speed manual, final drive ratio 4.021, 3.941.
c) Automatic, hydraulic torque converter and 3–speed Planetary gear set, final drive ratio 4.062.
Gear ratios: a) 4–speed manual: 1st 3.363; 2nd 1.947; 3rd 1.285; 4th 0.939; R 3.083.
b) 5–speed manual: 1st 3.363; 2nd 1.947; 3rd 1.285; 4th 0.939; 5th 0.777; R 3.083.
c) Automatic: Max torque multiplication in converter approx 2 times, Planetary gear set ratios: 1st 2.846; 2nd 1.581; 3rd 1; R 2.176.
Chassis: Integral body; front McPherson struts with lower A–arms and antiroll bar, rear compound axle (longitudinal arms, axle tube) with Panhard rod and coil springs, some models antiroll bar, telescopic dampers. Servo/power assisted brakes, front ventilated, disc diamater 24.2cm, rear drums, mechanical hand brake to rear wheels; rack and pinion steering; fuel tank 50L (11Gal) [13.2US Gal]; tyres 155 SR 13, wheel rims 4.5 or 5J.
Dimensions: 3–door Saloon/Sedan: Wheelbase 238.5cm, track 143/143cm, clearance 15.5cm, turning circle 10.6m, load space (VDA) 7.8-37cu ft (222-1050dm3). Length 395cm, width 167cm, height 138–141cm. 4/5–door Saloon/Sedan: Wheelbase 245.5cm, track 143/143cm. Load space (VDA) 4-door 11.9cu ft (337dm3). Length 423.5cm, width 167cm, height 140.5cm.
Performance: (67hp) Max speed approx 98mph/157kmh, speed at 1000rpm in 5th gear (4.021) 21.1mph/33.9kmh; power to weight ratio from 17.3kg/kW (12.7kg/PS); consumption ECE (59hp) 5.2/7.1/8.2L/100km (54.3/39.8/34.4mpg) [45.2/33.1/28.7US mpg].

Mitsubishi Lancer

1.5 Litre
60/54kW–80.5/72hp–82/73PS
Fuel Injection/2V Carb

As 1.3 Litre, except:

Weight: 3–door Saloon/Sedan, kerbweight 870-1035kg, USA from 1015kg, gross vehicle weight 1465kg.
4–door Saloon/Sedan, kerbweight from 900-1025kg, USA from 1030kg, 4WD 1010kg, gross vehicle weight 1465kg.
5-door Saloon/Sedan, kerbweight from 960kg.
4WD from approx 1070kg.
Engine data (JIS): 4–cylinder in–line (75.5 x 82mm), 1468cm3; compression ratio 9.4:1; 60kW (80.5hp) [82PS] at 5500rpm, 40.9kW/L (54.8hp/L) [55.9PS/L]; 124Nm (91.5lbft) at 3000rpm.
With Catalyst (DIN): 62kW (83hp) [84PS] at 5500rpm; 122Nm (90lbft) at 3000rpm; unleaded grade.
USA Version (SAE net): 60kW (80hp) [82PS]; 126Nm (93lbft).
Also with Carb (JIS net): 54kW (72hp) [73PS] at 5500rpm; 117Nm (86.3lbft) at 3500rpm.
Export Version (DIN): 60kW (80hp) [82PS] at 5500rpm; 120Nm (88.6lbft) at 3500rpm.
Engine construction: 4G 15 designation. Electronic fuel injection, 72hp version with electronically controlled 2V carb, 65Ah battery, 65A alternator.
Transmission (to front or all wheels): a) 4-speed manual (USA), final drive ratio 3.454.
b) 5–speed manual, final drive ratio 4.021.
c) Automatic, final drive ratio 3.600.
d) 4-speed automatic (only injection) with Program E/P, final drive ratio 4.367 or 4.062.
4WD (only 4–door, 72hp): Permanent all–wheel–drive, central differential (50/50% power distribution) with viscous coupling. 5– speed manual, final drive ratio 5.084.
Gear ratios: a) 4–speed manual: As 1.3 Litre.
b) 5–speed manual: As 1.3 litre.
For 4WD: 1st 3.083; 2nd 1.684; 3rd 1.115; 4th 0.806; 5th 0.651; R 3.166.
c) Automatic: As 1.3 Litre.
d) 4-speed automatic, Planetary gear set ratios: 1st 2.846; 2nd 1.581; 3rd 1; 4th 0.685; R 2.176.
Chassis: Optional power assisted steering; tyres 155 SR 13 or 175/70 SR 13. 4WD: Rear rigid axle with double longitudinal arms, Panhard rod, coil springs and antiroll bar; tyres 165 SR 14 or 175/70 SR 13.
Dimensions: Length USA 3-door 403cm, 4-door 432cm.
4WD: Track 142.5/142cm. Height 142.5cm.
Performance: (Catayst version) Max speed 103mph/165kmh, with Automatic 97mph/156kmh (manufacturers test specification) speed at 1000rpm in 5th gear 21.1mph/33.9kmh; acceleration 0 - 62mph/100kmh 11.9secs, automatic 14secs; power to weight ratio from 15.4kg/kW (11.3kg/PS); consumption ECE 5.5/7.6/8.5L/100km (51.4/37.2/33.2mpg) [42.8/30.9/27.7US mpg], automatic 6.5/8.7/9.0L/100km (43.5/32.5/31.4 mpg) [36.2/27/26.1US mpg].

Mitsubishi Lancer

1.6 DOHC
107/92kW–143/123hp–145/125PS
Turbo/Fuel Injection

As 1.3 Litre, except:

Weight: 3–door Saloon/Sedan, kerbweight from 970-1140kg, Turbo from 1000kg, USA from 1130kg; gross vehicle weight 1550kg.

Mitsubishi

4-door Saloon/Sedan, kerbweight from 1010kg, USA from 1140kg, Turbo 4WD from 1120kg.
5-door Saloon/Sedan, kerbweight from 1070kg, Turbo 4WD from 1180kg.

Engine data (JIS net): 4-cylinder in-line (82.3 x 75mm), 1595cm3; compression ratio 8:1; 107kW (143hp) [145PS] at 6000rpm, 67.1kW/L (89.9hp/L) [90.9PS/L]; 206Nm (151.9lbft) at 2500rpm.
USA Version (SAE net): 101kW (135hp) [136PS] at 6000rpm; 191Nm (141lbft) at 3000rpm.
Without turbocharger (JIS net): Compression ratio 9.2:1; 92kW (123hp) [125PS] at 6500rpm, 57.7kW/L (77.3hp/L) [78.4PS/L]; 137Nm (101.1lbft) at 5200rpm.
With Catalyst (DIN): Compression ratio 10:1; 91kW (122hp) [124PS] at 6500rpm; 142Nm (104.8lbft) at 5000rpm; unleaded grade.
USA Version (SAE net): Compression ratio 9.2:1; 84kW (113hp) [114PS] at 6000rpm; 137Nm (101.1lbft) at 3000rpm.
Without Catalyst (DIN): Compression ratio 10:1; 92kW (123hp) [125PS] at 6500rpm; 142Nm (104.8lbft) at 5000rpm.

Engine construction: 4G 61 DOHC designation. 4 valves (in V 57deg) per cylinder, hydraulic tappets, 2 overhead camshafts (toothed belt); oil capacity 4.9L (4.6US qt), without Turbo 4.4L (4.2US qt). oil-cooler (Turbo); electronic fuel injection; 143hp version: 1 exhaust turbocharger, charger-air cooler. 65Ah battery, alternator 65-75A, cooling system capacity 6L (5.7US qt).

Mitsubishi Colt GTi-16V

Transmission (to front or all wheels): a) 5-speed manual, final drive ratio 4.589 or 4.322.
b) 4-speed automatic (not for Turbo) with Program E/P, final drive ratio 4.062.
4WD (only 4/5 door turbo): Permanent all-wheel-drive, central differential (50/50% power distribution) with viscous coupling, rear limited slip differential (viscous or mechanical), 5-speed manual, final drive ratio 5.084.

Gear ratios: a) 5-speed manual: 1st 3.083; 2nd 1.833; 3rd 1.240; 4th 0.896; 5th 0.731; R 3.166.
Non-turbo version: 1st 3.083; 2nd 1.947; 3rd 1.285; 4th 0.939; 5th 0.777 (USA 0.756); R 3.083.
For 4WD: 1st 2.846; 2nd 1.684; 3rd 1.115; 4th 0.806; 5th 0.651; R 3.166.
b) Automatic, Planetary gear set ratios: 1st 2.846; 2nd 1.581; 3rd 1; 4th 0.685; R 2.176.

Chassis: Front and rear antiroll bar. Four-wheel disc brakes (ventilated at front), front disc diameter 26.6cm, rear 26.5cm, optional ABS; power assisted steering; tyres 195/60 HR 14, without turbo 185/60 HR 15, wheel rims 5 or 5.5J. 4WD: rear rigid axle with double longitudinal arms, Panhard rod, coil springs and antiroll bar.

Dimensions: Length USA 3-door 403cm, 4-door 432cm. 4WD track 142/142cm, height 142.5cm.

Performance: Max speed approx 130.5mph/210kmh, speed at 1000rpm in 5th gear (0.731, axle 4.322) 21.3mph/34.2kmh, 4WD 20.3mph/32.6kmh; power to weight ratio from 9.3kg/kW (6.9kg/PS); consumption approx 8-14L/100km (35.3-20.2mpg) [29.4- 16.8US mpg].
Catalyst Version: Max speed 121mph/195kmh (manufacturers test specification), speed at 1000rpm in 5th gear (axle 4.589) 19.3mph/31.1kmh; acceleration 0 - 62mph/100kmh 9.2secs; power to weight ratio 11.4kg/kW (8.4kg/PS); consumption ECE 6.3/8.1/10.5L/100km (44.8/34.9/26.9mpg) [37.3/29/22.4US mpg].

1.8 Diesel
45kW-60hp-61PS
Injection Pump

As 1.3 Litre, except:

Body, Weight: Saloon/Sedan 3-door, kerbweight 960-1060kg, gross vehicle weight 1465kg.
Saloon/Sedan 4-door, kerbweight 980-1080kg, gross vehicle weight 1500kg.
Saloon/Sedan 5-door, kerbweight from 1030kg.

Engine data (JIS net): 4-cylinder in-line (80.6 x 88mm), 1796cm3; compression ratio 22.2:1; 45kW (60hp) [61PS] at 4500rpm, 26.6kW/L (35.6hp/L) [36.2PS/L]; 111Nm (81.9lbft) at 2500rpm.
European Version (DIN): 44kW (59hp) [60PS] at 4500rpm; 113Nm (83.4lbft) at 3000rpm.

Engine construction: Swirl chamber turbulence diesel engine, 4D 65 designation. Parallel valves; 2 counter-balance shafts; oil capacity 5.6L (5.3US qt), oil-cooler; diesel injection pump VE4. Battery 64-80Ah; alternator 65A; cooling system capacity 6L (5.7US qt).

Transmission: 5-speed manual, final drive ratio 3.752.

Gear ratios: 1st 3.363; 2nd 1.947; 3rd 1.285; 4th 0.939; 5th 0.756; R 3.083.

Chassis: Tyres 155 SR 13 or 175/70 SR 13.

Performance: Max speed approx 93mpg/148kmh, speed at 1000rpm in 5th gear 23.2mph/37.4kmh; power to weight ratio from 21.3kg/kW (15.7kg/PS); consumption ECE 4.6/6.6/6.5L/100km (61.4/42.8/43.5mpg) [51.1/35.6/36.2US mpg].

Mitsubishi Lancer Wagon

Estate/Station Wagon based on the old model Colt/Lancer. Also permanent four wheel drive version. In USA also sold as the Dodge/Plymouth Colt Wagon.

1.5/1.3 Litre
60/53kW-80/71hp-82/72PS
Injection/Compound Carb

Body, Weight: Estate/Station Wagon 5-door, 5-seater; kerbweight (DIN) from 900, USA from 1030kg.

Engine data (DIN): 4-cylinder in-line (75.5 x 82mm), 1468cm3; compression ratio 9.4:1; 60kW (80hp) [82PS] at 5500rpm 40.9kW/L (54.8hp/L) [55.9PS/L]; 120Nm (88.6lbft) at 3500rpm.
Also 61kW (82hp) [83PS].
USA Version (SAE net): 56kW (75hp) [76PS] at 5500rpm; 118Nm (87lbft) at 2500rpm.
With Carb:
With Catalyst (DIN): 51kW (68hp) [70PS] at 5500rpm; 115Nm (84.9lbft) at 3500rpm;
Without Catalyst: 54kW (72hp) [73PS]; 117Nm (86.3lbft).
1.3 Litre (DIN): (71 x 82mm), 1299cm3; compression ratio 9.7:1; 53kW (71hp) [72PS] at 5500rpm, 40.8kW/L (54.7hp/L) [55.4PS/L]; 105Nm (77.5lbft) at 4000rpm.

Engine construction: Designated G 13/15B. Overhead valves in V, 1 overhead camshaft (toothed belt); light-alloy cylinder head; 5 bearing crankshaft; oil capacity 3.4L (3.2US qt); electronic fuel injection or downdraught carb (Catalyst version 68hp electronically regulated). 12V 45-64Ah battery, alternator 50-75A; cooling system capacity approx 5.65L (5.3US qt).

Transmission (to front wheels): a) 4-speed manual, final drive ratio 4.021, 3.941.
b) 5-speed manual, final drive ratio 4.322. 4.021. 3.941.
c) Automatic, hydraulic torque converter with 3-speed Planetary gear set, final drive ratio 3.943 or 3.598.

Gear ratios: a) 4-speed manual: 1st 3.363; 2nd 1.947; 3rd 1.285; 4th 0.939; R 3.083.
b) 5-speed manual: 1st 3.363; 2nd 1.947; 3rd 1.285; 4th 0.939; 5th 0.777; R 3.083.
c) Automatic; max torque multiplication in converter 2.17 times, Planetary gear set ratios: 1st 2.846; 2nd 1.581; 3rd 1; R 2.176.

Chassis: Integral body; front McPherson struts with lower A arm, rear semi-rigid axle (trailing arm, torsion bar) with Panhard rod and coil springs, some models front antiroll bar, telescopic damper. Servo/power assisted brakes, front discs, rear drums, handbrake to rear wheel; power assisted rack and pinion steering, fuel tank 47L (10.3Gal) [12.4US Gal]; tyres 155 SR 13, optional 175/70 SR 13, wheel rims 4.5 or 5J.

Dimensions: Wheelbase 238cm, track 141/134cm, clearance 15cm, turning circle 9.6m, load space 16.2-42.7cu ft (460-1210dm3), length 413.5-418.5cm, USA 130cm, width 163.5cm, height 141.5-143cm.

Performance: (1.5 Litre, 82hp) Max speed 96mph/155kmh (manufacturers test specification), speed at 1000rpm in 5th gear (axle 4.021) 21.1mph/33.9kmh; power to weight ratio from 15.9kg/kW (11.6kg/PS); consumption approx 6-10L/100km (47.1-28.2mpg) [39.2US mpg].

Mitsubishi

```
1755cm3
61kW-82hp-83PS
1 Compound Carb
```

Engine for Lancer Wagon 4WD

As 1.3 Litre, except:

Body, Weight: Kerbweight (DIN) from 1045kg, USA 1160kg.

Engine data (Catalyst DIN): 4-cylinder in-line (80.6 x 86mm), 1755cm3; compression ratio 9:1; 61kW (82hp) [83PS] at 5500rpm, 34.8kW/L (46.6hp/L) [47.3PS/L]; 135Nm (99.6lbft) at 3500rpm; Regular unleaded grade.
Japanese Version (JIS net): 62kW (83hp) [85PS]; 138Nm (101.8lbft).
With Injection (SAE net): 65kW (87hp) [88PS] at 5000rpm; 138Nm (101.8lbft) at 3000rpm.

Engine construction: Designated G 37 B. 2 counter-balance shafts; Catalyst with 1 electronic downdraught compound carb. 12 V 60Ah battery, 55A alternator; cooling system capacity approx 7.65L (7.2US qt).

Transmission (to all wheels): Permanent all wheel drive, central differential lock. 5-speed manual, final drive ratio 5.084.

Gear ratios: 1st 3.083; 2nd 1.684; 3rd 1.115; 4th 0.806; 5th 0.651; R 3.166.

Chassis: Rear rigid axle with 4 trailing arms, Panhard rod and coil springs, antiroll bar front and rear, ventilated front disc brakes; tyres 185/60 HR 14, USA 185/70 SR 14.

Dimensions: Wheelbase 238.5cm, track 141/136cm, clearance 16.5-18cm. Length 418.5cm, USA 430cm, height 146.5-148cm.

Performance: Max speed 96mph/155kmh (manufacturers test specifications), speed at 1000rpm in 5th gear 19.9/32.0kmh; power to weight ratio from 16.1kg/kW (11.9kg/PS); consumption approx 7-12L/100km (40.4-23.5mpg) [33.6-19.6US mpg].

Mitsubishi Lancer Wagon Diesel

```
1.8 Diesel
44kW-59hp-60PS
Injection Pump
```

As 1.3 Litre, except:

Weight: Kerbweight from 1000kg.

Engine data (DIN): 4-cylinder in-line (80.6 x 88mm),1796cm3; compression ratio 21.5:1; 44kW (59hp) [60PS] at 4500rpm, 24.5kW/L (32.8hp/L) [33.4PS/L]; 113Nm (83.4lbft) at 3000rpm.

Engine construction: Swirl chamber turbulence - diesel engine. Designated 4 D 65. Parallel valves; 2 counter-balance shafts; oil capacity 5.6L (5.3US qt), oil cooler; diesel injection pump. 64 or 80Ah battery; cooling system capacity approx 6.65L (6.2US qt).

Transmission: 5-speed manual, final drive ratio 3.412, 3.752.

Gear ratios: 1st 3.363; 2nd 1.947; 3rd 1.285; 4th 0.939; 5th 0.756 (or 0.777); R 3.083.

Chassis: Some models front ventilated disc brakes.

Performance: Max speed 90mph/145kmh (manufacturers test specifications), speed at 1000rpm in 5th gear (axle 3.421) 25.4mph/40.9kmh; acceleration 0 - 62mph/100kmh 15.4secs; power to weight ratio from 22.7kg/kW (16.7kg/PS); consumption ECE 4.7/6.8/7.1L/100km (60.1/41.5/39.8mpg) [50/34.6/33.1US mpg].

Mitsubishi Precis

3 or 5-door Saloon/Sedan with tail gate and transverse front engine; derived from the Hyundai Pony model constructed by Hyundai for the US market. For sale through Mitsubishi. For technical data see Hyundai.

Mitsubishi Precis

Mitsubishi Sapporo

Middle class Saloon/Sedan with front wheel drive. Launched August 1983 also Galant and Eterna. Summer 1987: Marketed under the name of Sapporo in Europe. From Autumn 1987 replaces Galant/Eterna. Sapporo and Sigma (USA) in Australia (Magna). In USA now available with V6 engine.

Mitsubishi Sapporo

```
2351cm3
91/95kW-122/127hp-124/129PS
Fuel Injection
```

As 2000 V6, except:

Body, Weight: Saloon/Sedan 4-door, 5-seater; kerbweight from 1245kg, Magna (Australia) from 1220kg.
Estate/Station Wagon (Magna, AUS) 5-door, 5-seater; kerbweight (DIN) from 1325kg.

Engine data (Catalyst DIN): 4-cylinder in-line (86.5 x 100mm), 2351cm3; compression ratio 9.5:1; 91kW (122hp) [124PS] at 5000rpm, 38.7kW/L (51.9hp/L) [52.7PS/L]; 189Nm (139.5lbft) at 3500rpm; unleaded regular grade.
Without Catalyst: 95kW (127hp) [129PS] at 5000rpm; 193Nm (142.4lbft) at 4000rpm.
Engine for Magna, Australia: (91.1 x 98mm), 2555cm3; compression ratio 8.8:1; 93kW (125hp) [127PS] at 4800rpm; 205Nm (151.3lbft) at 2400rpm.
With Carb: 83kW (111hp) [113PS] at 5200rpm; 195Nm (143.9lbft) at 2800rpm.

Engine construction: Designated 4G 64. Transverse front engine. Valves in V, 1 overhead camshaft (toothed belt); light-alloy cylinder head; 5 bearing crankshaft; 2 counter-balance shafts; oil capacity 4L (3.8US qt); electronic fuel injection. 52 or 64Ah battery, 65, 70 or 85A alternator, cooling system capacity approx 9L (8.5US qt).

Transmission (to front wheels): a) 5-speed manual, final drive ratio 3.625, Magna 4.067.
b) Automatic, hydraulic torque converter with 4-speed Planetary gear set, final drive ratio 3.466; Magna 3.986, 3.705, 3.665 or 3.466.

Gear ratios: a) 5-speed manual, 1st 3.166; 2nd 1.833; 3rd 1.240; 4th 0.896; 5th 0.690 (Magna 0.666); R 3.166.
b) Automatic: 1st 2.551; 2nd 1.488; 3rd 1; OD 0.685; R 2.176.
Magna (Carb): 1st 2.846; 2nd 1.581; 3rd 1; OD 0.685; R 2.176.

Chassis: Integral body; front McPherson struts with lower A arm, rear composite axle (trailing arm, torsion tube) with Panhard rod and coil springs, front and rear antiroll bar, telescopic damper, some models electronically regulated shock absorber with level control system. Servo/power assisted disc brakes (ventilated, Magna not front), optional with ABS, mechanical handbrake to rear wheels; power assisted rack and pinion steering.

Mitsubishi

Fuel tank 60L (13.2Gal) [15.9US Gal], Magna 64L (14.1Gal) [16.9US Gal]; tyres 195/60 HR 15, Magna 175/75 HR 14, wheel rims 5.5 or 6J.

Dimensions: Wheelbase 260cm, track 144.5/141.5cm, Magna 151/147cm, clearance 15.5cm, turning circle 12m, load space VDA 15.4cu ft (436dm3), Magna Wagon 30.2-51.1cu ft (856-1448dm3). Length 466cm, Magna 462cm, Wagon 472.5cm, width 169.5cm, Magna 176.5cm, height 137cm, Magna 139.5cm, Wagon 143.5cm.

Performance (Catalyst Version): Max speed 118mph/190kmh, Automatic 115mph/185kmh (manufacturers test specification), speed at 1000rpm in 5th gear 28mph/45kmh; power to weight ratio from 13.1kg/kW (9.7kg/PS); consumption ECE 6.8/8.3/13.0L/100km (41.5/34/21.7mpg) [34.6/28.3/18.1US mpg], Automatic 7.3/8.8/12.9L/100km (38.7/32.1/21.9mpg) [32.2/26.7/18.2US mpg].

Mitsubishi Magna Station Wagon

```
2972cm3 V6
106kW-142hp-144PS
Fuel Injection
```

Engine for Sigma (USA)

As 2.4 Litre, except:

Weight: Kerbweight from 1395kg.

Engine data (SAE net): 6-cylinder in V 60deg (91.1 x 76.0mm), 2972cm3; compression ratio 8.9:1; 106kW (142hp) [144PS] at 5000rpm, 35.7kW/L (47.8hp/L) [48.5PS/L]; 228Nm (305.5lbft) at 2500rpm.

Engine construction: Designated 6G 72. Valves in V, hydraulic tappets, 1 overhead camshaft (toothed belt) per cylinder; 4 bearing crankshaft; oil capacity 4.3L (4.1US qt); electronic fuel injection. 75A alternator; cooling system capacity approx 8L (7.6US qt).

Transmission: Automatic, final drive ratio 3.705.

Chassis: Tyres 195/60 HR 15, wheel rims 6J.

Dimensions: Length 472cm, height 131cm.

Performance: Max speed approx 124mph/200kmh, speed at 1000rpm in 4th gear 27.5mph/44.3kmh; power to weight ratio from 13.2kg/kW (9.7kg/PS); consumption approx 11-16L/100km (25.7-17.7mpg) [21.4-14.7US mpg].

Mitsubishi Galant/Eterna

Middle range Saloon/Sedan with front wheel drive and engine from 1.6 to 2 Litre displacement. October 1987: New body and four valve DOHC engine with and without turbocharger as well as version with permanent all wheel drive, independent front and rear suspension and all-wheel steering. Autumn 1988: Also 5-door hatchback available (marketed in Japan as Eterna).

```
1800/1600
69/82kW-93/83hp-94/85PS
Injection/1 Downdraught Carb
```

Body, Weight: Saloon/Sedan 4-door, 5-seater; kerbweight (DIN) from 1060kg. Saloon/Sedan 5-door, 5-seater; kerbweight (DIN) from 1100kg.

Engine data (JIS net): 4-cylinder in-line (80.6 x 86mm), 1755cm3; compression ratio 9:1; 69kW (93hp) [94PS] at 5000rpm, 39.3kW/L (52.7hp/L) [53.6PS/L]; 143Nm (105.5lbft) at 500rpm.
With Carb: 62kW (83hp) [85PS] at 5500rpm; 138Nm (101.8lbft) at 3500rpm.
With Catalyst (Carb, DIN): 63kW (84hp) [86PS] at 5500rpm; 133Nm (98.2lbft) at 3500rpm; premium unleaded grade.
European Version (Carb, DIN): Compression 9.5:1; 66kW (88hp) [90PS] at 5500rpm; 137Nm (101lbft) at 3500rpm.
1.6 Litre: (76.9 x 86mm), 1597cm3; compression ratio 9.1:1; 60kW (80hp) [82PS] at 5500rpm; 125Nm (92lbft) at 3500rpm.

Engine construction: Transverse front engine, inclined 10deg to right. Designated 4G 37, 1600 4G 32. Overhead valves in V, 1 overhead camshaft (toothed belt); light-alloy cylinder head, 2 counter-balance shafts (not for 1600); 5 bearing crankshaft; oil capacity 3.9L (3.7US qt); version 93hp electronic. Fuel injection, also 1 downdraught carb (some electronically regulated). 12 V 36-65Ah, 45-75A; cooling system capacity approx 6.1L (5.8US qt).

Transmission (to front wheels): a) 4-speed manual (1600 only), final drive ratio 4.018 (1.096 x 3.666).
b) 5-speed manual, final drive ratio 4.322 (1.097 x 3.941), 1600: 4.018 (1.096 x 3.666).
c) Automatic with Overdrive, hydraulic torque converter with 4-speed Planetary gear set. Final drive ratio, 4.007 (1.125 x 3.562), 4.062 (1.125 x 3.611), 1600: 3.600 (1.125 x 3.200).

Gear ratios: a) 4-speed manual: 1st 3.363; 2nd 1.947; 3rd 1.285; 4th 0.939; R 3.083.
b) 5-speed manual: 1st 3.363; 2nd 1.947; 3rd 1.285; 4th 0.939; 5th 0.756; R 3.083.
c) Automatic: Max torque multiplication with converter 2.17 times, Planetary gear set ratios: 1st 2.846; 2nd 1.581; 3rd 1; OD 0.685; R 2.176.

Chassis: Integral body; front McPherson struts with lower A arm, rear semi-rigid axle (A arm, torsion tube axle) with Panhard rod and coil springs, front antiroll bar (some versions to rear), telescopic damper. Servo/power assisted brakes, front discs ventilated, disc diameter 26.6cm, rear drums, handbrake to rear wheels; power assisted rack and pinion steering (except 1600); fuel tank 60L (13.2Gal) 15.9US Gal]; tyres 165 SR 14 or 185/70 SR/HR 14, 1600: 165 SR 13, wheel rims 5 or 5.5J, 1600 4.5 or 5J.

Dimensions: Wheelbase 260cm, track 146/145cm, clearance 17cm, turning circle 10.6m, load space VDA 14.8cu ft (420dm3), hatchback 14.1cu ft (400dm3), length 453cm, width 169.5cm, height 141.5-143cm, hatchback 140.5-141.5cm.

Performance (Catalyst Version): Max speed 104mph/168kmh (manufacturers test specification), speed at 1000rpm in 5th gear (4.322) 21.8mph/35kmh; acceleration 0 - 62mph/100kmh 12.7secs; power to weight ratio from 16.1kg/kW (11.8kg/PS); consumption ECE 5.9/7.7/10.0L/100km (51.4/36.7/28.2mpg) [39.9/30.5/23.5US mpg].

Mitsubishi Galant 1800

```
2000
82/80kW-110/107hp-112/109PS
Fuel Injection
```

Engine for Export

As 1800, except:

Weight: Kerbweight from 1130kg, USA from 1180kg.

Engine data (DIN): 4-cylinder in-line (85 x 88mm), 1997cm3; compression ratio 9:1; 82kW (110hp) [112PS] at 5500rpm, 41.1kW/L (55.1hp/L) [56.1PS/L]; 160Nm (118.1lbft) at 4500rpm.
With Catalyst: 80kW (107hp) [109PS] at 5500rpm; 159Nm (117.3lbft) at 4500rpm; unleaded premium grade.
USA Version (SAE net): Compression ratio 8.5:1; 76kW (102hp) [103PS] at 5000rpm; 157Nm (115.8lbft) at 4000rpm.

Engine construction: Designated 4G 63. Hydraulic valve lash adjustment; electronic fuel injection. Cooling system capacity 6.5L (6.1US qt).

Transmission: a) 5-speed manual, final drive ratio 4.018 (1.096 x 3.666).
b) Automatic, final drive ratio 4.214 (1.125 x 3.666) or 4.350 (1.25 x 3.867), USA 4.007 (1.125 x 3.562).

Chassis: Four disc brakes (front ventilated), USA rear drums, optional ABS; tyres 195/65 HR 14, USA 185/70 HR 14, wheel rims 5.5J.

Mitsubishi

Dimensions: Length USA 467cm.

Performance (Catalyst version): Max speed 116mph/186kmh, Automatic 112mph/180kmh (manufacturers test specification), speed at 1000rpm in 5th gear 22.8mph/36.7kmh; acceleration 0 - 62mph/100kmh 10.6secs, Automatic 12.2secs; power to weight ratio from 14.2kg/kW (10.4kg/PS); consumption ECE 6.2/8.1/10.0L/100km (45.6/34.9/28.2mpg) [37.9/29/23.5US mpg], automatic 7.0/9.0/10.8L/100km (40.4/31.4/26.2mpg) [33.6/26.1/21.8US mpg].

Mitsubishi Galant 2000 GLSi

2000 DOHC
103kW-138hp-140PS
Fuel Injection

As 1.8 Litre, except:

Weight: Kerbweight from 1140kg, USA from 1270kg, hatchback from 1180kg; 4WD from 1300kg, hatchback from 1370kg.

Engine data (JIS net): 4-cylinder in-line (85 x 88mm), 1997cm3; compression ratio 9:1; 103kW (138hp) [140PS] at 6000rpm, 51.6kW/L (69.1hp/L) [70.1PS/L]; 172Nm (126.9lbft) at 5000rpm.
With Catalyst (DIN): Compression ratio 9.8:1; 106kW (142hp) [144PS] at 6500rpm; 170Nm (125.5lbft) at 5000rpm; unleaded premium grade.
USA Version (SAE net): Compression ratio 9:1; 101kW (135hp) [137PS] at 6000rpm; 170Nm (125.5lbft) at 5000rpm.
Without Catalyst (ECE): Compression ratio 9.8:1; 107kW (143hp) [145PS] at 6500rpm; 170Nm (125.5lbft). at 5000rpm.

Engine construction: Designated 4G 63 DOHC. 4 valves in V 57deg per cylinder; hydraulic valve lash adjustment, 2 overhead camshafts (toothed belt); oil capacity 4.7L (4.4US qt), oil cooler; electronic fuel injection MPI. 12V 48-65Ah; alternator 65-75A, cooling system capacity 6.5L (6.1US qt).

Transmission (to front wheels, 4WD to all wheels): a) 5-speed manual, final drive ratio 4.592 (1.097 x 4.187), 4WD 5.208 (1.680 x 3.166).
b) Automatic (not 2WD), final drive ratio, 4.007 (1.125 x 3.562).

Gear ratios:a) 5-speed manual, 1st 3.038; 2nd 1.947; 3rd 1.285; 4th 0.939; 5th 0.756; R 3.083.
For 4WD: 1st 2.846; 2nd 1.684; 3rd 1.115; 4th 0.833; 5th 0.690; R 3.166.
b) Automatic: As 1.8 Litre.

Chassis: Four wheel disc brakes, front ventilated, optional with ABS; optional regulated damper and level control system; tyres 195/60 HR 15 or 195/65 HR 14, wheel rims 6 or 5.5J.
For 4WD: Rear independent suspension with semi-trailing arm, upper and lower A arm, antiroll bar; hydraulic four wheel steering.

Mitsubishi Galant 2000 DOHC

Dimensions: Length USA 467cm. 4WD: Clearance 16.5cm, length 456-457cm, height 143.5-144cm, hatchback 141.5cm.

Performance (Catalyst version): Max speed 127mph/205kmh, 4WD 124mph/200kmh (manufacturers test specification), speed at 1000rpm in 5th gear 20.1mph/32.4kmh, 4WD 19.5mph/31.3kmh; acceleration 0 - 62mph/100mph 8.8secs, 4WD 9.9secs; power to weight ratio from 11.3kg/kW (8.3kg/PS); consumption ECE 6.6/8.3/11.2L/100km (42.8/34/25.2mpg) [35.6/28.3/21mph], 4WD 6.9/8.9/12.3L/100km (40.9/31.7/23mpg) [34.1/26.4/19.1US mpg].

2000 DOHC
151kW-202hp-205PS
Turbo/Fuel Injection

As 1.8 Litre, except:

Weight: Kerbweight from 1340kg, hatchback 1410kg.

Engine data (JIS net): 4-cylinder in-line (85 x 88mm), 1997cm3; compression ratio 7.8;1; 151kW (202hp) [205PS] at 6000rpm, 75.6kW/L (101.3hp/L) [102.7PS/L]; 294Nm (217lbft) at 3000rpm.

Engine construction: Designated 4G 63 DOHC. 4 valves in V 57deg per cylinder; hydraulic valve lash adjustment, 2 overhead camshafts (toothed belt); oil capacity 4.7L (4.4US qt), oil cooler; electronic fuel injection MPI; 1 turbocharger TC 05, charge-air cooler. 12V 48/65Ah; alternator 65/75A, cooling system capacity 6.5L (6.1US qt).

Transmission (to all wheels): Permanent all wheel drive, central differential with viscous coupling, 50/50% power distribution. 5-speed manual, final drive ratio 4.933 (1.275 x 3.866). Optional rear limited slip differential.

Gear ratios: 5-speed manual: 1st 2.846; 2nd 1.684; 3rd 1.115; 4th 0.833; 5th 0.666; R 3.166.

Chassis: Rear independent suspension with trailing arm, upper and lower control arm, antiroll bar; front disc brakes (ventilated) with ABS; hydraulic four-wheel steering; tyres 195/60 HR 15, wheel rims 6J.

Dimensions: Clearance 16.5cm, length 456cm, height 144cm, hatchback 141.5cm.

Performance: Max speed approx 143mph/230kmh, speed at 1000rpm in 5th gear 22mph/35.4kmh; power to weight ratio from 8.9kg/kW (6.5kg/PS); consumption approx 9-18L/100km (8.5-15.7mpg) [26.1-13.1US mpg].

1800 Diesel
56kW-75hp-76PS
Turbo/Injection Pump

As 1.8 Litre, except:

Weight: Kerbweight from 1140kg, hatchback from 1180kg.

Mitsubishi Galant Diesel

Engine data (JIS net): 4-cylinder in-line (80.6 x 88mm), 1796cm3; compression ratio 22.2:1; 56kW (75hp) [76PS] at 4500rpm, 31.2kW/L (41.8hp/L) [42.3PS/L]; 149Nm (110lbft) at 2500rpm.
European Version (DIN): 55kW (74hp) [75PS] at 4500rpm; 152Nm (112.1lbft) at 2500rpm.

Engine construction: Swirl chamber turbulence diesel engine. Designated 4 D 65 Turbo. Parallel valves; oil capacity 5.6L (5.3US qt), oil cooler; Nippon-Denso VE 4 diesel injection pump; 1 turbo-charger, max charge-air pressure 0.66 bar. 64-80Ah battery; 65A alternator, cooling system capacity 8.1L (7.7US qt).

Transmission: a) 5-speed manual, final drive ratio 4.322 or 4.471.
b) Automatic, final drive ratio 4.367.

Gear ratios: a) 5-speed manual: 1st 3.363; 2nd 1.947; 3rd 1.285; 4th 0.939; 5th 0.729; R 3.083.
Or: 1st 3.250; 2nd 1.833; 3rd 1.240; 4th 0.896; 5th 0.690; R 3.166.
b) Automatic: 1st 2.551; 2nd 1.488; 3rd 1; OD 0.685; R 2.176.

Mitsubishi

Performance: Max speed 101mph/162kmh (manufacturers test specification), speed at 1000rpm in 5th gear (0.690, axle 4.471) 23mph/37kmh; acceleration 0 – 62mph/100kmh 14.5secs; power to weight ratio from 20.4kg/kW (15kg/PS); consumption ECE 4.8/6.8/7.3L/100km (58.8/41.5/38.7mpg) [49/34.6/32.2US mpg].

Mitsubishi Starion

2 + 2 Coupe with hatchback, 2 Litre Turbo engine and rear wheel drive. Launched Geneva 1982. May 1984: Modifications to the body and new Turbo engine with 197hp (JIS). 1986: For export with 2.6 Litre with flared wheel arches. Available in the USA as Chysler Conquest.

2 Litre
132kW-177hp-180PS
Turbo/Central Single Point Injection

Body, Weight: 3–door Coupe, 2+2–seater; kerbweight (DIN) 1230– 1260kg.

Engine data (DIN): 4–cylinder in–line (85 x 88mm), 1997cm3; compression ratio 7.6:1; 132kW (177hp) [180PS] at 6000rpm, 66.1kW/L (89hp/L)[90.1PS/L]; 290Nm (214lbft) at 3500rpm.
Export version without charger–air cooler: 110kW (147hp) [150PS] at 5500rpm; 230Nm (169.7lbft) at 3000rpm.
Or 125kw (167.5hp) [170PS]; 245Nm (180.8lbft).
Japanese version (3 valves, JIS net): Compression ratio 7.5:1; 125kW (167.5hp) [170PS] at 5800rpm; 255Nm (188.2lbft) at 3000rpm.

Engine construction: 4 G 63 EC1 Turbo designation. Overhead valves (in V), Japanese version 3 valves per cylinder, 1 overhead camshaft (toothed belt); 2 counter–balance shafts; light–alloy cylinder head; crankshaft with 5 bearings; oil capacity 4.7L (4.4US qt), oil–cooler; electronic central/single point EC1 injection; Mitsubishi exhaust turbocharger, charger–air cooler. Battery 12V 45/65Ah, alternator 65A; cooling system capacity 7.2L (6.8US qt).

Transmission (to rear wheels): a) 5–speed manual, final drive ratio 3.545 or 3.909.
b) Automatic, hydraulic torque converter and 4–speed Planetary gear set, final drive ratio 3.909 or 3.545. Optional limited slip differential.

Gear ratios: a) 5–speed manual: 1st 3.369; 2nd 2.035; 3rd 1.360; 4th 1; 5th 0.856; R 3.635.
Or 1st 3.74; 2nd 2.136; 3rd 1.36; 4th 1; 5th 0.856; R 3.635.
b) Automatic: Max torque multiplication in converter 2 times, Planetary gear set ratios: 1st 2.452; 2nd 1.452; 3rd 1; 4th 0.688; R 2.212.

Chassis: Integral body; front and rear independent suspension, control arms, tension struts and antiroll bar, rear McPherson struts, A–arms and telescopic dampers. Servo/power assisted disc brakes (ventilated), optional ABS (only rear wheels), mechanical hand brake to rear wheels; recirculating ball steering, optional power assisted; fuel tank 75L (16.5Gal) [19.8US Gal]; tyres 215/60 HR 15, wider version 205/55 VR 16 front, 225/50 VR 16 rear, wheel rims 6.5J, large version 7 and 8J.

Dimensions: Wheelbase 243.5cm, track 141/139cm, wider version 147/140cm, clearance 9cm, turning circle 10.7m. Length 440–443cm, width 168.5–170.5cm, wider version 174.5cm, height 127.5–132cm.

Performance: Max speed 137mph/220kmh (manufacturers test specifications), speed at 1000rpm in 5th gear (3.909) 21.8mph/35.0kmh; acceleration 0 – 62mph/100km 7.6secs; power to weight ratio from 9.3kg/kW (6.8kg/PS); ECE consumption 7.3/9.6/11.9L/100km (38.7/29.4/23.7mpg) [32.2/24.5/19.8US mpg].

Mitsubishi Starion Turbo

2.6 Litre
114kW–153hp–155PS
Turbo/Fuel Injection

As 2 Litre, except:
Weight: Kerbweight (DIN) from 1320kg. USA from 1375kg.

Engine data (Catalyst, DIN): 4–cylinder in–line (91.1 x 98mm), 2555cm3; compression ratio 7:1; 114kW (153hp) [155PS] at 5000rpm, 44.6kW/L (59.8hp/L) [60.7PS/L]; 284Nm (209.6lbft) at 2500rpm; unleaded fuel.
With Intercooler:
USA version (SAE net): 140kW (188hp) [191PS] at 5000rpm; 317Nm (233.9lbft) at 2500rpm.
Japanese Version (JIS net): 129kW (173hp) [175PS] at 5000rpm; 314Nm (231.7lbft) at 3000rpm.

Engine construction: G 54 B designation. 1 overhead camshaft (chain); electronic fuel injection, Version 153hp without charge-air cooler. Battery 66/75Ah, alternator 65/75A; cooling system capacity 8.3– 8.5L (7.9–8US qt).

Transmission: a) 5–speed manual, final drive ratio 3.545.
b) Automatic, final drive ratio 3.545.
Limited slip differential.

Gear ratios: a) 5–speed manual: 1st 3.369; 2nd 2.035; 3rd 1.360; 4th 1; 5th 0.856; R 3.578.
Or: 1st 3.40; 2nd 2.016; 3rd 1.345; 4th 1; 5th 0.856; R 3.578.
b) Automatic, Max torque multiplication in converter approx 2 times, Planetary gear set ratios: 1st 2.458; 2nd 1.458; 3rd 1; 4th 0.686; R 2.182.

Chassis: Power assisted steering; tyres 205/55 VR 16 (front) and 225/50 VR 16 (rear), optional 225/50 VR 16 (front) and 245/45 VR 16 (rear), wheel rims (front/rear) 7/8J, optional 8/9J.

Dimensions: Track 147/140cm or 146.5/145.5cm. Width 173.5– 174.5cm.

Performance: (153hp) Max speed 134mph/215kmh (manufacturers test specifications), speed at 1000rpm in 5th gear 23.7/38:2kmh; acceleration 0 – 62mph/100kmh 8.2secs; power to weight ratio from 11.6kg/kW (8.6kg/PS); ECE consumption 8.0/10.1/13.6L/100km (35.3/28/20.8mpg) [29.4/23.3/17.4US mpg].

Mitsubishi Eclipse

New model. Sporty Coupe with front wheel drive based on the Mitsubishi Galant. Four cylinder with 90 SAE-hp, DOHC 16V Turbo with 190hp. All wheel drive in preparation. Is marketed as Diamond-Star (USA). Provisionally for the American market at the moment, available as Chrysler. Data see Plymouth Laser.

Mitsubishi Eclipse

Mitsubishi Debonair V

Luxury Saloon/Sedan with new V6 engine with 2 or 3 Litre engine capacity, automatic transmission and front wheel drive, not for export. Debut July 1986. From 1987 also available with supercharged 2 Litre V6 engine.

2 Litre V6
77kW–103hp–105PS
Fuel Injection

Body, Weight: 4–door Saloon/Sedan, 5/6–seater; kerbweight (DIN) 1350–1400kg.

Engine data (JIS net): 6–cylinder in 60deg V (74.7 x 76mm), 1998cm3; compression ratio 8.9:1; 77kW (103hp) [105PS] at 5000rpm, 38.6kW/L (51.7hp/L) [52.5PS/L]; 158Nm (116.5lbft) at 4000rpm.

Mitsubishi

Engine construction: Transverse mounted front engine. 6G 71 designation. Valves in V, hydraulic tappets, 1 overhead camshaft per cylinder bank (toothed belt); light–alloy cylinder head, crankshaft with 4 bearings; oil capacity 4.3L (4.1US qt); electronic fuel injection. Battery 12V 60Ah, alternator 70A; cooling system capacity approx 8L (7.6US qt).

Transmission (to front wheels): Automatic, hydraulic torque converter and 4–speed Planetary gear set, final drive ratio 4.446.

Gear ratios: Automatic, max torque multiplication in converter 2 times, Planetary gear set ratios: 1st 2.846; 2nd 1.581; 3rd 1; 4th 0.685; R 2.176.

Chassis: Integral body, front McPherson struts with lower A–arms, rear compound axle (longitudinal arms, torsion tube axle) with Panhard rod and coil springs, front and rear antiroll bar, telescopic dampers. Servo/power assisted disc brakes (ventilated at front). Mechanical handbrake to rear wheels; power assisted rack and pinion steering; fuel tank 72L (15.8Gal) [19US Gal]; tyres 175 SR 14, optional 185/70 SR 14 or 195 SR 14, wheel rims 5.5J.

Dimensions: Wheelbase 273.5cm, track 145.5/140.5cm, clearance 17cm, turning circle 10.6m. Length 469cm, width 169.5cm, height 144cm.

Performance: Max speed approx 106mph/170kmh, speed a 1000rpm in 4th gear 23.7mph/38.1kmh; power to weight ratio from 17.5kg/kW (12.9kg/PS); consumption (touring) approx 10–15L/100km (28.2– 18.8mpg) [23.5–15.7US mpg].

Mitsubishi Debonair V Supercharger

```
2 Litre V6
110kW–147hp–150PS
Supercharger/Fuel Injection
```

As 103hp, except:

Weight: Kerbweight (DIN) 1440kg.

Engine data (JIS net): 6–cylinder in 60deg V (74.7 x 76.0mm), 1998cm3; compression ratio 8:1; 110kW (147hp) [150PS] at 5500rpm, 55.1kW/L (73.8hp/L) [75.1PS/L]; 221Nm (163lbft) at 3000rpm.

Engine construction: 6G 71 Supercharger designation. Oil–cooler; 1 mechanical supercharger (Rootes type); charge–air cooler (water/air).

Transmission: Automatic, final drive ratio 4.350.

Gear ratios: Automatic: Max torque multiplication in converter 2 times, Planetary gear set ratios: 1st 2.551; 2nd 1.488; 3rd 1; 4th 0.685; R 2.176.

Chassis: Tyres 195/70 SR 14.

Performance: Max speed approx 118mph/190kmh, speed at 1000rpm in 4th gear 24.3mph/39.1kmh; power to weight ratio from 13.1kg/kW (9.6kg/PS); consumption (touring) approx 10– 15L/100km (28.2–18.8mpg) [23.5–15.7US mpg].

```
3 Litre V6
110kW–147hp–150PS
Fuel Injection
```

As 103hp, except:

Weight: Kerbweight (DIN) 1470–1510kg.

Engine data (JIS net): 6–cylinder in 60deg V (91.1 x 76.0mm), 2972cm3; compression ratio 8.9:1; 110kW (147hp) [150PS] at 5000rpm, 37kW/L (49.6hp/L) [50.5PS/L]; 231Nm (170.4lbft) at 2500rpm.

Engine construction: 6G 72 designation.

Transmission: Automatic, final drive ratio 3.9.

Gear ratios: Automatic: Max torque multiplication in converter 2 times, Planetary gear set ratios: 1st 2.551; 2nd 1.488; 3rd 1; 4th 0.685; R 2.176.

Chassis: Tyres 195/70 SR 14, AMG version 205/60 HR 15, wheel rims AMG 6J.

Dimensions: Length 486.5cm, AMG version 486cm, width 172.5cm, height 142.5–144cm.

Performance: Max speed approx 121mph/195kmh, speed at 1000rpm in 4th gear 27mph/43.5kmh; power to weight ratio from 13.3kg/kW (9.8kg/PS); consumption approx 12–17L/10km (23.5–16.6mpg) [19.6– 13.8US mpg].

Mitsubishi Space Wagon/Chariot

Roomy Saloon/Sedan with front wheel drive and variable interior, 7–seater. Four–cylinder engine with 1.6, 1.8 and 2 Litre engine capacities. Chariot designation in Japan, Colt Vista in the USA. Debut February 1983. June 1984: also available with 4WD. October 1984: 1.8 Litre turbodiesel.

```
1.6 Litre
58kW–78hp–79PS
1 2V Carb
```

Body, Weight: 5–door Estate/Station Wagon, 6–7–seater; kerbweight (DIN) 980–1030kg.

Engine data (JIS net): 4–cylinder in–line (76.9 x 86mm), 1598cm3; compression ratio 9.1:1; 58kW (78hp) [79PS] at 5500rpm, 36.3kW/L (48.6hp/L) [49.4PS/L]; 128Nm (171.5lbft) at 3500rpm.

Engine construction: Transverse mounted front engine. G 32 B designation. Overhead valves (in V), 1 overhead camshaft (toothed belt); light–alloy cylinder head; crankshaft with 5 bearings; oil capacity 4L (3.8US qt); 1 downdraught 2V carb (some models electronically controlled). Battery 12V 35/45Ah, alternator 45A; cooling system capacity 6.65L (6.3US qt).

Transmission (to front wheels): 5–speed manual, final drive ratio 4.018 (1.096 x 3.666).

Gear ratios: 5–speed manual: 1st 3.454; 2nd 1.947; 3rd 1.285; 4th 0.939; 5th 0.756; R 3.083.

Chassis: Integral body; front McPherson struts with lower single control arm and transverse torsion struts, rear independent suspension with longitundinal swinging arms and coil springs, front/rear antiroll bar, telescopic dampers. Servo/power assisted brakes, front discs, rear drums, mechanical handbrake to rear wheels; rack and pinion steering, optional power assisted; fuel tank 50L (11Gal) [13.2US Gal]; tyres 165 SR 13, wheel rims 4.5 or 5J.

Dimensions: Wheelbase 262.5cm, track 141/137.5cm, clearance 15cm, turning circle 10.6m. Length 429.5cm, width 164cm, height 152.5cm.

Performance: Max speed approx 93mph/150kmh speed at 1000rpm in 5th gear 22.3mph/35.9kmh; power to weight ratio from 16.9kg/kW (12.4kg/PS); consumption approx 7–11L/100km (40.4– 25.7mpg) [33.6–21.4US mpg].

Mitsubishi Space Wagon

```
1755cm3
62kW–83hp–85PS
1 2V Carb
```

As 1.6 Litre, except:

Weight: Kerbweight (DIN) 1030–1090kg.

Engine data (JIS net): 4–cylinder in–line (80.6 x 86mm), 1755cm3; compression ratio 9:1; 62kW (83hp) [85PS] at 5500rpm, 35.3kW/L (47.3hp/L) [48.4PS/L]; 138Nm (101.8lbft) at 3500rpm.
Export version (DIN): Compression ratio 9.5:1; 66kW (88.5hp) [90PS] at 5500rpm; 137Nm (101.1lbft) at 3500rpm.
Or: 70kW (94hp) [95PS]; 140Nm (103.3lbft).

Engine construction: G 37 B designation. 2 counter–balance shafts. Battery 12V 45/60Ah, alternator 60/65A.

Transmission: a) 5–speed manual, final drive ratio 4.018 (1.096 x 3.666).
b) Automatic, hydraulic torque converter and 3–speed Planetary gear set, final drive ratio 3.597 (1.136 x 3.166).

Mitsubishi

Gear ratios: a) 5-speed automatic: As 1600.
b) Automatic: Max torque multiplication in converter approx 2.3 times, Planetary gear set ratios: 1st 2.846; 2nd 1.581; 3rd 1; R 2.176.

Chassis: Front ventilated disc brakes. Optional tyres 185/70 SR 13.

Performance: Max speed 101mph/163kmh, automatic 98mph/157kmh (manufacturers test specifications), speed at 1000rpm in 5th gear 22.3mph/35.9kmh; power to weight ratio from 16.6kg/kW (12.2kg/PS); ECE consumption 6.3/8.5/10.7L/100km (44.8/33.2/26.4mpg) [37.3/27.7/22US mpg], automatic 7.5/9.7/10.4L/100km (37.7/29.1/27.2mpg) [31.4/24.2/22.6US mpg].

Mitsubishi Space Wagon 4x4

```
1997cm3
81kW-108.5hp-110PS
1 2V Carb
```

Engine for 4WD and Catalyst Version

As 1.6 Litre, except:

Weight: Kerbweight (DIN) 2WD 1160–1120kg, USA from 1195kg, 4WD 1200–1335kg, USA from 1340kg, gross vehicle weight 1850kg.

Engine data (JIS): 4-cylinder in-line (85 x 88mm), 1997cm3; compression ratio 8.5:1; 81kW (108.5hp) [110PS] at 5500rpm, 40.5kW/L (54.3hp/L) [55.1PS/L]; 164Nm (121lbft) at 3500rpm.
European version (DIN): Compression ratio 9.5:1; 75kW (100.5hp) [102PS] at 5500rpm, 37.6kW/L (50.4hp/L) [51.1PS/L]; 154Nm (115.8lbft) at 3500rpm.
With injection:
With Catalyst (DIN): Compression ratio 8.5:1; 74kW (99hp) [101PS] at 5000rpm; 157Nm (115.9lbft) at 4000rpm; unleaded regular grade.
USA version (fuel injection, SAE net): Identical data.
For BRD (Catalyst DIN): Compression ratio 9:1; 79kW (106hp) [107PS] at 5500rpm; 159Nm (117.3lbft) at 4500rpm.

Engine construction: G 63 B designation. Hydraulic tappets for Catalyst version. 2 counter-balance shafts; Compound carb or electronic fuel injection. Battery 12V 52–70Ah, alternator 65A, cooling system capacity 7L (6.6US qt).

Transmission (4WD to all wheels): a) 5-speed manual, final drive ratio 4.018; 3.466.
b) Automatic, final drive ratio 3.705, 3.466, 3.187.
4WD: Engageable rear-wheel-drive. a) 4-speed manual with Economy (reduction 1.238) and Power (reduction 1.611) positions, final drive ratio 3.714 front, 3.722 rear.
b) 5-speed manual, final drive ratio 3.714 front, 3.722 rear.
Optional rear limited slip differential.

Gear ratios: a) 4-speed manual E/P (only 4WD): 1st 3.083; 2nd 1.631; 3rd 0.961; 4th 0.758; R 2.916.
b) 5-speed manual: 1st 3.454; 2nd 1.947; 3rd 1.285; 4th 0.939; 5th 0.756; R 3.083.
For 4WD: 1st 4.967; 2nd 2.628; 3rd 1.549; 4th 1.166; 5th 0.896; R 4.699.
c) Automatic: Max torque multiplication in converter approx 2.17 times, Planetary gear set ratios: 1st 2.846; 2nd 1.581; 3rd 1; R 2.176.

Chassis: Front ventilated disc brakes; power assisted steering; tyres 165 SR 13 or 185/70 SR 13.
4WD: Rear semi-trailing arms and horizontal torsion bars; tyres 165 SR 14 or 185/70 SR/HR 14, wheel rims 5 or 5.5J.

Dimensions: 4WD; track 140.5/138.5cm, clearance 18cm, turning circle 11.4m. Length 444.5cm, height 158cm.

Performance: Max speed 99.5mph/160kmh, automatic 97mph/156kmh, 4WD 101mph/163kmh, 4WD Catalyst 102mph/165kmh (manufacturers test specifications), speed at 1000rpm in 5th gear (4.018 axle) 22.3mph/35.9kmh, 4WD 21.3mph/34.3kmh; power to weight ratio from 14.8kg/kW (10.9kg/PS); consumption DIN 6.7/8.9/11.2L/100km (42.2/31.7/25.2mpg) [35.1/26.4/21US mpg], 4WD 7.4/9.8/13.0L/100km (38.2/28.8/21.7mpg) [31.8/24/18.1US mpg].

```
1.8 Diesel
58kW-78hp-79PS
Turbo/Injection Pump
```

As 1.6 Litre, except:

Weight: Kerbweight from 1175kg.

Engine data (JIS net): 4-cylinder in-line (80.6 x 88mm), 1796cm3; compression ratio 21.5:1; 58kW (78hp) [79PS] at 4500rpm; 32.3kW/L (43.3hp/L) [44PS/L]; 165Nm (121.7lbft) at 2500rpm.
European version (DIN): 55kW (74hp) [75PS] at 4500rpm; 152Nm (112.1lbft) at 2500rpm.

Engine construction: Swirl chamber turbulence diesel engine. 4 D 65 designation. Parallel valves, 2 counter-balance shafts; oil capacity 4.3L (4.1US qt), oil-cooler; diesel injection pump; Mitsubishi exhaust turbocharger. Battery 12V 56/80Ah, alternator 55/65A.

Chassis: Front ventilated disc brakes; power assisted steering. Tyres 185/70 SR 13.

Performance: Max speed 93mph/150kmh (manufacturers test specifications), speed at 1000rpm in 5th gear 22.3mph/35.9kmh; power to weight ratio from 20.3kg/kW (14.9kg/PS); ECE consumption 5.8/8.0/7.9L/100km (48.7/35.3/35.8mpg) [40.6/29.4/29.8US mpg].

Mitsubishi Jeep

Off road vehicle. Available with 3 different wheelbases and 3 engines including 1 diesel. Marketed in Japan as 'Jeep'.

Mitsubishi Jeep

```
2/2.6 Litre
73/88kW-98/118hp-100/120PS
1 2V Carb
```

Body, Weight: Estate/Station Wagon, fabric roof, 4-seater, 9-seater, long wheelbase; kerbweight from 1150kg. 5-door Estate/Station Wagon, 5–6-seater; kerbweight from 1350kg.

Engine data (JIS): 4-cylinder in-line (84 x 90mm) 1995cm3; compression ratio 8.5:1; 73kW (98hp) [100PS] at 5000rpm, 36.6kW/L (49hp/L) [50.1PS/L]; 162Nm (119.5lbft) at 3000rpm. Or (91.1 x 98mm), 2555cm3; compression ratio 8.2:1; 88kW (118hp) [120PS] at 5000rpm, 34.4kW/L (46.1hp/L) [47PS/L]; 209Nm (154.2lbft) at 3000rpm.

Engine construction: 4 G 52/G 54 B designation. Valves in V; 1 overhead camshaft (chain); light-alloy cylinder head; crankshaft with 5 bearings; 2 counter-balance shafts; oil capacity 6L (5.7US qt); 1 downdraught 2V carb. Battery 12V 60Ah, alternator 48A; cooling system capacity approx 8L (7.6US qt).

Mitsubishi

Transmission (to rear wheels or all wheels): Engageable front-wheel-drive, reduction gears, optional front free-wheel hubs, 4-speed manual, final drive ratio 5.375.

Gear ratios: 1st 3.3; 2nd 1.795; 3rd 1.354; 4th 1; R 3.157; final drive ratio with reduction gears: 1st 0.903; and 2.306.

Chassis: Sub-frame with cross-members; front and rear rigid axle with semi-elliptical springs, telescopic dampers. Servo/power assisted drum brakes; mechanical handbrake to drive shaft; recirculating ball steering; fuel tank 45/60L (9.9-13.2Gal) [11.9-15.9US Gal]; tyres 6.00-14, 7.60-15 or 215 R 15.

Dimensions: Wheelbases 203/222.5/264cm, track 130.5/130.5cm, clearance 21cm, turning circle 11.6-13.4m. Lengths 345.5/368/410/429cm, widths 166.5/162cm, height 189-194cm.

Performance: Max speed 62-75mph/100-120kmh (manufacturers test specifications), speed at 1000rpm in 4th gear 17.2mph/27.6kmh; power to weight ratio from 15.7kg/kW (11.5kg/PS).

2.7 Litre Diesel
69kW-93hp-94PS
Turbo/Injection Pump

As petrol/gasoline engine, except:

Weight: Estate/Station Wagon (fabric roof) from 1350kg, 5-door (solid construction) from approx 1600kg.

Engine data (JIS net); 4-cylinder in-line (92 x 100mm), 2659cm3; compression ratio 17.5:1; 69kW (93hp) [94PS] at 3500rpm; 25.9kW/L (34.7hp/L) [35.4PS/L]; 206Nm (151.9lbft) at 2000rpm.

Engine construction: 4 DR 6 designation. Parallel valves, side-mounted camshaft; grey cast-iron cylinder head; oil capacity approx 6L (5.7US qt), oil-cooler; diesel injection pump; 1 exhaust turbocharger. Battery 2 x 40Ah, cooling system capacity approx 10L (9.5US qt).

Transmission: Final drive ratio 4.777.

Performance: Max speed approx 81mph/130kmh, speed at 1000rpm in 4th gear 19.3mph/31.1kmh; power to weight ratio from 19.6kg/kW (14.4kg/PS).

Mitsubishi Pajero

Off road vehicle with engageable four wheel drive, front independent suspension, petrol/gasoline or diesel engine. Debut Tokyo 1982, production from September 1982. Designated Montero in the USA. 1986: turbodiesel now with 2.5 Litre engine capacity. 1988: Turbodiesel with intercooler, 3 Litre V6 fuel engine.

Mitsubishi Pajero

2.6 Litre
76kW-102hp-103PS
1 2V Carb

Engine for export

Body, Weight: 3-door canvas top Estate/Station Wagon, 4-5-seater; kerbweight (DIN) 1380-1515kg, gross vehicle weight 2115kg. 3-door canvas top Estate/Station Wagon, 4-5-seater; kerbweight 1450-1570kg, USA 1450-1500kg, gross vehicle weight 2115kg. 5-door Estate/Station Wagon, 5-7-seater; kerbweight (DIN) 1560-1780kg, gross vehicle weight 2450kg.

Engine data (DIN): 4-cylinder in-line (91.1 x 98mm), 2555cm3; compression ratio 8.2:1; 76kW (102hp) [103PS] at 4500rpm, 29.6kW/L (39.5hp/L) [40.3PS/L]; 192Nm (141.6lbft) at 2500rpm; lead regular grade.

With Catalyst: 76kW (102hp) [103PS] at 5000rpm; 183Nm (113.7lbft) at 3000rpm. USA version (SAE net): Compression ratio 8.7:1; 81kW (108.5hp) [110PS] at 5000rpm, 193Nm (120lbft) at 3000rpm.

Engine construction: 4 G 54 designation; valves in V, Catalyst engine hydraulic tappets; 1 overhead camshaft (chain); light-alloy cylinder head; crankshaft with 5 bearings; 2 counter-balance shafts; oil capacity 5L (4.7US qt); 1 downdraught 2V carb. Battery 12V 45/70Ah, alternator 45/50A; cooling system capacity 8.6L (8.1US qt).

Transmission (to rear wheels or all wheels); Engageable front wheel drive, reduction gears, automatic free-wheel hubs.
a) 5-speed manual, final drive ratio 4.875, USA 4.625.
Optional 4-speed manual, final drive ratio 4.875.
b) Automatic, hydraulic torque converter and 4-speed Planetary gear set, final drive ratio 4.875, USA 4.625.
Optional limited slip differential.

Gear ratios: Reduction gears: 1st 1; 2nd 1.944.
a) 5-speed manual: 1st 3.967; 2nd 2.136; 3rd 1.36; 4th 1; 5th 0.856; R 3.578.
Optional 4-speed manual: 1st 3.74; 2nd 2.136; 3rd 1.36; 4th 1; R 3.578.
b) Automatic: Max torque multiplication in converter 2.02 times. Planetary gear set ratios: 1st 2.826; 2nd 1.493; 3rd 1.000; 4th 0.688; R 2.703.

Chassis: Sub-frame. Front independent suspension with lower and upper A arms, torsion struts, antiroll bar, rear rigid axle with leaf springs, telescopic dampers. Servo/power assisted brakes, front discs (ventilated), rear drums; recirculating ball steering, optional power assisted; fuel tank 60L (13.2Gal) [15.9US Gal], 5-door 92L (20.2Gal) [24.3US Gal]; tyres 215 SR 15, USA 225/75 SR 15, optional 6.50-16 or 7.00-16, wheel rims 5.5 or 6J.

Dimensions: 3-door; wheelbase 235cm, track 140/137.5cm, clearance 18cm, turning circle 11m. Length 399.5cm, width 168cm, height 182/184cm. 5-door; wheelbase 269.5cm, turning circle 11.8m. Length 460cm, width 168cm, height 186.5/194.5cm.

Performance: Max speed 81-87mph/130-140kmh (manufacturers test specifications), speed at 1000rpm in 4th gear 16.9mph/27.2kmh; power to weight ratio from 18.2kg/kW (13.4kg/PS); ECE consumption 10.2/15.1/16.0L/100km (27.7/18.7/17.7mpg) [23.1/15.6/14.7US mpg], 5-door 10.9/16.1/16.5L/100km (25.9/17.5/17.1mpg) [21.6/14.6/14.3US mpg].

---

2 Litre
81kW-108.5hp-110PS
1 2V Carb

Only 3-door

As 2555cm3, except:

Weight: Kerbweight from 1340kg.

Engine data (JIS): (85 x 88mm), 1997cm3; compression ratio 8.5:1; 81kW (108.5hp) [110PS] at 5500rpm, 40.5kW/L (54.3hp/L) [55.1PS/L]; 164Nm (121lbft) at 3500rpm.

Engine construction: G 63 B designation. 1 overhead camshaft (toothed belt).

Transmission: 5-speed manual, final drive ratio 4.875.

Chassis: Tyres 7.60-15.

Dimensions: Length 387cm.

Performance: Max speed approx 75mph/120kmh, power to weight ratio from 16.5kg/kW (12.2kg/PS); consumption approx 10-16L/100km (28.2-17.7mpg) [23.5-14.7US mpg].

---

2 Litre
107kW-143hp-145PS
Turbo/Central Single Point Injection

As 2555cm3, except:

Weight: Kerbweight from 1360kg.

Engine data (JIS): 4-cylinder in-line (85 x 88mm), 1997cm3; compression ratio 7.5:1; 107kW (143hp) [145PS] at 5500rpm, 53.6kW/L (71.8hp/L) [72.6PS/L]; 216Nm (134.2lbft) at 3000rpm.

Engine construction: G 63 Turbo EC1 designation; 1 overhead camshaft (toothed belt); oil capacity 4.2L (4US qt), oil-cooler; electronic EC1 central/single point injection, Mitsubishi exhaust turbocharger. Battery 12V 60Ah; alternator 65A.

Transmission: 5-speed manual, final drive ratio 4.625.

Chassis: Four-wheel disc brakes (ventilated at front).

Dimensions: Length 393cm, 5-door 459cm.
Performance: Max speed approx 90kmh/145kmh, speed at 1000rpm in 5th gear 20.8mph/33.5kmh; power to weight ratio from 12.8kg/kW (9.4kg/PS); consumption approx 12-20L/100km (23.5-14.1mpg) [19.6- 11.8US mpg].

```
2.5 Litre Diesel
70/62kW-94/83hp-95/84PS
Turbo/Injection Pump
```

As 2555cm3, except:
Weight: 3-door; kerbweight (DIN) 1520-1640kg, gross vehicle weight 2115kg. 5-door; kerbweight (DIN) 1780-1875kg; gross vehicle weight 2450kg.
Engine data (DIN): 4-cylinder in-line (91.1 x 95mm), 2477cm3; compression ratio 21:1; 70kW (94hp) [95PS] at 4200rpm, 28.3kW/L (37.9hp/L) [38.3PS/L]; 235Nm (173lbft) at 2000rpm.
With charge-air cooler: 62kW (83hp) [85PS]; 201Nm (148lbft).
Japanese version (JIS net): 62kW (83hp) [85PS]; 196Nm (144.6lbft).
Engine construction: 4 D 56 designation. Swirl chamber turbulence diesel engine. Parallel valves, 1 overhead camshaft (toothed belt); oil capacity 6.4L (6.1US qt), oil-cooler; VE diesel injection pump; Mitsubishi exhaust turbocharger. Battery 12V 64/80Ah or 2 x 55Ah, alternator 45/65A.
Transmission: a) 5-speed manual, final drive ratio 4.625 or 4.875.
b) 4-speed automatic, final drive ratio 4.625 or 4.875.
Gear ratios: a) 4-speed manual; 1st 4.33; 2nd 2.355; 3rd 1.574; 4th 1; R 4.142.
b) 5-speed manual; as 2.6 Litre.
c) Automatic: As 2.6 Litre.
Chassis: Some models four-wheel disc brakes (ventilated at front).
Dimensions: Length (Japan) 393-396cm, 5-door 447.5-459cm.
Performance: Max speed 87mph/140kmh (manufacturers test specifications), speed at 1000rpm in 5th ger (axle 4.625) 22.6mph/36.3kmh; power to weight ratio from 22kg/kW (16.2kg/PS); consumption ECE [83hp] 3-door 8.4/9.6/13.2L/100km (33.6/29.4/21.4mpg) [28/24.5/17.8US mpg], 5-door 9.1/10.5/14.1L/100km (31/26.9/20mpg) [25.8/22.4/16.7US mpg].

Mitsubishi Pajero

```
3.0 V6
107kW-143hp-145PS
Fuel Injection
```

As 2555cm3, except:
Weight: 3-door: Kerbweight (DIN) USA 1585-1600kg.
5-door: Kerbweight (DIN) from 1820kg.
Engine data (SAE net): 6-cylinder in V 60deg (91.1 x 76mm), 2972cm3; compression ratio 8.7:1; 107kW (143hp) [145PS] at 5000rpm, 36kW/L (48.2hp/L) [48.8PS/L]; 228Nm (168.3lbft) at 2500rpm.
European Version (with or without Catalyst DIN): 104kW (139hp) [141PS] at 5000rpm; 225Nm (166lbft) at 3000rpm.
Engine construction: Designated 6G 72. Valves in V, hydraulic tappets, 1 overhead camshaft (toothed belt) per cylinder bank; 4 bearing crankshaft; oil capacity 4.3L (4.1US qt); electronic fuel injection. 12V 65Ah, alternator 75A; cooling system capacity approx 8L (7.6US qt).
Transmission: a) 5-speed manual, final drive ratio 4.625.
b) 4-speed automatic, final drive ratio 4.625.
Gear ratios: a) 5-speed manual: 1st 3.918; 2nd 2.261; 3rd 1.395; 4th 1; 5th 0.829; R 3.925.
b) Automatic: As 2.6 Litre.
Chassis: Rear rigid axle with coil springs, two trailing arms, Panhard rod and antiroll bar. Power/assisted steering; tyres 235/75 R 15 (USA) or 205 R 15, wheel rims 6J.

Dimensions: Track 140/141.5cm, length USA 3-door 400cm.
Performance: Max speed 99mph/160kmh (manufacturers test specification), speed at 1000rpm in 5th gear (axle 4.625) 22.6mph/36.3mph; power to weight ratio from 14.8kg/kW (10.9kg/PS); consumption approx 12-20L/100km (23.5-14.1mpg) [19.6-11.8US mpg].

```
MIURA                                    BR
```

Besson Gobbi SA, Av. Sertorio 113, 90 000 Porto Alegre, Brazil.
Small Brazilian vehicle manufacturer.

Miura

Saga - 787 - X8 - Targa Spider

Two-seater Coupe with synthetic body. Targa debut 1982, Spider 1983, Saga November 1984. From end of 1988 all models available with 2 Litre VW engine. Ford engine for export to the USA.

Miura Saga 787

```
2000cm3
82/73kW-110/98hp-112/99PS
1 Compound Carb
```

Body, Weight: 2-door Targa and Saga Coupe, 2-seater; kerbweight 975-1070kg.
Engine data (DIN): 4-cylinder in-line (82.5 x 92.8mm), 1984cm3.
a) For operation on Ethyl alcohol (DIN): Compression ratio 12:1; 82kW (110hp) [112PS] at 5200rpm, 41.3kW/L (55.3hp/L) [56.4PS/L]; 170Nm (125.5lbft) at 3400rpm.
b) Petrol/Gasoline engine: Compression ratio 8:1; 73kW (98hp) [99PS] at 5200rpm, 36.8kW/L (49.3hp/L) [49.9PS/L]; 159Nm (117.3lbft) at 3400rpm; unleaded regular grade.
Engine construction: Front engine (longitudinal), 1 overhead camshaft (toothed belt); light-alloy cylinder head; 5 main bearing crankshaft; oil capacity 3.5L (3.3US qt); 1 Brosol Pierburg 2E7 downdraught compound carb. Battery 12V 54Ah, Alternator 65A; cooling system capacity 6.7L (6.3US qt).
Transmission (to front wheels): 5-speed manual, final drive ratio 4.11.
Gear ratios: 1st 3.45; 2nd 1.99; 3rd 1.29; 4th 0.97; 5th 0.8; R 3.166.
Chassis: VW-Passat platform; front McPherson struts with control arms, antiroll bar and coil springs, rear rigid axle with longitudinal arms, control arm struts, coil springs and telescopic dampers. Brakes optional servo/power assisted, front discs, rear drums, discs 23.8cm diameter; Saga with all round disc brakes; mechanical handbrake to rear wheels; rack and pinion steering; fuel tank 65L (14.3Gal) [17.2US Gal]; tyres 195/70 HR 14, wheel rims 6.5J.
Dimensions: Wheelbase 248cm, track 141/141.5cm, clearance 21cm, turning circle 13m, length 436cm, width 169cm, height 125cm.
Performance (without turbo): Max speed approx 118mph/190kmh (manufacturers test specifications), speed at 1000rpm in 5th gear 22mph/35.4kmh; power to weight ratio from 11.9kg/kW (8.7kg/PS); consumption approx 8-12L/100km (35.3-23.5mpg) [29.4-19.6US mpg].

Miura • Moretti • Morgan

Miura Saga X8

MORETTI   I

Moretti, Fabbrica Automobili et Stabilimenti Carozzerie S.A.S., Via Monginevro 278-282, 10142 Turin, Italy

Small specialist Italian body manufacturer building prototypes and special bodies based on Fiat models.

Moretti Panda Rock

Multi-purpose vehicle based on Fiat Panda. Debut Turin 1982, 4 x 4 July 1984.

As Fiat Panda 750/1000, except:

Body, Weight: 2-door convertible, 4/5-seater; kerbweight (DIN) from 690kg; 4x4 790kg.

Dimensions: Wheelbase 216cm, 4 x 4 217cm, track 126/126cm. Length 341cm, width 150cm, height 142cm, 4 x 4 147cm.

Fiat Panda Rock

Moretti Uno Folk

Moretti Uno Folk

Vehicle with folding roof based on Fiat Uno. Debut January 1984.

As Fiat Uno 45 SL 'Fire' or diesel S, except:

Body, Weight: 2-door Convertible, 5-seater; kerbweight (DIN) 710-800kg.

Dimensions: Length 364cm, width 155cm, height 145cm.

Moretti Uno Country

Multi-purpose vehicle based on the Fiat Uno 45/SL 'Fire'. Debut January 1988.

As Fiat Uno Fire or Diesel, except:

Body, Weight: 2-door Convertible, 5-seater; kerbweight (DIN) 710-800kg.

Dimensions: Wheelbase 236cm, track 133/139cm. Length 364.5cm, width 155.5cm, height 142.5cm.

MORGAN   GB

Morgan Motor Company Ltd., Pickersleigh Road, Malvern Link, Worcestershire WR14 2LL, England.

Small English sports car manufacturer with long history/tradition. Early pioneer of three-wheel vehicles.

MODEL RANGE
4/4 1600 - Plus Four - Plus 8

Morgan 4/4 1600

Roadster – Tourer

Roadster with sub-frames, front disc brakes and Ford 1.6 Litre engine. Winter 1981/82: with Ford CVH engine.

Morgan 4/4 1600 Tourer

```
1.6 Litre
71kW-95hp-96PS
1 2V Carb
```

Body, Weight: 2-door Roadster, 2-seater; kerbweight from 865kg. 2-door Tourer, 4-seater; kerbweight from 920kg.

Engine data (DIN): 4-cylinder in-line (80 x 79.5mm), 1598cm3; compression ratio 9.5:1; 71kW (95hp) [96PS] at 5750rpm, 44.2kW/L (59.2hp/L) [60.1PS/L]; 132Nm (97.4lbft) at 4000rpm.

Engine construction: Ford CVH designation. Hydraulic tappets; 1 overhead camshaft (toothed belt); light-alloy cylinder head; crankshaft with 5 bearings; oil capacity 3.5L (3.3US qt); 1 Weber 28/32 TLDM downdraught 2V carb. Battery 12V 40Ah, alternator 45/55A; cooling system capacity 7.3L (6.9US qt).

Transmission (to rear wheels): 5-speed manual, floor shift; final drive ratio 4.1 (10/41), optional 4.56 (9/41).

Gear ratios: 1st 3.65; 2nd 1.97; 3rd 1.37; 4th 1; 5th 0.83; R 3.66.

Chassis: Sub-frame with cross members; front guide tube and coil springs, rear rigid axle with semi-elliptical springs, front telescopic dampers, rear piston dampers. Front disc brakes, rear drums, disc diameter 27.9cm, hand brake to rear wheels; worm and wheel steering; fuel tank 45/56L (9.9/12.3Gal) [11.9/14.8US Gal]; tyres 165 SR 15 or 195/60 VR 15, wheel rims 5 or 6.5".

Dimensions: Wheelbase 244cm, track 122/124cm, clearance 15cm, turning circle 10m. Length 389cm, width 150cm, height 129cm, 4-seater 135cm.

Morgan · Moskvich

Performance: Max speed 115mph/185kmh (manufacturers test specifications), speed at 1000rpm in 4th gear 18.3mph/29.5kmh; acceleration 0 – 60mph/97kmh 8secs; power to weight ratio from 12.2kg/kW (9.0kg/PS); consumption (touring) 8–9L/100km (35.3– 31.4mpg) [29.4–26.1US mpg], manufacturers test specifications.

Morgan 4/4 1600 Roadster

Morgan Plus Four

Roadster with box section frame, available with 2 Litre Rover engine since Spring 1988.

> 2 Litre
> 103kW–138hp–140PS
> Fuel Injection

Body, Weight: 2-door Roadster, 2/4 seater; kerbweight from 900kg.

Engine data (DIN): 4-cylinder in-line (84.5 x 89mm), 1996cm3; compression ratio 10:1; 103kW (138hp) [140PS] at 6000rpm, 51.6kW/L (69.1hp/L) [70.1PS/L]; 178Nm (131.4lbft) at 4500rpm.
With Catalyst: 98kW (131hp) [133PS] at 5900rpm; 176Nm (129.9lbft) at 4400rpm.

Engine construction: Designated M16i. 4 valves per cylinder; 2 overhead camshafts (toothed belt); light-alloy cylinder blocks; 5 main bearing crankshaft; Lucas L electronic fuel injection. Battery 12V 55/60Ah, Alternator 65/80A; cooling system capacity 6L (5.7US qt).

Transmission (to rear wheels): 5-speed manual, floor shift, final drive ratio 3.73.

Gear ratios: 1st 3.32; 2nd 2.09; 3rd 1.40; 4th 1; 5th 0.79; R 3.43.

Chassis: Box section frame with cross members; front vertical leading tube and coil springs, rear rigid axle with semi elliptic springs, front telescopic damper, rear piston dampers. Front disc brakes, rear drums, disc diameter 27.9cm, mechanical handbrake to rear wheels; recirculating ball steering; fuel tank capacity 57L (12.5Gal) [15.1US Gal]; tyres 190/60 HR 15, wheel rims 6".

Dimensions: Wheelbase 244cm, track 119/124cm, clearance 15cm, turning circle 10m, length 389cm, width 150cm, height 127cm.

Performance: Max speed 170mph/172kmh (manufacturers test specifications), speed at 1000rpm in 4th gear 23.7mph/38.1kmh; acceleration 0-60mph/97kmh 8.7secs; power to weight ratio from 6.4kg/kW (6.5kg/PS); consumption ECE (touring) 8-11L/100km (35.3-25.7mpg) [29.4-21.4US mpg].

Morgan Plus 8

Roadster with 3.5 Litre V8 Rover engine. High performance. Debut September 1968. October 1976: more power, 5-speed Rover transmission. May 1984 also with fuel injection and rack and pinion steering.

> 3.5 Litre V8
> 142kW–190hp–193PS
> Fuel Injection

Body, Weight: 2-door Roadster, 2-seater; kerbweight from 940kg, gross vehicle weight 1200kg.

Engine data: 8-cylinder in 90deg V (88.9 x 71.12mm), 3532cm3; compression ratio 9.75:1; 142kW (190hp) [193PS] at 5280rpm, 40.2kW/L (53.9hp/L) [54.6PS/L]; 298Nm (219.9lbft) at 4000rpm; leaded premium grade.
With Catalyst: In preparation.

Engine construction: Hydraulic tappets, central camshaft (chain); light-alloy cylinder head and block, dry cylinder liners; crankshaft with 5 bearings; oil capacity 5.7L (5.4US qt); Lucas LE electronic fuel injection. Battery 12V 50, 57/68Ah, alternator 55/65A; cooling system capacity 11.1L (10.5US qt).

Transmission (to rear wheels): 5-speed manual, floor shift; final drive ratio 3.31; limited slip differential.

Gear ratios: 1st 3.321; 2nd 2.087; 3rd 1.396; 4th 1; 5th 0.79; R 3.428.

Chassis: Sub-frame with cross members; front guide tube and coil springs, rear rigid axle with semi-elliptical springs, front telescopic dampers, rear piston dampers. Servo/power assisted brakes, front disc, rear drums, disc diameter 27.9cm, handbrake to rear wheels; rack and pinion steering; fuel tank 61L (13.4Gal) [16.1US Gal], tyres 205/60 VR 15, wheel rims 6.5J.

Dimensions: Wheelbase 249cm, track 138/137.5cm, clearance 14cm, turning circle 11.5m. Load space 4.9cu ft (140dm3). Length 396cm, width 160cm, height 122cm.

Performance: Max speed 123mph/197kmh (manufacturers test specifications), speed at 1000rpm in 5th gear 27.2mph/43.8kmh; acceleration 0 – 62mph/100kmh 7secs; power to weight ratio 6.6kg/kW (4.9kg/PS); consumption (DIN) 11.8L/100km (25.7mpg) [21.4US mpg].

Morgan Plus 8

MOSKVICH   SU

AZLK, V/O Autoexport, 14, Volkhonka ST.l, 119902, Moscow, USSR
Russian vehicle manufacturer based in Moscow

Moskvich 2140

Middle of the range car with 1479cm3 OHC four-cylinder engine, 412/427 original editions; end 1974: modern Saloon/Sedan body for 2140.

Moskvich 2140

> 1479cm3
> 53kW–71hp–72PS
> 1 2V Carb

Body, Weight: 4-door Saloon/Sedan, 5-seater; kerbweight (DIN) 1045–1100kg, gross vehicle weight approx 1500kg.

Engine data (DIN): 4-cylinder in-line (82 x 70mm), 1479cm3; compression ratio 8.8:1; 53kW (71hp) [72PS] at 5800rpm, 35.8kW/L (48hp/L) [48.7PS/L]; 112Nm (82.6lbft) at 3400rpm; leaded premium grade.
With reduced compression 7.1:1; 48kW (64hp) [65PS] at 5200rpm.

Moskvich • MVS

Engine construction: Engine inclined 20deg. Valves in 52deg V, 1 overhead camshaft (chain); light–alloy cylinder head; wet cylinder liners; crankshaft with 5 bearings; oil capacity 5L (4.7US qt); 1 downdraught 2V compound carb. Battery 12V 45/55Ah, alternator 40A; cooling system capacity 7.5/10L (7.1/9.5US qt).
Transmission (to rear wheels): Full synchromesh 4–speed manual, final drive ratio 4.22, 3.89 or 4.55.
Gear ratios: 1st 3.49; 2nd 2.04; 3rd 1.33; 4th 1; R 3.39.
Chassis: Integral body; front trapeze A–arms and coil springs, rear rigid axle with semi–elliptical springs, front antiroll bar, telescopic dampers. Servo/power assisted brakes, front discs, rear drums, mechanical hand brake to rear wheels; worm and wheel steering; fuel tank 46L (10.1Gal) [12.2US Gal]; tyres 6.45–13/165 SR 13 or 6.95–13/175 SR 13, wheel rims 4, 4.5 or 5J.
Dimensions: Wheelbase 240cm, track 127/127cm, clearance 20cm, turning circle 11.5m. Load space 21.2cu ft (600dm3). Length 421– 425cm, width 155cm, height 148cm.
Performance: Max speed 84–88mph/135–142kmh (manufacturers test specifications), speed at 1000rpm in 4th gear 16.2mph/26kmh; power to weight ratio from 19.7kg/kW (14.5kg/PS); ECE consumption 7.4/10.2/10.3L/100km (38.2/27.7/27.4mpg) [31.8/22.8/23.1US mpg].

Moskvich Ish–2126

New model. Five–seater middle of the range Saloon/Sedan with tail gate and rear wheel drive. Mechanically based on the Moskvich 2140 but with some of the new 2141 chassis elements. Length approx 400cm, width approx 165cm, engine approx 1500cm3, 5–speed manual. Prototype debut Autumn 1987.

Moskvich Ish–2126

Moskvich 2141

21412 - 2141
Middle of the range Saloon/Sedan with longitudinal engine (1.5 or 1.6 Litre), front wheel drive and tail gate. Production start up December 1986. Provisional data; 1700cm3 engine (84hp 102.5mph/165kmh) under preparation. Export version also known as "Aleko".

```
1479cm3
54kW–72hp–73PS
1 2V Carb
```

Engine for 21412
Body, Weight: 5–door Saloon/Sedan, 5–seater; kerbweight (DIN) 1080kg, gross vehicle weight 1480kg.
Engine data (DIN): 4–cylinder in–line (82 x 70mm), 1479cm3; compression ratio 9.5:1; 54kW (72hp) [73PS] at 5500rpm, 36.5kW/L (48.9hp/L) [49.4PS/L]; 108Nm (79.7lbft) at 3300rpm; leaded premium grade.
With reduced 7.2:1 compression: 48kW (64hp) [65PS] at 5200rpm.
Engine construction: In–line engine positioned in front of the front axle. Valves in 52deg V, 1 overhead camshaft (chain); light–alloy cylinder head; wet cylinder liners; crankshaft with 5 bearings; oil capacity 3.5L (3.3US qt); 1 downdraught 2V carb. Battery 12V 55Ah, alternator 55A; cooling system capacity approx 8L (7.6US qt).
Transmission (to front wheels): 5–speed manual, final drive ratio 4.1.

Gear ratios: 1st 3.31; 2nd 2.05; 3rd 1.37; 4th 0.95; 5th 0.73; R 3.36.
Chassis: Integral body; front independent suspension with McPherson struts, lower control arms and antiroll bar, rear compound axle (longitudinal arms with control arms), coil springs, telescopic damper. Servo/power assisted brakes, front discs, rear drums, handbrake to rear wheels; rack and pinion steering; fuel tank approx 55/52L (12.1/11.4Gal) [14.5/15.3US Gal]. Tyres 165 SR 13 or 155 SR 13, wheel rims 5J.
Dimensions: Wheelbase 258cm, track 144/142cm, clearance approx 16cm, turning circle 11.3m. Load space 14.1–49.4cu ft (470– 1270dm3). Length 435cm, width 169cm, height 140cm.
Performance: Max speed 92mph/147kmh (manufacturers test specifications); speed at 1000rpm in 5th gear 22.7mph/36.5kmh; acceleration 0 – 62mph/100kmh 18.7secs; power to weight ratio from 20kg/kW (14.8kg/PS); ECE consumption 6.3/8.6/10.0L/100km (44.8/32.8/28.2mpg) [37.3/27.4/23.5US mpg].

Moskvich 21412

```
1569cm3
52kW–70hp–71PS
1 2V Carb
```

As 1479cm3, except:
Weight: Kerbweight (DIN) approx 1070–1090kg, gross vehicle weight approx 1470/1530kg.
Engine data (DIN): 4–cylinder in–line (79 x 80mm), 1569cm3; compression ratio 8.5:1; 52kW (70hp) [71PS] at 5400rpm, 33.1kW/L (44.4hp/L) [45.2PS/L]; 118Nm (87lbft) at 3100rpm; leaded regular grade.
Also: 59kW (79hp) [80P].
Performance: Max speed 96mph/155kmh (manufactuers test specifications); acceleration 0 – 62mph/100kmh 15.7secs; power to weight ratio 20.6kg/kW (15.1kg/PS); consumption (ECE) 6.1/8.3/9.4L/100km (46.3/34/30.1mpg) [38.6/28.3/25US mpg].

MVS F

MVS Manufacture de Voitures de Sport, 89–91 Rue du Faubourg Saint Honore, 75008 Paris, France

Company founded in 1985 by two finance companies for the production of high–value limited series vehicles.

MVS Venturi

Two–door Coupe with two seats, 2.5 Litre PRV turbo engine, 5– speed manual transmission, prototype exhibited at the 1984 Paris Motor Show. Debut Paris 1986. Cabriolet/Convertible Paris 1988.

MVS Venturi Cabriolet

MVS • Nissan

2.5 Litre V6
147kW–197hp–200PS
Fuel Injection/Turbo

Body, Weight: 2–door Coupe/Convertible, 2 seater; kerbweight (DIN) 1255kg.

Engine data (DIN): 6–cylinder in 90deg V (91 x 63mm), 2458cm3; compression ratio 8.6:1; 147kW (197hp) [200PS] at 5750rpm, 59.8kW/L (80.1hp/L) [81.4PS/L]; 290Nm (214lbft) at 2500rpm.
With Catalyst: Compression ratio 8:1; 136kW (182hp) [185PS].

Engine construction: Mid–engine mounted longitudinally. Z7U–730 desgination. 2x1 overhead camshafts (chain); light-alloy cylinder head and block; wet cylinder liners; crankshaft with 4 bearings; oil capacity 7.5L (7.1US qt); Renix A.E.I electronic fuel injection; 1 Garrett T3 exhaust turbocharger; max boost pressure 0.85bar; Intercooler. Battery 12V 50Ah, alternator 90/105A; cooling system capacity 14L (13.2US qt).

Transmission (to rear wheels); 5–speed manual (without direct drive), final drive ratio 3.889.

Gear ratios: 5–speed manual: 1st 3.364; 2nd 2.059; 3rd 1.381; 4th 0.964; 5th 0.756; R 3.545.

Chassis: Steel chassis with front and rear supports; front lower and upper A–arms, coil springs with coaxial telescopic dampers, rear independent suspension with 2 longitudinal struts and control arms, coil springs and telescopic dampers, front and rear antiroll bar. Servo/power assisted disc brakes (ventilated), front and rear disc diameter 28.0cm; mechanical hand brake to rear wheels; rack and pinion steering; fuel tank 90L (19.8Gal) [23.8US Gal]; front tyres 205/55 VR 16, rear 245/45 VR 16.

Dimensions: Wheelbase 240cm, track 146/147cm, clearance 16cm, turning circle 10m. Load space 5.3cu ft (150dm3). Length 409cm, width 170cm, height 117cm.

Performance: Max speed 152mph/245kmh (manufacturers test specifications), speed at 1000rpm in 5th gear 24.9mph/40.1kmh; acceleration 0-60mph/100kmh 6.9secs; standing km 26.8secs; power to weight ratio 8.5kg/kW (6.3kg/PS); consumption (ECE) 6.5/9.1/13.2L/100km (43.5/31/21.4mpg) [36.2/25.8/17.8US mpg].

MVS Venturi

NISSAN   J

Nissan Motors Co., Ltd., 17–1, Ginza 6–chome, Chuo–ku, Tokyo 104, Japan

Car brand of a large Japanese commercial vehicle manufacturer. 1966 agreement with Prince Motors Ltd. The former 'Datsun' export designation was dropped.

MODEL RANGE
Pao – March/Micra – Sunny – Prairie/4WD – Silvia/200 SX – Bluebird/Auster/Stanza – New Bluebird – Maxima – Skyline – Leopard – Laurel – Cedric/Gloria – Fairlady Z – President – Patrol/Safari – New Safari – Terrano/Pathfinder

Nissan Pao

New model. Successor of the Be-1. Small car with an air of nostalgia. Based on the March/Micra. Part of the body in synthetic materials, 1 litre engine, front wheel drive, five speed manual or automatic. Launched at the Tokyo show 1987. Production began January 1989, an export version is not planned.

1 Litre
38kW–51hp–52PS
1 2V Carb

Body, Weight: Saloon/Sedan 3-door, 4–seater; kerbweight (DIN) approx 720kg, with folding roof from 730kg.

Engine data (JIS net): 4–cylinder in-line (68 x 68mm), 988cm3, compression ratio 9.5:1; 38kW (51hp) [52PS] at 6000rpm, 38.7kW/L (51.9hp/L) [52.6PS/L]; 75Nm (55.4lbft) at 3600rpm.

Engine construction: Designated MA 10. Transverse front engine. Valves in V; 1 overhead camshaft (toothed belt); light-alloy cylinder head and block; 5 bearing crankshaft; oil capacity 2.8L (2.6US qt); 1 electronic downdraught carb. 12V 45Ah battery; 40/50A alternator; cooling system capacity approx 4L (3.8US qt).

Transmission (to front wheels): a) 5-speed manual, final drive ratio 4.05. b) Automatic, hydraulic torque converter with 3-speed Planetary gear set, final drive ratio 3.889.

Gear ratios: a) 5-speed manual: 1st 3.412; 2nd 1.958; 3rd 1.258; 4th 0.921; 5th 0.721; R 3.385.
b) Automatic; max torque multiplication in converter 2 times; Planetary gear set ratios: 1st 2.826; 2nd 1.542; 3rd 1; R 2.364.

Chassis: Integral body; front McPherson struts, A arm and antiroll bar, rear rigid axle with trailing arm, coil springs, telescopic damper. Servo/power assisted disc brakes, front discs, rear drums, handbrake to rear wheel; power assisted rack and pinion steering; fuel tank 40L (8.8Gal) [10.6US Gal]; tyres 155 SR 12, wheel rims 4J.

Dimensions: Wheelbase 230cm, track 136.5/135.5cm, turning circle 9.2m, length 374m, width 157cm, height 148cm.

Performance: Max speed approx 87mph/140kmh, speed at 1000rpm in 5th gear 21.2mph/34.1kmh; power to weight ratio from 18.9kg/kW (13.8kg/PS); consumption approx 5-9L/100km (47.9-31.4mpg) [47-26.1US mpg].

Nissan Pao

Nissan March/Micra

Compact small car with front wheel drive and tailgate, new 1 Litre engine, 4/5–speed or automatic transmission. Debut October 1982. 'Micra' export designation. January 1985: sporty version with turbocharger and 83hp.

Nissan March/Micra

Nissan

1/1.2 Litre
37/42kW–49.5/56hp–50/57PS
1 Carb

Body, Weight: 3/5–door Saloon/Sedan, 4/5–seater; kerbweight (DIN) from 630kg, Europe 700–770kg.

Engine data (DIN): 4–cylinder in–line (68 x 68mm), 988cm3, compression ratio 9.5:1; 37kW (49.5hp) [50PS] at 6000rpm, 37.4kW/L (50.1hp/L) [50.6PS/L]; 72Nm (53.1lbft) at 3600rpm; leaded regular grade.
With automatic: Compression ratio 10.3:1, 40kW (53.5hp) [54PS]; 76Nm (56.1lbft).
With Catalyst: (71 x 78mm), 1235cm3; compression ratio 9:1; 42kW (56hp) [57PS] at 5200rpm, 34kW/L (45.6hp/L) [46.2PS/L]; 93Nm (68.6lbft) at 3200rpm.
With unregulated Catalyst: 44kW (59hp) [60PS] at 5200rpm.
Japanese version (JIS net): 38kW (51hp) [52PS] at 6000rpm; 75Nm (55.3lbft) at 3600rpm.

Engine construction: Designated MA 10. Transverse mounted front engine; valves in V; 1 overhead camshaft (toothed belt); light–alloy cylinder head and block; crankshaft with 5 bearings; oil capacity 2.8L (2.6US qt); 1 Hitachi downdraught compound carb. Battery 12V 45Ah; alternator 40/50A; cooling system capacity 4L (3.8US qt).

Transmission (to front wheels): a) 4–speed manual, final drive ratio 4.05; 3.81.
b) 5–speed manual, final drive ratio 4.05; 3.81; 3.591.
c) Automatic, hydraulic torque converter with 3–speed Planetary gear set, final drive ratio 3.737; 3.889.

Gear ratios: a) 4–speed manual: 1st 3.412; 2nd 1.958; 3rd 1.258; 4th 0.921; R 3.385.
b) 5–speed manual: 1st 3.412; 2nd 1.731; 3rd 1.121; 4th 0.85; 5th 0.721; R 3.385.
Or: 1st 3.412; 2nd 1.958; 3rd 1.258; 4th 0.921; 5th 0.721; R 3.385.
c) Automatic: Max torque multiplication in converter 2 times; Planetary gear set ratios: 1st 2.826; 2nd 1.542; 3rd 1; R 2.364.

Chassis: Integral body, front McPherson struts and control arm, rear rigid axle with longitudinal and diagonal struts and coil springs, a few models with front antiroll bar, telescopic dampers. Servo/power assisted brakes, front discs, rear drums, mechanical handbrake to rear axle; rack and pinion steering, optional power assisted steering; fuel tank 40L (8.8Gal) [10.6US Gal]; tyres 5.95–12 145 SR 12 or 155 SR 12, 155/70 SR 13, wheel rims 4, 4.5J, or 5J.

Dimensions: Wheelbase 230cm, track 134.5/133cm, turning circle 9.2m, load space 6–13.2cu ft (170/375dm3), length 364/376cm, width 156cm, height 139.5cm.

Performance: (1 Litre) Max speed 88mph/142kmh, automatic 87mph/140kmh (manufacturers test specifications). Speed at 1000rpm in 5th gear (4.05:1) 21.4mph/34.5kmh. Acceleration 0 – 62mph/100kmh 15.9secs; power to weight ratio from 16.6kg/kW (12.1kg/PS); fuel consumption ECE 5.0/6.6/6.4L/100km (56.5/42.8/44.1mpg) [47/35.6/36.8US mpg], 5–speed 4.8/6.4/6.3L/100km (58.5/44.1/44.8mpg) [49/36.8/37.3US mpg].

---

1 Litre
62kW–83hp–85PS
Turbo/Fuel Injection

As 49.5/56hp model except:

Body, Weight: 3–door Saloon/Sedan; kerbweight 710–730kg.

Engine data (JIS): 4–cylinder in–line (68 x 68mm), 988cm3; compression ratio 8:1; 62kW (83hp) [85PS] at 6000rpm, 62.7kW/L (84hp/L) [86PS/L]; 118Nm (87lbft) at 4400rpm.

Engine construction: Designated MA 10 ET. Electronic fuel injection ECCS; 1 exhaust turbocharger.

Transmission: a) 5–speed manual, final drive ratio 4.353.
b) Automatic, final drive ratio 3.737.

Gear ratios: a) 5–speed manual: 1st 3.063; 2nd 1.826; 3rd 1.207; 4th 0.902; 5th 0.733; R 3.417.
b) Automatic: As 56hp model.

Chassis: Front and rear antiroll bars. Front ventilated discs brake; tyres 165/70 HR 12; 175/60 HR 133, wheels 5J.

Dimensions: Track 135/133cm, length 373cm, width 157cm, height 138.5cm.

Performance: Max speed approx 99.5mph/160kmh, speed at 1000rpm in 5th gear 19.4mph/31.2kmh; power to weight ratio from 11.4kg/kW (8.4kg/PS); consumption approximately 6–11L/100km (47.1–25.7mpg) [39.2–21.4US mpg].

Nissan Sunny

Pulsar – EXA – Langley – Laurel Spirit – Liberta Villa – Sentra

---

Extensive lower/middle class range with identical technology, transverse mounted front engine, front wheel drive, 1, 1.3, 1.5, 1.6 or 1.7 Litre diesel engine. Some models with permanent 4WD. New edition Sunny/Pulsar May 1986. October 1986 EXA Coupe. February 1987: Pulsar hatchback 4WD with viscous coupling in both axle differentials. Autumn 1987: New 1.5 Litre engine with 12 valves. 1989: Powerful engine for Catalyst version.

Nissan Sunny

1.0/1.3 Litre
44/37kW–59/49hp–60/50PS
1 Carb

Body, Weight: 3–door Saloon/Sedan kerbweight 890–945kg. 4–door Saloon/Sedan kerbweight 905–950kg. 5–door Saloon/Sedan kerbweight 890–960kg. 5–door Estate/Station Wagon kerbweight 955–960kg.

Engine data (DIN): 4–cylinder in–line (76 x 70mm), 1270cm3; compression ratio 9:1; 44kW (59hp) [60PS] at 5600rpm, 34.7kW/L (46.5hp/L) [47.2PS/L]; 100Nm (73.8lbft) at 3600rpm.
Japanese version (JIS net): 49kW (66hp) [67PS] at 6000rpm; 98Nm (72.3lbft) at 3600rpm.
For some countries (DIN): (73 x 59mm), 988cm3; compression ratio 9:1; 37kW (49hp) [50PS] at 6000rpm, 37.2kW/L (49.8hp/L) [50.6PS/L]; 75Nm (55.4lbft) at 4000rpm.

Engine construction: Designated E 13/10 S. Transverse engine; valves in V; 1 overhead camshaft (toothed belt); light–alloy cylinder block; 5 bearing crankshaft; oil capacity 3.2L (3US qt); 1 compound carb (some models electronic control). 12V 44–60Ah battery, 50–60A alternator; cooling system capacity 4.3L (4.1US qt).

Transmission: a) 4–speed manual, final drive ratio 4.353 or 3.895, 1.0 4.471.
b) 5–speed manual, final drive ratio 4.353 or 3,895.
c) Automatic, hydraulic torque converter with 3–speed Planetary gear set, final drive ratio 3.737 or 3.600.

Gear ratios: a) 4–speed manual: 1st 3.333; 2nd 1.955; 3rd 1.286; 4th 0.902; R 3.417.
b) 5–speed manual: 1st 3.333; 2nd 1.955; 3rd 1.286; 4th 0.902; 5th 0.756 or 0.733; R 3.417.
c) Automatic: Max torque multiplication in converter 2 times; Planetary gear set ratios: 1st 2.826; 2nd 1.543; 3rd 1; R 2,364.

Chassis: Integral body; front McPherson struts, A arm and antiroll bar, rear independent suspension with McPherson struts, 2 parallel control arms and antiroll bar, telescopic damper. Servo/power assisted brakes, front discs, rear drums, handbrake to rear wheels; rack and pinion steering optional power assistance; fuel tank 50L (11Gal) [13.2US Gal]; tyres 145 SR 13 or 155 SR 13, wheel rims 4.5J.

Dimensions: Wheelbase 143cm, track 143.5/143cm, clearance 15cm, turning circle 10.2m, load space hatchback 9.8–40.3cu ft (278–1140dm3), Saloon/Sedan 14.4cu ft (409dm3), length 403cm, 4–door 421.5cm, Wagon 427cm, width 164cm, height 138cm.

Performance: Max speed 97mph/156kmh, 1.0 litre 84mph/135kmh (manufacturers test specifications), speed at 1000rpm in 5th gear 20.6mph/33.2kmh; acceleration 0 – 62mph/100kmh 14.9secs; power to weight ratio from 20.6kg/kW (15.1kg/PS); consumption approx 6–10L/100km (47.1–28.2mpg) [39.2–23.5US mpg].

1.5 Litre
71/62kW–95/83hp–97/85PS
Fuel Injection/Carb

As 1.3 Litre model, except:

Nissan

Body, Weight: 3-door Saloon/Sedan, from 890kg, 4WD 1060kg. 4-door Saloon/Sedan, from 920kg, 4WD 1080kg. 5-door Saloon/Sedan, from 920kg. 3-door Coupe, from 985kg. 5-door Estate/Station Wagon, from 975kg.

Engine data (JIS net): 4-cylinder in-line (73.6 x 88mm), 1497cm3; compression ratio 9:1; 71kW (95hp) [97PS] at 6000rpm, 47.2kW/L (63.2hp/L) [64.8PS/L]; 129Nm (95.2lbft) at 4400rpm.
With carb: Compression ratio 9.5:1; 62kW (83hp) [85PS] at 6000rpm; 123Nm (90.7lbft) at 3600rpm.
Export version (Carb, DIN): 1392cm3; 55 or 59kW (74 or 79hp) [75 or 80PS] at 6200rpm.
With E 15 (2 valves): (76 x 82mm), 1488cm3; compression ratio 9:1; 51kW (68hp) [70PS] at 5600rpm; 121Nm (89.3lbft) at 2800rpm.

Engine construction: Designated GA 15S/E (Export E 15). 3 valves (in V) per cylinder, 1 overhead camshaft (chain); electronic fuel injection, 83hp and export version compound carb. Cooling system capacity approx 5L (4.7US qt).

Transmission (4WD to all wheels): a) 5-speed manual, final drive ratio 4.353 or 4.167.
b) Automatic, final drive ratio 3.476 or 3.600.
c) Automatic with OD, final drive ratio 3.876.
4WD: engageable or permanent all-wheel drive (with viscous coupling in central differential) 5-speed manual, final drive ratio 4.471. Automatic, final drive ratio 4.059. 'Triple viscous' model with viscous limited slip on both axle differentials.

Gear ratios: a) 5-speed manual: 1st 3.063; 2nd 1.826; 3rd 1.207; 4th 0.902; 5th 0.756; R 3.417.
Or (83hp): 1st 3.333; 2nd 1.955; 3rd 1.286; 4th 0.902; 5th 0.733; R 3.417.
b) Automatic; Max torque multiplication in converter 2 times; Planetary gear set ratios: 1st 2.826; 2nd 1.543; 3rd 1; R 2.364.
With OD: 1st 2.785; 2nd 1.545; 3rd 1; OD 0.694; R 2.272.

Chassis: Some models front ventilated disc brakes; tyres 155 SR 13 or 175/70 SR 13, optional 185/60 HR 14. With 4WD: Rear independent suspension with McPherson struts, control arms, longitudinal arms and antiroll bar, front ventilated disc brakes; fuel tank 47L (10.3Gal) [12.4US Gal]; tyres 175/70 SR 13.

Dimensions: 4WD Saloon/Sedan; track 143/141.5cm. Height 139.5cm. Coupe; length 423.5cm, width 166.5cm, height 132.5cm. Estate/Station Wagon; length 427cm.

Performance: Max speed approx 106mph/170kmh, speed at 1000rpm in 5th gear 20mph/32.2kmh; power to weight ratio from 13.4kg/kW (9.8kg/PS); consumption approx 6-11L/100km (47.1-25.7mpg) [39.2-21.4US mpg].

Nissan Sunny

1.6 Litre
66kW–88hp–90PS
Central/Single Point Injection

As for Export engine

As 1.3 Litre model except:

Body, Weight: 2-door Saloon/Sedan (USA), 1000kg.
3-door Saloon/Sedan, 940-1020kg, USA 1015kg, gross vehicle weight 1415kg.
4-door Saloon/Sedan, 935-1020kg, USA 1010-1200kg, 4WD 1080-1160kg, gross vehicle weight 1415, 4WD 1575kg.
5-door Saloon/Sedan, 945-1020kg, gross vehicle weight 1415kg.
3-door Coupe, 985-1025kg, USA 1025kg.
5-door Estate/Station Wagon, 990-1020kg, USA 1045kg, 4WD 1120-1200kg, USA 1240kg, gross vehicle weight 1515kg, 4WD 1575kg.

Engine data (Catalyst DIN): 4-cylinder in-line (76 x 88mm), 1597cm3; compression ratio 9.4:1; 66kW (88hp) [90PS] at 6000rpm, 41.3kW/L (55.3hp/L) [56.4PS/L]; 130Nm (95.9lbft) at 4000rpm.

USA version (SAE net): 67kW (90hp) [91PS]; 130Nm (95.9lbft) at 3200rpm.
Export Version (2 valves, Carb (DIN): Compression ratio 9.6:1; 62kW (83hp) [84PS] at 5600rpm; 132Nm (97.4lbft) at 3200rpm.

Engine construction: Designated GA 16i, 2 valves CA 16. 3 valves per cylinder, hydraulic valve play compensation, 1 overhead camshaft (toothed belt); electronic fuel injection. 12V 60Ah battery, 65A alternator, cooling system capacity 5.4L (5.1US qt).

Nissan Sunny Wagon

Transmission (to front wheels, 4WD to all wheels):
a) 4-speed manual (USA), final drive ratio 4.167.
b) 5-speed manual, final drive ratio 4.167.
c) Automatic, final drive ratio 3.600 or 3.476.
d) Automatic with OD, final drive ratio 3.600.
4WD: Engageable all wheel drive, 5-speed manual, final drive ratio 4.471.
Or: Permanent all wheel drive (with viscous coupling in central differential), 5-speed manual, final drive ratio 4.471.
Optional rear limited slip differential (viscous).

Gear ratios: a) 4-speed manual (USA): As 1 Litre.
b) 5-speed manual: 1st 3.333; 2nd 1.955; 3rd 1.286; 4th 0.902; 5th 0.756 (or 0.733); R 3.417.
or (4WD): 1st 3.063; 2nd 1.826; 3rd 1.207; 4th 0.902; 5th 0.756; R 3.417.
c) Automatic; max torque multiplication with converter 2 times; Planetary gear set: 1st 2.826; 2nd 1.543; 3rd 1; R 2.364.
d) Automatic with OD: 1st 2.785; 2nd 1.545; 3rd 1; OD 0.694; R 2.272.

Chassis: Ventilated front disc brakes; tyres 155 SR 13 or 175/70 SR 13, optional 185/60 HR 14, wheel rims 5J.
4WD: Rear independent suspension with McPherson struts, A arm, trailing arm and antiroll bar. Fuel tank 47L (10.3Gal) [12.4US Gal].

Dimensions: Length USA: Saloon/Sedan 3-door 412.5cm, Saloon/Sedan 2/4-door 428.5cm.
Coupe: Length 423.5cm, width 166.5cm, height 132.5cm.
Estate/Station Wagon: 10.5-42.4cu ft (load space 297-1202dm3), length 427cm, USA 437.5cm.
4WD: Track 143/141.5cm, load space Sedan 10.5cu ft (297dm3), height 139cm, Wagon 140cm.

Performance: (Catalyst Version) Max speed 109mph/175kmh, automatic 103mph/165kmh, 4WD 99mph/160kmh (manufacturers test specification), speed at 1000rpm in 5th gear (0.756) 20.9mph/33.7kmh, 4WD 19.5mph/31.4kmh; power to weight ratio from 15.2kg/kW (11.1kg/PS); consumption ECE 5.6/7.5/9.3L/100km (50.4/37.7/30.4mpg) [42/31.4/25.3US mpg], automatic 6.6/8.7/9.8L/100km (42.8/32.5/28.8mpg) [35.6/27/24US mpg].

1.8/1.6 DOHC
92/90kW–123/121hp–125/122PS
Fuel Injection

As 1.3 Litre, except:

Body, Weight: 3-door Saloon/Sedan; kerbweight from 1020kg. 1.8 Catalyst from 1100kg, gross vehicle weight 1575kg.
4-door Saloon/Sedan; kerbweight from 1030kg. 3-door Coupe 3-door; kerbweight 1070-1120kg, USA approx 1180kg, gross vehicle weight 1520kg.

Engine data (Catalyst, DIN): 4-cylinder in-line (83 x 83.6mm), 1809cm3; compression ratio 10.5:1; 92kW (123hp) [125PS] at 6400rpm, 50.9kW/L (68.2hp/L) [69.1PS/L]; 150Nm (110.7lbft) at 4800rpm.
USA Version (SAE net): 93kW (125hp) [127PS]; 152Nm (112.2lbft).
Without Catalyst: (78 x 83.6mm) 1598cm3; compression ratio 10:1; 90kW (121hp) [122PS] at 6600rpm; 138Nm (101.8lbft) at 5200rpm.
Japanese version (JIS net): 1598cm3; 88kW (118hp) [120PS] at 6400rpm; 129Nm (95.2lbft) at 5200rpm.

R20

Nissan

Nissan Sunny 1.6 GTI

Engine construction: Designated CA18DE/CA16DE. (USA CA18DE). 4 valves per cylinder, 1800 hydraulic tappets, 2 overhead camshafts (toothed belt), oil capacity 3.8L (3.6US qt), some versions with oil cooler; Bosch L-Jetronic electronic fuel injection. Battery 12V 60Ah, 70A alternator; cooling system capacity 5.2L (4.9US qt).

Transmission: a) 5-speed manual, final drive ratio 4.471; 1800 4.167.
b) Automatic with OD, final drive ratio 4.133.
Optional limited slip differential (Viscous).

Gear ratios: a) 5-speed manual; 1st 3.285; 2nd 1.850; 3rd 1,273; 4th 0.954; 5th 0.796; R 3.429.
1.6 Litre with: 1st 3.063; 2nd 1.826; 3rd 1.286; 4th 0.975; 5th 0.810; R 3.417.
b) Automatic; max torque multiplication in converter 2 times; Planetary gear set ratios: 1st 2.785; 2nd 1.545; 3rd 1; OD 0.694; R 2.272.

Chassis: Four-wheel disc brakes, ventilated at front; tyres 185/60 HR 14, wheel rims 5.5J.

Dimensions: Track 142.5/143cm. Coupe: Track 142.5/142.5cm, load space 9.6-18.1cu ft (273-514dm3). Length 423.5cm, width 166.5cm, height 132.5cm

Performance: (Catalyst version) Max speed 124mph/200kmh (manufacturers test specifications), speed at 1000rpm in 5th gear 19.8mph/31.9kmh; power to weight ratio from 12.0kg/kW (8.8kg/PS); consumption ECE 6.3/8.1/8.9L/100km (44.8/34.9/31.7mpg) [37.3/29/26.4US mpg].

Nissan EXA

```
1.7 L Diesel
40kW-53.5hp-54PS
Injection Pump
```

As 1.3 Litre model except:

Body, Weight: Saloon/Sedan 3-door, kerbweight from 1015kg.
Saloon/Sedan 4-door, kerbweight from 970kg.
Saloon/Sedan 5-door, kerbweight from 990kg.
Estate/Station Wagon: 5-door; kerbweight from 1055kg.

Engine data (DIN): 4-cylinder in-line (80 x 83.6mm), 1681cm3; compression ratio 21.8:1; 40kW (53.5hp) [54PS] at 4800rpm, 23.8kW/L (31.9hp/L) [32.1PS/L]; 104Nm (76.7lbft) at 2800rpm.
Japanese Version (JIS net): Identical data.

Engine construction: Designated CD 17. Swirl chamber diesel engine. Parallel valves; oil capacity 3.8L (3.6US qt); diesel injection pump.

Transmission: a) 5-speed manual, final drive ratio 3.789.
b) Automatic, final drive ratio 3.476.

Gear ratios: a) 5-speed manual; 1st 3.333; 2nd 1.955; 3rd 1.286; 4th 0.902; 5th 0.756; R 3,417.
b) Automatic; max torque multiplication in converter 2 times; Planetary gear set ratios: 1st 2.826; 2nd 1.543; 3rd 1; R 2.364.

Chassis: Tyres 155 SR 13, optional 175/70 SR 13.

Dimensions: Estate/Station Wagon; length 427cm

Performance: Max speed 93mph/150kmh (manufacturers test specification), speed at 1000rpm in 5th gear 23mph/37kmh; acceleration 0 – 62mph/100kmh 18.1secs; power to weight ratio from 24.2kg/kW (18kg/PS); consumption ECE 4.6/6.5/6.5L/100km (61.4/43.5/43.5mpg) [51.1/36.2/36.2US mpg].

Nissan Prairie

New model. Large capacity Estate/Station wagon with transverse engine and front wheel drive, 5-door (2 from sliding doors), 5 as well as 8-seater. Launched August 1982. September 1985 version with engageable all wheel drive and 2 litre engine. August 1988: Model renovated, 4x4 now with integral permanent all wheel drive. 1989 introduced in the USA under the name of Axxess.

Nissan Prairie 4x4

```
2 Litre
67kW-90hp-91PS
Carb/Injection
```

Body, Weight: Estate/Station Wagon 5-door, 5/8-seater; kerbeight (DIN) from 1180kg, 4x4 from 1300kg

Engine data (JIS net): 4-cylinder in-line (84.5x88mm), 1974 cm3; compression ratio 8.5:1; 67kW (90hp) [91PS] at 5200rpm, 33.9kW/L (45.4hp/L) [46.1PS/L]; 145Nm (107lbft) at 2800rpm.
European Version (DIN): 73kW (98hp) [99PS] at 5600rpm; 161Nm (118.8lbft) at 3200rpm.
With Catalyst (DIN): 72kW (97hp) [98PS] at 5200rpm; 150Nm (110.7lbft) at 2400rpm.

Engine construction: Designated CA20S/CA20E. Transverse front engine, valves in V, 1 overhead camshaft (toothed belt); light-alloy cylinder head; 5 bearing crankshaft; oil capacity 3.6-3.9L (3.4-3.7US qt); 1 electronic compound carb, with Catalyst electronic fuel injection. 12V 50-60Ah, alternator 50 or 60A; cooling system capacity approx 9L (8.5US qt).

Transmission (to front wheels, 4x4 to all wheels):
a) 5-speed manual, final drive ratio 4.167, 4x4 4.471.
b) Automatic, hydraulic torque converter with 4-speed Planetary gear set, final drive ratio 3.876, 4x4 4.420.
4x4: Permanent all wheel drive, central differential (power distribution 50/50%) with viscous coupling, optional with rear limited slip differential.

Gear ratios: a) 5-speed manual: 1st 3.400; 2nd 1.955; 3rd 1.272; 4th 0.954; 5th 0.795; R 3.428.
4x4: 1st 3.714; 2nd 2.095; 3rd 1.343. 4th 0.954; 5th 0.740; R 3.428.
b) Automatic: Max torque multiplication in converter 2 times; Planetary gear set ratios: 1st 2.785; 2nd 1.545; 3rd 1; 4th 0.694; R 2.272.

Chassis: Integral body, all round independent suspension; front McPherson struts, lower A arm and antiroll bar (not for 4x4), rear McPherson struts, lower parallel control arm, single trailing arm and antiroll bar, telescopic damper. Servo/power assisted brakes, front discs ventilated, rear drums, mechanical handbrake to rear wheels; power assisted rack and pinion steering; fuel tank 65L (14.3Gal) [17.2US Gal], for 4x4 60L (13.2Gal) [15.9US Gal]; tyres 165 SR 14 or 185/70 SR 14, for Europe 195/70 SR 14 or 195/65 SR 14, wheel rims 5 or 5.5J.

Dimensions: Wheelbase 261cm, 4x4 259.5cm, track 146/143cm, clearance 16.5-17cm, turning circle 10.6-10.8m, length 435-436cm, width 169cm, height 162.5-163.4cm, 4x4 165-166cm.

Performance: Max speed 106mph/170kmh, (4x4 103mph/165kmh), with Automatic 103mph/165kmh (4x4 96mph/155kmh) (manufacturers test specification), speed at 1000rpm in 5th gear (195/70 SR 14) 21.8mph/35.1kmh, 4x4 21.9mph/35.2kmh; power to weight ratio from 16.3kg/kW (12.0kg/PS); consumption ECE 7.3/9.6/11.1L/100km (38.7/29.4/25.4mpg) [32.2/24.5/21.2US mpg], 4x4 Automatic 7.9/10.2/12.6L/100km (35.8/27.7/22.4mpg) [29.8/23.1/18.7US mpg].

Nissan Prairie 4x4

Nissan Silvia/200 SX

New model. Sporty Coupe convertible with rear wheel drive. 1.8 Litre DOHC 4 cylinder engine with and without turbocharger. Convertible only with automatic transmission. Launched May 1988. Autumn 1988: Export version 200 SX with tail gate.

Nissan 200 SX

1.8 Litre
99kW–133hp–135PS
Fuel Injection

Not available for Convertible

Body, Weight: Coupe 2-door, 2+2-seater; kerbweight (DIN) 1090-1130kg.

Engine data (JIS net): 4-cylinder in-line (83 x 83.6mm), 1809cm3; compression ratio 9.5:1; 99kW (133hp) [135PS] at 6400rpm, 54.7kW/L (73.3hp/L) [74.6PS/L] at 5200rpm.

Engine construction: Designated: CA 18DE. Valves in V, 4 valves per cylinder. 2 overhead camshafts (toothed belt); light-alloy cylinder head; 5 bearing crankshaft; oil capacity 3.5L (3.3US qt); electronic fuel injection ECCS. 12 V 40-60Ah battery, 50A alternator; cooling system capacity approx 7L (6.6US qt).

Transmission (to rear wheels): a) 5-speed manual, final drive ratio 4.375 or 4.363. b) Automatic, hydraulic torque converter with 4-speed Planetary gear set, final drive ratio 4.375 or 4.363.

Gear ratios: a) 5-speed manual: 1st 3.592; 2nd 2.057; 3rd 1.361; 4th 1; 5th 0.821; R 3.657.
b) Automatic; max torque multiplication in converter 2 times; Planetary gear set ratios; 1st 3.027; 2nd 1.619; 3rd 1; 4th 0.694; R 2.272.

Chassis: Integral body; front McPherson struts, control arm, torsion struts and antiroll bar, rear multi suspension (lower A arm, axial struts, upper single control arm and diagonal struts), coil springs and coaxial telescopic damper, antiroll bar. Servo/power assisted four wheel disc brakes (front ventilated), optional ABS; handbrake to rear wheels; power assisted rack and pinion steering; optional hydraulic four wheel steering; fuel tank 60L (13.2Gal) [15.9US Gal]; tyres 185/70 SR 14, optional 195/60 HR 15, wheel rims 5J, optional 6J.

Dimensions: Wheelbase 247.5cm, track 146.5/146cm, clearance 13.5cm, turning circle 10.4m, length 447cm, width 169cm, height 129cm.

Performance: Max speed approx 124mph/200kmh, speed at 1000rpm in 5th gear 19.8mph/31.8kmh; power to weight ratio from 11kg/kW (8.1kg/PS); consumption approx 7-11L/100km (40.4-25.7mpg) [33.6-21.4US mpg].

1.8 Litre
129kW–173hp–175PS
Turbo/Fuel Injection

As 133hp, except:

Body, Weight: Coupe 2-door, 2+2-seater; kerbweight (DIN) from 1120-1160kg, USA (240SX) 1205kg.
Coupe 200 SX 3-door, 2+2-seater; kerbweight (DIN) from 1190kg, USA (240SX) 1220kg.
Convertible 2-door, 2+2-seater; kerbweight (DIN) 1250kg.

Nissan Silvia 240 SX

Engine data (JIS net): 4-cylinder in-line (83 x 83.6mm), 1809cm3; compression ratio 8.5:1; 129kW (173hp) [175PS] at 6400rpm, 71.3kW/L (95.5hp/L) [96.7PS/L]; 226Nm (166.8lbft) at 4000rpm.
With Catalyst (DIN): 124kW (166hp) [169PS] at 6400rpm; 224Nm (165.3lbft) at 4000rpm; unleaded regular grade.
Without Catalyst: 126kW (168hp) [169PS] at 6400rpm; 228Nm (168.3lbft) at 4000rpm.
USA Version (Not Turbo, SAE net): 4-cylinder in-line (89 x 96mm), 2388cm3; compression ratio 9.1:1; 104kW (139hp) [142PS] at 5600rpm; 206Nm (152lbft) at 4400rpm.

Engine construction: Designated CA 18 DET. Oil cooler; 1 exhaust turbo-charger; charge-air cooler. 12 V 55Ah, 80A alternator. USA version: 3 valves per cylinder; 1 overhead camshaft (toothed belt).

Transmission: a) 5-speed manual, final drive ratio 4.363 (Japan) or 3917, 4.111 (USA).
b) 4-speed automatic, final drive ratio 4.363 (Japan) or 3.917.
Optional limited slip differential.

Gear ratios: a) 5-speed manual: 1st 3.321; 2nd 1.902; 3rd 1.308; 4th 1; 5th 9.838; R 3.382.
Europe: As 133hp.
b) Automatic: As 133hp.

Chassis: Tyres 195/60 VR/HR 15, wheel rims 6J.

Dimensions: Coupe 200 SX: Track 146.6/146.5cm. Length 453.3cm. 240 SX (USA): Length 452cm.

Performance: Max speed 140mph/225kmh, with Catalyst 137mph/220kmh (manufacturers test specification), speed at 1000rpm in 5th gear (0.821, axle 3.917) 21.8mph/35kmh; acceleration 0 - 62mph/100kmh 7.5secs; power to weight ratio from 8.7kg/kW (6.4kg/PS); consumption ECE 6.2/8.1/10.7L/100km (45.6/34.9/26.4mpg) [37.9/29/22US mpg], with automatic 6.6/8.4/12L/100km (42.8/33.6/23.5mpg) [35.6/28/19.6US mpg].

Nissan Silvia Turbo Convertible

Nissan

Nissan Auster–Stanza–Bluebird (Export)

Middle of the range cars with engines ranging from 1.6 to 2.0 Litre. Debut August 1971. Since 1983 (Tokyo) with front wheel drive. 1985 also with transversely mounted V6 engine, designation 'Maxima'. Autumn 1985 new 16–valve turbo engine. October 1985: Auster revised (sold as Bluebird for export). Also assembled in England since 1987. January 1989: 1.8 Litre 16V (Catalyst) also produced in England.

1.6 Litre
58kW–78hp–79PS
1 Compound Carb

Body, Weight: 4/5-door Saloon/Sedan, 5-seater; kerbweight (DIN) from 1070kg. 5-door Estate/Station Wagon, 5-seater; kerbweight (DIN) from 1040kg.

Engine data (JIS): 4-cylinder in-line (78 x 83.6mm), 1598cm3; Compression ratio 9:1; 58kW (78hp) [79PS] at 5200rpm, 36.3kW/L (48.6hp/L) [49.4PS/L]; 123Nm (90.8lbft) at 3200rpm.
European version (DIN): 62kW (83hp) [84PS] at 5200rpm; 131Nm (96.7lbft) at 3600rpm.

Engine construction: Designated CA 16S. Front transverse engine. Valves in V, 1 overhead camshaft (toothed belt); light-alloy cylinder-heads; 5 bearing crankshaft; oil capacity 4L (3.8US qt); 1 downdraught carb. Battery 12 V 33-60 Ah, Alternator 60 A; cooling system capacity 6.8L (6.4US qt).

Transmission (to front wheels): a) 4-speed manual, final drive ratio 3.895, 4.056. b) 5-speed manual, final drive ratio 3.895 or 4.056. c) Automatic, hydraulic torque converter with 3-speed Planetary gear set, final drive ratio 3.476 or 3.737.

Gear ratios: a) 4-speed manual: 1st 3.333; 2nd 1.955; 3rd 1.286; 4th 0.902; R 3.417. b) 5-speed manual: 1st 3.333; 2nd 1.955; 3rd 1.286; 4th 0.902; 5th 0.733; R 3.417. c) Automatic: Max torque multiplication in converter 2 times; Planetary gear set ratios: 1st 2.826; 2nd 1.543; 3rd 1; R 2.364.

Chassis: Integal body; front and rear independent suspension, front McPherson struts, A-arm, some models with antiroll bar, rear McPherson struts, twin control arms and semi trailing arm, Estate/Station Wagon with rigid axle and leaf spring, telescopic dampers. Servo/power assisted brakes, front discs (ventilated), rear drums, handbrake to rear wheels; rack and pinion steering with optional power assistance; fuel tank capacity 60L (13.2Gal) [15.9US Gal] (Estate/Station Wagon 53L (11.6Gal) [14US Gal]; tyres 165 SR 13 (Estate/Station Wagon 5.50-13).

Dimensions: Wheelbase 255cm, track 145.5/145.5, Wagon 146.5/140cm, clearance 15-17cm, turning circle 10m.
Saloon/Sedan: Load space 14.5cu ft (410dm3). Length 436-453cm, width 169cm, height 139-140cm.
Hatchback: Load space 11.4–40.4cu ft (324-1145dm3). Length 436.5-447.5cm, height 139-139.5cm.
Estate/Station Wagon: Length 440.5-444.5cm, height 142-143.5cm.

Performance: Max speed 102mph/165kmh (manufacturers test specifications), speed at 1000rpm in 4th gear 19.3mph/31.1kmh; power to weight ratio from 18.1kg/kW (13.3kg/PS); consumption ECE 6.6/8.4/10.3L/100km (42.8/33.6/27.4mpg) [35.6/28.0/22.8US mpg].

1.8 Litre
65kW–87hp–88PS
Central/Single Point Injection

As 1.6 Litre, except:

Body, Weight: 4/5-door Saloon/Sedan, kerbweight 1040–1220kg; gross vehicle weight 1720kg. 4-door Hardtop, kerbweight 1100–1250kg. Estate/Station Wagon, kerbweight 1080–1170kg, gross vehicle weight 1750kg.

Engine data (JIS net): 4-cylinder in-line (83 x 83.6mm), 1809cm3; compression ratio 8.8:1; 65kW (87hp) [88PS] at 5200rpm, 35.9kW/L (48.1hp/L) [48.6PS/L]; 142Nm (104.7lbft) at 3200rpm.
Export version (Carb, DIN): 66kW (89hp) [90PS] at 5200rpm; 150Nm (106.2lbft) at 3200rpm.
With turbocharger (JIS): Compression ratio 8:1; 88kW (118hp) [120PS] at 5600rpm; 181Nm (133.6lbft) at 3600rpm.
European version (DIN): 99kW (133hp) [135PS]; 191Nm (141lbft).

Engine construction: Designated CA 18i/CA 18S/CA 18 E-Turbo. Electronic central/single point fuel injection. Export 1 compound carb; Turbo with electronic fuel injection.

Transmission: a) 4-speed manual (export), final drive ratio 3.895, 4.056. b) 5-speed manual, final drive ratio 4.167, turbo 3.895; export 3.895, 4.056. c) Automatic (export and Estate/Station Wagon), final drive ratio 3.476; 3.737. d) 4-speed automatic, final drive ratio 3.876, turbo 3.642.

Gear ratios: a) 4-speed manual: 1st 3.063; 2nd 1.826; 3rd 1.207; 4th 0.902; R 3.417. b) 5-speed manual: 1st 3.063; 2nd 1.826 or 1.955; 3rd 1.207 or 1.286; 4th 0.902; 5th 0.733; R 3.417. Turbo: 1st 3.400; 2nd 1.955; 3rd 1.272; 4th 0.911; 5th 0.740; R 3.428. c) 3-speed automatic: As 1.6 Litre model. d) 4-speed automatic: Planetary gear set ratios: 1st 2.785; 2nd 1.545; 3rd 1; OD 0.694; R 2.364.

Chassis: Front antiroll bar, optional rear; Estate/Station Wagon with rear independent suspension; tyres also 165 SR 14 or 185/70 SR 14.
Turbo: Four wheel disc brakes (front ventilated); power assisted steering; tyres (Export) 195/60 HR 15.

Dimensions: Track 146/146cm.

Performance: Max speed 106–112mph/170–180kmh, turbo 121mph/195kmh (manufacturers test specifications), speed at 1000rpm in 5th gear (165 SR 13, 4.056:1) 22.8mph/36.7kmh, turbo 24.7/39.7kmh; power to weight ratio from 12.1kg/kW (8.9kg/L); consumption ECE 6.5/8.7/10.6L/100km (43.5/32.5/26.6mpg) [36.2/27/22.2US mpg], turbo 6.7/9.0/10.3L/100km (42.2/31.4/27.4mpg) [35.1/26.1/22.8US mpg].

Nissan Bluebird 16V

1.8 DOHC
95kW–127hp–129PS
Fuel Injection

Engine for Export

As 1.6 Litre, except:

Body, Weight: 4/5-door Saloon/Sedan, kerbweight (DIN) from 1270kg, gross vehicle weight 1760kg.

Engine data (Catalyst DIN): (83 x 83.6mm), 1809cm3; compresssion ratio 10.5:1; 95kW (127hp) [129PS] at 6400rpm, 52.5kW/L (70.3hp/L) [71.3PS/L]; 153Nm (112.9lbft) at 5200rpm.

Engine construction: Designated CA 18DE. 4 valves (in V) per cylinder, hydraulic tappets, 2 overhead camshafts (toothed belt); electronic fuel injection, Bosch LH-Jetronic licence. Cooling system capacity approx 8L (7.6US qt).

Transmission: 5-speed manual, final drive ratio 4.471.

Gear ratios: 5-speed manual: 1st 3.400; 2nd 1.955; 3rd 1.273; 4th 0.954; 5th 0.796; R 3.429.

Chassis: Antiroll bar front and rear; four wheel disc brakes (front ventilated); power assisted steering; tyres 195/60 HR 15, wheel rims 6 J.

Dimensions: 4-door Saloon/Sedan; track 146/146cm, turning circle 10.3m, length 446cm, width 169cm, height 139.5cm. 5-door Saloon/Sedan; length 441cm.

Performance: Max speed 121mph/195kmh (manufacturers test specifications), speed at 1000rpm in 5th gear 19.6mph/31.6kmh; power to weight ratio from 13.4kg/kW (9.8kg/PS); consumption (town/country/mixed) 9.9/7.0/8.6L/100km (28.5/40.4/32.8mpg) [23.8/33.6/27.4US mpg].

1.8 DOHC
107kW–143hp–145PS
Turbo/Fuel Injection

As 1.6 Litre model, except:

Body, Weight: 4-door Saloon/Sedan, kerbweight from 1210kg. 4-door Hardtop, kerbweight from 1230kg.

Engine data (JIS net): (83 x 83.6mm), 1809cm3; compression ratio 8.5:1; 107kW (143hp) [145PS] at 6400rpm, 59.1kW/L (79.2hp/L) [80.2PS/L]; 201Nm (148.3lbft) at 4000rpm.

Engine construction: Designated CA 18DET. 4 valves (in V) per cylinder, hydraulic tappets, 2 overhead camshafts (toothed belt), oil-cooler; electronic fuel injection; Garrett T25 exhaust turbocharger. Cooling system capacity approx 8L (7.6US qt).

Transmission: a) 5-speed manual, final drive ratio 4.167.
b) 4-speed automatic, final drive ratio 4.133.

Gear ratios: a) 5-speed manual: 1st 3.285; 2nd 1.850; 3rd 1.272; 4th 0.954; 5th 0.795; R 3.428.
b) Automatic: Max torque multiplication in converter 2.1 times, Planetary gear set ratios: 1st 2.785; 2nd 1.545; 3rd 1; 4th 0.694; R 2.272.

Chassis: Front and rear antiroll bars, optional level control system. All round disc brakes (ventilated at front); power assisted steering; tyres 195/60 HR 15, wheels 6J.

Dimensions: Track 146/146cm.

Performance: Max speed approx 124mph/200kmh. Speed at 1000rpm in 5th gear 21.1mph/34.0kmh; power to weight ratio from 11.3kg/kW (8.3kg/L); consumption approx 8–15L/100km (35.3–18.8mpg) [29.4–15.7US mpg].

Nissan Bluebird Wagon

```
2 Litre
85/75kW-114/101hp-115/102PS
Injection/Carb
```

Engine for export

As 1.6 Litre, except:

Body, Weight: 4/5-door Saloon/Sedan, kerbweight 1160-1240kg; gross vehicle weight 1720kg; Estate/Station Wagon, kerbweight 1190-1250kg, gross vehicle weight 1750kg.

Engine data (DIN): 4-cylinder in-line (84.5 x 88mm), 1974cm3; Compression ratio 9:1; 85kW (114hp) [115PS] at 5600rpm, 43kW/L (57.6hp/L) [58.3PS/L]; 172Nm (130lbft) at 2800rpm; regular unleaded grade.
With catalyst (DIN): Compression ratio 8.5:1; 76kW (102hp) [104PS] at 5200rpm; 156Nm (209lbft) at 4000rpm.
Export version (carb): 75kW (101hp) [102PS] at 5200rpm, 162Nm (119.6lbft) at 3600rpm.
Or: 71kW (95hp) [96PS]; 155Nm (114.4lbft)

Engine construction: Designated CA 20E/CA 20S. Electronic fuel injection, some versions with 1 carb.

Nissan Bluebird Hatchback

Transmission: a) 5-speed manual, final drive ratio 4.167
b) Automatic, final drive ratio 4.134

Gear ratios: a) 5-speed manual: 1st 3.285; 2nd 1.850; 3rd 1.206; 4th 0.911; 5th 0.795; R 3.428.

b) 4-speed Automatic, Planetary gear set ratios: 1st 2.785; 2nd 1.545; 3rd 1; OD 0.694; R 2.272.

Chassis: Antiroll bars front and rear; Estate/Station Wagon with rear independent suspension; tyres 185/70 SR 14, wheel rims 5.5 J.

Dimensions: a) 4-door Saloon/Sedan: Track 146/146cm, turning circle 10.3m. Length 440cm, width 169cm, height 139.5cm.
b) 5-door Saloon/Sedan: Turning circle 10.8m, length 436cm.
c) Estate/Station Wagon: Track 145.5/145.5cm. Length 444.5cm, height 143.5cm.

Performance: Max speed approx 115mph/185kmh, speed at 1000rpm in 5th gear 21.4mph/34.5kmh; power to weight ratio from 14.1kg/kW (10.4kg/PS); consumption ECE (114hp) 6.4/8.5/10.7L/100km (44.1/33.2/26.4mpg) [36.8/27.7/22US mpg], Automatic 6.9/8.6/11.4L/100km (40.9/32.8/24.8mpg) [34.1/27.4/20.6US mpg].

```
2 Litre Diesel
49kW-66hp-67PS
Injection Pump
```

Only for Estate/Station Wagon and Bluebird export

As 1.6 Litre model except:

Weight: Saloon/Sedan from 1240kg, Estate/Station Wagon from 1265kg.

Engine data (JIS net): 4-cylinder in-line (85 x 86mm), 1952cm3, compression ratio 21.3:1; 49kW (66hp) [67PS] at 4600rpm, 25.1 kW/L (33.6hp/L) [34.3PS/L]; 128Nm (94.4lbft) at 2400rpm.
Export version (DIN): Identical data.

Engine construction: Designated LD 20-11. Parallel valves; grey cast iron cylinder head; oil capacity 4L (3.8US qt), oil-cooler; diesel injection pump. Battery 12V 70Ah, alternator 60/80A; cooling system capacity 10L (9.5US qt).

Transmission: a) 5-speed manual, final drive ratio 4.071, or 4.167.
b) 4-speed automatic, final drive ratio 3.876; 3.900.

Gear ratios: a) 5-speed manual: 1st 3.4; 2nd 1.955; 3rd 1.272; 4th 0.911; 5th 0.74; R 3.428.
b) Automatic: Max torque multiplication in converter 2.1 times, Planetary gear set ratios: 1st 2.785; 2nd 1.545; 3rd 1; OD 0.694; R 2.272.

Chassis: Estate/Station Wagon export with rear independent suspension, tyres 165 SR 14 or 185/70 SR 14.

Dimensions: Estate/Station Wagon 145.5/144.5cm track.

Performance: Max speed 98mph/150kmh (manufacturers test specifications), speed at 1000rpm in 5th gear (165 SR 14, 4.167) 22.9mph/36.9kmh; power to weight ratio from 25.3kg/kW (18.5kg/PS); consumption ECE 5.6/7.8/8.2L/100km (50.4/36.2/34.4mpg) [42/30.2/28.7US mpg].

Nissan New Bluebird

Middle of the range with 1.6 to 2 Litre capacity four-cylinder engines. Debut August 1971, with front wheel drive since 1983. September 1987: model series revised and expanded with a four-valve turbo-engined flagship. Currently available only on domestic market. Previous model for export (see Nissan Auster – Stanza).

```
1.6 Litre
58kW-78hp-79PS
1 Carb
```

Body, Weight: 4-door Saloon/Sedan, 5-seater; kerbweight (DIN) 990–1050kg.

Engine data (JIS net): 4-cylinder in-line (78 x 83.6mm), 1598cm3; compression ratio 9:1; 58kW (78hp) [79PS] at 5200rpm, 36.3kW/L (48.6hp/L) [49.4PS/L]; 123Nm (90.7lbft) at 3200rpm.

Engine construction: Designated CA 16S. Transverse mounted front engine. Valves in V. 1 overhead camshaft (toothed belt); light-alloy cylinder head; crankshaft with 5 bearings; oil capacity 4L (3.8US qt); 1 downdraught compound carb. Battery 12V 45/60Ah, alternator 50/60A; cooling system capacity approx 6.5L (6.1US qt).

Transmission (to front wheels): a) 5-speed manual, final drive ratio 3.895.
b) Automatic, hydraulic torque converter and 3-speed Planetary gear set, final drive ratio 3.476.

Gear ratios: a) 5-speed manual: 1st 3.333; 2nd 1.955; 3rd 1.286; 4th 0.902; 5th 0.733; R 3.417.
b) Automatic: Max torque multiplication in converter 2 times; Planetary gear set ratios: 1st 2.826; 2nd 1.543; 3rd 1; R 2.364.

Nissan

Chassis: Integral body; front and rear independent suspension, front McPherson struts, control arms and antiroll bar, rear McPherson struts, double control arm and longitudinal arms, telescopic dampers. Servo/power assisted brakes, front discs (ventilated), rear drums, handbrake to rear wheels; rack and pinion steering, optional power assisted steering; fuel tank 60L (13.2Gal) [15.9US Gal], tyres 165 SR 13, wheels 5J.

Dimensions: Wheelbase 255cm, track 146/144cm, clearance 14.5–16cm, turning circle 10.8m. Length 452cm, width 169cm, height 137.5–139.5cm.

Performance: Max speed approx 102.5mph/165kmh, speed at 1000rpm in 5th gear 23.7mph/38.2kmh; power to weight ratio from 17.1kg/kW (12.5kg/PS); consumption approx 7–10L/100km (40.4–28.2mpg) [33.6–23.5US mpg].

Nissan Bluebird

```
1.8 Litre
65kW–87hp–88PS
Central/Single Point Injection
```

As 1.6 Litre model, except:

Body, Weight: 4–door Saloon/Sedan, kerbweight 1000–1090kg, 4WD 1160–1220kg. 4–door Hardtop, 5–seater, kerbweight 1040–1120kg, 4WD 1200–1240kg.

Engine data (JIS net): 4–cylinder in–line (83 x 83.6mm), 1809cm3; compression ratio 8.8:1; 65kW (87hp) [88PS] at 5200rpm, 35.9kW/L (48.1hp/L) [48.6PS/L]; 142Nm (104.7lbft) at 3200rpm.

Engine construction: Designated CA 18i. Electronic central/single point fuel injection.

Transmission (to front or all wheels): a) 5–speed manual, final drive ratio 3.895; 4WD 4.471.
b) 4–speed automatic, hydraulic torque converter and 4–speed Planetary gear set: final drive ratio 3.642 or 4.133; 4WD 4.420.
4WD: Permanent all–wheel–drive, central differential (50/50% power distribution) with viscous coupling.
Optional rear limited slip differential.

Gear ratios: a) 5–speed manual: 1st 3.063; 2nd 1.1826; 3rd 1.207; 4th 0.902; 5th 0.733; R 3.417.
For 4WD: 1st 3.400; 2nd 1.955; 3rd 1.272; 4th 0.954; 5th 0.740; R 3.428.
b) 4–speed automatic, Planetary gear set ratios: 1st 2.785; 2nd 1.545; 3rd 1; OD 0.694; R 2.272.

Chassis: Some models with rear antiroll bar; tyres 165 SR 13 or 185/70 SR 13, SSS version 185/65 HR 14, wheels 5 or 5.5J. 4WD: rear anti roll bar, four–wheel disc brakes (ventilated at front); tyres 185/70 SR 14, wheels 5.5J.

Dimensions: Hardtop height 134.5–136.5cm.

Performance: Max speed approx 109mph/175kmh, speed at 1000rpm in 5th gear 23.7mph/38.2kmh. 4WD 21.5mph/34.6kmh; power to weight ratio from 15.4kg/kW (11.4kg/PS); consumption approx 6–11L/100kmh (47.1–25.7mpg) [39.2–21.4US mpg].

```
1.8 DOHC
99kW–133hp–135PS
Fuel Injection
```

As 1.6 Litre model, except:

Body, Weight: 4–door Saloon/Sedan, kerbweight 1110–1170kg, 4WD 1250–1280kg. 4–door Hardtop, 5–seater, kerbweight 1140–1200kg, 4WD 1280–1310kg.

Engine data (JIS net): (83 x 83.6mm), 1809cm3, compression ratio 9.5:1; 99kW (133hp) [135PS] at 6400rpm, 54.7kW/L (73.3hp/L) [74.6PS/L]; 159Nm (117.3lbft) at 5200rpm.

Engine construction: Designated CA 18DE. 4 valves (in V) per cylinder, hydraulic tappets, 2 overhead camshafts (toothed belt); electronic fuel injection. Cooling system capacity approx 8L (7.7US qt).

Transmission (to front or all wheels): a) 5–speed manual, final drive ratio 4.471.
b) 4–speed automatic, hydraulic torque converter and 4–speed Planetary gear set; final drive ratio 4.420.
4WD: Permanent all wheel drive, central differential (50/50% power distribution) with viscous coupling.
Optional rear limited slip differential, front 2WD.

Gear ratios: a) 5–speed manual: 1st 3.400; 2nd 1.955; 3rd 1.272; 4th 0.954; 5th 0.795; R 3.428.
b) 4–speed automatic, Planetary gear set ratios: 1st 2.785; 2nd 1.545; 3rd 1; OD 0.694; R 2.272.

Chassis: Rear antiroll bar; all round disc brakes (ventilated at front), optional ABS; power assisted steering; tyres 195/65 HR 14, wheels 5.5 or 6J.

Dimensions: Hardtop height 134.5/136.5cm.

Performance: Max speed approx 121mph/195kmh, speed at 1000rpm in 5th gear 19.5mph/31.4kmh; power to weight ratio from 11.1kg/kW (8.1kg/PS); consumption approx 8–13L/100km (35.3–21.7mpg) [29.4–18.1US mpg].

Nissan Bluebird SSS Attesa

```
1.8 DOHC
129kW–173hp–175PS
Turbo/Fuel Injection
```

As 1.6 Litre model, except:

Body, Weight: 4–door 4WD Saloon/Sedan, kerbweight 1280–1310, competition version SSS–R 1190kg. 4–door 4WD Hardtop, 5–seater, kerbweight 1310–1340kg.

Engine data (JIS net): (83 x 83.6mm), 1809cm3; compression ratio 8.5:1; 129kW (173hp) [175PS] at 6400rpm, 71.3kW/L (95.5hp/L) [96.7PS/L]; 226Nm (166.7lbft) at 4000rpm.
DET–R version: Compression ratio 8:1; 136kW (182hp) [185PS] at 6400rpm; 240Nm (177lbft) at 4400rpm.

Engine construction: Designated CA 18DET/DET–RR, 4 valves (in V) per cylinder, hydraulic tappets, 2 overhead camshafts (toothed belt); oil–cooler; electronic fuel injection, 1 exhaust turbocharger, charge–air cooler. Cooling system capacity approx 8L (7.6US qt).

Transmission (to all wheels): a) 5–speed manual, final drive ratio 4.471, SSS–R 4.167.
b) 4–speed automatic, hydraulic torque converter and 4–speed Planetary gear set; final drive ratio 4.420.
4WD: Permanent all–wheel drive, central differential (50/50% power distribution) with viscous coupling and rear limited slip differential.

Gear ratios: a) 5–speed manual: 1st 3.400; 2nd 1.955; 3rd 1.272; 4th 0.954; 5th 0.740; R 3.428. SSS–R: 1st 3.281; 2nd 2.095; 3rd 1.653; 4th 1.272; 5th 0.795; R 3.428.
b) 4–speed automatic, Planetary gear set ratios: 1st 2.785; 2nd 1.545; 3rd 1; OD 0.694; R 2.272.

Chassis: Rear antiroll bar; all round disc brakes (ventilated at front), optional ABS; power assisted steering,; tyres 195/65 HR 14; wheels 5.5 or 6J.

Dimensions: Hardtop height 134.5/136.5cm.

Performance: Max speed over 130mph/210kmh, speed at 1000rpm in 5th gear 20.9mph/33.7kmh; power to weight ratio (without SSS–R) from 9.9kg/kW (7.3kg/PS); consumption approx 9–18L/100km (31.4–15.7mpg) [26.1–13.1US mpg].

```
2.0 Diesel
49kW–66hp–67PS
Injection Pump
```

As 1.6 Litre model, except:

Weight: Kerbweight 1100–1150kg.

Engine data (JIS net): 4–cylinder in–line (85 x 86mm), 1952cm3; compression ratio 21.3:1; 49kW (66hp) [67PS] at 4600rpm, 25.1kW/L (33.6hp/L) [34.3PS/L]; 128Nm (94.4lbft) at 2400rpm.

Engine construction: Designated LD 20–11. Grey cast–iron cylinder head; oil capacity 4.5L (4.3US qt), oil–cooler; diesel–injection pump. Battery 12V 70Ah, alternator 60/80A; cooling system capacity 10L (9.5US qt).

Transmission: a) 5–speed manual, final drive ratio 4.167.
b) 4–speed automatic, final drive ratio 3.876.

Gear ratios: a) 5–speed manual: 1st 3.400; 2nd 1.955; 3rd 1.272; 4th 0.911; 5th 0.740; R 3.428.
b) 4–speed automatic: Planetary gear set ratios: 1st 2.785; 2nd 1.545; 3rd 1; OD 0.694; R 2.272.

Performance: Max speed approx 90mph/145kmh, speed at 1000rpm in 5th gear 22.9mph/36.9kmh; power to weight ratio from 22.4kg/kW (16.4kg/PS); consumption approx 6–9L/100km (47.1–31.4mpg) [39.2– 26.1US mpg).

Nissan Maxima

New model. Four door, middle class Saloon/Sedan with transverse 3 Litre V6 engine, four speed automatic transmission and front wheel drive. Launched in October 1988. Exported to Europe and the USA.

Nissan Maxima

3000 V6
125kW–158hp–170PS
Fuel Injection

Body, Weight: 4-door Saloon/Sedan, 5-seater; kerbweight (DIN) from 1360, USA from 1400kg.

Engine data (Catalyst DIN): 6-cylinder in V 60deg (87 x 83mm), 2960cm3; Compression ratio 10:1; 125kW (168hp) [170PS] at 5600rpm, 42.2kW/L (56.5hp/L) [57.4PS/L]; 248Nm (183lbft) at 2800rpm.
Japanese version (JIS): Compression ratio 9:1; 118kW (158hp) [160PS] at 5200rpm; 248Nm (183lbft) at 3200rpm.
USA Version (SAE): 119kW (160hp) [162PS] at 5200rpm; 245Nm (180.8lbft) at 3200rpm.

Engine construction: Designated VG 30E. Transverse front engine. Valves in V, hydraulic tappets, 1 overhead camshaft (toothed belt); light-alloy cylinder heads; 4 main bearing crankshaft; oil capacity 3.9L (3.7US qt); electronic fuel injection. 12V 60Ah Battery, Alternator 70A; cooling system capacity 9L (8.5US qt).

Transmission (to front wheels): a) 5-speed manual, final drive ratio 3.650.
b) Automatic with P/H Programme, hydraulic torque converter with 4-speed Planetary gear set, final drive ratio 3.642

Gear ratios: a) 5-speed manual: 1st 3.285; 2nd 1.850; 3rd 1.272; 4th 0.954; 5th 0.795; R 3.428.
Automatic: Max torque multiplication in converter 2 times; Planetary gear set ratios: 1st 2.785; 2nd 1.545; 3rd 1; OD 0.694; R 2.272.

Chassis: Integral body; front and rear indepedent suspension, front McPherson struts, A-arm and antiroll bar, rear McPherson struts, twin control arms, semi-trailing arm and anti roll bar, electronically regulated telescopic damper. Servo/power assisted four wheel disc brakes (front ventilated) with ABS, handbrake to rear wheels; power assisted rack and pinion steering; fuel tank capacity 70L (15.4Gal) [18.5US Gal]; tyres 205/65 VR 15 or 205/60 HR 15, wheel rims 6.5 or 6 J.

Dimensions: Wheelbase 265cm, track 151/149cm, clearance 14.5-16cm, turning circle 11m, length 476.5-478cm, width 176cm, height 139.5-140.5cm.

Performance: Max speed 140mph/225kmh, Automatic 130mph/210kmh (manufacturers test specifications), speed at 1000rpm in 5th gear 25.3mph/40.8kmh; power to weight ratio from 11.5kg/kW (8.5kg/PS); consumption (town/country/mixed) 11.4/7.4/9.6L/100km (24.8/38.2/29.4mpg) [20.6/31.8/24.5US mpg].

Nissan Skyline

Middle of the range car with 4 or 6–cylinder engine. August 1981: new body and new engine range. 1982: new 2 Litre DOHC engine. August 1985: new body, modified rear suspension and new six–cylinder engine. Autumn 1987: evolutionary version of the GTS for motor racing (group A).

1.8 Litre
62kW–83hp–85PS
1 Carb

Body, Weight: 4–door Saloon/Sedan, 5–seater; kerbweight (DIN) from 1170kg. 4-door Hardtop, 5–seater; kerbweight (DIN) from 1200kg. 5–door Estate/Station Wagon, 5–seater; kerbweight (DIN) from 1180kg.

Engine data (JIS net): 4–cylinder in–line (83 x 83.6mm), 1809cm3; compression ratio 8.8:1; 62kW (83hp) [85PS] at 5200rpm, 34.3kW/L (46hp/L) [47PS/L]; 132Nm (97.4lbft) at 3200rpm.
Export version (DIN): (84.5 x 88mm), 1974cm3; compression ratio 8.5:1; 66kW (88.5hp) [90PS] at 5200rpm; 148Nm (109.2lbft) at 3200rpm.

Engine construction: Designated CA 18S. Valves in V; 1 overhead camshaft (toothed belt); light–alloy cylinder head; crankshaft with 5 bearings; oil capacity 4.3L (4.1US qt); 1 downdraught compound carb. Battery 12V 45/60Ah, alternator 50/60A; cooling system capacity 7L (6.6US qt).

Transmission (to rear wheels): a) 5-speed manual, final drive ratio 3.889.
b) Automatic, hydraulic torque converter and 3-speed Planetary gear set and OD, final drive ratio 3.899.

Gear ratios: a) 5-speed manual: 1st 3.321; 2nd 1.902; 3rd 1,308; 4th 1; 5th 0.838; R 3.382.
b) Automatic: Max torque multiplication in converter 2 times; Planetary gear set ratios: 1st 2.842; 2nd 1.542; 3rd 1; OD 0.686; R 2.40.

Chassis: Integral body; front McPherson struts with control arms; tension struts and antiroll bar, rear rigid axle with double longitudinal arms, Panhard rod and coil springs, telescopic damper. Servo/power assisted brakes, front discs (ventilated), rear drums, mechanical handbrake to rear wheels; rack and pinion steering, optional power assisted steering; fuel tank 65L (14.3Gal) [17.2US Gal] Estate/Station Wagon 62L (13.6Gal) [16.4US Gal]; tyres 165 SR 14 or 185/70 SR 14, wheels 5 or 5.5J.

Dimensions: Wheelbase 261.5cm, track 142.5/140cm, clearance 14cm, turning circle 9.8m. Length 459–466cm, width 169cm, height 139.5– 142.5cm.

Performance: Max speed 106mph/170kmh (manufacturers test specifications), speed at 1000rpm in 5th gear (3.899) 21.7mph/34.9kmh; power to weight ratio from 17.7kg/kW (13kg/PS); consumption approx 8–13L/100km (35.3–21.7mpg) [29.4–18.1US mpg].

Nissan Skyline

2.0 6-cylinder
85kW–114hp–115PS
Fuel Injection

As 1.8 Litre model, except:

Body, Weight: 4–door Saloon/Sedan, weight from 1250kg. 4–door Hardtop, weight from 1290kg. 5–door Estate/Station Wagon, weight from 1350kg. 2–door Coupe, 5–seater, weight from 1270kg.

Engine data (JIS net): 6–cylinder in–line (78 x 69.7mm), 1998cm3; compression ratio 9.5:1; 85kW (114hp) [115PS] at 5600rpm, 42.5kW/L (57hp/L) [57.6PS/L]; 167Nm (123.2lbft) at 4000rpm.
Export Version (DIN): (86 x 85mm), 2962cm3; 105kW (141hp) [143PS] at 4800rpm; 233Nm (172lbft) at 3200rpm.

Engine construction: Designated RB 20 E (Export RB 30S). Hydraulic tappets; crankshaft with 7 bearings; oil capacity 4.3 (4.1US qt); electronic fuel injection (3 Litre with carb). Battery 45/70Ah, alternator 50/60A; cooling system capacity 9L (8.5US qt).

Nissan

Transmission: a) 5-speed manual, final drive ratio 4.111, export 3.900.
b) Automatic, final drive ratio 4.111.

Gear ratios: a) 5-speed manual: 1st 3.592; 2nd 2.057; 3rd 1.361; 4th 1; 5th 0.821; R 3.657.
Export: 1st 3.321; 2nd 1.902; 3rd 1.308; 4th 1; 5th 0.759; R 3.382.
b) Automatic; Planetary gear set ratios: 1st 3.027; 2nd 1.619; 3rd 1; OD 0.694; R 2.272.

Chassis: Rear independent suspension (except Estate/Station Wagon) with diagonal arms, coil springs and antiroll bar. All round disc brakes (front ventilated); power assisted steering; tyres 185/70 SR 14, turbo 195/60 HR 15, wheels 5.5J.

Dimensions: Track 142.5/141.5cm. Estate/Station Wagon 142.5/140cm. Coupe height 136.5cm.

Performance: Max speed approx 112mph/180kmh, speed at 1000rpm in 5th gear (4.111) 21.1mph/33.9kmh; power to weight ratio from 12.4kg/kW (9.1kg/PS); consumption approx 8–13L/100km (35.3–21.7mpg) [29.4–18.1US mpg].

```
2.0 24V
110/140kW–147/188hp–150/190PS
Fuel Injection/Turbo
```

As 1.8 Litre model, except:

Body, Weight: 4-door Hardtop, weight from 1390kg, turbo from 1440kg. 2-door Coupe, 5-seater, weight from 1280kg, turbo from 1320kg.

Engine data (JIS net): 6-cylinder in-line (78 x 69.7mm), 1998cm3; compression ratio 10.2:1 110kW (147hp) [150PS] at 6400rpm, 55.1kW/L (73.7hp/L) [75.1PS/L]; 181Nm (133.5lbft) at 5200rpm.
With exhaust turbocharger: Compression ratio 8.5:1; 140kW (188hp) [190PS] at 6400rpm, 70.1kW/L (93.9hp/L) [95.1PS/L]; 240Nm (177lbft) at 4800rpm.
Evolution version DET-R: 154kW (206hp) [210PS]; 245Nm (180.7lbft).

Engine construction: Designated RB 20DE/RB 20DET. 4 valves (in V 46deg) per cylinder, hydraulic tappets, 2 overhead camshafts (toothed belt); crankshaft with 7 bearings; oil capacity 4.4L (4.2US qt) oil-cooler (turbo); electronic fuel injection, 188hp version with 1 Garrett T3 (DET-R Garrett T04E) turbocharger and charge-air cooler. Battery 45/70Ah, alternator 60/90A; cooling system capacity 11L (10.4US qt).

Transmission: a) 5-speed manual, final drive ratio 4.375.
b) Automatic, final drive ratio 4.625, turbo 4.375.
Turbo: Limited slip differential.

Gear ratios: a) 5-speed manual: 1st 3.592; 2nd 2.057; 3rd 1.361; 4th 1; 5th 0.821; R 3.657.
Turbo: 1st 3.321; 2nd 1.902; 3rd 1.308; 4th 1; 5th 0.838; R 3.382.
b) Automatic, Planetary gear set ratios: 1st 3.027; 2nd 1.619; 3rd 1; OD 0.694; R 2.272.

Chassis: Rear independent suspension with diagonal arms, coil springs and antiroll bar. All round disc brakes (turbo – front/rear ventilated), optional ABS; power assisted steering; tyres 205/60 HR 15, wheels 6, optional 6.5J.

Dimensions: Track 142.5/142cm, length 466cm, height 138.5cm. Coupe 136.5cm.

Performance: Max speed approx 124–137mph/200–220kmh, speed at 1000rpm in 5th gear (0.838) 19.5mph/31.3kmh; power to weight ratio from 9.4kg/kW (6.5kg/PS); consumption approx 10–18L/100km (28.2–15.7mpg) [23.5–13.1US mpg].

Nissan Skyline Twincam 24 V Coupe GTS

```
2.8 Diesel
69kW–92hp–94PS
Injection Pump
```

As 1.8 Litre model, except:

Body, Weight: 4-door Saloon/Sedan, weight from 1330kg.

Engine data (JIS net): 6-cylinder in-line (85 x 83mm), 2825cm3, compression ratio 21.1:1; 69kW (92hp) [94PS] at 4800rpm, 24.4kW/L (32.7hp/L) [33.3PS/L]; 177Nm (130.6lbft) at 2400rpm.

Engine construction: Designated RD 28. Pre-combustion chamber diesel engine. Parallel valves, hydraulic tappets; grey cast-iron cylinder head; crankshaft with 7 bearings; oil capacity approx 5L (4.7US qt); diesel injection pump. Battery 70Ah, alternator 60A, cooling system capacity 9L (8.5US qt).

Transmission: a) 5-speed manual, final drive ratio 3.900.
b) Automatic with OD, final drive ratio 3.700.

Gear ratios: a) 5-speed manual: 1st 3.321; 2nd 1.902; 3rd 1.308; 4th 1; 5th 0.759; R 3.382.
b) Automatic: As 1800 model.

Chassis: Rear independent suspension with diagonal arms, coil springs and antiroll bar. All round disc brakes (ventilated at front); power assisted steering; tyres 185/70 SR 14, wheels 5.5J.

Dimensions: Track 142.5/141.5cm.

Performance: Max speed approx 99.5mph/160kmh, speed at 1000rpm in 5th gear 24mph/38.6kmh; power to weight ratio from 19.3kg/kW (14.1kg/PS); consumption approx 6–10L/100km (47.1–28.2mpg) [39.2–23.5US mpg].

Nissan Leopard

Luxury Coupe with rear wheel drive. 2 and 3 Litre V6 engine capacity. Not available for export. Launched in April 1986. Spring 1988: modified body and enlarged engine.

```
2.0 V6
85kW–114hp–115PS
Fuel Injection
```

Body, Weight: 2-door Coupe, 5-seater; kerbweight from 1310kg.

Engine data (JIS net): 6-cylinder V 60deg (78 x 69.7mm), 1998cm3; compression ratio 9.5:1; 85kW (114hp) [115PS] at 6000rpm, 42.5kW/L (57hp/L) [57.5PS/L]; 163Nm (120.2lbft) at 3200rpm.

Engine construction: Designated VG 20E. Valves in V, hydraulic tappets; 1 overhead camshaft (toothed belt); light-alloy cylinder head; crankshaft with 4 bearings; oil capacity 4.7L (4.4US qt); electronic fuel injection. Battery 12V 45/60Ah, alternator 50/60A; cooling system capacity 6.2L (5.9US qt).

Transmission (to rear wheels): Automatic, hydraulic torque converter and 4-speed Planetary gear set, final drive ratio 4.111.

Gear ratios: Automatic, max torque multiplication in converter 2 times; Planetary gear set ratios: 1st 2.842; 2nd 1.542; 3rd 1; 4th 0.686; R 2.4.

Chassis: Integral body; front McPherson struts, control arms, tension struts and antiroll bar, rear independent suspension with diagonal arms, coil springs and antiroll bar, telescopic dampers. Servo/power assisted disc brakes (ventilated at front), handbrake to rear wheels; power assisted rack and pinion steering; fuel tank 65L (14.3Gal) [17.2US Gal]; tyres 205/60 HR 14, wheels 6 J, optional 6.5 J.

Dimensions: Wheelbase 261.5cm, track 142.5/142.5cm, clearance 13.5cm, turning circle 10.4m. Length 469.5cm, width 169cm, height 137cm.

Performance: Max speed approx 112mph/180kmh, speed at 1000rpm in 4th gear 25.2mph/40.6kmh; power to weight ratio from 16kg/kW (11.8kg/PS); consumption approx 8–12L/100km (35.3–23.5mpg) [29.4–19.6US mpg].

```
2.0 24V
154kW–206hp–210PS
Turbo/Fuel Injection
```

As 114hp, except:

Weight: Kerbweight from 1440kg.

Engine data (JIS): 6-cylinder in V 60deg (78 x 69.7mm), 1998cm3; compression ratio 8.5:1; 154kW (206hp) [210PS] at 6800rpm, 77.1kW/L (103hp/L) [105.1PS/L]; 265Nm (195.6lbft) at 3600rpm.

Engine construction: Designated VG 20 DET. 4 valves per cylinder; 2 overhead camshafts (toothed belt); oil cooler; 1 Garrett turbocharger, charge-air cooler. Cooling system capacity approx 9L (8.5US qt).

Transmission: Automatic with Programme, final drive ratio 4.363; limited slip differential.

Gear ratios: 1st 3.027; 2nd 1.619; 3rd 1; 4th 0.694; R 2.272.

Nissan

Chassis: Optional electronically regulated dampers; disc brakes (ventilated), with optional ABS; tyres 215/60 HR 15, wheel rims 6.5 J.

Dimensions: Track 143.5/143.5cm.

Performance: Max speed over 137mph/220kmh, speed at 1000rpm in 4th gear 24mph/38.6kmh; power to weight ratio from 9.4kg/kW (6.9kg/PS); consumption approx 11-17L/100km (25.7–16.6mpg) [21.4–13.8US mpg].

Nissan Leopard

```
3.0 24V
187/147kW–251/197hp–255/200PS
Turbo/Fuel Injection
```

As 114hp model, except:

Weight: Kerbweight from 1520kg, without Turbo from 1460kg.

Engine data (JIS net): 6–cylinder in V 60deg (87 x 83mm), 2960cm3; compression ratio 8.5:1; 187kW (251hp) [255PS] at 6000rpm, 63.2kW/L (84.7hp/L) [62.5PS/L]; 343Nm (253lbft) at 3200rpm.
Without Turbo: Compression ratio 10.5:1; 147kW (197hp) [200PS] at 6000rpm; 260Nm (192lbft) at 4400rpm.

Engine construction: Designated VG 30 DET/DE. 4 valves per cylinder; 2 overhead camshafts (toothed belt). Oil cooler; 1 Garrett CNR-1 Turbocharger; Cooling system capacity approx 9L (8.5US qt).

Transmission: Automatic with Programme, final drive ratio 3.916, without Turbo 4.083. Limited slip differential.

Gear ratios: 1st 2.784; 2nd 1.544; 3rd 1; 4th 0.694; R 2.275.

Chassis: Electronically regulated dampers; rear brake discs, (ventilated), ABS; tyres 215/60 HR 15, wheels 6.5J.

Dimensions: Track 143.5/143.5cm, Length 480.5cm.

Performance (Turbo): Max speed over 143mph/230kmh, speed at 1000rpm in 4th gear 26.8mphmph/43.1kmh; power to weight ratio from 8.1kg/kW (6.0kg/PS); consumption approx 12–20L/100km (23.5–14.1mpg) [19.6–11.8US mpg].

Nissan Laurel

New model. Middle class Saloon/Sedan with engine from 1.8 to 2.8 Litre capacity and rear wheel drive. Launched in 1968. Winter 1977 and November 1980: new body. For 1985: a modified 6-cylinder engine and further improvements. December 1988: reworked model range, new body and suspension. Not available for export.

```
1.8 Litre
67kW–90hp–91PS
Central/Single Point Injection
```

Body, Weight: 4–door Hardtop Saloon/Sedan, 5–seater, kerbweight (DIN) from 1170kg.

Engine data (JIS net): 4–cylinder in–line (83 x 83.6mm), 1809cm3; compression ratio 8.8:1; 67kW (90hp) [91PS] at 5200rpm, 37.0kW/L (49.6hp/L) [50.3PS/L]; 142Nm (104.8lbft) at 3200rpm.

Engine construction: Designated CA 18S/CA 20S. Valves in V; 1 overhead camshaft (toothed belt); light–alloy cylinder head; crankshaft with 5 bearings; oil capacity 3.9L (3.7US qt); electronic central/single point injection. Battery 12V 45/60Ah, alternator 50/60A; cooling system capacity approx 7L (6.6US qt).

Transmission (to rear wheels): a) 5–speed manual, final drive ratio 3.900.
b) Automatic, hydraulic torque converter and 4–speed Planetary gear set, final drive ratio 4.111.

Gear ratios: a) 5–speed manual: 1st 3.592; 2nd 2.057; 3rd 1.361; 4th 1; 5th 0.821; R 3.382.
b) Automatic, max torque multiplication in converter 2 times; Planetary gear set ratios: 1st 2.785; 2nd 1.545; 3rd 1; 4th 0.694; R 2.272.

Chassis: Integral body; front McPherson struts, control arms, torsion struts and antiroll bar, rear compound linkage axle (lower A-arm, axial strut, upper single control arm, diagonal strut) coil springs and co–axial telescopic dampers, antiroll bar. Servo/power assisted disc brakes (front ventilated), handbrake to rear wheels; power assisted rack and pinion steering; fuel tank 65L (14.3Gal) [17.2US Gal]; tyres 165 SR 14 or 185/70 SR 14 optional 195/65 HR 15, wheels 5.5 or 6 J.

Dimensions: Wheelbase 267cm, track 146/145.5cm, clearance 15cm, turning circle 10m. Length 469cm, width 169.5cm, height 136.5cm.

Performance: Max speed 109mph/175kmh, (manufacturers test specifications), speed at 1000rpm in 5th gear 22mph/35.5kmh; power to weight ratio from 17.5kg/kW (12.8kg/PS); consumption approximately 8–13L/100km (35.3–21.7mpg) [29.4–18.1US mpg].

```
2.0 6–cylinder
92kW–123hp–125PS
Fuel Injection
```

As 1.8 Litre model, except:

Weight: Kerbweight (DIN) from 1230kg.

Engine data (JIS net): 6–cylinder in–line (78 x 69.7mm), 1998cm3; compression ratio 9.5:1; 92kW (123hp) [125PS] at 5600rpm, 46.0kW/L (61.6hp/L) [62.5PS/L]; 172Nm (127lbft) at 4400rpm.

Engine construction: Designated RB 20. Hydraulic tappets; crankshaft with 7 bearings; oil capacity 4.7L (4.4US qt); electronic fuel injection. Cooling system capacity approx 10L (9.5US qt).

Transmission: a) 5–speed manual, final drive ratio 3.900 or 3.916.
b) Automatic, final drive ratio 3.900 or 3.916.
Optional limited slip differential

Gear ratios: a) 5–speed manual, 1st 3.321; 2nd 1.902; 3rd 1.308; 4th 1; 5th 0.838; R 3.382.
b) Automatic, 1st 3.027; 2nd 1.619; 3rd 1; 4th 0.694; R 2.272.

Chassis: Brakes with optional ABS; tyres 185/70 SR 14.

Performance: Max speed 118mph/190kmh (manufacturers test specifications), speed at 1000rpm in 5th gear 21.7mph/35.0kmh; power to weight ratio from 13.4kg/kW (9.8kg/PS); consumption approx 9–15L/100km (31.4–18.8mpg) [26.1–15.7US mpg].

Nissan Laurel Hardtop

```
2.0 24V
151/114kW–202/153hp–205/155PS
Turbo/Fuel Injection
```

As 1.8 Litre model, except:

Weight: Kerbweight (DIN) from 1380kg, without Turbo from 1330kg.

Engine data (JIS net): 6–cylinder in–line (78 x 69.7mm), 1998cm3; compression ratio 8.5:1; 151kW (202hp) [205PS] at 6400rpm, 75.6kW/L (101.3hp/L) [103.5PS/L]; 265Nm (195.6lbft) at 3200rpm.
Without Turbo: Compression ratio 10.2:1; 114kW (153hp) [155PS] at 6400rpm, 57.1kW/L (76.5hp/L) [77.6PS/L]; 184Nm (135.8lbft) at 5200rpm.

Engine construction: Designated RB 20DE/ RB 20DET. 4 valves (in V 46deg) per cylinder, hydraulic valve tappets; 2 overhead camshafts (toothed belt); crankshaft with 7 bearings; oil capacity approx 5L (4.7US qt); oil–cooler; electronic fuel injection, Garrett T3 turbocharger and charge–air cooler. Batter 45-70Ah, Alternator 60-90A; cooling system capacity approx 11L (10.4US qt).

Transmission: 5–speed manual (not for Turbo), final drive ratio 4.363
b)Automatic with Programme, final drive ratio 4.363, without Turbo 4.363. Limited slip differential (153hp optional).

Gear ratios: a) 5–speed manual: As 1.8 Litre.
b)Automatic: 1st 2.785; 2nd 1.545; 3rd 1; 4th 0.694; R 2.272.
Without Turbo: 1st 3.027; 2nd 1.619; 3rd 1; 4th 0.694; R 2.272.

Nissan

Chassis: Optional electronically regulated dampers; rear disc brakes (ventilated) and ABS (turbo only); optional Hicas II hydraulic four wheel steering; tyres 205/60 HR 15, without Turbo 195/65 HR 15, wheel rims 6 J.

Dimensions: Track 142/141.5cm. Length 469cm.

Performance: Max speed approx 137mph/220kmh, speed at 1000rpm in 4th gear (Automatic) 23.5mph/37.8kmh; power to weight ratio from 9.1kg/kW (6.7kg/PS); consumption approx 11–18L/100km (25.7–15.7mpg) [21.4–13.1US mpg].

Nissan Laurel Hardtop

```
2.8 Diesel
69kW–92.5hp–95PS
Injection Pump
```

As 1.8 Litre model, except:

Weight: Kerbweight (DIN) from 1310kg.

Engine data (JIS net): 6–cylinder in–line (85 x 83mm), 2825cm3; compression ratio 21.2:1; 69kW (92.5hp) [94PS] at 4800rpm, 24.4kW/L (32.7hp/L) [33.3PS/L]; 177Nm (130.6lbft) at 2400rpm.

Engine construction: Designated RD 28. Pre–combustion diesel engine. Parallel valves, hydraulic tappets; grey cast–iron cylinder head; crankshaft with 7 bearings; oil capacity 5.4L (5.1US qt); diesel injection pump. Battery 70Ah, alternator 60A. Cooling system capacity 9L (8.5US qt).

Transmission: a) 5-speed manual, final drive ratio 3.916
b) Automatic, final drive ratio 3.692.

Gear ratios: a) 5-speed manual: 1st 3.321; 2nd 1.902; 3rd 1.308; 4th 1; 5th 0.759.
b) Automatic: As 1800 model.

Chassis: Optional ABS; tyres 185/70 SR 14 or 195/65 HR 15.

Performance: Max speed approx 102mph/165kmh (manufacturers test specifications), speed at 1000rpm in 5th gear 23.8mph/38.4kmh; power to weight ratio from 19.0kg/kW (13.9kg/PS); consumption approx 7-11L/100km (40.4-25.7mpg) [33.6–21.4US mpg].

Nissan Cefiro

New model. Four door Saloon/Sedan of superior class with 2 Litre engine of 123 and 202hp and rear wheel drive. Priority suspension Hicas 11. Not for export. Launched September 1988.

```
2000
92kW–123hp–125PS
Fuel Injection
```

Body, Weight: Saloon/Sedan 4-door, 5-seater; kerbweight (DIN) from 1240kg.

Engine data (JIS net): 6-cylinder in-line (78 x 69.7mm), 1998cm3; compression ratio 9.5:1; 92kW (123hp) [125PS] at 5600rpm, 46kW/L (61.6hp/L) [62.6PS/L]; 172Nm (126.9lbft) at 4400rpm.

Engine construction: Designated RB 20E. Valves in V, hydraulic tappets, 1 overhead camshaft (toothed belt); light-alloy cylinder head; 7-bearing crankshaft; oil capacity 4.4L (4.2US qt); electronic fuel injection. 12V 45-60Ah battery, alternator 50-70A; cooling system capacity approx 9L (8.5US qt).

Transmission (to rear wheels): a) 5-speed manual, final drive ratio 3.900.
b) Automatic, hydraulic torque converter and 4-speed Planetary gear set, final drive ratio 3.900.

Gear ratios: a) 5-speed manual: 1st 3.321; 2nd 1.902; 3rd 1.308; 4th 1; 5th 0.838; R 3.382.
b) Automatic; max torque multiplication in converter approx 2 times, Planetary gear set ratios: 1st: 3.027; 2nd 1.619; OD 0.694; R 2.272.

Chassis: Integral body; front McPherson struts, control arm, torsion strut and antiroll bar, rear control arm (lower A arm, axial strut, top single A arm and diagonal support arm), coil springs and coaxial telescopic damper, antiroll bar, optional electronically controlled damping. Servo/power assisted disc brakes (front ventilated), optional ABS; hand brake to rear wheels; power assisted rack and pinion steering, optional hydraulic four wheel steering; fuel tank 65L (14.3gal) [17.2US Gal]; tyres 195/65 HR 15 or 205/60 HR 15, wheel rims 5.5 - 6J.

Dimensions: Wheelbase 267cm, track 146/145.5cm, clearance 15cm, turning circle approx 10m, length 469cm, width 169.5cm, height 137.5cm.

Performance: Max speed approx 118mph/190kmh, speed at 1000rpm in 5th gear 22.2mph/35.8kmh; power to weight ratio from 13.5kg/kW (9.9kg/PS); consumption approx 8-12L/100km (35.3-23.5mpg) [29.4-19.6US mpg].

Nissan Cefiro

```
2.0 24V
114kW–153hp–155PS
Fuel Injection
```

As 123hp, except:

Weight: Kerbweight from 1290kg.

Engine data (JIS net): 6-cylinder in-line (78 x 69.7mm), 1998cm3; compression ratio 10.2:1; 114kW (153hp) [155PS] at 6400rpm, 57.1kW/L (76.5hp/L) [77.6PS/L]; 184Nm (135.8lbft) at 5200rpm.

Engine construction: Designated RB 20DE; 4 valves in V 46deg per cylinder, hydraulic tappets, 2 overhead camshafts (toothed belt). 45-70Ah battery, 60-90A alternator; cooling system capacity approx 10L (9.5US qt).

Transmission: a) 5-speed manual, final drive ratio 4.363.
b) Automatic, final drive ratio 4.363.
Optional limited slip differential.

Gear ratios: a) 5-speed manual: 1st 3.592; 2nd 2.057; 3rd 1.361; 4th 1; 5th 0.821; R 3.657.
b) Automatic: As 123hp.

Performance: Max speed approx 131mph/210kmh, speed at 1000rpm in 5th gear 20.1mph/32.4kmh; power to weight ratio from 11.3kg/kW (8.3kg/PS); consumption approx 9-14L/100km (31.4-20.2mpg) [26.1-16.8US mpg].

Nissan Cefiro

```
2.0 24V
151kW–202hp–205PS
Fuel Injection/Turbo
```

As 123hp, except:

Weight: Kerbweight (DIN) from 1320kg.

Engine data (JIS net): 6-cylinder in-line (78 x 69.7mm), 1998cm3; compression ratio 8.5:1; 151kW (202hp) [205PS] at 6400rpm, 75.6kW/L (101.3hp/L) [103.5PS/L]; 265Nm (195.6lbft) at 3200rpm.

Engine construction: Designated RB 20DET. 4 valves in V 46deg per cylinder, hydraulic tappets, 2 overhead camshafts (toothed belt); oil cooler; 1 turbocharger and charge-air cooler. 45-70Ah battery, 60-90A alternator, cooling system capacity approx 11L (10.4US qt).

Transmission: a) 5-speed manual; final drive ratio 4.363.
b) Automatic; final drive ratio 4.363.
Limited slip differential.

Gear ratios: a) 5-speed manual, 1st 3.321; 2nd 1.902; 3rd 1.308; 4th 1; 5th 0.759; R 3.382.
b) Automatic, Planetary gear set ratios: 1st 2.785; 2nd 1.545; 3rd 1; OD 0.694; R 2.272.

Chassis: Tyres 205/60 HR 15, wheel rims 6, optional 6.5J.

Performance: Max speed over 143mph/230kmh, speed at 1000rpm in 5th gear 21.5mph/34.6kmh; power to weight ratio from 8.7kg/kW (6.4kg/PS); consumption approx 10-18L/100km (28.2-15.7mpg) [23.5-13.1US mpg].

Nissan Cedric/Gloria

Upper middle of the range Saloon/Sedan with 2 to 3 Litre capacity 6-cylinder engines and rear wheel drive. June 1983: new generation of engines. June 1987: revised V6-engines, new body, rear independent wheel suspension. January 1988: luxury fittings (extended) Cima with powerful 3 Litre engine.

```
2 Litre V6
92kW-123hp-125PS
Fuel Injection
```

Body, Weight: 4-door Saloon/Sedan, 5/6-seater; kerbweight (DIN) from 1310kg. 4-door Hardtop Saloon/Sedan, 5/6-seater, kerbweight (DIN) from 1360kg.

Engine data (JIS net): 6-cylinder in V 60deg (78 x 69.7mm), 1998cm3; compression ratio 9.5:1; 92kW (123hp) [125PS] at 6000rpm, 46kW/L (61.6hp/L) [62.6PS/L]; 167Nm (123.2lbft) at 3200rpm.

Engine construction: Designated VG 20E. Valves in V, hydraulic tappets, 2x1 overhead camshaft (toothed belt); light-alloy cylinder head; crankshaft with 4 bearings; oil capacity 4.5L (4.3US qt); electronic fuel injection. Battery 12V 45/60Ah, alternator 50/70A; Cooling system capacity approx 9L (8.5US qt).

Transmission (to rear wheels): a) 5-speed manual, final drive ratio 4.625.
b) Automatic, hydraulic torque converter and 4-speed Planetary gear set, final drive ratio 4.625.

Gear ratios: a) 5-speed manual: 1st 3.592; 2nd 2.057; 3rd 1.361; 4th 1; 5th 0.821; R 3.657.
b) Automatic; Max torque multiplication in converter 2 times, Planetary gear set ratios: 1st 2.785; 2nd 1.545, 3rd 1; OD 0.694; R 2.272.

Chassis: Integral body; all-round independent suspension; front McPherson struts with control arms, torsion struts and antiroll bar; rear diagonal arms, spring coils, some models with antiroll bar, telescopic dampers. Servo/power assisted disc brakes (ventilated at front), mechanical handbrake to rear wheels; power assisted rack and pinion steering; fuel tank 72L (15.8Gal) [19US Gal]; tyres 185 SR 14 or 195/70 SR 14, wheels 5 or 5.5, optional 6J.

Dimensions: Wheelbase 273.5cm, track 144/145-145.5cm, clearance 15cm, turning circle 11m. Length 469cm, width 169.5cm, height 140-142.5cm.

Performance: Max speed approx 115mph/185kmh, speed at 1000rpm in 5th gear 19.5mph/31.4kmh; power to weight ratio from 14.2kg/kW (10.5kg/PS); consumption approx 8-13L/100km (35.3-21.7mpg) [29.4-18.1US mpg].

```
2 Litre V6 24V
136kW-182hp-185PS
Turbo/Fuel Injection
```

As 123hp, except:

Weight: Saloon/Sedan from 1470kg; Hardtop from 1440kg.

Engine data (JIS net): 6-cylinder in V 60deg (78 x 69.7mm), 1998cm3; compression ratio 8.5:1; 136kW (182hp) [185PS] at 6800rpm, 68.1kW/L (91.2hp/L) [92.6PS/L]; 216Nm (159.3lbft) at 4800rpm.

Engine construction: Designated VG 20 DET. 4 valves (in V) per cylinder, 2x1 overhead camshafts (toothed belt); oil-cooler; 1 CNR-1 exhaust turbocharger.

Transmission: 4-speed automatic, with 2 programmes, final drive ratio 4.375. Optional limited slip differential (viscous).

Gear ratios: Planetary gear set ratios: 1st 3.027, 2nd 1.619; 3rd 1; OD 0.694: R 2.272.

Chassis: Front and rear antiroll bars; optional ABS brakes; tyres 205/65 HR 15, wheels 6J.

Dimensions: Track 144/145cm

Performance: Max speed approx 130mph/210kmh, speed at 1000rpm in OD 24.2mph/39.0kmh; power to weight ratio from 10.6kg/kW (7.8kg/PS); consumption approx 10-16L/100km (28.2-17.7mpg) [23.5-14.7US mpg].

Nissan Gloria V 20 Twin Cam Turbo

```
3 Litre V6
143/118kW-192/158hp-195/160PS
Turbo/Fuel Injection
```

As 123hp, except:

Weight: Saloon/Sedan from 1520kg, without Turbo 1450kg, Hardtop from 1530kg, without Turbo 1470kg.

Engine data (JIS net): 6-cylinder in V 60deg (87 x 83mm), 2960cm3; compression ratio 8.3:1; 143kW (192hp) [195PS] at 5200rpm, 48.3kW/L (64.7hp/L) [65.9PS/L]; 294Nm (217lbft) at 3200rpm.
Without Turbo: Compression ratio 9:1; 118kW (158hp) [160PS] at 5200rpm; 39.9kW/L (53.5hp/L) [54.1PS/L]; 248Nm (183lbft) at 3200rpm.

Engine construction: Designated VG 30 ET/E. Oil-cooler, Garrett exhaust turbocharger. Cooling system capacity 11L (10.4US qt).

Transmission: 4-speed automatic, with 2 programmes, final drive ratio 3.700. Turbo optional limited slip differential (viscous).

Gear ratios: Automatic; as 2 Litre V6.

Chassis: Front and rear antiroll bars; ABS; air suspension with sport/normal programme. Turbo; disc brakes to rear ventilated, tyres 205/65 HR 15, wheel rims 6J.

Dimensions: Track 144/145cm or 144.5/146cm. Length 486cm, width 172cm.

Performance: Max speed approx 130mph/210kmh, speed at 1000rpm in OD 28.7mph/46.1kmh; power to weight ratio from 10.6kg/kW (7.8kg/PS); consumption approx 11-18L/100km (25.7-15.7mpg) [21.4-13.1US mpg].

Nissan Gloria V 30 Turbo Brougham VIP

```
3 Litre 24V
187/147kW-251/197hp-255/200PS
Turbo/Fuel Injection
```

Engine for Gloria Cima

As 123hp model except:

Body, Weight: 4-door Hardtop kerbweight from 1630kg, without turbo 1550kg.

Engine data (JIS net): 6-cylinder in V 60deg (87 x 83mm), 2960cm3; compression ratio 8.5:1; 187kW (251hp) [255PS] at 6000rpm, 63.2kW/L (84.7hp/L) [86.1PS/L]; 343Nm (253.1lbft) at 3200rpm.

Nissan

Without turbo: Compression ratio 10.5:1; 147kW (197hp) [200PS] at 6000rpm; 260Nm (191.9lbft) at 4400rpm.

Engine construction: Designated VG 30 DET/DE. 4 valves (in V) per cylinder, 2x1 overhead camshafts (toothed belt); oil cooler; 1 CNR–1 exhaust turbocharger.

Transmission: 4–speed automatic; with 2 programmes, final drive ratio 3.900, without turbo 4.111. Limited slip differential.

Gear ratios: Automatic; 1st 2.784; 2nd 1.544; 3rd 1; 4th 0.694; R 2.275. Without turbo: As 2 Litre V6.

Chassis: Front and rear antiroll bars; rear brake discs also ventilated, ABS; air suspension with sport/normal programme; tyres 205/65 HR 15, turbo also 215/60 HR 15, wheels 6J, turbo also 6.5J.

Dimensions: Track 150/152cm or 151.5/149.5cm. Length 489cm, width 177cm, height 138–140cm.

Performance: Max speed approx 127–140mph/205–225kmh, speed at 1000rpm in OD (turbo) 27.2mph/43.8kmh; power to weight ratio from 8.7kg/kW (6.4kg/PS); consumption approx 12–20L/100km (23.5– 14.1mpg) [19.6–11.8US mpg].

Nissan Cima

```
2.8 Litre Diesel
69kW–92.5hp–94PS
Injection Pump
```

As 123hp model except:

Weight: Saloon/Sedan from 1390kg, Hardtop from 1430kg.

Engine data (JIS net): 6–cylinder in–line (85 x 83mm), 2825cm3; compression ratio 21.2:1; 69kW (92.5hp) [94PS] at 4800rpm, 24.4kW/L (32.4hp/L) [33.3PS/L]; 177Nm (130.6lbft) at 2400rpm.

Engine construction: Designated RD 28. Pre–combustion chamber diesel engine. Parallel valves; grey cast–iron cylinder head; crankshaft with 7 bearings; oil capacity 5.5L (5.2US qt); diesel injection pump. Battery 70Ah, alternator 60A, cooling system capacity 9L (8.5US qt).

Transmission: a) 5–speed manual, final drive ratio 4.083.
b) Automatic, final drive ratio 4.083.

Performance: Max speed approx 96mph/155kmh, speed at 1000rpm in 5th gear 22.1mph/35.5kmh; power to weight ratio from 20.1kg/kW (14.8kg/PS); consumption approx 7–12L/100km (40.4–23.5mpg) [33.6– 19.6US mpg].

Nissan Fairlady Z

Nissan 280 ZX successor; new V6–engine with turbocharger and 2 and 3 Litre engine capacities. Available as coupe with 2 and 2+2– seater. 300 ZX export designated. Debut September 1984. October 1986: body retouches and 4–valve–version of the 3 Litre V6 engine without turbo.

```
2 litre 6–cylinder
132kW–177hp–180PS
Turbo/Fuel Injection
```

Body, Weight: 3–door Coupe, 2–seater; kerbweight (DIN) 1310–1360kg. 3–door Coupe 2+2–seater; kerbweight (DIN) 1350–1400kg.

Engine data (JIS net): 6–cylinder in–line (78 x 69.7mm), 1998cm3; compression ratio 8.5:1; 132kW (177hp) [180PS] at 6400rpm, 66.1kW/L (88.6hp/L) [90.1PS/L]; 226Nm (166.7lbft) at 3600rpm.

Some countries: 6–cylinder in V 60deg (78 x 69.7mm), 1998cm3; compression ratio 8.0:1; 125kW (167.5hp) [170PS] at 6000rpm, 216Nm (159.3lbft) at 4000rpm.

Engine construction: Designated RB 20DET. 4 valves (in V 46deg) per cylinder, hydraulic tappets, 2 overhead camshafts (toothed belt); crankshaft with 7 bearings; oil capacity 4.7L (4.4US qt); oil–cooler; electronic fuel injection, Garrett T3 turbocharger and charger–air cooler. Battery 12V 45Ah, alternator 60/70A; cooling system capacity approx 9L (8.5US qt).

Transmission (to rear wheels): a) 5–speed manual, final drive ratio 4.375.
b) Automatic, hydraulic torque converter and 3–speed Planetary gear set with OD, final drive ratio 4.625.
Optional limited slip differential.

Gear ratios: a) 5–speed manual: 1st 3.321; 2nd 1.902; 3rd 1.308; 4th 1; 5th 0.838; R 3.382.
b) Automatic, Max torque multiplication in converter 2 times, Planetary gear set ratios: 1st 2.842; 2nd 1.542; 3rd 1; OD 0.686; R 2.4

Chassis: Integral body, front McPherson struts with control arm, compression struts and antiroll bar, rear independent suspension with diagonal arms, coil springs and antiroll bar, telescopic dampers. Servo/power assisted discs brakes (ventilated at front), mechanical handbrake to rear wheels; power assisted rack and pinion steering; fuel tank 72L (15.8Gal) [19US Gal]; tyres 215/60 HR 15, wheels 6.5J.

Dimensions: Wheelbase 232cm, track 141.5/143.5cm, clearance 15cm, turning circle 9.8m. Length 440.5cm, width 169cm, height 129.5cm. 2+2: Wheelbase 252cm, turning circle 10.6m. Length 460.5cm, height 131cm.

Performance: Max speed approx 137mph/220kmh, speed at 1000rpm in 5th gear 19.8mph/31.9kmh; power to weight ratio from 9.9kg/kW (73.kg/PS); consumption approx 9–17L/100km (31.4–16.6mpg) [26.1– 13.8US mpg].

```
3 Litre V6
143kW–192hp–195PS
Turbo/Fuel Injection
```

As 2 Litre model except:

Weight: Kerbweight from 1440kg, 2+2 from 1480kg, USA from 1425kg (without turbo), 2+2 from 1480kg.

Engine data (JIS net): 6–cylinder in V 60deg (87 x 83mm), 2960cm3; compression ratio 7.8:1; 143kW (192hp) [195PS] at 5200rpm, 48.3kW/L (64.7hp/L) [65.9PS/L]; 309Nm (228lbft) at 3600rpm.
Export version (DIN): 168kW (225hp) [228PS] at 5400rpm; 326Nm (240.6lbft) at 4400rpm or 177kW (237hp) [241PS] at 5400rpm; 342Nm (252.4lbft).
With Catalyst (DIN): 149kW (200hp) [203PS] at 5200rpm; 309Nm (228lbft) at 3600rpm.
USA version (SAE net): Compression ratio 8.3:1; 153kW (205hp) [208PS] at 5300rpm.
Without turbocharger (DIN): Compression ratio 9.1; 125kW (167.5hp) [170PS] at 5600rpm; 236Nm (174.1lbft) at 4400rpm.
USA version (SAE net): 123kW (165hp) [167PS] at 5200rpm; 293Nm (216.2lbft) at 4000rpm.

Engine construction: Designated VG 30ET. 2 valves per cylinder, 2x1 overhead camshaft; oil capacity 4.5L (4.3US qt); max boost pressure 0.49bar. Battery 60Ah, alternator 70A.

Transmission: a) 5–speed manual, final drive ratio 3.545, without turbo 3.9.
b) Automatic, final drive ratio 3.545, without turbo 3.9.

Gear ratios: a) 5–speed manual: 1st 3.350; 2nd 2.056; 3rd 1.376; 4th 1; 5th 0.779; R 3.153.
Or (without turbo) 1st 3.321; 2nd 2.090; 3rd 1.308; 4th 1; 5th 0.759; R 3.382.
b) Automatic, 1st 2.458; 2nd 1.458. 3rd 1; 4th 0.686; R 2.182.

Chassis: Ventilated brake discs on all wheels, optional ABS; tyres 215/60 HR/VR 15 or 225/50 VR 16, wheels 6.5J or 7J.

Dimensions: Track 145.5/147.5cm, width 172.5cm.

Performance (Turbo): Max speed 155mph/250kmh, with Catalyst 143mph/230kmh (manufacturers test specification), speed at 1000rpm in 5th gear 26.4mph/42.4kmh; acceleration from 0 – 62mph/100kmh in 7.9secs; power to weight ratio from 8.2kg/kW (6.0kg/PS); consumption approx 7.0/8.7/14.5L/100km (40.4/32.5/19.5mpg) [33.6/27/16.2US mpg].

Nissan 300 ZX

New model. Sports car with V6 engine and rear wheel drive. Also Coupe with 2 or 2+2–seater. February 1989: Model fully renovated, world premiere in Chicago Motor Show. At present no data for US version, exports to Europe in 1990. Version with twin Turbo, 297hp and approx 295lbft in preparation.

Nissan

Nissan 300 ZX

3.0 V6 24V
165kW–222hp–225PS
Fuel Injection

Body, Weight: Coupe 3-door, 2-seater; kerbweight (DIN) from 1460kg. Coupe 3-door, 2 + 2 seater; kerbweight (DIN) from 1505kg.

Engine data (SAE net): 6-cylinder in V 60deg (87 x 83mm), 2960cm3, compression ratio 10.5:1; 165kW (222hp) [225PS] at 6400rpm, 55.7kW/L (74.6hp/L) [76PS/L]; 269Nm (198.5lbft) at 4800rpm; unleaded regular grade.

Engine construction: Designated VG 30DE, 4 valves in V 46deg per cylinder, hydraulic tappets, 2 overhead camshafts (toothed belt) per range; light-alloy cylinder head; 4 bearing crankshaft; oil capacity 4L (3.8US qt); oil cooler; electronic fuel injection. 12V battery, cooling system capacity approx 9L (8.5US qt).

Transmission (to rear wheels): a) 5-speed manual, final drive ratio 4.083. b) Automatic with programme, hydraulic torque converter and 4-speed Planetary gear set, ratio 4.083. Limited slip differential (Visco).

Nissan 300 ZX

Gear ratios: a) 5-speed manual, 1st 3.314; 2nd 1.925; 3rd 1.302; 4th 1; 5th 0.752; R 3.382.
b) Automatic, max torque multiplication with converter 2 times, Planetary gear set ratios: 1st 2.785; 2nd 1.545; 3rd 1; OD 0.694; R 2.272.

Chassis: Integral body; all round independent suspension with coil springs and coaxial telescopic damper, front lower A arm with torsion strut, top semi-trailing arm, articulating arm, rear lower A arm, axial arm, lower single A arm and diagonal support arm, antiroll bar front and rear. Servo/power assisted front disc brakes (ventilated) and ABS, disc diameter front 28cm, rear 29.7cm, handbrake to rear wheels; power assisted rack and pinion steering, optional power assisted steering Super HICAS; fuel tank 70L (15.4Gal) [18.5US Gal]; tyres 225/50 VR 16, wheel rims 7.5J.

Dimensions: Wheelbase 245cm, track 149.5/153.5cm, length 430.5cm, width 179cm, height 127cm.

Performance: Max speed 146mph/235kmh (manufacturers test specification), speed at 1000rpm in 5th gear 23.4mph/37.7kmh; power to weight ratio from 8.9kg/kW (6.5kg/PS); consumption approx 10-16L/100km (28.2-17.7mpg) [23.5-14.7US mpg].

Nissan President

Official vehicle with 4.4 Litre V8 engine and automatic. Tokyo debut in 1965. October 1973: body and interior modifications.

4.4 Litre V8
147kW–197hp–200PS
Fuel Injection

Body, Weight: 4-door Saloon/Sedan 5/6-seater; kerbweight (DIN) 1905–1990kg.

Engine data (JIS): 8-cylinder in V 90deg (92 x 83mm), 4414cm3; compression ratio 8.6:1; 147kW (197hp) [200PS] at 4800rpm, 33.3kW/L (44.6hp/L) [45.3PS/L]; 338Nm (249.4lbft) at 3200rpm; leaded premium grade.

Engine construction: Designated Y 44. Hydraulic tappets, central camshaft (chain); light-alloy cylinder head; crankshaft with 5 bearings; oil capacity 4.1L (3.9US qt); electronic fuel injection ECCS. Battery 12V 60Ah, alternator 80A; cooling system capacity 16L (15.1US qt).

Transmission (to rear wheels): Automatic, hydraulic torque converter and 3-speed Planetary gear set, transmission selector lever on steering wheel, final drive ratio 3.364.

Gear ratios: Max torque multiplication in converter 2 times. Planetary gear set ratios: 1st 2.458; 2nd 1.458; 3rd 1; R 2.182.

Chassis: Integral body; front double A-arm and coil springs, rear rigid axle with coil springs and longitudinal arms, front and rear antiroll bars, telescopic dampers. Servo/power assisted brakes, front discs (ventilated), rear drums, mechanical handbrake to rear wheels; power assisted steering; fuel tank 95L (20.9Gal) [25.1US Gal]; tyres 205 SR 14, wheels 6J.

Dimensions: Wheelbase 285cm, track 152/150cm, clearance 18.5cm, turning circle 11.6m. Length 525/528cm, width 183cm, height 148/149cm.

Performance: Max speed 121mph/195kmh (manufacturers test specification), speed at 1000rpm in direct gear 23.3mph/37.5kmh; power to weight ratio from 13kg/kW (9.5kg/PS); consumption (touring) approx 15–20L/100km (18.8–14.1mpg) [15.7–11.8US mpg].

Nissan President

Nissan Patrol/Safari

Off-road Estate/Station Wagon. 2 and 4-wheel drive with reduction gear. 1980: new body. 2.75 Litre petrol/gasoline and 3.25 Litre diesel engine. Summer 1981: new body; 1983 turbo diesel engine. Production under licence in Spain. Production continues on parallel to the new Patrol GR.

2.8 Litre
98kW–131hp–134PS
1 Carb

Body, Weight: 3-door Hardtop, 4–5-seater; kerbweight (DIN) from 1635kg. 5-door Estate/Station Wagon, 5–10-seater; kerbweight (DIN) from 1760kg.

Engine data (JIS): 6-cylinder in-line (86 x 79mm), 2753cm3; compression ratio 8.6:1; 98kW (131hp) [134PS] at 5200rpm, 35.6kW/L (47.7hp/L) [48.7PS/L]; 213Nm (157.1lbft) at 3600rpm.
European version (DIN): 88kW (118hp) [120PS] at 4800rpm, 201Nm (148.3lbft) at 3200rpm.
Also 4 Litre OHV (export, SAE net): (85.7 x 114.3mm), 3956cm3; compression ratio 8.2:1; 110kW (147hp) [150PS] at 3800rpm, 294Nm (217lbft) at 2400rpm. Or (DIN): 84.5kW (113hp) [115PS]; 270Nm (199.3lbft).

Nissan

Engine construction: 1 overhead camshaft (chain), light-alloy cylinder head; crankshaft with 4 bearings; oil capacity 5.3L (5US qt); 1 downdraught Hitachi VC 42-4A carb, oil bath air filter. Battery 12V 65Ah, alternator 35/50A; cooling system capacity 11L (10.4US qt).

Transmission (to rear wheels or to all wheels): Engageable all-wheel drive, reduction 2.22, Estate/Station Wagon 2.074.
a) 4-speed manual, final drive ratio 4.375 or 4.625 (4 Litre: 3.900, 4.111).
b) 5-speed manual, final drive ratio 4.375 (4 Litre: 3.900, 4.111).
c) Automatic, hydraulic torque converter and 3-speed Planetary gear set, transmission selector lever on steering wheel, final drive ratio 4.875; 4.625; 4.375. Optional rear limited slip differential.

Gear ratios: a) 4-speed manual: 1st 4.222 or 3.897; 2nd 2.37; 3rd 1.44; 4th 1; R 4.622.
b) 5-speed manual: 1st 3.897; 2nd 2.37; 3rd 1.44; 4th 1; 5th 0.825; R 4.267.
c) Automatic; Max torque multiplication in converter 2 times, Planetary gear set ratios: 1st 2.458; 2nd 1.458; 3rd 1; R 2.182.

Chassis: Chassis with frame rails and cross members, front and rear rigid axle with semi-elliptic springs, front cornering stabiliser, telescopic dampers. Servo/power assisted brakes, front discs (ventilated), rear drums, some models four-wheel drum brakes, mechanical handbrake to propellor shaft; recirculating ball steering with optional power assisted; fuel tank 82L (18Gal) [21.7US Gal]; tyres 6.50-16 or 7.00-16, optional 205 R 16, wheels 5.5J or 6J.

Dimensions: Hardtop; wheelbase 235cm, track 141/141cm, clearance 21cm, turning circle 11.2m. Length 407-423cm, width 169cm, height 183.5-185cm. Estate/Station Wagon; wheelbase 297cm, turning circle 13.3m, length 469cm, height 180.5-198.5cm.

Performance: Max speed 118mph/150kmh (manufacturers test specification), speed at 1000rpm in 4th gear 19.1mph/30.8kmh; power to weight ratio from 15.3kg/kW (11.2kg/PS), Hardtop ECE fuel consumption 11.1/15.8/17.0L/100km (25.4/17.9/16.6mpg) [21.2/14.9/13.8US mpg], Estate/Station Wagon 12.7/17.2/18.9L/100km (22.2/16.4/14.9mpg) [18.5/13.7/12.4US mpg].

Performance (Turbo D): Max speed 90mph/145kmh (manufacturers specifications); power to weight ratio from 21.4kg/kW (15.7kg/PS); consumption ECE 10.2/15.1/13.5L/100km (27.7/18.7/20.9mpg) [23.1/15.6/17.4US mpg].

Nissan New Safari/Patrol GR

Off-road Estate/Station Wagon with 6-cylinder 4.2 Litre diesel engine, 2 and 4-wheel drive with reduction. Launched October 1987. Autumn 1988: Version for export with Turbodiesel 2.8 Litre with direct injection.

Nissan Patrol GR

Nissan Patrol

```
3.25 Litre Diesel
70/88kW-94/118hp-95/120PS
Injection Pump/Turbo
```

As petrol/gasoline engine except:
Weight: Kerbweight (DIN) from 1880kg.
Engine data (JIS net): 6-cylinder in-line (83 x 100mm), 3246cm3; compression ratio 21.6:1; 70kW (94hp) [95PS] at 3600rpm, 21.5kW/L (28.8hp/L) [29.3PS/L]; 216Nm (159.3lbft) at 1800rpm.
European version (DIN): Identical data.
With turbocharger: 88kW (118hp) [120PS] at 4000rpm, 27.1kW/L (36.3hp/L) [37PS/L]; 265Nm (195.6lbft) at 2000rpm.
European version (DIN): 81kW (108.5hp) [110PS] at 4000rpm; 255Nm (188.2lbft) at 2000rpm.
Spanish version (DIN): 4-cylinder in-line (92 x 101.6mm), 2702cm3; 51kW (68.3hp) [70PS] at 3600rpm; 152Nm (112.1lbft) at 2000rpm.
Engine construction: Diesel engine. Designated SD 33/SD 33T. Side mounted camshaft; grey cast-iron cylinder head; injection pump under licence Bosch, wet air-cleaner. Battery 12 or 2x12V 80Ah, alternator 60A, cooling system capacity 9L (8.5US qt).
Transmission: 5-speed manual, final drive ratio 4.375; 4.625 (Spanish also 4.111).
Gear ratios: 1st 4.222; 2nd 2.370; 3rd 1.440; 4th 1; 5th 0.825; R 4.622.
Or: 1st 3.897; 2nd 2.370; 3rd 1.440; 4th 1; 5th 0.825; R 4.267.
For 4-cylinder: 1st 4.431; 2nd 2.560; 3rd 1.726; 4th 1.269; 5th 1.
Chassis: Also tyres 31x10.50-15.
Dimensions: Estate/Station Wagon also track 146.5/145.5cm, length 508cm, width 181cm.

```
2.8 Litre 6-cylinder Diesel
85kW-114hp-115PS
Turbo/InjectionPump
```

Body, Weight: Estate/Station Wagon 3-door, 4/5-seater; kerbweight (DIN) from 1835kg, gross permissible 2450kg.
Estate/Station Wagon 5-door, 4/7-seater; kerbweight (DIN) from 1885kg, gross permissible 2700kg.
Engine data (JIS net): 6-cylinder in-line (85 x 83mm), 2826cm3; compression ratio 21.2:1; 85kW (114hp) [115PS] at 4400rpm, 30.1kW/L (40.3hp/L) [40.7PS/L]; 235Nm (173.4lbft) at 2400rpm.
Engine construction: Swirl chamber diesel engine. Designated RD 28T. Hydraulic tappets; 1 overhead camshaft (toothed belt); grey cast iron cylinder head; 7 bearing crankshaft; oil capacity 5.7L (5.4US qt); diesel injection pump; 1 turbocharger. 12V 80Ah battery, 60A alternator. Cooling system capacity approx 10L (9.5US qt).
Transmission (to rear wheels or to all wheels): Engageable all-wheel-drive, free-wheel hubs (automatic/manual), cross country reduction.
a) 5-speed manual, final drive ratio 4.63.
b) Automatic, hydraulic torque converter and 4-speed Planetary gear set. Rear limited slip differential and additional differential locking device.
Gear ratios: Reduction: 1st 1; 2nd 2.02.
a) 5-speed manual: 1st 4.061; 2nd 2.357; 3rd 1.490; 4th 1; 5th 0.862; R 4.245.
b) Automatic, max torque multiplication in converter 2 times, lower in Planetary gear set: 1st 2.784; 2nd 1.544; 3rd 1; 4th 0.694; R 2.275.
Chassis: Chassis with frame rails and cross members, front and rear rigid axles with coil springs, trailing arms and front Panhard rods, optional antiroll bar, double rear trailing arms, Panhard rods and antiroll bar, telescopic dampers. Servo/power assisted disc brakes (ventilated), mechanical handbrake to propellor shaft; power assisted recirculating ball steering; fuel tank 95L (20.9Gal) [25.1US Gal]; tyres 215 R 16 or 31 x 10 R 15 LT, wheel rims 6 or 7J.
Dimensions: Wheelbase 240cm, long version wheelbase 297cm, track 153/153.5cm or 158/158.5cm, clearance 20.5cm, turning circle 13.4m-14.2m. Length 424cm, long version 481cm, width 180cm or 193cm, height 180cm-199.5cm.
Performance: Max speed approx 93mph/150kmh (manufacturers test specification); speed at 1000rpm in 5th gear 21.5mph/34.6kmh; power to weight ratio from 21.6kg/kW (16.0kg/PS); consumption ECE 8.9/13.5/12.4L/100km (31.7/20.9/22.8mpg) [26.4/17.4/19US mpg].

```
4.2 Litre 6-cylinder Diesel
92kW-123hp-125PS
Injection Pump
```

Japanese Version
As 2.8 Litre, except:

Weight: Estate/Station Wagon 3-door from 1920kg, 5-door from 2010kg.

Engine data (JIS net): 6-cylinder in-line (96 x 96mm), 4169cm3; compression ratio 22.7:1; 92kW (123hp) [125PS] at 4000rpm, 22.1kW/L (29.6hp/L) [30.0PS/L]; 273Nm (201.5lbft) at 2000rpm.

Engine construction: Designated TD 42. Side camshaft; with Turbo. 12 V 2x55 or 2x64Ah battery.

Transmission: a) 5-speed manual, final drive ratio 4.111.
b) Automatic, final drive ratio 4.111.

Gear ratios: a) 5-speed manual: 1st 4.556; 2nd 2.625; 3rd 1.519; 4th 1; 5th 0.836; R 4.245.
b) Automatic, as 2.8 Litre.

Chassis: Fuel tank 80L (17.6Gal) [21.1US Gal]; tyres also 6.50-16.

Dimensions: Length 423.5-442cm, long version 480.5-499cm, height 179-198.5cm.

Performance: Max speed approx 93mph/150kmh; speed at 1000rpm in 5th gear 24.7mph/39.7kmh; power to weight ratio from 20.9kg/kW (15.4kg/PS); consumption approx 10-19L/100km (28.2-14.9mpg) [23.5-12.4US mpg].

Nissan New Safari

Nissan Terrano/Pathfinder

Based on light duty off-road leisure time vehicle with engageable all wheel drive and reduction gearbox. Basic model in Japan with 2.6 Litre diesel engine, 2.4 or 3 Litre petrol/gasoline engine for export. Convertible luxury interior with 5-seater. Marketed in the USA as 'Pathfinder'. Debut August 1986.

2.7 Litre Diesel
73/62kW-98/83hp-100/85PS
Turbo/Injection Pump

Body, Weight: 3-door Estate/Station Wagon, 5-seater; kerbweight (DIN) from 1670kg.

Engine data (JIS net): 4-cylinder in-line (96 x 92mm), 2663cm3; compression ratio 21.9:1; 73kW (98hp) [100PS] at 4000rpm, 27.4kW/L (36.7hp/L) [37.6PS/L]; 216Nm (159.4lbft) at 2200rpm.
Without Turbo: Compression ratio 21.8:1; 62kW (83hp) [85PS] at 4300rpm; 177Nm (130.6lbft) at 2200rpm.

Engine construction: Designated TD 27 T/TD 27. Swirl chamber diesel engine. Side-mounted camshaft; grey cast iron cylinder head; crankshaft with 5 bearings; oil capacity approx 5L (4.7US qt); diesel injection pump. Turbocharger. Battery 12V 64Ah, alternator 50/60A; cooling system capacity approx 9L (8.5US qt).

Transmission (to rear wheels or all wheels): Engageable front wheel drive with automatic free-wheel hub. Transfer case with off-road reduction.
a) 5-speed manual, final drive ratio 4.625; without Turbo 4.875.
b) For Turbo: Automatic, hydraulic torque converter and 4-speed Planetary gear set, final drive ratio 4.625.
Optional rear limited slip differential.

Gear ratios: Reduction gear: 1st 1; 2nd 2.020.
a) 5-speed manual: 1st 3.592; 2nd 2.246; 3rd 1.415; 4th 1; 5th 0.821; R 3.657.
b) Automatic: max torque multiplication in converter 2 times, Planetary gear set: 1st 3.027; 2nd 1.619; 3rd 1; OD 0.694; R 2.272.

Chassis: Box-section frame with cross members; front independent suspension with double A-arms and longitudinal torsion bar springs, rear rigid axle with coil springs, double trailing arms and Panhard rod, front and rear antiroll bars, telescopic dampers. Servo/power assisted brakes, front discs (ventilated), rear drums, mechanical handbrake to rear wheels; power assisted recirculating ball steering; fuel tank 80L (17.6Gal) [21.1US Gal]; tyres 215 SR 15, wheels 5.5J.

Dimensions: Wheelbase 265cm, track 144.5/143cm, clearance 21cm, turning circle 11.2m. Length 436.5cm, width 169cm, height 168cm.

Performance: (Turbodiesel) Max speed approx 93mph/150kmh; speed at 1000rpm in 5th gear 21.7mph/34.9kmh; power to weight ratio from 23.6kg/kW (17.2kg/PS); consumption approx 8-15L/100km (35.3-18.8mpg) [29.4- 15.7US mpg].

Nissan Terrano

2.4 Litre
76/74kW-102/99hp-103/101PS
Central-Single Point Injection/Carb

Export model engine:

As 83hp model except:

Weight: Kerbweight (DIN) from 1540kg, gross vehicle weight 2250kg.

Engine data (Catalyst DIN): 4-cylinder in-line (89 x 96cm), 2388cm3; compression ratio 8.3:1; 76kW (102hp) [103PS] at 4800rpm, 31.8kW/L (42.6hp/L) [43.1PS/L]; 186Nm (137.2lbft) at 2400rpm; unleaded regular grade.
Export version: 74kW (99hp) [101PS] at 4800rpm; 177Nm (130.6lbft) at 2800rpm.

Engine construction: Designated Z 24. 1 overhead camshaft (chain); light-alloy cylinder head; oil capacity 5L (4.7US qt); Catalyst version electronic central/single point fuel injection, others 1 downdraught compound carb. Battery 60Ah, alternator 50A, cooling system capacity approx 8L (7.6US qt).

Transmission: 5-speed manual, final drive ratio, 4.625.

Chassis: Tyres 215/70 R 15 or 6.50-15.

Dimensions: Track 142.5/140cm or 142.5/138.5cm. Height 169cm.

Performance: Max speed 93mph/150kmh (manufacturers test specification), speed at 1000rpm in 5th gear 20.4mph/32.9kmh; power to weight ratio from 20.3kg/kW (27.2hp/L) [15.0kg/PS]; consumption ECE 9.6/12.5/16L/100km (29.4/22.6/17.7mpg) [29.4/18.8/14.7US mpg].

3 Litre V6
108kW-145hp-147PS
Central/Single Point Fuel Injection

As 83hp, except:

Weight: Kerbweight (DIN) from 1695kg, gross vehicle weight 2300kg.

Engine data (Catalyst, DIN): 6-cylinder in V 60deg (87 x 83mm), 2960cm3; compression ratio 9.1; 100kW (134hp) [136PS] at 4800rpm, 33.8kW/L (45.3hp/L) [45.9PS/L]; 213Nm (157.2lbft) at 2800rpm.
USA Version (SAE net): 108kW (145hp) [147PS] at 4800rpm; 226Nm (166.8lbft) at 2800rpm.
Japanese Version (JIS net): 103kW (138hp) [140PS] at 4800rpm; 226Nm (166.8lbft) at 2800rpm.

Engine construction: Designated VG 30i. Valves in V, hydraulic tappets, 1 overhead camshaft (toothed belt); light-alloy cylinder head, crankshaft with 4 bearings; oil capacity 4.4L (4.2US qt); electronic central/single point fuel injection. Battery 60Ah, alternator 60A; cooling system capacity approx 10.5L (9.9US qt).

Transmission: a) 5-speed manual, final drive ratio 4.375.
b) Automatic, hydraulic torque converter and 4-speed Planetary gear set, final drive ratio 4.375 or 4.625.

Gear ratios: a) 5-speed manual: 1st 4.061; 2nd 2,357; 3rd 1.490; 4th 1; 5th 0.862; R 4.13.
b) Automatic: Max torque multiplication in converter 2 times, Planetary gear set ratios: 1st 2.842; 2nd 1.542; 3rd 1; OD 0.686; R 2.182.

Chassis: Some models with rear disc brakes; tyres 215 R 15, 215/75 R 15, optional 235/75 R 15 or 31x10.5 R 15, wheels 5.5J or 6J, optional 7J.

Nissan • Oldsmobile

Dimensions: Track 142.5/141cm, 144.5/143cm or 145.5/144cm. Height 167–169.5cm.

Performance: Max speed approx 99mph/160kmh, speed at 1000rpm in 5th gear 21.9mph/35.2kmh; power to weight ratio from 15.7kg/kW (11.5kg/PS); consumption (town/country/mixture) 14.1/9.7/12.1L/100km (20/29.1/23.3mpg) [16.7/24.2/19.4US mpg].

Nissan Terrano V6

OLDSMOBILE — USA

Oldsmobile Division, General Motors, Lansing 21, Michigan USA
Marque affiliated to the General Motors Corporation.

MODEL RANGE
Cutlass Calais – Cutlass Ciera – Cutlass Supreme – Delta 88 – Ninety-Eight Custom Cruiser – Toronado/Trofeo – Silhouette

Oldsmobile Cutlass Calais

Cutlass Calais–Cutlass Calais SL–Cutlass Calais International

Sporty front wheel drive vehicle, with a 2.5 Litre 4–cylinder engine or a 3 Litre V6, 5–speed manual or automatic transmission. Launched August 1984. Modifications to the front and revisions to the 2.5 Litre engine in 1987. 16–valve 2.3 Litre engine introduced in 1988. 1989 with new 3.3 Litre V6 "3300".

Oldsmobile Cutlass Calais SL Coupe

```
2.5 Litre
82kW-110hp-112PS
Central/Single Point Injection
```

Body, Weight (laden):
Cutlass Calais: Coupe 2–door, 5–seater; approx 1140kg. Saloon/Sedan 4–door, 5–seater; approx 1165kg.
Cutlass Calais SL: Coupe 2–door, 5–seater; approx 1150kg. Saloon/Sedan 4–door, 5–seater; approx 1180kg.
Cutlass Calais International; Coupe 2–door, 5–seater; approx 1245kg. Saloon/Sedan 4–door, 5–seater; approx 1270kg.

Engine data (SAE net): 4–cylinder in–line (101.6 x 76.2mm), 2471cm3; compression ratio 8.3:1; 82kW (110hp) [112PS] at 5200rpm, 33.2kW/L (44.5hp/L) [45.3PS/L]; 183Nm (135.1lbft) at 3200rpm; unleaded regular grade.

Engine construction: Designated L68. Transverse front engine; hydraulic tappets, side camshaft (toothed belt); 5 bearing crankshaft; oil capacity 3.8L (3.6US qt); TBI Rochester electronic central/single point injection. Battery 12V 54Ah, alternator 74A; cooling system capacity approx 7.4L (7.0US qt).

Transmission (to all wheels): a) 5–speed manual, final drive ratio 3.35.
b) Automatic THM 125, hydraulic torque converter and 3–speed Planetary gear set, central selector lever, final drive ratio 2.84.

Gear ratios: a) 5–speed manual: 1st 3.73; 2nd 2.04; 3rd 1.45; 4th 1.03; 5th 0.74; R 3.5.
b) Automatic: Max torque multiplication in converter 2.5 times, Planetary gear set ratios: 2.84; 1.6; 1; R 2.07.

Chassis: Integral body. Front auxiliary frame, front McPherson struts and lower A arm, antiroll bar with longitudinal swinging arms, optional antiroll bar, coil springs and telescopic damper front and rear. Servo/power assisted brakes, front discs (ventilated), diameter 24.7cm, rear drums; pedal operated parking brake to rear wheels; power assisted rack and pinion steering; fuel tank 51.5L (11.3Gal) [13.6US qt]; tyres 185R 13, optional 195/70R 14, 205/70R 13, 215/60 R 14, wheel rims 5.5 or 6".

Dimensions: Wheelbase 263.5cm, track 141/40cm, clearance 16cm, turning circle approx 11.9m, load space 13.2cu ft (375dm3). Length 454cm, width 169.5cm, height 133cm.

Performance: Max speed approx 112mph/180kmh, speed at 1000rpm in top gear 28.6mph/46kmh; power to weight ratio from 13.9kg/kW (10.2kg/PS); consumption approx 8–14L/100km (35.3–20.2mpg) [29.4– 16.8US mpg].

Oldsmobile Cutlass Calais SL Sedan

```
2.3 16V
112/138kW-150/185hp-152/187PS
Fuel Injection
```

As 2.5 Litre, except:

Weight: Increased weight 20kg.

Engine data (SAE net): 4–cylinder in–line (92 x 85mm), 2260cm3, compression ratio 9.5:1; 112kW (150hp) [152PS] at 5200rpm, 49.6kW/L (66.5hp/L) [67.3PS/L]; 217Nm (160.1lbft) at 4000rpm; regular grade. Optional compression: 10:1; 138kW (185hp) [187PS] at 6200rpm 217Nm (160lbft) at 5200rpm.

Engine construction: Designated LD 2/LGO.. 4–Valves per cylinder; 2 overhead camshaft (chain); light-alloy cylinder head; Rochester fuel injection. Spark plugs AC FR 3LS; alternator 85/100A; cooling system capacity approx 7.2L (6.8US qt).

Transmission: a) 5–speed manual, final drive ratio 3.61.
b) Automatic, final drive ratio, 2.84; 3.06.

Gear ratios: a) 5–speed manual: 1st 3.50; 2nd 2.05/2.19; 3rd 1.38; 4th 0.94/1.03; 5th 0.72: R 3.41.
b) Automatic: Max torque multiplication in converter 2.5 times, Planetary gear set ratios: 2.84; 1.6; 1; R 2.07.

Performance: Max speed approx 124–137mph/200–220kmh, speed at 1000rpm in 5th gear 27.3mph/43.9kmh; power to weight ratio from 8.4kg/kW (6.2kg/PS); consumption approx 8–15L/100km (35.3– 18.8mpg) [29.4–15.7US mpg].

```
3 Litre V6
119kW-160hp-162PS
Fuel Injection
```

As 2.5 Litre, except:

Weight: Inceased weight 40kg.

Oldsmobile

Engine data (SAE net): 6–cylinder in V 90deg (93.98 x 80.26mm), 3340cm3; compression ratio 9:1; 119kW (160hp) [162PS] at 5200rpm, 35.6kW/L (47.7hp/L) [48.5PS/L]; 251Nm (185.2lbft) at 3200rpm.

Engine construction: Designated LG7. Central camshaft (chain); 4 bearing crankshaft; oil capacity 3.8L (3.6US qt); Rochester electronic fuel injection. Spark plugs AC R44-LTS6; alternator 74A; cooling system capacity approx 9.4L (8.9US qt).

Transmission: Automatic, final drive ratio 2.39.

Chassis: Front and rear antiroll bar.

Performance: Max speed approx 131mph/210kmh, speed at 1000rpm in top gear 29.6mph/47.7kmh; power to weight ratio from 10.1kg/kW (7.4kg/PS); consumption approx 9–15L/100km (31.4–18.8mpg) [26.1–12.5US mpg].

Oldsmobile Cutlass Calais International Series Coupe

Oldsmobile Cutlass Ciera

Ciera SL–Ciera Brougham – Wagon

Front wheel drive with 4–cylinder or V6 engines and automatic transmission. Designated "A–Body", mechanics based on the Compact and X–Bodies. Launched December 1981. Introduction of the Estate/Station Wagon and the 3.8 Litre engine. 1986; 2.8 Litre V6 to replace the 3 Litre V6. For 1989: Modifications to body and new 3.3 Litre V6.

```
2.5 Litre
82kW–110hp–112PS
Central/Single Point Injection
```

Body, Weight: Cutlass Ciera SL: Saloon/Sedan 4–door, 6–seater; kerbweight (DIN) 1255kg. Coupe 2–door, 6–seater; kerbweight (DIN) 1240kg. Estate/Station Wagon 5–door, 6–seater; kerbweight (DIN) 1320kg.

Engine data (SAE net): 4–cylinder in–line (101.6 x 76.2mm), 2471cm3; compression ratio 8.3:1. 82kW (110hp) [112PS] at 5200rpm, 33.2kW/L (44.5hp/L) [45.3PS/L]; 183Nm (135.1lbft) at 3200rpm; unleaded regular grade. Also 73kW (98hp) [99PS].

Engine construction: Designated LR 8. Transverse front engine. Hydraulic tappets, side camshaft (toothed belt); 5 bearing crankshaft; oil capacity 3.8L (3.6US qt); Rochester electronic central/single point injection. Spark plugs AC R44TSX; Battery 12V 45/55Ah, alternator 56–78A; cooling system capacity approx 9.3L (8.8US qt).

Transmission (to all wheels): Automatic THM 125, hydraulic torque converter and 3–speed Planetary gear set, central selector lever or to steering wheel with centre console, final drive ratio 2.84.

Gear ratios: Max torque multiplication in converter 2.35 times, Planetary gear set ratios: 2.84; 1.6; 1; R2.07.

Chassis: Integral body. Front auxiliary frame, front McPherson struts and lower A arm, antiroll bar; rear rigid axle with trailing arm and Panhard rod, coil springs and telescopic damper, antiroll bar. Servo/power assisted brakes, front disc (ventilated), diameter 24.7 or 26.0cm, rear drums; pedal operated parking brake to rear wheels; power assisted rack and pinion steering; fuel tank 59L (13Gal) [15.6US Gal]; tyres 185/75 R 14, optional 195/70 R 14, 215/60 R 14, wheel rims 5.5 or 6".

Dimensions: Wheelbase 266.5cm, track 149/144.5cm, clearance min 14.5cm, turning circle 12.5m, load space 15.9cu ft (450dm3), length 483.5cm, width 176.5cm, height 137.5cm. Estate/Station Wagon: Load space 74.3cu ft (2105dm3), length 493.5cm, height 138.5cm.

Performance: Max speed approx 103-109mph/165-175kmh, speed at 1000rpm in top gear 25.3mph/40.7kmh; power to weight ratio from 15.1kg/kW (11.1kg/PS); consumption approx 9–14L/100km (31.4–20.2mpg) [26.1–16.8US mpg].

Oldsmobile Cutlass Ciera Cruiser Wagon

```
2.8 Litre V6
93kW–125hp–127PS
Fuel Injection
```

As 2.5 Litre, except:

Weight: Increased weight 35kg.

Engine data (SAE net): 6–cylinder in V 60deg (88.9 x 76.2mm), 2838cm3; compression ratio 8.9:1; 93kW (125hp) [127PS] at 4500rpm, 32.8kW/L (44.1hp/L) [44.8PS/L]; 217Nm (160.1lbft) at 3600rpm.

Engine construction: Designated LB 6. 4 bearing crankshaft; central camshaft; Rochester electronic fuel injection. Spark plugs AC R43CTLSE; alternator 66–97A; cooling system capacity 11.8L (11.2US qt).

Transmission: a) Automatic (not available for Estate/Station Wagon) final drive ratio 2.84.
b) 4-speed automatic, final drive ratio 3.33.

Gear ratios: a) Automatic: Max torque multiplication in converter 2.35 times, Planetary gear set ratios; 2.84; 1.6; 1; R 2.07.
b) 4-speed automatic: Max torque multiplication in converter 1.95 times, Planetary gear set ratios: 1st 2.92; 2nd 1.57; 3rd 1; 4th 0.7; R 2.38.

Performance: Max speed approx 112mph/180kmh, speed at 1000rpm in top gear (3.33.1) 30.8mph/49.6kmh; power to weight ratio from 13.7kg/kW (10kg/PS); consumption approx 11–16L/100km (25.7– 17.7mpg) [21.4–14.7US mpg].

Oldsmobile Cutlass Ciera SL Coupe

```
3.3 Litre V6
119kW–160hp–162PS
Fuel Injection
```

As 2.5 Litre, except:

Weight: Increased weight 45kg.

Engine data (SAE net): 6–cylinder in V 90deg (93.98 x 80.26mm), 3340cm3; compression ratio 9:1; 119kW (160hp) [162PS] at 5200rpm, 35.6kW/L (47.7hp/L) [48.5PS/L]; 251Nm (185.2lbft) at 3200rpm.

Oldsmobile

Engine construction: Designated LG 7. Central camshaft (chain); 4 bearing crankshaft; Rochester electronic fuel injection. Spark plugs AC R44-LTS6; alternator 74A; cooling system capacity approx 9.4L (8.9US qt).

Transmission: a) Automatic (for Estate/Station Wagon not available), final drive ratio 2.84.
b) 4-speed manual, final drive ratio 2.84; 3.06.

Gear ratios: a) Automatic, max torque multiplication in converter 2.35 times, Planetary gear set ratios: 2.84; 1.6; 1; R 2.07.
b) 4-speed automatic: max torque multiplication in converter 1.95times, Planetary gear set: 1st 2.92; 2nd 1.57; 3rd 1; 4th 0.7; R 2.38.

Performance: Max speed approx 131mph/210kmh, speed at 1000rpm in 4th gear 36.1mph/58.1kmh; power to weight ratio from 10.8kg/kW (7.9kg/PS); consumption approx 9–15L/100km (31.4–18.8mpg) [26.1– 15.7US mpg].

Oldsmobile Cutlass Ciera International Series Sedan

Oldsmobile Cutlass Supreme

New 2–door Coupe from Oldsmobile with front wheel drive and V6 engine. Launched Autumn 1987. For 1989 with 3.1 Litre V6.

Oldsmobile Cutlass Supreme SL

> 2.8/3.1 Litre V6
> 97/103kW–130/138hp–132/140PS
> Fuel Injection

Body, Weight (laden); Coupe 2–door, 4/6–seater; approx 1400kg.

Engine data (SAE net): 6–cylinder in V 60deg (88.9 X 76.2mm), 2838cm3; compression ratio 8.9:1; 97kW (130hp) [132PS] at 4500rpm, 34.2kW/L (45.8hp/L) [46.5PS/L]; 231Nm (170.1lbft) at 3600rpm; unleaded regular grade.
Latest: (88.9 x 84mm), 3128cm3; compression ratio 8.8:1; 103kW (138hp) [140PS] at 4800rpm, 32.9kW/L (44.1hp/L) [44.8PS/L]; 248Nm (183lbft) at 3600rpm.

Engine construction: Designated LB 6/LH O. Transverse front engine; hydraulic tappets, central camshaft (chain); 4 bearing crankshaft; light–alloy cylinder head; oil capacity 3.8L (3.6US qt); Rochester electronic fuel injection. Spark plugs AC R43CTLSE; battery 12V 54/69Ah, alternator 108/120A, cooling system capacity, 10.7L (10.1US qt).

Transmission (to all wheels): a) 5–speed manual, final drive ratio 3.61.
b) Automatic THM 440-T4; hydraulic torque converter and 4-speed Planetary gear set, final drive ratio 3.33.

Gear ratios: a) 5–speed manual: 1st 3.50; 2nd 2.05; 3rd 1.38; 4th 0.94; 5th 0.72; R 3.42.
b) Automatic: Max torque multiplication in converter 1.95 times, Planetary gear set ratios: 2.92; 1.56; 1; 0.7 R 2.38.

Chassis: Integral body with front auxiliary frame; independent suspension front and rear; front McPherson struts (coil springs), lower A arm and antiroll bar, rear control arm, shock absorber strut, transverse leaf spring (fibre glass), antiroll bar, optional level control system; telescopic damper. Servo/power assisted disc brakes (ventilated), optional with ABS (Delco/Moraine), diameter front 26.7cm, rear 25.6cm; pedal operated parking brake to rear wheels, power assisted rack and pinion steering, fuel tank 64.5L (14.2Gal) [17.0US Gal], tyres 195/75 R 14; 205/70 R 14, 215/65 R 15, 215/60 VR 16, wheel rims 5.5 or 6".

Dimensions: Wheelbase 273cm, track 151/147cm, clearance 15cm, turning circle 11.9m, load space 15.5cu ft (440dm3), length 488cm, width 180.5cm, height 134cm.

Performance: Max speed approx 112-118mph/180-190kmh; speed at 1000rpm in 5th gear 28.2mph/45.4kmh; power to weight ratio from 13.6kg/kW (10kg/PS); consumption approx 9–16L/100km (31.4– 17.7mpg) [26.1-14.7US mpg].

Oldsmobile Cutlass Supreme International Series

Oldsmobile 88 Royale

Saloon/Sedan and Coupe, with V6 engine and front wheel drive, automatic transmission and overdrive. 1987: 3.8 Litre V6. 1989: also available with 165hp engine.

Oldsmobile Delta 88 Royale Coupe

> 3.8 Litre V6
> 123kW–165hp–167PS
> Fuel Injection

Body, Weight (laden):
Delta 88 Royale: Coupe 2–door, 6–seater; 1460kg. Saloon/Sedan 4–door, 6–seater; 1480kg.
Delta 88 Royale Brougham: Coupe 2–door, 6–seater; 1475kg. Saloon/Sedan 4–door, 6–seater; 1490kg.

Engine data (SAE net): 6–cylinder in V 90deg (96.52 x 86.36mm), 3791cm3; compression ratio 8.5:1; 123kW (165hp) [167PS] at 5200rpm, 32.4kW/L (43.4hp/L) [44.1PS/L]; 285Nm (210.3lbft) at 2000rpm; unleaded regular grade.

Engine construction: Designated LN 3 "3800". Transverse front engine. Hydraulic tappets, central camshaft (chain); 4 bearing crankshaft; 1 counter-balance shaft; oil capacity 3.8L (3.6US qt); Bosch electronic fuel injection. Spark plugs AC R44LTS; battery 12V 54/69Ah, alternator 105a; cooling system capacity 11.1 (10.5US qt).

Transmission (to front wheels): Automatic; "Turbo–Hydra–Matic" 440 T4, hydraulic torque converter and Planetary gear set, 4–speed/overdrive, central selector lever or steering wheel, final drive ratio 2.84; 2.97.

Gear ratios: Max torque multiplication in converter 1.64 times, Planetary gear set ratios: 2.92; 1.57; 1; OD 0.7; R 2.38.

Oldsmobile

Chassis: Integral body with front auxiliary frame; independent suspension front and rear; front McPherson strut, lower A arm and antiroll bar, rear shock absorber strut, lower A arm and antiroll bar; coil springs and telescopic damper, optional level control system. Servo/power assisted brakes, optional with ABS (ITT Teves), front discs (ventilated), diameter 25.6cm, rear drums, optional ABS; pedal operated parking brake to rear wheels; power assisted rack and pinion steering; fuel tank 68L (14.9Gal) [18.0US Gal]; tyres 205/70 R 14, 215/65 R 15, wheel rims 6J.

Dimensions: Wheelbase 281.5cm, track 153/152cm, clearance 15cm, turning circle 13.0m, load space 16.2cu ft (460dm3), length 499cm, width 184cm, height 138cm, Coupe 137cm.

Performance: Max speed approx 121mph/195kmh, speed at 1000rpm in top gear 26.5mph/42.6kmh; power to weight ratio from 11.9kg/kW (8.7 kg/PS); consumption approx 11–17L/100km (25.7–16.6mpg) [21.4–13.8US mpg].

Oldsmobile Delta 88 Royale Brougham

Oldsmobile Ninety-Eight

Regency – Touring – Brougham

Luxury Saloon/Sedan, front wheel drive, V6 engine, automatic and overdrive. 1986: 3.8 Litre engine. 1988: with increased performance. 1989 with improvements to equipment.

Oldsmobile Ninety-Eight Regency Sedan

```
3.8 Litre V6
123kW–165hp–167PS
Fuel Injection
```

Body, Weight (laden):
Regency: Saloon/Sedan 4–door, 6–seater; 1510kg.
Brougham: Saloon/Sedan 4–door, 6–seater; 1520kg.
Touring: Saloon/Sedan 4-ddor, 6–seater; 1590kg.

Engine data (SAE net): 6–cylinder in V 90deg (96.52 x 86.36mm), 3791cm3; compression ratio 8.5:1; 123kW (165hp) [167PS] at 5200rpm, 32.4kW/L (43.4hp/L) [44.1 PS/L]; 285Nm (210.3lbft) at 2000rpm; unleaded regular grade.

Engine construction: Designated LN 3 "3800". Transverse front engine. Hydraulic tappets, central camshaft (chain); 4 bearing crankshaft; 1 counter–balance shaft; oil capacity 3.8L (3.6US qt); Bosch electronic fuel injection. Spark plugs AC R44LTS; battery 12V 54/69Ah, alternator 105A; cooling system capacity 11.7L (11.1US qt).

Transmission (to front wheels): Automatic; "Turbo Hydra–Matic" 440 T4, hydraulic torque converter and 4-speed Planetary gear set, central selector lever or to steering wheel, final drive ratio 2.84; 2.97.

Gear ratios: Max torque multiplication in converter 1.68 times, Planetary gear set ratios: 2.92; 11.57; 1; OD 0.7; R 2.38.

Chassis: Integral body with front auxiliary frame; independent suspension front and rear; front McPherson struts, lower A arm and antiroll bar, rear shock absorber strut, lower A arm and antiroll bar; coil springs, telescopic damper, optional level control system. Servo/power assisted brakes, front discs (ventilated), diameter 25.6cm, rear drums, optional with ABS (ITT Teves); pedal operated parking brake to rear wheels; power assisted rack and pinion steering; fuel tank 68L (14.9Gal) [18.0US Gal] ; tyres 205/75R 14, for touring 215/65 R 15, 215/60 VR 16, wheel rims 6/7J.

Dimensions: Wheelbase 281.5cm, track 153/152cm, clearance 15cm, turning circle 13.0m, load space 16.4cu ft (465dm3), length 499cm, width 184cm, height 139cm.

Performance: Max speed approx 121mph/195kmh; speed at 1000rpm in direct gear 26.5mph/42.6kmh; power to weight ratio from 12.3kg/kW (8.7kg/PS); consumption approx 11–17L/100km (25.7–16.6mpg) [21.4– 13.8US mpg].

Oldsmobile Ninety-Eight Touring Sedan

Oldsmobile Custom Cruiser Wagon

Estate/Station Wagon base on the Delta 88 Custom Cruiser, rear wheel drive, 5 Litre V8 engine.

```
5 Litre V8
104kW–140hp–142PS
1 4V Carb
```

Body, Weight (laden): Estate/Station Wagon 5–door, 6–seater 1915kg.

Engine data (SAE net): 8–cylinder in V 90deg (96.52 x 85.98mm), 5033cm3, compression ratio 8:1; 104kW (140hp) [142PS] at 3200rpm, 20.7kW/L (27.7hp/L) [28.2PS/L]; 346Nm (255.3lbft) at 2000rpm; unleaded regular grade.

Engine construction: Designated LV 2. Hydraulic tappets, central camshaft (toothed belt); 5 bearing crankshaft; oil capacity 4.7L (4.4US qt); 1 Rochester downdraught carb, spark plugs AC FR3LS6. Battery 12V 54Ah, alternator 100A; cooling system capacity, approx 14.5L (13.7US qt).

Transmission (to rear wheels): Automatic; "Turbo Hydra–Matic" 440 T4, hydraulic torque converter and Planetary gear set, 4 speed/overdrive, central selector lever or to steering wheel, final drive ratio 2.93; 3.23.

Gear ratios: Max torque multiplication in converter 1.9 times; Planetary gear set ratios: 2.74; 1.57; 1; OD 0.67; R 2.07.

Chassis: Box section frame; front overhead trapeze A arm, lower control arm with elastic positional tension strut and coil springs, front antiroll bar; rear rigid axle with coil springs, lower trailing arm and upper differential leading semi trailing arm, telescopic damper. Optional pneumatic level control system to rear. Servo/power assisted brakes, front discs (ventilated), diameter 30.1cm, rear drums; pedal operated parking brake to rear wheels; power assisted recirculating ball steering, with variable gear reduction, fuel tank 83L (18.2Gal) [21.9US Gal]; tyres 225/75 R 15, wheel rims 7J.

Dimensions: Wheelbase 294.5cm, track 158/1163cm, clearance 16cm, turning circle 13m, load space 87.2cu ft (2470dm3), length 559.5cm, width 203cm, height 148.5cm.

Oldsmobile

Performance: Max speed approx 99–106mph/160–170kmh, speed at 1000rpm in top gear 41.5mph/66.9kmh; power to weight ratio from 18.4kg/kW (13.5kg/PS); consumption approx 12–19L/100km (23.5–14.9mpg) [19.6–12.4US mpg].

Oldsmobile Custom Cruiser Wagon

Oldsmobile Toronado/Trofeo

Luxury Coupe with front wheel drive. Autumn 1985: new compact body, transverse V6 engine. 1988: improved performance. 1989 with sporty luxurious version "Trofeo".

```
3.8 Litre V6
123kW–165hp–167PS
Fuel Injection
```

Body, Weight (laden): Coupe 2-door, 4/5-seater; approx 1525kg, Trofeo 1555kg.
Engine data (SAE net): 6-cylinder in-line in V 90deg (96.52 x 86.36mm), 3791cm3; compression ratio 8.5:1; 123kW (165hp) [167PS] at 5200rpm, 32.4kW/L (43.4hp/L) [44.1PS/L]; 285Nm (210.3lbft) at 2000rpm; unleaded regular grade.
Engine construction: Designated LN 3 "3800". Transverse front engine. Hydraulic tappets, central camshaft (chain); 4 bearing crankshaft; 1 counter-balance shaft; oil capacity 3.8L (3.6US qt); electronic fuel injection. Battery 12V 54/69Ah, alternator 120A; cooling system capacity, approx 11.3L (10.7US qt).
Transmission (to front wheels): Automatic; "Turbo Hydra-Matic" 440 T4; hydraulic torque converter and Planetary gear set, 4 speed/overdrive, central selector lever or to steering wheel, final drive ratio 2.84; 2.97.
Gear ratios: Max torque multiplication in converter 1.67 times, Planetary gear set ratios: 2.92; 1.57; 1; OD 0.67; R 2.38.
Chassis: Integral body with front auxiliary frame; independent suspension front and rear; front McPherson struts (coil springs), lower semi trailing and control arm, rear control arm, shock absorber strut, fibre glass transverse leaf spring, optional antiroll bar, level control system; telescopic damper. Servo/power assisted disc brakes (ventilated), optional with ABS (Teves), front disc diameter 26.0cm, rear 25.4cm, optional ABS; pedal operated parking brake to rear wheels; power assisted rack and pinion steering; fuel tank 71L (15.6Gal) [18.8US Gal]; tyres 205/70R 15, 215/65R 15, wheel rims 6J.
Dimensions: Wheelbase 274.5cm, track 152/152cm, clearance 15cm, turning circle 12.8m, load space 14.1cu ft (400dm3), length 476cm, width 180cm, height 134.5cm.
Performance: Max speed 121mph/195kmh; speed at 1000rpm in top gear (2.84) 26.7mph/43kmh; power to weight ratio from 12.4kg/kW (9.1kg/PS); consumption approx 11-17L/100km (25.7-16.6mpg) [21.4-13.8US mpg].

Oldsmobile Toronado

Oldsmobile Silhouette

New model. Pilot build and multi-purpose body of GM. Fibre glass body, 3 side doors and 1 tail gate, 5-7 seater; 3.1 Litre V6 front wheel drive, automatic. Provisional details and data incomplete.

Oldsmobile Silhouette

```
3.1 Litre V6
90kW-120hp-122PS
Central/Single Point Injection
```

Body, Weight: Estate/Station Wagon 3-door with tail gate, 5/7-seater; kerbweight approx 1570kg.
Engine data (SAE net): 6-cylinder in V 60deg (88.9 x 84mm), 3128cm3; compression ratio 8.8:1; 90kW (120hp) [122PS] at 4500rpm, 28.8kW/L (38.6hp/L) [39PS/L]; 231Nm (170.1lbft) at 3200rpm; unleaded regular grade.
Engine construction: Transverse front engine. Hydraulic tappets, central camshaft (chain); 4 bearing crankshaft; light-alloy cylinder head; 4 bearing crankshaft; light-alloy cylinder block; oil capacity 3.8L (3.6US qt); Rochester electronic central fuel injection. Spark plugs AC R43 CTLSE; battery 12V 54/69Ah, alternator 108/120A; cooling system capacity approx 10.7L (10.1US qt).
Transmission (to front wheels): Automatic THM 125, hydraulic torque converter and 3-speed Planetary gear set, selector lever to centre console, final drive ratio 2.84.
Gear ratios: Max torque multiplication 2.35times, Planetary gear set: 2.84; 1.6; R 2.07.
Chassis: Box type frame with cross member; front independent suspension with coil springs, A arm and antiroll bar; rear coil springs, trailing arm, optional rear antiroll bar; telescopic damper. Servo/power assisted brakes ventilated, front disc diameter 26.7cm, rear drums, pedal operated parking brake to rear wheels; Power assisted rack and pinion steering; fuel tank 76L (16.7Gal) [20.1US Gal]; tyres 205/70 R 14, 195/70 R 15, wheel rims 6J.
Dimensions: Wheelbase 279cm, track 155/152cm, clearance 18cm, turning circle 12.5m, load space 123.6cu ft (3500dm3), length 491cm, width 183cm, height 164cm.
Performance: Max speed over 103mph/165kmh, speed at 1000rpm in top gear 26mph/41kmh; power to weight ratio from 17.4kg/kW (12.9kg/PS); consumption (touring) approx 10-16L/100km (28.2-17.7mpg) [23.5-14.7US mpg].

Oldsmobile Silhouette

Opel

OPEL   D

Adam Opel AG, Russelsheim, Germany

Part of General Motors. American–European market vehicles

MODEL RANGE

Corsa – Kadett – Vectra – Omega - Senator

Opel Corsa

Small car, with front wheel drive, engines from 1 to 1.6 Litre, 4 or 5–speed transmission, hatchback or notchback. Launched September 1982. April 1985: available with 4 or 5–doors. Frankfurt 1987: also available with a 99hp 1.6 Litre engine and 1.5 Litre diesel engine. 1988: introduction of the turbodiesel.

1 Litre S
33kW–44hp–45PS
1 Carb

Body, Weight: Saloon/Sedan Corsa 3/5–door, 5–seater; kerbweight (DIN) 740 – 765kg, gross vehicle weight 1220 – 1245kg. Saloon/Sedan Corsa 22/4–door, 5–seater; kerbweight (DIN) 740 – 765kg, gross vehicle weight 1220 – 1245kg.

Engine data (DIN): 4–cylinder in–line (72 x 61mm), 993cm; compression ratio 9.2:1; 33kW (44hp) [45PS] at 5400rpm, 33.3kW/L (44.6hp/L) [45.3PS/L]; 68Nm (50.2lbft) at 2600 – 3800rpm; leaded premium grade.

Engine construction: Transverse engine, side camshaft (chain); 3 bearing crankshaft; oil capacity 2.75L (2.6US qt); 1 Weber downdraught carb 32 TL. Battery 12V 36Ah, alternator 55A; cooling system capacity, approx 5.5L (5.2US qt).

Transmission (to front wheels): a) 4–speed manual, floor shift, final drive ratio, 3.94.
b) 5–speed manual, final drive ratio 4.18.

Gear ratios: a) 4–speed manual: 1st 3.55; 2nd 1.96; 3rd 1.3; 4th 0.89; R 3.18 or 3.31.
b) 5–speed manual: 1st 3.55; 2nd 1.96; 3rd 1.3; 4th 0.89; 5th 0.71; R 3.18 or 3.31.

Chassis: Integral body, front control arm and trailing arm and McPherson struts (negative camber), rear trailing arm, front and rear coil springs, telescopic damper. Servo/power assisted brakes, front discs, diameter 23.6cm, rear drums; mechanical handbrake to rear wheels; rack and pinion steering; fuel tank 42L (9.2Gal) [11.1US Gal]; tyres 145 SR 13, optional 165/70 SR 14, wheel rims 4.5/5J.

Dimensions: Wheelbase 234.5cm, track 132/130.5cm, clearance 14cm, turning circle 10m, load space (VDA) 8/29.8cu ft (225/845dm3), length 362cm, width 153cm, height 136.5cm. Corsa notchback; load space 18.2cu ft (430dm3); length 395.5cm, width 154cm, height 136cm.

Performance: Max speed 89mph/143kmh (manufacturers test specification), speed at 1000rpm in 4th gear 18.3mph/29.4kmh; acceleration 0 – 62mph/100kmh 19.5secs, 5–speed 19secs; power to weight ratio from 22.4 kg/kW (16.4kg/PS); consumption ECE 4.9/6.6/7.2L/100km (57.6/42.8/39.2mpg) [48.0/35.6/32.7US mpg], 5–speed 4.7/6.4/7.3L/100km (60.1/44.1/38.7mpg) [50.0/36.8/32.2US mpg].

Opel Corsa GL

1.2 Litre S/N
40/33kW–53/44hp–54/45PS
1 Carb

As 1 litre, except:

Weight: Unladen weight from 755/780kg, gross vehicle weight 1235/1260kg.

Engine data (DIN): 4–cylinder in–line (77.8 x 62.9mm), 1196cm3; 40kW (53hp) [54PS] at 5600rpm, 33.4kW/L (44.8hp/L) [45.1PS/L]; 90Nm (66.4lbft) at 2200rpm. Version for regular grade: (79 x 61mm), 1196cm3, compression ratio 8:1; 33kW (44hp) [45PS] at 5000rpm, 27.7kW/L (37.1hp/L) [37.6PS/L]; 80Nm (59lbft) at 2200-2600rpm.

Engine construction: Light–alloy cylinder head, hydraulic tappets, 1 overhead camshaft (toothed belt); 5 bearing crankshaft; (Version regular grade: side camshaft with chain, 3 bearing crankshaft); oil capacity 3L (2.8US qt); 1 Pierburg downdraught carb 1B1. Alternator 55, optional 65A; cooling system capacity, approx 6.1L (5.8US qt).

Transmission: a) 4–speed manual, final drive ratio 3.74; 3.94.
b) 5–speed manual, final drive ratio 3.94; 4.18.

Chassis: 2–4 door; front and rear antiroll bars.

Performance: Max speed 95mph/152kmh, 1.2N 89mph/143kmh (manufacturers test specification), speed at 1000rpm in 4th gear 19.3mph/31.1kmh; acceleration 0 – 62mph/100kmh 16.5secs, 5–speed 16secs, 1.2N 18.0secs; power to weight ratio from 18.9kg/kW (14kg/PS); consumption ECE 4.9/6.5/7.7L/100km (57.6/43.5/36.7mpg) [48.0/36.2/30.5US mpg], 5–speed 4.7/6.3/7.91L/100km (60.1/44.8/35.8mpg) [50.0/37.3/29.8US mpg], 1.2N – 5.4/7.2/8.1 L/100km (52.3/39.2/34.9mpg) [43.6/32.7/29.0US mpg].

Opel Corsa GL

1.3 Litre S
51/44kW–68/59hp–69/60PS
1 2V Carb/Central–Single Point Injection

As 1 Litre, except:

Weight: Unladen weight from 765/805kg, gross vehicle weight 1245/1270kg.

Engine data (DIN): 4–cylinder in–line (75 x 73.4mm), 1297cm3; compression ratio 9.2:1; 51kW (68hp) [69PS] at 5800rpm, 39.3kW/L (45.4hp/L) [53.2PS/L]; 101Nm (74.5lbft) at 3800–4200rpm.
With Catalyst: (central/single point injection); compression ratio 9.01, 44kW (59hp) [60PS] at 5600rpm, 33.9kW/L (45.4hp/L) [46.3PS/L]; 96Nm (70.8lbft) at 3400rpm; unleaded regular grade.
Without Catalyst (with carb): Compression ratio 8.2:1.

Engine construction: Light–alloy cylinder head, hydraulic tappets, 1 overhead camshaft (toothed belt); 5 bearing crankshaft; oil capacity 3L (2.8US qt); 1 Pierburg/Solex downdraught compound carb 2E3. Catalyst, Multec central injection. Cooling system capacity, approx 6.1L (5.8US qt).

Transmission: a) 4-speed manual, final drive ratio 3.94.
b) 5-speed manual, final drive ratio 3.94; 4.18.

Chassis: Front and rear antiroll bar.

Performance: Max speed 102mph/165kmh, Catalyst 96mph/155kmh (manufacturers test specification), speed at 1000rpm in 5th gear 23mph/37.1kmh; acceleration 0 – 62mph/100kmh 13secs, Catalyst 15.0secs; power to weight ratio from 14.8kg/kW (11.1kg/PS); consumption ECE 4.7/6.3/8.6L/100km (60.1/44.8/32.8mpg) [50.0/37.3/27.4US mpg], Catalyst 5.0/6.6/8.9L/100km (56.5/42.8/31.7mpg) [47.0/35.6/26.4US mpg].

1.6 Litre
74/53kW–99/71hp–100/72PS
Fuel Injection

As 1 litre, except:

Weight: Unladen weight from 820kg, gross 1260kg.

Engine data (DIN): 4–cylinder in–line (79 x 81.5mm), 1598cm3; compression ratio 10:1; 74kW (99hp) [100PS] at 5600rpm, 46.3kW/L (62hp/L) [62.6PS/L]; 135Nm (99.6lbft) at 3400rpm; unleaded premium grade.

Opel

With Catalyst (central/single point injection): Compression 9.2:1; 53kW (71hp) [72PS] at 5200rpm, 33.2kW/L (44.5hp/L) [45.1PS/L]; 125Nm (92.3lbft) at 3200rpm; unleaded regular grade.

Engine construction: Light–alloy cylinder head; hydraulic tappets; 1 overhead camshaft (toothed belt); 5 bearing crankshaft; oil capacity 3.5L (3.3US qt); electronic Bosch LE– Jetronic fuel injection 3.1L (2.9US qt). Alternator 55A optional 65A; cooling system capacity, approx 6.1L (5.8US qt).

Transmission: 5–speed manual, final drive ratio 3.74; 3.94.

Gear ratios: 1st 3.55; 2nd 1.96; 3rd 1.3; 4th 0.89; 5th 0.71; R 3.18 or 3.31.

Chassis: Front and rear antiroll bar; tyres 175/65 HR 14, wheel rims 5J.

Performance: Max speed 117mph/188kmh, Catalyst 104mph/168kmh, speed at 1000rpm in 5th gear 19.9mph/32.0kmh; acceleration 0 – 62mph/100kmh 9.5secs, Catalyst 12.0secs; power to weight ratio from 11.1kg/kW (8.2kg/PS); consumption DIN 5.5/7.0/9.2L/100km (51.4/40.4/30.7mpg) [42.8/33.6/25.6US mpg], Catalyst 5.6/7.5/8.7L/100km (50.4/37.7/32.5mpg) [42.0/31.4/27.0US mpg].

Opel Corsa GSi

```
1.5L Diesel
37/49kW–49/66hp–50/67PS
Injection Pump/Turbo
```

As 1 litre, except:

Weight: Unladen weight from 835/875kg, gross 1315/1340kg.

Engine data (JIS): 4–cylinder in–line (76 x 82mm), 1488cm3; compression ratio 23:1; 37kW (49hp) [50PS] at 4800rpm, 24.9kW/L (33.4hp/L) [33.6PS/L]; 90Nm (66.4lbft) at 3000rpm.

With Turbo: Compression ratio 22:1; 49kW (66hp) [67PS] at 4600rpm; 32.9kW/L (44.1hp/L) [45PS/L]; 132Nm (97.4lbft) at 2600rpm.

Opel Corsa 1.5 TD

Engine construction: Designated Isuzu 4EC1. Diesel engine pre–combustion chamber; 1 overhead camshaft (toothed belt); 5 bearing crankshaft; Bosch diesel injection pump VE. Battery 12V 66Ah, alternator 70A. Optional: Exhaust turbocharger.

Transmission: 5–speed manual, final drive ratio 3.74.

Gear ratios: 1st 3.55; 2nd 1.96; 3rd 1.3; 4th 0.89; 5th 0.71; R 3.18 or 3.31.

Performance: Max speed 94mph/151kmh, TD 103mph/166kmh (manufacturers test specification), speed at 1000rpm in 5th gear 24.2mph/39.2kmh; acceleration 0 – 62mph/100kmh 17.5secs, TD 13.0secs; power to weight ratio from 17.0kg/kW (12.5kg/PS); consumption ECE 3.9/5.5/5.6L/100km (72.4/51.4/50.4mpg) [60.3/42.8/42.0US mpg]. TD 4.0/5.6/5.8L/100km (70.6/50.4/48.7mpg) [58.8/42.0/40.6US mpg].

Opel Kadett

LS – GL – GLS – GT – GSi – Caravan – Diesel

Spacious middle class car, with transverse engine and front wheel drive. Available as Saloon/Sedan or Estate/Station Wagon, 3/5– doors. Available with engines from 1.3 to 2 Litre and 1.6 Litre diesel. Launched August 1984. Frankfurt 1985: introduction of the 4–door notchback, in 1985 introduction of the GSi convertible. Autumn 1986: 2 Litre IAA. 1987: 16V engine. January 1989 with modifications to body and interior, 1.7 Litre diesel.

Opel Kadett LS

```
1.3 Litre S
44kW–59hp–60PS
Carb/Central–Single Point Injection
```

Body, Weight: Saloon/Sedan, 3/5door, 5–seater; kerbweight (DIN) from 850/870kg, gross vehicle weight 1345/1365kg. Saloon/Sedan, 4–door, 5–seater; kerbweight (DIN) 855kg, gross vehicle weight 1365kg. Estate/Station Wagon 3/5–door, 5–seater; kerbweight (DIN) 895/915kg, gross vehicle weight 1420kg. Automatic heavier by 35kg.

Engine data (Catalyst, DIN): 4–cylinder in–line (75 x 73.4mm), 1297cm3; compression ratio 9:1; 44kW (59hp) [60PS] at 5600rpm, 33.9kW/L (45.4hp/L) [46.3PS/L]; 96Nm (71lbft) from 3400rpm; unleaded regular grade.
Without Catalyst (OHV, carb): Compression ratio 8.2.1.
Certain countries: (79 x 61mm), 1196cm3; compression ratio 9:1; 40kW (54hp) [55PS] at 5600rpm; 84Nm (62bft) at 3600rpm; leaded premium grade.

Engine construction: Transverse front engine. Light–alloy cylinder head, hydraulic tappets, 1 overhead camshaft (toothed belt); 5 bearing crankshaft; (version 49hp) side camshaft with chain, 3 bearing crankshaft); oil capacity 3L (2.8US qt); Rochester electronic central injection, without Catalyst; 1 Pierburg 1B1 carb. Battery 12V 36/44Ah; alternator 55/65A; cooling system capacity, approx 7L (6.6US qt).

Transmission (to front wheels): a) 4–speed manual, final drive ratio 3.94, Estate/Station Wagon 4.18; optional limited slip differential.
b) 5–speed manual, final drive ratio 4.18.

Gear ratios: a) 4–speed manual: 1st 3.55; 2nd 1.96; 3rd 1.3; 4th 0.89; R 3.18 or 3.31.
b) 5–speed manual: 1st 3.55; 2nd 1.96; 3rd 1.3; 4th 0.89; 5th 0.71; R 3.31.

Chassis: Integral body; front transverse arm and A arm, McPherson struts and coil springs (negative camber), rear semi–rigid axle (trailing arms), front and rear coil springs, telescopic damper, front and rear antiroll bar. Servo/power assisted brakes, front discs, diameter 23.6cm, rear drums; mechanical handbrake to rear wheels; rack and pinion steering; fuel tank 52L (11.4Gal) [13.7US Gal], Estate/Station Wagon 50L (11.0Gal) [13.2US mpg]; tyres 155 TR 13, 175/70 TR 13, 175/65 TR 14, wheel rims 5, 5.5J.

Dimensions: Wheelbase 252cm, track 140/140.5cm, clearance min 13.5cm, turning circle 10.5m, load space (VDA) 13.8–35.3cu ft (390–1000dm3), length 400cm, width 166.5cm, height 140cm. Notchback Saloon/Sedan: Load space 19.4cu ft (550dm3), length 422cm, width 166cm. Estate/Station Wagon: Load space (VDA) 16.6–53.7cu ft (470– 1520dm3), length 423cm, height 143cm.

Opel

Performance: Max speed 99mph/160kmh (manufacturers test specification), speed at 1000rpm in 5th gear 22.2mph/35.8kmh; acceleration 0 – 62mph/100kmh 15secs, Catalyst 16.5secs, power to weight ratio from 19.3kg/kW (14.2kg/PS); consumption DIN 5th gear 5.2/6.8/9.1L/100km (54.3/41.5/31mpg) [45.2/34.6/25.8US mpg], Catalyst 5.2/6.8/8.9L/100km (54.3/41.5/31.7mpg) [45.2/34.6/26.47US mpg].

```
1.3 Litre S
55kW–74hp–75PS
1 2V Carb
```

As 1.3 Litre, except:

Engine data (DIN): 4–cylinder in–line (75 x 73.4mm), 1297cm3; compresion ratio 9.2:1; 55kW (74hp) [75PS] at 5800rpm, 42.4kW/L (56.8hp/L) [57.8PS/L]; 101Nm (74.5lbft) at 4200rpm; leaded premium grade.
Optional for certain exports: 51kW (68hp) [69PS] at 5800rpm; 97Nm (71.6lbft) at 4200rpm; or 52kW (70hp) [71PS].

Engine construction: 1 Pierburg downdraught compound carb 2 E. Cooling system capacity, approx 7L (6.6US qt).

Transmission: a) 4–speed manual, final drive ratio 3.94; Estate/Station Wagon 4.18.
b) 5–speed manual, final drive ratio 4.18.
Optional limited slip differential for 4 and 5-speed.

Performance: Max speed 106mph/170kmh (automatic 103mph/165kmh) (manufacturers test specification); acceleration 0 – 62mph/100kmh, 13.0secs, automatic 15.5secs; power to weight ratio from 15.5kg/kW (11.4kg/PS); consumption DIN 5.2/6.7/8.7L/100km, (54.3/42.2/32.5mpg) [45.2/35.1/27.0US mpg], 5-speed 5.0/6.5/8.9L/100km (56.5/43.5/31.7mpg) [47.0/36.2/26.4US mpg]. Automatic 6.2/7.7/9.2L/100km (45.6/36.7/30.7mpg) [37.9/30.5/25.6US mpg].

Opel Kadett GL Caravan

```
1.6 Litre S
60/55kW–80/74hp–82/75PS
1 2V Carb
```

As 1.3 Litre, except:

Body, Weight: Cabriolet/Convertible 2–door, 5–seater; kerbweight (DIN) from 985kg; Remaining 1.6 Litre engine derivatives add 35kg.

Engine data (Catalyst DIN): 4–cylinder in–line (79 x 81.5mm), 1598cm3; compression ratio 9.2:1; 55kW (74hp) [75PS] at 5200rpm, 34.4kW/L (46.1hp/L) [46.9PS/L]; 125Nm (92lbft) at 3200rpm; unleaded premium grade.
Without Catalyst : 125Nm (92.2lbft) at 3200rpm.
Certain countries: Compression ratio 10:1; 60kW (80hp) [82PS] 130Nm (96lbft); leaded premium grade.

Engine construction: Oil capacity 3.5L (3.3US qt); 1 Pierburg downdraught compound carb 2E. Battery 12V 44/55Ah; cooling system capacity approx 6.4L (6.1US qt).

Transmission: a) 5-speed manual, final drive ratio 3.43.
b) Automatic THM 125 hydraulic torque converter and 3-speed Planetary gear set; final drive ratio 3.74, Estate/Station Wagon 3.94.

Gear ratios: a) 5-speed manual: 1st 3.55; 2nd 1.96; 3rd 1.3; 4th 0.89; 5th 0.71; R 3.31.
b) Automatic: Max torque multiplication in converter 2.4 times, Planetary gear set 2.84; 1.6; 1; R 2.07.

Performance: Max speed 106mph/170kmh, Catalyst and automatic 103mph/165kmh, speed at 1000rpm in 5th gear 27mph/43.5kmh; acceleration 0 – 62mph/100kmh 13.0secs, automatic 15.5secs; power to weight ratio from 15.8kg/kW (11.6kg/PS); consumption DIN 5.0/6.8/8.3L/100km (56.5/41.5/34mpg) [47/34.6/28.3US mpg], automatic 6.1/8.2/9.2L/100km (46.3/34.4/30.7mpg) [38.6/28.7/25.6US mpg].

Opel Kadett GL

```
1.8 Litre
62/82kW-83/110hp-84/112PS
Fuel Injection/Carb
```

Export engine

As 1.2 Litre, except:

Body, Weight: Saloon/Sedan 3/5–door, kerbweight (DIN) 905/925kg, gross vehicle weight 1425kg. Saloon/Sedan 4–door, kerbweight (DIN) 955kg, gross vehicle weight 1425kg. Estate/Station Wagon 3/5–door, kerbweight (DIN) 945/965kg, gross vehicle weight 1480kg.

Engine data (DIN): 4–cylinder in–line (84.8 x 79.5mm), 1796cm3; compression ratio 9.2:1; 62kW (83hp) [84PS] at 5400rpm, 34.5kW/L (46.2hp/L) [46.8PS/L]; 143Nm (105.5lbft) at 2600rpm; leaded premium grade.
With Fuel Injection: Compression ratio 10:1; 82kW (110hp) [112PS] at 5600rpm; 158Nm (116.6lbft) at 3000rpm; premium grade.

Engine construction: Oil capacity 4 L (3.8US qt); Bosch electronic LE3 Jetronic/1 Pierburg 2 EE/BPS regulated downdraught Pierburg EE. Battery 12V 44/55Ah; cooling system capacity approx 7.5L (7.1 US qt).

Transmission: a) 5–speed manual, final drive ratio 3.72.
b) Automatic, final drive ratio 3.43.

Gear ratios: a) 5-speed manual: 1st 3.42; 2nd 1.95; 3rd 1.28; 4th 0.89; 5th 0.71; R 3.33.
b) Automatic: Max torque multiplication in converter 2.48 times, Planetary gear set ratios; 2.84; 1.6; 1; R 2.07.

Performance: Max speed 110mph/178kmh, Automatic 107mph/173kmh, speed at 1000rpm in 5th gear 20.7mph/33.3kmh; acceleration 0 – 62mph/100kmh 11.5secs, Automatic 13secs; power to weight ratio from 14.6kg/kW (10.8kg/PS); consumption DIN 5.1/6.7/9.6L/100km (55.4/42.2/29.4mpg) [46.1/35.1/24.5US mpg], Automatic 6.3/8.0/10.1L/100km. ((44.8/35.3/28mpg) [37.3/29.4/23.3US mpg].

Opel Kadett Cabriolet GSi

```
2 Litre
85/95kW-114/128hp-115/130PS
Fuel Injection
```

As 1.3 Litre, except:
Body, Weight:
Saloon/Sedan GSi 3/5–door, kerbweight (DIN) 965/985kg, gross vehicle weight 1460kg.
Saloon/Sedan GT 4–door, kerbweight (DIN) 970kg, gross vehicle weight 1440kg.
Cabriolet/Convertible 2–door, kerbweight (DIN) 1040kg, gross vehicle weight 1455kg.

Opel

Estate/Station Wagon Club 5-door, kerbweight (DIN) 1010kg, gross vehicle weight 1500kg.

Engine data (Catalyst, DIN): 4-cylinder in-line (86 x 86mm), 1998cm3; compression ratio 9:2; 85kW (114hp) [115PS] at 5400rpm, 42.5kW/L (57hp/L) [57.6PS/L]; 170Nm (125.5lbft) at 3000rpm; leaded premium grade.
Without Catalyst: 175Nm (129lbft).
GSi: Compression ratio 10:1; 95kW (128hp) [130PS] at 5600rpm, 47.6kW/L (63.8hp/L) [65.1PS/L]; 180Nm (18.3mkp) at 4600rpm; premium grade.

Engine construction: Oil capacity 3.75L (3.5US qt); Bosch Motronic electronic fuel injection ML 4.1. Battery 12V 44/55Ah, alternator 55/65A; cooling system capacity approx 6.9L (6.5US qt).

Transmission: a) 5-speed manual, final drive ratio 3.55.
b) Automatic (not for Estate/Station Wagon with Catalyst), final drive ratio 3.33.

Gear ratios: a) 5-speed manual: 1st 3.42 (Estate/Station Wagon 3.55); 2nd 2.16; 3rd 1.48; 4th 1.13; 5th 0.89; R 3.33.
b) Automatic: Max torque multiplication in converter 2.35 times, Planetary gear set ratios: 2.84; 1.6; 1; R 2.07.

Chassis: Front discs ventilated; tyres 175/65 HR 14 or 185/60 HR 14, wheel rims 5.5J.

Performance: Max speed 121mph/195kmh (manufacturers test specifications), speed at 1000rpm in 5th gear 21mph/33.8kmh; acceleration 0 - 62mph/100kmh 9.0secs; power to weight ratio from 11.3kg/kW (8.4kg/PS); consumption DIN 6.1/7.8/10.7L/100km (46.3/36.2/26.4mpg) [38.6/30.2/22US mpg].

Opel Kadett GT

---
2 Litre DOHC 16V
110kW–147hp–150PS
Fuel Injection

Engine for GSi 16V

As 1.3 Litre, except:

Body, Weight: Saloon/Sedan 3/5-door, kerbweight (DIN) 1010/1030kg, gross vehicle weight 1490kg.

Engine data (Catalyst, DIN): 4-cylinder in-line (86 x 88mm), 1998cm3; compression ratio 10.5:1; 110kW (147hp) [150PS] at 6000rpm, 55.1kW/L (73.8hp/L) [75.1PS/L]; 196Nm (144.6lbft) at 4800rpm; unleaded premium grade.
For export also without Catalyst: 115kW (154hp) [156PS]; 203Nm (149.8lbft); leaded premium grade.

Opel Kadett GSi 16V

Engine construction: Valves in V 46deg. 4 valves per cylinder; 2 overhead camshafts (toothed belt); oil capacity 4.5L (4.3US qt); electronic Bosch Motronic M 2.5 fuel injection 2.5L (2.4US qt). Battery 12V 44Ah, alternator 55A; cooling system capacity approx 6.9L (6.5US qt).

Transmission: 5-speed manual, final drive ratio 3.42.

Gear ratios: 1st 3.55; 2nd 2.16; 3rd 1.48; 4th 1.12; 5th 0.89; R 3.33.

Chassis: Front disc brakes ventilated, diameter front 25.6cm, rear 23.6cm; tyres 185/65VR 14, wheel rims 5.5J.

Performance: Max speed 135mph/217kmh (manufacturers test specification), speed at 1000rpm in 5th gear 22.3mph/35.9kmh; acceleration 0 – 62mph/100kmh 8.0secs; power to weight ratio from 9.2kg/kW (6.7kg/PS); consumption DIN 5.7/7.0/9.9L/100km (49.6/40.4/28.5mpg) [41.3/33.6/23.8US mpg].

1.7 D/1.5 TD
42/49kW-55/66hp-57/67PS
Injection Pump

As 1.3 Litre, except:

Body, Weight: Saloon/Sedan 3/5-door, kerbweight (DIN) 920/940kg, gross vehicle weight 1445kg. Saloon/Sedan 4-door, kerbweight (DIN) 950kg, gross vehicle weight 1445kg. Estate/Station Wagon 3/5-door, kerbweight (DIN) 975/995kg, gross vehicle weight 1500kg.

Engine data (DIN): 4-cylinder in-line (82.5 x 79.5mm), 1700cm3; compression ratio 23:1; 42kW (55hp) [57PS] at 4600rpm, 24.7kW/L (33hp/L) [33.5PS/L]; 105Nm (77.5lbft) from 2400-2600rpm.
For some countries with Isuzu-Diesel and Turbocharger: (76 x 79.5mm), 1488cm3; compression ratio 22:1; 49kW (66hp) [67PS] at 4600rpm; 32.9kW/L (44.1hp/L) [45PS/L]; 132Nm (44.1hp/L) at 2600rpm.

Engine construction: Diesel engine swirl chamber. Bosch diesel injection pump; oil capacity 5L (4.7US qt). Battery 66Ah, alternator 65A; cooling system capacity approx 7.6L (7.2US qt).

Transmission: 5-speed manual, final drive ratio 3.74.

Gear ratios: 1st 3.55; 1.96; 3rd 1.30; 4th 0.89; 5th 0.71 R 3.31.

Performance: Max speed 95mph/153kmh, TD 107mph/170kmh (manufacturers test specification), speed at 1000rpm in 5th gear 24.8mph/39.9kmh; acceleration 0–62mph/100kmh 18.5secs, TD 13secs; power to weight ratio from 21.9kg/kW (16.1kg/PS); consumption DIN 4.0/5.7/6.7L/100km (70.6/49.6/42.2mpg) [58.8/41.3/35.1US mpg], TD 4.7/6.6/6.0L/100km (60.1/42.8/47.1mpg) [50/35.6/39.2US mpg].

Opel Kadett Caravan Diesel

Opel Vectra

New model. Successor to the Ascona. 4/5-door Saloon/Sedan with front or all wheel drive. Launched in August 1988.

1.6 Litre
55kW-74hp-75PS
Central/Single Point Injection

Body, Weight: 4-door Saloon/Sedan, 5-seater; kerbweight (DIN) 1005kg, gross vehicle weight 1550kg. 5-door Saloon/Sedan, 5-seater; kerbweight (DIN) 1035kg, gross vehicle weight 1550kg.

Engine data (Catalyst DIN): 4-cylinder in-line (79 x 81.5mm), 1598cm3; compression ratio 9.2:1; 55kW (74hp) [75PS] at 5200rpm, 34.4kW/L (46.1hp/L) [46.9PS/L]; 125Nm (92.3lbft) at 2600rpm; regular unleaded.
Euronorm:127Nm (93.8lbft)
With Carb: Compression ratio 10:1; 60kW (80hp) [82PS] at 5400rpm; 130Nm (96lbft) at 2600rpm; premium grade.

Opel

Opel Vectra GL

Engine construction: Transverse engine. Light-alloy cylinder head. Hydraulic tappets, 1 overhead camshaft (toothed belt); 5 main bearing crankshaft; oil capacity 3.5L (3.3US qt); Rochester TB1 700 electronic central/single point injection. Battery 12V 44Ah, alternator 55/70/90A; cooling system capacity approx 5.8L (5.5US qt).

Transmission (to front wheels): a) 5-speed manual, final drive ratio 4.18, 3.94. b) Automatic Aisin Warner, hydraulic torque converter and 4-speed Planetary gear set, final drive ratio 2.81.

Gear ratios: a) 5-speed manual: 1st 3.55; 2nd 1.96; 3rd 1.3; 4th 0.89; 5th 0.71; R 3.31. b) Automatic, max torque multiplication in converter 2.5 times, Planetary gear set ratios: 3.883; 2.118; 1.364; 1; R 4.853.

Chassis: Integral body; front McPherson struts with lower A-arm (negative steering offset); rear compound axle (trailing arm with cross members) with coil springs, antiroll bar front and rear, telescopic dampers. Servo/power assisted brakes with optional ABS (Teves), disc diameter front 23.6cm, rear drums; handbrake to rear wheels; rack and pinion steering with optional power assistance; fuel tank capacity 61L (13.4Gal) [16.1US Gal]; tyres 175/70 TR 14 or other dimensions up to 195/60 HR 14, wheel rims 5.5 J.

Dimensions: Wheel base 260cm, track 142.5/142.5cm, clearance min approx 14cm. Turning circle 11m. Load space 18.7-29.7cu ft (530/840dm3). Length 443cm, width 170cm, height 140cm.
Fastback: Load space 16.2/30/45.6cu ft (460/850/1290dm3). Length 435cm.

Performance: Max speed 109mph/176kmh (manufacturers test specifications), speed at 1000rpm in 5th gear 22.2mph/35.8kmh; acceleration 0 - 62mph/100kmh 14.0secs; power to weight ratio from 18.3kg/kW (13.4kg/PS); consumption DIN 5.2/6.8/8.9L/100km (54.3/41.5/31.7mpg) [41.5/34.6/26.4US mpg].

1.4 Litre
55kW-74hp-75PS
1 Compound Carb

Engine for Export

As 1.6 Litre, except:

Body, Weight: 4-door Saloon/Sedan, 5-seater; kerbweight (DIN) 990kg, gross vehicle weight 1530kg. 5-door Saloon/Sedan, 5-seater; kerbweight (DIN) 1020kg, gross vehicle weight 1530kg.

Engine data (DIN): 4-cylinder in-line (77.6 x 73.4mm), 1389cm3; compression ratio 9.4:1; 55kW (74hp) [75PS] at 5600rpm, 35.6kW/L (47.7hp/L) [48.4PS/L]; 108Nm (79.7lbft) at 3000rpm. Regular grade.

Opel Vectra CD

Engine construction: Oil capacity 3L (2.8US qt); 1 Pierburg downdraught compound carb. Battery 12V 36Ah, alternator 55A; cooling system capacity approx 5.6L (5.3US qt).

Transmission: 5-speed manual, final drive ratio 4.29.
Gear ratios: 1st 3.55; 2nd 1.96; 3rd 1.3; 4th 0.89; 5th 0.71; R 3.31.
Performance: Max speed 109mph/176kmh (manufacturers test specifications), speed at 1000rpm in 5th gear 21.7mph/34.9kmh; acceleration 0 - 62mph/100kmh 14.5secs; power to weight ratio from 18kg/kW (13.2kg/PS); consumption DIN 5.0/6.3/9.2L/100km (50.5/44.8/30.7mpg) [47/37.3/25.6US mpg].

1.8 Litre
65kW-87hp-88PS
Electronic Carb

As 1.6 Litre, except:

Body, Weight: 4-door Saloon/Sedan; kerbweight (DIN) 1040kg, gross vehicle weight 1590kg. 4-door 4 x 4 Saloon/Sedan; kerbweight (DIN) 1195kg, gross vehicle weight 1695kg. 5-door Saloon/Sedan; kerbweight (DIN) 1070kg, gross vehicle weight 1590kg.

Engine data (DIN): 4-cylinder in-line (84.8 x 79.5mm), 1796cm3; compression ratio 9:2; 65kW (87hp) [88PS] at 5400rpm, 36.2kW/L (48.5hp/L) [49.0PS/L]; 143Nm (105.5lbft) at 3000rpm.

Engine construction: Oil capacity 4L (3.8US qt); Bosch/Pierburg 2EE electronic carb. Cooling system capacity 6.7L (6.3US qt).

Transmission (to front wheels, 4 x 4 to all wheels):
a) 5-speed manual, final drive ratio 3.72.
b) Automatic, hydraulic torque converter and 4 speed Planetary gear set, final drive ratio 2.81.
4 x 4: 5-speed manual, final drive ratio 3.94; variable power distribution between front and rear, viscous coupling, electronically regulated multiplate clutch.

Gear ratios: a) 5-speed manual: 1st 3.55; 2nd 1.95; 3rd 1.28; 4th 0.89; 5th 0.71; R 3.33.
Or Sports gears (GT and 4 x 4): 1st 3.55; 2nd 2.16; 3rd 1.48; 4th 1.13; 5th 0.89; R 3.33.
b) Automatic, max torque multiplication in converter approx 2.3 times, Planetary gear set ratios: 1st 3.672; 2nd 2.098; 3rd 1.391; 4th 1; R 4.022.

Chassis 4 x 4: Rear independent suspension with semi-trailing arm, coil springs and antiroll bar, all round disc brakes; fuel tank 65L (14.3Gal) [17.2US Gal].

Dimensions: 4 x 4: Track 142.5/144.5cm, load space 13.4-24.4cu ft (380-690dm3).

Performance: Max speed 113mph/182kmh (manufacturers test specifications), speed at 1000rpm in 5th gear 24mph/38.6kmh; acceleration 0 - 62mph/100kmh 12.5secs; power to weight ratio from 16.0kg/kW (11.8kg/PS); consumption ECE 5.3/6.8/9.6L/100km (53.3/41.5/29.4mpg) [44.4/34.6/24.5US mpg].
4 x 4: No details available.

Opel Vectra GT

---

2 Litre
85kW-114hp-115PS
Fuel Injection

As 1.6 Litre, except:

Body, Weight: 4-door Saloon/Sedan; kerbweight (DIN) 1085kg, gross vehicle weight 1645kg. 4 x 4 Saloon/Sedan; kerbweight (DIN) 1210kg, gross vehicle weight 1715kg. 5-door Saloon/Sedan; kerbweight (DIN) 1115kg, gross vehicle weight 1645kg.
Automatic heavier by 35kg.

Engine data (Catalyst DIN): 4-cylinder in-line (86 x 86mm), 1998cm3; compression ratio 9:2; 85kW (114hp) [115PS] at 5200rpm, 42.5kW/L (57hp/L) [57.6PS/L]; 170Nm (125.5lbft) at 2600rpm.
Also: 74kW (99hp) [100PS]; 158Nm (116.6lbft)
Without Catalyst: 95kW (127hp) [130PS]; 180Nm (132.8lbft); premium grade.

Opel

Engine construction: Oil capacity 4.0L (3.8US qt); Bosch Motronic ML fuel injection 4.1. Cooling system capacity approx 7.2L (6.8US qt)
Transmission (to front wheels, 4 x 4 to all wheels):
a) 5-speed manual, final drive ratio 3.55.
b) Automatic, hydraulic torque converter and 4-speed Planetary gear set, final drive ratio 2.4.
4 x 4: 5-speed manual, final drive ratio 3.72; variable power distribution between front and rear, viscous coupling, electronically regulated multiplate clutch.
Gear ratios: a) 5-speed manual: 1st 3.55; 2nd 1.95; 3rd 1.28; 4th 0.89; 5th 0.71; R 3.33.
Or Sports gears (GT and 4 x 4): 1st 3.55; 2nd 2.16; 3rd 1.48; 4th 1.13; 5th 0.89; R 3.33.
b): Automatic, max torque multilplication in converter approx 2.35 times, Planetary gear set ratios: 1st 3.672; 2nd 2.098; 3rd 1.391; 4th 1; R 4.022.
Chassis: All round disc brakes (front ventilated); power assisted steering; tyres 195/60 HR 14.
4 x 4: rear independent steering with semi-trailing arms, coil springs and antiroll bar. Fuel tank capacity 65L (14.3Gal) [17.2US Gal].
Dimensions: 4 x 4: Track 142.5/144.5cm. Load space 13.4-24.4cu ft (380-690dm3).
Performance: Max speed 123mph/198kmh, Automatic 120mph/193kmh (manufacturers test specifications), speed at 1000rpm in 5th gear 26.6mph/42.8kmh; acceleration 0 - 62mph/100kmh 10.5secs; power to weight ratio from 12.8kg/kW (9.4kg/PS); consumption ECE 5.6/7.1/10.3L/100km (50.4/39.8/27.4mpg) [42/33.1/22.8US mpg], Automatic 6.0/7.5/10.8L/100km (47.1/37.7/26.2mpg) [39.2/31.4/21.8US mpg].
4 x 4: Max speed 119mph/192kmh (manufacturers test specifications); acceleration 0 - 62mph/100kmh 11secs; consumption ECE 7.2/8.6/11.9L/100km (39.2/32.8/23.7mpg) [32.7/27.4/19.8US mpg].

Opel Vectra 4 x 4

```
2 Litre DOHC 16V
110kW-147hp-150PS
Fuel Injection
```

As 1.6 Litre, except:
Body, Weight: 4-door Saloon/Sedan; kwerbweight (DIN) 1175, gross vehicle weight 1675kg. 4 x 4 4-door Saloon/Sedan; kerbweight (DIN) 1265kg, gross vehicle weight 1765kg.
Engine data (Catalyst DIN): 4-cylinder in-line (86 x 86mm), 1998cm3; compression ratio 10.5:1; 110kW (147hp) [150PS] at 6000rpm, 55.1kW/L (73.8hp/L) [75.1PS/L]; 196Nm (144.6lbft) at 4800rpm.
Engine construction: Valves in V 46deg; 4 valves per cylinder; 2 overhead camshafts (toothed belt); oil capacity 4.5L (4.3US qt); Bosch Motronic M 2.5 fuel injection. Cooling system capacity approx 7.2L (6.8US qt).
Transmission (to front wheels, 4 x 4 to all wheels):
5-speed manual, final drive ratio 3.42.
4 x 4: 5-speed manual, final drive ratio 3.55; variable power distribution between front and rear, viscous coupling, electronically regulated multiplate clutch.
Gear ratios: 1st 3.55; 2nd 2.16; 3rd 1.48; 4th 1.13; 5th 0.89; R 3.33.
Chassis: Rear independent suspension with semi-trailing arms, coil springs and antiroll bar. All round disc brakes (front ventilated) with ABS; power assisted steering; fuel tank capacity 65L (14.3Gal) [17.2US Gal]; tyres 195/60 HR 15, wheel rims 6J also tyres 205/55 VR 15.

Dimensions: Track 142.5/144.5cm. Load space 4 x 4 13.4-24.4cu ft (380-690dm3).
Performance: Max speed 135mph/217kmh (manufacturers test specifications), speed at 1000rpm in 5th gear 23mph/37.0kmh; acceleration 0 - 62mph/100kmh approx 9secs; power to weight ratio from 10.7kg/kW (7.8kg/PS); consumption ECE 5.8/7.4/10.3L/100km (48.7/38.2/27.4mpg) [40.6/31.8/22.8US mpg].
4 x 4: Max speed 129mph/208kmh (manufacturers test specifications); acceleration 0 - 62mph/100kmh approx 9.5secs; consumption ECE 6.5/8.1/10.9L/100km (43.5/34.9/25.9mpg) [36.2/29/21.6US mpg].

Opel Vectra 2000 16V

```
1.7 Litre Diesel
42/60kW-56/80hp-57/82PS
Injection Pump/Turbo
```

As 1.6 Litre, except:
Body, Weight: 4-door, Saloon/Sedan, 5-seater; kerbweight (DIN) 1070kg, gross vehicle weight 1610kg. 5-door Saloon/Sedan, 5-seater; kerbweight (DIN) 1100kg, gross vehicle weight 1610kg.
Engine data (DIN): 4-cylinder in-line (82.5 x 79.5mm) 1700cm3; compression ratio 23.1; 42kW (56hp) [57PS] at 4600rpm, 24.7kW/L (33.1hp/L) [33.5PS/L]; 105Nm (77.5lbft) from 2400-2600rpm.
With turbocharger: 60kW (80hp) [82PS].
Engine construction: Swirl chamber with direct injection. Bosch diesel injection pump. Battery 70Ah; cooling system capacity approx 9.1L (8.6US qt).
Transmission: 5-speed manual, final drive ratio 3.94.
Chassis: Tyres 175/70 TR 14.
Performance: Max speed 94mph/152kmh, Turbodiesel 109mph/175kmh (manufacturers test specifications), speed at 1000rpm in 5th gear 24.7mph/39.7kmh; acceleration 0 - 62mph/100kmh 20.0secs, Turbodiesel 14.0secs; power to weight ratio from 25.5kg/kW (18.8kg/PS); consumption ECE 4.4/6.0/6.7L/100km (64.2/47.1/42.2mpg) [53.5/39.2/35.1US mpg].

Opel Vectra 1.7 D

Opel Omega

LS–GL–GLS–CD–3000

Successor to the Rekord, 4–door Saloon/Sedan and 5–door Caravan., independent suspension. New generation of engines. Launched August 1986. From Autumn 1988 also available with 2.4-Litre engine.

```
1.8N/1.8S
65/66kW-87/88.5hp-88/90PS
1 Carb
```

Opel 331

Body, Weight: Saloon/Sedan 4-dooor, 5-seater; kerbweight (DIN) from 1215kg, gross vehicle weight 1770kg. Estate/Station Wagon "Caravan" 5-door, 5-seater; kerbweight (DIN) from 1230kg, gross vehicle weight 1865kg. Increased weight for automatic transmission 25kg.

Engine data (DIN): 1.8N: 4–cylinder in–line (84.8 x 79.5mm), 1796cm3; compression ratio 9.2:1; 65 kW (87hp) [88PS] at 5200rpm, 36.2kW/L (48.5hp/L) [49PS/L]; 143Nm (105.5lbft) at 3200rpm; unleaded premium grade.
1.8S: Compression ratio 10.0:1; 66kW (88.5hp) [90PS] at 5200rpm, 36.9kW/L (49.4hp/L) [50.1PS/L]; 148Nm (109.2lbft) at 3400rpm; leaded premium grade.

Engine construction: Hydraulic tappets; 1 overhead camshaft (toothed belt); light–alloy cylinder head; 5 bearing crankshaft; oil capacity 4.5L (4.3US qt); 1 Pierburg 2EE downdraught compound carb (11.8SV:2E3). Battery 12V 55/44Ah, alternator 55/70A; cooling system capacity 6.4L (6.1US qt).

Transmission (to rear wheels): a) 5–speed manual, final drive ratio 3.7; 3.9.
b) Automatic, hydraulic torque converter and 4–speed Planetary gear set, final drive ratio 3.9.
Optional limited slip differential.

Gear ratios: a) 5–speed manual: 1st 4.044; 2nd 2.265; 3rd 1.434; 4th 1; 5th 0.842; R 3.748.
b) Automatic: Max torque multiplication in converter 2.35 times, Planetary gear set ratios: 1st 2.45; 2nd 1.45; 3rd 1; 4th 0.69; R 2.21.

Chassis: Integral body; front and rear independent suspension; front McPherson struts and lower A arm, coil springs, front and rear antiroll bar and telescopic damper; optional electronic shock absorber adjustment. Servo/power assisted disc brakes, front and rear diameter 25.8cm; optional ABS; mechanical handbrake to rear wheels; power assisted rack and pinion steering (except some basic models); fuel tank 75L (16.5Gal) [20.1US Gal], Estate/Station Wagon 70L (15.4Gal) [18.5US Gal]; tyres 175 TR/HR 14 or tyres 185/70TR/HR 14 195/65 TR/HR 14; wheel rims 5.5/6J.

Dimensions: Wheelbase 273cm, track 145/147cm, clearance 14cm, turning circle 10.8m, load space 18.4–30.7cu ft (520–870dm3), length 469cm, width 177cm, height 144.5cm.
Estate/Station Wagon: Track 145/146cm, load space 19-65.3cu ft (540-1850dm3). Length 473cm, height 148cm.

Performance: 1.8 S, Saloon/Sedan: Max speed 114mph/183kmh, automatic 110mph/177kmh (manufacturers test specification), speed at 1000rpm in 5th gear 23.2mph/37.3kmh; acceleration 0 – 62mph/100kmh 14.0secs, automatic 15.5secs; power to weight ratio from 18.4kg/kW (13.5kg/PS); consumption ECE 5.6/7.1/9.8L/100km (50.4/39.8/28.8mpg) [42.0/33.1/24.0US mpg], automatic 5.7/7.3/10.1L/100km (49.6/38.7/28.0mpg) [41.3/32.2/23.3US mpg]. Caravan: Max speed 111mph/175kmh, automatic 106mph/170kmh (manufacturers test specification); acceleration 0 – 62mph/100kmh 15.0secs, automatic 16.5secs; consumption ECE 6.1/7.8/9.8L/100km (46.3/36.2/28.8mpg) [38.6/30.2/24.0US mpg], automatic 6.1/7.8/10.1L/100km (46.3/36.2/28.0mpg) [38.6/30.2/23.3US mpg].

Opel Omega GL

```
1.8i
85kW–114hp–115PS
Fuel Injection
```

As 87/88.5hp, except:

Weight: Saloon/Sedan, kerbweight (DIN) from 1235kg, gross vehicle weight 1795kg. Estate/Station Wagon "Caravan", kerbweight (DIN) from 1255kg, gross vehicle weight 1885kg.

Engine data (DIN) 4–cylinder in–line (84.8 x 79.5mm), 1796cm3; compression ratio 10:1; 85kW (114hp) [115PS] at 5600rpm 47.3kW/L (63.4hp/L) [64.0PS/L]; 160Nm (118.1lbft) at 4600rpm; leaded premium grade.

Engine construction: Electronic Bosch L–Jetronic fuel injection L3.1.

Transmission: a) 5-speed manual, final drive ratio 3.7.
b) Automatic, final drive ratio 3.9.

Performance: Saloon/Sedan: Max speed 121mph/195kmh, automatic 118mph/190kmh (manufacturers test specification); acceleration 0 – 62mph/100kmh 12.0secs, automatic 13.5secs; power to weight ratio from 14.5kg/kW (10.7kg/PS); consumption ECE 5.4/7.0/10.5L/100km (52.3/40.4/26.9mpg) [43.6/33.6/22.4US mpg], automatic 5.7/7.1/11.0L/100km (49.6/39.8/25.7mpg) [41.3/33.6/21.4US mpg]. Caravan: Max speed 116mph/187kmh, automatic 112mph/180kmh (manufacturers test specification); acceleration 0 – 62mph/100kmh 13.0secs, automatic 14.5secs; consumption ECE 5.8/7.7/10.5L/100km (48.7/36.7/26.9mpg) [40.6/30.5/22.4US mpg], automatic 6.1/7.8/11.0L/100km (46.3/36.2/25.7mpg) [38.6/30.2/21.4US mpg].

Opel Omega Caravan GLS

```
2.0i
90/85kW–121/114hp–122/115PS
Fuel Injection
```

As 87/99hp, except:

Weight: Saloon/Sedan, kerbweight (DIN) from 1255kg, gross vehicle weight 1790kg. Estate/Station Wagon "Caravan", kerbweight (DIN) from 1275kg, gross vehicle weight 1885kg.

Engine data (DIN): 4–cylinder in–line (86 x 86mm), 1998cm3; compression ratio 10:1; 90kW (121hp) [122PS] at 5400rpm, 45kW/L (60.3hp/L) (61.1PS/L); 170Nm (125.5lbft) at 2600rpm; leaded premium grade.
With Catalyst: Compression ratio 9.2.1; 85kW (114hp) [115PS] at 5400rpm, 42.5kW/L (57.1hp/L) [57.6PS/L]; 117Nm (86.3lbft) at 2600rpm; unleaded premium grade.
Certain Countries: 74kW (99hp) [100PS]; 158Nm (116.6lbft).

Engine construction: Electronic Bosch fuel injection, digital regulator (Motronic).

Transmission: a) 5–speed manual, final drive ratio 3.7.
b) Automatic, final drive ratio 3.7.

Chassis: Front disc brakes (ventilated).

Performance (With Catalyst): Saloon/Sedan: Max speed 121mph/195kmh, automatic 118mph/190kmh (manufacturers test specification); acceleration 0–62mph/100kmh 11.8secs, automatic 13.0secs; power to weight ratio from 14.8kg/kW (10.9kg/PS); consumption ECE 5.9/7.7/11.5L/100km (47.9/36.7/24.6mpg) [39.9/30.5/20.5US mpg], automatic 5.9/7.5/11.7L/100km (47.9/37.7/24.1mpg) [39.9/31.4/20.1US mpg].
Caravan: Max speed 116mph/187kmh, automatic 112mph/180kmh (manufacturers test specification); acceleration 0 – 62mph/100kmh 13.0secs, automatic 14.0secs; consumption ECE 6.4/8.5/11.5L/100km (44.1/33.2/24.6mpg) [36.8/27.7/20.5US mpg], automatic 6.4/8.3/11.7L/100km (44.1/34/24.1mpg) [36.8/28.3/20.1US mpg].

```
2.4i
92kW-123hp-125PS
Fuel Injection
```

As 87/89hp, except:

Weight: Saloon/Sedan, kerbweight (DIN) from 1275kg, gross vehicle weight 1830kg. Estate/Station Wagon "Caravan", kerbweight (DIN) from 1295kg, gross vehicle weight 1925kg.

Engine data (Catalyst DIN): 4-cylinder in-line (95 x 85mm), 2410cm3; compression ratio 9.2:1; 92kW (123hp) [125PS] at 4800rpm, 38.2kW/L (51.2hp/L) [51.9PS/L]; 240Nm (177lbft) from 2400-2600rpm; regular unleaded grade.

Engine construction: Grey cast iron cylinder head; side camshaft (chain) in cylinder head; oil capacity 4.5L (4.3US qt); Bosch Motronic electronic fuel injection. Cooling system capacity approx 7.8L (7.4US qt).

Transmission: a) 5-speed manual, final drive ratio 3.45.
b) Automatic, final drive ratio 3.7

Opel

Chassis: Disc brakes, front ventilated; tyres 195/65 HR 15.

Performance: Saloon/Sedan: Max speed 124mph/200kmh, Automatic 123mph/198kmh (manufacturers test specifications); acceleration 0 - 62mph/100kmh 10.8secs, Automatic 11.5secs; power to weight ratio from 13.9kg/kW (10.2kg/PS); consumption ECE 6.8/8.3/12.8L/100km (41.5/34/22.1mpg) [34.6/28.3/18.4US mpg], Automatic 6.9/8.3/12.8L/100km (40.9/34/22.1mpg) [34.1/28.3/18.4US mpg]. Caravan: Max speed 119mph/192kmh, Automatic 118mph/190kmh (manufacturers test specifications); acceleration 0-62mph/100kmh 12.0secs (Automatic 12.5secs); consumption ECE 7.1/8.8/12.8L/100km (39.8/32.1/22.1mpg) [33.1/26.7/18.4US mpg], Automatic 7.2/8.8/12.8L/100km (39.2/32.1/22.1mpg) [32.7/26.7/18.4US mpg].

Opel Omega CD 2.4i

3.0i
130kW-174hp-177PS
Fuel Injection

Engine for Omega 3000 and Caravan 3.0i

As 87/89hp, except:

Weight: Saloon/Sedan, kerbweight (DIN) from 1410kg, gross vehicle weight 1930kg. Estate/Station Wagon "Caravan", kerbweight (DIN) from 1435kg, gross vehicle weight 2065kg.

Engine data (with and without Catalyst, DIN): 6-cylinder in-line (95 x 69.8mm), 2969cm3; compression ratio 9.4:1; 130kW (174hp) [177PS] at 5600rpm, 43.9kW/L (58.8hp/L) [59.6 PS/L]; 240Nm (177.1lbft) with 4000rpm; unleaded premium grade.

Engine construction: Side camshaft (chain) in cylinder head; 7 bearing crankshaft; grey cast iron cylinder head; oil capacity 5L (4.7US qt); electronic Bosch Motronic fuel injection; electronic digital control. Battery 12V 55Ah, alternator 70A; cooling system capacity approx 10.2L (9.6US qt).

Transmission: a) 5-speed manual, final drive ratio 3.7.
b) Automatic, final drive ratio 3.7.
Limited slip differential.

Chassis: Front ventilated disc brakes, diameter 28cm, rear 27cm; tyres 195/65 VR 15; 205/65 VR 15; wheel rims 7J.

Dimensions: Track 145/147cm, length 474cm, height 142cm.

Performance: Max speed 141mph/227kmh, Automatic 138mph/222kmh (manufacturer test specification); acceleration 0 – 62mph/100kmh 8.8secs, automatic 9.8secs; power to weight ratio from 10.8kg/kW (8.0kg/PS); consumption ECE 7.9/9.6/15.6L/100km (35.8/29.4/18.1mpg) [29.8/24.5/15.1US mpg], Automatic 7.4/9.0/15.2L/100km (38.2/31.4/18.6mpg) [31.8/26.1/15.5US mpg]. Caravan: Max speed 137mph/220kmh, Automatic 133mph/214kmh (manufacturers test specifications); acceleration 0 - 62mph/100kmh 9.3secs, Automatic 10.5secs; consumption ECE 8.1/10.1/15.6L/100km (34.9/28/18.1mpg) [29.0/23.3/15.1US mpg], Automatic 7.6/9.5/15.2L/100km (37.2/29.7/18.6mpg) [30.9/24.8/15.5US mpg].

Opel Omega 3000

2.3D
53.5kW-72hp-73PS
Injection Pump

As 87/89hp, except:

Weight: Saloon/Sedan, kerbweight (DIN) from 1315kg, gross vehicle weight 1870kg. Estate/Station Wagon "Caravan", kerbweight (DIN) from 1335kg, gross vehicle weight 1965kg.

Engine data (DIN): 4-cylinder in-line (92 x 85mm), 2260cm3; compression ratio 23:1; 54kW (72hp) [73PS] at 4400rpm, 23.9kW/L (32hp/L) [32.3PS/L]; 138Nm (101.8lbft) at 2400rpm.

Engine construction: Turbulence chamber diesel engine; grey cast iron cylinder head; 1 overhead camshaft (chain); oil capacity 5.5L (5.2US qt); Bosch injection pump; oil filter. Battery 12V 70Ah, alternator 70A; cooling system capacity approx 10.8L (10.2US qt).

Transmission: a) 5 speed manual, final drive ratio 3.7.
b) Automatic, final drive ratio 3.7.

Performance: Saloon/Sedan: Max speed 101mph/163kmh, automatic 96mph/155kmh (manufacturers test specification); acceleration 0 – 62mph/100kmh 19.0secs, automatic 21.5secs; power to weight ratio from 24.3kg/kW (18kg/PS); consumption ECE 5.2/7.0/7.9L/100km (54.3/40.4/35.8mpg) [45.2/33.6/29.8US mpg], automatic 5.1/6.7/8.3L/100km (55.4/42.2/34.0mpg) [46.1/35.1/28.3US mpg]. Caravan: Max speed 96mph/155kmh, automatic 90mph/145kmh (manufacturers test specification); acceleration 0 – 62mph/100kmh 20.5secs, automatic 23.0secs; consumption ECE 5.4/7.5/7.9L/100km (52.3/37.7/35.8mpg) [43.6/31.4/29.8US mpg] automatic 5.3/7.3/8.3L/100km (53.3/38.7/34.0mpg) [44.4/32.2/28.3US mpg].

2.3TD
74kW-99hp-100PS
Injection Pump/Turbo

As 88/90PS, except:

Weight: Saloon/Sedan, kerbweight (DIN) from 1335kg, gross vehicle weight 1870kg. Estate/Station Wagon "Caravan", kerbweight (DIN) from 1355kg, gross vehicle weight 1965kg.

Engine data (DIN): 4-cylinder in-line (92 x 85mm), 2260cm3; compression ratio 23:1; 74kW (99hp) [100PS] at 4200rpm, 32.7kW/L (43.8hp/L) [44.2PS/L]; 215Nm (158.7lbft) at 2200rpm.

Engine construction: Turbulence chamber diesel engine; grey cast iron cylinder head; 1 overhead camshaft (chain); oil capacity 5.5L (5.2US qt); Bosch injection pump; 1 turbocharger KKK K24; intercooler; oil bath air filter. Battery 12V 70Ah, alternator 70A; cooling system capacity approx 10.8L (26.2US qt).

Transmission: a) 5-speed manual, final drive ratio 3.45.
b) Automatic, final drive ratio 3.7.

Performance: Saloon/Sedan: Max speed 114mph/184kmh, automatic 112mph/180kmh (manufacturers test specification), speed at 1000rpm in direct gear 24.9mph/40.0kmh; acceleration 0 – 62mph/100kmh 14secs, automatic 15.5secs; power to weight ratio from 18kg/kW (13.3kg/PS); consumption ECE 5.4/7.2/8.5L/100km (52.3/39.2/33.2mpg) [43.6/32.7/27.7US mpg], automatic 5.3/7.1/9.0L/100km (53.3/39.8/31.4mpg) [44.4/33.1/26.1US mpg]. Caravan: Max speed 109mph/176kmh, automatic (manufacturers test specification); acceleration 0 – 62mph/100kmh 15secs, automatic 16.5secs; consumption ECE 5.5/7.7/8.5L/100km (51.4/36.7/33.2mpg) [42.8/30.5/27.7US mpg], automatic 5.6/7.6/9.0L/100km (50.4/37.2/31.4mpg) [42/30.9/26.1US mpg].

Opel Omega Caravan 2.3 TD

Opel • Otosan

Opel Senator

5-seater Saloon/Sedan, based on the Omega, 3 Litre 6-cylinder engine, 5-speed manual or automatic transmission. Power assisted steering and ABS. For some countries a 2.5 Litre engine is also available.

Opel Senator

```
3.0i Litre
130kW-174hp-177PS
Fuel Injection
```

Body, Weight: Saloon/Sedan 4-door, 5-seater; kerbweight (DIN) 1435–1500kg, gross vehicle weight 1985kg.

Engine data (with and without Catalyst, DIN): 6-cylinder in-line (95 x 69.8mm), 2969cm3; compression ratio 9.4:1; 130kW (174hp) [177PS] at 5600rpm, 43.9kW/L (58.8hp/L) [59.6PS/L]; 240Nm (177.1lbft) from 4400rpm; unleaded premium grade. Or: Compression ratio 8.6:1; 115kW (154hp) [156PS] at 5400rpm; 230Nm (169.7lbft) from 3800-3400rpm.

Engine construction: Hydraulic tappets; 1 side camshaft (chain) in cylinder head; 7 bearing crankshaft; oil capacity 5.5L (5.2US qt); digital regulated Bosch fuel injection Motronic. Battery 12V 55Ah, alternator 70A; cooling system capacity approx 10.2L (9.6US qt).

Transmission (to rear wheels): a) 5-speed manual, final drive ratio 3.45, 3.7; optional limited slip differential.
b) Automatic, hydraulic torque converter and 4-speed Planetary gear set; central selector lever, final drive ratio 3.45. Optional limited slip differential.

Gear ratios: a) 5 speed manual: 1st 4.044; 2nd 2.265; 3rd 1.434; 4th 1; 5th 0.842; R 3.748.
b) Automatic: Max torque multiplication in converter 2.3 times, Planetary gear set ratios: 1st 2.45; 2nd 1.45; 3rd 1; 4th 0.69; R 2.21.

Opel Senator CD

Chassis: Integral body; front and rear independent suspension; front McPherson struts and lower A arm and trailing arm, rear A arm, coil springs, front and rear antiroll bar and telescopic damper, optional electronic shock absorber adjustment. Servo/power assisted disc brakes (front ventilated), diameter front 28cm, rear 27cm; mechanical handbrake to rear wheels; power assisted (Servotronik) recirculating ball steering; fuel tank 75L (16.5Gal) [19.8US Gal], tyres 205/65 VR 15; 195/65 VR 15, wheel rims 6J.

Dimensions: Wheelbase 273cm, track 145/147cm, clearance 14cm, turning circle 10.8m, load space 18.7–32.8cu ft (530/930dm3), length 484.5cm, width 176.5cm, height 145cm.

Performance (With Catalyst): Max speed 140mph/225kmh, automatic 134mph/215kmh (manufacturers test specification), speed at 1000rpm in 5th gear 25.3mph/40.7kmh; acceleration 0 – 62mph/100kmh 9.3secs, automatic 10.3secs; power to weight ratio from 11kg/kW (8.1kg/PS); consumption ECE 7.9/9.6/15.6L/100km (35.8/29.4/18.1mpg) [29.8/24.5/15.1US mpg], automatic 7.4/9.0/15.2L/100km (38.2/31.4/18.6mpg) [31.8/26.1/15.5US mpg].

```
2.5 Litre E
103kW-138hp-140PS
Fuel Injection
```

As 3 Litre, except:

Weight: Kerbweight (DIN) from 1425kg.

Engine data (DIN): 6-cylinder in-line (87 x 69.8mm), 2490cm3; compression ratio 9.2.:1; 103kW (138hp) [140PS] at 5200rpm, 41.4kW/L (55.5hp/L) [56.2PS/L]; 205Nm (151.3lbft) at 4200rpm; leaded premium grade.

Engine construction: Oil capacity 5.5L (5.2US qt); electronic LE 2 Jetronic fuel injection.

Transmission: a) 5-speed manual, final drive ratio 3.45.
b) Automatic, final drive ratio 3.7.

Chassis: Tyres 195/70 R 14; 205/60 VR 15.

Performance: Max speed 210kmh, automatic 200kmh (manufacturers test specification); acceleration 0 – 62mph/100kmh 11.0secs, automatic 12secs; power to weight ratio from 13.8kg/kW (10.2kg/PS); consumption ECE 7.0/8.6/13.8L/100km (40.4/32.8/20.5mpg) [33.6/27.4/17.0US mpg].

OTOSAN TR

Otosan Otomobil Sanayi As, PK 102 Kadikoy–Istanbul, Turkey

First Turkish vehicle manufacturer. First produced cars under licence from Reliant (England) in 1967. Production of the Anadol–16 suspended, and production of the Ford Taunus/Cortina commenced.

Otosan Ford Taunus

Production of the old Ford Taunus/Cortina with a 1.6 Litre engine.

```
1.6 Litre
51.5kW-69hp-70PS
1 Carb
```

Body, Weight: Saloon/Sedan 4-door, 5-seater; kerbweight (DIN) 1060kg, gross vehicle weight 1520kg.

Engine data (DIN): 4-cylinder in-line (87.65 x 66mm), 1593cm3; compression ratio 8.2:1; 51.5kW (69hp) [70PS] at 5300rpm, 32.3kW/L (43.2hp/L) [44PS/L]; 113Nm (70.2lbft) at 2700rpm; leaded regular grade.

Engine construction: Designated Ford. 1 overhead camshaft (toothed belt); 5 bearing crankshaft; oil capacity 3.75 L (3.6US qt); 1 Ford downdraught carb VV. Battery 12V 60Ah, alternator 55A; cooling system capacity approx 5.8L (5.5US qt).

Transmission (to rear wheels): 4-speed manual, final drive ratio 3.89.

Gear ratios: 1st 3.58; 2nd 2.01; 3rd 1.397; 4th 1; R 3.324.

Chassis: Integral body: front overhead A arm, lower single control arm with tension strut, coil springs; rear rigid axle with lower A arm and overhead semi trailing arm, coil springs, front and rear antiroll bar and telescopic damper. Servo/power assisted front disc brakes, rear drums, disc diameter 24.4cm, mechanical handbrake to rear wheel; rack and pinion steering; fuel tank 54L (11.9Gal) [14.3US Gal]; tyres 165 SR 13, wheel rims 5.5J.

Dimensions: Wheelbase 258cm, track 142.5/144.5cm, track 142.5/144.5cm, clearance 16.5cm, turning circle 10.6m, load space 15.9cu ft (450dm3), length 437cm, width 170cm, height 138cm.

Performance: Max speed 92mph/148kmh (manufacturers test specification), speed at 1000rpm in 4th gear 17.3mph/27.9kmh; power to weight ratio 20.6kg/kW (15.2kg/PS); consumption approx 7–12 L/100km (40.4–23.5mpg) [33.6–19.6US mpg].

Otosan • Pag • Panther

Otosan Ford Taunus 1.6

PAG   BR

Projets de'Avant Garde Ltda, Estrada Sitio do Morro, 151 (Caixa Postal 91), 06500 Santana do Parnaiba SP, Brazil

Small factory, working on the base of the VW Saveiro (pickup). A small synthetic Nick vehicle. Linked to VW's represensive in Sao Paulo, Dacon.

Pag Nick

New model. A small 2-door vehicle with 2-seats, 1.6 or 1.8 litre engine. Sheet steel roof and doors with the rest of the body synthetic. Launched Summer 1988.

```
1.6 Litre
66kW–88hp–90PS
1 2V Carb
```

Body, Weight: 2–door Saloon/Sedan, 2–seater; kerbweight (DIN) 830kg, gross vehicle weight 1240kg.

Engine data (DIN): 4–cylinder in–line (81 x 77.4mm), 1595cm3; compression ratio 12:1, 66kW (88hp) [90PS] at 5600rpm, 41.4kW/L (54.4hp/L) [56.4PS/L]; 128Nm (94.5lbft) at 2600rpm; ethyl alcohol.
Petrol/gasoline: Compression ratio 8.5:1; 58kW (78hp) [79PS] at 5600rpm, 124Nm (91.5lbft) at 2600rpm.

Engine construction: Front engine inclined 20deg to the right. 1 overhead camshaft (toothed belt); light-alloy cylinder head; 5 bearing crankshaft; oil capacity 3.5L (3.3US qt); 1 Wecarbras (weber) downdraught 2V carb. 12V 54Ah battery, 35A battery; cooling system capacity 5.1L (4.8US qt).

Transmission (to front wheels): 5–speed manual, final drive ratio 4.11 (9/37).

Gear ratios: 1st 3.45; 2nd 1.94; 3rd 1.29; 4th 0.91; V 0.73; R 3.17.

Chassis: Integral body; front A arm and McPherson struts with coil springs (negative off-set steering), antiroll bar, rear semi trailing arms and coil springs, telescopic dampers. Servo/Power assisted brakes; front disc diameter 23.9cm, rear drums; mechanical handbrake on rear; power assisted rack and pinion steering; fuel tank 55L (12.1Gal) [14.5US Gal]; tyres 175/70 SR 13, Felgen 5J.

Dimensions: Wheelbase 202cm, track 135/137cm, clearance 13.5cm, turning circle 9.5cm. Length 318cm, width 160cm, height 135cm.

Performances: Max speed 109mph/175kmh (manufacturers test specifications), speed at 1000rpm in 5th gear 22mph/35.4kmh; acceleration 0–62mph/100kmh 9.7secs; power to weight ratio from 12.6kg/kW (9.2kg/PS); consumption 7–11L/100km (40.4–25.7mpg) [33.6–21.4US mpg].

Pag Nick

```
1.8 Litre
73kW–98hp–99PS
1 2V Carb
```

As 1.6 Litre, except

Engine data (DIN): 4–cylinder in–line (81 x 86.4mm), 1781cm3; compression ratio 12:1; 73kW (98hp) [99PS] at 5600rpm, 41kW/L (54.9hp/L) [55.6PS/L]; 149Nm (110lbft) at 3200rpm; also available with petrol/gasoline engine.

Engine construction: 1 Brosol Pierburg 2E7 downdraught 2V carb. 45A alternator; cooling system capacity 6.6L (6.2US qt).

Chassis: Tyres 185/60 HR 14, wheel rims 6J.

Performances: Max speed 115mph/185kmh (manufacturers test specifications), speed at 1000rpm in 5th gear 20mph/32.2kmh; acceleration 0–62mph/100kmh 9.2secs; power to weight ratio from 11.4kg/kW (8.4kg/PS); consumption approx 8–12L/100km (35.3–23.5mpg) [29.4–19.6US mpg].

PANTHER   GB

The Panther Car Company Ltd, Horsecroft Road, The Pinnacles, Harlow, Essex CM19 5BA, England.

Small manufacturer of sports cars, some in the old style. Part of the South Korean Jindo Group.

Panther Kallista

2-seater Roadster with aluminium body, mechanical components from Ford, 2.3 4-cylinder or 2.8 6-cylinder engine. Launched October 1982, Autumn 1983; available with injection. Autumn 1988; 1.6 and 2.3 litre engine.

```
1.6 Litre
68kW–91hp–93PS
1 2V Carb
```

Body, Weight: 2–door Roadster; 2–seater; Kerbweight (DIN) 900kg; gross vehicle weight 1260kg.

Engine data (DIN): 4–cylinder in–line (80 x 79.5mm), 1598cm3; compression ratio 9.5:1; 68kW (91hp) [93PS] at 5750rpm, 42.6kW/L (57.1hp/L) [58.2PS/L]; 133Nm (98.1lbft) at 4000rpm; leaded premium grade.

Engine construction: Designation Ford CVH, hydraulic tappets, 1 overhead camshaft (toothed belt); light-alloy cylinder; 5 bearing crankshaft; oil capacity 3.5L (3.3US qt); 1 Weber 32/34 DFT. downdraught 2V carb; 12V 40Ah, battery, 45/55A alternator; cooling system capacity approx 7.3L (6.9US qt).

Transmission: (to rear wheels): 5–speed manual, final drive ratio 3.73.

Gear ratios: 1st 3.65; 2nd 1.95; 3rd 1.37; 4th 1; 5th 0.82; R 3.66.

Chassis: Integral body, front A arm and coil springs, rear rigid axle with coil springs, upper and lower trailing arms and Panhard rod, front antiroll bar, telescopic damper. Servo/power assisted brakes, disc diameter 24.8cm, rear drum brakes, mechanical handbrake on rear; power assisted rack and pinion steering; 45.5L (10 Gal) [12US Gal] fuel tank or 50L (11Gal) [13.2US Gal]; tyres 185/70 HR 13, 5.5J wheels.

Dimensions: Wheelbase 255cm, track 148/143cm, clearance approx 12cm, turning circle approx 10.5m, length 389cm, width 169.5cm, height 127cm.

Panther Kallista 1.6

Panther • Paykan • Peugeot

Performance: Max speed 95mph/153kmh (manufacturers test specification), speed at 1000rpm in top gear 22.7mph/35.6kmh; acceleration 0 – 60mph/97kmh 12.5secs; power to weight ratio 13.2kg/kW (9.7kg/PS); consumption approx 6–10L/100km (47.1– 28.2mpg) [39.2–23.5US mpg].

```
2.8 Litre V6
99.5kW–133hp–135PS
1 2V Carb
```

As 1.6 Litre, except:

Weight: Kerbweight (DIN) 995kg.

Engine data (DIN): 6–cylinder in 60deg V (93 x 68.5mm) 2792cm3; compression ratio 9.2:1; 99.5kW (133hp) [135PS] at 5200rpm, 35.6kW/L (47.7hp/L) [48.4PSL]; 216Nm (159.3lbft) at 3000rpm.

Engine construction: Ford V6, parallel valves, mechanical, tappets, central camshaft (gear wheel); 4 bearing crankshaft; oil capacity 4.5L (4.3US qt); 1 downdraught 2V carb, Solex 35/35 EEIT. Cooling system capacity 7.7L (7.3US qt)

Transmission: a) 5–speed manual, final drive ratio 3.31
b) Automatic, hydraulic torque converter and 3–speed Planetary gear set, central gear lever; final drive ratios 3.31.

Gear ratios: a) 5–speed manual: 1st 3.36; 2nd 1.81; 3rd 1.26; 4th 1; 5th 0.82; R 3.37.
b) Automatic: Max torque multiplication in converter 2.22 times; Planetary gear set ratios: 1st 2.47; 2nd 1.47; 3rd 1; R 2.11.

Performance: Max speed 110mph/177kmh (manufacturers test specification), speed at 1000rpm in top gear 26.2mph/40kmh; acceleration 0 – 60mph/97kmh 7.8secs; power to weight ratio 10kg/kW (7.4kg/PS); consumption (touring) 10–15L/100km (28.2– 18.8mpg) [23.5–15.7US mpg].

Panther Kallista 2.8

```
2.9 Litre V6
110.5kW–148hp–150PS
Fuel injection
```

As 1.6 Litre, except.

Weight: Kerbweight (DIN) 1020kg

Engine data (DIN): 6–cylinder in 60deg V (93 x 72mm), 2935cm3, compression ratio 9.5:1; 110.5 kW (148hp) [150PS] at 5700rpm, 37.6kW/L (50.4hp/L) [51.1PS/L]; 233Nm (171.9lbft) at 3000rpm.
With Catalyst: Compression ratio 9:1; 106.5kW (143hp) [145PS] at 5500rpm; 36.3kW/L (48.6hp/L) [49.4PS/L]; 222Nm (22.6lbft) at 3000rpm; unleaded regular grade.

Engine construction: Ford V6, parallel valves, central camshaft (toothed belt) 4 bearing crankshaft; oil capacity 4.5L (4.3US qt); fuel injection Bosch K–Jetronic. Cooling system capacity approx 8L (7.6US qt).

Transmission: a) 5–speed manual, final drive ratio 3.31.
b) Automatic, hydraulic torque converter and 4–speed Panetary gear set, central selector lever with final drive ratio 3.31.

Gear ratios: a) 5–speed manual: 1st 3.36; 2nd 1.81; 3rd 1.26; 4th 1; 5th 0.82; R 3.37.
b) Automatic: Max torque multipication in converter 2 times; Planetary gear set ratios: 1st 2.47; 2nd 1.47; 3rd 1; 4th 0.75; R 2.11.

Performance: Max speed 112mph/180kmh (manufacturers test specification), speed at 1000rpm in 5th gear 24.8mph/40kmh; acceleration 0 – 60mph/97kmh approx 7.7secs; power to weight ratio 9.2kg/kW (6.8kg/PS); consumption (touring) 10–15L/100km (28.2–18.8mpg) [23.5–15.7US mpg].

Panther Solo

Four wheel drive 2 + 2–seater Coupe, with a Ford 2 Litre Turbocharged engine and 5–speed transmission, mechanics supplied by Ford. First shown at Birmingham 1984. 2 + 2 version Frankfurt 1987. A 2.9 V6 engine is in preparation for the USA.

```
2 Litre Turbo
152kW–204hp–207PS
Fuel injection
```

Body, Weight: 3–door Coupe, 2 + 2–seater; kerbweight approx (DIN) 1100kg.

Engine data (DIN): 4–cylinder in–line (90.82 x 76.95mm), 1994cm3; compression ratio 8:1; 152kW (204hp) [207PS] at 6000rpm, 76.2kW/L (102.1hp/L) [103.8PS/L]; 276Nm (203.7lbft) at 4500rpm; leaded premium grade.

Engine construction: Mid engined car. Valves in V 45deg (4 per cylinder), hydraulic tappets; 2 overhead camshafts (toothed belt); light-alloy cylinder head; oil cooler. Electronic fuel injection, Weber Marelli; 1 exhaust turbocharger Garrett T31/TO4, max boost pressure approx 0.55bar, charge–air cooler.

Transmission: (to all wheels) 5–speed manual, 4WD Ferguson system with viscous coupling (distribution front 36%, rear 64%), final drive ratio 3.52.

Gear ratios: 1st 2.952; 2nd 1.937; 3rd 1.336; 4th 1; 5th 0.804; R 2.755.

Chassis: Integral body; front and rear independent suspension, front McPherson struts, control arm and antiroll bar, rear semi– trailing arm, control arm, antiroll bar, coil springs and telescopic damper. Servo/power assisted disc brakes (front ventilated), disc diameter front 21.2cm, rear 23.6cm, ABS system ATE, mechanical handbrake to rear wheels; rack and pinion steering; fuel tank 57L (12.5Gal) [15.1US Gal); tyres 195/170 VR 15, wheel rims 6J.

Dimensions: Wheelbase 253cm, track 153/151.5cm, clearance 15cm. Length 434.5cm, width 178cm, height 118cm.

Performance: Max speed 178mph/241kmh (manufacturers test specifications), speed at 1000rpm in 5th gear 26.4mph/42.4kmh; acceleration 0 – 60mph/97kmh 5.7secs; power to weight ratio from 7.2kg/kW (5.3kg/PS); consumption approx 8–13L/100km (35.3– 21.7mpg) [29.4–18.1US mpg]

Panther Solo

PAYKAN   IR

Iran Khodro Co., Karadl Road, Teheran, Iran.

Licence manufacturer of vehicles in the PSA Group. Production of the ancient Hillman Hunter with a Peugeot engine has now ceased, currenlty producing a model based on the Peugeot 405.

PEUGEOT   F

Automobiles Peugeot–Talbot, 75 Avenue de la Grande Armee, 75116 Paris, France.

MODEL RANGE
205 – 309 – 305 – 405 – 505

Peugeot 205

Compact Saloon/Sedan with 5–seats, front wheel drive, 2/4–door with tail gate. Debut January 1983. Summer 1983 with diesel engine, January 1984 model GTI with 103hp. February 1986: available as a convertible and with automatic transmission. Paris 1986: GTI 1.9 with 129hp. 1988: new engine range "TU".

Peugeot

954cm3
33kW–44hp–45PS
1 Carb

Body, Weight: Saloon/Sedan 3/5–door, 5–seater; kerbweight (DIN) 760kg, gross vehicle weight 1140kg.

Engine data (DIN): 4–cylinder in–line (70 x 62mm). 954cm3, compression ratio 9.4:1; 33kW (44hp) [45PS] at 5200rpm, 34.7kW/L (46.5hp/L) [47.1PS/L]; 69Nm (50.9lbft) at 2400rpm; leaded premium grade.
In some countries: 31kW (41.5hp) [42PS]

Engine construction: Designated TU 9. Engine block with transmission and differential tilted 6deg to front. Overhead valves in V (approx 35deg), 1 overhead camshaft (chain) light– alloy cylinder and wet cylinder liner; 5 bearing crankshaft; oil capacity 3.5L (3.3US qt); 1 horizontal draft carb Solex 32 PBISA 16/412 Battery 12V 25Ah, alternator 750W; cooling system capacity 5.8L (5.5US qt).

Peurgoet 205 GR

Transmission (to front wheels): 4–speed manual (without direct drive), final drive ratio 4.286.

Gear ratios: 1st 3.42; 2nd 1.81; 3rd 1.13; 4th 0.81; R 3.58.

Chassis: Integral body, front McPherson strut (coil spring and co–axial telescopic damper) with control arm and antiroll bar, rear independent suspension with trailing arms, transverse torsion bar, and telescopic dampers. Servo/power assisted brakes, front discs, 24.7cm diameter, rear drums; mechanical handbrake on rear; rack and pinion steering; fuel tank 50L (11Gal) [13.2US Gal]; tyres 135 SR 13, 4.5 inch wheels.

Dimensions: Wheelbase 242cm, track 135/130cm, clearance 12cm, turning circle 10.5m. Load space 7.6–42.4cu ft (215–1200dm3). Length 370.5cm, width 156/157cm, height 137.5cm.

Performance: Max speed 89mph/143kmh (manufacturers test specifications), speed at 1000rpm in 4th gear 17.8mph/28.7kmh; acceleration 0 – 62mph/100kmh 18.8secs; standing km 39.4secs; power to weight ratio 23kg/kW (16.9kg/PS); consumption ECE 4.6/6.3/6.8L/100km (61.4/44.8/41.5mpg) [51.1/37.3/34.6US mpg].

1124cm3
40kW–54hp–55PS
1 Carb

As 954cm3, except for:

Weight: Kerbweight (DIN) 765kg, gross vehicle weight 1195kg.

Engine data (DIN): 4–cylinder in–line (72 x 69mm), 1124cm3; compression ratio 9.4:1; 40kW (54hp) [55PS] at 5800rpm, 35.6kW/L (47.7hp/L) [48.9PS/L]; 89Nm (65.6lbft) at 3200rpm.

Peugeot 205 XL

Engine construction: Designated TU 1.
Transmission: a) 4–speed manual, final drive ratio 3.765.
b) 5–speed manual, final drive ratio 3.938.
Gear ratios: a) 4–speed manual: 1st 3.418; 2nd 1.81; 3rd 1.129; 4th 0.814; R 3.584.
b) 5–speed manual: 1st 3.418; 2nd 1.81; 3rd 1.276; 4th 0.975; 5th 0.767; R 3.584.
Chassis: Tyres 145 SR 13.
Performance: Max speed 98mph/157kmh (manufacturers test specifications), speed at 1000rpm in 5th gear 21.3mph/34.2kmh; acceleration 0 – 62mph/100kmh 14.6secs; standing km 36.2secs; power to weight ratio from 19.1kg/kW (13.9kg/PS); consumption ECE 5–speed 4.5/5.9/6.7L/100km (62.8/47.9/42.2mpg) [52.3/39.9/35.1US mpg].

1294cm3
76kW–102hp–103PS
2 2V Carbs

As 954cm3, except:

Weight: Kerbweight (DIN) approx 790kg, gross vehicle weight 1220kg.

Engine data (DIN): 4–cylinder in–line (75 x 73.2mm), 1294cm3: compression ratio 9.6:1; 76kW (102hp) [103PS] at 6800rpm, 58.7kW/L (78.6hp/L) [79.6PS/L]; 120Nm (88.5lbft) at 5000rpm.

Engine construction: Designated TU 2.4. 2 downdraught 2V carbs Weber 40 DCOM 10; alternator 1000W.

Transmission: 5–speed manual, final drive ratio 4.286.

Gear ratios: 1st 3.418; 2nd 1.95; 3rd 1.357; 4th 1.054; 5th 0.854; R 3.584.

Chassis: Front ventilated discs; tyres 165/70 HR 13, 5.5J wheels.

Performance: Max. speed 118mph/190kmh (manufacturers test specification), speed at 1000rpm in 5th gear 17.6mph/28.3kmh: acceleration 0–62mph/100kmh 9.6secs; standing km 31.4secs; power to weight ratio from 10.4kg/kW (7.7kg/PS); consumption ECE 5.5/7.6/9.6L/100km (51.4/37.2/29.4mpg) [42.8/30.9/24.5US mpg].

Peugeot 205 Raylle

1361cm3
48/45kW–68/60hp–70/61PS
1 Carb

As 954cm3, except:

Weight: Saloon/Sedan 3/5–door; kerbweight (DIN) 790kg, gross vehicle weight 1220kg. Convertible/Cabriolet 2–door, 4–seater; kerbweight (DIN) 885kg, gross vehicle weight 1215kg.

Engine data (DIN): 4–cylinder in–line (75 x 77mm), 1361cm3: compression ratio 9.3:1; 51kW (68hp) [70PS] at 5600rpm, 37.5kW/L (50.3hp/L) [51.4PS/L]; 111Nm (81.9lbft) at 3400rpm.
With Catalyst: Compression ratio 8.4:1; 45kW (60hp) [61PS] at 5200rpm, 33.1kW/L (44.3hp/L) [44.8PS/L]; 103Nm (76lbft) at 3000rpm.

Engine construction: Designated TU3. 1 downdraught carb Weber 34 PBISA 17/481. Battery 12V 29Ah.

Transmission: 5–speed gear, final drive ratio 3.765.

Gear ratios: 1st 3.418; 2nd 1.81; 3rd 1.276; 4th 0.975; 5th 0.767; R 3.584.

Chassis: Rear antiroll bar; tyres 145 SR 13.

Dimensions: Convertible/Cabriolet: Load space 7.6–20cu ft (215–565dm3), height 138cm.

Performance: Max speed 104mph/167kmh, Convertible/Cabriolet 101mph/162kmh, with Catalyst 99mph/159kmh (manufacturers test specifications), speed at 1000rpm in 5th gear 22.2mph/35.8kmh; acceleration 0 – 62mph/100kmh 12.2secs; standing km 34.2secs; power to weight ratio from 15.5kg/kW (11.3kg/PS); consumption ECE 4.6/6.6/7.2L/100km (61.4/44.1/39.2mpg) [51.1/36.8/32.7US mpg], Convertible/Cabriolet 4.8/6.6/7.2L/100km (58.8/42.8/39.2mpg) [49/35.6/32.7US mpg].

Peugeot

Peugeot 205 CJ

```
1361cm3
63/59kW–79/84hp–85/80PS
2V Carb/Central–Single Point Injection
```

As 954cm3, except:

Body, Weight: Saloon/Sedan 3/5–door; kerbweight (DIN) 820kg, gross vehicle weight 1230kg. Convertible 2–door, 4–seater, kerbweight (DIN) 885kg, gross vehicle weight 1215kg.

Engine data (DIN): 4–cylinder in–line (75 x 77mm), 1361cm3; compression ratio 9.3:1; 63kW (84hp) [85PS] at 6400rpm, 46.3kW/L (62hp/L) [62.5PS/L]; 116Nm (85.6lbft) at 4000rpm.
With Catalyst (central/single point injection): 59kW (79hp) [80PS] at 6200rpm; 42.3kW/L (56.7hp/L) [58.8PS/L]; 111Nm (81.9lbft) at 4000rpm.

Engine construction: Designated TU 3S. Oil capacity 4L (3.8US qt); 1 downdraught 2V carb Solex 3234 Z2. Battery 12V 29Ah; cooling system capacity 8.7L (8.2US qt).

Transmission: 5–speed manual, final drive ratio 4.286.

Gear ratios: 1st 3.418; 2nd 1.95; 3rd 1.357; 4th 1.054; 5th 0.854; R 3.584.

Chassis: Rear antiroll bar; tyres 165/70 SR 13, wheels 5J.

Dimensions: Track 136.5/131.5cm. Width 157cm. Convertible: Load space 7.6–20cu ft (215–565dm3), height 138cm.

Performance: Max speed 111mph/178kmh, Convertible 108mph/174kmh, Catalyst 109mph/175kmh (manufacturers test specifications), speed at 1000rpm in 5th gear 17.6mph/28.3kmh; acceleration 0 – 62mph/100kmh 10.6secs (11.4secs); standing km 32.5secs (32.7secs); power to weight ratio from 13.0kg/kW (9.6kg/PS); consumption ECE 5.2/7.0/9.5L/100/km (54.3/40.4/29.7mpg) [45.2/33.6/24.8US mpg], Convertible 5.5/7.3/8.9L/100km (51.4/38.7/31.7mpg) [42.8/32.2/26.4US mpg].

Peugeot 205 XS

```
1580cm3
59/55kW–79/74hp–80/75PS
1 Carb
```

As 954cm3, except:

Weight: Kerbweight (DIN) 880kg, gross vehicle weight 1300kg.

Engine data (DIN): 4–cylinder in–line (83 x 73mm), 1580cm3, compression ratio 9.4:1; 59kW (79hp) [80PS] at 5600rpm, 37.2kW/L (49.8hp/L) [50.6PS/L]; 132Nm (97.3lbft) at 2800rpm.
With Catalyst: 55kW (74hp) [75PS] at 5800rpm; 34.8kW/L (46.6hp/L) [47.5PS/L] at 3000rpm.
Or: (83 x 88mm), 1905cm3; compression ratio 8.4:1; 73kW (98hp [100PS] at 6000rpm, 38.6kW/L (51.7hp/L) [52.5PS/L]; 137Nm (101.1lbft) at 3000rpm.

R22

Engine construction: Designated XU 5 IC, in–line engine inclined 30deg to rear, parallel valves, 1 overhead camshaft (toothed belt); oil capacity 4.5L (4.3US qt); 1 Weber downdraught carb 36 TLC 1. 1.9 Litre: Electronic fuel injection. Battery 12V 29Ah; cooling system capacity approx 6.7L (6.3US qt).

Transmission: Automatic ZF 4 HP 14, hydraulic torque converter and 4–speed Planetary gear set. Final drive ratio 3.824.

Gear ratios: Automatic: Max torque multiplication in converter 2 times, Planetary gear set ratios: 1st 2.511; 2nd 1.425; 3rd 1.041; 4th 0.769; R 2.943.

Chassis: Rear antiroll bar; power assisted steering; tyres 165/70 SR 13, Wheel rims 5 J.

Dimensions: Track 136.5/131.5cm. Width 157cm.

Performance: Max speed 104mph/167kmh, Catalyst 101mph/162kmh (manufacturers test specifications), speed at 1000rpm in 4th gear 21.9mph/35.2kmh; acceleration 0 – 62mph/100kmh 13.6secs, standing km 35.3secs; power to weight 14.9kg/kW (11kg/PS); consumption ECE 5.6/7.5/8.5L/100km (50.4/37.7/33.2mpg) [42/31.4/27.7US mpg].
1.9 Litre: Max speed approx 112mph/180kmh.

Peugeot 205 GTI

```
1580cm3
85kW–114hp–115PS
Fuel Injection
```

Engine for GTI and CTI

As 954cm3, except:

Body, Weight: 3–door Saloon/Sedan, 5–seater; kerbweight (DIN) 850kg, gross vehicle weight 1275kg. Convertible 2–door, 4–seater; kerbweight (DIN) 935kg, gross vehicle weight 1265kg.

Engine data (DIN): 4–cylinder in–line (83 x 73 mm), 1580cm3; compression ratio 9.8:1 85kW (114hp) [115 PS] at 6250rpm, 53.8kW/L (72hp/L) [72.8PS/L]; 134Nm (98.9lbft) at 4000rpm.
Certain countries: 76kW (102hp) [104PS].

Engine construction: Designated XU 5J, engine inclined 30deg to rear. Parallel valves, 1 overhead camshaft (toothed belt). Oil capacity 5L (4.7US qt); Bosch L–Jetronic electronic fuel injection. 12V 29Ah Battery; cooling system capacity, approx 6.6L (6.2US qt).

Peugeot 205 CTI

Peugeot

Transmission: 5-speed manual, final drive ratio 4.063.

Gear ratios: 1st 3.251; 2nd 1.85; 3rd 1.36; 4th 1.069; 5th 0.865; R 3.333.

Chassis: Front A arm (not for Convertible). Front and rear antiroll bar; front ventilated disc brakes; tyres 185/60 HR 14, wheel rims 5.5J.

Dimensions: Track 139/133ccm, width 157cm, height 135.5cm. Convertible; load space 7.6–20cu ft (215–565dm3), height 138cm.

Performance: Max speed 122mph/196kmh, Convertible 118mph/190kmh (manufacturers test specifications), speed at 1000rpm in 5th gear 18.7mph/30.1kmh 9.1secs (9.7secs); standing km 30.4secs (31.2secs); power to weight ratio from 10kg/kW (7.4kg/PS); Consumption ECE 5.9/7.5/9.2L/100km (47.9/37.7/30.7mpg) [39.9/31.4/25.6US mpg], Convertible 6.0/7.8/9.2L/100km (47.1/36.2/30.7mpg) [39.2/30.2/25.6US mpg].

```
1905 cm3
96/90/76kW–129/120/102hp–
130/122/105PS
Fuel Injection
```

Engine for GTI 1.9

As 954 cm3, except:

Body, Weight: Saloon/Sedan 3-door, 5-seater; kerbweight (DIN) 880kg gross vehicle weight 1300kg. Convertible/Cabriolet (Catalyst only 104PS) 2-door, 4-seater; kerbweight 935kg, gross vehicle weight 1295kg.

Engine data (DIN): 4-cylinder in-line (83 x 88mm), 1905cm3, compression ratio 9.6:1 96KW (129hp) [130PS] at 6000rpm, 50.4kW/L (67.5hp/L) [68.3PS/L]; 165Nm (122.1lbft) at 4750rpm.
With Catalyst: Compression ratio 9.2:1; 90kW (120hp) [122PS] at 6000rpm, 47.2kW/L (63.2hp/L) [64PS/L]; 147Nm (105lbft) at 3000rpm.
Or: Compression ratio 8.4:1; 76kW (102hp) [104PS] at 6000rpm, 39.9kW/L (53.4hp/L) [54.6PS/L]; 139Nm (103.1lbft) at 3000rpm.

Engine construction: Fuel injection XU 9. Engine inclined 30deg to rear; parallel valves, 1 overhead camshaft (toothed belt); Oil capacity 5L (4.7US qt); Bosch LE2 Jetronic electronic fuel injection, 120hp Bosch Motronic M1.3. 12V 29Ah Battery; cooling system capacity approx 6.6L (6.2US qt).

Transmission: 5-speed manual, final drive ratio 3.688.

Gear ratios: 1st 2.923; 2nd 1.85; 3rd 1.36; 4th 1.069; 5th 0.865; R 3.333.

Chassis: Front A arm (not available for Convertible/Cabriolet), front and rear anti-roll bar; Servo/power assisted disc brakes (ventilated at front), 102hp version, rear drums. Tyres 185/55 VR 15, wheel rims 6J, 102hp version 185/60 HR 14, wheel rims 5.5J.

Dimensions: Track 139/133cm, width 157cm, height 135.5cm. Convertible/Cabriolet: Load space 7.6–20cu ft (215/565dm3). Height 138cm.

Performance: Max speed 128mph/206kmh, Catalyst 118mph/202kmh, (102hp, 118mph/190kmh) (manufacturers test specifications). Speed at 1000rpm in 5th gear 20.9mph/33.7kmh; acceleration 0 – 62mph/100kmh 7.8secs, Catalyst 8.5secs (102hp, 9.5secs); standing km 29.2scs; power to weight ratio 9.2 kg/kW (6.8kg/PS). Consumption ECE 5.9/7.7/9.7L/100km (47.9/36.7/29.1mpg) [39.9/30.5/24.2US mpg].

```
1.8/1.9 Litre Diesel
44/48kW–59/64hp–60/65PS
Injection Pump
```

As 954 cm3, except:

Weight: Kerbweight (DIN) 880kg, gross vehicle weight 1300kg.

Engine data (DIN): 4-cylinder in-line (80 x 88mm), 1769cm3; compression ratio 23:1; 44kW (59hp) [60PS] at 4600rpm, 24.9kW/L (33.4hp/L) [33.9PS/L]; 108Nm (80lbft) at 2000rpm.
1.9 Litre: (83 x 88mm), 1905cm3; compression ratio 23:1; 48kW (64hp) [65PS] at 4600rpm, 25.2kW/L (33.7hp/L) [34.1PS/L]; 121Nm (89.3lbft) at 2000rpm.

Engine construction: Fuel injection XUD 7. Transverse engine. Parallel valves, grey cast iron cylinder block; 1 open camshaft (toothed belt); oil capacity 5L (4.7US qt); Diesel injection pump. 12V 42Ah battery; 50A alternator; cooling system capacity approx 8.3L (7.9US qt).

Transmission: a) 4-speed manual, final drive ratio 3.471.
b) 5-speed manual, final drive ratio 3.588.

Gear ratios: a) 4-speed manual: 1st 3.308; 2nd 1.882; 3rd 1.148; 4th 1.148; 5th 0.8; R 3.333.
b) 5-speed manual: 1st 3.308; 2nd 1.882; 3rd 1.28; 4th 0.969; 5th 0.757; R 3.333.

Chassis: Rear antiroll bar; optional power assisted steering; tyres 155/70 SR 13 or 165/70 SR 13.

Dimensions: Width 157cm.

Performance: Maximum speed 97mph/156kmh, 1.9D 101mph/162kmh (manufacturers test specifications), speed at 1000rpm in 5th gear 23.7mph/38.1kmh; acceleration 0 – 62mph/100kmh 15.1secs, 1.9D 14.2secs; standing km 36.5secs; power to weight ratio at 20.0kg/kW (14.7kg/PS); consumption ECE 3.9/5.2/5.4L/100km (72.4/54.3/52.3mpg) [60.3/45.2/43.6US mpg].

Peugeot 309

5-door Saloon/Sedan between 205 and 305, chassis as 205, with 1.1, 1.3, 1.6 and 1.9 Litre displacement engines, 4 or 5-speed transmission. Launched September 1985. From Autumn 1986 also with 1.9 Litre diesel. December 1986: Also with 3 door saloon/sedan. GTI with 129hp.

```
1118 cm3
40.5kW–54hp–55PS
1 Carb
```

Body, Weight: 3/5-door Saloon/Sedan, 5-seater; kerbweight (DIN) 850/870kg, gross vehicle weight 1290kg.

Engine data (DIN): 4-cylinder in-line (74 x 65mm), 1118cm3; compression ratio 9.6:1; 40.5kW (54hp) [55PS] at 6000rpm, 36.2kW/L (49hp/L) [49.2PS/L]; 88Nm (64.9lbft) at 3000rpm; leaded premium grade.

Engine construction: Fuel injection E1A. Transverse front engine, inclined to the rear. Side camshaft (chain); Light-alloy cylinder head. 5 bearing crankshaft. Oil capacity 3.3L (3.1US qt); 1 Weber downdraught carb 32 IBSH 13. 12V 24Ah Battery, alternator 55A; cooling system capacity approx 6.6L (6.23US qt).

Transmission: (to front wheels): a) 4-speed manual, (without direct drive), final drive ratio 4.429.
b) 5-speed manual, final drive ratio 4.063.

Gear ratios: a) 4-speed manual: 1st 3.251; 2nd 1.85; 3rd 1.148; 4th 0.800; R 3.333.
b) 5-speed manual: 1st 3.251; 2nd 1.85; 3rd 1.28; 4th 0.969; 5th 0.757; R 3.333.

Chassis: Integral body. Front McPherson struts (coil springs and coaxial telescopic damper) with lower control arm and antiroll bar, rear independent suspension with semi trailing arm, torsion bar and telescopic damper. Servo/power assisted disc brakes, front disc diameter 24.7cm, rear drums; mechanical hand brake on rear wheels; rack and pinion steering; Fuel tank 55L (12.1Gal) [14.5US Gal]; tyres 145 SR 13, wheel rims 4.5 inch.

Dimensions: Wheelbase 247cm. Track 141/137.5, clearance 13cm, turning circle 11.0m, load space 10.4/16/21.7cu ft (295/455/615dm3). Length 405cm, width 163cm, height 138cm.

Performance: Max speed 93mph/150kmh (manufacturers test specifications), speed at 1000rpm in 4th gear 20.9mph/33.6kmh; acceleration 0 – 62mph/100kmh 17.3secs; standing km 38.1secs; power to weight ratio 21kg/kW (15.5kg/PS); consumption ECE 5.3/6.9/7.4L100km (53.3/40.9/38.2mpg) [44.4/34.1/31.8US mpg].

```
1.3/1.4cm3
47/59kW–63/79hp–64/80PS
1 Carb
```

As 1118cm3, except:

Engine data (DIN): 4-cylinder in-line (76.7 x 70mm), 1294cm3, compression ratio 9.5:1; 47kW (63hp) [64PS] at 5600rpm, 36.4kW/L (48.8hp/L) [49.5PS/L]; 108Nm (79.71bft) at 2800rpm.
With Catalyst (Central injection, OHC engine TU3M): (75 x 77mm), 1361cm3; 59kW (79hp) [80PS] at 6200rpm, 42.3kW/L (56.7hp/L) [58.8PS/L]; 111Nm (81.9lbft) at 4000rpm.

Engine construction: Fuel injection G1A. 1 Weber 32 IBSCH 14 downdraught carb. 12V 29 Ah battery.

Peugeot 309 XL

Peugeot

Transmission: 5-speed manual, final drive ratio 4.063.
Gear ratios: 1st 3.251; 2nd 1.85; 3rd; 1.28; 4th 0.969; 5th 0.757; R 3.333.
Performance: Max speed 103mph/165kmh, Catalyst 106mph/170kmh (manufacturers test specifications), speed at 1000rpm in 5th gear 20.9mph/33.7kmh; acceleration 0 – 62mph/100kmh 14.8secs; standing km 36.0secs; power to weight ratio from 18.1kg/kW (13.3kg/PS); consumption ECE 4.8/6.3/7.7L/100km (58.8/44.8/36.7mpg) [49/37.3/30.5US mpg].

> 1580 cm3
> 69/55kW–93/74hp–94/75PS
> 1 2V Carbs

As 1118cm3, except:

Weight: Kerbweight (DIN) 870/890, Automatic 910kg, gross vehicle weight 1310/1330kg.
Engine data (DIN): 4-cylinder in-line (83 x 73mm) 1580cm3, compression ratio 8.95:1; 69kW (93hp) [94PS] at 6250rpm, 43.7kW/L (58.6hp/L) [59.5PS/L]; 137Nm (101lbft) at 3250rpm.
With automatic: Compression ratio 9.4:1; 59kW (79hp) [80PS] at 5600rpm; 130Nm (95.9lbft) at 2800rpm.
With Catalyst: Compression ratio at 8.35:1 55kW (74hp) [75PS] at 5800rpm, 34.8kW/L (46.6hp/L) [47.5PS/L]; 115Nm (84.91bft) at 3000rpm.
Engine construction: Designation XU 5 2C. 1 overhead camshaft (toothed belt); light-alloy cylinder block; oil capacity 4.5L (4.3US qt); 1 Weber 34/34 Z1 twin barrel carb; automatic Weber 36 TLC1 carb. 12V 33 Ah battery; cooling system capacity 7.5L (7.1US qt).
Transmission: a) 5-speed manual, final drive ratio 4.06.
b) Automatic ZF 4 HP 14, hydraulic torque converter and 4-speed Planetary gear set. Central selector lever, final drive ratio 3.824.
Gear ratios: a) 5-speed manual: 1st 3.251; 2nd 1.85; 3rd 1.28; 4th 0.969; 5th 0.757; R 3.333.
b) Automatic: Max torque multiplication in converter 2 times. Planetary gear set ratios 2.51; 1.42; 1.04; 0.77; R 2.94.
Chassis: Rear antiroll bar; tyres 165/70 SR 13, wheel rims 5J.
Performance: Max speed 112mph/180kmh, automatic 103mph/165kmh (manufacturers test specifications), speed at 1000rpm in 5th gear 20.9mph/33.7kmh; acceleration 0 – 62mph/100kmh 10.5secs, automatic 16.0secs; standing km 32.4secs, automatic 36.9secs; power to weight ratio from 12.6kg/kW (9.3kg/PS); consumption ECE 5.3/6.8/8.8 (53.3/41.5/32.1mpg) [44.4/34.6/26.7US mpg]. Automatic 5.8/7.4/8.5L/100km (48.7/38.2/33.2mpg) [40.6/31.8/27.7US mpg].

> 1905cm3
> 81/73.5kW–109/99hp–110/100PS
> Fuel Injection

As 1118cm3, except:

Weight: Kerbweight (DIN) 920kg, gross vehicle weight 1350kg.
Engine data (DIN): 4-cylinder in-line (83 x 88mm), 1905cm3.
With central/single point injection: Compression ratio 9.2:1; 81kW (109hp) [110PS] at 6000rpm, 42.5kW/L (56.9hp/L) [57.7PS/L]; 161Nm (118.8lbft) at 3000rpm.
Automatic (with fuel injection): Compression ratio 8.4:1; 73.5kW (99hp) [100PS] at 6000rpm, 38.6kW/L (51.7hp/L) [52.5PS/L]; 143Nm (105.5lbft) at 3000rpm; unleaded fuel.
Engine construction: Designated XU9. 1 overhead camshaft (toothed belt); light-alloy cylinder block; oil capacity 4.5L (4.3US qt); Solex/electronic central injection. Bosch LU2-Jetronic electronic fuel injection. 12V33 Ah Battery; 750W alternator; cooling system capacity approx 8.0L (7.6US qt).
Transmission: a) 5 speed manual, final drive ratio 3.69.
b) Automatic ZF 4 HP, hydraulic torque converter and 4-speed Planetary gear set, central selector lever, final drive ratio 3.15.
Gear ratios: a) 5-speed manual: 1st 3.251 2nd 1.85; 3rd 1.28; 4th 0.969; 5th 0.757; R 3.333.
b) Automatic; max torque multiplication in converter 2 times, Planetary gear set ratios: 2.51; 1.42; 1.04; 0.77; R 2.94.
Chassis: Rear antiroll bar; tyres 175/65 HR 14, wheel rims 5.5J.
Dimensions: Track 140/137cm.
Performance: Max speed 119mph/191kmh, automatic 112mph/180kmh (manufacturers test specifications), speed at 1000rpm in top gear 23.7mph/38.2kmh; acceleration 0 – 62mph/100kmh 9.9secs automatic 12.7secs; power to weight ratio from 11.4kg/kW (8.4kg/PS); consumption approx 7-10L/100km (40.4-28.2mpg) [33.6-23.5US mpg], automatic 7-11L/100km (40.4-25.7mpg) [33.6-21.4US mpg].

Peugeot 309 XS

> 1905cm3
> 96/90kW–129/121hp–130/122PS
> Fuel Injection

As 1118cm3, except:

Weight: Kerbweight (DIN) 930/950kg, gross vehicle weight 1350kg.
Engine data (DIN): 4-cylinder in-line (83 x 88mm); 1905cm3; compression ratio 9.6:1; 96kW (129hp) [130PS] at 6000rpm, 50.4kW/L (67.5hp/L) [68.2PS/L]; 165Nm (121.81bft) at 4750rpm.
With Catalyst: Compression ratio 9.2:1; 90kW (121hp) [122PS] at 6000rpm, 47.2kW/L (63.2hp/L) [64PS/L]; 153Nm (112.9lbft) at 3000rpm; unleaded regular grade.
Certain countries: 88kW (118hp) [120PS].
Engine construction: Designated XUD 9. 1 overhead camshaft (toothed belt); light-alloy cylinder block; Oil capacity 4.5L (4.3US qt); Bosch LE2-Jetronic fuel injection; Catalyst Bosch Motronic M1.3. 12V 33Ah battery; 750W alternator; cooling system capacity approx 8.0L (7.6US qt).
Transmission: 5-speed manual, final drive ratio 3.69.
Gear ratios: 1st 2.923; 2nd 1.85; 3rd 1.360 4th 1.069; 5th 0.865; R 3.333.
Chassis: Front A arm, power/assisted steering, front ventilated disc brakes; tyres 185/55 VR15, wheel rims 6J.
Dimensions: Track 141/138cm.
Performance: Max speed 128mph/206kmh, Catalyst 126mph/202kmh (manufacturers test specifications), speed at 1000rpm in top gear 21mph/33.7kmh; acceleration 0 – 62mph/100kmh 8secs Catalyst 8.1secs; standing km 29.8secs; power to weight ratio from 9.7kg/kW (7.1kg/PS); consumption ECE 6.1/7.8/10L/100km (46.3/36.2/28.2mpg) [38.6/30.2/23.5US mpg].

Peugeot 309 GTI

> 1905cm3 Diesel
> 48kW-64hp-65PS
> Injection Pump

As 1118cm3, except:

Weight: Kerbweight (DIN) 930/950kg, gross vehicle weight 1350/1370kg.
Engine data (DIN): 4-cylinder in-line (83 x 88mm), 1905cm3; compression ratio 23.5:1; 48kW (64hp) [65PS] at 4600rpm, 25.1kW/L (33.6hp/L) [34.1PS/L]; 120Nm (88.6lbft) at 2000rpm.
Engine construction: Designated XUD 9. Parallel valves; 1 overhead camshaft (toothed belt); grey cast iron cylinder block; oil capacity 5L (4.7US qt); diesel injection pump. 12V 42Ah battery; 750 W alternator; cooling system capacity 8.5L (8US qt).
Transmission: 5-speed manual, final drive ratio 3.814.
Gear ratios: 1st 3.251; 2nd 1.850; 3rd 1.28; 4th 0.969; 5th 0.757; R 3.333.
Chassis: Tyres 165/70 SR 14.

Peugeot

Performance: Max speed 99mph/160kmh (manufacturers test specification), speed at 1000 rpm in top gear 22.2mph/35.8kmh; acceleration 0 - 62mph/100kmh 15.3secs; standing km 36.2secs; power to weight ratio from 19.4kg/kW (14.3kg/PS); consumption ECE 4.4/5.9/7.0L/100km (64.2/47.9/40.4mpg) [53.5/39.9/33.6US mpg].

Peugeot 309 Diesel

Peugeot 305

Four-door Saloon/Sedan with front transverse engine and front wheel drive. Launched November 1977. Geneva 1980; new Export Break (Estate/Station Wagon). 1988 only with 1.6 Litre fuel and 1.9 Litre diesel.

Peugeot 305 Break GR

```
1.6 Litre
59kW–79hp–80PS
1 Carb
```

Body, Weight: Break (Estate/Station Wagon) 5–door, 5–seater; Kerbweight (DIN) 985kg, gross vehicle weight 1495kg.

Engine data (DIN): 4–cylinder in–line (83 x 73 mm), 1580cm3; compression ratio 9.4:1; 59kW (79hp) [80PS] at 5600rpm, 37.2kW/L (49.8hp/L) [50.6PS/L]; 132Nm (97.41bft) at 2800rpm; leaded premium grade.

Engine construction: Designated XL5. Transverse engine and transmission inclined at 30deg to rear. 1 overhead camshaft (toothed belt); light–alloy cylinder block and head; 5 bearing crankshaft; oil capacity 4.5L (4.3US qt); 1 Weber downdraught carb 34 TL 8 or Solex 36 FY 2. 12V 40Ah battery, alternator 750W; cooling system capacity approx 5.8L (5.5US qt).

Transmission (to all front wheels): 5–speed manual, final drive ratio, 4.188.

Gear ratios: 1st 3.251; 2nd 1.85 3rd 1.28 4th 0.969 5th 0.757; R 3.333.

Chassis: Integral body; front McPherson struts with A arm and coil spring, rear independent suspension with trailing arms. McPherson struts and coil springs, front and rear antiroll bar, telescopic damper. Servo/power assisted brakes, front discs, diameter 26.6cm, rear drums; mechanical and brake on rear wheels; rack and pinion steering; fuel tank Break 50L (11.0Gal) [13.2US Gal]; tyres 165/70TR 14 or 155 SR 14, wheel rims 5J.

Dimensions: Wheelbase 262cm; track 142/135cm, clearance 12cm, turning circle 11m. Load space 14.5-53.3cu ft (410-1510dm3). Length 428.5cm, width 163.5cm, height 143cm.

Performance: Max speed (manufacturers test specifications) 102mph/164kmh. Speed at 1000rpm in 5th gear 21.2mph/34.1kmh; acceleration 0 – 62mph/100kmh 14secs; power to weight ratio 16.7kg/kW (12.3kg/PS); consumption ECE 5.5/7.5/8.9L/100km (51.4/37.7/31.7mpg) [42.8/31.4/26.4 mpg US].

```
1.9 Litre Diesel
48kW–64hp–65PS
Injection Pump
```

As 1.3 Litre, except:

Body, Weight: Break (Estate/Station Wagon) 5–door, 5–seater; kerbweight (DIN) 1060kg, gross vehicle weight 1565kg.

Engine data (DIN): 4-cylinder in-line (83 x 88mm), 1905cm3; compression ratio 23.5:1 48kW (64hp) [65PS] at 4600rpm, 25.1kW/L (33.6hp/L) [34.1PS/L]; 120Nm (88.61bft) at 2000rpm.

Engine construction: Designated XUD 9. Parallel valves; 1 overhead camshaft (toothed belt); grey cast iron cylinder head and block; oil capacity 5L (4.7US qt); diesel injection pump. 12V 60Ah battery; 750W alternator; cooling system capacity 9.5L (9US qt).

Dimensions: Track 142/133cm.

Performance: Max speed at 95mph/152kmh (manufacturers test specifications), acceleration 0 – 62mph/100kmh, 17.4secs; standing km 37.6secs; power to weight ratio from 22.1kg/kW (16.3 kg/PS); consumption ECE 4.8/6.8/6.8L/100km (58.8/41.5/41.5mpg) [49.0/34.6/34.6US mpg].

Peugeot 405

New model: Four–door Saloon/Sedan; Transverse front engine from 1.4 to 1.9 Litre displacement. 4 or 5–speed manual transmission and independent suspension. Launched May 1987. Geneva 1988; introduction of diesel and turbodiesel engine, also automatic transmission, also later Break - Estate/Station Wagon. Geneva 1989: Saloon/Sedan 1.9 Litre 109hp also with permanent four wheel drive. M1 16 4x4 with viscous coupling and Torsen differential for the Spring of 1989.

Peugeot 405 Break GL

```
1361cm3
47kW–63hp–64PS
1 Carb
```

Body, Weight: Saloon/Sedan 4–door, 5–seater; kerbweight (DIN) 970kg, gross vehicle weight 1400kg.

Engine data (ECE); 4–cylinder in–line (75 x 77mm), 1361cm3, compression ratio 9.3:1; 51kW (68hp) [69PS] at 5600rpm, 37.5kW/L (50.2hp/L) [50.7PS/L]; 109Nm (80.41bft) at 3400rpm; leaded premium grade.

Engine construction: Designated TU–3. Transverse engine inclined at 6deg to rear. Valves in V 35deg. 1 overhead camshaft (toothed belt); light–alloy cylinder head and block; 5 bearing crankshaft. Oil capacity 3.5L (3.3US qt); 1 Solex downdraught carb 34 PBISA 17/481. 12V 29/35Ah, 55A alternator; cooling system capacity approx 6.6L (6.2US qt).

Transmission (on front wheel): 4–speed manual, central gear lever. Final drive ratio. 4.286 (14/60).

Gear ratios: 1st 3.418 2nd 1.810 3rd 1.129 4th 0.814; R 3.584.

Chassis: Integral body; front and rear sub-frame; front McPherson strut (coil spring and coaxial telescopic damper) with lower control arm and antiroll bar, rear independent suspension with trailing arm, transverse torsion bar and telescopic damper; front and rear antiroll bar. Servo/power assisted brakes, front discs, diameter 26.6cm, rear drums; mechanical handbrake to rear wheels; rack and pinion steering; fuel tank 70L (15.4Gal) [18.5US Gal]; tyres 165/70 TR 14, wheel rims 5J

Peugeot

Dimensions: Wheelbase 267cm, track 145/143.5cm, clearance 12.5cm, turning circle 11m. Load space 16.6 cu ft (470dm3). Length 441cm, width 171.5cm, height 140.5cm. Break (Estate/Station Wagon): Clearance 14cm, load space 13.7-26.3cu ft (390-745dm3), length 440cm, height 144.5cm.

Performance: Max speed at 103mph/165kmh (manufacturers test specifications), speed at 1000rpm in 4th gear 19.2mph/30.9kmh; acceleration 0 – 62mph/100 15.5secs, standing km 36.2secs; power to weight ratio 19kg/kW (14.1kg/PS); consumption ECE 5.4/7.0/8.3L/100km (52.3/40.4/34mpg) [43.6/33.6/28.3US mpg].

1580cm3
68/53kW–91/71hp–92/72PS
1 2V Carb

As 1361cm3, except:

Weight: Saloon/Sedan 4-door, 5-seater; Kerbweight (DIN) 1020kg, gross vehicle weight 1500kg.
Break (Estate/Station Wagon), 5-door, 5-seater; kerbweight (DIN) from 1120kg, gross vehicle weight 1620kg.

Engine data (ECE): 4–cylinder in–line (83 x 73mm), 1580cm3; compression ratio 8.95:1; 68kW (91hp) [92PS] at 6000rpm, 43kW/L (57.6hp/L) [58.2PS/L]; 132Nm (97.41bft) at 2600rpm.
With Catalyst and electronically regulated carb: Compression ratio 8.6:1; 53kW (71hp) [72PS] at 5600rpm, 33.5kW/L (44.9hp/L) [45.6PS/L]; 123Nm (90.81bft) at 2800rpm; unleaded fuel.

Engine construction: Designated XU 5 2C. Engine inclined 30deg towards rear. Parallel valves; oil capacity 5L (4.7US qt); 1 Solex downdraught carb 34/34Z1.

Transmission: 5 speed manual, final drive ratio. 4.188(16/67).

Gear ratios: 1st 3.251 2nd 1.1850 3rd 1.280 4th 0.969 5th 0.757 R 3.333.

Chassis: Optional power assisted steering; tyres Break (Estate/Station Wagon) GR 175/70TR 14.

Performance: Max speed 112mph/180kmh, Break (Estate/Station Wagon) 109mph/175kmh (manufacturers test specifications); speed at 1000rpm in 5th gear 21.2mph/34.1kmh; acceleration 0 – 62mph/100kmh 11.6secs, Break (Estate/Station Wagon) 12.1secs, standing km 33.4secs; power to weight ratio from 15kg/kW (11.1kg/PS); consumption ECE 5.5/6.9/9.0L/100km (51.4/40.9/31.4mpg) [42.8/34.1/26.1US mpg]. Break (Estate/Station Wagon) 5.7/7.3/9.0L/100km (49.6/38.7/31.4mpg) [41.3/32.2/26.1US mpg].

Peugeot 405 GR

1905 cm3
81kW–109hp–110PS
1 2V Carb/Fuel Injection

As 1361cm3, except:

Weight: Saloon/Sedan 4-door, 5-seater; Kerbweight (DIN) 1020kg, gross vehicle weight 1500kg.
Break: 5-door Estate/Station Wagon, 5-seater; kerbweight (DIN) from 1120kg, gross vehicle weight 1620kg.

Engine data (ECE): 4–cylinder in–line (83 x 88mm), 1905cm3, compression ratio 9.3:1; 81kW (109hp) [110PS] at 6000rpm, 42.5kW/L (56.9hp/L) [57.8PS/L]; 160Nm (118.11bft) at 3000rpm.
Some Countries: 70kW (94hp) [95PS].
With Catalyst and fuel injection: Identical data; unleaded fuel.

Engine construction: Designated XU9 2C. Engine inclined 30deg towards rear. Parallel valves; oil capacity 5L (4.7US qt); 1 Solex twin barrel carb or Bosch LU2-Jetronic fuel injection.

Transmission: a) 5–speed manual, final drive ratio; 4.063, GR 3.938.
b) Automatic ZF 4 HP 14, hydraulic torque converter and 4-speed Planetary gear set. Central selector lever, final drive ratio 3.824.
4x4: Permanent four wheel drive (front and rear distribution 53/47%), manual locked front and rear differential, final drive ratio 4.43.

Gear ratios: a) 5–speed manual: 1st 3.251 (4x4 3.454); 2nd 1.85; 3rd 1.28; 4th 0.969; 5th 0.757; R 3.333.
GR: 1st 3.251; 2nd 1.85; 3rd 1.148; 4th 0.829; 5th 0.658; R 3.333.
b) Automatic: Max torque multiplication in converter 2 times, Planetary gear set ratios: 2.511; 1.425; 1.041; 0.769; R 2.943.

Chassis: Power assisted steering; tyres 185/65 HR 14 or 175/70 TR 14 wheel rims 5.5J. 4x4: Rear level control system.

Performance: a) Final drive ratio 4.063: Max speed 118mph/190kmh, automatic 114mph/184kmh, Catalyst 115mph/185kmh (manufacturers test specifications), speed at 1000rpm in 5th gear 22mph/35.4kmh; acceleration 0 – 62mph/100kmh 10.2secs, automatic 13secs, Catalyst 11.4secs, standing km 31.8secs; power to weight ratio 12.6kg/kW (9.3hp/PS); consumption ECE 5.8/7.5/9.5L/100km (48.7/37.7/29.7mpg) [40.6/31.4/24.8US mpg]. Automatic 6.2/7.7/9.7L/100km (45.6/36.7/29.1mpg) [37.9/30.5/24.2US mpg].
b) Final drive ratio 3.938: Max speed 117mph/188kmh (manufacturers test specifications), speed at 1000rpm in 4th gear 26.6mph/42.8kmh; acceleration 0 – 62mph/100kmh 10.3secs, standing km 32.0secs; consumption ECE 5.5/7.0/9.3L/100km (51.4/40.4/30.4mpg) [42.8/33.6/25.3US mpg].

Peugeot 405 SRI

1905cm3
90kW–121hp–122PS
Fuel Injection

Engine for GRI and SRI

As 1361cm3, except:

Weight: Saloon/Sedan 4-d0or, 5-seater; kerbweight (DIN) 1040kg, gross vehicle weight 1550kg.
Break (Estate/Station Wagon): 5-door, 5-seater; kerbweight (DIN) from 1120kg, gross vehicle weight 1620kg.

Engine data (ECE): 4–cylinder in–line (83 x 88mm), 1905cm3; compression 9.3:1; 90kW (121hp) [122PS]) at 5500rpm, 47.2kW/L (63.2hp/L) [64PS/L]; 170Nm (125.51bft) at 4500rpm.
With Catalyst and fuel injection (DIN): Identical data; unleaded fuel.
Certain countries: 88kW (118hp) [120PS].

Engine construction: Designated XU9 J2. Engine inclined 30deg towards rear. Parallel valves; oil capacity 5L (4.7US qt); Bosch LE3–Jetronic, electronic fuel injection; Catalyst: Bosch Motronic 1.3.

Transmission: a) 5–speed manual, final drive ratio 4.063.
b) Automatic ZF 4 HP 14, hydraulic torque converter and 4-speed Planetary gear set. Central selector lever. Final drive ratio 3.824.

Gear ratios: a) 5–speed manual: 1st 3.251 2nd 1.85 3rd 1.28 4th 0.969 5th 0.757; R 3.333.
b) Automatic: Max torque multicplication in converter 2 times, Planetary gear set: 2.511; 1.425; 1.041; 0.769; R 2.943.

Chassis: Power assisted steering; four wheel disc brakes, front ventilated discs, rear disc diameter 25cm, optional Bendix ABS system; tyres 195/60 HR 14, wheel rims 6J.

Dimensions: Width 171.5cm.

Performance: a) Max speed 124mph/200kmh, Automatic 121mph/194kmh (manufacturers test specifications), speed at 1000rpm in 5th gear 22mph/35.4kmh; acceleration 0 – 62mph/100kmh 9.7secs, automatic 11.9secs; standing km 31secs; power to weight ratio 11.6kg/kW (8.5kg/PS) consumption ECE 6.0/7.8/10.4L/100km (47.1/36.2/27.2mpg) [39.2/30.2/22.6US mpg].

Peugeot

b) Break (Estate/Station Wagon): Max speed 121mph/195kmh (manufacturers test specification); acceleration 0 - 62mph/100mph, 10.2secs, standing km 31.5secs; consumption ECE 6.1/8.1/10.4L/100km (46.3/34.9/27.2mpg) [38.6/29/22.6US mpg].

```
1905cm3 16V
116/110kW-155/147hp-158/150PS
Fuel Injection
```

Engine for Ml 16

As 1361cm3, except:

Weight: Kerbweight (DIN) 1110kg, gross vehicle weight 1560kg.

Engine data (ECE): 4–cylinder in-line (83 x 88mm), 1905cm3; compression 10.4:1; 116kW (155hp) [158PS] at 6500rpm, 60.9kW/L (81.6hp/L) [82.9PS/L]; 177Nm (130.6lbft) at 5000rpm.
With Catalyst: Compression ratio 9.7:1; 110kW (1147hp) [150PS] at 6400rpm, 57.7kW/L (77.3hp/L) [78.7PS/L]; 166Nm (122.5lbft) at 5000rpm.
Certain countries: 108kW (145hp) [147PS].

Peugeot 405 MI 16

Engine construction: Designated XUD 9 J4. Engine inclined 30deg to the rear; 4 valves per cylinder (V 49deg 30'), hydraulic tappets, 2 overhead camshaft(toothed belt); oil capacity 5.3L (5US qt); oil cooler. Bosch Motronic ML4 1 electronic fuel injection. 12V 45Ah Battery; 750W alternator; cooling system capacity approx 7.2L (6.8US qt).

Transmission: 5–speed manual. Final drive ratio, 4.429 (14/62).
4x4: Permanent four wheel drive (distribution front/rear 53/47%), central differential with viscous coupling, Torsen rear differential, final drive ratio 4.43.

Gear ratios: 1st 2.923 (4x4 3.455); 2nd 1.85; 3rd 1.28; 4th 0.969; 5th 0.757 (4x4 0.8); R.3.333.

Chassis: Front lower A arm; power/assisted steering; front disc brakes (ventilated), disc diameter rear 25cm, optional ABS (Bendix); tyres 195/60 VR 14, wheel rims 6J.
4x4: Rear level control system.

Performance: Max speed 137mph/220kmh, Catalyst 133mph/214kmh (manufacturers test specifications); speed in 5th gear at a 1000rpm 20mph/32.2kmh; acceleration 0–62mph/100kmh 8.6secs, Catalyst 9secs; standing km 29.5secs. Power to weight ratio 9.6kg/kW (7.0kg/PS); consumption ECE 6.5/8.0/11.3L/100km (43.5/35.3/25mpg) [36.2/29.4/20.8US mpg].

```
1905cm3 Diesel
51kW–68hp–70PS
Injection
```

As 1361cm3, except:

Weight: Saloon/Sedan 4-door, 5-seater; kerbweight (DIN) from 1080kg, gross vehicle weight 1560kg.
Break 5-door, 5-seater; kerbweight (DIN) from 1120kg, gross vehicle weight 1620kg.

Engine data (ECE): 4–cylinder in–line (83 x 88mm), 1905cm3; compression ratio 23:1; 51kW (68hp) [70PS] at 4600rpm, 26.8kW/L (35.9hp/L) [36.7PS/L]; 120Nm (88.6lbft) at 2000rpm.
With internal EGR-system: 48kW (64hp) [65PS].

Engine construction (ECE): Designated XUD 9A. Parallel valves, grey cast iron cylinder block; oil capacity 5L (4.7US qt); diesel injection pump. 12V 42Ah Battery; alternator 750 W; cooling system capacity approx 7.8L (7.4US qt).

Transmission: 5–speed manual, final drive ratio 4.063, Saloon/Sedan GLD 3.938.

Gear ratios: 1st 3.251; 2nd 1.850; 3rd 1.28 4th 0.969; 5th 0.757 R 3.333

Chassis: Tyres 165/70 SR 14, GRD 175/70 SR 14.

Performance: Max speed 103mph/165kmh, Break (Estate/Station Wagon) 101mph/162kmh (manufacturers test specifications), speed at 1000rpm in top gear 22.4mph/36.1kmh; power to weight ratio from 21.2kg/kW (15.4kg/PS); consumption ECE 4.6/6.2/7.0 (61.4/45.6/40.4mpg) [51.1/37.9/33.6US mpg], Break (Estate/Station Wagon) 4.8/6.5/7.0L/100km (58.8/43.5/40.4mpg) [49.0/36.2/33.6US mpg].

Peugeot 405 GRD Break

```
1769cm3 Diesel
66kW-88hp-90PS
Injection Pump/Turbo
```

As 1361cm3, except:

Body, Weight: Saloon/Sedan 4-door, 5-seater; kerbweight (DIN) from 1080kg, gross vehicle weight 1560kg.
Break (Estate/Station Wagon) 5-door, 5-seater; kerbweight (DIN) from 1120kg, gross vehicle weight 1620kg.

Engine data (ECE): 4-cylinder in-line (80 x 88mm), 1769cm3; compression ratio 22:1; 66kW (88hp) [90PS] at 4300rpm, 37.3kW/L (50hp/L) [50.9PS/L]; 180Nm (132.8lbft) at 2100rpm.

Engine construction: Designated XUD 7TE. Transverse engine. Parallel valves, greycast iron cylinder block; oil capacity 5L (4.7US qt); diesel injection pump; 1 turbocharger KKK K14 or Garrett T2; max charge-air pressure 0.8 bar; charge-air cooler. 12V 42Ah, alternator 50A, cooling system capacity approx 8.8L (8.3US qt).

Transmission: 5-speed manual, final drive ratio 4.063.

Gear ratios: 1st 3.251; 2nd 1.850; 3rd 1.148; 4th 0.829; 5th 0.658; R 3.333.

Chassis: Tyres 185/65 HR 14.

Performance: Max speed 112mph/180kmh, Break (Estate/Station Wagon) 109mph/175kmh (manufacturers test specification), speed at 1000rpm in top gear 25.3mph/40.7kmh; power to weight ratio from 16.3kg/kW (12kg/PS); consumption ECE 4.6/6.2/7.5L/100km (61.4/45.6/37.7mpg) [51.1/37.9/31.4US mpg], Break (Estate/Station Wagon) 4.9/6.5/7.5L/100km (57.6/43.5/37.7mpg) [48.0/36.2/31.4US mpg].

Peugeot 505

Saloon/Sedan with 2 Litre or 2,3 Litre diesel engine; manual or automatic transmission. Launched May 1979, Paris 1980. Turbodiesel version. 1982; new engine range and automatic transmission, also Estate/Station Wagon. 1987 Turbodiesel with charge–air cooler; 2.85 Litre V6 with 167hp.

```
1796cm3
62kW–83hp–84PS
1 2V Carb
```

Body, Weight: 4–door Saloon/Sedan, 5–seater; kerbweight (DIN) 1215kg, gross vehicle weight 1640kg.

Engine data (ECE): 4–cylinder in–line (84 x 81mm); 1796cm3; compression ratio 8.8:1; 62kW (83hp) [84PS] at 5250rpm, 34.3kW/L (46hp/L) [46.8PS/L]; 144Nm (106.3lbft) at 2750rpm; leaded premium grade.
Some Countries (DIN): 66kW (88hp) [90PS].

Engine construction: Designated XM 7A. Engine inclined towards 45deg to right; Light–alloy cylinder head; side camshaft (chain); wet cylinder liners; 5 bearing crankshaft; oil capacity 4L (3.8US qt); 1 Solex 32/34 CISAC downdraught twin barrel carb. 12V 45Ah battery, 500W alternator; cooling system capacity approx 7.1L (6.7US qt).

Transmission (to rear wheels); 5–speed manual; final drive ratio 3.7.

Gear ratios: 1st 3.592; 2nd 2.088; 3rd 1.368; 4th 1; 5th 0.823; R 3.634.

Chassis: Integral body; front McPherson struts with coil springs and coaxial telescopic damper, control arm with longitudinal compression struts, antiroll bar, rear independent suspension with A arm, coil springs and inboard telescopic damper, antiroll bar. Break (Estate/Station Wagon) rear rigid axle, coil springs and antiroll bar. Servo/power assisted brakes, front disc brakes, diameter 27.3cm, rear drums; mechanical handbrake to rear wheel; power assisted steering; fuel tank 70L (15.4Gal) [18.5US Gal]; tyres 175 SR; wheel rims 5J.

Peugeot 343

Dimensions: Wheelbase 274.5cm, track 146/144cm, clearance min 12cm, turning circle 11.8m. Load space 17.1cu ft (485dm3). Length 458cm, width 173.5cm. GL 172.5cm, height 144cm. Break: Wheelbase 290cm. Load space 39.5/79.1cu ft (1120/2240dm3). Length 490cm, width 173cm, height 154cm. Familial: Load space 21.9–68.5cu ft (620–1940dm3).
Performance: Max speed at 98mph/157kmh (manufacturers test specifications), speed at 1000rpm in 5th gear 23.6mph/38.0kmh; acceleration 0 – 62mph/100kmh 14.5secs; power to weight ratio from 19.6kg/kW (14.5kg/PS); consumption ECE 6.3/8.3/11.3L/100km (44.8/34.0/25.0mpg) [37.3/28.3/20.8US mpg].

```
1971cm3
87/72kW–105/96hp–106/98PS
1 2V Carb
```

As 1796cm3, except:

Body, Weight: 4–door Saloon/Sedan, 5–seater; unladen weight (DIN) 1215/1240kg, gross vehicle weight 1655kg. Break/Family 5–door, 5/7–seater; unladen weight (DIN) 1300kg, gross vehicle weight 1980kg.
Engine data (ECE): 4–cylinder in–line (88 x 81mm); 1971cm3; compression ratio 8.8:1; 78kW (105hp) [106PS] at 5250rpm, 39.6kW/L (53hp/L) [53.8PS/L]; 161Nm (118.8lbft) at 3000rpm.
For Break (Estate/Station Wagon)/Familial: 72kW (96hp) [98PS] at 5200rpm.
Engine construction: Designated XN 1A. 1 Solex 34/34 downdraught twin barrel carb.
Transmission: a) 5–speed manual, final drive ratio 3.889; Break 4.222.
b) Optional GR ZF automatic transmission 4 HP 22, hydraulic torque converter and 4–speed Planetary gear set. Central selector lever, final drive ratio 4.111.
Gear ratios: a) 5–speed manual: 1st 3.592; 2nd 2.088; 3rd 1.368; 4th 1; 5th 0.823; R 2.634.
b) Automatic; max torque multiplication in converter 2 times, Planetary gear set ratios: 1st 2.48; 2nd 1.48; 3rd 1; 4th 0.728; R 2.086.
Chassis: Tyres 185/65 HR 14, Break (Estate/Station Wagon) 185 SR 14.
Performance (Saloon/Sedan): Max speed 109mph/175kmh, automatic 103mph/165kmh (manufacturers test specifications), speed at 1000rpm in 5th gear 22.1mph/35.5kmh; acceleration 0 – 62mph/100kmh 12.2secs, automatic 15.9secs; power to weight ratio from 16.6kg/kW (11.5kg/PS); consumption ECE 6.4/8.5/11.8L/100km (44.1/33.2/23.9mpg) [36.8/27.7/19.5US mpg]. Automatic 6.9/9.6/11.8L/100km (40.9/29.4/23.9mpg) [34.1/24.6/19.9US mpg].

Peugeot 505 GR Break

```
2165cm3
90/85.5kW–121/115hp–122/116PS
Fuel Injection
```

As 1796cm3, except:

Body, Weight: 4–door Saloon/Sedan, 5–seater; Kerbweight (DIN) 1265kg. Gross vehicle weight 1715kg. Break/Family 5–door, 5/7–seater; kerbweight (DIN) 1365/1400kg, gross vehicle weight 1965/1985kg.
Engine data (ECE): 4–cylinder in–line (88 x 89mm); 2165cm3, compression ratio 9.8:1; 90kW (121hp) [122PS] at 5750rpm, 41.6kW/L (55.7hp/L) [56.4PS/L]; 180Nm (132.8) at 4250rpm.
With Catalyst: Compression 8.8.1; 85.5kW (115hp) [116PS] 39.5kW/L (52.9hp/L) [53.6PS/L].
USA Version (SAE net) with turbo-charger: 135kW (181hp) [183PS]; 278Nm (205.2lbft).
Engine Construction: Designated ZDJ–L. Engine inclined to right. Parallel valves; light–alloy engine block and cylinder head; 1 overhead camshaft (toothed belt); oil capacity 5L (4.7US qt), mechanical Bosch L-Jetronic, electronic fuel pump. 750W Alternator; cooling system capacity approx 7.5L (7.1US qt).

Transmission: a) 5–speed manual, final drive ratio 3.889; Break 4.111.
b) Automatic transmission, final drive ratio 4.111. Limited slip differential.
Gear ratios: a) 5–speed manual: 1st 3.592 2nd 2.088 3rd 1.368 4th 1; 5th 0.823; R 3.634.
b) Automatic: Max torque multiplication in converter 2 times, Planetary gear set ratios: 1st 2.48; 2nd 1.48; 3rd 1; 4th 0.728; R 2.086.
Chassis: Servo/power assisted disc brakes, rear disc diameter 27.3cm; Tyres 185/70 TR 14, wheel rims 5.5J.
Dimensions: Track 148/145cm.
Performance (Saloon/Sedan): Max speed at 115mph/185kmh, automatic transmission 113mph/182kmh, Catalyst 111/109mph-178/176kmh (manufacturers test specifications), speed at 1000rpm in 5th gear 22.1mph/35.5kmh; acceleration 0 – 62mph/100km 10.0secs, automatic 11.7secs, Catalyst 12.5/12.8secs; standing km 31.8secs, automatic 33.6secs; power to weight ratio 14.1kg/kW (10.4kg/PS); consumption ECE 6.6/8.4/11.0L/100km (42.8/33.6/25.7mpg) [35.6/28.0/21.4US mpg], automatic 6.8/8.9/11.8L/100km (41.5/31.7/23.9mpg) [34.6/26.4/19.9US mpg]..

Peugeot 505 GTI

```
2.85 Litre V6
122/107kW–164/143hp–166/146PS
Fuel Injection
```

As 1796cm3, except:

Body, Weight: 4–door Saloon/Sedan, 5–seater; Kerbweight (DIN) 1335kg, gross vehicle weight 1795kg.
Engine data (DIN): 6–cylinder in V 90deg. (91 x 73mm) 2849cm3, compression ratio 10:1; 122kW (164hp) [166PS] at 5600rpm, 42.9kW/L (57.5hp/L) [58.3PS/L]; 235Nm (173.4lbft) at 4250rpm; leaded premium grade.
With Catalyst: 107kW (143hp) [146PS] at 5000rpm, 37.6kW/L (50.4hp/L) (51.2PS/L); 235Nm (173.4lbft) at 3750rpm.
Engine construction: Designated ZN3J. Parallel valves; 1 overhead camshaft (chain); light–alloy cylinder head and block; wet cylinder liners; 4 bearing crankshaft; oil capacity 6L (5.7US qt); Bosch LH–Jetronic 2.2 fuel injection. 12V 45Ah Battery; 1000W alternator; cooling system capacity approx 9.5L (9.0US qt).
Transmission: a) 5–speed manual, final drive ratio 3.7.
b) ZF–Automatic transmission 4 HP 22, hydraulic torque converter and 4–speed Planetary gear set. Central selector lever, final drive ratio 3.889.
Gear ratios: a) 5–speed manual: 1st 3.845; 2nd 2.183; 3rd 1.451; 4th 1; 5th 0.845; R 3.587.
b) Automatic: Max torque multiplication in converter 2 times, Planetary gear set: 1st 2.48; 2nd 1.48; 3rd 1; 4th 0.728; R 2.086.
Chassis: Servo/power assisted disc brakes (front ventilated), rear diameter 27.3cm, optional Teves ABS System; tyres 195/60 HR 15.
Performance: Max speed 127mph/205kmh, Catalyst 122mph/197kmh, automatic 123mph/198kmh (manufacturers test specifications), speed at 1000rpm in 5th gear 22.4mph/36.0kmh; power to weight ratio 10.9kg/kW (8.0kg/PS); consumption ECE 7.6/10.0/12.8L/100km (37.2/28.2/22.1mpg) [30.9/23.5/18.4US mpg]. Automatic 7.8/9.9/13.6L/100km (36.2/28.5/20.8mpg) [30.2/23.8/17.3US mpg].

Peugeot 505 V6 S

Peugeot F • Peugeot RA • Pininfarina

2498cm3 Diesel
51kW–68hp–69PS
Fuel Pump

As 1796cm3, except:

Weight: Kerbweight (DIN) 1270/1300kg, gross vehicle weight 1725kg. Break (Estate/Station Wagon): Kerbweight (DIN) 1375/1415kg, gross vehicle weight 2055kg. Familial; kerbweight (DIN) 1410/1445kg, gross vehicle weight 2085kg.
Engine data(ECE): 4–cylinder in–line (94 x 90mm), 2498cm3, compression ratio 21:1; 51kW (68hp) [69PS] at 4500rpm, 20.4kW/L (27.3hp/L) [27.6PS/L]; 148Nm (109.2lbft) at 2000rpm.
Engine construction: Designated XD3. Cylinder block inclined to right. Side camshaft (chain); oil capacity 5L (4.7US qt); Bosch injection pump EP/VAC. 12V 60Ah Battery, 750W alternator; cooling system capacity approx 10L (9.5US qt).
Transmission: 5–speed manual, final drive ratio 3.308. Break (Estate/Station Wagon) 4.222.
Limited slip differential.
Gear ratios: 1st 3.592; 2nd 2.088; 3rd 1.368; 4th 1; 5th 0.823; R 3.634.
Chassis: Tyres 185/70 TR 14.
Performance: a) Saloon/Sedan: Max speed at 93.2mph/150kmh, speed at 1000rpm in 5th gear 26.4mph/42.5kmh; acceleration 0 – 62mph/100kmh 18.2secs; power to weight ratio from 24.9kg/kW (18.4kg/PS); consumption ECE 5.4/7.5/8.4L/100km (52.3/37.7/33.6mpg) [43.6/31.4/28.0US mpg].
b) Break (Estate/Station Wagon): Max speed at 91mph/146kmh; acceleration 0 – 62mph/100kmh 19.5secs; consumption ECE 6.4/9.0/9.3L/100km (44.1/31.4/30.4mpg) [36.8/26.1/25.3US mpg].

2408cm3 Diesel
76/66kW–102/88hp–104/90PS
Injection Pump/Turbo

As 1796cm3, except:

Weight: Saloon/Sedan; kerbweight (DIN) 1345/1375kg, gross vehicle weight 1820/1825kg. Break (Estate/Station Wagon); kerbweight (DIN) 1480kg, gross vehicle weight 2080kg. Familial: Kerbweight (DIN) 1510kg, gross vehicle weight 2095kg.
Engine data (DIN): 4–cylinder in–line (94 x 90mm), 2498cm3; compression ratio 21:1; 76kW (102hp) [104PS] at 4150rpm, 30.4kW/L (40.7hp/L) [41.6PS/L]; 235Nm (173.4bft) at 2000rpm.
SRD: 66kW (88hp) [90PS]; 204Nm (150.51bft).
Engine construction: Designated XD 3TE/3T. Diesel engine. Side camshaft (chain), 5 bearing crankshaft; Bosch EP/VAC injection; exhaust turbocharger KKK K16 (SRD: Garrett), max boost pressure 0.8bar; charge–air cooler; oil capacity 5L (4.7US qt). 12V 60Ah Battery, 750W alternator; cooling system capacity approx 10L (9.5US qt).
Transmission: a) 5–speed manual (except Break and Familial), final drive ratio 3.182.
b) Automatic, final drive ratio 3.308. Break/Family 3.889.
Gear ratios: a) 5–speed manual: 1st 3.845; 2nd 2.183; 3rd 1.451; 4th 1; 5th 0.845; R 3.587.
b) Automatic: Max torque multiplication in converter 2.29 times; Planetary gear set ratios: 1st 2.48; 2nd 1.48; 3rd 1; R 2.09.
Chassis: Servo/power assisted disc brakes (front ventilated), rear diameter 27.3cm; tyres 185/70TR 14.
Performance: a) Saloon/Sedan GTD: Max speed 111mph/178kmh, automatic 108mph/174kmh, speed at 1000rpm in 5th gear 27.7mph/44.5kmh; acceleration 0 – 62mph/100kmh 13.0secs automatic 14.1secs; power to weight ratio from 17.7 kg/kW (12.9kg/PS); consumption ECE 5.5/7.7/8.6L/100km (51.4/36.7/32.8mpg) [42.8/30.5/27.4US mpg], automatic 5.8/8.6/9.6L/100km (48.7/32.8/29.4mpg) [40.6/27.4/24.5US mpg].
b) Break (Estate/Station Wagon): Max speed 101mph/162kmh; acceleration 0 – 62mph/100kmh 16.1secs; consumption ECE 7.6/10.4/9.9L/100km (37.2/27.2/28.5mpg) [30.9/22.6/23.8US mpg].

PEUGEOT RA

Safrar–Peugeot, Bonpland 2349, Buenos Aires, Casilla de Correo No. 102, Sucursal 25.

Argentinian branch of Peugeot France. Fiat Automobiles and Safrar Peugeot merged in Autumn 1981 now known as Sevel Argentina SA.

Peugeot 504

Argentinian version of Peugeot 504 with 2 Litre engine. 1985: More powerful engine. 1988 refinements to body.

2 Litre
73.5kW–99hp–100PS
1 2V Carb

As Peugeot 504 (France) 1983, except:

Body, Weight: Saloon/Sedan 4–door, 5–seater; kerbweight (DIN) 1165kg, gross vehicle weight 1675kg.
Engine data (DIN): 4–cylinder in–line (88 x 81mm), 1971cm3, compression ratio 8.8:1; 73.5kW (99hp) [100PS] at 5000rpm, 164Nm (121lbft) at 2750rpm; leaded premium grade.
Transmission: Final drive ratio 3.70.
Dimensions: Wheelbase 274cm, track 142/133cm, clearance 12cm, turning circle 10.4m, load space 16.2cu ft (460dm3). Length 453cm, width 169cm, height 146cm.

Peugeot 504

Peugeot 505

Argentinian version of Peugeot 505 with 2 Litre engine. Various modifications on the basic model.

2 Litre
73.5kW–99hp–100PS
1 2V Carb

As Peugeot 505 (France), except:

Engine data (DIN): 4–cylinder in–line (88 x 81mm), l971cm3, compression ratio 8.8:1; 73.5kW (99hp) [100PS] at 5000rpm, 164Nm (121lbft) at 2750rpm. Leaded premium grade.
With fuel injection: 78.5kW (105hp) [107PS].
Transmission: Final drive ratio 3.70.
Gear ratios: a) 4–speed manual: 1st 3.591; 2nd 2.104; 3rd 1.366; 4th 1; R 3.634.
b) 5–speed manual: As French version.
c) Automatic: As French version.
Chassis: Rear rigid axle with 2 coil springs, drive shaft in torque tube, compression strut, transverse tie rod, antiroll bar and telescopic damper. Fuel tank 50L (11.0Gal) [13.2US Gal].

PININFARINA I

Industrie Pininfarina SpA Via Lesna 78/80, 10095 Grugliasco (TO), Italia.
Pininfarina Studi e Ricerche SpA. Via Nazionale 30, 10020 Cambiano (TO), Italia.

Car body design studio. Construction and development of vehicles, industrial design for complete vehicle production. "Pininfarina Studi e Richerche": Designed vehicles include; Alfa Romeo Spider, Cadillac Allante, Ferrari Testarossa, Ferrari 412, Lancia Thema Estate/Station Wagon (including some mechanical components) and Peugeot 205 Convertible. Production: 150 vehicles per day, approx 33000 units per annum.

Pininfarina • Plymouth

Cadillac Allante

PLYMOUTH   USA

Chrysler–Plymouth Division, Chrysler Corporation, Detroit, Michigan 48231, USA.

Product of the Chrysler Corporation.
MODEL RANGE
Laser - Horizon – Sundance – Reliant – Acclaim– Gran Fury – Voyager.

Plymouth Laser

New model. 2 + 2 seater Sports Coupe with 2-doors and a hatchback, 1.8 Litre Turbo engine, technically related to Mitsubishi Galant. Launched December 1989.

1.8 Litre
68kW-92hp-93PS
Fuel Injection

Body, Weight: Coupe 3-door, 2 + 2-seater; kerbweight (DIN) from 1135kg, RS 1210kg.

Engine data (SAE net): 4-cylinder in-line (80.6 x 86mm), 1755cm3; compression ratio 9:1; 68kW (91hp) [93PS] at 5000rpm, 38.8kW/L (51.9hp/L) [53PS/L]; 142Nm (104.8lbft) at 3500rpm; regular grade.

Engine construction: Front transverse engine, inclined 10deg to the right. Designated Mitsubishi 4G 37. Overhead valves in V, hydraulic valve lash adjustment; 1 overhead camshaft (toothed belt); 2 counter-balance shafts; light-alloy cylinder head; 5 bearing crankshaft; oil capacity approx 4L (3.8US qt); electronic fuel injection. 12V 45Ah battery, alternator 65A; cooling system capacity approx 6L (5.7US qt).

Transmission (to all wheels): a) 5-speed manual, final drive ratio 4.322 (1.097x3.941).
b) Automatic, hydraulic torque converter with 4-speed Planetary gear set, final drive ratio 4.007 (1.125x3.562).

Gear ratios: a) 5-speed manual: 1st 3.363; 2nd 1.947; 3rd 1.285; 4th 0.939; 5th 0.756; R 3.083.
b) Automatic; max torque multiplication in converter 2.17times, Planetary gear set: 1st 2.846; 2nd 1.581; 3rd 1; OD 0.685; R 2.176.

Chassis: Integral body; front McPherson struts with lower A arm, rear semi-rigid axle (trailing arm, torsion tube) with Panhard rod and coil springs, front and rear antiroll bar, telescopic damper. Servo/power assisted brakes, front discs ventilated 21.8cm, rear 22.2cm, handbrake to rear wheels; rack and pinion steering, optional with servo; fuel tank 60L (13.2Gal) [15.9US Gal]; tyres 185/70 HR 14, optioal 205/55 HR 16, wheel rims 5.5 optional 6J.

Dimensions: Wheelbase 247cm, track 146.5/145cm, clearance 17cm, turning circle 10.4m, load space 10.2cu ft (290dm3). Length 433cm, width 169cm, height 126.5cm.

Performance: Max speed 109mph/175kmh, automatic 106mph/170kmh (manufacturers test specification), speed at 1000rpm in 5th gear 21.8mph/35kmh; acceleration 0 - 60mph/97kmh 11.4secs, automatic 13.7secs; power to weight ratio from 16.7kg/kW (12.2kg/PS); consumption approx 6-10L/100km (47.1-28.2mpg) [39.2-23.5US mpg].

2 Litre DOHC
100kW-135hp-136PS
Fuel Injection

As 1.8 Litre, except:

Weight: Kerbweight from 1230kg.

Engine data (SAE net): 4-cylinder in-line (85 x 88mm), 1997cm3; compression ratio 9:1; 100kW (135hp) [136PS] at 6000rpm, 50.1kW/L (67.1hp/L) [68.1PS/L]; 170Nm (125.5lbft) at 5000rpm.

Engine construction: Designated Mitsubishi 4G 63 DOHC. 4 valves in 57deg per cylinder; 2 overhead camshafts (toothed belt); oil capacity 4.7L (4.4US qt). 75A alternator; cooling system capacity 6.5L (6.1US qt).

Chassis: Power steering; tyres 205/55 HR 16, wheel rims 6J.

Performance: Max speed 121mph/195kmh, automatic 113mph/182kmh (manufacturers test specification); acceleration 0 - 60mph/97kmh 8.7secs, automatic 11.4secs; power to weight ratio from 12.3kg/kW (9.0kg/PS); consumption approx 8-13L/100km (35.3-21.7mpg) [29.4-18.1US mpg].

2 Litre DOHC
142kW-190hp-193PS
Turbo/Fuel Injection

As 1.8 Litre, except:

Weight: Kerbweight from 1250kg.

Engine data(SAE net): 4-cylinder in-line (85 x 88mm), 1997cm3; compression ratio 7.8:1; 142kW (190hp) [193PS] at 6000rpm 71.2kW/L (95.4hp/L) [96.7PS/L]; 275Nm (203lbft) at 5000rpm; unleaded premium grade.

Engine construction: Designated Mitsubishi 4G 63 DOHC. 4 valves in V 57deg per cylinder; 2 overhead camshafts (toothed belt); oil capacity 4.7L (4.4US qt), oil cooler; electronic fuel injection. 1 exhaust turbo-charger TC O5, charge-air cooler. 75A alternator; cooling system capacity 6.5L (6.1US qt).

Transmission: 5-speed manual, final drive ratio 4.153.

Gear ratios: 5-speed manual: 1st 3.083; 2nd 1.833; 3rd 1.240; 4th 0.896; 5th 0.731; R 3.166.

Chassis: Power assisted steering; tyres 205/55 VR 16, wheel rims 6J.

Performance: Max speed 143mph/230kmh (manufacturers test specification), speed at 1000rpm in 5th gear 23.7mph/38.1kmh; acceleration 0 - 60mph/97kmh 6.9secs; power to weight ratio from 8.8kg/kW (6.5kg/PS); consumption approx 9-18L/100km (31.4-15.7mpg) [26.1-13.1US mpg].

Plymouth Laser

Plymouth Laser SR Turbo

Plymouth

Plymouth Horizon

Compact front wheel drive model with a 2.2 Litre engine, technically identical to the Dodge Omni. Launched December 1977. For 1988; fuel injection version.

2.2 Litre
69kW–93hp–94PS
Fuel Injection

Body, Weight (laden): 5–door Saloon/Sedan, 5–seater; approx 1040kg.
Engine data (SAE net): 4–cylinder in–line (87.5 x 92mm), 2213cm3; Compression ratio 9.5:1; 69kW (93hp) [94PS] at 4800rpm, 31.2kW/L (41.8hp/L) [42.5PS/L]; 165Nm (121.8lbft) at 3200rpm; unleaded regular grade.
Engine construction: Transverse and rear inclined front engine. Hydraulic tappets; 1 overhead camshaft (toothed belt); light–alloy cylinder head; 5 bearing crankshaft; oil capacity 3.8L (3.6US qt); Bosch/Holley electronic central/single point fuel injection. 12V 60/66Ah Battery, 90A alternator; cooling system capacity approx 8.5L (8.0US qt).
Transmission (to front wheel): a) 5–speed manual, final drive ratio 2.55.
b) Automatic (Torqueflite), hydraulic torque converter and 3– speed Planetary gear set. Final drive ratio 2.78.
Gear ratios: a) 5–speed manual: 1st 3.29; 2nd 2.08; 3rd 1.45; 4th 1.04; 5th 0.72; R 3.14.
b) Automatic: Max torque multiplication in converter 2 times. Planetary gear set ratios: 2.69; 1.55; 1; R 2.1.
Chassis: Integral body (Frame–Floor–Installation with bolt on body; front A arm and McPherson strut with coil springs, rear independent suspension with trailing arms and coil springs, front antiroll bar; telescopic damper. Servo/power assisted brakes, front disc (ventilated), diameter 22.8cm, rear drums; mechanical handbrake to rear wheels; rack and pinion steering, optional power assisted; fuel tank 49L (10.8Gal) [12.9US Gal]; tyres 165 R 13, wheel rims 5J.
Dimensions: Wheelbase 251.5cm, track 142.5/141.5cm, clearance 12cm, turning circle 12.2m, load space 10.4/33cu ft (295/935dm3). Length 414.5cm, width 168cm, height 134.5cm.
Performance: Max speed approx 96–103mph/155–165kmh, speed at 1000rpm in 5th gear 36.5mph/58.8kmh; power to weight ratio from 14.9kg/kW (10.9kg/PS); consumption approx 8–13L/100km (35.3– 21.7mpg) [29.4–18.1US mpg].

Plymouth Horizon

Plymouth Sundance

Compact Saloon/Sedan with 3/5–door, 2.2 Litre naturally aspirated or turbocharged engine. Identical model to the Dodge Shadow. Launched March 1986. For 1989 with 2.5 Litre engine.

2.2 Litre
69kW–93hp–94PS
Central/Single Point Injection

Body, Weight (laden): Saloon/Sedan 3–door, 5–seater; approx 1180kg. Saloon/Sedan 5–door, 5–seater; approx 1200kg.
Engine data (SAE net): 4–cylinder in–line (87.5 x 92mm), 2213cm3; compression ratio 9.5:1; 69kW (93hp) [94PS] at 4800rpm, 31.2kW/L (41.8hp/L) [42.5PS/L]; 165Nm (121.8lbft) at 3200rpm; unleaded regular grade.
Engine construction: Transverse front engine. Hydraulic tappets, 1 overhead camshaft (toothed belt); light–alloy cylinder head; 5 bearing crankshaft; oil capacity 3.8L (3.6US qt); Bosch/Holley central/single point injection. 12V 60/66Ah Battery, 90A alternator. Cooling system capacity, approx 8.5L (8.0US qt).
Transmission (to front wheels): a) 5–speed manual, final drive ratio 2.51.
b) Automatic (Torqueflite), hydraulic torque converter and 3– speed Planetary gear set, final drive ratio 3.02.
Gear ratios: a) 5–speed manual: 1st 3.29; 2nd 2.08; 3rd 1.45; 4th 1.04; 5th 0.72; R 3.14.
b) Automatic: Max torque multiplication in converter 2.1 times, Planetary gear set ratios: 2.69; 1.55; 1; R 2.1.
Chassis: Integral body. Front McPherson strut and A arm, rear rigid axle with trailing arm and Panhard rod, front and rear coil springs, telescopic damper and antiroll bar. Servo/power assisted brakes, front disc (ventilated), diameter 25.5cm, rear drums; pedal operated parking brake to rear wheels; Servo/power assisted rack and pinion steering; fuel tank 53L (11.6Gal) [14.0US Gal]; tyres 175R 13 or 185/70 R 14, wheel rims 5/5.5J, optional tyres 195/60 VR 15, wheel rims 6J.
Dimensions: Wheelbase 246.5cm, track 146.5/145.5cm, clearance min 11.5cm, turning circle 11.0m. Load space 13.2/33.4cu ft (375/945dm3), Hatchback 370/935dm3). Length 436cm, width 171cm, height 134cm.
Performance: Max speed approx 99–103mph/160–165kmh, speed at 1000rpm in 5th gear 82.3mph/61.4kmh; power to weight ratio from 17.1kg/kW (12.6kg/PS); consumption approx 7–12L/100km (40.4– 23.5mpg) [33.6–19.6US mpg].

Plymouth Sundance

2.5 Litre
74kW–100hp–101PS
Central/Single Point Injection

As 2.2 Litre, except:
Weight: Increased weight 15kg.
Engine data (SAE Net): 4–cylinder in–line (87.5 x 104mm), 2501cm3; compression 9:1; 74kW (100hp) [101PS] at 4800rpm, 29.6kW/L (39.7hp/L) [40.4PS/L]; 184Nm (135.8lbft) at 2800rpm. Export Version: 77kW (103hp) [105PS] at 4800rpm or 71kW (94.5hp) [95PS].
Engine construction: 2 counter–balance shafts.
Performance: Max speed approx 106–112mph/170–180kmh. Power to weight ratio from 16.1kg/kW (11.8kg/PS); consumption, approx 9– 14L/100km (31.4–20.2mpg) [26.1–16.8US mpg].

Plymouth Sundance

2.5 Litre Turbo
112kW–150hp–152PS
Fuel Injection

As 2.2 Litre, except:

Plymouth 347

Body, Weight (laden): Excess weight 25kg.

Engine data (SAE net): 4–cylinder in–line (87.5 x 104mm), 2501cm3; compression ratio 7.8:1; 112kW (150hp) [152PS] at 4800rpm, 44.8kW/L (60hp/L) [60.8PS/L]; 244Nm (180lbft) at 2000rpm; unleaded regular/premium grade.
Certain countries: 107kW (143hp) [146PS].

Engine construction: 2 counter-balance shafts; Holley electronic fuel injection, 1 turbocharger M.H.I.

Performance: Max speed approx 115–121mph/185–195kmh. Power to weight ratio from 10.8kg/kW (7.9kg/PS); consumption approx 9–14L/100km (31.4– 20.2mpg) [26.1–16.8US mpg].

Plymouth Reliant

Small American compact with front wheel drive, 4–cylinder engine, 5–speed manual or automatic transmission, 2/4–door Saloon/Sedan or 5–door Estate/Station Wagon. Launched Autumn 1980. Introduction of the 2.5 Litre engine in 1986. 1989 available only as saloon.

2.2 Litre
69kW–93hp–94PS
Central/Single Point Injection

Body, Weight (laden): Saloon/Sedan 2–door, 6–seater; approx 1100kg.
Saloon/Sedan 4–door, 6–seater; approx 1110kg.

Engine data (SAE net): 4–cylinder in–line (87.5 x 92mm) 2213cm3, compression ratio 9.5:1; 69kW (93hp) [94PS] at 4800rpm, 31.2kW/L (41.8hp/L) [42.5PS/L]; 165Nm (121.8lbft) at 3200rpm; unleaded regular grade.

Engine construction: Transverse front engine. Hydraulic tappets, 1 overhead camshaft (toothed belt); light–alloy cylinder head; 5 bearing crankshaft; oil capacity 3.8L (3.6US qt); Bosch/Holley electronic central/single point injection. 12V 60/66Ah Battery, alternator 90A; cooling system capacity approx 8.5L (8.0US qt).

Transmission (to front wheels): a) 5–speed manual, final drive ratio 2.51.
b) Automatic (Torqueflite), hydraulic torque converter and 3– speed Planetary gear set, selector lever either positioned centrally or on the steering wheel. Final drive ratio 3.02.

Gear ratios: a) 5–speed manual: 1st 3.29; 2nd 2.08; 3rd 1.45; 4th 1.04; 5th 0.72; R 3.14.
b) Automatic: Max torque multiplication in converter 2.1 times, Planetary gear set ratios: 2.69; 1.55; 1; R 2.1.

Chassis: Integral body. Front McPherson strut and A arm, rear rigid axle with trailing arm and Panhard rod, front and rear coil springs, telescopic damper and antiroll bar. Servo/power assisted brakes, front discs (ventilated), rear drums, disc diameter 23.6 or 25.5cm; pedal operated parking brake to rear wheels; rack and pinion steering, optional power assisted. Fuel tank 53L (11.6Gal) [14.0US Gal]; tyres 175 R13, wheel rims 5J, optional tyres 185/70 R 14, wheel rims 5.5J.

Dimensions: Wheelbase 255cm, track 146/145.5cm, clearance min 12cm, turning circle 11.4m, load space 15cu ft (425dm3), length 454cm, width 173cm, height 133–134cm.

Performance: Max speed approx 96–99mph/160–165kmh, speed at 1000rpm in 5th gear 38.1mph/61.4kmh; power to weight ratio from 15.9kg/kW (11.7kg/PS); consumption approx 8–13L/100km (35.3– 21.7mpg) [29.4–18.1US mpg].

Plymouth Reliant

2.5 Litre
74kW–100hp–101PS
Central/Single Point Injection

As 2.2 Litre, except:
Weight: Increased weight 30kg.

Engine data (SAE net): 4–cylinder in–line (87.5 x 104mm), 2501cm3; compression ratio 9:1; 74kW (100hp) [101PS] at 4800rpm, 29.7kW/L (39.8hp/L) [40.4PS/L]; 180Nm (132.8lbft) at 2800rpm.

Engine construction: 2 counter–balance shafts.

Transmission: Automatic, final drive ratio 3.02.

Performance: Max speed at 106–112mph/170–180kmh, speed at 1000rpm in top gear 22.8mph/36.7kmh; power to weight ratio from 15.3kg/kW (11.2kg/PS); consumption from 9–14L/100km (31.4–20.2mpg) [26.1– 16.8US mpg].

Plymouth Reliant

Plymouth Acclaim

New model. Four door Saloon/Sedan with front wheel drive on A-car basis, 2.5 or 3 Litre engine, replacing the Caravelle. Launched January 1989.

2.2 Litre
72kW-97hp-98PS
Central/Single Point Injection

Not available for LX

Body, Weight (laden): 4–door Saloon/Sedan, 5/6-seater; approx 1250kg.

Engine data (SAE net): 4–cylinder in–line (87.5 x 104mm) 2501cm3; compression ratio 8.9:1; 74kW (99hp) [101PS] at 4800rpm, 29.6kW/L (39.7hp/L) [40.4PS/L]; 183Nm (135lbft) at 2800rpm; unleaded regular grade.

Engine construction: Transverse front engine. Hydraulic tappets, 1 overhead camshaft (toothed belt); light–alloy cylinder head; 2 counter-balance shafts; 5 bearing crankshaft; oil capacity 3.8L (3.6US qt); Holley central injection. 12V 66Ah Battery, 90A alternator; cooling system capacity approx 8.5L (8.0US qt).

Plymouth Acclaim LE

Transmission (to front wheel): a) 5-speed manual, final drive ratio 2.51.
b) Automatic "Torqueflite", hydraulic torque convertible and 3-speed Planetary gear set, central selector lever or steering wheel, final drive ratio 3.02.

Gear ratios: a) 5-speed manual: 1st 1.329; 2nd 2.08; 3rd 1.45; 4th 1.04; 5th 0.72; R 3.14.
b) Automatic; max torque multiplication 2.1 times, Planetary gear set: 2.69; 1.55; 1; R 2.1.

Chassis: Integral body. Front McPherson strut and A arm, rear rigid axle with trailing arm and Panhard rod, front and rear coil springs, telescopic damper and antiroll bar. Servo/power assisted brakes, front discs (ventilated), rear drums, disc diameter 25.5cm; pedal operated parking brake to rear wheels; Power/assisted rack and pinion steering; fuel tank 61L (13.4Gal) [16.1US Gal]; tyres 185/70R 14, LE 195/70 R 15, wheel rims 5.5/6J.

Dimensions: Wheelbase 262.5cm, track 146/145.5cm, clearance min 12cm, turning circle 11.9m. Load space 14.5cu ft (410dm3). Length 460cm, width 173cm, height 141cm.

Plymouth

Performance: Max speed approx 103mph/165kmh, 1000rpm in 5th gear 38.5mph/62kmh; power to weight ratio from 16.9kg/kW (12.4kg/PS); consumption approx 10-15L/100km (28.2-18.8mpg) [23.5-15.7US mpg].

```
2.5 Litre
112kW-150hp-152PS
Central/Single Point Injection
```

Not available for LX

As 2.5 Litre, except:

Weight: Kerbweight from 1265kg.

Engine data (SAE net): 4–cylinder in-line (87.5 x 104mm), 2501cm3; compression ratio 7.8:1; 112kW (150hp) [152PS] at 4800rpm, 44.8kW/L (60hp/L) [60.8PS/L]; 244Nm (180lbft) at 2000rpm; premium or regular grade.
Certain countries: 107kW (144hp) [146PS].

Engine construction: Holley electronic fuel injection, 1 M.H.I. turbocharger.

Performance: Max speed approx 115/121mpg–185/195kmh; power to weight ratio from 11.3kg/kW (8.3kg/PS); consumption approx 9-15L/100km (31.4-18.8mpg) [26.1-15.7US mpg].

Plymouth Acclaim LX

```
3 Litre V6
105kW-141hp-143PS
Fuel Injection
```

Engine for LX

As 2.5 Litre, except:

Weight: Kerbweight (DIN) approx 1345kg.

Engine data (SAE net): 6–cylinder in V 60deg (91.1 x 76mm), 2972cm3, compression ratio 8.9:1; 105kW (141hp) [143PS] at 5000rpm, 35.3kW/L (47.3hp/L) [48.1PS/L]; 232Nm (171.2lbft) at 2800rpm.

Engine construction: Designated Mitsubishi 6G 72. Valves in V; 1 overhead camshaft (toothed belt); without 2-counter balance shafts; Holley electronic fuel injection. Cooling system capacity approx 9L (8.5US qt).

Transmission: Automatic "Torqueflite", hydraulic torque converter and 4-speed Planetary gear set, central selector lever 2.36.

Gear ratios: Automatic: Max torque multiplication 1.8 times, Planetary gear set 2.84; 1.57; 1; 0.69; R 2.21.

Chassis: Tyres 205/60 R 15, wheel rims 6J.

Performance: Max speed approx 121mph/195kmh, speed at 1000rpm in top gear 93.9mph/70.1kmh; power to weight ratio from 12.8kg/kW (9.4kg/PS); consumption approx 12-17L/100km (23.5-16.6mpg) [19.6-13.8US mpg].

Plymouth Gran Fury

Large Saloon/Sedan with 6–cylinder V8 engine. Parallel model to the Dodge Diplomat and Chrysler New Yorker. Launched October 1979. Produced by AMC in 1987 in Kenosha. 1989: Latest production.

```
5.2 Litre V8
104kW-140hp-142PS
1 2V Carb
```

Body, Weight (laden): 4–door Saloon/Sedan, 6–seater; approx 1630kg.

Engine data (SAE net): 8–cylinder in-line V 90deg (99.31 x 84.07mm), 5210cm3; compression ratio 9.0:1; 104kW (140hp) [142PS] at 3600rpm, 20.0kW/L (26.8hp/L) [27.3PS/L]; 360Nm (266.1lbft) at 2000rpm; unleaded regular grade.
Police version (with 4V carb): 130kW (174hp) [177PS] at 4000rpm, 25.0kW/L (33.5hp/L) [34.0PS/L]; 339Nm (250.2lbft) at 3200rpm.

Plymouth Gran Fury

Engine construction: Hydraulic tappets, central camshaft (chain); 5 bearing crankshaft; oil capacity 3.8L (3.6US qt); 1 Holley 6280 downdraught twin carb. 12V 66/70Ah Battery, 90A alternator; cooling system capacity approx 14.7L (13.9US qt).

Transmission (to rear wheels): Automatic (Torqueflite), hydraulic torque converter and 3–speed Planetary gear set; selector lever either positioned centrally or on the steering wheel, final drive ratio 2.26; 2.24; 2.76; 2.94. Optional limited slip differential.

Gear ratios: Automatic: Max torque multiplication in converter 2 times, Planetary gear set ratios, 2.74; 1.54; 1; R 2.22.

Chassis: Integral body; front upper keystone A arm; lower single control arm with elastic position tension strut and two control arms. Antiroll bar, rear rigid axle with semi–elliptic spring, telescopic damper. Servo/power assisted brakes, front discs (ventilated), rear drums, disc diameter 27.5cm; parking brake to rear wheels; servo/power assisted recirculating ball steering; fuel tank 68L (14.9Gal) [18.0US Gal], tyres 205/75R 15, wheel rims 7".

Dimensions: Wheelbase 286cm, track 153.5/152.5cm, clearance 15cm, turning circle 13.3m, load space 15.5cu ft (440dm3). Length 519.5cm, width 184cm, height 140cm.

Performance: Max speed approx 106mph/170kmh, speed at 1000rpm in top gear 34.5mph/55.5kmh; power to weight ratio from 15.5kg/kW (11.4kg/PS); consumption (touring) approx 13–18L/100km (21.7– 15.7mpg) [18.1–13.1US mpg].

Plymouth Gran Fury (Police)

Plymouth Voyager

Large Saloon/Sedan, front wheel drive, 5/8–seater, with 2.5 or 3.0 Litre engine. Available in 2 wheelbases. Parallel model to the Dodge Caravan. Export version the Chrysler Voyager; refer there for Technical Data.

Plymouth Voyager LX

PONTIAC — USA

Pontiac Motor Division, General Motors Corporation, Pontiac, Michigan 48053, USA.

Affiliated to General Motors Corporation.

MODEL RANGE
LeMans – Sunbird – Grand Am – 6000 – Firebird – Grand Prix – Bonneville – Safari Wagon - Trans Sport.

Pontiac LeMans

Replica of the Opel Kadett, manufactured under license by Daewoo in South Korea. Refer to Daewoo LeMans for Technical Data.

Pontiac Le Mans

Pontiac Sunbird

Sunbird – Sunbird SE – Sunbird GT

Compact front wheel drive vehicle, with transverse engine, 4- speed manual or automatic transmission, part of the General Motors J–Car family. Launched April 1981. 1984 introduction of the Convertible and 1.8 Litre Turbo engine. Modifications to the body in 1989.

Pontiac Sunbird SE

2 Litre
71kW–96hp–97PS
Central/Single Point Injection

Body, Weight (laden):
Sunbird LE: Saloon/Sedan 4/5-seater; approx 1090kg.
Coupe 2-door, 4/5-seater; approx 1080kg.
Sunbird SE: Coupe 2-door, 4/5-seater; approx 1185kg.
Sunbird GT: Coupe 2-door, 4/5-seater; approx 1140kg.
Convertible 2-door, 4/5-seater; approx 1220kg.

Engine Data (SAE net): 4–cylinder in–line (86 x 86mm), 1998cm3; compression ratio 8.8:1; 71kW (96hp) [97PS] at 4800rpm, 35.5kW/L (47.6hp/L) [48.5PS/L]; 160Nm (118.1lbft) at 3600rpm; unleaded regular grade.

Engine Construction: Designated LT 2. Transverse front engine. Hydraulic tappets; 1 overhead camshaft (toothed belt); 5 bearing crankshaft; light-alloy cylinder head; oil capacity 3.5L (3.3US qt); electronic central/single point injection (TBI). Battery 12V 54Ah, alternator 74A; cooling system capacity approx 7.4L (7.0US qt).

Transmission (to front wheels): a) 5-speed manual, final drive ratio 3.45.
b) Automatic THM 125, hydraulic torque converter and 3-speed Planetary gear set, final drive ratio 3.18.

Gear ratios: a) 5-speed manual: 1st 3.91; 2nd 2.15; 3rd 1.45; 4th 1.03; 5th 0.74; R 3.58.
b) Automatic: Max torque multiplication in converter 2.4 times, Planetary gear set ratios: 2.84; 1.6; 1; R 2.07.

Chassis: Integral body. Front sub-frame, front McPherson strut and lower A arm, antiroll bar; rear independent suspension with longitudinal swinging arms, antiroll bar, front and rear coil springs and telescopic damper. Servo/power assisted brakes, front disc (ventilated), diameter 24.7cm, rear drums; parking brake to rear wheels; rack and pinion steering, optional power assisted; fuel tank 51L (11.2Gal) 13.5US Gal]; tyres 185 R 13, optional 195/70 R 14; 215/60 R 14, wheel rims 5.5" or 6".

Dimensions: Wheelbase 257cm, track 141/140cm, clearance min 14cm, turning circle approx 11.3m. Load space 13.4cu ft (380dm3), Coupe 12.5cu ft (355dm3), length 460cm, width 169cm, height 136cm, Coupe 132cm.

Performance: Max speed approx 103-108mph/165–175kmh, speed at 1000rpm in 5th gear 26.3mph/42.3kmh; power to weight ratio from 15.2kg/kW (11.1kg/PS); consumption, approx 9–14L/100km (31.4–20.2mpg) [26.1–16.8US mpg].

Pontiac Sunbird LE Coupe

2 Litre Turbo
123kW–165hp–167PS
Fuel Injection

Not available for Estate/Station Wagon.

As 96hp, except:

Weight: Increased weight 20kg.

Engine data (SAE net); 4–cylinder in–line (86 x 86mm), 1998cm3, compression ratio 8:1; 123kW (165hp) [167PS] at 5600rpm, 61.5kW/L (82.4hp/L) [83.6PS/L]; 237Nm (175lbft) at 4000rpm.

Engine construction: Designated LT 3. Bosch electronic fuel injection; 1 Garrett turbocharger; max boost pressure 0.6bar.

Transmission: a) 5-speed manual, final drive ratio 3.61.
b) Automatic THM 125, hydraulic torque converter and 3-speed Planetary gear set, central selector lever, final drive ratio 3.18.

Gear ratios: a) 5-speed manual: 1st 3.50; 2nd 2.19; 3rd 1.38; 4th 0.94; 5th 0.72; R 3.41.
b) Automatic: Max torque multiplication in torque converter 2.08 times, Planetary gear set ratios: 2.84; 1.6; 1; R 2.07.

Performance: Max speed approx 131mph/210kmh, speed at 1000rpm in 5th gear 25.9mph/41.6kmh; power to weight ratio 8.9kg/kW (6.6kg/PS); consumption, approx 9–16L/100km (31.4–17.7mpg) [26.1–14.7US mpg].

Pontiac Sunbird GT Convertible

Pontiac

Pontiac Grand Am

Grand Am LE – Grand Am SE
Compact Coupe with front wheel drive, 2.5 Litre engine and 5-speed manual or automatic transmission. Launched August 1984. Summer 1985: available as 4-door Saloon/Sedan. 1987 introduction of turbocharged engine. 1988: 2.3 Litre "Quad 4" instead of 3 Litre V6. 1989: 2.5 Litre with increased more performance and body modifications.

Body, Weight (laden): 4-door Saloon/Sedan, 5-seater; LE 1170kg, E 1235kg. Coupe, 2-door, 5-seater; LE 1145kg, SE 1210kg.

2.5 Litre
82kW–110hp–112PS
Central/Single Point Injection

Engine data (SAE net): 4-cylinder in-line (101.6 x 76.2mm), 2471cm3; compression ratio 9:1. 82kW (110hp) [112PS] at 5200rpm, 33.2kW/L (44.5hp/L) [45.3PS/L]; 183Nm (135.1lbft) at 3200rpm; unleaded regular grade.

Engine construction: Designated L 68, transverse front engine. Hydraulic tappets. Side camshaft (toothed belt); 5 bearing crankshaft; Oil capacity 3.8L (3.6US qt); Rochester electronic central/single point injection. Spark plugs AC R44TSX; battery 12V 54Ah, alternator 74A; cooling system capacity approx 7.4L (7.0US qt).

Transmission (to front wheel): a) 5-speed manual, final drive ratio 3.35. b) Automatic THM 125, hydraulic torque converter and 3-speed Planetary gear set, final drive ratio 2.84.

Gear ratios: a) 5-speed manual: 1st 3.73; 2nd 2.04; 3rd 1.45; 4th 1.03; 5th 0.74; R 3.58.
b) Automatic: Max torque multiplication in converter 2.5 times, Planetary gear set ratios: 2.84; 1.6; 1; R 2.07.

Chassis: Integral body. Front sub-frame, front McPherson strut and lower A arm, antiroll bar; rear independent suspension with longitudinal swinging arms, optional antiroll bar, coil springs and telescopic damper front and rear. Servo/power assisted brakes, front discs (ventilated), diameter 24.7cm, rear drums; Parking brake to rear wheels; power assisted rack and pinion steering; Fuel tank 51.5L (11.3Gal) [13.6US Gal]; tyres 185 R 13, 195/70 R 14, wheel rims 5.5 or 6J.

Dimensions: Wheelbase 262.5cm, track 141/140cm, clearance 15cm, turning circle approx 10.7m. Load space 13.1cu ft (370dm3). Length 461cm, width 169cm, height 133.5cm.

Performance: Max speed approx 112mph/180kmh, speed at 1000rpm in 5th gear 28.6mph/46.0kmh; power to weight ratio from 14kg/kW (10.2kg/PS); consumption, approx 8–14L/100km (35.3–20.2mpg) [29.4–16.8US mpg].

Pontiac Grand Am LE Sedan

2.3 Litre DOHC 16V
112kW–150hp–152PS
Fuel Injection

As 2.5 Litre, except:
Weight: Increased weight 25kg.

Engine data (SAE net): 4-cylinder in-line (92 x 85mm), 2260cm3, compression ratio 9.5:1; 112kW (150hp) [152PS] at 5200rpm, 49.6kW/L (66.5hp/L) [67.3PS/L]; 217Nm (160.1lbft) at 4000rpm.
Optional high output: Compression ratio 10:1; 134kW (180hp) [182PS] at 6200rpm; 244Nm (180lbft) at 5200rpm.

Engine construction: Designated LD 2. 4 valves per cylinder; 2 overhead camshafts (chain); Light-alloy cylinder head; Rochester electronic fuel injection. Spark plugs AC FR3LS; alternator 85/100A; cooling system capacity approx 7.2L (6.8US qt).

Transmission: a) 5-speed manual, final drive ratio 3.61. b) Automatic, final drive ratio 2.84.

Gear ratios: a) 5-speed manual: 1st 3.50; 2nd 2.05; 3rd 1.38; 4th 0.94; 5th 0.72; R 3.41.
b) Automatic: Max torque multiplication in converter 2.5 times, Planetary gear set ratios: 2.84; 1.6; 1; R 2.07.

Performance: Max speed approx 124-137mph/200-220kmh, speed at 1000rpm in 5th gear 27.3mph/43.9kmh; acceleration 0 - 60mph/97kmh 8.5secs; power to weight ratio from 10.4kg/kW (7.7kg/PS); consumption approx 8–15L/100km (35.3–18.8mpg) [29.4– 15.7US mpg].

Pontiac Grand Am LE Coupe

2 Litre Turbo
123kW–165hp–167PS
Fuel Injection

As 95hp, except:
Weight: Increased weight 10kg.

Engine data (SAE net): 4-cylinder in-line (86 x 86mm), 1998cm3; compression ratio 8:1; 123kW (165hp) [167PS] at 5600rpm, 61.5kW/L (82.4hp/L) [83.6PS/L]; 237Nm (174.9lbft) at 4000rpm.

Engine construction: Designated LT 3. 1 overhead camshaft (toothed belt); light-alloy cylinder head; Bosch electronic fuel injection; 1 exhaust turbocharger AiResearch T2; maximum charge-air pressure 0.6bar. Spark plugs AC R44CXLS; alternator 85/100A; cooling system capacity approx 7.6L (7.2US qt).

Transmission: a) 5-speed manual, final drive ratio 3.61. b) Automatic, final drive ratio 3.18.

Gear ratios: a) 5-speed manual: 1st 3.50; 2nd 2.05 3rd 1.38 4th 0.94 5th 0.72; R 3.41.
b) Automatic: Max torque multiplication in converter 2.84 times, Planetary gear set ratios: 2.84; 1.6; 1; R 2.07.

Performance: Max speed approx 131mph/210kmh, speed at 1000rpm in 5th gear 27.3mph/43.9kmh; power to weight ratio 9.2kg/kW (6.8kg/PS); consumption approx 9–16L/100km (31.4–17.7mpg) [26.1– 13.3US mpg].

Pontiac Grand Am SE Coupe

Pontiac 6000

6000 – 6000 LE – 6000 S/E – 6000 STE – 6000 STE/AWD
V6 or 4-cylinder engine, manual or automatic transmission and front wheel drive. Designated "A–Body", mechanicals based on the A–Body. Launched December 1981, 1984; Estate/Station Wagon. 1988: 3.1 Litre V6 with four wheel drive. 1989 with more power and body modifications.

Pontiac 351

Pontiac 6000 LE

2.5 Litre
82kW–110hp–112PS
Central/Single Point Injection

Not available for S/E and STE

Body, Weight:
6000 LE: 4–door Saloon/Sedan, 6–seater; kerbweight (DIN) 1260kg.
Estate/Station Wagon, 5–door, 8–seater; kerbweight (DIN) 1320kg.
6000 SE: 4–door Saloon/Sedan, 5–seater; approx 1265kg.
Estate/Station Wagon, 5–door, 7–seater; kerbweight (DIN) 1325kg.
6000STE: 4–door Saloon/Sedan, 5–seater; approx 1375kg.
Increased weight for air conditioning 25kg.

Engine data (SAE net): 4–cylinder in–line (101.6 x 76.2mm), 2471cm3; compression ratio 9:1; 82kW (110hp) [112PS] at 5200rpm, 33.2kW/L (44.5hp/L) [45.3PS/L]; 183Nm (135.1lbft) at 3200rpm; unleaded regular grade.

Engine construction: Designated LR 8. Transverse front engine. Hydraulic tappets, side camshaft (toothed belt); 5 bearing crankshaft; Oil capacity 2.8L (2.6US qt); Rochester electronic central/single point injection. Spark plugs AC R44TSX; battery 12V 54AH, alternator 56/78A; cooling system capacity approx 9.2L (8.7US qt).

Transmission (to front wheels): Automatic THM 125, hydraulic torque converter and 3–speed Planetary gear set, selector lever either positioned centrally or on the steering wheel, final drive ratio 2.84.

Gear ratios: Automatic: Max torque multiplication in converter 2.35 times, Planetary gear set ratios: 2.84; 1.6; 1; R 2.07.

Chassis: Integral body. Front sub–frame, front McPherson strut and lower A arm, antiroll bar; rear rigid axle with trailing arm, Panhard rod, coil springs and telescopic damper, level control system for STE. Servo/power assisted brakes, front disc brakes (ventilated) diameter 24.7 or 26.0cm, rear drums, STE with four wheel disc brakes and ABS system, Teves MK 11; parking brake to rear wheels; power assisted rack and pinion steering; fuel tank 59L (13.0Gal) [15.6US Gal]; Tyres 185/75 R 14, 195/70 R 14, wheel rims 5.5 or 6".

Dimensions: Wheelbase 266.5cm, track 149/144.5cm, clearance min 16cm, turning circle 12.2m. Load space 16.2cu ft (460dm3), length 479.5cm, width 183cm, height 136.5cm. Station Wagon: Load space 74.3cu ft (2105dm3), length 491cm, height 137.5cm.

Performance: Max speed approx 103mph/165kmh, speed at 1000rpm in top gear 25.3mph/40.7kmh; power to weight ratio from 15.4kg/kW (11.2kg/PS); consumption approx 9–14L/100km (31.4–20.2mpg) [26.1– 16.8US mpg].

Pontiac 6000 SE Station Wagon

2.8 Litre V6
97kW–128hp–132PS
Fuel Injection

As 2.5 Litre, except:

Weight: Increased weight 40kg.

Engine data (SAE net): 6–cylinder in V 60deg (88.9 x 76.2mm), 2838cm3; compression ratio 8.9:1; 97kW (128hp) [132PS] at 4500rpm, 43.2kW/L (57.9hp/L) [46.5PS/L]; 231Nm (170.5lbft) at 3600rpm.

Engine construction: Designated LB 6. 4 bearing crankshaft; central camshaft (chain); light-alloy cyllinder head; oil capacity 3.8L (3.6US qt); Rochester electronic fuel injection. Spark plugs AC R43CTLSE; alternator 66–97A; cooling system capacity approx 11.8L (11.2US qt).

Transmission: a) 5-speed manual, final drive ratio 2.84; 3.18.
b) 4-speed Automatic, final drive ratio 3.33.

Gear ratios: a) Automatic; max torque multiplication with converter 2.35 times, Planetary gear set: 2.84; 1.6; 1; R 2.07.
b) Automatic with OD: Max torque multiplication in converter 1.95 times, Planetary gear set ratios: 1st 2.92; 2nd 1.56; 3rd 1; OD 0.7; R 2.38.

Performance: Max speed at 112mph/180kmh, power to weight ratio from 13.4kg/kW (9.8kg/PS); consumption approx 10–15L/100km (28.2–18.8mpg) [23.5–15.7US mpg].

Pontiac 6000 SE

3.1 Litre V6
104kW–140hp–142PS
Fuel Injection

Engine for STE/AWD

As 2.5 Litre, except:

Body, Weight: Saloon/Sedan STE/4WD 4-door, 6-seater; approx 1530kg.

Engine data (SAE net): 6–cylinder in V 60deg (88.9 x 84mm), 3128cm3; compression ratio 8.8:1; 104kW (140hp) [142PS] at 4800rpm, 33.2kW/L (44.5hp/L) [45.4PS/L]; 251Nm (185.2lbft) at 3200rpm.

Engine construction: Designated LH 0. 4 bearing crankshaft; central camshaft (chain); light-alloy cylinder head; oil capacity 3.8L (3.6US qt); Rochester electronic fuel injection. Alternator 66/97A; cooling system capacity approx 11.8L (11.2US qt).

Transmission (Permanent four wheel drive with locked central differential, power distribution front/rear 60/40deg): Automatic "Turbo Hydra-Matic", hydraulic torque converter and 3– speed Planetary gear set, final drive ratio 3.42; 3.33.

Gear ratios: Automatic: Max torque multiplication with converter 2.22times, Planetary gear set ratios: 1st 2.84; 2nd 1.6; 3rd 1; R 2.07.

Chassis: Rear suspension with control arm, shock absorber strut, transverse leaf spring, antiroll bar and telescopic damper. Servo assisted brakes ABS (Teves), front disc (ventilated) diameter and rear 26cm; tyres 195/70 R 15 wheel rims J.

Performance: Max speed approx 118mph/190kmh, speed at 1000rpm in top gear 23.9mph/38.5kmh; acceleration 0 - 60mph/97kmh 10.6secs; power to weight ratio from 14.7kg/kW (10.8kg/PS); consumption approx 11–17L/100km (25.7–16.6mpg) [21.4– 13.8US mpg].

Pontiac 6000 STE All Wheel Drive

Pontiac Firebird

Firebird – Formula – TransAm – TransAm GTA

4–seater rear wheel drive sports car, with 2.5, 2.8 or 5 Litre engine and manual or automatic transmission. Launched December 1981. 1989 modifications to the body and interior.

> 2.8 Litre
> 101kW–135hp–137PS
> Fuel Injection

Not available for TransAm and Formula

Body, Weight: Sport Coupe 3–door, 4–seater; kerbweight (DIN) 1400kg. Increased weight for air conditioning 18–24kg.

Engine data (SAE net): 6–cylinder in V 60deg (88.9 x 76.2mm), 2838cm3; compression ratio 8.9:1; 101kW (135hp) [137PS] at 4900rpm, 35.5kW/L (47.6hp/L) [48.3PS/L]; 217Nm (160.1lbft) at 3900rpm; unleaded regular grade.

Engine construction: Designated LB 8. Hydraulic tappets, central camshaft (chain); 4 bearing crankshaft; Oil capacity 3.8L (3.6US qt); Rochester electronic fuel injection. Spark plugs AC R42CTS; battery 12V 54Ah, alternator 85/100A; cooling system capacity approx 12.3L (11.6US qt).

Transmission (to rear wheels): a) 5–speed manual, final drive ratio 3.42. b) Automatic, hydraulic torque converter and 4–speed Planetary gear set, final drive ratio 3.42. Optional limited slip differential.

Gear ratios: a) 5–speed manual: 1st 4.03; 2nd 2.37; 3rd 1.50; 4th 1; 5th 0.76; R 3.76. b) Automatic; max torque multiplication in converter 2.35 times, Planetary gear set ratios: 1st 3.06; 2nd 1.63; 3rd 1; OD 0.7; R 2.29.

Chassis: Integral body; lower front A arm, shock absorber strut, coil springs and antiroll bar, rear rigid axle with trailing arm, coil springs and Panhard rod, antiroll bar, front and rear telescopic damper. Servo/power assisted brakes, front disc brakes (ventilated), diameter 26.7cm, rear drums, optional disc brake; mechanical handbrake to rear wheel; power assisted recirculating ball steering; Fuel tank 59L (13.0Gal) [15.6US Gal]; Tyres 215/65R, wheel rims 7J.

Dimensions: Wheelbase 256.5cm, track 154/156.4cm, clearance min 12cm, turning circle 12.6m, load space 12.4/31.1cu ft (350/880dm3). Length 484cm, width 184cm, height 126.5cm.

Performance: Max speed approx 106–112mph/170–180kmh. Speed at 1000rpm in 5th gear 28.8mph/46.4kmh; power to weight ratio from 13.9kg/kW (10.2kg/PS); consumption approx 10–15L/100km (28.2–18.8mpg) [23.5–15.7US mpg].

Pontiac Firebird Formula

> 5 Litre V8
> 127kW–170hp–172PS
> Central/Single Point Injection

As 2.8 Litre, except:

Weight: Kerbweight from 1475kg.

Engine data (SAE net): 8–cylinder in V 90deg (94.89x88.39mm), 5001cm3; compression ratio 9.3:1; 127kW (170hp) [172PS] at 4000rpm, 25.4kW/L (34hp/L) [34.4PS/L]; 346Nm (255.3lbft) at 2400rpm.

Engine construction: Designated LO 3. 5 bearing crankshaft; Oil capacity 4.5L (4.3US qt); Rochester electronic central injection. AC R45TS spark plugs; cooling system capacity approx 15.7L (14.9US qt).

Transmission: a) 5–speed manual, final drive ratio 3.08. b) Automatic, final drive ratio 2.73.

Gear ratios: a) 5–speed manual: 1st 2.95; 2nd 1.94; 3rd 1.34; 4th 1; 5th 0.63; R 2.76. b) Automatic with OD: Max torque multiplication in converter 2.15 times, Planetary gear set ratios: 1st 3.06; 2nd 1.63; 3rd 1; OD 0.7; R 2.29.

Chassis: Tyres for Formula 245/50 VR 16, wheel rims 8J.

Performance: Max speed approx 118–124mph/190–200kmh. Speed at 1000rpm in 5th gear 38mph/61.2kmh; power to weight ratio from 11.6kg/kW (8.5kg/PS); consumption approx 10–17L/100km (28.2– 16.6mpg) [23.5–13.8US mpg].

Pontiac Firebird TransAm

> 5 Litre V8
> 142/160/168kW–190/215/225hp– 193/218/227PS
> Fuel Injection

As 2.8 Litre, except:

Weight: Kerbweight (DIN) from 1485kg.

Engine data (SAE net): 8–cylinder in V 90deg (94.89 x 88.39mm), 5001cm3; compression ratio 9.3:1; 142kW (190hp) [193PS] at 4000rpm, 28.4kW/L (38.1hp/L) [38.6PS/L]; 400Nm (295lbft) at 2800rpm.
With 5–speed manual: 160kW (215hp) [218PS] at 4400rpm, 32.0kW/L (42.9hp/L) [43.6PS/L]; 387Nm (285.6lbft) at 3200rpm.
With dual exhaust: 168kW (225hp) [228PS] at 4600rpm, 33.6kW/L (45hp/L) [45.6PS/L]; 407Nm (300.4lbft) at 3200; premium unleaded grade.

Engine construction: Designated LB 9. 5 bearing crankshaft; Oil capacity 4.5L (4.3US qt); Bosch electronic fuel injection. Spark plugs AC R45TS; dual exhaust. Alternator 105A; cooling system capacity approx 16.8L (15.9US qt).

Transmission: a) 5–speed manual, final drive ratio 3.08; 225hp 3.45. b) Automatic, final drive ratio 2.73.

Gear ratios: a) 5–speed manual: 1st 2.95; 2nd 1.94; 3rd 1.34; 4th 1; 5th 0.63; R 2.76. 225hp: 1st 2.75; 2nd 1.94; 3rd 1.34; 4th 1; 5th 0.74; R 2.76. b) Automatic with OD: Max torque multiplication in converter 2.15 times, Planetary gear set ratios: 1st 3.06; 2nd 1.63; 3rd 1; OD 0.7; R 2.29.

Chassis: Tyres for Formula and GTA 245/50 VR16, wheel rims 8".

Performance: Max speed approx 124-137mph/200-220kmh, speed at 1000rpm in 5th gear 28.9mph/46.5kmh; power to weight ratio from 8.8kg/kW (6.5kg/PS); consumption approx 11–20L/100km (25.7– 14.1mpg) [21.4–11.8US mpg].

Pontiac Firebird TransAm GTA

Pontiac

```
5.7 Litre V8
168/175kW-225/235hp-228/238PS
Fuel Injection
```

Engine for Formula and GTA

As 2.8 Litre, except:

Weight: Kerbweight (DIN) from 1595kg.

Engine data (SAE net): 8-cylinder in V 90deg (101.6 x 88.39mm), 5733cm3; compression ratio 9.3:1; 168kW (225hp) [228PS] at 4400rpm, 29.3kW/L (39.3hp/L) [39.8 PS/L]; 448Nm (330.6lbft) at 3200rpm.
With dual exhaust: 175kW (235hp) [238PS] at 4400rpm, 30.5kW/L (40.9hp/L) [41.5PS/L]; 461Nm (340.2lbft) at 3200rpm.

Engine construction: Designated L 98. 5 bearing crankshaft; oil capacity 4.5L (4.3US qt); Bosch electronic fuel injection; spark plugs AC R45TS; battery 12V 62Ah, alternator 105A; cooling system capacity approx 16.8L (15.9US qt).

Transmission: Automatic, final drive ratio: 2.77; 235hp 3.27. Limited slip differential.

Gear ratios: Max torque multiplication in converter 1.91 times. Planetary gear set ratios: 1st 3.06; 2nd 1.63; 3rd 1; OD 0.7; R 2.29.

Chassis: Tyres 215/65R 15, optional (for GTA series) 245/50 VR 16, wheel rims 8".

Performance: Max speed over 140mph/225kmh. Speed at 1000rpm in 4th gear (2.77) 38.1mph/61.3kmh; acceleration 0 - 60mph/97kmh 6.5secs; power to weight ratio from 9.1kg/kW (6.7kg/PS); consumption approx 11-22L/100km (25.7-12.8mpg) [21.4-10.7US mpg].

Pontiac Firebird TransAm GTA

```
3.8L V6 Turbo
182kW-245hp-248PS
Fuel Injection
```

As 2.8 Litre, except:

Body, Weight: Kerbweight approx 1600kg.

Engine data (SAE net): 6-cylinder in V 90deg (96.52 x 86.36mm), 3791cm3; compression ratio 8:1; 182kW (245hp) [248PS] at 4400rpm, 48kW/L (64.3hp/L) [65.4PS/L]; 461Nm (340.2lbft) at 2800rpm.

Engine construction: 1 Garrett turbocharger T3; intercooler.

Transmission: Automatic, final drive ratio 2.77; or 3.27. Limited slip differential.

Gear ratios: Max torque multiplication in converter 1.91 times, Planetary gear set: 1st 3.06; 2nd 1.63; 3rd 1; OD 0.7; R 2.29.

Chassis: Tyres 215/65 R 15, optional (for GTA series), 245/50 VR 16, wheel rims 8".

Performance: Max speed over 140mph/225kmh, speed at 1000rpm in 4th gear (2.77) 38mph/61.3kmh; acceleration 0 - 60mph/97kmh 6.5secs; power to weight ratio from 9.1kg/kW (6.7kg/PS); consumption approx 11-22L/100km (25.7-12.8mpg) [21.4-10.7US mpg].

Pontiac Grand Prix

Grand Prix - Grand Prix LE - Grand Prix SE - Grand Prix Turbo

New model, 2-door Coupe, wheel drive and V6 engine. Launched Autumn 1987. For 1988 with 3.1 litre V6/Turbo.

```
2.8 Litre V6
97kW-130hp-132PS
Fuel Injection
```

Body, Weight (laden): Coupe 2 door, 4/6-seater; approx 1405kg.

R23

Engine data (SAE net): 6-cylinder in V 60deg (89 x 76mm), 2837cm3; compression ratio 8.8:1; 97kW (130hp) [132PS] at 4500rpm, 34.2kW/L (45.8hp/L) [46.5PS/L]; 230Nm (169.7lbft) at 3600rpm; unleaded regular grade.

Engine construction: Designated LB 6. Transverse front engine. Hydraulic tappets, central camshaft (chain); 4 bearing crankshaft; light-alloy cylinder head; oil capacity 3.8L (3.6US qt); Rochester electronic fuel injection. Spark plugs AC R43CTLSF; battery 12V 54/69Ah, alternator 108/120A; cooling system capacity 10.7L (10.1US qt).

Transmission (to front wheel): a) 5-speed manual, final drive ratio 3.61. b) Automatic THM 440-T4, hydraulic torque converter and 4-speed Planetary gear set, final drive ratio 2.33.

Gear ratios: a) 5-speed manual: 1st 3.50; 2nd 2.05; 3rd 1.38; 4th 0.94; V 0.72; R 3.41.
b) Automatic: Max torque multiplication in converter 1.95 times, Planetary gear set ratios: 2.92; 1.56; 1; 0.7 R 2.38.

Chassis: Integral body with front sub-frame; front and rear independent suspension; front McPherson strut (coil springs), lower A arm, antiroll bar, rear control arm, shock absorber strut, transverse leaf spring (fibreglass), antiroll bar and optional level control system; telescopic damper. Servo/power assisted disc brakes with optional ABS (Delco/Moraine), disc diameter front 26.7cm, rear 25.6cm; pedal operated parking brake to rear wheels; power assisted rack and pinion steering; Fuel tank 64.5L (14.2Gal) [17.0US Gal]; tyres 195/75 R 14, SE optional 215/60 R 15, wheel rims 5.5 or 6".

Dimensions: Wheelbase 273cm, track 151/147cm, clearance 15cm, turning circle 12.5m. Load space 15.2cu ft (430dm3). Length 492.5cm, width 182.5cm, height 134cm.

Performance: Max speed approx 112/115mph/180/185kmh; speed at 1000rpm in 5th gear 65.4mph/48.8kmh, acceleration 0 - 60mph/97kmh 10.4secs; power to weight ratio from 14.5kg/kW (10.6kg/PS); consumption approx 9-15L/100km (31.4-18.8mpg) [26.1-15.7US mpg].

Pontiac Grand Prix LE

```
3.1 Litre V6
104kW-140hp-142PS
Fuel Injection
```

As 2.8 Litre, except:

Weight: Kerbweight (DIN) from 1460kg.

Engine data (SAE net): 6-cylinder in V 60deg (88.9 x 84mm), 3128cm3; compression ratio 8.8:1; 104kW (140hp) [142PS] at 4500rpm, 33.2kW/L (44.5hp/L) [45.4PS/L]; 251Nm (185.2lbft) at 3600rpm.

Transmission: Automatic, final drive ratio 3.33.

Gear ratios: Max torque multiplication in converter 2.31 times, Planetary gear set ratios 2.92; 1.56; 1; 0.7; R 2.38.

Performance: Max speed approx 118mph/190kmh; speed at 1000rpm in 4th gear 32mph/51.5kmh; power to weight ratio from 14.0kg/kW (10.3kg/PS); consumption approx 10-15L/100km (28.2-18.8mpg) [23.5-15.7US mpg].

Pontiac Grand Prix SE

Pontiac

3.1 Litre V6
153kW–205hp–208PS
Fuel Injection/Turbo

As 2.8 Litre, except:

Weight: Kerbweight (DIN) from 1565kg.

Engine data (SAE net): 6-cylinder in V 60deg (88.9 x 84mm), 3128cm3; compression ratio 8.75:1; 153kW (205hp) [208PS] at 4800rpm, 48.9kW/L (65.5hp/L) [66.5PS/L]; 298Nm (219.9lbft) at 3200rpm; unleaded premium grade.

Engine construction: Garrett turbocharger T25; intercooler.

Transmission: Automatic, final drive ratio 3.33.

Gear ratios: Max torque multiplication in converter 1.72 times, Planetary gear set ratios: 2.92; 1.56; 1; 0.7; R 2.38.

Chassis: ABS; tyres 245/50 ZR 16, wheel rims 8J.

Performance: Max speed approx 134mph/215kmh, speed at 1000rpm in 4th gear 31.9mph/51.5kmh; power to weight ratio from 10.2kg/kW (7.5kg/PS); consumption approx 10–17L/100km (28.2-16.6mpg) [23.5-13.8US mpg].

Pontiac Grand Prix Turbo

Pontiac Bonneville

Bonneville LE – Bonneville SE – Bonneville SSE

Luxury car with front wheel drive, transverse 3.8 Litre V6 engine and automatic transmission with overdrive. Launched Autumn 1986: For 1989 with more powerful engine.

Pontiac Bonneville LE

3.8 Litre V6
123kW–165hp–167PS
Fuel Injection

Body, Weight (laden): Saloon/Sedan 4–door, 5/6–seater; approx 1495kg, SE 1520kg, SSE 1615kg.

Engine data (SAE net): 6–cylinder in V 90deg (96.52 x 86.36mm), 3791cm3; compression ratio 8.5:1; 123kW (165hp) [167PS] at 5200rpm, 32.4kW/L (43.4hp/L) [44.1PS/L]; 285Nm (210.3lbft) at 2000rpm; unleaded regular grade.

Engine construction: Designated LN 3 "3800". Transverse front engine. Hydraulic tappets, central camshaft (chain); 4 bearing crankshaft; oil capacity 3.8L (3.6US qt); Bosch electronic fuel injection. Spark plugs AC R44LTS; battery 12V 54/69Ah, alternator 120A; cooling system capacity approx 11.7L (11.1US qt).

Transmission (to front wheels): Automatic "Turbo Hydra–Matic" 440–T4, hydraulic torque converter and 4-speed Planetary gear set, central selector lever or on steering wheel, final drive ratio LE 2.84; SE 2.97; SSE 3.33.

Gear ratios: Max torque multiplication in converter 1.67 times, Planetary gear set ratios: 2.92; 1.57; 1; OD 0.7; R 2.38.

Chassis: Integral body with front sub–frame; front and rear independent suspension, front McPherson struts, lower A arm and antiroll bar; coil springs, telescopic damper, level control system for SSE. Servo/power assisted brakes, optional ABS (ITT Teves), front disc brakes (ventilated), diameter 25.6cm, rear drums; pedal operated parking brake to rear wheels; power assisted rack and pinion steering; fuel tank 68L (14.9Gal) [18.0US Gal]; tyres LE 205/75 R 14, SE 215/65 R 15, wheel rims 6J, SSE 215/60 R 16, wheel rims 7J.

Dimensions: Wheelbase 281.5cm, track 153/152cm, clearance 15cm, turning circle 13m. Load space 15.4cu ft (435dm3). Length 504/505cm, width 184cm, height 140cm.

Performance: Max speed approx 118-124mph/190-200kmh; speed at 1000rpm in OD 39.4mph/63.4kmh; acceleration 0 60mph/97kmh 10.7secs; power to weight ratio from 12.1kg/kW (8.9kg/PS); consumption approx 10–16L/100km (28.2-17.7mpg) [23.5– 13.3US mpg].

Pontiac Bonneville SSE

Pontiac Safari Wagon

Special vehicle from Pontiac, derived from the Chevrolet Impala/Caprice. 1987: Estate/Station Wagon and 5.8 Litre V8 engine.

Pontiac Safari Wagon

5 Litre V8
104kW–140hp–142PS
1 4V Carb

Body, Weight (laden): Estate/Station Wagon 5–door, 8–seater, approx 1910kg.

Engine data (SAE net): 8–cylinder in V 90deg (94.89 x 88.39mm), 5001cm3; compression ratio 8:1; 104kW (140hp) [142PS] at 3200rpm, 20.8kW/L (27.9hp/L) [28.4PS/L]; 346Nm (255.3lbft) at 2000rpm; unleaded regular grade.

Engine construction: Designated LG4. Hydraulic tappets, central camshaft (chain); 5 bearing crankshaft; Oil capacity 4.5L (4.3US qt); 1 Rochester downdraught 4V Carb. Spark plugs AC FR3LS6; battery 12V 54Ah, alternator 78A; cooling system capacity approx 14.8L (14.0US qt).

Transmission (to rear wheels): 4–speed Overdrive–automatic, hydraulic torque converter and 4– speed Planetary gear set, central selector lever on steering wheel, final drive ratio 2.93; 3.23.
Optional limited slip differential "Positraction".

Gear ratios: Automatic with OD: Max torque multiplication in converter 1.9 times, Planetary gear set ratios: 1st 2.74; 2nd 1.57; 3rd 1; OD 0.67; R2.07.

Chassis: Box section frame with cross member; front overhead trapeze A arm, lower single control arm with elastic positioned tension strut and coil springs, front antiroll bar; rear rigid axle with coil springs, lower and upper trailing arm, differential and leading semi–trailing arm, telescopic damper, optional level control system. Servo/power assisted brakes, front discs (ventilated), diameter 30.1cm, rear drums, pedal operated parking brake to rear wheels; Servo assisted ball and nut steering; Fuel tank 83L (18.2Gal) [21.9US Gal]; tyres 225/75 R 15, Wheel rims 7".

Pontiac USA • Pontiac CDN • Porsche

Dimensions: Wheelbase 294.5cm, track 157.5/163cm, clearance 16cm, turning circle 13.8m. Load space 89cu ft (2490dm3), length 546.5cm, width 201.5cm, height 145.5cm.

Performance: Max speed approx 112mph/180kmh; speed at 1000rpm in OD 41.4mph/66.7kmh; power to weight ratio from 18.4kg/kW (13.4kg/PS); consumption (touring) approx 13–20L/100km (21.7–14.1mpg) [18.1–11.8US mpg].

Pontiac Trans Sport

LE - SE

New model. Pilot run model, general purpose vehicle from GM. Fibre glass body, 3 side doors and tail gate, 5 or 7-seater; 3.1 Litre V6 engine, front wheel drive, automatic. Data incomplete.

Pontiac Trans Sport

3.1 Litre V6
90kW–120hp–122PS
Central/Single Point Injection

Body, Weight: Estate/Station Wagon, 3-door with tailgate, 5/7-seater; kerbweight approx 1585kg.

Engine data (SAE net): 6-cylinder in V 60deg (88.9 x 84mm), 3128cm3; compression ratio 8.8:1; 90kW (120hp) [122PS] at 4500rpm; 28.8kW/L (38.6hp/L) [39PS/L]; 231Nm (170.5lbft) at 3200rpm; unleaded regular grade.

Engine construction: Designated LH 0. Transverse front engine. Hydraulic tappets, central camshaft (chain); 4 bearing crankshaft; light-alloy cylinder head: oil capacity 3.8L (3.6US qt); Rochester electronic central injection. Spark plugs AC R43CTLSE; 12V 54/69Ah battery, 108/120A alternator; cooling system capacity 10.7L (10.1US qt).

Transmission (to front wheels): Automatic THM 125, hydraulic torque converter and 3-speed Planetary gear set, central selector lever to steering wheel or central console, final drive ratio 2.84.

Gear ratios: Max torque multiplication in converter 2.35 times, Planetary gear set 2.84; 1.6; 1; R 2.07.

Pontiac Trans Sport

Chassis: Box type frame with cross member; front independent suspension with coil springs, A arm and antiroll bar; rear coil springs, trailing arm, optional rear antiroll bar; telescopic damper. Servo/power assisted disc brakes ventilated, 26.7cm, rear drums, pedal operated parking brake to rear wheel; power assisted rack and pinion steering; fuel tank 76L (16.7Gal) [20.1US Gal]; tyres 205/70 R 14; 195/70 R 15, wheel rims 6J.

Dimensions: Wheelbase 279cm, track 155/152cm, clearance 18cm, turning circle 12.5m, load space max 123.6cu ft (3500dm3), length 494cm, width 188cm, height 166cm.

Performance: Max speed over 103mph/165kmh, speed at 1000rpm in top gear 25.5mph/41kmh; power to weight ratio from 17.6kg/kW (13.0kg/PS); consumption approx 10-16L/100km (28.2-17.7mpg) [23.5-14.7US mpg].

PONTIAC CDN

General Motors of Canada Ltd., Oshawa, Ontario, Canada.

Canadian badge for GM Canada. Based on the American Chevrolet and Pontiac models with minor modifications.

PORSCHE D

Dr.Ing.h.c.F. Porsche KG, Porschestrasse 42, 7000 Stuttgart– Zuffenhausen, West Germany

Manufacturer of Sports Cars, originally produced by VW.
MODEL RANGE
944–911–928.

Porsche 944

944 - 944 S2 - 944 Turbo

Sports Coupe based on the 924, with 2.5 Litre 4–cylinder light– alloy engine and two vibration dampers. Launched June 1981. February 1985: 944 Turbo with 217hp engine. July 1986: four valves per cylinder. Production of the 944S convertible scheduled for Summer 1988. July 1988: 2.7 and 3 Litre engine.

Porsche 944

2.7 Litre
121kW–162hp–165PS
Fuel Injection

Engine for 944

Body, Weight: Coupe 2–door with tailgate, 2 + 2–seater; kerbweight (DIN) 1290kg, gross vehicle weight 1630kg.

Engine data (Catalyst ECE): 4–cylinder in–line (104 x 78.9mm), 2681cm3; compression 10.9:1; 121kW (162hp) [165PS] at 5800rpm, 45.1kW/L (60.4hp/L) [61.5PS/L]; 225Nm (166lbft) at 4200rpm; unleaded premium grade.
Without Catalyst: Identical Data.

Engine construction: Engine inclined to right. Hydraulic tappets; 1 overhead camshaft (toothed belt); 2 counter–balance shafts; light-alloy cylinder head and block; 5 bearing crankshaft. Oil capacity 6.5L (6.1US qt); Bosch L-Jetronic digital electronic fuel injection. Battery 12V 63Ah, alternator 115A; cooling system capacity approx 8.5L (8.0US qt).

Transmission (to rear wheels); a) 5–speed manual (without direct drive), mounted in rear with differential assembly; floorshift; final drive ratio 3.889 (9/35).
b) Automatic, hydraulic torque converter and 3–speed Planetary gear set, final drive ratio 3.083.
Optional limited slip differential.

Gear ratios: a) 5–speed manual: 1st 3.6; 2nd 2.125; 3rd 1.458; 4th 1.071; V 0.829; R 3.5.
b) Automatic: Max torque multiplication in converter 2.4 times, Planetary gear set ratios: 1st 2.714; 2nd 1.5; 3rd 1; R 2.428.

Porsche

Chassis: Integral body; front (negative steering off-set) McPherson struts (coil springs, coaxial, telescopic damper) and single control arm, rear independent suspension with semi trailing arm and transverse torsion bars, telescopic damper front and rear. Servo/power assisted disc brakes (ventilated), optional ABS (Bosch), disc diameter front 28.2cm, rear 28.9cm, optional Bosch ABS System; mechanical handbrake to rear wheel; power/assisted rack and pinion steering; fuel tank 80L (17.6Gal) [21.1US Gal], with 8L (1.8Gal) [2.1US Gal] reserve; tyres 195/65 VR 16, rear 225/50 VR 15, optional 215/60 VR 16 front, wheel rims 7J, optional rear 8J.

Dimensions: Wheelbase 240cm, track 147.5/145cm, clearance 12.5cm, turning circle 10.7m, load space approx 8.8–17.6cu ft (250–500dm3), length 420cm, US 432cm, width 173.5cm, height 127.5cm.

Performance: Max speed 136mph/220kmh, automatic 135mph/218kmh (manufacturers test specifications), speed at 1000rpm in 5th gear 22.4mph/36kmh; acceleration 0 – 62mph/100kmh 8.2secs, automatic 9.4secs; consumption ECE 7.0/8.4/13.5L/100km (40.4/33.6/20.9mpg) [33.6/28.3/17.4US mpg].

Porsche 944 S2 Cabriolet

```
3 Litre
155kW–208hp–211PS
Fuel Injection
```

Engine for 944 S2

As 2.7 Litre, except:

Weight: Coupe or Convertible 2-door, 2+2-seater; Kerbweight (DIN) from 1310kg; gross vehicle weight 1650kg.

Engine data (Catalyst ECE): 4-cylinder in-line (104 x 88mm), 2990cm3; compression ratio 10.9:1; 155kW (208hp) [211PS] at 5800rpm, 51.8kW/L (69.4hp/L) [70.6PS/L]; 280Nm (206.6lbft) at 4000rpm.
Without Catalyst: Identical Data.

Engine construction: 4 valves per cylinder; 2 overhead camshafts; oil cooler.

Transmission: 5-speed manual, final drive ratio 3.875.

Gear ratios: 1st 3.500; 2nd 2.059; 3rd 1.400; 4th 1.034; 5th 0.829; R 3.500.

Chassis: Tyres front 205/55 ZR 16, rear 225/50 ZR 16, wheel rims 7/8J.

Dimensions: Length 423cm.

Performance: Max speed 149mph/240kmh (manufacturers test specifications), speed at 1000rpm in 5th gear 22.4mph/36.0kmh; acceleration 0 – 62mph/100kmh 7.1secs; power to weight ratio 8.4kg/kW (6.2kg/PS); consumption ECE: no data available.

Porsche 944 S2

```
2.5 Litre Turbo
184kW–247hp–250PS
Fuel Injection
```

Engine for 944 Turbo

As 2.7 Litre, except:

Weight: Kerbweight (DIN) 1350kg; gross vehicle weight 1670kg.

Engine data (Catalyst DIN): 4-cylinder in-line (100 x 78.9mm), 2479 cm3; compression ratio 8:1; 184kW (247hp) [250PS] at 6000rpm, 74.2kW/L (99.4hp/L) [100.8PS/L]; 350Nm (258.3lbft) at 4000rpm; leaded premium grade.

Engine construction: Oil cooler; oil capacity 7L (6.6US qt); 1 exhaust turbocharger (KKK K 26 26/70), inter-cooler; max boost pressure 0.75bar.

Transmission: 5-speed manual, final drive ratio 3.375. Limited slip differential.

Gear ratios: 1st 3.500; 2nd 2.059; 3rd 1.400; 4th 1.034; 5th 0.829; R 3.500.

Chassis: ABS; front tyres 225/50 ZR 16, rear 245/45 ZR 16, wheel rims 7/9J.

Dimensions: Track 145.5/143.5cm, length 423cm.

Performance: Max speed 162mph/260kmh (manufacturers test specifications), speed at 1000rpm in 5th gear 25.5mph/41kmh; acceleration 0 – 62mph/100kmh 5.9secs; standing km 25.5secs; power to weight ratio 7.3kg/kW (5.4kg/PS); consumption ECE 7.1/9.3/13.3L/100km (39.8/30.4/21.1mpg) [33.1/25.3/17.7US mpg].

Porsche 944 Turbo

Porsche 911 Carrera

Coupe – Targa – Cabriolet – Speedstar

Luxury 2 + 2-seater sports car with 6-cylinder rear mounted engine. Launched as the 901 in 1963. Autumn 1980; 3 Litre 202hp engine. Geneva 1982: Cabriolet/Convertible made available. Autumn 1983; engine power increased. Autumn 1987; 2-seater Speedster with folding roof or hardtop.

Porsche 911 Carrera

```
3.2 Litre
170/159.5kW–228/214hp–231/217PS
Fuel Injection
```

Body, Weight: Coupe, Targa with safety frame or Cabriolet/Convertible 2-door, 2 + 2-seater; Kerbweight (DIN) from 1210kg, USA 1250kg, gross vehicle weight 1530kg. Speedster 2-door, 2-seater with folding roof or hardtop; kerbweight approx 1140kg.

Engine data (DIN): 6-cylinder Boxer engine (95 x 74.4mm), 3164cm3; compression ratio 10.3:1; 170kW (228hp) [231PS] at 5900rpm, 53.7kW/L (72hp/L) [73PS/L]; 284Nm (209.6lbft) at 4800rpm; leaded premium grade.
With Catalyst: Compression ratio 9.5:1; 160kW (214hp) [217PS] at 5900rpm; 265Nm (195.6lbft) at 4800rpm; unleaded regular grade.

Porsche

Porsche 911 Carrera Cabriolet

Engine construction: Rear engine. Valves (in V), 1 overhead camshaft per cylinder bank (chain); light–alloy cylinder head and crankcase; 8 bearing crankshaft; dry sump system, oil cooler, oil capacity 13L (12.3US qt); Bosch L–Jetronic digital electronic fuel injection. Battery 12V 66Ah, alternator 90A. Air cooled with axial fan.

Transmission (to rear wheels): 5–speed manual, final drive ratio 3.444. Optional limited slip differential.

Gear ratios: 1st 3.500; 2nd 2.059; 3rd 1.409; 4th 1.074; 5th 0.861; R 2.857.
Swiss version: 1st 3.154; 2nd 1.895; 3rd 1.333; 4th 1.036; 5th 0.861; R 2.857.

Chassis: Integral body; with all round independent suspension, front single control arm with longitudinal antiroll bar and shock absorber struts, rear semi trailing arm, single control arm, torsion bar and telescopic damper; front and rear antiroll bar. Servo/power assisted disc brakes (ventilated). Handbrake to rear wheels; rack and pinion steering; fuel tank 85L (18.7Gal) [22.5US Gal], with 8L (1.8Gal) [2.1US Gal] reserve; front tyres 205/55 ZR 16, rear 225/50 ZR 16, with wheel rims 6 or 8J; optional 245/45 ZR 16 rear, wheel rims 7/8J.

Dimensions: Wheelbase 227cm, track 137/140.5cm, clearance 13cm, turning cirle 10.9m. Load space 7cu ft (200dm3). Length 429cm, width 165cm, height 132cm. Optional with 911 Turbo body; track 143/149cm, width 177.5cm, height 131cm.

Performance: Max speed 152mph/245kmh, Catalyst 149mph/240kmh (manufacturers test specifications), speed at 1000rpm in top gear 24.3mpg/39.1kmh; acceleration 0 – 62mph/100kmh 6.1secs, Catalyst version 6.3secs; standing km 26.1secs, Catalyst 26.3secs; power to weight ratio from 7.1kg/kW (5.2kg/PS); consumption ECE 6.8/9.0/13.6L/100km (41.5/31.4/20.8mpg) [34.6/26.1/17.3US mpg], Catalyst version 7.9/9.8/14.9L/100km (35.8/28.8/19.0mpg) [29.8/24.0/12.4US mpg] Turbo–look 7.8/10.1/13.6L/100km (36.2/28.0/20.8mpg) [30.2/23.3/17.3US mpg].

Porsche 911 Carrera Speedster

Porsche 911 Turbo

High performance sports car with a 3.3 Litre Turbocharged engine and Bosch K–Jetronic fuel injection. Launched Paris 1974. Frankfurt 1977: improved performance 296hp.

> 3.3 Litre Turbo
> 220.5kW–296hp–300PS
> Fuel Injection

As 911 Carrera, except:

Porsche 911 Turbo

Weight: Coupe; Kerbweight (DIN) 1335kg, gross vehicle weight 1680kg.

Engine data (ECE): (97 x 74.4mm), 3299cm3; compression ratio 7:1; 220.5kW (296hp) [300PS] at 5500rpm, 66.9kW/L (89.6hp/L) [91PS/L]; 430Nm (317.3lbft) at 4000rpm. Leaded premium grade.
With Catalyst: 210.5kW (282hp) [286PS]; 377Nm (278.2lbft).

Engine construction: Bosch K–Jetronic fuel injection. Exhaust turbocharger KKK 3 LDZ, inter-cooler; boost pressure 0.8bar.

Transmission: 4–speed manual, final drive ratio 4.222 (9/38), optional limited slip differential.

Gear ratios: 1st 2.25; 2nd 1.304–CH 1.250; 3rd 0.893; 4th 0.625; R 2.437.

Chassis: Disc diameter front 28.3cm, rear 29cm, front tyres 205/55 VR 16, rear 225/50 VR 16, front wheel rims 7", rear 8".

Dimensions: Track 143/149cm, width 177.5cm, height 131cm.

Performance: Max speed 162mph/260kmh (manufacturers test specifications), speed at 1000rpm in 4th gear 27.7mph/44.5kmh; acceleration 0 – 62mph/100kmh 5.2secs; standing km 24secs; power to weight ratio 6.1kg/kW (4.5kg/PS); consumption ECE 10.7/13.0/14.3L/100km (26.4/21.7/19.8mpg) [22/18.1/16.4US mpg].

Porsche 911 Turbo Targa/Cabriolet

Porsche 911 Carrera 4

New model. 2 + 2-seater sports car with 3.6 Litre, rear mounted 6 cylinder Boxer engine and permanent all wheel drive. Launched November 1988.

Porsche 911 Carrera 4

Porsche • Portaro

> 3.6 Litre
> 184kW–247hp–250PS
> Fuel Injection

Body, Weight: Coupe 2-door. 2+2-seater; kerbweight (DIN) from 1450kg, gross vehicle weight 1790kg.

Engine data (Catalyst, ECE): 6-cylinder Boxer engine (100 x 76.4mm), 3600cm3; compression ratio 11.3:1; 184kW (247hp) [250PS] at 6100rpm, 51.1kW/L (68.5hp/L) [69.4PS/L]; 310Nm (228.8lbft) at 4800rpm; unleaded regular grade.

Engine construction: Rear engine. Valves in V, 1 overhead camshaft per cylinder bank (chain); light-alloy cylinder head and crankcase, light-alloy cylinders; 8 bearing crankshafts; dry sump system, oil cooler, oil capacity 11.5L (10.9US qt); Bosch Motronic electronic injection, M 2.1 electronic digital engine. 12V 72Ah battery, 150A alternator; air cooling with axial blower.

Transmission (to all wheels): 5-speed manual, power distribution front 31%, central Planetary-differential and rear electro-hydraulic regulated differential. Multi plate clutch, final drive ratio 3.444.

Gear ratios: 1st 3.500; 2nd 2.118; 3rd 1.444; 4th 1.086; 5th 0.868; R 2.857.

Chassis: Integral body; all round independent suspension, front McPherson struts with A arm, rear semi-trailing arm, front and rear antiroll bar. Servo/power assisted disc brakes ventilated, disc diameter 29.8cm front, rear 29.9cm, mechanical handbrake to rear wheels, ABS (Bosch); Power assisted rack and pinion steering; fuel tank 77L (16.9Gal) [20.3US Gal]. Front tyres 225/55 ZR 16, rear 225/50 ZR 16, wheel rims 6J or 8J.

Dimensions: Wheelbase 227cm, track 138/137.5cm, clearance min 12cm, turning circle 11.8m, load space 3.2cu ft (90dm3), length 425cm, width 165cm, height 132cm.

Performance: Max speed 162mph/260kmh (manufacturers test specification), speed at 1000rpm in 5th gear 24.1mph/38.7kmh; acceleration 0 - 62mph/100kmh 5.9secs; standing km 25.6secs; power to weight ratio from 7.9kg/kW (5.8kg/PS); consumption ECE 8.0/9.5/17.9L/100km (35.3/29.7/15.8mpg) [29.4/24.8/13.1US mpg].

Porsche 911 Carrera 4

Porsche 928 S4

High performance Coupe with a V8 engine and 5-speed manual or automatic transmission (rear mounted and incorporating differential). Launched March 1977, 928S August 1979. Summer 1982 production of the 928 with a 4.5 Litre engine suspended. Autumn 1986; 5 Litre, 316hp, 4 valves per cylinder engine. February 1989: GT with 326hp.

Porsche 928 S4

> 5 Litre V8
> 235.5/243kW–316/326hp–320/330PS
> Fuel Injection

Body, Weight: Coupe 2-door with tailgate, 2 + 2-seater; kerbweight (DIN) from 1580kg, gross vehicle weight 1920kg.

Engine data (ECE): 8-cylinder in V 90deg (100 x 78.9mm), 4957cm3; compression ratio 10:1; 235.5kW (316hp) [320PS] at 6000rpm, 47.5kW/L (63.7hp/L) [64.5PS/L]; 431Nm (318.1lbft) at 3000rpm; leaded premium grade.
With Catalyst: Identical Data.
GT: 243kW (326hp) [330PS] at 6200rpm; 49kW/L (65.7hp/L) [66.6PS/L]; 430Nm (317.3lbft) at 4100rpm.

Engine construction: Hydraulic tappets; 4 valves per cylinder; 2 overhead camshafts for each cylinder bank (toothed belt); light-alloy cylinder head and crankcase; 5 bearing crankshaft; oil capacity 7.5L (7.1US qt); twin fuel injectors; Bosch LH Jetronic; electronic fuel pump. Battery 12V 72Ah, alternator 115A; cooling system capacity approx 16L (15.1US qt).

Transmission (to rear wheels): a) 5-speed manual, in rear with differential assembly, final drive ratio 2.636, USA 2.267.
b) Automatic, hydraulic torque converter and 4-speed Planetary gear set, central selector lever, final drive ratio 2.538 (USA 2.20).
Optional limited slip differential.

Gear ratios: a) 5 speed manual: 1st 3.765; 2nd 2.512; 3rd 1.790; 4th 1.354; 5th 1; R 3.305.
b) Automatic: Max torque multiplication in converter 2 times, Planetary gear set ratios: 1st 3.676; 2nd 2.412; 3rd 1.436; 4th 1; R 5.139.

Chassis: Integral body; front lower and upper A arm, McPherson struts (Coil springs and coaxial telescopic damper), rear compound axle with lower single control arm, longitudinal compression strut, coil springs and coaxial telescopic damper, front and rear antiroll bar. Servo/power assisted disc brakes (ventilated) with ABS (Bosch), disc diameter, front 28.2cm, rear 28.9cm, optional Bosch ABS System; handbrake to rear wheels; power assisted rack and pinion steering; fuel tank 86L (18.9Gal) [22.7US Gal], with 8L (1.8Gal) [2.11US Gal] reserve. Front tyres 225/50 ZR 16, rear 245/45 ZR 16, wheel rims, front 7J, rear 8J.

Dimensions: Wheelbase 250cm, track 155/154.5cm, clearance min 12cm, turning circle 11.5m, load space 7/14cu ft (200/400dm3). Length 452cm, width 183.5cm, height 128cm.

Performance: Max speed 168mph/270kmh, GT 171mph/275mph, automatic 165mph/265kmh, (manufacturers test specifications), speed at 1000rpm in 5th gear 27mph/43.5kmh; acceleration 0 – 62mph/100kmh 5.9secs, GT 5.8secs, automatic 6.3secs; standing km 25.5secs; power to weight ratio 6.7kg/kW (4.9kg/PS). Consumption ECE 9.4/10.8/19.6L/100km (30.1/26.2/14.4mpg) [25.0/21.8/12.0US mpg], Catalyst version 9.8/11.2/19.8L/100km (28.8/25.2/14.3mpg) [24.0/21.0/11.9US mpg], GT 9.7/12.0/21.9L/100km (29.1/23.5/12.9mpg) [24.2/19.6/10.7US mpg]. Automatic 9.0/10.9/17.1L/100km (31.4/25.9/16.5mpg) [26.1/21.6/13.8US mpg], Catalyst version 9.4/11.3/17.5L/100km (30.1/25.0/16.1mpg) [25.0/20.8/13.4US mpg].

Porsche 928 S4 GT

PORTARO P

GV, Sociedade Electro–Mecanica de Automove is, LDA., Rua Nova de S. Mamede, 3 to 9 Lisboa 2, Portugal.

Portuguese manufacturer of specialist vehicles.

Portaro Pampas 260

Rough terrain vehicle built under license for ARO, with a Daihatsu diesel engine or Volvo engine. Launched 1976.

Portaro • Premier

2.5 Litre Diesel
55kW–74hp–75PS
Injection Pump

Body, Weight: Estate/Station Wagon, 3-door, 3 to 9-seater; kerbweight (DIN) 1790kg. Gross vehicle weight 2550kg.

Engine data (DIN): 4–cylinder in-line (88 x 104mm) 2530cm3; compression ratio 21:1; 55kW (74hp) [75PS] at 3600rpm, 21.7kW/L (29.1hp/L) [29.6PS/L]; 172Nm (127.1lbft) at 2200rpm.
With Turbo: 70.5kW (95hp) [96PS].

Engine construction: Designated Daihatsu NDG 80. Side camshaft, 5 bearing crankshaft; optional oil cooler, oil capacity 6.5L (6.1US qt); Nippon Denso (Bosch) injection pump. Battery 12V 120Ah, alternator 300W; cooling system capacity approx 12L (11.4US qt).

Transmission (to rear wheels or all wheels): 4 or 5–speed manual, final drive ratio 4.71, optional 4.66 or 5.14; two or four wheel drive; final drive ratio in auxilliary transmission 2.18.

Gear ratios: a) 4–speed manual: 1st 4.921; 2nd 2.781; 3rd 1.654; 4th 1; R 5.08. b) 5–speed manual: 1st 3.717; 2nd 2.177; 3rd 1.408; 4th 1; 5th 0.876; R 4.434.

Chassis: Main chassis beam and cross members; front independent suspension with single control arm and coil springs, rear rigid axle with laminated spring, telescopic damper. Front drum brakes, mechanical handbrake to rear wheels; worm and wheel steering, optional power assisted; fuel tank 95L (20.9Gal) [25.1US Gal]; tyres 6.50–16 or 7.50–16, wheel rims 5", optional tyres 185–15, wheel rims 6".

Dimensions: Wheelbase 235cm, track 144.5/144.5, clearance min 22cm, turning circle 12m. Length 400cm, width 184cm, height 194cm.

Performance: Max speed 72–81mph/115–130kmh (manufacturers test specifications), speed at 1000rpm in 4th gear 17.3mph/27.9kmh; power to weight ratio from 32.5kg/kW (23.9kg/PS); consumption approx 10–20L/100km (28.2–14.1mpg) [23.5–11.8US mpg].

Portaro Pampas 260

2.3 Litre
82.5kW–111hp–112PS
1 Carb

As 2.5 Litre, except:

Weight: Kerbweight (DIN) 1690kg.

Engine data (DIN): 4–cylinder in-line (96 x 80mm), 2316cm3; compression ratio 10.3:1; 82.5kW (111hp) [112PS] at 5000rpm, 35.6kW/L (47.7hp/L) [48.4PS/L]; 185Nm (136.5lbft) at 2500rpm; leaded premium grade.

Engine construction: Designated Volvo B 23 A. 1 overhead camshaft (toothed belt), light–alloy cylinder head; 5 bearing crankshaft; oil capacity 3.8L (3.6US qt); 1 horizontal carb Stromberg 175CD. Battery 12V 60Ah, alternator 55A; cooling system capacity approx 9.5L (9.0US qt).

Performance: Max speed 75mph/120kmh (manufacturers test specifications); power to weight ratio 20.5kg/kW (15.5kg/PS); consumption approx 11–20L/100km (25.7–14.1mpg) [21.4–11.8US mpg].

2.1 Litre Turbo
114kW–153hp–155PS
Fuel Injection

As 2.5 Litre, except:

Engine data (DIN): (92 x 80mm), 2127 cm3; compression ratio 7.5:1; 114kW (153hp) [155PS] at 5500rpm, 53.6kW/L (71.8hp/L) [72.9PS/L]; 240Nm (177.1lbft) at 3750rpm; leaded premium grade.

Engine construction: Designated B 21 ET. 1 overhead camshaft (toothed belt), light–alloy cylinder head; 5 bearing crankshaft; oil capacity 3.8L (3.6US qt) 1 exhaust turbocharger, Garrett AiResearch TB O3; max boost pressure 0.67bar. Bosch K Jetronic fuel injection. Battery 12V 60Ah, alternator 55A; cooling system capacity approx 9.5L (9.0US qt).

Performance: Max speed 99mph/160kmh (manufacturers test specifications); power to weight ratio 15.7kg/kW (11.5kg/PS); consumption approx 12–22L/100km (23.5–12.8mpg) [19.6–10.7US mpg].

PREMIER   IND

The Premier Automobiles Limited, LB Shastri Marg, Kurla, Bombay 400 070, India

Indian manufacturer of vehicles based on the Fiat 1100 and 124, for home market only.

Premier Padmini – President

Medium size vehicle with a 1.1 Litre engine and 4–speed manual transmission.

1.1 Litre
32.5/29.5kW–43/39hp–44/40PS
1 Carb

Body, Weight: 4–door Saloon/Sedan, 4/5–seater; kerbweight 895kg. Gross vehicle weight 1125/1295kg. Optional other body variants.

Engine Data (DIN): 4–cylinder in-line (68 x 75mm), 1089cm3; compression ratio 7.8:1; 32.5kW (43hp) [44PS] at 5000rpm, 29.8kW/L (39.9hp/L) [40.4PS/L]; 73Nm (53.9lbft) at 3000rpm; leaded regular grade.
Or: 29.5kW (39hp) [40PS] at 5000rpm; 68Nm (50.2lbft) at 3000rpm.

Engine construction: Side camshaft (chain), light–alloy cylinder head; 3 bearing crankshaft; oil capacity 3.9L (3.7US qt); 1 Solex M 32 PBIC IBX downdraught carb. Battery 12V 45Ah, Dynamo 264W; cooling system capacity approx 4.5L (4.3US qt).

Transmission (to rear wheels): 4–speed manual, 2nd, 3rd and 4th gear synchromesh, steering wheel or floor shift; final drive ratio 4.3 (10/43).

Gear ratios: 1st 3.86; 2nd 2.38; 3rd 1.57; 4th 1; R 3.86.

Chassis: Integral body, front swinging A arm and coil springs, rear rigid axle with semi elliptic spring, front and rear antiroll bar, telescopic damper. Drum brakes, mechanical handbrake to rear wheels; worm and wheel steering. Fuel tank 38L (8.4Gal) [10.0US Gal]; tyres 5.20–14, wheel rims 3.5J.

Dimensions: Wheelbase 234cm, track 123/121.5cm, clearance 13cm, turning circle 10.5m, load space 10.9cu ft (310dm3). Length 393cm, width 146cm, height 147cm.

Performance: Max speed 78-74mph/125-119kmh (manufacturers test specifications), speed at 1000rpm in 4th gear 16.2mph/26kmh; power to weight ratio from 27.5kg/kW (20.3kg/PS); consumption approx 7–10L/100km (40.4-28.2mpg) [33.6-23.5US mpg].

Premier Padmini

Premier 118 NE

Body based on the early Fiat 124. Engine and transmission as the Nissan Cherry. Launched Autumn 1985.

Premier • Proton

```
1172cm3
39kW–52hp–53PS
1 2V Carb
```

Body, Weight: Saloon/Sedan 4-door, 5-seater; kerbweight (DIN) 900kg, gross vehicle weight 1300kg.

Engine data (DIN): 4-cylinder in-line (73 x 70mm), 1172cm3; compression ratio 9:1; 39kW (52hp) [53PS] at 5600rpm, 33.3kW/L (44.6hp/L) [45.2PS/L]; 79Nm (58.3lbft) at 4000rpm; leaded regular grade.

Engine construction: Designated Nissan A 12. Side camshaft (chain); light-alloy cylinder head; 5 bearing crankshaft; oil capacity 3.2L (3.0US qt); 1 Hitachi downdraught 2V carb. Battery 12V 45Ah, alternator 36A; cooling system capacity approx 6.4L (6.1US qt).

Transmission (to rear wheels): 4-speed manual, final drive ratio 3.9 (10/39).

Gear ratios: 1st 3.757; 2nd 2.167; 3rd 1.404; 4th 1; R 3.64.

Chassis: Integral body; front swinging A arm, coil springs, rear rigid axle with coil springs, Panhard rod, front and rear antiroll bar, telescopic damper. Optional servo/power assisted brakes, front disc brakes, rear drums, brake disc diameter 22.7cm, mechanical handbrake to rear wheels; worm and wheel steering; fuel tank 39L (8.6Gal) [10.3US Gal], tyres 5.60-13, wheel rims 4.5".

Dimensions: Wheelbase 242cm, track 133/130cm, clearance 15.5cm, turning circle 10.7m, load space 13.6cu ft (385dm3), length 405cm, width 161cm, height 143.5cm.

Performance: Max speed 100mph/135kmh (manufacturers test specifications), speed at 1000rpm in 5th gear 17.3mph/27.8kmh; power to weight ratio from 23.1kg/kW (17.0kg/PS); consumption approx 7–10L/100km (40.4–28.2mpg) [33.6–23.5US mpg].

Premier 118 NE

PROTON — MAL

Perusahaan Otomobil Nasional Sdn Bhd, Hicom Industrial Estate, Batu Tiga, Shah Alam, Selangor, Malaysia

Malaysian manufacturer of vehicles under license from Mitsubishi.

Proton Aeroback-Saloon

Car works of Colt/Lancer also Hyundai Pony/Excel with 1.3 Litre [67hp] or 1.5 Litre four-cylinder [74hp], 5-speed manual or Automatic.

```
1.3 Litre
50kW–67hp–68PS
1 Compound Carb
```

Body, Weight: Saloon/Sedan 4-door, 4-seater; kerbweight (DIN) approx 920kg. Saloon/Sedan 5-door, 4-seater; kerbweight (DIN) approx 925kg.

Engine data (DIN): 4-cylinder in-line (71 x 82mm), 1299cm3; compression ratio 9.8:1; 50kW (67hp) [68PS] at 6000rpm, 38.5kW/L (51.6hp/L) [52.3PS/L]; 102Nm (75.3lbft) at 4000rpm; premium grade.

Engine construction: Designated Mitsubishi G 13 B. Overhead valves in V, 1 overhead camshaft (toothed belt); light-alloy cylinder head; 5 bearing crankshaft; oil capacity 4L (3.8US qt); 1 downdraught carb. 12V 40Ah battery, alternator 50A; cooling system capacity approx 7.3L (6.9US qt).

Transmission (to front wheels): 5-speed manual, final drive ratio 3.166.

Gear ratios: 1st 4.226; 2nd 2.365; 3rd 1.467; 4th 1.105; 5th 0.855; R 4.109.

Chassis: Integral body; front McPherson struts (coil springs) with lower A arm, rear independent suspension with trailing arm and coil springs, front and rear antiroll bar, telescopic damper. Servo/power assisted brakes, front discs, rear drums; handbrake to rear wheels; power assisted rack and pinion steering; fuel tank 45L (9.9Gal) [11.9US Gal]; tyres 155 SR 13, wheel rims 4.5J.

Dimensions: Wheelbase 238cm, track 139/134cm, clearance 15cm, turning circle 10.4m, load space 5-door max, 26.6cu ft (753dm3), 4-door 11.1cu ft (315dm3), length 413.5cm, 4-door 431cm, width 163cm, height 136cm.

Performance: Max speed 96mph/155kmh (manufacturers test specification), speed at 1000rpm in 5th gear 24.3mph/39.1kmh; acceleration 0 - 60mph/97kmh 14.1secs; power to weight ratio from 18.4kg/kW (13.5kg/PS); consumption approx 6–9L/100km (47.1–31.4mpg) [39.2–26.1US mpg].

Proton Saloon

```
1.5 Litre
55kW–74hp–75PS
1 Compound Carb
```

As 1.3 Litre, except:

Body, Weight: Saloon/Sedan 4-door, 4-seater; kerbweight (DIN) from 925-950kg. Saloon/Sedan 5-door, 4-seater; kerbweight (DIN) 925-950kg.

Engine data: 4-cylinder in-line (75.5 x 82mm), 1468cm3; compression ratio 9.5:1; 55kW (74hp) [75PS] at 5500rpm, 37.5kW/L (50.1hp/L) [51.1PS/L]; 118Nm (87.1lbft) at 3500rpm.

Engine construction: Designated Mitsubishi G 15 B.

Transmission (to front wheels): a) 5-speed manual, final drive ratio 3.166. b) Automatic, hydraulic torque converter with 3-speed Planetary gear set, final drive ratio 3.166.

Gear ratios: a) 5-speed manual: 1st 4.226; 2nd 2.365; 3rd 1.467; 4th 1.105; 5th 0.855; R 4.109.
b) Automatic; max torque multiplication in converter 2 times, Planetary gear set ratios: 1st 2.846; 2nd 1.581; 3rd 1; R 2.176.

Chassis: Tyres 175/70 HR 13, wheel rims 5J.

Performance: Max speed 97mph/156kmh, automatic 89mph/143kmh (manufacturers test specification), speed at 1000rpm in 5th gear 21.1mph/33.9kmh; acceleration 0 - 60mph/97kmh 13.1secs, automatic 17.6secs; power to weight ratio from 16.8kg/kW (12.3kg/PS); consumption approx 7–11L/100km (40.4-25.7mpg) [33.6-21.4US mpg].

PUCH — A

See Mercedes-Benz/Puch

Puch G

PUMA BR

Alfa Metais Veiculos Ltda., Av. Joscelino Kubitschek 3291, 81000 Curitiba, Brasil.

New badge under the direction of Alfa Metais, successor to Puma which closed in 1985. Construction of sports cars with VW Boxer or with Chevrolet-Opala engine, plus later Variants with Passat engine.

Puma AM 1 · AM 2

Coupe and Convertible based on the VW beetle.

```
1.6 Litre
32kW-43hp-44PS
2 Carbs
```

Body, Weight: Convertible AM 1/Coupe AM 2-door, 2-seater; kerbweight (DIN) 750kg, gross vehicle weight 1000kg.

Engine data (DIN): 4-cylinder Boxer engine (85.5 x 69mm), 1584cm3, compression ratio 7.5:1; 32kW (43hp) [44PS] at 3600rpm, 20.2kW/L (27hp/L) [27.8PS/L]; 99Nm (73lbft) at 2000rpm; regular grade.

Engine construction: Rear engine, central camshaft (gear wheel); light-alloy cylinder head and block; 4 bearing crankshaft; oil cooler, oil capacity 2.5L (2.4US qt); 2 Solex 32 PDSIT downdraught carbs. 12V 36Ah battery, alternator 50A; air cooled with blower.

Transmission (to rear wheels): 4-speed manual, final drive ratio 4.121.

Gear ratios: 1st 3.78; 2nd 2.06; 3rd 1.32; 4th 0.89; R 3.88.

Chassis: Central frame, rear forked with platform super structure; front twin cranked arm with transverse torsion bar. Rear independent suspension with swing axle, trailing arm, transverse torsion bar and diagonal arms; front antiroll bar; telescopic damper. Front disc brakes, rear drums; handbrake to rear wheels; worm and wheel steering; fuel tank 40L (8.8Gal) [10.6US Gal], from 5L (4.7US qt) reserve; tyres 195/60 HR 14, wheel rims 6J.

Dimensions: Wheelbase 215cm, track 139/140cm, clearance 15cm, turning circle 10.5m. Length 400cm, width 166.5cm, height 120cm.

Performance: Max speed approx 87mph/140kmh (manufacturers test specification), speed at 1000rpm in 4th gear 29.4kmh; acceleration 0 - 62mph/100kmh 20.4secs; power to weight ratio from 23.4kg/kW (17kg/PS); consumption approx 8-10L/100km (35.3-28.2mpg) [29.4-23.5US mpg].

Puma AM2

```
4.1 Litre
99kW-133hp-135PS
1 2V Carb
```

As 1.6 Litre, except:

Body, Weight: Coupe 2-door, 2-seater; kerbweight (DIN) 980kg, gross vehicle weight 1260kg.

Engine data (for operating on ethyl alcohol, SAE net): 6-cylinder in-line (98.4 x 89.6mm), 4093cm3; compression ratio 10:1; 99kW (133hp) [135PS] at 4000rpm, 24.3kW/L (32.6hp/L) [33PS/L]; 295Nm (217.7lbft) at 2000rpm.

Engine construction: Designated: GMB 251. Hydraulic tappets, side camshaft (gear wheel); 7 bearing crankshaft; oil capacity 5L (4.7US qt); 1 Weber downdraught twin carb. 12V 45Ah battery, alternator 32A; cooling system capacity approx 10.2L (9.6US qt).

Transmission: 5-speed manual, final drive ratio 2.73.

Gear ratios: 1st 3.4; 2nd 2.16; 3rd 1.38; 4th 1; 5th 0.84; R 3.81.

Chassis: Box type frame with cross member; front lower A arm, upper single control arm with transverse torsion bar, coil springs, telescopic damper, rear leaf springs, telescopic damper. Servo/power assisted brakes; power steering; fuel tank 70L (15.4Gal) [18.5US Gal]; tyres 225/60 HR 14, wheel rims 7J.

Performance: No details available.

Puma

RAYTON FISSORE I

Rayton Fissore, spa., Via Fondovalle, 12602 Cherasco (CN), Italy.

Italian manufacturer of luxury rough terrain vehicles.

Rayton Fissore 3.5 – 2.4 td

Rough terrain four wheel drive vehicle; with a super–charged 2 Litre engine or 2.4 Litre turbodiesel from Fiat. Launched July 1984. Turin 1988: with engines supplied by BMW, modifications to body and interior. Marketed as "Laforza" in the USA.

```
3.5 Litre
155kW–208hp–211PS
Fuel Injection
```

Body, Weight: Saloon/Sedan 4–door, 7–seater; kerbweight (DIN) approx 1850kg, gross vehicle weight 2750kg.

Engine data (DIN): 6–cylinder in–line (92 x 86mm), 3430cm3; compression ratio 9.0:1; 155kW (208hp) [211PS] at 5700rpm, 45.2kW/L (60.6hp/L) [61.5PS/L]; 305Nm (225lbft) at 4000rpm; unleaded regular grade.

Engine construction: Designated BMW 3.5. Valves in V 52deg, 1 overhead camshaft (chain); light–alloy cylinder head; 7 bearing crankshaft; oil capacity 5.75L (5.5US qt), oil cooler; Bosch Motronic digital electronic engine (fuel injection/ignition) control. 12V battery 66Ah, 90A alternator; cooling system capacity 12L (11.4US qt).

Transmission (to rear wheels or all wheels): 5–speed manual and 2–speed reduction gear, engeable four wheel drive; final drive ratio, front and rear 4.44, reduction gear set ratios 1 (town) and 2.74 (country).
Rear limited slip differential, also available at the front.

Gear ratios: 1st 3.83; 2nd 2.20; 3rd 1.40; 4th 1; V 0.81; R 3.46.

Chassis: Integral body; front independent suspension with shock absorber strut (rear twin), single control arm, compression strut and torsion spring rod; rear rigid axle with semi–elliptic spring, telescopic damper. Servo/power assisted brakes, front disc, rear drums, mechanical handbrake to rear wheels; power assisted rack and pinion steering; fuel tank 80L (17.6Gal) [21.1US Gal]; tyres 6.00–16, wheel rims 5J.

Dimensions: Wheelbase 270cm, track 172/172cm, turning circle 10.5m, clearance 19cm, length 457cm, width 201cm, height 178cm.

Performance: Max speed 112mph/180kmh (manufacturers test specifications), speed at 1000rpm in 5th gear 23.1mph/37.2kmh; power to weight ratio 11.9kg/kW (8.8kg/PS); consumption approx 12–20L/100km (23.5–14.1mpg) [19.6–11.8US mpg].

Rayton Fissore • Reliant

Rayton Fissore 3.5

2.4 Litre Diesel
92kW–123hp–125PS
Turbo/Injection Pump

Engine for 2.4 td

As 3.5 Litre, except:

Engine data (DIN): 6–cylinder in–line (80 x 81mm), 2443cm3; compression ratio 22:1; 92kW (123hp) [125PS] at 4800rpm, 37.7kW/L (50.5hp/L) [51.2PS/L]; 226Nm (23mkp) at 2300rpm.

Engine construction: Designated BMW 2.4 td. Swirl chamber diesel engine. Parallel valves, 1 overhead camshaft (toothed belt); light–alloy cylinder head; oil capacity 5.25L (5US qt); Bosch injection electronically regulated Pump; 1 exhaust turbocharger. 12V battery 85Ah, 80A alternator; cooling system capacity approx 12L (11.4US qt).

Transmission: 5–speed manual, final drive ratio 3.9.

Performance: Max speed 96mph/155kmh (manufacturers test specifications), speed at 1000rpm in 5th gear 27.1mph/43.6kmh, power to weight ratio 20.1kg/kW (14.8kg/PS); consumption approx 8–15L/100km (35.3–18.8mpg) [29.4–15.7US mpg].

2.4 Litre Diesel
77kW–103hp–105PS
Turbo/Injection pump

Not for Italy

As 3.5 Litre, except:

Weight: Kerbweight (DIN) approx 1850kg.

Engine data (DIN): (93 x 90mm), 2445cm3; compression ratio 22:1; 77kW (103hp) [105PS] at 4100rpm, 31.6kW/L (42.3hp/L) [42.9PS/L]; 216Nm (159.4lbft) at 2400rpm.
Or: 66kW (88hp) [90PS] at 4100rpm, 27.1kW/L (36.3hp/L) [36.8PS/L]; 196Nm (144.6lbft) at 2400rpm.
Some Countries: 81kW (108hp) [110PS].

Engine construction: Swirl chamber diesel engine. 1 overhead camshaft (toothed belt), light–alloy cylinder block; oil capacity 6.7L (6.3US qt) Bosch injection pump; 1 exhaust turbocharger (KKK); max charge–air pressure 0.87 bar. Battery 12V 88Ah, alternator 55A; cooling system capacity approx 11L (10.4US qt).

Performance: Max speed above 111mph/150kmh (manufacturers test specifications), power to weight ratio 24kg/kW (17.6kg/PS); consumption approx 10–14L/100km (28.2–20.2mpg) [23.5–16.8US mpg].

Rayton Fissore Turbo D

RELIANT GB

Reliant Motor PLC, Tamworth, Staffordshire B77 IHN, England
English vehicle manufacturer of passenger cars. In 1969 amalgamated with Bond.

Reliant Scimitar

Sports car with front engine and rear wheel drive. Available with 1.4 or 1.6 Litre Ford engine. Launched Autumn 1984. Geneva 1986; 1.8 Litre (Nissan) made available.

1.4 Litre
55kW–74hp–75PS
1 Carb

Body, Weight: Convertible 2–door, 2–seater; kerbweight (DIN) 840kg, gross vehicle weight 1120kg.

Engine data (DIN): 4–cylinder in–line (77.24 x 74.3mm), 1392cm3; compression ratio 9.5:1; 55kW (74hp) [75PS] at 5600rpm, 39.5kW/L (52.9hp/L) [53.9PS/L]; 109Nm (80.4lbft) at 4000rpm; leaded premium grade.
Some countries: 52kW (68hp) [69PS].

Engine construction: Designated CVH. Front engine. Valves in V 45deg, hydraulic tappets, 1 overhead camshaft (toothed belt), light–alloy cylinder block; 5 bearing crankshaft; oil capacity 3.5L (3.3US qt); 1 Weber downdraught carb 28/30 DFTM. Battery 12V 60Ah; alternator 45A; cooling system capacity approx 8L (7.6US qt).

Transmission (to rear wheels): 4–speed manual, final drive ratio 3.92.

Gear ratios: 1st 3.65 2nd 1.97; 3rd 1.37; 4th 1; R 3.66.

Chassis: Box section frame with sub frame, plastic body. Front under and lower A arm and coil springs, rear independent suspension with semi trailing arm and coil springs, front and rear antiroll bar, telescopic damper. Servo/power assisted brakes, front disc brake, rear drums, disc diameter 22.6cm, mechanical handbrake to rear wheel; rack and pinion steering; fuel tank 45 L (9.9Gal) [11.9US Gal]; tyres 175/70 SR 13, optional 185/60 HR 14, wheel rims 5 or 5.5J.

Dimensions: Wheelbase 213.5cm, track 130/132cm, clearance 15cm, turning circle 9.1m, load space 6.7cu ft (190dm3), length 388.5cm, width 158cm, height 124cm.

Performance: Max speed 99mph/160kmh (manufacturers test specifications), speed at 1000rpm in 4th gear 16.8mph/27.1kmh, acceleration 0 – 62mph/100kmh 13.4secs; power to weight ratio 15.9kg/kW (11.7kg/PS); consumption ECE 6.7/8.5/10.3L/100km (42.2/33.2/27.4mpg) [35.1/27.7/22.8US mpg].

1.6 Litre
70kW–94hp–95PS
1 2V Carb

As 1.4 Litre, except:

Engine data (DIN); 4–cylinder in–line (80 x 79.5mm), 1598cm3; compression ratio 9.5:1; 70kW (94hp) [95PS] at 5600rpm, 43.7kW/L (58.6hp/l) [59.4PS/L]; 132Nm (97.4lbft) at 4000rpm; leaded premium grade.

Engine construction: 1 Weber downdraught carb 28/32 TLDM.

Transmission: 5–speed manual, final drive ratio 3.92.

Gear ratios: 1st 3.65; 2nd 1.97; 3rd 1.37; 4th 1; 5th 0.82; R 3.66.

Chassis: Tyres 175/70 HR 13, wheel rims 5J.

Performance: Max speed 111mph/179kmh (manufacturers test specifications), speed at 1000rpm in 5th gear 20.5mph/33.0kmh, acceleration 0 – 62mph/100kmh 10.3secs; power to weight ratio from 12.0 kg/kW (8.8kg/PS); consumption ECE 6.1/7.9/10.4L/100km (46.3/35.8/27.2mpg) [38.6/29.8/22.6US mpg].

1.8 Litre Turbo
99.4kW–133hp–135PS
Fuel Injection

As 1.4 Litre, except:

Engine data (DIN): 4–cylinder in–line (83 x 83.6mm), 1809cm3; compression ratio 8.0:1; 99.4kW (133hp) [135PS] at 6000rpm, 54.9kW/L (73.6hp/L) [74.6PS/L]; 191Nm (141lbft) at 4000rpm.
With Catalyst: 89.5kW/L (120hp) [122PS] at 5200rpm; 184Nm (135.8lbft) at 3200rpm.

Engine construction: Designated Nissan CA 18 E-T. Electronic fuel injection ECCS; Garrett exhaust turbocharger; max charge-air pressure 0.5 bar. Battery 12V 60Ah, alternator 70A; cooling system capacity approx 8L (7.6US qt).

Transmission: 5-speed manual, final drive ratio 3.92.

Gear ratios: 1st 3.592; 2nd 2.057; 3rd 1.361; 4th 1; 5th 0.813; R 3.657.

Chassis: Tyres 185/60 HR 14, wheel rims 5.5J.

Performance: Max speed 127mph/205kmh (manufacturers test specifications), speed at 1000rpm in 5th gear 20.8mph/33.4kmh, acceleration 0 – 62mph/100kmh 7.9secs; power to weight ratio from 8.4kg/kW (6.2kg/PS); consumption ECE 6.7/8.6/10.8L/100km (42.2/32.8/26.2mpg) [35.1/27.4/21.8US mpg].

Reliant Scimitar 1800 Ti

RENAULT   F

Regie Nationale des Usines Renault, Billancourt (Seine), France

French producer of vehicles.

MODEL RANGE
4 – 5 – 9 – 11 – 19 – 21/21 Nevada – 25 – Alpine – Espace

Renault 4

Front wheel drive Estate/Station Wagon with 956cm3 engine. Launched Frankfurt 1961. GTL 1978 with 1.1 Litre engine.

Renault 4 Savane

```
956cm3
25kW–33hp–34PS
1 Carb
```

Body, Weight: Saloon/Sedan 5-door, 4-seater; kerbweight (DIN) 695kg, gross vehicle weight 1030kg.

Engine data (DIN): 4-cylinder in-line (65 x 72mm), 956cm3; compression ratio 8.3:1; 25kW (33hp) [34PS] at 5000rpm, 26.2kW/L (35.1hp/L) [35.6PS/L]; 62Nm (45.8lbft) at 2500rpm; leaded regular grade.

Engine construction: Side camshaft (chain); light-alloy cylinder block, wet cylinder liners; 5 bearing crankshaft; gauze filter, oil capacity 2.75L (2.6US qt); 1 Zenith downdraught carb 28 IF. Battery 12V 28Ah, alternator 40A; cooling system capacity approx 5.5L (5.2US qt).

Transmission (to front wheels, optional to all wheels): Front wheel drive, 4-speed manual, gear shift lever to dashboard; final drive ratio 3.44.

Gear ratios: 1st 3.83; 2nd 2.24; 3rd 1.46; 4th 1.03; R 3.55.

Chassis: Platform type frame with front and rear side rails, independent body; front control arm and front reactor strut, controllable longitudinal torsion strut, rear indpendent suspension with trailing arm and controllable tie bar, front antiroll bar, telescopic damper. Front disc brakes, diameter 22.8cm, rear drums; handbrake to front wheels; rack and pinion steering; fuel tank 34L (7.5Gal) [9.0US Gal]; tyres 135 SR 13 or 145 SR 13, wheel rims 4".

Dimensions: Wheelbase right 245cm, left 240cm, track 128/124.5cm, clearance min 17.5cm, turning circle 10.1m, load space 9–33.5cu ft (255–950dm3), length 367cm, width 148.5–151cm, height 155cm.

Performance: Max speed 73mph/118kmh (manufacturers test specifications), speed at 1000rpm in 5th gear 17.6mph/28.3kmh; standing km 43.5secs; power to weight ratio from 27.8kg/kW (20.4kg/PS); consumption ECE 6.0/–/7.1L/100km (47.1/–/39.8mpg) [39.2/–/33.1US mpg].

```
1108cm3
25kW–33hp–34PS
1 Carb
```

As 956cm3, except:

Weight: Kerbweight (DIN) 720kg, gross vehicle weight 1050kg.

Engine data (DIN): 4-cylinder in-line (70 x 72mm), 1108cm3; compression ratio 9.5:1; 25kW (33hp) [34PS] at 4000rpm, 22.6kW/L (30.3hp/L) [30.7PS/L]; 74Nm (54.6lbft) at 2500rpm; leaded premium grade.

Engine construction: Oil capacity 3.25L (3.1US qt), cooling system capacity approx 5.9L (5.6US qt).

Transmission: Final drive ratio 3.1.

Performance: Max speed 75mph/120kmh (manufacturers test specification), speed at 1000rpm in top gear 19.6mph/31.5kmh; standing km 42.5secs; power to weight ratio 28.8kg/PS; consumption ECE 5.4/–/6.3L/100km (52.3/–/44.8mpg) [43.6/–/37.3US mpg].

Renault 5

Successor to the original Renault 5, launched January 1972 with transverse front engine and all round independent suspension, larger and more spacious. Launched September 1984. July 1985 5-door made available, November 1985 1.6 Litre diesel. 1988 new engine range.

Renault 5 Five

```
1108cm3
35kW–46hp–47PS
1 Carb
```

Body, Weight: Saloon/Sedan 3/5-door; kerbweight (DIN) from 715–730kg, gross vehicle weight 1130–1145kg.

Engine data (DIN): 4-cylinder in-line (70x72mm), 1108cm3; compression ratio 9.5:1; 35kW (46hp) [47PS] at 5250rpm, 31.6kW/L (42.3hp/L) [42.4PS/L]; 80Nm (59lbft) at 2500rpm; leaded premium grade.
Some Countries: 33kW (44hp) [45PS].
Also: (65 x 72mm), 956cm3; compression ratio 9.2:1; 31kW (41.5hp) [42PS]; 65Nm (48lbft).

Engine construction: Transverse front engine. Side camshaft (chain); light-alloy cylinder block; wet cylinder liners; 5 bearing crankshaft; gauze filter, oil capacity 3.25L (3.1US qt); 1 Solex downdraught carb 32 IF2. Battery 12V 28/35Ah, alternator 50A; cooling system capacity, approx 5.5L (5.2US qt).

Transmission (to front wheels): a) 4-speed manual, final drive ratio 3.294. b) 5-speed manual, final drive ratio 3.438.

Gear ratios: a) 4-speed manual: 1st 3.727; 2nd 2.053; 3rd 1.32; 4th 0.903; R 3.545.

Renault

...ed manual: 1st 3.727; 2nd 2.053; 3rd 1.32; 4th 0.967; 5th 0.794; R 3.545.

Chassis: Integral body, front and rear independent suspension, front (negative camber) McPherson strut (coil springs and coaxial telescopic damper) with lower A arm, antiroll bar, rear trailing arm, tie bar and antiroll bar, telescopic damper. Servo/power assisted brakes, front discs, diameter 23.8cm, rear drums; mechanical handbrake to rear wheels; rack and pinion steering; fuel tank 43L (9.5Gal) [11.4US Gal]. Tyres 145/70 SR 13, wheel rims 4.5".

Dimensions: Wheelbase 240.5cm, 5–door 246.5cm, track 133/129cm, clearance min 12cm, turning circle 11.1m, 5-door 11.6m; load space 8.3–32.3cu ft (235–915dm3), 5–door 33.7cu ft (955dm3); length 359cm, 5–door 365cm, width 158.5, height 139cm.

Performance: Max speed 89mph/143kmh (manufacturers tested specification), speed at 1000rpm in 5th gear; acceleration 0 – 62mph/100kmh 16secs; power to weight ratio from 20.7kg/kW (15.4kg/PS); consumption ECE 4.5/6.1/5.8L/100km (62.8/46.3/48.7mpg) [52.3/38.6/40.6mpg], 5–speed 4.1/5.6/5.8L/100km (57.4/50.4/48.7mpg) [57.4/42.0/40.6US mpg].

```
1237cm3
40kW–54hp–55PS
1 Carb
```

As 1108cm3, except:

Weight: Kerbweight (DIN) 735–760kg, gross vehicle weight 1175/1190kg.

Engine data (DIN): 4–cylinder in–line (71.5 x 77mm), 1237cm3; compression ratio 9.25:1; 40kW (54hp) [55PS] at 5250rpm, 32.3kW/L (43.3hp/L) [44.5PS/L]; 90Nm (120.6lbft) at 3000rpm.

Engine construction: 1 Solex downdraught carb 32 BIS or Zenith 32 IFS.

Gear ratios: a) 4–speed manual, final drive ratio 3.438.
b) 5–speed manual, final drive ratio 3.563; 3.294.

Performance: Max speed 96mph/155kmh (manufacturers test specifications), speed at 1000rpm in 5th gear 21.8–23.5mph/35– 37.8kmh; acceleration 0–62mph/100kmh 14.3secs; power to weight ratio 18.4kg/kW (13.4kg/PS); consumption ECE 4.7/6.5/6.8L/100km (60.1/43.5/41.5mpg) [50.0/36.2/34.6US mpg], 5–speed 4.5/6.3/6.8L/100km (62.8/44.8/41.5mpg) [52.3/37.3/34.6US mpg].

```
1397cm3
44kW–59hp–60PS
1 Carb/Injection
```

As 1108cm3, except:

Weight: Kerbweight 745–760kg, gross vehicle weight 1170–1285kg.

Engine data (DIN): 4–cylinder in–line (76 x 77mm), 1397cm3; compression rati0 9.25:1; 44kW (59hp) [60PS] at 5250rpm, 31.5kW/L (44.1hp/L) [42.9PS/L]; 105Nm (76.7lbft) at 2500rpm
With Catalyst (and central/single point injection): (75.8 x 77mm), 1390cm3; compression ratio 9:1; 44kW (59hp) [60PS] at 4750rpm, 100Nm (73.8lbft) at 3000rpm; unleaded regular grade.

Engine construction: 1 Weber 32DRT carb, cooling system capacity 6.2L (5.9US qt).

Transmission: 5–speed manual, final drive ratio 3.29.

Gear ratios: 1st 3.727; 2nd 2.053; 3rd 1.32; 4th 0.967; 5th 0.794; R 3.545

Chassis: Tyres 155/70 SR 13.

Performance (Catalyst): Max speed 98mph/158kmh (manufacturers test specifications); speed at 1000rpm in 5th gear 23.4mph/37.7kmh; acceleration 0–62mph/100kmh 14secs; power to weight ratio 18.9kg/kW (12.4kg/PS); consumption ECE 5.2/6.8/8.3L/100km (54.3/41.5/34mpg) [45.2/34.6/28.3US mpg]

```
1397cm3
50/44kW–67/59hp–68/72PS
1 2V Carb
```

As 1108cm3, except:

Weight: Kerbweight (DIN) 765–815kg, gross vehicle weight 1195– 1235kg.

Engine data (DIN): 4–cylinder in–line (76 x 77mm), 1397cm3; compression ratio 9.25:1; 50kW (67hp) [68PS] at 5250rpm, 37.4kW/L (50.1hp/L) [48.7PS/L]; 106Nm (78.2lbft) at 3000rpm.
For GTS: 53kW (71hp) [72PS] at 5750rpm.

Engine construction: 1 Weber downdraught carb 32 DRT. Cooling system capacity 6.2L (5.9US qt).

Transmission: a) 5–speed manual, final drive ratio 3.438.
b) Automatic, electronically controlled, hydraulic torque converter and 3–speed Planetary gear set, central selector lever. Final drive ratio (3.294 x 0.853) 2.81.

Gear ratios: a) 5-speed manual: 1st 3.727; 2nd 2.053; 3rd 1.32; 4th 0.967; 5th 0.794; R 3.545.
b) Automatic: Max torque multiplication in converter 2 times, Planetary gear set ratios: 1st 2.5; 2nd 1.5; 3rd 1; R 2.

Chassis: Tyres 155/70 SR 13.

Performance: Max speed 103mph/165kmh, automatic 96mph/154kmh (manufacturers test specifications), speed at 1000rpm in 5th gear 22.6mph/36.3kmh; acceleration 0 – 62mph/100kmh 12.2secs, automatic 16.5secs; power to weight ratio from 15.3kg/kW (11.3kg/PS); consumption ECE 4.6/6.3/7.2L/100km (61.4/44.8/39.2mpg) [51.1/37.3/32.7US mpg], automatic 5.4/7.5/7.5L/100km (52.3/37.7/37.7mpg) [43.6/31.4/31.4US mpg].

Renault 5 GTS

```
1397cm3 Turbo
88kW–118hp–120PS
1 Carb
```

Engine for GT Turbo

As 1108cm3, except:

Weight: Kerbweight (DIN) 830kg, gross vehicle weight 1255kg.

Engine data (DIN): 4–cylinder in–line (76 x 77mm), 1397cm3, compression ratio 7.9:1; 88kW (118hp) [120PS] at 5750rpm, 63kW/L (84.4hp/L) [85.9PS/L]; 165Nm (121.8lbft) at 3750rpm; leaded premium grade.

Engine construction: Oil capacity 3.7L (3.5US qt); oil cooler 1 Solex downdraught carb 32 DIS T2; 1 Garrett exhaust turbocharger, charge-air cooler. Battery 37Ah; cooling system capacity approx 6.8L (6.4US qt).

Transmission: 5–speed manual, final drive ratio 3.733.

Gear ratios: 1st 3.091; 2nd 1.842; 3rd 1.320; 4th 0.967; 5th 0.758; R 3.545.

Chassis: All round disc brakes, front discs ventilated, diameter 23.8cm; fuel tank 50L (11.0Gal) [13.2US Gal]; tyres 175/60 HR 13, wheel rims 5.5J.

Dimensions: Track 132.5/131cm, width 159.5cm, height 136.5cm.

Performance: Max speed 127mph/204kmh (manufacturers test specifications), speed at 1000rpm in 5th gear 21.8mph/35.0kmh; acceleration 0 – 62mph/100kmh 8.0secs; power to weight ratio 9.4kg/kW (6.9 kg/PS); consumption ECE 5.6/7.6/8.7L/100km (50.4/37.2/32.5mpg) [42.0/30.9/27 US mpg].

Renault 5 GT Turbo

```
1721cm3
66/55/70kW–88/74/94hp–90/75/95PS
1 Carb/Fuel Injection
```

As 1108cm3, except:

Weight: Kerbweight (DIN) 825–840kg, gross vehicle weight 1240– 1255kg.

Renault

Renault 5 GTE

Engine data (DIN): 4–cylinder in–line (81 x 83.5mm), 1721cm3, compression ratio 10.1; 66kW (88hp) [90PS] at 5500rpm, 38.3kW/L (51.3hp/L) [52.3PS/L]; 138Nm (101.8lbft) at 3500rpm.
Some countries: 64kW (86hp) [87PS].
With Catalyst and electronic fuel injection: Compression ratio 9.5.1; 55kW (74hp) [75PS]; 129Nm (95.2lbft).
Engine for GTE (Turbo–Look electronic fuel injection): 70kW (94hp) [95PS] at 5250rpm, 40.7kW/L (54.4hp/L) [55.2PS/L]; 143Nm (105.5lbft) at 3000rpm; unleaded regular grade.

Engine construction: 1 overhead camshaft (toothed belt); oil capacity 5L (4.7US qt); 1 Solex downdraught carb 28–34 Z10. Battery 12V 50Ah; cooling system capacity approx 6.1L (5.8US qt).

Transmission: a) 5–speed manual, final drive ratio 3.563. GTE 3.867.
b) Automatic transmission, electronically controlled, hydraulic torque converter and 3–speed Planetary gear set, central selector lever, final drive ratio (3.294 x 0.853) 2.81.

Gear ratios: a) 5–speed manual: 1st 3.091; 2nd 1.842; 3rd 1.32; 4th 0.967; 5th 0.794; R 3.545.
b) Automatic: Max torque multiplication in converter 2 times, Planetary gear set ratios: 1st 2.5; 2nd 1.5; 3rd 1; R 2.

Chassis: GTE with 4 disc brakes (front ventilated), diameter 23.8cm; fuel tank 50L (11.0Gal) [13.2US Gal]; tyres 195/55HR 13, wheel rims 5.5J.

Dimensions: GTE; Track 134/131.5cm, width 159.5cm, height 136cm.

Performance: Max speed 114mph/184kmh (manufacturers test specifications), speed at 1000rpm in 5th gear 22.8mph/36.7kmh; acceleration 0 – 62mph/100kmh 9.4secs; power to weight ratio from 12.5kg/kW (9.2kg/PS); consumption ECE 5.0/6.6/9.3L/100km (56.5/42.8/30.4mpg) [47.0/35.6/25.3US mpg]. With Catalyst: Max speed 106mph/170kmh, GTE 115mph/185kmh acceleration 0 – 62mph/100kmh 11.2secs, GTE 9.3secs.

Renault 5 Baccara

```
1596cm3 Diesel
40.5kW–54hp–55PS
Injection Pump
```

Engine for TD and GTD

As 1108cm3, except:
Weight: Kerbweight (DIN) 795–810kg, gross vehicle weight 1235–1250kg.
Engine data (DIN): 4–cylinder in–line (78 x 83.5mm), 1596cm3; compression ratio 22.5:1; 40.5kW (54hp) [55PS] at 4800rpm, 25.3kW/L (33.9hp/L) [34.5PS/L]; 102Nm (75.3lbft) at 2250rpm.
Engine construction: Pre–combustion chamber diesel engine; oil capacity 5L (4.7US qt); Bosch injection pump. Battery 12V 65Ah; cooling system capacity, approx 6.3L (6.0US qt).
Transmission: 5–speed manual, final drive ratio 3.294.
Gear ratios: 1st 3.727; 2nd 2.053; 3rd 1.32; 4th 0.967; 5th 0.794; R 3.545.
Chassis: Front antiroll bar; servo/power assisted brakes; tyres 155/70 SR 13.
Performance: Max speed 93mph/150kmh (manufacturers test specifications), speed at 1000rpm in 5th gear 23.8mph/38.3kmh; acceleration 0 – 62mph/100kmh 16.5secs; power to weight ratio from 19.6kg/kW (14.5kg/PS); consumption ECE 3.9/5.7/5.7L/100km (72.4/49.6/49.6mpg) [60.3/41.3/41.3US mpg].

Renault 9

4–door Saloon/Sedan, front wheel drive, 1.1 or 1.4 Litre engine, 4/5–speed manual or automatic transmission and independent suspension. Launched 15 September 1981. 1983: New 1.6 Litre diesel engine. July 1985: Turbo version. 1988: New engine range.

```
1.2 Litre
40kW–54hp–55PS
1 Carb
```

Engine for C and TC

Body, Weight: Saloon/Sedan 4–door, 5–seater; kerbweight (DIN) 825kg, gross vehicle weight 1265kg.

Engine data (DIN): 4–cylinder in–line (71.5 x 77mm), 1237cm3; compression ratio 9.25:1; 40kW (54hp) [55PS] at 5250rpm, 32.3kW/L (43.3hp/L) [44.5PS/L]; 90Nm (66.4lbft) at 3000rpm; leaded premium grade.

Engine construction: Transverse mounted engine block with transmission and differential assembly. Side camshaft (chain); light–alloy cylinder head; wet cylinder liners; 5 bearing crankshaft; oil capacity 3.25L (3.1US qt); 1 Solex downdraught carb 32 BIS. Battery 12V 30Ah, alternator 50/70A, cooling system capacity approx 6.1L (5.8US qt).

Transmission (to all wheels): a) 4–speed manual (without direct drive), final drive ratio 3.867.
b) 5–speed manual, final drive ratio 4.067.

Gear ratios: a) 4–speed manual: 1st 3.727; 2nd 2.053; 3rd 1.32; 4th 0.903; R 3.545.
b) 5–speed manual: 1st 3.727; 2nd 2.053; 3rd 1.32; 4th 0.967; 5th 0.794; R 3.545.

Renault 9 C

Chassis: Integral body, front and rear independent suspension, front (negative camber) McPherson struts (coil springs and coaxial telescopic damper) with lower A arm and antiroll bar; rear trailing arm and transverse torsion bar, antiroll bar, telescopic damper. Servo/power assisted brakes, front disc brakes, diameter 23.8cm, rear drums; mechanical handbrake to rear wheels; rack and pinion steering; fuel tank 47L (10.3Gal) [12.4US Gal]; tyres 145 SR 13, wheel rims 4.5J.

Renault

Dimensions: Wheelbase 248.5cm, track 140/135.5cm, clearance 12cm, turning circle 10.9m, load space 14.2cu ft (400dm3), length 413cm, width 166.5cm, C 163.5cm, height 141cm.

Performance: Max speed 91mph/146kmh (manufacturers test specifications), speed at 1000rpm in 5th gear 19.9mph/32kmh; acceleration 0 – 62mph/100kmh 16secs; power to weight ratio from 20.6kg/kW (15kg/PS); consumption ECE 5.3/7.3/7.6L/100km (53.3/38.7/37.2mpg) [44.4/32.2/30.9US mpg], 5- speed 5.1/7.0/7.6L/100km (55.4/40.4/37.2mpg) [46.1/33.6/30.9US mpg].

1.4 Litre
50kW–67hp–68PS
1 2V Carb

Engine for TL and GTL and Automatic

As 1.2 Litre, except:

Weight: Kerbweight (DIN) 840–865kg, gross vehicle weight 1295kg.

Engine data (DIN): 4–cylinder in–line (76 x 77mm), 1397cm3; compression ratio 9.25:1; 50kW (67hp) [68PS] at 5250rpm, 35.8kW/L (48.1hp/L) [48.7PS/L]; 108Nm (79.7lbft) at 3000rpm.
Some countries: 44kW (59hp) [60PS].

Engine construction: 1 Weber downdraught 2V carb 32 DRT. Battery 12V 35Ah; cooling system capacity approx 5.8L (5.5US qt).

Transmission: a) 4–speed manual, final drive ratio 3.867.
b) 5–speed manual, final drive ratio 4.067.
c) Automatic, electronically controlled, hydraulic torque converter and 3–speed Planetary gear set, final drive ratio (3.563 x 0.92) 3.278.

Gear ratios: a) 4–speed manual: 1st 3.727; 2nd 2.053; 3rd 1.32; 4th 0.903; R 3.545.
b) 5–speed manual: 1st 3.727; 2nd 2.053; 3rd 1.32; 4th 0.967; 5th 0.794; R 3.545.
c) Automatic, max torque multiplication in converter 2 times, Planetary gear set ratios: 1st 2.5; 2nd 1.5; 3rd 1; R2.

Chassis: Tyres 155 SR 13.

Performance: Max speed 99mph/160kmh, automatic 95mph/153kmh (manufacturers test specifications), speed at 1000rpm in 5th gear 20.3mph/32.7kmh; acceleration 0 – 62mph/100kmh 13.1secs, automatic 17.5secs. Power to weight ratio from 16.8kg/kW (12.4kg/PS); consumption ECE 5.3/7.3/8.3L/100km (53.3/38.7/34.0mpg) [44.4/32.2/28.3US mpg], 5-speed manual 5.1/7.1/8.3L/100km (55.4/39.8/34.0mpg) [46.1/33.1/28.3US mpg], automatic 6.0/7.9/8.2L/100km (47.1/35.8/34.4mpg) [39.2/29.8/28.7US mpg].

1.7 Litre
66/55/70kW–88/74/94hp–90/75/95PS
1 2V Carb/Injection

Engine for GTX, TXE/GTE

As 1.1 Litre, except:

Weight: Kerbweight (DIN) 895–945kg, gross vehicle weight 1335– 1410kg.

Engine data (DIN): 4–cylinder in–line (81 x 83.5mm), 1721cm3; compression ratio 10:1; 66kW (88hp) [90PS] at 5500rpm, 38.3kW/L (51.3hp/L) [52.3PS/L]; 138Nm (101.8lbft) at 3500rpm.
Some countries: 64kW (86hp) [87PS].
With Catalyst and central/single point injection: Compression ratio 9.5:1; 55kW (74hp) [75PS] at 5000rpm; 129Nm (95.2lbft) at 2750rpm.
GTE (Turbo-Look, electronic fuel injection): 70kW (94hp) [95PS] at 5250rpm; 40.7kW/L (54.5hp/L) [55.2PS/L]; 143Nm (105.5lbft) at 3000rpm; regular unleaded grade.

Engine construction: 1 overhead camshaft (toothed belt); oil capacity 5.5L (5.2US qt); Zenith downdraught 2V carb 28/34Z 10. Battery 12V 35Ah; cooling system capacity approx 6.7L (6.3US qt).

Transmission: 5–speed manual, final drive ratio 3.563, GTE 4.21.

Gear ratios: 1st 3.727; 2nd 2.053; 3rd 1.32; 4th 0.967; 5th 0.794; R 3.545.
GTE: 1st 3.09; 2nd 1.84; 3rd 1.32; 4th 0.97; 5th 0.76; R 3.55.

Chassis: Tyres 175/70 SR 13 or 175/65 HR 14, wheel rims 5.5J.

Performance: Max speed 110mph/177kmh, 74hp version 101mph/164kmh, GTE 111mph/179kmh (manufacturers test specifications), speed at 1000rpm in 5th gear 23.2mph/37.3kmh; acceleration 0 – 62mph/100kmh 10.7secs, 74hp 12.6secs, GTE 10.0secs; standing km 32.4 secs; power to weight ratio from 13.5kg/kW (9.9kg/PS); consumption ECE 5.4/7.2/9.2L/100km (52.3/39.2/30.7mpg) [43.6/32.7/25.6 US mpg].

Renault 9 TXE

1.4 Litre
84.5kW–113hp–115PS
1 Carb/Turbo

As 1.2 Litre, except:

Body, Weight: Saloon/Sedan 4–door, 5–seater; kerbweight (DIN) 905kg, gross vehicle weight 1330kg.

Engine data (DIN): 4–cylinder in–line (76 x 77mm), 1397cm3; compression ratio 7.9:1; 85kW (114hp) [115PS] at 5750rpm, 60.8kW/L (81.5hp/L) [82.3PS/L]; 165Nm (121.8lbft) at 3000rpm.

Engine construction: Parallel valves; oil cooler; 1 Solex downdraught carb 32 DIS; 1 Garrett exhaust turbocharger T2, charge–air cooler.

Transmission: 5–speed manual, final drive ratio 4.07.

Gear ratios: 1st 3.09; 2nd 1.84; 3rd 1.32; 4th 0.97; 5th 0.758; R 3.45.

Chassis: All round disc brakes, front ventilated; disc diameter 23.8cm, tyres 175/65 HR, wheel rims 5.5J.

Dimensions: Track 141/137.5cm, height 138cm.

Performance: Max speed 118mph/190kmh (manufacturers test specifications), speed at 1000rpm in 5th gear 21.3mph/34.3kmh; acceleration 0 – 62mpg/100kmh 8.5secs, standing km 29.8secs; power to weight ratio 10.6kg/kW (7.9kg/kW); consumption ECE 6.0/8.1/8.6L/100km (47.1/34.9/32.8mpg) [39.2/29.0/27.4US mpg].

1.6 Litre Diesel
40.5kW–54hp–55PS
Injection pump

Engine for TD and GTD

As 1.2 Litre, except:

Weight: Kerbweight (DIN) 905kg, gross vehicle weight 1340kg.

Engine data (DIN): 4–cylinder in–line (78 x 83.5mm), 1596cm3; compression ratio 22.5:1; 40KW (54hp) [55PS] at 4800rpm, 25.1kW/L (33.6hp/L) [34.5PS/L]; 102Nm (75.3lbft) at 2250rpm.

Engine construction: Pre–combustion chamber diesel engine; oil capacity 5.5L (5.2US qt); Bosch injection pump. Battery 12V 65Ah; cooling system capacity approx 6.7L (6.3US qt).

Transmission: 5–speed manual, final drive ratio 3.867.

Gear ratios: 1st 3.727; 2nd 2.053; 3rd 1.32; 4th 0.967; 5th 0.794; R 3.545.

Chassis: Tyres 155 SR 13.

Performance: Max speed 91mph/146kmh (manufacturers test specifications), speed at 1000rpm in 5th gear 21.4mph/34.4kmh; acceleration 0 – 62mph/100kmh 16secs; power to weight ratio from 22.6kg/kW (16.5kg/PS); consumption ECE 4.4/6.3/6.4L/100km (64.2/44.8/44.1mpg) [53.5/37.3/36.8US mpg].

Renault 11

Hatchback Saloon/Sedan (3/5–door), front wheel drive with a 1108 or 1397cm3 engine. Technically similar to the Renault 9. Launched Geneva 1983. 1984: with 1.7, 1.4 Turbo or 1.6 Litre diesel engine. Summer 1985 available with a 1.3 Litre engine. 1987 new base engine range.

Renault

1.2 Litre
40kW–54hp–55PS
1 Carb

Body, Weight: Saloon/Sedan 3/5–door, 5–seater; kerbweight (DIN) 830-850kg, gross vehicle weight 1250-1285kg.

Engine data (DIN): 4–cylinder in–line (71.5 x 77mm), 1237cm3; compression ratio 9.25:1; 40kW (54hp) [55PS] at 5250rpm, 32.3kW/L (43.3hp/l) [44.5PS/L]; 90Nm (66.4lbft) at 3000rpm; leaded premium grade.

Engine construction: Engine block with transmission and differential transverse mounted and inclined towards rear. Side camshaft (chain); light–alloy cylinder head; wet cylinder liners; 5 bearing crankshaft; gauze filter, oil capacity 3.25L (3.1US qt); 1 Solex 32 BIS downdraught carb. Battery 12V 30Ah, alternator 60A; cooling system capacity approx 6.1L (5.8US qt).

Transmission (to all wheels): a) 4–speed manual (without direct drive), final drive ratio 3.867.
b) 5–speed manual, final drive ratio 4.067.

Gear ratios: a) 4–speed manual: 1st 3.727; 2nd 2.053; 3rd: 1.320; 4th 0.903; R 3.545.
b) 5–speed manual: 1st 3.727; 2nd 2.053; 3rd: 1.320; 4th 0.967; 5th 0.794; R 3.545.

Chassis: Integral body, front and rear independent suspension, front (negative camber) McPherson strut (coil springs and coaxial telescopic damper) with lower A arm and antiroll bar, rear trailing arm, transverse torsion bar and antiroll bar, telescopic damper. Servo/power assisted brakes, front discs, diameter 23.8cm, rear drums; mechanical handbrake to rear wheel; rack and pinion steering; fuel tank 47L (10.3Gal) [12.4US Gal]; tyres 145 SR 13, wheel rims 4.5J.

Dimensions: Wheelbase 248.5cm, track 140/135.5cm, clearance 12cm, turning circle 10.9m. Load space 12/30.7/42.4cu ft (340/870/1200dm3), length 404.5cm, width 166.5cm, height 141cm.

Performance: Max speed 92mph/148kmh (manufacturers test specifications), speed at 1000rpm in 5th gear 19.9mph/32kmh; acceleration 0 – 62mph/100kmh 16secs; power to weight ratio from 20.7kg/kW (15.1kg/PS); consumption ECE 5.1/7.0/7.6L/100km (55.4/40.4/37.2mpg) [46.1/33.6/30.9US mpg]. 5–speed 5.0/6.8/7.6L/100km (56.5/41.5/37.2mpg) [47.0/34.6/30.9US mpg].

1.4 Litre
50kW–67hp–68PS
1 2V Carb

As 1.2 Litre, except:

Weight: Kerbweight (DIN) 850–885kg, gross vehicle weight 1280-1315kg.

Engine data (DIN): 4–cylinder in–line (76 x 77mm), 1397cm3; compression ratio 9.25:1; 50kW (67hp) [68PS] at 5250rpm, 35.8kW/L (48hp/L) [48.7PS/L]; 108Nm (79.7lbft) at 3000rpm.
Some countries: 44kW (59hp) [60PS].

Engine construction: 1 Weber downdraught carb 32DRT. Battery 12V 35Ah; cooling system capacity approx 5.8L.

Transmission: a) 4–speed manual, final drive ratio 3.867.
b) 5–speed manual, final drive ratio 4.067.
c) Automatic, electronically controlled, hydraulic torque converter and 3–speed Planetary gear set, central selector lever, final drive ratio (3.563 x 0.92) 3.278.

Renault 11 TL

Gear ratios: a) 4–speed manual: 1st 3.727; 2nd 2.053; 3rd 1.32; 4th 0.903; R 3.545.
b) 5–speed manual: 1st 3.727; 2nd 2.053; 3rd 1.32; 4th 0.967; 5th 0.794; R 3.545.
c) Automatic, Max torque multiplication in converter 2 times, Planetary gear set ratios: 1st 2.5; 2nd 1.5; 3rd 1; R 2.

Chassis: Tyres 155 SR 13.

Performance: Max speed 101mph/162kmh, automatic 97mph/156kmh (manufacturers test specifications), speed at 1000rpm in 5th gear 20.3mph/32.7kmh; acceleration 0 – 62mph/100kmh 13.1secs, automatic 17.5secs; power to weight ratio from 17kg/kW (12.5kg/PS); consumption ECE 5.3/7.1/8.3L/100km (53.3/39.8/34.0mpg) [44.4/33.1/28.3US mpg], 5-speed 5.0/6.9/8.3L/100km (56.5/40.9/34.0mpg) [47.0/34.1/28.3US mpg], automatic 5.9/7.6/8.2L/100km (47.9/37.2/34.4mpg) [39.9/30.9/28.7US mpg].

1.7 Litre
66/55/70kW–88.5/74/94hp–90/75/95PS
1 2V Carb/Fuel Injection

As 1.2 Litre, except:

Weight: Kerbweight (DIN) 895/915kg, gross vehicle weight 1355kg.

Engine data (DIN): 4–cylinder in–line (81 x 83.5mm), 1721cm3; compression ratio 10:1; 66kW (88.5hp) [90PS] at 5500rpm, 38.3kW/L (51.3hp/L) [52.3PS/L]; 138Nm (101.8lbft) at 3500rpm.
Certain countries: 64kW (86hp) [87PS].
With Catalyst and central/single point electronic injection: Compression ratio 9.5:1; 55kW (74hp) [75PS] at 5000rpm; 129Nm (95.2lbft) at 2750rpm.
GTE (Turbo-Look, electronic fuel injection): 70kW (94hp) [95PS] at 5250rpm; 40.7kW/L (54.5hp/L) [55.2PS/L]; 143Nm (105.5lbft) at 3000rpm; unleaded regular grade.

Engine construction: 1 overhead camshaft (toothed belt); oil capacity 5.5L (5.2US qt); 1 Zenith downdraught 2V carb 28/34 Z 10. Battery 12V 35Ah; cooling system capacity approx 6.7L (6.3US qt).

Transmission: 5–speed manual, final drive ratio 3.563, GTE 4.21.

Gear ratios: 1st 3.727; 2nd 2.053; 3rd 1.32; 4th 0.967; 5th 0.794; R 3.545.
GTE: 1st 3.09; 2nd 1.84; 3rd 1.32; 4th 0.97; 5th 0.76; R 3.55.

Chassis: Tyres 175/70 SR 13 or 175/65 HR 14, wheelbase 5.5J.

Performance: Max speed 111mph/179kmh, 103mph/166kmh, GTE 113mph/181kmh (manufacturers test specifications), speed at 1000rpm in 5th gear 23.2mph/37.3kmh; acceleration 0 – 62mph/100kmh 10.7secs, 12.6secs, GTE 10.0secs; standing km 32.4secs; power to weight ratio from 13.6kg/kW (9.9kg/PS); consumption ECE 5.2/6.9/9.2L/100km (54.3/40.9/30.7mpg) [45.2/34.1/25.6US mpg].

1.4 Litre
84.5kW–113hp–115PS
1 Carb/Turbo

As 1.2 Litre, except:

Body, Weight: 3–door Saloon/Sedan, 5–seater; kerbweight (DIN) 905/925kg, gross vehicle weight 1330–1350kg.

Engine data (DIN): 4–cylinder in–line (76 x 77mm), 1397cm3; compression ratio 7.9:1; 85kW (114hp) [115PS] at 5750rpm, 60.8kW/L (881.5hp/L) [82.3PS/L]; 165Nm (121.8lbft) at 3000rpm.

Renault 11 Turbo

Engine construction: Parallel valves; oil cooler; 1 Solex downdraught carb 32 DIS; 1 Garrett exhaust turbocharger T2, charge–air cooler.

Transmission: 5–speed manual, final drive ratio 4.07.

Gear ratios: 1st 3.09; 2nd 1.84; 3rd 1.32; 4th 0.97; 5th 0.758; R 3.45.

Chassis: All round disc brakes, front ventilated; disc diameter 23.8cm; tyres 175/65 HR 14, wheel rims 5.5J.

Renault

Performance: Max speed 120mph/193kmh (manufacturers test specifications), speed at 1000rpm in 5th gear 21.3mph/34.3kmh; acceleration 0 – 62mph/100kmh 8.5secs; standing km 29.8secs; power to weight ratio 10.5kg/kW (7.9kg/kW); consumption ECE 5.8/7.7/8.6L/100km (48.7/36.7/32.8mpg) [40.6/30.5/27.4US mpg].

1.6 Litre Diesel
40.5kW–54hp–55PS
Injection Pump

As 1.2 Litre, except:

Weight: Kerbweight (DIN) 925/935kg, gross vehicle weight 1325kg.

Engine data (DIN): 4–cylinder in–line (78 x 83.5mm), 1596cm3; compression ratio 22.5:1; 40.5kW (54hp) [55PS] at 4800rpm, 25.3kW/L (33.9hp/L) [34.5PS/L]; 102Nm (75.3lbft) at 2250rpm.

Engine construction: Pre–combustion chamber diesel engine; 1 overhead camshaft (toothed belt); oil capacity 5.5L (5.2US qt); Bosch injection pump. Battery 12V 65Ah; cooling system capacity approx 6.7L (6.3US qt).

Transmission: 5–speed manual, final drive ratio 3.563.

Gear ratios: 1st 3.727; 2nd 2.053; 3rd 1.32; 4th 0.967; 5th 0.794; R 3.545.

Chassis: Tyres 155 SR 13, wheel rims 5.5J.

Performance: Max speed 92mph/148kmh (manufacturers test specifications), speed at 1000rpm in 5th gear 21.4mph/34.4kmh; acceleration 0 – 62mph/100kmh 16secs; power to weight ratio from 22.8kg/kW (16.8kg/PS); consumption ECE 4.4/6.3/6.4L/100km (64.2/44.8/44.1mpg) [53.5/37.3/36.8US mpg].

Renault 19

New model. Medium saloon/Sedan, front wheel drive, two or four door, tail gate, various engines from 54hp to 138hp; four or five speed manual transmission and Automatic, replacing the models 9/11. Launched June 1988.

1.4 Litre
44/50kW–59/67hp–60/68PS
Carb/Injection

Body, Weight: Saloon/Sedan 3-door, 5-seater; kerbweight (DIN) 900kg, gross vehicle weight 1350kg.
Saloon/Sedan 5-door, 5-seater; kerbweight (DIN) 920kg, gross vehicle weight 1370kg.

Engine data (DIN): 4-cylinder in-line (76 x 77mm), 1397cm3; compression ratio 9:1; 44kW (59hp) [60PS] at 5250rpm, 31.5kW/L (42.2hp/L) [42.9PS/L]; 103Nm (76lbft) at 2750rpm; Regular/premium unleaded grade.
With regular grade: 104Nm (76.8lbft) at 3000rpm.
For export: Compression ratio 9.25:1; 50kW (67hp) [68PS] at 5250rpm; 104Nm (76.8lbft) at 3000rpm.
With Catalyst (and central/single point injection): (75.8 x 77mm), 1390cm3; 44kW (59hp) [60PS] at 4750rpm; 31.7kW/L (43.2PS/L); 102Nm (75.3lbft) at 3000rpm.
For certain countries: (71.5 x 77mm), 1237cm3; 40kw (54hp) [55PS] at 5000rpm; 90Nm (66lbft) at 3000rpm.

Engine construction: Designated "C". Engine block with transmission and differential transverse. Side camshaft (chain); light-alloy cylinder head; wet cylinder liners; 5 bearing crankshaft; oil capacity 3L (2.8US qt); 1 Solex 32 IF2. downdraught carb. 12V 35/40Ah battery, alternator 60/70A; cooling system capacity approx 6.7L (6.3US qt).

Transmission (to all wheels): a) 4-speed manual, final drive ratio 3.56.
b) 5-speed manual, final drive ratio 3.56, Catalyst 3.87.

Gear ratios: a) 4-speed manual: 1st 3.727; 2nd 2.053; 3rd 1.32; 4th 0.903; R 3.545.
b) 5-speed manual: 1st 3.727; 2nd 2.053; 3rd 1.32; 4th 0.967; 5th 0.794; R 3.545.

Chassis: Integral body, front and rear independent suspension, front subframe, front (negative steering offset) McPherson struts (coil springs and coaxial telescopic damper) with lower A arm and antiroll bar, rear trailing arm and transverse torsion bar, antirollbar and telescopic damper. Servo/power assisted brakes, front discs, disc diameter 23.8cm, rear drums; handbrake to rear wheel; rack and pinion steering; fuel tank 55L (12.1gal) [14.5US Gal]; tyres 145SR 13, wheel rims 4.5J.

Dimensions: Wheel base 254.5cm, track 142/141.5cm, clearance 12cm, turning circle 11m, load space 13.6-30.5cu ft (385-865dm3). Length 415.5cm, width 167.5/169.5cm, height 141.5cm.

Performance: Max speed 99mph/160kmh (manufacturers test specification), speed at 1000rpm in 5th gear 19.9mph/32kmh; acceleration 0 – 62mph/100kmh 15secs; power to weight ratio from 20.9kg/kW (15kg/PS); consumption ECE 5.1/6.7/7.8L/100km (55.4/42.2/36.2mpg) [46.1/35.1/30.2US mpg], 5-speed manual 4.8/6.4/7.8L/100km (58.8/44.1/36.2mpg) [49/36.8/30.2US mpg]. With 1237-cm3-engine: Max speed 96mph/155kmh; acceleration 0 – 62mph/100kmh 16.1secs; consumption ECE 5.2/6.9/7.6L/100km (54.3/40.9/37.2mpg) [45.2/34.1/30.9US mpg], 5-speed 5.0/6.6/7.6L/100km (56.5/42.8/37.2mpg) [42/35.6/30.9US mpg].

Renault 19 GTS

1.4 Litre
59kW–79hp–80PS
1 2V Carb

As 59/67hp except:

Body, Weight: Saloon/Sedan 3-door, 5-seater; kerbweight (DIN) 920kg, gross vehicle weight 1380kg.
Saloon/Sedan 5-door, 5-seater; kerbweight (DIN) 940kg, gross vehicle weight 1400kg.

Engine data (DIN): 4-cylinder in-line (75.8 x 77mm), 1390cm3; compression ratio 9.5:1; 59kW (79hp) [80PS] at 5750rpm, 42.4kW/L (56.8hp/L) [57.6PS/L]; 108Nm (79.7lbft) at 2750rpm.

Engine construction: Designated "E". Valves in V. 1 overhead camshaft (toothed belt); oil capacity 4L (3.8US qt); 1 Weber 32 TIDR downdraught carb. 12V 40/60Ah battery; cooling system capacity 5.8L (5.5US qt).

Transmission: a) 4-speed manual, final drive ratio 3.563.
b) 5-speed manual, final drive ratio 4.067.
c) Automatic, electronic control, hydraulic torque converter and 3-speed Planetary gear set, final drive ratio 3.87.

Gear ratios: a) 4-speed manual: 1st 3.727; 2nd 2.048; 3rd 1.321; 4th 0.903; R 3.545.
b) 5-speed manual: 1st 3.727; 2nd 2.048; 3rd 1.321; 4th 0.967; 5th 0.795; R 3.545.
c) Automatic; max torque multiplication 2 times, Planetary gear set: 1st 2.5; 2nd 1.5; 3rd 1; R 2.

Chassis: Tyres 165/70 TR 13.

Performance: Max speed 108mph/173kmh, Automatic 104mph/167kmh (manufacturers test specification), speed at 1000rpm in 5th gear 19.9mph/32kmh; acceleration 0 - 62mph/100kmh 12.2secs; power to weight ratio 15.6kg/kW (11.5kg/PS); consumption ECE 5.1/6.6/7.6L/100km (55.4/42.8/37.2mpg) [46.1/35.6/30.9US mpg], 5-speed 5.1/6.6/7.9L/100km (55.4/42.8/35.8mpg) [46.1/35.6/29.8US mpg], automatic 5.7/7.1/7.7L/100km (49.6/39.8/36.7mpg) [41.3/33.1/30.5US mpg].

1.7 Litre
55/56kW–74/75hp–75/76PS
1 2V Carb/Injection

As 59/67hp, except:

Body, Weight: Saloon/Sedan 3-door, 5-seater; kerbweight (DIN) 920kg, gross vehicle weight 1380kg.
Saloon/Sedan 5-door, 5-seater; kerbweight (DIN) 940kg, gross vehicle weight 1400kg.

Engine data (Unregulated Catalyst (DIN): 4-cylinder in-line (81 x 83.5mm), 1721cm3; compression ratio 9.2:1; 55kW (74hp) [75PS] at 5000rpm, 32kW/L (42.9hp/L) [43.6PS/L]; 128Nm (94.5lbft) at 3250rpm; unleaded regular grade.
With Catalyst (and regulated Catalyst): Compression ratio 9.5:1; 130Nm (95.9lbft) at 2750rpm.
Export Version: 56kW (75hp) [76PS] at 5000rpm, 129Nm (95.2lbft) at 3000rpm; regular grade, or 54kW (72hp) [73PS].

Renault

Engine construction: Designated "F". 1 overhead camshaft (toothed belt); oil capacity 5L (4.7US qt); 1 Solex 32/34 downdraught 2V carb. 12V 50/60Ah, alternator 70A; cooling system capacity approx 6.6L (6.2US qt).

Transmission: a) 5-speed manual, final drive ratio 4.067.
b) Automatic, electronically controlled transmission, hydraulic torque converter and 3-speed Planetary gear set, final drive ratio 3.87.

Gear ratios: a) 5-speed manual: 1st 3.727; 2nd 2.048; 3rd 1.321; 4th 0.967; 5th 0.795; R 3.545.
b) Automatic: Max torque multiplication in converter 2 times, Planetary gear set ratios: 1st 2.5; 2nd 1.5; 3rd 1; R 2.

Chassis: Tyres 165/70 TR 13.

Performance: Max speed 106mph/171kmh, automatic 103mph/165kmh (manufacturers test specification), speed at 1000rpm in 5th gear 19.9mph/32kmh; power to weight ratio from 16.7kg/kW (12.3kg/PS); consumption approx 6-10L/100km (47.1-28.2mpg) [39.2-23.5US mpg].

```
1.7 Litre
68/66/70kW-91/88/94hp-92/90/95PS
1 2V Carb/Injection
```

As 59/67hp, except:

Body, Weight: Saloon/Sedan 3-door, 5-seater; kerbweight (DIN) 945kg, gross vehicle weight 1425kg.
Saloon/Sedan 5-door, 5-seater; kerbweight (DIN) 965kg, gross vehicle weight 1445kg.

Engine data (DIN): 4-cylinder in-line (81 x 83.5mm), 1721cm3; compression ratio 9.5:1; 68kW (91hp) [92PS] at 5750rpm, 38.8kW/L (52hp/L) [53.5PS/L] 138Nm (101.8lbft) at 3000rpm; regular grade
With unregulated Catalyst: 66kW (88hp) [90PS] at 5500rpm; 136Nm (100.4lbft) at 3000rpm.
With Catalyst (and fuel injection): 70kW (94hp) [95PS] at 5250rpm, 40.7kW/L (54.5hp/L) [55.2PS/L]; 143Nm (105.5lbft) at 3000rpm; unleaded regular grade.

Engine construction: Designated "F". 1 overhead camshaft (toothed belt); oil capacity 5L (4.7US qt); 1 Solex 32/34 downdraught 2V carb. 12V 50/60Ah, alternator 70A; cooling system capacity approx 6.6L (6.2US qt).

Transmission: 5-speed manual, final drive ratio 4.067, optional 3.563.

Gear ratios: 1st 3.091; 2nd 1.864; 3rd 1.321; 4th 0.967; 5th 0.756; R 3.545.
Or: 1st 3.091; 2nd 2.048; 3rd 1.321; 4th 0.967; 5th 0.795; R 3.55.

Chassis: Front ventilated disc brakes; optional ABS bendix system with rear disc brakes; tyres 175/70 TR 13 or 175/65 TR 14, wheel rims 5.5J.

Performance: Max speed 114-113mph/183-181kmh (manufacturers test specification), speed at 1000rpm in 5th gear 21.3/23.2mph/34.3/37.3kmh; acceleration 0 - 62mph/100kmh 10.7/11secs; power to weight ratio from 13.9kg/kW (10.3kg/PS); consumption ECE 5.5/7.2/9.8L/100km (51.4/39.2/28.8L/100km) [42.8/32.7/24.0US mpg] (3.563:1) 5.3/6.9/9.6L/100km (53.3/40.9/29.4mpg) [44.4/34.1/24.5US mpg].

Renault 19

```
1.8 Litre
103/97kW-138/130hp-140/132PS
Fuel Injection
```

Production date not set. Incomplete data.

As 59/67hp, except:

Body, Weight: Saloon/Sedan 3-door, 5-seater; kerbweight (DIN) 1050kg, gross vehicle weight 1495kg.
Saloon/Sedan 5-door, 5-seater; kerbweight (DIN) 1070kg, gross vehicle weight 1515kg.

Engine data (DIN): 4-cylinder in-line (82 x 83.5mm), 1764cm3; compression ratio 10:1; 103kW (138hp) [140PS] at 6500rpm, 58.4kW/L (78.2hp/L) [79.4PS/L]; 165Nm (121.8lbft) at 4250rpm.

With Catalyst: 97kW (130hp) [132PS] at 6500rpm, 55kW/L (73.7hp/L) [74.8PS/L]; 155Nm (114.4lbft) at 4500rpm.

Engine construction: 4 valves per cylinder; 1 overhead camshaft; electronic fuel injection.

Transmission: 5-speed manual, final drive ratio 3.563.

Gear ratios: 1st 3.091; 2nd 2.048; 3rd 1.321; 4th 0.967; 5th 0.795; R 3.55.

Chassis: Front ventilated disc brakes; optional ABS system Bendix with rear disc brakes; tyres 195/50 VR 15, wheel rims 6.5J.

Performance: Max speed 134mph/215kmh (manufacturers test specification), speed at 1000rpm in 5th gear 20.2mph/32.5kmh; acceleration 0 - 62mph/100kmh 7.9secs; power to weight ratio from 10.2kg/kW (7.5kg/PS); consumption ECE 6.0/7.4/10.1L/100km (47.1/38.2/28mpg) [39.2/31.8/23.3US mpg].

Renault 19 16V/16S

```
1.9 Litre Diesel
48kW-64hp-65PS
Injection Pump
```

As 59/67hp, except:

Body, Weight: Saloon/Sedan 3-door, 5-seater; kerbweight (DIN) 985kg, gross vehicle weight 1460kg.
Saloon/Sedan 5-door, 5-seater; kerbweight (DIN) 1005kg, gross vehicle weight 1480kg.

Engine data (DIN): 4-cylinder in-line (80 x 93mm), 1870cm3; compression ratio 21.5:1; 48kW (64hp) [65PS] at 4500rpm, 25.7kW/L (34.4hp/L) [34.8PS/L]; 121Nm (89.3lbft) at 2250rpm.

Renault 19 GTD

Engine construction: Designated F8Q. In-line engine, pre-combustion chamber engine; parallel valves, light-alloy cylinder head and block; oil capacity 5L (4.7US qt); diesel injection pump. 12V 70Ah battery; 70A alternator; cooling system capacity approx 7.4L (7.0US qt).

Transmission: 5-speed manual, final drive ratio 3.563.

Gear ratios: 1st 3.091; 2nd 2.048; 3rd 1.21; 4th 0.967; 5th 0.795; R 3.545.

Chassis: Tyres 165/70 TR 14, wheel rims 5.5J.

R24

Renault

Performance: Max speed 100mph/161kmh; speed at 1000rpm in 5th gear 22.7mph/36.6kmh; acceleration 0 - 62mph/100kmh 15.7secs; power to weight ratio 20.5kg/kW (15.2kg/PS); consumption ECE 4.6/6.2/7.3L/100km (61.4/45.6/38.7mpg) [51.1/37.9/32.2US mpg].

Renault 21 – 21 Nevada

Medium size car, available in 3 body styles. Front wheel drive, 5 engine versions. Launched Geneva 1986. Paris 1986; Estate/Station Wagon made available "Nevada". June 1987; Turbo 173hp. February 1988; four wheel drive Estate/Station Wagon made available. 1989 with four speed automatic.

```
1.7 Litre
56kW–75hp–76PS
1 2V Carb
```

Engine for TL and Nevada TL

Body, Weight: Saloon/Sedan 4–door, 5–seater; kerbweight (DIN) 955kg, gross vehicle weight 1385kg. Estate/Station Wagon, 5–door, 5/7–seater; kerbweight (DIN) 1010kg, gross vehicle weight 1530kg.

Engine data (DIN): 4–cylinder in–line (81 x 83.5mm), 1721cm3, compression ratio 9.2:1; 56kW (75hp) [76PS] at 5000rpm, 32.5kW/L (43.6hp/L) [44.2PS/L]; 129Nm (95.2lbft) at 3250rpm; unleaded regular grade.
Some countries: 53kW (71hp) [73PS].
In some countries for Saloon/Sedan: (76 x 77mm), 1397cm3; compression ratio 9.25:1; 50kW (67hp) [68PS] at 5250rpm, 37.4kW/L (50.1hp/L) [48.7PS/L]; 106Nm (78.3lbft) at 3000rpm.

Engine construction: Designated F2N B712. Engine block with transmission and differential, transverse mounted, inclined to the rear. 1 overhead camshaft (toothed belt); light–alloy cylinder head; wet cylinder liners; 5 bearing crankshaft; oil capacity 5.5L (5.2US qt); 1 Solex downdraught 2V carb 28-34Z. Battery 12V 50Ah, alternator 60A; cooling system capacity approx 5.6L (5.3US qt).

Transmission (to rear wheels): a) 4–speed manual (without direct drive), final drive ratio 3.294.
b) 5–speed manual, final drive ratio 3.563.

Gear ratios: a) 4–speed manual: 1st 3.727; 2nd 2.053; 3rd 1.32; 4th 0.903; R 3.545.
b) 5–speed manual: 1st 3.727; 2nd 2.053; 3rd 1.320; 4th 0.967; 5th 0.794; R 3.545.

Chassis: Integral body. Front and rear independent suspension; front (negative camber) McPherson struts (coil springs and coaxial telescopic damper) with lower A arm and antiroll bar, rear trailing arm and transverse torsion bar, antiroll bar, telescopic damper. Servo/power assisted brakes, front discs, diameter 23.8cm, rear drums; mechanical handbrake to rear wheels; rack and pinion steering; fuel tank 66L (14.5Gal) [17.4US Gal]; tyres 155 TR 13, optional 175/70 TR 13, wheel rims 5". Nevada; tyres 175/70 TR 13, wheel rims 5.5J.

Dimensions: Wheelbase 266cm, track 143/140cm, clearance 12cm, turning circle 10.2m. Load space 17.3cu ft (490dm3), length 446cm, width 170.5cm, height 141.5cm. Nevada: Wheelbase 281cm, track 143/140.5cm, clearance 12cm, turning circle 11.2m. Load space 32.8/60.4cu ft (930/1710dm3), length 464.5cm, width 171.5cm, height 143cm.

Performance: Max speed 108mph/109mph/173-176kmh (manufacturers test specifications), speed at 1000rpm in 5th gear 23.2mph/37.3kmh; acceleration 0 – 62mph/100kmh 12secs; standing km 33.7secs; power to weight ratio from 17.1kg/kW (12.6kg/PS); consumption ECE 5.4/6.9/8.8L/100km (52.3/40.9/32.1mpg) [43.6/34.1/26.7US mpg], 5-speed 5.3/6.8/9.1L/100km (53.3/41.5/31.0mpg) [44.4/34.6/25.8US mpg]. Nevada: Max speed 168/170mph; consumption ECE 5.6/7.6/8.8 L/100km (50.4/37.2/32.1mpg) [42.0/30.9/26.7US mpg], 5–speed 5.5/7.4/9.1L/100km (51.4/38.2/31.0mpg) [42.8/31.8/25.8US mpg].

Renault 21 TS

```
1.7 Litre
66/70kW–88/94hp–90/95PS
1 2V Carb/Fuel Injection
```

As 1.7 Litre 75hp, except:

Weight: Saloon/Sedan; kerbweight (DIN) 970–1000kg, gross vehicle weight 1440kg. Estate/Station Wagon; kerbweight (DIN) 1030–1060kg, gross vehicle weight 1565–1645kg.

Engine data (DIN): 4–cylinder in–line (81x83.5mm), 1721cm3; compression ratio 10:1; 66kW (88hp) [90PS] at 5500rpm, 38.5kW/L (51.6hp/L) [52.3PS/L]; 138Nm (101.8lbft) at 3500rpm; leaded premium grade.
With Catalyst (Fuel injection): Compression ratio 9.5:1; 70kW (94hp) [95PS] at 5250rpm, 143Nm (105.5lbft) at 3000rpm; unleaded regular grade.

Engine construction: Designated F2N-C710.

Transmission: 4–speed manual (for Saloon/Sedan), final drive ratio 3.56.
b) 5–speed manual, final drive ratio 3.56, GTS 4.07.

Gear ratios: a) 4–speed manual: 1st 3.727; 2nd 2.053; 3rd 1.32; 4th 0.967; R 3.545.
b) 5–speed manual: 1st 3.727; 2nd 2.053; 3rd 1.32; 4th 0.967; 5th 0.794; R 3.545.
GTS: 1st 3.091; 2nd 1.842; 3rd 1.32; 4th 0.967; 5th 0.758; R 3.545.

Chassis: Front disc brakes, ventilated; optional power assisted steering; tyres 175/70 TR 13, optional 175/65 HR 14, wheel rims 5.5J.

Performance: Max speed 115mph/185kmh, Nevada 111mph/179kmh (manufacturers test specification), speed at 1000rpm in 5th gear 23.2mph/37.3kmh; acceleration 0 – 62mph/100kmh 10.7/11.5secs; power to weight ratio from 14.1kg/kW (10.8kg/PS); consumption ECE 5.1/6.5/9.0L/100km (55.4/43.5/31.4mpg) [47.0/36.2/26.1US mpg], Nevada 5.2/6.9/9.0L/100km (54.3/40.4/31.4mpg) [45.2/33.6/26.1US mpg]. With Catalyst: Max speed 115–111mph/185–179kmh; acceleration 0 – 62mph/100kmh 10.7/11.5secs; consumption ECE 6.4/8.0/10.8L/100km (44.1/35.3/26.2mpg) [36.8/29.4/21.8US mpg], Nevada ECE 6.6/8.6/10.8L/100km (42.8/32.8/26.2mpg) [35.6/27.4/21.8US mpg].

Renault 21 Nevada GTS

```
2/2.2 Litre
88.5/81kW–119/109hp–120/110PS
Fuel Injection
```

As 1.7 Litre 76hp, except:

Weight: Saloon/Sedan kerbweight (DIN) 1075–1090kg, gross vehicle weight 1530–1560kg. Estate/Station Wagon kerbweight (DIN) 1135–1170kg, gross vehicle weight 1670–1750kg.

Engine data (DIN): 4–cylinder in–line (88 x 82mm), 1995cm3, compression ratio 10:1; 88.5kW (119hp) [120PS] at 5500rpm, 44.2kW/L (59.2hp/L) [60.2PS/L]; 168Nm (124.1lbft) at 4500rpm; leaded premium grade.
Some countries: 76kW (102hp) [103PS] or 79kW (106hp) [107PS].
With Catalyst: (88 x 89mm), 2165cm3; compression ratio 9.2:1; 81kW (109hp) [110PS] at 5000rpm, 174Nm (128.4lbft) at 3500rpm; unleaded regular grade.

Engine construction: Designated J7R-R750. Longitudinally mounted engine. Overhead valves (in V); light–alloy cylinder engine; Oil capacity 5.3L (5.0US qt); Renix electronic fuel injection. Cooling system capacity approx 7.4L (7.0US qt).

Transmission (to front or all wheels, Nevada 4x4 to all wheels):
a) 5–speed manual, final drive ratio 3.444.
b) Automatic, electronic controlled transmission, hydraulic torque converter and 4-speed Planetary gear set, central selector lever, (3.778x0.89) 3.362.

Gear ratios: a) 1st 4.091; 2nd 2.176; 3rd 1.409; 4th 1.030; 5th 0.861; R 3.545.
b) Automatic; max torque multiplication 2 times, Planetary gear set, 1st 2.71; 2nd 1.55; 3rd 1; 4th 0.679; R 2.21.

Renault

Chassis: Front disc brakes ventilated; optional rear wheel disc brakes and ABS System Teves; optional power assisted steering; tyres 185/65 HR 14, wheel rims 5.5J.

Dimensions: Wheelbase 260cm, Nevada 275cm.

Performance: Max speed 124mph/200kmh, Automatic 121mph/194kmh, Nevada 120mph/193kmh (manufacturers test specification), speed at 1000rpm in 5th gear 22.8mph/36.7kmh; acceleration 0 – 62mph/100kmh 9.7/10.5secs; power to weight ratio from 12.4kg/kW (9.1kg/PS); consumption ECE 5.8/7.1/10.7L/100km (48.7/39.8/26.4mpg) [40.6/33.1/22.0US mpg], Automatic 6.3/7.5/10.8L/100km (44.8/37.7/26.2mpg) [37.3/31.4/21.8US mpg], Nevada 6.0/7.6/10.6L/100km (47.1/37.2/26.6mpg) [39.2/30.9/22.2US mpg]. With Catalyst: Max speed at 119–122mph/192–196kmh, acceleration 0 – 62mph/100kmh 9.9/10.7secs; consumption ECE 6.6/8.3/11.8L/100km (42.8/34/23.9mpg) [35.6/28.3/19.9US mpg], Nevada 7.0/8.9/11.8L/100km (40.4/31.7/23.9mpg) [33.6/26.4/19.9US mpg].

Renault 21 Injection

2 Litre Turbo
129kW–172hp–175PS
Fuel Injection

As 1.7 Litre 76hp, except:

Body, Weight: Saloon/Sedan 4–door, 5–seater; kerbweight (DIN) 1190kg, gross vehicle weight 1635kg.

Engine data (DIN): 4–cylinder in–line (88 x 82mm), 1995cm3; compression ratio 8:1; 129kW (173hp) [175PS] at 5200rpm, 64.7kW/L (86.7hp/L) [87.7PS/L]; 270Nm (199.3lbft) at 3000rpm; unleaded/leaded premium grade.

Engine construction: Designated J7RC752. Longitudinally mounted engine tilted to left. 1 overhead camshaft (toothed belt); light–alloy cylinder head and block; wet cylinder liners; 5 bearing crankshaft; oil capacity 6.2L (5.9US qt); Renix electronic fuel injection; 1 Garrett exhaust turbocharger T3, max boost pressure 0.9bar; 2 charge–air coolers. Battery 12V 50Ah, alternator 70A; cooling system capacity approx 6.2L (5.9US qt).

Transmission (to all wheels): 5–speed manual (without direct drive), final drive ratio 3.444.

Renault 21 Turbo

Gear ratios: 1st 3.364; 2nd 2.059; 3rd 1.381; 4th 1.037; 5th 0.821; R 3.545.

Chassis: Front discs ventilated, optional four disc brakes and ABS System Teves; power assisted steering; tyres 195/55 VR 15, wheel rims 5.5J.

Dimensions: Wheelbase 259.5cm, track 145/140cm, clearance 12cm, turning circle 11.1m. Load space 17.3/29.7cu ft (490/840dm3), length 450cm, width 172cm, height 140cm.

Performance: Max speed 141mph/227kmh (manufacturers test specifications), speed at 1000rpm in 5th gear 23.9mph/38.5kmh; acceleration 0 – 62mph/100kmh 7.4secs; standing km 27.8secs; power to weight ratio from 9.3kg/kW (6.8kg/PS); consumption ECE 6.7/8.2/10.8L/100km (42.2/34.3/26.2mpg) [35.1/28.7/21.8US mpg].

2.1 Litre Diesel
49kW–66hp–67PS
Injection Pump

As 1.7 Litre 76hp, except:

Weight: Saloon/Sedan; kerbweight (DIN) 1075–1085kg, gross vehicle weight 1535kg. Estate/Station Wagon; kerbweight (DIN) 1130/1165kg, gross vehicle weight 1670/1750kg.

Engine data (DIN): 4–cylinder in–line (86 x 89mm), 2068cm3; compression ratio 21:1; 49kW (66hp) [67PS] at 4500rpm, 23.7kW/L (31.8hp/L) [32.4PS/L]; 127Nm (93.7lbft) at 2500rpm.

Engine construction: Designated J8SA704. Longitudinal mounted engine; pre–combustion chamber diesel engine; parallel valves; light–alloy cylinder head and block; oil capacity 6L (5.7US qt); Diesel injection pump. Battery 12V 65Ah; cooling system capacity approx 7.5L (7.1US qt).

Transmission: 5–speed manual, final drive ratio 3.222; Nevada 4x4 3.44.

Gear ratios: 1st 4.091; 2nd 2.176; 3rd 1.409; 4th 1.030; 5th 0.861; R 3.545.

Chassis: Front disc brakes ventilated; power assisted steering; tyres 175/70 HR 14, wheel rims 5.5J.

Dimensions: Wheelbase 260cm, Nevada 275cm.

Performance: Max speed 102mph/164kmh, Nevada 98mph/158kmh (manufacturers test specifications), speed at 1000rpm in 5th gear 23.7mph/38.1kmh; acceleration 0 – 62mph/100kmh 15.6/16.6secs; power to weight ratio 21.9kg/kW (16.0kg/PS); consumption ECE 4.6/6.0/7.9L/100km (61.4/47.1/35.8mpg) [51.1/39.2/29.8US mpg]. Nevada 5.0/6.8/7.9L/100km (56.5/41.5/35.8mpg) [47/34.6/29.8US mpg].

2.1 Litre Diesel
65kW–87hp–88PS
Injection Pump/Turbo

As 1.7 Litre 75hp, except:

Weight: Saloon/Sedan; kerbweight (DIN) 1135–1160kg, gross vehicle weight 1575kg. Estate/Station Wagon; kerbweight (DIN) 1185/1205, gross vehicle weight 1745/1800kg.

Engine data (DIN): 4–cylinder in–line (86 x 89mm), 2068cm3; compression ratio 21:1; 65kW (87hp) [88PS] at 4250rpm, 31.4kW/L (41.9hp/L) [42.6PS/L]; 181Nm (133.6lbft) at 2000rpm.

Engine construction: Designated J8SB714. Longitudinal mounted engine; pre–combustion chamber diesel engine; light–alloy cylinder block and head; oil capacity 6L (5.7US qt); Bosch diesel engine pump VE 9 F; Garrett turbocharger T3, charge–air cooler. Battery 12V 65Ah; cooling system capacity approx 7.7L (7.3US qt).

Renault 21 Turbo D

Renault

Transmission: 5–speed manual, final drive ratio 3.444.
Gear ratios: 1st 4.091; 2nd 2.176; 3rd 1.409; 4th 0.971; 5th 0.784; R 3.545.
Chassis: Front disc brakes ventilated; power assisted steering; tyres 185/70 HR 13, Nevada 185/65 TR 14, wheel rims 5.5J.
Dimensions: Wheelbase 260cm, Nevada 275cm.
Performance: Max speed 110kmh/177kmh, Nevada 106mph/172kmh (manufacturers test specifications), speed at 1000rpm in 5th gear 25mph/40.3kmh; acceleration 0 – 62mph/100kmh 11.8/12.5secs; power to weight ratio 17.5kg/kW (12.9kg/PS); consumption ECE 5.0/6.7/8.3L/100km (56.5/42.2/34.0mpg) [47.0/35.1/28.3US mpg]. Nevada 5.2/7.1/8.3L/100km (54.3/39.8/34.0mpg) [45.2/33.1/28.3US mpg].

Renault 25

Replaced the 20/30. Large Saloon/Sedan with front wheel drive and tailgate, engines from 2 to 2.7 Litre, also diesel and turbodiesel. Aerodynamic body with a drag coefficient of 0.28cd. Launched November 1983. Paris 1984; Turbo V6. Improved performance for 1988.

2 Litre
76kW–101hp–103PS
1 2V Carb

Body, Weight: Saloon/Sedan 5–door, 5–seater; kerbweight (DIN) 1145–1180kg, gross vehicle weight 1595-1605kg.
Engine data (DIN): 4–cylinder in-line (88 x 82mm), 1995cm3; compression ratio 9.2:1; 76kW (101hp) [103PS] at 5500rpm, 38.1kW/L (50.7hp/L) [51.6PS/L]; 162Nm (119.6lbft) at 3000rpm; leaded premium grade.
Some countries: 74kW (99hp) [101PS].
Engine construction: Designated J6R. Overhead valves (in V), 1 overhead camshaft (toothed belt); light-alloy cylinder block and head, wet cylinder liners; 5 bearing crankshaft, oil capacity 5.3L (5.0US qt); 1 Weber downdraught 2V carb 28/36 DARA. Battery 12V 50Ah, alternator 60A; cooling system capacity approx 7.3L (6.9US qt).
Transmission (to front wheels) a): 5–speed manual, final drive ratio TS 3.222, GTS 3.556.
b) Automatic, electronically controlled, hydraulic torque converter and 3–speed Planetary gear set, central selector lever, final drive ratio (4.111 x 0.808) 3.322.
Gear ratios: a) 5–speed manual TS: 1st 4.091; 2nd 2.176; 3rd 1.409; 4th 0.971; 5th 0.784; R 3.545. GTS: 1st 4.091; 2nd 2.176; 3rd 1.409; 4th 1.03; 5th 0.861; R 3.545.
b) Automatic: Max torque multiplication in converter 2.3 times, Planetary gear set ratios: 1st 2.5; 2nd 1.5; 3rd 1; R 2.
Chassis: Integral body; front lower A arm and upper control arm with tie bar, coil springs with coaxial telescopic damper, rear independent suspension with longitudinal tie bar and control arm, coil springs and telescopic damper, antiroll bar front and rear. Servo/power assisted brakes, front discs ventilated, diameter 25.9cm, rear drums, optional Bosch ABS System; mechanical handbrake to rear wheels; power assisted rack and pinion steering (except TS and TD); fuel tank 72L (14.7Gal) [17.7US Gal]; tyres 165 SR 14 or 185/70 R 14, wheel rims 5.5J.
Dimensions: Wheelbase 272.5cm, TS and TD 272cm, track 149.5/147.5cm, clearance 19.5/12cm, turning circle 11.6m, load space 15.5/43.8cu ft (440/1240dm3), length 471.5cm, width 181cm, height 141.5cm.
Performance: Max speed 113mph/182kmh, automatic 116mph/178kmh (manufacturers test specifications), speed at 1000rpm in top gear (GTS) 22.8mph/36.7kmh; acceleration 0 – 62mph/100kmh 11.5secs, automatic 12.7secs; standing km 32.3secs, automatic 33.5secs; power to weight ratio from 15.1kg/kW (11.1kg/PS); consumption ECE 5.3/7.0/9.6L/100km (53.3/40.4/29.4mpg) [44.4/33.6/24.5US mpg]. GTS 5.7/7.6/10.5L/100km (49.6/37.2/26.9mpg) [41.3/30.9/22.4US mpg]. Automatic 6.3/8.2/11.0L/100km (44.8/34.4/25.7mpg) [37.3/28.7/22.4US mpg].

Renault 25 TS

2 Litre
88kW–118hp–120PS
Fuel Injection

As 2 Litre 101hp, except:
Weight: Kerbweight (DIN) from 1180kg, gross vehicle weight 1635kg.
Engine data (DIN): 4–cylinder in–line (88 x 82mm), 1995cm3; compression ratio 10:1; 88kW (118hp) [120PS] at 5500rpm, 44.1kW/L (59.1hp/L) [60.2PS/L]; 168Nm (124.1lbft) at 4500rpm; leaded premium grade.
Engine construction: Designated J7R. Renix electronic injection pump.
Transmission: 5–speed manual, final drive ratio 3.556.
Gear ratios: 1st 4.091; 2nd 2.176; 3rd 1.409; 4th 1.03; 5th 0.861; R 3.545.
Chassis: Tyres 185/70 HR 14, wheel rims 5.5J.
Performance: Max speed 121mph/195kmh (manufacturers test specification), speed at 1000rpm in 5th gear 22.8mph/36.7kmh; acceleration 0 – 62mph/100kmh 10.7secs; power to weight ratio from 13.4kg/kW (9.8kg/PS); consumption ECE 6.0/7.4/10.9L/100km (47.1/38.2/25.9mpg) [39.2/31.8/21.6US mpg].

2.2 Litre
92.5/81kW–124/108hp–126/110PS
Fuel Injection

As 2 Litre 101hp, except:
Weight: Kerbweight (DIN) from 1215–1235kg, gross vehicle weight 1655/1675kg.
Engine data (DIN): 4–cylinder in–line (88 x 89mm), 2165cm3; compression ratio 9.9:1; 92.5kW (124hp) [126PS] at 5250rpm, 42.8kW/L (57.4hp/L) [58.2PS/L]; 189Nm (139.5lbft) at 2750rpm.
With Catalyst: Compression ratio 9.2:1; 81kW (108hp) [110PS] at 5000rpm; 174Nm (128.4lbft) at 3500rpm.
Some countries: 79kW (106hp) [108PS].
Engine construction: Designated J7. Renix electronic fuel injection. Alternator 60/105A.
Transmission: a) 5–speed manual, final drive ratio 3.44.
b) 4-speed automatic, final drive ratio (3.78 x 1.08) 4.072.
Gear ratios: a) 5–speed manual: 1st 4.09; 2nd 2.18; 3rd 1.54; 4th 1.16; 5th 0.93; R 3.545.
b) Automatic: Max torque multiplication in converter 2.3 times, Planetary gear set ratios: 1st 2.78; 2nd 1.56; 3rd 1; 4th 0.68; R 2.
Chassis: Tyres 195/60 HR 15, wheel rims 6J.
Performance: Max speed 122mph/197kmh, automatic 120mph/193kmh (manufacturers test specifications), speed at 1000rpm in top gear 21.8mph/35.1kmh, automatic 25.3mph/40.7kmh; acceleration 0 – 62mph/100kmh 10.3secs, automatic 10.5secs; power to weight ratio from 13.1kg/kW (9.6kg/PS); consumption ECE 6.2/7.9/11.3L/100km (45.6/35.8/25mpg) [37.9/29.8/20.8US mpg]. Automatic 6.7/8.1/11.9L/100km (42.2/34.9/23.7mpg) [35.1/29.0/19.8US mpg]. With Catalyst: Max speed 138mph/187kmh, automatic 135mph/183kmh; acceleration 0 – 62mph/100kmh 11.6secs, automatic 12.7secs.

Renault 25 V6 Injection

2.85 Litre V6
118/116kW–158/151hp–160/153PS
Fuel Injection

As 2 Litre 101hp, except:
Weight: Kerbweight (DIN) from 1300kg, gross vehicle weight 1755kg.
Engine data (DIN): 6–cylinder in V 90deg (91 x 73mm), 2849cm3; compression ratio 9.5:1; 118kW (158hp) [160PS] at 5400rpm, 41.4kW/L (55.5hp/L) [56.2PS/L]; 235Nm (173.4lbft) at 2500rpm; unleaded premium grade.

Renault

With Catalyst: 113kW (151hp) [153PS] at 5400rpm; 230Nm (170lbft) at 2500rpm; unleaded regular grade.
Some countries: 110kW (147hp) [150PS] or 104kW (139hp) [141PS].

Engine construction: Designated Z7W-B700. 2 x 1 overhead camshaft (chain); light-alloy cylinder head and block; wet cylinder liners; 4 bearing crankshaft; oil capacity 5.5L (5.2US qt); mechanical Bosch K Jetronic fuel injection. Battery 12V 50Ah, alternator 90/105A; cooling system capacity approx 9.5L (9.0US qt).

Transmission: 5-speed manual, final drive ratio 3.889.

Gear ratios: 1st 3.364; 2nd 2.059; 3rd 1.381; 4th 0.964; 5th 0.756; R 3.545.

Chassis: Servo/power assisted disc brakes, front ventilated, disc diameter front 28cm, rear 25.4cm, ABS; fuel tank 72L (15.8Gal) [19.0US Gal]; tyres 195/60 VR 15, wheel rims 6J.

Performance: Max speed 13mph/212kmh, Automatic 122mph/196kmh (manufacturers test specification), speed at 1000rpm in top gear 23.7mph/38.3kmh, Automatic 21.4mph/34.5kmh; acceleration 0-62mph/100kmh 9.2secs, Automatic 11.3secs; power to weight ratio from 11kg/kW (8.1kg/PS); consumption ECE 7.1/9.0/13.9L/100km (39.8/31.4/20.3mpg) [33.1/26.1/20.3US mpg], Automatic 8.2/9.8/14.5L/100km (34.4/28.8/19.5mpg) [28.7/24.8/16.2US mpg].
With Catalyst: Max speed 129mph/208kmh; acceleration 0 - 62mph/100kmh 9.3secs.

Renault 25 V6 Baccara

2.5 Litre V6
134kW-180hp-182PS
Fuel Injection/Turbo

As 2 Litre 101hp, except:

Weight: Kerbweight (DIN) from 1350kg, gross vehicle weight 1795kg.

Engine data (DIN): 6-cylinder in V 90deg (91 x 63mm) 2457cm3; compression ratio 8.6:1; 134kW (180hp) [182PS] at 5500rpm, 54.4kW/L (73.1hp/L) [74PS/L]; 281Nm (207.4lbft) at 3000rpm.

Engine construction: Designated Z7U. 2 x 1 overhead camshaft (chain); light-alloy cylinder head and block; wet cylinder liners, 4 bearing crankshaft; oil capacity 5.8L (5.5US qt); Renix fuel injection; 1 Garrett exhaust turbocharger T3; charge-air cooler. Battery 12V 50Ah, alternator 90/105A; cooling system capacity approx 9.8L (9.3US qt).

Transmission: 5-speed manual, final drive ratio 3.889.

Gear ratios: 5-speed manual: 1st 3.364; 2nd 2.059; 3rd 1.381; 4th 0.964; 5th 0.756; R 3.545.

Chassis: Servo/power assisted disc brakes (front ventilated), front disc diameter 28cm, rear 25.4cm, ABS; fuel tank 72L (15.8Gal) [19.0US Gal]; tyres 205/60 VR 15, wheel rims 6J.

Renault 25 V6 Turbo

Dimensions: Length 470cm.

Performance: Max speed under 140mph/225kmh (manufacturers test specifications), speed at 1000rpm in 5th gear 24.4mph/39.2kmh; acceleration 0 - 62mph/100kmh 7.7secs; standing km 27.9secs; power to weight ratio 10.1kg/kW (7.4kg/PS); consumption ECE 6.8/8.9/12.9L/100km (41.5/31.7/21.9mpg) [34.6/26.4/18.2US mpg].

2.1 Litre Diesel
51kW-69hp-70PS
Injection Pump

As 2 Litre 101hp, except:

Weight: Kerbweight (DIN) from 1190kg, gross vehicle weight 1650kg.

Engine data (DIN): 4-cylinder in-line (86 x 89mm), 2068cm3; compression ratio 21.5:1; 51kW (69hp) [70PS] at 4500rpm, 24.7kW/L (32.9hp/L) [33.8PS/L]; 137Nm (101lbft) at 2250rpm.

Engine construction: Designated J8S. Pre-chamber diesel engine; parallel valves, 1 overhead camshaft; oil capacity 6L (5.7US qt); diesel injection pump. Battery 12V 65Ah; cooling system capacity approx 7.2L (6.8US qt).

Transmission: 5-speed manual, final drive ratio 3.778.

Gear ratios: 1st 4.091; 2nd 2.176; 3rd 1.409; 4th 1.030; 5th 0.861; R 3.545.

Performance: Max speed 102.5mph/165kmh (manufacturers specifications), speed at 1000rpm in 5th gear 21.5mph/34.6kmh; acceleration 0-62mph/100kmh 17.5secs; power to weight ratio 23.3kg/kW (17kg/PS); consumption ECE 5.0/7.0/8.8L/100km (56.5/40.4/32.1mpg) [47/33.6/26.7US mpg].

2.1 Litre Diesel
63kW-84hp-85PS
Injection Pump/Turbo

As 2 Litre 101hp, except:

Weight: Kerbweight (DIN) from 1250kg, gross vehicle weight 1715kg.

Engine data (DIN): 4-cylinder in-line (86 x 89mm), 2068cm3; compression ratio 21.5:1; 63kW (84hp) [85PS] at 4250rpm, 30.5kW/L (40.5hp/L) [41.1PS/L], 181Nm (134.1lbft) at 2000rpm.

Engine construction: Designated J8S. Pre-combustion diesel engine; parallel valves, 1 overhead camshaft; 5 bearing crankshaft; oil capacity 6L (5.7US qt); Bosch diesel injection pump VE 9F; Garrett turbocharger T3, charge-air cooler. Battery 12V 65Ah, alternator 70/105A; cooling system capacity approx 7.4L (7.0US qt).

Transmission: 5-speed manual, final drive ratio 3.556.

Gear ratios: 1st 4.091; 2nd 2.176; 3rd 1.409; 4th 0.971; 5th 0.784; R 3.545.

Chassis: Tyres 195/60 R 15, wheel rims 6J.

Performance: Max speed 107mph/172kmh (manufacturers test specification), speed at 1000rpm in 5th gear 25mph/40.4kmh; acceleration 0 - 62mph/100kmh 13.1secs; power to weight ratio 19.8kg/kW (14.7kg/PS); consumption ECE 5.0/6.9/8.4L/100km (56.5/40.9/33.6mpg) [47.0/34.1/28.0US mpg].

Renault Espace

Large front wheel drive passenger vehicles. Available with 2 Litre engines or 2068cm3 turbodiesel. Launched Summer 1984. Brussels 1988: "Quadra" with permanent four wheel drive.

2 Litre
76kW-101hp-103PS
1 2V Carb

Body, Weight: Saloon/Sedan 5-door, 5/7-seater; kerbweight (DIN) 1190kg, gross vehicle weight 1820kg.

Engine data (DIN): 4-cylinder in-line (88 x 82mm), 1995cm3; compression ratio 9.2:1; 76kW (101hp) [103PS] at 5500rpm, 38.1kW/L (50.7hp/L) [51.6PS/L]; 162Nm (119.6lbft) at 3000rpm; leaded premium grade.

Engine construction: Front mounted engine; designated J6R; overhead valves (in V), 1 overhead camshaft (toothed belt); light-alloy cylinder block and head, wet cylinder liners; 5 bearing crankshaft; oil capacity 6.2L (5.9US qt); 1 Weber downdraught 2V carb 28-36 DARA 0. Battery 12V 50Ah, alternator 60A; cooling system capacity approx 7.2L (6.8US qt).

Transmission (to front wheels): 5-speed manual, final drive ratio 3.44.

Gear ratios: 1st 4.091; 2nd 2.176; 3rd 1.409; 4th 1.030; 5th 0.861; R 3.545.

Renault

Chassis: Integral steel structure with synthetic body, front lower A arm, upper control arm with torsion bars and coil springs, antiroll bar with trailing arm, Panhard rod and coil springs, telescopic damper. Servo/power assisted brakes, front ventilated, disc diameter 25.9cm, rear drums; handbrake to rear wheels; power assisted rack and pinion steering; fuel tank 63L (13.8Gal) [16.6US Gal]; tyres 185/65 TR 14, wheel rims 5.5J.

Dimensions: Wheelbase 258cm, track 146.5/149cm, clearance 15cm, turning circle 12.4m, load space 10.9-108cu ft (310-3060dm3); length 436.5cm, width 178cm, height 166cm.

Performance: Max speed over 106mph/170kmh (manufacturers test specification), speed at 1000rpm in 5th gear 22.8mph/36.7kmh; acceleration 0 – 62mph/100kmh 12.6secs; standing km in 34.5secs; power to weight ratio 15.7kg/kW (11.6kg/PS), consumption ECE 6.3/8.4/10.7L/100km (44.8/33.6/26.4mpg) [37.3/28.0/22.0US mpg].

Renault Espace 2000 GTS

2/2.2 Litre
88/81kW–119/109hp–120/110PS
Fuel Injection

As 2 Litre 101hp, except:

Weight: Kerbweight (DIN) from 1215kg, Quadra 1290kg, gross vehicle weight 1835kg, Quadra 1960kg.

Engine data (DIN): 4-cylinder in-line (88 x 82mm), 1995cm3, compression ratio 10:1; 88kW (119hp) [120PS] at 5500rpm, 44.1kW/L (59.2hp/L) [60.2PS/L]; 168Nm (124.1lbft) at 4500rpm; leaded premium grade.
With Catalyst: (88 x 89mm), 2165cm3; compression ratio 9.2:1; 81kW (109hp) [110PS] at 5000rpm; 174Nm (128.4lbft) at 3500rpm; unleaded regular grade. Some countries: 79kW (106hp) [107PS].

Engine construction: Designated J7R. Renix electronic fuel injection.

Transmission (to front wheels, Quadra to all wheels): 5-speed manual, final drive ratio 3.778; Quadra with permanent four wheel drive, central differential with viscous coupling, variable power distribution front/rear.

Renault Espace 2000-1 Quadra

Gear ratios: 1st 4.091; 2nd 2.176; 3rd 1.409; 4th 1.03; 5th 0.861; R 3.545.

Chassis: Quadra rear De-Dion-axle with rear disc brakes, diameter rear 25.5cm; fuel tank 63L (13.8Gal) [16.6US Gal], Quadra 58L (12.7Gal) [15.3US Gal]; tyres 195/65 TR 14, wheel rims 5.5J.

Performance: Max speed 111mph/178kmh, Quadra 108mph/175kmh (manufacturers specifications), speed at 1000rpm in 5th gear 21.1mph/34.1kmh; acceleration 0 – 62mph/100kmh 11.5secs; Quadra 11.4secs; power to weight ratio from 13.8kg/kW (10.1kg/PS); consumption ECE 6.8/8.7/11.1L/100km (41.5/32.5/25.4mpg) [34.6/27.0/21.2US mpg], Quadra 7.6/9.9/11.7L/100km (37.2/28.5/24.1mpg) [30.9/23.8/20.1US mpg].
With Catalyst: Max speed 109mph/175kmh; consumption ECE 7.2/9.0/11.7L/100km (39.2/31.4/24.2mpg) [32.7/26.1/20.1US mpg], Quadra 7.4/10.1/12.1L/100km (38.2/28/23.3mpg) [31.8/23/19.4US mpg].

2.1 Litre Turbodiesel
65kW–87hp–88PS
Injection Pump

Engine for Espace Turbo D/DX:

As petrol/gasoline engine, except:

Weight: Kerbweight (DIN) 1255kg, gross vehicle weight 1880kg.

Engine data (DIN): 4-cylinder in-line (86 x 89mm), 2068cm3; compression ratio 21.5:1; 65kW (87hp) [88PS] at 4250rpm, 31.4kW/L (42hp/L) [42.6PS/L]; 181Nm (133.6lbft) at 2000rpm.

Engine construction: Swirl chamber diesel engine. Designated J8S. 1 overhead camshaft (toothed belt); oil capacity 6.3L (6.0US qt); Bosch diesel injection pump VE; Garrett exhaust T3 turbocharger, max boost pressure 0.6bar; charge-air cooler. Battery 12V 66Ah; alternator 70A; cooling system capacity approx 8.5L (8.0US qt).

Gear ratios: 1st 4.091; 2nd 2.176; 3rd 1.409; 4th 0.971; 5th 0.784; R 3.545.

Performance: Max speed 103mph/165kmh (manufacturers test specifications), speed at 1000rpm in 5th gear 25mph/40.3kmh; acceleration 0 – 62mph/100kmh 13.2secs; power to weight ratio 19.3kg/kW (14.3kg/PS); consumption ECE 5.1/7.2/8.0L/100km (55.4/39.2/35.3mpg) [46.1/32.7/29.4US mpg].

Renault Alpine V6 GT – V6 Turbo

2 + 2-seater Coupe with a synthetic body, available with a 2.85 Litre PRV engine giving 158hp or a 2.5 Litre V6 turbocharged engine giving 197hp. Launched Geneva 1985.

Renault Alpine V6 Turbo

2.85 Litre V6
118kW–158hp–160PS
Multiple Carbs

Engine for V6 GT

Body, Weight: Coupe 2-door (with tailgate), 2+2-seater; kerbweight (DIN) 1140kg, gross vehicle weight 1460kg.

Engine data (DIN): 6-cylinder in V 90deg (91 x 73mm), 2849cm3; compression ratio 9.5:1; 118kW (158hp) [160PS] at 5750rpm, 41.4kW/L (55.5hp/L) [56.2PS/L]; 226Nm (166.8lbft) at 3500rpm; leaded premium grade.

Engine construction: Rear engine, designated Z6W-A 700. Valves in V; 1 overhead camshaft (chain); light-alloy cylinder head and block; wet cylinder liners; 4 bearing crankshaft; oil capacity 7.0L (6.6US qt); 1 Solex downdraught carb 34 TB1A and 1 2V; electronic fuel pump. Battery 12V 50Ah, alternator 90A; breakerless ignition system; cooling system capacity approx 12L (11.4US qt).

Transmission (to rear wheels); 5-speed manual final drive ratio 3.444 (9/31).

Gear ratios: 1st 3.364; 2nd 2.059; 3rd 1.381; 4th 1.037; 5th 0.821; R 3.545.

Chassis: Integral body with glass fibre reinforced polyester and central frame chassis; independent suspension front and rear with double A arm, coil springs, telescopic damper and antiroll bar; servo/power assisted brakes (ventilated), disc diameter front and rear 26.9cm, optional ABS; mechanical handbrake to rear wheels; rack and pinion steering; fuel tank 72L (15.8mpg) [19.0US mpg]; front tyres 190/55 VR 365, rear 220/55 VR 365, wheel rims 135mm or 195mm.

Dimensions: Wheelbase 234cm, track 149.5/146cm, clearance min 12.5cm, turning circle 11.9m, load space 3.2–7.8cu ft (90–220dm3), length 433cm, width 175.5cm, height 119.5cm.

Performance: Max speed 146mph/235kmh (manufacturers test specifications), speed at 1000rpm in 5th gear 24.4mph/39.3kmh; acceleration 0 – 62mph/100kmh 8.0secs, standing km 28.0secs; power to weight ratio 9.7kg/kW (7.7kg/PS); consumption ECE 7.0/7.9/14.7L/100km (40.4/35.8/19.2mpg) [33.6/29.8/16.0US mpg].

Renault F • Renault RA

```
2.5 Litre V6
147/136kW–197/182hp–200/185PS
Fuel Injection/Turbo
```

Engine for V6 Turbo

As 2.85 Litre, except:

Weight: Kerbweight (DIN) 1210kg, gross vehicle weight 1550kg.

Engine data (DIN): 6–cylinder in V 90deg (91 x 63mm) 2458cm3; compression ratio 8.6:1; 147kW (197hp) [200PS] at 5750rpm, 59.8kW/L (80.1hp/L) [81.4PS/L]; 290Nm (214lbft) at 2500rpm.
With Catalyst: Compression ratio 8:1; 136kW (182hp) [185PS] at 5500rpm; 292Nm (215.5lbft) at 2250rpm.

Engine construction: Designated Z7U–T30; Renix electronic fuel injection A.E.I. 1 Garrett exhaust turbocharger T3; charge–air cooler; cooling system capacity approx 15L (14.2US qt).

Transmission: 5–speed manual, final drive ratio 3.444.

Gear ratios: 5–speed manual: 1st 3.364; 2nd 2.059; 3rd 1.381; 4th 0.964; 5th 0.756; R 3.545. With Catalyst: 4th 1.037; 5th 0.821.

Chassis: Fuel tank 73L (16Gal) [19.3US Gal]; front tyres 195/50 VR 15, rear 225/45 VR 15, wheel rims 6 or 8.5J.

Performance: Max speed 155mph/250kmh, Catalyst version 148mph/238kmh (manufacturers tested specifications), speed at 1000rpm in 5th gear 26.5mph/42.6kmh, Catalyst version 24.4mph/39.3kmh; acceleration 0 – 62mph/100kmh 7.0secs, standing km 26.8secs, Catalyst version 27.4secs; power to weight ratio 8.2kg/kW (6.0kg/PS); consumption ECE 6.4/8.1/12.8L/100km (44.1/34.9/22.1mpg) [36.8/29.0/18.4US mpg].

RENAULT RA

Renault Argentina S.A., Sarmiento 1230, 1041 Buenos Aires, Argentina

Leading manufacturer of vehicles in Argentina, production started in 1956 and consists different models made up of various elements from differing marques. Part of Renault since 1967. Vehicles produced are the Renault 4, 9, 11, 12, 18, and Fuego.

Renault 4

F – GTL

Argentine version of the Renault 4 with a 1118cm3 engine, 40hp. For Technical data refer to the French Renault 4.

Renault 9

Argentine version of the Renault 9 with a 1397cm3 engine, developing 70hp. For Technical data refer to the French Renault 9.

Renault 11

TI – TS

5–door version of the Renault 11, with a 1.4 Litre 58/70hp engine. August 1986; available with a turbocharger (94hp). For Technical data refer to the French Renault 11.

Renault 12

TL – GTS – Break – Break GTS

Medium size, 5–door, front wheel drive, with a 1.4 Litre 4– cylinder engine. Available in TL and GTS.

```
1.4 Litre
46.5/56.5kW–62/75hp–63/77PS
1 Carb
```

Body, Weight: Saloon/Sedan 4–door, 5–seater; kerbweight (DIN) from 905kg, gross vehicle weight 1350kg. Estate/Station Wagon, 5–door, 5–seater; kerbweight (DIN) 950kg, gross vehicle weight 1435kg.

Engine data (DIN): For TL: 4–cylinder in–line (76 x 77mm), 1397 cm3; compression ratio 9.5:1; 46.5kW (62hp) [63PS] at 5200rpm, 33.2kW/L (44.5hp/L) [45.1PS/L]; 108Nm (80lbft) at 3000rpm; leaded premium grade.
For GTS: Compression 9.5:1; 56.5kW (75hp) [77PS] at 5500rpm, 40.4kW/L (54.1hp/L) [55.1PS/L]; 113Nm (83.4lbft) at 3500rpm.

Engine construction: Engine placed in front of front axle; side camshaft (chain); light–alloy cylinder head; wet cylinder liners; 5 bearing crankshaft; oil capacity 3L (2.8US qt); 1 downdraught carb – Carter CS–32–2067–S (TS: Solex C EIES 2). Battery 12V 40Ah, alternator 38A; cooling system capacity approx 5L (4.7US qt).

Transmission (to front wheels): 4–speed manual (without direct drive), final drive ratio 3.78 (9/34).

Gear ratios: 1st 3.61; 2nd 2.26; 3rd 1.48; 4th 1.03; R 3.08.

Chassis: Integral body, front lower A arm, upper control arm with torsion bar and coil springs, rear rigid axle with trailing arm, central A arm and coil springs, front and rear antiroll bar, telescopic damper. Servo/power assisted brakes, front discs, diameter 23.8cm and rear drum brakes; mechanical handbrake to rear wheels; rack and pinion steering; fuel tank 45L (9.9Gal) 11.9US Gal]; tyres 145 SR 13 or 5.60 S 13, Estate/Station Wagon 155 SR 13, wheel rims 4.5".

Dimensions: Wheelbase 244cm, track 131/131cm, clearance 12cm, turning circle 10m. Load space 14.8cu ft (420dm3), Estate/Station Wagon 32.1–58.3cu ft (910–1650dm3), length 439cm, Estate/Station Wagon 449cm, width 161.5cm, height 143cm, Estate/Station Wagon 151cm.

Performance: Max speed 87mph/140kmh (manufacturers test specifications), speed at 1000rpm in 5th gear 17.9mph/28.8kmh; power to weight ratio from 16.0kg/kW (11.8kg/PS); consumption 8– 9L/100km (35.3–31.4mpg) [29.4–26.1US mpg].

Renault 12 GTS

Renault 18

LX – GTX – GTXII – GTX II Break

5–seater rear wheel drive, with a 2 Litre 4–cylinder engine. Break (Estate/Station Wagon) also available with four wheel drive.

```
2 Litre
76/70kW–102/94hp–103/95PS
1 2V Carb
```

Body, Weight: Saloon/Sedan 4–door, 5–seater; kerbweight (DIN) 1045kg, gross vehicle weight 1455kg. Break (Estate/Station Wagon), 5–door, 5–seater; kerbweight (DIN) 1125kg, gross vehicle weight 1500kg.

Engine data (DIN): 4–cylinder in–line (88 x 82mm), 1995cm3; compression ratio 8.7:1; 76kW (102hp) [103PS] at 5700rpm, 38kW/L (50.9hp/L) [51.6PS/L]; 159Nm (117.3lbft) at 3000rpm; leaded premium grade.
Engine for LX: Compression ratio 7.5:1; 70.0kW (94hp) [95PS] at 5700rpm, 35.0kW/L (46.9hp/L) [47.6PS/L]; 157Nm (116.1lbft) at 3000rpm.
Engine for GTL: (76 x 77mm), 1397cm3; compression ratio 9.5:1; 56.5kW (76hp) [77PS] at 5500rpm, 40.4kW/L (54.1hp/L) [55.1PS/L]; 113Nm (83.4lbft) at 3500rpm.

Engine construction: Engine mounted in front of front axle. Designated 829.00/01. Overhead valves (in V); 1 overhead camshaft (toothed belt); light–alloy cylinder head and block; 5 bearing crankshaft; oil capacity 5.3L (5US qt); 1 Weber downdraught 2V carb 32 DARA 55. Battery 12V 45Ah, alternator 70A; cooling system capacity approx 8L (7.6US qt).

Transmission (to front wheels, 4x4 with engageable rear wheel drive): 4/5–speed manual (without direct drive), final drive ratio 3.778.

Renault RA • Rolls-Royce

Gear ratios: 1st 4.090; 2nd 2.176; 3rd 1.409; 4th 0.97; GTX: 5th 0.810; R 3.545.
4x4: 1st 4.090; 2nd 2.176; 3rd 1.409; 4th 1.030; 5th 0.861; R 3.545.
Chassis: Integral body; front lower A arm, upper control arm with torsion bar and coil springs, rear rigid axle with trailing arm, central A arm and coil springs, front and rear antiroll bar, telescopic damper. Servo/power assisted brakes, front disc, diameter 22.8cm, rear drums; mechanical handbrake to rear wheels; rack and pinion steering; fuel tank 53L (11.6Gal) [14US Gal], Break (Estate/Station Wagon) 57L (12.5Gal) [15.1US Gal]. Tyres 185/70 HR 13, wheel rims 5.5".
Dimensions: Wheelbase 244cm, track 143/134.5cm, clearance min 12cm, turning circle 10.2m. Load space 14cu ft (395dm3): Break 16.8/55cu ft (475/1560dm3). Length 447cm, Break 451cm, width 168cm, height 142cm.
Performance: Max speed approx 106mph/170kmh speed at 1000rpm in 5th gear 17.3mph/27.9kmh; power to weight ratio from 13.8kg/kW (10.1kg/PS); consumption approx 8–12L/100km (35.3–23.5mpg) [29.4–19.6US mpg].

Renault 18 Break 4x4

Renault Fuego GTX

Argentine version of the early Fuego. 2.2 Litre engine (88 x 89mm), 114hp, max speed 118mph/190kmh.

ROLLS ROYCE — GB

Rolls-Royce Motors Limited, Crewe, Cheshire, CW1 3PL, England.
English manufacturer of vehicles and engines.
MODEL RANGE
Silver Spirit – Silver Spur – Corniche – Phantom VI

Rolls Royce Silver Spirit

High class Saloon/Sedan with a 6.75 Litre V8 light-alloy engine. Successor of the Silver Shadow. Independent self levelling suspension. Launched Paris 1980. Autumn 1986: Available with fuel injection and ABS.

```
6.75 Litre V8
Fuel Injection
```

Body, Weight: Saloon/Sedan 4-door, 5-seater; kerbweight (DIN) 2250-2320kg, gross vehicle weight 2700kg.
Engine data: 8-cylinder in V 90deg (104.14 x 99.06mm), 6750cm3; compression ratio 9:1; leaded premium grade (some countries: compression ratio 8:1 or 7.3:1). No official details for power and torque. Compression ratio 9:1; approx 173kW (232hp) [233PS] at approx 4300rpm; approx 450Nm (332.1lbft) at approx 1600rpm. With Catalyst: Compression ratio 8:1; approx 158kW (212hp) [215PS] at approx 4200rpm; approx 460Nm (339.5lbft) at 1500rpm.
USA Version: Approx 147kW (197hp) [200PS].
Engine construction: Designated L4101. Hydraulic tappets; central camshaft (gear); light-alloy cylinder head and cylinder block; wet cylinder liners; 5 bearing crankshaft; oil cooler, oil capacity 9.9L (9.4US qt); Bosch K/KE Jetronic fuel injection, 2 electronic fuel pumps. Spark plugs NGK BPR 5 EV; Battery 12V 68/71Ah, alternator 108A; cooling system capacity approx 18L (17US qt).
Transmission (to rear wheels): Turbo Hydra-Matic Automatic GM 400, hydraulic torque converter and 3-speed Planetary gear set, central selector lever or to steering wheel with positions P-R-N-D-I-L; final drive ratio, 2.69.
Gear ratios: Max torque multiplication in converter 2 times, Planetary gear set ratios; 2.48; 1.48; 1; R 2.08.
Chassis: Integral body, front and rear sub frame; front twin A arm, coil springs and telescopic damper, rear independent suspension with semi trailing arm, coil springs and hydro pneumatic strut/shock absorber strut, automatic level control system; front and rear antiroll bar. Servo/power assisted disc brakes (front ventilated) and ABS (Bosch system), disc diameter 27.9cm, foot operated parking brake to rear wheels; power assisted rack and pinion steering; fuel tank 108L (23.7Gal) [28.5US qt); tyres 235/70 HR/VR 15, wheel rims 6".
Dimensions: Wheelbase 306cm, track 153.5/153.5cm, clearance 16.5cm, turning circle 13.1m, load space cu ft (410-550dm3), length 527cm, width 188.5cm, height 148.5cm.
Performance: Max speed 129mph/208kmh, Catalyst version approx 121mph/195kmh (manufacturers test specification), speed at 1000rpm in top 29.8mph/48.3kmh; acceleration 0 – 62mph/97kmh 10secs; consumption (ECE) 15.6/17.5/23.6L/100km (18.1/16.1/12mpg) [15.1/13.4/10US mpg].

Rolls Royce Silver Spirit

Rolls-Royce Silver Spur

Saloon/Sedan extra-long wheelbase vehicle with optional separater; successor to the Silver Wraith II. Launched Paris 1980. 1984: available with a 407.5cm wheelbase.

```
6.75 Litre V8
Fuel Injection
```

As Silver Spirit, except:
Body, Weight: Saloon/Sedan 4-door, 5-seater; kerbweight (DIN) 2295kg-2350kg, with Separation 2385kg-2440kg, gross vehicle weight 2725/2815/2870kg.
Dimensions: Wheelbase 316cm, turning circle approx 13.4m, length 537cm.

Rolls Royce Silver Spur

Rolls-Royce Corniche II

2-door Convertible from H J Mulliner/Park Ward, based on the Silver Spirit. Launched March 1971; rack and pinion steering. For 1985; modifications to body and interior. Autumn 1986; fuel injection and ABS.

```
6.75 Litre V8
Fuel Injection
```

As Silver Spirit, except:

Rolls-Royce • Rover

Body, Weight: Cabriolet 2-door, 4/5-seater (H.J. Mulliner/Park Ward); kerbweight (DIN) 2360-2420kg, gross vehicle weight 2760kg.

Engine data: As Silver Spirit.

Dimensions: Wheelbase 306cm, track 153.5/153.5cm, turning circle 12.9m, clearance 15m, load space 14.1cu ft (400dm3) net 9.5cu ft (270dm3), length 520/530cm, width 183.5cm, height 152cm.

Performance: Max speed 127mph/205kmh, Catalyst version approx 121mph/195kmh (manufacturers test specification), speed at 1000rpm in direct drive 30mph/48.3kmh; consumption (ECE) 15.6/18.2/25.4L/100km (18.1/15.5/11.1mpg) [15.1/12.9/9.3US mpg].

Rolls Royce Corniche II

Rolls-Royce Phantom VI

Large vehicle, long wheelbase and drum brakes. Separate front and rear climate control. Launched October 1968. Birmingham 1978: larger engine, servo/power assisted brakes and GM (Turbo-Hydra-Matic) transmission.

> 6.75 Litre V8
> 1 4V Carb

Body, Weight: Saloon/Sedan (H.J. Mulliner/Park Ward), 4-door, 7-seater; kerbweight (DIN) 2740kg. State Landaulette (H.J.Mulliner/Park Ward) 5-seater.

Engine data: 8-cylinder in V 90deg (104.1 x 99.1mm), 6750cm3; compression ratio 8:1 for premium grade (optional compression 7.3:1). No details for power and torque.

Engine construction: Hydraulic tappets, central camshaft (gear); light-alloy cylinder block and cylinder head; wet cylinder liners; 5 bearing crankshaft; oil capacity 9.4L (8.9US qt); 1 Solex 2V downdraught carb 4A1 or 2 horizontal carbs SU HIF 7; 2 electronic SU injection pump. Spark plugs Champion RN 12 Y; Battery 12V 68/71Ah, alternator 75A; cooling system capacity approx 20L (18.9US qt).

Transmission (to rear wheels): Turbo-Hydra-Matic-Transmission GM 400, hydraulic torque converter and 3-speed Planetary gear set, central selector lever with positions P-R-N-D-I-L; final drive ratio 3.89.

Rolls Royce Phantom VI

Gear ratios: Max torque multiplication in converter 2 times, Planetary gear set ratios: 2.48; 1.48; 1; R2.08.

Chassis: Box type frame, longitudinal supports and cross member, front trapeze A arm, coil springs and antiroll bar, rear rigid axle with semi elliptic springs, auxilliary Z formed stabilizer, hydraulic piston dampers (rear electrically adjustable). Servo/power assisted drum brakes, foot operated parking brake to rear wheels; power assisted worm and wheel steering; fuel tank 104.5 L (23Gal) [27.6US Gal]; tyres 8.90 S 15. wheel rims 6".

Dimensions: Wheelbase 368.5cm, track 154.5/162.5cm, clearance 18.5cm, turning circle 15.8m, load space 13.1cu ft (370dm3), length 604.5cm, width 200.5cm, height 175cm.

Performance: Max speed approx 106mph/170kmh, speed at 1000rpm in direct drive 22.5mph/36.2kmh; consumption ECE 22.2/25.6/28.2L/100km (12.7/11.0/10.0mpg) [10.6/9.2/8.3USmpg].

ROVER   GB

Austin Rover Group Ltd., Canley, Coventry, CV4 9DB, England.

Producer of passenger vehicles and rough terrain vehicles. Constructer of the first Gas Turbine vehicle.

MODEL RANGE
Rover 213/216 – Rover 800

Rover 213 – 216

213 – 213S – 213SE – 216SE – 216 Vanden Plas EFi – 216 Vitesse

Replacement for the Triumph Acclaim. As the Honda Civic/Ballade built under license in England. Launched June 1984, March 1985; new 216 version with a 1.6 Litre engine.

> 1342cm3
> 52kW-70hp-71PS
> 1 2V Carb

Engine for 213, 213S and 213SE

Body, Weight: Saloon/Sedan 4-door, 5-seater; kerbweight (DIN) from 860kg, gross vehicle weight 1400kg.

Engine data (DIN): 4-cylinder in-line (74 x 78mm), 1342cm3; compression ratio 8.7:1; 52kW (70hp) [71PS] at 6000rpm, 38.7kW/L (51.9hp/L) [52.9PS/L]; 106Nm (78.2lbft) at 3500rpm; leaded regular grade.
Some countries: 53.5kW (72hp) [73PS].

Engine construction: Designated EV. Transverse front engine, 3 valves per cylinder, 1 overhead camshaft (toothed belt); light-alloy cylinder head and block, dry cylinder liners, 5 bearing crankshaft; oil capacity 3.8L (3.6US qt); 1 downdraught registered carb. Battery 12V 45Ah, alternator 55A; cooling system capacity approx 5.1L (4.8US qt).

Transmission (to front wheels): a) 5-speed manual, final drive ratio 4.428.
b) Automatic, hydraulic torque converter and 3-speed Planetary gear set, final drive ratio 3.933.

Gear ratios: a) 5-speed manual: 1st 2.916; 2nd 1.764; 3rd 1.181; 4th 0.846; 5th 0.714; R 2.916.
b) Automatic: Max torque multiplication in converter 2.3 times, Planetary gear set ratios; 1st 2.42; 2nd 1.50; 3rd 0.91; R 1.954.

Chassis: Integral body; front independent suspension with shock absorber strut, lower control arm, rear rigid axle with trailing arm, Panhard rod and coil springs, telescopic damper. Servo/power assisted brakes, front discs, rear drums, disc diameter 23.1cm, mechanical handbrake to rear wheels; rack and pinion steering; fuel tank 46L (10.1Gal) [12.2US Gal]; tyres 155 SR 13, 165 SR 13, wheel rims 4.5J.

Dimensions: Wheelbase 245cm, track 140/141cm, clearance 16.5cm, turning circle 9.6m, load space 15.2cu ft (430dm3), length 415.5cm, width 162.5cm, height 138cm.

Performance: Max speed 96mph/155kmh (manufacturers test specification), speed at 1000rpm in 5th gear 20.8mph/33.5kmh; acceleration 0 – 60mph/97kmh 11.7secs; power to weight ratio from 16.5kg/kW (12.1kg/PS); consumption ECE 5.4/7.4/7.4L/100km (52.3/38.2/38.2mpg) [43.6/31.8/31.8US mpg], automatic 5.8/8.5/7.6L/100km (48.7/33.2/37.2mpg) [40.6/27.7/30.9US mpg].

Rover

Rover 216 Vanden Plas EFI

```
1598cm3
63kW–84hp–86PS
1 Carb
```

Engine for 216S and 216SE

As 1342cm3, except:

Weight: Kerbweight (DIN) 940–945kg, gross vehicle weight 1400kg.

Engine data (DIN): 4–cylinder in–line (76.2 x 87.6mm), 1598cm3; compression ratio 9.6:1; 63kW (84hp) [86PS] at 5600rpm, 39.4kW/L (52.8hp/L) [53.8PS/L]; 132Nm (97.4lbft) at 3500rpm; leaded premium grade.
Certain countries: 61kW (82hp) [83PS]; 129Nm (95.2lbft).

Engine construcion: Designated "S" Series (2 valves per cylinder); grey cast iron cylinder block and head; 1 semi downdraught carb ARG. Alternator 65A; cooling system capacity approx 6.5L (6.1US qt).

Transmission: 5–speed manual, final drive ratio 4.062.

Gear ratios: 1st 2.923; 2nd 1.75; 3rd 1.142; 4th 0.848; 5th 0.648; R 3.0.

Chassis: Tyres 165 SR 13, wheel rims 5J.

Performance: Max speed 102mph/164kmh (manufacturers test specification), speed at 1000rpm in 4th gear 19.7mph/31.7kmh in 5th gear 25.7mph/41.4kmh; acceleration 0 – 60mph/97kmh 10.1secs; power to weight ratio from 14.0kg/kW (10.9kg/PS); consumption ECE 5.1/6.7/8.8L/100km (55.4/42.2/32.1mpg) [46.1/35.1/26.7US mpg].

```
1598cm3
76.5kW–103hp–104PS
Fuel Injection
```

As 1342cm3, except:

Weight: Kerbweight (DIN) 945–975kg, gross vehicle weight 1400kg.

Engine data: 4–cylinder in–line (76.2 x 87.6mm) 1598cm3; compression ratio 9.7:1; 76.5kW (103hp) [104PS] at 6000rpm, 47.9kW/L (64.2hp/L) [65.1PS/L]; 137Nm (101.1lbft) at 3500rpm; leaded premium grade.
Some countries: 75kW (101hp) [102PS]; 135Nm (99.6lbft).

Engine construction: Designated "S" series (2 valves per cylinder; grey cast iron cylinder block and head; electronic fuel injection (Lucas "L"). Alternator 65A; cooling system capacity approx 6.5L (6.1US qt).

Transmission: a) 5–speed manual, final drive ratio 4.062, Vitesse 3.937.
b) 4–speed automatic ZF 4 HP 14, hydraulic torque converter and Planetary gear set; central selector lever; final drive ratio (3.688 x 1.157) 4.267.

Gear ratios: a) 5–speed manual: 1st 3.25; 2nd 1.75; 3rd 1.142; 4th 0.848; 5th 0.648; R 3. Vitesse: 1st 3.25; 2nd 1.894; 3rd 1.346; 4th 1.033; 5th 0.848; R 3.
b) Automatic: Max torque multiplication in converter 2 times, Planetary gear set ratios: 1st 2.41 2nd 1.37; 3rd 1; 4th 0.739; R 2.83.

Chassis: Rear antiroll bar (Vitesse only); front disc brakes (ventilated); tyres 165 SR 13, Vitesse 175/65 TR 14, wheel rims 5J.

Performance: Max speed 108mph/174kmh, Vitesse 112mph/180kmh (manufacturers test specification), speed at 1000rpm in 5th gear 25.7mph/41.4kmh, Vitesse 19.9mph/32.0kmh; acceleration 0 – 60mph/97kmh 9.4secs, Vitesse 9.2secs; power to weight ratio from 12.4kg/kW (9.1kg/PS); consumption ECE 5.2/6.8/8.1L/100km (54.3/41.5/34.9mpg) [45.2/34.6/29.0US mpg], Vitesse 5.6/7.1/8.5L/100km (50.4/39.8/33.2mpg) [42.0/33.1/27.2US mpg] automatic 6.2/8.4/9.4L/100km (45.6/33.6/30.1mpg) [37.9/28/25.0US mpg].

Rover 216 Vitesse

Rover 800

820/SE – 820Si – 825i/Sterling – 827Si/Sterling

Medium size 4–door vehicle; front wheel drive, with a transverse 2 Litre 4–cylinder or 2.5 Litre 6–cylinder engine. Produced as a joint venture with Honda. Launched July 1986. February 1988: available with 2.7 Litre engine.

```
2 Litre
73.5kW–98hp–100PS
1 Carb
```

Engine for 820 Fastback

Body, Weight: Saloon/Sedan 5–door, 5–seater; kerbweight (DIN) 1300–1315kg, gross vehicle weight 1850kg.

Engine data (ECE): 4–cylinder in–line (84.5 x 89mm), 1996cm3; compression ratio 9.1:1; 73.5kW (98hp) [100PS] at 5400rpm, 36.8kW/L (49.3hp/L) [50.1PS/L]; 163Nm (120.3lbft) at 3000rpm; 95/97 regular grade.

Engine construction: Designated "0" Series. 1 overhead camshafts (toothed belt); light–alloy cylinder head, 5 bearing crankshaft; oil capacity 5.8L (5.5US qt); electronic injection ARG. 12V 55/60Ah, alternator 65/80A; cooling system capacity approx 6L (5.7Us qt).

Transmission (to front wheels): a) 5–speed manual, final drive ratio 4.200.
b) Automatic ZF 4 HP 14, hydraulic torque converter and 4–speed Planetary gear set, central selector lever. Final drive ratio 4.405.

Gear ratios: a) 5–speed manual: 1st 3.250; 2nd 1.894; 3rd 1.222; 4th 0.935; 5th 0.764; R 3.
b) Automatic: Planetary gear set ratios: 1st 2.412; 2nd 1.369; 3rd 1; 4th 0.739; R 2.828.

Chassis: Integral body; front and rear indpendent suspension, front with McPherson struts, upper and lower A arm as well as lower longitudinal tie bar. Rear, lower control arm and longitudinal tie bar, shock absorber strut and coil springs, front and rear antiroll bar. Servo/power assisted disc brakes optional ABS (Bosch), front discs (ventilated), diameter front 26.2cm, rear 26.0cm; mechanical handbrake to rear wheels; power assisted rack and pinion steering; fuel tank 68L (14.9Gal) [18.0US Gal]; tyres 175 HR 14, wheel rims 5.5J.

Dimensions: Wheelbase 276cm, track 149/145cm, clearance 14.5cm, turning circle 11.1m, load space 15.5cu ft (445dm3) Fastback 16.6/34.3/49.6cu ft (470/970/1405dm3), length 469.5cm, width 173cm, height 140cm.

Rover 820 Fastback

True value is timeless

**Rolls-Royce Motor Cars
International S.A.
Au Glapin
CH - 1162 St-Prex
Telefon 021 806 2731
Telex 454 216**

EVEN IF IT RAINS, IT SHINES.

JAGUAR

JAGUAR CARS LTD., COVENTRY, ENGLAND.

The Jaguar XJ-S is, above all, a rather British convertible.

Designed to capitalise on the sunshine. But with a weather eye on the downside.

Which is why Jaguar's engineers ensured that the powered hood glides swiftly, securely into place within twelve seconds of your touching the button. We've also raised the roof itself to new levels of comfort. It's thickly padded, fully lined, and has a tinted, heated glass rear screen.

So you're perfectly insulated against the British summer.

The sinuous quality of the XJ-S on the road, also, is impressive in the wet. Advanced anti-lock braking with anti-yaw control provides assurance and authority in the most demanding conditions.

And whatever the weather, the awesome power of the silent electronically managed 12 cylinder engine, the car's matchless handling characteristics, and the unbridled luxury of its appointments are a constant reminder to its occupants.

Every cloud has a silver lining.

XJS
THE V12 CONVERTIBLE

WORLD SPORTSCAR CHAMPIONS —1987-1988—

Rover

Performance: Max speed 112mph/180kmh, Automatic 110mph/177kmh (manufacturers test specification) speed at 1000rpm in 5th gear 22.4mph/36kmh; acceleration 0 - 62mph/100kmh 12.4secs, automatic 14.5secs, standing km 33.8secs, automatic 35.5secs; power to weight ratio from 17.7kg/kW (13.0kg/PS); consumption ECE 6.2/7.9/10.6L/100km (45.6/35.8/26.6mpg) [37.9/29.8/22.2US mpg], Automatic 6.4/8.2/11.1L/100km (44.1/34.4/25.4mpg) [36.8/28.7/21.2US mpg].

```
2 Litre
88.5kW–119hp–120PS
Central/Single Point Injection
```

Engine for 820e/Se

As 98hp, except:

Body, Weight: Saloon/Sedan 4-door, 5-seater; kerbweight (DIN) 1305-1340kg, gross vehicle weight 1850kg.
Saloon/Sedan 5-door, 5-seater; kerbweight (DIN) 1335-1370kg, gross vehicle weight 1850kg.

Engine data (ECE): 4-cylinder in-line (84.5 x 89mm), 1996cm3, compression ratio 10:1; 88.5kW (119hp) [120PS] at 5600rpm, 44.2kW/L (59.2hp/L) [60.1PS/L]; 162Nm (119.6bft) at 3500rpm.

Engine construction: Designated M16e. 4 valves per cylinder; 2 overhead camshafts (toothed belt); light-alloy cylinder head, 5 bearing crankshaft; oil capacity 5.8L (5.5US qt); electronic central injection ARG.

Chassis: Tyres 195/70 HR 14 or 195/65 VR, wheel rims 6J.

Performance: Max speed 119-120mph/191-193kmh, Automatic 117-118mph/188-190kmh (manufacturers test specification), speed at 1000rpm in 5th gear 22.4mph/36kmh; acceleration 0 - 62mph/100kmh 11.0secs, automatic 12.7secs, standing km 32.8, automatic 34.0secs; power to weight ratio from 14.8kg/kW (10.9kg/PS); consumption ECE 6.0/7.8/10.5L/100km (47.1/36.2/26.9mpg) [39.2/30.2/22.4US mpg], automatic 6.5/8.4/12.0L/100km (43.5/33.6/23.5mpg) [36.2/33.6/19.6US mpg].

Rover 820i

```
2 Litre
103/98kW–138/131hp–140/133PS
Fuel Injection
```

Engine for 820i/Si

As 98hp, except:

Weight: Saloon/Sedan 4-door, 5-seater; kerbweight (DIN) 1300–1320kg, gross vehicle weight 1850kg.
Saloon/Sedan 5-door, 5-seater; kerbweight (DIN) 1330-1350kg, gross vehicle weight 1850kg.

Engine data (ECE): 4-cylinder in line (84.5 x 89mm), 1996cm3; compression ratio 10:1; 103kW (138hp) [140PS] at 6000rpm, 51.6kW/L (69.1hp/L) [70.1PS/L]; 178Nm (131.4lbft) at 4500rpm.
With Catalyst: 98kW (131hp) [133PS] at 5900rpm, 49.2kW/L (65.9hp/L) [66.7PS/L]; 176Nm (129.9lbft) at 4400rpm.

Engine construction: Designated M16i. 4 valves per cylinder; 2 overhead camshafts (toothed belt); light-alloy cylinder head, 5 bearing crankshaft; oil capacity 5.8L (5.5US qt); Lucas electronic fuel injection.

Transmission: 5-speed manual, final drive ratio 4.200.

Chassis: Tyres 195/70 HR 14 or 195/65 VR 15, wheelbase 6J.

Performance: Max speed 126-127mph/202-204kmh (manufacturers test specifications), speed at 1000rpm in 5th gear 22.4mph/36kmh, acceleration 0 - 62mph/100kmh 9.8secs, standing km 31.2secs; power to weight ratio from 12.6kg/kW (9.3kg/PS); consumption ECE 6.6/8.2/10.5L/100km (42.8/34.4/26.9mpg) [35.6/28.7/22.4US mpg]. With Catalyst: Max speed 124-126mph/199-202kmh (manufacturers test specification), acceleration 0 - 62mph/100kmh 9.8secs.

```
2.7 Litre V6
130/124kW–174/166hp–177/169PS
Fuel Injection
```

Engine for 827 Si/SLi/Vitesse/Sterling

As 98hp, except:

Weight: Saloon/Sedan 4-door, 5-seater; kerbweight (DIN) 1375–1475kg, gross vehicle weight 1910kg.
Saloon/Sedan 5-door, 5-seater; kerbweight (DIN) 1405-1445kg, gross vehicle weight 1910kg.

Rover 827 Vitesse

Engine data (ECE); 6-cylinder in V 90deg (87 x 75mm), 2675cm3; compression 9.4:1; 130kW (174hp) [177PS] at 6000rpm, 48.6kW/L (65.1hp/L) [66.2PS/L]; 228Nm (168.3lbft) at 4500rpm.
With Catalyst: Compression ratio 9:1; 124kW (166hp) [169PS] at 5900rpm, 46.4kW/L (62.2hp/L) [63.2PS/L]; 225Nm (166.1lbft) at 4500rpm.

Engine construction: Designated C27A V6. Overhead valves in V; hydraulic tappets, 4 valves per cylinder, 1 overhead camshaft (toothed belt); light-alloy cylinder block and head, dry cylinder liners; 4 bearing crankshaft; oil capacity 5.5L (5.2US qt); oil cooler; Honda electronic fuel injection PGM-FI. Battery 12V 75Ah, alternator 65/80A; cooling system capacity approx 8L (7.6US qt).

Transmission: a) 5-speed manual, final drive ratio 4.200.
b) Automatic, final drive ratio 4.266.

Gear ratios: a) 5-speed manual: 1st 2.923; 2nd 1.789; 3rd 1.222; 4th 0.909; 5th 0.75; R 3.
b) Automatic: Planetary gear set ratios: 1st 2.647; 2nd 1.555; 3rd 1.058; 4th 0.794; R 1.904.

Chassis: Front disc diameter 28.5cm, tyres 195/65 VR 15 or 205/60 VR 15, wheel rims 6J.

Performance: Max speed 137-140mph/220-225kmh, automatic 134-136mph/215-217kmh (manufacturers test specification), speed at 1000rpm in 5th gear 22.7mph/36.6kmh, acceleration 0 – 62mph/100kmh 8.2secs, automatic 8.9secs, standing km 29.1secs, automatic 30.0secs; power to weight ratio 10.6kg/kW (7.8kg/PS); consumption ECE 7.4/9.0/12.3L/100km (38.2/31.4/23.0mpg) [31.8/26.1/19.1US mpg], automatic 8.4/10.0/12.7L/100km (33.6/28.2/22.2mpg) [28.0/23.5/18.5US mpg]. With Catalyst: Max speed 134-137mph/215-220kmh, automatic 132-134mph/212-215kmh; acceleration 0 – 62mph/100kmh 8.4secs, automatic 9.2secs; standing km 29.4secs, automatic 30.6secs, consumption ECE 8.2/9.3/12.9L/100km (34.3/30.4/21.9mpg) [28.7/25.3/18.2US mpg], automatic 9.1/10.2/14.0L/100km (31/27.7/20.2mpg) [25.8/23.1/16.8US mpg].

Rover 827 Sterling

Saab

SAAB	S

Saab–Scania AB, Saab Car Division, Head Office Nykoeping (Factory Trollhaetten), Sweden

Swedish aeroplane, car, commercial vehicle and electronics manufacturer.

MODEL RANGE
900 – 900 i – 900 Turbo – 900 Turbo 16 – 9000 i – 9000 Turbo 16 – 9000 CD

Saab 900

900 – i – Turbo – Turbo 16 – Turbo 16 S – Turbo 16 Cabriolet

2, 3, 4 or 5–door car; 2 Litre engines with various power output. Debut May 1978. Geneva 1980: also available as notchback. Brussels 1984: Turbo 16 model with 4 valves per cylinder, Turbo 16 S with aerodynamic features. 900 Turbo 16 Cabriolet available in the USA since Spring 1986.

Saab 900i

2 Litre
81/85kW–108.5/114hp–110/115PS
Fuel injection

Engine for 900i

Body, Weight: Saloon/Sedan 2/3/4/5–door, 5–seater; kerbweight approx 1175–1290kg; gross vehicle weight 1640–1720kg.

Engine data (Catalyser, ECE): 4–cylinder in–line (90 x 78mm), 1985cm3; compression ratio 9.25:1; 81kW (108.5hp) [110PS] at 5250rpm, 40.8kW/L (54.7hp/L) [55.4PS/L]; 161Nm (118.8lbft) at 3000rpm; leaded regular grade.
Without Catalyst: Compression ratio 9.5:1; 85kW (114hp) [115PS] at 5500rpm, 42.8kW/L (54.7hp/L) [57.9PS/L]; 167Nm (123.2lbft) at 3000rpm.

Engine construction: Engine block tilted 45deg. 1 overhead camshaft (chain); light–alloy cylinder head; crankshaft with 5 bearings; oil 3.5L (3.3US qt); 1 Pierburg horizontal carb or Bosch mechanical fuel injection. Battery 12V 60Ah, alternator 70/80A; cooling system capacity 10L (9.5US qt).

Transmission: a) 5–speed manual for Catalyst, final drive ratio 3.89.
b) 5–speed manual without Catalyst, final drive ratio 3.89.
c) Borg–Warner automatic, hydraulic torque converter and 3–speed Planetary gear set, final drive ratio 3.89.

Gear ratios: a) 5–speed manual for Catalyst: 1st 3.73; 2nd 2.22; 3rd 1.46; 4th 1.05; 5th 0.84; R 4.20.
b) 5–speed manual without Catalyst: 1st 3.56; 2nd 2.07; 3rd 1.35; 4th 0.98; 5th 0.78; R 3.91.
c) Automatic; max torque multiplication in converter 2.38 times, Planetary gear set ratios: 1st 2.06; 2nd 1.25; 3rd 0.86; R 1.80.

Chassis: Integral body; front lower swinging A arms and coil springs, upper control arms, rear rigid axle with longitudinal arms and Panhard rods, coil springs, telescopic dampers. Servo/power assisted disc brakes, front disc diameter 28cm, rear 25.8cm; handbrake to front wheels; rack and pinion steering; fuel tank 63L (13.8Gal) [16.6US Gal]; tyres 185/65 TR/HR 15, wheel rims 5.5J.

Dimensions: Wheelbase 251.5cm, track 143/144cm, clearance 14cm, turning circle 10.3m. Load space 2/4–door 21.7–53cu ft (615–1500dm3), 3/5–door 21.2–56.5cu ft (600–1600dm3). Length 468/469cm, width 169cm, height 142cm.

Performance: Max speed 106mph/170kmh, Automatic 99mph/160kmh (manufacturers test specifications), speed at 1000rpm in 5th gear 21.7mph/35kmh; acceleration 0–62mph/100kmh 13.0secs, Automatic 16secs; power to weight ratio from 14.5kg/kW (10.7kg/PS); consumption ECE 7.5/10.4/13.1L/100km (37.7/27.2/21.6mpg) [31.4/22.6/18US mpg], Automatic 8.2/12.1/13.0L/100km (34.4/23.3/21.7mpg) [28.7/19.4/18.1US mpg].
Without Catalyst: Max speed 109–102mph/175–165kmh (manufacturers test specifications), speed at 1000rpm in 5th gear 23mph/37kmh; acceleration 0–62mph/100kmh 12/15secs; consumption ECE 6.8/10.1/13.5L/100km (41.5/28/20.9mpg) [34.6/23.3/17.4US mpg], Catalyst 8.7/11.6/14.1L/100km (32.5/24.4/20mpg) [27/20.3/16.7US mpg].

Saab 900i

2 Litre
93/96kW–126/129hp–125/130PS
Fuel Injection

Engine for 900i 16

As 2 Litre 108.5/114hp, except:

Body, Weight: 3/4/5–door Saloon/Sedan, 5 seats; kerbweight (DIN) 1185–1300kg, gross vehicle weight 1670–1740kg.

Engine data (Catalyst, DIN): 4–cylinder in–line (90 x 78mm), 1985cm3; compression ratio 10:1; 93kW (126hp) [125PS] at 6000rpm, 46.8kW/L (63.5hp/L) [63PS/L]; 170Nm (125.4lbft) at 3000rpm.
Without Catalyst: 96kW (129hp) [130PS], 48.4kW/L (64.9hp/L) [65.5PS/L].

Engine construction: Transverse engine, tilted 20deg to front. Hydraulic tappets, 4 valves per cylinder, 2 overhead camshafts (chain); oil–cooler, oil capacity approx 4L (4.2US qt); Bosch LH–Jetronic electronic fuel injection; without Catalyst K–Jetronic.

Transmission: a) 5–speed manual, final drive ratio 3.89.
b) Automatic, final drive ratio 3.89.

Gear ratios: a) 5–speed manual; 1st 3.56; 2nd 2.07; 3rd 1.35; 4th 0.98; 5th 0.78; R 3.91.
b) Automatic: Max torque multiplication in converter 2.38 times; Planetary gear set ratios: 1st 2.06; 2nd 1.25; 3rd 0.86; R 1.8.

Performance: Max speed 109mph/175kmh, Automatic 106mph/170kmh (manufacturers test specifications), speed at 1000rpm in 5th gear 23mph/37kmh; acceleration 0–62mph/100kmh 11.5secs, Automatic 14.5secs; power to weight ratio from 12.7kg/kW (9.4kg/PS); consumption ECE 6.9/9.4/12.6L/100km (40.9/30.1/22.4mpg) [34.1/25/18.7US mpg], Automatic 7.9/10.7/13.4L/100km (39.8/26.4/21.1mpg) [33.1/22/17.6US mpg].
Without Catalyst: Max speed 112–109mph/180–175kmh (manufacturers test specifications); acceleration 0–62mph/100kmh 11.5/14.5secs; consumption ECE 7.1/9.9/11.9L/100km (34/25.7/23.9mpg) [28.3/21.4/19.9US mpg], Automatic 8.3/11.0/11.8L/100km.

2 Litre Turbo
114/103kW–153/138hp–155/140PS
Fuel Injection

Engine for Turbo 8

As 108.5/114hp, except:

Body, Weight: 2–door 900 Turbo, 5–seater; kerbweight (DIN) from 1205kg, gross vehicle weight 1630kg. 3–door 900 Turbo, 5–seater; kerbweight (DIN) from 1215kg, gross vehicle weight 1670/1720kg. 4–door 900 Turbo, 5–seater; kerbweight (DIN) from 1240kg, gross vehicle weight 1690–1740kg. 5–door 900 Turbo, 5–seater; kerbweight from 1250kg, gross vehicle weight 1690–1740kg.

Engine data (DIN): 4–cylinder in–line (90 x 78mm), 1985cm3; compression ratio 8.5:1; 114kW (153hp) [155PS] at 5000rpm, 57.4kW/L (76.9hp/L) [78.1PS/L]; 235Nm (173.3lbft) at 3000rpm; leaded regular grade.
With Catalyst: 103kW (138hp) [140PS] at 5000rpm, 235Nm (173.3lbft) at 2500rpm.

Engine construction: Boost through exhaust turbocharger, boost pressure 0.7bar; charger–air cooler; oil capacity 4L (3.8US qt), Bosch K–Jetronic mechanical fuel injection. Alternator 70/80A; cooling system capacity 10L (9.5US qt).

Saab

Transmission: a) 5–speed manual, final drive ratio (3.667 x 0.839) 3.075.
b) Automatic, final drive ratio (3.667 x 0.878) 3.22.

Chassis: Tyres 185/65 HR 15, wheel rims 5.5J.

Performance: Max speed 124mph/200kmh, Catalyst 118mph/190kmh, automatic 121mph/195kmh (manufacturers test specifications), speed at 1000rpm in 5th gear 22.8mph/36.7kmh; acceleration 0 – 62mph/100kmh 9secs, Catalyst 9.8secs, automatic 10.5secs; power to weight ratio from 10.6kg/kW (7.8kg/PS); ECE consumption 7.9/10.9/13.5L/100km (35.8/25.9/20.9mpg) [29.8/21.6/17.4US mpg], Catalyst 7.5/10.1/13.5L/100km (37.7/28/20.9mpg) [31.4/23.3/17.4US mpg], automatic 8.3/11.6/12.7L/100km (34/24.4/22.2mpg) [28.3/20.3/18.5US mpg].

Saab 900 Turbo

```
2 Litre Turbo 16
118/129kW–158/173hp–160/175PS
Fuel Injection
```

Engine for Turbo 16/Turbo 16 S/CD 16 and Turbo 16 Cabriolet

As 108.5/114hp, except:

Body, Weight: Saloon/Sedan 3/4/5–door, 5–seater; kerbweight (DIN) approx 1245–1315kg, gross vehicle weight 1720–1760kg; Convertible/Cabriolet approx 1325–1370kg, gross vehicle weight 1720–1740kg.

Saab 900 Turbo 16 Cabriolet

Engine data (Catalyst ECE): 4–cylinder in–line (90 x 78mm), 1985cm3; compression ratio 9:1; 118kW (158hp) [160PS] at 5500rpm, 59.4kW/L (79.6hp/L) [80.1PS/L]; 255Nm (188.2lbft) at 3000rpm.
Without Catalyst: 129kW (173hp) [175PS] at 5300rpm, 274Nm (202lbft) at 3000rpm.

Engine construction: Hydraulic tappets; 4 valves per cylinder; 2 overhead camshafts (chain); boost through exhaust turbocharger, boost pressure 0.85bar, charger–air cooler; oil capacity 4L (3.8US qt); Bosch LH–Jetronic fuel injection. Alternator 70/80A; cooling system capacity 10L (9.5US qt).

Transmission: a) 5–speed manual, final drive ratio 3.89.
b) Automatic (for Convertible/Cabriolet), final drive ratio 3.89.

Gear ratios: a) 5–speed manual for Catalyst: 1st 3.56; 2nd 2.07; 3rd 1.35; 4th 0.98; 5th 0.78; R 3.91.
b) 5–speed manual without Catalyst: 1st 3.31; 2nd 1.93; 3rd 1.26; 4th 0.91; 5th 0.73; R 3.64.
c) Automatic; max torque multiplication 2.38 times, Planetary gear set ratios: 1st 2.39; 2nd 1.45; 3rd 1; R 2.09.

Chassis: Tyres 196/60 VR 15, wheel rims 5.5J.

Performance: Max speed 127mph/205kmh, Convertible/Cabriolet 124mph/200kmh (manufacturers test specifications), speed at 1000rpm in 5th gear 20.3mph/37.1kmh; acceleration 0–62mph/100kmh 9.6secs; power to weight ratio from 10.5kg/kW (7.8kg/PS); consumption ECE 7.4/10.6/11.9L/100km (38.2/26.6/23.7mpg) [31.8/22.2/19.8US mpg].
Without Catalyst: Max speed 130–127mph/210–205kmh (manufacturers test specifications); acceleration 0–62mph/100kmh 8.7secs; consumption ECE 6.9/10.0/11.2L/100km (40.9/28.2/25.2mpg) [34.1/23.5/21US mpg].

Saab 900 Turbo 16 S

Saab 9000 i – Turbo 16 – CD

9000 i – Turbo 16 – CD

Luxury Saloon/Sedan with 2 Litre 16V turbo transverse engine and front wheel drive, aerodynamic body with tailgate. Debut May 1984. 1986 model year: 900 i version with turbocharger. 1987 also with automatic transmission. January 1988 4–door CD edition.

Saab 9000i

```
2 Litre
94/98kW–126/131hp–128/133PS
Fuel Injection
```

Engine for 9000 i and CD

Body, Weight: Saloon/Sedan 4/5–door, 5–seater; kerbweight (DIN) approx 1300–1370kg, gross vehicle weight 1780–1840kg.

Engine data (Catalyst ECE): 4–cylinder in–line (90 x 78mm), 1985cm3; compression ratio 10:1; 94kW (126hp) [128PS] at 5500rpm, 47.4kW/L (63.5hp/L) [64.5PS/L]; 173Nm (127.7lbft) at 3750rpm. Premium or regular unleaded.
Without Catalyst: 98kW (131hp) [133PS] at 5500rpm.

Engine construction: Transverse engine, tilted 20deg forwards. Hydraulic valve tappets, 4 valves per cylinder, 2 overhead camshafts (chain); light–alloy cylinder head; crankshaft with 5 bearings; oil–cooler, oil capacity approx 4.4L (4.2US qt); Bosch LH–Jetronic electronic fuel injection. Cooling system capacity 10L (9.5US qt).

Transmission (to front wheels): a) 5–speed manual, final drive ratio 4.45.
b) ZF automatic, hydraulic torque converter and 4–speed Planetary gear set, final drive ratio 4.19.

Gear ratios: a) 5–speed manual: 1st 3.38; 2nd 1.76; 3rd 1.18; 4th 0.89; 5th 0.70; R 3.21.
b) Automatic: Max torque multiplication in converter 2.57 times, Planetary gear set ratios: 1st 2,58; 2nd 1.41; 3rd 1; 4th 0.74; R 2.88.

Chassis: Integral body with front sub–frames; front independent suspension with McPherson struts and control arms, rear rigid axle with 2 front and 2 rear positioned longitudinal arms and Panhard rods, front and rear antiroll bars, coil springs and telescopic dampers. Servo/power assisted disc brakes, also available with ABS+3, front disc diameter (ventilated) 27.8cm, rear 25.6cm, mechanical handbrake to rear wheels; power assisted rack and pinion steering; fuel tank 68L (14.9Gal) [18US Gal]; tyres 185/65 HR 15; wheel rims 6J.

Saab • Sbarro • Seat

Dimensions: Wheelbase 267cm, track 152/149cm, clearance 15cm, turning circle 10.9m. Load space 22–56.5cu ft (625–1600dm3). Length 462cm, CD 478cm, width 176.5cm, height 143cm.

Performance: Max speed over 115mph/185kmh (manufacturers test specifications), speed at 1000rpm in 5th gear 22.6mph/36.2kmh; acceleration 0–62mph/100kmh 9secs, automatic 9.4secs; power to weight ratio from 13.8kg/kW (10.2kg/PS); ECE fuel consumption 6.7/8.8/12.4L/100km (42.2/32.1/22.8mpg) [35.1/26.7/19US mpg], Automatic 7.1/9.1/13.9L/100km (39.8/31/20.3mpg) [33.1/25.8/16.9US mpg].
Without Catalyst: Max speed 118–115mph/190–185kmh (manufacturers test specifications); acceleration 0–62mph/100kmh 8.4/8.9secs; consumption ECE 7.2/8.8/12.2L/100km (39.2/32.1/23.2mpg) [32.7/26.7/19.3US mpg], Automatic 8.4/8.9/15.5L/100km (33.6/31.7/18.2mpg) [28/26.4/15.2US mpg].

Saab 9000 CD

---
2 Litre Turbo
120kW–161hp–163PS
Fuel Injection

Engine for Turbo 16 and CD

As 9000 i, except:

Body, Weight: Saloon/Sedan 4/5–door, 5–seater; kerbweight (DIN) approx 1340–1440kg, gross vehicle weight 1785–1870kg.

Engine data (Catalyst ECE): 4–cylinder in–line (90 x 78mm), 1985cm3; compression ratio 9:1; 120kW (161hp) [163PS] at 5300rpm, 60.4kW/L (80.9hp/L) [82.1PS/L]; 257Nm (201.5lbft) at 3000rpm.
Without Catalyst: 129kW (173hp) [175PS] at 5500rpm; 273Nm (27.8mkp) at 3000rpm.

Engine construction: Oil capacity approx 5L (4.7US qt); 1 exhaust turbocharger, boost pressure 0.75bar (without Catalyst 0.85bar), charger–air cooler.

Transmission: a) 5–speed manual, final drive ratio 4.05.
b) ZF 4–speed automatic, final drive ratio 3.85.

Chassis: Tyres 205/55 VR 15, CD 195/65 VR 15.

Dimensions: CD length 478cm.

Performance: Max speed 134mph/215kmh, Automatic 130mph/210kmh (manufacturers test specifications), speed at 1000rpm in 5th gear 24.2mph/39kmh; acceleration 0–62mph/100kmh 8.9secs, Automatic 9.3secs; power to weight ratio from 11.2kg/kW (8.2kg/PS); consumption ECE 6.5/8.6/12.2L/100km (43.5/32.8/23.2mpg) [36.2/27.4/19.3US mpg], Automatic 6.9/10.0/14.3L/100km (40.9/28.2/19.8mpg) [34.1/23.5/16.4US mpg].
Without Catalyst: Max speed 137–134mph/220–215kmh (manufacturers test specifications); acceleration 0–62mph/100kmh 8.3/8.8secs; consumption ECE 7.0/8.5/12.1L/100km (40.4/33.2/23.3mpg) [33.6/27.7/19.4US mpg], Automatic 7.9/9.5/14.3L/100km (35.8/29.7/19.8mpg) [29.8/24.8/16.4US mpg].

Saab 9000 CD
R25

SBARRO   CH

ACA Atelier de construction automobile, Franco Sbarro, CH–1422 Les Tuileries–de–Grandson, Switzerland

Manufacturer of one–off customised luxury vehicles according to plans discussed with its clients. Basic models: currently the Windhound luxury off–road vehicle (based either on US or European version according to the customer's wishes); limited editions of the Mercedes–Benz S–class (sometimes with turbo V8 engines); wedge–coupe Challenge (based on Porsche 911 Convertible/Cabriolet, other mechanical bases and chassis also available); further replicas of various historical constructions combined with modern drive mechanics (technical data differs from one case to the next).

Sbarro Robur

SEAT   E

Seat SA, Avda. Gran Via Corts Catalanes, 140 Barcelona, Spain

Spanish car manufacturer. Manufacturer of Seat and VW models for both the domestic and export markets.

MODEL RANGE
Marbella – Ibiza – Malaga

Seat Marbella

Two–door compact car with tail gate, technically related to Fiat Panda. Debut 1982/83. December 1986: also with 850cm3 engine.

Seat Marbella

903/843cm3
29/26kW–39/34hp–40/34PS
1 Carb

Body, Weight: 3–door Saloon/Sedan, 5–seater; kerbweight (DIN) 680kg, gross vehicle weight 1150kg.

Seat

Engine data (DIN): 4–cylinder in–line (65 x 68mm), 903cm3; compression ratio 8.5:1; 29kW (39hp) [40PS] at 5400rpm, 32.1kW/L (43hp/L) [44.3PS/L]; 66Nm (48.7lbft) at 3000rpm; leaded regular grade.
Or: (65 x 63.5mm), 843cm3; compression ratio 7.8:1; 26kW (34hp) [35PS] at 5400rpm, 30.8kW/L (41.2hp/L) [41.5PS/L]; 56Nm (41.3lbft) at 2800rpm.

Engine construction: Transverse mounted front engine. Side mounted camshaft (chain); light–alloy cylinder head; crankshaft with 3 bearings; oil capacity 3.9L (3.7US qt); 1 Bressel/Weber 32 ICEV downdraught carb. Battery 12V 32Ah, alternator 45A; cooling system capacity 5.2L (4.9US qt).

Transmission (to front wheels): a) 4–speed manual (without direct drive, fully synchronised), final drive ratio 4.071 (14/57).
b) For 903cm3: 5–speed manual, final drive ratio 4.5.

Gear ratios: a) 4–speed manual: 1st 3.90; 2nd 2.05; 3rd 1.34; 4th 0.97; R 3.72.
b) 5–speed manual: 1st 3.50; 2nd 1.95; 3rd 1.32; 4th 0.97; 5th 0.76; R 3.64.

Chassis: Integral body; front independent suspension with McPherson struts (coil springs), single control arms and longitudinal struts, rear rigid axle with semi–elliptical springs, telescopic dampers. Front disc diameter 22.7cm, rear drums; handbrake to rear wheels; rack and pinion steering; fuel tank 35L (7.7Gal) [9.2US Gal] including 7–8L (1.5–1.8Gal) [1.8–2.1US Gal] reserve; tyres 135 SR 13 or 145/70 SR 13, wheel rims 4 or 4.5J.

Dimensions: Wheelbase 216cm, track 125.5/125cm, clearance 13cm, turning circle 9.2m. Load space 9.5–38.5cu ft (270–1090dm3). Length 347.5cm, width 146cm, height 144.5cm.

Performance: Max speed 81mph/131kmh (manufacturers test specifications), speed at 1000rpm in 4th gear (4.071:1) 15.8mph/25.4kmh; acceleration 0 – 62mph/100kmh 20.2secs; power to weight ratio from 23.4kg/kW (17.0kg/PS); ECE consumption 4.9/6.9/7.3L/100km (57.6/40.9/38.7mpg) [48/34.1/32.2US mpg], 5–speed 4.7/6.7/7.5L/100km (60.1/42.2/37.7mpg) [50/35.1/31.4US mpg].

Seat Ibiza

Compact three or five door middle–class Saloon/Sedan with front wheel drive. 1.2 and 1.5 Litre engines developed from Porsche petrol/gasoline engines, Fiat diesel engine. Guigiaro body. Debut summer 1984. January 1986: 'Junior' with 903cm3 engine. October 1986: also with 5 doors. Febuary 1987: SXI with fuel injection. Winter 88/89: modifications to the body and interior.

Seat Ibiza

```
1.2 Litre
46.5kW–62hp–63PS
1 Carb
```

Body, Weight: 3–door Saloon/Sedan, 5–seater; kerbweight (DIN) 875–900kg, gross vehicle weight 1400kg. 5–door Saloon/Sedan, 5–seater; kerbweight (DIN) 905–920kg, gross vehicle weight 1400kg.

Engine data (DIN): 4–cylinder in–line (75 x 67.5mm), 1193cm3; compression ratio 9.5:1; 46kW (62hp) [63PS] at 5800rpm, 38.6kW/L (52.3hp/L) [52.8PS/L]; 86Nm (63.5lbft) at 3500rpm; regular grade.
For some countries: 44kW (59hp) [60PS].

Engine construction: Transverse mounted front engine. Hydraulic tappets, 1 overhead camshaft (toothed belt); light–alloy cylinder head; crankshaft with 5 bearings; oil capacity 4L (3.8US qt); 1 Pierburg 36–1B–3 downdraught carb. Battery 12V 45Ah, alternator 55A; cooling system capacity approx 7.5L (7.1US qt).

Transmission (to front wheels): a) 5–speed manual, final drive ratio 4.294.

Gear ratios: 1st 3.50; 2nd 1.95; 3rd 1.32; 4th 0.97; 5th 0.76; R 3.64.

Chassis: Integral body; front suspension with McPherson struts, lower single control arms and torsion bars, rear independent suspension with A arms, shock absorber struts and self– stabilising transverse leaf springs, telescopic dampers. Servo/power assisted brakes, front discs, rear drums, disc diameter approx 23cm, mechanical handbrake to rear wheels; rack and pinion steering; fuel tank 50L (10.3/11Gal) [12.4/13.2US Gal] including 4.5–7L (1–1.5Gal) [1.2–1.8US Gal] reserve, tyres 155 SR 13, GLX 165/65 SR 14, wheel rims 5J.

Dimensions: Wheelbase 244.5cm, track 142/139cm, turning circle 10.2m; load space 11.3–42.4cu ft (320–1200dm3). Length 364cm, width 161cm, height 139.5cm.

Performance: Max speed 96mph/155kmh (manufacturers test specifications), speed at 1000rpm in 5th gear 20.7mph/33.3kmh; acceleration 0 – 62mph/100kmh 16.0secs; standing km 37.2secs; power to weight ratio 19kg/kW (13.9kg/PS); ECE consumption 4.9/6.6/9.0L/100km (57.6/42.8/31.4mpg) [48/35.6/26.1US mpg].

```
903cm3
32.5kW–43.5hp–44PS
1 Carb
```

Engine for Junior

As 1.2 Litre, except:

Body, Weight: 3–door Saloon/Sedan, 5–seater; kerbweight (DIN) 825–860kg, gross vehicle weight 1315kg. 5–door Saloon/Sedan, 5–seater; kerbweight (DIN) 860–880kg, gross vehicle weight 1315kg.

Engine data (DIN): 4–cylinder in–line (65 x 68mm), 903cm3; compression ratio 9:1; 32kW (43.5hp) [44PS] at 5800rpm, 35.4kW/L (48.1hp/L) [48.7PS/L]; 64Nm (47.2lbft) at 3000rpm; leaded premium grade.
Some countries: 56Nm (41.3lbft).

Engine construction: Side mounted camshaft (chain); crankshaft with 3 bearings; oil capacity 3.6L (3.4US qt); 1 Bressel/Solex downdraught carb. Cooling system capacity 5L (4.7US qt).

Transmisson: 5–speed manual, final drive ratio 4.785.

Chassis: Tyres 145 SR 13, wheel rims 4.5J.

Performance: Max speed 80mph/129kmh (manufacturers test specifications), speed at 1000rpm in 5th gear mph/28.1kmh; acceleration 0-62mph/100kmh 22secs; power to weight ratio from 25.8kg/kW (18.7kg/PS); ECE consumption 5.3/–/8.8L/100km (53.3/–/32.1mpg) [44.4/–/26.7US mpg].

Seat Ibiza

```
1.5 Litre
62.5/66kW–84/88.5hp–85/90PS
Carb/Fuel Injection
```

As 1.2 Litre, except:

Body, Weight: 3–door Saloon/Sedan, 5–seater; kerbweight (DIN) 890–925kg, gross vehicle weight 1450kg. 5–door Saloon/Sedan, 5–seater; kerbweight (DIN) 925–945kg, gross vehicle weight 1450kg.

Engine data (DIN): 4–cylinder in–line (83 x 67.5mm), 1461cm3; compresson ratio 10.5:1; 63kW (84hp) [85PS] at 5600rpm, 43.1kW/L (57.7hp/L) [58.2PS/L]; 116Nm (85.6lbft) at 3500rpm.
With Catalyst (Bosch LU-Jetronic fuel injection): Compression ratio 10.2:1; 66kW (88.5hp) [90PS] at 6000rpm, 45.3kW/L (60.7hp/L) [61.6PS/L]; 119Nm (87.8lbft) at 5000rpm.

Engine construction: 1 Weber 22 DSTA 100 or 32 DSTA 150 downdraught carb.

Transmisson: 5–speed manual, final drive ratio 3.737 or (Catalyst) 4.29.

Chassis: Tyres 155 SR 13 or 165/65 SR 14, wheel rims 5/5.5J.

Seat

Performance: Max speed 109mph/175kmh (manufacturers test specifications), speed at 1000rpm in 5th gear mph/36.8kmh; acceleration 0 – 62mph/100kmh 13secs, Catalyst 12.5secs; power to weight ratio 14.1kg/kW (10.5kg/PS); ECE consumption 4.9/6.5/9.1L/100km (mpg) [US mpg].

Seat Ibiza

```
1.5 Litre
74/66kW–99/88.5hp–100/90PS
Fuel Injection
```

Engine for SXI

As 1.2 Litre, except:

Body, Weight: 3–door Saloon/Sedan, 5–seater; kerbweight (DIN) 925kg, gross vehicle weight 1450kg. 5–door Saloon/Sedan, 5–seater; kerbweight (DIN) 945kg, gross vehicle weight 1450kg.

Engine data (DIN): 4–cylinder in–line (83 x 67.5mm), 1461cm3; compression ratio 11:1; 74kW (99hp) [100PS] at 5900rpm, 50.7kW/L (67.9hp/L) [69.9PS/L]; 128Nm (94.4lbft) at 4700rpm.
With Catalyst: Compression ratio 10.2:1, 66kW (88.5hp) [90PS] at 6000rpm, 45.3kW/L (60.7hp/L) [61.6PS/L]; 119Nm (87.8lbft) at 5000rpm; unleaded premium grade.

Engine construction: Bosch LE2–Jetronic electronic fuel injection, with Catalyst LU-Jetronic.

Transmission: 5–speed manual, final drive ratio 4.294.

Chassis: Front antiroll bar; tyres 185/60 HR 14, wheel rims 5.5J.

Performance: Max speed 115mph/185kmh, with Catalyst 109mph/175kmh (manufacturers test specifications), speed at 1000rpm in 5th gear 19.8mph/31.9kmh; acceleration 0 - 62mph/100kmh 10.8secs; power to weight ratio 12.5kg/kW (9.2kg/PS); ECE consumption 5.1/6.9/8.9L/100km (55.4/40.9/31.7mpg) [46.1/34.1/26.4US mpg].

Seat Ibiza

```
1714cm3 Diesel
40.5kW–53hp–55PS
Injection Pump
```

As 1.2 Litre, except:

Body, Weight: 3–door Saloon/Sedan, 5–seater; kerbweight (DIN) 950kg, gross vehicle weight 1450kg. 5–door Saloon/Sedan, 5–seater; kerbweight (DIN) 970kg, gross vehicle weight 1450kg.

Engine data (DIN): 4–cylinder in–line (83 x 79.2mm), 1714cm3; compression ratio 20:1; 40kW (54hp) [55PS] at 4500rpm, 23.3kW/L (31.6hp/L) [32.1PS/L]; 98Nm (72.3lbft) at 2300rpm.
Some countries: 92Nm (67.9lbft) at 3000rpm.

Engine construction: Designated 138A 5.000. Diesel engine; mechanical tappets; 1 overhead camshaft (toothed belt); Bosch diesel injection pump. Battery 12V 60Ah, alternator 55A; cooling system capacity 8L (7.6US qt).

Transmission: 5–speed manual, final drive ratio 4.294.

Performance: Max speed 93mph/148kmh (manufacturers test specifications), speed at 1000rpm in 5th gear 20.7mph/33.3kmh; acceleration 0 – 62mph/100kmh 20.2secs; power to weight ratio 23.7kg/kW (17.3kg/PS); ECE consumption 4.9/6.9/8.4L/100km (57.6/40.9/33.6mpg) [48/34.1/28 US mpg].

Seat Malaga

Notchback Saloon/Sedan based on the Ronda with 1.2 and 1.5 Litre engines developed by Porsche as well as diesel engines by Fiat. Debut Barcelona Motor Show May 1985. For 1988 injection with 99hp.

```
1.2 Litre
46.5kW–62hp–63PS
1 Carb
```

Body, Weight: 4–door Saloon/Sedan, 5–seater; kerbweight (DIN) 910–975kg, gross vehicle weight 1450kg.

Engine data (DIN): 4–cylinder in–line (75 x 67.5mm), 1193cm3; compression ratio 9.5:1; 46.5kW (62.5hp) [63PS] at 5800rpm, 39.0kW/L (52.3hp/L) [52.8PS/L]; 88Nm (64.9lbft) at 3500rpm; leaded regular grade.
For some countries: 44kW (59hp) [60PS].

Engine construction: Transverse mounted front engine. Hydraulic tappets, 1 overhead camshaft (toothed belt); light–alloy cylinder head; crankshaft with 5 bearings, oil capacity 4L (3.8US qt), 1 Pierburg 36–1B–3 downdraught carb. Battery 12V 45Ah, alternator 55A; cooling system capacity approx 7L (6.6US qt).

Transmission (to front wheels): a) 4–speed manual, final drive ratio 4.294. b) 5–speed manual, final drive ratio 4.294.

Gear ratios: a) 4–speed manual: 1st 3.50; 2nd 1.95; 3rd 1.32; 4th 0.97.
b) 5–speed manual: 1st 3.50; 2nd 1.95; 3rd 1.32; 4th 0.97; 5th 0.76.

Chassis: Integral body; front independent suspension with McPherson struts, lower single control arms and torsion bars, antiroll bar, rear independent suspension with A arms, shock absorber struts and self–stabilising transverse leaf springs, telescopic dampers. Servo/power assisted brakes, front discs, rear drums, disc diameter 22.7cm; mechanical handbrake to rear wheels; rack and pinion steering; fuel tank 47/50L (10.3/11Gal) [12.4/13.2US Gal] including 4.5–7L (1–1.5Gal) [1.2–1.8US Gal] reserve, tyres 155 SR 13, optional 165/65 SR 13, wheel rims 5J.

Dimensions: Wheelbase 244.3cm, track 142/139cm, clearance 14.5cm, turning circle 10.3m. Load space 18.2cu ft (515dm3). Length 427.5cm, width 165cm, height 140cm.

Performance: Max speed 93mph/150kmh (manufacturers test specifications), speed in 5th gear at 1000rpm 20.7mph/33.3kmh, acceleration 0 – 62mph/100kmh 17.0secs; power to weight ratio 19.6kg/kW (14.4kg/PS); ECE consumption 5.0/7.0/9.3L/100km (56.5/40.4/30.4mpg) [47/33.6/25.3US mpg].

```
1.5 Litre
63kW-84hp-85PS
12V Carb
```

As 1.2 Litre, except:

Weight: Kerbweight (DIN) 975kg, gross vehicle weight 1450kg.

Engine data (DIN): 4–cylinder in–line (83 x 67.5mm), 1461cm3; compression ratio 10.5:1; 63kW (84hp) [85PS] at 5600rpm, 43.1kW/L (57.7hp/L) [58.6PS/L]; 116Nm (85.6lbft) at 3500rpm. Premium grade.

Engine construction: 1 Weber 22 DSTA 100 or 32 DSTA 150 downdraught 2V carb.

Transmission: 5–speed manual, final drive ratio 3.737.

Gear ratios: 1st 3.50; 2nd 1.95; 3rd 1.32; 4th 0.97; 5th 0.76; R 3.64.

Chassis: Tyres 155 SR 13 or 165/65 SR 14, wheel rims 5/5.5J.

Performance: Max speed 102mph/165kmh (manufacturers test specifications), speed at 1000rpm in 5th gear 22.9mph/36.8kmh; acceleration 0 – 62mph/100kmh 13secs, Catalyst 12.6secs; standing km 34.7secs; power to weight ratio 15.5kg/kW (11.5kg/PS); ECE consumption 4.9/6.5/9.1L/100km (57.6/43.5/31mpg) [48/36.2/25.8US mpg].

SAAB

LITTLE WONDER OUR CARS
ARE EXCITING TO DRIVE.

A Saab Turbo's sheer power shrinks the mileage and stretches the imagination.

These front-wheel drive cars effortlessly sweep the curves, flatten the hills and calmly move the needle up the speedometer. This renowned performance not only makes driving more pleasurable, it also makes it safer.

The 16-valve turbocharged engine with APC engine management, intercooler and Saab Direct Ignition system* develops an impressive 273 Nm torque. This enables you to surge past traffic and accelerate out of trouble without having to shift down.

According to a test conducted by Germany's *Auto, Motor und Sport*, Saab's engine provides the best 5th-gear 60–120 km/h performance in its class.

*Our unique Saab Direct Ignition system is fitted on the Saab 9000 CD and Saab 9000 Turbo 16 on some markets.

A Saab Turbo is distinguished as much for its handling characteristics as for its sheer power.

And for its driving comfort systems. All instruments and controls are in your natural field of vision and reach: it's the type of ergonomics we built into our supersonic aircraft.

The firm chassis and large, well-appointed interior makes a Saab Turbo as pleasurable to travel in as it is to drive.

Our long distance cruisers combine power, panache and practicality. With the type of individuality and man-machine interaction that fires the imagination. And makes driving exciting.

Excitement that you can sample for yourself by test driving the Saab Turbo of your choice at your nearest Saab dealership.

SAAB SCANIA **SAAB**

Seat • Shiguli/Lada

Seat Malaga

1.5 Litre
74/66kW–99/88.5hp–100/90PS
Fuel injection

As 1.2 Litre, except:

Weight: Kerbweight (DIN) 975kg, gross vehicle weight 1450kg.

Engine data (DIN): 4–cylinder in–line (83 x 67.5mm), 1461cm3; compression ratio 11:1; 74kW (99hp) [100PS] at 5900rpm, 50.7kW/L (67.9hp/L) [68.9PS/L]; 128Nm (94.4lbft) at 4700rpm.
With Catalyst: Compression ratio 10.2:1; 66kW (88.5hp) [90PS] at 6000rpm, 45.3kW/L (60.7hp/L) [61.6PS/L]; 119Nm (87.8lbft) at 5000rpm; unleaded regular grade.

Engine construction: Bosch LE2–Jetronic electronic fuel injection, Catalyst LU-Jetronic

Transmission: 5–speed manual, final drive ratio 4.29 or 3.737.

Gear ratios: 1st 3.50; 2nd 1.95; 3rd 1.32; 4th 0.97; 5th 0.76; R 3.64.

Chassis: Tyres 185/60 SR 14, 165/65 SR 14 or 155 SR 13, wheel rims 5.5J.

Performance: Max speed 108mph/174kmh, Catalyst 102mph/165kmh (manufacturers test specifications), speed at 1000rpm in 5th gear 20.2–22.9mph/32.5–36.8kmh; acceleration 0 – 62mph/100kmh 11.6secs, Catalyst 12.6secs; standing km 32.2secs; power to weight ratio 13.2kg/kW (9.8kg/PS); ECE consumption 5.3/7.0/8.9L/100km (53.3/40.4/31.7mpg) [44.4/33.6/26.4US mpg].

Seat Malaga Diesel

1714cm3
Diesel 40.5kW–54hp–55PS
Injection pump

As 1.2 Litre, except:

Weight: Kerbweight (DIN) 975–1015kg, gross vehicle weight 1450kg.

Engine data (DIN): 4–cylinder in–line (83 x 79.2mm), 1714cm3; compression ratio 20:1; 40kW (54hp) [55PS] at 4500rpm, 23.3kW/L (31.2hp/L) [32.1PS/L]; 98Nm (72.3lbft) at 3000rpm.

Engine construction: Designated 138A 5.000. Diesel engine; mechanical tappets; 1 overhead camshaft (toothed belt); Bosch diesel injection pump. Battery 12V 66Ah, alternator 55A; cooling system capacity 8.9L (8.4US qt).

Transmission: 5–speed manual, final drive ratio 4.294.

Gear ratios: 1st 3.50; 2nd 1.95; 3rd 1.32; 4th 0.97; 5th 0.76; R 3.64.

Chassis: Tyres 155 SR 13, wheel rims 5J, optional tyres 165/65 SR 14, wheel rims 5.5J.

Performance: Max speed 90mph/145kmh (manufacturers test specifications), speed at 1000rpm in 5th gear 19.9mph/32.0kmh; acceleration 0 – 62mph/100kmh 22.9secs; power to weight ratio 25.4kg/kW (18.4kg/PS); ECE consumption 5.1/6.9/8.4L/100km (55.4/40.9/33.6mpg) [46.1/34.1/28US mpg].

SHIGULI/LADA SU

Shiguli, V/O Autoexport, 14 Volkhonka St., 119902, Moscow, USSR

Car manufacturer in Togliatti aided by Fiat.

Shiguli VAZ 2108 – Lada Samara

Compact Saloon/Sedan with transverse engine, front wheel drive and tail gate. Four–cylinder engines with 54, 64 and 74hp power from 1.1, 1.3 and 1.5 Litre capacities. Debut end 1984, 5–door Saloon/Sedan Autumn/Winter 1987/88.

1.1 Litre
40.5kW–54hp–55PS
1 2V Carb

Body, Weight: 3–door Saloon/Sedan, 5–seater: kerbweight (DIN) 900–925kg, gross vehicle weight 1325–1375kg. 5–door Saloon/Sedan, 5–seater; kerbweight (DIN) 915–940kg, gross vehicle weight 1340–1380kg.

Engine data (DIN): 4–cylinder in–line (76 x 60.6mm), 1100cm3; compression ratio 9.6/9.9:1; 40.5kW (54hp) [55PS] at 5600rpm, 36.8kW/L (49.2hp/L) [50PS/L]; 77Nm (56.8lbft) at 3400rpm; leaded regular grade.
Or 39kW (52hp) [53PS].

Engine construction: Transverse mounted front engine, 1 overhead camshaft (toothed belt); light–alloy cylinder head; crankshaft with 5 bearings; oil capacity 3.5L (3.3US qt); 1 Solex downdraught 2V carb. Battery 12V 45/55Ah, alternator 55A; cooling system capacity 7.8L (7.4US qt).

Transmission (to front wheels): a) 4–speed manual, final drive ratio 4.13 or 4.3. b) 5–speed manual, final drive ratio 4.13 or 4.3.

Gear ratios: a) 4–speed manual: 1st 3.636; 2nd 1.95; 3rd 1.357; 4th 0.941; R 3.53. b) 5–speed manual: 1st 3.636; 2nd 1.95; 3rd 1.357; 4th 0.941; 5th 0.784; R 3.53.

Chassis: Integral body; front independent suspension with McPherson struts, lower control arms and antiroll bar, rear compound steering axle (longitudinal arms with cross linkage), coil springs, telescopic dampers. Servo/power assisted brakes, front discs, rear drums, disc diameter approximately 23.9cm, mechanical handbrake to rear wheels; rack and pinion steering; fuel tank 43L (9.5Gal) [11.4US Gal]; tyres 155 SR 13, 165 SR 13, 165/70 SR 13 or 175/70 SR 13, wheel rims 4.5 or 5J.

Dimensions: Wheelbase 246cm, track 139/138cm or 140/137cm, clearance 16/12cm, turning circle 10/11m. Load 11.7/23/42.4cu ft (330/650/1200dm3). Length 400.5cm, width 162/165cm, height 140cm.

Performance: Max speed 87mph/140kmh (manufacturers test specifications), speed at 1000rpm in 4th gear (4.13:1) 15.9mph/25.6kmh; acceleration 0 – 62mph/100kmh 17–20secs; power to weight ratio from 22.2kg/kW (16.4kg/PS); ECE consumption 5.7/7.9/8.2L/100km (49.6/35.8/34.4mpg) [41.3/29.8/28.7US mpg].

Shiguli/Lada Samara

1.3 Litre
48kW–64hp–65PS
1 2V Carb

As 1.1 Litre, except:

Engine data (DIN): 4–cylinder in–line (76 x 71mm), 1288cm3; compression ratio 9.6/9.9:1; 48kW (64hp) [65PS] at 5600rpm, 37.2kW/L (49.8hp/L) [50.4PS/L]; 94Nm (69.3lbft) at 3600rpm.
With closed–loop Catalyst: 46kW (62hp) [63PS] at 5800rpm; 93Nm (68.6lbft) at 3500rpm.

Shiguli/Lada

Transmission: a) 4–speed manual, final drive ratio 4.13, 3.94 or 3.7.
b) 5–speed manual, final drive ratio 4.13, 3.94, 3.7.

Performance: Max speed 90–95mph/145–152kmh (manufacturers test specifications), speed at 1000rpm in 5th gear (4.13:1); 20.3mph/32.7kmh; acceleration 0 – 62mph/100kmh 14.5–16secs; power to weight ratio from 18.8kg/kW (13.8kg/PS); ECE consumption 6.0/8.1/7.9L/100km (47.1/34.9/35.8mpg) [39.2/29/29.8US mpg], 5– speed 5.4/8.0/7.9L/100km (52.3/35.3/35.8mpg) [43.6/29.4/29.8US mpg].

Shiguli/Lada Samara

```
1.5 Litre
55kW–74hp–75PS
1 2V Carb
```

As 1.1 Litre, except:

Engine data (DIN): 4–cylinder in–line (82 x 71mm), 1500cm3; compression ratio 9.6/9.9:1; 55kW (74hp) [75PS] at 5600rpm, 36.8kW/L (49.3hp/L) [50PS/L]; 106Nm (78.2lbft) at 3200rpm.
With closed–loop Catalyst: 54kW (72hp) [73PS].

Transmission: a) 4–speed manual, final drive ratio 3.94 or 3.7.
b) 5–speed manual, final drive ratio 3.94 or 3.7.

Performance: Max speed over 114mph/155kmh (manufacturers test specifications), speed at 1000rpm in 5th gear (3.94:1) 21.4mph/34.4kmh; acceleration 0 – 62mph/100kmh 13.5–15secs; power to weight ratio from 16.4kg/kW (12.0kg/PS); ECE consumption 6.1/8.1/8.7L/100km (46.3/34.9/32.5mpg) [38.6/29/27US mpg], 5– speed 5.7/7.7/8.7L/100km (49.6/36.7/32.5mpg) [41.3/30.5/27US mpg].

Shiguli – Lada

Based on Fiat 124 Saloon/Sedan with 1.2 Litre OHC 4–cylinder engine. Summer 1972: also available as Estate/Station Wagon (VAZ–2102). Export designation: Lada. 2105 and 2107 models with modernised body and interior. 1986: some models also available with 5–speed manual or automatic from GM.

```
1198cm3
45.5/44/47kW–61/59/63hp–62/60/64PS
1 2V Carb
```

Body, Weight: 4–door Saloon/Sedan, 5–seater; kerbweight (DIN) from 955kg, gross vehicle weight 1395/1460kg. 5–door Estate/Station Wagon, 5–seater; kerbweight (DIN) 980– 1010kg, gross vehicle weight 1440/1460kg.

Engine data (DIN): 4–cylinder in–line (76 x 66mm), 1198cm3; compression ratio 8.5:1; 45.5kW (61hp) [62PS] at 5600rpm, 38.0kW/L (50.9hp/L) [51.8PS/L]; 87Nm (64.2lbft) at 3400rpm; leaded premium grade.
For some countries: 44kW (59hp) [60PS], 47kW (63hp) [64PS] or 49kW (66hp) [67PS].

Engine construction: 1 overhead camshaft (chain/toothed belt); light–alloy cylinder head; crankshaft with 5 bearings; oil capacity 3.75L (3.6US qt); 1 Weber 32 DCR downdraught compound carb. Battery 12V 55Ah, alternator 42/45/47A; cooling system capacity 10L (9.5US qt).

Transmission (to rear wheels): 4–speed manual, floor shift; final drive ratio 4.1, 4.3 or 4.44.

Gear ratios: 1st 3.75; 2nd 2.3; 3rd 1.49; 4th 1; R 3.87.
Or 1st 3.667; 2nd 2.1; 3rd 1.361; 4th 1; R 3.526.

Chassis: Integral body; front trapeze A arms and coil springs, rear rigid axle with coil springs, longitudinal push and reactor struts, Panhard rods, front and rear antiroll bar, telescopic dampers. Brakes, optional with servo/power assistance, front discs, rear drums, disc diameter 25.3cm, mechanical handbrake to rear wheels; worm and wheel steering; fuel tank 39L (8.6Gal) [10.3US Gal], Estate/Station Wagon 45L (9.9Gal) [11.9US Gal]; tyres 6.15–13, 155 SR 13, 165 SR 13 or 175/70 SR 13 on 4.5, 5 or 5.5J wheel rims, Estate/Station Wagon 6.45–13 or 165 SR 13.

Dimensions: Wheelbase 242.5cm, track 135/130.5 and 136.5/132cm, clearance 17cm, turning circle 11.4m. Load space 13.6–14.8cu ft (385–420dm3), Estate/Station Wagon 22.2–20.1cu ft (630 + 570dm3), length 404.5–414.5cm, Estate/Station Wagon 406–412cm, width 161/162cm, height 144cm, Estate/Station Wagon 146cm.

Performance: Max speed 84–89mph/135–142kmh (manufacturers test specifications), speed at 1000rpm in 4th gear 16mph/25.7kmh; acceleration 0 – 62mph/100kmh 18.9–20secs; power to weight ratio from 21kg/kW (15.4kg/PS); ECE consumption 6.9/9.4/9.2L/100km (40.9/30.1/30.7mpg) [34.1/25/25.6US mpg], Estate/Station Wagon 8.0/10.8/10.8L/100km (35.3/26.2/26.2mpg) [29.4/21.8/21.8US mpg].

Shiguli/Lada 1200

```
1294cm3
51.5/48/50kW–69/64/67hp–70/65/68PS
1 2V Carb
```

As 1198cm3, except:

Engine data (DIN): (79 x 66mm), 1294cm3; compression ratio 8.5:1; 51.5kW (69hp) [70PS] at 5600rpm, 39.8kW/L (53.3hp/L) [54.1PS/L]; 94Nm (69.3lbft) at 3400rpm.
Some countries: 48kW (64hp) [65PS], 50kW (67hp) [68PS] or 53kW (71hp) [72PS].

Transmission: a) 4–speed manual, final drive ratio 4.1; 4.3.
b) 5–speed manual, final drive ratio 4.1; 4.3.
c) Automatic THM 125, hydraulic torque converter and 3–speed Planetary gear set; central selector lever with P–R–N–D–2–1 positions; final drive ratio 4.1; 4.3.

Gear ratios: a) 4–speed manual: 1st 3.667; 2nd 2.1; 3rd 1.361; 4th 1; R 3.526.
b) 5–speed manual: 1st 3.667; 2nd 2.1; 3rd 1.361; 4th 1; 5th 0.82; R 3.667.
c) Automatic: Max torque multiplication in converter 2.4 times, Planetary gear set ratios: 2.84; 1.6; 1; R 2.07.

Performance: Max speed 90–95mph/145–153kmh (manufacturers test specifications); acceleration 0 – 62mph/100kmh 15.9–17.9secs (manufacturers test specifications); power to weight ratio from 19.3kg/kW (14.2kg/PS); ECE consumption 7.1/9.5/9.5L/100km (39.8/29.7/29.7mpg) [33.1/24.8/24.8US mpg].

```
1452cm3
56.5/55kW–76/74hp–77/75PS
1 2V Carb
```

As 1198cm3, except:

Body, Weight: 4–door Saloon/Sedan, 5–seater; kerbweight (DIN) 995–1060kg, gross vehicle weight 1345/1460kg. 5–door Estate/Station Wagon, 5–seater; kerbweight (DIN) 1055kg, gross vehicle weight 1510kg.

Engine data (DIN): (76 x 80mm), 1452cm3; compression ratio 8.5:1; 56.5kW (76hp) [77PS] at 5600rpm, 38.9kW/L (52.1hp/L) [53PS/L]; 106Nm (78.2lbft) at 3500rpm.
Some countries: 55kW (74hp) [75PS] or 52kW (70hp) [71PS].

Transmission: a) 4–speed manual, final drive ratio 4.1; 4.3.
b) 5–speed manual, final drive ratio 4.1; 3.9; 4.3.

Gear ratios: a) 4–speed manual: 1st 3.667; 2nd 2.1; 3rd 1.361; 4th 1; R 3.526.
b) 5–speed manual: 1st 3.667; 2nd 2.1; 3rd 1.361; 4th 1; 5th 0.82; R 3.667.

Chassis: Servo/power assisted brakes.

Performance: Max speed 91–96mph/147–155kmh (manufacturers test specifications), speed at 1000rpm in 4th gear 15.5mph/25kmh; acceleration 0 – 62mph/100kmh (manufacturers test specifications) 15–18secs; power to weight ratio 17.6kg/kW (12.9kg/PS); consumption (ECE) 7.3/9.6/9.8L/100km (38.7/29.4/28.8mpg) [32.2/24.5/24US mpg], 5–speed 7.0/9.6/9.2L/100km (40.4/29.4/30.7mpg) [33.6/24.5/25.6US mpg].

Shiguli/Lada • Sipani

Shiguli/Lada 2104/Nova

```
1569cm3
57.5kW–77hp–78PS
1 2V Carb
```

As 1198cm3, except:

Body, Weight: 4–door Saloon/Sedan, 5–seater; kerbweight (DIN) 1015–1045kg, gross vehicle weight 1445kg.

Engine data (DIN): (79 x 80mm), 1569cm3; compression ratio 8.5:1; 57.5kW (77hp) [78PS] at 5400rpm, 36.6kW/L (49hp/L) [49.2PS/L]; 123Nm (90.7lbft) at 3400rpm; leaded regular grade.
Some countries: 59kW (79hp) [80PS] or 62kW (84hp) [85PS].

Transmission: a) 4–speed manual, final drive ratio 4.1.
b) 5–speed manual, final drive ratio 4.1.

Gear ratios: a) 4–speed manual: 1st 3.667; 2nd 2.1; 3rd 1.361; 4th 1; R 3.526.
Or: 1st 3.24; 2nd 1.98; 3rd 1.28; 4th 1; R 3.94.
b) 5–speed manual: 1st 3.667; 2nd 2.1; 3rd 1.361; 4th 1; V 0.82; R 3.667.

Chassis: Servo/power assisted brakes

Performance: Max speed 96–98mph/154–157kmh (manufacturers test specifications), speed at 1000rpm in 4th gear 15.5mph/25kmh; acceleration 0–62mph/100kmh (manufacturers test specifications) 14secs; power to weight ratio 17.7kg/kW (13.0kg/PS); ECE consumption 7.4/9.9/9.7L/100km (38.2/28.5/29.1mpg) [31.8/23.8/24.2US mpg].

Shiguli/Lada 2107

Shiguli VAZ–2121 – Lada Niva

Off–road–going vehicle with four wheel drive, 1.6 Litre 4– cylinder engine. Debut Winter 1976. Autumn 1985: 5–speed manual.

```
1.6 Litre
59/56/57.5kW–79/75/77hp–80/76/78PS
1 2V Carb
```

Body, Weight: 3–door Estate/Station Wagon – Convertible, 4/5– seater; kerbweight (DIN) 1150/1185kg, gross vehicle weight 1550/1590kg.

Engine data (DIN): 4–cylinder in–line (79 x 80mm), 1569cm3; compression ratio 8.5:1; 59kW (79hp) [80PS] at 5400rpm, 37.6kW/L (50.4hp/L) [51PS/L]; 122Nm (90lbft) at 3200rpm; leaded regular grade.
Or: 56/57.5kW (75/77hp) [76/78PS] at 5400rpm; 118Nm (87lbft) at 3400rpm.
Or: 54kW (72hp) [73PS] to 62kW (84hp) [85PS].

Engine construction: 1 overhead camshaft (chain); light–alloy cylinder head; crankshaft with 5 bearings; oil capacity 3.75L (3.6US qt); 1 Weber 32 DCR downdraught carb. Battery 12V 56Ah, alternator 42/45A; cooling system capacity 10.7L (10.1US qt).

Transmission (to all wheels): 4 or 5–speed manual, 2–speed reduction gears; final drive ratio 4.1 or 4.3.

Gear ratios: 1st 3.667; 2nd 2.10; 3rd 1.36; 4th 1; 5th 0.82; R 3.526/3.34; reduction gears: 1st 1.2; 2nd 2.135.

Chassis: Integral body; front trapeze A arms, coil springs, rear rigid axle, coil springs, longitudinal compression struts, Panhard rods, front antiroll bar; telescopic dampers. Servo/power assisted brakes, front discs, rear drums, disc diameter 27.3cm, mechanical handbrake to rear wheels; worm and wheel steering; optional power assisted; fuel tank 45L (9.9Gal) [11.9US Gal]; tyres 6.95–16/175 SR 16, 185 SR 16, 195 SR 16, 205/75 R 14 or 220/70 R 15, wheel rims 5/5.5J.

Dimensions: Wheelbase 220cm, track 143/140cm, clearance 22cm, turning circle 11.6m. Load space 10.6/40.6cu ft (300/1150dm3). Length 372cm, width 168cm, height 164cm.

Performance: Max speed 81–83mph/130–134kmh (manufacturers test specifications), speed at 1000rpm in 4th gear 16.1mph/25.9kmh; acceleration 0–62mph/100kmh 23secs; power to weight ratio 19.5kg/kW (14.4kg/PS); ECE consumption 9.8/14.7/11.6L/100km (28.8/19.2/24.4mpg) [24/16/20.3US mpg], 5–speed 9.2/14.0/11.6L/100km (30.7/20.2/24.4mpg) [25.6/16.8/20.3US mpg].

Shiguli/Lada Niva

SIPANI   IND

Sipani Automobiles Ltd, 25/26 Industrial Suburb, 2nd Stage, Tumkur Road, Bangalore 560 022, India

Indian car manufacturer producing the original Reliant Kitten as the Dolphin.

Sipani Dolphin/Montana

Saloon/Sedan or Estate/Station Wagon with synthetic body, 850cm3 engine, 4–speed manual transmission. Successor to the original Reliant Kitten from Great Britain. Montana with new front and as a four–door Saloon/Sedan.

```
848cm3
28.5kW–38hp–39PS
1 Carb
```

Body, Weight: 2–door Saloon/Sedan, 4–seater; kerbweight (DIN) 505kg; gross vehicle weight 835kg. 3–door Estate/Station Wagon, 4–seater; kerbweight (DIN) 525kg; gross vehicle weight 840kg.

Engine data (DIN): 4–cylinder in–line (62.5 x 69.1mm), 848cm3; compression ratio 8.5:1; 28.5kW (38hp) [39PS] at 5500rpm, 33.8kW/L (45.3hp/L) [46.0PS/L]; 63Nm (46.5lbft) at 3500rpm; leaded regular grade.

Engine construction: Side–mounted camshaft (chain); light–alloy cylinder head and block, wet cylinder liners; crankshaft with 3 bearings; oil capacity 3.1L (2.9US qt); 1 SU HS2 downdraught carb. Battery 12V 35Ah, alternator 35A; cooling system capacity 3.7L (3.5US qt).

Transmission (to rear wheels): 4–speed manual, final drive ratio 3.23.

Gear ratios: 1st 3.88; 2nd 2.046; 3rd 1.32; 4th 1; R 3.25.

Chassis: Steel frame; front A arms, coil springs and telescopic dampers, antiroll bar, rear rigid axle with semi–elliptical springs, telescopic dampers. Dual circuit disc brakes, mechanical handbrake to rear wheels; rack and pinion steering; fuel tank 27.5L (6Gal) [7.3US Gal]; tyres 145 SR 10 or 5.20–10, wheel rims 350B x 10.

Dimensions: Wheelbase 214.5cm, track 124.5/124.5, minimum clearance 12.5cm, turning circle 7.3m. Load space 8.5–30cu ft (240–850dm3), Estate/Station Wagon 9.5–40cu ft (270–1130dm3). Length 333/344cm, Estate/Station Wagon 335/348cm, width 142cm, height 139.5cm.

Performance: Max speed 67mph/108kmh (manufacturers test specifications), speed at 1000rpm in 4th gear 15.5mph/25.0kmh; acceleration 0 – 50mph/80kmh 11.8secs (manufacturers test specifications); power to weight ratio 17.6kg/kW (12.9kg/PS); consumption (touring) 4.8L/100km (58.8mpg) [49US mpg], (manufacturers test specifications).

Sipani Dolphin

SKODA   CS

AZNP (Skoda), Trida Rude armady 294, PSC 293 60 Mlada Boleslav, Czechoslovakia

MODEL RANGE
120 - Coupe Rapid - Favorit

Skoda 120 – Coupe Rapid 136

105 L – 105 S – 120 L – 120 LS – 120 GLS – 130 L – Coupe Rapid 130
Saloon/Sedan with, 1174 and 1289cm3 rear mounted engine. Launched in Autumn 1976. September 1981; new Coupe models based on the Saloon/Sedan 105/120.

```
1174cm3
38kw–51hp–52PS
1 2V Carb
```

Engine for 120 L

Weight: 4-door Saloon/Sedan, 5-seater; kerbweight (DIN) 875kg, gross vehicle weight 1275kg.

Engine data (DIN): 4-cylinder in-line (72 x 72mm), 1174cm3; 38kW (51.5hp) [52PS] at 5000rpm, 32.4kW/L (45hp/L) [44.3PS/L]; 85Nm (62.7lbft) at 3000rpm. Regular unleaded grade.

Engine construction: Rear engine inclined 30deg to the right. Side camshaft (chain); cast iron cylinder head and light-alloy cylinder block, wet cylinder liners; 3 main bearing crankshaft; oil capacity 4L (3.8US qt); 1 Jikov 32 SEDR downdraught twin carb. Battery 12V 40Ah, Alternator 55A; cooling system, front cooler capacity 11.5L (10.9US qt).

Transmission (to rear wheels): a) 4-speed manual (without direct gear), final drive ratio 4.222.
b) 5-speed manual, final drive ratio 4.222.

Gear ratios: a) 4–speed manual; 1st 3.8; 2nd 2.12; 3rd 1.41; 4th 0.96; R 3.27.
b) 5–speed manual: 1st 3.8; 2nd 2.12; 3rd 1.41; 4th 1.08; 5th 0.83; R 3.27.

Chassis: Integral body; front swinging arm and coil springs, rear independent suspension with swinging axle, longitudinal compression strut, semi trailing arms, front antiroll bar, telescopic dampers. Servo/power assisted brakes, front discs, rear drums, disc diameter 25.2cm; mechanical handbrakes to rear wheels; rack and pinion steering; fuel tank capacity 37L (8.1Gal) [9.8US Gal], with 4L (0.9Gal) [1US Gal] reserve; tyres 165 SR 13, wheel rims 4.5 J.

Dimensions: Wheelbase 240cm, track 139/135cm, clearance 12cm, turning circle 11m. Load space 9.9 + 4.2cu ft (280 + 120dm3). Length 420cm, width 161cm, height 140cm.

Performance: Max speed 87mph/140kmh (manufacturers test specification); acceleration 0 – 62mph/100kmh 19secs; power to weight ratio 23kg/kW (16.8kg/PS); consumption ECE 6.3/–/8.7L/100km (44.8/–/32.5mpg) [37.3/–27US mpg], 5–speed manual 6.0/–/8.7L/100km (47.1/–/32.5mpg) [39.2/–/27 US mpg].

Skoda 120 L

```
1289cm3
46kW–61.5hp–62PS
1 2V Carb
```

Engine for Coupe Rapid 136

As 120, except:

Body, Weight: 2-door Coupe, 4-seater; kerbweight (DIN) 890kg, gross vehicle weight 1240kg.

Engine data (DIN): 4-cylinder in-line (75.5 x 72mm), 1289cm3; compression ratio 9.7:1; 46kW (61.5hp) [62PS] at 5000rpm, 35.7kW/L (47.8hp/L) [48.1PS/L]; 100Nm (73.8lbft) at 3000rpm; leaded regular grade.

Engine construction: Light-alloy cylinder head. Oil capacity 4L (3.8US qt).

Transmission: 5-speed manual, final drive ratio 3.9.

Gear ratios: 1st 3.8; 2nd 2.12; 3rd 1.41; 4th 1.08; 5th 0.83; R 3.27.

Chassis: Rear semi-trailing arm, disc brakes diameter 24.7cm.

Dimensions: Height 138cm.

Performance: Max speed 93mph/153kmh (manufacturer's test specification); speed at 1000rpm in 5th gear 20.7mph/33.4kmh; acceleration 0–62mph/100kmh 14secs, power to weight ratio from 19.3kg/kW (15.3kg/PS); consumption ECE 5.7/7.9/8.7L/100km (49.6/35.8/32.5mpg) [41.3/29.8/27.0US mpg].

Skoda Coupe Rapid 136

Skoda Favorit 1.3

New model. Front mounted 1.3 Litre engine and front wheel drive, rear torsion crank axle. Body from Bertone. First shown September 1987, production commenced Summer 1988.

```
1289cm3
46/43kW–61/57hp–62/58PS
1 2V Carb
```

Body, Weight: Saloon/Sedan 5–door, 5–seater; kerbweight (DIN) 840kg, gross vehicle weight 1290kg.

Skoda • Standard • Stutz • Subaru

Skoda Favorit 1.3

Engine data (DIN): 4–cylinder in–line (75.5 x 72mm), 1289cm3;
a) Engine for 136L: Compression ratio 9.7:1; 46kW (61hp) [62PS] at 5000rpm, 35.7kW/L (47.8hp/L) [48.1PS/L]; 100Nm (73.6lbft) at 3000rpm; leaded premium grade.
b) Engine for 135L: Compression ratio 8.8:1; 43kW (57hp) [58PS] at 5000rpm, 33.4kW/L (44.8hp/L) [45PS/L]; 94Nm (69.4lbft) at 3000rpm; regular unleaded. With Catalyst: 41kW (55hp) [56PS].

Engine construction: Front engine inclined 20deg towards right, side camshaft (chain); cast iron and light–alloy cylinder head and block, wet cylinder liners; 3 bearing crankshaft; oil capacity 4L (3.8US qt); 1 Pierburg downdraught 2V carb 2E3. Battery 12V 40Ah, alternator 55A; cooling system capacity approx 6L (5.7US qt).

Transmission (to front wheels): 5–speed manual, final drive ratio 3.895 (74/17).

Gear ratios: 1st 3.308; 2nd 1.913; 3rd 1.267; 4th 0.927; 5th 0.717; R 2.923.

Chassis: Integral body; front McPherson struts with A arm, rear torsion crank axle (trailing arm, suspension tube) and coil springs, telescopic damper. Servo/power assisted brakes, front discs, diameter 23.6cm, rear drums, mechanical handbrake to rear wheels; rack and pinion steering; fuel tank 47L (10.3Gal) [12.4US Gal], 5L (1.1Gal) [1.3US Gal] reserve; tyres 165/70 SR 13, wheel rims 4.5J.

Dimensions: Wheelbase 245cm, track 140/136.5cm, clearance 12cm, turning circle 11.3m, load space 8.8–19.4cu ft (240-550dm3), length 381.5cm, width 162cm, height 141.5cm.

Performance: Max speed 93mph/150kmh (manufacturers test specification) speed at 1000rpm in 5th gear 23mph/37.2kmh; acceleration 0 – 62mph/100kmh 14secs; power to weight ratio 18.3kg/kW (13.5kg/PS); consumption ECE 5.2/7.0/7.6L/100km (54.3/40.4/37.2mpg) [45.2/33.6/30.9US mpg].
135L: Acceleration 0-62mph/100kmh 15secs; consumption ECE 5.5/7.3/7.9L/100km (51.4/38.7/35.8mpg) [42.8/32.2/29.8US mpg].

Skoda Favorit 1.3

STANDARD — IND

Standard Motor Products of India Ltd., 134 Anna Road, Madras 600 002, India.

Standard 2000

Indian Company, working under licence producing the early Rover 2000.

2.1 Litre
61kW–82hp–83PS
1 Carb

Body, Weight: 5-door Saloon/Sedan, 5-seater; kerbweight (DIN) 1335kg, gross vehicle weight 1785kg.

Engine data (DIN): 4-cylinder in-line (81 x 100mm), 2061cm3; Compression ratio 8:1; 61kW (82hp) [83PS] at 4250rpm, 29.6kW/L (39.7hp/L) [40.3PS/L]; 147Nm (108.5lbft) at 2500rpm; regular grade

Engine construction: Side camshaft (chain); 3 main bearing crankshaft; oil capacity 4.25L (4US qt); 1 downdraught carb. Battery 12V 60 Ah, Dynamo 500W; cooling system capacity (without heating) 8L (7.6US qt).

Transmission (to rear wheels): 4-speed manual, final drive ratio 3.9.

Gear ratios: 1st 3.807; 2nd 2.253; 3rd 1.506; 4th 1; R 3.807.

Chassis: Integral body; front McPherson struts with coil springs and co axial telescopic dampers, lower control arm and antiroll bar, rear rigid axle with semi trailing arm, coil springs, Watt linkage, level control system, telescopic dampers. Servo/power assisted brakes, front diameter 25.8cm, rear drums; parking brakes to rear wheels; rack and pinion steering with optional power assistance; fuel tank capacity 69L (15.2Gal) [18.2US Gal]; tyres 175 SR 14, wheel rims 5 J.

Dimensions: Wheelbase 281.5cm, track 150/150cm, clearance 15.5cm, turning circle 11.2m, load space 12–44cu ft (340/1245dm3). Length 470cm, width 177cm, height 138.5cm.

Performance: Max speed approx 90mph/145kmh (manufacturers test specifications), speed at 1000rpm in 4th gear 13.6mph/21.9kmh; power to weight ratio from 16.4kg/kW (16.1kg/PS); consumption approx 8-13L/100km (35.3/21.7mpg) [29.4/18.1US mpg].

Standard 2000

STUTZ — USA

Stutz Motor Car of America, Inc., 230 West 55th Street, New York 10019, USA
American manufacturer of Luxury vehicles. No longer in production.

Stutz Bearcat II Convertible

SUBARU — J

Fuji Heavy Industries Ltd., Subaru Bldg., Tsunohazu, Shinjuku–ku Tokyo, Japan
Japanese vehicle manufacturer and heavy industry company.

Subaru Rex – Rex Turbo – 700

Small vehicle with a 2-cylinder water cooled engine. Launched July 1972. August 1981: front wheel drive, new body and front and rear independent suspension. 1983: also available with four wheel drive; 1984: more powerful Turbocharged engine. 1987: modified new editions also with continuously variable automatic transmission. Export name is Mini Jumbo. 1988 also available with compressor.

ŠKODA FAVORIT

EXPORT
MOTOKOV
Na strži 63   140 62 Praha   Czechoslovakia   Phone: 42 2 414 2838   Fax: 42 2 42 53 84

Subaru

```
544cm3
22/26kW–29/35hp–30/36PS
1 2V Carb
```

Engine for Rex

Body, Weight: Saloon/Sedan 3–door, 4–seater; kerbweight (DIN) 520–550kg. 4WD 640-650kg. Saloon/Sedan 5–door, 4–seater; kerbweight (DIN) 550–560kg.

Engine data (JIS net): 2–cylinder in–line (76 x 60mm), 544cm3; compression ratio 9.5:1; 22kW (29hp) [30PS] at 6000rpm, 40.4kW/L (54.1hp/L) [55.1PS/L]; 41Nm (30.1lbft) at 3500rpm; regular grade.
With 3 valves per cylinder: Compression ratio 9:1; 26kW (35hp) [36PS] at 7000rpm; 43Nm (31.6lbft) at 4500rpm.

Engine construction: Designated EK 23. Transverse front engine; valves in V; 1 overhead camshaft (toothed belt); 2 counter– balance shafts; light–alloy cylinder head; 3 bearing crankshaft; oil capacity 2.5L (2.4US qt); 1 Hitachi downdraught compound carb. Battery 12V 21-35Ah, alternator 40 A.

Transmission (to front wheels or all wheels): a) 4–speed manual, final drive ratio 4.352; 4.529.
b) 5–speed manual, final drive ratio 5.571.
c) Automatic, hydraulic torque converter with 2–speed Planetary gear set, final drive ratio (1.257 x 4.444) 5.586.
d) Continuously variable automatic, with metal drive belt; final drive ratio (1.954 x 4.352) 8.504.
4WD: Engageable rear wheel drive, 5-speed manual, final drive ratio 6.166.

Gear ratios: a) 4–speed manual: 1st 4.083; 2nd 2.437; 3rd 1.666; 4th 1.115; R 4.
b) 5–speed manual: 1st 3.383; 2nd 2.263; 3rd 1.520; 4th 1.032; 5th 0.878; R 3.641.
for 4WD: 1st 4.181; 2nd 2.444; 3rd 1.52; 4th 1.032; 5th 0.823; R 4.09.
c) Automatic: Max torque multiplication in converter 1.9 times, Planetary gear set ratios: 1st 1.821; 2nd 1; R 1.821.
d) Continuously variable automatic: From 2.503 to 0.497; R 2.818.

Chassis: Integral body; front McPherson struts with control arm, tension struts and coil springs, rear independent suspension with semi trailing arm and coil springs. Four wheel drum brakes, 3 valve engine with front disc brakes, mechanical handbrake to rear wheels; rack and pinion steering; fuel tank 32L (8.8mpg) [7.33US mpg]; tyres 5.20–10; 5.65–12; 135 SR 10, 4WD 135 SR 12.

Dimensions: Wheelbase 229.5cm, track 122/122cm, clearance 17.5cm, turning circle 9m, length 319.5cm, width 139.5cm, height 141/142cm.

Performance: Max speed approx 68mph/110kmh, speed at 1000rpm in 5th gear 11mph/18kmh; power to weight ratio from 20kg/kW (14.4kg/PS); consumption (touring) 3.5–7L/100km (80.7–40.4mpg) [67.2–33.6US mpg], manufacturers test specification.

Subaru Rex ECVT

```
544cm3
40kW–54hp–55PS
Compressor/Injection
```

Body, Weight: 3-door Saloon/Sedan; kerbweight (DIN) from 600kg.

Engine data (JIS): 2-cylinder in-line (76 x 60mm), 544cm3; compression ratio 8.0:1; 40kW (54hp) [55PS] at 6400rpm, 73.5kW/L (98.5hp/L) [101.1PS/L]; 73Nm (53.9lbft) at 4400rpm.

Engine construction: Designated EK 23 Super Charger. 3 valves per cylinder. 1 mechanical compressor, charge-air cooler.

Transmission (to front wheels): a) 5-speed manual, final drive ratio 5.285;
b) Continuously variable automatic ECVT, final drive ratio (1.708 x 4.352), 7.433.

Gear ratios: a) 5-speed manual: 1st 3.538; 2nd 2.262; 3rd 1.520; 4th 1.032; 5th 0.852; R 3.461.
b) ECVT: continuously variable between 2.503 and 0.497; R 2.633.

Chassis: Front antiroll bar; front disc brakes; tyres 155/70 SR 12.
Dimensions: Track 122.5/122.5cm.
Performance: Max speed approx 87mph/140kmh, speed at 1000rpm in 5th gear 13.2mph/21.3kmh; power to weight ratio from 15kg/kW (10.9kg/PS); consumption approx 5-9L/100km (56.5–31.4mpg) [47–26.1US mpg].

Subaru 700

```
665 cm3
27kW–36hp–37PS
1 2V Carb
```

Engine for 700

As 544cm3, except:
Body, Weight: Saloon/Sedan 3/5–door, 4–seater; kerbweight (DIN) 570–615kg.
Engine data (DIN): 2–cylinder in–line (78 x 69.6mm), 665cm3; compression ratio 9.5:1; 27kW (36hp) [37PS] at 6000rpm, 40.9kW/L (54.8hp/L) [55.6PS/L]; 54Nm (40lbft) at 3000rpm; premium grade.
Some countries: Compression ratio 8.5:1; 25.5kW (34hp) [35PS]; 52Nm (38.2lbft); regular grade.
Engine construction: Designated EK 42. 2 Counter–balance shafts; 1 Zenith–Stromberg downdraught compound carb.
Transmission: 4–speed manual, final drive ratio 4.222.
Gear ratios: 1st 4.083; 2nd 2.437; 3rd 1.666; 4th 1.115; R 4.
Chassis: Some models; front antiroll bar, front disc brakes, tyres 135 SR 12.
Performance: Max speed 77mph/125kmh (manufacturers test specification), speed at 1000rpm in 4th gear 12.6mph/20.3kmh; power to weight ratio 21.1kg/kW (15.4kg/PS); consumption ECE 5.1/-/6.1L/100km (55.4/-/46.3mpg) [46.1/-/38.6US mpg].

Subaru Justy – Justy 4WD

Compact Saloon/Sedan with 3-cylinder engine. In some countries designated "J 10", 4WD with engageable all wheel drive. Launched as a prototype in Tokyo, 1983. 1986: 1.2 Litre, 3 valve engine. 1987: 1-Litre FWD also with continuously variable gears. Autumn 1988: modified front and rear, ECVT also for 1.2 Litre 4WD and Export.

Subaru Justy 1.2 4WD ECVT

```
998cm3
40.5kW–54hp–55PS
1 2V Carb
```

Weight: Saloon/Sedan 3-door, kerbweight (DIN) from 690kg; 4WD from 750kg. Saloon/Sedan 5-door, kerbweight (DIN) from 705kg; 4WD 765kg.

Subaru

Engine data (DIN): 3-cylinder in-line (78 x 69.6mm), 998cm3; compression ratio 9.5:1; 40.5kW (54hp) [55PS] at 6000rpm, 40.1kW/L (54.3hp/L) [55.1PS/L]; 80Nm (59lbft) at 3600rpm; regular grade.
Japanese Version (JIS): 46kW (62hp) [63PS]: 83Nm (61.1lbft).
Basic Model: 42kW (56hp) [57PS]; 81Nm (59.6lbft).

Engine construction: Front engine, transverse, valves in V; 1 overhead camshaft (toothed belt); counter-balance shaft, 4 bearing crankshaft, light-alloy cylinder head; oil capacity 3L (2.8US qt), 1 Zenith-Stromberg downdraught compound carb. Battery 12V 27-45Ah; alternator 45A; cooling system capacity approx 6.5L (6.1US qt).

Transmission (to front wheels or with engageable four wheel drive): a) 5-speed manual, floorshift, final drive ratio 5.2, Japan also with 4.37, 4.058.
b) ECVT continuously variable automatic with metal drive belt, final drive ratio (1.357 x 4.352) 5.906.

Gear ratios: a) 5-speed manual: 1st 3.071; 2nd 1.695; 3rd 1.137; 4th 0.794; 5th 0.631; or 0.675; R 3.461.
b) Continuously variable automatic: From 2.503 to 0.497; R 2.475.

Chassis: Integral body, all round independent suspension, front McPherson struts, single control arm, tensions struts and antiroll bar, rear trailing arm and control arm, coil springs, telescopic damper. Servo/power assisted brakes, front discs (ventilated), rear drums, mechanical handbrake to rear wheels; rack and pinion steering; fuel tank 35L (7.7Gal) [9.2US Gal]; tyres 145 SR 12.

Dimensions: Wheelbase 228.5cm, track 133/129cm, clearance 15cm, turning circle 9.8m, load space 5.6/34.6cu ft (160/980dm3), length 369.5cm, width 153.5cm, height 142cm.

Performance: Max speed 90mph/145kmh (manufacturers test specification), speed at 1000rpm in top gear 18.8mph/30.2kmh; acceleration 0 – 62mph/100kmh 15.4secs; power to weight ratio from 17.3kg/kW (12.5kg/PS); consumption ECE 5.4/7.2/7.2L/100km (52.3/39.2/39.2mpg) [43.6/32.7/32.7US mpg], 4WD 6.8/7.2/7.2L/100km (41.5/39.2/39.2mpg) [34.6/32.7/32.7US mpg].

Subaru Justy 1.2 4WD ECVT

```
1190cm3
50kW–67hp–68PS
1 2V Carb
```

As 998cm3, except:

Weight: 3-door Saloon/Sedan, kerbweight (DIN) from 740kg, USA 790kg; 4WD from 810kg. 5-door Saloon/Sedan, kerbweight (DIN) from 755kg, 4WD from 825kg.

Engine data (DIN): 3-cylinder in-line (78 x 83mm), 1190cm3; compression ratio 9.1:1; 50kW (67hp) [68PS] at 5600rpm, 42kW/L (56.2hp/L) [57.2PS/L]; 95Nm (127.3lbft) at 3600rpm.
With Catalyst (DIN): 49kW (66hp) [67PS] at 5200rpm; 95Nm (70.1lbft) at 3600rpm.
Japanese Version (JIS): Compression ratio 9.5:1; 54kW (72hp) [73PS] at 6000rpm; 98Nm (72.3lbft) at 3600rpm.

Engine construction: 3 valves per cylinder.

Transmission: a) 5-speed manual, final drive ratio 4.437, 4.800, 4WD 5.200.
b) Continuously variable Automatic, final drive ratio (1.275 x 4.352), 5.549 or (1.275 x 4.666) 5.949; 4WD (1.357 x 4.352) 5.906.

Gear ratios: 5-speed manual: 1st 3.071; 2nd 1.695; 3rd 1.137; 4th 0.823; 5th 0.675; R 3.461. 4WD: 4th 0.771; 5th 0.631.
b) Automatic ECVT: as 1 Litre.

Chassis: Optional rear antiroll bar, optional power assisted steering; tyres 165/65 SR 13, USA also 145 SR 12.

Performance: Max speed 91-96mph/147-155kmh (manufacturers test specification), speed at 1000rpm in 5th gear (4WD) 18.9mph/30.4kmh; acceleration 0 – 62mph/100kmh 13.2secs, power to weight ratio from 13.7kg/kW (10.1kg/PS); consumption (town/country/mixed) 7.6/5.8/6.7L/100km (37.2/48.7/42.2mpg) [30.9/40.6/35.1US mpg]. ECVT 6.9/5.7/6.2L/100km (40.9/49.6/45.6mpg) [34.1/41.3/37.9US mpg].

Subaru Leone

Mid range vehicle with Boxer engine and front or four wheel drive. May 1979: dimensions enlarged and new body developed. Since 1983 available with Turbo engine. Autumn 1984: new body, and engine modifications. Autumn 1985: new Coupe. 1987, some models with permanent all wheel drive.

```
1.6 Litre
56kW–75hp–76PS
1 Compound Carb
```

As 1.3 Litre, except:

Body, Weight: 4-door Saloon/Sedan, 5-seater; kerbweight (DIN) from 950kg. 4WD from 1000kg. 3-door Coupe, 5-seater; kerbweight (DIN) from 975kg; 4WD from 1050kg. 5-door Estate/Station Wagon, 5-seater; kerbweight (DIN) from 1015kg, 4WD from 1090kg.

Engine data (JIS): 4-cylinder Boxer engine (92 x 60mm), 1595cm3; Compression ratio 9:1; 56kW (75hp) [76PS] at 5200rpm, 35.1kW/L (47hp/L) [47.6PS/L]; 118Nm (87.1lbft) at 3200rpm; regular unleaded grade.
European version (DIN): Compression ratio 9:1; 54.5kW (73hp) [74PS] at 5200rpm, 123Nm (90.8lbft) at 3200rpm.
Also 1.3 Litre (DIN): (83 x 60mm), 1299cm3; 48kW (64hp) [65PS] at 5600rpm; 98Nm (72.3lbft) at 3600rpm.

Engine construction: Designated EA 71/EA 65. Central camshaft (cogwheel); light-alloy cylinder head and block; 3 bearing crankshaft; oil capacity 4L (3.8US qt); 1 Zenith-Stromberg downdraught compound carb. Battery 12V 40-52Ah, alternator 60A; cooling system capacity approx 5.5L (4.7US qt).

Transmission (to front wheels, 4WD with engageable rear wheel drive): a) 5-speed manual, final drive ratio 3.889.
b) Automatic, hydraulic torque converter with 3-speed Planetary gear set, final drive ratio 3.796.
Optional reduction gears, 1.592.

Gear ratios: a) 5-speed manual: 1st 3.636; 2nd 1.950; 3rd 1.344; 4th 0.971; 5th 0.783; R 3.583.
for 4WD: 1st 3.545; 2nd 2.111; 3rd 1.448; 4th 1.088; 5th 0.871; R 3.416.
b) Automatic (also for 2WD): Max torque multiplication in converter 1.9 times; Planetary gear set ratio: 1st 2.821; 2nd 1.559; 3rd 1; R 2.257.

Chassis: Integral body; all round independent suspension; front McPherson struts, control arm and coil springs; torsion struts, rear semi-trailing arms; certain models front and rear antiroll bar; telescopic damper. Servo/power assisted brakes, front disc (ventilated), rear drums, mechanical handbrake to front wheels; rack and pinion steering, optional power assisted; fuel tank 60L (13.2Gal) [15.9US Gal]; tyres 155 SR 13 or 175/70 SR 13, wheel rims 4.5J.

Dimensions: Wheelbase 247cm, Estate/Station Wagon 246.5cm, track 142.5/142.5cm, 4WD 141.5/142.5cm, clearance 16.5-18cm, turning circle 9.6m. Length 437cm, Estate/Station Wagon 441cm, width 166cm, height 138.5-142cm, Coupe 136.5-138.5cm, Estate/Station Wagon 142-149cm.

Performance: Max speed 99mph/160kmh, automatic 96mph/155kmh (manufacturers test specification); power to weight ratio 17.9kg/kW (13.2kg/PS); consumption ECE 5-speed 6.3/8.3/8.7L/100km (44.8/34/32.5mpg) [37.3/28.3/27US mpg], automatic 7.1/9.5/9.1L/100km (39.8/29.7/31mpg) [33.1/24.8/25.8US mpg].

Subaru Leone

Subaru

**1.8 Litre
66kW–88hp–90PS
1 2V Carb**

As 1.6 Litre, except:

Body, Weight: Saloon/Sedan kerbweight (DIN) from 990kg, Coupe from 1030kg. Estate/Station Wagon 5-door from 1110kg.

Engine data (DIN): 4-cylinder Boxer engine (92 x 67mm), 1782cm3; compression ratio 9.0:1; 66kW (88hp) [90PS] at 5600rpm, 37.2kW/L (49.8hp/L) [50.5PS/L]; 137Nm (101.1lbft) at 3600rpm.
Japanese Version (JIS net): 62.5kW (84hp) [85PS] at 5600rpm; 135Nm (99.6lbft) at 3200rpm.

Engine construction: Designated EA 82. Hydraulic tappets; 2 x 1 overhead camshaft (toothed belt).

Transmission (To all wheels, 4WD with engageable rear wheel drive or permanent 4WD):
a) 5-speed manual, final drive ratio 3.700; 4WD 3.9.
b) Automatic, final drive ratio 3.793, 3.364.
4WD:
5-speed: Permanent or engageable 4WD, central differential with manual lock bar and power distribution 50/50%
Automatic: Permanent electronically regulated multi plate clutch with variable power distribution to both axles.
Optional rear limited slip differential.

Chassis: 4WD with optional level control system; tyres 175/70 HR 13.

Performance: Maximum speed 109mph/175kmh, automatic 106mph/170kmh (manufacturers test specification), speed at 1000rpm in 5th gear (155 SR 13) 22.7mph/36.6kmh; power to weight ratio from 15kg/kW (11kg/PS); consumption ECE 6.1/7.9/9.1L/100km (46.3/35.8/31mpg) [38.6/29.8/25.8US mpg], automatic 7.1/9.2/8.7L/100km (39.8/30.7/32.5mpg) [33.1/25.6/27US mpg].

Subaru 4WD Station Wagon

**1.8 Litre
77/72kW–103/96hp–105/98PS
Fuel Injection**

As 1.6 Litre, except:

Body, Weight: Saloon/Sedan kerbweight (DIN) from 1100kg. Coupe from 1030kg, 4WD from 1120kg. Estate/Station Wagon, from 1060kg, 4WD 1140kg.

Engine data (DIN): 4-cylinder Boxer engine (92 x 67mm), 1782cm3; compression ratio 10:1; 77kW (103hp) [105PS] at 6000rpm, 43.3kW/L (58hp/L) [58.9PS/L]; 142Nm (104.8lbft) at 3600rpm.
With Catalyst: Compression ratio 9.5:1; 72kW (96hp) [98PS] at 5600rpm; 140Nm (103.3lbft) at 2800rpm.
USA Version (SAE net): 67kW (90hp) [91PS] at 5200rpm; 137Nm (101.1lbft) at 2800rpm.

Engine construction: Designated EA 82E. Hydraulic tappets; 2 x 1 overhead camshaft (toothed belt); electronic fuel injection or central/single point injection (USA).

Transmission (4WD with engageable rear wheel drive or permanent 4WD):
a) 5-speed manual, final drive ratio 3.7 or 3.9; 4WD 3.9.
b) Automatic, final drive ratio 3.454, 3.6.
c) Automatic with OD, hydraulic torque converter with 4-speed Planetary gear set, final drive ratio 3.796, 3.7, 4WD 3.9
4WD:
5-speed: Permanent or engageable 4WD, central differential with manual lock bar, power distribution 50/50%
Automatic: Permanent electronically regulated multi plate clutch with variable power distribution to both axles, USA also engageable.
Optional reduction and/or rear limited slip differential.

Gear ratios: 5-speed manual, 2WD: 1st 3.636; 2nd 2.105; 3rd 1.428; 4th 1.093; 5th 0.885; R 3.583.
4WD: 1st 3.545; 2nd 1.947; 3rd 1.366; 4th 0.972; 5th 0.780; R 3.416.
Or: 1st 3.545; 2nd 2.111; 3rd 1.448; 4th 1.088; 5th 0.871; R 3.416.
b) 3-speed automatic: As 1.6 Litre
c) Automatic with OD: 1st 2.785; 2nd 1.545; 3rd 1; OD 0.694; R 2.272.

Chassis: Some versions with electro-pneumatic spring/damper units (level control system with height adjustment), as well as four wheel disc brakes (front ventilated); power assisted steering; tyres 175/70 HR 13 or 185/70 HR 13, wheel rims 5 J.

Dimensions: Length, USA Saloon/Sedan and Coupe 443cm, Estate/Station Wagon 449cm

Performance (2WD): Max speed 112mph/180kmh (manufacturers specification), speed at 1000rpm in 5th gear (Axle 3.7) 20.1mph/32.4kmh; power to weight ratio from 13kg/kW (9.5kg/PS); consumption ECE 6.1/7.8/9.1L/100km (46.3/36.2/31mpg) [38.6/30.2/25.8US mpg].

Subaru 1.8 Sedan 4WD

**1.8 Litre
88/96kW–118/129hp–120/131PS
Turbo/Fuel Injection**

Only available as 4WD, except in the USA.

As 1.6 Litre, except:

Body, Weight: Saloon/Sedan kerbweight (DIN) from 1090kg. Coupe from 1110kg. Estate/Station Wagon from 1160kg.

Engine data (Catalyst DIN): 4-cylinder boxer engine (92 x 67mm), 1782cm3; compression ratio 7.7:1; 88kW (118hp) [120PS] at 5200rpm, 49.4kW/L (66.2hp/L) [67.3PS/L]; 183Nm (135lbft) at 3200rpm.
Japanese Version (JIS): 88kW (118hp) [120PS]; 179Nm (132lbft) at 2400rpm.
Without Catalyst (DIN): 96kW (129hp) [131PS] at 5600rpm; 196Nm (144.6lbft) at 2800rpm; also 100kW (134hp) [136PS].

Engine construction: Designated EA82. Hydraulic tappets; 2 x 1 overhead camshaft (toothed belt); electronic fuel injection; 1 exhaust turbocharger IHI.

Subaru 4WD Super Station Turbo

Transmission (to all wheels): Permanent all wheel drive, with central differential and manual lock bar, power distribution 50/50%. Automatic; variable power distribution between front and rear (through electronically regulated multi plate clutch).
a) 5-speed manual, final drive ratio 3.7.
b) Automatic with OD, final drive ratio 3.9 or 3.7; USA 2WD with 2-speed automatic, final drive ratio 3.36.
Reduction gears, optional limited slip differential.

Gear ratios: a) 5-speed manual: 1st 3.545; 2nd 1.947; 3rd 1.366; 4th 0.972; 5th 0.780; R 3.416.
Or: 1st 3.545; 2nd 2.111; 3rd 1.448; 4th 1.088; 5th 0.871; R 3.416.
b) Automatic with OD: 1st 2.785; 2nd 1.545; 3rd 1; OD 0.694; R 2.272.

Subaru

Chassis: Some versions with electro-pneumatic spring/damper units (level control system with height adjustment) as well as four wheel disc brakes (front ventilated); power assisted steering; tyres 175/70 HR 13 or 185/70 HR 13 optional 185/70 HR 14, wheel rims 5 J or 5.5 J.

Performance: Maximum speed 121mph/195kmh, speed at 1000rpm in 5th gear 24.6mph/39.6kmh; power to weight ratio from 12.0kg/kW (8.8kg/PS); consumption approx 6.7/8.7/10L/100km (42.2/32.5/28.2mpg) [35.1/27/23.5US mpg].

Subaru 4WD Coupe Turbo

Subaru XT Coupe

2–door Coupe, based on the Leone/4WD, front wheel drive or permanent 4WD, 1.8 Litre Boxer engine. Launched Spring 1985. Designated "Alcyone" for the Japanese market. 1987: New 4WD system, also available with 2.7 Litre, 6-cylinder engine.

```
1.8 Litre Turbo
88kW–118hp–120PS
Fuel Injection
```

Body, Weight: Coupe 2–door, 5–seater; kerbweight (DIN) from 1050kg, USA from 1115kg.

Engine data (Catalyst, DIN): 4–cylinder boxer engine (92 x 67mm), 1782cm3; compression ratio 7.7:1; 88kW (118hp) [120PS] at 5200rpm, 49.4kW/L (66.2hp/L) [67.3PS/L]; 183Nm (135lbft) at 3200rpm.
Japanese Version (JIS net): 88kW (118hp) [120PS]; 179Nm (132lbft) at 2400rpm.
Without Catalyst (DIN): 100kW (134hp) [136PS] or 96kW (129hp) [131PS] at 5600rpm; 196Nm (144.6lbft) at 2800rpm.
USA Version (Without Turbo, SAE net): Compression ratio 9.5:1; 72kW (96hp) [98PS] at 5200rpm, 140Nm (103.3lbft) at 3200rpm.

Engine construction: Designated EA 82. Hydraulic tappets; 2 x 1 overhead camshaft (toothed belt); light–alloy cylinder head and block; 3 bearing crankshaft; oil capacity 4L (3.8US qt), 1 exhaust turbocharger IHI; electronic fuel injection. Battery 12V 28–52Ah, alternator 60-65A, cooling system capacity approx 5.5L (5.2US qt).

Transmission (to front wheels, 4WD with engageable rear wheel or permanent all wheel drive): a) 5–speed manual, final drive ratio 3.454, USA 3.7; 4WD 3.7.
b) Automatic, hydraulic torque converter with 4–speed Planetary gear set, central selector lever, final drive ratio 3.7, USA 3.9.
4WD:
5-speed manual: Permanent or engageable 4WD, central differential with manual lock bar, power distribution 50/50%.
Automatic: Variable power distribution between front and rear (through electronically regulated multi plate clutch).
Optional rear limited slip differential.

Gear ratios: a) 5–speed manual: 1st 3.545; 2nd 1.947; 3rd 1.366; 4th 0.972; 5th 0.780; R 3.416.
Or: 1st 3.545; 2nd 2.111; 3rd 1.45; 4th 1.088; 5th 0.87; R 3.416
Or (2WD): 1st 3.636; 2nd 2.105; 3rd 1.428; 4th 1.093; 5th 0.885; R 3.583.
b) Automatic with OD: 1st 2.785; 2nd 1.545; 3rd 1; OD 0.694; R 2.272.

Chassis: Integral body; front and rear independent suspension with front McPherson struts, front control arm and antiroll bar, rear semi trailing arm with coil springs, antiroll bar, telescopic dampers. Some models with electro–pneumatic spring/damper units. Servo/power assisted disc brakes (front ventilated), optional ABS, USA rear drums; mechanical handbrake to front wheels; power assisted rack and pinion steering; fuel tank 60L (13.2Gal) [15.9US Gal]; tyres 185/70 HR 13; 185/65 HR 14, wheel rims 5J.

Dimensions: Wheelbase 246.5cm, track 143.5/142.5cm, 4WD 142/142.5 clearance 17/20.5cm, turning circle 9.8m, load space 11.1cu ft (315dm3). Length 445cm (USA 451cm), width 169cm, height 129.5/133.5cm.

Performance: (134hp) Maximum speed 124mph/200kmh (manufacturers test specification), speed at 1000rpm in 5th gear 22.9mph/36.8kmh; acceleration 0 – 62mph/100kmh 9.5secs; power to weight ratio from 11kg/kW (8.1kg/PS); consumption approx 8–12L/100km (35.3– 23.5mpg) [29.4–19.6US mpg].

Subaru XT Coupe

```
2.7 Litre
110kW–147hp–150PS
Fuel Injection
```

As 1.8 Litre, except:

Body, Weight: Kerbweight (DIN) 1300kg, USA 2WD from 1275kg, 4WD 1310kg.

Engine data (JIS net): 6–cylinder Boxer engine (92 x 67mm), 2672cm3; compression ratio 9.5:1; 110kW (147hp) [150PS] at 5200rpm, 41.2kW/L (55.2hp/L) [56.1PS/L]; 211Nm (156lbft) at 4000rpm.
USA Version (SAE net): 108kW (145hp) [147 PS] at 5200rpm; 211Nm (155.7lbft) at 4000rpm

Engine construction: Designated ER 27. 4 bearing crankshaft; oil capacity 5L (4.7US qt); without exhaust turbocharger. Alternator 90A, cooling system capacity approx 8L (7.6US qt).

Transmission (to front wheels or permanent all wheel drive): a) 5–speed manual, final drive ratio 3.9; USA (2WD) 3.7.
b) Automatic, final drive ratio 3.7.
4WD: Permanent all wheel drive as 1.8 Litre.

Gear ratios: a) 5–speed manual: 1st 3.545; 2nd 1.947; 3rd 1.366; 4th 0.972; 5th 0.780; R. 3.416.
b) Automatic: As 1.8 Litre.

Chassis: Tyres 205/60 HR 14.

Dimensions: Track 144.5/142.5cm, 4WD 143.5/144cm.

Performance: Maximum speed approx 137mph/220kmh, speed at 1000rpm in 5th gear 22.5mph/36.2kmh; power to weight ratio from 11.8kg/kW (8.7kg/PS); consumption from 9–14 L/100km (31.4–20.2mpg) [26.1–16.8US mpg].

Subaru XT 6 Coupe

Subaru Legacy

New model. 4-door Saloon/Sedan with notchback and Estate/Station Wagon. Front wheel drive or permanent all wheel drive. Four-cylinder Boxer engine with four valves per cylinder, from 1.8 Litre with 108hp to 2 Litre Turbo with 217hp in the case of the RS Sports version. Launched in January 1989, exported to Europe in Autumn.

Subaru • Suzuki

1800 OHC
81kW–108hp–110PS
Central/Single Point Injection

Body, Weight: 4-door Saloon/Sedan, 5-seater; kerbweight (DIN) from 1060kg, 4WD from 1150kg. 5-door Estate/Station Wagon, 5-seater, kerbweight (DIN) from 1210kg.

Engine data (JIS net): 4-cylinder Boxer engine (87.9 x 75mm), 1820cm3; Compression ratio 9.7:1; 81kW (108hp) [110PS] at 6000rpm, 44.5kW/L (59.6hp/L) [60.4PS/L]; 149Nm (110lbft) at 3200rpm; regular grade unleaded.
USA Version (SAE net): (96.9 x 75mm), 2211cm3; Compression ratio 9.5:1; 97kW (130hp) [132PS] at 5600rpm.

Engine construction: Designated EJ 18. 4 valves (in V 30deg) per cylinder, hydraulic valve lash adjustment, 1 overhead camshaft (toothed belt), per bank; light–alloy cylinder head and block; 5 bearing crankshaft; oil capacity approx 4.5L (4.3US qt); electronic central/single point injection. Battery 12V 40-52Ah, Alternator 60A, cooling system capacity approx 6L (5.7US qt).

Transmission (to front wheels, 4WD to all wheels): a) 5-speed manual, final drive ratio 3.700, 4WD 3.900.
b) Automatic, hydraulic torque converter with 4-speed Planetary gear set, final drive ratio 4.111.
4WD: Permanent all wheel drive; with 5-speed manual, with central differential (power distribution 50/50%) with viscous coupling (exception is the 1800 Mi with engageable 4WD); with Automatic permanent electronically regulated multi plate clutch with variable power distribution to both axles.
Optional rear limited slip differential (Viscous).

Gear ratios: a) 5-speed manual: 1st 3.636; 2nd 2.105; 3rd 1.428; 4th 1.093; 5th 0.885; R 3.583.
4WD: 1st 3.545; 2nd 2.111; 3rd 1.488; 4th 1.088; 5th 0.871; R 3.416.
b) Automatic, max torque multiplication in converter approx 2 times; Planetary gear set ratios: 1st 2.785; 2nd 1.545; 3rd 1; 4th 0.694; R 2.272.

Chassis: Integral body; all round independent suspension, front McPherson struts, lower A-arm and antiroll bar, rear McPherson struts with two lower control arms, trailing arms and antiroll bars, telescopic damper. Servo/power assisted four wheel disc brakes (front ventilated), handbrake to rear wheels; power assisted rack and pinion steering; fuel tank capacity 60L (13.2Gal) [15.9US Gal]; tyres 165 SR 13 also 175/70 SR 14, wheel rims 5 J.

Dimensions: Wheelbase 258cm, track 147.5/146cm or 146.5/145cm, 4WD 147/146cm or 146/145cm. Clearance 16.5-17cm, turning circle 10.1m. Length 451cm, Estate/Station Wagon 460cm, width 169cm, height 138.5cm, 4WD 139.5cm, Estate/Station Wagon 147cm.

Performance: Max speed approx 115mph/185kmh; speed at 1000rpm in 5th gear 20.7mph/33.3kmh, 4WD 19.9mph/32.1kmh; power to weight ratio from 13.1kg/kW (9.6kg/PS); consumption approx 7-12L/100km (40.4–23.5mpg) [33.6–19.6US mpg].

Subaru Legacy 2.0

2000 DOHC
110kW–147hp–150PS
Fuel Injection

As 1.8 Litre, except:

Weight: Saloon/Sedan, kerbweight (DIN) from 1170kg, 4WD from 1220kg. 4WD Estate/Station Wagon, kerbweight (DIN) from 1280kg.

Engine data (JIS net): 4-cylinder Boxer engine (92 x 75mm), 1994cm3; Compression ratio 9.7:1; 110kW (147hp) [150PS] at 6800rpm, 55.2kW/L (74hp/L) [75.2PS/L]; 172Nm (126.9lbft) at 5200rpm; regular grade unleaded.

Engine construction: Designated EJ 20. 4 valves (in V 52deg) per cylinder, 2 overhead camshafts (toothed belt) per bank; electronic fuel injection.

Transmission: a) 5-speed manual, final drive ratio 3.700, 4WD 3.900.
b) Automatic 4.111

Gear ratios: a) 5-speed manual 2WD and 4WD: 1st 3.545; 2nd 2.111; 3rd 1.488; 4th 1.088; 5th 0.871; R 3.416.
b) Automatic, as 1.8 Litre

Chassis: Estate/Station Wagon also with electro-pneumatic spring/damper units (level control system and adjustable height control); also optional ABS; tyres 175/70 HR 14 or 185/65 HR 14.

Dimensions: Track 146.5/145cm, 4WD 146/145cm. Height Estate/Station Wagon also 149 or 150cm.

Performance: Max speed above 124mph/200kmh, speed at 1000rpm in 5th gear 21.4mph/34.4kmh, 4WD 20.3mph/32.7kmh; power to weight ratio from 10.6kg/kW (7.8kg/PS); consumption approx 8-13L/100km (35.3/21.7mpg) [29.4/18.1US mpg].

Subaru Legacy 2.0 Wagon

2000 DOHC
162kW–217hp–220PS
Turbo/Injection

As 1.8 Litre, except:

Body, Weight: 4WD Saloon/Sedan, kerbweight (DIN) from 1290kg.

Engine data (JIS net): 4-cylinder, Boxer engine (92 x 75mm), 1994cm3; compression ratio 8.5:1; 162kW (217hp) [220PS] at 6400rpm, 81.2kW/L (108.8hp/L) [110.3PS/L]; 270Nm (199lbft) at 4000rpm.

Engine construction: Designated EJ 20 Turbo. 4 valves (in V 52deg) per cylinder, 2 overhead camshafts (toothed belt) per bank; oil cooler; electronic fuel injection; 1 exhaust turbocharger, charge–air cooler.

Transmission (to all wheels): 5-speed manual, final drive ratio 4.111. Optional rear limited slip differential (Viscous).

Gear ratios: 5-speed manual: 1st 3.545; 2nd 2.111; 3rd 1.448; 4th 1.088; 5th 0.825; R 3.416.

Chassis: Rear disc brakes also ventilated, optional ABS; tyres 205/60 HR 15, wheel rims 6 J.

Dimensions: Track 146.5/145.5cm.

Performance: Max speed approx 143mph/230kmh, speed at 1000rpm in 5th gear 21mph/33.8kmh; power to weight ratio from 8.0kg/kW (5.9kg/PS); consumption approx 9-18L/100km (31.4–15.7mpg) [26.1–13.1US mpg].

SUZUKI J

Suzuki Motor Co. Ltd., Hamamatsu–Nishi, P.O.Box 1, 432–91 Hamamatsu, Japan.
Japanese manufacturer of motorcycles and automobiles.

Suzuki Alto/Fronte/Cervo

New model. Small front wheel drive, 3–cylinder vehicle. Launched June 1982. October 1984, available with 4 wheel drive. Summer/Autumn 1985, new body. 1987; available with DOHC, 4 valves per cylinder and Turbo ("Works"), Turbo version with permanent 4 wheel drive. Summer 1988: new body and modified engine.

547cm3
25/43kW–33.5/57.5hp–34/58PS
1 Carb/Injection/Turbo

Body, Weight: 3/5-door Saloon/Sedan, 4-seater: kerbweight (DIN) 540kg. 3-door Turbo Saloon/Sedan, kerbweight from 600kg, 4WD from 650kg.

Engine data (JIS net): 3–cylinder in–line (65 x 55mm), 547cm3; compression ratio 9.7:1; 25kW (33.5hp) [34PS] at 6500rpm, 45.7kW/L (61.2hp/L) [62.2PS/L]; 42Nm (31lbft) at 4000rpm; leaded premium grade.

Suzuki

Turbo EPI: Compression ratio 8.1:1; 43kW (57.5hp) [58PS] at 6500rpm, 78.6kW/L (105.3hp/L) [106PS/L]; 73Nm (53.9lbft) at 4000rpm.
Engine construction: Designated F 5 B. Transverse front engine; valves in V; 1 overhead camshaft (toothed belt), light-alloy cylinder head; 4 bearing crankshaft; oil capacity 3L (2.8US qt); 1 Mikuni-Solex downdraught compound carb. Turbo "Works" Version, oil cooler, electronic Fuel Injection, 1 exhaust turbocharger and charge-air cooler. Battery 12V 42Ah, alternator 300W; cooling system capacity approx 4L (3.8US qt).
Transmission (to front wheels, 4WD to all wheels): a) 4-speed manual, final drive ratio 5.941.
b) 5-speed manual (Turbo), final drive ratio 4.705.
c) Automatic, hydraulic torque converter and 3-speed Planetary gear set, central selector lever, final drive ratio 5.353 (1.302 x 4.111) Turbo 4.386 (1.113 x 3.941).
4WD: Permanent all wheel drive with central viscous coupling, 5-speed manual, final drive ratio 5.705, Turbo 4.705.
Gear ratios: a) 4-speed manual: 1st 3.384; 2nd 2.055; 3rd 1.28; 4th 0.892; R 3.272.
b) 5-speed manual (4WD): 1st 4.300; 2nd 2.470; 3rd 1.608; 4th 1.093; 5th 0.903; R 4.000
Turbo (FF and 4WD): 1st 4.100; 2nd 2.470; 3rd 1.608; 4th 1.093; 5th 0.966; R 4.000.
c) Automatic: Max torque multiplication in converter 2 times, Planetary gear set ratios: 1st 2.659; 2nd 1.530; 3rd 1; R 2.129; Turbo 1st: 2.727; 2nd 1.536; 3rd 1; R 2.222.
Chassis: Integral body; front McPherson struts, trailing arm and antiroll bar, rear torsion crank axle (rear rigid axle) with trailing arm and Panhard rod, telescopic damper. Four wheel drum brakes, Turbo and 4WD with front discs, mechanical handbrake to rear wheels; rack and pinion steering; fuel tank 30L (6.6Gal) [7.9US Gal]; tyres 5.20-10; 135 SR 12; 4WD and Turbo 155/70 SR 12.
Dimensions: Wheelbase 233.5cm, track 122-120cm, 4WD 121.5/120cm, clearance 15.5cm, turning circle 8.8m, length 319.5cm, width 139.5cm, height 138-138.5cm. 4WD 141cm.
Performance: Maximum speed approx 74.5mph/120kmh, Turbo approx 87mph/140kmh, speed at 1000rpm in 4th gear 11.1mph/18.0kmh, Turbo in 5th gear 13.1mph/21.1kmh; power to weight ratio from 14kg/kW (10.3kg/PS); consumption approx 4-9L/100km (70.6-31.4mpg) [58.8-26.1US mpg].

Suzuki Alto

547cm3 12V
29/31kW-39/41hp-40/42PS
1 Carb

As 33.5hp, except:
Body, Weight: 3/5-door Saloon/Sedan, 4-seater; kerbweight (DIN) from 570kg, 4WD from 620kg. Saloon/Sedan with 2 side sliding doors, weight 590kg, 4WD 640kg. 3-door Cervo Coupe, 4-seater; kerbweight (DIN) 590kg.
Engine data (JIS net): 3-cylinder in-line (65 x 55mm), 547cm3; Compression ratio 10:1; 29kW (39hp) [40PS] at 7500rpm, 53kW/L (71hp/L) [73.1PS/L]; 42Nm (31lbft) at 6000rpm.
Or: 31kW (41hp) [42PS] at 7500rpm; 43Nm (31.7lbft) at 6000rpm.
Engine construction: Designated F 5 B12. 4 valves in V per cylinder; 1 overhead camshaft (toothed belt); 1 downdraught compound carb.
Transmission (to front wheels, 4WD to all wheels): a) 4-speed manual, final drive ratio 5.941.
b) 5-speed manual, final drive ratio 5.941, Cervo 5.937, 4WD 5.705.
c) Automatic, final drive ratio 5.353 (1.302 x 4.111).
Gear ratios: a) 4-speed manual: As 33.5hp.
b) 5-speed manual: 1st 3.384; 2nd 2.055; 3rd 1.28; 4th 0.892; 5th 0.774; R 3.272.
Cervo: 1st 3.384; 2nd 2.055; 3rd 1.375; 4th 0.962; 5th 0.833; R 2.916.
4WD: As 33.5hp.
c) Automatic: As 33.5hp.

Chassis: Front disc brakes, tyres 135 SR 12, 145/70 SR 12 or 155/70 SR 12.
Dimensions: Coupe Cervo; wheelbase 217.5cm, height 133cm.
Performance: Max speed approx 77.6mph/125kmh, speed at 1000rpm in 5th gear (0.774, Axle 5.941) 12.8mph/20.7kmh; power to weight ratio from 18.4kg/kW (13.6kg/PS); consumption approx 4-7L/100km (70.6-40.4mpg) [58.8-33.6US mpg].

Suzuki Fronte

547cm3 DOHC
47/35kW-63/45hp-64/46PS
Fuel Injection/Turbo

As 33.5hp, except:
Body, Weight: 3-door Saloon/Sedan, 4-seater; kerbweight (DIN) from 610kg, 4WD from 660kg.
Engine data (JIS net): 3-cylinder in-line (65 x 55mm), 547cm3; Compression ratio 8:1; 47kW (63hp) [64PS] at 7500rpm, 85.9kW/L (115hp/L) [118PS/L]; 77Nm (56.8lbft) at 4000rpm.
Without turbo: Compression ratio 10:1; 34kW (45hp) (46PS) at 7500rpm; 44Nm (32.5lbft) at 6000rpm.
Engine construction: 4 valves (in V) per cylinder, hydraulic valve lash adjustment; 2 overhead camshafts (toothed belt); oil cooler; EPI electronic fuel injection; 1 turbocharger and charge-air cooler.
Transmission (to front wheels, 4WD to all wheels): a) 5-speed manual, final drive ratio, Turbo and Turbo 4WD, 4.705; without Turbo 5.941.
b) Automatic, final drive ratio 4.386 (1.113 x 3.941), without Turbo 5.213 (1.268 x 4.111).
Gear ratios: a) 5-speed manual: 1st 4.100; 2nd 2.470; 3rd 1.608; 4th 1.093; 5th 0.966; R 4.000.
Without turbo: 1st 3.384; 2nd 2.055; 3rd 1.375; 4th 0.962; 5th 0.833; R 3.272
b) Automatic: 1st 2.727; 2nd 1.536; 3rd 1; R 2.222.
Chassis: Front disc brakes; tyres 155/65 HR 13, without Turbo 155/70 SR 12.
Dimensions: Turbo Track 122.5-120, 4WD 122/120cm, height 137.5, 4WD 140cm.
Performance: Max speed approx 87-99mph/140-160kmh, speed at 1000rpm in 5th gear (0.966, Axle 4.705), 13.5mph/21.7kmh; power to weight ratio from 13.0kg/kW (9.5kg/PS); consumption approx 5-9L/100km (56.5-31.4mpg) [47-26.1US mpg].

Suzuki Alto Works Twincam RS-R

Suzuki Cultus/Swift

New Model. Compact Saloon/Sedan, front wheel drive, 3-cylinder 993cm3 engine. Launched Autumn 1983. September 1984; available with a 1.3 Litre 4-cylinder engine. Summer 1986; GTi/GXi with 16 valve DOHC engine. New body, modifications to the engine and rear independent suspension. Available in the USA as Chevrolet's Geo Metro.

Suzuki

Suzuki Cultus/Swift

993cm3
43kW–57.5hp–58PS
1 Carb/Central–Single Point Injection

Body, Weight: 3-door, Saloon/Sedan, 5-seater; kerbweight (DIN) 680–740kg, USA from 720kg. 5-door Saloon/Sedan, 5-seater; kerbweight (DIN) 720-770kg, USA from 745kg.

Engine data (DIN): 3–cylinder in–line (74 x 77mm), 993cm3; compression ratio 9.5:1; 43kW (57.5hp) [58PS] at 6000rpm, 43.3kW/L (58hp/L) [58.4PS/L]; 78Nm (57.7lbft) at 3500rpm.
European version (DIN): 39kW (52hp) (53PS) at 5800rpm; 80Nm (59lbft) at 3000rpm.
With Catalyst (Central/Single Point Injection DIN): Compression ratio 9:1; 41kW (55hp) [56PS] at 5700rpm; 80Nm (59lbft) at 3000rpm.
USA (SAE net): Also 36kW (48hp) [49PS] at 4700rpm; 79Nm (58.3lbft) at 3300rpm; Or with Turbocharger: Compression ratio 8.3:1; 52kW (70hp) [71PS] at 5500rpm; 108Nm (79.7lbft) at 3500rpm.

Engine construction: Designated G 10. Transverse front engine. Hydraulic tappets. Valves in V; 1 overhead camshaft (toothed belt); light–alloy cylinder head and engine block; 4 bearing crankshaft; oil capacity 3.5L (3.3US qt); 1 Hitachi downdraught compound carb or central/single point injection; turbo engine (USA) with electronic fuel injection and charge air cooler. Battery 12V 36-45Ah, alternator 45-50A; cooling system capacity approx 3.9-4.1L (4.1US qt).

Transmission (to front wheels): a) 4–speed manual, final drive ratio 4.388.
b) 5–speed manual, final drive ratio 4.388; 4.105; 3.950.
c) Automatic, hydraulic torque converter and 3–speed Planetary gear set (0.98 x 3.950) 3.871, 3.950.

Gear ratios: a) 4–speed manual: 1st 3.416; 2nd 1.894; 3rd 1.280; 4th 0.914; R 3.272.
b) 5–speed manual: 1st 3.416; 2nd 1.894; 3rd 1.280; 4th 0.914; 5th 0.757; R 3.272
c) Automatic: Max torque multiplication in converter 2.1 times; Planetary gear set ratios: 1st 2.810; 2nd 1.549; 3rd 1; R 2.296.

Chassis: Integral body; all round independent suspension front McPherson struts, lower single control arm, rear trailing arms and coil springs, Turbo (USA) also with rear antiroll bar and telescopic damper. Servo assisted brakes, front discs, rear drums, mechanical handbrake to rear wheels; rack and pinion steering; fuel tank 40L (8.8Gal) [10.6US Gal]; tyres 155/70 SR 13, USA 145 SR 12, Turbo 165/65 HR 13, wheel rims 4 or 4.5 J.

Dimensions: Wheelbase 226.5cm, 5–door 236.5cm, track 136.5/134cm, clearance 16cm, turning circle 9.2m, length 371cm, 5–door 381cm, width 157.5–159cm, height 135cm, 5-door 138cm.

Performance: Max speed 90mph/145kmh, (manufacturers test specification), speed at 1000rpm in 5th gear (4.105) 20.1mph/32.4kmh; power to weight ratio from 15.8kg/kW (11.7kg/PS); consumption ECE (52hp) 4.0/5.9/5.9L/100km (70.6/47.9/47.9mpg) [58.8/39.9/39.9US mpg].

Suzuki Swift 1.3

1299cm3
54kW–72hp–73PS
1 Compound Carb

As 993cm3, except:

Weight: 3/5-door Saloon/Sedan; kerbweight (DIN) 740-800kg, USA 5-door from 790kg.

Engine data (JIS): 4-cylinder in-line (74 x 75.5mm), 1299cm3; compression ratio 9.5:1; 54kW (72hp) [73PS] at 6000rpm, 41.6kW/L (55.7hp/L) [56.2PS/L]; 100Nm (73.8lbft) at 3700rpm.
European Version (DIN): 49kW (66hp) [67PS] at 6000rpm, 101Nm (74.5lbft) at 3500rpm.
With Catalyst (Central Injection DIN): 52kW (70hp) [71PS] at 6000rpm; 101Nm (74.5lbft) at 3500rpm

Engine construction: Designated G 13 B. Valves in V, mechanical tappets; 5 main bearing crankshaft.

Transmission: a) 5-speed manual, final drive ratio 3.789; 3.684; 3.523.
b) Automatic, final drive ratio 3.684.

Performance (66hp): Max speed 101mph/163kmh (manufacturers test specification), speed at 1000rpm in 5th gear (3.523), 23.5mph/37.8kmh; power to weight ratio from 13.7kg/kW (10.1kg/PS); consumption ECE 4.2/5.8/6.3L/100km (67.3/48.7/44.8mpg) [56/40.6/37.3US mpg], Automatic 5.5/7.5/7.2L/100km (51.4/37.7/39.2mpg) [42.8/31.4/32.7US mpg].

1299cm3 16V
85kW–114hp–115PS
Fuel Injection

Engine for GTi

As 993cm3, except:

Body, Weight: 3-door Saloon/Sedan; kerbweight (DIN) 770-790kg, USA from 800kg.

Engine data (JIS): 4-cylinder in-line (74 x 75.5mm), 1299cm3; Compression ratio 11.5:1; 85kW (114hp) [115PS] at 7500rpm, 65.4kW/L (87.6hp/L) [88.5PS/L]; 110Nm (81.2lbft) at 6500rpm.
With Catalyst (DIN): Compression ratio 10:1; 74kW (99hp) [101PS] at 6450rpm; 113Nm (83.4lbft) at 4950rpm.

Engine construction: Designated G 13 B. 4 valves (in V) per cylinder; 2 overhead camshafts (toothed belt); 5 main bearing crankshaft, electronic fuel injection.

Transmission: a) 5-speed manual, final drive ratio 4.105.
b) Automatic, final drive ratio 3.684
Optional limited slip differential.

Gear ratios: a) 5-speed manual: 1st 3.416; 2nd 1.894; 3rd 1.375; 4th 1.030; 5th 0.870; R 3.272.
b) Automatic, as 993cm3.

Chassis: Rear antiroll bar, four wheel disc brakes (front ventilated); tyres 175/60 HR 14.

Performance (Catalyst version): Max speed 113mph/182kmh (manufacturers test specification), speed at 1000rpm in 5th gear 18mph/29kmh; power to weight ratio from 9.1kg/kW (6.7kg/PS); consumption ECE 5.6/7.1/7.3L/100km (50.4/39.8/36.2mpg) [42/33.1/30.2US mpg].

Suzuki Jimny 550 – SJ 410 – SJ 413

Rough terrain four wheel drive vehicle, with 539cm3 or 970cm3 engines, reduction gear, two body styles and two wheelbases. Model 413 with 1.3 Litre from Autumn 1984. For 1987 also available with 543cm3 Turbo engine.

539cm3
20.5kW–27hp–28PS
1 Carb

Body, Weight: Roadster with fabric top; 2–door, 4–seater; kerbweight (DIN) 740kg. Estate/Station Wagon, 3–door, 4–seater; kerbweight (DIN) 770kg.

Engine data (JIS): 3–cylinder in–line (61 x 61.5mm), 539cm3; compression ratio 6.2:1; 20.5kW (27hp) [28PS] at 4500rpm, 38kW/L (50.9hp/L) [51.9PS/L]; 53Nm (39.1lbft) at 2500rpm; regular grade.

Engine construction: Two stroke engine with pressure lubrication system, light–alloy cylinder head; oil capacity 4L (3.8US qt); 4 bearing crankshaft; 1 horizontal compound carb. Battery 12V 42Ah, dynamo 175W; cooling system capacity approx 5L (4.7US qt).

Suzuki

Transmission (to rear wheels or all wheels): 4-speed manual (without direct drive), final drive ratio 4.777, rear wheel drive with engageable front wheel drive; reduction gear.
Gear ratios: 1st 3.834; 2nd 2.358; 3rd 1.542; 4th 1; R 4.026. Reduction gear: 1st 1.741; 2nd 3.052.
Chassis: Box section frame with cross member; front and rear rigid axle with laminated springs, telescopic damper. Front drum brakes, optional front disc brakes, mechanical handbrake on propeller shaft; ball and nut steering; fuel tank 40L (8.8Gal) [10.6US Gal]; tyres 6.00-16, optional 195 SR 15.
Dimensions: Wheelbase 203cm, track 119/120cm, clearance 24cm, turning circle 9.8m, length 319.5cm, width 139.5cm, height 169/170cm.
Performance: Maximum speed approx 62mph/100kmh, speed at 1000rpm in top gear 13.4mph/21.6kmh; power to weight ratio from 36.1kg/kW (26.4kg/PS); consumption approx 4-9L/100km (70.6-31.4mpg) [58.8-26.1US mpg].

Suzuki Jimny 550

```
543cm3 Turbo
31kW-41.5hp-42PS
Fuel Injection
```

As 27hp, except:
Body, Weight: Roadster with fabric top, 2-door, 4-seater; kerbweight (DIN) 780kg. Estate/Station Wagon 3-door, 4-seater; kerbweight (DIN) 810kg.
Engine data (JIS): 3-cylinder in-line (62 x 60mm), 543cm3; compression ratio 8.3:1; 31kW (41.5hp) [42PS] at 6000rpm, 57.1kW/L (76.5hp/L) [77.3PS/L]; 58Nm (43lbft) at 4000rpm.
Engine construction: Electronic fuel injection EPI, turbocharger and charge-air cooler.
Transmission: 5-speed manual, final drive ratio 5.375.
Gear ratios: 1st 4.063; 2nd 2.361; 3rd 1.469; 4th 1; 5th 0.877; R 3.809. Reduction gear: 1st 1.58; 2nd 2.511.
Chassis: Front disc brakes; tyres 175 R 16.
Performance: Maximum speed approx 68.4mph/110kmh, speed at 1000rpm in top gear 16.5mph/26.5kmh; power to weight ratio from 25.2kg/kW (18.6kg/PS); consumption approx 5-10L/100km (56.5-28.2mpg) [47-28.2US mpg].

```
970cm3
33kW-44hp-45PS
1 Compound Carb
```

Engine for SJ 410

As 27hp, except:
Body, Weight: Roadster with fabric top, 2-door, 4-seater; kerbwight (DIN) 870kg, gross vehicle weight 1300kg. Estate/Station Wagon, 3-door, 4-seater; kerbweight (DIN) 890kg, gross vehicle weight 1300kg.
Engine data (DIN): 4-cylinder in-line (65.5 x 72mm), 970cm3; compression ratio 8.8:1; 33kW (44hp) [45PS] at 5500rpm, 34kW/L (45.6hp/L) [56.4PS/L]; 74Nm (55lbft) at 3000rpm.
Japanese Version (JIS): 38kW (51hp) [52PS].
Engine construction: Four stroke engine. Designated F 5 A. Valves in V; 1 overhead camshaft (toothed belt), light-alloy cylinder head; 5 bearing crankshaft; oil capacity 3L (2.8US qt); 1 Mikuni-Solex downdraught compound carb. Battery 12V 30Ah, alternator 35A; cooling system capacity approx 7.2L (6.8US qt).
Transmission: 4-speed manual, final drive ratio 4.11, reduction gear.

Gear ratios: 1st 3.138; 2nd 1.947; 3rd 1.423; 4th 1; R 3.466. Reduction gear: 1st 1.58; 2nd 2.511.
Chassis: Front disc brakes; tyres 195 SR 15.
Dimensions: Wheelbase 203cm, track 121/122cm, clearance 23cm, turning circle 11m, length 343/344cm, width 146cm, height 169cm.
Long wheelbase: Wheelbase 237.5cm, turning circle 13.2m, length 401cm.
Performance: Maximum speed 66-70mph/107-112kmh (manufacturers test specification), speed at 1000rpm in top gear 12.3mph/19.8kmh; power to weight ratio from 26.4kg/kW (19.3kg/PS); consumption ECE 8.5/-/10.4L/100km (33.2/-/27.2mpg) [27.7/-/22.6US mpg].

Suzuki Jimny SJ 413

```
1325cm3
47kW-63hp-64PS
1 Compound Carb
```

Engine for SJ 413

As 27hp, except:
Body, Weight: Roadster with fabric top, 2-door, 4-seater; kerbweight (DIN) 890kg. Estate/Station Wagon, 3-door, 4-seater; kerbweight (DIN) 940kg. Estate/Station Wagon long, 2-door, 4-seater; kerbweight (DIN) 1010kg; max overall weight 1330-1400kg.
Engine data (DIN): 4-cylinder in-line (74 x 77mm), 1325cm3; compression ratio 8.9:1; 47kW (63hp) [64PS] at 6000rpm, 35.5kW/L (47.6hp/L) [48.3PS/L]; 100Nm (73.8lbft) at 3500rpm.
With Catalyst: Identical data.
Engine construction: Four stroke engine. Designated G 13 A. Valves in V: 1 overhead camshaft (toothed belt), light-alloy cylinder head; 5 bearing crankshaft; oil capacity 3L (2.8US qt); 1 Mikuni-Solex downdraught 2V carb. Battery 12V 30/42Ah, alternator 35A; cooling system capacity approx 7.2L (6.8US qt).
Transmission: 5-speed manual, final drive ratio 3.909, reduction gear.
Gear ratios: 1st 3.652; 2nd 1.947; 3rd 1.423; 4th 1; 5th 0.795; R 3.466. Reduction gear: 1st 1.409; 2nd 2.268.
Chassis: Servo/power assisted front disc brakes; tyres 195 SR 15.
Dimensions: Wheelbase 203cm, track 121/122cm, clearance 23cm, turning circle 11m, length 343/344cm, width 146cm, height 169/184cm. Long wheelbase: Wheelbase 237.5cm, turning circle 13.2m, length 401cm.
Performance: Maximum speed 79mph/127kmh (manufacturers test specification), speed at 1000rpm in 4th gear 12mph/19.3kmh; power to weight ratio from 18.9kg/kW (13.9kg/PS); consumption ECE 7.9/8.4/8.9L/100km (35.8/33.6/31.7mpg) [29.8/28.0/26.4US mpg].

Suzuki Escudo/Vitara

New model. Compact three door all-terrain vehicle with four wheel drive and reduction gears. 1.6 Litre, 4-cylinder engine, also available as Hardtop or Convertible. Launched in Summer 1988. European designation is Vitara, USA is Geo Tracker.

```
1.6 Litre
60kW-80hp-82PS
Central/Single Point Injection
```

Suzuki • Tatra

Suzuki Escudo/Vitara

Body, Weight: 2-door convertible Saloon/Sedan, 4-seater; kerbweight (DIN) from 970kg, USA 1015kg, gross vehicle weight 1450kg. 3-door Estate/Station Wagon, 4-seater; kerbweight (DIN) from 990kg, USA 1030kg, gross vehicle weight 1450kg.

Engine data (JIS): 4-cylinder in-line (75 x 90mm), 1590cm3; compression ratio 8.9:1; 60kW (80hp) [82PS] at 5500rpm, 37.7kW/L (50.5hp/L) [51.6PS/L]; 129Nm (95.2lbft) at 3000rpm; regular unleaded grade.
With Catalyst (DIN): 59kW (79hp) [80PS] at 5400rpm; 127Nm (99.5lbft) at 3000rpm; or 60kW (80hp) [82PS] at 5300rpm; 131Nm (96.7lbft) at 2750rpm;
With Carb (DIN): 55kW (74hp) [75PS] at 5250rpm; 123Nm (90.8lbft) at 3100rpm.

Engine construction: Designated G 16 A. Valves in V; 1 overhead camshaft (toothed belt), light-alloy cylinder head; 5 main bearing crankshaft; oil capacity 4.2L (4US qt); EPI electronic central/single point injection, some versions with downdraught carb. Battery 12V 36-50 Ah, Alternator 50-55 A; cooling system capacity 5.3-5.6L (5-5.3US qt).

Transmission (to rear or all wheels): Engageable all-wheel drive, reduction gears, free wheel hubs to front wheels.
a) 5-speed manual, final drive ratio 5.125.
b) Automatic, hydraulic torque converter with 3-speed Planetary gear set, final drive ratio 4.625.

Gear ratios: a) 5-speed manual: 1st 3.652; 2nd 1.947; 3rd 1.379; 4th 1; 5th 0.864; R 3.670.
b) Automatic: Max torque multiplication in converter 2.4 times; Planetary gear set ratios: 1st 2.4; 2nd 1.479; 3rd 1; R 1.92.
Reduction gear ratios: 1st 1; 2nd 1.816.

Chassis: Box section frame with cross members; front shock absorbers, rear A-arm, short coil springs, antiroll bar, rear rigid axle with semi trailing arm, reaction arm, coil springs, telescopic damper. Servo/power assisted brakes, front discs (diameter 29cm), rear drums, mechanical handbrake to rear wheels; recirculating ball steering with optional power steering; fuel tank capacity 42L (9.2Gal) [11.1US Gal]; tyres 195 SR 15 or 205/75 SR 15, wheel rims 5.5 J.

Dimensions: Wheelbase 220cm, track 139.5/140cm, clearance 20cm, turning circle 9.8m. Length 356-365cm, width 163-163.5cm, height 166.5cm.

Performance: Max speed 87mph/140kmh (manufacturers test specification), speed at 1000rpm in top gear 18mph/29.0kmh; power to weight ratio from 16.2kg/kW (11.8kg/PS); consumption ECE 7.8/11.4/10.4L/100km (36.2/24.8/27.2mpg) [30.2/20.6/22.6US mpg].

Suzuki Vitara/Geo Tracker

TATRA   CS

Tara Kombinat, 742 21 Koprivnice, Czechoslovakia
Vehicle manufacturer.

Tatra 613-3

Luxury touring vehicle, with air conditioning, V8 engine and rear wheel drive. Long wheelbase version 613 S. 1984; modifications to the body and interior.

Tatra 613-3

```
3.5 Litre V8
123.5kW-166hp-168PS
2 2V Carbs
```

Body, Weight: a) 4-door Saloon/Sedan, 5-seater; kerbweight (DIN) 1690kg, gross vehicle weight 2160kg.
b) Long wheelbase "S" Saloon/Sedan; kerbweight (DIN) 1840kg.
c) Landaulette; kerbweight (DIN) 1800kg.

Engine data (DIN): 8-cylinder in V 90deg (85 x 77mm), 3495cm3; compression ratio 9.3:1; 123.5kW (166hp) [168PS] at 5200rpm, 35.3kW/L (47.3hp/L) [48.1PS/L]; 265Nm (195.6lbft) at 3330rpm; leaded premium grade.

Engine construction: Rear engine. Valves in V 52deg, 2 x 2 overhead camshaft (toothed belt); light-alloy cylinder head; crankshaft with 5 bearings; oil cooler; oil capacity 9.5L (9.0US qt); 2 Jikov 32-34 EDSR downdraught 2 stage carbs. Battery (2 x 6V) 12V 75Ah, alternator 55/75A, air cooling with axial blower.

Transmission (to rear wheels): 4-speed manual, floor shift; final drive ratio 3.15, S 3.909.

Gear ratios: 1st 3.394; 2nd 1.889; 3rd 1.165; 4th 0.862; R 3.244.

Chassis: Integral body; front McPherson struts with lower control arms, tension struts and stabiliser; rear independent suspension with semi-trailing A arm, coil springs, telescopic damper. Servo/power assisted disc brakes, front disc diameter 28cm, rear 26.8cm; rear mechanical handbrake; rack and pinion steering; fuel tank 2 x 36L (7.9Gal) [9.5US Gal] including approx 8L (1.76Gal) [2.1US Gal] Reserve; tyres 205/70 HR 14, wheels 6J.

Dimensions: Wheelbase 298cm, track 152/152cm, clearance 16cm, turning circle 12.5m; load space 15.2cu ft (430dm3); length 500cm, width 180cm, height 144cm. Long wheelbase Saloon/Sedan and Landaulette: Wheelbase 315cm, length 515cm.

Performance: Max speed 118-124mph/190-200kmh (manufacturers test specifications), speed at 1000rpm in 4th gear 27.3-22.0mph/44-35.4kmh; acceleration 0 - 62mph/100kmh in 10.5-12secs; standing km 33.6secs; power to weight ratio 13.7kg/kW (10.1kg/PS); consumption ECE 10.6/12.8/16.2L/100km (26.6/22.1/17.4mpg) [22.2/18.4/14.5US mpg], S 11.2/14.1/18.3 L/100km (25.2/20.0/15.4US mpg) [21.0/16.7/12.9US mpg].

Tatra 613 S

THUNDERBIRD	USA

See under Ford USA.

TOFAS	TR

Tofas Oto Ticaret A.S, Tofas Han, Kat 1–2–3, Buyukdere Caddesi 145, Zincirlikuyu, 80622 Istanbul, Turkey

Turkish vehicle manufacturer, producing vehicles under licence from Fiat.

Tofas Murat 131

Dogan – Sahin – Kartal

Based on the Fiat 131, Saloon/Sedan or Estate/Station Wagon, 1.6 Litre engine, also available with a 1.3 Litre 4–speed manual transmission.

> 1585cm3
> 55kW–74hp–75PS
> 1 2V Carb

Body, Weight: 4–door Sahin Saloon/Sedan, 6–seater; kerbweight (DIN) 945kg, gross vehicle weight 1410kg. 4–door Dogan Saloon/Sedan, 5–seater; kerbweight (DIN) 985kg, gross vehicle weight 1450kg. 5–door Kartal Estate/Station Wagon, 5–seater; kerbweight (DIN) 1060kg, gross vehicle weight 1550kg.

Engine data (DIN): 4–cylinder in–line (84 x 71.5mm), 1585cm3; compression ratio 8:1; 55kW (74hp) [75PS] at 5400rpm, 34.8kW/L (46.6hp/L) [47.3PS/L]; 124Nm (91.5lbft) at 3000rpm; leaded regular grade.

Engine construction: Designated: 131 C.2000. Valves in V 6deg, 1 overhead camshaft (toothed belt); light–alloy cylinder head; crankshaft with 5 bearings; oil capacity 4.25L (4.1US qt); 1 Weber 32 ADF 21/250 downdraught 2V carb. Battery 12V 45Ah, alternator 55A; cooling system capacity 7.4L (7.0US qt).

Transmission (to rear wheels): a) 4–speed manual, final drive ratio 4.1 (10/41), Sahin 3.727.
b) 5–speed manual, only available for Dogan, final drive ratio 4.1 (10/41).

Gear ratios: a) 4–speed manual: 1st 3.612; 2nd 2.045; 3rd 1.357; 4th 1; R 3.244.
b) 5–speed manual: 1st 3.612; 2nd 2.045; 3rd 1.357; 4th 1; 5th 0.834; R 3.244.

Chassis: Integral body; front McPherson struts, coil springs and coaxial telescopic damper, control arm and antiroll bar, rear rigid axle and coil springs, longitudinal thrust and reaction struts, Panhard rod, telescopic damper. Servo/power assisted brakes, front disc, diameter 22.7cm, rear drums; mechanical handbrake; rack and pinion steering; fuel tank 50L (11.0Gal) [13.2US Gal], including 5–7L(1.1–1.5Gal) [1.3–1.8US Gal] Reserve; tyres 165 SR 13, Kartal 175 SR 14, wheels 41/2J.

Tofas Murat 131 Sahin

Dimensions: Wheelbase 249cm, track 138/132.5cm, clearance 12cm, turning circle 10.3m; load space 22.6/41.3cu ft (640/1170dm3), length 424cm, Estate/Station Wagon 432cm, width 163/164cm, height 136cm, Estate/Station Wagon 152.5cm.

Performance: Max speed 99mph/160kmh (manufacturers test specifications), speed at 1000rpm in 4th gear (165 SR 13) 16.5mph/26.5kmh; acceleration 0 – 62mph/100kmh in 14.5–16.5 secs; power to weight ratio 17.1kg/kW (12.6kg/PS); consumption ECE 7.6/10.8/9.4L/100km (37.2/26.2/30.1mpg) [30.9/21.8/25.0US mpg].

> 1297cm3
> 48kW–64hp–65PS
> 1 2V Carb

As 1585cm3, except:

Engine data (DIN): 4–cylinder in–line (76 x 71.5mm), 1297cm3; compression ratio 8.2:1; 48kW (64hp) [65PS] at 5400rpm, 36.8kW/L (49.3hp/L) [50.1PS/L]; 102Nm (75.3lbft) at 3000rpm.

Engine construction: 1 Weber 32 ADF 7/250 downdraught 2V carb.

Performance: Max speed 93mph/150kmh (manufacturers test specifications), power to weight ratio from 19.8kg/kW (14.5kg/PS); consumption (touring) approx 6–11L/100km (47.1– 25.7mpg) [39.2–21.4US mpg].

Tofas Murat 131 Kartal

Tofas Murat Serce

Based on the early Fiat 124, with a 1.3 Litre engine and 4–speed transmission.

> 1297cm3
> 48kW–64hp–65PS
> 1 2V Carb

Body, Weight: 4–door Saloon/Sedan, 5–seater; kerbweight (DIN) from 895kg, gross vehicle weight 1320kg.

Engine data (DIN): 4–cylinder in–line (76 x 71.5mm), 1297cm3; compression ratio 8.2:1; 48kW (64hp) [65PS] at 5400rpm, 36.8kW/L (49.3hp/L) [50.1PS/L]; 102Nm (75.3lbft) at 3000rpm.

Engine construction: Valve in V 6deg, 1 overhead camshaft (toothed belt); light–alloy cylinder head; crankshaft with 5 bearings; oil capacity 4.2L (4.0US qt); 1 Weber 32 ADF 7/250 downdraught carb. Battery 12V 45Ah, alternator 55A; cooling system capacity 7.4L (7.0US qt).

Transmission (to rear wheels): 4–speed manual, final drive ratio 3.727.

Gear ratios: 1st 3.75; 2nd 2.3; 3rd 1.49; 4th 1; R 3.87.

Chassis: Integral body; front keystone A arm and coil springs, rear rigid axle with coil springs, longitudinal thrust and reaction struts, Panhard rod, front and rear antiroll bars, telescopic damper. Servo/power assisted brakes, front disc, rear drums, disc diameter 25.3cm, rear mechanical handbrake; rack and pinion steering; fuel tank 39L (8.6Gal) [10.3US Gal]; tyres 155 SR 13, wheels 4.5.

Dimensions: Wheelbase 242cm, track 134/131cm, clearance 17cm, turning circle 11.4m; load space 13.6–14.8cu ft (385–420dm3), length 400cm, width 161.5cm, height 136.5cm.

Performance: Max speed 93mph/150kmh (manufacturers test specifications), speed at 1000rpm in 4th gear 17.7mph/28.4kmh; acceleration 0 – 62mph/100kmh in 19.0secs; power to weight ratio from 18.6kg/kW (13.8kg/PS); consumption ECE 7.1/9.5/11.1L/100km (39.8/29.7/25.4mpg) [33.1/24.8/21.2US mpg].

Tofas Murat Serce

de TOMASO I

de Tomaso Modena S.p.A. Automobili, Viale Virgilio M9, 41100 Modena, Italia

Italian manufacturer of special and high performance vehicles.

de Tomaso Pantera

Sports Coupe with a Ford V8 engine, body by Ghia. Launched New York 1970.

```
5.8 Litre V8
198.5/220.5kW-266/296hp-270/300PS
1 4V Carb
```

Body, Weight: 2–door Coupe, 2–seater; kerbweight (DIN) from 1420kg, gross vehicle weight 1600kg.

Engine data (DIN): 8–cylinder in V 90deg (101.65 X 88.9mm), 5769cm3; compression ratio 8.5:1; 156kW (209hp) [212PS] at 4200rpm, 27.1kW/L (36.3hp/L) [36.PS/L]; 441Nm (325.5lbft) at 2500rpm.
Optional: 182kW (244hp) [247PS]; 198kW (265hp) [270PS]; 220kW (295hp) [300PS]; 242kW (324hp) [330PS].

Engine construction: Ford mid–engine, hydraulic tappets, central camshaft (chain); crankshaft with 5 bearings; (optional) oil cooler, oil capacity 5.5L (5.2US qt); 1 Motorcraft downdraught 4V carb. Battery 12V 70/90Ah, alternator 61A; cooling system capacity 24L (22.7US qt).

Transmission (to rear wheels): 5–speed manual ZF, final drive ratio 4.22 (9/38); limited slip differential.

Gear ratios: 1st 2.23; 2nd 1.47; 3rd 1.04; 4th 0.85; 5th 0.71; R 2.865.

Chassis: Integral body; front keystone A arm, coil springs, rear independent suspension with keystone control arms, coil springs with coaxial telescopic damper, front and rear antiroll bars. Servo/power assisted (ventilated) disc brakes, front disc diameter 28.8cm, rear 29.7cm, rear mechanical handbrake; rack and pinion steering; fuel tank 80/85L (17.6/18.7Gal) [21.1/22.5US Gal]; front tyres 185/70 VR 15, rear 215/70 VR 15, front wheels 7", rear 8", (optional) 8" or 10" or front tyres C 60/15, rear H 60/15 or front 225/50 VR 15, rear 285/50 VR 15; (optional) 285/40 VR 15, rear 345/35 VR 15, tyres 10/13".

Dimensions: Wheelbase 251.5cm, track 145/146 or 151/157cm, clearance 13/12cm, turning circle 12m; length 427–445cm, width 183–197cm, height 110cm.

Performance: Max speed [212PS] 137mph/220kmh, [270PS] 155mph/250kmh, [330PS] 174mph/280kmh (manufacturers test specification), speed at 1000rpm in 5th gear 24mph/38kmh; acceleration 0 - 62mph/100kmh approx 6secs [212PS] standing km 27.7secs; consumption (touring) 15-25L/100km (18.8-11.3mpg) [15.7-9.4US mpg]

de Tomaso Pantera

de Tomaso Deauville – Longchamp

Luxury Saloon/Sedan and Coupe with a Ford V8 engine. Launch of the Deauville Turin 1970, Longchamp Turin 1972, Longchamp GTS and Convertible summer 1980.

```
5.8 Litre V8
198.5/220kW-266/296hp-270/300PS
1 4V Carb
```

Body, Weight: 4–door Deauville Saloon/Sedan, 5–seater; kerbweight (DIN) 1940kg, gross vehicle weight 2340kg. 2–door Longchamp Coupe, 4/5–seater; kerbweight (DIN) 1700kg, gross vehicle weight 2100kg. 2–door Longchamp Convertible, 2+2–seater; kerbweight (DIN) approx 1750kg.

Engine data (DIN): 8–cylinder in V 90deg (101.65 x 88.9mm) 5769cm3; compression ratio 8.5:1; 198.5kW (266hp) [270PS] at 5600rpm, 34.4kW/L (46.1hp/L) [46.8PS/L]; 441Nm (325.5bft) at 3500rpm.
Optional: 220kW (296hp) [300PS] at 6000rpm.

Engine construction: Hydraulic tappets; central camshaft (chain); crankshaft with 5 bearings; optional oil cooler; oil capacity 5.5L (5.2US qt); 1 Motocraft downdraught 4V carb. Battery 12V 70/72Ah, alternator 61A, cooling system capacity 18L (17US qt).

Transmission (to rear wheels): a) 5-speed manual, final drive ratio 3.54 or 3.31. b) Automatic (Cruise–O–Matic): hydraulic torque converter and 3-speed Planetary gear set, selector lever in the middle, final drive ratio 3.07.

Gear ratios: a) 5-speed manual: 1st 2.91; 2nd 1.78; 3rd 1.22; 4th 1; 5th 0.845; R 2.70.
b) Automatic: Max torque multiplication in converter 2.05 times, Planetary gear set ratios: 1st 2.46; 2nd 1.46; 3rd 1; R 2.1.

Chassis: Integral body, front keystone–A arm, coil springs, rear independent suspension with control arm, coil springs, front antiroll bar, telescopic damper. Servo/power assisted (ventilated) disc brakes, front disc diameter 28.8cm, rear 27.5cm, rear mechanical handbrake; power assisted rack and pinion steering, fuel tank 100L (22.0Gal) [26.4US Gal]; tyres 215/70 VR 15, wheels 7"; front 225/50 VR 15, rear 285/50 VR 15, wheels front 8", rear 10".

Dimensions: Wheelbase 260cm, track 152/152cm, or 157/162cm, clearance 15cm, or 12cm, turning circle 12m; length 460cm, width 183cm, GTS 195.5cm, height 130cm.

Performance: Max speed 137-149mph/220-240kmh (manufacturers test specifications), speed at 1000rpm in 5th gear (3.54:1) 26.1/42kmh, automatic (3.07:1) 25.5mph/41kmh; power to weight ratio from 7.7kg/kW (5.7kg/PS); consumption (touring) approx 17-25L/100km (16.6-11.3mpg) [13.8-9.4US mpg].

de Tomaso Longchamp

TOYOTA J

Toyota Motor Co Ltd, Toyota-shi, Aichi-ken, Japan

Japanese producer of vehicles since 1937.

MODEL RANGE
Starlet – Corolla – Sprinter – Tercel – Corsa – Corona – Carina – Celica – MR 2 – Camry/Vista – Mark II Cressida/Chaser/Cresta – Crown – Soarer – Century – Blizzard – Land Cruiser - 4-Runner.

Toyota Starlet

Medium size vehicle with tailgate, new generation 4-cylinder engines and front wheel drive. Launched October 1984. Summer 1986; available with turbocharger and 103hp.

```
1 Litre
40kW-53hp-54PS
1 2V Carb
```

Engine for Export

Toyota

Body, Weight: 3-door Saloon/Sedan, 4/5-seater; kerbweight (DIN) 745-765kg, gross vehicle weight 1225kg. 5-door Saloon/Sedan, 4/5-seater; kerbweight (DIN) 755-775kg, gross vehicle weight 1225kg.

Engine data (DIN): 4-cylinder in-line (70.5 x 64mm), 999cm3; compression ratio 9:1; 40kW (53hp) [54PS] at 6000rpm, 40.1kW/L (53.7hp/L) [54.0PS/L]; 75Nm (55.4lbft) at 3800rpm, regular grade.

Engine construction: Transverse front engine. Designated 1-EL. 3 valves per cylinder; 1 overhead camshaft (toothed belt); light-alloy cylinder head; crankshaft with 5 bearings; oil capacity 3.2L (3.0US qt); 1 Aisan downdraught 2V carb. Battery 12V 40/60Ah, alternator 40A, cooling system capacity 4.6L (4.4US qt).

Transmission (to front wheels): a) 4-speed manual, final drive ratio 4.312 or 4.058.
b) 5-speed manual, final drive ratio 4.312 or 4.058.

Gear ratios: a) 4-speed manual: 1st 3.545; 2nd 1.904; 3rd 1.310; 4th 0.969; R 3.250.
b) 5-speed manual: 1st 3.545; 2nd 1.904; 3rd 1.310; 4th 1.031; 5th 0.864; R 3.250.

Chassis: Integral body; front McPherson struts, A arm and antiroll bars, rear semi-rigid axle (trailing arm, axle tube) with McPherson struts: Panhard rod and antiroll bars, telescopic damper. Servo/power assisted brakes, front disc, rear drum, rear mechanical handbrake; rack and pinion steering; fuel tank 40L (8.8Gal) [10.6US Gal]; tyres 145 SR 13, optional 155 SR 13, wheels 4.5J.

Dimensions: Wheelbase 230cm, track 138.5/134.5cm, clearance 16.5cm, turning circle 9.8m; load space VDA 11.7/32cu ft (331/906dm3), length 370cm, width 159cm, height 139.5cm.

Performance: Max speed 93mph/150kmh (manufacturers test specifications), speed at 1000rpm in 5th gear (4.312) 17.3mph/27.8kmh; acceleration 0 – 62mph/100kmh in 13.5secs; power to weight ratio from 18.6kg/kW (13.8kg/PS); consumption ECE 5.1/7.3/6.5L/100km (55.4/38.7/43.5mpg) [46.1/32.2/36.2US mpg].

Toyota Starlet 1.3

```
1.3 Litre
55kW-74hp-75PS
1 Carb
```

As 1 Litre, except:

Weight: Kerbweight 710-785kg.

Engine data (DIN): 4-cylinder in-line (73 x 77.4mm), 1296cm3; compression ratio 9.0:1; 55kW (74hp) [75PS] at 6200rpm, 42.6kW/L (57.1hp/L) [57.9PS/L]; 103Nm (76lbft) at 4200rpm.
With unregulated Cataylst: Identical.
With Catalyst (DIN): 53kW (71hp) [72PS] at 6000rpm; 103Nm (76lbft) at 3600rpm.
Japanese version (JIS net): Compression ratio 9.5:1; 54kW (72hp) [73PS] at 6000rpm; 101Nm (74.5lbft) at 4000rpm.

Engine construction: Designation 2E-LU. 1 Aisan constant pressure carb.

Transmission: a) 4-speed manual, final drive ratio 3.722 or 3.526.
b) 5-speed manual, final drive ratio 3.941 or 3.722.
c) Automatic, hydraulic torque converter and 3-speed Planetary gear set, final drive ratio 3.333.

Gear ratios: a) 4-speed manual; As 1 Litre.
b) 5-speed manual: 1st 3.545; 2nd 1.904; 3rd 1.310; 4th 0.969; 5th 0.815; R 3.250.
c) Automatic, Max torque multiplication in converter 2.5 times, Planetary gear set ratios: 1st 2.810; 2nd 1.549; 3rd 1; R 2.296.

Chassis: For Japan also without front antiroll bars, optional power assisted steering; also tyres 165/70 SR 13 and wheels 5J.

Performance: Max speed 106mph/170kmh (manufacturers test specifications), speed at 1000rpm in 5th gear (3.941, 165/70 SR 13) 20.1mph/32.3kmh; acceleration 0 – 62mph/100kmh in 10.5secs; power to weight from 13.1kg/kW (9.7kg/PS); consumption ECE 5.3/7.4/6.8L/100km (53.3/38.2/41.5mpg) [44.4/31.8/34.6US mpg], 5-speed 4.9/6.8/6.8L/100km (57.6/41.5/41.5mpg) [48/34.6/34.6US mpg].

```
1.3 Litre
77kW-103hp-105PS
Turbo/Fuel Injection
```

As 1 Litre, except:

Weight: Kerbweight 770kg.

Engine data (JIS net): 4-cylinder in-line (73 x 77.4mm), 1296cm3; compression ratio 8.2:1; 77kW (103hp) [105PS] at 5600rpm, 59.4kW/L (80hp) [81PS/L]; 149Nm (110lbft) at 3600rpm.

Engine construction: Designated 2E-ELU Turbo. Oil cooler. Electronic fuel injection, 1 exhaust turbocharger, charge-air cooler.

Transmission: 5-speed manual, final drive ratio 3.722.

Gear ratios: 1st 3.166; 2nd 1.904; 3rd 1.310; 4th 0.969; 5th 0.816; R 3.250.

Chassis: Front ventilated disc brakes: tyres 175/60 HR 14, wheels 5J.

Performance: Max speed approx 112mph/180kmh, speed at 1000rpm in 5th gear 21.2mph/34.1kmh; power to weight from 10kg/kW (7.3kg/PS); consumption approx 7-12L/100km (40.4-23.5mpg) [33.6- 19.6US mpg].

```
1.45 Litre Diesel
40kW-54hp-55PS
Injection Pump
```

As 1 Litre, except:

Weight: Kerbweight 770-865kg.

Engine data (JIS net): 4-cylinder in-line (74 x 84.5mm); 1453cm3; compression ratio 22:1; 40kW (54hp) [55PS] at 5200rpm, 27.5kW/L (36.9hp/L) [37.9PS/L]; 91Nm (67.2lbft) at 3000rpm.
European version (DIN): Identical Data.

Engine construction: Designated 1N. Turbulence chamber diesel engine, 2 valves per cylinder, oil capacity 3.8L (3.6US qt); diesel injection pump. Battery 60Ah, alternator 55A, cooling system capacity 5.7L (5.4US qt).

Transmission: 5-speed manual, final drive ratio 3.722.

Gear ratios: 1st 3.545; 2nd 1.904; 3rd 1.310; 4th 0.969; 5th 0.864 or 0.815; R 3.250.

Performance: Max speed 93mph/150kmh (manufacturers test specifications), speed at 1000rpm in 5th gear 20mph/32.2kmh; acceleration 0 – 62mph/100kmh in 14.5secs; power to weight ratio from 19.2kg/kW (14kg/PS); consumption ECE 3.9/5.7/4.7L/100km (72.4/49.6/60.1mpg) [60.3/41.3/50US mpg].

Toyota Corolla – Sprinter

Corolla – Corolla FX – Corolla Levin – Sprinter – Sprinter Cielo – Sprinter Trueno

Medium size vehicle (revised edition), front wheel drive, 1.3 and 1.6 Litre petrol/gasoline engine with multi-valves, 1.8 Litre diesel engine, all round independent suspension. Sprinter for Japan only. Launched May 1987. Spring 1988: Corolla RV 4WD Estate/Station Wagon successosr to the Tercel 4x4.

```
1300
53.5kW-72hp-73PS
1 Carb
```

Body, Weight: 3/5-door FX Saloon/Sedan, 5-seater; kerbweight (DIN) from 880kg. 4-door Saloon/Sedan, 5-seater; kerbweight (DIN) from 880kg. 5-door Saloon/Sedan, 5-seater; kerbweight (DIN) from 900kg. 5-door Estate/Station Wagon, 5-seater; kerbweight (DIN) from 900kg.

Engine data (JIS net): 4-cylinder in-line (73 x 77.4mm), 1296cm3; compression ratio 9.5:1; 53.5kW (72hp) [73PS] at 6000rpm, 41.4kW/L (55.5hp/L) [56.3PS/L]; 101Nm (74.5lbft) at 4000rpm.
European version (DIN): 55kW (74hp) [75PS] at 6200rpm; 103Nm (76lbft) at 4200rpm.
With unregulated Catalyst: Identical data.
With Catalyst (DIN): 53kW (71hp) [72PS] at 6000rpm; 103Nm (76lbft) at 4000rpm; unleaded regular grade.

Toyota

Estate Station/Wagon also with 1.45L (JIS net): (73 x 87mm), 1456cm3; compression ratio 9.3:1; 58kW (78hp) [79PS] at 6000rpm; 118Nm (87.1lbft) at 4000rpm.

Engine construction: Designated 2E. 3 valves per cylinder, 1 camshaft overhead (toothed belt); light–alloy cylinder head; crankshaft with 5 bearings; oil capacity 3.2L (3.0US qt); 1 constant pressure carb. Battery 12V 40–60Ah, alternator 40–60A; cooling system capacity 5.0L (4.7US qt).

Transmission (to front wheels): a) 4–speed manual, final drive ratio 3.722.
b) 5–speed manual, final drive ratio 3.722, 4.058, 4.312.
c) Automatic, hydraulic torque converter and 3–speed Planetary gear set, final drive ratio 3.519, 3.722.

Gear ratios: a) 4–speed manual: 1st 3.545; 2nd 1.904; 3rd 1.310; 4th 0.969; R 3.25.
b) 5–speed manual: 1st 3.545; 2nd 1.904; 3rd 1.310; 4th 0.969; 5th 0.815; R 3.25.
c) Automatic: Max torque multiplication in converter 2.1 times, Planetary gear set ratios: 1st 2.810; 2nd 1.549; 3rd 1; R 2.296.

Chassis: Integral body, front and rear independent suspension with McPherson struts, front lower A arm, rear parallel control arm and trailing arm, front antiroll bars, some models also rear; Estate/Station Wagon (also Van) rear rigid axle with leaf springs. Servo/power assisted brakes, front disc, rear drums, rear mechanical handbrake; rack and pinion steering, fuel tank 50L (11.0Gal) [13.2US Gal] tyres 155 SR 13, optional 175/70 SR 13, wheels 5J, Estate/Station Wagon also tyres 145 SR 13, wheels 4 or 4.5J.

Dimensions: Wheelbase 243cm, track 143/141cm, Van (with rigid axle) 143/143cm, clearance 15.5cm, turning circle 10.2m; load space (VDA) FX 9.9cu ft (281dm3), Hatchback 13.6cu ft (385dm3), Saloon/Sedan 15.5cu ft (440dm3), Estate/Station Wagon 15cu ft (426dm3); Length FX 399.5cm, 4–door 419.5cm, 5–door 321.5cm, Estate/Station Wagon 420.5cm, width 165.5cm, height 136–136.5cm, Estate/Station Wagon 143cm.

Performance: Max speed 96-99mph/155-160kmh (manufacturers test specifications), speed at 1000rpm in 5th gear (4.312) 18.7mph/30.1kmh; acceleration 0 – 62mph/100kmh in 11.7secs; power to weight ratio from 16.4kg/kW (12.1kg/PS); consumption 5.7/7.6/8L/100km (49.6/37.2/35.3mpg) [41.3/30.9/29.4US mpg].

Toyota Corolla FX

1500 DOHC
69/62kW–93/83hp–94/85PS
Fuel Injection/2V Carb

As 1300, except:

Body, Weight: 3/5–door FX Saloon/Sedan, kerbweight from 920kg. 4–door Saloon/Sedan, kerbweight from 910kg. 5–door Saloon/Sedan, 5–seater, kerbweight from 950kg. 5–door Estate/Station Wagon, kerbweight (DIN) from 980kg. 2–door Coupe, 5–seater, kerbweight (DIN) from 910kg.

Engine data (JIS net): 4–cylinder in–line (78.7 x 77mm), 1498cm3; compression ratio 9.8:1; 69kW (93hp) [94PS] at 6000rpm, 46.1kW/L (61.8hp/L) [62.7PS.L]; 129Nm (95.2lbft) at 4400rpm.
With Carb: 62kW (83hp) [85PS] at 6000rpm; 123Nm (90.8lbft) at 3600rpm.

Engine construction: Designated 5A–F/FE. 4 valves (in V) per cylinder; 2 overhead camshaft (toothed belt/toothed wheel); electronic fuel injection, 83hp version, 1 Aisan two stage carb. Cooling system capacity 5.2L (4.9US qt).

Transmission: a) 5–speed manual, final drive ratio 4.058. 83hp: 3.722.
b) 3–speed automatic (83hp only), final drive ratio 3.333.
c) 4–speed automatic, final drive ratio 2.821.

Gear ratios: a) 5–speed manual, as 1300.
b) 3–speed automatic, as 1300.
c) 4–speed automatic, Planetary gear set ratios: 1st 3.643; 2nd 2.008; 3rd 1.296; OD 0.892; R 2.977.

Chassis (93hp): Front and rear antiroll bars; front ventilated disc brakes; optional power assisted steering; tyres 175/70 SR 13, optional 185/60 HR 14, wheels 5, optional 5.5J; Estate/Station Wagon (83hp) tyres 155 SR 13 or 175 SR 13, wheels 5J.

Dimensions: Track also 144.5/142.5cm; Coupe length 422.5cm, width 166.5cm, height 130cm.

Performance (93hp): Max speed approx 109–115mph/175–185kmh. power to weight ratio from 14.2kg/kW (10.4kg/PS); consumption approx 6–11L/100km (47.1–25.7mpg) [39.2–21.4US mpg].

Toyota Corolla Liftback

1600 DOHC
67/77kW–90/103hp–91/105PS
1 2V Carb/Fuel Injection

Engine for the Export and 4WD

As 1300, except:

Body, Weight: 3/5–door FX Saloon/Sedan, kerbweight (DIN) 960/1015kg. 4–door Saloon/Sedan, kerbweight (DIN) 970–1025kg, USA from 1000kg, 4WD 1060-1220, USA from 1180kg. 5–door Saloon/Sedan, kerbweight (DIN) 995–1050kg. 5–door Estate/Station Wagon, kerbweight (DIN) 1025kg, USA 1035kg, RV 4WD 1120-1200 (USA from 1220kg). 2–door Coupe (USA only), 5–seater, kerbweight (DIN) from 1015kg. 4–door four wheel drive Saloon/Sedan, kerbweight (DIN) 1060– 1220kg.

Engine data (Catalyst, DIN): 4–cylinder in–line (81 x 77mm), 1587cm3; compression ratio 9.5:1; 66kW (88hp) [90PS] at 6000rpm, 42kW/L (56.3hp/L) [56.7PS/L]; 132Nm (97.4lbft) at 3600rpm; unleaded regular grade.
USA version (SAE net): Identical data.
Without Catalyst (also 4WD, DIN): 70kW (94hp) [95PS] at 6000rpm; 135Nm (99.6lbft) at 3600rpm.
For 4WD (with injection): 77kW (103hp) [105PS] at 5600rpm, 48.5kW/L (64.9hp/L) [66.2PS/L]; 142Nm (104.8lbft).
Japanese version, four wheel drive (JIS net): 67kW (90hp) [91PS] at 6000rpm; 132Nm (97.4lbft) at 3600rpm.

Engine construction: Designated 4A–F/FE. 4 valves (in V) per cylinder; 2 overhead camshafts (toothed belt/toothed wheel); 88/90/94hp; 1 downdraught carb, electrically regulated, 103hp; electronic fuel injection. Battery 40Ah, four wheel drive 60Ah, alternator 60A, cooling system capacity 5.2/5.6L (4.9/5.3US qt).

Transmission (to all wheels, 4WD to all wheels): a) 5–speed manual, final drive ratio 4.058, USA 3.722, 4WD 4.235 or 4.562 (RV).
b) 3–speed automatic, final drive ratio 3.526.
c) 4–speed automatic, final drive ratio 2.821, USA 2.962, four wheel drive 3.034.
4WD: Permanent all wheel drive, central differential (50/50%), manual lock bar or (in connection with automatic) hydraulic multi-plate clutch limited slip differential.

Gear ratios: a) 5–speed manual: 1st 3.166 (USA 3.545); 2nd 1.904; 3rd 1.310; 4th 0.969; 5th 0.815; R 3.25. With 4WD: 1st 3.538; 2nd 2.045; 3rd 1.333; 4th 0.972; 5th 0.820; R 3.583.
RV Wagon: 1st 3.833; 2nd 2.045; 3rd 1.333; 4th 0.918; 5th 0.755; R 3.583.
b) 3–speed automatic, as 1300.
c) 4–speed automatic, Planetary gear set ratios: 1st 3.643; 2nd 2.008; 3rd 1.296; OD 0.892; R 2.977.

Chassis: Front and rear antiroll bars, front ventilated disc brakes; optional power assisted steering; tyres 155 SR 13 or 175/70 SR 13, wheels 5J. 4WD: Rear rigid axle with coil springs, 4 trailing arms, Panhard rod; tyres 165 SR 13 or 185/70 SR 13, wheels 5J.

Toyota

Dimensions: Length (USA) Saloon/Sedan 432cm, Estate/Station Wagon 435.5cm. Coupe (USA): Track 144.5/142.5cm; length 437.5cm, width 166.5cm, height 126cm. 4WD: Track 144/138cm; clearance 17cm, turning circle 10.6m. Load space RV Wagon 11.5-21.8cu ft (327-618dm3), length RV Wagon 425cm, height Saloon/Sedan 138cm, RV Wagon 145-148.5cm.

Performance: Max speed 109mph/175kmh, automatic 106mph/170kmh, 4WD (103hp) 112mph/180kmh, RV Wagon 129mph/175kmh (manufacturers test specification) speed at 1000rpm in 5th gear 19.9mph/32.0kmh, 4WD 19.5mph/31.4kmh; acceleration 0 – 62mph/100kmh 10.8secs, automatic 13.1secs, 4WD in 12secs; power to weight ratio from 14.5kg/kW (10.7kg/PS); consumption ECE 5.6/7.6/8.6L/100km (50.4/37.2/32.8mpg) [42/30.9/27.4US mpg].

Toyota Corolla RV/Carib 4WD

```
1600 DOHC
88kW–118hp–120PS
Fuel Injection
```

As 1300, except:

Body, Weight: 3–door FX Saloon/Sedan, kerbweight from 1020kg. 4–door Saloon/Sedan, kerbweight from 1020kg. 2–door Coupe, 5–seater, kerbweight from 990kg, USA 1075kg.

Engine data (JIS net): 4–cylinder in–line (81 x 77mm), 1587cm3; compression ratio 9.4:1; 88kW (118hp) [120PS] at 6600rpm, 55.5kW/L (74.4hp/L) [75.6PS/L]; 142Nm (104.8lbft) at 5200rpm.
With Catalyst (DIN): 85kW (114hp) [116PS] at 6600rpm; 138Nm (101.8lbft) at 5000rpm; unleaded premium grade.
USA version (SAE net): Identical data.
Without Catalyst (DIN): Compression ratio 10:1; 92kW (123hp) [125PS] at 6600rpm; 145Nm (107lbft) at 5000rpm.

Toyota Corolla 1600 Compact GTi

Engine construction: Designated 4A–GE. 4 valves (in V) per cylinder; 2 overhead camshafts (toothed belt); oil capacity 3.7L (3.5US qt), oil cooler; electronic fuel injection (Bosch). Battery 12V 60Ah, alternator 60A; cooling system capacity 6L (5.7US qt).

Transmission: a) 5–speed manual, final drive ratio 4.312.
b) 4–speed automatic, final drive ratio 2.821.

Gear ratios: a) 5–speed manual: 1st 3.166; 2nd 1.904; 3rd 1.310; 4th 0.969; 5th 0.815; R 3.25.
b) 4–speed automatic, Planetary gear set ratios: 1st 3.643; 2nd 2.008; 3rd 1.296; OD 0.892; R 2.997.

Chassis: Front and rear antiroll bars; all round disc brakes, front ventilated; optional power assisted steering; tyres 185/60 HR 14, wheels 5.5J.

Dimensions: Track 144.5/142.5cm. Coupe; length 422.5cm, USA 437.5cm, width 166.5cm, height 130cm, USA 126cm.

Performance: Max speed 118mph/190kmh (manufacturers test specifications), speed at 1000rpm in 5th gear 18.8mph/30.2kmh; acceleration 0 – 62mph/100kmh in 8.5secs; power to weight ratio from 11.2kg/kW (8.2kg/PS); consumption (urban, town, combination) 6.0/8.3/7.3L/100km (47.1/34.0/38.7mpg) [39.2/28.3/32.2US mpg].

Toyota Corolla Twin Cam 16 Coupe (USA)

```
1600 DOHC
107kW–143hp–145PS
Compressor/Fuel Injection
```

As 1300, except:

Body, Weight: 2–door Coupe, 5–seater, kerbweight (DIN) 1070kg.

Engine data (JIS net): 4–cylinder in–line (81 x 77mm), 1587 cm3; compression ratio 8:1; 107kW (143hp) [145PS] at 6400rpm, 67.4kW/L (90.3hp/L) [91.4PS/L]; 186Nm (137.3lbft) at 4400rpm.

Engine construction: Designated 4A–GZE. 4 valves (in V) per cylinder; 2 overhead camshaft (toothed belt); oil capacity 3.7L (3.5US qt), oil cooler; 1 SC 12 mechanical compressor, type Roots, charge–air cooler; Bosch L–Jetronic electronic fuel injection (under license). Battery 12V 60Ah, alternator 60A; cooling system capacity approx 6L (5.7US qt).

Transmission: 5–speed manual, final drive ratio 3.993.

Gear ratios: 1st 3.230; 2nd 2.045; 3rd 1.333; 4th 0.972; 5th 0.820; R 3.583.

Chassis: Front and rear antiroll bars; all round disc brakes, front ventilated; optional power assisted steering; tyres 195/60 HR 14, wheels 5.5J.

Dimensions: Track 145.5/143.5cm; length 422.5cm, width 168cm, height 130cm.

Performance: Max speed over 124mph/200kmh, speed at 1000rpm in 5th gear 20.8mph/33.5kmh; power to weight ratio from 10.0kg/kW (7.4kg/PS); consumption approx 8–14L/100km (35.3–20.2mpg) [29.4– 16.8US mpg].

```
1800 Diesel
47kW–63hp–64PS
Injection Pump
```

As 1300, except:

Body, Weight: 4–door Saloon/Sedan, kerbweight from 990kg.

Engine data (JIS net): (83 x 85mm), 1840cm3; compression ratio 23:1; 47kW (63hp) [64PS] at 4700rpm, 25.6kW/L (34.3hp/L) [34.8PS/L]; 118Nm (87.1lbft) at 2600rpm.
European Version (DIN): Identical.

Engine construction: Designated 1C–L. 2 valves per cylinder; oil capacity 4.3L (4.1US qt); diesel injection pump. Battery 12V 65Ah, alternator 55A; cooling system capacity 7.3L (6.9US qt).

Transmission: a) 5–speed manual, final drive ratio 3.736.
b) Automatic, hydraulic torque converter and 4–speed Planetary gear set; final drive ratio 2.724.

Gear ratios: a) 5–speed manual: 1st 3.538; 2nd 2.041; 3rd 1.322; 4th 0.945; 5th 0.731; R 3.153.
b) 4–speed automatic: Planetary gear set ratios: 1st 3.643; 2nd 2.008; 3rd 1.296; OD 0.892; R 2.977.

Chassis: Optional power assisted steering; tyres 165 SR 13.

Toyota

Performance: Max speed approx 99mph/160kmh, speed at 1000rpm in 5th gear 24.9mph/40.0kmh; acceleration 0 - 62mph/100kmh 14.5secs; power to weight ratio from 21.0kg/kW (15.5kg/PS); consumption ECE 4.4/6.2/6.4L/100km (64.2/45.6/44.1mpg) [53.5/37.9/36.8US mpg].

Toyota Tercel – Corsa – Corolla II

Front wheel drive medium size vehicle. 3/5–door Saloon/Sedan (Hatchback) with transverse 4–cylinder 1.3 or 1.45 Litre engines and Turbodiesel. Launched May 1986.

```
1300
54kW–72hp–73PS
1 Carb
```

Body, Weight: 3–door Saloon/Sedan, 5–seater; kerbweight (DIN) from 800kg. 5–door Saloon/Sedan, 5–seater; kerbweight (DIN) from 820kg.

Engine data (JIS net): 4–cylinder in–line (73 x 77.4mm), 1296cm3; compression ratio 9.5:1; 54kW (72hp) [73PS] at 6000rpm, 41.7kW/L (55.9hp/L) [56.3PS/L]; 101Nm (74.5lbft) at 4000rpm.
Or compression ratio 10:1; 49kW (66hp) [67PS] at 6000rpm; 98Nm (72.3lbft) at 3600rpm.

Engine construction: Transverse front engine. Designated 2E-LU. 3 valves per cylinder; 1 overhead camshaft (toothed belt); light– alloy cylinder head; crankshaft with 5 bearings; oil capacity 3.2L (3US qt); 1 Aisan constant pressure carb. Battery 12V 40/60Ah, alternator 40/50A; cooling system capacity 4.9L (4.6US qt).

Transmission (to front wheels): a) 4–speed manual, final drive ratio 3.722 or (66hp) 3.095.
b) 5–speed manual, final drive ratio 3.722.
c) Automatic, hydraulic torque converter and 3–speed Planetary gear set, final drive ratio 3.519.

Gear ratios: a) 4–speed manual: 1st 3.545; 2nd 1.904; 3rd 1.310; 4th 0.969; R 3.25. Or: 1st 3.545; 2nd 1.904; 3rd 1.233; 4th 0.885; R 3.25.
b) 5–speed manual: 1st 3.545; 2nd 1.904; 3rd 1.310; 4th 0.969; 5th 0.815; R 3.25.
c) Automatic: Max torque multiplication in converter 2.1 times, Planetary gear set ratios: 1st 2.810; 2nd 1.549; 3rd 1; R 2.296.

Chassis: Integral body; front McPherson struts, A–arm and antiroll bar, rear laminated compound axle (trailing arm, torsion tube axle) with McPherson struts, Panhard rod and antiroll bar, telescopic damper. Servo/power assisted brakes, front disc, rear drums, rear mechanical handbrake; rack and pinion steering; fuel tank 45L (9.9Gal) [11.9US Gal]; tyres 145 SR 13, optional 155 SR 13, tyres 41/2J.

Dimensions: Wheelbase 238cm, track 138.5/137.5cm, clearance 16cm. Turning circle 9.8m, length 386.5cm, width 162.5cm, height 137– 138cm.

Performance: Max speed approx 99mph/160kmh; speed at 1000rpm in 5th gear (3.722) 21.2mph/34.1kmh; power to weight ratio from 14.8kg/kW (11kg/PS); consumption approx 5–9L/100km (56.5–31.4mpg) [47.0–26.1US mpg].

Toyota Corsa

```
1450
81/57kW–109/87hp–110/88PS
Turbo/Fuel Injection
```

As 1300, except:

Body, Weight: 3–door Saloon/Sedan; kerbweight (DIN) from 850kg, USA from 895kg, Turbo from 890kg. 5–door Saloon/Sedan; kerbweight (DIN) from 840kg, USA from 920kg. 2–door Coupe (USA only), 4–seater; kerbweight (DIN) from 910kg.

Engine data (JIS net): 4–cylinder in–line (73 x 87mm), 1456cm3; compression ratio 8.0:1; 81kW (109hp) [110PS] at 5600rpm, 55.6kW/L (74.5hp/L) [75.5PS/L]; 169Nm (124.7lbft) at 3200rpm.
Without Turbocharger: Compression ratio 9.3:1; 57kW (87hp) [88PS] at 6000rpm; 120Nm (88.6lbft) at 4800rpm.
USA Version (Carb, SAE net): 58kW (78hp) [79PS] at 6000rpm; 118Nm (87lbft) at 4000rpm.

Engine construction: Designated 3 E-TE/3E-E. Turbo: Oil cooler; Bosch electronic fuel injection. 1 exhaust turbocharger, charge–air cooler. 87hp: electronic central/single point injection (USA carb).

Transmission: a) 4-speed manual (USA), final drive ratio 3.095.
b) 4-speed manual, final drive ratio 3.722.
c) 3-speed Automatic (USA), final drive ratio 3.722.
d) Automatic, hydraulic torque and 4-speed Planetary gear set, final drive ratio 2.821, without Turbo 2.962.

Gear ratios: a) 4–speed manual (USA): As 1300.
b) 5–speed Automatic: 1st 3.166; 2nd 1.904; 3rd 1.310; 4th 0.969; 5th 0.815; R 3.250. Without Turbo: As 1300.
c) 3-speed Automatic (USA): As 1300
d) 4-speed Automatic: 1st 3.643; 2nd 2.008; 3rd 1.296; OD 0.892; R 2.977.

Chassis: All round disc brakes (turbo only, front ventilated); optional power assisted steering; tyres 185/60 HR 14 (Turbo), 165/70 SR 13, USA also 145 SR 13, wheel rims 5.5J (Turbo), 4.5 or 5.5J.

Dimensions: Turbo; track 139.5/136.5cm. USA: Hatchback; length 399.5cm. Coupe: Length 423.5cm, width 162.5cm, height 131.5cm.

Performance (Turbo): Max speed approx 115mph/185kmh; speed at 1000rpm in 5th gear 21.7mph/34.9kmh; power to weight ratio from 11.0kg/kW (8.1kg/PS); consumption approx 7–13L/100km (40.4–21.7mpg) [33.6– 18.1US mpg].

Toyota Tercel II

```
1450 Diesel
49kW–66hp–67PS
Turbo/Injection Pump
```

As 1300, except:

Weight: Kerbweight (DIN) from 870kg.

Engine data (JIS net): 4–cylinder in–line (74 x 84.5mm), 1453cm3; compression ratio 22:1; 49kW (66hp) [67PS] at 4700rpm, 33.7kW/L (45.2hp/L) [46.1PS/L]; 130Nm (95.9lbft) at 2600rpm.

Engine construction: Designated 1N–T. Turbulence chamber diesel engine. 2 valves per cylinder; oil capacity approx 4L (3.8US qt); diesel injection pump; 1 exhaust turbocharger.

Transmission: a) 5–speed manual, final drive ratio 3.526.
b) Automatic, hydraulic torque converter and 4–speed Planetary gear set, final drive ratio 2.655.

Gear ratios: a) 5–speed manual: 1st 3.545; 2nd 1.904; 3rd 1.310; 4th 0.969; 5th 0.725; R 3.250.
b) Automatic: 1st 3.643; 2nd 2.008; 3rd 1.296; OD 0.892; R 2.977.

Chassis: Optional power assisted steering; tyres 155 SR 13 or 175/60 HR 14, wheels 4.5 or 5J.

Performance: Max speed approx 93mph/150kmh; speed at 1000rpm in 5th gear 25.7mph/41.4kmh; power to weight ratio from 17.7kg/kW (13.0kg/PS); consumption approx 4–9L/100kmh (70.6–31.4mpg) [58.8– 26.1US mpg].

Toyota Corona/Carina II - Celica

Medium size Saloon/Sedan, Estate/Station Wagon (Corona) and soprts Coupe (Corona and Celica); engines from 1.5 to 2.0 Litre. 1983: New Corona with front wheel drive.

August 1985: Coupe Celica remodelled, with front wheel drive. **October 1986:** Celica - high powered version with permanent all wheel drive and turbo engine; Celica also available as convertible (also in the USA). **January 1988:** Corona Saloon/Sedan (in Europe known as the Carina II) and Estate/Station Wagon now with front wheel drive. **Summer 1988:** Carina parallel model and Corona (1.6 Litre) rejuvenated and available with 4WD.

1600 DOHC
74/66kW-100/89hp-102/90PS
Carb/Injection

Engine for Corona 4-door, 1-OHC Version for Estate/Station Wagon.

Body, Weight: 4-door Saloon/Sedan, 5-seater; kerbweight (DIN) from 970kg. 4WD from 1180kg.
5-door Saloon/Sedan, 5-seater; kerbweight (DIN) from 1050kg.
5-door Estate/Station Wagon, 5-seater; kerbweight (DIN) from 960kg; a simple "Van" is also planned.

Engine data (DIN): 4-cylinder in-line (81 x 77mm), 1587cm3, compression ratio 9.5:1; 75kW (100hp) [102PS] at 5800rpm, 47.3kW/L (63.4hp/L) [64.3PS/L]; 142Nm (104.8lbft) at 3000rpm.
For 4WD (JIS): 74kW (99hp) [100PS] at 5600rpm; 137Nm (101lbft) at 4400rpm.
With Catalyst (Carb DIN): 66kW (89hp) [90PS] at 6000rpm; 135Nm (99.6lbft) at 3600rpm.
1.5 Litre (Carb JIS): (78.7 x 77mm), 1498cm3; Compression ratio 9.8:1; 62kW (84hp) [85PS] at 6000rpm; 123Nm (90.8lbft) at 3600rpm.
For Estate/Station Wagon and "Van" (1 OHC, 3 valves): (73 x 87mm), 1456cm3; compression ratio 9.3:1; 58kW (78hp) [79PS] at 6000rpm; 118Nm (87lbft) at 4000rpm.

Engine construction: Designated 4A-F/FE 5A-F (100hp with lean burn). Front transverse engine. 4 valves (in V 22deg) per cylinder, 2 overhead camshaft (toothed belt/toothed wheel); light-alloy cylinder head; crankshaft with 5 bearings; oil capacity 3.2L (3US qt); electronic fuel injection or 1 downdraught 2V carb, electronically controlled. Battery 12V 40-60 Ah, alternator 40-70A; cooling system capacity approx 5L (4.9US qt).

Transmission (to front wheels, 4WD to all wheels): a) 5-speed manual, final drive ratio 3.722, 3.941 or 4.058, 4WD 4.235; Estate/Station Wagon also 3.736; Van also with 4-speed manual, final drive ratio 4.058.
b) Automatic, hydraulic torque converter and 4-speed Planetary gear set, final drive ratio 2.821 or 2.962, 4WD 3.034
4WD: Permanent all wheel drive, central differential (distribution 50/50%), with manual lock bar, with Automatic transmission, automatic limited slip differential (multi plate clutch, electronically regulated).

Gear ratios: a) 5-speed manual: 1st 3.545 (Catalyst 3.166); 2nd 1.904; 3rd 1.310; 4th 0.969; 5th 0.815; R 3.250. Estate/Station Wagon also: 1st 3.538; 2nd 2.041; 3rd 1.322; 4th 0.945; 5th 0.731; R 3.153. 4WD (Van) 4-speed: 1st 3.545; 2nd 1.904; 3rd 1.310; 4th 0.969; R 3.250.
b) Automatic: Max torque multiplication in converter 2.1 times, Planetary gear set ratios: 1st 3.643; 2nd 2.008; 3rd 1.296; OD 0.892; R 2.977.

Chassis: Integral body; front and rear independent suspension, front McPherson struts, lower A-arm, rear McPherson struts, parallel control arm, trailing arm, front and rear antiroll bars; Estate/Station Wagon rear rigid axle with leaf springs. Servo/power assisted brakes, front ventilated disc, rear drums, 4WD with rear discs and optional ABS; handbrake to rear wheels; rack and pinion steering, optional power assisted; fuel tank 60L (13.2Gal) [15.9US Gal], Estate/Station Wagon 55L (12.1Gal) [14.5US Gal]; tyres 165 SR 13, Van 155 SR 13; optional 185/70 SR 13, wheels 5J.

Toyota Carina II

Performance (Catalyst version): Max speed approx 112mph/180kmh speed at 1000rpm in 5th gear (axle 4.058) 24.5mph/33.0kmh; power to weight ratio from 15.6kg/kW (11.4kg/PS); acceleration 0 - 62mph/100kmh 11.5secs; power to weight ratio from 15.6kg/kW (11.4kg/PS); consumption approx ECE 5.4/6.9/8.8L/100km (52.3/40.9/32.1mpg) [43.6/34.1/26.7US mpg].

1600 DOHC
91kW-122hp-124PS
Fuel Injection

Engine for Coupe Celica (Export) and Carina.

As 100/89hp, except:

Body, Weight: 4-door Saloon/Sedan (Japan); kerbweight (DIN) from 1020kg; 2-door Coupe, 4-seater; kerbweight (DIN) 1090kg. 3-door Coupe, 4-seater; kerbweight (DIN) 1110kg.

Engine data (DIN): 4-cylinder in-line (81 x 77mm), 1587cm3; compression ratio 10:1; 91kW (122hp) [124PS] at 6600rpm, 57.3kW/L (76.8hp/L) [78.1PS/L]; 142Nm (104.8lbft) at 5000rpm.
Version for export (ECE): 88kW (118hp) [120PS]; 138Nm (101.8lbft).
Japanese Version (JIS): Compression ratio 9.4:1; 88kW (119hp) [120PS] at 6600rpm; 142Nm (104.8lbft) at 5200rpm.

Engine construction: Designated 4A-GELU. Camshaft drive, toothed belt only; oil capacity 3.7L (3.5US qt), oil cooler; electronic fuel injection. Battery 60Ah, alternator 60A; cooling system capacity 6L (5.7US qt).

Transmission: a) 5-speed manual, final drive ratio 4.312.
b) Automatic (Carina), final drive ratio 2.892.

Gear ratios: a) 1st 3.166; 2nd 1.904; 3rd 1.310; 4th 0.969; 5th 0.815; R 3.25.
b) Automatic: As 1600.

Chassis: All round disc brakes, front ventilated; tyres 185/70 HR 14 or 195/60 HR 14; wheels 5.5 or 6J.

Dimensions (Celica): Track 146.5/143cm; load space 14-33cu ft (395-935dm3), length 436.5cm, width 171cm, height 129cm.

Performance (Celica): Max speed 124mph/200kmh (manufacturers test specifications), speed at 1000rpm in 5th gear 19.4mph/31.2kmh; acceleration 0 - 62mph/100kmh 8.9secs; power to weight ratio from 12kg/kW (8.8kg/PS); consumption (ECE) 5.4/7.1/8.4L/100km (52.3/39.8/33.6mpg) [43.6/33.1/28US mpg].

1800 DOHC
77kW-103hp-105PS
Central/Single Point Injection

As 100/89hp, except:

Body, Weight: 4-door Saloon/Sedan; kerbweight (DIN) from 1020kg. 5-door Saloon/Sedan, 5-seater; kerbweight (DIN) from 1070kg. 2-door Coupe, 4-seater; kerbweight (DIN) 1005-1060kg. 3-door Coupe, 4-seater; kerbweight (DIN) 1010-1080kg.

Engine data (JIS net): 4-cylinder in-line (82.5 x 86mm), 1838cm3; compression ratio 9.3:1; 77kW (103hp) [105PS] at 5600rpm, 41.9kW/L (56.1hp/L) [57.1PS/L]; 149Nm (110lbft) at 2800rpm.
For Coupe Corona/Celica (1 OHC 2 valves, JIS): (80.5 x 90mm), 1832cm3; compression ratio 9:1; 77kW (103hp) [105PS] at 5400rpm; 157Nm (115.9lbft) at 3000rpm.

Engine construction: Designated 4S-Fi. Electronic central/single point injection.

Transmission: a) 5-speed manual, final drive ratio 3.736.
b) Automatic, final drive ratio 3.534.

Gear ratios: a) 5-speed manual: 1st 3.538; 2nd 2.041; 3rd 1.322; 4th 0.945; 5th 0.731; R 3.153.
b) Automatic: Planetary gear set ratios: 1st 2.810; 2nd 1.549; 3rd 1; OD 0.706; R 2.296.

Dimensions: Track also 147/144cm. Coupe: Track 146.5/143cm; load space 14-33cu ft (395-935dm3), length 436.5-441.5cm, width 169-171cm, height 126.5-129.5cm.

Performance: Max speed approx 109-115mph/175-185kmh, speed at 1000rpm in 5th gear 24.9mph/40.0kmh; power to weight ratio from 13.1kg/kW (9.6kg/PS); consumption approx 7-11L/100km (40.4- 25.7mpg) [33.6-21.4US mpg].

2000 DOHC
88kW-118hp-120PS
Fuel Injection

As 89/100hp, except:

Toyota

Body, Weight: 4–door Saloon/Sedan, kerbweight (DIN) from 1100kg. 5–door Saloon/Sedan, 5–seater; kerbweight (DIN) from 1120kg. 2–door Coupe, 4–seater; kerbweight (DIN) from 1100kg, USA from 1105kg. 3–door Coupe, 4–seater; kerbweight (DIN) from 1120kg, USA from 1145kg. 2–door Convertible, 2+2–seater; kerbweight (DIN) from 1220kg, USA from 1215kg.

Engine data (JIS net): 4–cylinder in–line (86 x 86mm), 1998cm3; compression ratio 9.3:1; 88kW (118hp) [120PS] at 5600rpm, 44kW/L (59hp/L) [60.1PS/L] 169Nm (124.7lbft) at 4400rpm.
With Catalyst (Carina II, DIN): Compression ratio 9.8:1; 89kW (119hp) [121PS] at 5600rpm; 176Nm (129.9lbft) at 4400rpm; unleaded premium grade.
USA version (Celica, SAE net): 86kW (115hp) [117PS] at 5200rpm, 170Nm (125.5lbft) at 4400rpm.
Without Catalyst (Carina II, DIN): Compression ratio 9.8:1; 94kW (126hp) [128PS] at 5600rpm; 176Nm (129.9lbftmkp) at 4400rpm.

Engine construction: Designated 3S–FE. Oil capacity 4.2L (4US qt); Bosch L–Jetronic electronic fuel injection. Battery 12V 50Ah, alternator 840W, cooling system capacity 6.5L (6.1US qt).

Transmission: a) 5–speed manual, final drive ratio 3.736 or 3.944.
b) Automatic, final drive ratio 3.358, 3.534 or 3.736 (Celica USA), 4.176.

Gear ratios: a) 5–speed manual: 1st 3.538; 2nd 1.960; 3rd 1.250; 4th 0.945; 5th 0.731; R 3.153.
Or: 1st 3.285; 2nd 2.041; 3rd 1.322; 4th 0.945; 5th 0731; R 3.153.
Or: 1st 3.285; 2nd 2.041; 3rd 1.322; 4th 1.028; 5th 0.820; R 3.153.
b) Automatic: Planetary gear set ratios: 1st 2.81; 2nd 1.549; 3rd 1; OD 0.706; R 2.296.

Chassis: Power assisted steering. Tyres 185/65 HR 14, optional 195/60 HR 14 (Celica USA also 165 SR 13 or 185/70 SR 13), wheels 5, 5.5J, optional 6J.

Dimensions: Track 147/144cm; Coupe/Convertible, track 146.5/143cm; load space (Coupe) 14–33cu ft (395–935dm3), length of 3–door Coupe 436.5cm, 2–door Coupe and Convertible 441.5cm, width 169–171cm, height 126.5–129.5cm.

Performance: (Carina II, Catalyst version): Max speed approx 121mph/195kmh, speed at 1000rpm in 5th gear (0.820, Axle 3.944) 21mph/33.8kmh; acceleration 0 - 60mph/100kmh 9.3secs power to weight ratio from 12.9kg/kW (9.5kg/PS); consumption (town/country/mixed) 8.8/5.8/7.5L/100km (32.1/48.7/37.7mpg) [26.7/40.6/31.4US mpg].

Toyota Carina II Liftback

```
2000 DOHC
103kW–138hp–140PS
Fuel Injection
```

As 89/100hp, except:

Body, Weight: 4–door Saloon/Sedan, kerbweight (DIN) from 1120kg. 5–door Saloon/Sedan; kerbweight (DIN) from 1140kg. 2–door Coupe, 4–seater; kerbweight (DIN) from 1130kg, USA 1180kg. 3–door Coupe, 4–seater; kerbweight (DIN) from 1150kg, USA 1210kg. 2–door Convertible, 2+2 seater; kerbweight (DIN) from 1240kg.

Engine data (JIS net): 4–cylinder in–line (86 x 86mm); 1998cm3; compression ratio 9.2:1; 103kW (138hp) [140PS] at 6200rpm, 51.6kW/L (69.1hp/L) [70.1PS/L]; 172Nm (126.9lbft) at 4800rpm.
European version (only Celica, DIN): Compression ratio 9.8:1; 110kW (147hp) [150PS]; 180Nm (132.8lbft) at 4800rpm; premium grade.
With Catalyst (for Celica, DIN): Compression ratio 9.2:1; 103kW (138hp) [140PS] at 6000rpm; 173Nm (127.7lbft) at 4800rpm; unleaded premium grade.
USA version (SAE net): 101kW (135hp) [137PS] at 6000rpm; 170Nm (125.5lbft) at 4800rpm.

Engine construction: Designated 3S–GELU. Camshaft drive, toothed belt only; oil capacity 4.7L (4.4US qt); oil cooler; Bosch L–Jetronic electronic fuel injection. Battery 12V 60Ah, alternator 660W; cooling system capacity 6.2L (5.9US qt).

Transmission: a) 5–speed manual, final drive ratio 4.176 or 3.944.
b) Automatic, final drive ratio 3.731 or 3.944.

Gear ratios: a) 5–speed manual: 1st 3.285; 2nd 2.041; 3rd 1.322; 4th 1.028; 5th 0.820; R 3.153.
b) Automatic: Planetary gear set ratios: 1st 2.81; 2nd 1.549; 3rd 1; OD 0.706; R 2.296.

Chassis: All round disc brakes, front ventilated; power assisted steering; tyres 195/60 HR/VR 14, Celica optional 225/50 VR 15 (USA 205/60 HR 14), wheel rims 5.5, 6J, Celica optional 7J.

Dimensions: Track Corona 147/144cm. Coupe/Convertible: Track 146.5/143cm; load space (Coupe) 14–33cu ft (395–935dm3), length of 3–door Coupe 436.5cm, 2–door Coupe and Convertible 441.5cm, width 171cm, height 126.5–129.5cm.

Performance (Celica): Max speed 131mph/210kmh, with Catalyst 124mph/200kmh (manufacturers test specifications), speed at 1000rpm in 5th gear (3.944) 19.6mph/31.5kmh; acceleration 0 – 62mph/100kmh 8.7secs, Catalyst 9.0secs; power to weight ratio from 10.5kg/kW (7.7kg/PS); consumption (ECE) 5.9/7.5/9.8L/100km (47.9/37.7/28.8mpg) [39.9/31.4/24US mpg], with Catalyst 6.5/8.3/10.1L/100km (43.5/34/28mpg) [36.2/28.3/23.3US mpg].

Toyota Celica

```
2000 DOHC
136kW–182hp–185PS
Turbo/Fuel Injection
```

Engine for Celica Turbo 4WD

As 89/100hp, except

Body, Weight: 3–door Coupe, 4–seater; kerbweight (DIN) 1360–1450kg, USA 1450kg, gross vehicle weight 1835kg.

Engine data (JIS net): 4–cylinder in–line (86 x 86mm), 1998cm3; compression ratio 8.5:1; 136kW (182hp) [185PS] at 6000rpm, 68.1kW/L (91.3hp/L) [92.6PS/L]; 240Nm (177.1lbft) at 4000rpm.
With Catalyst (DIN): 136kW (182hp) [185PS] at 6000rpm; 250Nm (184.5lbft) at 3600rpm; unleaded premium grade.
USA version (SAE net): 142kW (190hp) [193PS] at 6000rpm; 258Nm (190.4lbft) at 3200rpm.

Engine construction: Designated 3S–GTE. Camshaft drive, toothed belt only; oil capacity 4.7L (4.4US qt), oil cooler, Bosch L–Jetronic electronic fuel injection; 1 exhaust turbocharger, charge–air cooler (water/air). Battery 12V 60Ah, alternator 840W, cooling system capacity 8L (US qt).

Transmission (to all wheels): Permanent all wheel drive, central differential with viscous coupling, power distribution 50/50%; 5–speed manual; final drive ratio 4.285 or 3.933.

Gear ratios: 1st 3.583; 2nd 2.045; 3rd 1.333; 4th 0.972; 5th 0.731; R 3.583.

Toyota Celica Cabriolet

Chassis: All round disc brakes, front ventilated, optional ABS; power assisted steering, tyres 205/60 VR 14, or 195/60 HR/VR 14; wheels 6J.
Dimensions: Track 146.5/144cm, turning circle 11.8m; load space 14–33cu ft (395–935dm3), length 436.5–438cm, width 171cm, height 129cm.
Performance: Max speed 137mph/220kmh (manufacturers test specifications), speed at 1000rpm in 5th gear (3.933) 23.8mpg/38.3kmh; acceleration 0 – 62mph/100kmh 8.1secs; power to weight ratio from 10.0kg/kW (7.4kg/PS); consumption (ECE) 7.1/8.8/11.4L/100km (39.8/32.1/24.8mpg) [33.1/26.7/20.6US mpg].

Toyota Celica Turbo 4WD

```
2000 Diesel
54kW–72hp–73PS
Injection Pump
```

As 89/100hp, except:
Body, Weight: 4–door Saloon/Sedan; kerbweight (DIN) from 1060kg. 5–door Estate/Station Wagon; kerbweight (DIN) from 1050kg.
Engine data (JIS net): 4–cylinder in–line (86 x 85mm), 1974cm3; compression ratio 23:1; 54kW (72hp) [73PS] at 4700rpm, 27.4kW/L (36.7hp/L) [37PS/L]; 132Nm (97.4lbft) at 3000rpm.
European Version (DIN): Identical data.
Engine construction: Designated 2C. 2 valves per cylinder, 1 overhead camshaft (toothed belt), grey cast iron cylinder head; oil capacity 5L (4.7US qt); diesel injection pump. Battery 80Ah, alternator 60A; cooling system capacity 7.5L (7.1US qt).
Transmission: a) 5–speed manual, final drive ratio 3.736.
b) Automatic (Estate/Station Wagon 3–speed), final drive ratio 2.821, Estate/Station Wagon 3.837.
Gear ratios: a) 5–speed manual: 1st 3.538; 2nd 2.041; 3rd 1.322; 4th 0.945; 5th 0.731; R 3.153.
b) Automatic: As 1500.
Performance: Max speed approx 102mph/165kmh, speed at 1000rpm in 5th gear 24.9mph/40.0kmh; power to weight ratio from 19.4kg/kW (14.4kg/PS); consumption ECE 4.5/6.2/7.2L/100km (62.8/45.6/39.2mpg) [52.3/37.9/32.7US mpg].

Toyota Carina Wagon Diesel

Toyota MR2

1500 S – 1600 G – 1600 G Limited – 1600 Super Charger
Sports Coupe, 2–seater with a 1.5 or 1.6 Litre transverse mounted engine, 5–speed manual or automatic transmission with overdrive. Front and rear independent suspension. Launched June 1984. August 1986; 1600 DOHC with removeable roof (T–roof) and supercharger.

```
1500
61kW–82hp–83PS
1 2V Carb
```

Engine for 1500 S
Body, Weight: 2–door Coupe, 2–seater; kerbweight (DIN) 960– 1000kg.
Engine data (JIS): 4–cylinder in–line (77.5 x 77mm), 1453cm3; compression ratio 9.3:1; 61kW (82hp) [83PS] at 5600rpm, 42kW/L (56.3hp/L) [57.1PS/L]; 118Nm (87lbft) at 3600rpm.
Engine construction: Designated 3A–LU. Transverse central mounted engine. 1 overhead camshaft (toothed belt); light–alloy cylinder head; crankshaft with 5 bearings; oil capacity 3.2L (3US qt); 1 Aisan downdraught 2V carb. Battery 12V 32/40/45Ah, alternator 50A; cooling system capacity 10L (9.5US qt).
Transmission (to rear wheels): a) 5–speed manual, final drive ratio 3.941.
b) Automatic with overdrive, hydraulic torque converter and 4– speed Planetary gear set, final drive ratio 2.962.
Gear ratios: a) 5–speed manual: 1st 3.545; 2nd 1.904; 3rd 1.31; 4th 0.969; 5th 0.815; R 3.25.
b) Automatic: Max torque multiplication in converter 2.1 times, Planetary gear set ratios: 1st 3.643; 2nd 2.008; 3rd 1.296; 4th 0.892; R 2.977.
Chassis: Integral body, front and rear independent suspension, front McPherson struts, lower control arm, antiroll bar, rear McPherson struts, control arm, adjustable supplementary control arms, trailing arms, transverse arms and antiroll bar. Servo/power assisted disc brakes, rear mechanical handbrake; rack and pinion steering; fuel tank 41L (9Gal) [10.8US Gal]; tyres 185/60 HR 14, wheels 5.5J.
Dimensions: Wheelbase 232cm, track 144/144cm, clearance 14cm, turning circle 10.4m; load space (VDA) 2.5 + 5cu ft (70 + 142dm3), length 395cm, width 166.5cm, height 125cm.
Performance: Max speed approx 106–112mph/170–180kmh, speed at 1000rpm in 5th gear 20.6mph/33.1kmh; power to weight from 16.6kg/kW (12.2kg/PS); consumption approx 7–11L/100km (40.4– 25.7mpg) [33.6–21.4US mpg].

```
1600 DOHC
88kW–118hp–120PS
Fuel Injection
```

As 1500, except:
Weight: Kerbweight (DIN) from 1010kg, USA from 1065kg.
Engine data (JIS net): 4–cylinder in–line (81 x 77mm), 1587cm3; compression ratio 9.4:1; 88kW (118hp) [120PS] at 6600rpm, 55.5kW/L (74.4kW/L) [75.6PS/L]; 142Nm (104.8lbft) at 5000rpm.
European version (DIN): Compression ratio 10:1; 91kW (122hp) [124PS] at 6600rpm; 142Nm (104.8lbft) at 5000rpm.
With Catalyst (DIN): Compression ratio 9.4:1; 85kW (114hp) [116PS] at 6600rpm; 134Nm (98.9lbft) at 4800rpm.

Toyota MR2 T–Roof

Engine construction: Designated 4A–GELU. 4 valves (in V) per cylinder; 2 overhead camshafts (toothed belt); oil capacity 3.7L (3.5US qt); oil cooler; Bosch D–Jetronic, Catalyst L–Jetronic electronic fuel injection. Battery 12V 40/60Ah, alternator 70A; cooling system capacity 12.8L (12.1US qt).
Transmission: a) 5–speed manual, final drive ratio 4.312.
b) Automatic, final drive ratio 2.962.
Gear ratios: a) 5–speed manual: 1st 3.166; 2nd 1.904; 3rd 1.31; 4th 0.969; 5th 0.815; R 3.25.
b) Automatic: As 1500.

Toyota

Chassis: Front ventilated disc brakes; wheels 5.5 or 6J.
Performance: Max speed 121–124mph/195–200kmh (manufacturers test specifications), speed at 1000rpm in 5th gear 18.7mph/30.1kmh; acceleration 0–62mph/100kmh 8.1secs, with Catalyst in 9secs; power to weight ratio from 11.3kg/kW (8.3kg/PS); consumption ECE 6.0/7.7/8.1L/100km (47.1/36.7/34.9mpg) [39.2/30.5/29US mpg] with Catalyst 6.2/8.0/8.4L/100km (45.6/35/33.6mpg) [37.9/29.4/28US mpg].

1600 DOHC
107kW–143hp–145PS
Supercharger/Fuel Injection

As 1500, except:

Weight: Kerbweight (DIN) 1060–1120kg, USA from 1130kg.
Engine data (JIS net): 4–cylinder in–line (81 x 77mm), 1587cm3; compression ratio 8:1; 107kW (143hp) [145PS] at 6400rpm, 67.4kW/L (90.3hp/L) [91.4PS/L]; 186Nm (137.3lbft) at 4400rpm.
USA version (SAE net): 108kW (145hp) [147PS] at 6400rpm, 190Nm (140.2lbft) at 4000rpm.
Engine construction: Designated 4A–GZE. 4 valves (in V) per cylinder; 2 overhead camshafts (toothed belt); oil capacity 3.7L (3.5US qt), oil cooler; 1 SC 12 mechanical supercharger, Roots type, charge–air cooler; Bosch L–Jetronic electronic fuel injection. Battery 12V 40/60Ah, alternator 60/70A; cooling system capacity 12.8L (12.8US qt).
Transmission: a) 5–speed manual, final drive ratio 4.285.
b) Automatic, final drive ratio 2.892 or 3.034
Gear ratios: a) 5–speed manual: 1st 3.230; 2nd 1.913; 3rd 1.258; 4th 0.918; 5th 0.731; R 3.583.
b) Automatic: As 1500.
Chassis: Front ventilated disc brakes; wheels 5.5 or 6J.
Performance: Max speed over 130mph/210kmh, speed at 1000rpm in 5th gear 21mph/33.8kmh; power to weight ratio from 9.9kg/kW (7.3kg/PS); consumption approx 8–14L/100km (35.3–20.2mpg) [29.4–16.8US mpg].

Toyota Camry/Vista

Front wheel drive, medium size vehicle with transverse mounted front engine. Launched April 1982. August 1986; new body and new 2.0 Litre engine with 4 valves per cylinder and Estate/Station Wagon. April 1987; available with a 2.0 Litre V6 DOHC. October 1987; permanent four wheel drive. 1988: 2.5 Litre V6 for export.

1800
62kW–83hp–85PS
Central/Single Point Injection

Body, Weight: 4–door Saloon/Sedan, 5–seater; kerbweight (DIN) 1050–1150kg. 4–door Hardtop (Vista); 5–seater; kerbweight (DIN) 1100–1170kg. 5–door Estate/Station Wagon, 5–seater; kerbweight (DIN) from approx 1110kg.
Engine data (JIS net): 4–cylinder in–line (80.5 x 90mm), 1832cm3; compression ratio 9:1; 62kW (83hp) [85PS] at 5200rpm, 33.8kW/L (45.3hp/L) [46.4PS/L]; 142Nm (104.8lbft) at 3000rpm.
European version (2V carb, DIN): 66kW (88hp) [90PS] at 5200rpm, 36kW/L (48.2hp/L) [49.1PS/L]; 141Nm (104.1lbft) at 3400rpm.
Engine construction: Transverse engine. Designated 1S–Ci. 1 overhead camshaft (toothed belt), hydraulic tappets, light–alloy cylinder head; crankshaft with 5 bearings; oil capacity 4L (3.8US qt); electronic central/single point injection. Battery 12V 45/60Ah, alternator 60/75A; cooling system capacity 7L (6.6US qt).
Transmission (to front wheels): a) 5–speed manual, final drive ratio 3.736.
b) Automatic, hydraulic torque converter and 3–speed Planetary gear set, with OD, final drive ratio 3.731.
Gear ratios: a) 5–speed manual: 1st 3.538; 2nd 1.960; 3rd 1.250; 4th 0.945; 5th 0.731; R 3.153.
Or: 1st 3.538; 2nd 2.041; 3rd 1.322; 4th 0.945; 5th 0.731; R 3.153.
b) Automatic: Max torque multiplication in converter 1.92 times, Planetary gear set ratios: 1st 2.81; 2nd 1.549; 3rd 1; OD 0.734 or 0.706; R 2.296.
Chassis: Integral body; front and rear independent suspension, front McPherson struts with lower control arm and antiroll bar, rear McPherson struts with parallel control arms and longitudinal struts, some models rear antiroll bar; telescopic damper. Servo/power assisted brakes, front ventilated discs, rear drums, rear mechanical handbrake; rack and pinion steering, optional power assisted; fuel tank 60L (13.2Gal) [15.9US Gal]; tyres 165 SR/HR 13 or 185/70 SR 13, wheels 5J.

Dimensions: Wheelbase 260cm, track 147.5/144.5cm; clearance 16cm, turning circle 10.6m; load space 17.8cu ft (505dm3), Estate/Station Wagon 23.3–45.9cu ft (633–1300dm3), length 452cm, Estate/Station Wagon 461cm, height 169–171cm, height 137/140cm, Estate/Station Wagon 144cm.
Performance: Max speed approx 106mph/170kmh, speed at 1000rpm in 5th gear 25.1mph/40.4kmh; power to weight ratio from 16.8kg/kW (12.4kg/PS); consumption approx 6–11L/100km (47.1–25.7mpg) [39.2–21.4US mpg].

Toyota Camry 2000 Station Wagon

2000 16V
88kW–118hp–120PS
Fuel Injection

As 1800, except:

Body, Weight: 4–door Saloon/Sedan, kerbweight (DIN) from 1150kg, USA 1220kg, 4WD 1290kg. 4–door Hardtop, kerbweight (DIN) from 1180kg, 4WD 1300kg. 5–door Estate/Station Wagon, 5–seater; kerbweight (DIN) from 1235kg, USA 1295kg.
Engine data (JIS net): 4–cylinder in–line (86 x 86mm), 1998cm3; compression ratio 9.3:1; 88kW (118hp) [120PS] at 5600rpm, 44kW/L (59hp/L) [60.1PS/L]; 169Nm (124.7lbft) at 4400rpm.
European version (DIN): Compression ratio 9.8:1; 94kW (126hp) [128PS] at 5600rpm; 179Nm (132.1lbft) at 4400rpm.
With Catalyst (DIN): Compression ratio 9.3:1; 89KW (120hp) [121PS] at 5600rpm; 176Nm (129.9lbft) at 4400rpm.
4WD and USA: 86kW (115hp) [117PS] at 5200rpm, 171Nm (126.2lbft) at 4400rpm.
Engine construction: Designated 3S–FE. 4 valves (in V 22.3deg) per cylinder, mechanical tappets, 2 overhead camshafts (toothed belt/toothed wheel); oil capacity 4.2L (4US qt); Bosch L–Jetronic electronic fuel injection. Battery 50Ah, alternator 70A, cooling system capacity 6.5L (6.1US qt).
Transmission (to front wheels, 4WD to all wheels): a) 5–speed manual, final drive ratio 3.944 or 3.736.
b) 4–speed automatic, optional S/E programme, final drive ratio 4.176 or 3.534; USA 3.625 or 3.736.
4WD: Permanent all wheel drive, central differential (power distribution 50/50%) with viscous coupling and mechanical lock; 5–speed manual, final drive ratio 4.235 or 4.562
Gear ratios: a) 5–speed manual: 1st 3.285; 2nd 2.041; 3rd 1.322; 4th 1.028; 5th 0.820; R 3.153.
Or: 1st 3.538; 2nd 1.960; 3rd 1.250; 4th 0.945; 5th 0.731; R 3.153. 4WD: 1st 3.583; 2nd 2.045; 3rd 1.333; 4th 1.028; 5th 0.820; R 3.583.
b) Automatic: As 1800.
Chassis: Front and rear antiroll bars; 4WD and versions with ABS all round disc brakes, front ventilated; tyres 185/70 SR/HR 14, Estate/Station Wagon also 175/70 HR 14, tyres 5.5J.

Toyota Camry 4WD

Toyota

Dimensions: 4WD; track 147.5/143.5-144cm. Load space 13cu ft (370dm3). USA variants: Length 462.5cm, Estate/Station Wagon 465cm, height 137.5cm, Estate/Station Wagon 138.5cm.

Performance (Catalyst version): Max speed 118mph/190kmh, Estate/Station Wagon and 4WD 115mph/185kmh (manufacturers test specifications), speed at 1000rpm in 5th gear (0.820, axle 3.944) 21.9mph/35.3kmh; acceleration 0 – 62mph/100kmh 9.7secs, 4WD 12.2secs; power to weight ratio from 12.5kg/kW (9.2kg/PS); consumption ECE 6.0/7.9/8.9L/100km (47.1/35.8/31.7mpg) [39.2/29.8/26.4US mpg], Automatic 6.8/8.3/9.4L/100km (41.5/34/30.1mpg) [34.6/28.3/25.0US mpg].

```
2000 16V
103kW–138hp–140PS
Fuel Injection
```

As 1800, except:

Body, Weight: 4–door Saloon/Sedan, kerbweight (DIN) from 1190kg. 4–door Hardtop, kerbweight (DIN) from 1210kg.

Engine data (JIS net): 4–cylinder in–line (86 x 86mm), 1998cm3; compression ratio 9.2:1; 103kW (138hp) [140PS] at 6200rpm, 51.6kW/L (69.1hp/L) [70.1PS/L]; 172Nm (126.9lbft) at 4800rpm.

Engine construction: Designated 3S-GE. 4 valves (in V) per cylinder, mechanical tappets; 2 overhead camshafts (toothed belt); electronic fuel injection. Cooling system capacity 6.2L (5.9US qt).

Transmission: a) 5–speed manual, final drive ratio 4.176.
b) 4–speed automatic with E/S–programme, final drive ratio 3.731.

Gear ratios: a) 5–speed manual: 1st 3.285; 2nd 2.041; 3rd 1.322; 4th 1.028; 5th 0.820; R 3.153.
b) Automatic: As 1800.

Chassis: Front and rear antiroll bars, level control system; all round disc brakes, front ventilated, optional ABS; power assisted steering; tyres 195/60 HR 15, wheels 5.5J.

Dimensions: Track 147/144cm.

Performance: Max speed approx 124mph/200kmh, speed at 1000rpm in 5th gear 20.4mph/32.9kmh; power to weight ratio from 11.6kg/kW (8.5kg/PS); consumption approx 8–13L/100km (35.3–21.7mpg) [29.4–18.1US mpg].

```
2.5 V6 24V
118kW–158hp–160PS
Fuel Injection
```

As 1800, except:

Body, Weight: 4–door Saloon/Sedan, kerbweight (DIN) 1310–1360kg (USA), kerbweight from 1420kg.

Engine data (Catalyst DIN): 6–cylinder in V 60deg (87.5 x 69.5mm), 2507cm3; compression ratio 9:1; 118kW (158hp) [160PS] at 5800rpm, 47.1kW/L (63.1hp/L) [63.8PS/L]; 206Nm (152lbft) at 4600rpm. Regular unleaded grade.
USA Version (SAE net): 114kW (153hp) [155PS] at 5600rpm, 210Nm (155lbft) at 4400rpm.
Japanese version (JIS net): (78 x 69.5mm), 1993cm3; Compression ratio 9.6:1; 103kW (138hp) [140PS] at 6000rpm, 174Nm (128.4lbft) at 4600rpm.

Engine construction: Designated 2 VZ-FE/1-VZ-FE. 4 valves (in V 22.3deg) per cylinder, mechanical tappets; 2 overhead camshafts (toothed belt/toothed wheel); crankshaft with 4 bearings; oil capacity 3.9L (3.7US qt); Bosch L–Jetronic electronic fuel injection. 12V 60Ah battery, 840w alternator, cooling system capacity 8.5L (8US qt).

Transmission: a) 5–speed manual, final drive ratio 3.933, 4.285.
b) 4–speed automatic with E/S–programme, final drive ratio 3.933, USA 3.625.

Gear ratios: a) 5–speed manual: 1st 3.230; 2nd 2.045; 3rd 1.333; 4th 0.972; 5th 0.820; R 3.583.
For 2-Litre: 1st 3.583; 2nd 2.045; 3rd 1.333; 4th 1.028; 5th 0.820; R 3.583.
b) Automatic: As 1800.

Chassis: Front and rear antiroll bars, level control system; all round disc brakes, front ventilated, optional ABS; power assisted steering; tyres 195/60 VR 15, for Japan 185/70 SR 14 or optionally 195/60 HR 15, tyres 5.5J.

Dimensions: Track 147-147.5/144cm; length 450-462.5cm, Estate/Station Wagon (USA) 465cm.

Performance(Catalyst version): Max speed approx 130mph/210kmh, Automatic 124mph/200kmh (manufacturers test specifications) speed at 1000rpm in 5th gear (Axle 3.933) 22.4mph/mph/36.0kmh; acceleration 0 - 62mph/100kmh 9secs; power to weight ratio from 11.2kg/kW (8.2kg/PS); consumption approx 7.2/9.0/12.9L/100km (39.2/31.4/21.9mpg) [32.7/26.1/18.2US mpg].

Toyota Camry V6

```
2000 D
60kW–80hp–82PS
Turbo/Injection Pump
```

As 1800, except:

Body, Weight: 4–door Saloon/Sedan; kerbweight (DIN) from 1150kg. 5–door Estate/Station Wagon, kerbweight (DIN) from 1220kg.

Engine data (JIS net): 4–cylinder in–line (86 x 85mm), 1974cm3; compression ratio 23:1; 60kW (80hp) [82PS] at 4500rpm, 30.4kW/L (40.7hp/L) [41.5PS/L]; 160Nm (118.1lbft) at 2400rpm.
European version (DIN): 62kW (83hp) [84PS] at 4500rpm; 164Nm (121lbft) at 3000rpm.

Engine construction: Designated 2C-T. Valves parallel, mechanical tappets; oil capacity 4.6L (4.4US qt); oil cooler; diesel injection pump, exhaust turbocharger. Battery 80Ah, alternator 60A; cooling system capacity 8.5L (8.0US qt).

Transmission: a) 5–speed manual, final drive ratio 3.736.
b) Automatic, final drive ratio 3.731.

Chassis: Tyres 185/70 SR 13 or 185/70 SR 14.

Performance: Max speed 106mph/170kmh (manufacturers test specifications), speed at 1000rpm in 5th gear (tyres 185/70-14) 26mph/41.9kmh; acceleration 0 – 62mph/100kmh 14.4secs; power to weight ratio from 19.0kg/kW (14.0kg/PS); consumption ECE 4.7/6.7/6.8L/100km (60.1/42.2/41.5mpg) [50/35.1/34.6US mpg].

Toyota Mark II (Cressida) – Chaser

New model. Saloon/Sedan and Station Wagon. Launched January 1977. Chaser; luxury parallel model. August 1988: new body, modified suspension and engine.

```
1.8 Litre
77kW–103hp–105PS
Central/Single Point Injection
```

Body, Weight: 4–door Saloon/Sedan/Hardtop, 5/6 seater; kerbweight (DIN) from 1170kg.

Engine data (JIS): 4–cylinder in–line (82.5 x 86mm), 1838cm3; compression ratio 9.3:1; 77kW (103hp) [105PS] at 5600rpm, 41.9kW/L (56.1hp/L) [57.1PS/L]; 149Nm (110lbft) at 2800rpm.

Engine construction: Designated 4S-Fi. 4 valves (in V 22.3deg) per cylinder. 2 overhead camshafts (toothed belt/toothed wheels), light alloy cylinder heads; crankshaft with 5 bearings; oil capacity 4.2L (4US qt); electronic central/single point injection. Battery 12V 35-60Ah, alternator 40-60A; cooling system capacity 6.5L (6.1US qt).

Transmission (to rear wheels): a) 5–speed manual, final drive ratio 3.727.
b) 3–speed automatic with overdrive, final drive ratio 4.100.

Gear ratios: a) 5–speed manual: 1st 3.566; 2nd 2.056; 3rd 1.384; 4th 1; 5th 0.85; R 4.091.
b) Automatic: Max torque multiplication in converter 2.4 times, Planetary gear set ratios: 1st 2.45; 2nd 1.45; 3rd 1; OD 0.688; R 2.222.

Chassis: Integral body; front McPherson struts, control arm, tension strut, rear rigid axle with double trailing arms, Panhard rod and coil springs, some models front and rear antiroll bars, telescopic damper. Servo/power assisted brakes, front ventilated discs, rear drums, mechanical handbrake to rear wheels; power assisted rack and pinion steering; fuel tank 65L (14.3Gal) [17.2US Gal]; tyres 175 SR 14, wheels 5-5.5J.

Dimensions: Wheelbase 268cm, track 145.5/140cm, clearance 15.5cm, turning circle approx 10.7m; length 459-469cm, width 169.5cm, height 137.5-140.5cm.

Toyota

Performance: Max speed approx 102mph/165kmh, speed at 1000rpm in 5th gear 22.7mph/36.6kmh; power to weight ratio from 15.2kg/kW (11.1kg/PS); consumption (touring) approx 8–13L/100km (35.3–21.7mpg) [29.4–18.1US mpg].

Toyota Mark II

```
2.0 24V
99kW-133hp-135PS
Fuel Injection
```

As 1.8 Litre, except:

Weight: Saloon/Sedan/Hardtop, kerbweight from 1290kg.

Engine data (JIS): 6-cylinder in-line (75 x 75mm), 1988cm3; Compression ratio 9.6:1; 99kW (133hp) [135PS] at 5600rpm, 49.8kW/L (66.7hp/L) [67.9PS/L]; 177Nm (130.6lbft) at 4400rpm.

Engine construction: Designated 1G-FE. 7 bearing crankshaft; oil capacity 4.3L (4.1US qt); electronic fuel injection. Cooling system capacity approx 9L (8.5US qt).

Transmission: a) 5-speed manual, final drive ratio 3.909.
b) Automatic, final drive ratio 4.100.

Gear ratios: a) 5-speed manual: 1st 3.285; 2nd 1.894; 3rd 1.275; 4th 1; 5th 0.86; R 3.768.
b) Automatic: As 1800.

Chassis: Rear independent suspension, with lower control arm, tapered strut, upper A-arm, coil springs, coaxial shock absorbers and antiroll bar, optional level control system. Four wheel disc brakes (front ventilated), with optional ABS; tyres 185/70 SR/HR 14.

Dimensions: Track 145.5/145.5cm.

Performance: Max speed approx 118mph/190kmh, speed at 1000rpm in 5th gear 21.1mph/34.0kmh; power to weight ratio from 13.0kg/kW (9.6kg/PS); consumption approx 8-14L/100km (35.3-20.2mpg) [29.4-16.8US mpg].

Toyota Chaser

```
2.0 24V
110/125kW-147/168hp-150/170PS
Fuel Injection/Compressor
```

As 1.8 Litre, except:

Weight: Saloon/Sedan/Hardtop, kerbweight from 1360kg, with Compressor from 1480kg.

Engine data (JIS): 6-cylinder in-line (75 x 75mm), 1988cm3; Compression ratio 9.5:1; 110kW (147hp) [150PS] at 6200rpm, 55.3kW/L (74.1hp/L) [75.5PS/L]; 182Nm (134.3lbft) at 5600rpm.
With Roots Compressor: Compression ratio 8:1; 125kW (168hp) [170PS] at 6000rpm, 62.9kW/L (84.3hp/L) [85.5PS/L]; 226Nm (166.8lbft) at 3600rpm.

Engine construction: Designated 1G-GE/1G-GEZ. Camshaft drive only with toothed belt; 7 main bearing crankshaft; oil capacity 4.3L (4.1US qt), oil cooler; electronic fuel injection.
168hp Version: Mechanical Roots Compressor.
Battery 12V 45-60 Ah, Alternator 50-70A; cooling system capacity approx 8L (7.6US qt).

Transmission: a) 5-speed manual (only 148hp), final drive ratio 4.300.
b) Automatic, final drive ratio 4.556, Compressor 4.300.

Gear ratios: a) 5-speed manual: 1800.
b) Automatic: 1st 2.804; 2nd 1.531; 3rd 1; OD 0.705; R 2.393.

Chassis: Rear independent suspension, with lower control arm, tapered strut, upper A-arm, coil springs, coaxial shock absorbers and antiroll bar, optional level control system. Four wheel disc brakes (front ventilated, Compressor at rear), optional ABS; tyres 195/70 HR 14, with Compressor 195/65 HR 15, wheel rims 6J.

Dimensions: Track 145.5/145.5cm.

Performance: Max speed approx 124-130mph/200-210kmh, speed at 1000rpm in 5th gear 19.7mph/31.8kmh, Compressor in OD 23.8mph/38.3kmh; power to weight ratio from 11.8kg/kW (8.7kg/PS); consumption approx 8-14L/100km (35.3-20.2mpg) [29.4-16.8US mpg], Compressor 10-16L/100km (28.2-17.7mpg) [23.3-14.7US mpg].

```
2.0 24V
154kW-206hp-210PS
Fuel Injection/2 Turbos
```

As 1.8 Litre, except:

Weight: Saloon/Sedan (USA), kerbweight from 1550kg; 4-door Hardtop, kerbweight from 1420kg.

Engine data (JIS): 6-cylinder in-line (75 x 75mm), 1988cm3; Compression ratio 8.5:1; 154kW (206hp) [210PS] at 6200rpm, 77.5kW/L (103.9hp/L) [105.6PS/L]; 275Nm (203lbft) at 3800rpm.
USA Version with 3-Litre induction engine (SAE): (83 x 91mm), 2954cm3; Compression ratio 9.2:1; 142kW (190hp) [193PS] at 5600rpm; 251Nm (185.2lbft) at 4400rpm.

Engine construction: Designated 1G-GTE (USA 7M-GE). 2 overhead camshafts (toothed belt); 7 main bearing crankshaft; oil capacity 4.3L (4.1US qt), oil cooler; electronic fuel injection; 2 parallel turbochargers and charge air cooler (air/air). Battery 12V 60 Ah, Alternator 60-70 A; cooling system capacity approx 8L (7.6US qt).

Transmission: a) 5-speed manual, final drive ratio 4.300.
b) Automatic, final drive ratio 4.556, Cressida USA 3.909.
Optional limited slip differential.

Gear ratios: a) 5-speed manual: 1st 3.285; 2nd 1.894; 3rd 1.275; 4th 1; 5th 0.783; R 3.768.
b) Automatic; Planetary gear set ratios: 1st 2.804; 2nd 1.531; 3rd 1; OD 0.705; R 2.393.

Chassis: Rear independent suspension with lower control arm, tapered strut, upper A-arm, coil springs, coaxial shock absorbers and antiroll bar, optional level control system. Four wheel disc brakes (ventilated), ABS (optional in USA.); tyres 205/60 HR 15 (USA 195/65 HR 15), wheel rims 6-6.5J.

Dimensions: Track 145.5/145.5cm. Length USA 481cm.

Performance: Max speed above 137mph/220kmh, speed at 1000rpm in 5th gear 21.1mph/34kmh; power to weight ratio from 9.2kg/kW (6.8kg/PS); consumption approx 12-18L/100km (23.5-15.7mpg) [19.6-13.1US mpg].

Toyota Cressida (USA)

```
2.45 D
69/62kW-92/83hp-94/85PS
Turbo/Injection Pump
```

As 1.8 Litre, except:

Weight: Kerbweight from 1300kg.

Engine data (JIS net): 4–cylinder in–line (92 x 92mm), 2446cm3; compression ratio 21:1; 69kW (92hp) [94PS] at 4000rpm, 28.2kW/L (37.4hp/L) [38.4PS/L]; 216Nm (159.4lbft) at 2400rpm.
Without Turbo: Compression ratio 22.2:1; 62kW (83hp) [85PS] at 4200rpm; 165Nm (121.8lbft) at 2400rpm.

Engine construction: Designated 2L/2L–T. Valves in parallel; grey cast iron cylinder head; oil capacity 5.8L (5.5US qt), oil cooler; Denso diesel injection pump; version 92hp with exhaust turbocharger. Battery 12V 60-70Ah, alternator 60A; cooling system capacity 9L (8.5US qt).

Transmission: a) 5–speed manual, final drive ratio 3.583, without Turbo 3.909.
b) Automatic, final drive ratio 3.727.

Gear ratios: a) 5–speed manual: As 1800.
b) Automatic: 1st 2.452; 2nd 1.452; 3rd 1; OD 0.688; R 2.212.

Performance (Turbodiesel): Max speed approx 106mph/170kmh, speed at 1000rpm in 5th gear 23.7mph/38.1kmh; power to weight ratio from 18.8kg/kW (13.8kg/PS); consumption approx 6-9L/100km (47.1-31.4mpg) [39.2-26.1US mpg].

Toyota Crown

Spacious vehicle with rear wheel drive and box frame chassis. Tokyo 1983: new chassis and engine. Autumn 1985; supercharged 2.0 Litre 24 valve engine and 6–cylinder in–line 3.0 Litre DOHC engine. Autumn 1987; revised model range, improved mechanics.

```
2 Litre
77kW–103hp–105PS
Fuel Injection
```

Body, Weight: 4–door Saloon/Sedan, 5/6–seater; kerbweight (DIN) 1320–1410kg. 4–door Hardtop, 5–seater; kerbweight (DIN) 1370–1430kg. 5–door Estate/Station Wagon, 5/6 or 7/8–seater; kerbweight (DIN) 1370–1460kg.

Engine data (JIS net): 6–cylinder in–line (75 x 75mm), 1988cm3; compression ratio 9.2:1; 77kW (103hp) [105PS] at 5200rpm, 38.7kW/L (51.9hp/L) [52.8PS/L]; 157Nm (115.9lbft) at 4000rpm. Estate/Station Wagon (also van): 74kW (99hp) [100PS]; 153Nm (112.9lbft).

Engine construction: Designated 1G–E. Valves in V, hydraulic tappets; 1 overhead camshaft (toothed belt); light–alloy cylinder head; crankshaft with 7 bearings; oil capacity 5.6L (5.3US qt); electronic fuel injection. Battery 12V 45/60Ah, alternator 50–70A; cooling system capacity approx 8L (7.6US qt).

Transmission (to rear wheels): a) 4–speed manual (3 + E) with steering column shift, final drive ratio 4.556.
b) 5–speed manual with floor shift, final drive ratio 4.556.
c) Automatic, hydraulic torque converter and 3–speed Planetary gear set with OD, final drive ratio 5.125.

Gear ratios: a) 4–speed manual: 1st 3.352; 2nd 1.627; 3rd 1; OD 0.802; R 4.059.
b) 5–speed manual: 1st 3.566; 2nd 2.056; 3rd 1.384; 4th 1; 5th 0.850; R 4.091.
c) Automatic: Max torque multiplication in converter 1.92 times, Planetary gear set ratios:1st 2.452; 2nd 1.452; 3rd 1; OD 0.688; R 2.212.

Chassis: Box type frame with cross members; front upper A arm, lower single control arm and tension strut, coil springs, some models with antiroll bar, rear rigid axle with double trailing arm, Panhard rod and coil springs (Estate/Station Wagon with leaf springs), Hardtop also with independent suspension (semi–trailing arm), telescopic damper. Servo/power assisted brakes, front ventilated discs, rear drums (Standard model with front drums), rear mechanical handbrake; recirculating ball steering, fuel tank 72L (15.8Gal) [19US Gal], Estate/Station Wagon 64L (14.1Gal) [16.9US Gal]; tyres 185 SR 14, Standard 6.40-14, optional 195/70 SR 14; tyres 5J.

Dimensions: Wheelbase 273cm, track 145.5/140cm, Standard 143/138cm, Hardtop also 145.5/144.5cm, clearance 16.5–18cm, turning circle 11m; length 469cm, width 169.5cm, height Saloon/Sedan 143.5–145cm, Hardtop 141cm, Estate/Station Wagon 151.5–154cm.

Performance: Max speed approx 99mph/160kmh, speed at 1000rpm in 5th gear (4.556:1) 19.1mph/30.8kmh; power to weight ratio from 17.1kg/kW (12.6kg/PS); consumption approx 9–13L/100km (31.4– 21.7mpg) [26.1–18.1US mpg].

```
2.0 DOHC
103/118kW–138/158hp–140/160PS
Fuel Injection/Supercharger
```

As 103hp, except:

Weight: Saloon/Sedan, kerbweight from 1500kg, with supercharger 1570kg. Hardtop, kerbweight from 1480kg, with supercharger 1580kg. Estate/Station Wagon (with supercharger), kerbweight 1590kg.

Engine data (JIS net): 6–cylinder in–line (75 x 75mm), 1988cm3; compression ratio 9.1:1; 103kW (138hp) [140PS] at 6200rpm, 51.8kW/L (69.4hp/L) [70.4PS/L]; 173Nm (127.7lbft) at 4000rpm.
With supercharger: Compression ratio 8.0:1; 118kW (158hp) [160PS] at 6000rpm; 206Nm (152lbft) at 4000rpm.

Engine construction: Designated 1G–GE/1G–GZE. 4 valves (in V) per cylinder, mechanical tappets, 2 overhead camshafts (toothed belt); oil capacity 4.5L (4.3US qt), oil cooler; electronic fuel injection. Supercharged version with mechanical Roots compressor.

Transmission: Automatic, final drive ratio 5.125, supercharger 4.556. Optional limited slip differential.

Gear ratios: Automatic, as 103hp.
Supercharger: 1st 2.804; 2nd 1.531; 3rd 1; OD 0.705; R 2.393.

Chassis: Rear independent suspension (except Estate/Station Wagon) with semi–trailing arm and coil springs, front and rear antiroll bars, also with air suspension; four wheel ventilated disc brakes, optional ABS; power assisted steering; tyres 195/70 SR 14, wheels 5.5 or 6J.

Dimensions: Track 145.5/144.5cm, Estate/Station Wagon 145.5/140cm.

Performance: Max speed approx 118–131mph/190–210kmh, speed at 1000rpm in OD 20mph/32.2kmh, supercharger 19.8mph/31.9kmh; power to weight ratio from 13.3kg/kW (9.8kg/PS); consumption approx 10– 18L/100km (28.2–15.7mpg) [23.5–13.1US mpg].

Toyota Crown Supercharger

```
3.0 DOHC
140kW–188hp–190PS
Fuel Injection
```

As 103hp, except:

Body, Weight: Saloon/Sedan, kerbweight from 1590kg. Hardtop, kerbweight from 1620kg.

Engine data (JIS net): 6–cylinder in–line (83 x 91mm), 2951cm3; compression ratio 9.2:1; 140kW (188hp) [190PS] at 5600rpm, 47.4kW/L (63.5hp/L) [64.3PS/L]; 255Nm (188.2lbft) at 3600rpm.

Engine construction: Designated 7M–GE. 4 valves (in V) per cylinder, mechanical tappets, 2 overhead camshafts (toothed belt); oil capacity 5.1L (4.8US qt); electronic fuel injection.

Transmission: Automatic, final drive ratio 4.100.
Optional drive slip regulation (ASR).

Gear ratios: Automatic; 1st 2.804; 2nd 1.531; 3rd 1; OD 0.705; R 2.393.

Chassis: Rear independent suspension with semi–trailing arms, air suspension, front and rear antiroll bars; four wheel ventilated disc brakes with ABS; power assisted steering; tyres 195/70 SR 14, Hardtop 205/65 HR 15, wheels 5.5 or 6J.

Dimensions: Track 145.5/145.5cm, Hardtop 148/147–148cm; length 486cm, width 172cm, Hardtop 174.5cm, height 142cm, Hardtop 140– 141cm.

Performances: Max speed approx 131mph/210kmh, speed at 1000rpm in OD 25mph/40.3kmh; power to weight ratio from 11.4kg/kW (8.4kg/PS); consumption approx 10–18L/100km (28.2-15.7mpg) [23.5– 13.1US mpg].

Toyota Crown Turbodiesel Wagon

2.45 D
69/62/54kW–93/83/72hp–94/85/73PS
Turbo/Injection Pump

As 103hp, except:

Weight: Saloon/Sedan, kerbweight from 1470kg, naturally aspirated diesel from 1400kg. Hardtop, kerbweight from 1460kg. Estate/Station Wagon, kerbweight from 1550kg, naturally aspirated diesel from 1450kg.

Engine data (JIS net): 4–cylinder in–line (92 x 92mm), 2446cm3; With automatic: Compression ratio 21:1; 69kW (93hp) [94PS] at 4000rpm, 28.2kW/L (37.8hp/L) [38.4PS/L]; 201Nm (148.3lbft) at 2400rpm.
With 5–speed manual: Compression ratio 20:1; 62kW (83hp) [85PS]; 188Nm (138.7lbft).
Without turbo: Compression ratio 22.3:1; 54kW (72hp) [73PS] at 4000rpm; 149Nm (110lbft) at 2400rpm.
For van: 56kW (75hp) [76PS]; 154Nm (113.7lbft).

Engine construction: Designated 2L–THE/21–T/2L. Parallel valves, mechanical tappets; grey cast iron cylinder head; crankshaft with 5 bearings; oil capacity 5.8L (5.5US qt), oil cooler; diesel injection pump; exhaust turbocharger. Cooling system capacity approx 9L (8.5US qt).

Transmission: a) 4–speed manual (3 + E, not for turbo), final drive ratio 4.100.
b) 5–speed manual, final drive ratio 3.909; without turbo 4.100, van 4.300.
c) Automatic, final drive ratio 4.300.

Gear ratios: a) 4–speed manual: As 103hp.
b) 5–speed manual: As 103hp.
c) Automatic: 1st 2.452; 2nd 1.452; 3rd 1; OD 0.688; R 2.212.

Chassis: Turbodiesel four drive disc brakes; power assisted steering, tyres 185 SR 14 or standard diesel 6.40–14.

Performance: Max speed approx 90–103mph/145–165kmh, speed at 1000rpm in 5th gear (final drive ratio 3.909) 22.2mph/35.8kmh; power to weight ratio from 21.3kg/kW (15.6kg/PS); consumption approx 6–11 L/100km (47.1–25.7mpg) [39.2–21.4US mpg].

Toyota Soarer/Supra

Sports Coupe with a 6–cylinder engine and rear wheel drive. Launched February 1981. January 1986: revised models, modified body, independent suspension. February 1986: Coupe Supra base model, revised wheelbase; also with detachable roof. Summer 1989: light facelift for the Supra, modified engine.

2.0 24V
99kW–133hp–135PS
Fuel Injection

Body, Weight: 2–door Coupe Soarer, 4–seater; kerbweight (DIN) 1310–1340kg. 3–door Coupe Supra, 4–seater; kerbweight (DIN) 1370–1390kg.

Engine data (JIS net): 6–cylinder in–line (75 x 75mm), 1988cm3; compression ratio 9.6:1; 99kW (133hp) [135PS] at 5600rpm, 49.8kW/L (66.7hp/L) [67.9PS/L]; 177Nm (130.6lbft) at 4400rpm.
For Soarer (1 OHC, 12 valves): Compression ratio 9.2:1; 77kW (105PS) at 5200rpm; 157Nm (16.0mkp) at 4000rpm.

Engine construction: Designated 1G–FE. 4 valves in V 22.3deg per cylinder; 2 overhead camshaft (toothed belt gear wheels); light–alloy cylinder head; oil capacity 5.6L (5.3US qt); electronic fuel injection. Battery 12V 45/60Ah, alternator 50–70A; cooling system capacity approx 8L (7.6US qt).

Transmission (to rear wheels): a) 5–speed manual, final drive ratio 3.909.
b) 3–speed automatic with overdrive, final drive ratio 4.300.

Gear ratios: a) 5–speed manual: 1st 3.285; 2nd 1.894; 3rd 1.275; 4th 1; 5th 0.86; R 3.768.
b) Automatic: Max torque multiplication in converter 2.4 times, Planetary gear set ratios: 1st 2.45; 2nd 1.45; 3rd 1; OD 0.688; R 2.222.

Chassis: Integral body; front and rear independent suspension, front lower and upper A arm, coil springs with coaxial shock absorber, antiroll bar, rear lower double control arm, upper A arm, coil springs with coaxial shock absorber and some models antiroll bar. Servo/power assisted disc brakes, front ventilated, rear mechanical handbrake; rack and pinion steering; fuel tank 61L (13.4Gal) [16.1US Gal], Supra 70L (15.4Gal) [18.5US Gal]; tyres 185/70 SR or 195/70 SR 14 (Soarer), 195/60 HR 15 (Supra), wheels 5.5 or 6J.

Dimensions: Soarer: Wheelbase 267cm, track 146/145.5cm, clearance approx 15cm; length 467.5cm, width 169.5cm, height 134.5cm. Supra: Wheelbase 259.5cm, track 146/145.5cm; length 462cm, width 169cm, height 130cm.

Performance (Supra): Max speed approx 124mph/200kmh, speed at 1000rpm in 5th gear 21.1mph/34.0kmh; acceleration from 13.8kg/kW (10.1kg/PS); consumption approx 8–12L/100km (35.3–23.5mpg) [29.4–19.6US mpg].

Toyota Soarer

2.0 DOHC
110/154kW–147/206hp–150/210PS
2 Turbo/Fuel Injection

As 133hp, except:

Body, Weight: Coupe Soarer, kerbweight 1340–1430kg. Coupe Supra, kerbweight 1400–1480kg.

Engine data (JIS net): 6–cylinder in–line (75 x 75mm), 1988cm3; compression ratio 9.5:1; 110kW (147hp) [150PS] at 6200rpm, 55.3kW/L (74.1hp/L) [75.4PS/L]; 183Nm (18.6mkp) at 5600rpm.
Version with 2 turbochargers: Compression ratio 8.5:1; 154kW (206hp) [210PS] at 6200rpm, 77.5kW/L (103.9hp/L) [105.6PS/L]; 275Nm (203lbft) at 3800rpm.

Engine construction: Designated 1G–GEU/1G–GTEU. Camshaft drive only with toothed belt; oil capacity 4.3L (4.1US qt); oil cooler.
Version 206hp with 2 parallel turbochargers and charge-air cooler.

Transmission: a) 5–speed manual, final drive ratio 4.300.
b) Automatic, final drive ratio 4.556.
Some models limited slip differential.

Gear ratios: a) 5–speed manual: 1st 3.566; 2nd 2.056; 3rd 1.384; 4th 1; 5th 0.85; R 4.091. Turbo: As 133hp.
b) Automatic: As 133hp.

Chassis: Front and rear antiroll bars; front and rear ventilated disc brakes, turbo with twin discs, optional ABS; tank capacity Soarer/Twin turbo 70L (15.4Gal) [18.5US Gal]; tyres 205/60 HR 15, wheels 6J.

Performance: Max speed approx 130-143mph/210–230kmh, speed at 1000rpm in 5th gear 19.3mph/31kmh (turbo) or 19.5mph/31.4kmh; power to weight ratio from 9.5kg/kW (7kg/PS); consumption approx 9–18L/100km (31.4–15.7mpg) [26.1–13.1US mpg].

Toyota Supra Turbo

3.0 DOHC
176kW–236hp–240PS
Turbo/Fuel Injection

As 133hp, except:

Body, Weight: Soarer, kerbweight (DIN) 1490–1520kg. Supra, kerbweight (DIN) 1480–1600kg, USA from 1570kg, turbo from 1600kg.

Engine data (JIS net): 6–cylinder in–line (83 x 91mm), 2954cm3; compression ratio 8.4:1; 176kW (236hp) [240PS] at 5600rpm, 59.5kW/L (79.7hp/L) [81.2PS/L]; 343Nm (253.1lbft) at 3200rpm.

Evolution Version (larger turbo): 198kW (265hp) [270PS] at 5600rpm; 358Nm (36.5mkp) at 4400rpm.
With Catalyst (DIN): 173kW (232hp) [235PS] at 5600rpm; 344Nm (253.9lbft) at 3200rpm.
USA version (SAE net): Identical data.
Without turbocharger: European version (DIN): Compression ratio 9.2:1; 150kW (201hp) [204PS] at 6000rpm; 254Nm (187.5lbft) at 4800rpm.
USA version (SAE net): 149kW (199hp) [203PS] at 6000rpm; 255Nm (188.2lbft) at 3600rpm.

Engine construction: Designated 7M-GTEU/&M-GEU. Camshaft drive only with toothed belt; oil capacity 5.1L (4.8US qt), oil cooler; turbocharger and charge-air cooler. Battery 12V 60/70Ah, alternator 60 or 70A; cooling system capacity 8.1L (7.7US qt).

Transmission: a) 5-speed manual, final drive ratio 3.727, 3.909; without turbo 3.909 or 4.300.
b) Automatic, final drive ratio 3.727, 3.909, 4.100 or 4.300.
Some models limited slip differential.

Gear ratios: a) 5-speed manual: 1st 3.251; 2nd 1.955; 3rd 1.310; 4th 1; 5th 0.753; R 3.180.
Also turbo: 1st 3.285; 2nd 1.894; 3rd 1.275; 4th 1; 5th 0.783 (USA 0.768); R 3.768.
b) Automatic: 1st 2.804; 2nd 1.531; 3rd 1; OD 0.705; R 2.393.

Chassis: Front and rear antiroll bars, some versions Soarer with level control system; front and rear ventialted disc brakes, optional ABS; tank capacity Soarer 70L (15.4Gal) [18.5US Gal]; tyres 225/50 VR 16 or 215/60 HR 15, wheels 6 or 7J.

Dimensions: Track (Supra) also 147/147.5cm or 148.5/148cm; length Supra (USA) 467.5cm, width Soarer 172.5cm, Supra 174.5cm.

Performance (Catalyst version): Max speed 152.3mph/245kmh (manufacturers test specifications), speed at 1000rpm in 5th gear (3.727) 25.7mph/41.3kmh; acceleration 0 – 62mph/100kmh in 6.3secs; power to weight ratio from 8.7kg/kW (6.4kg/PS); consumption ECE 8.5/10.5/14.9L/100km (33.2/26.9/19mpg) [27.7/22.4/15.8US mpg]. Without turbo: Max speed 137mph/220kmh (manufacturers test specifications), acceleration 0 – 62mph/100kmh in 8.2secs; power to weight ratio 10.6kg/kW (7.8kg/PS); consumption ECE 7.7/9.5/13.1L/100km (36.7/29.7/21.6mpg) [30.5/24.8/18US mpg].

Toyota Supra Turbo

Toyota Century

5/6-seater luxury vehicle, air suspension and V8 engine. For 1983: larger engine.

```
4 Litre V8
121kW-162hp-165PS
Fuel Injection
```

Body, Weight: 4-door Saloon/Sedan, 5/6-seater; kerbweight (DIN) 1790–1830kg.

Engine data (JIS net): 8-cylinder in V 90deg (87 x 84mm), 3995cm3; compression ratio 8.6:1; 121kW (162hp) [165PS] at 4400rpm, 30.3kW/L (40.6hp/L) [41.3PS/L]; 289Nm (213.3lbft) at 3600rpm.

Engine construction: Designated 5V-EU. Central camshaft (toothed wheel); light-alloy cylinder head and block, dry cylinder liners; crankshaft with 5 bearings; oil capacity 5L (4.7US qt); electronic fuel injection. Battery 12V 60Ah, alternator 960W; cooling system capacity 13.4L (12.7US qt).

Transmission (to rear wheels): Automatic, hydraulic torque converter and 4-speed Planetary gear set, selector lever on steering column; final drive ratio 3.583.

Gear ratios: Max torque multiplication in converter 2.2 times, Planetary gear set ratios: 1st 2.804; 2nd 1.531; 3rd 1; 4th 0.705; R 2.393.

Chassis: Integral body; front McPherson struts, A arm and antiroll bar, rear rigid axle with trailing arms and coil springs, antiroll bar, optional rear level control system, telescopic damper. Four wheel ventilated servo/power assisted disc brakes, rear mechanical handbrake; power assisted recirculating ball steering; fuel tank 95L (20.9Gal) [25.1US Gal]; tyres 205/70 SR 14.

Dimensions: Wheelbase 286cm, track 155/155.5cm, clearance 15.5/16.5cm, turning circle 12.6m; length 512cm, width 189cm, height 143–145cm.

Performance: Max speed 112mph/180kmh (manufacturers test specifications), speed at 1000rpm in 5th gear 29.3/47.2kmh; acceleration from 14.8kg/kW (10.8kg/PS); consumption approx 13– 20L/100km (21.7–14.1mpg) [18.1–11.8US mpg].

Toyota Century

Toyota Blizzard

Rough terrain vehicle with body and mechanics from Daihatsu, diesel engine from Toyota. Launched March 1980. 1983: 5-speed manual transmission. Summer 1984: Based on the Daihatsu Rugger, 2.45 Litre engine.

```
2.45 Litre Diesel
62kW-83hp-85PS
Turbo/Injection Pump
```

Body, Weight: 3-door Estate/Station Wagon, 5/7-seater; kerbweight (DIN) from 1450kg, without turbo 1360kg. 3-door soft-top, 4/5-seater; kerbweight (DIN) from 1430kg, without turbo 1350kg.

Engine data (JIS net): 4-cylinder in-line (92 x 92mm), 2446cm3; compression ratio 20:1; 62kW (83hp) [85PS] at 4000rpm, 25.3kW/L (33.9hp/L) [34.8PS/L]; 188Nm (138.7lbft) at 2400rpm.
Without turbocharger: Compression ratio 22.3:1; 56kW (75hp) [76PS] at 4000rpm; 154Nm (113.6lbft) at 2400rpm.

Engine construction: Designated 2L-T. 1 overhead camshaft (toothed belt); grey cast iron cylinder head; crankshaft with 5 bearings; oil capacity 5.8L (5.5US qt); Bosch VE diesel injection pump; exhaust turbocharger. Battery 12V 65Ah, alternator 50A; cooling system capacity approx 9L (8.5US qt).

Transmission (to rear or all wheels): Rear wheel drive with engageable four wheel drive, front-free wheel hub. Reduction gear: Final drive ratio road 1.295, cross county 2.367. 5-speed manual, final drive ratio 3.700. Some models with limited slip differential rear or mechanical lock.

Gear ratios: 1st 3.477; 2nd 2.037; 3rd 1.317; 4th 1; 5th 0.82; R 4.148.
Or (without turbo): 1st 3.647; 2nd 2.136; 3rd 1.382; 4th 1; 5th 0.86; R 4.351.

Chassis: Box section frame with transverse crossmembers; front and rear rigid axle with leaf springs, front Panhard rod and antiroll bar, telescopic damper. Servo/power assisted brakes, front discs, rear drums, parking brake to rear wheels; power assisted recirculating ball steering (except 75hp); fuel tank 60L (13.2Gal) [15.9US qt]; tyres 6.00– 16, H78–15 or 215 R 15, wheels 6J, optional 7J.

Toyota Blizzard

Toyota

Dimensions: Wheelbase 220.5cm, track 132/130cm, clearance 21cm; length 365.5–396.5cm, width 158cm, height 183–184cm.
Performance: Max speed approx 84mph/135kmh, speed at 1000rpm in 5th gear 20.9mph/33.7kmh; power to weight ratio from 23.1kg/kW (16.8kg/PS); consumption approx 8–13L/100km (35.3–21.7mpg) [29.4– 18.1US mpg].

Toyota Land Cruiser/Land Crusier II

Rough terrain four wheel drive vehicle with variable body styles and wheelbase. 1985: New body and mechanical modifications, Land Cruiser II available with 2.4 Litre engine or 2.45 Litre Diesel/Turbo engine. 1987: Modified body and mechanics. 1988: For Italy the 2.5 litre Turbodiesel from VM also available.

4 Litre
107kW–143hp–145PS
1 2V Carb

Body, Weight: 3–door Hardtop SWB, 5–seater; kerbweight (DIN) from 1680kg, gross vehicle weight 2380kg. 3–door Soft–top SWB, 5–seater; kerbweight (DIN) from 1670kg, gross vehicle weight 2380kg. 3–door Hardtop/Soft–top MWB, 5–seater; kerbweight (DIN) from 1720kg, gross vehicle weight 2410kg. 5–door Estate/Station Wagon, 5/8–seater; kerbweight (DIN) from 1865kg, gross vehicle weight 2760–2910kg. 3–door Hardtop LWB, 5/12–seater; kerbweight (DIN) from 1930kg, gross vehicle weight 3035kg.
Engine data (JIS net): 6–cylinder in–line (94 x 95mm), 3956cm3; compression ratio 8.1:1; 107kW (143hp) [145PS] at 4200rpm, 27.1kW/L (36.3hp/L) [36.7PS/L]; 275Nm (203lbft) at 3000rpm; regular grade.
Export version (SAE net): 108kW (144hp) [147PS] at 4200rpm; 275Nm (203lbft) at 2200rpm. Or 101kW (135hp) [137PS].
With Catalyst (Injection DIN): 115kW (154hp) [156PS] at 4000rpm; 298Nm (220lbft) at 3000rpm.
Engine construction: Designated 3F. Side camshaft; grey cast iron cylinder head; crankshaft with 7 bearings, oil capacity 8L (7.6US qt); 1 Aisan downdraught 2V carb; Catalsyt version with electronic fuel injection. Battery 12V or 24V 50/70Ah, alternator 50/60A; cooling system capacity 17L (16.1US qt).
Transmission (to rear or all wheels): Engageable front wheel drive, optional free-wheel hub; 2–speed reduction gear.
a) 4–speed manual, final drive ratio 3.7 or 4.1.
b) 5–speed manual, final drive ratio 3.7 or 4.1.
c) Automatic, hydraulic torque converter and 3–speed Planetary gear set with OD, final drive ratio 4.111.
Optional rear limited slip or lock differential.

Toyota Land Cruiser

Gear ratios: Reduction gears: 1st 1; 2nd 1.963.
a) 4–speed manual: 1st 4.843; 2nd 2.618; 3rd 1.516; 4th 1; R 4.843.
b) 5–speed manual: 1st 4.843; 2nd 2.618; 3rd 1.516; 4th 1; 5th 0.845; R 4.843.
c) Automatic: Max torque multiplication in converter 1.92 times, Planetary gear set ratios: 1st 2.950; 2nd 1.530; 3rd 1; OD 0.717; R 2.678.
Chassis: Box section frame with transverse crossmembers; front and rear rigid axle with semi elliptic spring, some models front antiroll bar, telescopic damper. Servo/power assisted brakes, front ventilated discs, rear drums, some versions four wheel drum brakes, rear mechanical handbrake; recirculating ball steering, optional power assisted; fuel tank 90L (19.8Gal) [23.8US Gal]; tyres 7.00–15, 7.00–16, 7.50–16, 215 SR 15, 10 R 15 LT or 205 SR 16, wheels 6J.

Dimensions: a) 3–door Hardtop: Wheelbase 231cm, track 141.5/141cm, clearance 21cm, turning circle 10.6m; length 397.5–406cm, width 169cm, height 186.5–190cm.
b) Hardtop MWB: Wheelbase 260cm, turning circle 11.6m; length 423.5–435cm, height 191–195.5cm.
c) Estate/Station Wagon: Wheelbase 273cm, track 147.5/146cm or 151/150cm, turning circle 12.4m; length 467.5–475cm, width 180cm, height 180–196.5cm.
d) Hardtop LWB with or without side window: Wheelbase 298cm, turning circle 13m; length 488.5–499.5cm, height 193.5–208cm.
Performance: Max speed approx 99mph/160kmh (manufacturers specifications), speed at 1000rpm in 4th gear (3.700, 205 SR 16) 22.5mph/36.2kmh; power to weight ratio from 15.6kg/kW (11.5kg/PS); consumption approx 10–20L/100km (28.2–14.1mpg) [23.5–11.7US mpg].

2.4 Litre
81kW–109hp–110PS
1 2V Carb

Engine for Land Cruiser II (Export)
As 143hp, except:
Body, Weight: 3–door Estate/Station Wagon Hardtop, 5–seater; kerbweight (DIN) from 1495kg, gross vehicle weight 2110kg. 3–door Soft–top, 5–seater; kerbweight (DIN) from 1520kg, gross vehicle weight 2110kg.
Engine data (DIN): 4–cylinder in–line (92 x 89mm), 2367cm3; compression ratio 9.0:1; 81kW (109hp) [110PS] at 5000rpm, 34.2kW/L (45.9hp/L) [46.5PS/L]; 187Nm (138lbft) at 3400rpm; regular grade.
Engine construction: Designated 22 R. Valves in V, 1 overhead camshaft (chain); light-alloy cylinder head; crankshaft with 5 bearings, oil capacity 4.3L (4.1US qt); 1 Asian downdraught 2V carb. Battery 12V 50/70Ah, alternator 45/55A; cooling system capacity 10L (9.5US qt).
Transmission: a) 4–speed manual, final drive ratio 4.300.
b) 5–speed manual, final drive ratio 4.555 or 4.300.
c) Automatic, hydraulic torque converter and 3–speed Planetary gear set with OD, final drive ratio 4.300.
Optional limited slip differential or lock for rear axle.
Gear ratios: Reduction gears: 1st 1; 2nd 2.276.
a) 4–speed manual: 1st 3.928; 2nd 2.333; 3rd 1.451; 4th 1; R 4.743.
b) 5–speed manual: 1st 3.928; 2nd 2.333; 3rd 1.451; 4th 1; 5th 0.851; R 4.743.
c) Automatic: As 143hp.
Chassis: Front and rear rigid axle with coil springs, trailing arms and Panhard rod. Front disc brakes, rear drums; tyres 7.00–15, 215 SR 15 or 205 SR 16, optional 10 R 15, wheels 6J.
Dimensions: Wheelbase 231cm, track 141.5/141cm, clearance 22.5cm, turning circle 11.4m; length 397–406cm, width 169cm, height 188.5/192cm. Also wheelbase 260cm, length 435cm, height 193cm.
Performance: Max speed 90mph/145kmh (manufacturers test specifications), speed at 1000rpm in 5th gear (4.555) 21.3mph/34.2kmh; acceleration 0–62mph/100kmh in 20.7secs; power to weight ratio from 18.5kg/kW (13.6kg/PS); consumption ECE 10.4/16/15.5L/100km (27.2/17.7/18.2mpg) [22.6/14.7/15.2US mpg].

2.45 Diesel
63/53kW–84/71hp–86/72PS
Turbo/Injection Pump

Engine for Land Cruiser II
As 143hp, except:
Body, Weight: Hardtop, kerbweight (DIN) from 1580kg, long wheelbase from 1660kg, without turbo from 1550kg. Soft top, kerbweight 1550kg, without Turbo 1520kg.
Engine data (DIN): 4–cylinder in–line (92 x 92mm), 2446cm3; compression ratio 20:1; 63kW (84hp) [86PS] at 4000rpm, 25.8kW/L (34.6hp/L) [35.2PS/L]; 188Nm (138.7lbft) at 2400rpm.
Japanese version (JIS net): 62kW (83hp) [85PS]; 188Nm (138.7lbft).
Without turbocharger (DIN): Compression ratio 22.3:1; 53kW (71hp) [72PS] at 4000rpm; 155Nm (114.4lbft) at 2200rpm.
Engine construction: Designated 2L. Turbulence chamber diesel engine. Valves in parallel, 1 overhead camshaft (toothed belt); crankshaft with 5 bearings; oil capacity 5.8L (5.5US qt), oil cooler; diesel injection pump, turbocharger. Battery 1–2 x 12V 60/94Ah, alternator 45/50A; cooling system capacity 11.3L (10.7US qt).
Transmission: a) 4–speed manual, final drive ratio 4.875.
b) 5–speed manual, final drive ratio 4.875.
c) Automatic, final drive ratio 4.875.

Toyota

Gear ratios: Reduction gears: 1st 1; 2nd 2.295 or 2.276.
a) 4-speed manual: 1st 3.928; 2nd 2.333; 3rd 1.451; 4th 1; R 4.743.
b) 5-speed manual: 1st 3.928; 2nd 2.333; 3rd 1.451; 4th 1; 5th 0.851; R 4.743. Or 1st 4.313; 2nd 2.33; 3rd 1.436; 4th 1; 5th 0.838; R 4.22.
c) Automatic: As 143hp.

Chassis: Front and rear rigid axle with coil springs, trailing arms and Panhard rod. Front disc brakes, rear drums; power assisted steering; tyres 205 SR 16, 215 SR 15 or 78 H 15.

Dimensions: Wheelbase 231cm, track 141.5/141cm, clearance 22.5cm, turning circle 11.4m; length 397/406cm, width 169cm, height 188.5/192cm; Also wheelbase 260cm; length 435cm, height 193cm.

Performance: Max speed 81mph/130kmh (manufacturers test specifications), speed at 1000 in 4th gear 17mph/27.4kmh; acceleration 0 – 62mph/100kmh in 25.0secs; power to weight ratio from 25kg/kW (18.2kg/PS); consumption ECE 10.0/16.9/12.1L/100km (28.2/16.7/23.3mpg) [23.5/13.9/19.4US mpg].

Toyota Land Cruiser II

```
2.5 Litre Turbodiesel
73kW–98hp–99PS
Injection Pump
```

As 143hp, except:

Body, Weight: 3-door Estate/Station Wagon Hardtop, 5-seater; kerbweight (DIN) from 1835kg, gross vehicle weight 2450kg.

Engine data (DIN): 5-cylinder in-line (88 x 82mm), 2494cm3; Compression ratio 22:1; 73kW (98hp) [99PS] at 4000rpm, 29.3kW/L (39.3hp/L) [39.7PS/L]; 220Nm (162.4lbft) at 1600rpm.

Engine construction: Designated VM 66 A. Diesel precombustion chamber. 1 overhead camshaft (toothed belt); parallel valves, 6 main bearing crankshaft; oil capacity 7.2L (5.7US qt); Bosch diesel injection pump, turbocharger KKK, max boost pressure 0.9bar; charge air cooler. Battery 2 x 12V 55Ah, alternator 600W; cooling system capacity approx 10L (9.5US qt).

Transmission: 5-speed manual, final drive ratio 4.555.

Gear ratios: Reduction gear, 1st 1; 2nd 1.963.
5-speed manual: 1st 4.843; 2nd 2.618; 3rd 1.516; 4th 1; 5th 0.845; R 4.843.

Chassis: Fuel tank capacity 80L (17.6 Gal) [21.1US Gal].

Toyota Land Cruiser Turbodiesel

Dimensions: Wheelbase 260cm, track 141.5/140cm, clearance 19.5cm, turning circle 10.4m, length 435cm, width 169cm, height 192cm.

Performance: Max speed 90mph/145kmh (manufacturers test specifications), speed at 1000rpm in 5th gear 47.3mph/35.3kmh; power to weight ratio from 25.1kg/kW (18.5kg/PS); consumption ECE 10.2/14.7/14.4L/100km (27.7/19.2/19.6mpg) [23.1/16/16.3US mpg].

```
3.4 Diesel
91/66kW–122/88hp–124/90PS
Turbo/Injection Pump
```

As 143hp, except:

Weight: Increased weight approx 50–80kg. Turbodiesel (Hardtop SWB and MWB only) 1820–1900kg, gross vehicle weight 2410kg.

Engine data (DIN): 4-cylinder in-line (102 x 105mm), 3432 cm3; compression ratio 17.6:1; 91kW (122hp) [124PS] at 3400rpm, 26.6kW/L (35.6hp/L) [(36.1PS/L]; 280Nm (206.6lbft) at 2000rpm.
Japanese version (JIS net): 88kW (118hp) [120PS]; 284Nm (209.6lbft).
Without turbocharger (DIN): Compression ratio 20:1; 66kW (88hp) [90PS] at 3500rpm; 216Nm (159.4lbft) at 2100rpm.
Export version (SAE net): 69kW (93hp) [94PS]; 221Nm (163.1lbft).
Japanese version (JIS): 72kW (96hp) [98PS] at 3500rpm; 226Nm (166.8lbft) at 2200rpm.

Engine construction: Designated 13B–T/3B. Turbulence chamber diesel engine. Crankshaft with 5 bearings; oil capacity 6.7L (6.3US qt), oil cooler; injection pump; 1 exhaust turbocharger, boost pressure 0.42–0.56bar. Battery 2 x 12V 60–70Ah, alternator 720W; cooling system capacity 12.1/14.2L (11.4/13.4US qt).

Transmission: a) 4-speed manual (diesel), final drive ratio 4.111.
b) 5-speed manual, final drive ratio 4.111.
c) Automatic (turbo diesel), final drive ratio 4.111.

Performance: Max speed approx 93mph/150kmh, without turbo 75mph/120kmh, speed at 1000rpm in 4th gear 20.2mph/32.5kmh; power to weight ratio from 20.8kg/kW (15.3kg/PS); consumption ECE (TD) 8.9/12.6/12.7L/100km (31.7/22.4/22.2mpg) [26.4/18.7/18.5US mpg].

Toyota Land Cruiser Turbodiesel

```
4.0 Diesel
100/76kW–134/102hp–136/103PS
Turbo/Injection Pump
```

As 143hp, except:

Weight (none for SWB models): Increased weight approx 65kg.

Engine data (DIN): 6-cylinder in-line (91 x 102mm), 3980cm3; compression ratio 18.6:1; 100kW (134hp) [136PS] at 3500rpm, 25.1kW/L (33.6hp/L) [34.2PS/L]; 315Nm (232.5lbft) at 1800rpm.
Japanese version (JIS net): 99kW (133hp) [135PS]; 314Nm (231.7lbft) at 2000rpm.
Without turbo (DIN): Compression ratio 20.7:1; 76kW (102hp) [103PS] at 3500rpm; 241Nm (177.9lbft) at 1800rpm.
Export version (SAE net): 79kW (106hp) [107PS]; 246Nm (181.5lbft).
Japanese version (JIS net): 77kW (103hp) [105PS]; 250Nm (184.5lbft) at 2200rpm.

Engine construction: Turbulence chamber diesel engine. Designated 12H. Oil capacity 10.7L (10.1US qt), oil cooler; injection pump, 134hp with turbocharger. Battery 2 x 12V 48/70Ah, alternator 30/50A; cooling system capacity 15.4L (14.6US qt).

Transmission: a) 4-speed manual (not for TD), final drive ratio 4.111 or 3.700.
b) 5-speed manual, final drive ratio 4.111 or 3.700.
c) Automatic, final drive ratio 4.111, without turbo also 4.555.

Toyota J • Toyota BR

Performance (102hp): Max speed 90mph/145kmh (manufacturers test specifications), speed at 1000rpm in 4th gear (3.700, 205 SR 16) 22.5mph/36.2kmh; acceleration 0 – 62mph/100kmh in 26secs; power to weight ratio from 25.6kg/kW (18.0kg/PS); consumption ECE 9.8/13.8/15.4L/100km (28.8/20.5/18.3mpg) [24/17/15/13US mpg]. With turbocharger: Max speed approx 99mph/160kmh; power to weight ratio from 21.7kg/kW (16.1kg/PS).

Toyota 4-Runner

Engageable four wheel drive and reduction gears, 5- seater with luxury interior. Available with a 4-cylinder engine and V6 for the USA. Launched 1987.

2.4 Litre
82kW-110hp-112PS
Fuel Injection

Body, Weight: 3–door Estate/Station Wagon, 5–seater; kerbweight (DIN) 1620kg, USA 1635kg, gross vehicle weight 2305kg.

Engine data (Catalyst, DIN): 4–cylinder in–line (92 x 89mm), 2366cm3; compression ratio 9.3:1; 82kW (110hp) [112PS] at 4800rpm, 34.7kW/L (46.5hp/L) [47.3PS/L]; 187Nm (138lbft) at 3600rpm; unleaded regular grade. USA version (SAE net): 87kW (117hp) [118PS] at 4800rpm; 190Nm (140.2lbft) at 2800rpm.

Engine construction: Designated 22 REC. Valves in V. 1 overhead camshaft (chain); light–alloy cylinder head, crankshaft with 5 bearings; oil capacity 4.3L (4.1US qt); electronic fuel injection. Battery 45/60Ah, alternator 50/60A, cooling system capacity 8.4L (7.9US qt).

Transmission (to rear wheels or all wheels): Engageable front wheel drive with free-wheel hub, transfer box with off road reduction.
a) 5-speed manual, final drive ratio 4.100.
b) Automatic with OD, hydraulic torque converter and 4-speed Planetary gear set, final drive ratio 4.300.
Optional rear limited slip differential.

Gear ratios: Reduction gears: 1st 1; 2nd 2.276.
a) 5-speed manual: 1st 3.954; 2nd 2.141; 3rd 1.384; 4th 1; 5th 0.850; R 4.091.
b) Automatic: Max torque multiplication in converter 1.92 times, Planetary gear set ratios: 1st 2.804; 2nd 1.531; 3rd 1; OD 0.705; R 2.393.

Chassis: Box type frame with transverse cross members; front independent suspension with double A arm, longitudinal torison bar and antiroll bar, rear rigid axle semi elliptic spring, telescopic damper. Servo/power assisted brakes, front ventilated discs, rear drums, rear mechanical handbrake; power assisted recirculating ball steering fuel tank 65L (14.3Gal) [17.2US Gal]; tyres 215 R 15, USA 225/75 R 15, optional 235/70 R 15, wheels 6J, optional 7J.

Dimensions: Wheelbase 262.5cm, track 143/141cm, clearance 27cm, turning circle approx 11.5m; length 444cm, width 169cm, height 170.5cm, USA 168cm.

Performance: Max speed 96mph/155kmh (manufacturers test specifications), speed at 1000rpm in 5th gear 23.6mph/38kmh; acceleration 0 – 62mph/100kmh in 18.4secs; power to weight ratio from 19.8kg/kW (14.5kg/PS); consumption (urban, town, combination) 11.3/8.7/10.1L/100km (25.0/32.5/28mpg) [20.8/27/23.3US mpg].

Toyota 4-Runner

3 Litre V6
112kW-150hp-152PS
Fuel Injection

Model for the USA

As 2.4 Litre, except:

Weight: Kerbweight (DIN) from 1695kg.

Engine data (SAE net): 6–cylinder in V 60deg (87.5 x 82mm), 2958cm3; compression ratio 9:1; 112kW (150hp) [152PS] at 4800rpm, 37.9kW/L (50.8hp/L) [51.4PS/L]; 244Nm (180.1lbft) at 3200rpm.

Engine construction: 1 overhead camshaft (toothed belt); crankshaft with 4 bearings; oil capacity 4.5L (4.3US qt). Cooling system capacity approx 10L (9.5US qt).

Transmission: a) 5-speed manual, final drive ratio 4.100.
b) Automatic, final drive ratio 4.300.

Gear ratios: a) 5-speed manual: 1st 3.830; 2nd 2.062; 3rd 1.436; 4th 1; 5th 0.838; R 4.220.
b) Automatic: As 2.4 Litre.

Performance: Max speed approx 103mph/165kmh, speed at 1000rpm in 5th gear 23.9mph/38.4kmh; power to weight ratio from 15.1kg/kW (11.2kg/PS); consumption approx 10–18L/100km (28.2–15.7mpg) [23.5–13.0US mpg].

TOYOTA   BR

Toyota do Brasil S/A, Ind E Com, Estrada de Piraporinha, km 23, 9720 Sao Bernardo do Campo, Brasil.

Brazilian Toyota Motor Co manufacturing plant.

Toyota Bandeirante

Estate/Station Wagon rough terrain vehicle, with four wheel drive and Mercedes–Benz diesel engine.

3.8 Litre Diesel
62.5kW-84hp-85PS
Injection Pump

Body, Weight: 3–door Estate/Station Wagon, 5–seater; kerbweight (DIN) 1580–1710kg, gross vehicle weight 2000–2130kg.

Engine data (DIN) 4–cylinder in–line (97 x 128mm), 3784 cm3; compression ratio 17:1; 62.5kW (84hp) [85PS] at 2800rpm, 16.5kW/L (22.1hp/L) [22.5PS/L]; 235Nm (173.4lbft) at 1800rpm.

Engine construction: Mercedes-Benz diesel engine, type OM–314 with direct injection; oil capacity 7L (6.6US qt); Bosch injection pump, oil bath air cleaner. Battery 12V 126Ah, alternator 35A; cooling system capacity 14.5L (13.7US qt).

Transmission (to all wheels): 4-speed manual with transfer case (1.992/1), 3rd and 4th gear synchronized, final drive ratio 3.7 (10/37).

Gear ratios: 4-speed manual: 1st 4.925; 2nd 2.643; 3rd 1.519; 4th 1; R 4.925.

Chassis: Box type frame with transverse cross members; front and rear rigid axle with semi elliptic springs, telescopic damper. Servo/power assisted drum brakes; rear mechanical handbrake; fuel tank 52L (11.4Gal) [13.7US Gal]; tyres 6.70-16.

Dimensions: Wheelbase 228.5cm, optional 275.5cm, track 141.5/140cm, clearance 21cm, turning circle 10.6m; length 383.5/430.5cm, width 166.5cm, height 192/196.5cm.

Performance: Max speed 65mph/105kmh (manufacturers test specifications), power to weight ratio from 25.3kg/kW (18.6kg/PS); consumption (DIN) 9–10L/100km (31.4–28.2mpg) [26.1– 23.5US mpg].

Toyota Bandeirante

Trabant • Tschika • TVR

TRABANT — GDR

VEB Sachsenring Automobilwerke, 9541 Zwickau, GDR

Manufacturer of small vehicles, based in Zwickau, German Democratic Republic (DDR).

Trabant 601 Limousine

Trabant 601

Coach – Cabriolet (tramp) – Universal

Small 4–seater vehicle, with a 2–cylinder engine and front wheel drive. September 1985; electronic fuel injection. April 1988; rear coil springs.

```
595cm3
19kW–25hp–26PS
1 Carb
```

Body, Weight: 2–door Saloon/Sedan, 4–seater; kerbweight (DIN) 615kg, gross vehicle weight 1000kg. Cabriolet/Convertible (tramp) 4–seater; kerbweight (DIN) 645kg, gross vehicle weight 1020kg. 3–door Universal Estate/Station Wagon, 4–seater; kerbweight (DIN) 650kg, gross vehicle weight 1040kg.

Engine data (DIN): 2–cylinder in–line (72 x 73mm), 594.5cm3; compression ratio 7.8:1; 19kW (25hp) [26PS] at 4200rpm, 32kW/L (42.8hp/L) [43.7PS/L]; 54Nm (39.9lbft) at 3000rpm; leaded regular grade.

Trabant 601 Universal

Engine construction: Front engine, transverse two stroke engine with inlet rotary disc valve, two stroke mixture lubrication (2%); light–alloy cylinder head and block, dry cylinder liners; crankshaft with 3 bearings; 1 Horizontal carb; BVF 28 H 1–1. Battery 12V 38Ah, alternator 42A; air cooling with fan.

Transmission (to front wheels): Optional automatic clutch Hycomat; 4–speed manual (without direct drive), free-wheel in 4th gear, gear shift mechanism on dash board; final drive ratio 3.95 (19/75).

Gear ratios: 1st 4.08; 2nd 2.32; 3rd 1.52; 4th 1.103; R 3.83.

Chassis: Integral body (platform and framework wielded with Duroplast body tray); front lower A arm and upper transverse leaf spring, rear independent suspension with longitudinal arms as soon as coil springs, telescopic damper. Four wheel drum brakes, rear mechanical handbrake; rack and pinion steering; fuel tank 26L (5.7Gal) [6.9US Gal], including 6.5L (1.4Gal) [1.7US Gal] Reserve; tyres 5.20–13, optional 145 SR 13, wheels 4J.

Dimensions: Wheelbase 202cm, track 120.5/125.5cm, clearance 15.5cm, turning circle 10m; load space 14.8cu ft (420dm3), Estate/Station Wagon 15.9–49.4cu ft (450–1400dm3).
a) Coach (Saloon/Sedan): Length 351–359.5cm, tramp 348cm, width 150.5cm, height 144cm, tramp 146.5cm.
b) Estate/Station Wagon: Length 351–359.5cm, width 151cm, height 147cm.

Performance: Max speed 62mph/100kmh (manufacturers specifications), speed at 1000rpm in 4th gear 14.9mph/24kmh; acceleration 0 – 50mph/80kmh in 18secs; standing km in 49secs; power to weight ratio from 32.4kg/kW (23.7kg/PS); consumption (DIN) 6.8L/100km (41.5mpg) [34.6US mpg], (touring) 7–9L/100km (40.4–31.4mpg) [33.6–26.1US mpg] (manufacturers test specifications).

TSCHAIKA — SU

Tschaika, v/o Autoexport, 14 Volkhonka St, 119902 Moscow, USSR

Russian manufacturer based in Gorky.

Tschaika GAZ–14

Large vehicle with a 5.5 Litre V8 engine and automatic transmission, length 611cm.

Tschaika GAZ–14

```
5.5 Litre V8
147kW–197hp–200PS
1 4V Carb
```

Body, Weight: 4–door Saloon/Sedan, 5/7–seater; kerbweight (DIN) 2605kg, gross vehicle weight 3165kg.

Engine data (DIN): 8–cylinder in V 90deg (100 x 88mm), 5529cm3; compression ratio 8.5:1; 147kW (197hp) [200PS] at 4200rpm, 26.6kW/L (35.6hp/L) [36.2PS/L]; 451Nm (332.8lbft) at 2750rpm; leaded premium grade.

Engine construction: Central camshaft; crankshaft with 5 bearings; oil capacity 8.5L (8US qt); downdraught 4V carb, electic fuel pump. Battery 12V 108Ah (2 x 54Ah), alternator 500W; cooling system capacity 21.5L (20.3US qt).

Transmission (to rear wheels): Automatic, hydraulic torque converter and 3–speed Planetary gear set, selector lever in the middle; final drive ratio 3.38.

Gear ratios: Max torque multiplication in converter 2.35 times, Planetary gear set ratios: 1st 2.64; 2nd 1.55; 3rd 1; R 2.

Chassis: Box type frame with transverse crossmembers; front independent suspension with A–arms and coil springs, rear rigid axle with semi–elliptic springs, front antiroll bar, telescopic damper. Servo/power assisted brakes, front disc, rear drums, brake power limiter, rear parking brakes; power assisted worm and wheel steering; fuel tank 100/120L (22/26.4Gal) [26.4/31.7US Gal]; tyres 9.35–15 or 235–380.

Dimensions: Wheelbase 345cm, track 158/158cm, clearance 18cm, turning circle 16.4m; length 611.5cm, width 202cm, height 158cm.

Performance: Max speed 109mph/175kmh (manufacturers test specifications); acceleration 0 – 62mph/100kmh in 15secs; power to weight ratio 17.7kg/kW (13.0kg/PS); consumption 19L/100km (14.9mpg) [12.4US mpg].

TVR — GB

TVR Engineering Limited, Bristol Avenue, Blackpool, FY2 0JF England

TVR

English manufacturer of Sports vehicles with, synthetic body/chassis and mechanical components from Ford and Rover.

TVR S Convertible

New edition of the early TVR Roadster. 2-seater Sports car with a 2.8 Litre Ford engine. Launched Birmingham 1986. Birmingham 1988: 2.9 Litre V6 engine.

2.9 Litre V6
125kW-168hp-170PS
Fuel Injection

Body, Weight: 2-door Cabriolet/Convertible, 2-seater; kerbweight 940kg, gross vehicle weight 1100kg.
Engine data (DIN): 6-cylinder in V 60deg (93 x 72mm), 2935cm3; compression ratio 9.5:1; 125kW (168hp) [170PS] at 5700rpm, 42.6kW/L (57.1hp/L) [57.9PS/L]; 223Nm (164.6lbft) at 3000rpm; leaded premium grade.
With Catalyst: In preparation.
Engine construction: Designated Ford V6. Central camshaft (toothed wheel); crankshaft with 4 bearings; oil capacity 4.7L (4.4US qt); Bosch L-Jetronic fuel injection. Battery 12V 60Ah, alternator 45A; cooling system capacity 10L (9.5US qt).
Transmission (to rear wheels); 5-speed manual, final drive ratio 3.64.
Gear ratios: 1st 3.36; 2nd 1.81; 3rd 1.26; 4th 1; 5th 0.82; R 3.365.
Chassis: Steel tubular frame, independent suspension, front double A arm and rear semi-trailing arm, front and rear antiroll bars, coil springs and telescopic damper. Servo/power assisted brakes, front ventilated discs, rear drums, disc diameter 23.9cm, rear handbrake; rack and pinion steering; fuel tank 54.5L (12Gal) [14.4US Gal]; tyres 205/60 VR 15, wheels 7J.
Dimensions: Wheelbase 228.5cm, track 140/140cm, turning circle 14cm, clearance 9.6m; load space 9.4cu ft (225dm3), length 396cm, width 166.5cm, height 122.5cm.
Performance: Max speed 141mph/226kmh (manufacturers test specifications), speed at 1000rpm in 5th gear 24mph/38.6kmh; acceleration 0 – 60mph/97kmh 6.8secs; power to weight ratio from 7.5kg/kW (5.5kg/PS); consumption 9-13L/100km (31.4-21.7mpg) [26.1-18.1US mpg] (manufacturers specifications).

TVR S Convertible

TVR Tuscan

Protype October 1988, Production commences in 1989. Based on the S model with 3.5 to 5 litre V8 engine, suitable for street and circuit racing (Challenge).

3.5 Litre V8
168kW-225hp-228PS
Fuel Injection

As S Convertible, except:
Body, Weight: 2-door Convertible, 2-seater; kerbweight 1000kg, gross vehicle weight 1250kg.
Engine data (DIN): 8-cylinder in V 90deg (88.9 x 71.12mm), 3532cm3; Compression ratio 10:1; 168kW (225hp) [228PS] at 5280rpm, 47.6kW/L (63.8hp/L) [64.5PS/L]; 319Nm (235.4lbft) at 4000rpm; premium grade.

Challenge: 4.45 Litre V8; 268kW (359hp) [365PS] at 7000rpm; 475Nm (350lbft) at 6000rpm.
Optionally with 5 Litre V8 from Holden.
Engine construction: Designated Rover V8 Vitesse. Hydraulic tappets, central camshaft (chain); light-alloy cylinder head and block, dry cylinder liners; 5 main bearing crankshaft; oil capacity 5.5L (5.2US qt); Lucas L electronic fuel injection; cooling system capacity approx 11L (10.4US qt).
Transmission (to rear wheels): 5-speed manual, final drive ratio 3.31.
Gear ratios: 1st 3.32; 2nd 2.09; 3rd 1.40; 4th 1; 5th 0.79; R 3.43.
Chassis: Tyres 225/50 VR 15, wheel rims 8J.
Dimensions: Wheelbase 233.5cm, track 148/148cm, clearance 13cm, turning circle 9.6m. Length 394cm, width 174cm, height 118cm.
Performance: Max speed 156mph/251kmh (manufacturers test specifications); speed at 1000rpm in 5th gear 26mph/42kmh; acceleration 0-97kmh 5.5secs; power to weight ratio from 5.9kg/kW (4.4kg/PS); consumption 10-18L/100km (28.2-15.7mpg) [23.5-13.1US mpg] (manufacturers test specifications).

TVR Tuscan

TVR 350 - 400 - 450

2-door, 2-seater Coupe with all round independent suspension and Rover V8 engine. Launched Brussels 1980, Cabriolet/Convertible Autumn 1980, 390 SE Autumn 1984 and 420 Covertible/Sports Saloon/Sedan October 1986. 1989, 400/450 SE model with increased engine displacement.

TVR 350i

3.5 Litre V8
147kW-197hp-200PS
Fuel Injection

Engine for 350i
Body, Weight: 2-door Convertible/Cabriolet, 2-seater; kerbweight approx 1120kg, gross vehicle weight 1425kg.
Engine data (DIN): 8-cylinder in V 90deg (88.9 x 71.12mm), 3532cm3; Compression ratio 9.75:1; 147kW (197hp) [200PS] at 5280rpm, 41.7kW/L (55.9hp/L) [56.6PS/L]; 298Nm (219.9lbft) at 4000rpm; premium grade.
Engine construction: Designated Rover V8 Vitesse. Hydraulic tappets, central camshaft (chain); light-alloy cylinder head and block, dry cylinder liners; 5 main bearing crankshaft; oil capacity 5.5L (5.2US qt); Lucas L electronic fuel injection. Battery 12V 60 Ah, alternator 55A; cooling system capacity approx 11L (10.4US qt).

TVR · UAZ · Umm

Transmission (to rear wheels): 5–speed manual, final drive ratio 3.54.
Gear ratios: 1st 3.32; 2nd 2.09; 3rd 1.40; 4th 1; 5th 0.79; R 3.43.
Chassis: Steel tubular frame, front upper A arm, lower control arm, coil springs, rear control arm and trailing arm, coil springs, front antiroll bar, front and rear telescopic damper. Servo/power assisted disc brakes, rear inboard, disc diameter front 26.9cm, rear 27.7cm, rear mechanical handbrake; rack and pinion steering optional power assisted steering; fuel tank 61L (13.4Gal) [16.1US Gal]; tyres 205/60 HR/VR 15, wheels 6/7J.
Dimensions: Wheelbase 238.5cm, track 143.5/144cm, clearance 15cm, turing circle 9.6m; load space 7.9cu ft (225dm3), length 401.5cm, width 173cm, height 120.5cm.
Performance: Max speed 140mph/225kmh (manufacturers test specifications), speed at 1000 in 5th gear 24.5mph/39.5kmh; acceleration 0 – 60mph/97kmh in 6.2secs; power to weight ratio from 7.6kg/kW (5.6kg/PS); consumption 10–15L/100km (28.2-18.8mpg) [23.5-15.7US mpg]

4.3 Litre V8
205kW-319hp-279PS
Fuel Injection

Engine for 400 SE

As 3.5 Litre, except:

Body, Weight: 2–door Cabriolet/Convertible, 2-seater; kerbweight approx 1130kg, gross vehicle weight 1415kg.
Engine data (DIN): 8-cylinder in V 90deg (94 x 71.12mm), 4282cm3; compression ratio 10.5:1; 205kW (275hp) [279PS] at 5500rpm, 47.9kW/L (64.2hp/L) [65.2PS/L]; 366Nm (270.1lbft) at 3500rpm.
Transmission: 5–speed manual; final drive ratio 3.31. Limited slip differential.
Gear ratios: 1st 3.321; 2nd 2.087; 3rd 1.396; 4th 1; 5th 0.79; R 3.428.
Chassis: Front ventilated disc brakes; tyres 225/50 VR 15, wheel rims 7J.
Performance: Max speed over 149mph/240kmh (manufacturers test specifications), speed at 1000rpm in 5th gear 28.4-24.6mph/45.8-39.6kmh; acceleration 0-60mph/97kmh 5 secs; power to weight ratio from 5.5kg/kW (4.1kg/PS); consumption approx 10-15L/100km (28.2-18.8mpg) [23.5-15.7US mpg] (manufacturers specifications).

4.45 Litre V8
238kW-319hp-324PS
Fuel Injection

Engine for 450 SE

As 3.5 Litre, except:

Body, Weight: 2-door Convertible, 2-seater; kerbweight approx 1130kg, gross vehicle weight 1415kg.
Engine data (DIN): 8-cylinder in V 90deg (94 x 80mm), 4441cm3; compression ratio 9.75:1; 238kW (319hp) [324PS] at 5700rpm, 53.6kW/L (71.8hp/L) [73PS/L]; 421Nm (310.7lbft) at 4000rpm.
Transmission: 5-speed manual, final drive ratio 3.43. Optional limited slip differential.
Gear ratios: 1st 3.321; 2nd 2.087; 3rd 1.396; 4th 1; 5th 0.79; R 3.428.
Chassis: Front ventilated discs; power assisted steering; tyres 225/50 VR 15, wheel rims 8.5J, also tyres 245/45 VR 16, wheel rims 9J.

TVR 420 SE

Performance: Max speed above 164.7mph/265kmh (manufacturers test specifications), speed at 1000rpm in 5th gear 28.5mph/45.8kmh; acceleration 0-60mph/97kmh 5secs; power to weight ratio from 4.7kg/kW (3.5kg/PS); consumption approx 12-18L/100km (23.5-15.7mpg) [19.6-13.1US mpg].

UAZ   SU

UAZ, v/o Autoexport, 14 Volkhonka st, 119902, Moscow, USSR
Based in Oualinovsk, producing rough terrain and utility vehicles.

UAZ 31512

Four wheel drive rough terrain vehicle with a 2.4 Litre engine.

UAZ 31512

2.4 Litre
53kW–71hp–72PS
1 2V Carb

Body, Weight: 4–door Estate/Station Wagon with soft top, 7– seater; kerbweight (DIN) 1650–1920kg, gross vehicle weight from 2650kg.
Engine data (DIN): 4–cylinder in–line (92 x 92mm), 2446cm3; compression ratio 6.7:1; 53kW (71hp) [72PS] at 4000rpm, 21.7kW/L (29hp/L) [29.4PS/L]; 169Nm (124.7lbft) at 2200rpm; leaded regular grade.
For Italy also with diesel engine from Peugeot (2304cm3, 64hp; 2498cm3, 75hp) and VM Turbo diesel (2393cm3, 98.5hp) or Fiat engine (1995cm3, 111hp).
Engine construction: Side camshaft (gear); light–alloy cylinder head and block, wet cylinder liners; crankshaft with 5 bearings; bypass oil filter, oil capacity 5.8L (5.5US qt); 1 K–126B downdraught 2V carb, oil bath air cleaner. Battery 12V 60Ah, alternator 40A; cooling system capacity 13L (12.3US qt).
Transmission (to all wheels): Rear wheel drive with engageable four wheel drive; 4–speed manual, 3rd and 4th gear synchromesh; central differential with reduction gear, final drive ratio 5.125.
Gear ratios: 1st 4.124; 2nd 2.641; 3rd 1.58; 4th 1; R 5.224.; Reduction gear: 1st 1; 2nd 1.94.
Chassis: Box type frame with cross members; front and rear rigid axle with semi elliptic leaf springs, front and rear hydraulic telescopic damper. Four wheel drum brakes, front wheel parking brake; worm and wheel steering; fuel tank 2 x 39L (8.6Gal) [10.3US qt]; tyres 8.40-15 or 215-380, wheels 6J.
Dimensions: Wheelbase 238cm, track 144.5/144.5cm, clearance 22cm, turning circle 13.6m, length 402.5cm, width 178.5cm, height 190/199cm.
Performance: Max speed 65mph/105kmh (manufacturers test specifications), speed at 1000rpm in 4th gear 16.1mph/25.9kmh; power to weight ratio from 17.6kg/kW (12.9kg/PS); consumption (touring) approx 11–18L/100km (25.7–15.7mpg) [21.4–13.1US mpg].

UMM   P

Umm, Uniao mecanica, Lda, R das Flores, 71–2 D, Sogusa P, Lisboa 1200, Portugal.

Umm • Vauxhall • Volga

Portuguese manufacturer.

Umm Alter

Four wheel drive rough terrain vehicle with, 2, 2,3 or 2.5 Litre engines. Paris 1986; Turbodiesel made available.

> 2/2.3/2.5 Litre
> 64/49.5/56kW—86/66/75hp—87/67/76PS
> Petrol/Gasoline – Diesel

Body, Weight: Roadster with canvas top, 6-seater; kerbweight (DIN) 1590/1630kg, gross vehicle weight 2600kg.

Engine data (DIN): a) Diesel engine: 4-cylinder in-line (94 x 83mm), 2304cm3; compression ratio 22.2:1; 49.5kW (66hp) [67PS] at 4500rpm, 21.4kW/L (28.7hp/L) [29.1PS/L]; 134Nm (98.9lbft) at 2000rpm.
Or: (94 x 98mm), 2498cm3; 56kW (75hp) [76PS] at 4500rpm, 22.4kW/L (30hp/L) [30.4PS/L]; 148Nm (109.2lbft) at 2000rpm.
Or: 49kW (66hp) [66PS].
b) Petrol/Gasoline engine: (88 x 81mm), 1971cm3; compression ratio 8:1; 64kW (86hp) [87PS] at 5000rpm, 32.5kW/L (43.6hp/L) [44.1PS/L]; 162Nm (119.6lbft) at 2500rpm; leaded regular grade.

Engine construction: Diesel engine: Designated Indenor (Peugeot). Side camshaft (chain); light-alloy cylinder head; wet cylinder liners; crankshaft with 5 bearings; oil capacity 5L (4.7US qt); Bosch EP/VAC injection pump. Battery 12V 95Ah, alternator 500W; cooling system capacity 10L (9.5US qt).
Petrol/Gasoline engine: Engine tilted 12 degree to the right. Engine block and cylinder head in light-alloy; 1 overhead camshaft (toothed belt); oil capacity 5L (4.7US qt), 1 carb. Battery 12V 95Ah, alternator 500W; cooling system capacity, 6.3L (6US qt).

Transmission (to all wheels): 4-speed manual, front and rear final drive ratio 5.375, 5.86; engageable four wheel drive; rear limited slip differential.

Gear ratios: 1st 3.86; 2nd 2.18; 3rd 1.44; 4th 1; R 3.59.
For 66hp: 1st 3.864; 2nd 2.183; 3rd 1.445; 4th 1; R 3.587.
Reduction gear 0.966; 2.087.

Chassis: Box type frame with 4 cross members; front and rear rigid axle with semi elliptic springs, telescopic damper. Servo/power assisted drum brakes; rear mechanical handbrake; rack and pinion steering; fuel tank capacity 67L (14.7Gal) [17.7US Gal]; tyres 700 x 16, wheels 5.5J.

Dimensions: Wheelbase 254cm, track 134/134cm, clearance 23cm, turning circle 10.5m; length 413cm, width 163cm, height 198cm.

Performance: Max speed 68–81mph/110–130kmh (manufacturers test specifications), speed at 1000rpm in 4th gear 15.9mph/25.6kmh; power to weight ratio from 25.8kg/kW (19kg/PS); consumption road 10L/100km (28.2mpg) [23.5US mpg], cross country 12L/100km (23.5mpg) [19.6US mpg] (manufacturers test specifications).

Umm Alter

> 2498cm3 Diesel
> 81kW–109hp–110PS
> Turbocharger

As 2/2.3/2.5 Litres, except:

Weight: Kerbweight (DIN) 1610kg, gross vehicle weight 2720kg.

Engine data (DIN): 4-cylinder in-line (94 x 90mm), 2498cm3; compression ratio 21:1; 81kW (109hp) [110PS] at 4150rpm, 32.4kW/L (43.4hp/L) [44PS/L]; 237Nm (174.9lbft) at 2500rpm.

Engine construction: Designated XD 3T. Diesel engine. Side camshaft (chain), crankshaft with 5 bearings; Bosch EP/VAC injection; Garrett AiResearch TO 3 exhaust turbocharger; boost pressure 0.8bar; charge-air cooler; oil capacity 5L (4.7US qt); cooling system capacity 10L (9.5US qt).

Transmission: 5-speed manual, final drive ratio 4.88.

Gear ratios: 1st 3.862; 2nd 2.183; 3rd 1.445; 4th 1; 5th 0.844; R 3.587.

Performance: Max speed 87mph/140kmh (manufacturers test specifications), speed at 1000rpm in top gear 20.4mph/32.9kmh; power to weight ratio 19.9kg/kW (14.2kg/PS); consumption approx 10–15L/100km (28.2–18.8mpg) [23.5–15.7US mpg].

VAUXHALL   GB

Vauxhall Motors Ltd, Kimpton Road, Luton, LU2 0SY, Bedfordshire, England

Affiliated to General Motors. One of the largest automobile producers in Great Britain. Model range more or less identical to that of Opel: Nova (Corsa), Astra/Belmont (Kadett), Cavalier (Ventra), Carlton (Omega), Senator. For technical data see Opel.

Vauxhall Cavalier

VOLGA   SU

GAZ. V/O Autoexport, 14 Volkhonka St, 119902 Moscow, USSR Scaldia–Volga SA, 33 rue de l'Independence, Bruxelles 8, Belgium

Manufacturer based at Gorky, Russia and Belgium (Scaldia–Volga SA)

Volga GAZ–24–10

Medium size vehicle with a 2.5 Litre engine. Three types of engine are available with 4-speed manual transmission. Modified front end in 1986.

> 2.4 Litre
> 67kW–90hp–91PS
> 1 2V Carb

Body, Weight: 4-door Saloon/Sedan, 5-seater (Russia 6); kerbweight (DIN) from 1400kg, gross vehicle weight 1790–1940kg. 5-door Estate/Station Wagon, 5/7 seater; kerbweight (DIN) 1550–1590kg, gross vehicle weight 2040–2500kg.

Engine data (DIN): 4-cylinder in-line (92 x 92mm), 2446cm3; compression ratio 8.2:1; 67kW (90hp) [91PS] at 4500rpm, 27.4kW/L (36.7hp/L) [37.2PS/L]; 172Nm (127lbft) at 2200–2400rpm; leaded regular grade.
Or: 73.5kW (99hp) [100PS], 29.8kW/L (39.9hp/L) [40.9PS/L].

Engine construction: Side camshaft (toothed belt); light-alloy cylinder head and cylinder block, wet cylinder liners; crankshaft with 5 bearings; bypass filter, oil capacity 5.9L (5.6US qt); 1 downdraught 2V carb K–126 G. Battery 12V 54Ah, alternator 40A; cooling system capacity 11.5L (10.9US qt).

Transmission (to rear wheels): 4-speed manual, final drive ratio 3.9.

Gear ratios: 1st 3.5; 2nd 2.26; 3rd 1.45; 4th 1; R 3.54.

Volga • Volkswagen

Chassis: Intregal body; front keystone A arm and coil springs, rear rigid axle with semi elliptic springs; front antiroll bar, telescopic damper. Servo/power assisted drum brakes; rear mechanical handbrake; worm and wheel steering; fuel tank 55L (12.1Gal) [14.5US Gal]; tyres 205/70 R 14, wheels 5.5J.

Dimensions: Wheelbase 280cm, track 149.5/142.5cm, clearance 18cm, turning circle 12.4m, length 476cm Estate Station Wagon 473.5cm, width 180cm, height 149cm, Estate/Station Wagon 154cm.

Performance: Max speed 91mph/147kmh (manufacturers test specifications), speed at 1000rpm in 4th gear 19mph/30.6kmh; power to weight ratio from 19.0kg/kW (14.0kg/PS); acceleration 0 – 62mph/100kmh in 19secs; consumption ECE 9.3/12.9/15L/100km (30.4/21.9/18.8mpg) [25.3/18.2/15.7US mpg].

Volga GAZ–24–10 Wagon

Volga GAZ–24 Diesel

Fitted with Peugeot diesel engine.

```
2.3 Litre Diesel
51.5kW–69hp–70PS
Injection Pump
```

As GAZ 24–10, except:

Engine data (DIN): (94 x 83mm); 2304cm3; compression ratio 22.2:1; 51.5kW (69hp) [70PS] at 4500rpm, 22.3kW/L (29.9hp/L) [30.4PS/L]; 131Nm (96.7lbft) at 2200rpm.
Or (88 x 80mm), 1948cm3; compression ratio 21.8:1; 37kW (49hp) [50PS] at 4500rpm, 19kW/L (25.5hp/L) [25.7PS/L]; 107Nm (78.9lbft) at 2250rpm.

Engine construction: Designated Indenor XD 2 P. Engine inclined 20deg to the right, side camshaft (toothed belt); injection pump Roto–Diesel. Battery 12V 88Ah, alternator 50A.

Performance: Max speed 84mph/135kmh or 81mph/130kmh (manufacturers test specifications); power to weight ratio 28.8 or 34.6kg/kW (21.1 or 25.4kg/PS); consumption (touring) 8L/100km (35.3Gal) [29.4US mpg] (manufacturers test specifications).

Volga GAZ–3102

Volga GAZ–3102

Luxury Saloon/Sedan with stratified charged engine, 3 valves per cylinder.

```
2.4 Litre
72kW–97hp–98PS
1 2V Carb
```

As GAX–24, except:

Weight: Kerbweight (DIN) 1470kg.

Engine data (DIN): Compression ratio 8:1; 72kW (97hp) [98PS] at 4500rpm, 29.4kW/L (39.4hp/L) [40.1PS/L]; 175Nm (129.1lbft) at 2500rpm.
Or: 77kW (103hp) [105PS].

Engine construction: Stratified charged engine with pre–chamber, 3 valves per cylinder.

Transmission: Final drive ratio 3.9.

Chassis: Front disc brakes.

Dimensions: Length 496cm, width 182cm, height 147.5cm.

Performance: Max speed 93mph/150kmh (manufacturers test specifications); speed at 1000rpm in 4th gear 19.1mph/30.7kmh; power to weight ratio 19.1kg/kW (14kg/PS); consumption ECE 9.9/13.3/13.8L/100km (28.5/21.2/20.5mpg) [23.8/17.7/17US mpg].

VOLKSWAGEN D

Volkswagen AG, Wolfsburg, Deutschland.

Largest manufacturer of motor vehicles in Germany.

MODEL RANGE
Polo – Golf – Golf Cabrio – Golf Syncro – Golf Rallye - Jetta – Scirocco – Corrado – Passat

Volkswagen Polo

Polo–Polo Classic–Polo Coupe

Compact vehicle with transverse mounted engine, front wheel drive and tailgate. Polo and Derby launched Frankfurt 1981. Frankfurt 1985 Coupe G 40, with high performance 113hp engine and supercharger. October 1986: 1.3 Litre diesel engine.

```
1.05 Litre
33kW–44hp–45PS
1 Carb
```

Body, Weight: 3–door Saloon/Sedan and Coupe, 4/5 seater; kerbweight (DIN) 730/750kg, gross vehicle weight 1170kg. 4-door Saloon/Sedan, 4/5 seater, kerbweight (DIN) 740kg, gross vehicle weight 1190kg.

Volkswagen Polo Coupe

Engine data (Micro-Catalyst, DIN): 4–cylinder in–line (75 x 59mm), 1043cm3; compression ratio 9.5:1; 33kW (44hp) [45PS] at 5600rpm, 31.7kW/L (42.5hp/L) [43.2PS/L]; 74Nm (54.6lbft) at 3600rpm; unleaded regular grade.

Engine construction: Front inclined transverse engine, hydraulic tappets; 1 overhead camshaft (toothed belt); light–alloy cylinder head; crankshaft with 5 bearings, oil capacity 3.5L (3.3US qt); 1 Solex 35 PICT-5 downdraught carb. Battery 12V 36Ah, alternator 55/65A; cooling system capacity 6.5L (6.1US qt).

Transmission (to front wheels): a) 4–speed manual, final drive ratio 4.267.
b) 5-speed manual, final drive ratio 4.267.

Gear ratios: a) 4–speed manual: 1st 3.46; 2nd 1.95; 3rd 1.25; 4th 0.90; R 3.38.
b) 5-speed manual: 1st 3.46; 2nd 2.09; 3rd 1.47; 4th 1.12; 5th 0.89; R 3.38.

Chassis: Integral body; front (negative offset) control arm, McPherson struts, antiroll bar, rear longitudinal torsion bar with McPherson struts, front and rear telescopic damper. Brakes, front disc, rear drums, disc diameter 23.9cm, rear mechanical handbrake; rack and pinion steering; fuel tank 42L (9.2Gal) [11.1US Gal], including 6L (1.3Gal) [1.6US Gal] reserve; tyres 145 SR 13; 155/70 SR 13; 165/65 SR 13, wheels 4.5 or 5.5J.

Volkswagen

Dimensions: Wheelbase 233.5cm, track 130.5/133cm, clearance 10.5cm, turning circle 10.1m. Load space VDA 8.5/33.2cu ft (240/980dm3), length 365.5cm, width 158cm, height 135.5cm. Coupe: Load space 8.1/31.4cu ft (230/890dm3), width 159cm. Notchback: Track 132/134.5cm, load space 15.4cu ft (435dm3), length 397.5cm, width 159cm.

Performance: Max speed 88mph/142kmh (manufacturers test specifications), speed at 1000rpm in 4th gear 16.7mph/26.9kmh; acceleration 0 – 62mph/100kmh in 19.5secs (5th gear); power to weight ratio from 22.1kg/kW (16.2kg/PS); consumption ECE 5.7/7.8/8.0L/100km (49.6/36.2/35.3mpg) [41.3/30.2/29.4US mpg].

```
1.3 Litre
40.5kW–54hp–55PS
1 2V Carb/Injection
```

As 1.05 Litre, except:

Body, Weight: 3–door Saloon/Sedan and Coupe, 5–seater; kerbweight (DIN) 750/770kg, gross vehicle weight 1170kg. 4–door Saloon/Sedan 4/5–seater; kerbweight (DIN) 760kg, gross vehicle weight 1190kg.

Engine data (Unregulated Catalyst, DIN): 4–cylinder in–line (75 x 72mm), 1272cm3; compression ratio 9.5:1; 40.5kW (54hp) [55PS] at 5200rpm, 31.4kW/L (42.6hp/L) [43.3PS/L]; 96Nm (70.8lbft) at 3400rpm; leaded regular grade. With Catalyst (and injection): 97Nm (71.6lbft) at 3000rpm.

Engine construction: 1 downdraught 2V carb, Catalyst variants electronic fuel injection Digijet.

Transmission: a) 4–speed manual, final drive ratio 4.06.
b) 4 + E manual, final drive ratio 4.06.

Gear ratios: a) 4–speed manual: 1st 3.46; 2nd 1.95; 3rd 1.25; 4th 0.90; R 3.38.
b) 4 + E manual: 1st 3.46; 2nd 1.96; 3rd 1.25; 4th 0.89; 5th 0.74; R 3.38.

Chassis: Servo/power assisted brakes.

Performance: Max speed 95mph/153kmh (manufacturers test specifications), speed at 1000rpm in 4th gear 17.6mph/28.3kmh; acceleration 0 – 62mph/100kmh in 14.8secs; power to weight ratio from 18.7kg/kW (13.6kg/PS); consumption ECE 5.5/7.4/7.9L/100km (51.4/38.2/35.8mpg) [42.8/31.8/29.8US mpg], with 4 + E 5.0/6.9/7.9L/100km (56.5/40.9/35.8mpg) [47.0/34.1/29.8US mpg]. Catalyst 4 + E 5.0/6.9/7.9L/100km (56.5/40.9/35.8mpg) [47/34.1/29.8US mpg].

Volkswagen Polo CL

```
1.3 Litre
55kW–74hp–75PS
1 2V Carb
```

Engine for Coupe GT

As 1.05 Litre, except:

Weight: Kerbweight (DIN) 775/785kg, gross vehicle weight 1170kg.

Engine data (DIN): 4–cylinder in–line (75 x 72mm), 1272cm3; compression ratio 11:1; 55kW (74hp) [75PS] at 5800rpm, 43.4kW/L (58.2hp/L) [58.9PS/L]; 104Nm (76.8lbft) at 3600rpm; leaded premium grade.

Engine construction: Not hydraulic tappets (valves – rocker gear); 1 downdraught 2V carb.

Transmission: 5–speed manual, final drive ratio 4.06.

Gear ratios: 1st 3.46; 2nd 2.09; 3rd 1.47; 4th 1.12; 5th 0.89; R 3.38.

Chassis: Rear antiroll bar; servo/power assisted brakes; tyres 165/65 SR 13, wheels 5.5J.

Performance: Max speed 106mph/170kmh (manufacturers test specifications), speed at 1000rpm in 4th gear 17.8mph/28.7kmh; acceleration 0 – 62mph/100kmh in 11.9secs; power to weight ratio 14.1kg/kW (10.3kg/PS); consumption ECE 5.3/7.1/8.0L/100km (53.3/39.8/35.3mpg) [44.4/33.1/29.4US mpg].

Volkswagen Polo Coupe GT G 40

```
1.3 Litre
84.5kW–113hp–115PS
Fuel Injection/Supercharger
```

Engine for Coupe G40

As 1.05 Litre, except:

Weight: Kerbweight (DIN) 805kg.

Engine data (DIN): 4–cylinder in–line (75 x 72mm), 1272cm3, compression ratio 8.0:1; 84.5kW (113hp) [115PS] at 6000rpm, 66.4kW/L (89hp/L) [90.4PS/L]; 148Nm (109lbft) at 3600rpm; leaded premium grade fuel.
With Catalyst: 82.5kW (111hp) [112PS] at 6000rpm, 64.8kW/L (86.7hp/L) [88.0PS/L]; 148Nm (109.2lbft) at 3600rpm; unleaded premium grade.

Engine construction: Electronic fuel injection, central/single point electronic engine (Digifant), mechanical spiral supercharger G40, charge–air cooler.

Transmission: 5–speed manual, final drive ratio not known.

Gear ratios: 1st 3.46; 2nd 2.09; 3rd 1.47; 4th 1.12; 5th 0.89; R 3.38.

Chassis: Rear antiroll bar; servo/power assisted brakes, front ventilated discs, tyres 175/60 HR 13, wheels 5.5J.

Performance: Max speed 121mph/195kmh (manufacturers test specifications); acceleration 0 – 62mph/100kmh approx in 9secs; power to weight ratio 9.5kg/kW (7.0kg/PS); consumption ECE approx 5.5/7.5/8.5L/100km (51.4/37.7/33.2mpg) [42.8/31.4/27.7US mpg].

```
1.3 Litre Diesel
33kW–44hp–45PS
Injection Pump
```

As 1.05 Litre, except:

Body, Weight: 3–door Saloon/Sedan and Coupe, 5–seater; kerbweight (DIN) 800/810kg, gross vehicle weight 1230kg. 4–door Saloon/Sedan, 4/5 seater; kerbweight (DIN) 810kg, gross vehicle weight 1250kg.

Engine data (DIN): 4–cylinder in–line (75 x 72mm), 1272cm3; compression ratio 22:1; 33kW (44hp) [45PS] at 4900rpm, 26.0kW/L (34.8hp/L) [35.4PS/L]; 75Nm (55.4lbft) at 2500–3500rpm.

Engine construction: Turbulence chamber diesel engine; distributor injection pump Bosch VE, mechanical centrifugal governor, timing device, cold start enrichment. Battery 12V 50Ah; alternator 55A.

Transmission: 5–speed manual, final drive ratio 4.06.

Gear ratios: 1st 3.46; 2nd 2.09; 3rd 1.47; 4th 1.12; 5th 0.89; R 3.38.

Chassis: Servo/power assisted brakes.

Performance: Max speed 87mph/140kmh (manufacturers test specifications), speed at 1000rpm in 4th gear 14.4mph/23.2kmh; acceleration 0 – 62mph/100kmh in 21.2 ecs; power to weight ratio from 24.2kg/kW (17.8kg/PS); consumption ECE 4.4/6.4/6.1L/100km (64.2/44.1/46.3mpg) [53.5/36.8/38.6US mpg].

Volkswagen Golf

Compact Saloon/Sedan with transverse front engine, front wheel drive and tailgate. Available with a 1.3, 1.6 or 1.8 Litre engine, or a 1.6 Litre diesel engine. Launched August 1983. June 1985; Golf GTI 16V, February 1986 Golf Syncro. 1989: Syncro with more power.

```
1.3 Litre
40kW–54hp–55PS
1 2V Carb/Injection
```

Volkswagen

Body, Weight: 3/5–door Saloon/Sedan, 5–seater; kerbweight (DIN) 845/865kg Catalyst 855/875kg, gross vehicle weight 1360kg.

Engine data (Unregulated Catalyst, DIN): 4–cylinder in–line (75 x 72mm), 1272cm3; compression ratio 9.5:1; 40kW (53.6hp) [55PS] at 5200rpm, 31.4kW/L (42.0hp/L) [43.3PS/L]; 96Nm (70.8lbft) at 3400rpm; leaded regular grade. With Catalyst (and injection): 97Nm (71.6lbft) at 3000rpm.

Engine construction: Front inclined transverse engine, hydraulic tappets; 1 overhead camshaft (toothed belt); light–alloy cylinder head; crankshaft with 5 bearings; oil capacity 3.5L (3.3US qt); 1 downdraught 2V carb; with Catalyst Digijet electronic fuel injection. Battery 12V 36Ah, alternator 65A; cooling system capacity, approx 6.3L (6US qt).

Transmission (to rear wheels): a) 4–speed manual, final drive ratio 4.06. b) 4 + E–speed manual, final drive ratio 4.267.

Gear ratios: a) 4–speed manual: 1st 3.46; 2nd 1.95; 3rd 1.25; 4th 0.90; R 3.38. b) 4 + E manual: 1st 3.46; 2nd 1.96; 3rd 1.25; 4th 0.89; 5th 0.74; R 3.38.

Chassis: Integral body; front A arm and McPherson struts with coil springs (negative offset) rear longitudinal torsion bars with McPherson struts and coil springs, telescopic damper. Servo/power assisted brakes, front disc, rear drums, disc diameter 23.9cm; rear mechanical handbrake; rack and pinion steering, optional power assisted; fuel tank 55L (12.1Gal); tyres 155 SR 13, optional 175/70 SR 13, wheels 5/5.5J.

Dimensions: Wheelbase 247.5cm, track 142.5/142cm, clearance approx 13cm, turning circle approx 10.5m. Load space VDA 12.2/40.4cu ft (345/1145dm3), length 398.5cm, width 166.5cm, GT 168cm, height 141.5cm, GT 140.5cm.

Performance: Max speed 94mph/151kmh (manufacturers test specifications), speed at 1000rpm in 4th gear 18.2mph/29.3kmh; acceleration 0 – 62mph/100kmh in 16.5secs; power to weight ratio approx 20.9kg/kW (15.4kg/PS); consumption ECE 5.6/7.5/8.1L/100km (50.4/37.7/34.9mpg) [42.0/31.4/29.0US mpg], 4 + E 5.3/7.1/8.3L/100km (53.3/39.8/34.0mpg) [44.4/33.1/28.3US mpg], Catalyst 4 + E 5.5/7.5/8.7L/100km (51.4/37.7/32.5mpg) [42.8/31.4/27US mpg].

Volkswagen Golf CL

1.6 Litre
53/51kW–71/68hp–72/70PS
1 2V Carb

As 1.3 Litre, except:

Weight: Kerbweight (DIN) 870/890kg, gross vehicle weight 1400kg.

Engine data (Unregulated Catalyst, DIN): 4–cylinder in–line (81 x 77.4mm), 1595cm3; compression ratio 9.0:1; 53kW (71hp) [72PS] at 5000rpm, 33.1kW/L (44.4hp/L) [45.1PS/L]; 120Nm (88.5lbft) at 2700rpm; leaded regular grade. With Catalyst: 51kW (68hp) [70PS] at 5200rpm, 32kW/L (42.9hp/L) [43.9PS/L]; 118Nm (87.1lbft) at 2700rpm.

Engine construction: Oil capacity 4L (3.8US qt); Catalyst with electronic fuel injection. Compound carb.

Transmission: a) 4–speed manual, final drive ratio 3.67. b) 4 + E–speed manual, final drive ratio 3.67, Catalyst 3.17. c) Automatic, hydraulic torque converter and 3–speed Planetary gear set, final drive ratio 3.42.

Gear ratios: a) 4–speed manual: 1st 3.46; 2nd 1.94; 3rd 1.29; 4th 0.91; R 3.17. b) 4 + E manual: 1st 3.46; 2nd 1.94; 3rd 1.29; 4th 0.91; 5th 0.75; R 3.17. c) Automatic: Max torque multiplication in converter 2.4 times, Planetary gear set ratios: 1st 2.71; 2nd 1.50; 3rd 1; R 2.43.

Chassis: Tyres 175/70 SR 13, wheels 5.5J, optional tyres 185/60 SR 14, wheels 5.5 or 6J.

Performance: Max speed 102mph/164kmh, Catalyst 101mph/162kmh, automatic 99mph/159kmh (manufacturers test specifications), speed at 1000rpm in 4th gear 19.8mph/31.8kmh; acceleration 0 – 62mph/100kmh 13.5secs, Catalyst 13.8secs, automatic in 15.7secs; power to weight ratio 16.4kg/kW (12.1kg/PS); consumption ECE 5.9/8.0/8.9L/100km (47.9/35.3/31.7mpg) [39.9/29.4/26.4US mpg], 4 + E 5.4/7.3/8.9L/100km (52.3/38.7/31.7mpg) [43.6/32.2/26.4US mpg], automatic 6.5/8.3/9.3L/100km (43.5/34.0/30.4mpg) [36.2/28.3/25.3US mpg], Catalyst 4 + E 5.8/7.9/9.4L/100km (48.7/35.8/30.1mpg) [40.6/29.8/25.0US mpg].

Volkswagen Golf GL

1.8 Litre
62/66kW–83/88hp–84/90PS
1 2V Carb

Engine for Golf

As 1.3 Litre, except:

Weight: Kerbweight (DIN) 880/900kg, Catalyst 920/940kg, gross vehicle weight 1400kg, Catalyst 1500kg.

Engine data (Unregulated Catalyst, DIN): 4–cylinder in–line (81 x 86.4mm), 1781cm3, compression ratio 10.0:1; 62kW (83hp) [84PS] at 5000rpm, 34.8kW/L (46.6hp/L) [47.2PS/L]; 141Nm (104lbft) at 3300rpm. With Catalyst (Mono–Jetronic fuel injection): Compression ratio 9.1; 66kW (88hp) [90PS] at 5250rpm; 142Nm (104.8lbft) at 3000rpm. USA version (SAE net): Digifant fuel injection; 74kW (99hp) [101PS].

Engine construction: Oil capacity 4L (3.8US qt). Battery 12V 45Ah.

Transmission: a) 4 + E–speed manual, final drive ratio 3.67. b) Automatic, hydraulic torque converter and 3–speed Planetary gear set, final drive ratio 3.12.

Gear ratios: a) 4 + E manual: 1st 3.46; 2nd 1.94; 3rd 1.29; 4th 0.91; V 0.75; R 3.17. b) Automatic: Max torque multiplication in converter 2.44 times, Planetary gear set ratios: 1st 2.71; 2nd 1.50; 3rd 1; R 2.43.

Chassis: Power assisted steering; tyres 175/70 HR 13, wheels 5.5J, optional tyres 185/60 HR 14, wheels 6J.

Performance: Max speed 107mph/173kmh, automatic 104mph/168kmh, Catalyst 109mph/175kmh (manufacturers test specifications), speed at 1000rpm in 5th gear 24.0mph/38.7kmh; acceleration 0–62mph/100kmh 11.8secs, automatic 13.7secs, Catalyst 11.5secs; power to weight ratio from 14.2kg/kW (10.5kg/PS); consumption ECE 5.6/7.5/8.9L/100km (50.4/37.7/31.7mpg) [42.0/31.4/26.4US mpg], automatic 6.5/8.5/9.6L/100km (43.5/33.2/29.4mpg) [36.2/27.7/24.5US mpg], Catalyst 4 + E 5.8/7.8/9.8L/100km (48.7/36.2/28.8mpg) [40.6/30.2/24.0US mpg].

1.8 Litre
72kW–96hp–98PS
Fuel Injection

Engine for syncro

As 1.3 Litre, except:

Weight: Kerbweight (DIN) 1085/1105kg, gross vehicle weight 1540kg.

Engine data (Catalyst, DIN): 4–cylinder in–line (81 x 86.4mm), 1781cm3; compression ratio 9:1; 72kW (96hp) [98PS] at 5400rpm, 40.4kW/L (54.1hp/L) [55PS/L]; 143Nm (105.5lbft) at 3000rpm.

Engine construction: Oil capacity 4L (3.8US qt), Digifant electronic fuel injection.

Transmission (to all wheels): 4 + E manual, final drive ratio 4.47; variable power distribution front and rear via viscous coupling, rear automatic free–wheel.

Gear ratios: 1st 3.46; 2nd 1.94; 3rd 1.29; 4th 0.91; 5th 0.75; R 3.17.

Volkswagen

Chassis: Rear semi–trailing arm, front and rear antiroll bar; power assisted steering; tyres 175/70 HR 13, wheel rims 5.5J.

Dimensions: Load space 8.1/36.4cu ft (230/1030dm3).

Performances: Max speed 112mph/180kmh (manufacturers test specifications), speed at 1000rpm in 5th gear 19.7mph/31.7kmh; acceleration 0–62mph/100kmh 11.1secs; power to weight ratio from 15.1kg/kW (11.1kg/PS); consumption ECE 6.8/9.2/11.1L/100km (41.4/30.7/25.4mpg) [34.6/25.6/21.2US mpg].

Volkswagen Golf GT syncro

```
1.8 Litre
79kW–106hp–107PS
Fuel Injection
```

Engine for GTI

As 1.3 Litre, except:

Weight: Kerbweight (DIN) 920/940kg, USA 1000kg, gross vehicle weight 1400/1430kg.

Engine data (Catalyst, DIN): 4–cylinder in–line (81 x 86.4mm), 1781cm3; compression ratio 10:1; 79kW (106hp) [107PS] at 5400rpm, 44.4kW/L (59.5hp/L) [60.1PS/L]; 157Nm (115.9lbft) at 3800rpm.
USA version (SAE net): 78kW (105hp) [106PS].

Engine construction: Oil capacity 4L (3.8US qt); oil cooler; Digifant electronic fuel injection. Battery 12V 45Ah; alternator 55A.

Transmission: 5–speed manual; final drive ratio 3.67.

Gear ratios: 1st 3.46; 2nd 2.12; 3rd 1.44; 5th 1.13; 5th 0.89; R 3.17.

Chassis: Front and rear antiroll bars. Four wheel disc brakes (front ventilated), front disc diameter 23.9cm, rear 17.9cm; tyres 175/70 HR 13, wheels 5.5J, optional tyres 185/60 HR 14, tyres 5.5 or 6J.

Performance: Max 116mph/186kmh, (manufacturers test specifications), speed at 1000rpm in top gear 20.2mph/32.5kmh; acceleration 0 – 62mph/100kmh 10.3secs; power to weight ratio 11.6kg/kW (8.6kg/PS); consumption ECE 6.1/8.1/10.3L/100km (46.3/34.9/27.4mpg) [38.6/29.0/22.8US mpg].

Volkswagen Golf GTI

```
1.8 Litre
95kW–127hp–129PS
Fuel Injection
```

Engine for Golf GTI 16 V

As 1.3 Litre, except:

Body, Weight: 3–door Saloon/Sedan, 5–seater; kerbweight (DIN) 960/980kg, gross vehicle weight 1430kg.

Engine data (Catalyst, DIN): 4–cylinder in–line (81 x 86.4mm), 1781cm3; compression ratio 10:1; 95kW (127hp) [129PS] at 5800rpm, 53.3kW/L (71.4hp/L) [72.4PS/L]; 168Nm (124lbft) at 4250rpm; leaded premium grade.
USA version (SAE net): 92kW (123hp) [125PS].

Engine construction: Valves in V 25deg, 4 valves per cylinder, 2 overhead camshafts (toothed belt); oil cooler, oil capacity 4L (3.8US qt); Bosch KE–Jetronic mechanical/electronic fuel injection. Battery 12V 45Ah, alternator 65A.

Transmission: 5–speed manual; final drive ratio 3.67.

Gear ratios: 1st 3.46; 2nd 2.12; 3rd 1.44; 4th 1.13; 5th 0.91; R 3.17.

Chassis: Front and rear antiroll bars. All round disc brakes (front ventilated), front diameter 25.6cm, rear 17.9cm; tyres 185/60 VR 14, wheels 6J.

Dimensions: Clearance 10.5cm, width 168cm, height 139.5cm.

Performance: Max speed 124mph/200kmh (manufacturers specifications), speed at 1000rpm in 5th gear 19.7mph/31.7kmh; acceleration 0 - 62mph/100kmh 9secs; power to weight ratio from 10.1kg/kW (7.4kg/PS); consumption ECE 6.4/8.0/11.3L/100km (44.1/35.3/25mpg) [36.8/29.4/20.8US mpg].

Volkswagen Golf GTI 16 V

```
1.6 Litre Diesel
40kW–53hp–54PS
Injection Pump
```

As 1.3 Litre, except:

Weight: Kerbweight (DIN) 900/920kg, gross vehicle weight 1430kg.

Engine data (DIN): 4–cylinder in–line (76.5 x 86.4mm), 1588cm3; compression ratio 23:1; 40kW (53hp) [54PS] at 4800rpm, 25.2kW/L (33.4hp/L) [34PS/L]; 100Nm (73.8lbft) at 2300–2900rpm.

Engine construction: Turbulence chamber–diesel engine; oil capacity 4L (3.8US qt); distributor–Bosch VE injection pump, mechanical centrifugal governor, cold start enrichment. Battery 12V 63Ah, alternator 45A.

Transmission: a) 4–speed manual, final drive ratio 3.94.
b) 4 + E manual, final drive ratio 3.94.
c) Automatic, hydraulic torque converter and 3–speed Planetary gear set, selector lever in the middle, final drive ratio 3.42.

Gear ratios: a) 4–speed manual: 1st 3.46; 2nd 1.94; 3rd 1.29; 4th 0.88; R 3.17.
b) 4 + E manual: 1st 3.46; 2nd 1.94; 3rd 1.29; 4th 0.91; 5th 0.75; R 3.17.
c) Automatic: Planetary gear set ratios: 1st 2.71; 2nd 1.50; 3rd 1.00; R 2.43.

Volkswagen Golf Diesel

Performance: Max speed 92mph/148kmh, automatic 89mph/143kmh (manufacturers test specifications), speed at 1000rpm in 4th gear 19mph/30.5kmh; acceleration 0 – 62mph/100kmh 18.7secs, automatic 22.9secs; power to weight ratio from 22.5kg/kW (16.7kg/PS): consumption ECE 4.8/6.8/6.3L/100km (58.8/41.5/44.8mpg) [49/34.6/37.3US mpg], 4 + E 4.4/6.2/6.3L/100km (64.2/45.6/44.8mpg) [53.5/37.9/37.3US mpg], automatic 5.3/7.5/6.8L/100km (53.3/37.7/41.5mpg) [44.4/31.4/34.6US mpg].

Volkswagen

1.6 Litre Turbodiesel
51kW-69hp-70PS
Injection Pump

As 1.3 Litre, except:

Weight: Kerbweight (DIN) 920/940kg, gross vehicle weight 1430kg.

Engine data (DIN): 4-cylinder in-line (76.5 x 86.4mm), 1588cm3; compression ratio 23:1; 51kW (69hp) [70PS] at 4500rpm, 32.1kW/L (43.6hp/L) [44.1PS/L]; 133Nm (98.1lbft) at 2500-2900rpm.

Engine construction: Turbulence chamber-diesel engine; oil capacity 4L (3.8US qt); exhaust turbocharger, max boost pressure 0.7bar, distributor-Bosch VE fuel injection, mechanical centrifugal governor, cold start enrichment. Battery 12V 63Ah; alternator 45A.

Transmission: 4 + E manual, final drive ratio 3.67.

Gear ratios: 1st 3.46; 2nd 1.94; 3rd 1.29; 4th 0.91; 5th 0.75; R 3.17.

Chassis: GTD with rear antiroll bar; tyres 175/70 SR 13, optional 185/60 HR 14, wheels 5.5J.

Dimensions: Width (GTD) 168cm.

Performance: Max speed 99mph/160kmh (manufacturers specifications), speed at 1000rpm in 4th gear 19.8mph/31.8kmh in 5th 23.9mph/38.5kmh; acceleration 0 - 62mph/100kmh in 14.5secs; power to weight from 18kg/kW (13.1kg/PS); consumption ECE 4.3/6.1/6.1L/100km (65.7/46.3/46.3mpg) [54.7/38.6/38.6US mpg].

Volkswagon Golf Cabriolet

Convertible based on the Golf. Launched 1979.

1.6 Litre
53kW-71hp-72PS
1 2V Carb

As Golf 1.6/1.3, except:

Body, Weight: 2-door Convertible, 4/5-seater; kerbweight (DIN) 960kg, gross vehicle weight 1350kg.

Engine data (Unregulated Catalyst, DIN): 4-cylinder in-line (81 x 77.4mm), 1595cm3; compression ratio 9.0:1; 53kW (71hp) [72PS] at 5000rpm, 33.1kW/L (44.6hp/L) [45.1PS/L]; 120Nm (88.6lbft) at 2700rpm; leaded regular grade.

Transmission: a) 4-speed manual, final drive ratio 3.67.
b) 4 + E manual, final drive ratio 3.67.
c) Automatic, hydraulic torque and 3-speed Planetary gear set, final drive ratio 3.41.

Gear ratios: a) 4-speed manual: 1st 3.46; 2nd 1.94; 3rd 1.29; 4th 0.91; R 3.17.
4 + E manual: 1st 3.46; 2nd 1.94; 3rd 1.29; 4th 0.91; 5th 0.75; R 3.17.
c) Automatic, max torque multiplication in converter 2.4 times, Planetary gear set ratios: 1st 2.71; 2nd 1.50; 3rd 1; R 2.43.

Dimensions: Wheelbase 240cm, track 140.5/137cm, turning circle 10.3m, load space VDA 7.8/17.8cu ft (220/505dm3), length 389cm, width 164cm, height 141cm.

Performance: Max speed 93mph/150kmh, automatic 90mph/145kmh (manufacturers specifications); acceleration 0 - 62mph/100kmh 14secs, automatic 16.2secs; power to weight ratio 18.1kg/kW (13.3kg/PS); consumption ECE 6.4/9.2/8.9L/100km (44.1/30.7/31.7mpg) [36.8/25.6/26.4US mpg], 4 + E 5.9/8.6/8.9L/100km (47.9/32.8/31.7mpg) [39.9/27.4/26.4US mpg], automatic 7.2/10.0/9.3L/100km (39.2/28.2/30.4mpg) [32.7/23.5/25.3US mpg].

Volkswagen Golf Cabriolet

1.8 Litre
70kW-94hp-95PS
Fuel Injection

As Golf 1.8 83/89hp, except:

Body, Weight: 2-door Convertible, 4/5-seater; kerbweight (DIN) 1015kg, gross vehicle weight 1375kg.

Engine data (DIN): 4-cylinder in-line (81 x 86.4mm), 1781cm3, compression ratio 9:1; 70kW (94hp) [95PS] at 5500rpm, 39.3kW/L (52.3hp/L) [53.3PS/L]; 142Nm (104.8lbft) at 3000rpm.
USA version (SAE net): 67kW (90hp) [91PS].

Transmission: a) 4 + E manual, final drive ratio 3.67.
b) Automatic, hydraulic torque and 3-speed Planetary gear set, final drive ratio 3.41.

Gear ratios: a) 4 + E: 1st 3.46; 2nd 2.12; 3rd 1.44; 4th 1.13; 5th 0.89; R 3.17.
b) Automatic, max torque multiplication in converter 2.44 times, Planetary gear set ratios: 1st 2.71; 2nd 1.50; 3rd 1; R 2.43.

Dimensions: Wheelbase 240cm, track 140.5/137cm, turning circle 10.3m, load space VDA 7.8/17.8cu ft (220/505dm3), length 389cm, width 164cm, height 139.5cm.

Performance: Max speed 103mph/166kmh, Automatic 100mph/161kmh (manufacturers specifications); speed at 1000rpm in 5th gear 20.2mph/32.5kmh; acceleration 11.2secs, Automatic 13.4secs; power to weight ratio 14.5kg/kW (10.7kg/PS); consumption ECE 7.1/9.9/11.1L/100km (39.8/28.5/25.4mpg) [33.1/23.8/21.2US mpg], Automatic 8.3/11.2/11.2L/100km (34/25.2/25.2mpg) [28.3/21/21US mpgUS mpg].

Volkswagen Golf Cabriolet (USA)

Volkswagen Golf Rallye

New model. Sports version of the Golf with permanent all wheel drive, ABS and G-Lader Supercharger, 1.8 Litre engine with 118kW and 197hp power (as Corrado), tyres 205/50 R 15 with customised wheel rims. Performance: max speed 130mph/209kmh, 0 - 62mph/100kmh in 8.6secs. Prototype launched in Summer 1988 and at Geneva in 1989. Available in Summer 1989.

1.8 Litre
118kW-158hp-160PS
G-Turbocharger/Injection

Body, Weight: 3-door Saloon/Sedan, 5-seater; kerbweight (DINO) 1195kg, gross vehicle weight 1640kg.

Engine data (Catalyst DIN): 4-cylinder in-line (80.6 x 86.4mm), 1763cm3; Compression ratio 8.0:1; 118kW (158hp) [160PS] at 5600rpm, 66.8kW/L (89.5hp/L) [90.6PS/L]; 225Nm (166lbft) at 3800-4000rpm; unleaded regular grade.

Engine construction: Front transverse engine. Hydraulic tappets; 1 overhead camshaft (toothed belt); light-alloy cylinder head; 5 main bearing crankshaft; oil capacity 4L (3.8US qt); Digifant electronic fuel injection; G-60 mechanical spiral charger; Intercooler. Battery 12V 45Ah, 90A alternator; water cooled.

Transmission: Permanent all wheel drive with variable power distribution via viscous coupling; rear automatic free-wheel. 5-speed manual.

Chassis: Integral body; front A-arm and McPherson struts with coil springs (negative steering offset), rear semi-trailing arm, coil springs and telescopic damper, front and rear antiroll bar. Four wheel Servo/power assisted disc brakes (front ventilated) with ABS; handbrake to rear wheels; power assisted rack and pinion steering; fuel tank capacity 55L (12.1Gal) [14.5US Gal]; tyres 205/50 VR 15, wheel rims 6J.

Volkswagen

Dimensions: Wheelbase 248cm, track 143.5/143.5cm, clearance min 11cm, turning circle 10.8m, load space 9.9/4.3cu ft (280/1230dm3); length 403.5cm, width 170cm, height 140cm.

Performance: Max speed 130mph/209kmh (manufacturers test specifications), acceleration 0 - 62mph/100kmh 8.6secs; power to weight ratio 10.1kg/kW (7.5kg/PS); consumption ECE 7.1/9.5/12.5L/100km (39.8/29.7/22.6mpg) [33.1/24.8/18.8US mpg].

Volkswagen Golf Rallye

Volkswagen Jetta

Saloon/Sedan based on the Golf, with transverse front engine and front wheel drive. Available with a 1.3, 1.6 or 1.8 Litre engine, or 1.8 Litre Diesel. Launched January 1984. October 1984: Jetta GT. Amsterdam 1987; "16V" available.

```
1.3 Litre
40kW–54hp–55PS
1 2V Carb
```

Engine for Jetta, CL and GL

Body, Weight: 2/4door Saloon/Sedan, 5–seater; kerbweight (DIN) 875/895kg, Catalyst 885/905kg, gross vehicle weight 1400kg.

Engine data (Unregulated Catalyst DIN): 4–cylinder in–line (75 x 72mm), 1272cm3; compression ratio 9.5:1; 40kW (54hp) [55PS] at 5200rpm, 31.4kW/L (42.6hp/L) [43.3PS/L]; 96Nm (70.8lbft) at 3400rpm; leaded regular grade. With Catalyst (and fuel injection): 97Nm (71.6lbft) at 3000rpm.

Engine construction: Front inclined transverse engine, hydraulic tappets; 1 overhead camshaft (toothed belt); light-alloy cylinder head; crankshaft with 5 bearings; oil capacity 3.5L (3.3US qt); 1 downdraught two stage carb; Catalyst with electronic Digijet fuel injection. Battery 12V 36Ah, alternator 65A; cooling system capacity approx 6.3L (6US qt).

Volkswagen Jetta CL

Transmission (to front wheels): a) 4–speed manual, final drive ratio 4.06.
b) 4 + E manual, final drive ratio 4.267.

Gear ratios: a) 4–speed manual: 1st 3.46; 2nd 1.95; 3rd 1.25; 4th 0.90; R 3.38.
b) 4 + E manual: 1st 3.46; 2nd 1.96; 3rd 1.25; 4th 0.89; 5th 0.74; R 3.38.

Chassis: Integral body; front A–arm, antiroll bar and McPherson struts with coil springs (negative scrub radius), rear longitudinal arms, McPherson struts and coil springs, telescopic damper. Servo/power assisted brakes, front disc, rear drums, disc diameter 23.9cm; handbrake to rear wheels; rack and pinion steering, optional power assisted; fuel tank 55L (12.1Gal) [14.5US Gal]; tyres 175/70 SR 13, wheels 5.5 J.

Dimensions: Wheelbase 247.5cm, track 142.5/142cm, clearance approx 13cm, turning circle aprrox 10.5m, load space 19.4cu ft (550dm3), length 431.5cm, width 166.5cm, height 141.5cm.

Performance: Max speed 93mph/149kmh (manufacturers test specifications), speed at 1000rpm in 4th gear 18.3mph/29.4kmh; acceleration 0 – 62mph/100kmh in 17.0secs; power to weight from 21.6kg/kW (15.9kg/PS); consumption ECE 5.8/7.7/8.1L/100km (mpg) [US mpg], 4 + E 5.5/7.3/8.3L/100km (51.4/38.7/34mpg) [42.8/32.2/28.3US mpg], Catalyst 5.5/7.7/8.7L/100km (51.4/36.7/32.5mpg) [42.8/30.5/27US mpg].

```
1.6 Litre
53/51kW–71/69hp–72/70PS
1 Compound Carb
```

Engine for Jetta, CL and GL

As 1.3 Litre, except:

Weight: Kerbweight (DIN) 900/920kg, Catalyst 910/930kg, gross vehicle weight 1440kg.

Engine data (Unregulated Catalyst, DIN): 4–cylinder in–line (81 x 77.4mm), 1595cm3; compression ratio 9.0:1; 53kW (71hp) [72PS] at 5200rpm, 33.1kW/L (44.4hp/L) [45.1PS/L]; 120Nm (74.5lbft) at 2700rpm.
With Catalyst: 51kW (69hp) [70PS] at 5200rpm, 32kW/L (43.3hp/L) [43.9PS/L]; 118Nm (87.1lbft) at 2700rpm.

Engine construction: Oil capacity 4L (3.8US qt); Catalyst with electronic controlled compound carb.

Transmission: a) 4–speed manual, final drive ratio 3.67.
b) 4 + E manual, final drive ratio 3.67.
c) Automatic, hydraulic torque converter and 3–speed Planetary gear set, final drive ratio 3.42.

Gear ratios: a) 4–speed manual: 1st 3.46; 2nd 1.94; 3rd 1.29; 4th 0.91; R 3.17.
b) 4 + E manual: 1st 3.46; 2nd 1.94; 3rd 1.29; 4th 0.91; 5th 0.75; R 3.17.
c) Automatic: Max torque multiplication in converter 2.4 times, Planetary gear set ratios: 1st 2.71; 2nd 1.50; 3rd 1; R 2.43.

Chassis: Tyres 175/70 HR 13, optional 185/60 HR 14.

Performance: Max speed 101mph/162kmh, Catalyst 99mph/160kmh (manufacturers test specifications), speed at 1000rpm in 4th gear 19.8mph/31.8kmh; acceleration 0 – 62mph/100kmh 13.9secs, Catalyst 14.2secs, automatic 16.1secs; power to weight ratio 17kg/kW (12.5kg/PS); consumption ECE 6.1/8.3/8.9L/100km (46.3/34/31.7mpg) [38.6/28.3/26.4US mpg], 4 + E 5.6/7.6/8.9L/100km (50.4/37.2/31.7mpg) [42/30.9/26.4US mpg], automatic 6.7/8.6/9.3L/100km (42.2/32.8/30.4mpg) [35.1/27.4/25.3US mpg], Catalyst 4 + E 6.0/8.2/9.4L/100km (47.1/34.4/30.1mpg) [39.2/28.7/25US mpg].

```
1.8 Litre
62/66kW–83/88hp–84/90PS
1 2V Carb
```

Engine for Jetta, CL, GL and GT

As 1.3 Litre, except:

Weight: Kerbweight (DIN) 910/930kg, Catalyst 950/970kg, gross vehicle weight 1440/1470kg.

Engine data (Unregulated Catalyst DIN): 4–cylinder in–line (81 x 86.4mm), 1781cm3, compression ratio 10.0:1; 62kW (83hp) [84PS] at 5000rpm, 34.8kW/L (46.6hp/L) [47.2PS/L]; 141Nm (104lbft) at 3300rpm.
With Catalyst (Mono Jetronic central/single point injection): Compression ratio 9:1; 66kW (88hp) [90PS] at 5250rpm, 142Nm (104.8lbft) at 3000rpm.
USA version (Digifant Fuel Injection, SAE net): 74kW (99hp) [101PS].

Engine construction: Oil capacity 4L (3.8US qt). Battery 12V 45Ah.

Transmission: a) 4 + E manual, final drive ratio 3.67.
b) Automatic, hydraulic torque converter and 3–speed Planetary gear set, final drive ratio 3.12.

Gear ratios: a) 4 + E manual: 1st 3.46; 2nd 1.94; 3rd 1.29; 4th 0.91; 5th 0.75; R 3.17.
b) Automatic: Max torque multiplication in converter 2.44 times, Planetary gear set ratios: 1st 2.71; 2nd 1.50; 3rd 1; R 2.43.

Performance: Max speed 106mph/171kmh, automatic mph/166kmh, Catalyst 108mph/173kmh (manufacturers test specifications), speed at 1000rpm in 5th gear mph/38.7kmh; acceleration 0 – 62mph/100kmh 12.1secs, automatic 14.0secs; power to weight ratio from 14.7kg/kW (10.8kg/PS); consumption ECE 5.8/7.8/8.9L/100km (48.7/36.2/31.7mpg) [40.6/30.2/26.4US mpg], automatic 6.7/8.6/9.6L/100km (42.2/32.8/mpg) [35.6/27.4/mpg]. Catalyst 4 + E 5.9/8.0/10.1L/100km (47.9/35.3/28mpg) [39.9/29.4/23.3US mpg].

Volkswagen 433

Volkswagen Jetta Carat (USA)

1.8 Litre
72kW–97hp–98PS
Fuel Injection

Engine for syncro

As 1.3 Litre, except:

Weight: Kerbweight (DIN) 1115/1135kg, gross vehicle weight 1610kg.

Engine data (Catalyst DIN): 4-cylinder in-line (81 x 86.4mm), 1781cm3; Compression ratio 9:1; 72kW (97hp) [98PS] at 5400rpm, 40.4kW/L (54.1hp/L) [55PS/L]; 143Nm (105.5lbft) at 3000rpm

Engine construction: Oil capacity 4L (3.8US qt); Digifant electronic fuel injection.

Transmission (to all wheels): 4 + E manual, final drive ratio 4.47; variable power distribution front and rear via viscous coupling; rear automatic free-wheel.

Gear ratios: 1st 3.46; 2nd 1.94; 3rd 1.29; 4th 0.91; 5th 0.75; R 3.17.

Chassis: Rear semi trailing arm, front and rear antiroll bar; power assisted steering; tyres 175/70 HR 13, wheel rims 5.5J.

Dimensions: Load space 14.3/26cu ft (405/735dm3).

Performance: Max speed 110mph/178kmh (manufacturers test specifications), speed at 1000rpm in 5th gear 19.7mph/31.7kmh; acceleration 0 – 62mph/100kmh 11.4secs; power to weight ratio from 15.5kg/kW (11.4kg/PS); consumption ECE 6.9/11.1/11.1L/100km (40.9/25.4/25.4mpg) [34.1/21.2/21.2US mpg].

Volkswagen Jetta syncro

1.8 Litre
79kW–106hp–107PS
Fuel Injection

As 1.3 Litre, except:

Weight: Kerbweight (DIN) 950/970kg, gross vehicle weight 1470kg.

Engine data (DIN): 4-cylinder in-line (81 x 86.4mm), 1781cm3; compression ratio 10:1; 79kW (106hp) [107PS] at 5400rpm 44.4kW/L (59.5hp/L) [60.1PS/L]; 157Nm (115.9lbft) at 3100rpm.
USA version (SAE net): 78kW (105hp) [106PS].

Engine construction: Oil cooler, oil capacity 4L (3.8US qt). Digifant electronic fuel injection. Battery 12V 45Ah; alternator 55A.

Transmission: 5-speed manual; final drive ratio 3.67.

Gear ratios: 1st 3.46; 2nd 2.12; 3rd 1.44; 4th 1.13; 5th 0.89; R 3.17.

Chassis: Front and rear antiroll bars. All round disc brakes, front ventilated, rear diameter 17.9cm; tyres 175/70 HR 13, wheels 5.5J, optional tyres 185/60 HR 14, wheels 5.5 or 6J.

Dimensions: Clearance 10.5cm, width 168cm, height 139.5cm.

Performance: Max speed 114mph/184kmh, (manufacturers test specifications), speed at 1000rpm in top gear 20.2mph/32.5kmh; acceleration 0 – 62mph/100kmh 10.6secs; power to weight ratio from 12kg/kW (8.9kg/PS); consumption ECE 6.3/8.4/10.7L/100km (44.8/33.6/26.4mpg) [37.3/28/22US mpg].

1.8 Litre
95kW–127hp–129PS
Fuel Injection

Engine for Jetta GT 16 V

As 1.3 Litre, except:

Body, Weight: 4–door Saloon/Sedan, 5–seater; kerbweight (DIN) 1010kg, gross vehicle weight 1470kg.

Engine data (DIN): 4-cylinder in-line (81 x 86.4mm), 1781cm3; compression ratio 10:1; 95kW (127hp) [129PS] at 5800rpm, 53.3kW/L (71.4hp/L) [72.4PS/L]; 168Nm (124lbft) at 4250rpm.
USA version (SAE net): 92kW (123hp) [125PS].

Engine construction: Valves in V 25deg, 4 valves per cylinder, 2 overhead camshafts (toothed belt); oil cooler, oil capacity 4L (3.8US qt); Bosch KE–Jetronic mechanical/electronic fuel injection. Battery 12V 45Ah, alternator 65A.

Transmission: 5-speed manual; final drive ratio 3.67.

Gear ratios: 1st 3.46; 2nd 2.12; 3rd 1.44; 4th 1.13; 5th 0.91; R 3.17.

Chassis: Front and rear antiroll bars. All round disc brakes, front ventilated, rear diameter 17.9cm; tyres 185/60 VR 14, wheels 6J.

Dimensions: Clearance 10.5cm, width 168cm, height 139.5cm.

Performance: Max speed 122mph/196kmh, (manufacturers test specifications), speed at 1000rpm in 5th gear 19.7mph/31.7kmh; acceleration 0 – 62mph/100kmh 9.3secs; power to weight ratio from 10.6kg/kW (7.8kg/PS); consumption ECE 6.6/8.3/11.3L/100km (42.8/34/25mpg) [35.6/28.3/20.8US mpg].

Volkswagen Jetta GT 16V

1.6 Litre Diesel
39.5kW–53hp–54PS
Injection Pump

As 1.3 Litre, except:

Weight: Kerbweight (DIN) 930/950kg, gross vehicle weight 1470kg.

Engine data (DIN): 4-cylinder in-line (76.5 x 86.4mm), 1588cm3; compression ratio 23:1; 39.5kW (53hp) [54PS] at 4800rpm, 24.9kW/L (33.4hp/L) [34PS/L]; 100Nm (73.8lbft) at 2300–2900rpm.

Engine construction: Turbulence chamber–diesel engine; oil capacity 4L (3.8US qt); distributor–Bosch VE injection pump, mechanical centrifugal governor, cold start enrichment. Battery 12V 63Ah; alternator 45A.

Transmission: a) 4–speed manual, final drive ratio 3.94.
b) 4 + E manual, final drive ratio 3.94.
c) Automatic, hydraulic torque converter and 3–speed Planetary gear set, selector lever in the middle, final drive ratio 3.42.

Gear ratios: a) 4–speed manual: 1st 3.46; 2nd 1.94; 3rd 1.29; 4th 0.88; R 3.17.
b) 4 + E manual: 1st 3.46; 2nd 1.94; 3rd 1.29; 4th 0.91; 5th 0.75; R 3.17.
c) Automatic: Planetary gear set ratios: 1st 2.71; 2nd 1.50; 3rd 1.00; R 2.43.

Performance: Max speed 91mph/146kmh, automatic 88mph/141kmh (manufacturers test specifications), speed at 1000rpm in 4th gear 19mph/30.5kmh; acceleration 0 – 62mph/100kmh 19.3secs, automatic 23.5secs; power to weight from 23.5kg/kW (17.2kg/PS); consumption ECE 4.9/7.0/6.6L/100km (57.6/40.4/42.8mpg) [48/33.6/35.6US mpg], 4 + E 4.5/6.4/6.6L/100km (62.8/44.1/42.8mpg) [52.3/36.8/35.6US mpg], automatic 5.4/7.7/7.2L/100km (52.3/36.7/39.2US mpg) [43.6/30.5/32.7US mpg].

Volkswagen

1.6 Litre Diesel
51.5kW–69hp–70PS
Turbo/Injection Pump

As 1.3 Litre, except:

Weight: Kerbweight (DIN) 955/975kg, gross vehicle weight 1470kg.

Engine data (DIN): 4–cylinder in–line (76.5 x 86.4mm), 1588cm3; compression ratio 23:1; 51.5kW (69hp) [70PS] at 4500rpm, 32.5kW/L (43.5hp/L) [44.1PS/L]; 133Nm (98.2lbft) of 2500–2900rpm.

Engine construction: Turbulence chamber diesel engine; oil capacity 4L (3.8US qt); exhaust turbocharger, max boost pressure 0.7bar, distributor-Bosch VE injection pump, mechanical centrifugal governor, cold start enrichment. Battery 12V 63Ah, alternator 45A.

Transmission: 4 + E-speed manual; final drive rato 3.67.

Gear ratios: 1st 3.46; 2nd 1.94; 3rd 1.29; 4th 0.91; 5th 0.75; R 3.17.

Chassis: Tyres 175/70 HR 13, optional 185/60 HR 14.

Performance: Max speed 98mph/158kmh (manufacturers test specifications), speed at 1000rpm in 4th gear 19.8mph/31.8kmh, in 5th 23.9mph/38.5kmh; acceleration 0 – 62mph/100kmh in 15secs; power to weight ratio from 18.5kg/kW (13.6kg/PS); consumption ECE 4.4/6.3/6.4L/100km (64.2/44.8/44.1mpg) [53.5/37.7/36.8US mpg].

Volkswagen Scirocco

Coupe with tailgate, 74 and 137hp engines, front wheel drive. Launched Geneva 1974. Geneva 1981; new body. Summer 1982; 1.6 Litre injection replaced by 1.8 Litre. Autumn 1984; 1.8 Litre 88hp engine made available. June 1985; 16 valve, 137hp, 1.8 Litre engine.

1.6 Litre
53kW–71hp–72PS
1 2V Carb

Body, Weight: 3–door Coupe, 5–seater; kerbweight (DIN) 875kg, gross vehicle weight 1290kg.

Engine data (Unregulated Catalyst, DIN): 4–cylinder in–line (81.0 x 77.4mm), 1595cm3; compression ratio 9.0:1; 53kW (71hp) [72PS] at 5200rpm, 33.1kW/L (44.4hp/L) [45.1PS/L]; 120Nm (88.6lbft) at 2700rpm; unleaded regular grade.

Engine construction: Front engine, transverse mounted, hydraulic tappets; 1 overhead camshaft (toothed belt); light–alloy cylinder head; crankshaft with 5 bearings, oil capacity 4L (3.8US qt); 1 Solex downdraught 2V carb. Battery 12V 36Ah, alternator 65A; cooling system capacity 4.5L (4.3US qt).

Transmission (to front wheels): a) 4–speed manual, final drive ratio 3.67.
b) 4 + E-speed manual, final drive ratio 3.67.
c) Automatic, hydraulic torque converter and 3–speed Planetary gear set, final drive ratio 3.41.

Gear ratios: a) 4–speed manual: 1st 3.46; 2nd 1.94; 3rd 1.29; 4th 0.91; R 3.17.
b) 4 + E manual: 1st 3.46; 2nd 1.94; 3rd 1.29; 4th 0.91; 5th 0.74; R 3.17.
c) Automatic: Max torque multiplication in converter 2.4 times, Planetary gear set ratios: 1st 2.71; 2nd 1.50; 3rd 1; R 2.43.

Volkswagen Scirocco GT

Chassis: Integral body; front A arm and McPherson struts with coil springs, negative offset, rear longitudinal arms with McPherson struts and coil springs, telescopic damper. Servo/power assisted brakes, front discs, rear drums, disc diameter 23.9cm; rear mechanical hand brake; rack and pinion steering, optional power assisted; fuel tank 55L (12.1Gal) [14.5US Gal]; tyres 185/60 HR 14, wheel rims 6J.

Dimensions: Wheelbase 240cm, track 140.5/137cm, clearance 12.5cm, turning circle 10.5m, load space 12.2/32.5cu ft (345/920dm3), length 405cm, width 164.5cm, height 128cm.

Performance: Max speed 102mph/164kmh, automatic 99mph/159kmh (manufacturers test specifications), speed at 1000rpm in 5th gear 23.9mph/38.5kmh; acceleration 0 – 62mph/100kmh 12.7secs, automatic 14.9secs; power to weight 16.5kg/kW (12.1kg/PS); consumption ECE 5.8/7.9/8.9L/100km (48.7/35.8/31.7mpg) [40.6/29.8/26.4US mpg], 4 + E 5.3/7.2/8.9L/100km (53.3/39.2/31.7mpg) [44.4/32.7/26.4US mpg], Automatic 6.4/8.2/9.3L/100km (44.1/34.4/30.4US mpg) [36.8/28.7/25.3US mpg].

1.8 Litre
70kW–94hp–95PS
1 2V Carb

As 1.6 Litre, except:

Weight: Kerbweight (DIN) 890kg, Catalyst 950kg, USA 1005kg, gross vehicle weight 1320kg.

Engine data (Catalyst, DIN): 4–cylinder in–line (81 x 86.4mm), 1781cm3, compression ratio 9:1; 70kW (94hp) [95PS] at 5500rpm, 39.3kW/L (52.7hp/L) [53.3PS/L]; 142Nm (104.8lbft) at 3000rpm.

Engine construction: Oil capacity 4L (3.8US qt); Bosch mechanical fuel injection, K-Jetronic.

Transmission: a) 5–speed manual, final drive ratio 3.67.
b) Automatic, hydraulic torque converter and 3–speed Planetary gear set, final drive ratio 3.41.

Gear ratios: a) 5–speed manual: 1st 3.46; 2nd 2.12; 3rd 1.44; 4th 1.13; 5th 0.89; R 3.17.
b) Automatic: Max torque multiplication in converter 2.4 times, Planetary gear set ratios: 1st 2.71; 2nd 1.50; 3rd 1; R 2.43.

Chassis: Front and rear antiroll bars. Front ventilated disc brakes.

Performance: Max speed 113mph/181kmh, Catalyst 109mph/176kmh (manufacturers test specification), speed at 1000rpm in 5th gear 20.1mph/32.4kmh; acceleration 0 – 62mph/100kmh 10.2secs, automatic 12.4secs; power to weight ratio 13.6kg/kW (10kg/PS); consumption ECE 6.6/8.6/11.1L/100km (42.8/32.8/25.4mpg) [35.6/27.4/21.2US mpg], Automatic 7.7/9.8/11.2L/100km (36.7/28/25.2mpg) [30.5/24/21US mpg].

1.8 Litre
95kW–127hp–129PS
Fuel Injection

As 1.6 Litre, except:

Weight: Kerbweight (DIN) 970kg, gross vehicle weight 1320kg.

Engine data (DIN): 4–cylinder in–line (81 x 86.4mm), 1781cm3; compression ratio 10:1; 95kW (127hp) [129PS] at 5800rpm, 53.3kW/L (71.4hp/L) [72.4PS/L]; 168Nm (124lbft) at 4600rpm grade.
USA version (SAE net): 92kW (123hp) [125PS].

Engine construction: Valves in V 25deg, 4 valves per cylinder, 2 overhead camshafts (toothed belt); oil cooler, oil capacity 4L (3.8US qt); Bosch KE-Jetronic fuel injection. Battery 12V 45Ah, alternator 65A.

Transmission: 5–speed manual; final drive ratio 3.67.

Gear ratios: 1st 3.46; 2nd 2.12; 3rd 1.44; 4th 1.13; 5th 0.91; R 3.17.

Chassis: Front and rear antiroll bars. All round disc brakes, front ventilated, front disc diameter 25.6cm, rear 22.6cm.

Performance: Max speed 124mph/200kmh (manufacturers test specifications), speed at 1000rpm in 5th gear 19.7mph/31.7kmh; acceleration 0 – 62mph/100kmh 8.6secs, Catalyst 8.6secs; power to weight ratio 10.2kg/kW (7.5kg/PS); consumption ECE 6.3/7.9/11.3L/100km (44.8/35.8/25mpg) [37.3/29.8/20.8US mpg].

Volkswagen Scirocco GT 16V

Volkswagen

Volkswagen Corrado

New model. Two door Coupe with tail gate and front wheel drive, 1.8 Litre engine with mechanical spiral turbo charger G 60, 158hp. Launched August 1988.

Volkswagen Corrado

1.8 Litre
118kW-158hp-160PS
Injection/Supercharger

Body, Weight: Coupe 3-door, 5-seater: kerbweight (DIN) 1115kg, gross vehicle weight 1505kg.

Engine data (Catalyst DIN): 4-cylinder in-line (81 x 86.4mm), 1781cm3; compression ratio 8.0:1; 118kW (158hp) [160PS] at 5600rpm, 66.3kW/L (88.8hp/L) [89.8PS/L]; 225Nm (166.1lbft) at 4000rpm; unleaded premium grade.
For some countries: Without Catalyst, with 4 valves per cylinder, 100kW (134hp) [136PS].

Engine construction: Transverse inclined front engine. Hydraulic tappets; 1 overhead camshaft (toothed belt); light-alloy cylinder head; 5 bearing crankshaft; oil capacity 4L (3.8US qt); Digifant electronic fuel injection; mechanical spiral turbo-charger G 60, intercooler. 12V 45Ah battery, alternator 55A; cooling system capacity approx 5L (4.7US qt).

Transmission (to front wheels): 5-speed manual; final drive ratio 3.45.

Gear ratios: 1st 3.78; 2nd 2.11; 3rd 1.34; 4th 0.97; 5th 0.80; R 3.38.

Chassis: Integral body; front A arm and McPherson struts with coil springs (negative steering offset), rear compound axle longitudinal swinging arms and coil springs, telescopic damper, front and rear antiroll bar. Servo/power assisted front disc brakes (ventilated), ABS (Teves); handbrake to rear wheels; power/assisted rack and pinion steering; fuel tank 55L (12.1Gal) [14.5US Gal]; tyres 185/55 VR 15, wheel rims 6J.

Dimensions: Wheelbase 247cm, track 143.5/143cm, clearance min 11cm, turning circle 10.4m, load space 10.6/29.7cu ft (300/840dm3). Length 405cm, width 167.5cm, height 132cm.

Performance: Max speed 140mph/225kmh (manufacturers test specification), speed at 1000rpm in 5th gear 24.1mph/38.8kmh; acceleration 0 - 62mph/100kmh 8.3secs; power to weight ratio from 9.4kg/kW (7.0kg/PS); consumption ECE 6.0/7.5/11.8L/100km (47.1/37.7/23.9mpg) [39.2/31.4/19.9US mpg].

Volkswagen Corrado

Volkswagen Passat

Medium size front wheel drive vehicle, with 1.6 to 2.0 Litre engine and 1.6 Litre diesel. Available as Saloon/Sedan or Estate/Station Wagon. Launched Geneva 1988.

1.6 Litre
53hp-71hp-72PS
Fuel Injection/Carb

Body, Weight: 4-door Saloon/Sedan, 5-seater; kerbweight (DIN) 1100kg, gross vehicle weight 1620kg. 5-door Estate/Station Wagon, 5-seater; kerbweight (DIN) 1120kg, gross vehicle weight approx 1640kg.

Engine data (Catalyst, DIN): 4-cylinder in-line (81 x 77.4mm), 1595cm3; compression ratio 9.0:1; 53kW (71hp) [72PS] at 5200rpm, 33.2kW/L (44.5hp/L) [45.2PS/L]; 125Nm (92.3lbft) at 2750rpm; unleaded regular grade.
With unregulated Catalyst: 120Nm (88.6lbft) at 2700rpm.

Engine construction: Front A arm, transverse engine; hydraulic tappets; 1 overhead camshaft (toothed belt); light-alloy cylinder head; 5 bearing crankshaft; oil capacity 4L (3.8US qt); electronic fuel injection or 1 downdraught compound carb. 12V 36/44Ah battery, 65A alternator; cooling system capacity approx 5L (4.7US qt).

Transmission (to front wheels): a) 4-speed manual, final drive ratio 3.94. b) 5-speed manual, final drive ratio 3.68.

Gear ratios: a) 4-speed manual: 1st 3.78; 2nd 1.95; 3rd 1.19; 4th 0.82; R 3.38. b) 5-speed manual: 1st 3.78; 2nd 2.11; 3rd 1.34; 4th 0.97; 5th 0.80; R 3.38.

Chassis: Integral body; front A arm and McPherson struts with coil springs (negative steering offset), rear longitudinal swinging arms, compound axle and coil springs, telescopic damper. Servo/power assisted brakes, optional ABS (Teves) front discs, rear drums; handbrake to rear wheels; power/assisted rack and pinion steering; fuel tank 70L (15.4Gal) [18.5US Gal]; tyres 165/70 SR 14, 185/65 TR 14 or 195/60 HR 14, wheel rims 5.5/6J.

Dimensions: Wheelbase 262.5cm, track 148/142cm, clearance min 11cm, turning circle 10.7m. Saloon/Sedan: Load space 17.5/30.7cu ft (495/870dm3); length 457.5cm, width 170.5cm, height 143cm. Estate/Station Wagon: Load space 16.4/53cu ft (465/1500dm3); length 457cm, width 170.5cm, height 145/149cm.

Performance: Max speed 105mph/169kmh, Variant 100mph/161kmh (manufacturers test specifications), speed at 1000rpm in 5th gear 22.9mph/36.8kmh; acceleration 0 – 62mph/100kmh 16.1secs, Variant 16.3secs; power to weight ratio 20.7kg/kW (15.3kg/PS); consumption ECE 5.6/7.5/10.2L/100km (50.4/37.7/27.7mpg) [42/31.4/23.1US mpg], 5-speed 5.4/7.1/10L/100km (52.3/39.8/28.2mpg) [43.6/33.1/23.5US mpg]. Variant 5.6/7.4/10.0L/100km (50.4/38.2/28.2mpg) [42/31.8/23.5US mpg]

Volkswagen Passat CL

1.8 Litre
66kW-88hp-90PS
Central/Single Point Fuel Injection

As 1.6 Litre, except:

Body, Weight: Saloon/Sedan 4-door, 5-seater; kerbeight (DIN) 1125kg, gross vehicle weight 1650kg. Estate/Station Wagon 5-door, 5-seater; kerbweight (DIN) 1145kg, gross vehicle weight 1670kg.

Engine data (Catalyst, DIN): 4-cylinder in-line (81 x 86.4mm), 1781cm3, compression ratio 9:1; 66kW (88hp) [90PS] at 5250rpm, 37.1kW/L (49.7hp/L) [50.5PS/L]; 142Nm (104.8lbft) at 3000rpm.

Engine construction: Mono-Jetronic electronic central/single point fuel injection.

Transmission: 5-speed manual, final drive ratio 3.94, Variant 3.68.

Gear ratios: 1st 3.78; 2nd 2.11; 3rd 1.34; 4th 0.97; 5th 0.80; R 3.17.

Chassis: Tyres 185/65 TR 14 or 195/60 HR 14.

Performance: Max speed 110mph/177kmh, Variant 107mph/172kmh (manufacturers test specifications), speed at 1000rpm in 5th gear 23.1mph/37.1kmh; acceleration 0 – 62mph/100kmh 13.8secs, Variant 14.0secs; power to weight ratio 17.1kg/kW (12.5kg/PS); consumption ECE 6.1/7.8/10.7L/100km (46.3/36.2/26.4mpg) [38.6/30.2/22US mpg] Variant 6.2/7.9/10.5L/100km (45.6/35.8/26.9mpg) [37.9/29.8/22.4US mpg].

Volkswagen D • Volkswagen BR

Volkswagen Passat Variant

> 1.8 Litre
> 79kW–106hp–107PS
> Fuel Injection

As 1.6 Litre, except:

Body, Weight: 4–door Saloon/Sedan, 5–seater; kerbweight (DIN) approx 1150kg, gross vehicle weight 1660kg. 5–door Estate/Station Wagon, 5–seater; kerbweight (DIN) approx 1170kg, gross vehicle weight approx 1690kg.

Engine data (Catalyst, DIN): 4–cylinder in–line (81 x 86.4mm), 1781cm3; compression ratio 10:1; 79kW (106hp) [107PS] at 5400rpm, 44.4kW/L (59.5hp/L) [60.1PS/L]; 154Nm (113.7lbft) at 3800rpm.

Engine construction: Digifant electronic fuel injection.

Transmission: 5-speed manual, final drive ratio 3.68, Variant 3.45.

Gear ratios: 1st 3.78; 2nd; 2.11; 3rd 1.34; 4th 0.97; 5th 0.80; R 3.17.

Chassis: Front and rear antiroll bars. All round disc brakes, front ventilated; tyres 185/65 HR 14, 195/60 HR 14 or 195/55 VR 15, wheel rims 6J.

Performance: Max speed 118mph/190kmh, Variant 114mph/184kmh (manufacturers test specifications), speed at 1000rpm in 5th gear 24.6mph/39.6kmh; acceleration 0 – 62mph/100kmh 11.7secs, Variant 11.9secs; power to weight ratio 14.6kg/kW (10.7kg/PS); consumption ECE 5.7/7.4/10.3L/100km (49.6/38.2/27.4mpg) [41.3/31.8/22.8US mpg], Variant 5.9/7.7/10.7L/100km (47.9/36.7/26.4mpg) [39.9/30.5/22US mpg].

Volkswagen Passat GL

> 2 Litre 16V
> 100kW–134hp–136PS
> Fuel Injection

As 1.6 Litre, except:

Body, Weight: 4–door Saloon/Sedan, 5–seater; kerbweight (DIN) 1185kg, gross vehicle weight 1700kg. 5–door Estate/Station Wagon, 5–seater; kerbweight (DIN) 1205kg, gross vehicle weight 1730kg.

Engine data (Catalyst, DIN): 4–cylinder in–line (82.5 x 92.8mm), 1984cm3; compression ratio 10.8:1; 100kW (134hp) [136PS] at 5800rpm, 50.4kW/L (67.5hp/L) [68.5PS/L]; 180Nm (132.8lbft) at 4400rpm.

Engine construction: 4 valves per cylinder; Bosch K-Motronic fuel injection.

Transmission: 5-speed manual, final drive ratio 3.68, Variant 3.45.

Gear ratios: 1st 3.78; 2nd 2.11; 3rd 1.34; 4th 0.97; 5th 0.80; R 3.17.

Chassis: Front and rear antiroll bars. All round disc brakes, front ventilated, tyres 195/65 VR 14 or 185/65 VR 14 or 195/55 VR 15, wheel rims 6J.

Performance: Max speed 128mph/206kmh, Variant 124mph/199kmh (manufacturers test specifications), speed at 1000rpm in 5th gear 24.3mph/39.1kmh; acceleration 0 – 62mph/100kmh 9.9secs, Variant 10.1secs; power to weight ratio 11.8kg/kW (8.7kg/PS); consumption ECE 6.2/7.9/12.2L/100km (45.6/35.8/23.2mpg) [37.9/35.8/19.3US mpg], Variant 6.4/8.1/11.9L/100km (44.1/34.9/23.7mpg) [36.8/29/19.8US mpg].

Volkswagen Passat 16V

> 1.6 Turbodiesel
> 59kW–79hp–80PS
> Injection Pump

As 1.6 Litre, except:

Body, Weight: 4–door Saloon/Sedan, 5–seater; kerbweight (DIN) 1170kg, gross vehicle weight 1690kg. 5–door Estate/Station Wagon, 5–seater; kerbweight (DIN) 1190kg, gross vehicle weight (DIN) 1710kg.

Engine data (DIN): 4–cylinder in–line (76.5 x 86.4mm), 1588cm3; compression ratio 23:1; 59kW (79hp) [80PS] at 4500rpm, 37.2kW/L (49.8hp/L) [50.4PS/L]; 155Nm (114.4lbft) at 2500rpm.

Engine construction: Turbulence chamber diesel engine; oil capacity 3.5L (3.3US qt); exhaust turbocharger, max boost pressure 0.7bar, charge-air cooler; Bosch VE distributor injection pump, mechanical centrifugal governor, cold start enrichment. Battery 12V 63Ah; alternator 65A; cooling system capacity 7L (6.6US qt).

Transmission: 5-speed manual, final drive ratio 3.45.

Gear ratios: 1st 3.78; 2nd 2.11; 3rd 1.34; 4th 0.97; 5th 0.80; R 3.17.

Chassis: Tyres 185/65 TR 14 or 195/65 HR 14, wheel rims 6J.

Performance: Max speed 106mph/171kmh, Variant 103mph/165kmh (manufacturers test specifications), speed at 1000rpm in 5th gear 24.6mph/39.6kmh; acceleration 0 – 62mph/100kmh 15.6secs, Variant 15.8secs; power to weight ratio 19.8kg/kW (14.6kg/PS); consumption ECE 4.4/6.2/6.8L/100km (64.2/45.6/41.5mpg) [53.5/37.9/34.6US mpg], Variant 4.6/6.5/6.8L/100km (61.4/43.5/41.5mpg) [51.1/36.2/34.6US mpg].

Volkswagen Passat Variant

VOLKSWAGEN BR

Volkswagen do Brasil SA, Via Anchieta, km 23.5, Posto de Correio Volkswagen, 09 700 Sao Bernardo do Campo, Brasil.

Producer of Volkswagens in Brasil. Autumn 1986 amalgamated with Ford Brasil and Holding to form "Autolatina". Joint technical input.

MODEL RANGE
Gol – Voyage – Fox – Santana/Quantum

Volkswagen Gol – Voyage – Fox

Base model the Gol, front wheel drive and water cooled 4–cylinder engine. Saloo/Sedan launched June 1981, Estate/Station Wagon "Parati" May 1982, 4–door Saloon/Sedan January 1983. Export versions designated "Fox" and "Amazon". November 1985; Voyage with 1.8 Litre engine.

Volkswagen BR

1.6 Litre
58/65.5kW–78/88hp–79/89PS
1 2V Carb

Body, Weight: 2–door Saloon/Sedan, 5–seater; kerbweight (DIN) 820kg, gross vehicle weight 1240kg. 4–door Saloon/Sedan, 5–seater; kerbweight (DIN) 840kg, gross vehicle weight 1240kg. 3–door Saloon/Sedan, 5–seater; kerbweight (DIN) 850kg; gross vehicle weight 1240kg. 3–door (Parati) Estate/Station Wagon, 5–seater; kerbweight (DIN) 880kg, gross vehicle weight 1380kg.

Engine data (DIN): 4–cylinder in–line (81 x 77.4mm), 1595cm3; compression ratio 8.5:1, 59kW (79hp) [80PS] at 5600rpm, 37kW/L (49.6hp/L) [50.2PS/L]; 125Nm (92.3lbft) at 2600rpm; leaded regular grade.

Engine for ethyl alcohol: Compression ratio 12:1; 65kW (87hp) [89PS] at 5600rpm, 41kW/L (54.9hp/L) [55.8PS/L]; 128Nm (94.5lbft) at 2600rpm.

Volkswagen Gol

Engine construction: Front engine tilted 20deg to the right. 1 overhead camshaft (toothed belt); light–alloy cylinder head; crankshaft with 5 bearings; oil capacity 3.5L (3.3US qt); 1 Wecarbras (Weber) downdraught 2V carb. Battery 12V 36Ah, alternator 35A; cooling system capacity 5.1/5.6L (4.8/5.3US qt), electric cooling fan.

Transmission (to front wheels): a) 4–speed manual (without direct drive), final drive ratio 4.11 (9.37).
b) 5–speed manual, final drive ratio 4.11.

Gear ratios: a) 4–speed manual: 1st 3.45; 2nd 1.94; 3rd 1.29; 4th 0.91; R 3.17.
b) 5–speed manual: 1st 3.45; 2nd 1.94; 3rd 1.29; 4th 0.97; 5th 0.8; R 3.17.

Chassis: Integral body; front A arm and McPherson struts with coil springs (negative offset), antiroll bar, rear longitudinal arms with McPherson struts and coil springs, telescopic damper. Servo/power assisted brakes, front discs, rear drums, disc diameter 23.9cm, rear mechanical handbrake; rack and pinion steering; fuel tank 55L (12.1Gal) [14.5US Gal]; tyres 155 SR 13, wheel rims 5J, optional tyres 175/70 SR 13, wheels 5.5J.

Dimensions: Wheelbase 236cm, track 135/136.5cm, clearance 14.5cm, turning circle 10.2m; load space 16.2cu ft (460dm3), length 381–409cm, width 160cm, height 136.5cm. Estate/Station Wagon: Load space 18.7–54.4cu ft (530–1540dm3), width 162cm, height 138cm. Gol: Load space 11.7–40.6cu ft (330–1150dm3), length 379cm, height 137.5cm. Fox: Length 415cm.

Volkswagen Parati/Fox Wagon

Performance: Max speed 97mph/156kmh, alcohol engine 103mph/165kmh (manufacturers test specifications), speed at 1000rpm in 4th gear 17.6–20.5mph/28.3–33kmh; acceleration 0 – 62mph/100kmh in 12.8– 13.1secs; power to weight ratio from 12.6kg/kW (9.2kg/PS); consumption 8.5–12L/100km (33.2–23.5mpg) [27.7–19.6US mpg].

1.8 Litre
73kW–98hp–99PS
1 2V Carb

As 1.6 Litre, except:

Weight: Kerbweight (DIN) from 930kg, gross vehicle weight 1320kg.

Engine data (DIN): 4–cylinder in–line (81 x 86.4mm), 1781cm3.
a) Engine for operation on ethyl alcohol (DIN): Compression ratio 12:1; 73kW (98hp) [99PS] at 5200rpm, 41kW/L (54.9hp/L) [55.6PS/L]; 149Nm (110lbft) at 3200rpm.
b) Petrol/Gasoline engine for export to USA, with fuel injection (SAE net): Compression ratio 9.0:1; 60.5kW (81hp) [82PS] at 5500rpm, 33.9kW/L (45.4hp/L) [46.0PS/L]; 126Nm (93lbft) at 3250rpm; unleaded regular grade.

Engine construction: 1 Brosol Pierburg 2E7 downdraught 2V carb. Battery 12V 42Ah, alternator 45/65A; cooling system capacity 6.6L (6.2US qt).

Transmission: 5–speed manual, final drive ratio 4.11, Fox 3.89.

Gear ratios: 1st 3.45; 2nd 1.94; 3rd 1.29; 4th 0.97; 5th 0.8; R 3.17.
Fox: 1st 3.45; 2nd 1.7; 3rd 1.06; 4th 0.78; R 3.17.

Chassis: Servo/power assisted brakes; tyres 185/60 HR 14, wheels 6J; Fox: tyres 175/75 SR 13, wheels 5.5J.

Performance: Max speed 106mph/171kmh (manufacturers test specifications), speed at 1000rpm in 5th gear 20.1mph/32.3kmh; power to weight ratio from 12.7kg/kW (9.4kg/PS); consumption approx 9–11L/100km (31.4–25.7mpg) [26.1–21.4US mpg].

Volkswagen Voyage 1.8

2 Litre
88kW–118hp–120PS
Fuel Injection

As 1.6 Litre, except:

Weight: Kerbweight (DIN) from 980kg, gross vehicle weight 1320kg.

Engine data (DIN): 4-cylinder in-line (82.5 x 92.8mm), 1984cm3; compression ratio 10:1; 88kW (118hp) [120PS] at 5600rpm, 44.3kW/L (59.4hp/L) [60.5PS/L]; 181Nm (133.6lbft) at 3400rpm.

Engine construction: Hydraulic tappets; Bosch LE-Motronic fuel injection.

Transmission: 5-speed manual, final drive ratio 3.68.

Volkswagen Gol GTi/GTS

Volkswagen BR

Gear ratios: 1st 3.78; 2nd 2.11; 3rd 1.34; 4th 0.97; 5th 0.80; R 3.17.
Chassis: Tyres 185/60 HR 14, wheel rims 6J.
Performance: Max speed 115mph/185kmh (manufacturers test specification), speed at 1000rpm in 5th gear 21.3mph/34.2kmh; acceleration 0 - 62mph/100kmh 8.8secs; power to weight ratio from 11.1kg/kW (8.2kg/PS); consumption approx 7-10L/100km (40.4-28.2mpg) [33.6-23.5US mpg].

```
1.6 Litre Diesel
37kW–49hp–50PS
Injection Pump
```

Engine for export
As 1.6 Litre, except:
Weight: Kerbweight (DIN) 900kg.
Engine data (DIN): 4-cylinder in-line (76.5 x 86.4mm), 1588cm3, compression ratio 23.5:1; 37kW (49hp) [50PS] at 4500rpm, 23.2kW/L (31.1hp/L) (31.5PS/L); 93Nm (68.6lbft) at 3000rpm.
Engine construction: Turbulence chamber diesel engine, 1 overhead camshaft (toothed belt); light-alloy clyinder head; crankshaft with 5 bearings; oil capacity 3.5L (3.3US qt); Bosch VE distributor injection pump, mechanical centrifugal governor, cold start enrichment. Battery 12V 63Ah; alternator 45/65A.
Performance: Max speed 81mph/130kmh; power to weight ratio from 24.5kg/kW (18.0kg/PS); consumption approx 5-9L/100km (56.5- 31.4mpg) [47-26.1US mpg].

Volkswagen Santana – Quantum

C – CL – GL – GLS
Brasilian produced Santana, with a 1.8 Litre engine for operation on Petrol/Gasoline or Ethyl Alcohol; also available as a 2-door Saloon/Sedan. Launched June 1984. Estate/Station Wagon "Quantum" launched April 1985. Since Summer 1988 also with 2 Litre engine.

Volkswagen Santana

```
1800cm3
70/65.5kW-94/88hp-95/89PS
1 2V Carb
```

Body, Weight: 2-door Saloon/Sedan, 5-seater; kerbweight (DIN) from 1010kg, gross vehicle weight 1495kg. 4-door Saloon/Sedan, 5-seater; kerbweight (DIN) from 1035kg, gross vehicle weight 1520kg. 5-door Estate/Station Wagon (Quantum), 5-seater; kerbweight (DIN) from 1100kg, gross vehicle weight 1600kg.
Engine data (DIN): 4-cylinder in-line (81 x 86.4mm), 1781cm3.
a) Engine for operation on ethyl alcohol (DIN): Compression ratio 12:1; 70kW (94hp) [95PS] at 5200rpm, 39.2kW/L (52.5hp/L) [53.3PS/L]; 151Nm (111.4lbft) at 3400rpm.
b) Petrol/Gasoline engine: Compression ratio 8.5:1; 65.5kW (88hp) [89PS] at 5200rpm, 36.8kW/L (49.3hp/L) [50PS/L]; 143Nm (105.5lbft) at 3400rpm; leaded regular grade.
Engine construction: Front engine (longitudinal, tilted). 1 overhead camshaft (toothed belt); light-alloy cylinder head; crankshaft with 5 bearings; oil capacity 3.5L (3.3US qt); 1 Brosol Pierburg 2E7 downdraught 2V carb. Battery 12 V 54 or 42Ah, alternator 45/65A; cooling system capacity 6.6L (6.2US qt).
Transmission (to front wheels): a) 5-speed manual, final drive ratio 4.11.
b) Optional automatic, hydraulic torque converter and 3-speed Planetary gear set, selector lever in the middle, final drive ratio 3.727.
Gear ratios: a) 5-speed manual: 1st 3.45; 2nd 1.94; 3rd 1.29; 4th 0.97; 5th 0.80; R 3.17.
b) Automatic: Max torque multiplication in converter 2.5 times. Planetary gear set ratios: 1st 2.71; 2nd 1.50; 3rd 1; R 2.43.

Chassis: Integral body with sub-frame; front McPherson struts with A arm, antiroll bar and coil springs, (negative offset), rear rigid axle with longitudinal arms, coil springs, telescopic damper. Servo/power assisted brakes, front disc, rear drums, disc diameter 23.9cm, rear mechanical handbrake; rack and pinion steering; fuel tank 75L (16.5Gal) [19.8US Gal]; tyres 185/70 SR 13, wheels 5.5J.
Dimensions: Wheelbase 255cm, track 141.5/142cm, clearance 13cm, turning circle 10.2m; load space 17cu ft (480dm3), Estate/Station Wagon 20.8/60cu ft (590/1700dm3), length 455cm, Estate/Station Wagon 457cm, width 169.5cm, height 140cm, Estate/Station Wagon 138cm.
Performance: Max speed 101-108mph/163-174kmh (manufacturers test specifications), speed at 1000rpm in 5th gear 20.4mph/32.9kmh; acceleration 0 - 62mph/100kmh from 11.7secs, standing km from 33.5secs; power to weight from 14.4kg/kW (10.6kg/PS); consumption 8.4-15L/100km (33.6-18.8mpg) [28-15.7US mpg] (manufacturers test specifications).

Volkswagen Santana

```
1984cm3
82/73kW-110/98hp-112/99PS
1 Compound Carb
```

As 1800cm3, except:
Body, Weight: Saloon/Sedan 2-door, 5-seater; kerbweight (DIN) from 1035kg, gross vehicle weight 1520kg.
Saloon/Sedan 4-door, 5-seater; kerbweight (DIN) from 1055kg, gross vehicle weight 1540kg.
Estate/Station Wagon "Quantum" 5-door, 5-seater; kerbweight (DIN) from 1100kg, gross vehicle weight 1600kg.
Engine data (DIN): 4-cylinder in-line (82.5 x 92.8mm), 1984cm3.
a) Engine for operation on ethyl alcohol (DIN): Compression ratio 12:1; 82kW (110hp) [112PS] at 5200rpm, 41.3kW/L (55.3hp/L) [56.4PS/L]; 170Nm (125.5lbft) at 3400rpm.
b) Petrol/Gasoline engine: Compression ratio 8:1; 73kW (98hp) [99PS] at 5200rpm, 36.8kW/L (49.3hp/L) [49.9PS/L]; 159Nm (117.3lbft) at 3400rpm; regular grade.
Engine construction: 1 Brosol Pierburg 2E7 downdraught carb. 12V 54Ah, 65A alternator; cooling system capacity approx 6.7L (42.2mpg) [35.1US mpg].
Transmission: a) 5-speed manual, final drive ratio 4.11.
b) Optional Automatic, hydraulic torque converter and 3-speed Planetary gear set, central selector lever, final drive ratio 3.727 or 3.42.
Chassis: Tyres 185/70 SR 13, wheel rims 5.5J, optional 195/60 HR 14, wheel rims 6J.
Dimensions: Length 452.5cm, Estate/Station Wagon 454.5cm.

Volkswagen Quantum 2000

Volkswagen BR • Volkswagen MEX • Volkswagen RA

Performance: Max speed 126-134mph/171-182kmh (manufacturers test specification), speed at 1000rpm in 5th gear 20.4mph/32.9kmh; acceleration 0 - 62mph/100kmh from 10.5secs; standing km from 32.2secs; power to weight ratio from 12.6kg/kW (9.2kg/PS); consumption approx 8-15L/100km (35.3-18.8mpg) [29.4-15.7US mpg].

VOLKSWAGEN MEX

Volkswagen de Mexico, SA de C.V., Puebia/Pue., Mexico
Constructor of Volkswagens in Mexico.

Volkswagen 1200/1200L

Variant of the oldest series of vehicles in production. Air cooled, rear mounted engine. January 1978; production suspended in Europe.

```
1200cm3
25kW–33hp–34PS
1 Carb
```

Body, Weight: 2-door Saloon/Sedan, 5-seater; kerbweight (DIN) 760kg, L 780kg, gross vehicle weight 1140kg, L 1180kg.
Engine data (DIN): 4-cylinder Boxer engine (77 x 64mm), 1192cm3; compression ratio 7.3:1; 25kW (33hp) [34PS] at 3800rpm, 21kW/L (28.1hp/L) [28.5PS/L]; 75Nm (100.5lbft) at 1700rpm; regular grade.
Engine construction: Rear engine. Central camshaft (toothed wheel); light-alloy cylinder head; crankshaft with 4 bearings; screen oil fliter, oil cooler, oil capacity 2.5L (2.4US qt); 1 Solex 30 PICT-3 downdraught carb; oil bath air cleaner. Battery 12V 36Ah, optional 45Ah, alternator 30A; air cooled.
Transmission (to rear wheels): 4-speed manual (without direct drive), final drive ratio 4.375 (8/35); optional limited slip differential.
Gear ratios: 1st 3.78; 2nd 2.06; 3rd 1.26; 4th 0.93; R 3.78.
Chassis: Central tube frame, forked at rear forked with integral platform as body floor; front double cranked arm with transverse torsion bar; rear independent suspension with swing axle, trailing arms, transverse torsion bar and diagonal compensating springs above the axle; front antiroll bar and telescopic dampers. Four wheel drum brakes; rear mechanical handbrake; worm and wheel steering; fuel tank 40L (8.8Gal) [10.6US qt], including 5L (1.1Gal) [1.3US qt] reserve; tyres 155 SR 15 or 5.60–15, wheels 4–5J.
Dimensions: Wheelbase 240cm, track 131/135cm, clearance 15cm, turning circle 11m; load space, front 4.6cu ft (130dm3), rear 3.7cu ft (105dm3), length 406/409cm, width 155cm, height 150cm.
Performance: Max speed 72mph/115kmh (manufacturers test specifications), speed at 1000rpm in 4th gear 17.8mph/28.6kmh; acceleration 0 – 62mph/100kmh in 32secs; standing km 44secs; power to weight ratio from 30.4kg/kW (22.4kg/PS); consumption (ECE) 6.7–9.9L/100km (42.2–28.5mpg) [35.1–23.8US mpg].

Volkswagen 1200 L

```
1600
34kW–45hp–46PS
2 Carbs
```

As 1200, except:
Weight: Kerbweight (DIN) 820kg, gross vehicle weight 1200kg.
Engine data (DIN): (85.5 x 69mm), 1584cm3; compression ratio 6.6:1; 34kW (45hp) [46PS] at 4000rpm, 21.5kW/L (28.8hp/L) [29PS/L]; 98Nm (72.3lbft) at 2200rpm.
Engine construction: 2 Solex 32 PDSIT downdraught carbs.
Performance: Max speed 79mph/127kmh (manufacturers test specifications), power to weight ratio 24.1kg/kW (17.8kg/PS).

VOLKSWAGEN RA

Volkswagen Argentina S.A., Florencio Varela 1903, (1754) San Justo, Provincia de Buenos Aires, Argentina

Argentine copmany affiliated to the Chrysler Corporation; joint venture with Volkswagen since 1980.

Volkswagen Gacel

4–door Saloon/Sedan with front wheel drive, 1.6 Litre engine and 4–speed manual transmission. Technically similar to the Voyage produced in Brasil. Launched September 1983.

```
1.6 Litre
53.5kW–72hp–73PS
1 2V Carb
```

Body, Weight: 4-door Saloon/Sedan, 5-seater; kerbweight (DIN) 890kg, gross vehicle weight 1240kg.
Engine data (DIN): 4-cylinder in-line (79.5 x 80mm), 1588cm3; compression ratio 8.3:1, 53.5kW (72hp) [73PS] at 5200rpm, 33.4kW/L (44.8hp/L) [46PS/L]; 119Nm (87.8lbft) at 2600rpm; regular grade.
Engine construction: Front engine tilted 20deg to the right; 1 overhead camshaft (toothed belt); light-alloy cylinder head; crankshaft with 5 bearings; oil capacity 3.5L (3.3US qt); 1 Wecarbras (Weber) downdraught 2V carb. Battery 12V 36Ah, alternator 35A; cooling system capacity 5.1/5.6L (4.8/5.3US qt).
Transmission (to front wheels): 4-speed manual (without direct drive), floor shift; final drive ratio 4.11 (/37).
Gear ratios: 1st 3.45; 2nd 1.94; 3rd 1.29; 4th 0.91; R 3.17.
Chassis: Integral body; front A arm and McPherson struts with coil springs (negative offset), rear longitudinal arm with McPherson struts and coil springs, telescopic damper. Servo/power assisted brakes, front disc, rear drums, disc diameter 23.9cm, rear mechanical handbrake; rack and pinion steering; fuel tank 55L (12.1Gal) [14.5US Gal]; tyres 155 SR 13, wheels 5J.
Dimensions: Wheelbase 236cm, track 135/137cm, clearance 14.5cm, turning circle 10.2m; load space 16.2cu ft (460dm3), length 413.5cm, width 160cm, height 136.5cm.
Performance: Max speed 97mph/156kmh (manufacturers test specifications), speed at 1000rpm in 4th gear 17.6mph/28.3kmh; acceleration 0 – 62mph/100kmh approx 13secs; power to weight ratio from 16.6kg/kW (12.2kg/PS); consumption 8.5–12L/100km (33.2–23.5mpg) [27.7–19.6US mpg].

Volkswagen Gacel

Volkswagen 1500 – M 1.8

Saloon/Sedan derived from the early Chrysler Avenger with a 1.5 or 1.8 Litre 4–cylinder engine.

Volkswagen RA • Volkswagen SA • Volkswagen/Nissan

1.5/1.8 Litre
45/56kW–60/75hp–61/76PS
1 Carb

Body, Weight: 4–door Saloon/Sedan, 5–seater; kerbweight (DIN) 950/1.8Litre 960kg. 5–door Estate/Station Wagon, 5–seater; kerbweight (DIN) 1020kg.

Volkswagen 1500

Engine data (DIN): 4–cylinder in–line (86.1 x 64.3mm), 1498cm3; compression ratio 8:1; 45kW (60hp) [61PS] at 5000rpm, 30kW/L (40.2hp/L) [40.7PS/L]; 106Nm (78.2lbft) at 2800rpm; regular grade.
1.8 Litre engine: (86.1 x 77.2mm), 1798cm3; compression ratio 8.6:1; 56kW (75hp) [76PS] at 5000rpm, 31.1kW/L (41.7hp/L) [42.2PS/L]; 130Nm (95.9lbft) at 3200rpm.

Engine construction: Side camshaft (chain); crankshaft with 5 bearings; oil capacity 4.5L (4.3US qt); 1 Holley downdraught carb. Battery 12V 48Ah, alternator 38A; cooling system capacity 7.4L (7US qt).

Transmission (to rear wheels): a) 4–speed manual, final drive ratio 3.54.
b) Optional automatic, hydraulic torque converter and 4–speed Planetary gear set, selector lever in the middle with positions P–R–N–D–3–2/1.

Gear ratios: a) 4–speed manual: 1st 3.32; 2nd 2.03; 3rd 1.37; 4th 1; R 3.45.
b) Automatic: Max torque multiplication in converter approx 2.3 times, Planetary gear set ratios: 1st 3; 2nd 1.94; 3rd 1.35; 4th 1; R 4.69.

Chassis: Integral body; front McPherson struts, control arm and coil springs, rear rigid axle with trailing arm and coil springs, telescopic damper. Servo/power assisted brakes, front disc, diameter 24.1cm, rear drums, rear mechanical handbrake; rack and pinion steering; fuel tank 45L (9.9Gal) [11.9US Gal]; tyres 5.60–13, 155 SR 13 or 175/70 SR 13, wheels 4.5J.

Dimensions: Wheelbase 249cm, track 132/130.5cm, clearance 14cm, turning circle 9.9m; load space 14.1cu ft (400dm3), Estate/Station Wagon 32.5–60.7cu ft (920–1720dm3), length 426cm, Estate/Station Wagon 433cm, width 163/165cm, height 136cm.

Performance: Max speed 90–99mph/145–160kmh, speed at 1000rpm in direct gear 18.6mph/30kmh; power to weight ratio from 17.1kg/kW (12.6kg/PS); consumption (touring) approx 8–13L/100km (35.3–21.7mpg) [29.4–18.1US mpg].

Volkswagen Rural

Volkswagen Carat

New model. Argentine version of the Santana, available in three variants with 4–doors, 1.8 Litre engine and 5–speed transmission.

1800cm3
71kW–95hp–96PS
1 2V Carb

Body, Weight: 4–door Saloon/Sedan, 5–seater; kerbweight (DIN) from 1080kg, gross vehicle weight 1520kg.

Engine data (DIN): 4–cylinder in–line (81 x 86.4mm), 1781cm3; compression ratio 9:1; 71kW (95hp) [96PS] at 5500rpm, 39.9kW/L (53.5hp/L) [53.9kW/L]; 143Nm (105.5lbft) at 2700rpm; premium grade.

Engine construction: Front engine (longitudinal, tilted). 1 overhead camshaft (toothed belt); light–alloy cylinder head; crankshaft with 5 bearings; oil capacity 3.5L (3.3US qt); 1 Brosol Pierburg 2E7 downdraught 2V carb. Battery 12V 54Ah, alternator 55A; cooling system capacity 6.6L (6.2US qt).

Transmission (to front wheels): 5–speed manual, final drive ratio 4.11.

Gear ratios: 1st 3.45; 2nd 1.94; 3rd 1.29; 4th 0.97; 5th 0.80; R 3.17.

Chassis: Integral body with front sub–frame; front McPherson struts with A arm, antiroll bar and coil springs, negative offset, rear rigid axle with longitudinal, coil springs, telescopic damper. Servo/power assisted brakes, front disc, rear drums, disc diameter 23.9cm, rear mechanical handbrake; rack and pinion steering; fuel tank 75L (16.5Gal) [19.8US Gal]; tyres 185/70 SR 13, wheels 5.5J.

Dimensions: Wheelbase 255cm, track 141.5/142cm, clearance 13cm, turning circle 10.2m; load space 18.9cu ft (535dm3) (VDA 15.5cu ft/440dm3), length 452.5cm, width 171cm, height 140cm.

Performance: Max speed 112mph/180kmh (manufacturers test specifications), speed at 1000rpm in 5th gear 20.4mph/32.9kmh; power to weight ratio from 15.2kg/kW (11.3kg/PS); consumption approx 7–11L/100km (40.4–25.7mpg) [33.6–21.4US mpg].

Volkswagen Carat

VOLKSWAGEN SA

Volkswagen of South Africa (PTY) Ltd, P.O. Box 80, Uitenhage, 6230 South Africa

Manufacturing company in South Africa, producing Golf, Jetta and Passat under license from Volkswagen Germany. Carb versions with increased power, refer to Volkswagen Germany for technical data.

VOLKSWAGEN/NISSAN J

Nissan Motors Co Ltd, 17–1 Ginza 6–chome, Chuo–ku, Tokyo 104, Japan

Nissan producing Volkswagen under license only for the Japanese market.

Volkswagen Santana

Early Passat 4–door built under license by Nissan.

2.0 20V
103kW–138hp–140PS
Fuel Injection

As VW Passat 1987, except:

Body, Weight: 4–door Saloon/Sedan, kerbweight (DIN) 1180–1190kg.

Engine data (JIS net): 5–cylinder in–line (81.0 x 77.4mm), 1994cm3; compression ratio 10:1; 103kW (138hp) [140PS] at 6400rpm, 51.7kW/L (69.3hp/L) [70.2PS/L]; 172Nm (126.9lbft) at 4800rpm.

Engine construction: 4 valves (in V 25deg) per cylinder, 2 overhead camshafts (toothed belt/chain); crankshaft with 6 bearings; oil capacity approx 3.8L (3.6US qt); electronic fuel injection. Battery 12V 63Ah, alternator 90A; cooling system capacity 8L (7.6US qt).

Transmission: a) 5–speed manual, final drive ratio 4.700.
b) Automatic, final drive ratio 3.454.

Gear ratios: a) 5–speed manual: 1st 2,846; 2nd 1.523; 3rd 1.064; 4th 0.828; 5th 0.641; R 3.166.
b) Automatic: As 1.6 Litre.

Chassis: All round disc brakes, front ventilated; tyres 195/60 HR 14, tyres 6J.

Performance: Max speed approx 124mph/200kmh, speed at 1000rpm in 5th gear 23.2mph/37.3kmh; power to weight ratio from 11.5kg/kW (8.4kg/PS); consumption approx 7–13L/100km (40.4–21.7mpg) [33.6–18.1US mpg].

VOLVO S

Volvo Car Corporation, S–405 08 Goteborg, Sweden

Important industrial enterprise, producing motor vehicles and various other products. Production of the 300 and 480 series based in Holland.

MODEL RANGE
300 - 440 - 480 - 240 - 740 - 760 - 780

Volvo 300

340 – 360

Medium size Saloon/Sedan with tailgate, a 1.4 Litre Renault engine, constant variable transmission, 2 variants available. Launched February 1976. August 1980 available with a 2.0 Litre engine. August 1982; 360 series available with a 2.0 Litre injection engine. Summer 1983; Saloon/Sedan 360 with conventional boot/trunck. 1984; available with a 1.6 Litre diesel engine. Summer 1986; available with a 1.7 Litre Renault engine.

```
1.4 Litre
52/46.5kW–70/62hp–71/63PS
1 2V Carb
```

Body, Weight: 3–door Saloon/Sedan, 5–seater; kerbweight (DIN) from 950kg, gross vehicle weight 1430kg. 4/5–door Saloon/Sedan, 5–seater; kerbweight (DIN) from 995kg, gross vehicle weight 1455kg. Increased weight for automatic 25kg.

Engine data (DIN): 4–cylinder in–line (76 x 77mm), 1397cm3; compression ratio 9.25:1; 52kW (70hp) [71PS] at 5500rpm, 37.4kW/L (50.1hp/L) [50.8PS/L]; 108Nm (79.7lbft) at 3400rpm; premium grade.
Some countries: 45–48kW (60–64hp) [61–65PS].

Engine construction: Designated B14. Side camshaft (chain); light–alloy cylinder head; wet cylinder liners; crankshaft with 5 bearings; oil capacity 3.5L (3.3US qt); 1 Weber 32 DIR 109 downdraught 2V carb. Battery 12V 36/45Ah, alternator 50A; cooling system capacity approx 5.3L (5US qt).

Transmission (to rear wheels): a) 4–speed manual, final drive ratio 3.64.
b) 5–speed manual, final drive ratio 3.82.
Transmission and differential in rear as one assembly.
c) Automatic, two stage centrifugal clutch and constantly variable transmission (CVT), with kickdown, gear shift lever in the middle, vacuum controlled overdrive and engine brake, double belt drive with variable diameter pulleys, reduction gear and differential; final drive ratio 4.51.

Gear ratios: a) 4–speed manual: 1st 3.71: 2nd 2.16; 3rd 1.37; 4th 1; R 3.68.
b) 5–speed manual; 1st 3.71; 2nd 2.16; 3rd 1.37; 4th 1; 5th 0.83; R 3.68.
c) Continuously variable between 14.15 and 4.0; R 14.22.

Chassis: Integral body; front McPherson struts (coil springs and co–axial telescopic damper), lower keystone A arm, antiroll bar; rear De Dion axle with single leaf side springs and reaction arms, telescopic damper. Servo/power assisted brakes, front discs, diameter 23.9cm, rear drums; handbrake to rear wheels; rack and pinion steering; fuel tank 45L (9.9Gal) [11.9US Gal]; tyres 155 SR 13, wheels 4.5J or 175/70 SR 13 (5J).

Dimensions: Wheelbase 240cm, track 137/140cm, clearance 13.5cm, turning circle 9.2m, load space 13.4/42.4cu ft (380/1200dm3), length 432/443.5cm, width 166cm, height 139–143.5cm.

Volvo 340

Performance: Max speed 99mph/160kmh, automatic 96mph/155kmh (manufacturers test specifications), speed at 1000rpm in 4th gear 18mph/29kmh; acceleration 0 – 62mph/100kmh 15secs, automatic 15.5secs; power to weight ratio from 17.9kg/kW (13.2kg/PS); consumption ECE 5.8/7.8/8.8L/100km (48.7/36.2/32.1mpg) [40.6/30.2/26.7US mpg], 5–speed 6.0/8.1/8.8L/100km (47.1/34.9/32.1mpg) [39.2/29/26.7US mpg], automatic 6.6/8.6/9.2L/100km (42.8/32.8/30.7mpg) [35.6/27.4/25.6US mpg].

```
1.7 Litre
60kW–80hp–82PS
1 2V Carb
```

As 1.4 Litre, except:

Weight: Kerbweight (DIN) 1090kg.

Engine data: 4–cylinder in–line (81 x 83.5mm), 1721cm3; compression ratio 9:5:1; 60kW (80hp) [82PS]; 34.9kW/L (46.8hp/L) [47.6PS/L]; 131Nm (96.7lbft) at 3000rpm.
With Catalyst (fuel injection): 55kW (74hp) [75PS]; unleaded regular grade.

Engine construction: 1 overhead camshaft (toothed belt); oil capacity 5.5L (5.2US qt); 1 Solex 28–34 CLSAC Z 10 downdraught 2V carb. 12V 35Ah battery; cooling system capacity 8L (7.6US qt).

Transmission: 5–speed manual, final drive ratio 3.45.

Gear ratios: 1st 3.705; 2nd 2.156; 3rd 1.369; 4th 1; 5th 0.826; R 3.683.

Performance: Max speed 103mph/165kmh (manufacturers test specifications), speed at 1000rpm in 5th gear 23.1mph/37.1kmh; acceleration 0 – 62mph/100kmh in 12.4secs; standing km 34.0secs; power to weight ratio from 18.2kg/kW (13.3kg/PS); consumption ECE 5.4/7.3/9.3L/100km (52.3/38.7/30.4mpg) [43.6/32.2/25.3US mpg].

```
2 Litre
75kW–101hp–102PS
1 2V Carb
```

As 1.4 Litre, except:

Weight: Kerbweight (DIN) at 1075/1095kg, gross vehicle weight 1540kg.

Engine data (DIN): 4–cylinder in–line (88.9 x 80mm), 1986cm3; compression ratio 10:1; 75kW (101hp) [102PS] at 5700rpm, 37.8kW/L (50.7hp/L) [51.4PS/L]; 160Nm (118.1lbft) at 3300rpm.

Engine construction: Designated B 200K. 1 overhead camshaft (toothed belt); light–alloy cylinder head; crankshaft with 5 bearings; oil capacity 4L (3.8US qt); 1 Solex 34–34 CISAC Z11 horizontal 2V carb. Battery 12V 45/55Ah, alternator 55A; cooling system capacity 7L (6.6US qt).

Transmission: 5–speed manual, final drive ratio 3.36.

Gear ratios: 1st 3.71; 2nd 2.16, 3rd 1.37; 4th 1; 5th 0.83; R 3.68.

Chassis: Fuel tank 57L (12.5Gal) [15.1US Gal]; tyres 175/70 SR 13, wheels 5J, optional tyres 185/60 HR 14, wheels 5.5J.

Performance: Max speed 109mph/175kmh (manufacturers test specifications), speed at 1000rpm in 5th gear 23.6mph/38.0kmh; acceleration 0 – 62mph/100kmh in 12.5secs; power to weight ratio from 14.3kg/kW (10.5kg/PS); consumption ECE 5.5/7.1/9.4L/100km (51.4/39.8/30.1mpg) [42.8/33.1/25.0US mpg].

Volvo 360 GL

```
2 Litre
84.5/80kW–113/107hp–115/109PS
Fuel Injection
```

As 1.4 Litre, except:

Weight: Kerbweight (DIN) 1090/1120kg, gross vehicle weight 1555kg.

Volvo

Engine data (DIN): 4-cylinder in-line (88.9 x 80mm), 1986cm3; compression ratio 10:1; 84.5kW (113hp) [115PS] at 5700rpm, 42.6kW/L (57.1hp/L) [57.9PS/L]; 160Nm (118.1lbft) at 4200rpm; leaded premium grade.
Some countries: 82.5–87kW (111–117hp) [112–118PS].
With Catalyst: 80kW (107hp) [109PS]; 150Nm (110.7lbft).

Engine construction: Designated B 200E. 1 overhead camshaft (toothed belt); light-alloy cylinder head; crankshaft with 5 bearings; oil capacity 4L (3.8US qt); Bosch LE-Jetronic electronic fuel injection. Battery 12V 45/55Ah, alternator 55A; cooling system capacity 7L (6.6US qt).

Transmission: 5-speed manual, final drive ratio 3.82.

Gear ratios: 1st 3.71; 2nd 2.16; 3rd 1.37; 4th 1; 5th 0.83; R 3.68.

Chassis: Fuel tank 57L (12.5Gal) [15.1US Gal]; tyres 175/70 TR 13 or 185/60 HR 14, wheels 5.5J.

Performance: Max speed 115mph/185kmh (manufacturers test specifications), speed at 1000rpm in 5th gear 23.7mph/38.1kmh; acceleration 0 – 62mph/100kmh in 10.5secs; power to weight ratio from 12.9kg/kW (9.5kg/PS); consumption ECE 6.1/7.9/11.7L/100km (46.3/35.8/24.1mpg) [38.6/29.8/20.1US mpg].

Volvo 360 GLT

```
1.6 Litre Diesel
39.5kW-53hp-54PS
Injection Pump
```

As 1.4 Litre, except:

Weight: Kerbweight (DIN) 1050kg, gross vehicle weight 1500kg.

Engine data (DIN): 4-cylinder in-line (78 x 83.5mm), 1596cm3; compression ratio 22.5:1; 39.5kW (53hp) [54PS] at 4800rpm, 29.4k/L (33.4hp/L) [33.8PS/L]; 102Nm (73.5lbft) at 2250rpm.

Engine construction: Designated D 16. 1 overhead camshaft (toothed belt); CAV Rotodiesel injection pump. 12V 66Ah battery.

Transmission: 5-speed manual, final drive ratio 3.82.

Gear ratios: 1st 3.71; 2nd 2.16; 3rd 1.37; 4th 1; 5th 0.83; R 3.68.

Chassis: Fuel tank 48L (10.5Gal) [12.7US Gal]; tyres 175/70 SR 13 or 155 SR 13, tyres 5J.

Performance: Max speed 87mph/140kmh (manufacturers test specifications), speed at 1000rpm in 5th gear 20.8mph/33.5kmh; acceleration 0 - 62mph/100kmh 20secs; power to weight ratio 26kg/kW (19.4kg/PS); consumption ECE 4.7/7.4/7.0L/100km (60.1/38.2/40.4mpg) [50/31.8/33.6US mpg].

Volvo 440

New model. Middle of the range Saloon/Sedan with 1.7 Litre fuel engine from Renault with 78hp or 118hp front wheel drive, transverse engine. Chassis and suspension of Coupe 480. Launched June 1988.

```
1.7 Litre
60/58kW-80/78hp-82/79PS
1 2V Carb
```

Engine for DL and GL

Body, Weight: Coupe 5-door, 5-seater; kerbweight (DIN) approx 1010kg, gross vehicle weight 1500kg.

Engine data (DIN): 4-cylinder in-line (81 x 83.5mm), 1721cm3; compression ratio 9.2:1; 60kW (80hp) [82PS] at 5100rpm, 34.9kW/L (46.8hp/L) [47.6PS/L]; 130Nm (95.9lbft) at 3300rpm.
With unregulated Catalyst: 58kW (78hp) [79PS] at 5000rpm, 33.7kW/L (45.2hp/L) [45.9PS/L]; 128Nm (94.5lbft) at 3300rpm; unleaded regular grade.

Engine construction: Designated B18K/B18KD. Transverse engine block with transmission and differential transverse. 1 overhead camshaft (toothed belt); light-alloy cylinder head; wet cylinder liners; 5 bearing crankshaft; oil capacity 5.3L (5.0US qt); 1 downdraught 2V carb. 12V 55Ah, alternator 60A; cooling system capacity approx 7L (6.6US qt).

Transmission (to front wheels): 5-speed manual, final drive ratio 3.733.

Gear ratios: 1st 3.727; 2nd 2.053; 3rd 1.320; 4th 0.967; 5th 0.794; (F 0,758); R 3.545.

Chassis: Integral body; front sub frame; front McPherson struts (coil springs and coaxial telescopic damper), lower A arm; antiroll bar, rear rigid axle, Watt linkage, Panhard rod, coil springs, telescopic damper. Servo/power assisted brakes, optional ABS (Teves), front disc diameter 26cm, rear drums; handbrake to rear wheel; rack and pinion steering, GL with optional power assistance; fuel tank 48/50L (10.5/11Gal) [12.7/13.2US Gal]; tyres 165/70 TR 14, wheel rims 5.5".

Dimensions: Wheelbase 250.5cm, track 142/142.5cm, clearance 12.5cm, turning circle 11.1m. Load space 11.7-36.2cu ft (330-1025dm3). Length 431cm, width 168cm, height 138/140.5cm.

Performance: Max speed 106mph/170kmh (manufacturers test specification), speed at 1000rpm in 5th gear 22.7mph/36.5kmh; acceleration 0 - 62mph/100kmh 12.5secs; power to weight ratio from 16.8kg/kW (12.3kg/PS); consumption approx 6-10L/100km (47.1-28.2mpg) [39.2-23.5US mpg].

Volvo 440 GL

```
1.7 Litre
66/64kW-88/86hp-90/87PS
1 2V Carb
```

Engine for DL, GL, GLE and GLT

As 80/78hp, except:

Weight: Kerbweight (DIN) approx 1015kg, gross vehicle weight 1510kg.

Engine data (DIN): 4-cylinder in-line (81 x 83.5mm), 1721cm3; compression ratio 9.5:1; 66kW (88hp) [90PS] at 5800rpm, 38.5kW/L (51.6hp/L) [52.3PS/L]; 131Nm (96.7lbft) at 3600rpm.
With unregulated Catalyst: Compression ratio 9.5:1; 64kW (86hp) [87PS] at 5700rpm, 37.2kW/L (49.8hp/L) [50.6PS/L]; 130Nm (95.9lbft) at 3600rpm.

Engine construction: Designated B18KP/B18kPD. 1 downdraught compound carb.

Chassis: GLE with power assisted steering; tyres for GLE and GLT 175/65 TR 14.

Performance: Max speed 109mph/175kmh (manufacturers test specification), speed at 1000rpm in 5th gear 23.2mph/37.3kmh; acceleration 0 - 62mph/100kmh 11.5secs; power to weight ratio from 15.4kg/kW (11.3kg/PS); consumption ECE 5.1/6.9/9.4L/100km (55.4/40.9/30.1mpg) [46.1/34.1/25US mpg].

Volvo 440 GLT

Volvo

1.7 Litre
80/70kW–107/94hp–109/95PS
Fuel Injection

Engine for GL/GLE/GLT Injection

As 80/78hp, except:

Weight: Kerbweight (DIN) from 1030kg, gross vehicle weight: 1520kg.

Engine data (DIN): 4-cylinder in-line (81 x 83.5mm), 1721cm3; compression ratio 10.5:1; 80kW (107hp) [109PS] at 5800rpm, 46.5kW/L (62.3hp/L) [63.3PS/L]; 140Nm (103.3lbft) at 4100rpm.
With Catalyst: Compression ratio 9.5:1; 70kW (94hp) [95PS] at 5400rpm, 40.7kW/L (54.5hp/L) [55.2PS/L]; 140Nm (103.3lbft) at 4100rpm.

Engine construction: Designated B18E/B18ED/B18F. Electronic fuel injection. 70A alternator.

Transmission: 5-speed manual, final drive ratio 4.067, Catalyst 3.733.

Gear ratios: 1st 3.727; 2nd 2.053; 3rd 1.32; 4th 0.967; 5th 0.794; R 3.545.

Chassis: For 107hp GLE/GLT front disc brakes; GLE with power assisted steering; tyres for GLE and GLT 175/65 TR 14.

Performance: Max speed 115mph/185kmh, Catalyst 112mph/180kmh (manufacturers test specification), speed at 1000rpm in 5th gear 21.3mph/34.2kmh; acceleration 0 - 62mph/100kmh 10.8secs, Catalyst 11secs; power to weight ratio from 12.9kg/kW (9.4kg/PS); consumption ECE 5.8/7.5/10.8L/100km (48.7/37.7/26.2mpg) [40.6/31.4/21.8US mpg].

Volvo 440 Turbo

1.7 Litre Turbo
88kW–118hp–120PS
Fuel Injection

Engine for Turbo

As 80/78hp, except:

Weight: Kerbweight (DIN) approx 1065kg, gross vehicle weight 1540kg.

Engine data (DIN): 4-cylinder in-line (81 x 83.5mm), 1721cm3; compression ratio 8.1:1; 88kW (118hp) [120PS] at 5400rpm, 51.1kW/L (68.5hp/L) [69.7PS/L]; 175Nm (129.2lbft) at 1800-4600rpm.
With Catalyst: Identical data.

Engine construction: Designated B18FTM/B18FT. Bosch LH-Jetronic electronic fuel injection. 1 Garrett T2 turbocharger, max charge-air pressure 0.28 bar, intercooler. 70A alternator.

Transmission: 5-speed manual, final drive ratio 3.733.

Gear ratios: 1st 3.091; 2nd 1.842; 3rd 1.32; 4th 0.967; 5th 0.758; R 3.545.

Chassis: Front disc brakes; power assisted steering; tyres 185/60 HR 14.

Performance: Max speed approx 124mph/200kmh (manufacturers test specification), speed at 1000rpm in 5th gear 23.2mph/37.4kmh; acceleration 0 - 62mph/100kmh 9 secs; power to weight ratio from 12.1kg/kW (8.9kg/PS); consumption ECE 6.4/8.3/11L/100km (44.1/34/25.7mpg) [36.8/28.3/21.4US mpg].

Volvo 480

4-seater Coupe with tailgate, front wheel drive and 1.7 Litre injection engine; first model of a new generation of medium size vehicles from Volvo. Launched Geneva 1986, Turbo version for 1988.

1.7 Litre
80/70kW–107/94hp–109/95PS
Fuel Injection

Body, Weight: 3-door Coupe, 4-seater, kerbweight (DIN) 1010kg, gross vehicle weight 1355kg.

Engine data (Unregulated Catalyst, DIN): 4-cylinder in-line (81 x 83.5mm). 1721cm3; compression ratio 10.5:1; 80kW (107hp) [109PS] at 5800rpm, 46.5kW/L (62.3hp/L) [63.3PS/L]; 140Nm (103.3lbft) at 4000rpm.
With Catalyst: Compression ratio 9.5:1; 70kW (94hp) [95PS] at 5400rpm, 40.7kW/L (54.5hp/L) [55.2PS/L]; 140Nm (103.3lbft) at 4100rpm; unleaded regular grade.

Engine construction: Transverse mounted engine block and transmission assembly, 1 overhead camshaft (toothed belt); light-alloy cylinder head, wet cylinder liners; crankshaft with 5 bearings; oil capacity 5.3L (5US qt). Renix electronic fuel injection, Catalyst variants Bosch L4-Jetronic 12V 55Ah battery, 70A alternator; cooling system capacity 7L (6.6US qt).

Transmission (to front wheels): 5-speed manual, final drive ratio 4.067, Catalyst 3.73.

Gear ratios: 1st 3.091; 2nd 1.842; 3rd 1.320; 4th 0.967; 5th 0.758; R 3.545.

Chassis: Integral body; front McPherson struts (coil springs and co-axial telescopic damper), lower control arm, antiroll bar, rear rigid axle, Watt linkage, Panhard rod, coil springs, telescopic damper. Servo/power assisted disc brakes, disc diameter front 26cm, rear 22.8cm optional ABS (Teves); rear mechanical handbrake; power assisted rack and pinion steering; fuel tank 46/48L (10.1/10.5Gal) [12.2/12.7US Gal), tyres 185/60 HR 14, wheels 5.5J.

Dimensions: Wheelbase 250.5cm, track 141.5/142.5cm, clearance 11cm, turning circle 11.1m, load space 5.6/23.3cu ft (160/660dm3), length 426cm, width 168.5/171cm, height 132cm.

Performance: Max speed 118mph/190kmh, Catalyst 112mph/180kmh (manufacturers test specifications), speed at 1000rpm in 5th gear 20.3mph/32.7kmh; acceleration 0 - 62mph/100kmh 9.8secs, Catalyst 10.5secs; standing km 31secs; power to weight ratio from 12.6kg/kW (9.3kg/PS); consumption ECE 5.9/7.3/10.6L/100km (47.9/38.7/26.6pg) [39.9/32.2/22.2US mpg].

Volvo 480 ES

1.7 Litre Turbo
88kW–118hp–120PS
Fuel Injection

As 107hp, except:

Body, Weight: 3-door Coupe, 4-seater; kerbweight (DIN) 1025kg, gross vehicle weight 1410kg.

Engine data (DIN): 4-cylinder in-line (81 x 83.5mm), 1721cm3, compression ratio 8.1:1; 88kW (118hp) [120PS] at 5400rpm, 51.1kW/L (68.5hp/L) [69.7PS/L]; 175Nm (129.1lbft) at 4600rpm; leaded premium grade.
With Catalyst: 170Nm (125.5lbft) at 4000rpm.
Japanese Version: 85kW (114hp) [115PS] a 5400rpm; 175Nm (129lbft) at 4200rpm.

Engine construction: Bosch LH-Jetronic electronic fuel injection; 1 Garrett T2 Turbocharger, max boost pressure 0.28bar, charge-air cooler.

Transmission: 5-speed manual, final drive ratio 3.73.

Chassis: ABS (System Teves).

Performance: Max speed 124mph/200kmh, Catalyst 121mph/195kmh (manufacturers test specifications), speed at 1000rpm in 5th gear 23.2mph/37.4kmh; acceleration 0 - 62mph/100kmh 9.0secs, power to weight from 11.6kg/kW (8.5kg/PS); consumption ECE 6.3/8.1/11.0L/100km (44.8/34.9/25.7mpg) [37.3/29/21.4US mpg].

Volvo

Volvo 480 Turbo

Volvo 240

240 – 240 Turbo – 240 Diesel

Medium size vehicle with a 2.0 or 2.1 Litre engine. Launched August 1974. Paris 1978; 244 and 245 available with a diesel engine. August 1979; 2.3 Litre engine. Paris 1980; available with a 2.3 Litre carb engine, Estate/Station Wagon with Turbo.

```
2 Litre
74.5kW–100hp–101PS
1 Carb
```

Body, Weight: 2–door Saloon/Sedan, kerbweight 1235kg, gross vehicle weight 1780kg. 4–door Saloon/Sedan, 5–seater; kerbweight 1250kg, gross vehicle weight 1780kg. 5–door Estate/Station Wagon, 5–seater, kerbweight 1310kg, gross vehicle weight 1930kg.

Engine data (DIN): 4–cylinder in–line (88.9 x 80mm), 1986cm3; compression ratio 10:1; 74.5kW (100hp) [101PS] at 5400rpm, 37.4kW/L (50.1hp/L) [50.8PS/L]; 160Nm (118.1lbft) at 2400rpm; leaded premium grade.
Some countries (with electronic fuel injection): Compression ratio 10:1; 85kW (114hp) [116PS].

Engine construction: Designated B 20 K; engine inclined 20deg to the right; 1 overhead camshaft (toothed belt), light–alloy cylinder head; crankshaft with 5 bearings; oil capacity 3.8L (3.6US qt); 1 Solex CISAC W 7 DC downdraught carb. Battery 12V 60Ah; alternator 55A; cooling system capacity 9.5L (9US qt).

Transmission (to rear wheels): a) 4–speed manual, final drive ratio 3.31; 3.54.
b) 5–speed manual, final drive ratio 3.31.

Gear ratios: a) 4–speed manual: 1st 4.33; 2nd 2.32; 3rd 1.47; 5th 1; R 3.96.
b) 5–speed manual. 1st 4.03; 2nd 2.16; 3rd 1.37; 4th 1; 5th 0.83; R 2.21.

Chassis: Integral body; front keystone A arm, McPherson struts, antiroll bar, rear rigid axle, semi–trailing arms, Panhard rod, antiroll bar; coil springs, telescopic damper. Servo/power assisted disc brakes, hand brake to separate rear drums; rack and pinion steering, optional power assisted; fuel tank 60L (13.2Gal) [15.9US Gal]; tyres 185 SR 14, wheels 5.5".

Dimensions: Wheelbase 265cm, track 143/136cm, clearance 18cm, turning circle 9.8m; load space 14.9cu ft (395dm3), Estate/Station Wagon 42.4cu ft (1200dm3), length 479cm, width 172cm, height 143cm, Estate/Station Wagon 146cm.

Volvo 240 GL

Performance: Max speed 99mph/160kmh (manufacturers test specifications), speed at 1000rpm in 4th gear 21.8mph/35.1kmh; acceleration 0 – 62mph/100kmh 14secs; power to weight ratio from 16.6kg/kW (12.2kg/PS); consumption ECE 6.6/9.1/11.6L/100km (42.8/31/24.4mpg) [35.6/25.8/20.3US mpg].

```
2.3 Litre
83kW–111hp–113PS
1 Carb
```

As 2 Litre, except:

Body, Weight: 4–door Saloon/Sedan, 5–seater; kerbweight (DIN) 1280kg, gross vehicle weight 1780kg. 5–door Estate/Station Wagon, 5–seater; kerbweight (DIN) 1330kg, gross vehicle weight 1950kg.

Engine data (Catalyst, DIN): 4–cylinder in–line (96 x 80mm), 2316cm3, compression ratio 9.8:1; 83kW (111hp) [113PS] at 5100rpm, 35.8kW/L (48hp/L) [48.8PS/L]; 185Nm (136.5lbft) at 3000rpm; unleaded premium grade.

Engine construction: Designated B 23 A. 1 Solex CISAC horizontal carb.

Transmission: a) 4–speed manual with overdrive, final drive ratio 3.54.
b) Aisin–Warner Type 71 automatic, hydraulic torque converter and 4–speed Planetary gear set, selector lever in the middle, final drive ratio 3.73.

Gear ratios: a) 5–speed manual: 1st 4.03; 2nd 2.16; 3rd 1.37; 4th 1; 5th 0.83; R 2.21.
b) Automatic: Max torque multiplication in converter 2 times, Planetary gear set ratios: 1st 2.45; 2nd 1.45; 3rd 1; 4th 0.69; R 2.21.

Chassis: Optional power assisted steering; tyres 175 SR 14, wheels 5J; Estate/Station Wagon 185 SR 14, wheels 5.5J.

Performance: Max speed 106mph/170kmh, automatic 103mph/165kmh (manufacturers test specifications), speed at 1000rpm in 4th gear 20.4mph/32.8kmh; acceleration 0 – 62mph/100kmh 12.5secs, automatic 13.5secs. power to weight ratio from 15.4kg/kW (11.3kg/PS); consumption ECE 6.7/9.3/13.0L/100km (42.2/30.4/21.7mpg) [35.1/25.3/18.1US mpg], automatic 7.6/10.1/12.9L/100km (37.2/28/21.9mpg) [30.9/23.5/18.2US mpg].

Volvo 240 GL

```
2.3 Litre
96/85.5kW–129/115hp–131/116PS
Fuel Injection
```

As 2 Litre, except:

Body, Weight: 4–door Saloon/Sedan, 5–seater; kerbweight 1300kg, gross vehicle weight 1780kg. 5–door Estate/Station Wagon, 5–seater; kerbweight 1360kg, gross vehicle weight 1850kg.

Engine data (DIN): 4–cylinder in–line (96 x 80mm), 2316cm3; compression ratio 10.3:1; 96kW (129hp) [131PS] at 5400rpm, 41.4kW/L (55.5hp/L) [56.6PS/L]; 190Nm (140.2lbft) at 3600rpm, leaded premium grade.
With Catalyst: 85.5kW (115hp) [116PS] at 5100rpm, 36.8kW/L (49.3hp/L) [50.1PS/L]; 192Nm (141.7lbft) at 3000rpm; unleaded premium grade.
Some countries: Compression ratio 9.8:1; 83kW (111hp) [113PS]; 185Nm (136.5lbft).

Engine construction: Designated B 23 E. Bosch K–Jetronic mechanical fuel injection.

Transmission: a) 4–speed manual with overdrive, final drive ratio 3.73.
b) Aisin–Warner Type 71 automatic, hydraulic torque converter and 4–speed Planetary gear set, selector lever in the middle, final drive ratio 3.73.

Gear ratios: a) 4–speed + OD: 1st 4.03; 2nd 2.16; 3rd 1.37; 4th 1; OD 0.797; R 3.68.
b) Automatic: Max torque multiplication in converter 2 times, Planetary gear set ratios: 1st 2.45; 2nd 1.45; 3rd 1; 4th 0.69; R 2.21.

Chassis: Power assisted steering; tyres 185/70 HR 14 or 195/60 HR 14, wheels 5.5J.

Performance: Max speed 112mph/180kmh, automatic 106mph/170kmh (manufacturers test specifications), speed at 1000rpm in 4th gear 19mph/30.5kmh, in OD 23.4mph/37.6kmh; acceleration 0 – 62mph/100kmh 11secs, automatic 12secs; power to weight ratio 13.5kg/kW (9.9kg/PS); consumption ECE 6.7/9.5/12.9L/100km (42.2/29.7/21.9mpg) [35.1/24.8/18.2US mpg], automatic 7.1/10.0/12.9L/100km (39.8/28.2/21.9mpg) [33.1/23.5/18.2US mpg].

```
            2.1 Litre Turbo
           114kW–153hp–155PS
              Fuel Injection
```

As 2 Litre, except:

Body, Weight: 4–door Saloon/Sedan, 5–seater; kerbweight (DIN) 1340kg, gross vehicle weight 1780kg. 5–door Estate/Station Wagon, 5–seater; kerbweight (DIN) 1390kg, gross vehicle weight 1900kg.

Engine data (DIN): 4–cylinder in–line (92 x 80mm), 2127cm3; compression ratio 7.5:1; 114kW (153hp) [155PS] at 5500rpm, 53.6kW/L (71.8hp/L) [72.9PS/L]; 240Nm (177.1lbft) at 3750rpm; leaded premium grade.
Some countries: (88.9 x 80mm), 1986cm3; 106.5kW (143hp) [145PS].
USA version (SAE net): 2316cm3; 119kW (160hp) [162PS]; 254Nm (187.5lbft).

Engine construction: Designated B 21 ET. 1 Garrett AiResearch TB 03 exhaust turbocharger; max boost pressure 0.7bar; Bosch K– Jetronic fuel injection.

Transmission: 4–speed manual and overdrive, final drive ratio 3.73, USA 3.91.

Gear ratios: 1st 4.03; 2nd 2.16; 3rd 1.37; 4th 1; OD 0.798; R 3.68.

Chassis: Power assisted steering, tyres 195/60 HR 15, wheels 6J.

Performance: Max speed 118mph/190kmh (manufacturers test specifications), speed at 1000rpm in OD 23.5mph/37.8kmh, acceleration 0 – 62mph/100kmh 9secs; power to weight ratio 11.4kg/kW (8.4kg/PS); consumption ECE 7.5/10.3/15.0L/100km (37.7/27.4/18.8mpg) [31.4/22.8/15US mpg], Estate/Station Wagon 7.8/11.0/15.5L/100km (36.2/25.7/18.2mpg) [30.2/21.4/15.2US mpg].

```
            2.4 Litre Diesel
           60.5kW–81hp–82PS
             Injection Pump
```

As 2 Litre, except:

Body, Weight: 4–door Saloon/Sedan, 5–seater; kerbweight (DIN) 1360kg, gross vehicle weight 1850kg. 5–door Estate/Station Wagon, 5–seater, kerbweight (DIN) 1400kg, gross vehicle weight 2000kg.

Engine data (DIN): 6–cylinder in–line (76.5 x 86.4mm), 2383cm3, compression ratio 23.0:1; 60.5kW (81hp) [82PS] at 4800rpm, 25.4kW/L (34hp/L) [34.4PS/L], 140Nm (103.3lbft) at 2800rpm.
Some countries: 58kW (78hp) [79PS].

Engine construction: Designated D 24, turbulence chamber diesel engine, 1 overhead camshaft (toothed belt), light–alloy cylinder head; crankshaft with 7 bearings; oil capacity 7L (6.6US qt); Bosch VE distributor injection pump, mechanical centrifugal governor, timing device, cold start enrichment. Battery 12V 88Ah, alternator 55A; cooling system capacity 9.5L (9.0US qt).

Transmission: 4–speed manual with OD, final drive ratio 3.73.

Performance: Max speed 93mph/150kmh, automatic 90mph/145kmh (manufacturers test specifications), speed at 1000rpm in top gear 18.6mph/29.9kmh; acceleration 0 – 62mph/100kmh 17.5secs, automatic 20secs; power to weight ratio from 22.5kg/kW (16.6kg/PS); consumption ECE 5.6/8.1/8.9L/100km (50.4/34.9/31.7mpg) [42/29/26.4US mpg].

```
           Volvo 740 – 760
```

Large 4–door Saloon/Sedan, with 5–speed manual or automatic transmission. 760 launched February 1983, January 1984, 740. Chicago, February 1985; new Estate/Station Wagon. Autumn 1987; 760 with rear independent suspension and revised front end. Geneva 1988: 2.3 Litre engine 16V with 157hp.

```
               2.3 Litre
           86kW–115hp–117PS
              1 2V Carb
```

Engine for 740 GL

Body, Weight: 4–door Saloon/Sedan, 5–seater; kerbweight (DIN) from 1250kg; gross vehicle weight 1800kg. 5–door Estate/Station Wagon, 5/7–seater; kerbweight (DIN) from 1320kg; gross vehicle weight 1920kg.

Engine data (DIN): 4–cylinder in–line (96 x 80mm), 2316cm3; compression ratio 10.5:1; 86kW (115hp) [117PS] at 5200rpm, 37.2kW/L (49.8hp/L) [50.5PS/L]; 194Nm (143.2lbft) at 2500rpm, regular grade.
Some countries (with fuel injection): (88.9 x 80mm), 1986cm3; compression ratio 10:1; 87kW (117hp) [118PS]; 160Nm (118.1lbft); unleaded premium grade.

Engine construction: Designated B 23 A, 1 overhead camshaft (toothed belt); light–alloy cylinder head; crankshaft with 5 bearings; oil capacity 3.8L (3.6US qt); 1 Pierburg 2B5 horizontal 2V carb. Battery 12V 55Ah, alternator 55A, cooling system capacity 9.5L (9.0US qt).

Transmission (to rear wheels): a) 4–speed manual with overdrive, final drive ratio 3.31.
b) 5–speed manual, final drive ratio 3.54.
c) Aisin–Warner 71, 3–speed automatic with overdrive, hydraulic torque converter and Planetary gear set, selector lever in the middle, final drive ratio 3.91.

Gear ratios: a) 4–speed manual + OD: 1st 4.03; 2nd 2.16; 3rd 1.37; 4th 1; OD 0.79; R 3.68.
b) 5–speed manual: 1st 4.03; 2nd 2.16; 3rd 1.37; 4th 1; 5th 0.82; R 3.68.
c) Automatic: 1st 2.45; 2nd 1.45; 3rd 1; OD 0.69; R 2.21.

Chassis: Integral body; front McPherson struts with A arm, antiroll bar, rear rigid axle with semi–trailing arms and reaction strut, Panhard rod, antiroll bar, coil springs, telescopic damper. Servo/power assisted disc brakes, front ventilated; rear mechanical handbrake; power assisted rack and pinion steering; fuel tank 60L (13.2Gal) [15.9US Gal]; tyres 185/70 TR 14, Estate/Station Wagon 195/65 TR, wheels 5.5/6J.

Dimensions: Wheelbase 277cm, track 147/146cm, clearance 10.5cm, turning circle 9.9m, load space 17.7cu ft (500dm3), Estate/Station Wagon 35/75cu ft (990/2125dm3), length 478.5cm, width 175cm, height 141cm, Estate/Station Wagon 143.5cm.

Performance: Max speed 111mph/178kmh, automatic 106mph/170kmh (manufacturers test specifications), speed at 1000rpm in 5th gear 24.5mph/39.4kmh; acceleration 0 – 62mph/100kmh 12.5secs, automatic 13.0secs (manufacturers test specifications); power to weight ratio 14.5kg/kW (10.7kg/PS); consumption ECE 6.6/8.9/11.8L/100km (42.8/31.7/23.9mpg) [35.6/26.4/19.9US mpg], automatic 6.9/9.2/12.1L/100km (40.9/30.7/23.3mpg) [34.1/25.6/19.4US mpg].

Volvo 740 GL

```
               2.3 Litre
       96.5/85.5kW–129/115hp–131/116PS
              Fuel Injection
```

Engine for 740 GL/GLE

As 115hp, except:

Engine data (DIN): 4–cylinder in–line (96 x 80mm), 2316cm3, compression ratio 10.3:1; 96.5kW (129hp) [131PS] at 5500rpm, 41.6kW/L (55.7hp/L) [56.6PS/L]; 190Nm (140.2lbft) at 3600rpm.
With Catalyst: Compression ratio 9.8:1; 85.5kW (115hp) 116PS at 5400rpm; 185Nm (136.5lbft) at 2750rpm, unleaded regular grade.
Some countries: 83kW (111hp) [113PS].

Engine construction: Designated B 23 E. Bosch K–Jetronic mechanical fuel injection (Catalyst, LH–Jetronic). Alternator 80A.

Transmission: a) 4–speed manual with overdrive, final drive ratio 3.54.
b) Automatic ZF 4 HP–22, 3–speed with overdrive, hydraulic torque converter and Planetary gear set, final drive ratio 3.91.

Gear ratios: a) 4–speed manual: 1st 4.03; 2nd 2.16; 3rd 1.37; 4th 1; OD 0.79; R 3.68.
b) Automatic: Max torque multiplication in converter 2 times, Planetary gear set ratios: 1st 2.478; 2nd 1.478; 3rd 1; 4th 0.73; R 2.09.

Chassis: Fuel tank 82L (18Gal) [21.7US Gal]

Volvo

Performance: Max speed 112mph/180kmh, automatic and Catalyst 107mph/172kmh (manufacturers test specifications), speed at 1000rpm in OD gear 25.4mph/40.9kmh, acceleration 0 – 62mph/100kmh 10.0secs, Catalyst 12.2secs, automatic 11.0secs (manufacturers test specifications); power to weight ratio 13.5kg/kW (9.9kg/PS); consumption ECE 7.0/9.2/13.0L/100km (40.4/30.7/21.7mpg) [33.6/25.6/18.1US mpg], Catalyst 6.6/8.9/11.3L/100km (42.8/31.7/25mpg) [35.6/26.4/20.8US mpg], automatic 6.8/9.0/13.0L/100km (41.5/31.4/21.7mpg) [34.6/26.1/18.1US mpg].

Volvo 740 GLE

2.3 Litre DOHC 16V
117kW-157hp-159PS
Fuel Injection

As 115hp, except:

Body, Weight: 4-door, Saloon/Sedan, 5-seater. Kerbweight (DIN) from 1340kg; gross vehicle weight 1840kg; 5-door Estate/Station Wagon, 5/7-seater; kerbweight (DIN) from 1400kg; gross vehicle weight 1930kg.

Engine data (Catalyst DIN): 4-cylinder in-line (96 x 80mm), 2316cm3; compression ratio 10:1; 117kW (157hp) [159PS] at 5800rpm; 50.5kW/L (67.7hp/L) [68.7PS/L]; 210Nm (155lbft) at 4450rpm; unleaded regular grade.
For some countries: 114kW (153hp) [155PS].
Italian version: (88.9 x 80mm), 1986cm3; 100kW (134hp) [136PS].

Engine construction: Designated B234F. Hydraulic tappets, valves in V 38deg, 4 valves per cylinder; 2 overhead camshafts (toothed belt); 2 anti vibration arms; Bosch fuel injection. Battery 12V 55Ah, alternator 70A.

Transmission (to rear wheels): 4-speed manual with OD, final drive ratio 3.73.

Gear ratios: 1st 4.03; 2nd 2.16; 3rd 1.37; 4th 1; OD 0.79; R 3.68.

Chassis: Optional ABS (Bosch system); tyres 185/65 HR 15, Estate/Station Wagon 195/65 HR 15, wheel rims 6J.

Performance: Max speed 118mph/190kmh, Estate/Station Wagon 121mph/195kmh (manufacturers test specification), speed at 1000rpm in OD 24mph/38.6kmh, acceleration 0 - 62mph/100kmh 10.0secs, Estate/Station Wagon 10.5secs; power to weight ratio 11.5kg/kW (8.4kg/PS); consumption approx 9-12L/100km (31.4-23.5mpg) [26.1-19.6US mpg].

Volvo 740 GLT

2.3 Litre Turbo
134/115kW–180/154hp–182/156PS
Fuel Injection

Engine for 740/760 Turbo

As 115hp, except:

Body, Weight: 4-door Saloon/Sedan, 5-seater; kerbweight (DIN) from 1330kg, gross vehicle weight 1820kg. 5-door Estate/Station Wagon, 5/7-seater; kerbweight (DIN) from 1390kg; gross vehicle weight 1920kg.

Engine data (DIN): 4-cylinder in-line (96 x 80mm), 2316cm3; compression ratio 9.0:1; 134kW (180hp) [182PS] from 5800rpm; 57.8kW/L (77.5hp/L) [78.6PS/L]; 260Nm (191.8lbft) from 3400rpm; leaded premium grade.

With Catalyst: Compression ratio 8.7:1; 115kW (154hp) [156PS] at 4800rpm; 242Nm (178.6lbft) at 3300rpm.
Other countries: 110.5–132kW (148–177hp) [150– 179PS].

Engine construction: Designated B 23 ET; 1 Garrett T 03 exhaust turbocharger, charge–air cooler; max boost pressure 0.53bar; Bosch Motronic DME–L fuel injection. Battery 12V 55Ah, alternator 70A.

Transmission: a) 4–speed manual with overdrive, final drive ratio 3.54.
b) Automatic ZF 4 HP-22, 3–speed with overdrive, hydraulic torque converter and Planetary gear set, selector lever in the middle, final drive ratio 3.73.

Gear ratios: a) 4-speed manual: 1st 4.03; 2nd 2.16; 3rd 1.37; 4th 1; OD 0.79; R 3.68.
b) Automatic: Max torque multiplication in converter 2 times, Planetary gear set ratios: 1st 2.478; 2nd 1.478; 3rd 1; 4th 0.73; R 2.09.

Chassis: Fuel tank 82L (18Gal) [21.7US Gal]; tyres 195/60 HR 15, wheels 6J.

Performance: Max speed 124mph/200kmh, automatic and Catalyst 121mph/195kmh (manufacturers test specifications), speed at 1000rpm in 4th gear 19.8mph/31.8kmh, acceleration 0 – 62mph/100kmh 8.5secs, Catalyst 9.5secs, automatic 8.5secs (manufacturers test specifications), power to weight ratio 9.9kg/kW (7.3kg/PS); consumption ECE 7.6/9.8/14.2L/100km (37.2/28.8/19.9mpg) [30.9/24/16.6US mpg], Catalyst 7.3/9.8/13.2L/100km (38.7/28.8/21.4mpg) [32.2/24/17.8US mpg], automatic 8.2/10.3/15.1L/100km (34.4/27.4/18.7mpg) [28.7/22.8/15.6US mpg].

Volvo 740 Turbo

2.85 Litre V6
125/108kW–168/145hp–170/147PS
Fuel Injection

Engine for 760 GLE

As 115hp, except:

Body, Weight: 4–door Saloon/Sedan, 5–seater; kerbweight (DIN) from 1475kg; gross vehicle weight 1820kg. 5–door Estate/Station Wagon, 5/7–seater; kerbweight (DIN) from 1415kg; gross vehicle weight 1920kg.

Engine data (DIN): 6–cylinder in V 90deg (91 x 73mm), 2849cm3; compression ratio 10:1; 125kW (168hp) [170PS] at 5400rpm; 43.9kW/L (58.8hp/L) [59.7PS/L]; 240Nm (177.1lbft) at 4500rpm.
For some countries: 123kW (165hp) [167PS].
With Catalyst: Compression ratio 8.8:1; 108kW (145hp) [147PS] at 5100rpm; 235Nm (173.4lbft) at 3750rpm; unleaded regular grade.
For some countries: 105kW (141hp) [143PS].

Engine construction: Designated B 28 E. Valves in V; 2 x 1 overhead camshaft (chain); light–alloy cylinder head and block, crankshaft with 4 bearings; oil capacity 6.5L (6.1US qt), Bosch K–Jetronic fuel injection. Battery 12V 66Ah, alternator 90A.

Volvo 760 GLE

Transmission: Automatic, 3–speed with overdrive, hydraulic torque converter and Planetary gear set, final drive ratio 3.54.

Gear ratios: Automatic: 1st 2.45; 2nd 1.45; 3rd 1; OD 0.69; R 2.21.

Chassis: Rear transverse control arms and trailing arms; Bosch ABS System; fuel tank 80L (17.6Gal) [21.1US Gal]; tyres 195/60 HR 15.

Volvo

Dimensions: Saloon/Sedan; wheelbase 357cm, length 560cm, height 150cm.

Performance: Max speed 116mph/187kmh acceleration 0 – 62mph/100kmh 10secs (manufacturers test specifications), power to weight ratio 11.8kg/kW (8.7kg/PS); consumption ECE 8.8/11.3/15.7L/100km (32.1/25/18mpg) [26.7/20.8/15US mpg].

```
2.4 Litre Diesel
60kW-80hp-82PS
Injection Pump
```

Engine for 740 GL Diesel

As 115hp, except:

Body, Weight: 4–door Saloon/Sedan, 5–seater; kerbweight (DIN) from 1330kg; gross vehicle weight 1820kg.

Engine data (DIN): 6–cylinder in-line (76.5 x 86.4mm), 2383cm3; compression 23.0:1; 60kW (80hp) [82PS] at 4800rpm, 25.4kW/L (34hp/L) [34.4PS/L]; 140Nm (103.3lbft) at 2800rpm.

Engine construction: Designated D 24; turbulence chamber diesel engine; 1 overhead camshaft (toothed belt); light–alloy cylinder head; crankshaft with 7 bearings; oil capacity 6.5L (6.1US qt); Bosch VE distributor injection pump, mechanical centrifugal governor, timing device, cold starting enrichment. Battery 12V 90Ah.

Transmission: 5–speed manual, final drive ratio 3.73.

Performance: Max speed 96mph/155kmh (manufacturers test specifications), speed at 1000rpm in 4th gear 18.8mph/30.2kmh; acceleration 0 – 62mph/100kmh 17.5secs; power to weight ratio 22.2kg/kW (16.2kg/PS); consumption ECE 6.1/8.3/9.4L/100km (46.3/34/30.1mpg) [38.6/28.3/25US mpg].

```
2.4L Turbodiesel
90kW-121hp-122PS
Injection Pump
```

Engine for 760 GLE Turbodiesel

As 115hp, except:

Body, Weight: 4–door Saloon/Sedan, 5–seater, kerbweight (DIN) from 1500kg, gross vehicle weight 1950kg. 5–door Estate/Station Wagon, 5/7–seater, kerbweight (DIN) from 1445kg, gross vehicle weight 1920kg.

Engine data (DIN): 6–cylinder in-line (76.5 x 86.4mm), 2383cm3; compression ratio 23.0:1; 90kW (121hp) [122PS] at 4800rpm, 37.8kW/L (50.7hp/L) [51.2PS/L]; 235Nm (173.4lbft) at 2400rpm.
German and Italian version: 82.5kW (111hp) [112PS]; 205Nm (151.3lbft).
Switzerland and USA version (SAE net): 80kW (107hp) [109PS]; 205Nm (151.3lbft).
Also: 85kW (114hp) [116PS].

Engine construction: Designated D 24 TD. Turbulence chamber diesel engine; 1 overhead camshaft (toothed belt); light–alloy cylinder head, crankshaft with 7 bearings; oil capacity 6.5L (6.1US qt). Bosch VE distributor fuel injection pump, mechanical centrifugal governor, timing device, cold starting enrichment; Garrett T 03 exhaust turbocharger, max boost pressure 0.7bar.

Transmission: (to rear wheels) a) 4–speed manual with overdrive, final drive ratio 3.54.
b) ZF 4 HP–22 automatic, 3–speed with overdrive, hydraulic torque converter and Planetary gear set, selector lever in the middle, final drive ratio 3.73.

Gear ratios: a) 4–speed manual: 1st 4.03; 2nd 2.16; 3rd 1.37; 4th 1; OD 0.79; R 3.68.
b) Automatic: Max torque multiplication in converter 2 times, Planetary gear set ratios: 1st 2.478; 2nd 1.478; 3rd 1; 4th 0.73; R 2.09.

Chassis: ABS System Bosch; tyres 195/65 HR 15.

Volvo 760 GLE Turbodiesel

Performance: Max speed 113mph/181kmh, automatic 109mph/175kmh; acceleration 0 – 62mph/100kmh 12.0secs, automatic 13.0secs (manufacturers test specifications); power to weight ratio 16.7kg/kW (12.3kg/PS); consumption ECE 5.6/7.9/9.2L/100km (50.4/35.8/30.7mpg) [42/29.8/25.6US mpg] automatic 6.0/8.7/9.2L/100km (47.1/32.5/30.7mpg) [39.2/27/25.6US mpg].

Volvo 780

Coupe based on the Saloon/Sedan 760, body from Bertone, 2.85 Litre V6 or Turbodiesel engine and automatic transmission. Launched Geneva 1985. Catalyst and Turbodiesel with increased power for 1988.

```
2.85 Litre V6
125/108kW-168/145hp-170/147PS
Fuel Injection
```

Body, Weight: 2–door Coupe, 4/5–seater; kerbweight (DIN) 1420kg; gross vehicle weight approx 1800kg.

Engine data (DIN): 6–cylinder in V 90deg (91 x 73mm), 2849cm3, compression ratio 10:1; 125kW (168hp) [170PS] at 5400rpm; 43.9kW/L (58.8hp/L) [59.7PS/L]; 240Nm (177.1lbft) at 4500rpm.
With Catalyst: Compression ratio 8.8:1; 108kW (145hp) [147PS] at 5100rpm; 235Nm (173.4lbft) at 3750rpm; unleaded regular grade.
Some countries with 2 Litre turbo: 4–cylinder in–line (88.9 x 80mm), 1986cm3; compression ratio 8.5; 117.5kW (158hp) [160PS]; 245Nm (181lbft).

Engine construction: Designated B 28 E. Valves in V; 2 x 1 overhead camshaft (chain); light–alloy cylinder head and block; wet cylinder liners; crankshaft with 4 bearings; oil capacity 5.8L (5.5US qt); Bosch LH–Jetronic electronic fuel injection. Battery 12V 50/90Ah, alternator 90/105A; cooling system capacity 9.8L (9.3US qt).

Transmission (rear wheels): a) 5–speed manual with overdrive, final drive ratio 3.54.
b) Aisin–Warner Type 71 automatic, hydraulic torque converter and 4–speed Planetary set, selector lever in the the middle, final drive rato 3.91.

Gear ratios: a) 5–speed manual: 1st 4.03; 2nd 2.16; 3rd 1.37; 4th 1; 5th 0.79; R 2.21.
b) Automatic: Max torque multiplication in converter 2 times, Planetary gear set ratios: 1st 2.45; 2nd 1.45; 3rd 1; 4th 0.69; AR 2.21.

Chassis: Integral body; front McPherson struts with A arm, antiroll bar, rear rigid axle with semi–trailing arms and reaction struts, Panhard rod, antiroll bar; coil springs, telescopic damper. Servo/power assisted disc brakes, front ventilated; mechanical handbrake on rear wheels; power assisted steering; fuel tank 60L (13.2Gal) [15.9US Gal]; tyres 205/60 HR 15, wheel rims 6J.

Dimension: Wheelbase 277cm, track 146/146cm, clearance 10.5cm, turning circle 9.9m, load space 17.1cu ft (485dm3), length 479cm, width 175cm, height 140cm.

Performance: Max speed 117mph/188kmh, Catalyst 110mph/177kmh (manufacturers test specifications), speed at 1000rpm at the speed 18.2mph/29.3kmh; acceleration 0 – 62mph/100kmh 10.2secs Catalyst 11.2sec (manufacturers test specifications); power to weight ratio 11.4kg/kW (8.4kg/PS) consumption ECE 8.7/11.1/16.0L/100km (32.5/25.4/17.7mpg) [27/21.2/14.7US mpg], Catalyst 9.1/11.6/15.9L/100km (31/24.4/17.8mpg) [25.8/20.3/14.9US mpg].

Volvo 780

```
2.4 Litre Turbodiesel
95kW-127hp-129PS
Injection Pump
```

As 168/145hp, except:

Weight: Kerbweight (DIN) 1470kg, gross vehicle weight 1830kg.

Volvo • Wartburg • Yue Loong

Engine data (DIN): 6-cylinder in-line (76.5 x 86.4mm), 2383cm3; compression ratio 23.0:1; 95kW (127hp) [129PS] at 4650rpm, 39.9kW/L (53.5hp/L) [54.1PS/L]; 250Nm (184.5lbft) at 2400rpm.
Some countries: 90kW (121hp) [122PS].

Engine construction: Designated D 24 TD. Turbulence chamber diesel engine; parallel valves. 1 overhead camshaft (toothed belt); light-alloy cylinder head, crankshaft with 7 bearings; oil capacity 6.5L (6.1US qt); Bosch VE distributor injection pump, mechanical centrifugal govenor, cold starting enrichment; Garrett T 03 exhaust turbocharger, max boost pressure 0.7bar; charge-air cooler. Battery 12V 88Ah, alternator 70A.

Transmission: Automatic or 4-speed manual with overdrive, final drive ratio 3.54.

Gear ratios: 4-speed manual with overdrive: 1st 4.03; 2nd 2.16; 3rd 1.37; 4th 1; OD 0.79; R 3.69.

Performance: Max speed over 115mph/185kmh (manufacturers test specifications), speed at 1000rpm in OD 25.5mph/41.0kmh; acceleration 0 – 62mph/100kmh 10.5secs (manufacturers test specifications); power to weight ratio 15.5kg/kW (11.4kg/PS); consumption ECE 6.0/8.2/9.5L/100km (47.1/34.4/29.7mpg) [39.2/28.7/24.8US mpg].

Volvo 780

WARTBURG — GDR

VEB Automobilwerk Eisenach, Rennbahn 8, 5900 Eisenach, GDR
Famous vehicle manufacturer based in the German Democratic Republic.

Wartburg 1.3

Famous medium size vehicle. Saloon/Sedan and Kombi with front wheel drive. From Autumn 1988 modified version with 1.3 litre, 4-cylinder, 4-stroke engine from VW.

Wartburg 1.3

1.3 Litre
43kW-57hp-58PS
1 Carb

Body, Weight: 4-door Saloon/Sedan, 5-seater; kerbweight (DIN) 900kg, gross vehicle weight 1320kg. 5-door Estate/Station Wagon, 5/7-seater; kerbweight (DIN) 950kg, gross vehicle weight 1400kg.

Engine data (DIN): 4-cylinder in-line (75 x 72mm), 992cm3; compression ratio 9.5:1; 43kW (57hp) [58PS] at 5400rpm, 33.8kW/L (45.3hp/L) [45.6PS/L]; 96Nm (70.8lbft) at 3500rpm; leaded regular grade.

Engine construction: Transverse front engine. Hydraulic tappets; 1 overhead camshaft (toothed belt); light-alloy cylinder head; 5 main bearing crankshaft; oil capacity 3L (2.8US qt); 1 34 TLA downdraught carb. Battery 12V 44Ah, alternator 53A; cooling system capacity 6.5L (6.1US qt).

Transmission (to front wheels): 4-speed manual, final drive ratio 4.267.

Gear ratios: 1st 3.250; 2nd 2.053; 3rd 1.342; 4th 0.956; R 3.077.

Chassis: Box section frame; front and rear independent suspension with coil springs and rubber supplementary springs, front with twin control arms, rear swinging axle, rear antiroll bar, telescopic dampers. Front disc brakes, rear drum brakes, disc diameter 23.8cm, mechanical handbrake to rear wheels; rack and pinion steering; fuel tank 44L (9.7Gal) [11.6US Gal], including 3–4L (.66–.88Gal) [.79–1.1US Gal] reserve; tyres 165 SR 13; 175/70 SR 13, wheel rims 4.5J.

Dimensions: Wheelbase 245cm, track 136/136cm, clearance min 12cm, turning circle 10.8m. Saloon/Sedan: load space 18.5cu ft (525dm3). Saloon/Sedan: length 422cm, width 164cm, height 149.5cm. Estate/Station Wagon: length 428cm, width 164cm, height 149.5cm.

Performance: Max speed 84mph/135kmh (manufacturers test specifications), speed at 1000rpm in 4th gear 17.8mph/26.8kmh; power to weight ratio from 20.9kg/kW (15.5kg/PS); consumption ECE 6.4L/100km (44.1mpg) [36.8US mpg] (manufacturers test specifications)

Wartburg 1.3 Tourist

YUE LOONG — RC

Yue Loong Motor Company Ltd, 150 Nanking East Rd, Sec 2 Taipei, Taiwan
Taiwanese manufacturer of vehicles using components from Nissan.

Yue Loong 101

5-door Saloon/Sedan based on the Nissan Stanza, body elements from Yue Loong, 1.6 or 1.8 Litre engine.

1.6 Litre
65kW-87hp-89PS
1 2V Carb

Body, Weight: 5-door notchback Saloon/Sedan, 5-seater; kerbweight (DIN) 1040kg.

Engine data (SAE net): 4-cylinder in-line (78 x 83.6mm), 1598cm3; compression ratio 9:1; 65kW (87hp) [89PS] at 5200rpm, 40.7kW/L (54.5hp/L) [55.7PS/L]; 131Nm (96.7lbft) at 3200rpm.

Engine construction: Designated Nissan CA 16S. Front transverse mounted engine, valves in V, 1 overhead camshaft (toothed belt); light-alloy cylinder head; crankshaft with 5 bearings; oil capacity 4L (3.8US qt); 1 downdraught 2V carb. Battery 12V 33/60Ah, alternator 60A; cooling system capacity 6.8L (6.4US qt).

Transmission (to rear wheels): 4-speed manual, final drive ratio 4.056.

Gear ratios: 1st 3.333; 2nd 1.955; 3rd 1.286; 4th 0.902; R 3.417.

Chassis: Integral body; front and rear independent suspension, front McPherson struts, A arm, antiroll bar, rear McPherson struts, double control arm and trailing arm, front and rear telescopic damper. Servo/power assisted brakes, front ventilated discs, rear drums, handbrake to rear wheels; rack and pinion steering, optional power assisted; fuel tank 55L (12.1Gal) [14.5US Gal]; tyres 165 SR 13, wheels 5J.

Yue Loong • Zastava

Dimensions: Wheelbase 247cm, track 143/141cm, clearance 13cm, turning circle 10m, length 445.5cm, width 168cm, height 138cm.

Performance: Max speed 112mph/180kmh (manufacturers test specifications), speed at 1000rpm in 4th gear 18.5mph/29.8kmh; power to weight ratio 16kg/kW (11.7kg/PS); consumption approx 7– 10L/100km (40.4–28.2mpg) [33.6–23.5US mpg].

Yue Loong 101

```
1.8 Litre
72kW–97hp–98PS
1 2V Carb
```

As 1.6 Litre, except:

Body, Weight: 5–door notchback Saloon/Sedan, 5–seater; kerbweight (DIN) 1060– 1090kg. 5–door fastback Saloon/Sedan, 5–seater; kerbweight (DIN) 1060–1080kg.

Engine data (SAE net): 4–cylinder in–line (82.7 x 83.6mm), 1796cm3, compression ratio 8.8:1; 72kW (97hp) [98PS] at 5200rpm, 40.1kW/L (53.7hp/L) [54.6PS/L]; 146Nm (107.7lbft) at 3200rpm.

Transmission (to front wheels): a) 5–speed manual, final drive ratio 4.056. b) Automatic, hydraulic torque converter and 3–speed Planetary gear set, selector lever in the middle, final drive ratio 3.6.

Gear ratios: a) 5–speed manual: 1st 3.333; 2nd 1.955; 3rd 1.286; 4th 0.902; 5th 0.733; R 3.417.
b) Automatic: Max torque multiplication in converter 2 times; Planetary gear set ratios: 1st 2.826; 2nd 1.543; 3rd 1; R 2.364.

Chassis: Tyres 175/70 HR 14, wheels 5.5J.

Performance: Max speed, fastback 118mph/190kmh, notchback 115mph/185kmh, automatic 112mph/180kmh (manufacturers test specifications), speed at 1000rpm in 5th gear 23.2mph/37.3kmh; power to weight from 14.7kg/kW (10.8kg/PS); consumption approx 8– 12L/100km (35.3–23.5mpg) [29.4–19.6US mpg].

ZASTAVA   YU

Zavodi Crvena Zastava, Spanskih Boraca 4, 3400 Kragujevac, Yugoslavia

Old Yugoslavian manufacturer of arms and industrial machinery, producing vehicles under license from Fiat.

Zastava Yugo

3–door Saloon/Sedan with a 4–cylinder Fiat engine, front wheel drive, suspension as the Fiat 127. Launched April 1980. Summer 1985: Export to the USA. From Spring 1989 also available as convertible/cabriolet.

```
903 cm3
33kW–44hp–45PS
1 Carb
```

Engine for Yugo 45

Body, Weight: 3–door Saloon/Sedan, 5–seater; kerbweight (DIN) from 720kg, gross vehicle weight 1080–1220kg.

Engine Data (DIN): 4–cylinder in–line (65 x 68mm), 903cm3, compression ratio 9:1; 33kW (44hp) [45PS] at 5600rpm, 36.6kW/L (49hp/L) [49.9PS/L]; 62Nm (45.8lbft) at 3000rpm; leaded premium grade.

Zastava Yugo 45

Engine construction: Designated 100GL. 0.64. Front transverse engine. Side camshaft (chain); light–alloy cylinder head, crankshaft with 3 bearings; oil capacity 3.6/3.9L (3.4/3.7US qt); 1 Weber 32 ICEV 31 downdraught carb. Battery 12V 24/34/44Ah, alternator 33/55A; water cooled.

Transmission (to front wheels): 4–speed manual (without direct drive), final drive ratio 4.071.

Gear ratios: 1st 3.91; 2nd 2.055; 3rd 1.348; 4th 0.963; R 3.615.
Or: 1st 3.58; 2nd 2.234; 3rd 1.45; 4th 1.04; R 3.71.

Chassis: Integral body; front independent suspension with McPherson struts, lower single control arm and antiroll bar, rear independent suspension with A arm, damper and self stabilizing transverse leaf spring, telescopic damper. Servo/power assisted brakes (optional), front disc, diameter 27cm, rear drums; rear mechanical handbrake; rack and pinion steering; fuel tank 30L (6.6Gal) [7.9US Gal]; of which 3–5L (.7Gal–1.1Gal) [.8–1.3US Gal] reserve; tyres 135 SR 13, 145 SR 13 or 155/70 SR 13, wheels 4–5J.

Dimensions: Wheelbase 215cm, track 131/131cm, turning circle 10m, load space 9.5–27.5cu ft (270/780dm3). Length 349/353cm, width 154cm, height 139cm.

Performance: Max speed 84–87mph/135–140kmh (manufacturers test specifications); speed at 1000rpm in top gear 15.8mph/25.4kmh; acceleration from 0 – 62mph/100kmh in 21.7secs; power to weight ratio 22.7kg/kW (16.7kg/PS); consumption ECE 6.2/7.9/9.4L/100km (45.6/35.8/30.1mpg) [37.9/29.8/25.0US mpg].

Zastava Yugo 65

```
1100/1300cm3
40.5/48kW–54/64hp–55/65PS
1 Carb
```

Engine for Yugo 55 and Cabriolet/Convertible

As 903cm3 Version, except:

Body, Weight: 3–door Saloon/Sedan, 4/5 seater; kerbweight (DIN) from 790–810kg, gross vehicle weight 1220kg. 2–door Cabriolet/Convertible, 4–seater, kerbweight (DIN) approx 750kg, gross vehicle weight approx 1200kg.

Engine data (DIN): 4–cylinder in–line (80 x 55.5mm) 1116cm3; compression ratio 9.2:1; 40.5kW (54hp) [55PS] at 6000rpm, 36.3kW/L (48.6hp/L) [49.3PS/L]; 80Nm (59lbft) at 3000rpm.
With Catalyst: 39kW (52hp) [53PS] at 5000rpm; 70Nm (51.7lbft) at 4600rpm.
Engine for 65: (86 x 55.5mm), 1290cm3; compression ratio 9.2:1; 48kW (64hp) [65PS] at 5800rpm, 37.2kW/L (49.8hp/L) [50.4PS/L]; 100Nm (73.8lbft) at 3900rpm.
Engine for cabriolet/convertible (with Bosch Motronic Injection): (86 x 55.5mm), 1290cm3; compression ratio 9.1:1; 56kW (75hp) [76PS] at 5800rpm.

Zastava

Engine construction: Designated 128 A.000. 1 overhead camshaft (toothed belt); crankshaft with 5 bearings; oil capacity 4.25L (4.1US qt); 1 carb IPM 32 MGV or Weber 32 ICEV 14/250. Cooling system capacity 6.5L (6.1US qt).
Transmission: Final drive ratio 3.764.
Dimensions: Cabriolet/convertible: Length 353cm, height 140cm.
Performance: Max speed 90-96mph/145-155kmh (manufacturers test specifications); power to weight ratio from 16.9kg/kW (12.5kg/PS); consumption ECE 5.6/7.6/8.8L/100km (50.4/37.2/32.1mpg) [42.0/30.9/26.7US mpg], 64hp 5.1/7.7/10.9L/100km (55.4/36.7/25.9mpg) [46.1/30.5/21.6US mpg].

Zastava Yugo Cabrio

Zastava 101

Version of the Fiat 128 produced in Yugoslavia, rear independent suspension, with distinguishing equipment. Spring 1984: Available with 4-doors. Autumn 1988: Modifications to body details.

```
1100cm3
40.5/44kW-54/59hp-55/60PS
1 Carb
```

Body, Weight: 3-door Saloon/Sedan, 4/5-seater; kerbweight (DIN) 830kg, gross vehicle weight 1235kg. 4-door Saloon/Sedan, 5-seater; kerbweight (DIN) 850kg, gross vehicle weight 1235kg. 5-door Saloon/Sedan, 5-seater; kerbweight (DIN) 835 kg, gross vehicle weight 1235kg.
Engine data (DIN): 4-cylinder in-line (80 x 55.5mm), 1116cm3; compresson ratio 9.2:1; 40.5kW (54hp) [55PS] at 6000rpm, 36.3kW/L (48.6hp/L) [49.3PS/L]; 80Nm (59lbft) at 3000rpm; leaded premium fuel.
For some models: Compression ratio 9.2:1; 44kW (59hp) [60PS] or 47kW (63hp) [64PS]; 83Nm (61.2lbft) at 4400rpm.
Engine construction: Designated 128 A.000. Front transverse engine tilted forward at 20deg. 1 overhead camshaft (toothed belt); light-alloy cylinder head; crankshaft with 5 bearings; oil capacity 4.25L (4.1US qt); 1 carb IPM 32 MGV or Weber 32 ICEV 14/250. Battery 12V 34/36/45Ah, alternator 33/45A; cooling system capacity 6.5L (6.1US qt).
Transmission (to front wheels): 4-speed manual (without direct drive), final drive ratio 3.764 or 4.077.

Zastava 101

Gear ratios: 1st 3.583; 2nd 2.235; 3rd 1.46; 4th 1.034; R 3.714.
Chassis: Integral body; front independent suspension with McPherson strut, lower control arm and antiroll bar, rear independent suspension with A-arms, damper and self stabilizing transverse leaf spring, telescopic damper. Optional servo/power assisted brakes, front disc, rear drums, disc diameter 22.7cm; mechanical handbrake to rear wheels; rack and pinion steering; fuel tank 38L (8.4Gal) [10US Gal], of which 4.5-7L (1.0Gal) [1.4Gal] [1.2-1.8US Gal] Reserve; tyres 145 SR 13, optional 165/70 SR 13, wheels 4 1/2 or 5J.
Dimensions: Wheelbase 245cm, track 131/131.5cm, clearance 14.5cm, turning circle 10.3m. Load space 11.5-35.7cu ft (325-1010dm3), length 379-389cm, width 159cm, height 134,5/137cm.
Performance: Max speed approx 84-91mph/135-146kmh (manufacturers test specifications), speed at 1000rpm in 5th gear 16.5- 15.3mph/26.6-24.6kmh; acceleration 0 - 62mph/100kmh in 17secs; standing km 37.5secs; power to weight ratio from 17.7kg/kW (13kg/PS); consumption ECE 6.7/8.8/9.7L/100km (42.2/32.1/29.1mpg) [35.1/26.7/24.2US mpg] or 7.2/9.5/8.8L/100km (39.2/29.7/32.1mpg) [32.7/24.8/26.7US mpg].

```
1300cm3
53.5/48kW-72/64hp-73/65PS
1 2V Carb
```

As 1100cm3, except:
Engine data (DIN): (86 x 55.5mm), 1290cm3; compression ratio 9.2:1; 53.5kW (72hp) [73PS] at 6000rpm, 41.5kW/L (55.6kW/L) [56.6PS/L]; 100Nm (73.8lbft) at 3900rpm.
Or: compression ratio 9.1:1; 48kW (64hp) [65PS] at 5800rpm; 98Nm (72.3lbft) at 3500rpm.
Some countries: (86.4 x 55.5mm), 1301cm3.
Engine construction: 1 2V carb, Weber 32 DNTR 32/250 or Solex C 32 CIC 4; Battery 12V 54Ah.
Performance: Max speed 87-93mph/140-150kmh (manufacturers test specifications); acceleration 0 - 62mph/100kmh in 13.4secs; standing km 35.0secs; power to weight 15.5kg/kW (11.4kg/PS); consumption ECE 7.1/10.1/9.4L/100km (39.8/28/30.1mpg) [33.1/23.3/25US mpg], 64hp 6.3/8.5/10.3L/100km (44.8/33.2/27.4mpg) [37.3/27.7/22.8US mpg].

Yugo Florida

New Saloon/Sedan with front wheel drive and tailgate. Design by Giugiaro/Ital-Design. Fiat engine with 1.4 and latter also with 1.1 and 1.6 litre engine capacity as well as the 1.7 diesel. Launched at the Belgrade Show 1987. In production since Autumn 1988. All data provisional.

Yugo Florida

```
1372cm3
52kW-70hp-71PS
1 Twin Carb/Injection
```

Body, Weight: 5-door Saloon/Sedan, 5-seater; kerbweight (DIN) 875kg, gross vehicle weight approx 1420kg.
Engine data (DIN): 4-cylinder in-line (80.5 x 67.4mm), 1372cm3; compression ratio 9.2:1; 52kW (70hp) [71PS] at 6000rpm, 37.9kW/L (50.8hp/L) [51.8PS/L]; 108Nm (79.7lbft) at 2900rpm.
With Catalyst and Bosch Mono-Jetronic Central/Single Point Injection: Identical data.

Engine construction: Designated 160A1000. Transverse engine; 1 overhead camshaft (toothed belt); light-alloy cylinder head; 5 main bearing crankshaft; oil capacity 4.25L (4.0US qt); 1 Weber 32/34 downdraught carb. Battery 12V 40/45Ah, alternator 55A; cooling system capacity 6.5L (6.1US qt).

Transmission (to front wheels): 5-speed manual, final drive ratio 3.765.

Gear ratios: 1st 3.909; 2nd 2.267; 3rd 1.44; 4th 1.029; 5th 0.875; R 3.909.

Chassis: Integral body, with front and rear subframe; front independent suspension with McPherson struts and lower A arm, rear independent suspension with trailing arm, front and rear antiroll bars, coil springs and telescopic dampers. Servo/power assisted brakes, front discs, rear drums, disc diameter 24cm, mechanical handbrake to rear wheels; rack and pinion steering; fuel tank capacity 48L (10.5Gal) [12.7US Gal]; tyres 165/70 SR 13 or 165/65 SR 14, wheel rims 5".

Dimensions: Wheelbase 250cm, track 140/139.5cm, clearance approx 15cm, turning circle approx 10.5m, load space 14.5/45.2cu ft (410/1280dm3), length 396cm, width 164cm, height 143cm.

Performance: Max speed 99mph/160kmh manufacturers test specifications), speed at 1000rpm in 4th gear 16.6mph/26.7kmh, in 5th gear 19.5mph/31.4kmh; acceleration 0-62mph/100kmh 14.5secs, standing km 35secs; power to weight ratio from 16.8kg/kW (12.3kg/PS); consumption ECE 5.0/6.8/8.1L/100km (56.5/41.5/34.9mpg) [47.0/34.6/29.0US mpg].

ZAZ SU

Zaz, v/o Autoexport, 14, Volkhonka St, 11902, Moscow, USSR
Russian manufacturer, based in Saporoshje in the Ukraine.

Zaz 968 M

4-seater, V4 rear mounted 1196cm3 air cooled engine. Autumn 1987: modifications to the body and interior.

1196cm3
31/34kW–41/45hp–42/46PS
1 Carb

Body, Weight: 2-door Saloon/Sedan, 4-seater; kerbweight (DIN) 790–840kg, gross vehicle weight 1110cm3/1160kg.

Engine data (DIN): 4-cylinder in V 90deg (76 x 66mm), 1196cm3; compression ratio 7.2:1; 31kW (41hp) [42PS] at 4600rpm, 25.9kW/L (34.7hp/L) [35.1PS/L]; 75Nm (55.4lbft) at 2800rpm; leaded regular grade.
Or: Compression ratio 8.4:1; 34kW (45hp) [46PS] at 4800rpm.

Engine construction: Rear engine, overhead valves, central camshaft (gear driven); light-alloy cylinder head; crankshaft with 3 bearings; centrifugal oil filter; oil capacity 3.3/3.75L (3.1/3.6US qt); 1 downdraught carb (K-127), oil bath air filter. Battery 12V 42/55Ah, alternator 30A; axial cooling fan.

Transmission (to rear wheels): 4-speed manual, (without direct drive), 2nd, 3rd and 4th gear synchronized; final drive ratio 4/125.

Gear ratios: 1st 3.8; 2nd 2.12; 3rd 1.41; 4th 0.964; R 4.165.

Chassis: Integral body; front crank arm suspension and antiroll bar, rear independent suspension with wishbone, semi trailing arms and coil springs, telescopic damper. 4-wheel drum brakes (optional front disc brakes); mechanical handbrake to rear wheels; worm and wheel steering; fuel tank 30/40L (6.6/8.8Gal) [7.9/10.6US Gal]; tyres 6.15–13, 5.20/5.60–13 or 145 SR 13, optional 155 SR 13, wheel 4J.

Zaz 968 M

Dimensions: Wheelbase 216cm, track 122/120cm or 124/122.5cm, clearance 19cm, turning circle 11.8m. Length 373–376.5cm, width 149/157cm, height 137–140cm.

Performance: Max speed 73–81mph/118–130kmh (manufacturers test specifications), speed at 1000rpm in 5th gear 16.5mph/26.5kmh; power to weight ratio from 23.2kg/kW (17.2kg/PS); consumption ECE 6.5/–/9.5L/100km (43.5/–/29.7mpg) [36.2/–/24.8US mpg].

Zaz 1102 Tawrija

Compact Saloon/Sedan of lower/middle class with transverse engine, front wheel drive and tailgate. By 1990 will replace model with rear engine. Prototype first presented in Autumn 1987. Provisional data.

1091 cm3
37.5kW–50hp–51PS
1 2V Carb

Body, Weight: 3-door Saloon/Sedan, 5-seater; kerbweight (DIN) 710kg, gross vehicle weight 1100kg.

Engine data (DIN): 4-cylinder in-line (72 x 67mm), 1091cm3, compression ratio 9.5:1; 37.5kW (50hp) [51PS] at 5500rpm, 34.3kW/L (46hp/L) [46.7PS/L]; 76Nm (56.1lbft) at 3500rpm; leaded regular grade.
Or: 39kW (52hp) [53PS] from 5300-5600rpm; 80Nm (59lbft) at 3500rpm.

Engine construction: Front transverse engine, 1 overhead camshaft (toothed belt); light-alloy cylinder head; crankshaft with 5 bearings; oil capacity approx 3.5L (3.3US qt); 1 Solar downdraught 2V carb. Battery 12V 44Ah, alternator approx 45A; cooling system capacity 6L (5.7US qt).

Transmission (to front wheels): 5-speed manual, final drive ratio 4.13 or 4.3.

Gear ratios: 1st 3.454; 2nd 2.056; 3rd 1.333; 4th 0.969; 5th 0.828; R 3.358.

Chassis: Integral body; front independent suspension with McPherson struts, lower control arms and antiroll bar, fully floating rear axle, coil springs, telescopic damper. Servo/power assisted brakes, front disc, rear drums, disc diameter 23.5cm, mechanical handbrake to rear wheels; rack and pinion steering; fuel tank 39L (8.6Gal) [10.3US Gal]; tyres 155/70 SR 13, wheels 4.5J.

Dimensions: Wheelbase 232cm, track 131.5/129cm, clearance 16cm, turning circle 10m. Load space 8.8–26.1cu ft (250–740dm3), length 371cm, width 165cm, height 141cm.

Performance: Max speed 90mph/145kmh (manufacturers test specifications), speed at 1000rpm in 5th gear (4.13/1) 18.3mph/29.5kmh; acceleration 0–62mph/100kmh 17secs; power to weight ratio 18.9kg/kW (13.9kg/PS); consumption ECE 4.6/6.6/6.8L/100km (61.4/42.8/41.5mpg) [51.1/35.6/34.6US mpg].

Zaz 1102 Tawrija

ZIL SU

Zil v/o Autoexport, 14, Volkhonka St, 119902, Moscow, USSR

Manufacturer based in Moscow.

Zil

Large Saloon/Sedan with automatic transmission. 1978: new model 4104.

```
7/7.7 Litre V8
220.5/231.5kW–296/310hp–300/315PS
1 4V Carb
```

Body, Weight: 4–door Saloon/Sedan 4104, 5/7–seater; kerbweight (DIN) 3335kg.

Engine data: 8–cylinder in V 90deg (108 x 95mm), 6962cm3; compression ratio 9.5:1; 220.5kW (296hp) [300PS] at 4400rpm, 31.7kW/L (42.5hp/L) [43.1PS/L]; 569Nm (420lbft) at 2900rpm; leaded premium grade.
Engine for 4104: (108 x 105mm), 7695cm3; compression ratio 9.3:1; 231.5kW (310hp) [315PS] at 4600rpm, 30.1kW/L (40.3hp/L) [40.9PS/L]; 608Nm (448.7lbft) at 4000rpm.

Engine construction: Overhead valves, central camshaft; crankshaft with 5 bearings; full flow oil filter, oil capacity 9L (8.5US qt), 4104 12L (11.4US qt); 1 downdraught 4V carb, electric fuel pump. Battery 12V 108Ah (2 x 54Ah), 4104 120Ah (2 x 60Ah), Dynamo 500W; cooling system capacity 15L (14.2US qt), 4104 21.5L (20.3US qt).

Transmission (to rear wheels): Automatic, hydraulic torque converter and Planetary gear set, final drive ratio 3.54, 4104 3.62.

Gear ratios: Automatic, Planetary gear set ratios: 1st 2.02; 2nd 1.42; 3rd 1; R 1.42.

Chassis: Box type frame with cross members, front A arm and antiroll bar, rear rigid axle with semi–elliptic springs and trailing arms, front antiroll bar, telescopic damper. Servo/power assisted disc brakes, rear brake power limiting device, rear wheel parking brake; worm and wheel power steering system; fuel tank 120L (26.4Gal) [31.7US Gal]; tyres 9.35–15 or 235 HR 380.

Dimensions: Wheelbase 388cm, track 164.5/166.5cm, clearance 17.5cm, turning circle 16.5m, length 634cm, width 209cm, height 155cm.

Performance: Max speed over 118–124mph/190–200kmh (manufacturers test specifications), speed at 1000rpm in 3rd gear (3.54:1) 24.2mph/39kmh, (3.62:1) 23.7mph/38.1kmh; acceleration 0 – 62mph/100kmh 13–13.5secs; power to weight ratio from 13.1kg/kW (9.6kg/PS); consumption at 50mph/80kmh 18–22L/100km (15.7–12.8mpg) [13.1–10.7US mpg].

Zil

ZIMMER — USA

Zimmer Motor Cars Corporation, 777 Southwest 12 Avenue, P.O. Box 668, Pompano Beach, Florida 33061, USA

Luxury, low volume production vehicles.

Zimmer Quicksilver

Luxury Coupe based on the Pontiac Fiero, with a 2.8 Litre central mounted engine. Started production in March 1987.

```
2.8 Litre V6
104.5kW–140hp–142PS
Fuel Injection
```

Body, Weight: 2–door Coupe, 2–seater; kerbweight (DIN) at 1325kg.

Engine data (SAE net); 6–cylinder in V 60deg (88.9 x 76.2mm), 2838cm3; compression ratio 8.5:1; 104.5kW (140hp) [142PS] at 5200rpm, 36.8kW/L (49.2hp/L) [50.0PS/L]; 231Nm (170.5lbft) at 3600rpm, regular grade.

Engine construction: Designated Pontiac L44. Mid engine transverse mounted, central camshaft (chain) crankshaft with 4 bearings; oil capacity 3.8L (3.6US qt); electronic fuel injection Bosch; electric fuel pump in tank. Battery 12V 54Ah, alternator 94A; cooling system capacity 13L (12.3US qt).

Transmission (rear wheels): Automatic THM 125, hydraulic torque converter and 3–speed Planetary gear set, central shift control, final drive ratio 3.18.

Gear ratios: Max torque multiplication in converter 2.35 times, Planetary gear set ratios: 2.84; 1.6; 1; R 2.07.

Chassis: Intergal body; front A arm with coil springs and antiroll bar; rear sub–frame, McPherson struts and lower A arm, front and rear telescopic damper. Servo/power assisted discs brakes, diameter 24.7cm; parking brake to rear wheels; rack and pinion steering; fuel tank 38.5L (8.5Gal) [10.2US Gal]; tyres 205/70 R 14, wheels 6".

Dimensions: Wheelbase 278cm, track 148/150.5cm, clearance 15cm, turning circle 12.6m. Load space approx 10cu ft (285dm3), length 479.5cm, width 180cm, height 121cm.

Performance: Max speed approx 121mph/195kmh, speed at 1000rpm in 5th gear 23.3mph/37.5kmh; power to weight ratio from 12.7kg/kW (9.3kg/PS); consumption approx 10–15L/100km (28.2–18.8mpg) [23.5– 15.7US mpg].

Zimmer Quicksilver

PRS

PRS CONSULTANCY SERVICES

STRATEGIES FOR AUTOMOTIVE BUSINESS DEVELOPMENT

Through continuous original research across the Automotive Industry in three Continents, PRS can assist with:

- Strategy planning
- Technology tracking & forecasting
- Competitor analyses
- Acquisition search & evaluation
- Market & product planning

Areas of expertise:

- Engines/components
- New materials/plastics
- Electronics

For further information contact:

Vanessa Scholfield
PRS Business Consultancy Services Ltd
Premier House
44-48 Dover Street
London, W1X 4RF

Tel: 441 409 1635
Fax: 441 629 0221
Telex: 23442 PRSLON G

Vehicle Badging

Several manufacturers change vehicle badging for marketing reasons in various countries, although they are manufactured to identical specifications. Specifications contained in this publication are only quoted once. To assist in locating the data, the following table lists the vehicles by manufacturer: where the badge changes from country to country, refer to the **highlighted** vehicle badge for data.

Manufacturer/ Country of Origin	Domestic Badge	Western Europe Badge	Others	North America Badge
Daihatsu (Japan)	**Cuore**	Domino Cuore		N/A
	Rugger	**Rocky 4WD**	Fourtrak	Fourtrak
Daewoo (South Korea)	Le Mans	Le Mans		Pontiac Le Mans
Ford (Australia)	Ford Laser		Mazda 323	
	Ford Telstar		Mazda 626	
Holden (Australia)	Barina		Suzuki Swift	
	Gemini		Isuzu Gemini	
	Astra		Nissan Cherry (Or Opel for Engine)	
	Camira (Saloon/Sedan)		Opel Ascona	
	Camira (Estate/ StationWagon)		Vauxhall Cavalier	
Honda (Japan)	**Quint Integra**			Acura Integra
	Legend			Acura Legend
Hyundai (South Korea)	**Pony/Excel**			Mitsubishi Precis
Isuzu (Japan)	**Gemini**			Chevrolet Spectrum
	Piazza	Piazza		Impulse
Jeep (USA)	**Grand Daddy**	Grand Wagoneer	Grand Wagoneer	
Mazda (Japan)	Ford Festiva	121		Ford Festiva
	Ford Laser/ Meteor	323	Ford Laser/ Meteor	Mercury Tracer
	Ford Telstar	626	Ford Telstar	626/MX-6

Manufacturer/ Country of Origin	Domestic Badge	Western Europe Badge	Others	North America Badge
Mazda/cont Savannah/	**RX7** RX7		RX7	
	Luce/929	**929**	929	929
Mitsubishi (Japan)	**Minica**	Towny		
	Mirage	Colt/Lancer	Colt/Lancer	Dodge Colt/ Mirage
	Starion	Starion		Dodge Conquest Starion
	Chariot	**Space Wagon**		Dodge Colt/ Vista
	Pajero	**Pajero**		Montero
Nissan (Japan)	**March** **Sunny/** Pulsar	Micra	Micra Sunny/ Pulsar	Micra Sentra
	Praire	Praire		Stanza Wagon
	Silvia	Silvia		200 SX
	Auster	Bluebird		Stanza/Maxima
	Fairlady Z	300 ZX		300 ZX
	Terrano	**Terrano**	Terrano	Pathfinder
Subaru (Japan)	**Justy** **Leone**	Justy Subaru Leone	Justy/J10	J10/J12 DL/GL/GL–10
	Alcyone	**XT**	XT	XT
Suzuki (Japan)	**Cultus**	Swift		Chevrolet Sprint/ Swift Forsa
Toyota (Japan)	**Sprinter** **Corona**	Corolla Carina II		Corolla
	Mark II	Cressida		Cressida
Vauxhall (Great Britain)	Nova	**Opel Corsa**		
	Astra/ Belmont	**Opel Kadett**		
	Carlton	**Opel Omega**		
	Senator	**Opel Senator**		

UK Price Guide

The list quotes a price range from the base model to the highest standard specification model, exclusive of delivery charges or additional equipment costs. The prices, all inclusive of VAT are a guide only and may vary between Dealers.

Alfa Romeo
33	£8,650	– 11,100
Sprint	£9,200	– 10,200
75	£12,500	– 16,200
164	£17,925	– 20,250

Aston Martin
V8 Saloon	£81,500	– 87,000
Volante	£98,000	
Lagonda	£98,000	
Vantage Volante	£109,000	

Audi
80	£10,624	– 17,393
100	£13,134	– 23,526
90	£15,103	– 20,478
Coupe	£17,995	– 22,486
Quattro	£30,199	
200	£27,449	– 31,992

Bentley
Eight	£67,188	
Mulsanne S	£75,570	
Turbo R	£91,756	
Continental	£106,419	

BMW
316i	£10,750	– 11,245
318i	£11,880	– 12,375
320i	£13,480	– 17,395
325i	£16,125	– 20,175
520i	£15,985	– 17,540
525	£19,240	– 20,525
530i	£22,625	– 23,875
535i	£24,235	– 26,395
635 CSi	£36,860	
730i	£23,850	– 26,875
735i	£29,850	– 41,240
750i	£53,750	
M3	£23,550	
M635 CSi	£45,780	

Bristol
Britannia	£79,500	
Beaufighter Turbo	£79,500	
Brigand Turbo	£84,965	

Citroen
2CV	£3,685	– 4,103
AX	£4,103	– 7,003
Visa	£5,960	
BX	£6,532	– 13,443
CX	£11,554	– 17,397

Dacia
Duster	£6,500	

Daihatsu
Domino	£4,920	
Charade	£5,799	– 8,199
Fourtrak	£10,759	– 13,890

Daimler
3.6	£34,500	
Double Six	£35,000	

De Tomaso
Longchamp	£36,527	– 41,536
Pantera	£43,980	– 47,622

Ferrari
328	£44,999	– 46,501
Mondial	£48,899	– 53,403
412	£75,597	
Testarossa	£91,195	

Fiat
126	£2,789	
Panda	£4,060	– 6,201
Uno	£5,074	– 8,575
Tipo	£7,400	– 9,889
Regata	£7,175	– 10,050
X1/9	£8,926	
Croma	£10,550	– 15,700

Ford
Fiesta	£5,004	– 8,430
Escort	£6,121	– 11,874
Orion	£7,730	– 10,278
Sierra	£8,720	– 15,905
Granada	£11,995	– 23,250
RS Cosworth	£20,250	

FSO
1300	£2,999	
1500	£3,599	
Polonez	£3,899	– 5,349

Honda
Civic	£7,450	– 11,550
Ballade	£8,610	– 9,710
Integra	£9,190	– 11,030
Aerodeck	£10,300	– 12,670
Accord	£10,660	– 15,400
Prelude	£12,100	– 17,500
Legend	£21,990	– 26,500

Hyundai
Sonnet	£4,998	– 5,250
Pony	£5,799	– 6,999
Stellar	£6,500	– 7,649

Isuzu
Trooper	£11,798	– 17,298
Piazza	£12,498	– 13,499

Jaguar
XJ6	£19,200	– 22,200
XJS	£26,400	– 38,500
Sovereign	£27,500	– 31,000

Lada
Riva	£3,395	– 4,845
Samara	£4,595	– 5,695
Niva	£6,425	– 7,950

Lamborghini
Jalpa 3500	£43,656
Countach QV	£86,077

Lancia
Y10	£5,430	– 5,530
Delta	£6,995	– 16,995
Prisma	£8,375	– 9,675
Thema	£13,190	– 39,900

Land Rover
90	£12,493	– 13,911
110	£13,121	– 14,430

Lotus
Excel	£20,900	– 27,900
Esprit	£26,500	– 31,900

Maserati
Biturbo	£26,400	– 29,485

Mazda
121	£5,679	– 6,949
323	£7,049	– 13,999
626	£8,999	– 15,879
RX7	£17,499	

Mercedes
190	£14,200	– 29,900
200	£17,150	– 17,650
230	£18,900	– 25,200
250	£19,300	– 21,200
300	£21,700	– 32,800
260	£23,100	
420	£34,000	– 46,200
500	£39,650	– 51,400
560	£56,400	– 63,200

Mitsubishi
Colt	£6,999	– 10,469
Lancer	£8,639	– 11,719
Gallant	£9,679	– 13,599
Space Wagon	£10,029	– 11,299
Shogun	£12,899	– 16,299
Sapporo	£13,389	
Starion	£16,479	

Morgan
4/4 1600	£11,206	– 12,209
Plus 8	£16,856	

Nissan
Micra	£5,270	– 6,700
Sunny	£7,216	– 11,125
Bluebird	£8,789	– 12,570
Prairie	£9,790	– 11,340
Patrol	£12,599	– 15,695
Laurel	£13,745	
Silvia	£14,198	
300ZX	£19,185	– 22,941

Panther
Kallista	£10,975	– 12,995

Peugeot
205	£5,095	– 11,460
309	£5,995	– 10,645
405	£8,295	– 14,995
505	£11,120	– 19,250

Porsche
944	£25,991	– 39,893
911	£36,750	– 109,078
928	£55,441	

Range Rover
Turbo	£21,832	
Vogue	£23,029	– 28,855

Reliant
Scimitar	£8,575	– 11,425

Renault
5	£5,095	– 9,115
11	£6,305	– 9,710
9	£6,850	– 8,435
21	£8,700	– 16,900
25	£11,990	– 21,475
Espace	£13,485	– 17,790
GTA V6	£21,950	– 27,590

Rolls Royce
Silver Spirit	£77,827
Silver Spur	£91,943
Corniche II	£110,543

Rover
Mini	£4,299	– 5,149
Metro	£4,998	– 8,165
Maestro	£6,514	– 10,192

Montego	£8,347	– 12,455
Rover 213	£8,057	– 10,098
Rover 216	£9,068	– 10,984
Rover 820	£12,640	– 15,797
Rover 827	£17,200	– 18,765
Rover Vitesse	£20,443	
Rover Sterling	£22,550	

SAAB
900	£10,995	– 24,195
9000	£14,895	– 25,695

SEAT
Marbella	£3,949	– 4,549
Ibiza	£4,899	– 7,549
Malaga	£6,099	– 7,950

Skoda
105	£2,898	– 3,088
120	£3,249	– 3,699
130	£3,745	– 5,867

Subaru
Justy	£6,399	– 6,598
1.6	£7,399	– 8,999
1.8	£8,198	– 14,798
XT	£14,999	– 15,999

Suzuki
Auto	£5,250	
Swift	£5,699	– 6,899
Santana	£6,675	– 6,940
SJ4 13	£7,590	
Vitara	£9,000	– 9,750

Toyota
Starlet	£6,587	
Corolla	£7,598	– 12,040
Carina	£9,931	– 12,899
Space Cruiser	£11,954	
Camry	£12,250	– 16,864
MR2	£12,551	– 14,174
Land II Cruiser	£15,259	– 18,180
Celica	£15,917	– 20,701
Supra	£19,290	

TVR
S Convertible	£14,995	
350i Con.	£19,350	
400	£24,995	
450	£27,995	– 33,950

Vauxhall
Nova	£4,993	– 8,513
Astra	£6,310	– 12,992
Belmont	£6,927	– 10,145
Cavalier	£7,889	– 12,394
Carlton	£11,373	– 18,999
Senator	£16,079	– 20,972

Volkswagen
Golf	£7,186	– 13,425
Jetta	£7,598	– 12,298
Polo	£5,236	– 7,191
Passat	£10,230	– 16,131
Scirocco	£8,997	– 10,847

Volvo
340	£6,890	– 9,440
360	£10,525	– 11,370
240	£11,375	– 14,095
480	£12,345	
740	£12,695	– 19,425
760	£21,450	– 23,295

Yugo
311	£3,299	
511	£3,565	
45	£3,583	– 4,995
55	£3,940	– 4,472
513	£4,374	
65	£4,995	

USA Price Guide

The list quotes a price range from the base model to the highest standard specification model, exclusive of transportation or additional equipment costs. The prices are a guide only and may vary between Dealer or State.

Acura
Legend	$22,600 – 30,840
Integra	$11,260 – 14,510

Alfa–Romeo
Milano	$19,175 – 22,700
Spider	$16,700 – 23,400

Aston Martin
V8 Saloon	$142,000
V8 Volante	$168,000
V8 Vantage	$158,000
Lagonda	$187,500
Vantage Volante	$182,500

Audi
100	$24,980 – 30,805
200	$33,405 – 38,805

Bentley
Bentley Turbo R	$149,500
Mulsanne S	$118,900
Bentley Eight	$108,700
Continental	$204,800

Bertone
XI/9	$10,995

BMW
325i	$24,650 – 34,495
635csi	$47,000
M6	$55,950
525i	$37,000
535i	$43,600
735i	$54,000 – 58,000
750i	$70,000

Buick
Skyhawk	$9285 – 10,645
Skylark Custom	$11,115 – 11,825
Skylark Limited	$12,345 – 13,055
Century Custom	$12,199 – 13,866
Century Estate	$13,956 – 14,666
Regal Custom	$14,214
Regal Limited	$14,739
Le Sabre	$15,425
Le Sabre Custom	$15,330
Le Sabre Limited	$16,630 – 16,730
Le Sabre Wagon	$16,770
Electra Limited	$18,525
Electra T–Type	$21,325
Park Avenue	$29,460
Electra Estate	$19,850
Riviera	$22,540
Reatta	$26,700

Cadillac
Allante	$57,183
De Ville	$24,960 – 25,435
Fleetwood	$29,825 – 30,300
Fleetwood Sixty Special	$34,230
Seville	$29,750
El Dorado	$26,738
Brougham	$25,699

Chevrolet
Cavalier	$7,295 – 16,535
Camaro	$11,495 – 18,945
Corvette	$31,545 – 36,785
Tracker	$10,495 – 12,495
Metro	$5,995 – 7,195
Spectrum	$7,295 – 7,795
Chevrolet	$13,865 – 16,835
Celebrity	$11,495 – 12,225
Corsica	$9,985 – 12,825
Beretta	$10,575 – 12,685

Chrysler
Colt	$6,477 – 11,160
Colt Vista Wagon	$11,518 – 12,828
Sundance	$8,395 – 8,595
Horizon America	$6,595
Reliant K America	$7,595
Gran Fury Saloon	$11,995

Voyager	$11,312 – 16,362
Conquest	$18,974
New Yorker/Landau	$17,416 – 19,509
Le Baron Coupe/Convertible	$11,495 – 19,666
Le Baron	$11,495 – 17,095
Fifth Avenue	$18,345

Daihatsu
| Charade | $6,197 – 7,497 |

Dodge
Daytona	$9,295 – 13,295
Omni America	$6,595
Aries K America	$7,595
Spirit	$
Diplomat	$11,995 – 14,795
Caravan	$11,312 – 16,362
Colt	$6,477 – 11,145
Colt Vista Wagon	$11,518 – 12,828
Dynasty	$12,295 – 13,595
Shadow	$8,395 – 8,595
Lancer	$11,195 – 17,395

Ford
Tempo	$9,057 – 10,860
Mustang	$9,050 – 17,512
Probe	$10,943 – 14,077
Escort	$6,964 – 9,315
Festiva	$5,699 – 7,101
Ltd Crown Victoria	$15,851 – 17,556
Thunderbird	$14,612 – 19,823
Taurus	$11,778 – 19,739

Honda
Civic	$6,385 – 12,810
CRX	$8,895 – 10,930
Accord (Not including SEi)	$11,230 – 16,530
Prelude	$13,945 – 19,175

Hyundai
| Hatchback | $5,499 – 8,184 |
| Sedan | $6,199 – 8,234 |

Jaguar
XJS	$47,000 – 56,000
XJ6	$43,500
Vanden Plas	$47,500

Jeep–Eagle
Premier	$13,276 – 15,259
Medallion	$10,405 – 12,275
Summit	$9,347 – 10,364
Jeep Wrangler	$8,995 – 14,867
Jeep Cherokee	$13,657 – 24,151
Jeep Wagoneer	$23,220
Jeep Grand Wagoneer	$26,395
Jeep Comanche	$10,609 – 11,295
Jeep Cherokee(2WD)	$12,315 – 12,951
Jeep Comanche(2WD)	$7,646 – 8,469

Lincoln Mercury
Topaz	$9,577 – 11,980
Tracer	$8,556 – 9,726
Lincoln Town Car	$25,562 – 29,709
Lincoln Mark VII	$27,569
Lincoln Continental	$28,032 – 29,910
Merkur XR4 Ti	$19,759
Merkur Scorpio	$25,052
Grand Marquis	$16,701 – 17,922
Cougar	$15,448 – 19,650
Sable	$14,101 – 15,872

Lotus
| Esprit Turbo | $67,500 |

Maserati
Spyder	$44,995
228	$52,975
430	$41,500

Mazda
MPV	$12,909 – 13,759*
MX6	$11,399 – 15,499*
929	$21,920
626	$11,299 – 15,049*
323	$6,299 – 12,999*

*Manual only

Mercedes
190	$30,980 – 32,500
260	$39,200
300	$44,850 – 55,100
420	$61,210
560	$64,230 – 79,840

Mitsubishi
Precis	$5,499 – 8,089
Sigma	$17,069
Montero	$12,299 – 18,389
Mirage	$8,859 – 11,969
Galant	$10,971 – 15,269
Starion	$19,859

Nissan
Sentra	$6,849 – 12,444
Stanza	$11,849 – 14,549
Stanza (Wagon)	$12,599 – 14,864
Maxima	$16,999 – 18,899
Pulsar	$11,749 – 13,754

240 SX	$12,999	– 13,959
300 SX	$22,299	– 25,.449
Pathfinder	$15,399	– 19,349
Van	$14,799	– 17,099

Oldsmobile
Cutlass:

Calais	$10,420	– 14,920
Ciera	$12,145	– 17,245
Cruiser	$13,445	– 14,445
Supreme	$14,750	– 17,450

Eighty Eight:

Royale	$15,700	– 15,800
Royale Brougham	$16,800	– 16,900
Custom Cruiser	$17,300	

Ninety Eight:

Regency	$19,845	
Regency Brougham	$21,045	
Oldsmobile Touring Sedan	$26,545	
Toronado	$22,545	
Trofeo	$25,545	

Peugeot

405	$14,500	– 20,700
505	$17,590	– 26,985

Pontiac

Le Mans	$6,399	– 9,429
Sunbird	$8,849	– 16,899
Grand Am	$10,469	– 13,799
Firebird	$11,999	– 20,339
Pontiac 6000	$11,969	– 16,699
Grand Prix	$13,899	– 16,004
Safari	$15,659	
Bonnneville	$14,829	– 22,899

Porsche

911	$51,205	– 70,975
944	$36,360	– 52,650
928	$74,545	

Range Rover

Range Rover	$35,800	

Rolls Royce

Silver Spur	$142,600	
Corniche II	$205,500	
Silver Spur	$129,800	

Saab

900	$16,995	– 32,620
9000	$24,445	– 32,690

Subaru

Justy	$5,866	– 18,351
Hatchback	$8,596	
Sedan	$9,731	– 16,401
Coupe	$10,031	– 16,361
Wagon	$10,181	– 16,851
XT	$13,071	
XT6	$17,111	

Suzuki

Samurai	$8,495	– 9,495
Sidekick	$8,995	– 13,595
Swift	$7,495	– 9,995

Toyota

Tercel	$7,338	– 9,008
Corolla Family	$9,198	– 12,268
Corolla Sport	$10,628	– 12,728
Camry	$11,488	– 17,218
Cressida	$21,498	
MR2	$13,798	– 18,378
Celica	$11,808	– 20,878
Supra	$22,360	– 26,470

Volkswagen

Fox	$6,890	– 8,150
Golf	$8,465	– 9,885
Golf GTI	$13,650	
Jetta	$9,690	– 15,645
Cabriolet	$15,195	– 17,245
Vanagon	$17,035	– 20,560

Volvo

240	$17,250	– 20,775
740*	$19,985	– 26,086
760	$32,155	– 32,940
*Not 16V		
780	$37,790	– 38,975

Another Record

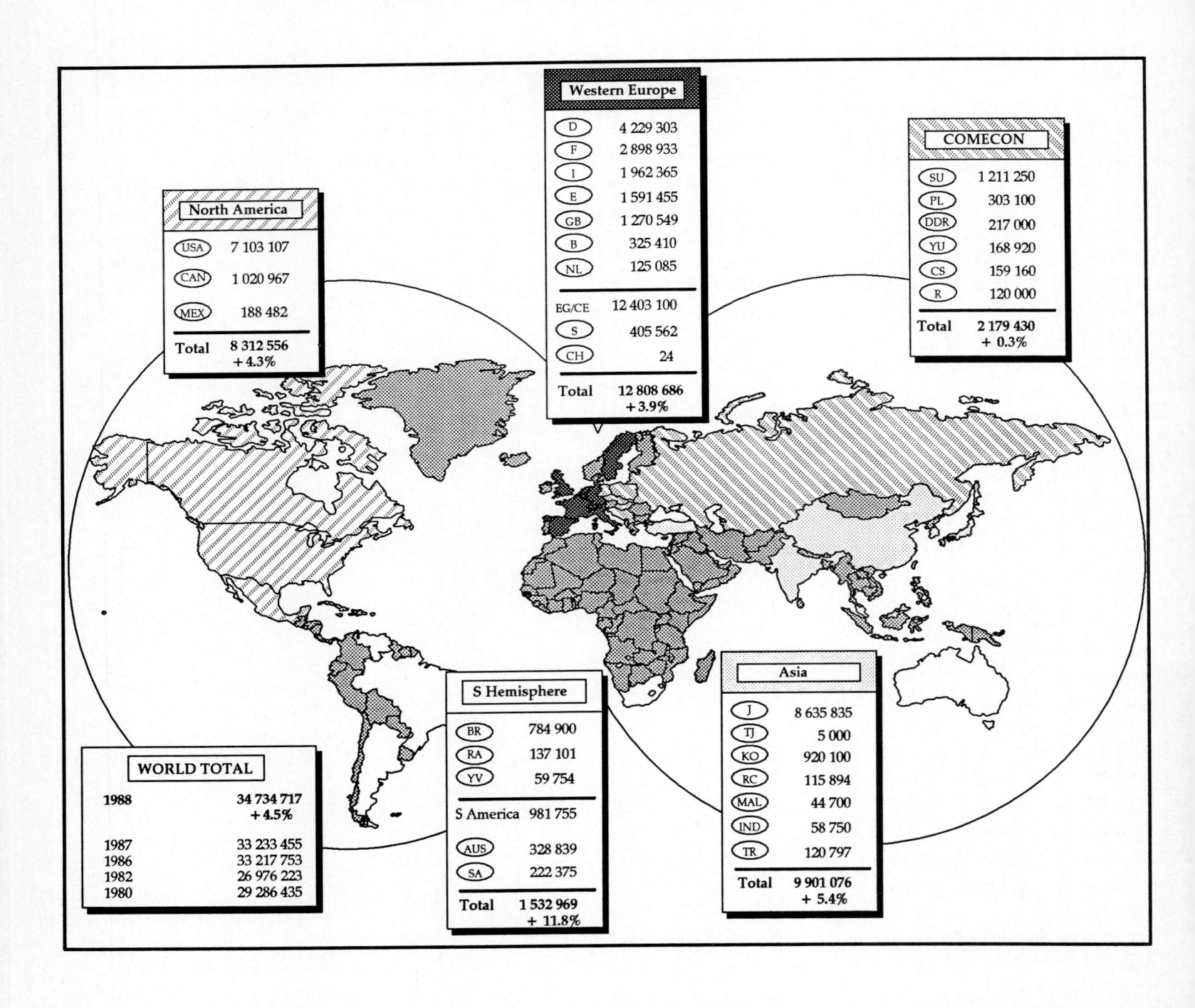

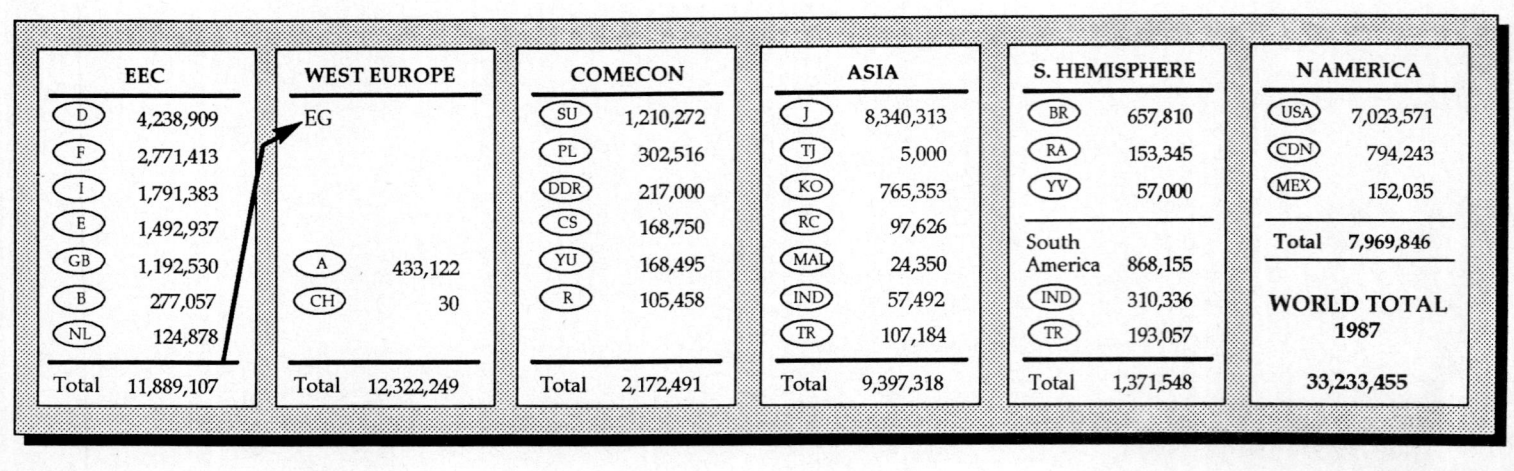

North America
USA	7 103 107
CAN	1 020 967
MEX	188 482
Total	8 312 556
	+4.3%

Western Europe
D	4 229 303
F	2 898 933
I	1 962 365
E	1 591 455
GB	1 270 549
B	325 410
NL	125 085
EG/CE	12 403 100
S	405 562
CH	24
Total	12 808 686
	+3.9%

COMECON
SU	1 211 250
PL	303 100
DDR	217 000
YU	168 920
CS	159 160
R	120 000
Total	2 179 430
	+0.3%

S Hemisphere
BR	784 900
RA	137 101
YV	59 754
S America	981 755
AUS	328 839
SA	222 375
Total	1 532 969
	+11.8%

Asia
J	8 635 835
TJ	5 000
KO	920 100
RC	115 894
MAL	44 700
IND	58 750
TR	120 797
Total	9 901 076
	+5.4%

WORLD TOTAL
1988	34 734 717
	+4.5%
1987	33 233 455
1986	33 217 753
1982	26 976 223
1980	29 286 435

EEC
D	4,238,909
F	2,771,413
I	1,791,383
E	1,492,937
GB	1,192,530
B	277,057
NL	124,878
Total	11,889,107

WEST EUROPE
EG	
A	433,122
CH	30
Total	12,322,249

COMECON
SU	1,210,272
PL	302,516
DDR	217,000
CS	168,750
YU	168,495
R	105,458
Total	2,172,491

ASIA
J	8,340,313
TJ	5,000
KO	765,353
RC	97,626
MAL	24,350
IND	57,492
TR	107,184
Total	9,397,318

S. HEMISPHERE
BR	657,810
RA	153,345
YV	57,000
South America	868,155
IND	310,336
TR	193,057
Total	1,371,548

N AMERICA
USA	7,023,571
CDN	794,243
MEX	152,035
Total	7,969,846

WORLD TOTAL 1987

33,233,455

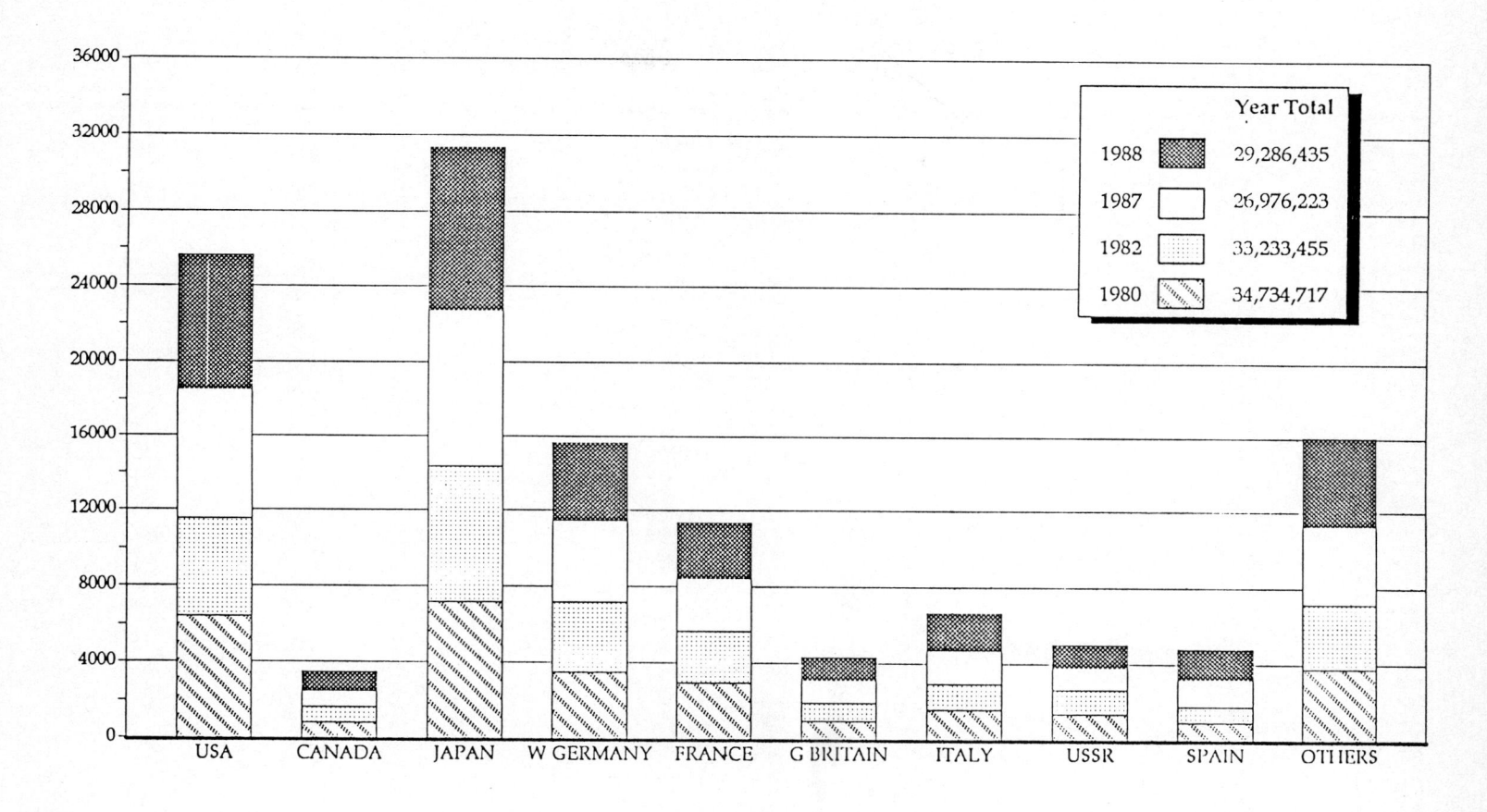

Year	Total
1988	29,286,435
1987	26,976,223
1982	33,233,455
1980	34,734,717

Worldwide production of cars and commercial vehicles reached a new high in 1988, the fourth successive rise. Our research into vehicle manufacturers shows that no less than 34,735 million cars rolled off the production line - 4.5% more than the previous year.

We include in this figure completed vehicles as well as more than 50% finished assemblies. These are defined as country of origin-produced, whereas purely assembled vehicles are excluded to avoid double-counting. Unfortunately there is no common definition as to what constitutes a passenger car. Japan does not include kombis in this sector. In North America the "large space" kombi is normally counted as a commercial vehicle, whilst the Espace is included in Renault figures. As a comparison, about 28,000 Renault Espace were built in 1988 as opposed to 833,000 units of this vehicle type in the USA and Canada. Also not included are the all-terrain kombis like Range Rover, Mercedes-Puch G, Lada Niva, Jeep Cherokee, Mitsubishi Pajero, etc

The world's largest producing country, Japan announced a 3.5% increase in output, while the USA increased production by only 1.1%. This rise was almost entirely due to increased Japanese production in the USA. In Europe, West Germany suffered a slight decline of 0.2%, whilst Italy, Spain, Great Britain and France recorded increases of 9.5%, 6.6%, 6.5% and 4.6% respectively. COMECON production remained at previous levels. Amongst the manufacturers (see table), General Motors further lost market share, whilst Ford, Toyota, Fiat and PSA increased their penetration of the passenger car market.

Car Production by Manufacturer

1988 Ranking	*	1987	%	1988	%	% +/-
1. GM	10	5,526,124	16.6	5,660,377	16.3	+ 2.4
2. Ford	13	4,090,344	12.3	4,299,302	12.4	+ 5.1
3. Toyota	4	2,842,159	8.6	3,145,484	9.1	+10.7
4. VAG	7	2,542,869	7.6	2,564,259	7.4	+ 0.8
5. Fiat	3	1,954,793	5.9	2,091,951	6.0	+ 7.0
6. Nissan	6	2,085,456	6.3	2,056,314	5.9	- 1.4
7. PSA	4	1,703,806	5.1	1,859,031	5.3	+ 9.1
8. Renault	5/4	1,798,572	5.4	1,778,248	5.1	- 1.1
Sub total		22,544,123	67.8	23,454,966	67.5	+ 4.0
Others		10,689,332	32.3	11,279,751	32.5	+ 5.5
Total		33,233,455	100	34,734,717	100	+ 4.5

* No of manufacturing countries (excluding assembly)
GM = General Motors; VAG = VW/Audi/Seat;
PSA = Peugeot/Talbot/Citroen

Car Production by Vehicle Badge

	1987 Actual	1988 Provisional
USA		
Chevrolet	1,359,093	1,303,478
Pontiac	645,064	799,416
Oldsmobile	593,162	563,005
Cadillac	272,486	265,687
Total General Motors	3,417,057	3,417,669
Ford	1,307,275	1,305,141
Mercury	326,883	294,174
Lincoln	182,289	207,107
Total Ford Motor Co	1,816,447	1,806,422
Plymouth	319,522	314,587
Dodge	410,474	512,779
Chrysler	354,584	248,335
Total Chrysler Corp	1,084,580	1,075,701
Honda	321,862	365,832
Mazda	4,326	163,714
Nummi Chevrolet	140,725	71,804
Nummi Toyota	42,065	55,043
Total Nummi	182,790	126,847
Nissan	113,272	109,975
Volkswagen	66,193	35,997
Renault (AMC)	15,994	0
Zimmer	400	200
Avanti	50	150
Excalibur	100	100
Others	500	500
Total USA	**7,023,571**	**7,103,107**
Canada		
Ford	266,000	300,197
Mercury	165,825	201,267
Total Ford MC	431,825	501,464
Chevrolet	50,000	20,130
Pontiac	80,000	29,690
Oldsmobile	169,303	219,687
Buick	35,000	139,613
Total General Motors	334,303	409,120
Eagle (Chrysler)	12,579	60,371
Honda	15,536	50,012
Total Canada	**794,243**	**1,020,967**
Mexico		
Nissan	57,830	72,632
Volkswagen	43,653	53,350
Chrysler/Dodge	23,174	27,500
Ford	15,860	20,000
Chevrolet (GM)	11,518	15,000
Total Mexico	**152,035**	**188,482**
West Germany		
Volkswagen	1,326,702	1,310,900
Audi	417,234	426,462
Total VAG	1,743,936	1,737,362
Opel (Vauxhall, GM)	849,610	842,087
Ford	551,669	597,389
Merkur (USA)	8,913	11,501
Total Ford	560,582	608,890
Mercedes-Benz	589,799	548,613
BMW	446,424	466,321
Porsche	48,520	25,969
Treser	0	20
GFG Elisar	12	15
Bitter	16	14
Isdera	6	8
Lorenz & Rankl	4	4
Total D	**4,238,909**	**4,229,303**
France		
Peugeot	858,400	971,900
Citroen	537,245	548,071
Total PSA	1,395,645	1,519,971
Renault	1,375,696	1,378,830
MVS	60	120
De la Chapelle	12	12
Total F	**2,771,413**	**2,898,933**
Italy		
Fiat	1,302,100	1,445,200
Alfa Romeo	191,500	230,300
Lancia	175,000	142,400
Autobianchi	99,300	122,800
Ferrari	3,902	4,001
Total Fiat	1,771,802	1,944,701
Innocenti	11,627	10,331
Maserati	3,496	3,130
De Tomaso	48	67
Total De Tomaso Gr	15,171	13,528
Bertone	1,555	1,651
Volvo (Bertone)	2,480	2,115
Lamborghini	314	320
Stutz (USA)	11	0
Others	50	50
Total I	**1,791,383**	**1,962,365**
Spain		
Seat	256,913	300,000
VW	116,020	105,000
Total Seat	372,933	405,000
Opel (Vauxhall, GM)	297,605	361,208
Fasa-Renault	307,927	304,361
Ford	276,611	281,726
Peugeot	108,100	105,900
Citroen	128,761	133,260
Talbot	1,000	0
Total PSA	237,861	239,160
Total E	**1,492,937**	**1,591,455**
Great Britain		
Austin	303,006	313,446
MG	27,216	14,551
Rover	130,708	140,773
Honda	5,500	4,979
Total Austin Rover	466,430	473,749
Ford	412,783	418,623
Vauxhall (GM)	184,138	182,553
Peugeot	43,700	80,100
Paykan (Iran)	2,600	0
Total PSA	46,300	80,100
Nissan	28,797	56,744
Jaguar	47,844	51,785
Daimler (Lim)	176	154
Total Jaguar	48,020	51,939
Rolls-Royce	1,907	1,737
Bentley	877	1,064
Total Rolls Royce	2,784	2,801
Lotus (GM)	799	1,300
TVR	550	701
Caterham	269	470
Morgan	411	430
Aston Martin (Ford)	225	235
Reliant	285	212
Panther	205	150
Evante	56	65
Marcos	31	45
Bristol	50	40
AC Cobra	30	25
Midas	17	17
Others	350	350
Total GB	**1,192,530**	**1,270,549**
Sweden		
Volvo	299,000	285,000
Saab	134,112	120,562
Total S	**433,112**	**405,562**
Belgium		
Ford	277,021	325,369
Apal	36	41
Total B	**277,057**	**325,410**
Netherlands		
Volvo	124,800	125,000
Donkervoort	78	85
Total NL	**124,878**	**125,085**
Switzerland		
Sbarro	30	24
Japan		
Toyota	2,708,069	2,982,922
Nissan	1,794,898	1,721,948
VW Santana	9,026	9,000
Total Nissan	1,803,924	1,730,948
Honda	1,241,000	1,280,000
Rover	800	1,000
Total Honda	1,241,800	1,281,000
Mazda	853,309	885,000
Mitsubishi	595,300	640,000
Subaru	482,139	480,000
Suzuki	296,979	296,413
Daihatsu	161,251	186,613
Isuzu	197,542	152,939
Total J	**8,340,313**	**8,635,835**
China		
Shanghai/Hongki	5,000	5,000
South Korea		
Hyundai	548,067	610,000
Daewoo	123,856	160,000
Kia	93,430	150,100
Total KO	**765,353**	**920,100**
Taiwan		
YLN	55,982	55,000
Ford	41,644	60,894
Total RC	**97,626**	**115,894**
Malaysia		
Proton Saga	24,350	44,700
India		
Premier	31,191	32,000
Hindustan	25,567	26,000
Standard	484	500
Sipani	250	250
Total IND	**57,492**	**58,750**
Turkey		
Tofas	53,796	60,017
Renault	43,056	49,188
Anadol	10,332	11,592
Total TR	**107,184**	**120,797**
Australia		
Ford	112,995	105,943
Holden (GM)	74,314	73,866
Toyota	44,032	54,944
Mitsubishi	43,000	47,200
Nissan	35,995	46,886
Total AUS	**310,336**	**328,839**
Brasil		
Volkswagen	259,765	315,000
Chevrolet (GM)	172,108	240,770
Ford	85,755	113,300
Fiat	137,048	112,900
Alfa Romeo	243	0
Total Fiat	137,291	112,900
Gurgel	2,014	1,700
Miura	248	260
Engesa	150	200
Farus	105	150
PAG	0	150
Lafer	74	70
Others	300	400
Total BR	**657,810**	**784,900**
Argentina		
Renault	55,899	45,869
Fiat	33,000	34,350
Peugeot	24,000	19,800
Ford	19,243	19,582
VW	19,021	16,000
IES	2,182	1,500
Total RA	**153,345**	**137,101**
Venezuela		
Chevrolet (GM)	27,947	30,000
Ford	16,353	11,854
Fiat	12,700	17,900
Total YV	**57,000**	**59,754**
South Africa		
Volkswagen	34,775	50,000
Audi	2,593	4,900
Total VAG	37,368	54,900
Toyota	47,903	52,575
Ford	23,000	25,000
Nissan	17,500	18,000
Mazda	17,000	18,000
BMW	14,916	17,800
Opel	16,000	15,000
Mercedes-Benz	8,280	11,100
Honda	11,000	10,000
Total SA	**193,057**	**222,375**
USSR		
Lada/Shiguli	658,831	660,000
Moskvich/Aleko	182,030	180,000
Saporoshez	167,495	168,000
Ish	130,397	130,000
Wolga	71,269	71,000
Oka	0	2,000
Tschaika	150	150
Zil	100	100
Total SU	**1,210,272**	**1,211,250**
Poland		
FSM	204,510	205,600
FSO	98,006	97,500
Total PL	**302,516**	**303,100**
East Germany		
Trabant	142,600	142,600
Wartburg	74,400	74,400
Total DDR	**217,000**	**217,000**
Yugoslavia		
Zastava	168,495	168,920
Czechoslovakia		
Skoda	168,398	158,760
Tatra	352	400
Total CS	**168,750**	**159,160**
Rumania		
Dacia	90,000	90,000
Oltcit	15,458	30,000
Total R	**105,458**	**120,000**
Grand Total	**33,233,455**	**34,734,717**

Car Parc

Table 1

World Car Population					
	1986/87 (mil)	%	1987/88 (mil)	%	%increase
W. Europe	125.3	32.7	129.0	32.6	3.0
Communist Europe	27.8	7.3	30.2	7.6	8.6
Europe Total	153.0	40.0	159.2	40.2	4.1
North America	151.6	39.7	156.1	39.4	3.0
South and Central America	19.5	5.1	20.1	5.1	3.1
Asia	42.6	11.1	44.2	11.2	3.8
Africa	7.3	1.9	7.6	1.9	4.1
Australia/ Oceania	8.5	2.2	8.9	2.2	4.7
World Total	**382.5**	**100**	**396.2**	**100**	**3.6**

Table 2

Cars in Circulation and Percentage Increase				
	1980	1987	1988	+%
W Germany	22,613,500	27,223,800	28,304,200	40
Italy	17,600,000	22,000,000	22,500,000	2.3
France	18,440,000	21,250,000	21,970,000	3.4
G Britain (inc N Ireland)	14,963,000	19,929,300	20,605,500	3.4
Spain	7,057,700	9,643,400	–	–
Netherlands	4,515,000	4,949,900	5,117,700	3.4
Belgium	3,158,700	3,360,300	3,457,400	2.9
Sweden	2,868,300	3,253,600	3,366,600	3.5
Switzerland	2,246,750	2,678,900	2,732,700	2.0
Austria	–	2,609,400	2,684,800	2.9
Finland	1,161,900	1,619,800	–	–
Norway	1,189,800	1,592,200	1,623,100	1.9
Denmark	1,423,400	1,558,100	1,587,600	1.9
Greece	–	1,339,200	1,435,100	7.2
Portugal	1,096,800	1,236,000	1,290,000	4.4
Eire	734,400	711,100	–	–
Luxembourg	157,000	162,500	–	–
Iceland	75,700	109,700	–	–
Total Europe	**83,605,000**	**113,363,600**	–	–
USA	–	135,671,000	139,041,000	2.5
Canada	10,300,000	10,780,700	11,900,000	–
Japan	22,667,300	28,653,700	29,478,300	2.9
Australia	5,712,500	6,842,500	7,072,800	3.4
New Zealand	1,277,100	1,533,000	–	–
Brazil	8,149,300	10,541,900	–	–
Argentina	2,950,000	3,857,500	–	–
Mexico	3,696,000	5,181,400	–	–
S Africa	2,330,900	3,012,000	–	–
USSR (1985)	8,254,700	13,225,000	–	–
Poland	2,117,100	3,962,000	–	–
DDR	2,392,300	3,462,200	–	–
CSSR	1,836,000	2,950,000	–	–
Yugoslavia	2,284,700	2,935,300	2,972,800	1.3

There are approximately 400 million passenger cars in circulation around the world. This figure is derived from the statistical year book "Facts and Figures" produced by the VDA in Frankfurt. A detailed analysis reveals that, as before, Eastern European growth in cars per capita is greatest, while developing countries such as Latin America, Asia and Africa show only small increases. In North America and Europe, car population increased by 3%. The largest parc is in the USA, with 139 million cars on the road. The UK is now a country showing over 20 million cars on the road.

At over 5 million units, the Netherlands currently has the fifth largest parc in Europe after West Germany, Italy, France and the UK.

In a comparison of individual national car populations (see table), no changes were reported at the top end of the league, headed, as before, by the USA, New Zealand, West Germany, Canada, Australia and Switzerland. Lower down, the UK regained its lead over Austria, while the Netherlands climbed one place, ousting Belgium.

The principalities, Liechtenstein and Monaco are not included in our comparison, despite very high car populations.

The two most heavily populated countries in the world, India and China, continue to show very low car populations. It remains to be seen whether the passenger car in these countries will ever assume its Western status as a standard personal belonging.

Data at the beginning of 1988

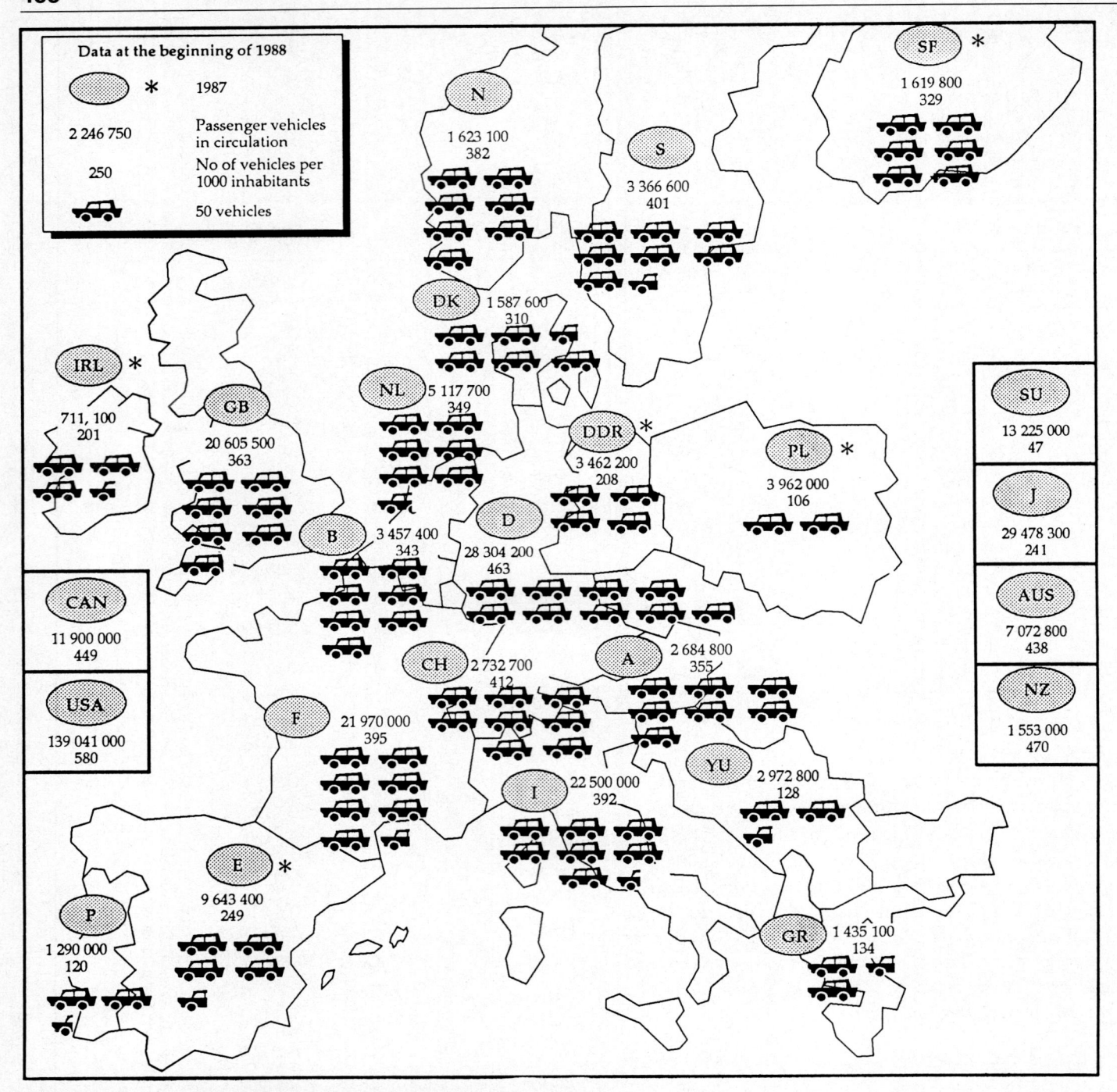

- ⬭ * 1987
- 2 246 750 — Passenger vehicles in circulation
- 250 — No of vehicles per 1000 inhabitants
- 🚗 — 50 vehicles

N 1 623 100 / 382
S 3 366 600 / 401
SF* 1 619 800 / 329
DK 1 587 600 / 310
IRL* 711 100 / 201
GB 20 605 500 / 363
NL 5 117 700 / 349
DDR* 3 462 200 / 208
PL* 3 962 000 / 106
SU 13 225 000 / 47
B 3 457 400 / 343
D 28 304 200 / 463
J 29 478 300 / 241
CAN 11 900 000 / 449
CH 2 732 700 / 412
A 2 684 800 / 355
AUS 7 072 800 / 438
USA 139 041 000 / 580
F 21 970 000 / 395
NZ 1 553 000 / 470
I 22 500 000 / 392
YU 2 972 800 / 128
E* 9 643 400 / 249
P 1 290 000 / 120
GR 1 435 100 / 134

Cars per 1000 inhabitants

	1970	1975	1980	1985	1986	1987	1988
USA	426	493	–	550	551	–	580
New Zealand	299	359	412	453	459	470	–
W Germany	218	280	369	415	428	446	463
Canada	306	371	430	427	447	–	449
Australia	294	353	389	–	427	–	438
Switzerland	221	278	353	391	406	410	412
Sweden	275	324	346	369	377	389	401
France	232	289	345	381	380	384	395
Italy	167	255	309	369	378	376	392
Norway	182	223	292	345	–	365	382
Austria	151	217	–	327	335	345	355
G Britain (inc N Ireland)	207	252	268	308	306	344	363
Belgium	190	256	315	–	343	–	343
Netherlands	173	219	299	331	340	340	349
Finland	–	201	244	302	315	329	–
Denmark	207	249	278	282	294	294	310
Spain	61	121	189	–	238	249	–
Japan	68	145	196	226	230	235	241
Eire	–	165	217	168	168	201	–
DDR	–	100	–	189	198	199	208
Greece	–	–	–	113	127	127	134
Yugoslavia	28	62	103	125	123	123	128
Portugal	42	86	110	113	118	116	120
Poland	–	–	–	93	99	106	–
USSR	–	–	–	42	–	47	–

ADVERTISERS

	Page		Page
Delco Products	I.F.C.	Hallwag AG	74/143
Saiag-SpA	4	Monroe Europa	78
Alfa Romeo	5	GenCorp	80
LUK Clutches	6	A C Rochester	54–55
UTC	11	Fiat	181
Libby-Owen Ford	12	Isuzu Motors Ltd	235
GE Plastics	16–17	General Motors Europe	120–121
Allied Signals	27	Siemens Bendix Automotive Electronics	196–197
ZF	28	SAAB-Scania	388–389
Mahle GmbH	29	Skoda	395
Alfred Teves GmbH	30	ECIA	46
Armstrong Equipment plc	31	Rolls Royce	379
Illinois Department of Commerce	40–41	Michelotti	160
The Easirider Co Ltd.	45	IBM Deutschland GmbH	275–277/B.C.
BMW GmbH	149–150	Jaguar	380–381
A B Automotive Electronics Ltd	63	Pirelli	I.B.C.
Längerer & Reich	243	Caro GmbH	243
		TRW	42

INDEX

	Page		
Cars International	1	A Sport Governed by Numerous Rules	32
Contents	3	Gags and Gadgets	38
Eastern Temptations for Western Markets	7	Power Trip	48
Concept Cars	13	Automobile Technology	56
Road Tests 1988	23	Sports Cars in View	64
		Specifications	81

A 85
- AC
- Acura
- Alfa Romeo
- Alpine
- ARO
- Aston Martin
- Audi
- Austin
- Autobianchi
- Avanti

B 107
- Bentley
- Bertone
- Bitter
- BMW D
- BMW SA
- Bristol
- Buick

C 124
- Cadillac
- Carbodies
- Caterham
- Chevrolet USA
- Chevrolet BR
- Chrysler
- Citroen F
- Citroen R
- Cizeta

D 156
- Dacia
- Daewoo
- Daihatsu
- Daimler
- De la Chapelle
- Dodge
- Donkervoort

E 171
- Eagle
- Ecosse
- Engesa
- Envemo
- Excalibur

F 174
- Farus
- Ferrari
- Fiat I
- Fiat BR
- Fiat RA
- Ford USA
- Ford EU
- Ford AUS
- Ford BR
- Ford RA
- Ford SA

G 215
- Geo
- Ginetta
- Gurgel

H 217
- Hindustan
- Hofstetter
- Holden
- Honda
- Hongki
- Hyundai

I 230
- Infinit
- Innocenti
- Irmscher
- Isuzu

J 237
- Jaguar
- Jeep
- Jensen

L 242
- Lada
- Lafa
- Laforza
- Lagonda
- Lamborghini
- Lancia
- Land Rover
- Lexus
- Lincoln
- Lotus
- Luaz

M 258
- Mahindra
- Maserati
- Mazda
- Mercedes-Benz
- Mercedes-Benz-Puch
- Mercury
- Merkur
- MG
- Middlebridge
- Mini GB
- Mini P
- Mitsubishi
- Miura
- Moretta
- Morgan
- Moskvich
- MVS

N 303
- Nissan

O 320
- Oldsmobile
- Opel
- Otosan

P 334
- Pag
- Panther
- Paykan
- Peugeot F
- Peugeot RA
- Pininfarina
- Plymouth
- Pontiac USA
- Pontiac CDN
- Porsche
- Portaro
- Premier
- Proton
- Puch
- Puma

R 361
- Rayton Fissore
- Reliant
- Renault F
- Renault RA
- Rolls-Royce
- Rover

S 383
- Saab
- Sbarro
- Seat
- Shiguli
- Sipani
- Skoda
- Standard
- Stutz
- Subaru
- Suzuki

T 404
- Tatra
- Thunderbird
- Tofas
- de Tomaso
- Toyota
- Trabant
- Tschaika
- TVR

U	425	**W**	448	Vehicle Badging	**454**
UAZ		Wartburg		UK Price Guide	**456**
Umm					
V	426	**Y**	448	US Price Guide	**459**
Vauxhall		Yue Loong		Another Record	**462**
Volga				Car Production by Vehicle Badge	**464**
Volkswagen D		**Z**	449		
Volkswagen BR				Car Parc	**465**
Volkswagen MEX		Zastava			
Volkswagen RA		Zaz		Advertisers	**467**
Volkswagen SA		Zil			
Volkswagen/Nissan		Zimmer			

PRS

PRS PUBLISHING LTD

OTHER PRS AUTOMOTIVE AND ENGINE YEARBOOKS

World Automotive Digest 1988 (Second Edition) - Price £195

The most comprehensive market reference to the world automotive industry. It provides detailed statistical information on production, demand and trade trends in the worldwide motor industry; analyses and comments on the main commercial and technical developments; identifies the main features which have shaped the individual companies within the automotive sector during the past year, and forecasts the automotive industry's future prospects.

World Components Digest 1989 (First Edition) Publication July 1989 - Price £195

A comprehensive review of important commercial and technical developments in the worldwide automotive components industry, together with an assessment of the current major issues. The Digest also contains top level viewpoints, company profiles and a statistical analysis.

Who's Who in Western European Automotive Components Markets 1988/89 (Second Edition) - Price £95

A unique reference containing information on over 500 automotive component manufacturers throughout Western Europe, including the materials and electronics field.

World Engine Digest 1989 (Ninth Edition) - Price £195

The World Engine Digest provides an up-to-date, comprehensive and detailed statement of world engine production with market data forecast to 1992. It also contains profiles of major engines and component companies; the major company, product and technical news in 1988; a world calendar of events for 1989/90 and a directory of companies.

Who's Who in World Engine and Component Markets 1988/89 (Fourth Edition) - Price £95

The standard company reference for engine and component manufacturers and their suppliers containing concise profiles of over 1500 engine and component companies.

For further information contact:

Elaine Boyden
PRS Publishing Ltd
44-48 Dover Street, London W1X 3RF
Tel: (01) 409 1635   Tlx: 23442   Fax: (01) 629 0221

ORDER FORM

	Quantity	Price	Total
Cars International 1989 ISBN No. 0 906237 45 9	☐	**£19.95**	£
World Automotive Digest 1988	☐	£195.00	£
World Components Digest 1989	☐	£195.00	£
Who's Who in Western European Automotive Component Markets 1988/89	☐	£ 95.00	£
World Engine Digest 1989	☐	£195.00	£
Who's Who in World Engine and Component Markets 1988/89	☐	£ 95.00	£
Plus postage and packing (per book: UK £5/Europe and rest of world £10): **Orders under £250 must be accompanied by payment**			£
I enclose a cheque for the total amount made payable to **PRS Publishing Ltd:**			£

I wish to pay by Visa/Access [VISA] [Access] [EUROCARD] [MasterCard]

To Visa/Access:–
I authorise you to debit my Visa/Access account with the amount of: £

My Visa/Access number is: ☐☐☐☐ ☐☐☐☐ ☐☐☐☐ ☐☐☐☐

Expiry date of card: ☐☐☐☐

Name (as on Visa/Access card):_____

Cardholder's Address:_____

Signature:_____

Name:_____ Position:_____

Company:_____

Address:_____

Tel/Tlx/Fax:_____ Date:_____

In Europe:

Elaine Boyden
PRS Business Publications
44-48 Dover Street
London W1X 3RF, England
Tel: (01) 409 1635
Tlx: 23442 Fax: (01) 629 0221

In the US:

Patricia Cresswell
PRS Consulting Group Inc
PO Box 1001, Darien
CT 06820, USA
Tel: (203) 656 1505
Tlx: 853750 Fax: (203) 655 1171